WINDOWS USER'S GUIDE TO DOS

USING THE COMMAND LINE
IN WINDOWS MILLENNIUM EDITION

CAROLYN Z. GILLAY
SADDLEBACK COLLEGE

BETTE A. PEAT
SOLANO COMMUNITY COLLEGE

FRANKLIN, BEEDLE & ASSOCIATES, INC. • 8536 SW ST. HELENS DRIVE, SUITE D
WILSONVILLE, OREGON • 97070 • 503-682-7668

DEDICATION

To Milton and Mary Hall, who are our best friends.

—C. Z. G.

———————

In loving memory of Barbara Turcotte, the kindest, wisest, most loving human being I have ever known. I am fortunate beyond measure to have been born to her.

—B. A. P.

President and Publisher	Jim Leisy (jimleisy@fbeedle.com)
Production	Stephanie Welch
	Tom Sumner
	Jeni Lee
Proofreader	Stephanie Welch
Cover	Ian Shadburne
Marketing	Chris Collier
Order Processing	Krista Brown

Printed in the U.S.A.

Rights and Permissions
Franklin, Beedle & Associates, Incorporated
8536 SW St. Helens Drive, Suite D
Wilsonville, Oregon 97070

Library of Congress Cataloging-in-Publication Data available from the publisher

CONTENTS

CHAPTER 2
COMMAND SYNTAX USING THE DIR COMMAND
WITH PARAMETERS AND WILDCARDS   **75**

CHAPTER 3
DISKS AND FORMATTING   128

CHAPTER 4
PROGRAM FILES, DATA FILES, AND SUBDIRECTORIES   159

CHAPTER 5
INTERNAL COMMANDS: COPY AND TYPE   221

CHAPTER 6
USING DEL, DELTREE, REN, AND MOVE   283

CHAPTER 7
USING ATTRIB, SUBST, XCOPY, DOSKEY,
AND THE MS-DOS TEXT EDITOR   344

CHAPTER 10
INTRODUCTION TO BATCH FILES   494

CHAPTER 11
ADVANCED BATCH FILES   559

CHAPTER 12
CONNECTIVITY   634

CHAPTER 13
PROTECTING YOUR SYSTEM   701

CHAPTER 14
ADVANCED TROUBLESHOOTING   754

PREFACE

Computer hardware, software, and operating system concepts are the focus of this textbook. It can be used in a wide variety of situations: in a course that focuses exclusively on the command line, as part of a course for the command line portion of a network or programming class, as an adjunct to a Windows Millennium Edition course, or in a class that follows the introduction to Windows Millennium Edition. This is not just a DOS textbook. Students will execute problem-solving exercises using the command line and learn operating system concepts. An existing installation of Windows Millennium Edition is necessary to use this book.

WHY STUDY DOS?

It is difficult to convince students with no experience in computing that they need the knowledge that DOS provides. Although DOS indeed is "dead" as a stand-alone operating system, command syntax, parameters, parsing commands, and troubleshooting all require the knowledge and skills that a command line interface can provide and that a GUI interface cannot. This text teaches these concepts using the MS-DOS window in Windows Millennium Edition. This text also deals with the commands and functions necessary to understand, maintain, and troubleshoot a system that are available only in the Windows Millennium Edition graphical user interface.

BEGINS WITH THE BASICS AND LEADS TO THE ADVANCED

This book will lead the student from a basic to a sophisticated use of the command line interface. Each chapter has questions for both novice and advanced students; the advanced students will be challenged, and the beginning students will also have their needs met. Furthermore, while this text does teach the various character-based commands specific to DOS, it also stresses the concepts, purpose, theory, and understanding of operating systems in general. Students will learn details about the command line interface, such as when and why one would use it instead of the graphical user interface of Windows Millennium Edition. Ample examples are provided to allow the student to master these concepts.

The command line interface lives on in Windows 95, Windows 98, Windows NT 4.0, Windows Millennium Edition, Windows 2000 Professional, Windows 2000 Server and Advanced Server, and Novell. Batch files are still used and useful in all of the above operating systems. The value of pipes, filters, and redirection used with batch files are covered in thorough step-by-step methodology. Advanced batch files are covered in detail, building on programming logic in an easily understood way. The student learns about all batch file commands and is introduced to DEBUG. These batch file skills are critical in the networking worlds of Novell and Windows as well as for the stand-alone computer system.

Setting up computer systems, optimizing performance, and troubleshooting require that students have command line skills. To this end, the student learns about creating an Emergency Repair Disk and the series of four Setup disks required to boot the system from floppies with Windows Millennium Edition.

This text also covers two major forms of connectivity: networking and the Internet. We have found that there is a gap in too many students' knowledge base. The student takes a Windows and/or DOS class and then, if he is on a networking career path, jumps into networking large systems. This can be an intimidating jump. Furthermore, there are many students who work in a small office that do not have a network administrator, work in an environment where they need to access a network, or simply want to know how to share files, folders, and devices on their own systems at home. These students are not going to follow the networking career path and take the networking classes. To address the needs of all of these types of students, this text introduces some basic networking concepts and then leads the student into setting up a peer-to-peer network (where possible), showing them how to share files, folders, and devices. The student will also learn network techniques, such as mapping drives.

The other aspect of connectivity covered deals with the Internet. The student will learn various options in connecting to the Internet and then do some simple activities using Internet Explorer to access the Internet. A brief introduction to TCP/IP concepts is included because when using the Internet, many students are exposed to terms such as "protocols" and "IP addresses" and become lost. This overview gives them an understanding of some of these important terms so that they better understand what it is they are doing when they are on the Internet. To further the students' knowledge of using the command line interface, this text covers some simple commands that can be run at the command line, such as FTP. In addition, certain troubleshooting commands such as Ping are included.

The last chapter covers a much-neglected topic, backing up a computer system. In addition, students learn the purpose and function of the Registry as well as what files make up the Registry. They learn advanced troubleshooting concepts, with understanding of the Registry and the CMOS setup. They learn about the tools available in Windows Millennium Edition, such as CHKDSK. They learn about the structure of the Registry, how files and the Registry interact, as well as learn about REGEDIT and how to do simple tasks using REGEDIT, when appropriate.

This book takes up where other Windows books leave off. Although no prior knowledge or experience with computers, software, operating systems, or Windows Millennium Edition is necessary, it helps if the students have completed a basic Windows Millennium Edition class.

ACTIVITIES DISK WITH SHAREWARE PROGRAMS AND DATA FILES

One of the most difficult parts of teaching the command line interface, as well as Windows Millennium Edition, to students is the esoteric nature of operating systems. Although students find the material interesting, the question that I repeatedly get is, "What good is DOS? It doesn't do anything." This is particularly true now as the world has moved to the GUI interface. This text demonstrates by discussion and example the importance of the command line interface. Furthermore, if instructors attempt to use a complex application program, such as Word, they spend their time teaching the application, not the operating system. Thus, two simple shareware applications are included: a simple database program (The Home-Phone-Book Program) and a simple spreadsheet program (The Thinker) that students work with. They will have the opportunity to load an application program and prewritten data files as well as to create simple data files. The student then can understand the differences between data files and program files and use operating system commands to manipulate both types of files. In addition, included are several educationally sound shareware games that reinforce certain DOS concepts in an enjoyable manner.

These files are on the Activities disk, included with this book, which provides files to be manipulated in the exercises in the book. The Activities disk's files are easily installed on a computer system's hard disk or on a network server. The exercises do not direct the student to save files to the hard disk or network server. Early on, the student creates a Data disk, and all files are written to the Data disk. This approach provides the real-life experience of working with the hard disk or server without risking damage to either. There are numerous warnings and cautions alerting a student when a possible network conflict could arise.

AN INTEGRATED PRESENTATION OF CONCEPTS AND SKILLS

Each section of the book is presented in a careful student-oriented step-by-step approach. Interspersed between the steps are the reasons for and results of each action. At the end of each chapter, there are application assignments that allow the student to apply his knowledge independently and to prove mastery of the subject area by using critical thinking skills. In addition, each command is presented in a syntactically correct manner so that when the students have finished the course, they will be able to not only use software documentation but also be comfortable in a network/internet environment that requires the use of syntax and commands. This also assists the students in their ability to learn how to solve problems independently using the documentation at hand. No matter what changes are made to future versions of the operating system, students will be able to use the new commands. This skill also transfers to the use of application packages and other operating system environments.

USES A SELF-MASTERY APPROACH

Each chapter includes a chapter overview, key terms list, chapter summary, discussion questions, true and false questions, completion questions, multiple choice questions, and writing the commands questions. In addition, each chapter includes application assignments. The application assignments vary depending on the activity that the student is pursuing. There are three sets of application assignments. The first two require the use of the computer, using the skills learned in the chapter. The first problem set requires the student to complete activities on the computer and write the resulting answers on a Scantron form. The second problem set also requires the student to use the computer but place the answers on a printout. The results that a student achieves are sent to a batch file provided with the Activities disk. The batch file is an easily followed program. The student supplies his solution to the problems. Then, the resulting printout includes not only the answers in a format that is consistent but also the student's name and other instructor-directed identifying information. The printout typically prints on two pages or fewer. The last set of application assignments are brief essay questions that encourage the student to merge what he has learned in the chapter with his improved understanding of the command line interface of the Windows Millennium Edition operating system. These three types of assignments reinforce critical thinking skills. The application assignments can also be turned in as homework. These features help to reinforce the material in the chapter. Where some hands-on assignments are not possible, such when as dealing with the Registry, the student still has an opportunity to answer brief essay questions that encourage the student to explain his understanding of the topic at hand.

SUPPLEMENTARY MATERIAL

This book comes with an Instructor's Manual that includes teaching suggestions for each chapter as well as the answers for every question and application exercise. There are additional chapter tests. A midterm and a final are included.

REFERENCE TOOLS

The book is useful as a reference to command line commands. The first appendix provides instructions for installing the subdirectory to the hard disk. This feature is particularly useful for those students who work at home or in an office. The rest of the appendices include a complete command reference, an ANSI table, and a tutorial on how to add any missing Windows components. There is also a glossary.

ACKNOWLEDGMENTS

My thanks to everyone who helped along the way. Special thanks to:
- My family, Parkers, Peats, and Farneths, for their continuous encouragement and their "You can do it" attitude. They believed when it wasn't practical to believe, and supported me through some rough roads.
- My friends and colleagues at Solano Community College, especially Jane Thompson, Donna Anderson, and Mary Ann Harris, for their unending support and friendship.
- The CIS students at Solano, for making me find answers for questions I never thought of, most particularly Jonathan Cerkoney and Janice Larsen.
- The "Covelo connection," Jean and Manny Macaraeg, for adjusting their schedule to accommodate mine so many times.
- All the crew at Franklin Beedle, for their patience and flexibility.
- And once again, most of all, to Carolyn—for the opportunity. Thank you, my dear, dear friend.

Anyone who wants to offer suggestions, improvements, or just share ideas can reach me at *bpeat@solano.cc.ca.us* or *wugbook@pacbell.net*.

—*B.A.P.*

A project of this scope is difficult to complete successfully without the contribution of many individuals. Special thanks go to:
- David Robinson of Pioneer Pacific College, for developing chapter questions and tests.

- Kathryn Maurdeff, for providing answers and PowerPoint presentations.
- Milton Hall, who lets me bounce ideas off of him to have a better book.
- All the authors of the shareware included with this textbook.
- My students at Saddleback College, who make writing worthwhile.
- My colleagues in the Computer Information Management Department at Saddleback College.
- The California Business Education Association and the National Business Education Association, for providing forums for professional growth as well as inviting me to make presentations sharing my teaching experiences.
- An especially big thanks to everyone at Franklin, Beedle & Associates. They somehow manage to turn my writing into a real book. Thank you Jeni Lee, Stephanie Welch, and Tom Sumner for making sure I say what I mean and for putting my words and graphics into an attractive format. Thank you Ian Shadburne, for designing the eye-catching cover. Thank you Sue Page, for the deft management of the preparation of instructor support materials. Thank you Christine Collier, for taking such good care of the professors who want our book. Thank you Krista Brown, for maintaining order in order processing.
- Thank you as well to Jim Leisy, who keeps me on my toes and makes sure I finish every book.
- To Bette Peat, my wonderful co-author, it's so fantastic to work with you.
- And, to my beloved Frank Panezich, who still does not understand that women cannot travel with one pair of black shoes.

Anyone who wants to offer suggestions or improvements or just share ideas can reach me at czg@bookbiz.com.

                                                                                                          —C.Z.G.

MICROCOMPUTER SYSTEMS

Hardware, Software, and the Operating System

LEARNING OBJECTIVES

1. Categorize the latest types of computers in use today.
2. Identify and explain the functions of basic hardware components.
3. Explain how a CPU functions.
4. Compare and contrast RAM, cache, and ROM.
5. Explain how the use of adapter boards increases the capabilities of a computer.
6. List and explain the functions of the various peripheral input and output devices of a computer.
7. Explain what external storage devices are.
8. Explain how to measure the capacity of a disk.
9. Explain how disk drives write information to and read information from a disk.
10. Explain the purpose and function of a hard disk.
11. Compare the purposes and functions of disks.
12. Explain how and why a disk is divided.
13. Explain how disk drives derive their names.
14. Compare and contrast system software and application software.
15. Explain the functions of an operating system.
16. Explain the advantages of using a network.

CHAPTER OVERVIEW

It is impossible to live today without being affected by computers. Computers are used in public and private industry and are found in every sector of the business world. Computer software is what makes computers

1

useful for all types of applications. There is specialized software for sophisticated scientific applications such as nuclear and atomic physics and for all forms of engineering and industrial research. The greatest use of application software is in business with all types of word-processing, accounting, and marketing packages. Computer use only continues to grow.

Application software makes a computer useful, but you must first understand how the operating system of a computer works. Foremost, the operating system manages all the basic functions of the computer and allows the computer to run application programs. When new technology appears in hardware and software, the operating system must keep pace. Thus, you must have a basic understanding of computer hardware to understand the role and function of the operating system. Hardware and technology are constantly changing so new versions of operating systems also appear. The operating system of choice today is Windows.

R.1   AN INTRODUCTION TO COMPUTERS

At the most basic level, computers are calculators; but this definition is very narrow. Computers are used to handle accounting chores (spreadsheets), write books (word-processing documents), organize and retrieve information (databases), create and manipulate graphics, and communicate with the world (the Internet). In the visual arts computers have revolutionized the way films are made, games are played, and reality is perceived (virtual reality).

R.2   CATEGORIES OF COMPUTERS

Computers are categorized by a variety of factors such as size, processing speed, information storage capacity, and cost. In the ever-changing technical world, these classifications are not absolute. Technical advancements blur some categories. For instance, many microcomputers today exceed the capabilities of mainframes manufactured five years ago. In addition, the microcomputer now is the dominant computer used by most businesses. These computers are available in sizes ranging from desktop to subnotebook. Table R.1 shows the major categories of computers.

Computer	Applications
Supercomputer: Very large computer	Sophisticated scientific applications such as nuclear physics, atomic physics, and seismology
Mainframe: Large computer	General purpose business machines. Typical applications include accounting, payroll, banking, and airline reservations
Minicomputer: Small mainframe computer	Specialized applications such as engineering and industrial research
Microcomputer: Small, general-purpose computer	General applications such as word processing, accounting for small businesses, and record keeping. Today, these computers are also known

as desktops, PCs, notebooks, subcompacts, and laptops.

TABLE R.1   COMPUTER TYPES

R.3   COMPUTER COMPONENTS

Although the range of computer types continues to grow, computers operate the same way, regardless of their category. Information is input, processed, and stored, and the resulting information is output. Figure R.1 is a graphic representation of this process.

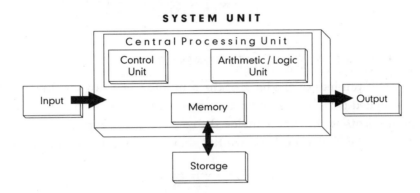

SYSTEM UNIT

FIGURE R.1   COMPONENTS OF A COMPUTER SYSTEM

Figure R.1 shows the process that occurs when using a computer. It represents the physical components of a computer system, referred to as **_hardware_**. All computer systems, from mainframes to notebooks, have the same basic hardware. Hardware by itself can do nothing—a computer system needs software. **_Software_** is a set of detailed instructions, called a **_program_**, that tells the hardware what operations to perform.

Data, in its simplest form, is related or unrelated numbers, words, or facts that, when arranged in a particular way, provide information. Software applications turn raw data into information.

R.4   MICROCOMPUTER HARDWARE COMPONENTS

This textbook is devoted to single-user computers—microcomputers. Microcomputers, today simply called computers, are also called micros, subcompacts, home computers, laptops, notebooks, personal computers (PCs), or desktop computers. Microcomputers are comprised of hardware components. Much like a stereo system, the basic components of a complete system, also called a system configuration, include an input device (typically a keyboard), a pointing device (a mouse or trackball), a system unit that houses the electronic circuitry for storing and processing data and programs (the central processing unit/CPU, adapter cards, power supply, and memory/RAM and ROM), an external storage unit that stores data and programs on disks (disk drives), and an output device such as a visual display unit (a monitor). Most people also purchase a printer for producing a printed version of the results. Typically today, a system also includes speakers for multimedia activities. Figure R.2 represents a typical microcomputer system.

FIGURE R.2   A TYPICAL MICROCOMPUTER SYSTEM

If you look at the back of the computer, you can see the input/output devices, called peripherals. Since they are "peripheral," or outside the case, they must communicate with what is inside the computer through cables attached to a connection that is called a *port*. Figure R.3 shows some examples of these connections.

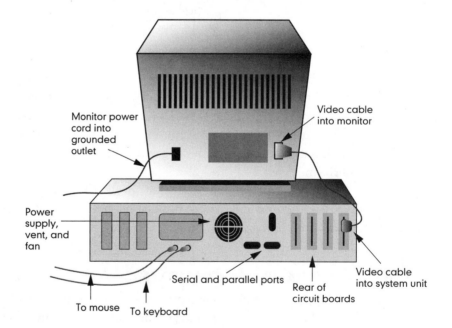

FIGURE R.3   CABLES ATTACHED TO A CASE

R.5   THE SYSTEM UNIT

The system unit, as shown in Figure R.4, is the "black box" that houses the electronic and mechanical parts of the computer. It contains many printed electronic circuit boards, also called interface cards, *cards*, or *adapter cards*. One of these is a special printed circuit board called the *system board* or the *motherboard*.

Attached to the system board is a microprocessor chip that is the central processing unit (CPU), random access memory (RAM), and read-only memory (ROM). The system unit is also referred to as the *chassis* or *case*. With the outer case removed, the unit looks like the diagram in Figure R.4.

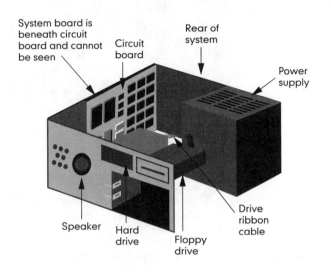

FIGURE R.4   INSIDE THE SYSTEM UNIT

Inside the typical system unit, you will find the following:

- A system board or motherboard that contains components such as a CPU, RAM, ROM, a chipset, and a system clock.
- Expansion slots that contain adapter cards such as a video card, a sound card, or a network interface card.
- Secondary storage units (disk drives)
- A power supply

A system unit has a power supply (to get power to every single part in the PC), disk drives (including CD-ROM drives, floppy disk drives, removable drives, and hard disk drives), and circuit boards. The motherboard, also called the system board, is the core of the system. Everything in the PC is connected to the motherboard so that it can control every part of in the system. Figure R.5 shows a system board.

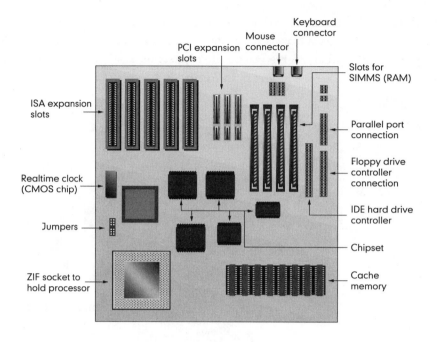

FIGURE R.5   COMPONENTS ON A SYSTEM BOARD

Most modern system boards have several components built in, including various sockets, slots, connectors, chips, and other components. Most system boards have the following components:

- A processor socket/slot is the place where the CPU is installed.
- A chipset is a single chip that integrates all the functions of older system chips such as the system timer, the keyboard controller, and so forth.
- A Super Input/Output chip integrates devices formerly found on separate expansion cards in older systems.
- All system boards must have a special chip containing software that is called BIOS (basic input/output system) or ***ROM-BIOS***. (***ROM*** is ***read-only memory***.) This chip contains the startup programs and drivers that are used to get your system up and running and acts as the interface to the basic hardware in your system. BIOS is a collection of programs embedded into a chip, called a flash ROM chip. It is nonvolatile, which means that, when you turn off the computer, none of the information stored in ROM is lost. ROM-BIOS has four main functions: POST (power-on self test), which tests a computer's critical hardware components such as the processor, memory, and disk controllers; the bootstrap loader, which finds the operating system and loads or boots your computer; BIOS, which is the collection of actual drivers used to act as a basic interface between the operating system and the hardware (when you run the Windows operating system in safe mode, you are running solely on BIOS drivers); and the CMOS (complementary metal-oxide semiconductor) setup, which contains the system configuration and setup programs. CMOS is usually a menu-driven program that allows you to configure the motherboard and chipset settings along with the date and time and passwords. You usually access the CMOS settings by pressing a special keystroke combination before the operating system loads. The keystroke, such as **F2**, depends on the com-

puter. Most ROM is located on the system board, but some ROM is located on adapter boards.

- SIMM/DIMM (single inline memory module/dual inline memory module) slots are for the installation of memory modules. These modules are small boards that plug into special connectors on the motherboard or memory card and replace individual memory chips. If one chip goes bad, the entire module must be replaced.
- System buses are the heart of every motherboard. A *bus* is a path across which data can travel within a computer. A data path is the communication highway between computer elements. The main buses in a system include:
  - The processor bus, the highest-speed bus in the system, is primarily used by the processor to pass information to and from memory.
  - The AGP (accelerated graphics port) bus is a high-speed bus specifically for a video card.
  - The PCI (peripheral component interconnect) bus is a collection of slots that high-speed peripherals such as SCSI (Small Computer System Interface) adapters, network cards, and video cards can be plugged into.
  - The ISA (Industry Standard Architecture) bus is an old bus which appeared in the first computers. Most people use it for plug-in modems, sound cards, and various other low-speed peripherals.
- The voltage regulator is used to drop the power supply signal to the correct voltage for the processor.
- A battery supplies power for the CMOS chip, which holds the system configuration information.

R.6   CENTRAL PROCESSING UNIT

A *central processing unit*, most commonly referred to as a *CPU*, is the brain of a computer and is composed of transistors on a silicon chip. It comprehends and carries out instructions sent to it by a program and directs the activity of the computer. The CPU is plugged into the motherboard. The CPU is described in terms of its central processing chip and its model designation. Intel manufactures many of the CPU chips in Windows-based PCs. Intel processors running Windows are commonly called *Wintel* machines. These chips were, for many years, designated by a model number such as 80386 or 80486. Typically the first two numbers were dropped so people referred to a computer as a 386 or 486. With the introduction of the 80586, Intel began referring to its chips as Pentiums, such as the Pentium 350. Since that time, Intel has released the Pentium II, the Pentium III, and the Pentium 4. The major competitors to Intel are AMD and Cyrix. A CPU is rated by the following items:

1. Speed. The system clock on the system board times the activities of the chips on the system board. This clock provides a beat that synchronizes all the activities. The faster the beat, the faster the CPU can execute instructions. This is measured in *megahertz* (*MHz*), where one MHz is equal to 1,000,000 beats of the clock per second. The original 8088 CPU had a MHz rating of 4.77 MHz. Today,

500 is a common speed, and speeds are available up to 866 MHz or more. In fact, a 1 GHz CPU has been developed, with even faster CPUs coming.

2. Efficiency of the program code built into the CPU chip.

3. Internal data path size (word size) is the largest number of bits the CPU can process in one operation. Word sizes range from 16 bits (2 bytes) to 64 bits (8 bytes).

4. Data path, the largest number of bits that can be transported into the CPU, ranges from 8 bits to 64 bits.

5. Maximum number of memory addresses that the CPU can assign. The minimum is 1 megabyte and the maximum is 4,096 megabytes (4 gigabytes).

6. Internal cache, which is memory included in the CPU. It is also referred to as primary cache or level 1 (L1) cache.

7. Multiprocessor ability. Some chips can accomplish more than one task at a time and thus are multiprocessors.

8. Special functionality. Some chips are designed to provide special services. For example, the Pentium MMX chip is designed to handle multimedia features especially well.

R.7   INPUT/OUTPUT (I/O) BUSES

Adapter cards are printed circuit boards, as mentioned previously. They are installed in a system unit either when the unit is purchased or later. Adapter cards allow a user to use a special video display, a mouse, a modem, or a fax-modem. These items are considered *peripheral devices* and are installed within a system unit in expansion slots. The number of adapter card options you can install depends on how many slots your system unit has. Inexpensive system units usually have only one or two expansion slots, but a costly system unit, especially one designed to be a network server, can have seven, eight, or more.

I/O buses allow your CPU to communicate with your peripheral devices. A peripheral device connected to your computer is controlled by the CPU. Examples of peripherals (also called peripheral device or devices) include such items as a disk drive, a printer, a mouse, or a modem. The original personal computers had nothing built into the computer except a CPU, memory, and a keyboard. Everything else such as floppy disk drives, hard disk drives, printers, and modems were provided by add-in cards. Nowadays, computer manufacturers have found that it is less expensive to build the most common peripherals into the motherboard. Connectors to which you connect the cables for your devices are called ports. Today, most computers include a parallel port for a printer, two serial ports for devices such as an external modem or a serial mouse, and controllers for up to two floppy disk drives and two hard disk drives.

However, not every peripheral has a built-in connection. Data paths often stop at an expansion slot. An *expansion slot* is a slot or plug where you can add an interface card to enhance your computer system. An *interface card* is a printed circuit board that enables a personal computer to use a peripheral device such as a CD-ROM drive, modem, or joystick, for which it does not already have the necessary connections, ports, or circuit boards. Interface cards are also called cards, adapter cards, or adapter boards. The size and shape of the expansion slot is dependent on the kind of bus your computer uses.

Remember, a bus is a set of hardware lines (conductors) used for data transfer among the components of the computer system. A bus is essentially a shared information highway that connects different parts of the system—including the CPU, the disk-drive controller, and memory. Buses are characterized by the number of bits that they can transfer at one time, which is equivalent to the number of wires within a bus. A computer with a 32-bit address bus and a 16-bit data bus can transfer 16 bits of data at a time from any of 2^{32} memory locations. Buses have standards—a technical guideline that is used to establish uniformity in an area of hardware or software development.

Common bus standards include ISA (Industry Standard Architecture), PCI (peripheral component interconnect), local bus, PC Card slots—formerly known as PCMCIA (Personal Computer Memory Card International Association)—primarily used on notebook computers, and VESA (Video Electronics Standards Association) local bus.

The newest bus standard is the *USB* (*Universal Serial Bus*). It is an external bus standard that brings plug-and-play standard capability to hardware devices outside the computer, eliminating the need to install cards into dedicated computer slots and reconfigure the system. Most new computers today include a USB connection. The advantage of USB is that you may daisy chain devices. This connectivity feature means that your first device plugs into the USB connector, then the next device plugs into the first device, and so forth. You only need one USB connection but can use it for many devices. In addition, USB devices can be "hot-plugged" or unplugged, which means that you can add or remove a peripheral device without needing to power down the computer. The device, however, must be USB compatible.

FireWire is a new bus technology. This bus was derived from the FireWire bus originally developed by Apple and Texas Instruments. It is now known as IEEE 1394 rather than FireWire. This bus is extremely fast and suits the demands of today's audio and video multimedia that must move large amounts of data quickly.

R.8   RANDOM ACCESS MEMORY

RAM (*random access memory*) is the workspace of the computer. It is often referred to simply as *memory*. The growth in the size of RAM in the last few years has been phenomenal. Whereas 4 MB of memory was more than satisfactory just a few years ago, the demand based on software needs has made 128 MB of RAM commonplace, and 256 or more MB of RAM desirable. Physically, RAM is contained in many electrical circuits. However, a computer's memory is not like a person's memory. RAM is not a permanent record of anything. RAM is the place where the programs and data are placed while the computer is working. Computer memory is temporary (volatile) and useful only while the computer is on. When the computer is turned off, what is in memory is lost.

There are two types of RAM, *dynamic RAM* (*DRAM*) and *static RAM* (*SRAM*). Dynamic RAM chips hold data for a short time whereas static RAM chips can hold data until the computer is turned off. DRAM is much less expensive than SRAM; thus most memory on a motherboard consists of DRAM. Dynamic RAM chips do not hold their data long and must be refreshed about every 3.86 milliseconds. To refresh means that the computer rewrites the data to the chip. The direct memory access (DMA) controller takes care of refreshing RAM. The DMA controller is on the system board and is part of the chipset. It provides faster memory access because it moves data in and out of RAM without involving the CPU. Today, you also see extended data output (EDO) memory on newer computers. This RAM module works about 20 percent faster then conventional RAM, but the system board must support EDO memory. Since the speed by which you and your computer work is driven by RAM, you can expect improvements in RAM speed to continue.

R.9   CACHE MEMORY

Caching is a method used to improve processing speed. It uses some of the more expensive static RAM chips to speed up data access. Basically, *cache memory* stores frequently used RAM data, thereby speeding up the process of data access. Whenever the CPU needs data from RAM, it visits the cache first to see if the data is available there. If it is, then rapid action occurs. If not, the CPU goes to RAM proper.

The cache will hold data or programming code that is often used or anticipated. This way the CPU has the instructions it needs ready and waiting without having to refresh RAM. Caches can be found in video and printer memory systems as well.

R.10   CONTROLLERS

A *controller* is a device on which other devices rely for access to a computer subsystem such as a disk drive. A disk controller, for example, controls access to one or more disk drives. What kind of controller interface you have will determine the number and kinds of devices you can attach to your computer. A common disk-drive controller is the Integrated Device Electronics (IDE), which resides on the drive itself, eliminating the need for a separate adapter card. Another type is the Small Computer System Interface (SCSI), pronounced "skuzzi," which is a very high-speed interface and is used to connect computers to many SCSI peripheral devices such as hard disks and printers. The original SCSI standard is now called SCSI-I, and the new enhanced SCSI standard is called SCSI-II. In addition, new developments include Fast SCSI, Fast/Wide SCSI, and UltraSCSI.

R.11   CONNECTORS

Most computers have both a serial port and a parallel port. See Figure R.6. These connections allow devices to be plugged in. *Serial ports* communicate in series, one data bit after another, and service serial devices such as modems and mouses. *Parallel ports* communicate in parallel, eight data bits at a time, and service parallel devices such as printers. The most common configuration for a personal computer is two serial ports and one parallel port. Serial ports are referred to as COM ports, and on a standard computer they are designated as COM1 and COM2. Parallel ports are called LPT ports. The first LPT port is called LPT1. COM stands for *com*munications and LPT stands for *line printer*.

A personal computer can have up to five I/O ports, usually three serial and two parallel. Although computers are limited to five ports, there can actually be more than five peripheral devices. Today, many devices, such as Zip drives and scanners, that plug into parallel ports have a "through port" so that one LPT port can service two devices. If you have a SCSI interface, you may also connect a series of devices, creating a daisy chain.

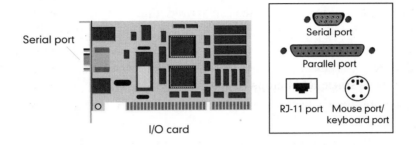

FIGURE R.6   I/O PORTS

Today, many computers come with a built-in modem. If that is the case, you will have a connector called an RJ-11 telephone plug, which is identical to the plug on the back of a telephone. Having an RJ-11 connector frees up a serial port.

R.12   PERIPHERALS—INPUT DEVICES

How do software programs and data get into RAM? The answer is input devices. The most common input device is the keyboard, which is attached to a system unit with a cable. By keying in instructions and data, you communicate with the computer. The computer places the information into RAM. Again, most modern computers have a keyboard port to connect the keyboard. See Figure R.6.

You can also input using a pointing device, such as a **mouse**, **trackball**, track pointer, or touchpad to get to the place to enter data. (In this textbook, all such devices will be collectively referred to as a *mouse*.) Data manipulation is as easy as moving the cursor to where you want it on the screen and pressing one of the mouse buttons. Most computers today have a connector for the mouse, most commonly called the PS/2 connector. See Figure R.6.

Other input devices include modems with which data can be downloaded directly into the computer, and scanners for inserting text through optical character recognition (OCR) software and graphics. Disk drives are both input and output devices.

R.13   PERIPHERALS—OUTPUT DEVICES

In addition to getting information into the CPU, you also want to get it out. You may want to see what you keyed in on the monitor, or you might desire a printed or "hard" copy of the data. These processes are known as output. Output devices refer to where information is sent. Thus, you read information in and write information out, commonly known as I/O for input and output.

R.14   OUTPUT DEVICES—MONITORS

A *monitor*, also called a terminal display screen, screen, cathode-ray tube (CRT), or video display terminal (VDT), looks like a television. The common monitor size standard used to be 14 inches (measured diagonally). However, today, most users opt for at least a 15-inch monitor. The new standard is becoming the 19-inch monitor, with the 21-inch monitor gaining ground. In addition, the liquid crystal display (LCD) used on notebook computers is now becoming available as a stand-alone monitor to accompany your desktop computer. These monitors take far less space since they are completely flat, but at this time, they are very new and very costly.

Another important facet to a monitor is the sharpness of its image, referred to as its *resolution*. Resolution is a measure of how many pixels on the screen are addressable by software. It is measured in the number of *pixels* (dots) on the screen. A resolution of 800 by 600 means 800 pixels per line horizontally and 600 pixels vertically. Multiplying 800 by 600 will give you the total number of pixels available (480,000 pixels). The resolution must be supported by the video card controller, and the software you are using must make use of the resolution capabilities of the monitor.

In addition, to determine the sharpness of your image, you must also know the dot pitch of the pixels. *Dot pitch* is the measurement in millimeters between pixels on the screen. The smaller the dot pitch, the sharper the image. Common sizes include .25 to .31. A dot pitch of .28 or .25 will give you the best results.

Another factor in choosing a monitor is the interlace factor. An *interlaced* monitor begins at the top of the screen and redraws (refreshes) every other line of pixels, then returns to the top and refreshes the rest of the lines. A *noninterlaced* monitor refreshes all the lines at one time, eliminating the wandering horizontal line and the flickering screen. Thus, a noninterlaced monitor is the preferred choice. The refresh rate (vertical scan rate) is the time it takes for the electronic beam to fill the screen with lines from top to bottom. Video Electronics Standards Association (VESA) has set a minimum refresh rate standard of 70 Hz (70 complete vertical refreshes per second) as one requirement of Super VGA monitors. Multiscan monitors are also available. These monitors offer a variety of vertical and horizontal refresh rates but cost much more than other monitors.

Information written to the screen by the CPU needs a special kind of circuit board—a video display adapter card, commonly called a video card or a graphics adapter card—which controls the monitor. In the early days of computing, the video adapters were only monochrome. The color graphics adapter (CGA) and the enhanced graphics adapter (EGA) came next, but only in 16 colors. Next was the video graphics array (VGA), which generated 256 colors. Today, most people have the Super VGA format, which generates sharper resolution and can display an almost unbelievable 16 million colors. Commonly, a video card has its own "on-board" memory, which is physically on the card. Today, eight megabytes of memory on a video card is common, and soon 16 megabytes will be the standard.

R.15 OUTPUT DEVICES—PRINTERS

A printer is attached to a system unit with a cable, usually to a parallel port. A printer allows a user to have a hard copy (unchangeable because it is on paper) of information.

In the past, **impact printers**, such as dot-matrix printers, were used. An impact printer works like a typewriter. The element strikes some kind of ribbon, which in turn strikes the paper and leaves a mark. A dot-matrix printer forms characters by selecting dots from a grid pattern on a movable print head and permits printing in any style of letters and graphics (pictures). Dot-matrix printers are still used today for multiple-part forms that use carbon paper.

Today, **nonimpact printers** are in general use. This category includes thermal printers that burn images into paper using a dot-matrix grid and **inkjet printers** that spray ionized drops of ink to shape characters. Today, inkjet printers that produce very good quality black and white as well as color images have become the most popular personal printer. The **laser printer** is more expensive, but produces fine quality black and white printing. Although laser color is available, it still remains very costly. Laser printers use a laser beam instructed by the computer to form characters with powdered toner fused to the page by heat, like a photocopying machine. Laser printers operate noiselessly at speeds up to 900 characters per second (cps), equivalent to 24 pages per minute.

R.16 MODEMS

A **modem** (**mo**dulator/**dem**odulator) translates the digital signals of the computer into the analog signals that travel over telephone lines. The speed at which the signal travels is called the baud rate—the unit of time for a signal to travel over a telephone line. The rate of transmission has increased to 56,000 baud, and will soon be even faster. The speed at which data packets travel is measured in bits per second (bps) and is usually very near the baud rate. For this transmission to occur, the party on the other end must also have a modem that translates the analog signals back into digital signals. In addition, the computer needs special instructions in the form of a software communication program.

Cable modems are also available in some areas. In this case, the cable company lays high-speed cable lines that require a special modem as well as a network interface card. This greatly increases the transmission speed. Another alternative is an Integrated Services Digital Network (ISDN) line—a high-speed telephone data line that also greatly increases speed. A digital subscriber line (DSL) is yet another choice, if available. Here users can purchase bandwidth that is potentially 10 times faster than ISDN lines but still slower than cable. **Bandwidth** can simply be described as a pipe that moves data from point A to point B. It is the data transfer capacity of a digital communications system.

Another choice for organizations such as businesses or educational institutions is a dedicated leased line that provides digital service between two locations at high speeds. A leased line is a permanent 24-hour connection to a specific location that can only be changed by the telephone company. Leased lines are used to connect local area networks to remote locations or to the Internet through a service provider. Leased lines include T-1 and T-3 connections. T-1 is a digital connection running at 1.55 megabits per second (Mbps) and costs several thousand dollars per month. A T-3 connection is equivalent to 30 T-1 lines and connections can run up to 45 Mbps. The cost limits the use to major companies or large universities. There are even satellite modems (wireless) that are incredibly fast and at this time quite costly.

The growth of online services has made a modem or a digital connection a necessity. CompuServe, America Online, and Internet service providers—all leading to the information superhighway—make all kinds of information available. These services are the libraries of the future.

R.17   CAPACITY MEASUREMENT—BITS AND BYTES

A computer is made primarily of switches. All it can do is turn a switch on or off: 0 (zero) represents an off state and 1 (one) represents an on state. A *bit* (short for *binary digit*) is the smallest unit a computer can recognize. Bits are combined in meaningful groups, much as letters of the alphabet are combined to make words. A common grouping is eight bits, called a *byte*. A byte can be thought of as one character.

Computer capacities, such as RAM and ROM, are measured in bytes, originally grouped by thousands of bytes or *kilobytes* (*KB*), but now by millions of bytes or *megabytes* (*MB*, sometimes called *megs*), and *gigabytes* (*GB*, sometimes called *gigs*). A computer is binary, so it works in powers of 2. A kilobyte is 2 to the tenth power (1,024), and K or KB is the symbol for 1,024 bytes. If your computer has 64KB of memory, its actual memory size is 64 x 1,024, or 65,536 bytes. For simplification, KB is rounded off to 1,000, so that 64KB of memory means 64,000 bytes. Rapid technological growth has made megabytes the measuring factor.

You should know the capacity of your computer's memory because it determines how much data the computer can hold. For instance, if you have 32 MB of RAM on your computer and you buy a program that requires 64 MB of RAM, your computer will not have the memory capacity to use that program. Furthermore, if your computer has a hard disk capacity of 100 MB and the application program you buy requires at least 125 MB of space on the hard disk, you won't be able to install the program. Today, of course, a computer that has a hard disk of only 100 MB is very unlikely, but the principle remains the same—you have a specific amount of space on your hard disk and you can exceed the size of your hard disk if you have many large programs.

Disk capacity is also measured in bytes. A 3½-inch double-density disk holds 720KB. Because high-density and hard disks hold so much more information, they are also measured in megabytes. A 3½-inch high-density disk holds 1.44 MB. Hard disks vary in size, commonly ranging from 1.2 GB to over 20 GB. Today, most people consider an 8 GB hard disk a minimum requirement; it has a capacity of over eight billion bytes. Most computer users, when referring to gigabytes, use the term "gig." An 8.2 GB hard drive is referred to as an "eight point two gig" hard drive.

R.18   DISKS AND DISK DRIVES

Since RAM is volatile and disappears when the power is turned off, ***secondary storage media*** or external storage media are necessary to save information permanently.

Disks and disk drives are magnetic media that store data and programs in the form of magnetic impulses. Such media include floppy disks, hard disks, compact discs (CD-ROMs), digital videodiscs (DVDs), removable drives such as Zip and Jaz drives, tapes, and tape cartridges. In the microcomputer world, the most common secondary storage media are floppy disks and hard disks, with removable drives and read/write CD-ROMs rapidly becoming a standard for most users.

Storing information on a disk is equivalent to storing information in a file cabinet. Like file cabinets, disks store information in files. When the computer needs the information, it goes to the disk, opens a file, reads the information from the disk file into RAM, and works on it. When the computer is finished working on that file, it closes the file and returns (writes) it back to the disk. In most cases, this process does not occur automatically. The application program in use will have instructions that enable the user to save or write to the disk.

R.19   FLOPPY DISKS

Floppy disks serve a dual purpose. First, disks provide a permanent way to hold data. When power is turned off, the disk retains what has been recorded on it. Second, floppy disks are transportable. Programs or data developed on one computer can be used by another merely by inserting the disk into the other computer. If it were not for this capability, programs such as the operating system or other application packages could not be used. Each time you wanted to do some work, you would have to write your own instructions.

Floppy disks come in two sizes: 3½ inch and 5¼ inch. The standard size used to be the 5¼ inch, but now the 3½ inch is the standard. The 5¼-inch floppy disk, technically known as a minifloppy diskette, is rarely used today. The 3½-inch diskette is a microfloppy diskette, but both are commonly referred to as floppy disks. Like a phonograph record, the 5¼-inch floppy disk has a hole (called a hub) in the center so that it can fit on the disk drive's spindle.

The disk drive spins the disk to find information on it or to write information to it. Once a disk is locked into a disk drive, it spins at about 300 revolutions per minute. The 3½-inch disk, made of a circular piece of plastic, polyurethane, or Mylar covered with magnetic oxide, is enclosed in a rigid plastic shell. The 3½-inch, 720 KB diskette has a plastic shutter–covered hole in the upper-right corner. When the plastic shutter covers the opening, the disk can be written to. When it does not cover the opening, the disk is "write protected" and cannot be written or saved to. The 3½-inch, 1.44 MB disk also works the same way. It has an opening in the upper-left corner, although this opening does not have a plastic shutter. There is a metal shutter over the area of the disk where the computer writes to the disk. The computer's disk drive opens the shutter only when it needs access. When the disk is not in the drive, the metal shutter is closed. Figure R.7 shows a 3½-inch disk.

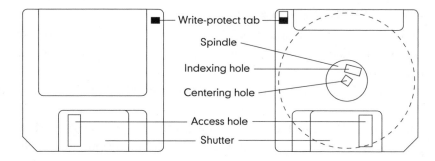

FIGURE R.7   A FLOPPY 3½-INCH DISK

R.20   CD-ROM

Today, a common transport device for software is a ***compact disc–read-only memory (CD-ROM)***. Borrowed from the music recording business, this disc can hold up to 600 MB of data and retrieves information by laser. Although originally a read-only device, CD-ROM drives are now readily available that both read from and write to a CD (CD-RWs). CD-ROM drives are commonplace, and most software companies are distributing their software via compact disc. The newest technology is ***DVD***. It is an enhancement of CD-ROM technology. It provides a new generation of optical-disc storage technology. It encompasses audio, video, and computer data. DVD was designed for multimedia applications with a key goal of being able to store a full-length feature film.

R.21   REMOVABLE DISKS

Recently, another type of external storage media has been developed—the removable disk. There are now hard disks that you can remove from a computer, making data portable. There are also other types of removable disk media. Two of the most common are Zip drives and Jaz drives. Zip drives come in two forms: permanent drives that are inside the computer, like a floppy drive, and portable drives that attach to the computer via a USB, serial, or SCSI port and can be moved from computer to computer easily. Zip drives use a diskette that is somewhat like a floppy disk in appearance. It can hold 100 MB of information—equivalent to more than 70 3½-inch floppy disks. Jaz drives use a cartridge rather than a disk. Currently, Jaz cartridges hold up to 2 gigabytes of data. The advent of these new disk types makes large amounts of data portable. Zip and Jaz drives read and write data more slowly than a hard disk. Zip drives in particular are becoming the popular alternative to floppy disks for storing and backing up user data.

R.22   HARD DISKS

A *hard disk*, also known as a fixed disk or a hard drive, is a nonremovable disk that is permanently installed in a system unit (see Figure R.8). A hard disk holds much more information than a removable floppy disk. If a floppy disk can be compared to a file cabinet that holds data and programs, a hard disk can be compared to a room full of file cabinets.

FIGURE R.8   A HARD DISK

A hard disk is composed of two or more rigid platters, usually made of aluminum and coated with oxide, which allow data to be encoded magnetically. Both the platters and the read/write heads are permanently sealed inside a box; the user cannot touch or see the drive or disks. These platters are affixed to a spindle that rotates at about 3,600 revolutions per minute (rpm), although this speed can vary. A hard disk drive is much faster than a standard floppy disk drive. The rapidly spinning disks in the sealed box create air pressure that lifts the recording heads above the surface of the platters. As the platters spin, the read/write heads float on a cushion of air.

Since a hard disk rotates faster than a floppy disk and since the head floats above the surface, the hard disk can store much more data and access it much more quickly than a floppy disk. Today, a common hard disk storage capacity is at least 10 gigabytes.

R.23   DIVIDING A DISK

A disk's structure is essentially the same whether it is a hard disk or a floppy disk. Data is recorded on the surface of a disk in a series of numbered concentric circles known as *tracks*, similar to the grooves in a phonograph record. Each track on the disk is a separate circle divided into numbered *sectors*. The amount of data that can be stored on a disk depends on the density of the disk—the number of tracks and the size of the sectors. Since a hard disk is comprised of several platters, it has an additional measurement, a *cylinder*. Two or more platters are stacked on top of one another with the tracks aligned. If you connect any one track through all the platters, you have a cylinder (see Figure R.9).

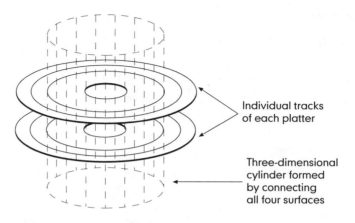

Individual tracks
of each platter

Three-dimensional
cylinder formed
by connecting
all four surfaces

FIGURE R.9   HARD DISK CYLINDERS

A *cluster* is the basic unit of disk storage. Whenever a computer reads from or writes to a disk, it always reads from and writes to a cluster, regardless of the space the data needs. Clusters are always made from adjacent sectors, from one to eight sectors or more. The location and number of sectors per cluster are determined by the software in a process known as formatting.

A disk is a random access medium, which does not mean that the data and/ or programs are randomly arranged on the disk. It means that the head of the disk drive, which reads the disk, does not have to read all the information on the disk to get a specific item. The CPU instructs the head of the disk drive to go directly to the track and sector that holds the specific item of information.

R.24   DISK DRIVES

A *disk drive* allows information to be written to and read from a disk. All disk drives have read/write heads, which read and write information back and forth between RAM and the disk, much like the ones on tape or video recorders.

A floppy disk drive is the device that holds a floppy disk. The user inserts a floppy disk into a disk drive (see Figure R.10). The hub of the disk fits onto the hub mechanism, which grabs the disk. When the disk drive door is shut, the disk is secured to the hub mechanism. The disk cover remains stationary while the floppy disk rotates. The disk drive head reads and writes information back and forth between RAM and the disk through the exposed head slot. Older disk drives are double-sided and can read from and write to both sides of a disk, but cannot read from or write to a high-density floppy disk. The current generation of high-density disk drives read from and write to both the old style floppy disk and the new style high-density disk.

3½-inch disk drive

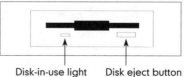

Disk-in-use light   Disk eject button

FIGURE R.10   A FLOPPY DISK DRIVE

R.25 DEVICE NAMES

A **device** is a place (a piece of hardware) for a computer to send information (write to) or a place from which to receive information (read from). In order for the system to know which device it is supposed to be communicating with at any given time, each device is given a specific and unique name. Device names, which are also known as reserved names, cannot be used for any other purpose. Disk drives are devices. A disk drive name is a letter followed by a colon.

Drive A: is the first floppy disk drive. Drive C: is the first hard disk drive. All other drives are lettered alphabetically from B: to Z:. You must be able to identify which disk drive you are using. There are certain rules that are *usually* followed. If you have two floppy drives that are stacked, the top one is Drive A. If you have two floppy drives side-by-side, the one on the left is Drive A. Today, usually users have one floppy disk (Drive A), one hard drive (Drive C), a removable drive (Drive D), and a CD-ROM drive (Drive E—although often the CD-ROM drive will have an assigned letter near the end of the alphabet such as R: to allow for the addition of more disk drives, both hard and removable, or for network drives). Some common examples are illustrated in Figure R.11.

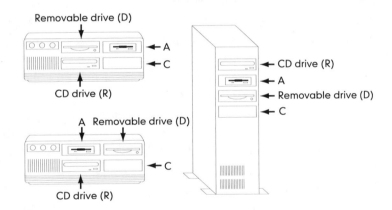

FIGURE R.11   DISK DRIVE CONFIGURATIONS

R.26 SOFTWARE

Up to this point, hardware is what has been discussed. However, software is what makes a computer useful. In fact, without software, hardware has no use. You can think of hardware as a box to run software. Software is the step-by-step instructions that tell the computer what to do. These instructions are called programs. Programs need to be installed or loaded into RAM, so that the CPU can execute them. Programs usually come stored on disks. A program is read into memory from a floppy disk, CD-ROM, or hard disk. Software can also be divided into categories. The most common division is application software and system software.

Application software, as its name suggests, is a set of instructions, a complete program, that directs the computer to solve a particular problem. Application software solves problems and handles information. It is a program designed to assist the user in the performance of a specific task, such as word processing, accounting, money management, or even games. Application software may also be called software packages, off-the-shelf software, canned software, or just software. There are thousands of commercially available application packages. You may have heard of application software by brand names such as WordPerfect (word processing), Excel (spreadsheet), Quicken (money management), or Doom (game). The reason most people purchase a computer is the availability of application software.

System software is also a set of instructions or programs. These programs coordinate the operations of all the various hardware components. System software is usually supplied by the computer manufacturer because it is necessary to run application software. System software is always computer-oriented rather than user-oriented; that is, it takes care of what the computer needs so the computer can run application software.

When you purchase a computer, you usually also purchase the operating system with it, preinstalled on the hard disk. The operating system supervises the processing of application programs and all the input/output of the computer. Running a computer is somewhat analogous to producing a concert. The hardware represents the musicians and their instruments. They do not change. The application software is like the score the musicians play, anything from Bach to Ricky Martin. The computer hardware can play any application software from an accounting program to a game. Like the conductor who tells the violins or trumpets when to play and how loudly, the operating system makes the computer work. It is the first and most important program on the computer and *must* be loaded into memory (RAM) before any other program.

Typically, operating systems are comprised of several important programs stored as system files. These include a program that transfers data to and from the disk and into and out of memory and that performs other disk-related tasks. Other important programs handle hardware-specific tasks. These programs check such things as whether a key has been pressed and, if it has, they encode it so that the computer can read it and then decode it so that it may be written to the screen. This program also encodes and decodes bits and bytes into letters and words.

The term *operating system* is generic. Brand names for microcomputer operating systems include System 7, Unix, Linux, MS-DOS, and UCSD-P. The most popular operating system for microcomputers has been Windows 98, which Microsoft Corporation developed and owns. It was the upgrade from Windows 95. Windows 98 is licensed to computer manufacturers, who tailor it to their specific hardware. In addition, users purchased Windows 98 commercially either as an upgrade to Windows 95 or as a complete package (if the user has purchased a computer with no operating system on it).

Microsoft also has a version of Windows called Windows NT Server that is designed for networked computers, with an iteration called Windows NT Workstation as a desktop interface.

In 2000, Microsoft introduced both Windows 2000 and Windows Millennium Edition (Windows Me). Windows Me is designed for the home computer user and can be considered an upgrade to Windows 98. Windows 2000 is a family of operating systems that consists of Windows 2000 Server, Windows 2000 Advanced Server, Windows 2000 Datacenter Server, and Windows 2000 Professional. Windows 2000 Server replaces Windows NT 4.0. Incorporating many new features and functions, Windows 2000 Server is powerful, yet easy to manage, and is designed for the small to medium business organization with many computers that need to share data and resouces. Windows 2000 Professional replaces Windows NT 4.0 Workstation, incorporating many new features and functions. Windows 2000 Professional is an operating system that is designed for corporate and high-end users who want a robust and powerful operating environment.

Most people who use a computer are interested in application software. They want programs that are easy to use. If you are going to use a computer and run application packages, you are going to need to know how to use the operating system first. No application program can be used without an operating system. Since Windows Millennium Edition is the newest microcomputer operating system in use today, this textbook is devoted to teaching the concepts of the operating system in general and Windows Millennium Edition operations in particular.

R.27   OPERATING SYSTEM FUNDAMENTALS

Windows Millennium Edition is a program that is always working. No computer hardware can work unless it has an operating system in RAM. When you ***boot the system***, you load the operating system software into RAM.

Some of the operating system (OS) software is built into the hardware. When you turn on the computer or "power up," the computer would not know what to do if there were no program directing it. The read-only memory chip called ROM-BIOS (read-only memory–basic input/output system), abbreviated to RIOS, is built into the hardware of the microcomputer system. ROM-BIOS programs provide the interface between the hardware and the operating system.

When you turn on the computer, the power goes first to ROM-BIOS. The first set of instructions is to run a self-test to check the hardware. The program checks RAM and the equipment attached to the computer. Thus, before getting started, the user knows whether or not there is a hardware failure. Once the self-test is completed successfully, the next job or program to execute is loading the operating system.

When the operating system loads, ROM-BIOS checks to see if a disk drive is installed. In today's computers, it is possible to tell the computer where you want it to load the operating system from. It can go first to the A drive to see if there is a disk there. If it finds none, it can then go to the C drive. The OS is looking for a special program called the ***boot record***. A computer can also be set up to boot from a CD-ROM or from another peripheral disk drive, such as a Zip or Jaz drive. These drives are attached to the computer by an internal interface card or a parallel port. If ROM-BIOS does not find the boot record in any of the drives it was set to look at or if there is something wrong with the boot record, you will get an error message. If the ROM-BIOS program does find the proper boot record, it reads the record from the disk into RAM and turns control over to this program. The boot record is also a program that executes; its job is to read into RAM the rest of the operating system, in essence, pulling the system up by its bootstraps. Thus, one boots the computer instead of merely turning it on.

The operating system files loaded into RAM manage the resources and primary functions of the computer, freeing application programs from worrying about how the document gets from the keyboard to RAM and from RAM to the screen. This whole process can be considered analogous to driving an automobile. Most of us use our cars to get from point A to point B. We would not like it if every time we wanted to drive we first had to open the hood and attach the proper cables to the battery and to all the other parts that are necessary to start the engine. The operating system is the engine of the computer that lets the user run the application as if driving a car.

R.28 WHY WINDOWS MILLENNIUM EDITION?

Previously, the most popular operating system was MS-DOS, a character-based operating system. In order to use it, you had to key in commands and did not use a pointing device such as a mouse. Each application program running under this operating system was installed as a separate entity—there was no sharing of resources, such as a printer, and no ability to run more than one application at a time.

In 1990 Microsoft released the first successful version of Windows, version 3.0—an "environment" that worked between the operating system and application programs. Windows introduced the PC user to a *graphical user interface*, referred to as a *GUI*. In the 3.0 version of Windows, commands could be issued by clicking a mouse. Peripheral devices such as printers were installed in Windows and were thus available to all the applications. Application programs were written to run under Windows. Windows offered the advantage of being able to run more than one program at a time in order to share data between programs. Windows for Workgroups was next introduced, which had built-in networking features for a peer-to-peer network. The last releases of these versions of Windows were Windows 3.1 and Windows for Workgroups 3.11.

In 1995, Microsoft introduced the Windows 95 operating system, an operating system that no longer required DOS as a stand-alone operating system. DOS and Windows became integrated into one operating system. The change from Windows 3.x to Windows 95 was dramatic. One of the biggest improvements was the change from a 16-bit operating system to a 32-bit operating system. This change took advantage of the power and speed of new microprocessors. Built with new architecture (design), Windows 95 was faster, handled computer resources better, improved the system capacity to run more applications, and was more robust. Robust means, among other things, that if an application program does not work, the system will not crash (cease to function). Instead, Windows 95 allowed you the opportunity to close an aberrant program so that you could continue your work.

Windows 95 introduced plug and play. Prior to the introduction of the Windows 95 plug-and-play standard, adding devices to a PC was a painful process. A lack of coordination between the hardware and software caused devices to conflict with one another. Furthermore, application software had no idea what devices were on the system. The different bus standards for different devices complicated the issue further. Plug and play lets devices "talk" to Windows 95, which then handles how the programs use the devices. This feature allows users to buy new devices, plug them into the computer, and allow Windows 95 to handle the "dirty" work.

Although the design of Windows 95 was important in terms of new hardware, for most users the change that they saw was in the user interface. The Windows 95 user interface was intended to be more intuitive and easier to use. Features like wizards led you through things you did not know how to do. Windows 95 also allowed you to use both the right and left mouse buttons and provided context-sensitive menus at a mere click of the mouse.

The move to Windows 98 from Windows 95 was less dramatic. Although the core operating system was improved for better performance, Windows 98 was essentially the same. In many ways it looked the same as Windows 95. What Windows 98 did was point the user into a new direction—the Internet. A basic design consideration for Windows 95 was a consistent visual and functional view of your computer system. Windows 98 and Internet Explorer Version 5.0 (the Windows 98 Web browser—Internet Explorer Version 5.5 has just been released) were intended to be integrated so that many of the Windows 98 functions work like a Web browser. This feature was designed to make users' transitions from their local computers to the Internet seamless and easy. There was another release of Windows called Windows 98 SE (Special Edition).

Windows Millennium Edition is designed specifically for home users and small businesses, whereas the family of Windows 2000 is designed for medium to large businesses that process large volumes of business transactions and that must maintain security. Windows Me is intended to make using a computer easier and to take advantage of new consumer technologies, such as interactive TV and digital photography.

Now that it is more common for home users to have more than one computer, Windows Me gives you the ability to network all of your home computers. It also lets you communicate more efficiently over the Internet and allows you to work with multimedia content, such as photos, videos, and music. It has many wizards, and Help has been improved, making troubleshooting problems easier. It includes a movie maker that lets you transfer video. It supports Universal Plug and Play, a developing technology that will allow future intelligent devices (such as specialized VCRs and thermostats) to be controlled from your computer.

Although Windows Me does not introduce any dramatic changes, such as those that differentiated Windows 3.1 from Windows 95, it does include of dozens of fixes, system tweaks, and upgrades to maximize the power of your computer. These improvements can be categorized as follows:

- **Computer safety and help**

  System File Protection is a feature that assists the user when installing new software. Some software installation programs would replace an important Windows Me file with an older version, which could cause your computer to malfunction. System File Protection prevents this from happening.

  System Restore is a feature that knows the condition of its own system files prior to installing new hardware or software. If your new addition causes your computer to malfunction, you may "roll back" to your earlier version when your computer worked properly.

Help in Windows Me has been greatly changed from previous versions of Windows. The new Help gathers all on-screen help systems into a single program called the Help and Support Center. In addition to Windows Help, it also has direct links to Web pages.

The Automatic Update feature will check the Microsoft Web site to check for updates, fixes, and patches to Windows Me, then downloads any it thinks your system needs and provides a menu that offers to install those fixes. This feature can be diabled.

Improved utilities, troubleshooting, and error messages are existing programs that have been improved to be faster and more reliable. Troubleshooters, first introduced in Windows 98, are step-by-step guides to assist you in solving problems. These troubleshooters have been improved and new ones have been added. In addition, many Windows error messages have been rewritten to provide better help.

- **Multimedia**
  Windows Me makes it easier to use the next generation of digital cameras and scanners. In addition, Windows Me includes Movie Maker, which allows you to get images from your camcorder, VCR, and so on. To use this feature, you must have special equipment—a video-capture card or the combination of a digital camcorder and a FireWire card. Windows Me also comes with version 7 of Media Player, which lets you play movies, listen to radio stations over the Internet, and transfer music files to your portable MP3 player.

- **Games**
  Windows Me has a new set of games, some of which even allow you to play other people over the Internet.

- **Connectivity**
  Windows Me provides an easy way to set up an Internet account and also comes with Internet Explorer 5.5 as its Web browser. IE 5.5 has better printing capabilities. Windows Me includes a Home Networking wizard that walks you through connecting two or more computers together.

The Windows Millennium Edition GUI is highly customizable. The user can choose to have the look of the desktop identical to Windows 95/98 or customized to each user's preferences. This textbook is a guide to understanding and using the Windows Millennium Edition operating system with its new features.

R.29 HARDWARE REQUIREMENTS FOR WINDOWS MILLENNIUM EDITION

Windows Millennium Edition is a powerful operating system. Although you can run your old programs under Windows Millennium Edition, you will find yourself buying the new, improved versions of your favorite application programs. However, these programs are powerful and large. To run Windows Millennium Edition, you need at least a Pentium or equivalent, 150 MHz or higher processor, at least 32 MB of RAM, a high-density disk drive, a CD-ROM or DVD drive, and a hard disk drive with at least 480 MB available. You might need up to 635 MB of free hard disk space, depending on what you install. A typical installation requires about 350 MB of available disk space. Furthermore, you need a VGA monitor and VGA display adapter or better. You will also need a pointing device, such as a mouse or trackball, and a keyboard. With this hardware, you can run Windows Millennium Edition and applications written for Windows Millennium Edition. This configuration is the absolute minimum.

A desirable configuration for Windows Millennium Edition is listed below:

Processor	Intel Pentium III 500 MHz or better
Cache	512 KB internal L2 cache
RAM	256 MB
Hard drive	14.4 GB with at least 1.5 GB free
Floppy drive	3½ inch
Removable drive	Zip drive
Monitor	19-inch high-resolution noninterlaced
Graphics	A video card with at least 32 MB of memory
CD	48X CD-ROM or better and DVD if you play many games
Modem	56K, unless you plan on using a cable or DSL modem
Sound system	Sound card with speakers and/or headphones
Input devices	Keyboard and mouse

Other features that you might want to use also require other hardware:
• Microphone to record sound files
• TV Tuner card and a TV antenna or cable connection if you want to receive TV stations on your computer
• Digital camera to move graphics to your computer
• Game controller to play certain video games
• Network Interface Card to set up a home network

In computers, and especially in Windows Millennium Edition, more is better—faster processor, more memory, more disk space.

R.30 NETWORKS

Today, it is likely that you will be using a network in a work or lab environment. A *network* is two or more connected computers, and it usually has various peripheral devices such as printers. A network allows users to communicate with each other and to share information and devices. Special operating system software and hardware are required for networking. Network software permits information exchange among users; the most common uses are electronic mail (email) and the sharing of files. With email, users can send and receive messages within the network system. Sharing files allows users to share information.

There are two kinds of networks. A *local area network (LAN)* encompasses a small area such as one office. The hardware components such as the server, the terminals, and printers are directly connected by cables. (See Figure R.12.) A *wide area network (WAN)* connects computers over a much larger area such as from building to building, state to state, or even worldwide. Hardware components of the WAN communicate over telephone lines, fiber-optic cables, or satellites. The Internet is an example of a WAN.

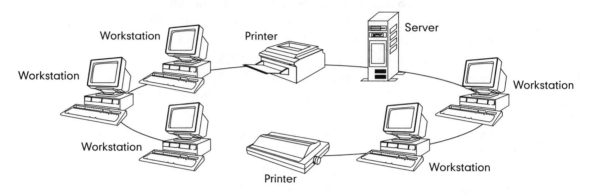

FIGURE R.12 A TYPICAL NETWORK CONFIGURATION

CHAPTER SUMMARY

This chapter discussed the fundamental operations of a computer. All computers function the same way. Data is input, processed, and stored. The results are the output. Hardware components include the system unit, the monitor, the keyboard, and the printer. The central processing unit (CPU) is the brain of the computer and can comprehend and carry out instructions sent to it by a program. RAM (random access memory) is the workspace of the computer. RAM is volatile. Cache memory is high-speed memory that stores the most recently used data. ROM (read-only memory) is a chip with programs written on it. ROM is not volatile. It usually holds the startup routines of a computer. CD-ROM drives are used to import data and install software from compact discs.

Adapter cards are printed circuit boards that allow a user to add various peripheral devices to a computer. Peripherals are devices that are attached to the system unit. All of these features are integrated by I/O buses, which are the connections through which data travels. The most common input devices are the keyboard and the mouse. The most common output devices are the monitor and the printer. Modems allow the transmission of data over telephone lines and allow computers to communicate.

Floppy disks, hard disks, removable disks, and compact discs are means of permanent storage for data and programs. A floppy disk is a piece of plastic inside a jacket. A hard disk is made of rigid platters that are permanently sealed inside a box. A compact disc can handle up to 600 MB of data, which makes it a great device for transporting information. All disks are divided into numbered tracks and sectors so that a computer can locate information.

A floppy disk drive is the device into which a floppy disk is inserted so that the computer can read from or write to it. Disk drives have reserved names that consist of a letter of the alphabet followed by a colon. The left or top disk drive is known as Drive A. The first hard disk drive is known as Drive C.

A byte represents a single character. The capacity of some floppy disks is measured in bytes, usually thousands of bytes, or kilobytes (KB). The capacity of RAM, ROM, and high-density floppy disks is measured in millions of bytes, or megabytes (MB), often referred to as megs. Hard drive capacity is referred to in gigabytes (GB).

Software is the step-by-step instructions that tell the computer what to do. These instructions are called programs. Programs are loaded into RAM, where the CPU executes each instruction. When programs are working in RAM, it is referred to as running or executing the program. Programs are stored on disks and loaded into RAM from disks. Software is divided into application software and system software. Application software solves problems, handles information, and is user-oriented. System software coordinates the operation of the hardware, is mandatory for running application software, and is computer-oriented. An operating system is comprised of programs, called system software, that perform the functions necessary to control the operations of the computer. The operating system interfaces with the user and tells the computer what to do.

Networks are two or more computers connected together that usually share peripheral devices such as printers. There are two basic types of networks: LANs and WANs. A LAN (local area network) is usually connected by cables within a small area. A WAN (wide area network) connects computers over a much larger area, from building to building to worldwide.

Windows Millennium Edition, the newest operating system in use today, is a graphical operating system that is user friendly, which makes the use of operating system commands easier.

KEY TERMS

adapter card	controller	hardware
application software	cylinder	impact printer
bandwidth	data	inkjet printer
bit	device	interface card
boot record	disk drive	interlaced
boot the system	dot pitch	kilobyte (KB)
bus	DVD	laser printer
byte	dynamic RAM (DRAM)	local area network (LAN)
cache memory	expansion slot	meg
card	floppy disk	megabyte (MB)
central processing unit	gig	megahertz (MHz)
(CPU)	gigabyte (GB)	memory
cluster	graphical user interface	modem
compact disc–read-only	(GUI)	monitor
memory (CD-ROM)	hard disk	motherboard

mouse	random access memory	static RAM (SRAM)
network	(RAM)	system board
nonimpact printer	read-only memory (ROM)	system software
noninterlaced	resolution	track
parallel port	ROM-BIOS	trackball
peripheral device	secondary storage media	Universal Serial Bus (USB)
pixel	sector	wide area network (WAN)
port	serial port	Wintel
program	software	

DISCUSSION QUESTIONS

1. Define hardware.
2. Define software.
3. What is data?
4. What is meant by the system configuration?
5. Describe a typical computer configuration.
6. What are interface cards? How may they be used?
7. What is the purpose and function of a bus?
8. Compare and contrast RAM, cache, and ROM.
9. Why are parallel and serial ports necessary? What are they used for?
10. List two input devices and two output devices and briefly explain how these devices work.
11. What purposes do disks serve?
12. What is the difference between disk storage and memory capacity?
13. What is a CD-ROM? A DVD?
14. What is the difference between a hard disk and a floppy disk?
15. What are tracks and sectors? Where are they found?
16. What is a cluster? What is it comprised of?
17. What is a device? Give three examples of devices.
18. Identify and define two types of modem connections.
19. Compare and contrast floppy disks, removable disks, CD-ROMs, DVDs, and hard disks.
20. Define an operating system.
21. Compare and contrast application software with system software.
22. Can application packages run without an operating system? Why or why not?
23. What is the function of an operating system?
24. What are the advantages of using Windows Millennium Edition?
25. What is the purpose and function of a network?

TRUE/FALSE QUESTIONS

For each question, circle the letter T if the statement is true or the letter F if the statement is false.

T   F   1. The system board contains components such as the CPU and RAM.

T   F   2. An interface card is a printed circuit board that enables a computer to use a peripheral device.

T   F   3. A monitor is a common input device.

T   F   4. A hard disk is a read-only device.

T   F   5. By themselves, the hardware components of a computer can do nothing.

COMPLETION QUESTIONS

Write the correct answer in each blank space.

6. A(n) _____ is a common path across which data can travel within a computer.

7. The components of a complete computer system are also called the _____.

8. Frequently used RAM data is stored in _____, which speeds up the process of data access.

9. The two most common ports available on computers are the _____ and _____ ports.

10. People purchase a computer because of the availability of _____.

MATCHING QUESTIONS

Match each term in the left-hand column with the proper definition in the right-hand column.

11. Hardware
12. Software
13. Floppy disk drive
14. RAM
15. Booting the system

a. Instructions that tell the computer what operations to perform
b. Tangible, physical part of a computer
c. Device where a floppy disk is inserted
d. Powering on a computer and loading the operating system
e. Workspace of the computer

MULTIPLE CHOICE QUESTIONS

For each question, write the letter for the correct answer in the blank space.

16. The physical components of a computer are called
    a. software.
    b. firmware.
    c. hardware.
    d. none of the above

17. Memory that disappears when the computer's power is turned off is considered
    a. volatile.
    b. nonvolatile.
    c. vital.
    d. nonvital.

18. The central processing unit
    a. is the workspace of the computer.
    b. comprehends and carries out instructions sent to it by a program.
    c. both a and b
    d. neither a nor b

19. Disks are divided into numbered
    a. tracks and sectors.
    b. bits and bytes.
    c. RAM and ROM.
    d. none of the above

20. An example of an input device is a
    a. monitor.
    b. keyboard.
    c. mouse.
    d. both b and c

APPLICATION ASSIGNMENT—BRIEF ESSAY

You are going to buy a computer system. You have a budget of $2,500. Write a report listing the features and specifications of the computer system you would like to purchase. (Do not include a printer in your system.) Be very specific in regards to the amount of RAM, the size of the hard drive or drives, the number and type of floppy drives and removable drives, monitor type, and so on.

GETTING STARTED WITH THE OPERATING SYSTEM

LEARNING OBJECTIVES

After completing this chapter, you will be able to:

1. Define *operating system*.
2. Define *enhancements*.
3. Explain the function and purpose of OS version numbers.
4. List some of the types of system configurations.
5. Explain the need and procedure for booting the system.
6. Explain the function of disk files.
7. Explain the function of and rules for file specifications.
8. List and explain the importance of the two types of computer files.
9. Describe the function and purpose of commands.
10. Compare and contrast internal and external commands.
11. Describe four keyboard groups and explain the purpose of each group of keys.
12. Explain the function and purpose of the DIR, VER, and CLS commands.
13. Explain the purpose of and the procedure for using the DATE and TIME commands.
14. Explain the legal and ethical ramifications of copying disks that were not purchased.
15. Explain the purpose and function of the DISKCOPY command.
16. Explain the necessary steps to end a work session.

STUDENT OUTCOMES

1. Identify your system configuration.
2. Boot the system.
3. Use the DIR command to display the files on the screen.
4. Cancel a command.
5. Use the VER command to determine which version of DOS is being used.
6. Use the CLS command to clear the screen.
7. Use the DATE and TIME commands to set or change the date and time on the computer.
8. Make a copy of a disk.
9. End a computer work session.

CHAPTER OVERVIEW

Most people who use computers are really interested in application software. They want programs that are easy to use and that help them solve specific problems. However, before you can use application software, you must know at least the basics of using the operating system. No computer can work without an operating system in RAM. The Windows operating system takes care of the mandatory functions for computer operations such as handling the input and output of the computer, managing computer resources, and running application software. It enables the user to communicate with the computer.

In this chapter you will learn about loading the operating system into the computer, familiarize yourself with the keyboard, use some basic commands, make a copy of the ACTIVITIES disk to use in future activities, learn your system configuration, and identify the version of Windows you are using.

1.1   WHAT IS AN OPERATING SYSTEM?

An ***operating system*** is a software program. If you have a microcomputer, commonly referred to as a PC, that conforms to the standards developed by IBM and uses a microprocessor in the Intel family, you are probably using a version of the Windows operating system. In fact, these computers are becoming known as ***Wintel*** machines because they use the Intel processor and run the Windows operating system.

You need to load the Windows operating system (the OS) into memory (RAM) before you can use other software programs. The OS is in charge of the hardware components of the computer. You, the user, communicate what you want the computer to do through the OS. These commands are issued by pointing and clicking in the graphical user interface (GUI) or by keying in commands such as TYPE or CLS at the command line prompt.

1.2　VERSIONS OF THE OPERATING SYSTEM (OS)

Microsoft periodically releases new versions of the OS to take advantage of new technology. These new upgrades contain enhancements. The term *enhancements* simply means that more functions and/or commands are available. In addition, new versions of software and operating systems fix problems, called *bugs,* that appeared in earlier versions. To keep track of these versions, each new version is assigned a number. The first version of Windows 95 was Windows 95 4.00.950, released in 1995. The last Windows 95 version was 95 4.00.1111, known as Windows 95B or OSR2. Also available is a major update of Windows 95 called Windows 98, SE version 4.10.1998. At this time, the most recent version of Windows is Windows Millennium Edition, referred to as Windows Me (Version 4.90.3000).

This text is generally applicable to all versions of the Windows operating system. It is assumed in this textbook that Windows Me is installed on the hard disk or the network server. If you are working on your own computer and have not installed or upgraded to Windows Me, refer to the documentation that came with the Windows software so you can initiate the installation or upgrade. If you are in a laboratory environment, a version of Windows will be available for you.

1.3　OVERVIEW OF FILES AND DISKS

You need a way to store information permanently. In the microcomputer world, the primary way to save data and programs permanently is to store them on a disk. After you have booted your computer, the OS reads the programs or data it needs from the disk into its memory. However, in order for Windows to find this information, it has to have a way of organizing it, which it does by keeping programs and data in files on the disk. Just as you organize your written work in files, Windows organizes computer information in disk files.

A *disk file* is much like a file folder stored in a file cabinet. The file cabinet is the floppy disk or the hard disk. A file consists of related information stored on the disk in a "folder" or directory with a unique name. Information with which a computer works is contained and stored in files on the disk. (See Figure 1.1.)

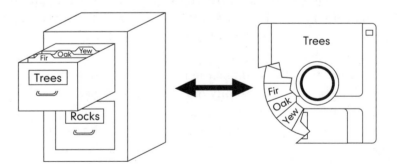

FIGURE 1.1　DISKS AND FILES

1.4   FILE NAMES, FILE TYPES, AND FOLDERS

Because computers must follow very specific rules, there is a specific format for file names. Technically, a file name is called the *file specification*. The first rule is that the file specification must be unique. Second, the file specification is broken into two parts, a *file name* and a *file extension*. The file name typically describes or identifies the file, and the file extension typically identifies the kind of data in the file. Since the term *file specification* is rather awkward, most people simply refer to the file name, meaning both the file name and its extension. In versions of the OS before Windows, referred to simply as DOS, you were limited in file name size. It was called the 8.3 rule (eight-dot-three rule), which was a limit of eight characters for the file name and three characters for the file extension. In Windows, those limits are gone. Now file names can have a maximum of 255 characters, referred to as LFNs (long file names). The three-letter file extension, known as the file type, remains in Windows. However, some software does not recognize long file names (LFNs), and some network operating systems have difficulty dealing with them. Because the storing of long file names takes additional space, consider using the 8.3 rule when saving to floppy disks with limited capacity.

There are two major types of computer files: *data files* and *program files*. Data files contain information that is usually generated by an application program. Most often, only an application program can use a data file directly. Program files are application programs that allow a user to perform specific tasks, for example, a payroll program that lets you create and maintain a payroll system for a company.

You do not purchase a computer to run the Windows operating system. You purchase a computer so that you may use application packages to help with tasks such as gaining access to the Internet, writing letters, managing your checkbook, doing your taxes, or creating a budget. If you needed to employ someone to do these tasks for you, you might go to a temporary employment agency and hire a secretary to write your letters or an accountant to manage your checkbook and taxes.

In the computer world, you purchase application packages, so that you can do the work. These application packages fall into generic categories such as word processing or spreadsheet programs. In the same way you would choose a specific temporary employee such as Mr. Woo for your letter writing, in the computer world, you choose application packages by their names. They have brand names such as WordPerfect, Quicken, or Lotus 1-2-3. These application packages are "employees" you choose to do the work.

In order for these application programs to do work, they must be copied from where they are installed (usually the hard drive, or perhaps the network drive) into RAM, the workspace of the computer. They are "temporary" employees because you call on them only when you need to do a specific task that they can accomplish. Windows is like an office manager who goes to the disk to get the correct file and place it in RAM. This process is known as loading the program from disk into memory. Windows then lets the program do its job. This process is known as executing the program. Program files are step-by-step instructions that direct the computer to do something.

Even though WordPerfect can create letters for anyone, you are interested only in the letters *you* create—the information that *you* want. Once you create your data, you also want to keep it. Remember, all the work occurs in RAM, and RAM is volatile (temporary). In order to keep information permanently, you direct WordPerfect to write (save) the information to disk as a data file. WordPerfect actually does not save the data; instead, it turns to the operating system, which does the actual work of writing the file to disk. When you need to retrieve the information to alter it, WordPerfect again turns to the OS to retrieve the file. Windows then reads the disk to retrieve the appropriate data file and gives it to WordPerfect.

A unique name must be assigned to each file so that it can be identified by the OS. Program files have predetermined names such as WPWIN.EXE for WordPerfect, QW.EXE for Quicken, or 123.EXE for Lotus 1-2-3. WPWIN is the file name and .EXE is the file extension. Clicking on the application icon tells Windows to retrieve the program from the disk and place it in memory so you may work. When you install the application program you wish to use, it creates the icon, which actually is a reference to the name and location of the program file so that Windows can find and load it. Data files, on the other hand, are named by you, the user. You may call the files anything that you want. For instance, a file name for a letter to your sister might be SISTER.LET or a name for your budget file might be BUDGET97.WK1. Typically, in the Windows environment, application programs assign a file extension such as .DOC or .WK1 to identify the data file as a document file belonging to a specific application program.

The above file specifications conform to the older DOS limitations of eight characters for a name and three characters for an extension. In Windows, the data file could have been named BUDGET FOR 1997.WK1. However, if you had an older version of Lotus 1-2-3 that was not able to handle long file names, Lotus would have generated an error message to you saying that the file name was invalid.

A file name is mandatory, but a file extension is not. A file name typically identifies the file, such as WP for word processing or SISTER for your letter. The file name tells you about the file, and the file type (extension) identifies the kind of data in a file. For instance, .EXE is reserved for programs so that Windows knows the file is a worker, not a data file; in a program like WPWIN.EXE, the extension .EXE stands for executable code.

Data files are generated by specific application programs, and the information or data in them can be altered or viewed only within the application package. You would not give your tax information to an administrative assistant to make changes. You would give that data to the accountant, who knows how to make the changes.

Data files do not stand alone. They can be used only in conjunction with an application program. Again, the job of the operating system is to fetch and carry both program files and data files in and out of memory and to and from the disk (reading and writing). In addition, since the OS is the "office manager," you may also use it to do office-related tasks such as copying or deleting a file. The OS does not know what is in the file folder, nor can it make changes to the information in the file folder. It can only manipulate the file folder by performing such tasks as copying the information in it or throwing it away.

To assist you in organizing your information further, the OS can divide or structure your disks into what are called folders or directories. Technically they are subdirectories, but the terms directory, subdirectory, and folder are used interchangeably. Folders allow you to group related program or data files so they will be easy to locate later. For instance, all the files related to a spreadsheet program such as Lotus 1-2-3 could be stored in a folder named LOTUS. You might then group any data files you created with Lotus, such as BUDGET93.WK1 and APRIL97.WK1, in another folder called BUDGETS.

A primary directory (root) is automatically created when you prepare a disk to store information. It is named and called the root directory, but its symbol is \ (the backslash). You can create additional folders (subdirectories) for storing related files. Directories, including the root, will be discussed in full detail in later chapters.

1.5   IDENTIFYING YOUR SYSTEM CONFIGURATION

All computers come with disk drives: the floppy disk drive, the hard or fixed disk drive, usually a CD-ROM drive, and sometimes a large capacity removable drive, such as a Zip drive or a DVD drive. Today there are many ways that computer systems can be configured:

- One hard disk drive, one CD-ROM drive, and one floppy disk drive.
- One hard disk drive, one CD-ROM drive, one floppy disk drive, and one ZIP drive.
- Two hard drives, one CD-ROM drive, and one floppy disk drive.
- One hard drive, one CD-ROM drive, one Read-Write CD-ROM, and one floppy disk drive.

The possibilities are numerous. Computers can be configured to suit the needs of the individual user.

1.6   COMPUTER CONFIGURATION GUIDE

This textbook is based on a specific computer configuration, the one that is most common to PC users.

Hard disk	C:
Floppy disk drive to be used	A:
Location of Windows utility files	C:\WINDOWS\COMMAND
Path set to (Include)	C:\WINDOWS\COMMAND
Windows files	C:\WINDOWS
Displayed screen prompt for Drive C	C:\>
Activities folder on Drive C	C:\WINDOSBK
Displayed prompt for floppy disk	A:\>

If your computer configuration conforms to the above listing, you can follow the textbook without making any adjustments. However, computer configuration setups vary, particularly on network systems. Thus, your system configuration may be different, and you might have to *substitute what is on your system* for the setups used in this textbook. Complete the following table so that the substitutions will be readily identifiable for your computer:

Description	Book Reference	Your System
Hard drive	C:	
Floppy drive	A:	
Location of OS utility files	C:\WINDOWS\COMMAND	
Path set to (Include)	C:\WINDOWS\COMMAND	
Windows Millennium files	C:\WINDOWS	
Displayed prompt for Drive C	C:\>	
Activities folder on Drive C	C:\WINDOSBK	
Prompt for floppy disk	A:\>	

1.7 BOOTING THE SYSTEM

You need to know how to get the operating system files from the bootable disk into memory (RAM) so that you can use the computer. With the Windows operating system, this happens automatically when you turn the system on. This process is known as ***booting the system***. These files reside on the hard disk; however, these files can be placed on a floppy disk so that you can boot the computer with minimum system files from Drive A. The following activity allows you to have your first hands-on experience with the computer. You are going to load Windows or "boot the system."

Note: Since laboratory procedures will vary, check with your instructor before proceeding with these activities. A special process may be needed to boot the system if you are on a network.

1.8 ACTIVITY: BOOTING THE SYSTEM

Step 1   Check to see if the monitor has a separate on/off switch. If it does, turn on the monitor.

Step 2   Be sure there is no disk in Drive A. If your Drive A has a door that shuts or latches, be sure it is open. (Remember that your instructions may be different if you are booting to a network.) Power on the computer by locating the Power button and pressing it. The Power button location can vary, depending on the design of the computer.

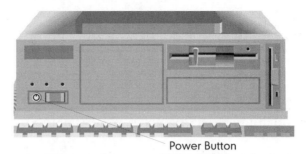

Power Button

FIGURE 1.2   POWERING ON THE COMPUTER

WHAT'S HAPPENING? ➤   The system checks itself in the diagnostic routine. You may see information on the screen about your computer. After the system check is complete, the computer loads the Windows operating system into RAM from the hard disk (or network server). It reads the hidden files, **IO.SYS** and **MSDOS.SYS**, as well as other system files. When this happens, the disk drive makes a buzzing noise and a light on the drive flashes on, letting you know that the system is reading the disk. This process will take time. While the operating system is loading, the screen displays the Windows logo screen. When the loading is complete, you will be looking at the Windows desktop.

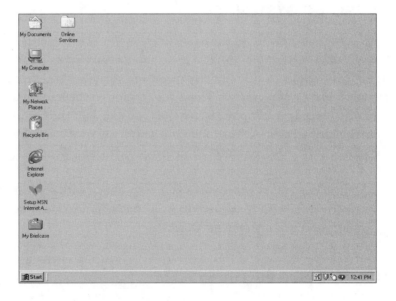

WHAT'S HAPPENING? ➤   You have successfully booted the system.

1.9   SHUTTING DOWN THE SYSTEM

It is very important that you shut down Windows Millennium computers correctly every time. When you go through the shut-down process, Windows writes certain information to the disk. If you simply turn off the computer, Windows will not have an opportunity to take care of the process it needs to go through to shut down.

Simply turning off the computer could "crash" the system, and you might be unable to boot the next time it is turned on.

1.10 ACTIVITY: THE WINDOWS SHUT-DOWN PROCEDURE

Step 1   Click the **Start** button on the lower-left corner of the screen. ("Click" means to place the point of the arrow over the word **Start** and press the left button on the mouse once.)

Step 2   Click **Shut Down**.

WHAT'S HAPPENING? ▶ Your dialog box may vary, depending on the version of Windows you are using or if you are on a network, or have set up profiles. If **Shut Down** does not appear in the drop-down window, click and hold on the down arrow and slide down to **Shut Down**.

Step 3   Click **OK**.

WHAT'S HAPPENING? ▶ On many computers today, the power will shut off automatically. On a computer that automatically shuts down, the screen will simply go blank, and you may not have to complete Step 4. On others, you will see a screen similar to the following:

Step 4   Turn off the Power switch. Turn off the monitor.

WHAT'S HAPPENING? ▶ You have successfully shut down Windows.

1.11 WHY DOS?

Since Windows is a GUI (graphical user interface), when you boot the system, you open the desktop with icons, menus, and pictures. You will run your programs and open your data files by clicking or double-clicking icons or menu choices. You accomplish tasks such as copying a file by opening the Windows Explorer window, selecting a file with your mouse, and dragging it to a different location, a procedure known as drag-and-drop. These are the reasons why a GUI is so popular. It is "user friendly."

In character-based operating systems, with DOS being the most common, all you would see on the screen after you booted would be a prompt such as C:\>—no picture, no icons, no drag-and-drop. In order to accomplish any task, you need to know what command to use. For instance, to copy a file in a character-based operating system, you would need to key in *COPY THIS.FIL THAT.FIL*. This means you would need to know the command and how to use it. Hardly as easy as a drag-and-drop operation!

Why then, you may ask yourself, would you ever need to learn the "hard, archaic way" of using your computer when you can easily use the new, improved way? In fact, if you talk to many people, they would say to you, "DOS is dead; long live Windows." They would also say, "You don't need to know DOS anymore because it is all Windows." Those people are only somewhat right. They are correct in saying that DOS as a stand-alone operating system is dead. A new computer comes with Windows as its operating system, not DOS. But they are wrong in assuming that you do not need to know DOS.

What they do not understand, and you will after completing this text, is that what they refer to as DOS is really the command line interface. In fact, the GUI is simply a pretty face on top of what is really going on under the hood. Windows is like the gauges on the dashboard of an automobile. When the red light goes on, there is trouble under the hood. The red light only alerts you to a problem. Sometimes, you may fix the problem simply by responding to the evidence given. For instance, if you see the red oil light come on, that information only requires you to put oil in your engine. Other times, you must dig deeper to solve the problem. You must go to the engine and run diagnostic tests to identify the problem. Then you can fix the problem.

The same is true in Windows. Windows will alert you to a problem like the red light on the dashboard. Sometimes you can fix it at the GUI level, and other times you must open the hood and go to the command line interface to run diagnostic software to identify the problem. Once you have identified the problem, you can fix it either by running the problem-solving software you are given with Windows or by making small fixes at the system level.

Microsoft, even though it expects you to use the GUI for your day-to-day computer operations, still knows the importance of a character-based interface—the command line. That is why, with Windows 95, Windows 98, Windows Me, Windows NT and even Windows 2000, one of the choices is the availability of the command line interface. In Windows, it is a menu choice called the MS-DOS Prompt. In Windows NT and Windows 2000, it is simply called the Command Prompt (with the MS-DOS icon). You open what is called a DOS window, but where you really are is right back to a character-based interface.

Why then did Microsoft leave this option available to the user? There are many reasons. For instance, you will find that there are many tasks that still cannot be accomplished from the GUI. In addition, Windows provides utility programs that can only be run at the command line to help you solve problems with Windows itself. Furthermore, there are other tasks that, although they can be done from the GUI, are accomplished easier and faster from the command line, and most users will use the command line in those instances. You will also find that even in the Windows environment, there is an assumption that the user "knows" DOS. For instance, you will find that error messages you receive are couched in DOS terms, such as "Path not found. Please check the location of your program and correct the path." Likewise, you will still find that there are programs, especially if you are involved in developing Web pages for use on the Internet, that can only be run from the "DOS system level" (another way of saying "command line interface").

Additionally, if you are a user of the Internet, which often runs on Unix- or Linux-based computers, you often find yourself at the command line. (Unix or Linux are command line interface operating system. Linux is based on Unix-like commands.) Although Unix and Linux do not use commands identical to DOS commands, they are in fact similar enough that, if you know one, you can figure out the other.

If you work with networks or plan a career in network administration, knowledge of the command line is a necessity. Network operating systems, such as Novell, rely on the command line interface. Even the Windows 2000 family of operating systems, Microsoft's GUI networking operating system, absolutely relies on command line interfaces. Novell, Windows 2000, and Windows allow you to write batch files, which are usually written, tested, and run at the command line interface, to automate many routine tasks. In fact, Windows 2000 has even more powerful batch file commands available to you than Windows. Furthermore, if a career in a computer-related field is in your future, you must know the command line interface. Almost all networking classes have as a prerequisite a working knowledge of DOS. Remember that DOS is used as a shorthand way of saying "command line interface."

You will also find that the knowledge that you gain in this text by learning the command line interface will help you understand what is going on in the Windows environment. Perhaps an analogy might be your automobile. Most of us are not auto mechanics and do not know how to do engine repair. Nonetheless, if you have an understanding of what is going on under the hood, you may be able to do minor repairs and preventative maintenance so you can avoid more costly major repairs. At the very least, you will be able to explain problems to professional auto technicians in intelligent terms that will allow them to identify problems so that they may spend their expensive time fixing, not identifying, them. In this text, you are going to use the command line prompt, and you will learn what's under the hood of Windows. This will give you, as with an automobile, the ability to do minor repairs and preventative maintenance as well as to explain complex problems to a software technician.

1.12   ACCESSING THE COMMAND LINE PROMPT

In order to use the command line interface, you first need to access it. You must open the DOS window. You may choose to open the DOS window from a menu, or you may create a shortcut to it. One thing you must remember is not to turn off the computer when you are in a DOS window. You must exit the window and then follow the Windows shut-down procedures.

Note: What you see on your screen may differ from the examples shown in this book. While most of the examples shown are done on a computer with Windows Me, some may be from Windows 95 or 98. You can ignore these minor differences. If there is a significant difference, it will be noted and explained.

1.13   ACTIVITY: THE COMMAND LINE PROMPT

Step 1   Boot the system.

Step 2   Click **Start**. Click **Programs**. Click **Accessories**. Click **MS-DOS Prompt**.
Note 1: In Windows 95 and 98, MS-DOS is on the Programs submenu.
Note 2: If you do not see the title bar, press [Alt] + [Enter]

WHAT'S HAPPENING? ➡ You have opened the MS-DOS Prompt window. This is the character-based interface. You may close this window and return to the desktop.

Step 3   Click the ☒ on the title bar in the right corner.

WHAT'S HAPPENING? ➡ You have returned to the desktop. You can also create a shortcut to the command line. A shortcut is an icon on the desktop that points to an application or command.
Note: If you are in a lab environment, check with your administrator or lab technician to see if there are any special instructions for creating shortcuts.

Step 4   Right-click the desktop.

Step 5   Point to **New**.

Step 6   Click **Shortcut**.

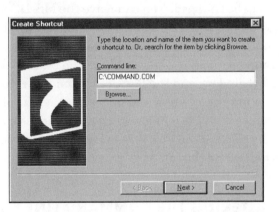

 You opened the wizard Create Shortcut dialog box. A wizard is a tool that leads you through the steps you need to take to accomplish your goal. In order to create a shortcut, you need to know the name and location of the program of interest.

Step 7   In the **Command line** text box, key in the following:
C:\COMMAND.COM

Step 8   Click **Next**.

 You may use any name you wish for your shortcut. However, in this example, Windows automatically gives the shortcut the name of MS-DOS Prompt. In this way, Windows is telling you that **COMMAND.COM** is the MS-DOS Prompt.

Step 9   Click **Finish**.

WHAT'S HAPPENING?   You have created a shortcut and placed it on the desktop. By double-clicking it, you can go to the command line, referred to as the "MS-DOS Prompt."

Note: In Windows Me, when you open the shortcut, you may be taken to either C:\WINDOWS\DESKTOP or to C:\, depending on what the setup was. This is determined by the working directory. The working directory becomes the directory from which the shortcut was executed.

1.14   CONTROLLING THE APPEARANCE OF THE COMMAND-LINE WINDOW

In Windows, everything initially appears in a window with a title bar and a toolbar, but this look can be changed. You can leave the MS-DOS Prompt in a window. When it is in a window, you can use the Minimize button ▬, the Maximize button ▢, or the Restore button ▣, all on the right side of the title bar. The Minimize button will make the window a button on the taskbar. The Maximize button will fill the entire screen with the window, and the Restore button will return the window to its previous size. While in window view, you may alter the size of the text in the window. You may also dispense with the window altogether and view the command line in full-screen mode by clicking the Full screen button on the toolbar ▣. To toggle (switch) between a window and the full-screen mode, you may press the **Alt** and **Enter** keys.

1.15   ACTIVITY: ALTERING THE COMMAND LINE WINDOW

Step 1   Double-click the **MS-DOS Prompt** shortcut on the desktop.

Step 2   Place and hold your mouse pointer over the Full screen button on the toolbar.

WHAT'S HAPPENING?   When you do not know what an icon represents, placing the mouse pointer over the object causes a brief description of the object to appear. This description is called a ***ToolTip***.

Step 3   Click the Minimize button on the toolbar.

WHAT'S HAPPENING?   The MS-DOS Prompt window has become a button on the toolbar. It is still open but not active.

Step 4   Click the **MS-DOS Prompt** button on the toolbar.

Step 5   Click the Maximize button on the title bar.

WHAT'S HAPPENING?   Now the MS-DOS Prompt window is at its maximum size. Depending on the resolution of your monitor and the text size setting, the display may fill the entire screen.

Step 6   Click the Restore button.

Step 7   Click the down arrow in the Font drop-down list box on the toolbar.

WHAT'S HAPPENING?   While you are in a window, you may choose a font size. The fonts that have **T** in front of them are called True Type fonts. The others are bitmapped fonts. Typically, a bitmapped font will be clearer and sharper in a MS-DOS window, and a True Type font is better for use in application programs such as Word or Excel. Your choices of font sizes will depend on your monitor and available resolutions.

Step 8   Click outside the Font box to close it. Click the Full screen button on the toolbar.

WHAT'S HAPPENING?   Now MS-DOS is no longer in a window and is in a full-screen mode. Toggling back and forth between the two views is done by pressing the **Alt** + **Enter** keys.

Step 9   Press the **Alt** + **Enter** keys.

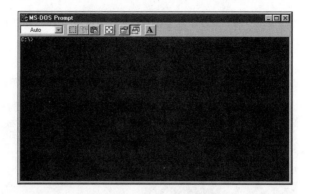

WHAT'S HAPPENING? You have returned the display to a window. The actual displays you will see on the screen are white text on a black background, but in this text, dark text on a lighter background will be used for easier reading. You may use the MS-DOS command line from a window or from a full screen. Choose whichever view suits you. Remember *never* turn off the computer when at the MS-DOS Prompt, whether you are using full screen or are in a window. You must first close the MS-DOS Prompt window and return to the Windows desktop, or type EXIT at the prompt in full screen view to return to the desktop. Then, you must shut down the computer using the Windows shut-down procedure, learned previously.

Step 10   Key in the following: C:\>**EXIT** Enter

WHAT'S HAPPENING? You have closed the MS-DOS Prompt window and returned to the desktop.

1.16   THE DEFAULT DRIVE AND DEFAULT DIRECTORY

The MS-DOS prompt, referred to as the command prompt, is where you key in your commands. You do not usually use a pointing device when in command prompt mode. Command prompt mode is character-based, which means that you must explicitly tell the operating system what you want it to do by keying in the instruction (command). Where you key in your command is indicated by a blinking *cursor* following the prompt. The prompt usually looks like C:\>_ or sometimes [C:\]_. (The _ represents the blinking cursor.) The letter and colon behind the greater-than sign or in brackets is the default drive. The \ is the default directory. The default drive and directory is your location. This will change depending on where you are. The default drive and directory that is displayed when you go to the command line prompt depends on the setup of your particular computer, how many hard drives you have, and what software is currently running. The most common prompt will be C:\; C:\WINDOWS> or C:\WINDOWS\DESKTOP>, but many other variations are possible. The operating system names drives using a letter followed by a colon, such as A:, C:, or J:. All drives, no matter the type—CD-ROM drives, floppy drives, removable drives such as Zip drives or Jaz drives, and hard drives—follow this naming rule. The default drive is the one where the operating system is currently pointing. It can be changed easily.

1.17   ACTIVITY: CHANGING THE DEFAULT DRIVE

Note 1: You should be at the Windows desktop.

Note 2: In this text, the prompt used will be C:\WINDOWS>.

Step 1   Click **Start, Programs, Accessories,** and **MS-DOS Prompt** or double-click the **MS-DOS Prompt** shortcut on the desktop.

Step 2   Get the disk labeled ACTIVITIES that came with the textbook.

Step 3   To insert a 3½-inch disk properly into the disk drive, place your thumb on the label with the metal shutter facing away from you and toward the floppy disk drive (see Figure 1.3). Slip the disk into the slot and gently push the disk into the drive until you hear it click and/or feel it snap into place. When properly in place, the small rectangular button at the bottom, left of the floppy drive will pop out.

FIGURE 1.3   INSERTING A DISK

Note 1: Remember, when you see the notation Enter, it means to press the Enter key located towards the right side and labeled Enter and/or Return.

Note 2: The prompt will be in the following font: C: What you key in will be in the following font: **C:** Key in only what follows the prompt, not the prompt itself.

Note 3: You will need to refer to your Configuration Table in Chapter 1.6 from time to time to ensure that your operating procedures for this, and all other activities, are correct for the computer you are using.

Step 4   Key in the following: C:\WINDOWS>**CD ** Enter

Step 5   Key in the following: C:\>**A:** Enter

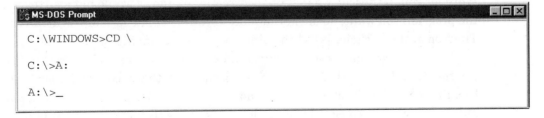

```
C:\WINDOWS>CD \

C:\>A:

A:\>_
```

> **WHAT'S HAPPENING?** You have changed or confirmed that the default directory is the root of C and changed the default drive to the A drive.

1.18 UNDERSTANDING COMMANDS

Windows operating system *commands* are programs and, like application programs, they perform specific tasks. OS commands are of two types: internal or external. When you boot the system, internal commands are automatically loaded and stored into memory (RAM). These internal commands are built into the command processor, COMMAND.COM. This file, and hence, these internal commands, are always placed in memory and remain in RAM the entire time your computer is on.

To use an internal command, you key in the command name at the command line or click the icon. For an internal command, Windows checks memory, finds the program, loads it into RAM, and executes it. These are called internal or resident commands because they reside in memory or inside the computer. Internal commands are limited in number because they take up valuable space in memory.

External commands are stored as files on a disk. When you wish to use an external command, you call upon the operating system to load the program into RAM by keying in the program's name or clicking its icon. Since it is an external command, the OS cannot find the program internally, so it must go to the disk, locate the file, load it into RAM, and then execute it. If the OS cannot find the file, the program cannot be run. These commands are called external or transient commands because they reside in a file on a disk and must be read into RAM each time you key them in.

You use your operating system, Windows, to load and execute programs such as Word or Quicken. When you click or double-click a program icon or choose a program from a menu, you are loading an external command. You do not have to key in a command name, but the process is the same. For instance, if you click the icon for Word, the icon stores the location and name of the program file such as C:\PROGRAM FILES\MICROSOFT OFFICE\WINWORD.EXE. The operating system looks first for the program in memory. When it cannot find it in memory, it goes to the specified location, including the disk drive as well as the directory. In the example given, Windows would look to Drive C in a folder called MICROSOFT OFFICE in a folder called PROGRAM FILES for a file called WINWORD.EXE. When it finds it, it loads it, and you have Word available to you. You are letting the GUI do the work. You could do the work yourself at the command prompt by simply keying in WINWORD.EXE. The end result would be the same. The OS would find and load Word for you. If the icon was set up incorrectly, Windows would not load (execute) the program you want, no matter how often you chose the icon or the menu choice. The icon or menu choice is only a pointer to the program file.

If the icon had stored incorrect information, such as an incorrect program location, Windows would give you the error message that it could not load Word because it could not find it. If you did not understand this process, you would not be able to use Word because all you would see would be the error message. If you did understand the operating system process, you would either correct the pointer or run Word from the command prompt.

Although all program files are external, including application programs, the term *external command* is reserved for the group of programs that perform operating system functions. These programs are files that come with Windows and are copied to a subdirectory called C:\WINDOWS\COMMAND on the hard disk when Windows is installed. This group of files is generically referred to as the command line utility files or system utility files.

In the MS-DOS Prompt window, unlike the Windows GUI environment, you have no icons. In order to use commands, you must know their file names. The DIR command, an internal command that stands for directory, is provided so that you may look for files on a disk from the command line. In Windows, Explorer is the equivalent of the DIR command. When you key in DIR and press the **Enter** key, you are asking the operating system to run the directory program. The purpose or task of the DIR command is to display the names of all the files in a directory on the disk onto the screen. You see what could be described as a table of contents of the disk. The DIR command is the first MS-DOS internal command you will use.

1.19 ACTIVITY: USING THE DIR COMMAND

Note: Be sure the disk labeled ACTIVITIES is in Drive A.

Step 1   Key in the following: A:\>**DIR** **Enter**

```
MS-DOS Prompt                                              _ □ ✕

    JAN        99              73   10-10-99   4:53p JAN.99
    TEST       TXT             65   12-11-99   4:03p TEST.TXT
    GETYN      COM             26   05-02-94  12:57a GETYN.COM
    WILD1      XXX             64   12-31-01   4:32p WILD1.XXX
    MAR        TMP             71   04-23-00   4:03p MAR.TMP
    MARCH      TMP             71   04-23-00   4:03p MARCH.TMP
    APR        TMP             72   04-23-00   4:18p APR.TMP
    NEWPRSON FIL           2,672   07-31-99  12:53p NEWPRSON.FIL
    Y          FIL              3   08-12-00   4:12p Y.FIL
    SANDYA~1 TXT              53   11-16-00  12:00p Sandy and Nicki.txt
    SANDYA~2 TXT              59   11-16-00  12:00p Sandy and Patty.txt
    EXP00JAN DAT             294   01-31-00  12:09p EXP00JAN.DAT
    DATA            <DIR>         07-03-00   1:50p DATA
    TEST            <DIR>         07-03-00   1:50p TEST
    GAMES           <DIR>         07-03-00   1:50p GAMES
    PHONE           <DIR>         07-03-00   1:51p PHONE
    FINANCE         <DIR>         07-03-00   1:51p FINANCE
    LEVEL-1         <DIR>         07-03-00   1:52p LEVEL-1
    SPORTS          <DIR>         07-03-00   1:52p SPORTS
    MEDIA           <DIR>         07-03-00   1:53p MEDIA
    WORKING         <DIR>         07-03-00   1:53p WORKING
           85 file(s)        28,537 bytes
            9 dir(s)        295,936 bytes free

    A:\>_
```

WHAT'S HAPPENING? You see text moving vertically on the screen. This movement is known as *scrolling*, the result of executing the DIR command. The operating system is displaying, or listing, all the files on the root of the disk in Drive A and stops scrolling when the list ends. The last subdirectory on the list is **WORKING**. You can tell it is a subdirectory by the **<DIR>** entry to the right of the name. The last file on the list is a file called **EXP00JAN.DAT**. The file name is **EXP00JAN**. The file extension is **DAT**. When you key in a file name, you must use a period between the name and its extension, but, when the file name is displayed in the directory listing on the screen, the period is omitted. Next is the number **294**, the size of the file in bytes; the date, **01-31-00**; and the time, **12:09p**. The date and time indicate either when this file was created or when it was last modified. Now look at the bottom two lines of the screen. One line states: **85 file(s) 28,537 bytes**. This line indicates how many files are in the current directory and how much room they occupy. The next line, **9 dir(s) 295,936 bytes free**, indicates first how many directories are below the current directory and second how much room is left on the disk for more files. All the files listed on the disk are practice files so that you may practice using the operating system commands without harming any of your own files.

1.20 SOFTWARE VERSIONS

Software companies regularly release new versions of software to take advantage of new technology. These upgrades also contain enhancements. The term *enhancements* simply means more features. In addition, new versions of software fix problems in older versions. This process is known as fixing bugs. To keep track of the versions, companies assign them version numbers. For instance, there is WordPerfect 8 and WordPerfect 9 and Word 97 and Word 2000.

As previously explained, version numbers are also assigned to operating systems. For MS-DOS, 1.0 was the first version, released in 1981, and DOS 6.22 was the last stand-alone, character-based operating system. Windows 95 replaced DOS 6.22. Windows 98 replaced Windows 95 and Windows Millennium Edition replaced Windows 98. Beginning with Windows 95, DOS has been integrated into the Windows operating system.

1.21 ACTIVITY: USING THE VER COMMAND

Step 1 Key in the following: A:\>**VER** [Enter]

```
MS-DOS Prompt                                                      _ □ ×

A:\>VER

Windows Millennium [Version 4.90.3000]


A:\>_
```

> **WHAT'S HAPPENING!** ➡ In this example, the computer is running the operating system Windows Millennium (Version 4.90.3000). The version number you see depends on the version of Windows that you have on your computer.

1.22 THE KEYBOARD

The keyboard on a microcomputer is similar to a typewriter keyboard, but it has at least 40 additional keys, many with symbols rather than alphabetic characters. Generally, the keyboard can be broken down into four major categories:

- **Alphanumeric keys.** These keys, located in the center of the keyboard, are the standard typewriter keys. They consist of the letters of the alphabet and Arabic numerals.
- **Function keys.** Keys labeled F1, F2, and so on, located across the top or on the left side of the keyboard, are known as "function keys." These keys are program-dependent, which means that their functions are dependent on the software in use. Often a notebook computer will have the function keys located in different spots on the keyboard due to space limitations.
- **Directional keys.** These keys, located between the alphanumeric keys and the number pad, are also known as the "cursor keys." These keys are also program-dependent and when used allow you to move the cursor in the direction of the arrows. There are additional keys labeled **Insert**, **Delete**, **Home**, **End**, **Page Up**, **Page Down**, **Num Lock**, **Print Screen**, and **Pause**, as well as others, depending on the keyboard and system. Notebook computers often have separate directional keys, but **Home**, **Page Up**, and other such keys share locations in the interest of saving space.
- **Numeric keys.** These keys, located to the right of the directional keys, are known as the number keypad or numeric keypad. Numeric keys can be used in two ways: like a calculator keypad or with the directional arrows and other commands. The directional arrows, in combination with other commands, are program-dependent. The user must activate the mode desired (numeric keypad or directional arrows) with the **Num Lock** key, which acts as a toggle switch. A *toggle switch* acts like an on/off switch. Press the key once and the numbers are turned on. Press the same key again and the numbers are turned off. Other toggle keys will be discussed later.

In addition, some of the newer keyboards come with what is called a **Windows key**. This key performs certain functions in the Windows environment. It cannot be used at the command line prompt. Some keyboards now also come with special keys for use with the Internet. These keys also cannot be used at the command line prompt.

The following activity will familiarize you with some of the special keys and features of a computer keyboard. Figure 1.4 shows one of the major types of keyboards used today.

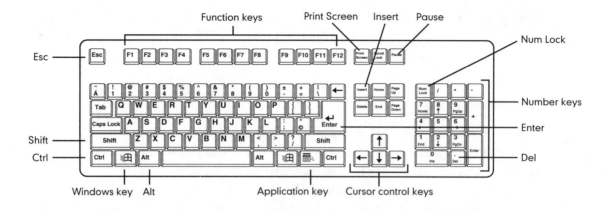

FIGURE 1.4   SAMPLE KEYBOARD LAYOUT FOR A WINDOWS NATURAL KEYBOARD

1.23   THE BACKSPACE KEY

The Backspace key, labeled **Backspace** or just the symbol ←, allows you to erase characters you have keyed in prior to pressing **Enter**.

1.24   ACTIVITY: CORRECTING ERRORS USING THE BACKSPACE KEY

Step 1   Key in the following: `A:\>`**The quick brown fox**

Step 2   Press the **Backspace** key until you reach the A prompt (A:\>). As you see, each time you press this key, you delete a character.

1.25   THE ESCAPE KEY

Esc is an abbreviation for Escape. Look for the key labeled **Esc**. When you press this key, it cancels a line you have keyed in, provided you have not yet pressed **Enter**. When you press the **Esc** key, the operating system eliminates the line of text and waits for you to key in something else.

1.26   ACTIVITY: USING THE ESCAPE KEY

Step 1   Key in the following: `A:\>`**The quick brown fox**

```
MS-DOS Prompt                                                _ □ ×
A:\>The quick brown fox_
```

WHAT'S HAPPENING?   To erase this line, you could repeatedly press the **Backspace** key. However, you can use the **Esc** key to cancel the line instead.

Step 2   Press the **Esc** key.

```
MS-DOS Prompt                                                    _ □ X

   A:\>_
```

WHAT'S
HAPPENING? ➤ Notice that the cursor is blinking at the beginning of the line. As stated previously, results will vary slightly, depending on the version of Windows you are using. In this text, the results shown will be from Windows Me.

1.27 THE SHIFT KEY

The Shift key is labeled **Shift** with an up arrow symbol ⇧ or just the up arrow symbol. This key allows the user to shift to uppercase letters and special characters such as the * above the number 8 key. There are usually two Shift keys, one on either side of the alphabet keys. To activate, you need only press one Shift key.

1.28 ACTIVITY: USING THE SHIFT KEY

Step 1   Press the key on the keyboard for the letter **m**.

Step 2   Hold down the Shift key and press the letter **m**.

```
MS-DOS Prompt                                                    _ □ X

   A:\>mM_
```

Step 3   Press either Backspace or Esc to delete the letters.

WHAT'S
HAPPENING? ➤ Windows is case *aware*, but not case *sensitive*. If you name a file **MyFile**, and later try to find it using **MYFILE** or **myfile**, the system will have no problem locating it. However, it will remember the case you used, and, when you use the DIR command, it will show you the file in the same case you used when you created it.

1.29 THE PRINT SCREEN KEY

In versions of DOS previous to Windows 95, the Print Screen key was used to send copy to the printer. Pressing this key along with the Shift key gave you a hard copy or printed version of what the screen displayed, like a snapshot of the screen at a specific moment in time. The Print Screen key in Windows does not function in this way. Pressing the Print Screen key still takes a snapshot of the screen, but you do not need to press the Shift key, but simply press the Print Screen key twice. Also, what you are capturing is a picture or graphic—not text to send to a printer. Pressing Print Screen captures an image of the entire screen. Pressing the Print Screen key once in conjunction with the Alt key captures an image of the active window only, not the entire screen. The image is copied to memory and can be pasted into a document to be printed, but it cannot be printed directly to the printer.

1.30   ACTIVITY: USING THE PRINT SCREEN KEY IN WINDOWS

Step 1   Click the Close button, ⊠, on the title bar of the MS-DOS Prompt window.

WHAT'S HAPPENING? ▶ You have closed the MS-DOS Prompt window and returned to the Windows desktop.

Step 2   Click **Start**. Point to **Programs**. Click **Accessories**. Click **WordPad**.

WHAT'S HAPPENING? ▶ You have opened the mini word-processing program WordPad that comes with Windows.

Step 3   Click the Minimize button on the WordPad title bar.

WHAT'S HAPPENING? ▶ You have minimized the WordPad program to a button on the taskbar. WordPad is still open and still running, but the window it is operating in has been minimized.

Step 4   Click **Start**. Point to **Programs**. Click **Accessories**. Click **MS-DOS Prompt**.

Step 5   Size the command line window to about four inches tall by five or six inches wide. Exact measurement is not important.

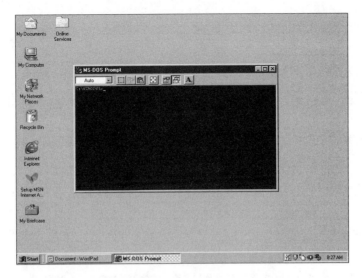

WHAT'S HAPPENING? ➤ You have opened the MS-DOS Prompt window.

Step 6   Hold down the key labeled [Alt] and while holding it down, press the [Print Screen] key once. Be sure you do not hold down the [Print Screen] key—just press it once.

Step 7   Open WordPad by clicking once on the **WordPad** button on the taskbar.

Step 8   On the WordPad toolbar, click **Edit**. Click **Paste**.

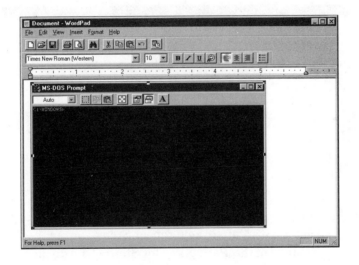

WHAT'S HAPPENING? ➤ You have captured a graphic image of the MS-DOS Prompt screen and pasted it into a document. You could save, print, or add text to this document.

Step 9   On the WordPad menu bar, click **File**. Click **Exit**.

Step 10   When asked to save changes, click **No**.

Step 11   Click the command line window to make it active.

Step 12   Key in the following: C:\WINDOWS>**EXIT** [Enter]

WHAT'S
HAPPENING?   You have returned to the desktop.

1.31   FREEZING THE DISPLAY

You have already seen that, when you use the DIR command, the display scrolls by so quickly on the screen that it is very difficult to read. There is a way to stop displays from rapidly scrolling on the screen. The Windows operating system allows you to read a long display by temporarily halting the scrolling. How you do it depends on what kind of computer you have. Most new computers have a key labeled **Pause**; all you need to do is press **Pause**. Nearly every kind of computer will let you use **Ctrl** + **S** for freezing the display. Most computers today are so fast that chances are the data will process much faster than you can manually pause the display.

1.32   ACTIVITY: USING THE PAUSE, CONTROL, AND S KEYS

Step 1   Double-click the **MS-DOS Prompt** shortcut on the desktop.

Step 2   Place the ACTIVITIES disk in Drive A.

Step 3   Key in the following: C:\WINDOWS>**A:** **Enter**

Step 4   Key in the following: A:\>**DIR** **Enter**

Step 5   Press the **Pause** key.

```
MS-DOS Prompt                                                      _ □ ×

A:\>DIR

 Volume in drive A is ACTIVITIES
 Volume Serial Number is 1508-190E
 Directory of A:\

BYE        TYP           45   05-30-00   4:32p BYE.TYP
CASES      FIL          314   08-12-00   4:12p CASES.FIL
APRIL      TMP           72   04-23-00   4:03p APRIL.TMP
BONJOUR    TMP           53   04-23-00   4:03p BONJOUR.TMP
FEB        TMP           75   04-23-00   4:03p FEB.TMP
```

WHAT'S
HAPPENING?   Pressing this key halts or "freezes" the display on the screen. If you do not have a **Pause** key, repeat Step 4, but press the **Ctrl** + **S** keys instead of the **Pause** key for Step 5. The display stops and the cursor remains blinking when you press these two keys. Again, a fast computer may process the data faster than you can pause the display.

Step 6   Press the **Enter** key. The display will continue.

1.33 CANCELING A COMMAND

If you keyed in a command and pressed [Enter], but you either made an error or changed your mind about executing the command, you could, in theory, cancel the command or cause it to stop executing. In reality, most computers execute commands so quickly that they cannot be canceled. To cancel an ongoing command after you have pressed [Enter], press the [Ctrl] key in conjunction with the [Break] key or the letter **C**. Look for the key labeled **Break**. It is often paired with the [Pause] key. This command is not the same as [Esc], which is used prior to pressing [Enter]. As previously stated, with today's fast computers, by the time you press these halting keys, the command may have already been completed.

1.34 ACTIVITY: USING DIR AND CANCELING A COMMAND

Step 1   Key in the following: A:\>**DIR** [Enter]

Step 2   As soon as the directory starts displaying on the screen, hold the [Ctrl] key down. While holding down the [Ctrl] key, press the [Break] key.

WHAT'S
HAPPENING! ➤ DOS stops running or executing the DIR command. You are returned to the A:\> prompt. You interrupted or stopped the program or the command from running, and, therefore, you see only a partial directory display. (Remember, don't be concerned if you cannot pause the display because the scroll action is too fast.) When you press the [Ctrl] key and the [Break] key, you see ^C displayed on your screen. [Ctrl] + **C** has the same function and meaning as [Ctrl] + [Break].

Step 3   Key in the following: A:\>**DIR** [Enter]

Step 4   As soon as the directory information starts displaying on the screen, hold the [Ctrl] key down and then simultaneously press the letter **C**.

WHAT'S
HAPPENING! ➤ This procedure worked exactly like [Ctrl] + [Break]. The system ceased executing the program or the DIR command and returned you to the A:\> prompt, ready for the next command.

1.35 THE CLS COMMAND

Your screen is filled with the display of the directory and other commands that you have keyed in. You may want to have a "fresh" screen, with nothing displayed except the A:\> prompt and the cursor in its "home" position (the upper left-hand corner of the screen). The internal command CLS clears the screen. Whatever is displayed on the screen will go away, as if you erased a chalkboard. The command erases the screen display, not your files.

1.36 ACTIVITY: USING THE CLS COMMAND

Step 1   Key in the following: A:\>**CLS** [Enter]

```
MS-DOS Prompt                                                    _ □ ✕

A:\>_
```

WHAT'S HAPPENING? ▶ The screen is now cleared, and the A:\> is back in the upper left-hand corner.

1.37 THE DATE AND TIME COMMANDS

The computer, via a battery, keeps track of the current date and time. Date and time are known as the *system date* and the *system time*. The system date and time are the date and time the computer uses when it opens and closes files (last date/time accessed) or when another program asks for the date and time. Today's computers have a built-in clock. It is simply a built-in, 24-hour, battery-operated clock that sets the date and time automatically when you boot the system. You can change or check the system date and system time whenever you wish by using the internal DATE and TIME commands at the command line, or from within the Windows desktop by clicking the time displayed at the far right of the taskbar.

1.38 ACTIVITY: USING DATE/TIME COMMANDS AT THE COMMAND LINE

Step 1   Key in the following: A:\>**DATE** [Enter]

```
MS-DOS Prompt                                                    _ □ ✕

A:\>DATE
Current date is Thu 07-05-2001
Enter new date (mm-dd-yy): _
```

WHAT'S HAPPENING? ▶ The date displayed on your screen is the current date, not the above example. If you did not wish to change the date, you would just press [Enter], retaining the date displayed and returning you to A:\>. However, if you do want to change the date, respond to the prompt. You must key in the date in the proper format such as **11-15-01**. You may not key in character data such as **November 15, 2001**. Furthermore, you are allowed to use some other separators that are not stated. You may key in **11/15/01** using the forward slash, or you may use periods such as **11.15.01**. No other characters can be used.

Step 2   Key in the following: **12-31-00** [Enter]

```
MS-DOS Prompt                                                    _ □ ✕

A:\>DATE
Current date is Thu 07-05-2001
Enter new date (mm-dd-yy): 12-31-00

A:\>_
```

 You did change the date, and we will examine this change in a moment. You can also change the time in the same fashion with the TIME command.

Step 3   Key in the following: A:\>**TIME** Enter

```
MS-DOS Prompt                                                    _ □ ✕
A:\>TIME
Current time is  1:12:13.78p
Enter new time: _
```

 The time displayed on your screen is the current time, not the above example. If you did not wish to change the time, you would just press Enter, retaining the time displayed and returning you to A:\>. However, if you do want to change the time, you respond to the prompt. You may use only the colon (:) to separate the numbers. Although in this case you are going to key in the seconds, most people usually key in only the hour and minutes. If you wish the time to be in the P.M., you add a "p" after the time. You may also use a 24-hour clock.

Step 4   Key in the following: **23:59:59** Enter

```
MS-DOS Prompt                                                    _ □ ✕
A:\>TIME
Current time is  1:12:13.78p
Enter new time: 23:59:59

A:\>_
```

 You have just reset the computer clock with the DATE and TIME commands. These are internal commands. How do you know the system date and time have been changed? You can check by keying in the commands.

Step 5   Key in the following: A:\>**DATE** Enter

Step 6   Press Enter

Step 7   Key in the following: A:\>**TIME** Enter

Step 8   Press Enter

```
MS-DOS Prompt                                                    _ □ ✕
A:\>DATE
Current date is Mon 01-01-2001
Enter new date (mm-dd-yy):

A:\>TIME
Current time is 12:01:45.20a
Enter new time:

A:\>_
```

WHAT'S HAPPENING? Your time display numbers may be slightly different. What have you done? You have changed the system date and time. You entered the date of December 31, 2000 (12-31-00), prior to changing the time. The date now displayed is Monday, January 1, 2001. How did that happen? Why is the displayed date different from the keyed-in date? After you entered the date of 12/31/00, you entered the time of 11:59 p.m. (23:59:59). Seconds went by; the time passed midnight, and, when you are past midnight, you are into a new day. Hence, the day "rolled over" from December 31, 2000 to January 1, 2001. In other words, the system keeps the date and time current based on the information you give.

The day of the week is displayed in the date. You can experiment with the DATE and TIME commands. For instance, you can find the day of your birthday in any future year by using the DATE command and entering your birthday.

Step 9   Key in the following: A:\>**DATE** [Enter]

Step 10   At the prompt on the screen—Enter new date (mm-dd-yy)—key in your birthday for 2002. In this example, I will use my birthday, 12-11-02. Key in the following: **12-11-02** [Enter]

Step 11   Key in the following: A:\>**DATE** [Enter]

Step 12   Key in the following: [Enter]

```
MS-DOS Prompt                                          _ □ ✕

A:\>DATE
Current date is Mon 01-01-2001
Enter new date (mm-dd-yy): 12-11-02

A:\>DATE
Current date is Wed 12-11-2002
Enter new date (mm-dd-yy):

A:\>_
```

WHAT'S HAPPENING? If you are using Windows 95 and have not added the Y2K patch, the OS will not know if you are referring to the year 1902 or the year 2002, and you will get an error message. In that case, you are required to enter a 4-digit year, 12-11-2002. However, if you have Windows Me or Windows 98, the OS knows that you mean the year 2002 and does not give an error message. The screen display shows you the day of your birthday in 2002. In this case, my birthday will fall on a Wednesday in 2002. If you wish to see or change the system date or time, you can also use the clock on the taskbar.

Step 13   Click the Close button in the MS-DOS Prompt window.

1.39 ACTIVITY: CHANGING THE DATE AND TIME USING THE TASKBAR

Step 1   Right-click the time display on the right of the taskbar. Click **Adjust Date/Time**.

WHAT'S
HAPPENING?➤ You have opened the Date/Time Properties dialog box. You can change the date by clicking on any one of the numbers in the calendar. You can change the time by either clicking in the box under the clock, deleting any part of the time, keying in the correct time, or by using the up and down arrows. This type of data-entry box is called a spin box, because the values go both up and down. You can change the year in the same way: key in the new value or use the spin box arrows. You can change the month by keying in the correct month or by using the down arrow and selecting the correct month. This type of data-entry box is called a drop-down list box.

Step 2   Change the date and time back to the correct values.

WHAT'S HAPPENING?⮞ You are returning the system time and date to their current values. Another feature of the clock on the taskbar is to show you the current date without opening the dialog box.

Step 3   Click **OK**.

Step 4   Place the mouse pointer over the time on the taskbar. Do not click, just point the arrow.

WHAT'S HAPPENING?⮞ The day and date are briefly displayed. The display remains only for a few seconds and then disappears.

1.40   MEDIA OBJECTS: THEIR PROPERTIES AND VALUES

What is an object? What is a property? To Windows, *everything* is an object. A file, the keyboard, a disk drive—all are objects. Each object has properties, and the properties may have values.

To explain the object-property-value relationship, you can use a person. A person is an object. All objects of that same type (human) have the same properties. Some *properties* of this person object are *name*, *height*, and *eye color*. The values of person objects, however, differ. One person's name property value is John Jones; another person's name property value is Olivia Wu. A newborn person has the property of name, but no value has been assigned to that property.

To discover information about an object in Windows, you examine that object's property sheet. Most objects' property sheets can be displayed by right-clicking on the object icon and choosing Properties from the shortcut menu. For example, when you copy a disk, it is very important that you know what type of media you are using. Furthermore, it is important to know what type of floppy disk drive or hard drive you have on your system. You need to know the "native" format of the disk drive, whether or not you have a high-density disk drive, and which drive is Drive A. In Windows, this information is ascertained by examining a drive's property sheet.

1.41   ACTIVITY: EXAMINING DISK PROPERTIES AND VALUES

Step 1   Double-click the **My Computer** icon on the desktop.

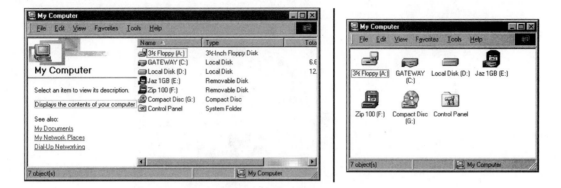

WHAT'S HAPPENING? You have opened the My Computer window. The view on the left is the default for Windows Me. This view enables Web contents in folders— it emulates what you see on the Web. In the view on the right, this feature is turned off, and you see only the contents as objects and folders. In this text, we will use the view on the right, without Web contents view enabled.

All the drives available to your system are displayed. On this system, there is one floppy drive: A. There are two hard drives or hard drive partitions, C and D. There are two removable drives and one CD-ROM drive. You are going to examine the properties of the A drive on your system, the drive where the ACTIVITIES disk is presently located.

Step 2   Right-click the A drive icon.

WHAT'S HAPPENING? A menu with options has "dropped down" from the A drive icon.

Step 3   Click **Properties**.

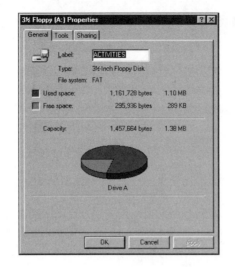

WHAT'S HAPPENING? ▶ The property sheet for the A drive is displaying the properties of the ACTIVITIES disk. You can see many things about the disk: the label or electronic name, the amount of used space, and the amount of free space displayed in numbers and in a graphic pie chart. You can also see the disk type and its total capacity. This is a 3½-inch diskette with a total capacity of 1,457,664 bytes.

Step 4   Click **Cancel**.

Step 5   Close **My Computer**.

1.42 ETHICAL CONSIDERATIONS IN COPYING DISKS

It is unethical and illegal to make a copy of a program or a disk that you did not purchase and do not own. Making a copy of a program or receiving a copy of a program is stealing someone else's work. If you did not personally purchase the program, even if you are using it at work, it is still illegal to copy it and use it. However, most software manufacturers allow you and encourage you to make backup copies of program disks for your own personal use in case something happens to the original. Remember, however, you need to have purchased the program or have permission to copy the disk in order to be both legal and ethical. If your program came on a CD-ROM, as is usually the case (such as with the Windows operating system), it is possible to copy it if you have a recording CD-ROM (CDRW) drive, but to record a CD you did not purchase is not ethical or legal.

In the following activity, you are going to copy the ACTIVITIES disk that comes with this book so that you have a working copy of the ACTIVITIES disk. You will work from a copy of the ACTIVITIES disk so that, if anything happens, you can use the original ACTIVITIES disk to make another copy. Whenever possible, always work from a copy, never an original. This copy of the ACTIVITIES disk will be used in all future exercises. It is legal to make a copy for your personal use only. If you are in a computer lab, check with your instructor for the procedures in your specific lab.

1.43   MAKING A COPY OF THE ACTIVITIES DISK: DISKCOPY

When making an exact copy of a disk, you must have like media. This means the disk you are copying from and the disk you are copying to must be *exactly* the same type and capacity. You are now going to make a working copy of the ACTIVITIES disk. You will use an external program called DISKCOPY. It is stored as a file called DISKCOPY.COM in the WINDOWS\COMMAND subdirectory. It does exactly what it says; it copies all the information, from one floppy disk to another. Before it copies a disk, it formats it. You can never use the DISKCOPY command to copy from a hard disk to a floppy disk or from a floppy disk to a hard disk. You could copy the disk from the desktop. Notice the menu in Activity 1.41, Step 2. One of the options is Copy Disk. In the following activity, you will use the command line method. Please follow the instructions precisely. The ACTIVITIES disk is a high-density, 3½-inch floppy disk. Your blank disk must be the same media type in order to do the next activity.

1.44   ACTIVITY: USING DISKCOPY

Note: If you are in a lab environment, check with your instructor to see if there are any special procedures in your lab.

Step 1   Get a new label. On the label write "ACTIVITIES Disk—Working Copy" and your name. Get a new disk or one that you no longer want the information on that is the same type and capacity as the ACTIVITIES disk. Affix the label to the disk. See Figure 1.5 for the correct location of the label.

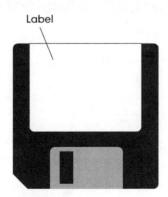

Label

FIGURE 1.5   FLOPPY DISK LABEL PLACEMENT

Step 2   Place the ACTIVITIES disk that came with the textbook in Drive A.

Step 3   Open the MS-DOS Prompt window.

Step 4   Key in the following: C:\WINDOWS>**CD \WINDOWS\COMMAND** Enter
Note: Refer to your configuration table, if necessary, to locate the correct directory.

Step 5   Key in the following: C:\WINDOWS\COMMAND>**DISKCOPY A: A:** Enter

```
MS-DOS Prompt                                                    _ □ ✕

C:\WINDOWS>CD \WINDOWS\COMMAND

C:\WINDOWS\COMMAND>DISKCOPY A: A:

Insert SOURCE diskette in drive A:

Press any key to continue . . .
```

WHAT'S HAPPENING? By keying in **DISKCOPY**, you asked the command processor to find a program called DISKCOPY. It first looked in memory in the internal table of commands. When it could not find a match, it went to the disk in Drive C and the subdirectory **WINDOWS\COMMAND**, found the program, loaded it into memory, and started executing it. This program has some prompts, which are instructions to follow. The program asks you to put the SOURCE disk that you wish to copy in Drive A. In this case, the ACTIVITIES disk, which you want to copy, is already in Drive A.

You are telling the operating system to make a copy from the disk in Drive A to the disk in Drive A. To make the copy or begin executing the command DISKCOPY, press any key. This instruction literally means any key on the keyboard. Typically, you use the `Space Bar` or the `Enter` key.

Step 6   Press `Enter`

```
MS-DOS Prompt                                                    _ □ ✕

C:\WINDOWS>CD \WINDOWS\COMMAND

C:\WINDOWS\COMMAND>DISKCOPY A: A:

Insert SOURCE diskette in drive A:

Press any key to continue . . .

Copying 80 tracks, 18 sectors per track, 2 side(s)

Reading from source diskette . . .
```

WHAT'S HAPPENING? Track and sector numbers will vary depending on the type of disk used. The DISKCOPY command tells the operating system to copy everything on the disk in Drive A (the SOURCE) to RAM. While this program is doing the copying, the cursor flashes onscreen. When the command is completed or the copying is finished, you will need to take another step. You see the following prompt:

```
MS-DOS Prompt                                                    _ □ ✕

Insert TARGET diskette in drive A:

Press any key to continue . . .
```

WHAT'S HAPPENING? This prompt tells you to remove the SOURCE disk from Drive A and insert the blank or TARGET disk in Drive A so the operating system has a place to copy the information.

Step 7 Remove the master ACTIVITIES disk from Drive A. Insert the blank disk labeled "ACTIVITIES Disk—Working Copy" into Drive A. Close or latch the drive door. Press **Enter**

```
MS-DOS Prompt                                                    _ □ ✕

C:\WINDOWS>CD \WINDOWS\COMMAND

C:\WINDOWS\COMMAND>DISKCOPY A: A:

Insert SOURCE diskette in drive A:

Press any key to continue . . .

Copying 80 tracks, 18 sectors per track, 2 side(s)

Reading from source diskette . . .

Insert TARGET diskette in drive A:

Press any key to continue . . .

Writing to target diskette . . .
```

WHAT'S HAPPENING? Again, you see the flashing cursor. After DISKCOPY formats the TARGET disk, whatever was copied into RAM is copied or written to the blank disk in Drive A. When the process is complete, you will see the following message:

```
MS-DOS Prompt                                                    _ □ ✕

Do you wish to write another duplicate of this disk (Y/N)? _
```

WHAT'S HAPPENING? The system wants to know if you wish to make multiple copies of the floppy diskette already in Drive A.

Step 8 Press **N**.

```
MS-DOS Prompt                                                    _ □ ✕

Do you wish to write another duplicate of this disk (Y/N)? N

Volume Serial Number is 1508-0C25

Copy another diskette (Y/N)? _
```

WHAT'S HAPPENING? ➤ The prompt tells you that the program has finished executing and asks you another question. Do you want to execute this program again to make another copy of another disk? In this case, you do not wish to make another copy, so you key in the letter **N** for no. The volume serial number changes with each DISKCOPY command and will not be the same as the example.

Step 9   Press **N**.

```
MS-DOS Prompt                                                    _ □ ✕

Volume Serial Number is 1508-0C25

Copy another diskette (Y/N)? N

C:\WINDOWS\COMMAND>_
```

WHAT'S HAPPENING? ➤ You are returned to the C:\WINDOWS\COMMAND> prompt. The operating system is now ready for a new command.

Step 10 Close the MS-DOS Prompt window.

1.45 HOW TO END THE WORK SESSION

You can stop working with the computer at any time. Since your programs are stored on disks, you will not lose them. However, you must always exit Windows properly and completely; otherwise you could do serious, sometimes irreparable, damage to the system.

1.46 ACTIVITY: ENDING THE WORK SESSION

Note: Check with your lab instructor to see what special procedures you might need to follow in your lab environment.

Step 1   Close any remaining open windows, including the MS-DOS window.

Step 2   Click **Start**.

Step 3   Click **Shut Down**. Be sure Shut down is the choice on the drop-down menu.

Step 4   Click **OK**.

WHAT'S HAPPENING? ➤ You have initiated the shut-down procedure.

Step 5   Wait until you see the screen telling you it is safe to turn off the computer. New computers will power down automatically. If this does not happen, wait until you see the screen telling you it is safe to turn off the computer.

Step 6   Turn off the monitor and the system unit (if necessary).

CHAPTER SUMMARY

1. An operating system is a software program that is required in order to run application software and to oversee the hardware components of the computer system.
2. Windows is the major operating system in use today on Wintel microcomputers.
3. All microcomputers come with disk drives. There are three basic types of disk drives: the floppy disk drive, the hard disk drive, and the CD-ROM drive.
4. Computer systems are configured in various ways, such as: 1) one hard disk drive, one CD-ROM drive, and one floppy disk drive, 2) one hard disk drive, one CD-ROM drive, one floppy disk drive, and one Zip drive, 3) two hard disk drives, one CD-ROM drive, and one floppy disk drive, or 4) one hard disk drive, one CD-ROM drive, one read/write CD-ROM drive, and one floppy disk drive.
5. Booting the system, also known as a cold start, means more than powering on the system. It loads the operating system into memory and executes the self-diagnostic test routine.
6. Internal commands are programs loaded in COMMAND.COM with the operating system. They remain in memory until the power is turned off.
7. External commands are stored on a disk and must be loaded into memory each time they are used. They are transient and do not remain in memory after being executed.
8. Programs and data are stored on disks as files. The formal name is file specification, which includes the file name and file extension.
9. A command is a program. A program is the set of instructions telling the computer what to do.
10. Programs (commands) must be loaded into memory in order to be executed.
11. To load a program into memory, the user can key in the command name at the system prompt or click on the command's icon.
12. The DIR command is an internal command that displays the directory (table of contents) of a disk.
13. The [Backspace] key deletes characters to the left.
14. The [Esc] key ignores what was previously keyed in before [Enter] is pressed.
15. The [Shift] key shifts letters to uppercase.
16. The [Print Screen] key can be used to "dump" an image of the screen so that it can be pasted into an application program and printed.
17. A toggle switch is like a light switch. In one position, the function is turned on. By pressing the same toggle switch again the function is turned off.
18. The [Ctrl] key and the [Pause] key, when held down together, freeze the screen display on older computers. Newer computers use the [Pause] key.
19. The [Ctrl] key and the [Break] key or the [Ctrl] key and the letter C when held down together cancel a command that was entered.
20. Minor internal commands include VER, CLS, DATE, and TIME.
    - VER displays the current version of the OS that is in memory.
    - CLS clears the screen.
    - DATE and TIME allow you to look at and/or change the system date and system time, a process that can also be done from the desktop taskbar.

21. DISKCOPY is an external command that makes an identical copy of any disk, track for track, sector for sector. It was used to make a working copy of the ACTIVITIES disk but can be used to make exact copies with any two floppy disks that are the same media type. It formats a disk prior to copying to it.

22. To end a work session with the computer, Windows must be shut down in the proper sequence and shouldn't be turned off until a message on the screen tells you it is safe to do so.

KEY TERMS

alphanumeric key	disk file	operating system
booting the system	enhancement	program file
bugs	file extension	scrolling
command	file name	system date
cursor	file specification	system time
data file	function key	toggle switch
directional key	numeric key	Wintel

DISCUSSION QUESTIONS

1. What is an operating system?
2. What are enhancements?
3. Define system configuration.
4. List two common ways that computer systems are configured.
5. Why is it necessary to boot the system?
6. How would you boot the system?
7. What is an object?
8. What is a property?
9. What is a value?
10. Identify and explain the function and purpose of the two parts of a file specification.
11. What is the difference between a command and a program?
12. Compare and contrast internal and external commands.
13. What is the purpose of the DIR command?
14. Name and describe the functions of the four parts of a keyboard.
15. What is the purpose and function of a toggle switch?
16. Identify one way to print what is on the screen.
17. How can you stop the display from rapidly scrolling on the screen?
18. How can you cancel a command after you have pressed Enter ?
19. What is the function of the VER command?
20. What is the function of the CLS command?
21. How can you set the date and time?
22. How do you set the time when using the TIME command?
23. What is the purpose of making a backup copy of a program?
24. Why should you work with a copy of a program rather than with the original?

25. Why is it important to know what type of media you are using when copying disks?
26. What is the purpose of the DISKCOPY command?
27. What are the necessary steps to end a work session?

TRUE/FALSE QUESTIONS

For each question, circle the letter T if the question is true and the letter F if the question is false.

T F 1. To identify what version of the operating system you are using, you could, at the command line, use the VER command.

T F 2. A correct way to key in a date would be **2/4/01**.

T F 3. When you see the computer notation Ctrl + **C**, it means you should key in the word **control** and then the letter **C**.

T F 4. LFN is an acronym for Last File Noted.

T F 5. DISKCOPY.COM is a program that is stored on the disk as a file.

COMPLETION QUESTIONS

Write the correct answer in each blank space.

6. One way to communicate with the computer is by _____ commands on the keyboard.

7. Programs, data, and text are stored on disks as _____.

8. The operating system is in charge of the _____ components of the computer.

9. If you wanted to see the table of contents of a disk in the MS-DOS command mode, you would key in _____.

10. If you wished to cancel a command line you keyed in prior to pressing Enter, you would press the _____ key.

MULTIPLE CHOICE QUESTIONS

For each question, write the letter for the correct answer in the blank space.

11. To display the contents of a disk, key in the following command:
    a. TOC
    b. DIR
    c. DIS
    d. Directory

12. To change the date to May 7, 2001, after you key in DATE, you could key in:
    a. 5/7/01
    b. 5-7-01
    c. 5.7.01
    d. all of the above

13. To clear the screen, key in:
    a. CLS
    b. CLR
    c. CLEAR
    d. Clear the screen
14. Which of the following is a type of disk drive?
    a. hard disk drive
    b. soft disk drive
    c. both a and b
    d. neither a nor b
15. To copy all the information from one floppy disk to another, you may use the command:
    a. DISKCOPY
    b. COPY
    c. DISKCMP
    d. D-COPY

APPLICATION ASSIGNMENTS

PROBLEM SET I—AT THE COMPUTER

PROBLEM A

A-a   Boot the system, if it is not booted.

A-b   Open the MS-DOS Prompt window.

A-c   Key in C:\WINDOWS>**CD ** Enter

A-d   Change the date to **5/8/01**.

A-e   Re-enter the same command.

1. The day of the week that appears on the screen is:
   a. Tue
   b. Wed
   c. Thu
   d. Fri

A-f   Change the date to the current date.

2. The command you used was:
   a. DATE
   b. TIME
   c. DISKCOPY
   d. none of the above

A-g   Key in **TIME** Enter

A-h   At the prompt, key in **27:00** Enter

3. What error message is displayed on the screen?
   a. Not a valid time
   b. Invalid time
   c. Please key in the correct time
   d. Do not use a colon

A-i   Press **Enter**

PROBLEM B

B-a   Place the working copy of the ACTIVITIES disk in Drive A.

B-b   Key in C:\>**A:** **Enter**

B-c   Key in A:\>**DIR** **Enter**

4. What date is listed for **Y.FIL**?
   a. 8-12-99
   b. 8-12-01
   c. 8-12-98
   d. 8-12-00

B-d   Press the **F3** key.

5. What appeared on the screen?
   a. DATE
   b. DIR
   c. Y.FIL
   d. none of the above

B-e   Press **Enter**

B-f   Immediately press **Ctrl** + **C**.

6. What symbols appeared on the screen?
   a. Ctrl + C
   b. Alt + C
   c. ^C
   d. :::C

B-g   If the MS-DOS Prompt is not in a window, place it in one now.
        (By pressing **Alt** + **Enter**)

B-h   Click the **A** button on the toolbar.

7. What Prompt Properties tab is on top?
   a. Program
   b. Font
   c. Memory
   d. Screen
   e. Misc

8. In Available types, which of the item(s) below are included in the list?
   a. Bitmap only
   b. TrueType only
   c. both a and b
   d. neither a nor b

B-i   Click **Cancel**.

PROBLEM C

C-a   Close the MS-DOS Prompt window.

9. You may close the MS-DOS Prompt window by clicking the
   a. ⬜ button on the title bar.
   b. 🅰 button on the toolbar.
   c. ⬛ button on the title bar.
   d. ✖ on the title bar.

C-b   Exit Windows properly.

10. The fastest way to exit Windows correctly is to
    a. turn off the computer.
    b. click Start, then click Shut Down.

C-c   Be sure to remove your ACTIVITIES Disk—Working Copy from Drive A.

PROBLEM SET II—BRIEF ESSAY

1. When DOS was a stand-alone operating system, file specifications were limited to the 8.3 file-naming rules. Windows 95 introduced the use of LFNs. Compare and contrast these two sets of rules. List any reasons for still retaining the use of 8.3 file names.

2. You can change the system time and date either from the command line or from Windows. List the advantages and disadvantages of each method. Which do you prefer? Explain your answer.

COMMAND SYNTAX

Using the DIR Command with Parameters and Wildcards

LEARNING OBJECTIVES

After completing this chapter you will be able to:
1. Define command syntax.
2. Explain what parameters are and how they are used.
3. Explain the purpose and use of the DIR command.
4. Define prompts and explain how they are used.
5. Explain the purpose of the CD command.
6. Explain the purpose and function of a device.
7. Explain the purpose and function of device names.
8. Explain the purpose and function of defaults.
9. Explain the function and purpose of subdirectories (paths).
10. Explain the use and purpose of wildcards.
11. Define global specifications and identify their symbols.
12. Explain the purpose and function of redirection.

STUDENT OUTCOMES

1. Read a syntax diagram and be able to name and explain what each part signifies.
2. Use both fixed and variable parameters with the DIR command.
3. Give the names of the disk drives on your computer.
4. Change the default drive and the directory.
5. Use subdirectories (paths) with the DIR command.
6. Use global specifications with the DIR command.
7. Use wildcards with the DIR command.

8. Redirect the output of the DIR command to either a file or a printer.
9. Use online Help.

CHAPTER OVERVIEW

To communicate with the computer at the command line prompt, you need to learn the computer's language. You must follow the syntax of the language and use punctuation marks the computer understands. As in mastering any new language, new vocabulary words must be learned, word order (syntax) must be determined, and the method of separating statements into syntactic units must be understood. The computer has a very limited use of language, so it is exceedingly important to be precise when you are speaking to it.

In this chapter you will learn some basic computer commands, the syntax or order of these commands, and where the commands begin and end. You will learn how to make your commands specific, how to use wildcards to affect a command, and how to determine which disk you want to write to or read from. You will also learn how to use the online Help feature.

2.1   COMMAND SYNTAX

All languages have rules or conventions for speaking and writing. The *syntax,* or word order, and punctuation, of a language is important. For example, in English the noun (person, place, or thing) is followed by the verb (the action). In Latin the verb most often ends a sentence, because Latin had no punctuation marks and the subject could be anywhere in the sentence, even within the verb. When you learn a language, you learn its syntax.

Anything you key into the computer must be a word the computer understands. The words you key in are actually commands ordering the computer to perform specific tasks. These commands must also be in the correct order; that is, they must have the proper syntax. The computer cannot guess what you mean. People can understand "Going I store," but if you key in an incorrect word or put correct words in the wrong order, a computer will respond with the message "Bad command or file name." This statement is the computer equivalent of "I do not understand."

In computer language, a command can be compared to a verb, the action you wish to take. In Chapter 1, you used the command DIR. In other words, when you keyed in DIR, you were asking the system to take an action: run the program called DIR that lets you see the directory (table of contents) of a disk.

Using the graphical user interface in the Windows OS does not change things—there are still syntax and rules. An icon that points to a program is based on the rules of syntax. Certainly, it is easier from a user's perspective to click an icon to accomplish a task rather than having to know the command and the appropriate syntax. However, when things do not work, you the user need to know how to go under the hood, so to speak, and fix the problem so that you can "click" on your desktop successfully.

2.2 WHAT ARE PARAMETERS?

A *parameter* is information you can use to modify or qualify a command. Some commands require parameters, while other commands let you add them when needed. Some parameters are *variable*. A *variable parameter* is one to which you the user supply the value. This process is similar to a math formula. For instance, $x + y = z$ is a simple formula. You can plug in whatever values you wish for x and y. If $x = 1$ and $y = 2$, you know the value of z, which is 3. These values can change or are *variable* so that x can equal 5 and y can equal 3, which makes z equal to 8. These variables can have any other numerical value you wish. You can also have $z = 10$ and $x = 5$ and mathematically establish the value of y. No matter what numbers x, y, or z are, you will be able to establish the value of each.

Other parameters are *fixed*. For instance, if the formula reads $x + 5 = z$, then x is the variable parameter and 5 is the fixed value. You can change the value of x but not the value of 5.

When you are working with some command line commands, you are allowed to add one or more parameters to make the action of a command more specific. This process is the same in English. If I give my granddaughter my Visa card and tell her, "Go buy," I have given her an open-ended statement—she can buy anything (making her one happy camper!). However, if I add a qualifier, "Go buy shoes," I have limited what she can do. The word "shoes" is the parameter. This pattern exemplifies precisely what parameters do to a command.

2.3 READING A SYNTAX DIAGRAM

A command line interface is a language that has a vocabulary, grammar, and syntax. To use the language of the command line, you must learn the vocabulary (commands) and understand the grammar (punctuation) and syntax (order). The syntax information is provided through online Help. The *command syntax* diagrams tell you how to enter a command with its optional or *mandatory parameters*. However, you need to be able to interpret these *syntax diagrams*.

Here is the formal command syntax diagram for the DIR command you used earlier:

```
DIR [drive:][path][filename][/P][/W][/A[[:]attributes]]
  [/O[[:]sortorder]][/S]/B][/L][/V][/4]
```

The first entry is the command name, DIR. You must use this name only. You cannot substitute another word such as DIRECTORY or INDEX. The parameters that follow the command are in brackets, [ ]. Brackets indicate that these parameters are optional—not required for the command. The DIR command has *optional parameters* only. There are no required, or mandatory, parameters for the DIR command.

2.4   USING FIXED PARAMETERS WITH THE DIR COMMAND

DIR is a command with optional parameters. Most often, a *fixed parameter* is referred to as a *switch* and typically begins with / (the slash).

In the DIR command syntax diagram, /W and /P are in brackets. You never key in the brackets, only / (the forward slash or slash) and the **W** or **P**. You must be careful; there is only one slash—the forward slash /. The \ is a *backslash* and is always referred to as the backslash. When a mark is referred to as a slash, it always means the forward slash.

When you key in **DIR** and the files scroll by, they move so quickly that you cannot read them. In the previous chapter, you learned that you could halt the display by pressing the Pause key or the Ctrl and **S** keys. However, there is a more efficient way to solve this problem by using the /P parameter. The /P parameter will display one screen of information at a time. It will also give you a prompt that you must respond to before it will display another screenful of information.

Note 1: There are times you may find it necessary to quit before you have completed the entire chapter. Each activity begins with a note indicating which diskette is in the drive, and what is the current directory and drive. Thus, if you complete an activity, you may pick up where you left off. When you stop working, be sure to return to the Windows desktop and initiate the Windows shut-down procedure.

Note 2: Be sure you know what your computer laboratory procedures are.

Note 3: If your system varies from the textbook, refer to the Configuration Table in section 1.6 in Chapter 1.

2.5   ACTIVITY: USING FIXED PARAMETERS WITH THE DIR COMMAND

Note: Whenever the textbook refers to the ACTIVITIES disk, you will use the working copy that you made in Chapter 1 and labeled "ACTIVITIES Disk—Working Copy."

Step 1   If it is not on, turn on the computer.

Step 2   Open an MS-DOS Prompt window.

Step 3   Key in the following: C:\WINDOWS>**CD ** Enter

Step 4   Key in the following: C:\>**CLS** Enter

```
MS-DOS Prompt                                        _ □ ✕

C:\>_
```

WHAT'S HAPPENING! ➡ You have successfully booted the system. You are at the root directory of Drive C.

Step 5   Insert the ACTIVITIES disk in Drive A. (Remember, this means your working copy.)

Step 6   Key in the following: C:\>**A:** Enter

```
MS-DOS Prompt                                            _ □ ☒

C:\>A:
A:\>_
```

WHAT'S HAPPENING?   The default drive is now Drive A. The default directory is the root of A.

Step 7   Key in the following: A:\>**DIR /P** Enter

```
MS-DOS Prompt                                            _ □ ☒

 Volume in drive A is ACTIVITIES
 Volume Serial Number is 1508-0C25
 Directory of A:\

 BYE       TYP        45   05-30-00   4:32p  BYE.TYP
 CASES     FIL       314   08-12-00   4:12p  CASES.FIL
 APRIL     TMP        72   04-23-00   4:03p  APRIL.TMP
 BONJOUR   TMP        53   04-23-00   4:03p  BONJOUR.TMP
 FEB       TMP        75   04-23-00   4:03p  FEB.TMP
 GOODBYE   TMP        34   01-01-02   4:32a  GOODBYE.TMP
 FEBRUARY  TMM        75   05-30-00   4:32p  FEBRUARY.TMM
 OLIVE     OIL        98   05-30-00   4:32p  OLIVE.OIL
 FILE3     FP         19   12-06-00   2:45p  FILE3.FP
 FILE3     SWT        19   12-06-00   2:45p  FILE3.SWT
 FILE4     FP         19   12-06-00   2:45p  FILE4.FP
 WILDONE   DOS       181   12-31-01   4:32p  WILDONE.DOS
 MIDDLE    UP         29   10-01-00   4:12p  MIDDLE.UP
 GOODBYE   TXT        34   01-01-02   4:32a  GOODBYE.TXT
 RIGHT     UP         26   10-01-00   4:12p  RIGHT.UP
 DRESS     UP         26   10-01-00   4:12p  DRESS.UP
 APRIL     TXT        72   06-16-00   4:32p  APRIL.TXT
 JANUARY   TXT        73   06-16-00   4:32p  JANUARY.TXT
 FEBRUARY  TXT        75   06-16-00   4:32p  FEBRUARY.TXT
 Press any key to continue . . .
```

WHAT'S HAPPENING?   You keyed in the command **DIR** followed by a slash / and the parameter **P**. The slash, which must be included with a fixed parameter, is commonly referred as a switch. However, the slash (/) is really a ***delimiter***. A delimiter is a signal that one thing is ending and another is beginning. The number of files on your screen may differ from the figure above, depending on the size of your open MS-DOS Prompt window. Command line commands use different punctuation marks such as delimiters, but the punctuation marks that they use are very specific. Remember, / is used only with fixed parameters.

In this example, the slash is the signal to the DIR command that additional instructions follow. The parameter P is the additional instruction. There can be no space between the slash and the P. The slash and the P stop the directory from scrolling. Thus, /P told the DIR command to fill the screen and then pause until the user takes some action. The message at the bottom of the screen tells you to press any key.

Step 8   Press Enter

```
 MS-DOS Prompt                                                    _ □ ×

(continuing A:\)
MARCH     TXT           71  06-16-00   4:32p MARCH.TXT
STEVEN    FIL           46  07-31-99  12:53p STEVEN.FIL
HELLO     TXT           53  05-30-00   4:32p HELLO.TXT
FILE2     CZG           19  12-06-00   2:45p FILE2.CZG
EXP01JAN  DAT          304  01-31-01  12:09p EXP01JAN.DAT
EXP01FEB  DAT          307  02-28-01  12:10p EXP01FEB.DAT
EXP99MAR  DAT          294  03-31-99  12:11p EXP99MAR.DAT
JAN       NEW           73  10-01-99   2:53p JAN.NEW
BYE       TXT           45  05-30-00   4:32p BYE.TXT
GO        BAT        4,530  05-27-98   1:47a GO.BAT
STATES    USA        1,228  07-31-00   4:32p STATES.USA
JANUARY   TMP           73  04-23-00   4:03p JANUARY.TMP
WILD2     YYY           64  12-31-01   4:32p WILD2.YYY
WILD3     ZZZ           64  12-31-01   4:32p WILD3.ZZZ
WILDONE                 93  12-31-01   4:32p WILDONE
WILDTHR   DOS          181  12-31-01   4:32p WILDTHR.DOS
APR       NEW           74  10-01-99   2:53p APR.NEW
WILDTWO   DOS          182  12-31-01   4:32p WILDTWO.DOS
RNS       EXE        7,269  11-22-89  10:35p RNS.EXE
EXP99JAN  DAT          294  01-31-99  12:09p EXP99JAN.DAT
EXP01MAR  DAT          302  03-31-01  12:11p EXP01MAR.DAT
EXP00MAR  DAT          292  03-31-00  12:11p EXP00MAR.DAT
Press any key to continue . . .
```

WHAT'S HAPPENING? When you pressed **Enter**, the display continued scrolling. Because there are still more files, the **DIR** command asks you to press any key again to continue the display. As you can see, the display stops each time the screen fills.

Step 9   Press **Enter**

Step 10   Press **Enter**

Step 11   Continue pressing **Enter** until you reach the end of the display.

```
 MS-DOS Prompt                                                    _ □ ×

WILD1     XXX           64  12-31-01   4:32p WILD1.XXX
MAR       TMP           71  04-23-00   4:03p MAR.TMP
MARCH     TMP           71  04-23-00   4:03p MARCH.TMP
APR       TMP           72  04-23-00   4:18p APR.TMP
NEWPRSON  FIL        2,672  07-31-99  12:53p NEWPRSON.FIL
Y         FIL            3  08-12-00   4:12p Y.FIL
SANDYA~1  TXT           53  11-16-00  12:00p Sandy and Nicki.txt
SANDYA~2  TXT           59  11-16-00  12:00p Sandy and Patty.txt
EXP00JAN  DAT          294  01-31-00  12:09p EXP00JAN.DAT
Press any key to continue . . .

(continuing A:\)
DATA           <DIR>       07-03-00   1:50p DATA
TEST           <DIR>       07-03-00   1:50p TEST
GAMES          <DIR>       07-03-00   1:50p GAMES
PHONE          <DIR>       07-03-00   1:51p PHONE
FINANCE        <DIR>       07-03-00   1:51p FINANCE
LEVEL-1        <DIR>       07-03-00   1:52p LEVEL-1
SPORTS         <DIR>       07-03-00   1:52p SPORTS
MEDIA          <DIR>       07-03-00   1:53p MEDIA
```

```
WORKING          <DIR>         07-03-00  1:53p WORKING
         85 file(s)        28,537 bytes
          9 dir(s)        295,936 bytes free


A:\>_
```

WHAT'S HAPPENING! ➡ You kept pressing **Enter** until there were no more files to display. The system prompt (A:\>) appears to signal that there are no more files on this disk and that the OS is waiting for you to key in the next command. There is another way to display the files on the screen. You may use the /W parameter to display the directory in a wide format.

Step 12 Key in the following: A:\>**DIR /W Enter**

```
╔══════════════════════════════════════════════════════════════════╗
║ ▓▓ MS-DOS Prompt                                       _ □ ✕ ║
╠══════════════════════════════════════════════════════════════════╣
║  Directory of A:\                                                  ║
║                                                                    ║
║ BYE.TYP        CASES.FIL     APRIL.TMP     BONJOUR.TMP   FEB.TMP    ║
║ GOODBYE.TMP    FEBRUARY.TMM  OLIVE.OIL     FILE3.FP      FILE3.SWT  ║
║ FILE4.FP       WILDONE.DOS   MIDDLE.UP     GOODBYE.TXT   RIGHT.UP   ║
║ DRESS.UP       APRIL.TXT     JANUARY.TXT   FEBRUARY.TXT  MARCH.TXT  ║
║ STEVEN.FIL     HELLO.TXT     FILE2.CZG     EXP01JAN.DAT  EXP01FEB.DAT║
║ EXP99MAR.DAT   JAN.NEW       BYE.TXT       GO.BAT        STATES.USA ║
║ JANUARY.TMP    WILD2.YYY     WILD3.ZZZ     WILDONE       WILDTHR.DOS║
║ APR.NEW        WILDTWO.DOS   RNS.EXE       EXP99JAN.DAT  EXP01MAR.DAT║
║ EXP00MAR.DAT   EMPLOYEE.ONE  EMPLOYEE.THR  APR.99        FEB.99     ║
║ CAROLYN.FIL    MAR.99        MIDDLE.RED    LEFT.RED      RIGHT.RED  ║
║ SECOND.FIL     PERSONAL.FIL  DANCES.TXT    MARK.FIL      GREEN.JAZ  ║
║ EMPLOYEE.TWO   AWARD.MOV     STATE.CAP     EXP00FEB.DAT  GRAMMY.REC ║
║ FRANK.FIL      FEB.NEW       OLDAUTO.MAK   MAR.NEW       FILE2.FP   ║
║ FILE2.SWT      BLUE.JAZ      FILE3.CZG     EXP99FEB.DAT  NAME.BAT   ║
║ NEWAUTO.MAK    STATE2.CAP    JAN.TMP       JAN.99        TEST.TXT   ║
║ GETYN.COM      WILD1.XXX     MAR.TMP       MARCH.TMP     APR.TMP    ║
║ NEWPRSON.FIL   Y.FIL         SANDYA~1.TXT  SANDYA~2.TXT  EXP00JAN.DAT║
║ [DATA]         [TEST]        [GAMES]       [PHONE]       [FINANCE]  ║
║ [LEVEL-1]      [SPORTS]      [MEDIA]       [WORKING]                ║
║          85 file(s)        28,537 bytes                            ║
║           9 dir(s)        295,936 bytes free                       ║
║                                                                    ║
║ A:\>_                                                              ║
╚══════════════════════════════════════════════════════════════════╝
```

WHAT'S HAPPENING! ➡ The directory display is now across the screen, five columns wide. In addition, the information about the files is not as comprehensive. All you see is the file specification—the file name and its extension. You do not see the file size, date, or time, but you still see the total number of files and the number of bytes free. You can also identify the directories by the brackets around them such as **[MEDIA]**. Thus, /W allows you to see the files side by side. You can use more than one parameter at a time. Since there are so many files on this disk, you did not see the entire directory.

Step 13 Key in the following: A:\>**DIR /P /W Enter**

```
╔══════════════════════════════════════════════════════════════════╗
║ ▓▓ MS-DOS Prompt                                       _ □ ✕ ║
╠══════════════════════════════════════════════════════════════════╣
║  Volume in drive A is ACTIVITIES                                   ║
║  Volume Serial Number is 1508-0C25                                 ║
```

```
Directory of A:\

BYE.TYP          CASES.FIL        APRIL.TMP        BONJOUR.TMP      FEB.TMP
GOODBYE.TMP      FEBRUARY.TMM     OLIVE.OIL        FILE3.FP         FILE3.SWT
FILE4.FP         WILDONE.DOS      MIDDLE.UP        GOODBYE.TXT      RIGHT.UP
DRESS.UP         APRIL.TXT        JANUARY.TXT      FEBRUARY.TXT     MARCH.TXT
STEVEN.FIL       HELLO.TXT        FILE2.CZG        EXP01JAN.DAT     EXP01FEB.DAT
EXP99MAR.DAT     JAN.NEW          BYE.TXT          GO.BAT           STATES.USA
JANUARY.TMP      WILD2.YYY        WILD3.ZZZ        WILDONE          WILDTHR.DOS
APR.NEW          WILDTWO.DOS      RNS.EXE          EXP99JAN.DAT     EXP01MAR.DAT
EXP00MAR.DAT     EMPLOYEE.ONE     EMPLOYEE.THR     APR.99           FEB.99
CAROLYN.FIL      MAR.99           MIDDLE.RED       LEFT.RED         RIGHT.RED
SECOND.FIL       PERSONAL.FIL     DANCES.TXT       MARK.FIL         GREEN.JAZ
EMPLOYEE.TWO     AWARD.MOV        STATE.CAP        EXP00FEB.DAT     GRAMMY.REC
FRANK.FIL        FEB.NEW          OLDAUTO.MAK      MAR.NEW          FILE2.FP
FILE2.SWT        BLUE.JAZ         FILE3.CZG        EXP99FEB.DAT     NAME.BAT
NEWAUTO.MAK      STATE2.CAP       JAN.TMP          JAN.99           TEST.TXT
GETYN.COM        WILD1.XXX        MAR.TMP          MARCH.TMP        APR.TMP
NEWPRSON.FIL     Y.FIL            SANDYA~1.TXT     SANDYA~2.TXT     EXP00JAN.DAT
[DATA]           [TEST]           [GAMES]          [PHONE]          [FINANCE]
[LEVEL-1]        [SPORTS]         [MEDIA]          [WORKING]
Press any key to continue . . .
```

WHAT'S HAPPENING? By using these parameters together, you could see the files in a wide display, one screenful at a time.

Step 14 Press Enter

```
MS-DOS Prompt                                                              _ □ ✕

GOODBYE.TMP      FEBRUARY.TMM     OLIVE.OIL        FILE3.FP         FILE3.SWT
FILE4.FP         WILDONE.DOS      MIDDLE.UP        GOODBYE.TXT      RIGHT.UP
DRESS.UP         APRIL.TXT        JANUARY.TXT      FEBRUARY.TXT     MARCH.TXT
STEVEN.FIL       HELLO.TXT        FILE2.CZG        EXP01JAN.DAT     EXP01FEB.DAT
EXP99MAR.DAT     JAN.NEW          BYE.TXT          GO.BAT           STATES.USA
JANUARY.TMP      WILD2.YYY        WILD3.ZZZ        WILDONE          WILDTHR.DOS
APR.NEW          WILDTWO.DOS      RNS.EXE        ' EXP99JAN.DAT     EXP01MAR.DAT
EXP00MAR.DAT     EMPLOYEE.ONE     EMPLOYEE.THR     APR.99           FEB.99
CAROLYN.FIL      MAR.99           MIDDLE.RED       LEFT.RED         RIGHT.RED
SECOND.FIL       PERSONAL.FIL     DANCES.TXT       MARK.FIL         GREEN.JAZ
EMPLOYEE.TWO     AWARD.MOV        STATE.CAP        EXP00FEB.DAT     GRAMMY.REC
FRANK.FIL        FEB.NEW          OLDAUTO.MAK      MAR.NEW          FILE2.FP
FILE2.SWT        BLUE.JAZ         FILE3.CZG        EXP99FEB.DAT     NAME.BAT
NEWAUTO.MAK      STATE2.CAP       JAN.TMP          JAN.99           TEST.TXT
GETYN.COM        WILD1.XXX        MAR.TMP          MARCH.TMP        APR.TMP
NEWPRSON.FIL     Y.FIL            SANDYA~1.TXT     SANDYA~2.TXT     EXP00JAN.DAT
[DATA]           [TEST]           [GAMES]          [PHONE]          [FINANCE]
[LEVEL-1]        [SPORTS]         [MEDIA]          [WORKING]
Press any key to continue . . .

(continuing A:\)
        85 file(s)         28,537 bytes
         9 dir(s)         295,936 bytes free

A:\>_
```

WHAT'S HAPPENING? You have returned to the command prompt.

2.6   USING FILE NAMES AS VARIABLE PARAMETERS

In the previous activities, you used the DIR command with two different optional fixed parameters, /P and /W. These optional fixed parameters have specific meanings. There is another parameter you can use with the DIR command: the name of the file.

File names are formally called file specifications. A file specification is broken into two parts, the file name and the file extension. When people refer to a *file* or file name, they really mean the file specification: the file name and file extension together. It is much like a person's name. When someone refers to Ramon, he usually means someone specific, such as Ramon Rodreiquez. In the computer world, when you refer to a file name, you must give both its first name (file name) and its last name (file extension). When you create files in an application program, you are allowed to name the file. On this disk the files already exist and are already named. You cannot call them anything else. However, when you have the opportunity for naming files, you must follow the rules. Windows has rules called *conventions* for naming files. These are:

1. All files in a directory (subdirectory) must have unique names.
2. File names are mandatory. All files must have file names that may be less than but no more than 215 characters long. However, it is recommended that you do not do this, as most programs cannot interpret very long file names.
3. File extensions are usually three characters long.
4. The following characters are illegal, and may NOT be used in a file name:
   \ / : * ? " < > ¦
5. All other characters, including periods and spaces, are legal in Windows file names.

Typically, a file name reflects the subject of the file, for example, EMPLOYEE or TAXES. The file extension is usually given by the application creating the file. For example, MS Word uses .DOC for its extension, Lotus 1-2-3 uses .WK1, and MS Excel uses .XLS.

Keep in mind that many older, 16-bit application packages created before Windows 95 cannot deal with long file names, spaces in file names, or periods in file names. These packages adhere to the older DOS rules, which limit the name to eight characters and the optional extension to three characters. You will also find that files on the Internet tend to adhere to the older DOS rules.

When a file has a long name, you will see two different versions of the name when you view it with the DIR command. On the right, you can see the name as created in the Windows operating system. On the left, you will see the name converted to the old DOS rules, called "eight-dot-three," referring to the length limits of the name and extension. Also, when you refer to a file name that does not adhere to the old eight-dot-three convention, you must enclose the name in quotation marks.

When you key in the DIR command, you get the entire table of contents of the disk, known as the directory. Usually, you do not care about all the files. Most often, you are interested only in whether or not one specific file is located or stored on the disk. If you use one of the parameters, /P or /W, you still have to look through all the files. You can locate a specific file quickly by using the file name. Simply give the DIR command specific information about what file you seek. Look at the syntax diagram:

```
DIR [drive:][path][filename] [/P] [/W]
```

The file name, indicated above in brackets, is a variable optional parameter. To use the optional parameter, you must plug in the value or the name of the file you are looking for [*filename*]. In some syntax diagrams, you will see [*filename*[.*ext*]]. The .*ext* is in separate brackets within the *filename* brackets because it is part of the file name syntax. A file may not have an extension, but if it does have an extension, you must include it. When you include it, there must be no spaces between the file name and the file extension.

The delimiter that is used between a file name and a file extension is a period, or what is called the ***dot***. A dot, as a delimiter, is used between a file name and a file extension. A file name is keyed in as MYFILE.TXT. To verbalize the name of this file, you would say "MY FILE dot TEXT." Remember, when you use the DIR command, you will not see the period or dot between the file name and the file extension on the screen. On the screen display, the dot is indicated by spaces. Since multiple periods are allowed in file names in Windows, the file extension follows the last period in the file name. Thus, in a file called MY.FIRST.FILE.TXT, the file extension is still .TXT.

2.7   ACTIVITY: USING A FILE NAME AS A VARIABLE PARAMETER

Note: You should be at the command line at the A:\> prompt.

Step 1   Key in the following: A:\>**DIR "Sandy and Nicki.txt"** Enter

```
MS-DOS Prompt                                                         _ □ ✕

A:\>DIR "Sandy and Nicki.txt"

 Volume in drive A is ACTIVITIES
 Volume Serial Number is 1508-0C25
 Directory of A:\

SANDYA~1 TXT                53  11-16-00 12:00p Sandy and Nicki.txt
         1 file(s)              53 bytes
         0 dir(s)          295,936 bytes free

A:\>_
```

WHAT'S HAPPENING?   The DIR command returned exactly what you asked for—a single file that met your criteria. In addition to the long file name, the file also has an eight-dot-three name on the left side of the directory display. The 8.3 file name is always derived from the long file name by removing any spaces from the file name, taking the first six characters of the file name, adding a tilde (~), and a number. But what if there were more than one file with the same first six characters in its name? Windows has a way to handle it.

Step 2   Key in the following: A:\>**DIR "Sandy and Patty.txt"** Enter

```
┌─────────────────────────────────────────────────────────────────┐
│ ▓▒ MS-DOS Prompt                                      _ □ X       │
├───────────────────────────────────────────────────────────────── │
│                                                                   │
│ A:\>DIR "Sandy and Patty.txt"                                     │
│                                                                   │
│  Volume in drive A is ACTIVITIES                                  │
│  Volume Serial Number is 1508-0C25                                │
│  Directory of A:\                                                 │
│                                                                   │
│ SANDYA~2 TXT            59  11-16-00 12:00p Sandy and Patty.txt    │
│          1 file(s)              59 bytes                           │
│          0 dir(s)          295,936 bytes free                     │
│                                                                   │
│                                                                   │
│ A:\>_                                                             │
│                                                                   │
└───────────────────────────────────────────────────────────────────┘
```

WHAT'S
HAPPENING! ➡ As the two files (**Sandy and Nicki.txt** and **Sandy and Patty.txt**) have
the same first six letters, the first file placed on the disk is given the
number 1 following the tilde, and the second file, the number 2. This
would be very confusing if you could not see the actual long file names on
the right. You want to be able to identify the contents of a file quickly by
looking at the file names. Older versions of DOS and older application
software will not allow you to use or view long file names. Furthermore,
you need to key in these eight-dot-three file names, even when using
programs that *can* handle long file names. In the real world, the more
you have to key in, the more likely you will make a typographical error.
Thus, even though you *can* use spaces and long names, it may be a
better idea to keep the file names short and concise. This is especially
important when using floppy disks. Long file names take up needed room
on floppies. This will be explained further in a later chapter.

Step 3   Key in the following: A:\>**CLS** [Enter]

Step 4   Key in the following: A:\>**DIR** [Enter]

```
┌─────────────────────────────────────────────────────────────────┐
│ ▓▒ MS-DOS Prompt                                      _ □ X       │
├───────────────────────────────────────────────────────────────── │
│    JAN      99            73   10-10-99  4:53p JAN.99              │
│    TEST     TXT           65   12-11-99  4:03p TEST.TXT            │
│    GETYN    COM           26   05-02-94 12:57a GETYN.COM           │
│    WILD1    XXX           64   12-31-01  4:32p WILD1.XXX           │
│    MAR      TMP           71   04-23-00  4:03p MAR.TMP             │
│    MARCH    TMP           71   04-23-00  4:03p MARCH.TMP           │
│    APR      TMP           72   04-23-00  4:18p APR.TMP             │
│    NEWPRSON FIL        2,672   07-31-99 12:53p NEWPRSON.FIL        │
│    Y        FIL            3   08-12-00  4:12p Y.FIL               │
│    SANDYA~1 TXT           53   11-16-00 12:00p Sandy and Nicki.txt │
│    SANDYA~2 TXT           59   11-16-00 12:00p Sandy and Patty.txt │
│    EXP00JAN DAT          294   01-31-00 12:09p EXP00JAN.DAT        │
│    DATA          <DIR>         07-03-00  1:50p DATA                │
│    TEST          <DIR>         07-03-00  1:50p TEST                │
│    GAMES         <DIR>         07-03-00  1:50p GAMES               │
│    PHONE         <DIR>         07-03-00  1:51p PHONE               │
│    FINANCE       <DIR>         07-03-00  1:51p FINANCE             │
│    LEVEL-1       <DIR>         07-03-00  1:52p LEVEL-1             │
│    SPORTS        <DIR>         07-03-00  1:52p SPORTS              │
│    MEDIA         <DIR>         07-03-00  1:53p MEDIA               │
│    WORKING       <DIR>         07-03-00  1:53p WORKING             │
└───────────────────────────────────────────────────────────────────┘
```

```
          85 file(s)        28,537 bytes
           9 dir(s)        295,936 bytes free

A:\>_
```

WHAT'S HAPPENING? First, you cleared the screen by using the internal command **CLS**. Then you keyed in **DIR**, and the entire table of contents of the disk in Drive A scrolled by on the screen. When there were no more files to display, you were returned to the A:\> prompt. You are looking at the file specifications on the disk in Drive A. You see the eight-dot-three file names on the left, separated by some spaces between the file names and the file extensions. The long file names appear on the right. The long file names use the period to separate the file extension from the file name, not spaces. The other information is the file size in bytes and the date and time the files were last updated. Any name followed by **<DIR>**, such as **DATA** in the previous screen, is a directory.

Step 5 Key in the following: A:\>**CLS** [Enter]

Step 6 Key in the following: A:\>**DIR STEVEN.FIL** [Enter]

```
MS-DOS Prompt                                                   _ □ ×

A:\>DIR STEVEN.FIL

 Volume in drive A is ACTIVITIES
 Volume Serial Number is 1508-0C25
 Directory of A:\

STEVEN    FIL          46  07-31-99 12:53p STEVEN.FIL
          1 file(s)            46 bytes
          0 dir(s)        295,936 bytes free

A:\>_
```

WHAT'S HAPPENING? This command tells you that it did find the file **STEVEN.FIL** on the disk in Drive A. Furthermore, **STEVEN.FIL** is the variable parameter. You substituted **STEVEN.FIL** for [*filename*[.*ext*]]. If there were no file by that name, you would get the response **File not found**. You are told the Volume name is ACTIVITIES; the file was last modified on July 31, 1999. The file is 46 bytes in size, and there are 295,936 bytes remaining on the disk.

Step 7 Key in the following: A:\>**DIR NOFILE.TXT** [Enter]

```
MS-DOS Prompt                                                   _ □ ×

A:\>DIR NOFILE.TXT

 Volume in drive A is ACTIVITIES
 Volume Serial Number is 1508-0C25
 Directory of A:\

File not found
                     295,936 bytes free
```

```
A:\>_
```

WHAT'S HAPPENING? → **File not found** is a system message. Sometimes it is referred to as an error message. DIR is telling you that it looked through the entire list of files in the root directory of the disk in Drive A and could not find a "match" for the file called **NOFILE.TXT**.

2.8   REPEATING COMMANDS USING THE FUNCTION KEYS

You may reuse the last command you keyed in on a line without rekeying it. When you key in a command, it is stored in a memory buffer until it is replaced by the next keyed in command. The last command line you keyed in can be recalled to the screen so you may edit it. To recall the command line one letter at a time, press the F1 key once for each keystroke you wish to repeat. To recall the entire command line, press the F3 key.

2.9   ACTIVITY: REPEATING A COMMAND USING THE FUNCTION KEYS

Note: The ACTIVITIES disk is in Drive A. You are at the MS-DOS Prompt screen. A:\> is the default drive and directory.

Step 1   Key in the following, including the error: A:\>**DIIR /p** [Enter]

```
MS-DOS Prompt                                            _ □ X

A:\>DIIR /p

Bad command or file name

A:\>_
```

WHAT'S HAPPENING? → Your command was keyed in incorrectly and was not understood by the system. You received the error message **Bad command or file name**. Note the differences in the error messages. In the previous activity, the error message was **File not found**. That message told you that the OS understood your command but could not find the answer to your question. In this example, the error message, **Bad command or file name**, informed you that the OS did not understand what it is you asked for. It is important to read the messages so that you understand what is happening.

Step 2   Press the F1 key twice.

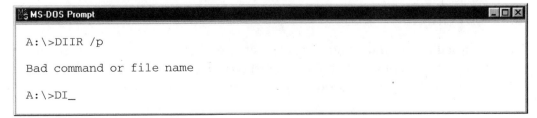

```
MS-DOS Prompt                                            _ □ X

A:\>DIIR /p

Bad command or file name

A:\>DI_
```

WHAT'S HAPPENING? ➤ The characters that you keyed in previously are being recalled from the buffer. If you were to press the [F1] key once more, the incorrectly entered second "I" would appear, the character error you want to eliminate.

Step 3   Press the [Delete] key once.

Step 4   Press the [F3] key.

```
┌──────────────────────────────────────────────────────────────────┐
│ ⬛ MS-DOS Prompt                                        _ □ ✕      │
├──────────────────────────────────────────────────────────────────┤
│ A:\>DIIR /p                                                        │
│                                                                    │
│ Bad command or file name                                          │
│                                                                    │
│ A:\>DIR /p_                                                        │
│                                                                    │
└──────────────────────────────────────────────────────────────────┘
```

WHAT'S HAPPENING? ➤ When you pressed the [Delete] key, nothing appeared to happen, but in fact the next character in the buffer was deleted. When you pressed the [F3] key, the remaining keystrokes in the buffer were added to the command line. Your correction was made.

Step 5   Press the [Esc] key to cancel the command.

Step 6   Press [Enter]

WHAT'S HAPPENING? ➤ You have returned the A:\> prompt.

Step 7   Click the [✕] on the title bar of the MS-DOS Prompt window.

WHAT'S HAPPENING? ➤ You have returned to the desktop.

2.10   DRIVES AS DEVICE NAMES

A disk drive is an example of a device. A device is a place to send information (write) or a place from which to receive information (read). Disk drives have assigned *device names*. These are letters of the alphabet followed by a colon. Using these names, Windows knows which disk drive to read from or write to. When you are at the command prompt, the prompt displayed on the screen tells you where the system is currently "pointing" and from which device data will be read from or written to. If you are using a stand-alone computer, your drive names will typically be A: or B: or C: However, if you are on a network, disk drive letters can vary. They can include such drive letters as J or P or W. Again, the displayed prompt will tell you on what drive (device) the operating system is going to take an action. Disk drives are not the only places where the system sends or receives information. Other common devices are the keyboard, the printer, and the monitor.

2.11   DEFAULTS

In addition to understanding names of devices, it is also important to understand the concept of *defaults*. Computers must have very specific instructions for everything they do. However, there are *implied* instructions that the system falls back to or defaults to in the absence of other instructions. Default, by computer definition, is the value used unless another value is specified. If you do not specify what you want, the system will make the assumption for you. For example, when A:\> is displayed on the screen, it is called the A prompt, but it is also the ***default drive***. When you want any activity to occur but do not specify where you want it to happen, the system assumes the activity will occur on the default drive, the A:\> that is displayed on the screen.

When you key in **DIR** after A:\>, how does the operating system know that you are asking for a table of contents of the disk in Drive A? When a specific direction is given, the operating system must have a specific place to look. A:\>, the default drive, is displayed on the screen. Since you did *not* specify which disk you wanted DIR to check, it defaulted to the default drive—the drive displayed in the prompt on the screen. It deduced that you want the table of contents or directory listing for the default drive, the disk in Drive A.

The prompt displayed on the screen is also known as the ***designated drive*** or the ***logged drive***. All commands, if given no other instructions to the contrary, assume that all reads and writes to the disk drive must take place on the default drive, the drive indicated by the prompt on the screen. When you are not in the MS-DOS Prompt window, the same rules apply. There is indeed a default drive, and in Explorer it is indicated on the title bar.

2.12 ACTIVITY: WORKING WITH DEFAULTS

Note: The ACTIVITIES disk should be in Drive A. You should be at the Windows desktop.

Step 1   Click **Start**. Point at **Programs**. Click **Accessories**. Click **MS-DOS Prompt**.

Step 2   Key in the following: C:\WINDOWS>**A:** (Enter)

```
MS-DOS Prompt                                                          [_][□][X]

C:\WINDOWS>A:

A:\>_

```

WHAT'S HAPPENING?   You have opened the MS-DOS Prompt window. Opening this window is often referred to as "shelling out to DOS" or "shelling out to the command line."

Step 3   Key in the following: A:\>**DIR** (Enter)

```
MS-DOS Prompt                                                          [_][□][X]

 JAN      99          73  10-10-99   4:53p  JAN.99
 TEST     TXT         65  12-11-99   4:03p  TEST.TXT
 GETYN    COM         26  05-02-94  12:57a  GETYN.COM
 WILD1    XXX         64  12-31-01   4:32p  WILD1.XXX
 MAR      TMP         71  04-23-00   4:03p  MAR.TMP
 MARCH    TMP         71  04-23-00   4:03p  MARCH.TMP
```

```
APR      TMP                72    04-23-00   4:18p  APR.TMP
NEWPRSON FIL             2,672    07-31-99  12:53p  NEWPRSON.FIL
Y        FIL                 3    08-12-00   4:12p  Y.FIL
SANDYA~1 TXT                53    11-16-00  12:00p  Sandy and Nicki.txt
SANDYA~2 TXT                59    11-16-00  12:00p  Sandy and Patty.txt
EXP00JAN DAT               294    01-31-00  12:09p  EXP00JAN.DAT
DATA            <DIR>             07-03-00   1:50p  DATA
TEST            <DIR>             07-03-00   1:50p  TEST
GAMES           <DIR>             07-03-00   1:50p  GAMES
PHONE           <DIR>             07-03-00   1:51p  PHONE
FINANCE         <DIR>             07-03-00   1:51p  FINANCE
LEVEL-1         <DIR>             07-03-00   1:52p  LEVEL-1
SPORTS          <DIR>             07-03-00   1:52p  SPORTS
MEDIA           <DIR>             07-03-00   1:53p  MEDIA
WORKING         <DIR>             07-03-00   1:53p  WORKING
         85 file(s)           28,537 bytes
          9 dir(s)           295,936 bytes free

A:\>_
```

WHAT'S HAPPENING? Displayed on the screen is the result of the DIR command you executed. Since you did not specify which disk drive DIR should look into, it assumed or defaulted to the disk in Drive A. Review the syntax diagram: The syntax diagram has [*drive*:], which is another optional variable parameter. You can substitute the letter of the drive you wish DIR to look into.

Step 4   Key in the following: A:\>**DIR A:** Enter

```
MS-DOS Prompt                                                    _ □ ✕

JAN      99                 73    10-10-99   4:53p  JAN.99
TEST     TXT                65    12-11-99   4:03p  TEST.TXT
GETYN    COM                26    05-02-94  12:57a  GETYN.COM
WILD1    XXX                64    12-31-01   4:32p  WILD1.XXX
MAR      TMP                71    04-23-00   4:03p  MAR.TMP
MARCH    TMP                71    04-23-00   4:03p  MARCH.TMP
APR      TMP                72    04-23-00   4:18p  APR.TMP
NEWPRSON FIL             2,672    07-31-99  12:53p  NEWPRSON.FIL
Y        FIL                 3    08-12-00   4:12p  Y.FIL
SANDYA~1 TXT                53    11-16-00  12:00p  Sandy and Nicki.txt
SANDYA~2 TXT                59    11-16-00  12:00p  Sandy and Patty.txt
EXP00JAN DAT               294    01-31-00  12:09p  EXP00JAN.DAT
DATA            <DIR>             07-03-00   1:50p  DATA
TEST            <DIR>             07-03-00   1:50p  TEST
GAMES           <DIR>             07-03-00   1:50p  GAMES
PHONE           <DIR>             07-03-00   1:51p  PHONE
FINANCE         <DIR>             07-03-00   1:51p  FINANCE
LEVEL-1         <DIR>             07-03-00   1:52p  LEVEL-1
SPORTS          <DIR>             07-03-00   1:52p  SPORTS
MEDIA           <DIR>             07-03-00   1:53p  MEDIA
WORKING         <DIR>             07-03-00   1:53p  WORKING
         85 file(s)           28,537 bytes
          9 dir(s)           295,936 bytes free

A:\>_
```

WHAT'S HAPPENING? You substituted **A:** for the variable optional parameter, [*drive*:]. The display, however, is exactly the same as DIR without specifying the drive because A:\> is the default drive. It is unnecessary to key in **A:** but not wrong to do so. If you want to see what files are on Drive C or Drive B, you must tell DIR to look on the drive you are interested in.

Note: Remember that if you are on a network, your hard drive letter may not be C:. Refer to your Configuration Table in section 1.6 for the correct drive letter for your system.

Step 5 Key in the following: A:\>**C:** Enter

Step 6 Key in the following: C:\WINDOWS>**CD ** Enter

```
MS-DOS Prompt                                              _ ☐ ☒

A:\>C:

C:\WINDOWS>CD \

C:\>_
```

WHAT'S HAPPENING! You have changed the default drive to the hard disk, Drive C. You then changed the directory to the root of C.

Step 7 Key in the following: C:\>**DIR A:** Enter

```
MS-DOS Prompt                                              _ ☐ ☒

JAN        99            73   10-10-99   4:53p  JAN.99
TEST       TXT           65   12-11-99   4:03p  TEST.TXT
GETYN      COM           26   05-02-94  12:57a  GETYN.COM
WILD1      XXX           64   12-31-01   4:32p  WILD1.XXX
MAR        TMP           71   04-23-00   4:03p  MAR.TMP
MARCH      TMP           71   04-23-00   4:03p  MARCH.TMP
APR        TMP           72   04-23-00   4:18p  APR.TMP
NEWPRSON   FIL        2,672   07-31-99  12:53p  NEWPRSON.FIL
Y          FIL            3   08-12-00   4:12p  Y.FIL
SANDYA~1   TXT           53   11-16-00  12:00p  Sandy and Nicki.txt
SANDYA~2   TXT           59   11-16-00  12:00p  Sandy and Patty.txt
EXP00JAN   DAT          294   01-31-00  12:09p  EXP00JAN.DAT
DATA            <DIR>         07-03-00   1:50p  DATA
TEST            <DIR>         07-03-00   1:50p  TEST
GAMES           <DIR>         07-03-00   1:50p  GAMES
PHONE           <DIR>         07-03-00   1:51p  PHONE
FINANCE         <DIR>         07-03-00   1:51p  FINANCE
LEVEL-1         <DIR>         07-03-00   1:52p  LEVEL-1
SPORTS          <DIR>         07-03-00   1:52p  SPORTS
MEDIA           <DIR>         07-03-00   1:53p  MEDIA
WORKING         <DIR>         07-03-00   1:53p  WORKING
         85 file(s)          28,537 bytes
          9 dir(s)          295,936 bytes free

C:\>_
```

WHAT'S HAPPENING! The display of files, which scrolled by quickly, is still of the files on Drive A, but this time you *had* to specify the drive because the default drive was no longer A. Keying in **DIR** and a drive letter, **A:**, told the command line, "I want a display of the directory (DIR), but this time I don't want you to display the files on the default drive. I want you to look only on the disk that is in Drive A." As long as you tell the command DIR where you want it to look, you can work *with* and *from* any drive you wish. If you are not specific, the command will execute on the default drive shown by the prompt on the screen (A:\>, B:\>, C:\>, etc.).

Step 8   Key in the following: C:\>**DIR HELLO.TXT** Enter

```
MS-DOS Prompt                                                    _ □ ×

C:\>DIR HELLO.TXT

 Volume in drive C is MILLENNIUM
 Volume Serial Number is 2B18-1301
 Directory of C:\

File not found
                         1,242,734,592 bytes free

C:\>_
```

Step 9   Key in the following: C:\>**DIR A:HELLO.TXT** Enter

```
MS-DOS Prompt                                                    _ □ ×

C:\>DIR A:HELLO.TXT

 Volume in drive A is ACTIVITIES
 Volume Serial Number is 1508-0C25
 Directory of A:\

HELLO    TXT            53   05-30-00  4:32p HELLO.TXT
         1 file(s)             53 bytes
         0 dir(s)         295,936 bytes free

C:\>_
```

WHAT'S HAPPENING? You first asked DIR to look on the default drive for a file called **HELLO.TXT**. The default drive is Drive C. The prompt displayed on the screen, C:\>, is the default drive. Since you did not specify which drive to check for the file called **HELLO.TXT**, DIR assumed the default drive. DIR could not find the **HELLO.TXT** file on the default drive, so it responded with **File not found**. The operating system is not smart enough to say, "Oh, this file is not on the default drive. Let me go check the ACTIVITIES disk in a different disk drive." The operating system followed your instructions exactly.

Your next step was more specific. You made a clearer request: "Look for a file called HELLO.TXT." However, you first told DIR what disk drive to look into—A:. The drive designator (**A:**) preceded the file name (**HELLO.TXT**) because you always tell DIR which "file cabinet" to look in (the disk drive **A:**) before you tell it which "folder" you want (**HELLO.TXT**). By looking at the syntax diagram, you see that you can combine optional variable parameters. You gave DIR [*drive*:][*path*][*filename*[.*ext*]] some specific values—**DIR A:HELLO.TXT**.

The **A:** was substituted for the [*drive*:], and **HELLO.TXT** was substituted for [*filename*[.*ext*]]. So far, you have used the optional variable parameters [*drive*:] and [*filename*[.*ext*]] and the optional fixed parameters [/P] and [/W]. You have not used [*path*].

2.13   A BRIEF INTRODUCTION TO SUBDIRECTORIES—THE PATH

Subdirectories are used primarily, but not exclusively, with hard disks. Hard disks have a large storage capacity (current common values are from 8 to 20 GB), and are therefore more difficult to manage than floppy disks. In general, users like to have similar files grouped together. Subdirectories allow a disk to be divided into smaller, more manageable portions. Windows refers to *subdirectories* as *folders*, and they are graphically represented with folder icons. In the command line shell, folders will be referred to as directories and subdirectories.

Subdirectories can contain other subdirectories. For example, you may have a subdirectory on the root directory of C: called MYFILES. Under MYFILES, you may have three subdirectories, LETTERS, REPORTS, and MISC. Graphically, this structure would appear as follows:

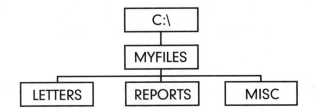

The full path name of a file called REP.DOC that is in the REPORTS directory is C:\MYFILES\REPORTS\REP.DOC. The first \ (backslash) always represents the root directory. The following backslashes without spaces are delimiters—separators between elements in the path, elements being subdirectories and the ending file.

Subdirectories can be used on floppy disks. If you think of a disk as a file cabinet, a subdirectory can be thought of as a drawer in the file cabinet. These file cabinet drawers (subdirectories) also hold disk files. Just as disk drives have a name, such as A:, B:, or C:, subdirectories must also have names so the system will know where to look. Since subdirectories are part of a disk, their names should not be a single letter of the alphabet. Single letters of the alphabet should be reserved for disk drives.

Every disk comes with one directory that is named by the operating system. This directory is called the *root directory* and is indicated by the backslash (\). The prompt displays the default directory as well as the default drive, as in A:\> or C:\>. Technically, there is only one *directory* on any disk—the root directory, referred to only as \. All others are *subdirectories*. However, the terms directories and subdirectories, folders and subfolders are used interchangeably. This textbook will also use the terms directory and subdirectory interchangeably. All subdirectories on a disk have names such as UTILITY or SAMPLE or any other name you choose. The rules for naming subdirectories are the same as for naming files, although subdirectory names do not usually have extensions.

When working with files on a disk, you need to perform certain tasks that can be summarized as finding a file, storing a file, and retrieving a file. Because there are subdirectories on a disk, simply supplying the DIR command with the drive that the file might be on is insufficient information. You must also tell DIR the path to the file. The ***path*** is the route followed by the operating system to locate, save, and retrieve a file. Thus, in a syntax diagram, the path refers to the course leading from the root directory of a drive to a specific file. Simply stated, when you see *path* in a syntax diagram, you substitute the directory name or names. In essence, you are being very specific by telling the DIR command not to go just to the file cabinet (the disk) but to go to a drawer (subdirectory) in the file cabinet.

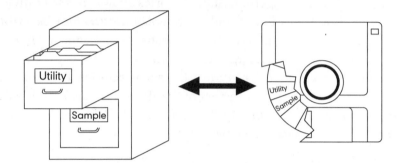

FIGURE 2.1   FILE CABINETS AND SUBDIRECTORIES

2.14   ACTIVITY: USING PATH WITH THE DIR COMMAND

Note: You are at the command line screen. The ACTIVITIES disk is in Drive A. C:\> is displayed as the default drive and the default directory.

Step 1   Key in the following: C:\>**DIR A:** ⌐Enter⌐

```
MS-DOS Prompt                                                      _ □ ✕

JAN       99              73   10-10-99   4:53p  JAN.99
TEST      TXT             65   12-11-99   4:03p  TEST.TXT
GETYN     COM             26   05-02-94  12:57a  GETYN.COM
WILD1     XXX             64   12-31-01   4:32p  WILD1.XXX
MAR       TMP             71   04-23-00   4:03p  MAR.TMP
MARCH     TMP             71   04-23-00   4:03p  MARCH.TMP
APR       TMP             72   04-23-00   4:18p  APR.TMP
NEWPRSON  FIL          2,672   07-31-99  12:53p  NEWPRSON.FIL
Y         FIL              3   08-12-00   4:12p  Y.FIL
SANDYA~1  TXT             53   11-16-00  12:00p  Sandy and Nicki.txt
SANDYA~2  TXT             59   11-16-00  12:00p  Sandy and Patty.txt
EXP00JAN  DAT            294   01-31-00  12:09p  EXP00JAN.DAT
DATA            <DIR>          07-03-00   1:50p  DATA
TEST            <DIR>          07-03-00   1:50p  TEST
GAMES           <DIR>          07-03-00   1:50p  GAMES
PHONE           <DIR>          07-03-00   1:51p  PHONE
FINANCE         <DIR>          07-03-00   1:51p  FINANCE
LEVEL-1         <DIR>          07-03-00   1:52p  LEVEL-1
SPORTS          <DIR>          07-03-00   1:52p  SPORTS
MEDIA           <DIR>          07-03-00   1:53p  MEDIA
WORKING         <DIR>          07-03-00   1:53p  WORKING
           85 file(s)          28,537 bytes
```

```
                 9 dir(s)          295,936 bytes free

    C:\>_
```

WHAT'S HAPPENING? On the screen display there are entries with **<DIR>** following their name, indicating subdirectories. How do you know what files are inside a subdirectory? Look at the beginning of the syntax diagram: DIR [*drive*:][*path*][*filename*[.*ext*]]. You will substitute the specific drive letter for [*drive*:] and substitute the specific subdirectory name for [*path*]. You include \ to indicate that you want to begin at the top of the directory and look down. You want to see what is in the **DATA** subdirectory.

Step 2   Key in the following: C:\>**DIR A:\DATA** Enter

```
MS-DOS Prompt                                                    _ □ ☒

 C:\>DIR A:\DATA

  Volume in drive A is ACTIVITIES
  Volume Serial Number is 1508-0C25
  Directory of A:\DATA

 .                <DIR>          07-03-00   1:50p .
 ..               <DIR>          07-03-00   1:50p ..
 GOOD     TXT           33   08-12-00   4:36p GOOD.TXT
 HIGHEST  TXT           32   08-12-00   4:36p HIGHEST.TXT
 MOTHER   LET          221   05-10-00   4:38p MOTHER.LET
 THIN     EST           83   07-04-00  11:29a THIN.EST
 TEA      TAX           52   07-04-00   4:37p TEA.TAX
 THANK    YOU          250   07-04-00  11:29a THANK.YOU
 BONJOUR  TXT           26   07-03-00   4:36p BONJOUR.TXT
          7 file(s)            697 bytes
          2 dir(s)       295,936 bytes free

 C:\>_
```

WHAT'S HAPPENING? You keyed in the command you wanted to execute, the drive letter you were interested in, the backslash to indicate that you wanted to start at the root directory, and finally the name of the subdirectory. Remember, the first backslash always indicates the root directory. The screen display shows you only what files are in the subdirectory (file drawer) called **DATA**. The third line of the display (**Directory of A:\DATA**) tells you the subdirectory you are looking in. What if you wanted to look for a specific file in a subdirectory? Once again, look at the syntax diagram: DIR [*drive*:][*path*][*filename*[.*ext*]]. You will substitute the drive letter, the path name, and the file name you wish to locate. You need to use a delimiter to separate the file name from the directory name. The delimiter reserved for path names is the backslash. It separates the path name from the file name so that DIR knows which is which.

Note: It is very important to remember that the first backslash always represents the root directory, and any subsequent backslashes are delimiters separating file names from directory names.

Step 3   Key in the following: C:\>**DIR A:\DATA\THIN.EST** Enter

```
  MS-DOS Prompt                                              _ □ ✕

  C:\>DIR A:\DATA\THIN.EST

   Volume in drive A is ACTIVITIES
   Volume Serial Number is 1508-0C25
   Directory of A:\DATA

  THIN      EST               83  07-04-00 11:29a THIN.EST
            1 file(s)                    83 bytes
            0 dir(s)              295,936 bytes free

  C:\>_
```

WHAT'S HAPPENING? ➡ You keyed in the command you wanted to execute, the drive letter you were interested in, the first backslash indicating the root directory, the name of the subdirectory, then a backslash used as a delimiter, and finally the name of the file. The screen display shows you only the file called **THIN.EST** located on the ACTIVITIES disk in the subdirectory DATA.

2.15 CHANGING DEFAULTS

Since you generally work on a specific drive, instead of keying in the drive letter every time, you can change the default drive so that the operating system *automatically* uses the drive displayed on the screen as the default drive.

   Refer to your Configuration Table in Chapter 1.6, or consult your instructor to see where the Windows system utility files are located. If they are in a subdirectory other than C:\WINDOWS\COMMAND, you will have to know the name of that location, and you will have to substitute that path for C:\WINDOWS\COMMAND. For example, if your system command files are located on a network in F:\APPS\WINDOWS\COMMAND, you would substitute that drive and path each time you see C:\WINDOWS\COMMAND in this text. If you have not filled out the information on your Configuration Table in section 1.6 in Chapter 1, you may wish to do so at this time.

2.16 ACTIVITY: CHANGING THE DEFAULT DRIVE

Note: You are in the MS-DOS Prompt window. The ACTIVITIES disk is in Drive A. C:\> is displayed as the default drive and the default directory.

Step 1   Key in the following: C:\>**A:** Enter

```
  MS-DOS Prompt                                              _ □ ✕

  C:\>A:

  A:\>_
```

WHAT'S
HAPPENING? → By keying in a letter followed by a colon, you are telling the system that
you want to change your work area to that designated drive. Thus, when
you keyed in **A:**, you changed the work area from the hard disk, Drive C,
to the floppy disk in Drive A. You have now made A: the default drive.
The assumption the DIR command will make is that all files will come
from the disk in Drive A. It will not look at the hard disk, Drive C.

Step 2   Key in the following: A:\>**DIR** Enter

```
MS-DOS Prompt                                                    _ □ ⊠

  JAN      99            73   10-10-99   4:53p  JAN.99
  TEST     TXT           65   12-11-99   4:03p  TEST.TXT
  GETYN    COM           26   05-02-94  12:57a  GETYN.COM
  WILD1    XXX           64   12-31-01   4:32p  WILD1.XXX
  MAR      TMP           71   04-23-00   4:03p  MAR.TMP
  MARCH    TMP           71   04-23-00   4:03p  MARCH.TMP
  APR      TMP           72   04-23-00   4:18p  APR.TMP
  NEWPRSON FIL        2,672   07-31-99  12:53p  NEWPRSON.FIL
  Y        FIL            3   08-12-00   4:12p  Y.FIL
  SANDYA~1 TXT           53   11-16-00  12:00p  Sandy and Nicki.txt
  SANDYA~2 TXT           59   11-16-00  12:00p  Sandy and Patty.txt
  EXP00JAN DAT          294   01-31-00  12:09p  EXP00JAN.DAT
  DATA          <DIR>        07-03-00   1:50p  DATA
  TEST          <DIR>        07-03-00   1:50p  TEST
  GAMES         <DIR>        07-03-00   1:50p  GAMES
  PHONE         <DIR>        07-03-00   1:51p  PHONE
  FINANCE       <DIR>        07-03-00   1:51p  FINANCE
  LEVEL-1       <DIR>        07-03-00   1:52p  LEVEL-1
  SPORTS        <DIR>        07-03-00   1:52p  SPORTS
  MEDIA         <DIR>        07-03-00   1:53p  MEDIA
  WORKING       <DIR>        07-03-00   1:53p  WORKING
           85 file(s)         28,537 bytes
            9 dir(s)         295,936 bytes free

  A:\>_
```

WHAT'S
HAPPENING? → DIR does not display the directory of the hard disk. It displays the
directory of the ACTIVITIES disk in Drive A. You have changed the
assumption or default, and, since you did not specify which drive you
wanted, the default directory was displayed. Since the default is now
A:\>, if you wish to locate any information on any other disk, you must
specify the parameters and include the letter of the drive and the
subdirectory, if necessary, where the file is located.

Step 3   Key in the following: A:\>**DIR DISKCOPY.COM** Enter

```
MS-DOS Prompt                                                    _ □ ⊠

  A:\>DIR DISKCOPY.COM

   Volume in drive A is ACTIVITIES
   Volume Serial Number is 1508-0C25
   Directory of A:\

  File not found
                        295,936 bytes free

  A:\>_
```

WHAT'S HAPPENING? ➤ Because the default drive is the drive with the ACTIVITIES disk, DIR looked for this file only on the ACTIVITIES disk in Drive A. You must be aware of where you are (what the default drive and subdirectory are) and where your files are located.

Step 4   Key in the following: A:\>**DIR C:\DISKCOPY.COM** [Enter]

```
MS-DOS Prompt                                                      _ □ X

A:\>DIR C:\DISKCOPY.COM

 Volume in drive C is MILLENNIUM
 Volume Serial Number is 2B18-1301
 Directory of C:\

File not found
                       1,242,808,320 bytes free

A:\>_
```

WHAT'S HAPPENING? ➤ Although you did tell DIR to look on Drive C, you were not specific enough. DIR looked only in the root directory of C and could not find the file of interest.

Step 5   Key in the following:
              A:\>**DIR C:\WINDOWS\COMMAND\DISKCOPY.COM** [Enter]
Note: Substitute your drive and/or subdirectory that contains your system utility files if it is different from this example.

```
MS-DOS Prompt                                                      _ □ X

A:\>DIR C:\WINDOWS\COMMAND\DISKCOPY.COM

 Volume in drive C is MILLENNIUM
 Volume Serial Number is 2B18-1301
 Directory of C:\WINDOWS\COMMAND

DISKCOPY COM          21,975  06-08-00  5:00p DISKCOPY.COM
        1 file(s)          21,975 bytes
        0 dir(s)   1,242,804,224 bytes free

A:\>_
```

WHAT'S HAPPENING? ➤ Your dates and times may vary depending on which version of Windows you are using. In this case, because you specified the drive and subdirectory as well as the file name, DIR knew where to look and located the file. You asked DIR not only to look on Drive C, but more specifically to look on Drive C in the subdirectory called **\WINDOWS\COMMAND** for the file called **DISKCOPY.COM**.

2.17 CHANGING DIRECTORIES

In addition to changing drives, you can also change directories. When you work on a hard disk, it is usually divided into subdirectories. Once you establish your default drive, you can also establish your default directory. Then, instead of keying in the path name every time, you can change the default directory so that the operating system will use the directory displayed on the screen as the default directory. To change directories, you key in the command **CD** (which stands for "change directory") followed by the directory (path) name. The partial command syntax is CD [*path*].

If you key in **CD** with no parameters, it tells you the directory that is currently the default. If you wish to change the default, you follow **CD** with a path name such as **CD \WINDOWS\COMMAND**.

2.18 ACTIVITY: CHANGING DIRECTORIES

Note: You are at the command line screen. The ACTIVITIES disk is in Drive A. A:\> is displayed as the default drive and the default directory.

Step 1   Key in the following: A:\>**C:** Enter

Step 2   Key in the following: C:\>**CD** Enter

```
MS-DOS Prompt                                                    _ □ ×

 A:\>C:

 C:\>CD
 C:\

 C:\>_
```

WHAT'S HAPPENING?   When you keyed in **CD**, C:\ displayed, telling you that your current default drive is C and the current default directory is the root or \. In the last activity, when you wanted to locate the file called **DISKCOPY.COM**, you had to precede it with the path name **\WINDOWS\COMMAND**. If you change to that directory, the only place that DIR will look for that file is in the current default directory.

Step 3   Key in the following: C:\>**CD \WINDOWS\COMMAND** Enter

```
MS-DOS Prompt                                                    _ □ ×

 C:\>CD \WINDOWS\COMMAND

 C:\WINDOWS\COMMAND>_
```

WHAT'S HAPPENING?   You told Windows to change from the current directory to a directory called **COMMAND** under a directory called **WINDOWS** under the root (\) of the default drive (C:). You changed directories so that **WINDOWS\COMMAND** is now the default directory. Notice how the prompt displays both the default drive and directory. Whenever you execute any command, the command will look only in the current directory for the file of interest.

Step 4   Key in the following: C:\WINDOWS\COMMAND>**DIR DISKCOPY.COM** Enter

```
┌─────────────────────────────────────────────────────────────────────────┐
│ MS-DOS Prompt                                                    _ □ ✕    │
├─────────────────────────────────────────────────────────────────────────┤
│ C:\WINDOWS\COMMAND>DIR DISKCOPY.COM                                       │
│                                                                           │
│  Volume in drive C is MILLENNIUM                                          │
│  Volume Serial Number is 2B18-1301                                        │
│  Directory of C:\WINDOWS\COMMAND                                          │
│                                                                           │
│ DISKCOPY COM          21,975  06-08-00  5:00p DISKCOPY.COM                │
│         1 file(s)            21,975 bytes                                 │
│         0 dir(s)    1,242,755,072 bytes free                             │
│                                                                           │
│ C:\WINDOWS\COMMAND>_                                                      │
└─────────────────────────────────────────────────────────────────────────┘
```

WHAT'S HAPPENING?   The DIR command looked only in the **\WINDOWS\COMMAND** directory and located the file called **DISKCOPY.COM**. Look at the line that states **Directory of C:\WINDOWS\COMMAND**. DIR always tells you where it has looked. This procedure works with any directory.

Step 5   Key in the following: C:\WINDOWS\COMMAND>**CD ** Enter

```
┌─────────────────────────────────────────────────────────────────────────┐
│ MS-DOS Prompt                                                    _ □ ✕    │
├─────────────────────────────────────────────────────────────────────────┤
│ C:\WINDOWS\COMMAND>CD \                                                   │
│                                                                           │
│ C:\>_                                                                     │
└─────────────────────────────────────────────────────────────────────────┘
```

WHAT'S HAPPENING?   Whenever you key in **CD **, it always takes you to the root directory of the drive you are on.

Step 6   Key in the following: C:\>**A:** Enter

Step 7   Key in the following: A:\>**CD DATA** Enter

Step 8   Key in the following: A:\DATA>**DIR** Enter

```
┌─────────────────────────────────────────────────────────────────────────┐
│ MS-DOS Prompt                                                    _ □ ✕    │
├─────────────────────────────────────────────────────────────────────────┤
│ C:\>A:                                                                    │
│                                                                           │
│ A:\>CD DATA                                                               │
│                                                                           │
│ A:\DATA>DIR                                                               │
│                                                                           │
│  Volume in drive A is ACTIVITIES                                          │
│  Volume Serial Number is 1508-0C25                                        │
│  Directory of A:\DATA                                                     │
│                                                                           │
│ .               <DIR>         07-03-00  1:50p .                           │
│ ..              <DIR>         07-03-00  1:50p ..                          │
│ GOOD     TXT            33    08-12-00  4:36p GOOD.TXT                     │
│ HIGHEST  TXT            32    08-12-00  4:36p HIGHEST.TXT                  │
└─────────────────────────────────────────────────────────────────────────┘
```

```
MOTHER      LET          221   05-10-00   4:38p  MOTHER.LET
THIN        EST           83   07-04-00  11:29a  THIN.EST
TEA         TAX           52   07-04-00   4:37p  TEA.TAX
THANK       YOU          250   07-04-00  11:29a  THANK.YOU
BONJOUR     TXT           26   07-03-00   4:36p  BONJOUR.TXT
            7 file(s)               697 bytes
            2 dir(s)           295,936 bytes free

A:\DATA>_
```

WHAT'S HAPPENING? You used three steps. First, you changed the default drive to A. Second, you changed from the root of the A drive to the **DATA** directory. Last, you executed the DIR command. All files in the **DATA** directory are displayed. You could have looked for a particular file, but, since there are only a few files in the **DATA** directory, you could find any file you are looking for easily.

Step 9   Key in the following: A:\DATA>**CD ** Enter

```
MS-DOS Prompt                                                  _ □ ×

A:\DATA>CD \

A:\>_
```

WHAT'S HAPPENING? You have now returned to the root directory of Drive A.

2.19   GLOBAL FILE SPECIFICATIONS: WILDCARDS, THE ?, AND THE *

Using the DIR command and a file specification, you can find one specific file that matches what you keyed in. Every time you wish to locate a file, you can key the entire file specification. Often, however, you wish to work with a group of files that have similar names or a group of files whose names you do not know. There is a "shorthand" system that allows you to operate on a group of files rather than a single file. This system is formally called *global file specifications*; informally, it is called using *wildcards*. Sometimes it is referred to as ambiguous file references. Conceptually, they are similar to playing cards, where the joker can stand for another card of your choice. In Windows, the question mark (?) and the asterisk (*) are the wildcards. These symbols stand for unknowns. The * represents or substitutes for a group or *string* of characters; the ? represents or substitutes for a *single* character. Many commands allow you to use global file specifications. You will use the DIR command to demonstrate the use of wildcards. You will find that the techniques you learn here will also apply when you use Search in the GUI (the Windows desktop).

2.20   ACTIVITY: DIR AND WILDCARDS

Note: The ACTIVITIES disk is in Drive A. A:\> is displayed as the default drive and the default directory.

Step 1   Key in the following: A:\>**C:** Enter

Step 2   Key in the following: C:\>**CD \WINDOWS\COMMAND** Enter

Note: Remember that if the system utility files are in a subdirectory with a different name, you will have to substitute your subdirectory name.

```
 MS-DOS Prompt                                                        _ □ ✕

A:\>C:

C:\WINDOWS>CD \WINDOWS\COMMAND

C:\WINDOWS\COMMAND>_

```

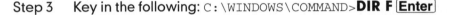 You have changed the default directory to where the system utility files are located. If you wanted to locate a file and all you remembered about the file name was that it began with the letter F and that it was located on the default drive and subdirectory, you would not be able to find that file. You have insufficient information.

Step 3   Key in the following: C:\WINDOWS\COMMAND>**DIR F** Enter

```
 MS-DOS Prompt                                                        _ □ ✕

C:\WINDOWS\COMMAND>DIR F

 Volume in drive C is MILLENNIUM
 Volume Serial Number is 2B18-1301
 Directory of C:\WINDOWS\COMMAND

File not found
                   1,247,850,496 bytes free

C:\WINDOWS\COMMAND>_

```

WHAT'S HAPPENING?   First, note how the prompt reflects the subdirectory **\WINDOWS\COMMAND** and shows the C:\WINDOWS\COMMAND> prompt. When you keyed in **DIR F**, you were correct, but only somewhat. You first entered the work you wanted done, the command DIR. You did not need to enter the drive letter. DIR assumed both the default drive and default subdirectory. However, DIR specifically looked for a file called **F**. There was no file called **F**; that was simply the first letter of the file name. You could find files that begin with F by using the wildcard symbol * to represent all other characters—both the file name (*) and the file extension (.*).

Step 4   Key in the following: C:\WINDOWS\COMMAND>**DIR F*.*** Enter

```
 MS-DOS Prompt                                                        _ □ ✕

C:\WINDOWS\COMMAND>DIR F*.*

 Volume in drive C is MILLENNIUM
 Volume Serial Number is 2B18-1301
```

```
Directory of C:\WINDOWS\COMMAND

FDISK     EXE        66,060  06-08-00  5:00p  FDISK.EXE
FORMAT    COM        49,415  06-08-00  5:00p  FORMAT.COM
FC        EXE        20,574  06-08-00  5:00p  FC.EXE
FIND      EXE         6,658  06-08-00  5:00p  FIND.EXE
          4 file(s)        142,707 bytes
          0 dir(s)   1,260,433,408 bytes free

C:\WINDOWS\COMMAND>_
```

WHAT'S HAPPENING? The files listed in the subdirectory vary, depending on the release or version of the OS, so do not worry if your screen display is different. You asked DIR to find files beginning with the letter F on the default drive and default subdirectory. You did not know anything else about the file names or even how many files you might have that begin with the letter F. You represented any and all characters following the letter F with the asterisk, separated the file name from the file extension with a period, and represented all the characters in the file extension with the second asterisk. Thus, **F*.*** (read as "F star dot star") means all the files that start with the letter F can have any or no characters following the letter F, and can have any or no file extension. Now DIR could look for a match.

In this example, the first file DIR found that had the F you specified was **FDISK.EXE**. DIR returned this file because the asterisk (*) following the F matched the remainder of the file name, DISK. Remember, * represents any group of characters. The second *, representing the file extension, matched **.EXE** because, again, the * represents any group of characters. The second file DIR found that began with F was **FORMAT.COM**. DIR displayed this file because the * following the F matched the remainder of the file name, ORMAT. The second * representing the file extension matched **.COM** because, again, the * represents any group of characters. The rest of the files match F*.* for the same reasons. You could have more or fewer files depending on how your system is set up.

There are other ways of requesting information using the *. If all you know about a group of files on the disk in the default drive is that the group has the common file extension **.SYS,** you could display these files on the screen using wildcards.

Step 5 Key in the following: C:\WINDOWS\COMMAND>**DIR *.SYS** Enter

```
MS-DOS Prompt                                          _ □ ×

C:\WINDOWS\COMMAND>DIR *.SYS

 Volume in drive C is MILLENNIUM
 Volume Serial Number is 2B18-1301
 Directory of C:\WINDOWS\COMMAND

ANSI      SYS         9,719  06-08-00  5:00p  ANSI.SYS
COUNTRY   SYS        30,742  06-08-00  5:00p  COUNTRY.SYS
```

```
KEYBOARD SYS         34,566  06-08-00  5:00p KEYBOARD.SYS
KEYBRD2  SYS         31,942  06-08-00  5:00p KEYBRD2.SYS
KEYBRD3  SYS         31,633  06-08-00  5:00p KEYBRD3.SYS
KEYBRD4  SYS         13,014  06-08-00  5:00p KEYBRD4.SYS
             6 file(s)          151,616 bytes
             0 dir(s)     1,260,449,792 bytes free

C:\WINDOWS\COMMAND>_
```

WHAT'S HAPPENING?   The * represented any file name, but all the files must have **.SYS** as a file extension. Again, the number of files displayed may vary. The next activities will demonstrate the differences between the two wildcards, * and ?.

Step 6   Key in the following: C:\WINDOWS\COMMAND>**DIR A:*.TXT** Enter

```
MS-DOS Prompt                                                    _ □ ×

C:\WINDOWS\COMMAND>DIR A:\*.TXT

 Volume in drive A is ACTIVITIES
 Volume Serial Number is 1508-0C25
 Directory of A:\

GOODBYE  TXT             34  01-01-02  4:32a GOODBYE.TXT
APRIL    TXT             72  06-16-00  4:32p APRIL.TXT
JANUARY  TXT             73  06-16-00  4:32p JANUARY.TXT
FEBRUARY TXT             75  06-16-00  4:32p FEBRUARY.TXT
MARCH    TXT             71  06-16-00  4:32p MARCH.TXT
HELLO    TXT             53  05-30-00  4:32p HELLO.TXT
BYE      TXT             45  05-30-00  4:32p BYE.TXT
DANCES   TXT             72  12-11-99  4:03p DANCES.TXT
TEST     TXT             65  12-11-99  4:03p TEST.TXT
SANDYA~1 TXT             53  11-16-00 12:00p Sandy and Nicki.txt
SANDYA~2 TXT             59  11-16-00 12:00p Sandy and Patty.txt
           11 file(s)         672 bytes
            0 dir(s)      295,936 bytes free

C:\WINDOWS\COMMAND>_
```

WHAT'S HAPPENING?   You asked DIR what files had an extension of **.TXT** and were located on the ACTIVITIES disk. You did not know anything about the file names, only the file extension. DIR searched the table of contents in Drive A since you placed an **A:** prior to ***.TXT**. It looked only in the root directory of the disk since you preceded ***.TXT** with \. The command found 11 files that matched ***.TXT**. Now how does the question mark differ from the asterisk?

Step 7   Key in the following: C:\WINDOWS\COMMAND>**DIR A:\?????.TXT** Enter

```
MS-DOS Prompt                                                    _ □ ×

C:\WINDOWS\COMMAND>DIR A:\?????.TXT

 Volume in drive A is ACTIVITIES
 Volume Serial Number is 1508-0C25
 Directory of A:\
```

```
APRIL    TXT              72  06-16-00  4:32p APRIL.TXT
MARCH    TXT              71  06-16-00  4:32p MARCH.TXT
HELLO    TXT              53  05-30-00  4:32p HELLO.TXT
         3 file(s)              196 bytes
         0 dir(s)          295,936 bytes free

C:\WINDOWS\COMMAND>_
```

WHAT'S HAPPENING? ➤ This time you asked your question differently. You still asked for files that had the file extension of **.TXT** in the root directory of the ACTIVITIES disk. However, instead of using the asterisk representing "any number of characters," you used the question mark (?) five times. For DIR, this means look for any file name that starts with any letter and that has a file name *exactly* five characters in length. This is a change from previous versions of DOS. In DOS 6.22 and previous versions, the same command would have referred to a file name that was five characters or fewer in length. The Windows wildcard is more specific. You asked for a file name with five characters and it displayed files with exactly five characters in their file name, no more and no less. You then separated the file name from the file extension with a period saying that the file not only needed to have a five-letter name, but the extension **.TXT**. This time only three files matched your request. Note how the above screen display differs from the screen display in Step 6. This time you do not see the files **GOODBYE.TXT**, **JANUARY.TXT**, **FEBRUARY.TXT**, **BYE.TXT**, **DANCES.TXT**, **TEST.TXT**, **SANDYA~1.TXT**, or **SANDYA~2.TXT** on the screen. Those file names were either longer or shorter than five characters.

Step 8 Key in the following: C:\WINDOWS\COMMAND>**DIR A:\EXP*.*** [Enter]

```
MS-DOS Prompt                                                    _ □ ×

C:\WINDOWS\COMMAND>DIR A:\EXP*.*

 Volume in drive A is ACTIVITIES
 Volume Serial Number is 1508-0C25
 Directory of A:\

EXP01JAN DAT             304  01-31-01  12:09p EXP01JAN.DAT
EXP01FEB DAT             307  02-28-01  12:10p EXP01FEB.DAT
EXP99MAR DAT             294  03-31-99  12:11p EXP99MAR.DAT
EXP99JAN DAT             294  01-31-99  12:09p EXP99JAN.DAT
EXP01MAR DAT             302  03-31-01  12:11p EXP01MAR.DAT
EXP00MAR DAT             292  03-31-00  12:11p EXP00MAR.DAT
EXP00FEB DAT             297  02-28-00  12:10p EXP00FEB.DAT
EXP99FEB DAT             295  02-28-99  12:10p EXP99FEB.DAT
EXP00JAN DAT             294  01-31-00  12:09p EXP00JAN.DAT
         9 file(s)            2,679 bytes
         0 dir(s)          295,936 bytes free

C:\WINDOWS\COMMAND>_
```

WHAT'S HAPPENING? ➤ This time you asked to see all the files located on the ACTIVITIES disk (Drive A) in the root directory (\) that start with the letters EXP

(EXP*.*). The *.* following the EXP represents the rest of the file name and the file extension. These file names were created with a pattern in mind. Budget files start with EXP which stands for expenses, followed by the last two digits of the year (99, 00, or 01), followed by the month (JANuary, FEBruary, or MARch). The file extension is .DAT to indicate these are data files, not program files. However, often you are not interested in all the files. You want only some of them. For example, you might want to know what expense files you have on the ACTIVITIES disk for the year 1999.

Step 9   Key in the following: C:\WINDOWS\COMMAND>**DIR A:\EXP99*.*** (Enter)

```
MS-DOS Prompt                                               _ □ ×

C:\WINDOWS\COMMAND>DIR A:\EXP99*.*

 Volume in drive A is ACTIVITIES
 Volume Serial Number is 1508-0C25
 Directory of A:\

EXP99MAR DAT            294   03-31-99 12:11p EXP99MAR.DAT
EXP99JAN DAT            294   01-31-99 12:09p EXP99JAN.DAT
EXP99FEB DAT            295   02-28-99 12:10p EXP99FEB.DAT
        3 file(s)              883 bytes
        0 dir(s)          295,936 bytes free

C:\WINDOWS\COMMAND>_
```

WHAT'S HAPPENING?   Here you asked for all the files on the ACTIVITIES disk in Drive A in the root directory that were expense files for 1999 (**EXP99**). The rest of the file names were represented by ***.***. On your screen display, you got only the 1999 files. However, suppose your interest is in all the January files. You no longer care which year, only which month.

Step 10   Key in the following: C:\WINDOWS\COMMAND>**DIR A:\EXP??JAN.*** (Enter)

```
MS-DOS Prompt                                               _ □ ×

C:\WINDOWS\COMMAND>DIR A:\EXP??JAN.*

 Volume in drive A is ACTIVITIES
 Volume Serial Number is 1508-0C25
 Directory of A:\

EXP01JAN DAT            304   01-31-01 12:09p EXP01JAN.DAT
EXP99JAN DAT            294   01-31-99 12:09p EXP99JAN.DAT
EXP00JAN DAT            294   01-31-00 12:09p EXP00JAN.DAT
        3 file(s)              892 bytes
        0 dir(s)          295,936 bytes free

C:\WINDOWS\COMMAND>_
```

WHAT'S HAPPENING?   The two question marks represented the two characters within the file name. The characters could have been any characters but they would be limited to two characters. You could have also keyed in **DIR EXP*JAN.***

because Windows will recognize characters entered after a wildcard. Previous versions of the operating system would have ignored all characters after the asterisk, allowing any and all characters to fill the remaining spaces. The command **DIR *JAN.*** would have resulted in the same display as **DIR *.***. Windows, however, does recognize characters following the asterisk wildcard, and the resulting display shows you the files you were looking for. However, if you had files such as **EXP2001JAN.DAT** and **EXP01JAN.DAT**, using **DIR EXP*JAN.DAT** would display both files but using **DIR EXP??JAN.DAT** would only display the **EXP01.DAT** file.

Step 11   Key in the following: C:\WINDOWS\COMMAND>**CD ** [Enter]

```
MS-DOS Prompt                                                    _ □ X

C:\WINDOWS\COMMAND>CD \

C:\>_
```

WHAT'S HAPPENING? ➤ You have returned to the root directory of C.

2.21 REDIRECTION

The system knows what you want to do when you key in commands. In the MS-DOS Prompt window, input is expected from the keyboard, which is considered the ***standard input*** device. In addition, the results of a command's execution are written to the screen. The screen, or monitor, is considered the ***standard output*** device.

You can change this through a feature called ***redirection***. Redirection allows you to tell the operating system to, instead of writing the output to the standard output device (the screen), write the information somewhere else. Typically, this is to a file or to a printer. Redirection does not work with all commands, only with commands that write their output to standard output. Redirection does work with the DIR command because DIR gets its input from the standard input device, the keyboard, and writes to the standard output device, the screen. The syntax is for redirection is: COMMAND > DESTINATION. The command is what you key in, such as **DIR *.TXT**. You then use the greater-than symbol (>) to redirect the results of that command to where you specify, instead of to the screen. A space is required on both sides of the greater-than sign (>). The command would be keyed in as **DIR *.TXT > MY.FIL** to send the results, or output of the DIR command, to a file named **MY.FIL**. The command would be keyed in as **DIR *.TXT > LPT1** if you wanted the output to go to the printer attached to the first printer port. You must use the device name for the printer, PRN for the default printer, or LPT1, LPT2, or LPT3 for a printer attached to a specific port or assigned to a specific port by your network.

2.22 ACTIVITY: REDIRECTING OUTPUT TO A FILE

Note: The system is booted. You have shelled out to the command prompt screen. The ACTIVITIES disk is in Drive A. C:\> is displayed as the default drive and the default directory.

Step 1   Key in the following: C:\>**A:** [Enter]

Step 2   Key in the following: A:\>**DIR *.NEW** [Enter]

```
MS-DOS Prompt                                                    _ □ ×

C:\>A:

A:\>DIR *.NEW

 Volume in drive A is ACTIVITIES
 Volume Serial Number is 1508-0C25
 Directory of A:\

JAN      NEW              73  10-01-99   2:53p JAN.NEW
APR      NEW              74  10-01-99   2:53p APR.NEW
FEB      NEW              75  10-01-99   2:53p FEB.NEW
MAR      NEW              71  10-01-99   2:53p MAR.NEW
         4 file(s)              293 bytes
         0 dir(s)          295,936 bytes free

A:\>_
```

WHAT'S HAPPENING? ➤ You changed the default drive to the A drive. You then asked for all the files on the ACTIVITIES disk that have the file extension of **.NEW**. You saw the output displayed on the screen. You have four files that meet the criteria. You keyed in a command and the results were sent to the screen.

You are now going to create a file on your ACTIVITIES disk using redirection. Remember that when the instructions in this text say "ACTIVITIES disk" they mean the copy of the ACTIVITIES disk you made in Chapter 1. It is this disk that is in the A drive.

Step 3   Key in the following: A:\>**DIR *.NEW > MY.HW** [Enter]

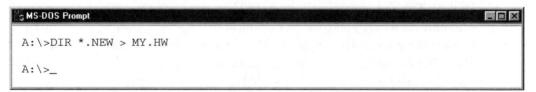

```
MS-DOS Prompt                                                    _ □ ×

A:\>DIR *.NEW > MY.HW

A:\>_
```

WHAT'S HAPPENING? ➤ This time you instructed the system to send the output of the DIR command to a file called **MY.HW**, instead of sending the output to the screen. Redirection is an "instead of" procedure. You either have the results of the DIR command displayed on the screen, or you send it to a file.

Note: If you get the message **Write protect error reading drive A Abort, Retry, Fail?**, your disk is write-protected. Remove the disk and move the sliding tab to cover the small hole in the corner to unprotect it. Reinsert the disk and press **A** (Abort) to return you to the command prompt. Then redo Step 3.

Step 4   Key in the following: A:\>**DIR MY.HW** [Enter]

```
MS-DOS Prompt                                                    _ □ ×

A:\>DIR MY.HW

 Volume in drive A is ACTIVITIES
 Volume Serial Number is 1508-0C25
 Directory of A:\

MY        HW            393   07-15-00  4:16p MY.HW
          1 file(s)              393 bytes
          0 dir(s)          295,424 bytes free


A:\>_
```

WHAT'S
HAPPENING? ➤   You now have a file that contains the output from the DIR command.

2.23   REDIRECTING OUTPUT TO THE PRINTER

You have seen that you can redirect output to a file. You can also redirect output to the printer. Since the DIR command normally writes to the screen, you can redirect the output of the DIR command to the printer to get a printout of what normally would be written to the screen. However, you cannot use just any name with a device, as you can with a file name. Windows has very specific names for its devices. You already know that a letter of the alphabet followed by a colon (:) is always a disk drive. Printers also have names. The printer device names are PRN, LPT1, LPT2, and sometimes LPT3. PRN is the default printer, usually LPT1.

CAUTION!   **BEFORE DOING THE NEXT ACTIVITY, CHECK WITH YOUR LAB INSTRUCTOR TO SEE IF THERE ARE ANY SPECIAL PRINTING PROCEDURES IN YOUR LAB. SOMETIMES, FOR INSTANCE, A NETWORK ENVIRONMENT WILL NOT LET YOU USE THE DEVICE NAME PRN. YOU MUST USE THE ALTERNATE NAME LPT1. BE SURE TO USE THE NUMBER ONE, NOT THE LOWER-CASE L. YOU MAY NEED TO USE LPT2 IN SOME INSTANCES. OFTEN, IN A NETWORK ENVIRONMENT, THERE IS A SHARED PRINTER AND YOU CANNOT REDIRECT THE OUTPUT TO THE PRINTER IN THE MANNER DESCRIBED.**

2.24   ACTIVITY: REDIRECTING THE OUTPUT TO THE PRINTER

Note 1: DO NOT do this activity until you have checked with your lab instructor for any special instructions. In fact, you may be unable to do the activity. If you cannot do it, read the activity.

Note 2: The ACTIVITIES disk is in Drive A. A: \> is displayed as the default drive and the default directory. Be sure the printer is turned on and online before beginning this activity.

Step 1   Key in the following: A: \>**DIR *.TXT** Enter

```
MS-DOS Prompt                                                    _ □ ✕

A:\>DIR *.TXT

 Volume in drive A is ACTIVITIES
 Volume Serial Number is 1508-0C25
 Directory of A:\

GOODBYE   TXT           34  01-01-02   4:32a GOODBYE.TXT
APRIL     TXT           72  06-16-00   4:32p APRIL.TXT
JANUARY   TXT           73  06-16-00   4:32p JANUARY.TXT
FEBRUARY  TXT           75  06-16-00   4:32p FEBRUARY.TXT
MARCH     TXT           71  06-16-00   4:32p MARCH.TXT
HELLO     TXT           53  05-30-00   4:32p HELLO.TXT
BYE       TXT           45  05-30-00   4:32p BYE.TXT
DANCES    TXT           72  12-11-99   4:03p DANCES.TXT
TEST      TXT           65  12-11-99   4:03p TEST.TXT
SANDYA~1 TXT            53  11-16-00  12:00p Sandy and Nicki.txt
SANDYA~2 TXT            59  11-16-00  12:00p Sandy and Patty.txt
        11 file(s)            672 bytes
         0 dir(s)         295,424 bytes free

A:\>_
```

WHAT'S HAPPENING? ➤ You asked for all the files on the ACTIVITIES disk that had the file extension of **.TXT**.

Step 2   Key in the following: A: \>**DIR *.TXT > PRN** Enter

WHAT'S HAPPENING? ➤ You instructed the operating system to send the output to an alternate output device, specifically the printer, instead of displaying it on the screen. The printer should be printing, and nothing should be on the screen. Remember, redirection is an "instead of" procedure. You either display the results of the DIR command on the screen, or send the results to the printer. See Figure 2.2.

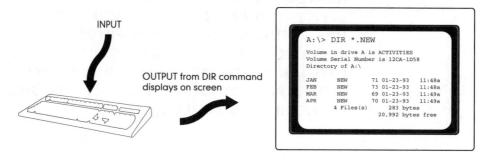

FIGURE 2.2   REDIRECTED OUTPUT

WHAT'S HAPPENING? ➤ If you have a dot-matrix printer, it printed the lines in the file and then it stopped. The printer did not advance to the beginning of a new page.

If you are on a network, your network administrator may have arranged to have a "form feed" message sent to the printer after each print job is sent to it. If this is the case, the paper will advance to a new page. If you are printing on a non-networked printer and you wanted this printout (hard copy), you would have to go to the printer and roll the platen until the perforated line appeared so that you could tear off the page. If you have an inkjet printer or a laser printer, the situation is even stranger. No paper appears at all. In order to feed the paper manually with an ink jet printer, you have to press the **Reset** button. With a laser printer, you have to go to the printer, turn the **Online** button off, press the form feed (**FF**) button, and then turn the **Online** button back on. In all these cases, you are providing what is called a *hardware solution* to a problem. You are manipulating the hardware to get the desired results.

With computers, there is always an easier way. What you want is a *software solution*, making the computer do the work. The problem in printing a page on a printer is that a computer has no idea what a page is or when it is finished printing. Thus, you want to send a signal to the printer that the page is over. You want the printer to eject the page that is printed and have the paper advance to a clean, empty sheet. This signal is known as a form feed, a page eject, or top of form. Most printers universally use Ctrl + **L** as the signal for a form feed. The problem is how to send this signal from the computer to the printer. Again, you will use redirection and a command called ECHO. ECHO is an internal command that you have not used before. ECHO can send a signal to the printer if you tell it to. Remember, when you see the notation of Ctrl + **L**, it means you are to hold down the Ctrl key and press the letter **L**.

Note: Many networks automatically send a form feed instruction to the shared printer after each print job. If this is so in your lab, do not do Step 3. Some printers will automatically eject the page as well. If that is true, skip Step 3.

Step 3   Key in the following: A:\>**ECHO** Ctrl + **L > PRN** Enter

```
MS-DOS Prompt                                          _ □ ×
A:\>DIR *.TXT > PRN

A:\>ECHO ^L > PRN

A:\>_
```

WHAT'S HAPPENING? The paper should eject. Look at the screen. When you keyed in Ctrl + **L**, it appeared on the screen as **^L**. If this procedure did not work for you, you will need to roll the paper manually on a dot-matrix printer. For an inkjet printer, press the **Reset** or **Clear** button. For a laser printer, turn the **Online** button off, press the form feed (**FF**) button, and then turn the **Online** button back on.

2.25 GETTING HELP

As you begin to use commands, their names, purposes, and proper syntax become familiar. Initially, however, these commands are new to users. Prior to DOS 5.0, the only way to become familiar with a command or to check the proper syntax was to locate the command in the manual. The reference manual that comes with any software package is called *documentation*. The completeness of the documentation can vary from software package to software package. The documentation that comes with an operating system consists of at least the installation instructions and occasionally a command reference manual, which is a list of commands with a brief description and syntax for each. For the Windows operating systems, documentation is in the form of text files on the CD. In DOS 6.0 and above, the documentation has been provided less and less in written form, and more and more online. There is a very good database of information that can be accessed via the Help choice on the Start menu from the desktop, but this help is for procedures and methods used in the Windows GUI, not the commands used from the MS-DOS Prompt screen. To get help with a command and its syntax, key in the name of the command, followed by a space, a forward slash (/), and a question mark (?). For reference, the commands and syntax resulting from this command are listed in Appendix B.

2.26 ACTIVITY: GETTING HELP WITH A COMMAND

Note: The ACTIVITIES disk is in Drive A. A:\> is displayed as the default drive and the default directory.

Step 1   Key in the following: A:\>**C:** Enter

Step 2   Key in the following: C:\>**CD \WINDOWS\COMMAND** Enter

```
MS-DOS Prompt                                              _ □ ×

A:\>C:

C:\>CD \WINDOWS\COMMAND

C:\WINDOWS\COMMAND>_
```

WHAT'S HAPPENING!   You have changed drives and directories to the directory containing the operating system commands on the hard disk.

Step 3   Key in the following: C:\WINDOWS\COMMAND>**DIR /?** Enter

```
MS-DOS Prompt                                              _ □ ×

        Displays a list of files and subdirectories in a directory.

DIR [drive:][path][filename] [/P] [/W] [/A[[:]attributes]]
  [/O[[:]sortorder]] [/S] [/B] [/L] [/V] [/4]

  [drive:][path][filename]
          Specifies drive, directory, and/or files to list.
          (Could be enhanced file specification or multiple filespecs.)
  /P      Pauses after each screenful of information.
```

```
  /W          Uses wide list format.
  /A          Displays files with specified attributes.
  attributes  D  Directories          R  Read-only files
              H  Hidden files         A  Files ready for archiving
              S  System files         -  Prefix meaning not
  /O          List by files in sorted order.
  sortorder   N  By name (alphabetic)   S  By size (smallest first)
              E  By extension(alphabetic) D  By date & time (earliest first)
              G  Group directories first  -  Prefix to reverse order
              A  By Last Access Date (earliest first)
  /S          Displays files in specified directory and all subdirectories.
  /B          Uses bare format (no heading information or summary).
  /L          Uses lowercase.
  /V          Verbose mode.
  /4          Displays year with 4 digits (ignored if /V also given).

Switches may be preset in the DIRCMD environment variable.  Override
preset switches by prefixing any switch with - (hyphen)—for example, /-W.


C:\WINDOWS\COMMAND>_
```

WHAT'S HAPPENING! ➤ On your screen, the first three lines of text will have scrolled off the screen. In this text, you see the entire display. This display is a complete syntax explanation for the DIR command. Previously, we looked at only a partial syntax diagram for the DIR command. Notice the first line of the complete diagram: **[/O[[:]sortorder]] [/S] [/B] [/L] [/V] [/4]**

Notice that the entire line is in brackets, **[ ]**, meaning that all of the parameters or switches are optional. The DIR command can stand alone—it requires no parameters. You may include the drive, path, and file name **[:]**, and you may specify the order (**/O**) in which you wish the files displayed. Look at the diagram around the twelfth line of the display, which begins with **/O List by files in sorted order**. Below that are the orders available. **N** is by name, **S** by size, **E** by extension, **D** by date, and so on.

Step 4   Key in the following: C:\WINDOWS\COMMAND>**A:** Enter

Step 5   Key in the following: A:\>**DIR /ON** Enter

```
MS-DOS Prompt                                               [_][□][X]

  RIGHT     RED            61   10-01-00   4:12p  RIGHT.RED
  RNS       EXE         7,269   11-22-89  10:35p  RNS.EXE
  SANDYA~1  TXT            53   11-16-00  12:00p  Sandy and Nicki.txt
  SANDYA~2  TXT            59   11-16-00  12:00p  Sandy and Patty.txt
  SECOND    FIL            75   08-12-00   4:12p  SECOND.FIL
  SPORTS          <DIR>         07-03-00   1:52p  SPORTS
  STATE     CAP           260   07-31-00   4:32p  STATE.CAP
  STATE2    CAP           265   07-31-00   4:32p  STATE2.CAP
  STATES    USA         1,228   07-31-00   4:32p  STATES.USA
  STEVEN    FIL            46   07-31-99  12:53p  STEVEN.FIL
  TEST      TXT            65   12-11-99   4:03p  TEST.TXT
  TEST            <DIR>         07-03-00   1:50p  TEST
  WILD1     XXX            64   12-31-01   4:32p  WILD1.XXX
  WILD2     YYY            64   12-31-01   4:32p  WILD2.YYY
  WILD3     ZZZ            64   12-31-01   4:32p  WILD3.ZZZ
  WILDONE   DOS           181   12-31-01   4:32p  WILDONE.DOS
```

```
WILDONE                   93  12-31-01   4:32p  WILDONE
WILDTHR  DOS             181  12-31-01   4:32p  WILDTHR.DOS
WILDTWO  DOS             182  12-31-01   4:32p  WILDTWO.DOS
WORKING        <DIR>          07-03-00   1:53p  WORKING
Y        FIL               3  08-12-00   4:12p  Y.FIL
         86 file(s)           28,930 bytes
          9 dir(s)           295,424 bytes free

A:\>_
```

WHAT'S HAPPENING? ➤ Notice that the files are displayed in alphabetical order. You can reverse the order.

Step 6　Key in the following: A:\>**DIR /O-N** Enter

```
MS-DOS Prompt                                          _ □ ✕

EXP00MAR DAT             292  03-31-00  12:11p  EXP00MAR.DAT
EXP00JAN DAT             294  01-31-00  12:09p  EXP00JAN.DAT
EXP00FEB DAT             297  02-28-00  12:10p  EXP00FEB.DAT
EMPLOYEE ONE              53  11-06-00   4:12p  EMPLOYEE.ONE
EMPLOYEE THR              57  11-06-00   4:12p  EMPLOYEE.THR
EMPLOYEE TWO              54  11-06-00   4:12p  EMPLOYEE.TWO
DRESS    UP               26  10-01-00   4:12p  DRESS.UP
DATA           <DIR>          07-03-00   1:50p  DATA
DANCES   TXT              72  12-11-99   4:03p  DANCES.TXT
CASES    FIL             314  08-12-00   4:12p  CASES.FIL
CAROLYN  FIL              47  07-31-99  12:53p  CAROLYN.FIL
BYE      TYP              45  05-30-00   4:32p  BYE.TYP
BYE      TXT              45  05-30-00   4:32p  BYE.TXT
BONJOUR  TMP              53  04-23-00   4:03p  BONJOUR.TMP
BLUE     JAZ              19  05-30-00   4:32p  BLUE.JAZ
AWARD    MOV              86  05-30-00   4:32p  AWARD.MOV
APRIL    TMP              72  04-23-00   4:03p  APRIL.TMP
APRIL    TXT              72  06-16-00   4:32p  APRIL.TXT
APR      NEW              74  10-01-99   2:53p  APR.NEW
APR      99               72  10-10-99   4:53p  APR.99
APR      TMP              72  04-23-00   4:18p  APR.TMP
         86 file(s)           28,930 bytes
          9 dir(s)           295,424 bytes free

A:\>_
```

WHAT'S HAPPENING? ➤ The file names scrolled by quickly, but they were in reverse alphabetical order, from Z to A. Thus, by using the parameters **/O-N** (**O** for order, the **-** for reverse, and **N** for file name), you accomplished your task.

Step 7　Key in the following: A:\>**DIR /S** Enter

```
MS-DOS Prompt                                          _ □ ✕

FOOT-PRO TMS             207  12-25-99  11:36a  FOOT-PRO.TMS
BSBALL-N TMS             222  02-24-00  11:36a  BSBALL-N.TMS
BASKETBL TMS             222  10-31-00   4:43p  BASKETBL.TMS
BSBALL-A TMS             211  02-24-00  11:36a  BSBALL-A.TMS
          5 file(s)            1,089 bytes

Directory of A:\TEST

.              <DIR>          07-03-00   1:50p  .
```

```
..                 <DIR>           07-03-00  1:50p  ..
NEW      FIL          32   01-01-02  4:43p  NEW.FIL
SAMPLE   FIL          24   01-01-02  4:43p  SAMPLE.FIL
         2 file(s)              56 bytes

Directory of A:\WORKING

.                  <DIR>           07-03-00  1:53p  .
..                 <DIR>           07-03-00  1:53p  ..
         0 file(s)               0 bytes

Total files listed:
     153 file(s)      1,098,110 bytes
      48 dir(s)         295,424 bytes free

A:\>_
```

WHAT'S HAPPENING? ▶ Again, the file names scrolled by quickly, but this time, all the files on the disk, including those in the subdirectories, were displayed. The /S parameter displays all the files from the specified directory and all its subdirectories.

Using the different parameters available with the DIR command, you can display files sorted by their *attributes* (covered in a later chapter), display only the names of the files with no additional information (/B), or display the information in lowercase (/L). You can display the directories at the beginning or end of the list (G or -G). The verbose (/V) parameter is very useful. It displays additional information about each directory entry.

Step 8   Key in the following: A:\>**DIR /V /P** Enter

```
MS-DOS Prompt                                            _ □ ×

  Volume in drive A is ACTIVITIES
  Volume Serial Number is 1508-0C25
  Directory of A:\
  File Name    Size   Allocated    Modified      Accessed    Attrib


  BYE      TYP    45        512   05-30-00  4:32p  07-03-00      A
  BYE.TYP
  CASES    FIL   314        512   08-12-00  4:12p  07-03-00      A
  CASES.FIL
  APRIL    TMP    72        512   04-23-00  4:03p  07-03-00      A
  APRIL.TMP
  BONJOUR  TMP    53        512   04-23-00  4:03p  07-03-00      A
  BONJOUR.TMP
  FEB      TMP    75        512   04-23-00  4:03p  07-03-00      A
  FEB.TMP
  GOODBYE  TMP    34        512   01-01-02  4:32a  07-03-00      A
  GOODBYE.TMP
  FEBRUARY TMM    75        512   05-30-00  4:32p  07-03-00      A
  FEBRUARY.TMM
  OLIVE    OIL    98        512   05-30-00  4:32p  07-03-00      A
  OLIVE.OIL
  Press any key to continue . . .
```

WHAT'S
HAPPENING? ▶ You are given much more information about each file and directory. You see the file creation date, as well as the last accessed date. You see the size of the file as well as the amount of space allocated to it on the disk. You also see the attribute of the file. (File attributes are switches that can be set and will be covered in fuller detail in a later chapter.)

Step 9   Press the **Enter** key as often as necessary to get to the end of the display.

```
MS-DOS Prompt                                                        _ □ ✕

PHONE        <DIR>                   07-03-00   1:51p   07-03-00        D
PHONE
FINANCE      <DIR>                   07-03-00   1:51p   07-03-00        D
FINANCE
LEVEL-1      <DIR>                   07-03-00   1:52p   07-03-00        D
LEVEL-1
SPORTS       <DIR>                   07-03-00   1:52p   07-03-00        D
SPORTS
MEDIA        <DIR>                   07-03-00   1:53p   07-03-00        D
MEDIA
WORKING      <DIR>                   07-03-00   1:53p   07-03-00        D
WORKING
MY        HW       393        512    07-15-00   4:16p   07-15-00        A
MY.HW
        86 file(s)          28,930 bytes
         9 dir(s)           63,488 bytes allocated
                          295,424 bytes free
Press any key to continue . . .

(continuing A:\)
  1,457,664 bytes total disk space,   79% in use

A:\>_
```

WHAT'S
HAPPENING? ▶ Notice the additional information in the last line of the display. You learn the total disk capacity and what percentage of the disk is used.

Step 10   Key in the following: A:\>**C:** **Enter**

Step 11   Key in the following: C:\>**EXIT** **Enter**

Step 12   Initiate and complete the Windows shut-down procedure.

CHAPTER SUMMARY

1. Command syntax means using the correct command and the proper order for keying in commands.
2. A parameter is some piece of information that you want to include in a command. It allows a command to be specific.
3. A delimiter indicates where parts of a command begin or end. It is similar to punctuation marks in English.
4. Some commands require parameters. They are called mandatory or required parameters. Other commands allow parameters; these are called optional parameters.

5. A variable parameter or switch is one that requires the user to supply a value. A fixed parameter or switch has its value determined by the OS.

6. A syntax diagram is a representation of a command and its syntax.

7. The DIR command is an internal command that displays the directory (table of contents) of a disk.

8. DIR has many parameters, all of which are optional.

9. A file specification has two parts, the file name and the file extension. A file name is mandatory; however, a file extension is optional. If you use a file extension, separate it from the file name by a period, called a dot.

10. A valid file name contains legal characters, most often alphanumeric characters. It cannot contain illegal characters.

11. Every device attached to the computer has a reserved, specific, and unique name so that the operating system knows what it is communicating with.

12. Disk drives are designated by a letter followed by a colon, as in A:. A printer has the device name of PRN, LPT1, LPT2, or LPT3.

13. Defaults are implied instructions the operating system falls back to when no specific instructions are given.

14. The root directory's name is \ (backslash).

15. Subdirectories allow a disk to be divided into areas that can hold files. Subdirectories are named by the user or by an application program.

16. The system prompt displayed on the screen is the default drive and directory.

17. You can change the default drive and default subdirectory.

18. To change the default drive, you key in the drive letter followed by a colon, as in **A:** or **C:**.

19. To change the default subdirectory, you key in **CD** followed by the subdirectory name, such as **CD \DATA** or **CD \WINDOWS\COMMAND**.

20. The subdirectory that contains the system utility files is usually \WINDOWS\COMMAND.

21. You can look for files on drives and subdirectories other than the default if you tell the OS where to look by prefacing the file names with a drive designator and/or path name.

22. If the file is in a subdirectory, the file name must be prefaced by the drive designator and followed by the subdirectory name. A user must include the subdirectory name in the command, as in **C:\WINDOWS\COMMAND\FILENAME.EXT**.

23. Global file specifications (* or ?) allow a user to substitute a wildcard for an unknown.

24. The ? represents one character in a file name; the * matches a string of characters.

25. A command's output that normally is displayed on the screen may be redirected to a file. You key in the command, add the redirection symbol (>), and then key in the file name.

26. A command's output that is normally displayed on the screen may be redirected to a printer. You key in the command, add the redirection symbol (>), and then key in the device name (PRN or LPT*n*).

27. To get help on a command, key in the name of the command followed by a forward slash and a question mark, such as **DIR /?**.
28. The DIR command allows you to sort the directory listing by use of the parameter /O followed by the sort order letter you are interested in. For instance, to sort by name, you would key in **DIR /ON**.

KEY TERMS

backslash	fixed parameters	root directory
command syntax	folders	standard input
default	global file specifications	standard output
default drive	logged drive	subdirectories
delimiter	mandatory parameter	switch
designated drive	optional parameters	syntax
device names	parameter	syntax diagram
documentation	path	variable parameter
dot	redirection	wildcards
file	required parameter	

DISCUSSION QUESTIONS

1. Define *command syntax*.
2. Why is syntax important when using a command?
3. Define *parameters*.
4. What is the difference between a variable and a fixed parameter?
5. How would you use a syntax diagram? Why is the diagram important?
6. Name two parameters that can be used with the DIR command. Explain why you would use the parameters.
7. Define *delimiters*. Give an example of a delimiter.
8. Define *file specifications*.
9. How do you separate a file name and a file extension?
10. What is used to separate a file specification from a path name?
11. What is the function and purpose of a device?
12. Explain the function and purpose of the default drive.
13. How can you tell which drive is the default drive?
14. Define *default subdirectory*.
15. How can you tell which directory is the default subdirectory?
16. What does A:\> mean?
17. What steps must be followed to change the default drive? Why would you change drives?
18. What steps must be followed to change a directory? Why would you change a directory?
19. What is the significance of the first backslash in a command?
20. Define *global file specifications*.
21. How are wildcards used?
22. If you see C:\WINDOWS\COMMAND> on the screen, what does it mean?

23. What is the purpose and function of redirection?
24. What would you do if you forgot the parameter for a wide DIR display?

TRUE/FALSE QUESTIONS

For each question, circle the letter T if the question is true and the letter F if the question is false.

T　F　1. Command syntax is the proper order or sequence for keying in commands.

T　F　2. When working at the command prompt, you are allowed to add one parameter to every command.

T　F　3. A device is a place to send information to (write) or receive information from (read).

T　F　4. The # is a wildcard and represents a group of characters.

T　F　5. If you see brackets in a syntax diagram, you do not use the parameters.

COMPLETION QUESTIONS

Write the correct answer in each blank space.

6. A variable parameter is one in which the _____ provides the value.
7. A mark (much like a punctuation mark in English) that separates characters is known as a(n) _____.
8. All files in a directory must have a(n) _____ name.
9. The \ symbol represents the _____.
10. If you keyed in _____, you would see all the files displayed across the screen, rather than down the screen.

MULTIPLE CHOICE QUESTIONS

For each question, write the letter for the correct answer in the blank space.

11. Which of the following is a global file specification?
   a. "
   b. /
   c. *
   d. .

12. In an MS-DOS Prompt window, the prompt displayed on the screen is
   a. the only drive the computer can ever use.
   b. the default drive.
   c. always the floppy disk drive.
   d. always the hard disk drive.

13. To display the directories for Drive A and Drive C at the same time, key in:
   a. DIR A: C:
   b. DIR A:/C

c. DIR A: DIR C:

d. Without an additional program running, you cannot have two commands on one command line.

14. The default drive can be changed by

a. pressing **Enter** twice.

b. using the DIR command.

c. entering the new drive letter followed by a colon.

d. The default drive cannot be changed.

15. If the system prompt is A:\> and you wanted to display all the files that are in the subdirectory called **CHAIRS** on Drive C, you would key in:

a. CHAIRS

b. DIR C:\CHAIRS

c. DIR CHAIRS

d. DIR A:\CHAIRS

WRITING COMMANDS

Write the correct steps or commands to perform the required action *as if you were at the computer*. The scenarios do not necessarily represent actual files on the disk. The prompt will indicate the default drive and directory.

16. A directory of all files that have the extension of **.TXT** on the root of Drive A.

```
C:\>
```

17. A directory listing of the file called **MYFILE.TXT** located in the subdirectory **NEWS** on Drive C.

```
A:\>
```

18. Clear the screen.

```
C:\WINDOWS\COMMAND>
```

19. Display all the file names on the default drive and directory so only the file names and extensions are listed. (*Hint:* See the syntax diagram.)

```
A:\>
```

20. Display all the files on the default drive that begin with the letter E, are five total characters in length, and have no extension.

```
A:\>
```

APPLICATION ASSIGNMENTS

PROBLEM SET I—AT THE COMPUTER

Open the MS-DOS Prompt window. Insert the ACTIVITIES Disk—Working Copy in Drive A.

1. On the ACTIVITIES disk in the root directory, find the file called **PERSONAL.FIL**. What is its size in bytes?
   a. 3
   b. 315
   c. 2,307
   d. 3,055

2. On the ACTIVITIES disk in the root directory, find all the files that have the file extension **.NEW**. How many files are there?
   a. one
   b. two
   c. three
   d. four

3. On the ACTIVITIES disk in the subdirectory called **GAMES**, find the file called **LS.PAS**. What is the file date?
   a. 6-23-89
   b. 8-13-98
   c. 3-1-97
   d. none of the above

4. Do a wide display of the root directory of the ACTIVITIES disk. The fourth file down in the second column is:
   a. FILE2.FP
   b. MAR.NEW
   c. APRIL.TXT
   d. DRESS.UP

5. Display the syntax diagram and help for the DIR command. What command did you use?
   a. DIR /HELP
   b. HELP /DIR
   c. DIR /?
   d. either a or b

6. From the root of the ACTIVITIES disk, change the default directory to **SPORTS**. What command did you use?
   a. CD :
   b. CD ..
   c. CD SPORTS or CD \SPORTS
   d. DIR \SPORTS

7. On the ACTIVITIES disk, to change back to the root from the
    SPORTS directory you would key in:
    a. CD ROOT
    b. CD \
    c. CD \ROOT
    d. none of the above

8. On the hard disk in the **WINDOWS\COMMAND** subdirectory, locate
    the file called **MEM**. What is the file extension?
    a. .BAT
    b. .COM
    c. .EXE
    d. .SYS

9. On the ACTIVITIES disk in the root directory, find all the files that
    have a file name that is four characters long and have the file exten-
    sion **.TXT**. What is displayed?
    a. YOUR.TXT
    b. MINE.TXT
    c. TEST.TXT
    d. NAME.TXT

10. On the ACTIVITIES disk in the root directory, how many files have a
    file name that is two characters in length and any file extension?
    a. two
    b. three
    c. six
    d. none of the above

11. On the ACTIVITIES disk in the subdirectory \ **DATA**, find all the files
    that have names beginning with the letter T and have any extension.
    What files are displayed?
    a. THIN.EST and TEA.TAX
    b. TEA.TAX and THANK.YOU
    c. THIN.EST and TEA.TAX and THANK.YOU
    d. none of the above

12. On the hard disk in the **WINDOWS\COMMAND** subdirectory, what
    file extension does *not* appear?
    a. .CZG
    b. .SYS
    c. .COM
    d. .EXE

13. When using the sort order parameter (/O), what additional parameter
    lets you sort files by file extension?
    a. X
    b. N

    c. D

    d. E

14. On the ACTIVITIES disk in the root directory, display all the files by file name in alphabetical order and pause the display. Which file appears first?

    a. APR.TXT

    b. BELLE.TXT

    c. APRIL.TXT

    d. APR.NEW

15. Key in the command to display the syntax and help for the DATE command. What is the last sentence to appear on the screen?

    a. Displays or sets the date.

    b. Press ENTER to keep the same date.

    c. Press ENTER to change the date.

    d. DATE [date]

PROBLEM SET II—AT THE COMPUTER

Note 1: Before proceeding with these assignments, check with your lab technician or instructor to see if there are any special procedures for your lab environment.

Note 2: The ACTIVITIES disk is in Drive A. The A:\> prompt is displayed as the default drive and directory. All work will occur from the root of the ACTIVITIES disk. You may not change drives or directories.

Note 3: The first homework activity may seem confusing and unclear. It is just a way to create a file containing your name and class information, which you will use for turning in your homework.

Step 1   Key in the following: A:\>**NAME** Enter

```
 MS-DOS Prompt                                          _ □ ✕

                 READ THESE INSTRUCTIONS!

    Key in your name and press the "<Enter>" key.
    Key in any other information your instructor requested
    such as class meeting time or section number.
    Each piece of information should go on a separate line.
    Press the "<Enter>" key each time you are done with a line.
    When you are completely through keying in information,
    press the F6 key and the "<Enter>" key.

    Once you press "<Enter>", you cannot return to a previous
    line to make corrections. Later you will be given an
    opportunity to correct errors.

    You will see a blank screen. Begin keying in data at the
    blinking cursor.

  _
```

Step 2 Here is sample information to key in. Your instructor will have other specific information that applies to your class. Key in the following:

Bette Peat　(*Your* name goes here) Enter
CIS 55　　(*Your* class goes here) Enter
M-W-F 8-9　(*Your* day and time go here) Enter
Chapter 2　(*Your* assignment goes here) Enter

Step 3 Press F6 Enter

> **WHAT'S HAPPENING?** You will see the following on the screen:

```
MS-DOS Prompt                                              _ □ X

         Your name and other information are

Bette Peat
CIS 55
M-W-F 8-9
Chapter 2


   Is this information correct? If it is, press Y for Yes.

   If it is incorrect, press N for No.

   If you press N, you will be given a chance to correct your errors.


_
```

> **WHAT'S HAPPENING?** This program gives you a chance to check your data entry—what you have keyed in. If it is correct, you press **Y**. If it is incorrect, you press **N**. In this case, the printout was correct.

Step 4 Press **Y**

```
MS-DOS Prompt                                              _ □ X

A:\>_
```

> **WHAT'S HAPPENING?** You have completed the program and returned to the command line prompt. You now have a file called **NAME.FIL** in the root directory of the working copy of the ACTIVITIES disk that contains the above data. (*Hint:* Remember redirection; see sections 2.21 and 2.22 to refresh your memory.) Now you are ready to complete Problem Set II. Remember to pay attention to the default directory. All the homework files need to be created in the root directory. If you do not create them there, you will not be able to find or print them.

TO CREATE 1.HW

❖　　The root directory of the ACTIVITIES disk is the default.

❖　　Locate all the files in the root directory that have a **.99** file extension.

❖　　Place the output in a file called **1.HW**.

TO CREATE 2.HW

❖   The root directory of the ACTIVITIES disk is the default.

❖   Locate all the files in the **GAMES** directory that begin with the letter A and have any file extension.

❖   Place the output in a file called **2.HW**.

TO CREATE 3.HW

❖   The root directory of the ACTIVITIES disk is the default.

❖   Find the files in the root directory that have file names five characters in length and have the file extension of **.TMP**.

❖   Place the output in a file called **3.HW**.

TO CREATE 4.HW

❖   The root directory of the ACTIVITIES disk is the default.

❖   Display all the files in the **PHONE** directory across the screen.

❖   Place the output in a file called **4.HW**.

TO CREATE 5.HW

❖   The root directory of the ACTIVITIES disk is the default.

❖   Display all the files with the file extension of **.TXT** in order by file name.

❖   Place the output in a file called **5.HW**.

CAUTION!   **DO NOT PROCEED WITH THIS STEP UNLESS IT IS OKAYED BY YOUR LAB INSTRUCTOR.**

TO PRINT YOUR HOMEWORK

Step 1   Be sure the printer is on and ready to accept print jobs from your computer.

Step 2   Key in the following (be very careful to make no typing errors):
          A:\>**GO NAME.FIL 1.HW 2.HW 3.HW 4.HW 5.HW** Enter

```
MS-DOS Prompt                                                    _ □ ×

A:\>GO NAME.FIL 1.HW 2.HW 3.HW 4.HW 5.HW

   Is there a message that says "File not found"?
   If so, press Y to find out what could be wrong.
   Otherwise, press N to continue.


 _
```

WHAT'S HAPPENING? → You should see the above message on your screen, telling you to press **N** if you received no error messages. You will get this message a total of five times in this example, because there are five *n*.HW files (*n* representing a number) that are being processed. If you do get an error message, press **Y** and follow the instructions on the screen. These steps assume you receive no error messages.

Step 3 Press **N** four more times. (The screen will appear as shown below.)

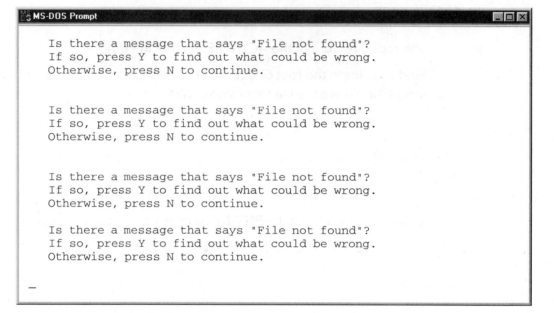

```
MS-DOS Prompt                                                    _ □ ✕

   Is there a message that says "File not found"?
   If so, press Y to find out what could be wrong.
   Otherwise, press N to continue.


   Is there a message that says "File not found"?
   If so, press Y to find out what could be wrong.
   Otherwise, press N to continue.


   Is there a message that says "File not found"?
   If so, press Y to find out what could be wrong.
   Otherwise, press N to continue.


   Is there a message that says "File not found"?
   If so, press Y to find out what could be wrong.
   Otherwise, press N to continue.


   _
```

WHAT'S HAPPENING? → There were no error messages so you continued to press **N**.

Step 4 Press **N** once more.

```
MS-DOS Prompt                                                    _ □ ✕

   You are about to delete any file with the .HW extension.

   Before you delete your homework files, check your hard copy or
   print out.

   If your homework printout is correct, press Y to delete the files.

   If your homework printout is incorrect, press N.

   Pressing N will prevent your homework files from being deleted.
   You can then begin again.


   _
```

WHAT'S HAPPENING? → Your homework was sent to the printer. Now the GO program gives you a chance to check your printed homework output. If it is correct, you press **Y**. If it is not, you press **N**. Your files will not be deleted if you press **N**. You will then have the opportunity to make any necessary corrections and begin printing again. In this case, the printout was correct.

Step 5   Press **Y**.

```
MS-DOS Prompt                                                          _ □ ✕

A:\>_
```

WHAT'S HAPPENING: ➤ You have completed the Application Assignments for Chapter 2 and have returned to the A prompt.

Step 6   Close the MS-DOS Prompt window. Initiate and complete the Windows shut-down procedure.

PROBLEM SET III—BRIEF ESSAY

Although the Windows operating system is a graphical user environment, it is still important to learn how to use the command line interface.

Agree or disagree with the above statement and defend your answer.

DISKS AND FORMATTING

LEARNING OBJECTIVES

After completing this chapter you will be able to:

1. Explain the need for formatting a disk.
2. Describe the structure of a disk.
3. Name and explain the purpose of each section of a disk.
4. Define *formatting*.
5. Explain the difference between internal and external commands.
6. List and explain the steps in formatting a floppy disk.
7. Explain the purpose and function of the /Q parameter and other parameters used with the FORMAT command.
8. Explain the difference between a bootable and a non-bootable disk.

STUDENT OUTCOMES

1. Format a floppy disk.
2. Use the LABEL command to change the volume label on a disk.
3. View the current volume label using the VOL command.
4. Use the /Q parameter to format a disk.
5. Create a bootable floppy disk.

CHAPTER OVERVIEW

Disks are the mainstay of the computer workstation. They are used for storing data and programs and for distributing data from one computer to another. In order to be used, disks must be formatted, a process by which an operating system sets up the guidelines for reading from and writing to a disk. In Windows, you can still format a disk by using the FORMAT command from the command line.

In this chapter you will learn how a disk is structured, how the operating system uses disks, and how to format and electronically label a disk. In addition, you will learn how to change the electronic label. Throughout, remember that formatting a disk is a dangerous operation because it removes all the data from a disk.

3.1   WHY FORMAT A DISK?

Each operating system has a unique way of recording information on a disk. This organizational scheme is known as a file system. One factor that makes a computer compatible with another is not the brand name such as Apple, IBM, or Compaq, but rather the operating system, part of which is the design of the file system that each computer uses. Disk formatting is based almost entirely on which operating system a computer uses. Operating systems prepare disks so that information can be read from and written to them. The disk manufacturers cannot prepare a disk in advance without knowing what kind of operating system it will be used on. The process of preparing a disk so that it will be compatible with an operating system is known as *formatting* or *initializing* the disk.

Since this is a textbook for Windows OS users, the only kind of formatting that you are interested in is Windows-based. Although there are many file systems in use, such as NTFS (Windows NT and Windows 2000) and HPFS (OS2), the one that Windows uses is called FAT, with FAT32 being an updated version of FAT that can be used by Windows 95 B (the second release of Windows 95), Windows 98, and Windows Me. FAT is short for *file allocation table*. So far, the disks that you have used with this text have been already prepared for your environment. Although most floppy disks come pre-formatted, you may still purchase unformatted disks. When you want to prepare a disk for use, you will use a system utility command called FORMAT.COM.

All disks, including hard disks, must be formatted. Even if you purchase preformatted disks, it is inevitable that you will want to reuse them. Disks that have been used but have information that is no longer needed can be erased or re-prepared with the FORMAT command. Hard disks are typically formatted once, when they are new, and are rarely reformatted because formatting eliminates what is on the disk. Although the FORMAT command works for both hard and floppy disks, this text deals only with formatting floppy disks.

3.2   STRUCTURE OF A DISK

Formatting a disk consists of two parts: *low-level formatting*, or *physical formatting*, and *high-level formatting*, or *logical formatting*. Low-level (physical) formatting creates and sequentially numbers tracks and sectors for identification purposes. (Tracks are concentric circles on a disk.) Each track is then divided into smaller units called sectors. A sector is the smallest unit on a disk and is 512 bytes in size. Sector size is usually 512 bytes—the industry standard. The number of tracks and sectors varies depending on the type of disk. When data needs to be written to or read from a disk, the identification number of the track and sector tells the read/write head where to position itself. This process accounts for every space on a disk. It is similar to assigning every house on a street a unique address so that it can be instantly identifiable. However, even after a disk is physically prepared to hold data, it still is not ready for use.

The second part of formatting is high-level (logical) formatting. In logical formatting, the operating system creates a file system on a disk so it can keep track of the location of files. Formatting a hard disk involves only logical formatting. Low-level formatting of a hard disk is usually done as part of the manufacturing process. Low-level formatting can also be done by the computer system vendor, or you may purchase special software programs to low-level format your hard disk. Most commonly, when you purchase a computer system, the high-level and low-level formatting of the hard disk is done. However, when you format a floppy disk, both the physical and logical formatting processes occur.

Logical formatting determines how the operating system uses a disk by building a structure to manage files on a disk so they can be easily saved and retrieved. The FORMAT command performs both high- and low-level formatting on a floppy disk. On a hard disk, only high-level formatting is performed. When you execute the FORMAT command, it first checks for any bad spots on the disk. If bad areas are found, called ***bad sectors***, they are marked as unusable. The formatting program then creates three critical elements: the boot record, the file allocation table (two copies), and the root directory. These elements occupy the first portion of the disk and take only about one to two percent of the disk space. The remainder of the disk is used for file storage. See Figure 3.1.

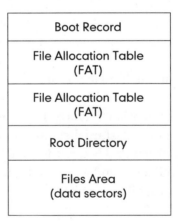

FIGURE 3.1   LOGICAL STRUCTURE OF A DISK

The order of the sections is always the same. The boot record, two copies of the FAT, and the root directory table are always located in the first sectors. These elements control how the files are stored on a disk and how Windows saves and retrieves files. The data sectors are where the data or files are actually stored.

BOOT RECORD

The boot record is a very short program on the first part of a disk. This program begins the process of loading the operating system from the disk into memory, which means that the necessary files are copied from the disk into memory. It does this by looking for a file called IO.SYS on the disk. If it finds it, it turns control over to that file, which continues to load itself and the other necessary files, MSDOS.SYS and COMMAND.COM.

Remember that starting a computer is called booting the system because the system pulls itself up by its bootstraps. If the disk does not have the necessary operating system files, the boot record cannot load the operating system into memory. It is a *non-bootable disk*. This program is smart enough to tell you so by displaying the following message:

```
Non-system disk or disk error
Replace and press any key when ready
```

Although every disk has a boot record, it must also have the operating system files on it (IO.SYS, MSDOS.SYS, and COMMAND.COM) in order to boot the system. Furthermore, the boot record contains information about the physical characteristics of a disk—the number of bytes per sector, sectors per track, and so forth. The boot record also includes information about which operating system was used to format the disk, the size of the FAT, the size of the root directory, and the volume serial number. From the boot record, disks can be identified by type—a hard disk, a 1.44 MB floppy disk, etc.

FILE ALLOCATION TABLE (FAT)

There needs to be a way to keep track of the status of all the data sectors on a disk so critical questions can be answered. For instance, does a sector already contain information, making it unusable? Is it a damaged sector that cannot be used, or is it empty and available for data storage? Since a disk, particularly a hard disk, can have so many sectors, managing them a sector at a time would be too time consuming and unwieldy. Therefore, one or more sectors are combined into logical units called clusters. When a file is written to a disk, the contents of the file are placed in unused clusters. The smallest unit that the operating system actually works with (reading from or writing to disk) is a cluster, also called an *allocation unit* because it allocates space on a disk.

The location of the file is tracked in the file allocation table (FAT). The FAT is a map of the data section and is made up of entries that correspond to every cluster on a disk. The number of clusters varies from one type of disk to another. Table 3.1 indicates the relationship between cluster size and disk size.

Disk Size	Number of Sectors in a Cluster	Cluster Size in Bytes	Cluster Size in Kilobytes
3½ inch 2.88 MB	Two sectors	1,024 bytes	1 kilobyte
3½ inch 1.44 MB	One sector	512 bytes	½ kilobyte

3½ inch 720 KB	Two sectors	1,024 bytes	1 kilobyte
5¼ inch 1.2 MB	One sector	512 bytes	½ kilobyte
5¼ inch 360 KB	Two sectors	1,024 bytes	1 kilobyte
32–63 MB	Two sectors	1,024 bytes	1 kilobyte
64–127 MB	Four sectors	2,048 bytes	2 kilobytes
128–255 MB	Eight sectors	4,096 bytes	4 kilobytes
256–511 MB	Sixteen sectors	8,192 bytes	8 kilobytes
512–1,023 MB	Thirty-two sectors	16,384 bytes	16 kilobytes
1,024 MB–2GB	Sixty-four sectors	32,768 bytes	32 kilobytes

TABLE 3.1   CLUSTER SIZE AND DISK SIZE

Since the smallest unit the OS can deal with is a cluster, a file that is only 100 bytes long saved to a 3½-inch 1.44 MB disk will actually occupy 512 bytes on the disk and, if it is saved to a 2 GB hard disk, it will actually occupy 32,768 bytes. Furthermore, as you can imagine, a data file is hardly ever *exactly* one cluster in size, nor is it necessarily an even number. Thus, to manage the data, each entry in the FAT is a number that indicates the status of the cluster. A 0 (zero) in the FAT means the cluster is empty and available for use. Other specific numbers indicate that a cluster is reserved (do not use) or bad (do not use). Any other number indicates that a cluster is in use.

To follow the trail of a data file longer than one cluster, the number in the FAT is a pointer to the next cluster that holds data for that file. That entry becomes a pointer to the next cluster that holds data in the same file. A special entry in the FAT indicates where the file ends and that no more data is in the file. Thus, the numbers in the FAT are used to link or chain clusters that belong to the same file. The FAT works in conjunction with the root directory table. Since the FAT is used to control the entire disk, two copies of the FAT are kept on the disk in case one is damaged. The FAT occupies as many sectors as it needs to map out the disk. However, the FAT file system can maintain a maximum of 65,525 clusters, which means that the largest hard drive that the original Windows 95 can support is 2.1 GB in size. If you have a hard drive larger than 2.1 GB, it must be logically divided into partitions that have their own drive letters. As Table 3.1 indicates, the larger the available space, the larger the cluster size must be on a disk. To overcome this limitation, FAT32 was introduced.

FAT32 is available on updated versions of Windows 95 (version 4.00.950.B and above). FAT32 is an enhancement of the FAT file system and is based on 32-bit file allocation table entries, rather than the 16-bit file entries the FAT file system used in DOS and the first version of Windows 95. As a result, FAT32 will support larger hard drives (up to two terabytes). A terabyte is a trillion bytes, or 1,000 billion bytes. FAT32 also uses smaller clusters than the FAT file system (for example, 4 KB clusters for an 8 GB hard drive). However, DOS, Windows 3.1, Windows NT, and the original version of Windows 95 will not recognize FAT32 and cannot boot or use files on any drive that has FAT32. If, for example, your C drive used FAT32 and you wanted to use another operating system such as DOS 6.22 by booting from the A drive, you would not be able to "see" the C drive at all.

ROOT DIRECTORY

Next on the disk is the root directory. The root directory is a table that records information about each file on the disk. When you key in **DIR**, the information displayed on the screen comes from this root directory table. The root directory stores information in a table about every file on a disk and includes the file name, the file extension, the size of the file in bytes, the date and time the file was created, the date and time the file was last modified, and the file attributes. A file can be flagged with these attributes: (R) read-only, which means the file normally cannot be erased; (H) hidden status, which means that a file will not be displayed when you issue the DIR command; (S) system status, which typically marks the file as a system file, such as IO.SYS; (V) *volume label*; and (A) archive status, which indicates that the file was modified since it was last backed up. In addition to these attributes, the starting cluster number indicates which cluster holds the first portion of the file, or the first FAT address. The root directory does not specify where a file is located on a disk; instead, it points to an entry in the FAT. Thus, the root directory table keeps track of what the files are, and the FAT keeps track of where the files are located.

FAT32 also makes changes in the root directory table. In FAT32, the root directory table can be any size and located in any place on the disk.

DATA PORTION OR FILES AREA

The rest of the disk, the largest part, is used for storing program, system, and data files. As far as the operating system is concerned, all files, programs, and data are just chains of bytes laid out in sequence. Space is allocated to files on an as-needed basis, one cluster at a time. When a file is written to a disk, the OS begins writing to the first available cluster. It writes in adjacent or *contiguous* clusters if possible but, if adjacent sectors are already in use (allocated by the FAT), the data is written to the next available space (unallocated). Thus, a file can be *noncontiguous*, that is, physically scattered over a disk in clusters that are not next to each other.

HOW THE FAT AND THE ROOT DIRECTORY TABLE INTERACT

To illustrate how the root directory table and the FAT work, imagine you want to create a file called MYFILE.TXT, which will occupy three clusters on a disk. Let us say that clusters 3, 4, and 6 are free. The operating system first creates an entry in the root directory table and fills in the file information (file name, file extension, date, time, etc.). Then, data is written to the first free cluster, number 3, as the starting cluster number in the root directory table. The OS knows it will need three clusters and must link or chain them. It does this by placing a 4 (a pointer) in the number 3 cluster pointing to the next available cluster. When it gets to cluster 4, it places a 6 (another pointer) pointing to the next available cluster. The FAT continues to cluster 6. When it gets to cluster 6, it places an end-of-file marker, a "note," indicating that the file ends there.

To make an analogy, imagine a self-storage facility comprised of storage bins that hold things (data). The front office that manages the self-storage facility does not care what is in the bins. The front office only has to know how many bins there are, where they are located, and if anything is in them. The front office has a map of all its numbered storage bins (FAT). The bins are numbered so that the front office knows where the bins are located. The front office also needs a list (directory) of all the people who have rented bins. Thus, I walk in and say I want the boxes stored for Gillay. The front office first looks up Gillay in the list to be sure they have stored my boxes. In this case, they find the name Gillay, so they know I have rented at least one bin. Besides my name, the directory list points to another list that says to go to the map (FAT), starting with bin 3. The front office goes to the map (FAT) and sees that storage bin 3 is linked to storage bin 4, which is linked to storage bin 6. Storage bin 6 has no links. Now the front office knows that Gillay has bins 3, 4, and 6 full of boxes. The front office can send someone (rotate the disk) to bins 3, 4, and 6 to retrieve the boxes. To look at this process graphically, see Figure 3.2.

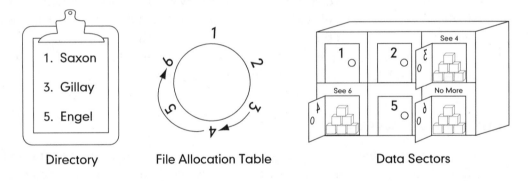

Directory   File Allocation Table   Data Sectors

FIGURE 3.2   STORING FILES

This analogy gives you some of the basic information you need in order to understand the structure of a disk.

3.3   FORMATTING A DISK

When a disk has already been formatted, formatting that disk again simply erases the record of the files from the root directory and the FAT. The data in the files is still on the disk because the low-level format was not performed. When you begin to write data to the disk, the old data is overwritten and irrevocably lost. Thus, when you format a previously used disk, you must know positively that you do not want the data on the disk. The data is still on the disk, but, when you format it, the root directory entries and FAT chains are gone, leaving no map to locate the data.

The important thing is to be cautious when using the FORMAT command. Since FORMAT can be used on any disk, including hard disks, be especially careful because, when you format a disk, everything on the disk, even a hard disk, will be gone—programs and data. In this text, you will be formatting only floppy disks. If you are working in a computer laboratory, please familiarize yourself with the proper laboratory procedures to avoid a computer tragedy.

You can format disks from the desktop using My Computer, but as this text is primarily concerned with the command line procedures, we will format from the command line.

3.4   CLARIFYING PROCEDURES

1. **System utility files subdirectory.** You will be at the MS-DOS Prompt screen. You will also have to change your directory so that you are in the subdirectory that has the system utility files. Remember to refer to your Configuration Table in Chapter 1.6 to ensure that all substitutions have been made before you begin this activity.
2. **A blank or new disk.** Whenever a new or blank disk is referred to, you may use a brand-new disk or an old disk containing information which you no longer wish to keep, because it will be written over in the format process.
3. If you are in a lab environment, you need to check with your instructor to see if there are any particular procedures that need to be followed in your lab. For instance, in some networked environments, you cannot format a floppy disk in Drive A.

3.5   ACTIVITY: FORMATTING A FLOPPY DISK

WARNING!   **NEVER FORMAT AN APPLICATION DISK OR A DISK THAT HAS DATA YOU WISH TO KEEP. ALSO, IF YOU HAVE A HARD DISK, YOU MUST BE *EXCEEDINGLY* CAREFUL. NEVER, *NEVER* KEY IN** c:\>FORMAT C:. **IF YOU DO, YOU MAY COMPLETELY ERASE, FOREVER, ALL THE INFORMATION ON THE HARD DISK.**

Step 1   "Shell out" to the command prompt screen. (This means to open an MS-DOS Prompt window.)

Note: Your starting prompt may differ from the examples in this text. Your initial prompt upon shelling out to the MS-DOS Prompt screen may be C:\WINDOWS> or perhaps a network drive, such as G:\>.

Step 2   Key in the following: c:\>**CD \WINDOWS\COMMAND** Enter

```
MS-DOS Prompt                                                          _ □ ✕

C:\>CD \WINDOWS\COMMAND

C:\WINDOWS\COMMAND>_
```

WHAT'S
HAPPENING?   You have changed the default directory to the **\WINDOWS\COMMAND** subdirectory. The prompt should now display C:\WINDOWS\COMMAND>.

To format a disk, you use the FORMAT command. FORMAT is another example of a system utility program, also called an external command, stored as a file in the **WINDOWS\COMMAND** subdirectory. The default drive and subdirectory, in this situation, become very important. Whenever you use an external command, you are telling the operating system to look for a file that matches what you keyed in.

Remember that the prompt on the screen represents the default drive and subdirectory. When the operating system looks for an external command, it will look on the default drive only (in this case, Drive C) and in the default subdirectory (in this case, **\WINDOWS\COMMAND**) for the command or file name that you keyed in. You can instruct the operating system to look or do something on a different disk drive or different subdirectory, but you must specify that disk drive and/or subdirectory. In this case, you are looking for the command FORMAT. You can see whether or not this command, stored as a file called **FORMAT.COM**, is located on the disk in the default drive and in the default subdirectory.

Step 3   Key in the following: C:\WINDOWS\COMMAND>**DIR FORMAT.COM** Enter

```
MS-DOS Prompt                                                    _ □ X

C:\WINDOWS\COMMAND>DIR FORMAT.COM

 Volume in drive C is MILLENNIUM
 Volume Serial Number is 2B18-1301
 Directory of C:\WINDOWS\COMMAND

FORMAT    COM        49,415  06-08-00  5:00p FORMAT.COM
          1 file(s)           49,415 bytes
          0 dir(s)   1,239,158,784 bytes free

C:\WINDOWS\COMMAND>_
```

WHAT'S
HAPPENING?   The screen display tells you that the FORMAT command, stored as the file named **FORMAT.COM**, is located on the default drive, Drive C. In addition, since your system utility files are in a subdirectory, you will not only be on Drive C but also in a subdirectory called **\WINDOWS\COMMAND**. To use (or execute or run) the FORMAT program, you key in the name of the command.

Step 4   Key in the following (be sure to include the drive letter A):
             C:\WINDOWS\COMMAND>**FORMAT A:** Enter

```
MS-DOS Prompt                                                    _ □ X

C:\WINDOWS\COMMAND>FORMAT A:
Insert new diskette for drive A:
and press ENTER when ready...
```

WHAT'S HAPPENING? ➤ In Step 3 you used the DIR command to locate the file. You called the program by keying in the name of the file. When you do that, you are asking the operating system to find the file called **FORMAT.COM** and load it into memory. **FORMAT** is the command that tells the system what work you want it to do. The **A:** tells the system that the disk you want to format is in Drive A. If you did not specify a lettered drive, A:, B:, or C:, you would receive a message that you were missing a parameter—the drive letter. In earlier versions of DOS, the FORMAT command would not ask for a drive letter and would format the default drive. Since the default drive is C and C is the hard disk, FORMAT would have unintentionally erased everything on the hard disk. You never want this to happen. *Never!*

In addition, you get a message or prompt that tells you what to do. Before you get involved in the following activity, it is exceedingly important that you know what kind of disk drive you have so that you can choose the correct disk with the correct format. It is assumed that you have a 3½-inch high-density disk drive and floppy disk. If you have any other type of floppy disk or drive, ask your instructor for further instructions. If you are not sure, refer to your Configuration Table in Chapter 1.6. If you do not use the correct floppy disk, you will have problems.

Step 5   Get a blank disk out and prepare a sticky paper label for it. Do not use either the ACTIVITIES disk or the ACTIVITIES Disk—Working Copy. Write your name and the words "DATA disk" on the label. Place the label on the disk. Insert the disk into Drive A. Be sure that this disk is either blank or contains data you no longer want. Everything on the disk will be eliminated after you press Enter

Step 6   Press Enter

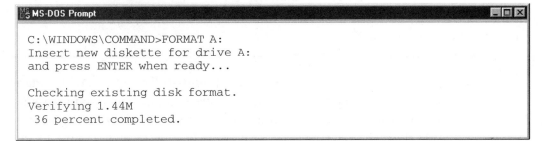

```
MS-DOS Prompt                                              _ □ ✕

C:\WINDOWS\COMMAND>FORMAT A:
Insert new diskette for drive A:
and press ENTER when ready...

Checking existing disk format.
Verifying 1.44M
 36 percent completed.
```

WHAT'S HAPPENING? ➤ The light on the floppy disk drive is glowing, indicating that activity is taking place on the disk you are formatting. The FORMAT command displays what media type it is formatting. The message will vary depending on whether the disk has or has not been formatted before. The **Verifying 1.44M** that appears in the above screen display will vary depending on the type of floppy disk you are formatting.

The message *nn* **percent completed** tells you that the formatting is taking place and, at that moment, *nn* percent of the formatting process is completed (the *nn* represents a number that changes as the disk is formatted) until it reaches 100 percent. Do not do anything until you see the following message displayed on the screen.

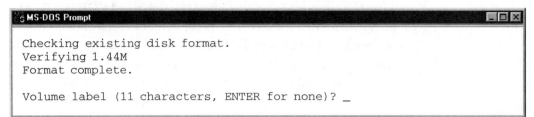

WHAT'S HAPPENING? You are being asked for a volume label, an electronic name. However, you are not going to place a volume label on the disk at this time.

Step 7   Press Enter

Step 8   Press N. Press Enter

```
MS-DOS Prompt                                              _ □ ×

Format another (Y/N)?N

C:\WINDOWS\COMMAND>_
```

WHAT'S HAPPENING? You have completed formatting your disk. The FORMAT command was executed, formatting the disk in Drive A. The bytes available will vary depending on what your disk capacity is. You also receive a status report that tells you how many spots were bad on the disk (if any). In addition, it tells you the allocation units on the disk. In this case, the allocation unit—the cluster—is 512 bytes so that you know that one sector on a 3½-inch high-density disk is a cluster. If you multiplied the size of the allocation unit by the number of allocations units available, you would come up with the number of available bytes (512 * 2,847 = 1,457,664 bytes). The OS can now read from and write to this disk because it has set up the tracks and sectors, boot record, FAT, root directory, and data section as needed. Notice the line **Volume Serial Number is 1F14-16D6**. This is a hexadecimal number, randomly generated by the formatting process. It is used for disk identification by application programs. For example, if you open a WordPerfect document file from a floppy disk and, while it is in memory, replace that disk with another, WordPerfect will be aware of the disk change by virtue of this number. Programmers can use *volume serial numbers* to identify the disks they use to distribute their programs.

Step 9   Key in the following: C:\WINDOWS\COMMAND>**CD \ Enter**

```
MS-DOS Prompt                                              _ □ ✕

C:\WINDOWS\COMMAND>CD \

C:\>_
```

> **WHAT'S HAPPENING?** ➤ You have returned to the root directory. The root directory of any disk is always the \.

3.6   FORMATTING A DISK WITH A VOLUME LABEL

You can use parameters other than the disk drive letter with the FORMAT command. The FORMAT command has many parameters, some of which are used more than others. The syntax for the FORMAT command is:

```
FORMAT drive: [/V[:label]] [/Q] [/F:size] [/C]
FORMAT drive: [/V[:label]] [/Q] [/T:tracks /N:sectors] [/C]
FORMAT drive: [/V[:label]] [/Q] [/1] [/4] [/C]
FORMAT drive: [/Q] [/1] [/4] [/8] [/C]

/V[:label]    Specifies the volume label.
/Q            Performs a quick format.
/F:size       Specifies the size of the floppy disk to format (such
              as 160, 180, 320, 360, 720, 1.2, 1.44, 2.88).
/T:tracks     Specifies the number of tracks per disk side.
/N:sectors    Specifies the number of sectors per track.
/1            Formats a single side of a floppy disk.
/4            Formats a 5.25-inch 360K floppy disk in a high-density drive.
/8            Formats eight sectors per track.
/C            Tests clusters that are currently marked "bad."
```

Although this syntax diagram may look intimidating, it really is not.

The parameters that are important to remember are as follows:

```
FORMAT drive: [/V[:label]] [/Q] [/F:size] [/C]
```

The other versions of the syntax show parameters that still work but have been superseded. Beginning with MS-DOS version 3.3, the *drive*: or drive letter is mandatory. It must be included. This mandatory drive letter prohibits you from accidentally formatting the disk in the default drive.

The /V allows you to place a volume label on a disk but, as you have already seen, the FORMAT command asks you for a volume label even if you don't include the /V. The /Q performs a quick format, but a quick format can be used only on a disk that has been previously formatted. It is "quick" because it simply deletes the entries from the FAT and the root directory and essentially leaves the files area untouched.

The /F:*size* parameter is an easy way to format floppy disks that do not match the capacity of a floppy disk drive. For instance, if you have a high-density disk drive but wish to format a 720 KB disk, you would inform the FORMAT command using /F:720. However, /F:*size* does not solve all your mismatching problems. If you have a 720 KB disk drive, you cannot format a high-density, 1.44 MB floppy disk in that drive. The 720 KB disk drive is older technology and does not recognize the new high-density media type. Do not format a floppy disk at a size higher than it was designed for. This means, for example, if you have a 720 KB disk, do not format it as a 1.44 MB disk. Table 3.2 shows the valid numbers that can be used. In general, however, the older capacity disks are disappearing and you will rarely have the need to use these numbers.

Disk Capacity	Number to Use with /F
160 KB	160
180 KB	180
360 KB	360
720 KB	720
1.2 MB	1.2
1.44 MB	1.44
2.88 MB	2.88

TABLE 3.2   VALID DISK SIZES

A parameter not listed, but still valid, is /U for unconditional. This is the most drastic type of formatting and, indeed, gets rid of everything on the disk as it completely rewrites the files area of the disk. When you have a problem with a disk, sometimes formatting with this parameter will solve the problem. The /U parameter can only be used at the command line. Usage would be FORMAT A: /U.

In the next activity, you are going to use the /V parameter to place a volume label on the disk you are formatting. A volume label is an electronic name. It is very much like labeling a file drawer so you know what it contains. The switch is /V, which tells the FORMAT command that it is to format a disk and place an electronic volume label on it. Whenever you format a disk in recent versions of the OS, you are automatically asked for a volume label, even if you do not include /V, so why use the parameter at all? When you don't use it, the formatting process stops and asks you for the volume label. When you use the /V (a fixed parameter), you can provide the label itself (a variable parameter) at the time you enter the command, rendering it unnecessary for the format command to ask you to enter it after the formatting process. In the partial command diagram FORMAT A: /V[:*label*], notice that the bracketed item [:*label*] includes both the colon and the label with no spaces between.

3.7   ACTIVITY: USING THE /V OPTION

Note: Your default directory is the root of C and C:\> is displayed. The disk just formatted is in Drive A.

Step 1   Key in the following: C:\>**CD \WINDOWS\COMMAND** [Enter]

```
MS-DOS Prompt                                                  _ □ ×

C:\>CD \WINDOWS\COMMAND
C:\WINDOWS\COMMAND>_
```

WHAT'S HAPPENING?   You made **\WINDOWS\COMMAND** the default subdirectory.

Step 2   Key in the following:
C:\WINDOWS\COMMAND>**FORMAT A: /V:SAMPLEDATA** [Enter]

```
MS-DOS Prompt                                                  _ □ ×

C:\>CD \WINDOWS\COMMAND
C:\WINDOWS\COMMAND>FORMAT A: /V:SAMPLEDATA
Insert new diskette for drive A:
and press ENTER when ready...
```

WHAT'S HAPPENING?   The FORMAT command was loaded from disk into memory. The data contained in any files on the disk is not actually deleted, but instead the FAT and the root directory table are "zeroed out." Also, the disk area is scanned for bad surfaces that might have appeared since the last time you formatted the disk.

Step 3   Press [Enter]

```
MS-DOS Prompt                                                  _ □ ×

C:\WINDOWS\COMMAND>FORMAT A: /V:SAMPLEDATA
Insert new diskette for drive A:
and press ENTER when ready...

Checking existing disk format.
Verifying 1.44M
 10 percent completed.
```

WHAT'S HAPPENING?   You have begun the process of formatting the DATA disk.

```
MS-DOS Prompt                                                  _ □ ×

Verifying 1.44M
Format complete.


   1,457,664 bytes total disk space
   1,457,664 bytes available on disk

        512 bytes in each allocation unit.
      2,847 allocation units available on disk.
```

```
Volume Serial Number is 3F76-10E8

Format another (Y/N)?_
```

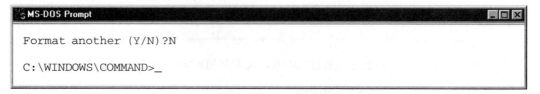 You were not asked to enter the volume label, as the label was provided within the command.

Step 4   Key in the following: **N** Enter

```
 MS-DOS Prompt                                                    _ □ ×

Format another (Y/N)?N

C:\WINDOWS\COMMAND>_
```

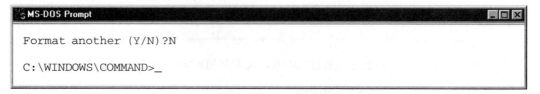 Since you do not want to format another disk, you pressed **N** for no. You named your disk SAMPLEDATA because on this disk you are going to store samples. Whenever you use a volume label, make it as meaningful as possible so that you do not have to look at all the files on the disk to know what is on the disk. Examples of meaningful names (volume labels) could include ENGLISH to indicate the disk is for your English home-work or INCOMETAX for a disk that contains your income tax data. There are two ways to see your volume label.

Step 5   Key in the following: C:\WINDOWS\COMMAND>**DIR A:** Enter

```
 MS-DOS Prompt                                                    _ □ ×

C:\WINDOWS\COMMAND>DIR A:

 Volume in drive A is SAMPLEDATA
 Volume Serial Number is 3F76-10E8
 Directory of A:\

File not found
                    1,457,664 bytes free

C:\WINDOWS\COMMAND>_
```

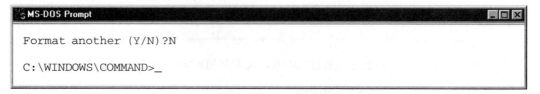 You can see displayed the label you entered, SAMPLEDATA. The inter-nal command VOL lets you look at the volume label on any disk or check to see if there is a label. By using this command, you can quickly see what is on a disk without having to execute the directory command. The syntax is:

```
VOL [drive:]
```

Step 6   Key in the following: C:\WINDOWS\COMMAND>**VOL** Enter

```
 MS-DOS Prompt                                                    _ □ ×

C:\WINDOWS\COMMAND>VOL

 Volume in drive C is MILLENNIUM
```

```
 Volume Serial Number is 2B18-1301

C:\WINDOWS\COMMAND>_
```

WHAT'S HAPPENING? ➤ The volume label on your hard disk may well be different depending on whether a volume label was entered when the hard disk was formatted. In this example, a volume label was placed on the hard disk, so you see the message **Volume in drive C is MILLENNIUM**. When you used the VOL command, the operating system looked only on Drive C, the default drive. To look at the volume label on Drive A, you must specifically request Drive A by giving VOL another parameter, the variable parameter [*drive:*] which represents the drive letter.

Step 7   Key in the following: C:\WINDOWS\COMMAND>**VOL A:** Enter

```
C:\WINDOWS\COMMAND>VOL A:

 Volume in drive A is SAMPLEDATA
 Volume Serial Number is 2436-14CD

C:\WINDOWS\COMMAND>_
```

WHAT'S HAPPENING? ➤ Since you placed a volume label on the DATA disk, you can see it with the VOL command. If a volume label is meaningful, it clearly identifies what files are on the disk.

3.8   THE LABEL COMMAND

It would be very inconvenient if every time you wanted to change the volume label on a disk you had to reformat the disk. Not only is this fatal to your data, but it takes time to format disks. In MS-DOS version 3.3, the LABEL command was introduced. It is an external command that lets you change the volume label without reformatting the disk. Remember, VOL, an internal command, lets you *see* the volume label, but LABEL lets you *change* the volume label. Bracketed items are always optional. The syntax is:

```
LABEL [drive:] [label]
```

3.9   ACTIVITY: USING THE LABEL COMMAND

Note: Your default directory is the **\WINDOWS\COMMAND** subdirectory on Drive C, and you have C:\WINDOWS\COMMAND> displayed. The disk you just formatted is in Drive A.

Step 1   Key in the following: C:\WINDOWS\COMMAND>**LABEL A:** Enter
Note: Be certain to include the A: parameter, or the OS will assume you want to change the electronic name of the C drive. This action can cause problems on networked computers.

```
MS-DOS Prompt                                                    _ □ ×

C:\WINDOWS\COMMAND>LABEL A:
Volume in drive A is SAMPLEDATA
Volume Serial Number is 2436-14CD
Volume label (11 characters, ENTER for none)? _
```

> **WHAT'S HAPPENING?** This message looks exactly like the one you saw when you used the /V parameter with the FORMAT command. At this point, you can key in a new volume label.

Step 2   Press Enter

```
MS-DOS Prompt                                                    _ □ ×

C:\WINDOWS\COMMAND>LABEL A:
Volume in drive A is SAMPLEDATA
Volume Serial Number is 2436-14CD
Volume label (11 characters, ENTER for none)?

Delete current volume label (Y/N)?_
```

> **WHAT'S HAPPENING?** The LABEL command knows that you already have a volume label, so it is asking you if you want to remove it.

Step 3   Key in the following: Y Enter

```
MS-DOS Prompt                                                    _ □ ×

Delete current volume label (Y/N)? Y

C:\WINDOWS\COMMAND>_
```

> **WHAT'S HAPPENING?** You deleted the current volume label.

Step 4   Key in the following: C:\WINDOWS\COMMAND>**VOL A:** Enter

```
MS-DOS Prompt                                                    _ □ ×

C:\WINDOWS\COMMAND>VOL A:

 Volume in drive A has no label
 Volume Serial Number is 2436-14CD

C:\WINDOWS\COMMAND>_
```

> **WHAT'S HAPPENING?** You no longer have a volume label on the disk. In the next step you are going to place a volume label on the DATA disk, but you are going to take a shortcut. You are going to use the volume label SAMPLEDATA. Since you already know what you want to key in, you do not have to wait for the LABEL command to ask you what label you want. The LABEL command allows the use of spaces, whereas the /V parameter with FORMAT does not allow spaces.

Step 5   Key in the following:

C:\WINDOWS\COMMAND>**LABEL A:SAMPLE DATA** Enter

    MS-DOS Prompt

    C:\WINDOWS\COMMAND>LABEL A:SAMPLE DATA

    C:\WINDOWS\COMMAND>_

WHAT'S HAPPENING?   You are returned to the system level prompt. Did your volume label change on the DATA disk?

Step 6   Key in the following: C:\WINDOWS\COMMAND>**VOL A:** Enter

---

    MS-DOS Prompt

    C:\WINDOWS\COMMAND>VOL A:

     Volume in drive A is SAMPLE DATA
     Volume Serial Number is 3F76-10E8

    C:\WINDOWS\COMMAND>_

WHAT'S HAPPENING?   Using the VOL command, you can see the new volume label.

3.10   FORMATTING A DISK USING THE /Q PARAMETER

Often you will want to clear a disk totally to ensure that there is really nothing on the disk and you know the tracks and sectors are already there from a previous formatting. There is no need to take the time to reformat the disk. You can use the /Q parameter. The /Q parameter stands for "quick" format. The /Q works *only* on a disk that has been previously formatted. It works like the usual FORMAT command, but skips the low-level formatting. It clears the FAT and root directory as it prepares a disk for new files. However, in order to clear the disk rapidly, /Q will not check for bad sectors on a disk. Using /Q is a very fast way to erase a disk.

3.11   ACTIVITY: USING THE /Q PARAMETER

Note: Your default directory is the **\WINDOWS\COMMAND** subdirectory on Drive C, and C:\WINDOWS\COMMAND> is displayed. The SAMPLE DATA disk is in Drive A.

Step 1   Key in the following: C:\WINDOWS\COMMAND>**FORMAT A: /Q** Enter

---

    MS-DOS Prompt

    C:\WINDOWS\COMMAND>FORMAT A: /Q
    Insert new diskette for drive A:
    and press ENTER when ready...

WHAT'S HAPPENING? FORMAT is asking you for a disk to format. Since you already have a disk in the drive, you may proceed.

Step 2   Be sure the SAMPLE DATA disk is in Drive A. Then press **Enter**

```
MS-DOS Prompt                                                    _ □ X

C:\WINDOWS\COMMAND>FORMAT A: /Q
Insert new diskette for drive A:
and press ENTER when ready...

Checking existing disk format.
QuickFormatting 1.44M
Format complete.

Volume label (11 characters, ENTER for none)? _
```

WHAT'S HAPPENING? Notice how fast the formatting occurred. FORMAT is asking you for a volume label.

Step 3   Press **Enter**

Step 4   Key in **N** **Enter** (you do not want to quick format another disk).

```
MS-DOS Prompt                                                    _ □ X

Volume label (11 characters, ENTER for none)?

    1,457,664 bytes total disk space
    1,457,664 bytes available on disk

        512 bytes in each allocation unit.
      2,847 allocation units available on disk.

Volume Serial Number is 0C3D-10F7

QuickFormat another (Y/N)?N


C:\WINDOWS\COMMAND>_
```

WHAT'S HAPPENING? The FORMAT command wanted to know if you had any more disks to quick format. You responded **N** for no. You returned to the system prompt. What happened to the SAMPLE DATA volume label?

Step 5   Key in the following: C:\WINDOWS\COMMAND>**VOL A:** **Enter**

```
MS-DOS Prompt                                                    _ □ X

C:\WINDOWS\COMMAND>VOL A:

 Volume in drive A has no label
 Volume Serial Number is 0C3D-10F7

C:\WINDOWS\COMMAND>_
```

WHAT'S HAPPENING? As you did not enter a new volume label, but just pressed **Enter** when you formatted the disk, the previous volume label was eliminated.

Step 6   Key in the following: C:\WINDOWS\COMMAND>**CD** \ [Enter]

```
MS-DOS Prompt                                              _ □ ×

C:\WINDOWS\COMMAND>CD \

C:\>_
```

WHAT'S HAPPENING? ➤ You returned to the root directory of the hard disk.

3.12   BOOTABLE AND NON-BOOTABLE DISKS

In previous versions of the OS, there was a /S fixed parameter, which allowed you to format a floppy disk with the operating system on it, making it bootable. With the increased size and complexity of Windows, this is no longer possible, and the /S parameter has been eliminated. If you key in FORMAT /S, you will receive the following error message:

```
MS-DOS Prompt                                              _ □ ×

C:\>FORMAT A: /S

Microsoft Windows no longer supports the format /s command.
To create a Startup Disk, click the Add/Remove Programs
icon in Control Panel.
Format terminated.

C:\>_
```

Having a ***bootable floppy disk*** is nonetheless *very* important. As shown in the error message, the only way to do this now is to create a ***startup disk***. This disk contains files needed to boot the computer, to run some diagnostic programs on a computer with problems, and to fix some possible errors.

The most important reason to have a startup disk is in case of emergencies. When you power on the computer, it looks to Drive A first for a disk with the operating system files. If it does not find them and if you have a hard disk, it next looks to Drive C. The disk in the A drive needs to have the system files on it in order to boot the system. The system files are COMMAND.COM, and the two hidden files, MSDOS.SYS and IO.SYS. COMMAND.COM is the command processor. It processes what the user keys in. When you boot the system, this file is one of the operating system files placed in memory. COMMAND.COM has internal commands that are resident in memory until the computer is turned off.

The reason for creating a startup disk is that, should you have a problem with your hard disk and not be able to boot from it, you will still have a way to boot the computer. You need a way to boot the computer because you may be able to solve the problem on the hard disk. However, if you cannot access the hard disk, you cannot boot from it. Windows takes care of this problem by encouraging you to create a startup disk during the installation process. However, you can create one at any time. By placing this bootable floppy disk in Drive A, where the computer first looks when booting, the computer will find the operating system files and boot the system.

Once you have booted the system, you then have the opportunity to access the hard disk and perhaps solve your problem.

3.13 ACTIVITY: CREATING A STARTUP DISK

Step 1   Key in the following: C:\>**EXIT** Enter

WHAT'S HAPPENING? ➤ You have returned to the desktop.

Step 2   Click **Start**. Click **Settings**. Click **Control Panel**.

Step 3   Double-click **Add/Remove Programs**.

WHAT'S HAPPENING? ➤ You have opened the windows where you can add or remove Windows programs, uninstall installed programs, and create a startup disk.

Step 4   Click the **Startup Disk** tab.

WHAT'S
HAPPENING? ▶ You have opened the window where the startup disk is created. Notice the message in the box. The disk created here is not only very valuable, but extremely necessary. What this disk contains and how you can use it will be examined in a later chapter.

Step 5   Click **Create Disk**.

WHAT'S
HAPPENING? ▶ You are prompted to insert a disk.

Step 6   The recently formatted, unlabeled disk should be in the A drive. If not, place it there now.

Step 7   Click **OK**.

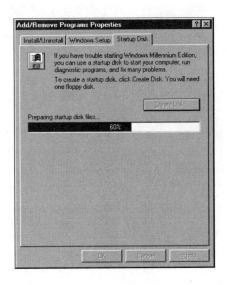

WHAT'S
HAPPENING? ▶ The percentage of completion is displayed in a sliding window. When 100 percent is completed, the buttons on the bottom of the window become active.

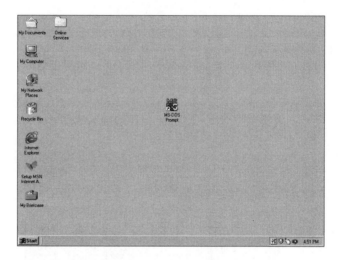

Step 8   Click **Cancel**.

Step 9   Close the Control Panel dialog box by clicking on ☒ in the upper-right corner.

WHAT'S HAPPENING?   You have returned to the desktop.

Step 10   Remove the startup disk from the A drive.

WHAT'S HAPPENING?   You now have a disk to use in case you need to recover from a problem with the operating system. Place this disk in a safe place, as we will come back to it in a later chapter.

3.14   ACTIVITY: MAKING A DATA DISK

As you have created a startup disk with the disk you have been using, you will need another DATA disk.

Step 1   Open an MS-DOS Prompt window.

Step 2   Place a new blank disk in the A drive.

Step 3   Key in the following: C:\>**CD \WINDOWS\COMMAND** Enter

Step 4   Key in the following: C:\WINDOWS\COMMAND>**FORMAT A: /V:DATA** Enter

```
MS-DOS Prompt                                                    _ □ X

C:\WINDOWS\COMMAND>FORMAT A: /V:DATA
Insert new diskette for drive A:
and press ENTER when ready...
```

WHAT'S HAPPENING? ➤ You are prompted to insert a disk, but a disk is already in the drive.

Step 5   Press Enter

```
MS-DOS Prompt                                                    _ □ X

C:\WINDOWS\COMMAND>FORMAT A: /V:DATA
Insert new diskette for drive A:
and press ENTER when ready...

Checking existing disk format.
Verifying 1.44M
Format complete.


    1,457,664 bytes total disk space
    1,457,664 bytes available on disk

         512 bytes in each allocation unit.
       2,847 allocation units available on disk.

Volume Serial Number is 174F-12F9

Format another (Y/N)?_
```

WHAT'S HAPPENING? ➤ You have formatted a disk and assigned a label, DATA, to the disk.

Step 6   Key in the following: **N** Enter

Step 7   Key in the following: C:\WINDOWS\COMMAND>**DIR A:** Enter

```
MS-DOS Prompt                                                    _ □ X

Format another (Y/N)?N


C:\WINDOWS\COMMAND>DIR A:

 Volume in drive A is DATA
 Volume Serial Number is 174F-12F9
 Directory of A:\

File not found
                    1,457,664 bytes free

C:\WINDOWS\COMMAND>_
```

WHAT'S HAPPENING? ➤ As you can see, the label or "name" on the disk is DATA, and there are
no files on the disk.

3.15 ACTIVITY: SHUTTING DOWN WINDOWS

Step 1   Key in the following: C:\WINDOWS\COMMAND>**EXIT** (Enter)

WHAT'S HAPPENING!▶   You have closed the MS-DOS Prompt window and have returned to the desktop. Remember, the appearance of the desktop will differ from computer to computer.

Step 2   Click **Start**. Click **Shut Down**. Be sure the **Shut down** option is showing in the drop-down list.

Step 3   Click the **OK** button and wait for the safe message before you turn off the power.

WHAT'S HAPPENING!▶   You have completed the Windows shut-down procedure.

3.16 HIGH-DENSITY DISKS AND DISK DRIVES

If you have a newer computer, you probably have what are called high-capacity or high-density 3½-inch disk drives. If so, whenever you use the FORMAT command, it will format any disk placed in the drive in its "native" format; it assumes that the disk to be formatted is a blank high-density disk. Thus, if you placed a 3½-inch, 720 KB, double-density disk in a 3½-inch high-density drive, FORMAT would prepare it as a high-density disk. Because a DS/DD (double-sided/double-density) disk was not designed as a DS/HD (double-sided/high-density) disk, it does not have as many magnetic particles and should not be formatted as a high-density disk. In fact, you will get an error message that will show many bytes as bad sectors.

   If you have high-density disk drives and use only high-density disks, you will have no problems. The problems begin to occur when you try to mix and match different density disks with different density drives.

   Double-density disk drives are found on older computers—most likely you will not run into these drives today. However, you do need to be aware of their limitations. A double-density disk drive *cannot* read from or write to a high-density diskette. High-density drives *can* both read from and write to either the DS/DD or DS/HD disks. This feature is one of the ways that hardware and software maintain what is called *downward compatibility*—something that was developed on an old computer can still be used on a new computer. The only problem you run into is in formatting disks. You can format a 720 KB disk in a DS/HD drive by using the following syntax:

```
FORMAT /F:720
```

   When you format a diskette, the FORMAT command report will tell you how many bytes it formatted. You can then place the information on your Configuration Table in Chapter 1.6. The important thing is to be aware of the type of floppy disk drive you have and what media type floppy disks you are using.

   This text will refer to 3½-inch diskettes. If you are using 5¼-inch diskettes, double-density disks have a capacity of 360 KB and high-density diskettes have a capacity of 1.2 MB. For formatting a double-density diskette in a high-density drive, the syntax is:

```
FORMAT /F:360
```

CHAPTER SUMMARY

1. Floppy disks that are purchased are sometimes not ready to use. They must first be prepared for use.
2. Each type of computer has its own specific way of recording information on a disk. This text is only concerned with Windows-based computers.
3. The command processor is stored as a file called COMMAND.COM. It processes what the user keys in. When you boot the system, this file is one of the operating system files placed in memory. COMMAND.COM has internal commands that are resident in memory until the computer is turned off.
4. Disks are the means to store data and programs permanently.
5. All disks must be formatted by a utility program stored as a file called FORMAT.COM so that data and programs can be read from and written to them.
6. Disks that have information on them can be formatted again.
7. If a disk has files on it, formatting the disk will remove all of those files.
8. Since the FORMAT command removes all data, formatting a hard disk can be dangerous.
9. Formatting a disk means that the physical layout of the disk is defined to determine how the information is stored on the disk so that the OS can locate what is stored.
10. The OS uses sections of a disk, whether it is a hard disk or a floppy disk. A disk is divided into concentric circles called tracks. Each track is divided into sectors. The number of tracks, sectors, and sides of a disk determine the capacity of the disk.
11. The smallest unit that the operating system will read from or write to is a cluster. A cluster is made up of one or more adjacent sectors depending on the type of disk.
12. Each disk has a root directory and two copies of a file allocation table (FAT).
13. When formatted, all disks have a boot record, a FAT, a directory, and data sectors.
14. A boot record loads the OS if it is a system disk or a message if it is not a system disk.
15. The FAT (file allocation table) is a map of every track and sector on the disk. The FAT tells the OS where files are on the disk. The FAT links a file together by pointing to the next cluster that holds the file's data.
16. The root directory has information about files including the file name and the file's starting cluster entry in the FAT.
17. The data sectors are where files are actually stored.
18. Files are chains of bytes laid out in sequence.

19. Files are written to a disk in the first available cluster and, if possible, in adjacent or contiguous clusters. If the adjacent clusters are already in use, the OS skips to the next available noncontiguous cluster.
20. A disk is formatted with the FORMAT command, an external utility program.
21. The basic syntax of the FORMAT command is:

```
FORMAT drive: [/V[:label]] [/Q] [/F:size] [/C]
```

22. The internal VOL command allows you to view the internal electronic label.
23. The external LABEL command allows you to change the internal electronic label.
24. The /Q parameter performs a quick format that does not check for bad sectors on a disk. In addition, it can be used only on a disk that has been previously formatted.
25. A bootable disk loads the operating system files. Typically, the hard disk is a bootable disk. You should also create a startup disk so that you may boot from Drive A if the need arises.
26. Always use the correct media type when formatting disks.

KEY TERMS

allocation unit	formatting	noncontiguous
bad sectors	high-level formatting	physical formatting
bootable disk	initializing	startup disk
contiguous	logical formatting	volume label
downward compatibility	low-level formatting	volume serial number
file allocation table (FAT)	non-bootable disk	

DISCUSSION QUESTIONS

1. What purpose do disks serve?
2. Why must you format a disk?
3. Compare and contrast physical (low-level) formatting with logical (high-level) formatting of a disk.
4. Define *tracks, sectors,* and *clusters.*
5. What is the purpose and function of the boot record?
6. Define *FAT.* How is it used on a disk?
7. Compare and contrast FAT and FAT32.
8. What is the purpose and function of the root directory?
9. Define *file attributes.* List at least two types of attributes and explain their purposes and functions.
10. How is space allocated to files?
11. FORMAT can be a dangerous command. Explain.
12. What does the prompt on the screen represent?
13. Compare and contrast internal and external commands.
14. What steps can you take when you see the message "Bad command or file name"?
15. What is a volume label?

16. When formatting a disk, the drive letter is a mandatory parameter. Why?
17. Give the syntax for the FORMAT command and explain each item.
18. Explain the purpose and function of a quick format.
19. When using the FORMAT command, what are the purpose and function of the parameter /V?
20. What is the purpose and function of the VOL command?
21. What is the purpose and function of the LABEL command?
22. When using the FORMAT command, when would you use the /Q parameter?
23. What makes a disk bootable?
24. How can you create a bootable floppy disk?
25. What is a high-density disk?
26. What is a double-density disk?
27. Can you use a 720 KB, 3½-inch disk in a 1.44 MB, 3½-inch drive? Why or why not?
28. Can you use a 1.44 MB, 3½-inch disk in a 720 KB, 3½-inch disk drive? Why or why not?

TRUE/FALSE QUESTIONS

For each question, circle the letter T if the question is true or the letter F if the question is false.

T   F   1. The root directory table keeps track of where files are located, while the FAT keeps track of what is in files.

T   F   2. You may format any disk with the FORMAT command.

T   F   3. **DIR FORMAT.COM** will execute the command FORMAT and format a disk.

T   F   4. Each disk is divided into tracks, which are then next divided into clusters.

T   F   5. Startup disks are bootable floppy disks.

COMPLETION QUESTIONS

Write the correct answer in each blank space.

6. The smallest unit of disk space the operating system will work with is called a(n) _____.

7. The information in files is stored in the _____ sectors of a disk.

8. Where the file is located is kept track of by the _____, while the _____ keeps track of the files and attributes.

9. A bootable disk that contains files to help you recover from problems is the _____ disk.

10. In order to use a disk, it must first be _____.

MULTIPLE CHOICE QUESTIONS

For each question, write the letter for the correct answer in the blank space.

11. When you format a disk, you
    a. erase everything on that disk.
    b. prepare it so the operating system can read from and write to it.
    c. both a and b
    d. neither a nor b

12. A non-bootable disk
    a. does not contain the operating system files.
    b. has more space for data files.
    c. cannot be used to boot the system.
    d. all of the above

13. To name a disk when you are formatting it, you can use
    a. the LABEL command.
    b. the VOL command.
    c. /V for volume label.
    d. /N for name.

14. To create a startup disk, begin with:
    a. Click Start, Click Programs
    b. Click My Computer, Click Create Startup Disk
    c. At the DOS Prompt window, key in CREATE A:
    d. Click Start, Click Settings, Click Control Panel

15. To change the volume label of the disk currently in Drive A without eliminating any information on it, key in:
    a. LABEL A:
    b. VOL A:
    c. VOLUME A:
    d. none of the above

WRITING COMMANDS

Write the correct steps or commands to perform the required action as if you were at the computer. The prompt will indicate the default drive and directory.

16. View the name of the disk in the default drive.

    ```
    A:\>
    ```

17. Format and place the volume label MYDISK on the disk in Drive A.

    ```
    C:\WINDOWS\COMMAND>
    ```

18. Display the volume label on Drive A.

    ```
    C:\>
    ```

19. Locate the FORMAT command on the hard drive.

    `A:\>`

20. Change the label on the disk in Drive A from DATA to ACTION.

    `C:\WINDOWS\COMMAND>`

APPLICATION ASSIGNMENTS

PROBLEM SET I—AT THE COMPUTER

Note 1: Your DATA disk is in Drive A. C:\> is displayed as the default drive and the default directory.

Note 2: Remember, be very careful when using the FORMAT command. *Never* issue the command without a drive parameter specified, A: or B:, and do not use the C drive as a parameter.

PROBLEM A

A-a   Format the DATA disk the fastest way.

A-b   Key in the following at the volume label prompt:
        MY_VERY_OWN_DATA_DISK Enter

1. In addition to the drive letter, what parameter did you use with the FORMAT command?
   a. /U
   b. /Q
   c. /S
   d. none of the above

A-c   Display the volume label of the DATA disk.

2. In addition to the drive letter, what command did you use?
   a. VOL
   b. NAME
   c. FORMAT
   d. all of the above

3. What volume label is displayed?
   a. MY_VERY_OWN_DATA_DISK
   b. MY_VERY_OWN_DATA
   c. MY_VERY_OWN
   d. MY_VERY

PROBLEM B

B-a   Change the name of the disk in the A drive without using the FORMAT command.

B-b   Use the name **CLASSDISK**.

☐   4. Which command did you use?
              a. NAME
              b. LABEL
              c. VOL
              d. none of the above

B-c   Check to see that the name has actually changed.

☐   5. What volume label is displayed?
              a. DATA
              b. CLASSDISK
              c. MY_VERY_OWN
              d. none of the above

B-d   Change the volume label to **DATA DISK**.

☐   6. In addition to the drive letter, what command did you use?
              a. VOL
              b. FORMAT
              c. LABEL
              d. none of the above

PROBLEM SET II—BRIEF ESSAY

You want to create a floppy disk that will boot your computer. Explain what steps you will take to do this.

PROGRAM FILES, DATA FILES, AND SUBDIRECTORIES

LEARNING OBJECTIVES

After completing this chapter you will be able to:

1. List and explain the major reasons for learning about the operating system.
2. Explain the difference between program files and data files.
3. Explain the difference between freeware and shareware programs.
4. Define real mode and protected mode operations.
5. Explain the hierarchical filing system of a tree-structured directory.
6. Define the CD, MD, and RD commands.
7. Explain the purpose and function of a root directory and tell how and when it is created.
8. Explain what subdirectories are and tell how they are named, created, and used.
9. Explain the purpose and use of subdirectory markers.
10. Identify the commands that can be used with subdirectories.
11. Explain the purpose of the PROMPT command.
12. Explain the purpose and function of the MOVE command.
13. List the steps to remove a directory.
14. Explain the purpose and function of the DELTREE command.
15. Explain the function of the PATH command.

STUDENT OUTCOMES

1. Load and use an application program.
2. Create subdirectories using the MD command.

3. Display the default directory using the CD command.
4. Change directories using the CD command.
5. Use subdirectory markers with commands.
6. Use the PROMPT command to change the display of the prompt.
7. Rename a directory using the MOVE command.
8. Use the RD command to eliminate a directory.
9. Use the DELTREE command to remove an entire tree structure.
10. Use the PATH command.

CHAPTER OVERVIEW

You do not purchase a computer to use the operating system. You purchase a computer to help you be more efficient in doing work you want to do. Work on a computer is comprised of two aspects—the programs that do the work and the information you create. When you work with a computer, you accumulate many programs and data files. If you are going to be an efficient user, you must have a way to manage these files. Part of the power of the Windows operating system is its ability to manage files. From the desktop, you can use Windows Explorer and My Computer to view the location of your files and to manage them. In this text, you will learn how to manage your files from the command prompt. There are things that you cannot do easily (and some things you cannot do at all) from the Windows GUI.

In this chapter you will learn to use a program file and a data file. You will also learn the subdirectory commands to help you manage your files.

4.1   WHY USE THE MS-DOS PROMPT SCREEN?

So far, you have used commands to prepare a disk for use (FORMAT), to copy a disk (DISKCOPY), to see what files are on a disk (DIR), and to clear the screen (CLS). Each of these commands is useful, but no one buys a computer to use the operating system. You purchase a computer to assist you in doing work, and the way you work on a computer is by using application programs. The four major categories of application programs include word processors to make writing easier, spreadsheets to manage budgets and do financial projections, databases to manage and manipulate collections of data, and graphics to create artistic drawings and designs. The application programs that use graphics include CAD (computer-aided design), desktop publishing, photo-editing programs, and scanning or camera programs. Each program has its own instructions that must be learned. If this is true, why are you learning about the operating system? There are two important reasons.

First and foremost, you cannot run an application program without first loading Windows. It is the manager of the system, supervising the hardware and software components and allowing you to load and execute specific application packages. All application programs run under the supervision of the operating system.

The second reason for learning about the operating system is that application programs are stored as files on disks and usually generate data files. Windows has a variety of commands that allow you to manage and manipulate program and data files. Be aware that the operating system manages the files—their location, movement, and so on—but not the information you put *into* files.

4.2 PROGRAM FILES, DATA FILES, AND THE OPERATING SYSTEM

On the hard disk is a subdirectory called **WINDOSBK**. This subdirectory was created by installing the files and directories from the ACTIVITIES disk to the hard disk. It was placed on the hard disk or network server by the lab technician or the instructor. If you are using your own computer, you will have to create the directory and place the files there yourself—see Appendix A for instructions on how to do this. The subdirectory WINDOSBK contains other subdirectories, among which are PHONE and FINANCE. These subdirectories have application programs, one called HPB and the other called Thinker, which will help you understand how operating systems work in the "real world."

HPB (Home Phone Book) is a simple application program that works much like a Rolodex. It is a database that allows you to keep track of names, addresses, and phone numbers. Designed to work under DOS, Thinker is a spreadsheet program that allows you to manipulate numbers in columns and rows. The Windows operating system, because it is downward compatible, allows for the use of older software, referred to as *legacy software*. You are going to use the MS-DOS Prompt window to execute these programs by loading the program and data files and listing the files that are there.

MS-DOS commands help you understand how the operating system works in conjunction with various types of files. An application or program file is an executable file that is loaded from disk into memory. The operating system then turns control over to the application program. With software written for DOS or earlier versions of Windows, when the application program needed to interface with the hardware, such as when it wanted to write a character to the screen, print, or respond to mouse movement, there were two choices. The application program could "talk" directly to the device, or it could talk to DOS and let DOS do the actual labor of writing to the screen or sending a job to the printer.. This is called *real mode* operation. With software written for the Windows operating system, this is not the case. Windows software runs in protected mode. In *protected mode,* no communication exists between the application software and the actual hardware itself. *Device drivers* (the software that comes with peripheral devices, such as a mouse or a modem) are called mini drivers. Instead of the having the manufacturer's device drivers talk to the hardware, or to the core of the operating system itself, these drivers talk to virtual device drivers, which are part of the Windows operating system. These virtual device drivers are outside of the core operations of the operating system, which remains "protected" from the actions of the devices and device drivers.

As an example, assume you bought a fancy ACME video card with all the new bells and whistles. It has the magic words "Plug and Play" on the package. When you install it, you may have to insert the disk that came with it in order to install a mini driver that talks to the Windows virtual video card driver and tells it how to blow the whistles and ring the bells. The core of the Windows operating system, however, is *not* touched by the software driver written by ACME. The Windows virtual video driver will make sure nothing gets through to the core of the operating system that could cause problems. Thus the term "protected mode."

An application program cannot load itself into memory. The operating system is the means by which the application program gets loaded into memory. Remember that work takes place only in memory. The operating system also assists in loading the data file into memory so that the application program can use the data. Ensuring the cooperative effort between the OS and the application program and its data files is the work of the operating system. You, the user, do not directly interface with the operating system at the application level.

There is another component: the MS-DOS commands that Windows provides. Commands are also programs. These commands allow you, the user, to interface directly with the operating system to manage your program and data files.

4.3   SHAREWARE

Some of you may have already purchased commercial application packages such as WordPerfect, Word, or PageMaker. There are hundreds of different programs to choose from that will meet almost any computer user's needs from managing a checkbook (such as Quicken) to playing a game (such as Flight Simulator).

The subdirectory WINDOSBK contains data files, freeware programs, and shareware programs. Freeware and shareware programs are available from a wide variety of sources. One of the most common sources today is the Internet. Friends and acquaintances may pass programs to you; members of computer clubs share their programs; or you can receive them from a source such as this textbook.

Freeware is software that is in the public domain. The authors (programmers) of these programs have donated the programs to anyone who wants to use them with the understanding that people will use them but not alter them. The programmers do not expect to be paid in any way—although sometimes they will ask for a small donation for expenses.

Shareware is a trial version of a program. The program is not distributed through commercial channels, thus saving the programmer the costs of marketing and distribution. After you purchase commercial software, if you do not like it or it does not meet your needs, you usually cannot return it. On the other hand, shareware is something you can try out. If you like it, you then register it with the programmer for a nominal fee. If you do not like it, you simply delete the file or files from your disk. Trying these programs costs you nothing. If you decide to retain and use the program, the programmer *does* expect to be paid. The programmer or programmers who write shareware are professional programmers, students, and people who just enjoy programming.

Sometimes, to encourage people to register, the program will be a limited version without all the features of the shareware program, will disable certain functions after a period of time, or will have annoying screens that pop up to remind you to register it. When you do register it, you receive the full version or the latest version of the program, the documentation (a manual of commands and instructions), and notices of updates and technical support. The update notices will provide you with the latest version of corrections to the programs. Technical support means you can call the programmer(s) for help if something is not working correctly.

This textbook includes both freeware and shareware. Appendix A lists all the shareware programs with the fees and addresses necessary to register them. If, after you complete the textbook, you wish to continue using the shareware programs, please pay the appropriate fees and register the programs. Otherwise, delete the files. Shareware provides some really great programs and by registering them, you are encouraging the programmer to write shareware. Who knows, you may be assisting the next Bill Gates or Steve Jobs.

4.4   ACTIVITY: USING DIR TO LOCATE THE HPB PROGRAM

Note 1: Check with your lab technician or network administrator to be sure that the subdirectory **WINDOSBK** has been installed for you, either on the C:\ drive or on a network drive. Be sure to fill in your Configuration Table in Chapter 1.6 with your specific location of this subdirectory. This text is written with the assumption that the **WINDOSBK** subdirectory is directly off the root of the C drive. If you are work-ing on your own computer, you will have to install the subdirectory **WINDOSBK**. Complete instructions on how to do this are in Appendix A.

Note 2: It is assumed that your computer is booted and Windows is loaded. You have shelled out to the MS-DOS Prompt screen. You have changed the directory to the root directory of C. C:\> is displayed on the screen as the default drive and directory.

Note 3: When keying in commands, you may use the function keys to correct typo-graphical errors. To edit command lines fully, you may use DOSKEY. (See Chapter 7.)

Step 1   Key in the following: C:\>**DIR WINDOS*.*** [Enter]

```
MS-DOS Prompt                                         _ □ ×

C:\>DIR WINDOS*.*

 Volume in drive C is MILLENNIUM
 Volume Serial Number is 2B18-1301
 Directory of C:\

WINDOSBK        <DIR>         07-20-01  4:25p WINDOSBK
        0 file(s)                 0 bytes
        1 dir(s)    1,199,734,784 bytes free

C:\>_
```

WHAT'S HAPPENING   You are verifying that you have a subdirectory called **WINDOSBK**. In this example, only one entry matches the criterion you requested. You asked DIR to find any file or any directory on the hard disk that begins with **WINDOS** and has any other characters in the file name and any file extension. Your display may vary depending on how many other files you have that begin with **WINDOS**. In this example, there is only the **WINDOSBK** subdirectory. If the entry named **WINDOSBK** is not displayed, refer to Appendix A and take the necessary steps before continuing.

Step 2   Key in the following: C:\>**CD \WINDOSBK\PHONE** [Enter]

Step 3   Key in the following: C:\WINDOSBK\PHONE>**DIR HPB.EXE** [Enter]

```
 MS-DOS Prompt                                                        _ □ ×

C:\>CD \WINDOSBK\PHONE

C:\WINDOSBK\PHONE>DIR HPB.EXE

 Volume in drive C is MILLENNIUM
 Volume Serial Number is 2B18-1301
 Directory of C:\WINDOSBK\PHONE

HPB        EXE        164,420  01-04-99  3:48a HPB.EXE
           1 file(s)          164,420 bytes
           0 dir(s)    1,199,730,688 bytes free

C:\WINDOSBK\PHONE>_
```

WHAT'S HAPPENING?   You changed the default directory to **WINDOSBK** and then to the **PHONE** subdirectory where the HPB program is located. You used the DIR command to see if the file called **HPB.EXE** is on the hard disk C: off of the *root directory* (\) in the subdirectory called **WINDOSBK\PHONE**. DIR is the command, **WINDOSBK\PHONE** is the *path,* and **HPB.EXE** is the file name of the program. The DIR command just allows you to see if the file is on the disk; it does not let you use the program. The name of the file is **HPB**. HPB stands for Home Phone Book. The name of the extension is **.EXE**. The **.EXE** file extension has a special meaning: executable code. This informs the OS the file is a program. The file extension **.EXE** always indicates an executable program.

Step 4   Key in the following: C:\WINDOSBK\PHONE>**DIR HPB.DAT** [Enter]

```
 MS-DOS Prompt                                                        _ □ ×

C:\WINDOSBK\PHONE>DIR HPB.DAT

 Volume in drive C is MILLENNIUM
 Volume Serial Number is 2B18-1301
 Directory of C:\WINDOSBK\PHONE

HPB        DAT          4,368  01-04-99  3:48a HPB.DAT
           1 file(s)            4,368 bytes
           0 dir(s)    1,199,730,688 bytes free

C:\WINDOSBK\PHONE>_
```

WHAT'S HAPPENING?   You used the DIR command to see if the file called **HPB.DAT** is in this subdirectory. DIR is the command, **HPB** is the file name, and **DAT** is the file extension. DIR does not let you use the data; it just lets you see if it is there.

4.5 USING APPLICATION PROGRAMS AND DATA FILES

In the above activity, you used the command DIR to see if there were two files on the disk, HPB.EXE and HPB.DAT. All DIR did was let you know that these files exist. To make use of these files, you have to load them into memory. Remember that the application program is HPB.EXE, which has the instructions to tell the computer what to do. The HPB.DAT data file cannot be used by itself. You must load the application program first; then you can get to the data.

4.6 ACTIVITY: USING APPLICATION PROGRAMS AND DATA FILES

Note: C:\WINDOSBK\PHONE> is displayed on your screen.

Step 1   Key in the following: C:\WINDOSBK\PHONE>**HPB.DAT** Enter

```
MS-DOS Prompt                                                    _□✗

C:\WINDOSBK\PHONE>HPB.DAT
Bad command or file name

C:\WINDOSBK\PHONE>_
```

WHAT'S HAPPENING   The file called **HPB.DAT** is a data file. It is not a program, so it cannot execute. It does not have a program file extension.**.EXE**, **.COM**, or **.BAT**. It is a data file. Data files cannot execute.

Step 2   Key in the following: C:\WINDOSBK\PHONE>**HPB** Enter

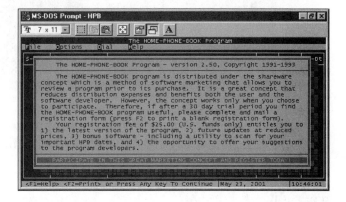

WHAT'S HAPPENING   When you keyed in **HPB**, the operating system was looking for a file with the name of **HPB** and an extension of **.COM**, **.EXE**, or **.BAT** because those are the extensions that mean "execute." Because **HPB** is a file with an **.EXE** file extension, it was found. It took an image copy of the program from the disk and loaded it into memory. Control was turned over to the HPB program. HPB is a shareware program with its own commands and instructions. You are looking at the registration information for the HPB program.

Step 3   Press Enter

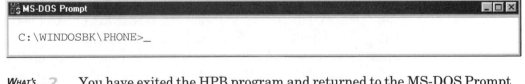

WHAT'S HAPPENING? You interfaced with the operating system when you keyed in the command **HPB**, and, by doing so, loaded the program. Control was given over to the HPB program. HPB can only work with one data file at a time. **HPB.EXE** asked the operating system to load its data file, **HPB.DAT**. The information on the screen, such as "Acme Fly-by-Night, Inc." with a phone number, is the data. If you wanted to add your own data, you would have to learn how to use the program.

Step 4   Press [Alt] + **O**.

WHAT'S HAPPENING? You have dropped down a menu that tells you how to perform tasks (Add, Erase, Find, and so on) with the information in this data file.

Step 5   Press [Esc]

Step 6   Press [Alt] + **F**. Press **X**.

```
MS-DOS Prompt                                              _ □ ×

C:\WINDOSBK\PHONE>_
```

WHAT'S HAPPENING? You have exited the HPB program and returned to the MS-DOS Prompt screen. You did not make any changes to the data file.

Step 7   Key in the following:
C:\WINDOSBK\PHONE>**CD \WINDOSBK\FINANCE** [Enter]

```
MS-DOS Prompt                                          _ □ ✕

C:\WINDOSBK\PHONE>CD \WINDOSBK\FINANCE

C:\WINDOSBK\FINANCE>_
```

WHAT'S HAPPENING? You have changed to another directory, **FINANCE**, which is under the **WINDOSBK** directory. It has different programs and data files.

Step 8 Key in the following: C:\WINDOSBK\FINANCE>**DIR TH*.EXE** Enter

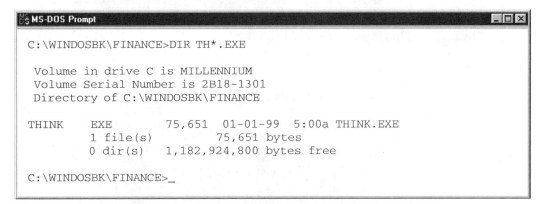

```
MS-DOS Prompt                                          _ □ ✕

C:\WINDOSBK\FINANCE>DIR TH*.EXE

 Volume in drive C is MILLENNIUM
 Volume Serial Number is 2B18-1301
 Directory of C:\WINDOSBK\FINANCE

THINK    EXE        75,651  01-01-99  5:00a THINK.EXE
        1 file(s)        75,651 bytes
        0 dir(s)   1,182,924,800 bytes free

C:\WINDOSBK\FINANCE>_
```

WHAT'S HAPPENING? You are looking at another program file called **THINK.EXE**.

Step 9 Key in the following: C:\WINDOSBK\FINANCE>**DIR *.TKR** Enter

```
MS-DOS Prompt                                          _ □ ✕

C:\WINDOSBK\FINANCE>DIR *.TKR

 Volume in drive C is MILLENNIUM
 Volume Serial Number is 2B18-1301
 Directory of C:\WINDOSBK\FINANCE

BALANCE  TKR         6,656  01-01-99  5:00a BALANCE.TKR
BUDGET   TKR        18,304  01-01-99  5:00a BUDGET.TKR
MORTGAGE TKR        10,624  01-01-99  5:00a MORTGAGE.TKR
HOMEBUD  TKR         8,064  01-01-99  5:00a HOMEBUD.TKR
        4 file(s)        43,648 bytes
        0 dir(s)   1,187,115,008 bytes free

C:\WINDOSBK\FINANCE>_
```

WHAT'S HAPPENING? This program uses the file extension **.TKR** to identify data files that belong to it. You have your choice of what data file you want to look at. Do not be concerned if the files are displayed in a different order.

Step 10 Key in the following: C:\WINDOSBK\FINANCE>**THINK** Enter

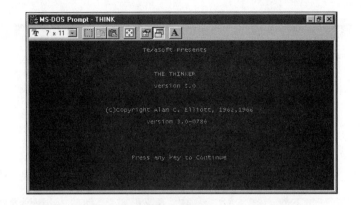

WHAT'S HAPPENING   This is also a shareware program.

Step 11   Press Enter

WHAT'S HAPPENING   This spreadsheet program allows you to manipulate numerical data. It has its own set of commands. You must tell it what data file you want to load. Each of the following keys you press will execute a command in this program. Be sure you begin by pressing the forward slash (/), not the backslash (\ ).

Step 12   Press /.

Step 13   Press **F**.

Step 14   Press **R**.

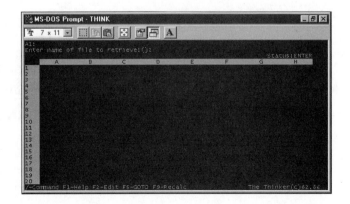

WHAT'S HAPPENING You went through a series of steps to get to the Retrieve command in this program. Programs that involve user-created data have different commands to load the data files, but in all cases, when you key in a data file name, the program will turn to the operating system to locate the data file and load it into memory.

Step 15 Key in the following: **HOMEBUD** [Enter]

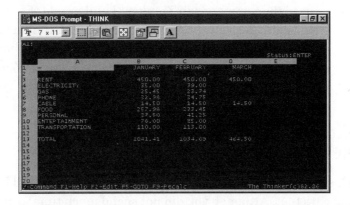

WHAT'S HAPPENING You have loaded the data file called **HOMEBUD.TKR**. The numbers and text displayed on the screen are the data you want to see.

Step 16 Press /.

Step 17 Press **F**.

Step 18 Press **R**.

WHAT'S HAPPENING By using the correct commands in this program, you have the opportunity to load another data file with different information. The data file that you are currently looking at is **HOMEBUD.TKR**. There are three other files, **BUDGET**, **MORTGAGE**, and **BALANCE**, that you could look at.

Step 19 Press [Enter]

Step 20 Press /.

Step 21 Press **Q**.

Step 22 Press **Y**.

```
MS-DOS Prompt                                              _ □ ×

C:\WINDOSBK\FINANCE>_
```

Step 23 Key in the following: C:\WINDOSBK\FINANCE>**CD ** [Enter]

```
MS-DOS Prompt                                              _ □ ×

C:\WINDOSBK\FINANCE>CD \

C:\>_
```

WHAT'S HAPPENING?   You exited the program Thinker and returned to the command prompt. You are now back to the system level. Next, you returned to the root directory. Thus, you used the operating system to load the application program called HPB, which can work with only one data file at a time, which you also loaded. You used the OS again to change to the directory where the Thinker program was located. You then used the commands of the Thinker program to load the data file, **HOMEBUD.TKR**. When you used the commands in Thinker, Thinker told the operating system to get the data files you specified so that Thinker could place the data files in memory to let you work with the information in them. You followed the instructions of the programs HPB and Thinker. When you were finished with each program, you returned to the MS-DOS Prompt window.

4.7   MANAGING PROGRAM AND DATA FILES AT THE COMMAND PROMPT

In the last few activities, you moved around the hard disk and loaded both program files and data files. Although you did not spend much time working with each program, the experience should give you some idea of how many different types of programs there are. With each new program, you generate new data files. Windows does a very good job of managing your program files so that you can launch them from the Start/Programs menu. You need to manage the data files you create in these programs so that you can quickly locate what you need and get to work.

As an example of what you are faced with, imagine that you own 10 books. By reading each spine, you can quickly peruse the authors and titles and locate the book you wish to read. Suppose your library grows, and you now have 100 books. You do not want to read every author and title looking for just one book, so you classify the information. A common classification scheme is to arrange the books alphabetically by the author's last name. Now you have shortened your search time. If you are looking for a book by Peat, you go to the letter P. You may have more than one book by an author that begins with P, but, by going to the letter P, you have narrowed your search. Now imagine you have 10,000 books—arranging alphabetically by author is still not enough. You may have 200 books by authors whose last names begin with P. So you further classify your books. You first divide them into categories like computer or fiction. Then, within the category, you arrange alphabetically by last name. So, if you wanted a computer book by Peat, you would first go to the computer section, then to the letter P. If you wanted a novel by Peters, you would first go to the fiction section and then the letter P. As you can see, you are classifying and categorizing information so that you can find it quickly.

This process is exactly what you want to do with files. Remember, you have many data files. You want to be able to locate them quickly by grouping them logically. The way you do this in the OS is by the means of subdirectories.

Some programs, upon installation, create a directory for your files. For example, Lotus 1-2-3 may create a directory called DATA beneath its program directory. Assuming Lotus resides in C:\123, your files would all go to C:\123\DATA. However, do you want all of your files together? What happens in a year or two, when you have created 200 more files? Some sort of organization becomes necessary.

4.8 HIERARCHICAL FILING SYSTEM OR TREE-STRUCTURED DIRECTORIES

As shown in Chapter 3, every disk must be formatted using a root directory. Formatting a disk automatically creates a directory known as the root directory. Every disk must have a root directory so that files can be located on the disk. The root directory table is the area of the disk that contains information about what is stored there. It is like an index to the disk. However, there is a limit to the number of files or entries that can be placed in the root directory table if your disk is formatted as FAT16. (See Table 4.1.) Under FAT16, the root directory is a fixed size and location on the disk. This is no longer true with FAT32. Under FAT32 the root directory is now free to grow as necessary and can be located anywhere on a disk. There is no longer a limit on the number of directory entries in the root directory because the root directory is now an ordinary cluster chain and can grow as large as needed, only limited by the physical size of your disk.

Disk Size	Number of Root Directory Entries
3½-inch and 5¼-inch DS/DD disks	112 root directory entries
3½-inch and 5¼-inch DS/HD disks	224 root directory entries
Hard disk	512 root directory entries

TABLE 4.1 FAT16 ROOT DIRECTORY FILE LIMITS

Although the limits of the root directory table on a floppy disk may be adequate, the limits on a FAT16 root directory of a hard disk were not. If you had a 1 GB hard disk, 512 entries were not enough space to store all the files the drive can accumulate. Normally, people work more efficiently when they group files and programs together logically. Subdirectories give you the capability of "fooling" the system so that you can create as many file entries as you need. The only limitation is the capacity of the disk. Even though FAT32 no longer limits the size of the root directory, nonetheless, subdirectories are still an important part of organizing a disk.

This capability is called the hierarchical or tree-structured filing system. In this system, the root directory has entries not only for files but also for other directories called subdirectories, which can contain any number of entries. Windows refers to the subdirectories as folders.

The root directory is represented by a backslash. (Do not confuse the backslash \ with the forward slash /.) All directories other than the root directory are technically called subdirectories, yet the terms directory and subdirectory are used interchangeably. Windows uses the terms folders and subfolders. All of these terms—folders, subfolders, directories, and subdirectories—are used interchangeably. Subdirectories are not limited to a specific number of files. Subdirectories may have subdirectories of their own. Subdirectories divide the disk into different areas.

The directory structure of a disk is like an inverted family tree with the root directory at the top and the subdirectories branching off from the root. The root directory is the point of entry in the hierarchical directory structure. In Figure 4.1, the example on the left is a family tree showing a parent who has two children; the one on the right is a root directory with two subdirectories. The two subdirectories contain all files and programs having to do with sales and accounting. Again, what you are doing is classifying and further classifying information.

FIGURE 4.1   A DIRECTORY IS LIKE A FAMILY TREE

A child can have only one biological mother, but a child can become a parent and have children. Those children can also become parents and have children. Likewise, ACCOUNTING can be a ***child directory*** of the root directory, but also a parent directory to subdirectories beneath it (see Figure 4.2).

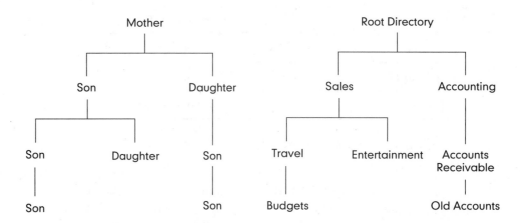

FIGURE 4.2   HIERARCHICAL STRUCTURE OF A DIRECTORY

The children are dependent on the parent above. Each subdirectory is listed in its ***parent directory*** but not in any directory above the parent. Note the absolute ***hierarchical structure***. You cannot skip a subdirectory any more than you can have a grandparent and grandchild with no parent in between. You move around in the directories via the path that tells the operating system where to go for a particular file.

Think of a disk as a building. When a structure is built, it has a finite size, which is also true of a disk. For example, you can have a 1.44 MB floppy disk or a 2 GB hard disk. The size is fixed. You cannot make it larger or smaller, but you can divide it into rooms. However, you have to get inside. To open the door you need a drive letter. Once inside, you are in a room that is equivalent to the fixed size of a disk. This undivided room is the root directory. Every disk has a root directory that may or may not be subdivided. The name of the root directory is always \ (backslash). Thus, the structure could look like Figure 4.3.

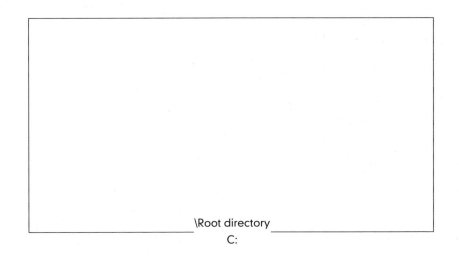

\Root directory
C:

FIGURE 4.3   A DISK AS A BUILDING

Since it is difficult to find things when they are scattered about a large room, you want to put up walls (subdirectories) so that like things can be grouped together. When the walls go up, the root directory becomes the main lobby—backslash (\ ). In the rooms (subdirectories) you plan to have games, names and addresses in phone books, and the operating system commands. You post a sign (label) indicating what you plan to put inside each room (see Figure 4.4).

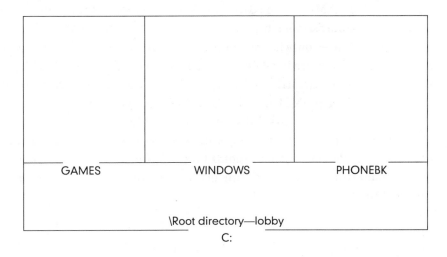

GAMES   WINDOWS   PHONEBK

\Root directory—lobby
C:

FIGURE 4.4   SUBDIRECTORIES AS ROOMS

Each room is off the main lobby, the \. You cannot go from the GAMES room to the PHONEBK room without first going through the main lobby (\ ). Furthermore, the lobby (\ ) only sees the entryways to the rooms. It does not know what is in the rooms, only that there are rooms (subdirectories). In addition, each room can be further divided (see Figure 4.5).

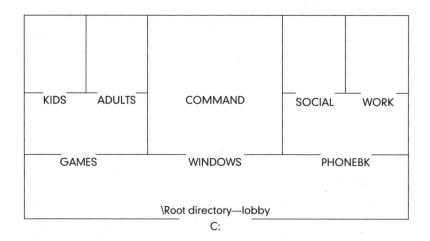

FIGURE 4.5   MORE SUBDIRECTORIES

Each new room (subdirectory) is off another room (subdirectory). The GAMES room, for example, now has two new rooms—KIDS and ADULTS. The GAMES room (subdirectory) now becomes a lobby. You can get to the KIDS and ADULTS rooms (subdirectories) only through the GAMES lobby. Furthermore, in order to get to the GAMES room, you must pass through the main lobby \ (root directory).

The GAMES lobby knows that there are two new rooms but does not know what is inside each. The main lobby (\) knows the GAMES room but does not know what is inside GAMES. The KIDS and ADULTS rooms know only the GAMES lobby.

The same relationship exists for all other new rooms (subdirectories). A subdirectory knows only its parent lobby and any children it may create. There are no shortcuts. If you are in the KIDS room and wish to go the SOCIAL room, you must return to the GAMES lobby, then you must pass through the main lobby (root directory) to the PHONEBK lobby. Only then can you enter the SOCIAL room.

You do not have to subdivide rooms. GAMES is subdivided, while COMMAND is not. Remember, you are not changing the size of the structure; you are merely organizing it. Presently, these rooms have nothing in them, but they are ready to receive something. That something is files. The files are like the furniture (see Figure 4.6).

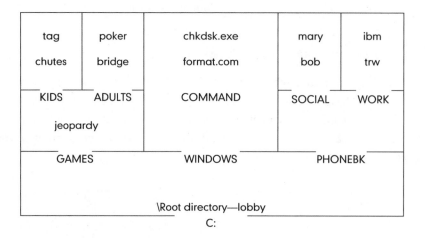

FIGURE 4.6   FILES IN SUBDIRECTORIES

You now have not only created the rooms (subdirectories), but you have also filled them with furniture (files). Thus, using subdirectories is a way to manage the numerous files and programs you collect and create. Again, this is a classification scheme, and you expect there to be some logic to it. Just as you would not expect to find a stove in a room called "bedroom," you would not expect to find a file called ADDRESS.EXE in a subdirectory called COMMAND. This does not mean there cannot be a mistake—that someone could, indeed, place the stove in the bedroom—but that would make the stove *very* hard to find.

There is another component to using subdirectories. When you use subdirectories, you can change your work area, much like using a room. If you are going to cook, you will go to the kitchen because you expect the tools that you need to be in that location. You expect not only the stove to be there but also all the tools you need—the sink, the spices, and the pots and pans. If you want to go to sleep, you will go to the bedroom because that is where you expect to find the bed. Subdirectories have names that you or a program choose. The only exception is the root directory, which is created when you format the disk and is always known as \ (backslash). The root directory *always* has the same name on every disk (\).

Because computers are so rigid, they must follow certain rules when naming anything. Subdirectories follow the same naming conventions as files. Usually, subdirectory names do not have extensions. Although the Windows operating system treats subdirectories as files, the subdirectories themselves cannot be manipulated with the standard file manipulation commands. Subdirectories have their own special commands. Table 4.2 lists the directory management commands.

Command	Function
CHDIR or CD	Changes a directory.
MKDIR or MD	Makes or creates a directory.
RMDIR or RD	Removes or erases a directory.
PATH	Defines the search paths.
PROMPT	Changes the look of the prompt to identify what subdirectory is the default.
DELTREE	Allows you to remove an entire tree with one command.
MOVE	Allows you to rename a directory.

TABLE 4.2   DIRECTORY MANAGEMENT COMMANDS

4.9   CREATING SUBDIRECTORIES

When you create a subdirectory, you are setting up an area where files can be stored. There is nothing in the subdirectory initially. The internal MD command creates a subdirectory. When you format a disk, you are preparing it to hold files. When you set up a subdirectory, you are preparing it to hold a logical group of files. The syntax of the command is:

```
MKDIR [drive:]path
```

or

```
MD [drive:]path
```

MD and MKDIR perform exactly the same function. You will use MD, because it requires less keystrokes. In the following activity, you will create two subdirectories under the root directory on the DATA disk. These subdirectories will be for two classes: one in political science and the other in physical education.

4.10 ACTIVITY: HOW TO CREATE SUBDIRECTORIES

Note: You are at the command prompt. C:\> is displayed as the default drive and directory.

Step 1   Place the DATA disk used in Chapter 3 into Drive A.

Step 2   Key in the following: C:\>**FORMAT A:/Q/V:DATA** Enter

```
MS-DOS Prompt                                                    _ □ ✕

C:\>FORMAT A:/Q/V:DATA
Insert new diskette for drive A:
and press ENTER when ready...
```

WHAT'S
HAPPENING   You are going to format the DATA disk again. In addition to using the /Q
                  parameter to format the disk quickly, you also used a shortcut to place a
                  volume label on the disk, so you do not have to wait for the volume label
                  prompt. If you want to include a volume label on a disk, you can do it at
                  the time of issuing the FORMAT command. However, when you use /V
                  (followed by a colon), you cannot have spaces in the volume label name.

Step 3   Press Enter

```
MS-DOS Prompt                                                    _ □ ✕

C:\>FORMAT A:/Q/V:DATA
Insert new diskette for drive A:
and press ENTER when ready...

Checking existing disk format.
QuickFormatting 1.44M
Format complete.

    1,457,664 bytes total disk space
    1,457,664 bytes available on disk

        512 bytes in each allocation unit.
      2,847 allocation units available on disk.

Volume Serial Number is 3330-1807

QuickFormat another (Y/N)?_
```

WHAT'S
HAPPENING?   You formatted the disk and placed a volume label on it.

Step 4   Press **N** Enter

Step 5   Key in the following: C:\>**A:** Enter

```
MS-DOS Prompt                                                    _ □ ×

C:\>A:

A:\>_
```

WHAT'S
HAPPENING?   You have changed the default drive. However, you are in more than a
                    default *drive*: you are in a default *directory*—the root of A. This is the
                    only directory that is on this disk and was created when you formatted it.
                    You can tell that you are in the root directory because when you look at
                    the prompt, it displays not just A: but also \, indicating the root.

Step 6   Key in the following: A:\>**MD POLYSCI** Enter

Step 7   Key in the following: A:\>**MD PHYSED** Enter

```
MS-DOS Prompt                                                    _ □ ×

A:\>MD POLYSCI

A:\>MD PHYSED

A:\>_
```

WHAT'S
HAPPENING?   You created two subdirectories called **POLYSCI** and **PHYSED** under the
                    root directory on the DATA disk. **POLYSCI** will hold all the files that
                    involve classes in political science, and **PHYSED** will hold files that
                    involve classes in physical education. Although you have created the
                    subdirectories to hold the files, they are now "empty" file cabinets. When
                    you used the MD command, all you saw on the screen was the system
                    prompt. How do you know that you created subdirectories? You can see
                    the subdirectories you just created by using the DIR command.

Step 8   Key in the following: A:\>**DIR** Enter

```
MS-DOS Prompt                                                    _ □ ×

A:\>DIR

 Volume in drive A is DATA
 Volume Serial Number is 3330-1807
 Directory of A:\

POLYSCI        <DIR>        07-20-01  4:57p POLYSCI
PHYSED         <DIR>        07-20-01  4:57p PHYSED
        0 file(s)              0 bytes
        2 dir(s)       1,456,640 bytes free
A:\>_
```

WHAT'S HAPPENING? The DIR command displayed the contents of the disk. In this case, there are only the two subdirectory files you just created. It is the **<DIR>** after each file name that indicates a subdirectory. **POLYSCI** and **PHYSED** are subdirectories. It is also important to note that the \ following the **Directory of A:** on the screen indicates the root directory of the disk.

One of the parameters for the DIR command is /A for attributes. The only attribute you are interested in is D for directories. If you look at the syntax diagram, it indicates the /A followed by a list of the attributes you can request. The D is for directories:

```
/A           Displays files with specified attributes.
attributes   D  Directories          R  Read-only files
             H  Hidden files         A  Files ready for archiving
             S  System files         -  Prefix meaning not
```

Step 9 Key in the following: A:\>**DIR /AD** Enter

```
MS-DOS Prompt                                              _ □ ✕

A:\>DIR /AD

 Volume in drive A is DATA
 Volume Serial Number is 3330-1807
 Directory of A:\

POLYSCI        <DIR>        07-20-01  4:57p POLYSCI
PHYSED         <DIR>        07-20-01  4:57p PHYSED
        0 file(s)              0 bytes
        2 dir(s)      1,456,640 bytes free

A:\>_
```

WHAT'S HAPPENING? You see displayed only the directories on the DATA disk because that is all that the disk contains. What if you want to look at a disk that already has directories and files on it?

Step 10 Key in the following: A:\>**DIR C:\WINDOSBK** Enter

```
MS-DOS Prompt                                              _ □ ✕

JAN      99              73  10-10-99  4:53p JAN.99
TEST     TXT             65  12-11-99  4:03p TEST.TXT
GETYN    COM             26  05-02-94 12:57a GETYN.COM
WILD1    XXX             64  12-31-01  4:32p WILD1.XXX
MAR      TMP             71  04-23-00  4:03p MAR.TMP
MARCH    TMP             71  04-23-00  4:03p MARCH.TMP
APR      TMP             72  04-23-00  4:18p APR.TMP
NEWPRSON FIL         2,672  07-31-99 12:53p NEWPRSON.FIL
Y        FIL              3  08-12-00  4:12p Y.FIL
SANDYA~1 TXT             53  11-16-00 12:00p Sandy and Nicki.txt
SANDYA~2 TXT             59  11-16-00 12:00p Sandy and Patty.txt
EXP00JAN DAT            294  01-31-00 12:09p EXP00JAN.DAT
DATA           <DIR>        07-20-01  4:25p DATA
TEST           <DIR>        07-20-01  4:25p TEST
GAMES          <DIR>        07-20-01  4:25p GAMES
PHONE          <DIR>        07-20-01  4:26p PHONE
FINANCE        <DIR>        07-20-01  4:26p FINANCE
LEVEL-1        <DIR>        07-20-01  4:26p LEVEL-1
```

```
SPORTS          <DIR>          07-20-01   4:26p SPORTS
MEDIA           <DIR>          07-20-01   4:26p MEDIA
WORKING         <DIR>          07-20-01   4:26p WORKING
         85 file(s)         28,537 bytes
         11 dir(s)     1,178,681,344 bytes free


A:\>_
```

WHAT'S HAPPENING?   As you can see, using DIR with no parameters shows you all files, not just directories.

Step 11   Key in the following: A:\>**DIR C:\WINDOSBK /AD** [Enter]

```
MS-DOS Prompt                                                          _ □ ✕

A:\>DIR C:\WINDOSBK /AD

 Volume in drive C is MILLENNIUM
 Volume Serial Number is 2B18-1301
 Directory of C:\WINDOSBK

.                <DIR>          07-20-01   4:25p .
..               <DIR>          07-20-01   4:25p ..
DATA             <DIR>          07-20-01   4:25p DATA
TEST             <DIR>          07-20-01   4:25p TEST
GAMES            <DIR>          07-20-01   4:25p GAMES
PHONE            <DIR>          07-20-01   4:26p PHONE
FINANCE          <DIR>          07-20-01   4:26p FINANCE
LEVEL-1          <DIR>          07-20-01   4:26p LEVEL-1
SPORTS           <DIR>          07-20-01   4:26p SPORTS
MEDIA            <DIR>          07-20-01   4:26p MEDIA
WORKING          <DIR>          07-20-01   4:26p WORKING
          0 file(s)                  0 bytes
         11 dir(s)     1,178,681,344 bytes free

A:\>_
```

WHAT'S HAPPENING?   The above command listed only the directories on the hard disk in the subdirectory called **WINDOSBK**. What if you wish to see the names of the files inside the directory? Since **POLYSCI** is a subdirectory, not just a file, you can display the contents of the directory with the DIR command. Remember, the terms *directory* and *subdirectory* are interchangeable. Actually there is only one directory—the root directory. Although others may be called directories, they are really subdirectories. Again, the syntax of the DIR command is DIR [*drive*:][*path*]. You use the subdirectory name for *path*.

Step 12   Key in the following: A:\>**DIR POLYSCI** [Enter]

```
MS-DOS Prompt                                                          _ □ ✕

A:\>DIR POLYSCI

 Volume in drive A is DATA
 Volume Serial Number is 3330-1807
 Directory of A:\POLYSCI

.                <DIR>          07-20-01   4:57p .
```

```
  ..            <DIR>          07-20-01  4:57p ..
      0 file(s)                     0 bytes
      2 dir(s)          1,456,640 bytes free

A:\>_
```

 The directory line, **Directory of A:\POLYSCI**, tells you the path. You are looking from the root directory into the subdirectory called **POLYSCI**. Even though you just created the subdirectory **POLYSCI**, it seems to have two subdirectories in it already, . (one period, also called the *dot*) and .. (two periods, also called the *double dot*) followed by **<DIR>**. Every subdirectory, except the root directory, has two named subdirectories, always. The subdirectory named . is another name or abbreviation for the current directory, **POLYSCI**. The subdirectory name .. is an abbreviation for the parent directory of the current directory, in this case the root directory \. The . (dot) and .. (double dot) are called *subdirectory markers* or *dot notation*. This always holds true—the single dot is the name of the subdirectory you are currently in, the default directory, and the double dot is the name of the directory immediately above the current directory, the parent directory.

Step 13   Key in the following: A:\>**DIR PHYSED** [Enter]

```
 MS-DOS Prompt                                          _ □ ×

A:\>DIR PHYSED

 Volume in drive A is DATA
 Volume Serial Number is 3330-1807
 Directory of A:\PHYSED

  .             <DIR>          07-20-01  4:57p .
  ..            <DIR>          07-20-01  4:57p ..
      0 file(s)                     0 bytes
      2 dir(s)          1,456,640 bytes free

A:\>_
```

 The line that reads **Directory of A:\PHYSED** tells you the path. You are looking from the root directory into the subdirectory called **PHYSED**, the same way you looked when you asked for a directory on another drive. If, for instance, you asked for a directory of the disk in Drive B, that line would read **Directory of B:**. If you had asked for a directory of Drive C, that line would have read **Directory of C:**. It tells you not only what drive but also what subdirectory is displayed on the screen.

4.11   THE CURRENT DIRECTORY

Just as the operating system keeps track of the default drive, it also keeps track of the *current directory,* or default directory of each drive. When you boot the system, the default drive is the drive you load the operating system from, usually C, and the default directory is the root directory of the current drive. You can change the directory just as you can change the drive. Doing so makes a specific subdirectory the default. In previous chapters you used the CD command to change the default directory to the \WINDOWS\COMMAND subdirectory on the hard disk. It was important to have that as the default subdirectory so that you could use the external commands.

The change directory command (CHDIR or CD) has two purposes. If you key in CD with no parameters, the name of the current default directory is displayed. If you include a parameter after the CD command, the default directory will be changed to the directory you request. This process is similar to changing drives by keying in the desired drive letter followed by a colon, i.e., A:, B:, and C:.

However, do not be fooled. If your default drive and directory is the root of A so that the displayed prompt is A:\> and you key in CD C:\WINDOSBK, you *will not* change drives. What you will do is change the default directory on Drive C from where you were to \WINDOSBK. Your current default drive and directory will still be the root of A and your displayed prompt will still be A:\>. However, if you change to the C drive by keying in C:, you will go to the current default directory on the C drive, which is now C:\WINDOSBK. The commands CHDIR and CD are exactly the same. You will use CD because it requires fewer keystrokes. The syntax for the CD command is as follows:

```
CD [drive:][path]
```

4.12 ACTIVITY: USING THE CD COMMAND

Note: The DATA disk is in Drive A. The default drive is Drive A, and A:\> is displayed on the screen.

Step 1   Key in the following: A:\>**CD** [Enter]

```
MS-DOS Prompt                                                    _ □ x
A:\>CD
A:\

A:\>_
```

WHAT'S HAPPENING   This display tells you that you are in the root directory of the DATA disk and that any command you enter will apply to this root directory, which is also the default directory. You can change this default using the CD command. You are going to change the default subdirectory from the root to the subdirectory called **POLYSCI**.

Step 2   Key in the following: A:\>**CD POLYSCI** [Enter]

Step 3   Key in the following: A:\POLYSCI>**CD** [Enter]

```
MS-DOS Prompt                                                    _ □ ✕

A:\>CD POLYSCI

A:\POLYSCI>CD
A:\POLYSCI

A:\POLYSCI>_
```

WHAT'S HAPPENING? In Step 2, CD followed by the name of the subdirectory changed the default from the root directory to the subdirectory **POLYSCI**. Since you changed the default directory, the prompt then said A:\POLYSCI>. However, you can always confirm that you changed the default directory by keying in **CD**. CD with no parameters always displays the default drive and default subdirectory. When you keyed in **CD**, it displayed **A:\POLYSCI**, which tells you that you are in the subdirectory **\POLYSCI** on the DATA disk in Drive A and that any command you enter with no parameters will apply to this default subdirectory. You can think of the command this way: CD with no parameters shows you the current drive and directory; CD followed by a subdirectory name changes the subdirectory. CD *cannot* be used to change drives.

Step 4 Key in the following: A:\POLYSCI>**DIR** [Enter]

```
MS-DOS Prompt                                                    _ □ ✕

A:\POLYSCI>DIR

 Volume in drive A is DATA
 Volume Serial Number is 3330-1807
 Directory of A:\POLYSCI

.               <DIR>         07-20-01   4:57p .
..              <DIR>         07-20-01   4:57p ..
        0 file(s)                  0 bytes
        2 dir(s)          1,456,640 bytes free

A:\POLYSCI>_
```

WHAT'S HAPPENING? You are displaying the contents of the current default directory, **\POLYSCI**. When you use a command, in this case DIR, it always assumes the default drive and default subdirectory, unless you specify another drive and/or subdirectory.

Step 5 Key in the following: A:\POLYSCI>**CD ** [Enter]

```
MS-DOS Prompt                                                    _ □ ✕

A:\POLYSCI>CD \

A:\>_
```

WHAT'S HAPPENING?   By keying in **CD **, you moved to the root directory of the DATA disk. The first backslash always means the root directory.

4.13   RELATIVE AND ABSOLUTE PATHS

You are going to add subdirectories to the ***tree structure*** so that the levels will look like those in Figure 4.7. To create these additional subdirectories, you use the MD, or make directory command (MKDIR or MD). The command syntax allows these parameters: MD [*drive:*]*path*.

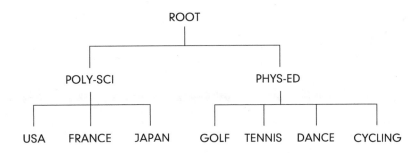

FIGURE 4.7   DIRECTORY WITH SUBDIRECTORIES

The drive: is the letter of the drive that contains the disk on which the subdirectory is to be created (such as A:, B:, or C:). If you omit the drive designator, the subdirectory will be created on the default or current drive. The path is the path name of the directory in which the subdirectory is to be created. If you omit the path name, the subdirectory is created in the default or current subdirectory.

It is important to understand the concept of the ***absolute path*** and the ***relative path***. The absolute path is the complete and total hierarchical structure. You start at the top and work your way down through every subdirectory without skipping a directory. The absolute path is *always* absolutely correct.

As an analogy, if you were living in Los Angeles, California, you could get a bus ticket to Santa Barbara. It would not be necessary to use the ***absolute path*** to ask for a ticket—the United States, California, Los Angeles, and then Santa Barbara—you could use the ***relative path*** of just Santa Barbara. If you were in London, England and were flying to Los Angeles and needed to buy your connecting bus ticket from the airport to Santa Barbara before you left England, you would indeed need to give the English ticket broker complete information about the ticket that you wanted. You would need to give the *absolute path* of where you wanted to leave from and where you wanted to go to—you would ask for a ticket to the USA, state of California, city of Los Angeles, and then a bus ticket from the airport to the city of Santa Barbara.

Just as the ticket salesperson in Los Angeles knows where Santa Barbara is, the current directory also knows information about its immediate surroundings. However, a directory knows *only* about the files and subdirectories within itself and the files and directory immediately above it. There can be many directories beneath it (many child directories) but only one directory above it (the parent directory). Each directory knows only its immediate child directories and its parent directory—no more. If you want to move to a different parent subdirectory, you must return to the root. The root is the common "ancestor" of all the directories on the disk.

Thus, if you wanted to go from the subdirectory GOLF in the above figure to the subdirectory FRANCE, you would need to go via ROOT. Once you get to the root, you can choose where you want to go. There are many places to go. It is like a subway—you must pass through all the stations along the path to get to your destination.

4.14 ACTIVITY: CREATING MORE SUBDIRECTORIES

Note: The DATA disk is in Drive A. A:\> is displayed as the default drive and the default directory.

Step 1   Key in the following: A:\>**CD** [Enter]

```
MS-DOS Prompt                                              _ □ ×

A:\>CD
A:\

A:\>_
```

WHAT'S
HAPPENING?
You confirmed that the default directory is the root of the DATA disk. To create three subdirectories under **POLYSCI**, you will use the MD command along with the subdirectory names. The subdirectories will be called **USA**, **JAPAN**, and **FRANCE**. You will begin with an absolute path and then use a relative path.

Step 2   Key in the following: A:\>**MD A:\POLYSCI\USA** [Enter]

```
MS-DOS Prompt                                              _ □ ×

A:\>MD A:\POLYSCI\USA

A:\>_
```

WHAT'S
HAPPENING?
You have given absolute instructions as to where to create the directory. You issued the command MD (make a directory) followed by the location (go to Drive A, under the root directory [\], under the directory called **POLYSCI**). The next backslash is a delimiter to separate **POLYSCI** from the next entry. Then you can add your new subdirectory called **USA**. You could not create **USA** until you created **POLYSCI** because it is a hierarchy. Looking at the screen, however, nothing seems to have happened.

Step 3   Key in the following: A:\>**DIR POLYSCI** [Enter]

```
MS-DOS Prompt                                              _ □ ×

A:\>DIR POLYSCI

 Volume in drive A is DATA
 Volume Serial Number is 3330-1807
 Directory of A:\POLYSCI
```

```
.                 <DIR>          07-20-01  4:57p .
..                <DIR>          07-20-01  4:57p ..
USA               <DIR>          07-20-01  5:19p USA
        0 file(s)                       0 bytes
        3 dir(s)          1,456,128 bytes free

A:\>_
```

What's Happening? You indeed have a subdirectory called **USA** under the root, under
POLYSCI. You are now going to create the subdirectory called **JAPAN**.
Here you can use a relative path. The default prompt shows you that you
are already in Drive A. If you are already in Drive A, it is the default
directory. Therefore, you do not need to include the drive letter because
the operating system assumes the default drive, unless you tell it otherwise. The default directory is the root. The \ is shown in the prompt,
which tells you that you are in the root directory and that it is your
default. Since you are already in the root, you do not need to include it.
The first backslash is implied.

Step 4   Key in the following: A:\>**MD POLYSCI\JAPAN** [Enter]

Step 5   Key in the following: A:\>**DIR POLYSCI** [Enter]

```
╔══════════════════════════════════════════════════════════════════════╗
║ MS-DOS Prompt                                              _ □ ✕       ║
╠══════════════════════════════════════════════════════════════════════╣
║ A:\>MD POLYSCI\JAPAN                                                   ║
║                                                                        ║
║ A:\>DIR POLYSCI                                                        ║
║                                                                        ║
║  Volume in drive A is DATA                                            ║
║  Volume Serial Number is 3330-1807                                    ║
║  Directory of A:\POLYSCI                                              ║
║                                                                        ║
║ .                 <DIR>          07-20-01  4:57p .                    ║
║ ..                <DIR>          07-20-01  4:57p ..                   ║
║ USA               <DIR>          07-20-01  5:19p USA                  ║
║ JAPAN             <DIR>          07-20-01  5:20p JAPAN                ║
║         0 file(s)                       0 bytes                       ║
║         4 dir(s)          1,455,616 bytes free                        ║
║                                                                        ║
║ A:\>_                                                                  ║
╚══════════════════════════════════════════════════════════════════════╝
```

What's Happening? You created the subdirectory **JAPAN** under **POLYSCI** and then you
used the DIR command to see that **JAPAN** was, indeed, created. As you
can see, in Step 2, you used the absolute path to create the directory. In
Step 4, you used the default values and created a subdirectory using the
relative path.

Step 6   Key in the following: A:\>**CD POLYSCI** [Enter]

```
╔══════════════════════════════════════════════════════════════════════╗
║ MS-DOS Prompt                                              _ □ ✕       ║
╠══════════════════════════════════════════════════════════════════════╣
║ A:\>CD POLYSCI                                                        ║
║                                                                        ║
║ A:\POLYSCI>_                                                          ║
╚══════════════════════════════════════════════════════════════════════╝
```

WHAT'S HAPPENING?   You have changed the default directory to **POLYSCI**, which is under the root directory. Using the relative path, you are going to create one more subdirectory, **FRANCE**, under **POLYSCI**. Remember, you are in **POLYSCI** under the root on the DATA disk, so all you need to use is a relative path name—relative to where you are.

Step 7   Key in the following: A:\POLYSCI>**MD FRANCE** [Enter]

Step 8   Key in the following: A:\POLYSCI>**DIR** [Enter]

```
MS-DOS Prompt                                                    _ □ ✕

A:\POLYSCI>MD FRANCE

A:\POLYSCI>DIR

 Volume in drive A is DATA
 Volume Serial Number is 3330-1807
 Directory of A:\POLYSCI

.                <DIR>         07-20-01   4:57p .
..               <DIR>         07-20-01   4:57p ..
USA              <DIR>         07-20-01   5:19p USA
JAPAN            <DIR>         07-20-01   5:20p JAPAN
FRANCE           <DIR>         07-20-01   5:21p FRANCE
        0 file(s)                 0 bytes
        5 dir(s)         1,455,104 bytes free

A:\POLYSCI>_
```

WHAT'S HAPPENING?   You needed only to key in **FRANCE**. The path was assumed from the position relative to where you were. In other words, as the current directory displayed, **A:\POLYSCI** was where the new directory **FRANCE** was added. Because you gave no other path in your command, the default drive and directory were assumed.

Step 9   Key in the following: A:\POLYSCI>**MD \MEXICO** [Enter]

Step 10 Key in the following: A:\POLYSCI>**DIR** [Enter]

```
MS-DOS Prompt                                                    _ □ ✕

A:\POLYSCI>MD \MEXICO

A:\POLYSCI>DIR

 Volume in drive A is DATA
 Volume Serial Number is 3330-1807
 Directory of A:\POLYSCI

.                <DIR>         07-20-01   4:57p .
..               <DIR>         07-20-01   4:57p ..
USA              <DIR>         07-20-01   5:19p USA
JAPAN            <DIR>         07-20-01   5:20p JAPAN
FRANCE           <DIR>         07-20-01   5:21p FRANCE
        0 file(s)                 0 bytes
        5 dir(s)         1,454,592 bytes free

A:\POLYSCI>_
```

WHAT'S HAPPENING? You created the subdirectory **MEXICO**, but where is it? Here is a common mistake users make. When you keyed in **MEXICO**, you were keying in an *absolute path*. Remember, the first backslash always means the root. You created the directory called **MEXICO** under the root,(\) not under **POLYSCI**. The term *first backslash* can be misleading. In the path statement **POLYSCI\USA**, some users would think that the first backslash is the one separating **POLYSCI** from **USA**. This is not true. You are separating **POLYSCI** from **USA**; hence, this backslash is a delimiter. The first backslash is the one that begins any path statement such as **POLYSCI\USA**. The backslash preceding **POLYSCI** is the first backslash.

Step 11 Key in the following: A:\POLYSCI>**DIR** \ [Enter]

```
MS-DOS Prompt                                              _ □ ×

A:\POLYSCI>DIR \

 Volume in drive A is DATA
 Volume Serial Number is 3330-1807
 Directory of A:\

POLYSCI        <DIR>          07-20-01  4:57p POLYSCI
PHYSED         <DIR>          07-20-01  4:57p PHYSED
MEXICO         <DIR>          07-20-01  5:22p MEXICO
          0 file(s)              0 bytes
          3 dir(s)      1,454,592 bytes free

A:\POLYSCI>_
```

WHAT'S HAPPENING? By keying in **DIR** \, you asked to look at the root directory. As you can see, looking at the screen display of the DATA disk, **MEXICO** is under the root directory. Windows simply followed your instructions. Remember, there are no files in the newly created subdirectories. You have made "rooms" for "furniture." As of now, they are empty. You can create subdirectories wherever you wish as long as the proper path is included. You *must* pay attention to where you are and to whether you are keying in an absolute path or a relative path. If you key in an absolute path of the directory you want to create, you will always be correct. If you key in a relative path, you must remember that you will create the subdirectory *relative* to where you are.

Step 12 Key in the following: A:\POLYSCI>**MD \PHYSED\TENNIS** [Enter]

```
MS-DOS Prompt                                              _ □ ×

A:\POLYSCI>MD \PHYSED\TENNIS

A:\POLYSCI>_
```

WHAT'S HAPPENING? Since the default, or current, directory is **POLYSCI**, you first had to tell the operating system to return to the root (\) and then go to the subdirectory called **PHYSED**. Remember, the relative path only looks down or under **POLYSCI**. Thus, the path is **\PHYSED**. You told the system that under **PHYSED** the name for the new subdirectory was **TENNIS**. The second backslash (**PHYSED\TENNIS**) is a separator or delimiter, separating the first subdirectory name from the second subdirectory name. The first backslash indicates the root. Any other backslash in the line is a delimiter. This is *always* true. The MD command does not change the current or default directory. You can verify that you created the subdirectory **TENNIS** under the subdirectory **\PHYSED** by using the DIR command with the path name.

Step 13   Key in the following: A:\POLYSCI>**DIR \PHYSED** Enter

```
 MS-DOS Prompt                                                    _ □ ✕

A:\POLYSCI>DIR \PHYSED

 Volume in drive A is DATA
 Volume Serial Number is 3330-1807
 Directory of A:\PHYSED

.               <DIR>        07-20-01   4:57p .
..              <DIR>        07-20-01   4:57p ..
TENNIS          <DIR>        07-20-01   5:26p TENNIS
        0 file(s)                  0 bytes
        3 dir(s)       1,454,080 bytes free

A:\POLYSCI>_
```

WHAT'S HAPPENING   The subdirectory **PHYSED** is displayed with the **TENNIS** subdirectory listed. It was very important to key in the backslash in **\PHYSED** in order to tell DIR to go up to the root and then down to the subdirectory **PHYSED**. If you had not included the backslash (\) and had keyed in **DIR PHYSED** only, you would have seen the message *File not found* because DIR would have looked below **POLYSCI** only. **PHYSED** is under the root directory, not under the subdirectory **POLYSCI**.

4.15   KNOWING THE DEFAULT DIRECTORY

Since Windows, and any operating system, always uses default values unless you specify otherwise, knowing the current default is very important. Recognizing the default drive and directory is easy because the screen displays the prompt or disk drive letter, A:\ or C:\. You know the default directory or subdirectory the same way. The screen displays the full path, but that was not always the case. In versions of DOS prior to DOS 6, the default prompt did not display the path—only the drive. If you were currently in C:\WINDOWS\COMMAND>, all you would have seen was C>—no path indicators at all. You change the way the prompt appears with the PROMPT command. The PROMPT command, issued without any parameters, still returns only the current drive and the greater-than sign (>). It eliminates the path display from the prompt. You also could key in the CD command, which would display the default or current drive *and* the directory you are in, but it is much easier to have the default subdirectory as well as the default drive always displayed in the prompt on the screen, which is the default setup in Windows.

4.16 THE PROMPT COMMAND

The system or command prompt is a letter of the alphabet designating the default or disk drive, followed by the greater-than sign, such as A> or C>. This was the prompt displayed automatically in versions of DOS prior to DOS 6.0. Since the introduction of DOS 6.0, if no prompt is specified, the prompt includes the path as well as the greater-than sign, such as A:\> or C:\>. However, the prompt can be changed to reflect what you want displayed. All you are changing with the PROMPT command is the way the prompt *looks*, not the function of the prompt. PROMPT is an *internal* command—it is contained in COMMAND.COM. The syntax for the PROMPT command is as follows:

```
Changes the Windows command prompt.

PROMPT [text]

    text     Specifies a new command prompt.
```

The PROMPT command also has some special characters called **metastrings** that mean specific things. When you include one of these metastrings, it establishes a specific value. Metastrings always have the syntax $x where x represents any of the following values:

```
Q   $   T   D   P   V   N   G   L   B   H   E   _
```

The following activity allows you to change the prompt and use text data as well as metastrings. PROMPT, when keyed in without any parameters, returns the displayed prompt to the old default value (A>, B>, or C>), which does not include the path.

4.17 ACTIVITY: CHANGING THE PROMPT

Note 1: The DATA disk is in Drive A. The default drive is Drive A. The default subdirectory is POLYSCI. The prompt A:\POLYSCI> is displayed.

Step 1   Key in the following: A:\POLYSCI>**PROMPT HELLO$G** Enter

```
A:\POLYSCI>PROMPT HELLO$G

HELLO>_
```

WHAT'S HAPPENING?   You changed the way the prompt looks. You no longer see A:\POLYSCI> but, instead, the text you supplied, HELLO. The greater-than sign, **>**, appeared because you keyed in **$G**. When the operating system sees **$G**, it returns the metastring value for G, which is **>**. The function of the prompt has not changed, only its appearance. The new prompt works just as if A>, B>, or C> were displayed. Any command keyed in works the same way.

Step 2   Key in the following: HELLO>**VOL** [Enter]

```
MS-DOS Prompt                                                    _ □ ✕

HELLO>VOL

 Volume in drive A is DATA
 Volume Serial Number is 3330-1807

HELLO>_
```

 As you can see, the VOL command works the same way. What if you change drives?

Step 3   Key in the following: HELLO>**C:** [Enter]

```
MS-DOS Prompt                                                    _ □ ✕

HELLO>C:

HELLO>_
```

You changed the default drive to C, but, by looking at the screen, there is no way to tell what the default drive is.

Step 4   Key in the following: HELLO>**VOL** [Enter]

```
MS-DOS Prompt                                                    _ □ ✕

HELLO>VOL

 Volume in drive C is MILLENNIUM
 Volume Serial Number is 2B18-1301

HELLO>_
```

You changed the designated drive. You can see, however, that having the default drive letter displayed on the screen is very important. You can return the prompt to the default value by keying in the command with no parameters.

Step 5   Key in the following: HELLO>**PROMPT** [Enter]

```
MS-DOS Prompt                                                    _ □ ✕

HELLO>PROMPT

C>_
```

WHAT'S HAPPENING Now you know what drive you are in. You can see the default drive, which is Drive C, displayed in the prompt.

Step 6   Key in the following: C>**A:** [Enter]

```
MS-DOS Prompt                                    _ ☐ ✕

C>A:

A>_
```

WHAT'S HAPPENING You know what drive you are in, but what subdirectory are you in? Knowing the default subdirectory is just as important as knowing the default drive.

Step 7   Key in the following: A>**CD** [Enter]

```
MS-DOS Prompt                                    _ ☐ ✕

A>CD
A:\POLYSCI

A>_
```

WHAT'S HAPPENING Keying in CD with no parameters showed that you are in the **POLYSCI** directory. However, rather than keying in CD every time you want to know the default drive and directory, you can change the prompt so it will display the default drive and directory automatically.

Step 8   Key in the following: A>**PROMPT PG** [Enter]

```
MS-DOS Prompt                                    _ ☐ ✕

A>PROMPT $P$G

A:\POLYSCI>_
```

WHAT'S HAPPENING You changed the prompt to display not only the default disk drive but also the default subdirectory (**PG**). The metastring **$P** returns the value of the path, and the metastring **$G** returns the value of the greater-than sign. Notice how you were returned to the last subdirectory you were in on the DATA disk. The operating system keeps track of which subdirectory you were in the last time you were on that drive.

4.18   SUBDIRECTORY MARKERS

The single . (one period) in a subdirectory is the specific name of the current directory, which is a way to refer to the current subdirectory. The .. (two periods) is the specific name of parent directory of the current subdirectory. The parent directory is the one immediately above the current subdirectory. You can use .. as a shorthand version of the parent directory name to move up the subdirectory tree structure. You can move up the hierarchy because a child always has only one parent. However, you cannot use a shorthand symbol to move down the hierarchy because a parent directory can have many child directories, and the operating system will have no way of knowing which child directory you are referring to.

4.19 ACTIVITY: USING SUBDIRECTORY MARKERS

Note: The DATA disk is in Drive A. The default drive is Drive A. The default subdirectory is **POLYSCI**. The prompt A:\POLYSCI> is displayed.

Step 1   Key in the following: A:\POLYSCI>**CD ..** ⸢Enter⸣
Note: With the CD or MD commands, the space after the command (CD) and before the backslash (\) or the directory marker (. or ..) is optional.

```
MS-DOS Prompt                                            _ □ ✕

A:\POLYSCI>CD ..

A:\>_
```

WHAT'S HAPPENING   You used **..** to move up to the root directory. The root directory is the parent of the subdirectory **POLYSCI**.

Step 2   Key in the following: A:\>**MD PHYSED\GOLF** ⸢Enter⸣

```
MS-DOS Prompt                                            _ □ ✕

A:\>MD PHYSED\GOLF

A:\>_
```

WHAT'S HAPPENING   You created a subdirectory called **GOLF** under the subdirectory called **PHYSED**. Since you were at the root directory of the DATA disk, you needed to include the relative path name, **PHYSED\GOLF**. Had you keyed in **MD \GOLF**, the **GOLF** subdirectory would have been created in the root directory because the root directory is the default directory. However, you do not need to include the path name of **PHYSED** if you change directories and make **PHYSED** the default directory.

Step 3   Key in the following: A:\>**CD PHYSED** ⸢Enter⸣

```
MS-DOS Prompt                                            _ □ ✕

A:\>CD PHYSED

A:\PHYSED>_
```

WHAT'S HAPPENING   **PHYSED** is now the default directory. Any activity that occurs will automatically default to this directory, unless otherwise specified. You may use a relative path name.

Step 4   Key in the following: A:\PHYSED>**MD DANCE** [Enter]

Step 5   Key in the following: A:\PHYSED>**DIR** [Enter]

```
MS-DOS Prompt                                                    _ □ ×

A:\PHYSED>MD DANCE

A:\PHYSED>DIR

 Volume in drive A is DATA
 Volume Serial Number is 3330-1807
 Directory of A:\PHYSED

 .              <DIR>          07-20-01   4:57p .
 ..             <DIR>          07-20-01   4:57p ..
 TENNIS         <DIR>          07-20-01   5:26p TENNIS
 GOLF           <DIR>          07-20-01   5:41p GOLF
 DANCE          <DIR>          07-20-01   5:42p DANCE
         0 file(s)                  0 bytes
         5 dir(s)         1,453,056 bytes free

A:\PHYSED>_
```

WHAT'S HAPPENING?   You used the relative path name. You did not have to key in the drive
letter or the first backslash (the root), only the name of the directory
DANCE that now is under the subdirectory called **PHYSED**.

Step 6   Key in the following: A:\PHYSED>**CD DANCE** [Enter]

```
MS-DOS Prompt                                                    _ □ ×

A:\PHYSED>CD DANCE

A:\PHYSED\DANCE>_
```

WHAT'S HAPPENING?   You used the relative path to move to the subdirectory **DANCE** under
PHYSED, which is under the root. You are going to create one more
directory under **PHYSED** called **CYCLING**, but you are going to use the
subdirectory markers.

Step 7   Key in the following: A:\PHYSED\DANCE>**MD ..\CYCLING** [Enter]

```
MS-DOS Prompt                                                    _ □ ×

A:\PHYSED\DANCE>MD ..\CYCLING

A:\PHYSED\DANCE>_
```

WHAT'S HAPPENING?   You used the markers to move up to the parent directory of DANCE,
which is PHYSED, and you created the directory CYCLING in that
directory.

Step 8   Key in the following: A:\PHYSED\DANCE>**DIR** [Enter]

```
MS-DOS Prompt                                                    _ □ ×

A:\PHYSED\DANCE>DIR

 Volume in drive A is DATA
 Volume Serial Number is 3330-1807
 Directory of A:\PHYSED\DANCE


.              <DIR>          07-20-01   5:42p .
..             <DIR>          07-20-01   5:42p ..
        0 file(s)                     0 bytes
        2 dir(s)          1,452,544 bytes free


A:\PHYSED\DANCE>_
```

WHAT'S HAPPENING?   When you keyed in the DIR command, you were looking at the default directory **DANCE**. **CYCLING** does not appear there because you did not put it there.

Step 9   Key in the following: A:\PHYSED\DANCE>**DIR ..** [Enter]

```
MS-DOS Prompt                                                    _ □ ×

A:\PHYSED\DANCE>DIR ..

 Volume in drive A is DATA
 Volume Serial Number is 3330-1807
 Directory of A:\PHYSED


.              <DIR>          07-20-01   4:57p .
..             <DIR>          07-20-01   4:57p ..
TENNIS         <DIR>          07-20-01   5:26p TENNIS
GOLF           <DIR>          07-20-01   5:41p GOLF
DANCE          <DIR>          07-20-01   5:42p DANCE
CYCLING        <DIR>          07-20-01   5:44p CYCLING
        0 file(s)                     0 bytes
        6 dir(s)          1,452,544 bytes free


A:\PHYSED\DANCE>_
```

WHAT'S HAPPENING?   When you keyed the DIR command followed by .. you looked at the parent directory of **DANCE**, which was **PHYSED**. **CYCLING**, indeed, appears there.

Step 10   Key in the following: A:\PHYSED\DANCE>**CD ..** [Enter]

```
MS-DOS Prompt                                                    _ □ ×

A:\PHYSED\DANCE>CD ..

A:\PHYSED>_
```

WHAT'S HAPPENING?   You used the subdirectory marker to move to the parent of **DANCE**, which is **PHYSED**.

Step 11   Key in the following: A:\PHYSED>**CD** [Enter]

```
MS-DOS Prompt                                                    _ □ ×

A:\PHYSED>CD\

A:\>_
```

WHAT'S HAPPENING You moved to the root directory of the DATA disk. (Notice there is not a space between CD and \ as there was in the above example. Remember, the space is optional.) Using the command **CD** or **CD ** will always take you to the root directory of the default disk. The following figures demonstrate what the DATA disk now looks like.

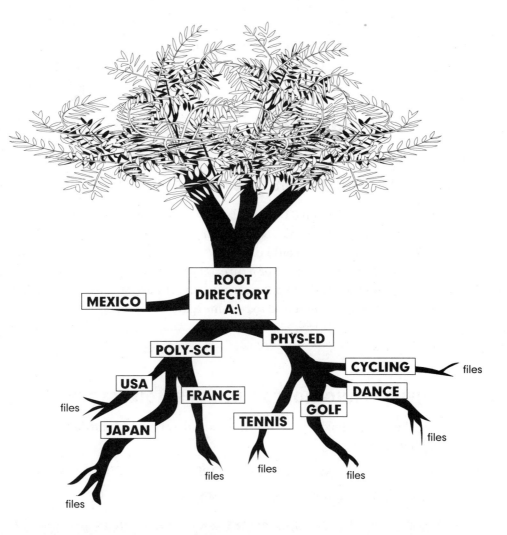

FIGURE 4.8   STRUCTURE OF THE DATA DISK

Another way to illustrate the subdirectory structure pictorially is as follows:

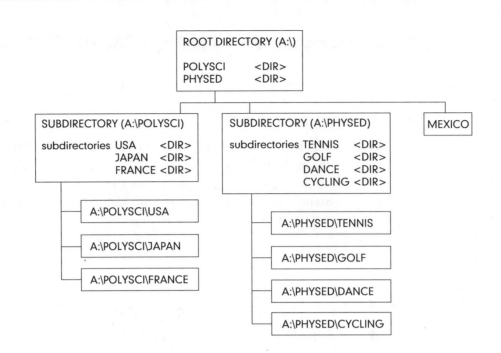

FIGURE 4.9 SUBDIRECTORIES: ANOTHER VIEW

4.20 CHANGING THE NAMES OF DIRECTORIES

Prior to MS-DOS version 6.0, the only way the operating system had to rename a directory was to eliminate the old directory and create a new one. Beginning with MS-DOS version 6.0, you could use the MOVE command. In the Windows operating system, you can rename a file or a directory from Windows Explorer. To rename a directory from the MS-DOS prompt, you can still use the MOVE command. The syntax of the MOVE command to rename a directory is:

```
To rename a directory:
MOVE [/Y ¦ /-Y] [drive:][path]dirname1 dirname2
```

4.21 ACTIVITY: USING MOVE TO RENAME A DIRECTORY

Note: The DATA disk is in Drive A. A:\> is displayed as the default drive and the default directory.

Step 1   Key in the following: A:\>**MOVE PHYSED GYM** [Enter]

Step 2   Key in the following: A:\>**DIR** [Enter]

```
MS-DOS Prompt                                               _ □ ✕

A:\>MOVE PHYSED GYM
A:\PHYSED => A:\GYM [ok]

A:\>DIR

 Volume in drive A is DATA
 Volume Serial Number is 3330-1807
```

```
Directory of A:\

POLYSCI         <DIR>         07-20-01  4:57p POLYSCI
MEXICO          <DIR>         07-20-01  5:22p MEXICO
GYM             <DIR>         07-20-01  4:57p GYM
          0 file(s)                 0 bytes
          3 dir(s)       1,452,544 bytes free

A:\>_
```

WHAT'S HAPPENING? You used the MOVE command to change the name of the **PHYSED** directory to **GYM**. You got a confirmation message on the screen that the rename process was successful. You then used DIR to confirm that the directory name was changed. Indeed, **PHYSED** is no longer there, but **GYM** is.

Step 3   Key in the following: A:\>**MOVE GYM\CYCLING GYM\BIKING** Enter

Step 4   Key in the following: A:\>**DIR GYM** Enter

```
┌── MS-DOS Prompt ──────────────────────────────────── _ □ × ┐

A:\>MOVE GYM\CYCLING GYM\BIKING
A:\GYM\CYCLING => A:\GYM\BIKING [ok]

A:\>DIR GYM

 Volume in drive A is DATA
 Volume Serial Number is 3330-1807
 Directory of A:\GYM

.               <DIR>         07-20-01  4:57p .
..              <DIR>         07-20-01  4:57p ..
TENNIS          <DIR>         07-20-01  5:26p TENNIS
GOLF            <DIR>         07-20-01  5:41p GOLF
DANCE           <DIR>         07-20-01  5:42p DANCE
BIKING          <DIR>         07-20-01  5:44p BIKING
          0 file(s)                 0 bytes
          6 dir(s)       1,452,544 bytes free

A:\>_
```

WHAT'S HAPPENING? You used the MOVE command to change the name of the **CYCLING** directory under **GYM** to **BIKING**. As long as you give the correct path name, either absolute or relative, you can be anywhere and rename a directory. You got a confirmation message on the screen that the rename process was successful. You then used DIR to confirm the name change. Indeed, **CYCLING** is no longer there, but **BIKING** is.

4.22 REMOVING DIRECTORIES

In the same way a disk can be cluttered with files, so can it be cluttered with subdirectories. Removing subdirectories requires a special command, the remove directory command (RD or RMDIR). As with CD and CHDIR, RD and RMDIR are exactly the same. RD is used because it requires less keystrokes. If a subdirectory has files in it, you cannot remove it with the RD or RMDIR command until it is empty of files or child directories. This two-step process prevents you from accidentally wiping out not only a directory but also the files inside. Thus, if a subdirectory has files in it, you can delete (DEL) the files first, then remove (RD) the subdirectory. You cannot delete a directory with the RD command that contains hidden or system files. In addition, you can never remove the default directory—the current directory. In order to remove a subdirectory, you must be in another directory. Furthermore, since you created the directories from the top down, to remove them, you must remove them from the bottom up. This means using RD one directory at a time. You cannot use wildcards with RD. The command syntax is:

```
Removes (deletes) a directory.

RMDIR [drive:]path
RD [drive:]path
```

If you do not include the drive designator, the default drive will be used. The remove directory command will not remove the directory you are currently in (the default directory), nor can it ever remove the root directory.

4.23   ACTIVITY: USING THE RD COMMAND

Note: The DATA disk is in Drive A. A:\> is displayed as the default drive and the default directory.

Step 1   Key in the following: A:\>**RD MEXICO** Enter

Step 2   Key in the following: A:\>**DIR** Enter

```
MS-DOS Prompt                                                    _ □ ✕

 A:\>RD MEXICO

 A:\>DIR

  Volume in drive A is DATA
  Volume Serial Number is 3330-1807
  Directory of A:\

 POLYSCI       <DIR>        07-20-01   4:57p POLYSCI
 GYM           <DIR>        07-20-01   4:57p GYM
         0 file(s)               0 bytes
         2 dir(s)       1,453,056 bytes free

 A:\>_
```

WHAT'S HAPPENING?   You, indeed, removed the directory called **MEXICO** from the root directory of the DATA disk.

Step 3   Key in the following: A:\>**CD POLYSCI\JAPAN** Enter

Step 4   Key in the following: A:\POLYSCI\JAPAN>**RD JAPAN** Enter

```
MS-DOS Prompt                                                    _ □ ✕

A:\>CD POLYSCI\JAPAN

A:\POLYSCI\JAPAN>RD JAPAN
Invalid path, not directory,
or directory not empty

A:\POLYSCI\JAPAN>_
```

WHAT'S HAPPENING?   **RD** did not remove the directory **\POLYSCI\JAPAN**. You got an error
message. In this case, the path is valid. **JAPAN** is a directory and it is
empty of files. The problem is that you cannot remove a directory you are
in. You can also never remove a directory that is above you as it would, of
course, never be empty. **RD** will never remove the default directory.
Remember, the root directory can never be removed.

Step 5   Key in the following: A:\POLYSCI\JAPAN>**CD ..** [Enter]

Step 6   Key in the following: A:\POLYSCI>**DIR** [Enter]

Step 7   Key in the following: A:\POLYSCI>**RD JAPAN** [Enter]

Step 8   Key in the following: A:\POLYSCI>**DIR** [Enter]

```
MS-DOS Prompt                                                    _ □ ✕

A:\POLYSCI\JAPAN>CD ..
A:\POLYSCI>DIR

 Volume in drive A is DATA
 Volume Serial Number is 3330-1807
 Directory of A:\POLYSCI

 .              <DIR>        07-20-01  4:57p .
 ..             <DIR>        07-20-01  4:57p ..
 USA            <DIR>        07-20-01  5:19p USA
 JAPAN          <DIR>        07-20-01  6:08p JAPAN
 FRANCE         <DIR>        07-20-01  5:21p FRANCE
        0 file(s)                0 bytes
        5 dir(s)        1,453,056 bytes free

A:\POLYSCI>RD JAPAN

A:\POLYSCI>DIR

 Volume in drive A is DATA
 Volume Serial Number is 3330-1807
 Directory of A:\POLYSCI

 .              <DIR>        07-20-01  4:57p .
 ..             <DIR>        07-20-01  4:57p ..
 USA            <DIR>        07-20-01  5:19p USA
 FRANCE         <DIR>        07-20-01  5:21p FRANCE
        0 file(s)                0 bytes
        4 dir(s)        1,453,568 bytes free

A:\POLYSCI>_
```

WHAT'S HAPPENING?   You moved to the parent of **JAPAN**, which is **POLYSCI**. You used the **DIR** command to see that **JAPAN** was there. You then used the **RD** command and the **DIR** command again. The subdirectory entry **JAPAN** **<DIR>** is not displayed. You did, indeed, remove it. Remember, you create directories in a hierarchical fashion, top-down, and you must remove directories bottom-up. If **JAPAN** had a subdirectory beneath it, such as **JAPAN\INDUSTRY**, you would have needed to remove the **INDUSTRY** subdirectory before you could remove the **JAPAN** subdirectory.

Step 9   Key in the following: A:\POLYSCI>**CD \ [Enter]**

```
MS-DOS Prompt                                          _ □ ✕

A:\POLYSCI>CD \

A:\>_
```

WHAT'S HAPPENING?   You have moved to the root directory of the DATA disk.

4.24   THE DELTREE COMMAND

As you can see, to remove directories one at a time can be a very laborious process when you have a complex directory structure. The **DELTREE** command was introduced with version 6.0 of MS-DOS. The **DELTREE** command, although useful, can also be *very* dangerous. It is a command that deletes the directory structure and all the files in the directories from the top down. It is fast, but it is also fatal! It is a good idea to use the **DIR /S** command before using **DELTREE** to ensure you do not delete files or remove directories you wish to keep. The syntax for **DELTREE** is:

```
Deletes a directory and all the subdirectories and files in it.

To delete one or more files and directories:
DELTREE [/Y] [drive:]path [[drive:]path[...]]

  /Y          Suppresses prompting to confirm you want to delete the
              subdirectory.
  [drive:]path  Specifies the name of the directory you want to delete.
```

4.25   ACTIVITY: USING DELTREE

Note: The DATA disk is in Drive A. The MS-DOS window is open, and A:\> is displayed as the default drive and the default directory.

Step 1   Key in the following: A:\>**DIR GYM /S [Enter]**

```
MS-DOS Prompt                                          _ □ ✕

 Volume in drive A is DATA
 Volume Serial Number is 3330-1807


Directory of A:\GYM
```

```
.                  <DIR>        07-20-01   4:57p .
..                 <DIR>        07-20-01   4:57p ..
TENNIS             <DIR>        07-20-01   5:26p TENNIS
GOLF               <DIR>        07-20-01   5:41p GOLF
DANCE              <DIR>        07-20-01   5:42p DANCE
BIKING             <DIR>        07-20-01   5:44p BIKING
            0 file(s)                 0 bytes


Directory of A:\GYM\BIKING

.                  <DIR>        07-20-01   5:44p .
..                 <DIR>        07-20-01   5:44p ..
            0 file(s)                 0 bytes


Directory of A:\GYM\DANCE

.                  <DIR>        07-20-01   5:42p .
..                 <DIR>        07-20-01   5:42p ..
            0 file(s)                 0 bytes


Directory of A:\GYM\GOLF

.                  <DIR>        07-20-01   5:41p .
..                 <DIR>        07-20-01   5:41p ..
            0 file(s)                 0 bytes


Directory of A:\GYM\TENNIS

.                  <DIR>        07-20-01   5:26p .
..                 <DIR>        07-20-01   5:26p ..
            0 file(s)                 0 bytes

Total files listed:
            0 file(s)                 0 bytes
           14 dir(s)       1,453,568 bytes free

A:\>_
```

WHAT'S HAPPENING? You will not be able to see all of this display on your screen; some of it
will scroll off. You can see that there are no files in **GYM** or any of its
subdirectories. Therefore, there is nothing in **GYM** that you wish to keep.

Step 2   Key in the following: A:\>**DELTREE GYM** [Enter]

```
MS-DOS Prompt                                                          _ □ ✕

A:\>DELTREE GYM
Delete directory "GYM" and all its subdirectories? [yn] _
```

WHAT'S HAPPENING? You get a chance to back out of the DELTREE command by pressing **N**
for No. In this case, you do want to proceed.

Step 3   Press **Y** [Enter]

```
MS-DOS Prompt                                                          _ □ ✕

Delete directory "GYM" and all its subdirectories? [yn] Y
Deleting GYM...

A:\>_
```

WHAT'S HAPPENING?   The DELTREE command informed you that it was deleting **GYM**. You can use the **DIR** command to confirm that **GYM** is gone.

Step 4   Key in the following: A:\>**DIR** [Enter]

```
MS-DOS Prompt                                                    _ □ ×

A:\>DIR

 Volume in drive A is DATA
 Volume Serial Number is 3330-1807
 Directory of A:\

POLYSCI        <DIR>         07-20-01  4:57p POLYSCI
        0 file(s)               0 bytes
        1 dir(s)         1,456,128 bytes free

A:\>_
```

WHAT'S HAPPENING?   You removed **GYM** and all its subdirectories with one command. **DELTREE** is very useful, very fast, very powerful, and *very dangerous*.

4.26   UNDERSTANDING THE PATH COMMAND

You have, so far, changed the current or default subdirectory using the CD command, which works well for locating various data files. In addition, in this chapter you executed two application programs, HPB and Thinker. You changed to the subdirectory where program files were located. You needed to do this in order to execute or run the programs.

The process of executing a program is simple and always the same. You key in the file name of the program, and the operating system looks first for the file in memory. If you key in DIR, for example, that program is in memory, and, since it is an internal program, the OS would need to look no further. If you key in THINK, it will not find it in memory, and the operating system will look for the file only in the current default drive and directory. First, it looks for THINK.COM. If no file by that name exists, it looks for THINK.EXE. If it finds no file by that name, its last search is for THINK.BAT. If it finds no file by any of those names, it returns a message, "Bad command or file name." That is the operating system's way of telling you it could not find a file by one of those names in the current drive or directory.

If DOS finds a file with the correct name, as it did with THINK.EXE, it takes a copy of the file, places it in memory, and turns control over to that application program. A program is executed in DOS this way. In the Windows GUI, you double-click the icon or choose an item off a menu to execute the program. However, the GUI is just a pretty face that does *exactly* what you did from the MS-DOS command prompt. When you work from the Windows interface, the Windows operating system first looks in memory and then on the disk for the selected program. The only difference is that when you install the program, it tells the Windows operating system where the program is being installed and what the path to the program is. Windows then keeps track of the location of the file. If there were an error in installation or a program file was somehow moved, Windows would not be able to execute the program because the path would be incorrect. Windows has a hard time fixing its mistakes; that is why managing Windows at the system level is so important.

The operating system's search for the correct file is limited to the file extensions .COM, .EXE, and .BAT. These are the only file extensions that indicate programs and are sometimes called *executables*. You have previously executed programs. You have also used external commands such as FORMAT, DISKCOPY, and MOVE which, being external commands, are also programs stored as files with either a .COM or .EXE file extension. These are examples of the system's utility files. They are just programs you want to execute (executables). When you use these programs, you do not have to key in C: and then CD \WINDOWS\COMMAND in order to execute them.

Why, then, when the root of the directory was the default drive and default directory, did those commands work? The files were not on the DATA disk. Based on this information, since those files were not in the default drive and subdirectory, you should have seen the message "Bad command or file name." Why didn't this happen? Because of the PATH command.

The PATH command sets a *search path* to other drives and directories. This command tells the system what other drives and directories you want it to look in for a program file not in the current drive or directory. The PATH command looks only for program files that can be executed—.COM, .EXE, or .BAT. All this means is that, when you key in a command and you have set the path, the operating system will search for the program first in memory, second in the current directory, and then in the subdirectories you have specified with the PATH command. When it finds the program, it will load and execute it. You can set the path for command files to another subdirectory or disk drive. In the Windows operating system, the default path includes the subdirectory where the system utility files are located—C:\WINDOWS\COMMAND. The command syntax for the path command is:

```
PATH [[drive:]path[;...]]
PATH ;

Type PATH ; to clear all search-path settings and direct Windows to
search only in the current directory.
Type PATH without parameters to display the current path.
```

PATH is the command. PATH with no parameters displays the current path. Choosing a *drive*: indicates which drive designator you want the path to follow. If you omit the drive designator, the default drive will be used. You can have more than one subdirectory in the search path by using the semicolon (;) between each path element (with no spaces between the semicolon and the paths). The semicolon (;) used as the only parameter, without the drive or path, cancels any paths you have set.

4.27   ACTIVITY: USING THE PATH COMMAND

CAUTION!   **DO NOT DO THIS ACTIVITY IF YOU ARE ON A NETWORK UNLESS YOU ARE TOLD TO DO SO BY YOUR INSTRUCTOR.**

Note: The DATA disk is in Drive A. A:\> is displayed as the default drive and the default directory.

Step 1   Key in the following: A:\>**PATH > HOLDPATH.BAT** Enter

```
[MS-DOS Prompt]                                          [_][□][X]

A:\>PATH > HOLDPATH.BAT

A:\>_
```

You have captured the current path and placed it in a batch file called **HOLDPATH.BAT**. Doing activities with the PATH command will destroy the path that is set up in your lab environment. By placing the current path in a batch file, you will be able to return to the proper path when the activities are done. Batch files will be discussed later in this text.

Step 2   Key in the following: A:\>**DIR** Enter

```
[MS-DOS Prompt]                                          [_][□][X]

A:\>DIR

 Volume in drive A is DATA
 Volume Serial Number is 3330-1807
 Directory of A:\

POLYSCI        <DIR>         07-20-01  4:57p POLYSCI
HOLDPATH BAT          36     07-20-01 10:41p HOLDPATH.BAT
        1 file(s)                36 bytes
        1 dir(s)         1,455,616 bytes free

A:\>_
```

You now have the file **HOLDPATH.BAT** on the root of the DATA disk. With this file, you will later be able to return the path to where it was set by your lab administrator.

Step 3   Key in the following: A:\>**PATH** Enter

```
[MS-DOS Prompt]                                          [_][□][X]

A:\>PATH
PATH=C:\WINDOWS;C:\WINDOWS\COMMAND

A:\>_
```

You have displayed the current search path. Your display may be different depending on what programs you have on your disk and their locations.

Step 4   Key in the following: A:\>**PATH;** Enter
         (Note that a semicolon follows the command PATH in this step.)

Step 5   Key in the following: A:\>**PATH** Enter

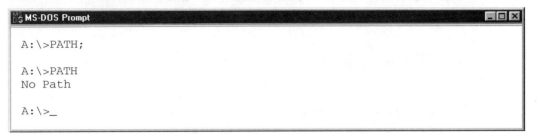

```
MS-DOS Prompt                                                    _ □ ✕

A:\>PATH;

A:\>PATH
No Path

A:\>_
```

WHAT'S HAPPENING   By using the semicolon (;) following the command word PATH, you
eliminated all possible existing search paths. The second PATH command, with no parameters, showed that there is now **No Path** set. You
will now attempt to move the file **HOLDPATH.BAT** into a subdirectory.

Step 6   Key in the following: A:\>**MD TEMP** Enter

Step 7   Key in the following: A:\>**MOVE HOLDPATH.BAT TEMP** Enter

```
MS-DOS Prompt                                                    _ □ ✕

A:\>MD TEMP

A:\>MOVE HOLDPATH.BAT TEMP
Bad command or file name

A:\>_
```

WHAT'S HAPPENING   You successfully used the MD command to create the **TEMP** directory off
of the root. You then attempted to use the MOVE command to move the
file **HOLDPATH.BAT** into the **TEMP** directory. MOVE is an external
command that resides in the **C:\WINDOWS\COMMAND** directory.
There is no longer a path to that directory, so the operating system
couldn't find the **MOVE.EXE** program. Hence, the message **Bad command or file name**. Windows could not execute the external command,
MOVE.EXE, because **MOVE.EXE** is not stored as a file in the root
directory of the DATA disk. Rather than having to key in **C:**, then **CD
\WINDOWS\COMMAND** for where the file is stored, usually you will
use the PATH command, which tells the operating system that, if it does
not find MOVE in the current drive and directory, it should continue the
search along the path. However, you tell it what drive and directories to
search.

Step 8   Key in the following: A:\>**PATH C:\WINDOWS\COMMAND** Enter
Note: Remember, if the system utility programs are in a subdirectory on the hard
disk other than **C:\WINDOWS\COMMAND**, you must key in the appropriate path
name. Refer to your Configuration Table in Chapter 1.6.

Step 9   Key in the following: A:\>**PATH** Enter

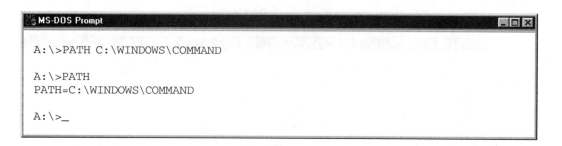

```
A:\>PATH C:\WINDOWS\COMMAND

A:\>PATH
PATH=C:\WINDOWS\COMMAND

A:\>_
```

WHAT'S HAPPENING?   When you first keyed in the **PATH C:\WINDOWS\COMMAND** command, it appeared that nothing happened, but something did. The second PATH command shows that you have set a path the operating system will search. If it does not find the command (file) in the default drive and subdirectory, in this case A:\, it will go to the path set, the subdirectory called **\WINDOWS\COMMAND** under the root directory of Drive C. There the file **MOVE.EXE** could be found.

Step 10   Key in the following: A:\>**MOVE HOLDPATH.BAT TEMP** [Enter]

```
A:\>MOVE HOLDPATH.BAT TEMP
A:\HOLDPATH.BAT => A:\TEMP\HOLDPATH.BAT [ok]

A:\>_
```

WHAT'S HAPPENING?   You did not get **Bad command or file name** this time. When **MOVE.EXE** could not be found in the root directory of the DATA disk, the operating system did not give up. Instead, it also searched the path that you set. It found the file on the hard disk in the subdirectory named **\WINDOWS\COMMAND**, loaded it into memory, and executed it. Furthermore, you can set more than one location in the search path.

Step 11   Key in the following: A:\>**THINK** [Enter]

```
A:\>THINK
Bad command or file name

A:\>_
```

WHAT'S HAPPENING?   Thinker is an application program, but it is not located in the root of the A drive nor in the **\WINDOWS\COMMAND** subdirectory. So, even though the search path is set, it is not set to the directory that holds the **THINK.EXE** file. In the beginning of this chapter, you found that this program was located in the **C:\WINDOSBK\FINANCE** directory and was called **THINK.EXE**. You had to change drives and directories in order to execute the program. If you do not want to change the default drive and subdirectory to use this program, you can use the PATH command instead.

Step 12 Key in the following: A:\>**PATH C:\WINDOSBK\FINANCE** Enter

Step 13 Key in the following: A:\>**PATH** Enter

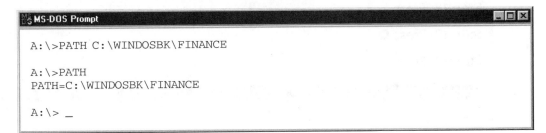

```
A:\>PATH C:\WINDOSBK\FINANCE

A:\>PATH
PATH=C:\WINDOSBK\FINANCE

A:\> _
```

WHAT'S HAPPENING? You set the search path to the **C:\WINDOSBK\FINANCE** subdirectory on the hard disk, but, by doing so, you canceled the path to the **C:\WINDOWS\COMMAND** subdirectory. In this example, you wanted to keep both search paths. In other words, instead of just searching the default drive and directory for the necessary program, you wanted the operating system to continue the search first in the **C:\WINDOWS\COMMAND** subdirectory and then to look in the **C:\WINDOSBK\FINANCE** directory. To instruct the operating system to do these two tasks, you have to include all the directories you want searched in your PATH command, and each directory has to be separated by a semicolon.

Step 14 Key in the following:
        A:\>**PATH C:\WINDOWS\COMMAND;C:\WINDOSBK\FINANCE** Enter

Step 15 Key in the following: A:\>**PATH** Enter

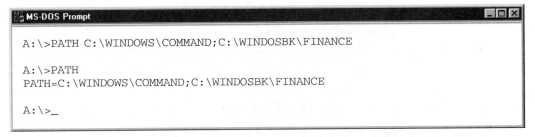

```
A:\>PATH C:\WINDOWS\COMMAND;C:\WINDOSBK\FINANCE

A:\>PATH
PATH=C:\WINDOWS\COMMAND;C:\WINDOSBK\FINANCE

A:\>_
```

WHAT'S HAPPENING? You set the path so that, if the operating system does not find the program you wish to execute in memory or in the default drive and subdirectory (A:\), it next will look in the **C:\WINDOWS\COMMAND** directory on the hard disk. If it does not find the file there, it will look on the hard disk in the subdirectory **C:\WINDOSBK\FINANCE**.

Step 16 Key in the following: A:\>**THINK** Enter

Step 17 Press Enter

WHAT'S HAPPENING? The operating system still did not find the **THINK.EXE** file in the default directory of the DATA disk. However, since you set the search path to the **C:\WINDOWS\COMMAND** subdirectory, it looked there, but **THINK.EXE** was not there either. The search continued on to

C:\WINDOSBK\FINANCE where the Thinker program, **THINK.EXE**, is located. Once the operating system found the program file, it loaded it.

Step 18 Press **/**.

Step 19 Press **Q**.

Step 20 Press **Y**.

```
MS-DOS Prompt                                          _ □ ×
A:\>_
```

WHAT'S HAPPENING? You are back at the system level. Now you want to return the path to its original setting.

Step 21 Key in the following: A:\>**CD TEMP** [Enter]

Step 22 Key in the following: A:\TEMP>**HOLDPATH** [Enter]

```
MS-DOS Prompt                                          _ □ ×
A:\>CD TEMP

A:\TEMP>HOLDPATH

A:\TEMP>PATH=C:\WINDOWS;C:\WINDOWS\COMMAND

A:\TEMP>

A:\TEMP>_
```

WHAT'S HAPPENING? The path has been returned to its original setting. The path is set for the duration of the time the computer is on or until the user changes it. Most users, as mentioned, have an **AUTOEXEC.BAT** file that automatically sets the search path each time they boot the system so that, unless the user wishes to make a change, the path is automatically set. You can now eliminate the **TEMP** directory from the DATA disk.

Step 23 Key in the following: A:\TEMP>**CD ** [Enter]

Step 24 Key in the following: A:\>**DELTREE TEMP** [Enter]

Step 25 Key in the following: **Y** [Enter]

```
MS-DOS Prompt                                          _ □ ×
A:\TEMP>CD \

A:\>DELTREE TEMP
Delete directory "TEMP" and all its subdirectories? [yn] y
Deleting TEMP...

A:\>_
```

WHAT'S HAPPENING? You have deleted the **TEMP** directory and with it the **HOLDPATH.BAT** file.

Step 26   Execute the Windows shut-down procedure.

CHAPTER SUMMARY

1. Software, under Windows, operates in protected mode when designed for the Windows operating system.
2. When running software created for older versions of DOS or Windows 3.x, Windows operates in real mode.
3. Subdirectories are created to help organize files on a disk as well as to defeat the number-of-files limitation of the root directory imposed by FAT16.
4. Whenever a disk is formatted, one directory is always created. It is called the root directory.
5. MD is an internal command that allows the user to create a subdirectory.
6. Subdirectory-naming conventions follow Windows file-naming conventions. Programs written for previous versions of MS-DOS and Windows follow the "eight-dot-three" file-naming convention.
7. A <DIR> following a file name indicates that it is a subdirectory.
8. CD is an internal command that, when keyed in by itself, will show the user the current or default directory.
9. CD followed by a directory name will change the current directory to the named directory.
10. When managing subdirectories and file names, you must use the backslash (\) as a delimiter to separate subdirectory and/or file names.
11. You may use either an absolute path name or a relative path name. The absolute path name is the entire subdirectory name or names. The relative path requires only the path name relative to your current directory.
12. The way the prompt looks can be changed using the PROMPT command. The PROMPT command followed by a text string will show that text.
13. The PROMPT command has metastrings. When included following the PROMPT command, the metastrings will return a value. For instance, the metastrings PG will set the prompt to display the default drive and subdirectory. To return the prompt to the default value, key in PROMPT with no parameters.
14. Subdirectory markers, also called dot notation, are shortcuts to using subdirectories. The single dot (.) represents the current directory itself. The double dot (..) represents the name of the parent directory.
15. You can move up the tree with subdirectory markers, but not down the tree.
16. The MOVE command allows you to rename subdirectories.
17. RD is an internal command that allows users to eliminate subdirectories.
18. Subdirectories must be empty of files before you can use the RD command.
19. The root directory can never be eliminated.
20. DELTREE is an external command that allows you to remove an entire directory including all its files and subdirectories with one command.

21. PATH is an internal command that allows you to tell the operating system on what disk and in what subdirectory to search for command files.
22. The operating system will search the path for executable files only, with the file extensions of .COM, .EXE, or .BAT.
23. PATH keyed in by itself will display the current path.
24. PATH keyed in with a semicolon following it will cancel the path.
25. If you have multiple search paths, subdirectory names are separated by semicolons.

KEY TERMS

absolute path	executable	real mode
child directory	hierarchical structure	relative path
current directory	legacy software	root directory
device driver	metastring	search path
dot (.)	parent directory	subdirectory marker
dot notation	path	tree structure
double dot (..)	protected mode	

DISCUSSION QUESTIONS

1. List three of the major categories of application software and briefly explain their functions.
2. What is the purpose and function of a program file (application program)?
3. Explain the purpose and function of the operating system when working with program files and data files.
4. Briefly explain the difference between real-mode and protected-mode operation.
5. Explain documentation, update notices, and technical support.
6. What file extensions indicate an executable program?
7. What is the purpose and function of the root directory? What symbol is used to represent the root directory?
8. What is a subdirectory?
9. Why would you want to create a subdirectory?
10. What is a parent directory?
11. Explain the purpose and function of three directory management commands.
12. Give the syntax for creating a subdirectory.
13. Give the syntax for the CD command.
14. What is the difference between an absolute path and a relative path?
15. If you wanted to create a subdirectory called JAIL under the subdirectory called COURT on Drive A:, would you get the same result by keying in either **MD A:\COURT\JAIL** or **MD A:\JAIL**? Why or why not?
16. What are subdirectory markers? How can they be used?
17. What are metastrings?
18. How can you return the prompt to the default value? Would you want to? Why or why not?

19. Explain the purpose and function of the MOVE command. Explain each part of the syntax.
20. Why will the RD command not remove a directory if there is a file in it?
21. What steps must be followed to remove a directory with RD?
22. What is the purpose and function of the DELTREE command?
23. What precautions might you want to take prior to using DELTREE? Why would you take them?
24. Give the syntax of the DELTREE command and explain each part of the syntax.
25. What is the purpose and function of the PATH command? Explain each part of the syntax.
26. How can you undo the path?
27. How can you set a multiple search path?
28. What is the difference between the path to a file and using the PATH command?

TRUE/FALSE QUESTIONS

For each question, circle the letter T if the question is true and the letter F if the question is false.

T   F   1. A subdirectory can hold a maximum of 112 files.

T   F   2. The DELTREE command deletes a specified directory structure and all the files and subdirectories beneath it.

T   F   3. The MOVE command allows you to delete subdirectories.

T   F   4. If the default directory is the root directory, you do not need to include the path name for creating a new subdirectory under a subdirectory called MEDIA.

T   F   5. The double dot is a shorthand name for the parent directory.

COMPLETION QUESTIONS

Write the correct answer in each blank space.

6. Two files can have the same name on the same disk so long as they are in _____ subdirectories.
7. When using MOVE to rename a directory, you need to use two parameters: the old directory name and the _____ directory name.
8. If the current default subdirectory is MEDIA, the directory directly above the current subdirectory is known as the _____ directory.
9. When looking at a directory display, you can identify a subdirectory because the name appears with _____ after it.
10. The extensions .COM, .EXE, and .BAT tell you that these files are _____.

MULTIPLE CHOICE QUESTIONS

For each question, write the letter for the correct answer in the blank space.

11. Formatting disks automatically creates
    a. subdirectories.
    b. a root directory.
    c. command files.
    d. none of the above

12. A subdirectory is created by using the
    a. MD command.
    b. CD command.
    c. MAKEDIR command.
    d. both a and c

13. When you create subdirectories under existing subdirectories,
    a. omitting the drive designator or path name means that the operating system will perform the task using the default values.
    b. omitting the new subdirectory name means that the operating system will name the new subdirectory after its parent directory.
    c. you must return to the root directory.
    d. no more than 32 subdirectories may be contained in any one subdirectory.

14. One of the major purposes in creating subdirectories is to be able to
    a. use the DIR command.
    b. use relative and absolute paths.
    c. group files together logically.
    d. none of the above

15. When you create subdirectories, you are allowed
    a. eight characters in the subdirectory name.
    b. to use the same naming conventions as for files.
    c. to save as many files as the disk space will allow.
    d. both b and c

WRITING COMMANDS

Write the correct steps or commands to perform the required action as if you were at the computer. The prompt will indicate the default drive and directory. Use the relative path whenever possible.

16. Locate the file called **BETTE.TXT** in the **ARCHIE** directory that is under **COMICS**.
    ```
    A:\COMICS>
    ```

17. Display the name of the current directory.
    ```
    A:\TEXT>
    ```

18. Change the prompt to = followed by the greater-than sign.

```
A:\>
```

19. Locate the file called **FISH.FIL** in the parent directory of the default directory using subdirectory markers.

```
C:\ZOO\AQUARIUM>
```

20. Set up a search path that will look in the root directory of Drive C, and then the **\BOOK** directory also located on Drive C.

```
A:\TEXT>
```

APPLICATION ASSIGNMENTS

Note 1: Remember, if you are logged on to a network, do not use the PATH command without instructions and/or assistance from your lab administrator.

Note 2: You will format a new disk, the APPLICATION disk.

CAUTION! **YOU WILL NOT USE THE DATA DISK. THE DATA DISK WILL BE USED ONLY FOR THE CHAPTER ACTIVITIES. THE APPLICATION DISK WILL BE USED ONLY FOR THE APPLICATION ASSIGNMENTS.**

Note 3: The homework problems will use Drive A as the drive where the APPLICATION disk is located.

Note 4: The homework problems will use the **WINDOWS\COMMAND** subdirectory as the directory where the operating system utility files are located. If you have a different drive or directory, substitute that drive or directory.

Note 5: Windows is running, and you have shelled out to the MS-DOS Prompt window. The visible prompt is C:\WINDOWS>.

PROBLEM SET I—AT THE COMPUTER

PROBLEM A

A-a **Do not use the DATA disk for these application problems.**

A-b Write your name and the word "APPLICATION" on a label for a blank disk or disk you no longer want; then insert the disk in Drive A. Be *sure* the disk is either blank or you no longer need the data it contains. Everything on it will be eliminated after you press the [Enter] key.

A-c Key in the following:
```
C:\WINDOWS>FORMAT A: /U /V:APPLICATION [Enter]
```

A-d Press [Enter]

A-e   When the message appears asking if you wish to format another disk, press **N** [Enter]

A-f   Key in the following: `C:\WINDOWS>`**A:** [Enter]

A-g   With the root directory of the APPLICATION disk as the default, use the relative path to create a directory called **NEW** on the APPLICATION disk.

        1. What command did you use to create the directory?
          a. MD NEW
          b. MD C:\NEW
          c. CD NEW
          d. CD C:\NEW

A-h   Using the relative path, make **NEW** the default directory.

        2. What command did you use to make **NEW** the default directory?
          a. MD NEW
          b. MD C:\NEW
          c. CD NEW
          d. CD C:\NEW

A-i   Do a directory listing of the default directory.

        3. Look at the directory display. How many bytes do the two directories occupy?
          a. 2,048
          b. 1,024
          c. 512
          d. 0

A-j   Remove the **NEW** directory.

        4. What command did you execute *first*?
          a. RD NEW
          b. CD NEW
          c. RD \
          d. CD \

PROBLEM B

B-a   Change the prompt so it reads only **HELLO THERE**.

        5. What command did you use?
          a. PROMPT pg
          b. PROMPT HELLO THERE
          c. PROMPT $HELLO $THERE
          d. none of the above

B-b   Key in the following: **PROMPT VG** [Enter]

6. What word is included in the prompt?
   a. Version
   b. Date
   c. Time
   d. Volume

B-c   Key in the following: **PROMPT PG** Enter

PROBLEM C

C-a   Get help on the PROMPT command.

7. What symbol will display the = sign in the prompt?
   a. $D
   b. $E
   c. $Q
   d. $T

C-b   Key in the following: A:>**PROMPT D_PG** Enter

8. What appears in the prompt?
   a. the current OS version
   b. the current date
   c. the current time
   d. the current volume label

C-c   Key in the following: A:>**PROMPT PG** Enter

C-d   Key in the following: A:>**CD POLY** Enter

9. What message appears?
   a. Incorrect DOS version
   b. Invalid subdirectory
   c. Invalid directory
   d. Invalid command

PROBLEM D

D-a   With the root directory of the APPLICATION disk as the default, create a directory called **HISTORY** off the root.

D-b   With the root directory of the APPLICATION disk as the default, create two subdirectories under **HISTORY**. One will be called **US**, and the other will be called **EUROPE**.

D-c   With the root directory of the APPLICATION disk as the default, create a directory called **OLD** off the root.

D-d   Make **OLD** the default directory.

D-e   With **OLD** as the default directory, create a subdirectory called **LET-TERS** under the **\HISTORY\US** subdirectory.

10. What command did you use?
    a. MD LETTERS
    b. MD HISTORY\LETTERS
    c. MD HISTORY\US\LETTERS
    d. MD \HISTORY\US\LETTERS

D-f   With **OLD** as the default directory, remove the subdirectory called **LETTERS** that you just created.

11. The command you used was:
    a. CD LETTERS
    b. CD HISTORY\LETTERS
    c. RD HISTORY\US\LETTERS
    d. RD \HISTORY\US\LETTERS

D-g   Use the subdirectory markers to move to the parent directory of **OLD**.

12. The command you used was:
    a. CD ..
    b. CD \
    c. MD..
    d. MD \

13. The parent of **OLD** is:
    a. HISTORY
    b. LETTERS
    c. the root of the APPLICATION disk—the \
    d. the root of the hard disk—the \

D-h   Remove the directory **OLD**.

14. Which of the following command(s) could you have used?
    a. RD OLD
    b. RD \OLD
    c. DELTREE OLD
    d. any of the above

PROBLEM E

E-a   Create a directory called **PHONE** under the root directory of the APPLICATION disk.

E-b   With the root directory as the default directory, create two subdirectories under the **PHONE** directory called **BUSINESS** and **PERSONAL**.

15. The command you used to create **PERSONAL** was:
    a. MD PERSONAL
    b. MD \PERSONAL
    c. MD PHONE\PERSONAL or MD \PHONE\PERSONAL
    d. MD PERSONAL\PHONE or MD \PERSONAL\PHONE

E-c   Do a directory listing of the **PHONE** directory.

16. How many files and directories are listed?
    a. 0 file(s)   2 dir(s)
    b. 0 file(s)   4 dir(s)
    c. 4 file(s)   4 dir(s)
    d. 2 file(s)   2 dir(s)

E-d   Using the relative path, change the default directory to **PHONE**.

17. The command you used was:
    a. CD PHONE
    b. MD PHONE
    c. RD PHONE
    d. DELTREE PHONE

E-e   With **PHONE** as the current default directory, use the relative path to change the default directory to **BUSINESS**.

18. The command you used was:
    a. CD \PHONE
    b. CD \BUSINESS
    c. CD BUSINESS
    d. RD BUSINESS

E-f   Use the subdirectory markers to move to the parent directory of **BUSINESS**.

19. The command you used was:
    a. CD ..
    b. CD \
    c. MD ..
    d. MD \

20. The parent of **BUSINESS** is:
    a. PERSONAL
    b. PHONE
    c. the root directory of the APPLICATION disk—the \
    d. none of the above

E-g   Move to the root directory of the APPLICATION disk.

21. The command you used was:
    a. CD ROOT
    b. CD \..
    c. CD ..\
    d. CD \

PROBLEM F

F-a With the root directory as the default directory, create a directory called **BOOKS** under the root of the APPLICATION disk.

22. Which of the following command(s) could you have used?
    a. MD BOOKS
    b. MD \BOOKS
    c. either a or b
    d. none of the above

F-b With the root directory as the default directory, create two subdirectories under the **BOOKS** directory called **MYSTERY** and **SCIFI**.

23. Which of the following command(s) could you have used to create the **MYSTERY** subdirectory?
    a. MD BOOKS\MYSTERY
    b. MD \BOOKS\SCIFI\MYSTERY
    c. either a or b
    d. none of the above

F-c With the root directory as the default directory and using the method learned in this chapter, rename the **SCIFI** directory to **HORROR**.

24. Which of the following command(s) could you have used to rename **SCIFI**?
    a. MOVE \BOOKS \BOOKS\HORROR
    b. MOVE SCIFI MYSTERY
    c. MOVE BOOKS\SCIFI BOOKS\HORROR
    d. either a or c

F-d Use the RD command to remove the **BOOKS** directory.

25. What steps do you have to complete *first*?
    a. Remove the HORROR directory.
    b. Remove the MYSTERY directory.
    c. Remove both the HORROR and MYSTERY directories.
    d. None. Just remove the BOOKS directory.

26. If you had used DELTREE to remove the **BOOKS** directory, what steps would you have had to complete *first*?
    a. Remove the HORROR directory.
    b. Remove the MYSTERY directory.
    c. Remove both the HORROR and MYSTERY directories.
    d. None. Just remove the BOOKS directory.

27. If you wanted to know what the current path was on your system, what command would you use?
    a. DIR
    b. PATH

        c. PATH /?

        d. PATH ?/

PROBLEM SET II—AT THE COMPUTER

PROBLEM A

A-a   With the root directory of the APPLICATION disk as the default, create a directory called **CLASS**.

        1. Write the command(s) you used to create the directory.

A-b   Make **CLASS** the default directory.

        2. Write the command(s) you used to change the default directory to **CLASS**.

A-c   With **CLASS** as the default directory, using the relative path, rename **CLASS** to **ORDERS**.

        3. Write any message(s) that appeared on the screen.

        4. Write the command(s) you used to accomplish renaming the directory.

A-d   Remove the directory called **ORDERS**.

        5. Write the command(s) you used to remove the directory.

PROBLEM B

B-a   Key in the following: A:\>**PROMPT TP$G** Enter

        6. Look at the screen display and write the displayed prompt.

B-b   Key in the following: **PROMPT PG** Enter

7. Look at the screen display and write the displayed prompt.

PROBLEM SET III—BRIEF ESSAY

A friend is watching you work at the command line. You key in the following:

```
C:\WINDOWS>CD \
C:\>A:
A:\>CD HOUSE\UTILS
A:\HOUSE\UTILS>DIR
A:\HOUSE\UTILS>DIR \HOMEWORK\PROBLEM
```

Your friend asks you how you know when and where to place the backslashes. Explain to her how to determine the positioning of the backslashes and the differences between the placements. Include a brief description of relative and absolute paths.

INTERNAL COMMANDS

COPY AND TYPE

LEARNING OBJECTIVES

After completing this chapter you will be able to:

1. Explain the purpose and function of internal commands.
2. Explain the purpose and function of the COPY command.
3. List the file-naming rules.
4. Explain the purpose and function of the TYPE command.
5. Explain when and how to use wildcards with the COPY command.
6. Explain the purpose and use of subdirectory markers.
7. Identify the commands that can be used with subdirectories.
8. Explain when and how files are overwritten.
9. Explain the function, purpose, and dangers of concatenating files.
10. Compare and contrast printing files using the TYPE and COPY commands.

STUDENT OUTCOMES

1. Copy a file on the same disk using the COPY command.
2. Use wildcards with the COPY command to copy files on the same disk.
3. Display a text file using the TYPE command.
4. Use the COPY command to make additional files on the same disk but in different subdirectories.

5. Use wildcards with the COPY command to copy files on the same disk to a different subdirectory.
6. Use the COPY and DIR commands with subdirectories.
7. Use subdirectory markers with commands.
8. Overwrite a file using the COPY command.
9. Combine the contents of two or more files using the COPY command.
10. Print files using the TYPE and COPY commands.

CHAPTER OVERVIEW

In this chapter you will review the Windows operating system rules used to create unique names for files and learn some essential internal commands that will help you manage and manipulate your files. You will learn about the COPY command, which allows you to make additional copies of files and back up files by copying them to another disk or directory, the consequences of overwriting files, and the consequences of combining the contents of files. You will copy dummy files that are in the WINDOSBK directory to your DATA disk so that you can have experience in naming, managing, manipulating, viewing, and printing files.

5.1   WHY LEARN COMMAND LINE COMMANDS?

In the last chapter, you learned how to manipulate subdirectories. You learned MD, CD, and RD, which are directory management commands that handle subdirectories. However, directories are places to hold files. With the directory management commands, you have built the bookshelves, but you have not as yet put any books on them. If shelves are directories, books are files. In a library, you are interested in locating, reading, and using books, not admiring the shelves. In the same way, on your computer, you are interested in locating, reading, and using files, not admiring the directories you created.

You will have many files and directories on a disk. The directories will be used to organize both your program and data files. Directories are the largest units of information management, but you need to manage information in smaller quantities—at the file level. You will generate many data files with your programs. You will need a way to perform "housekeeping tasks" such as copying files from one directory or one disk to another and eliminating files you no longer need. These tasks are different from creating or changing the data within the files. You must use the application program that created a data file to change the data in that file.

For instance, if you are the accountant who created Ms. Woo's tax return, you know how to manage the information correctly in her tax return. You also have other clients for whom you perform the same service. You, the accountant, are analogous to an application program such as TurboTax. The data for Ms. Woo's tax return is in a data file created by TurboTax. The other clients such as Mr. Rodriguez and Mr. Markiw also need separate data files, also generated in TurboTax. Those data files have to be named according to the rules of the operating system in which TurboTax works. If your version of TurboTax was created for the Windows OS, you will be able to use up to 255 characters in a file name, including blank spaces. If your version was created for DOS 6.22 or older operating systems, you will be limited to eight-character names with three-character extensions.

In addition to the accounting work, there are other tasks that must be performed. For instance, Ms. Woo might get married and want her data file under her married name. This does not require a change to the accounting data itself. You, as the accountant, do not need to perform these low-level tasks. You hire a clerk to perform them. In the computer world, you use the operating system to perform these tasks.

In Windows, you can use Windows Explorer and My Computer to manage your files. You can drag files from one place to another, cut and paste them, rename them, and delete them with the click of a mouse button. Using the command line will help you understand file manipulation as well as disk and subdirectory structure. You will also learn that there are some tasks that you can accomplish more easily and quickly at the command line rather than in the GUI. For instance, in the GUI, in order to copy a file and give it a new name, you must take two steps—first, copy the file; second, rename it. At the command line, you can accomplish this task with one step. The copy command allows you to change the name of the destination file as it is copied.

In addition, several major internal commands will help manage your files on disks and in directories. These file-management commands include DIR, COPY, REN, DEL, and TYPE. These commands are internal, meaning that once you have booted the system, they are always available to use. They are in the booting file COMMAND.COM; they are not separate files in the WINDOWS\COMMAND directory. These commands deal only with files as entities, as objects. You are not working with the *contents* of files, just manipulating the files. The commands allow you to see what files you have on a disk or in a directory (DIR), copy files from here to there (COPY), change their names (REN), throw files away (DEL), and take a quick peek at what is inside a file (TYPE). The following activities in this chapter will show you how to use the COPY and TYPE commands.

5.2   THE COPY COMMAND

COPY, one of the most frequently used internal commands, is used to copy files from one place to another. COPY does exactly what it says—it takes an original *source file*, makes an identical copy of that file, and places the copy where you want it—its destination. In a sense, it is similar to a photocopy machine. You place your original on the copy plate, press the appropriate button, and receive a copy of your document. Nothing has happened to your original document. If it has a smudge on it, so does your copy. The same is true with the COPY command—it makes an exact copy of the file, and the original file remains intact. Copying a file *does not* alter the original file in any way.

Why might you want to copy files? You might want to copy a file from one disk to another. For example, you might create an inventory of all your household goods for your homeowner's insurance policy. It would be stored as a file on your disk. If your home burned down, so would your disk with your inventory file. It makes sense to copy this file to another disk and store it somewhere else, perhaps in a safe-deposit box.

You might want to make a second copy of an existing file on the same disk. Why would you want to do this? If you are going to be making changes to a data file with the program that created it, you might like a copy of the original just in case you do not like the changes you make. You cannot have two files with the same name in the *same* directory, but you can have them in *different* directories.

You might want to copy a file to a device. One of the most common devices is the printer. You can use the COPY command to copy a file to the printer to get a hard copy, but it must be an ASCII file (a special kind of text file that contains no codes such as bold or italic—just keyed in characters).

You have used the HPB program and the Thinker program. You might wish to make another copy of those program files in case something happens to the original, presuming you are the legal owner. Those programs also had data files with information in them. You might like to have another copy, a backup copy of the various data files, so that if anything goes wrong, you still have a copy to work with.

COPY has a very specific syntax. Its basic syntax is always

```
COPY [drive:][path]filename [drive:][path]filename
```

or conceptually:

```
COPY source destination
```

COPY is the command or the work you want the system to do. The *source* is what you want copied, your original. The *destination* is where you want it copied to. The command, the source, and the destination are separated by spaces. In the formal syntax, the variables are as follows: [*drive:*] stands for the drive letter where the file is located; [*path*] is the subdirectory where the file is located; and *filename* is the name of the file you wish to copy. The file name is made up of two parts: the file name and the file extension. If a file has an extension, it is separated from the file name by the period or dot at the command line. If you are using a version of the operating system prior to Windows 95, when you key in a file name, you must have no spaces between the file name and the file extension. In Windows, if you wish to use a long file name (LFN) you must enclose the entire name in quotes. All three portions of the command—COPY, source, and destination—are mandatory. Drive and path do not need to be specified if you are using the default drive and subdirectory.

You use file-management commands to manage files. When you are learning how to use these commands, you do not want to worry about harming "real" programs or "real" data files. The WINDOSBK subdirectory, therefore, contains practice data files and program files. In the following activities, you will write data to your DATA disk only. You will never write to the hard disk. In this way you can enjoy the next activities and not worry about making mistakes. Mistakes are part of the learning process.

5.3   REVIEW OF FILE-NAMING RULES

To name any file, whether it is an application or a data file, you must follow the operating system file-naming rules. A file name is technically called a file specification. The file specification is comprised of two parts: the file name itself and the file extension. The file-naming rules are:

1. The names of files in a directory must be unique.
2. No file name can be longer than 255 characters, including the file extension.
3. File extensions are optional.
4. A file name must be separated from its extension with a period, called a dot.
5. All alphanumeric characters can be used in file names and file extensions except the following nine illegal or forbidden characters:

    "   /   \   : | <   >   *   ?

You cannot alter the rules. Usually, you will not get an opportunity to name program files. You purchase these programs, and the file names are those that were assigned by a programmer. Remember, a program file always has the file extension of .COM, .EXE, or .BAT. However, you will be naming your data files all the time. You name a data file from within the application program, usually when you save it to disk.

You should apply some common sense when you are naming files. For instance, naming a file ABCDEF.GHI does not tell you much about the contents of the file, but a file named TAXES99.TKR does give you a clear idea of what is in the data file. File names should reflect file contents. However, you must know how your application program works. Most application programs let you assign the file name, but not the file extension. The programs themselves usually assign the extension to data files.

5.4   ACTIVITY: MAKING COPIES OF FILES

Note 1: The DATA disk is in Drive A. Be sure it is the DATA disk and not the APPLICATION disk.

Note 2: C:\WINDOWS> is displayed as the default drive and the default directory. Remember to check your Configuration Table in Chapter 1.6 if your system configuration varies from the textbook.

Note 3: It is assumed that the **WINDOSBK** directory with its files has been installed on the hard disk. If it has not, refer to Appendix A for instructions on how to install it at home, or see your lab administrator.

CORRECTING KEYSTROKE ERRORS

When keying in commands, you may use the function keys to correct typographical errors. To edit command lines fully, you may use DOSKEY. For instructions on how to use DOSKEY, see Chapter 7, section 7.11.

Step 1   Key in the following: C:\WINDOWS>**CD \WINDOSBK** [Enter]

Step 2   Key in the following: C:\WINDOSBK>**DIR *.TMP** [Enter]

```
MS-DOS Prompt                                              _ □ ✕

C:\WINDOWS>CD \WINDOSBK

C:\WINDOSBK>DIR *.TMP
```

```
Volume in drive C is MILLENNIUM
Volume Serial Number is 2B18-1301
Directory of C:\WINDOSBK

APRIL      TMP           72    04-23-00   4:03p APRIL.TMP
BONJOUR    TMP           53    04-23-00   4:03p BONJOUR.TMP
FEB        TMP           75    04-23-00   4:03p FEB.TMP
GOODBYE    TMP           34    01-01-02   4:32a GOODBYE.TMP
JANUARY    TMP           73    04-23-00   4:03p JANUARY.TMP
JAN        TMP           73    04-23-00   4:03p JAN.TMP
MAR        TMP           71    04-23-00   4:03p MAR.TMP
MARCH      TMP           71    04-23-00   4:03p MARCH.TMP
APR        TMP           72    04-23-00   4:18p APR.TMP
           9 file(s)               594 bytes
           0 dir(s)    1,149,108,224 bytes free

C:\WINDOSBK>_
```

WHAT'S HAPPENING? ➤ You changed the default directory to **WINDOSBK**. You then used the DIR command to see what files had a **.TMP** file extension in this directory. You want to make a copy of the file called **JAN.TMP** and place it on the DATA disk. You are going to use the absolute path for both the *source file* and the *destination file*.

Step 3 Key in the following:

C:\WINDOSBK>**COPY C:\WINDOSBK\JAN.TMP A:\JAN.TMP** Enter

```
MS-DOS Prompt                                              _ □ ×

C:\WINDOSBK>COPY C:\WINDOSBK\JAN.TMP A:\JAN.TMP
        1 file(s) copied

C:\WINDOSBK>_
```

WHAT'S HAPPENING? ➤ You see a message on the screen telling you that the file was copied. If you look at your command, following the syntax diagram, **COPY** is the command and **JAN.TMP** is the source file or what you want to copy. It is located in the subdirectory called **WINDOSBK**, which is under the root directory of the hard disk. **C:** was substituted for [*drive*:]. The subdirectory name **\WINDOSBK** was substituted for [*path*] (remembering that \ indicates the root directory). The next \ is a delimiter separating the subdirectory name from the file name. The second backslash (\) is only a separator. **JAN.TMP** was substituted for the file name. A **.** (dot), not a space, separates the file name from the file extension.

The destination file also followed the syntax diagram. **A:** was substituted for [*drive*:]; \ was substituted for [*path*]; **JAN.TMP** was substituted for the file name. Each file followed the file-naming rules; each is a unique name with no illegal characters. Each file extension has no illegal characters. You used a period to separate the file name from the file extension. The period is not part of the file specification. It is a delimiter telling the operating system that you are done with the file name; get ready for the file extension. Thus, **JAN** is the source file name and **.TMP** is the source file extension. **JAN** is the destination file name, and **.TMP** is the destination file extension.

Step 4   Key in the following: C:\WINDOSBK>**DIR A:** Enter

```
 MS-DOS Prompt                                                    _ □ ✕

C:\WINDOSBK>DIR A:

 Volume in drive A is DATA
 Volume Serial Number is 3330-1807
 Directory of A:\

POLYSCI          <DIR>          07-20-01   4:57p POLYSCI
JAN       TMP              73   04-23-00   4:03p JAN.TMP
          1 file(s)               73 bytes
          1 dir(s)        1,455,616 bytes free

C:\WINDOSBK>_
```

You used the DIR command to confirm that you copied **JAN.TMP** to the DATA disk. You have one file and one subdirectory in the root directory of the DATA disk. Notice that on the directory display, the period or the dot is not displayed. However, remember that when you key in the file name, you must use the dot to separate the file name from the file extension. In Step 3 you used the absolute path name. You can save yourself a lot of time by using relative path names.

Step 5   Key in the following: C:\WINDOSBK>**COPY FEB.TMP A:** Enter

Step 6   Key in the following: C:\WINDOSBK>**COPY MAR.TMP A:** Enter

Step 7   Key in the following: C:\WINDOSBK>**COPY APR.TMP A:** Enter

Step 8   Key in the following: C:\WINDOSBK>**DIR A:** Enter

```
 MS-DOS Prompt                                                    _ □ ✕

C:\WINDOSBK>COPY FEB.TMP A:
        1 file(s) copied

C:\WINDOSBK>COPY MAR.TMP A:
        1 file(s) copied

C:\WINDOSBK>COPY APR.TMP A:
        1 file(s) copied

C:\WINDOSBK>DIR A:

 Volume in drive A is DATA
 Volume Serial Number is 3330-1807
 Directory of A:\

POLYSCI          <DIR>          07-20-01   4:57p POLYSCI
JAN       TMP              73   04-23-00   4:03p JAN.TMP
FEB       TMP              75   04-23-00   4:03p FEB.TMP
MAR       TMP              71   04-23-00   4:03p MAR.TMP
APR       TMP              72   04-23-00   4:18p APR.TMP
          4 file(s)              291 bytes
```

```
          1 dir(s)        1,454,080 bytes free

C:\WINDOSBK>_
```

WHAT'S HAPPENING? ➤ You executed several **COPY** commands and used **DIR** to confirm that you copied the files. You copied the file called **FEB.TMP** to the root directory of the DATA disk, but you did not need to key in all the information. Since the default drive and directory are already **C:\WINDOSBK**, the command will always look in the default drive and directory and no place else, unless you tell it otherwise. Since the destination you wanted the file copied to was the DATA disk, which in this case is Drive A, you had to key in the drive letter followed by a colon. The colon lets the operating system know the destination is a drive. If you just keyed in **A**, the COPY command would think that you wanted to name the file **A**. You did not give the destination file a name, because, if you do not supply a file name, the COPY command will use the source file name as the destination file name. In this case the source file name was **FEB.TMP**, and that is what the copy of the file on the DATA disk is called. You then proceeded to perform the same task with **MAR.TMP** and **APR.TMP**. Next, you will give the destination file a different name and override the defaults. Remember, in Windows Explorer or My Computer, you can copy files, but you cannot give them a new name when you copy them. Hence, you must copy the files, then rename each one. At the command line, you can copy and give the files a new name in one command. This is one of the reasons users like the command line.

Step 9   Key in the following:
          C:\WINDOSBK>**COPY MAR.TMP A:\MARCH.FIL** ⌷Enter⌷

Step 10   Key in the following: C:\WINDOSBK>**DIR A:** ⌷Enter⌷

```
MS-DOS Prompt                                                    _ □ ✕

C:\WINDOSBK>COPY MAR.TMP A:\MARCH.FIL
        1 file(s) copied

C:\WINDOSBK>DIR A:

 Volume in drive A is DATA
 Volume Serial Number is 3330-1807
 Directory of A:\

POLYSCI        <DIR>          07-20-01  4:57p POLYSCI
JAN      TMP            73    04-23-00  4:03p JAN.TMP
FEB      TMP            75    04-23-00  4:03p FEB.TMP
MAR      TMP            71    04-23-00  4:03p MAR.TMP
APR      TMP            72    04-23-00  4:18p APR.TMP
MARCH    FIL            71    04-23-00  4:03p MARCH.FIL
        5 file(s)              362 bytes
        1 dir(s)        1,453,568 bytes free

C:\WINDOSBK>_
```

WHAT'S HAPPENING? You executed the COPY command and used DIR to confirm that you copied the file. Following the syntax diagram, **COPY** is the command. **MAR.TMP** is the source file or what you want to copy. **MARCH.FIL** is the new destination file name. The destination file name followed the file-naming rules; it is a unique name with no illegal characters. You used a period to separate the file name from the file extension. The period is a delimiter, not part of the file specification. You did not need to use the drive letter or path name (subdirectory name) in the source file, but you did need to specify the drive letter in the destination. The default drive and subdirectory are always assumed unless you specify otherwise. In this case, you overrode the defaults by telling the COPY command to call the destination file on the DATA disk **MARCH.FIL**.

5.5   USING LONG FILE NAMES

You may consider using long files names (LFNs) with files on floppy disks, but only when really necessary. On a 1.44 MB floppy disk, the directory entry table has room for only 224 file names. In reality, you can rarely save more than 212 actual files or subdirectory names on the root of a floppy disk. Floppy disks were "designed" to hold files that complied with the old eight-dot-three naming convention based on the FAT. Even if the files are very small (not much data in them) and there is still ample room in the data sectors on the diskette for information, once the directory entry table is filled, you can no longer place more files on the disk, even though there is room. Once the root directory table is full, as far as the operating system is concerned, the disk is full regardless of how much actual space remains on the disk.

For example, assume you saved two files to the root of a floppy disk. One file is named FIRST.FIL, and the second is named TWENTY.FIL. If you saved the same files to another floppy disk, but with the names FIRST.FIL and TWENTYFIRST.FIL, the amount of space the actual data files would be the same. However, there would be a difference in the root directory table entries. Compare the two directory entry tables in Figure 5.1.

Disk 1 Directory Table	Disk 2 Directory Table
FIRST.FIL	FIRST.FIL
TWENTY.FIL	TWENTYF
	IRST.FIL

FIGURE 5.1 TWO DIRECTORY ENTRY TABLES

Notice that on the second disk, the long file name took two entries in the directory entry table. Disk 2 will "fill" faster than Disk 1, even though the amount of data is identical! A file with 20 characters in it can take the space of three eight-dot-three named files. Although it is possible to have files with up to 255 characters in their names, you can see how quickly the root directory entry table could be filled, thus limiting your ability to save files to a disk.

When viewing file names on the MS-DOS screen, you may have noticed that there are two listings of the names, one on each side of the size and date information. When a file name conforms to the eight-dot-three file-naming convention, both names are the same. When a file has a long file name, it appears in its entirety on the right side of the DIR display, and on the left side, it has an alias—an eight-dot-three file name.

When referring to files by their long file name at the command line, you need to enclose the entire file specification in quotes. The alias is created by removing spaces and other characters not accepted by older versions of the operating system. Then, the first six characters are used followed by the tilde (~) and a digit. The first file name alias gets digit 1. See Figure 5.2.

```
MS-DOS Prompt                                                    _ □ X

  MARCH     TXT            71  06-16-00   4:32p MARCH.TXT
  SANDYA~1 TXT             53  11-16-00 12:00p Sandy and Nicki.txt
```

FIGURE 5.2   DIRECTORY LISTING SHOWING ONE SHORT AND ONE LONG FILE NAME

Notice the second file listed. The file Sandy and Nicki.txt has an alias of SANDYA~1.TXT. The digit is assigned by the operating system. If you were to copy the file Sandy and Nicki.txt to a disk or directory where a file named Sandy and Patty.txt resided, it would be assigned the digit 2 following the tilde. See Figure 5.3.

```
MS-DOS Prompt                                                    _ □ X

  SANDYA~1 TXT            53  11-16-00 12:00p Sandy and Nicki.txt
  SANDYA~2 TXT            59  11-16-00 12:00p Sandy and Patty.txt
```

FIGURE 5.3   DIRECTORY LISTING CONTAINING SIMILAR FILE NAMES

Digits are assigned on a "first come-first named" basis. This can be confusing. If this same file were copied twice: first to a disk that had a name that had an alias of SANDYA~1 and second to a disk that did not, it would be assigned SANDYA~2 on the first disk and SANDYA~1 on the second disk. When dealing with long file names, it is helpful to have meaningful, unique characters within the first six characters of the name.

5.6   ACTIVITY: COPYING FILES WITH LONG FILE NAMES

Step 1   Key in the following:
          C:\WINDOSBK>**COPY "SANDY AND NICKI.TXT" A:** Enter

```
MS-DOS Prompt                                                    _ □ X

  C:\WINDOSBK>COPY "SANDY AND NICKI.TXT" A:
        1 file(s) copied

  C:\WINDOSBK>_
```

WHAT'S HAPPENING! You have successfully copied the file to the DATA disk.

Step 2   Key in the following: C:\WINDOSBK>**DIR A:** Enter

```
MS-DOS Prompt                                                    _ □ ✕

C:\WINDOSBK>DIR A:

 Volume in drive A is DATA
 Volume Serial Number is 3330-1807
 Directory of A:\

POLYSCI        <DIR>         07-20-01   4:57p  POLYSCI
JAN      TMP          73     04-23-00   4:03p  JAN.TMP
FEB      TMP          75     04-23-00   4:03p  FEB.TMP
MAR      TMP          71     04-23-00   4:03p  MAR.TMP
APR      TMP          72     04-23-00   4:18p  APR.TMP
MARCH    FIL          71     04-23-00   4:03p  MARCH.FIL
SANDYA~1 TXT          53     11-16-00  12:00p  Sandy and Nicki.txt
         6 file(s)              415 bytes
         1 dir(s)         1,453,056 bytes free

C:\WINDOSBK>_
```

WHAT'S HAPPENING? Notice the display on the right contains the entire file name **Sandy and Nicki.txt**, whereas the display on the left does not. The operating system has assigned the file name an alias in the eight-dot-three file-name format.

5.7 USING WILDCARDS WITH THE COPY COMMAND

In Chapter 2, you used global file specifications or wildcards (***** and **?**) with the DIR command so that you could display a group of files. You can also use wildcards to copy files. In the previous activity you copied one file at a time, for example, COPY JAN.TMP A:\. You then proceeded to key in a command line for each file you copied. Since each of the files you wished to copy had the same file extension, .TMP, instead of keying in each source file and destination file, you could have used the wildcards to key in the command line and reduced three commands to one. You can also use wild cards when changing the destination name.

5.8 ACTIVITY: USING WILDCARDS WITH THE COPY COMMAND

Note: The DATA disk is in Drive A. C:\WINDOSBK> is displayed.

Step 1 Key in the following: C:\WINDOSBK>**COPY *.TMP A:*.NEW** [Enter]

```
MS-DOS Prompt                                                    _ □ ✕

C:\WINDOSBK>COPY *.TMP A:*.NEW
APRIL.TMP
BONJOUR.TMP
FEB.TMP
GOODBYE.TMP
JANUARY.TMP
JAN.TMP
MAR.TMP
MARCH.TMP
APR.TMP
```

```
              9 file(s) copied

C:\WINDOSBK>_
```

WHAT'S HAPPENING? As each file is copied, it is displayed on the screen. Your command line instructed the operating system to copy any file in the **WINDOSBK** subdirectory that has the file extension **.TMP**, regardless of its file name, to a new set of files that will have the same file name but a different extension, **.NEW**. The * represented any file name. The operating system knew that you were referring to file extensions because you preceded the file extension with the delimiter, the period. These files will be copied to the DATA disk.

You could have keyed in the absolute path name, **COPY C:\WINDOSBK*.TMP A:*.NEW**, but once again, it is unnecessary to specify the source drive (default drive) and source subdirectory (default directory). Since you did not tell it otherwise, the COPY command assumed the default drive and subdirectory for the source. You needed to key in the destination drive and the destination file extension since you were not using the default values.

Step 2   Key in the following: C:\WINDOSBK>**DIR A:*.NEW** [Enter]

```
MS-DOS Prompt                                                    _ □ ✕

C:\WINDOSBK>DIR A:*.NEW

 Volume in drive A is DATA
 Volume Serial Number is 3330-1807
 Directory of A:\

APRIL     NEW        72   04-23-00   4:03p APRIL.NEW
BONJOUR   NEW        53   04-23-00   4:03p BONJOUR.NEW
FEB       NEW        75   04-23-00   4:03p FEB.NEW
GOODBYE   NEW        34   01-01-02   4:32a GOODBYE.NEW
JANUARY   NEW        73   04-23-00   4:03p JANUARY.NEW
JAN       NEW        73   04-23-00   4:03p JAN.NEW
MAR       NEW        71   04-23-00   4:03p MAR.NEW
MARCH     NEW        71   04-23-00   4:03p MARCH.NEW
APR       NEW        72   04-23-00   4:18p APR.NEW
          9 file(s)           594 bytes
          0 dir(s)      1,448,448 bytes free

C:\WINDOSBK>_
```

WHAT'S HAPPENING? You keyed in the command **DIR A:*.NEW**. You used the wildcards to display the **.NEW** files, instead of displaying the entire directory. You also used the wildcard * to make copies of the **.TMP** files. The file names are identical, but the extensions are different. You successfully copied nine files with the extension **.TMP** to nine new files with the extension **.NEW** from the hard disk to the DATA disk. However, the directory display merely shows that the files are there. How can you tell if the contents of the files are the same? You can use the TYPE command.

5.9   THE TYPE COMMAND

The DIR command allowed you to determine that, indeed, there are files with the .TMP and .NEW extensions on the DATA disk. Using the DIR command is like opening your file drawer (the disk) and looking at the labels on the files. DIR does not show you what is in the files. An internal command called TYPE opens a file and displays the contents of the file on the screen. However, although the TYPE command will display the contents of any file on the screen, a file must be an ASCII file for the data to be meaningful. The TYPE command displays the file on the screen without stopping (scrolling). If the file is longer than one full screen, you can stop the scrolling by pressing the **Pause** key. The syntax is:

```
TYPE [drive:][path]filename
```

TYPE is the command (the work) you want the system to perform. The brackets [ ] indicate that what is between the brackets is optional. You do not key in the brackets, only what is inside them. [*drive:*] represents the drive letter. You must substitute the drive letter where the file is located (A:, B:, or C:). Another name for the drive letter is *designated disk drive*. This letter tells the command on which disk drive to look for the information. [*path*] is the name of the subdirectory where the file is located. You do not key in "path." You substitute the name of the path or subdirectory name, as in \WINDOWS\COMMAND or \PHONE. The file name is mandatory. If the file has an extension, it must be included as part of the file name. You do not key in "filename" but substitute the actual name of the file. Filename is the parameter that the TYPE command expects. You can display only one file at a time on the screen. You *may not* use wildcards or global file specifications with the TYPE command. In addition, the file must be a text file to be readable. The TYPE command will not display the contents of a document file created with a word-processing program such as WordPerfect or Word.

5.10   ACTIVITY: DISPLAYING FILES USING THE TYPE COMMAND

Note: The DATA disk is in Drive A. C:\WINDOSBK> is displayed.

Step 1   Key in the following: C:\WINDOSBK>**TYPE** **Enter**

```
MS-DOS Prompt                                                    _ □ ×

C:\WINDOSBK>TYPE
Required parameter missing

C:\WINDOSBK>_
```

WHAT'S HAPPENING? ➤ The message displayed on the screen tells you that TYPE does not know what to do. The operating system is asking you, "TYPE or display what?" Since you did not give a file name as the parameter, as the syntax mandates, the TYPE command cannot show the contents of this file.

Step 2   Key in the following: C:\WINDOSBK>**TYPE PHONE\HPB.EXE** **Enter**

```
MS-DOS Prompt                                                    _ □ ×

C:\WINDOSBK>TYPE PHONE\HPB.EXE
MZD B@      á3   ¥[Ç   >  ♥&^  @




                              Ui∝q  Ü+~VWÜ W          Ü4
                                                  â>ΔΚΛτ94ΚΙΣΛΣΙ
ÄΠμ &¦ι- ¶  Ü  ε+⊥Äχμ &¦ - ¶ Äδερ &¦Θ¦e  +  PÜ14+
C:\WINDOSBK>_
```

WHAT'S HAPPENING? ▶ Your display may be slightly different, depending on your system. What you see on screen is, indeed, the contents of a file named **HPB.EXE** in the **PHONE** subdirectory—a program you executed in Chapter 4. This program or executable code is in machine language and not meaningful to you in this format. However, the TYPE command will display the contents of any file, even if it looks like nonsense characters to you. Remember, when you keyed in HPB, the program executed and allowed you to look at some data—names and addresses, but when you used TYPE, looking at the contents of the program was not meaningful. Because HPB is a program file and not a text file, using the TYPE command has no value.

Programs or executable code files are recognized by their file extensions. If you see the file extension **.COM**, **.EXE**, or **.SYS**, it tells you that the file is a program. **COM** stands for command file. **EXE** stands for executable code. **SYS** stands for system file. There are also other support files that programs need such as those files that have the **.DLL** (dynamic link library) extension. These types of files also are not text file and not readable using the TYPE command. However, the TYPE command will do whatever you ask, even if it means displaying nonsense. Remember, a file must be a text file to be readable.

Another name for a text file is an ASCII (pronounced "ask-ee") file. **ASCII** is an acronym for American Standard Code for Information Interchange. ASCII is a code that translates the bits of information into readable letters. All you need to remember is that an ASCII file is a readable text file. Another name for an ASCII file is an ***unformatted text file***. ASCII files are in a common language that almost all programs can recognize.

The data files that programs generate are usually not readable either. Each program has a special way of reading and writing the information in a data file so that the program knows what to do with the data. Usually, no other program can read the data file except the program that generated it. It would be like wanting to write a letter in Japanese if you didn't speak, read, or write Japanese. You would hire a translator (the program). He would write the letter (the data file). You still could not read the letter. You would give it to the translator to know what is in the letter. Furthermore, if you had another translator—say a French translator (another program), you could not give your Japanese letter (data file) to the French translator. She would not be able to read it either.

Step 3   Key in the following: C:\WINDOSBK>**TYPE PHONE\HPB.DAT** Enter

```
 MS-DOS Prompt                                                    _ □ ✕

04231994
        Smith                          Jane Doe
111119514162223334444Joh
n               12121952416555566667777123 Sunset Road
                                        Toronto           ON5H5
6Y2    Cana
da              416888888801011975Dear John & Jane,    X    Sample
record for co
uple with different last namesDelete it for practice!
Joe             01011971Joan            02021972
                                                         07041993
The
Book Biz
                     498 North Street
                             Orange            CA92669     USA
   7145559997                        B


                                     04231994            Tuttle
          Mary Brown    12201963               Steven
0514196371455593
77    444 Sweetheart Lane
             Tustin           CA92670      USA
714555888907
311994                     FX
                                        Walter
10121995

                         12121996
C:\WINDOSBK>_
```

WHAT'S
HAPPENING?   You are looking at the data file for the **HPB.EXE** program in its rawest form when you key in **TYPE PHONE\HPB.DAT**. This program has its data in a somewhat recognizable form, in that you can at least read some of it. But, as you can see, the format of the data is not correct, as it is when you use the data file with the program file, **HPB.EXE**.

Format, in this case, does not mean format as in format a disk but format in the sense of how the data is arranged. Only the program **HPB.EXE** knows how to arrange this data so it is meaningful to you. TYPE can be useful with data files like these because it gives you an idea of what information the file actually holds. Nearly all the files in the **WINDOSBK** directory are ASCII files, which means that you can read them using the TYPE command.

Step 4   Key in the following: C:\WINDOSBK>**TYPE JAN.TMP** Enter

```
MS-DOS Prompt                                                    _ □ ×

C:\WINDOSBK>TYPE JAN.TMP

This is my January file.
It is my first dummy file.
This is file 1.

C:\WINDOSBK>_
```

WHAT'S HAPPENING? In this case, the above is a text file (ASCII file), so you can read it. Using the TYPE command, you "opened" your file, **JAN.TMP**, and saw the contents displayed on the screen. Whenever a file is readable on the screen, as this one is, you know it is an ASCII file. You did not need to include the drive or path since **JAN.TMP** was on the hard disk in the **WINDOSBK** subdirectory and the TYPE command used the default values. You copied this file to the DATA disk in Activity 5.4. Is the content of the file the same on the DATA disk as it is in the **WINDOSBK** subdirectory? If it is, you will know that the COPY command makes no changes to any information in a file when it copies it.

Step 5   Key in the following: C:\WINDOSBK>**TYPE A:JAN.TMP** ⏎Enter

```
MS-DOS Prompt                                                    _ □ ×

C:\WINDOSBK>TYPE A:JAN.TMP

This is my January file.
It is my first dummy file.
This is file 1.

C:\WINDOSBK>_
```

WHAT'S HAPPENING? The contents of the two files are the same. Copying the file from one disk to another had no impact on the contents. This is also true no matter what type of file you copy. But, you would still need to include the drive designator **A:** in front of the file name **JAN.TMP** because that told the operating system which disk drive to select. Had you not included the drive designator, the operating system would have looked for the file **JAN.TMP** on the default hard disk and in the default subdirectory **\WINDOSBK**. After the TYPE command has executed, you are returned to the system prompt, ready for the next command.

Step 6   Key in the following: C:\WINDOSBK>**CD ** ⏎Enter

```
MS-DOS Prompt                                                    _ □ ×

C:\WINDOSBK>CD \

C:\>_
```

WHAT'S HAPPENING? You have returned to the root directory of the hard disk.

5.11 DUMMY FILES

You are going to use some dummy files. "Dummy" refers to the fact that that these files have no particular meaning and are of no importance. You can use these files to practice file-management commands without worrying about harming your "real" program and data files. The concept of dummy files and/or dummy data is common in data processing. Often data-processing professionals wish to test different portions of systems or programs. For instance, if you were writing a program about employee benefits, rather than looking at every employee, you would create dummy files and data in order to have a smaller representative sample that is manageable and easily tested. Not only are the files smaller, they are samples. If the data gets harmed in any way, it has no impact on the "real" data.

The following activities allow you to do the same. Following the instructions, you will use the COPY command to make copies of different files either on the DATA disk or from the WINDOSBK subdirectory to the DATA disk. You will then display the contents of the file on the screen with the TYPE command.

You sometimes want to have extra copies of the same files on the same disk. Often, you may wish to make copies of files created when you use other software application packages. You choose to make copies because you want to leave your original files intact. For instance, if you created an extensive client list with a database-management package and needed to update it, rather than working on the original file, you could re-key in the entire client list. If you made a mistake, you would still have your original list.

However, an easier method would be to copy the client list, stored as a file, to a new file with a new name and make changes to the new file. When you make a copy of a file on the same disk in the same subdirectory, you must give it a different name. Every file name in a directory must be unique.

5.12 ACTIVITY: USING THE COPY AND TYPE COMMANDS

Note 1: C:\> is displayed and the DATA disk is in Drive A.
Note 2: Remember that if your DATA disk is in a drive other than A, you will have to substitute the proper drive letter. Check your Configuration Table in Chapter 1.6 for the appropriate substitutions.

Step 1   Key in the following: C:\>**A:** Enter

```
MS-DOS Prompt                                          _ □ ×

C:\>A:

A:\>_
```

WHAT'S HAPPENING?   You changed the default drive so that all activities will automatically occur or default to the DATA disk.

Step 2   Key in the following: A:\>**COPY JAN.TMP JAN.OLD** Enter

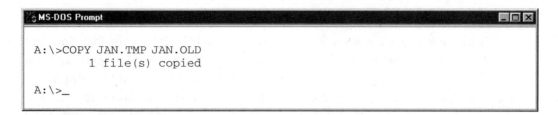

```
MS-DOS Prompt                                                    _ □ ✕

A:\>COPY JAN.TMP JAN.OLD
        1 file(s) copied

A:\>_
```

You keyed in the command and its required parameters to accomplish
the work you wanted done. You did not need to specify the drive letter or
the path name preceding either the source file or the destination file
name. Because you did not, the COPY command automatically read
JAN.TMP and wrote **JAN.OLD** to the default drive and directory, which
is the root directory of the DATA disk.

Step 3   Key in the following: A:\>**TYPE JAN.TMP** [Enter]

Step 4   Key in the following: A:\>**TYPE JAN.OLD** [Enter]

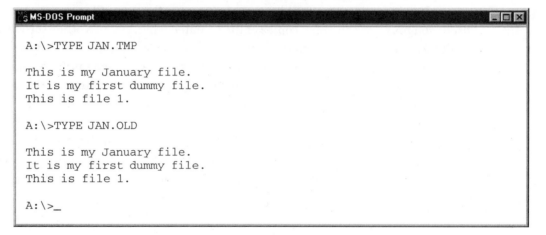

```
MS-DOS Prompt                                                    _ □ ✕

A:\>TYPE JAN.TMP

This is my January file.
It is my first dummy file.
This is file 1.

A:\>TYPE JAN.OLD

This is my January file.
It is my first dummy file.
This is file 1.

A:\>_
```

You can see that you made a copy of the **JAN.TMP** file to a new file
called **JAN.OLD**, but the contents of the files are identical.

Step 5   Key in the following: A:\>**COPY MAR.TMP MAR.TMP** [Enter]

```
MS-DOS Prompt                                                    _ □ ✕

A:\>COPY MAR.TMP MAR.TMP
MAR.TMP
File cannot be copied onto itself
        0 file(s) copied

A:\>_
```

You must give new files on the same disk and in the same subdirectory
unique names. Just as you should not label two file folders the same in a
file drawer, you would not label two disk files with the same names.

Step 6   Key in the following: A:\>**COPY MAR.TMP MARCH.TXT** [Enter]

```
MS-DOS Prompt                                                    _ □ ×

A:\>COPY MAR.TMP MARCH.TXT
        1 file(s) copied

A:\>_
```

WHAT'S HAPPENING? Here you are making a copy of the contents of the file on the DATA disk called **MAR.TMP**, copying the contents to the DATA disk, and calling this new file **MARCH.TXT**. You could have used the absolute path and filename keying in **COPY A:\MAR.TMP A:\MARCH.TXT**. Either is correct, but it is not necessary to specify the disk drive since the default drive is assumed. Nor is it necessary to specify the path or directory because the root directory (\) is the default directory.

Step 7   Key in the following: A:\>**TYPE MARCH.TXT** Enter

Step 8   Key in the following: A:\>**TYPE MAR.TMP** Enter

```
MS-DOS Prompt                                                    _ □ ×

A:\>TYPE MARCH.TXT

This is my March file.
It is my third dummy file.
This is file 3.

A:\>TYPE MAR.TMP

This is my March file.
It is my third dummy file.
This is file 3.

A:\>_
```

WHAT'S HAPPENING? The contents of each file are identical even though the file names are different. The COPY command does nothing to the original; the contents of the original file remain the same. As far as the system is concerned, what makes a file different is its unique file name. To the operating system, **MAR.TMP** and **MARCH.TXT** are unique, separate files.

Step 9   Key in the following: A:\>**COPY JAN.TMP JANUARY.TXT** Enter

Step 10   Key in the following: A:\>**COPY FEB.TMP FEBRUARY.TXT** Enter

Step 11   Key in the following: A:\>**COPY APR.TMP APRIL.TXT** Enter

```
MS-DOS Prompt                                                    _ □ ×

A:\>COPY JAN.TMP JANUARY.TXT
        1 file(s) copied

A:\>COPY FEB.TMP FEBRUARY.TXT
        1 file(s) copied

A:\>COPY APR.TMP APRIL.TXT
```

```
        1 file(s) copied

A:\>_
```

Step 12   Key in the following: A:\>**DIR *.TMP** [Enter]

Step 13   Key in the following: A:\>**DIR *.TXT** [Enter]

```
 MS-DOS Prompt                                                    _ □ ✕

   Volume Serial Number is 3330-1807
   Directory of A:\

JAN        TMP            73   04-23-00   4:03p JAN.TMP
FEB        TMP            75   04-23-00   4:03p FEB.TMP
MAR        TMP            71   04-23-00   4:03p MAR.TMP
APR        TMP            72   04-23-00   4:18p APR.TMP
           4 file(s)            291 bytes
           0 dir(s)       1,445,888 bytes free

A:\>DIR *.TXT

   Volume in drive A is DATA
   Volume Serial Number is 3330-1807
   Directory of A:\

SANDYA~1 TXT            53   11-16-00  12:00p Sandy and Nicki.txt
MARCH    TXT            71   04-23-00   4:03p MARCH.TXT
JANUARY  TXT            73   04-23-00   4:03p JANUARY.TXT
FEBRUARY TXT            75   04-23-00   4:03p FEBRUARY.TXT
APRIL    TXT            72   04-23-00   4:18p APRIL.TXT
           5 file(s)            344 bytes
           0 dir(s)       1,445,888 bytes free

A:\>_
```

WHAT'S HAPPENING!   You had four files with the extension **.TMP**. You still have those files,
but, in addition, you now have four more files you just "created" with the
copy command that have the extension **.TXT**. It is the operating system
that keeps track of all these files.

5.13   MAKING ADDITIONAL FILES ON THE SAME DISK

You often want to have extra copies of files on the same disk but in a different
subdirectory. You may want to keep your backup files in the same file cabinet (disk)
but in a different drawer (subdirectory). In this way you can group similar files
together. When you make a copy of a file on the same disk, in a different
subdirectory, it may have the same file name. Every file on a disk must have a
unique name. However, a copy of a file is in a different subdirectory, even though the
file name is the same, the different path name makes the file name different and
therefore unique.

5.14 ACTIVITY: USING THE COPY COMMAND

Note: The DATA disk is in Drive A. A:\> is displayed.

Step 1   Key in the following: A:\>**MD \CLASS** Enter

```
MS-DOS Prompt                                                    _ □ ×

A:\>MD \CLASS

A:\>_
```

WHAT'S HAPPENING? You created a subdirectory called **CLASS** on the DATA disk. Remember, MD, which means "Make Directory," is the command to create a place for additional files. The first backslash (\) is the name of the root directory. **CLASS** is the name of the subdirectory. The only reserved name for a directory is \. You may use any name for the subdirectory you create, provided that you follow the file-naming rules.

Step 2   Key in the following: A:\>**DIR** Enter

```
MS-DOS Prompt                                                    _ □ ×

JAN        TMP         73    04-23-00    4:03p  JAN.TMP
FEB        TMP         75    04-23-00    4:03p  FEB.TMP
MAR        TMP         71    04-23-00    4:03p  MAR.TMP
APR        TMP         72    04-23-00    4:18p  APR.TMP
MARCH      FIL         71    04-23-00    4:03p  MARCH.FIL
SANDYA~1   TXT         53    11-16-00   12:00p  Sandy and Nicki.txt
APRIL      NEW         72    04-23-00    4:03p  APRIL.NEW
BONJOUR    NEW         53    04-23-00    4:03p  BONJOUR.NEW
FEB        NEW         75    04-23-00    4:03p  FEB.NEW
GOODBYE    NEW         34    01-01-02    4:32a  GOODBYE.NEW
JANUARY    NEW         73    04-23-00    4:03p  JANUARY.NEW
JAN        NEW         73    04-23-00    4:03p  JAN.NEW
MAR        NEW         71    04-23-00    4:03p  MAR.NEW
MARCH      NEW         71    04-23-00    4:03p  MARCH.NEW
APR        NEW         72    04-23-00    4:18p  APR.NEW
JAN        OLD         73    04-23-00    4:03p  JAN.OLD
MARCH      TXT         71    04-23-00    4:03p  MARCH.TXT
JANUARY    TXT         73    04-23-00    4:03p  JANUARY.TXT
FEBRUARY   TXT         75    04-23-00    4:03p  FEBRUARY.TXT
APRIL      TXT         72    04-23-00    4:18p  APRIL.TXT
CLASS              <DIR>         07-24-01  12:26p  CLASS
        20 file(s)          1,373 bytes
         2 dir(s)       1,445,376 bytes free

A:\>_
```

WHAT'S HAPPENING? The directory display shows the subdirectory called **CLASS**. You know it is a subdirectory because it has <DIR> following the file name. To see what is inside that subdirectory, or "file cabinet," you must use DIR with the path name. A review of the syntax is:

```
DIR [drive:][path][filename]
```

You do not need to include the drive letter since the default drive is where
the DATA disk is. Nor do you need to include \ for the root directory,
since the root directory of the DATA disk is the default. You do need to
include the path name. The path name is the subdirectory name,
CLASS.

Step 3   Key in the following: A:\>**DIR CLASS** Enter

```
MS-DOS Prompt                                                    _ □ ✕

A:\>DIR CLASS

 Volume in drive A is DATA
 Volume Serial Number is 3330-1807
 Directory of A:\CLASS

 .               <DIR>          07-24-01 12:26p .
 ..              <DIR>          07-24-01 12:26p ..
         0 file(s)                   0 bytes
         2 dir(s)           1,445,376 bytes free

A:\>_
```

WHAT'S
HAPPENING? ▶ This directory listing is not for the root directory. The display tells you
what you are looking at. The third line of the display reads **Directory of
A:\CLASS**, telling you that you are looking at the subdirectory called
CLASS on the DATA disk. There is nothing yet in this subdirectory. The
. and the .. are created when you create a subdirectory. The . tells the
operating system that this is a subdirectory. The .. is a shorthand name
for the directory above **CLASS**, in this case the root directory (\). How do
you copy a file into this subdirectory? You can always correctly use the
absolute path. You do this by following the syntax of the COPY command:

```
COPY [drive:][path]filename [drive:][path]filename
```

Step 4   Key in the following: A:\>**COPY A:\JAN.TMP A:\CLASS\JAN.PAR** Enter

```
MS-DOS Prompt                                                    _ □ ✕

A:\>COPY A:\JAN.TMP A:\CLASS\JAN.PAR
        1 file(s) copied

A:\>_
```

WHAT'S
HAPPENING? ▶ You copied the source file, **JAN.TMP**, from the root directory on the
DATA disk, to the destination, the subdirectory **CLASS**; you also gave
the destination file a new name, **JAN.PAR**. By looking at the syntax
diagram, you can follow how you substituted the values you wanted:

```
COPY [drive:][path]filename [drive:][path]filename
COPY  A:       \    JAN.TMP    A:    \CLASS\ JAN.PAR
```

In the destination syntax, what is the second backslash? The first backslash is the name of the root directory. The second backslash is used as a delimiter between the subdirectory name and the file name. This delimiter tells the operating system that the subdirectory name is over and the file name is about to begin. Backslashes are used as delimiters separating subdirectory and file names.

Keying in the absolute path is not as easy as using the relative path. With the relative path, you don't have to key in the default drive and directory. The system will make these assumptions for you. You must include the command COPY. Since the DATA disk is the default drive, you do not need to include the drive letter, and, since the root directory is the default directory, you do not need to include the first \. However, you do need to include the source file name.

The same is true with the destination file. You do not need to include the drive letter or root directory, but you must include the path name and the new file name. The shorthand way of copying is done in Step 5.

Step 5   Key in the following: A:\>**COPY FEB.TMP CLASS\FEB.PAR** Enter

```
MS-DOS Prompt                                                        _ □ X

A:\>COPY FEB.TMP CLASS\FEB.PAR
       1 file(s) copied

A:\>_
```

WHAT'S HAPPENING?   In this case, you kept your typing to a minimum by using the relative path, observing your default drive and directory and keying in only what was necessary to execute the command.

Step 6   Key in the following: A:\>**DIR CLASS** Enter

```
MS-DOS Prompt                                                        _ □ X

A:\>DIR CLASS

 Volume in drive A is DATA
 Volume Serial Number is 3330-1807
 Directory of A:\CLASS

.              <DIR>        07-24-01 12:26p .
..             <DIR>        07-24-01 12:26p ..
JAN     PAR          73     04-23-00  4:03p JAN.PAR
FEB     PAR          75     04-23-00  4:03p FEB.PAR
        2 file(s)           148 bytes
        2 dir(s)      1,444,352 bytes free

A:\>_
```

WHAT'S HAPPENING?   You copied the files **JAN.TMP** and **FEB.TMP** from the root directory to the subdirectory **CLASS** on the DATA disk. You gave the copies new names, **JAN.PAR** and **FEB.PAR**. Are the files the same? You can use the TYPE command to compare the contents visually, but since TYPE does not support the use of wildcards, you must look at each file individually. Again, since you want to look at the contents of two files in different subdirectories, you must follow the TYPE syntax:

```
TYPE [drive:][path]filename[.ext]
```

Step 7   Key in the following: A:\>**TYPE JAN.TMP** [Enter]

Step 8   Key in the following: A:\>**TYPE CLASS\JAN.PAR** [Enter]

```
A:\>TYPE JAN.TMP

This is my January file.
It is my first dummy file.
This is file 1.

A:\>TYPE CLASS\JAN.PAR

This is my January file.
It is my first dummy file.
This is file 1.

A:\>_
```

WHAT'S HAPPENING? The contents of the files are the same, even though they are in different directories. The same is true for the **FEB** files.

Step 9   Key in the following: A:\>**TYPE FEB.TMP** [Enter]

Step 10   Key in the following: A:\>**TYPE CLASS\FEB.PAR** [Enter]

```
A:\>TYPE FEB.TMP

This is my February file.
It is my second dummy file.
This is file 2.

A:\>TYPE CLASS\FEB.PAR

This is my February file.
It is my second dummy file.
This is file 2.

A:\>_
```

WHAT'S HAPPENING? The file contents are the same.

5.15   USING WILDCARDS WITH THE COPY COMMAND

You can also use wildcards to copy files on the same drive to a different subdirectory. Again, the important point to remember when using the command line is that you can never violate syntax. It is always COPY *source destination*. Computers and commands always do what you tell them to. Users sometimes think that the "computer lost their files." More often than not, files are misplaced because the user gave an instruction that he or she thought meant one thing but, in reality, meant something else. For instance, the default drive and directory was A:\>, and you keyed in COPY THIS.FIL YOUR.FIL. You wanted YOUR.FIL to be copied to the root of Drive C. Since you did not key that in (C:\YOUR.FIL), the default drive and directory were used, and YOUR.FIL was copied to the default drive and directory (A:\) instead of where you wanted it to go.

5.16 ACTIVITY: USING WILDCARDS WITH THE COPY COMMAND

Note: The DATA disk is in Drive A. A:\> is displayed.

Step 1   Key in the following: A:\>**COPY *.TMP CLASS*.ABC** [Enter]

```
MS-DOS Prompt                                                    _ □ ✕

A:\>COPY *.TMP CLASS\*.ABC
JAN.TMP
FEB.TMP
MAR.TMP
APR.TMP
        4 file(s) copied

A:\>_
```

WHAT'S HAPPENING?   As each file is copied, it is displayed on the screen. Your command line says COPY any file on the DATA disk in the root directory (the default directory) that has the file extension **.TMP**, regardless of its file name, to a new set of files that will have the same file name but a different extension, **.ABC**. These files were copied to the DATA disk and to the subdirectory called **CLASS**.

You could have keyed in **COPY A:*.TMP A:\CLASS*.ABC**. Once again, for the source files (***.TMP**), it is unnecessary to specify the designated drive and directory. Since you did not tell it otherwise, the default drive and default directory were assumed. However, for the destination you had to include the subdirectory name, **CLASS**; otherwise, the files would have been copied to the default drive and directory instead of to the subdirectory **CLASS**.

This is another area where using the command line is much quicker and easier than using the GUI. In order to accomplish what you did with one command, you would have had to take many more steps in Explorer. You would have had to select the files individually, drag them to their new location, and then rename each file individually. You can see why users like the command line for certain tasks.

Step 2   Key in the following: A:\>**DIR *.TMP** [Enter]

Step 3   Key in the following: A:\>**DIR CLASS*.ABC** [Enter]

```
╔══════════════════════════════════════════════════════════════════════╗
║ ╦╗MS-DOS Prompt                                             _ □ ×     ║
╠══════════════════════════════════════════════════════════════════════╣
║ A:\>DIR *.TMP                                                          ║
║  Volume in drive A is DATA                                             ║
║  Volume Serial Number is 3330-1807                                     ║
║  Directory of A:\                                                      ║
║                                                                        ║
║ JAN      TMP          73   04-23-00   4:03p JAN.TMP                    ║
║ FEB      TMP          75   04-23-00   4:03p FEB.TMP                    ║
║ MAR      TMP          71   04-23-00   4:03p MAR.TMP                    ║
║ APR      TMP          72   04-23-00   4:18p APR.TMP                    ║
║          4 file(s)              291 bytes                              ║
║          0 dir(s)       1,442,304 bytes free                          ║
║                                                                        ║
║ A:\>DIR CLASS\*.ABC                                                    ║
║                                                                        ║
║  Volume in drive A is DATA                                             ║
║  Volume Serial Number is 3330-1807                                     ║
║  Directory of A:\CLASS                                                 ║
║                                                                        ║
║ JAN      ABC          73   04-23-00   4:03p JAN.ABC                    ║
║ FEB      ABC          75   04-23-00   4:03p FEB.ABC                    ║
║ MAR      ABC          71   04-23-00   4:03p MAR.ABC                    ║
║ APR      ABC          72   04-23-00   4:18p APR.ABC                    ║
║          4 file(s)              291 bytes                              ║
║          0 dir(s)       1,442,304 bytes free                          ║
║                                                                        ║
║ A:\>_                                                                  ║
╚══════════════════════════════════════════════════════════════════════╝
```

WHAT'S HAPPENING? ➤ You keyed in two separate commands, **DIR *.TMP** and **DIR CLASS*.ABC**. You used the wildcards to display the **.ABC** files in the subdirectory **CLASS** and the **.TMP** files in the root directory. You also used the wildcard * to make copies of the **.TMP** files. The file names are identical, but the extensions are different. The files were copied to the subdirectory **CLASS**. However, the directory display merely shows that the files are there. To see that the contents of the original files and copied files are the same, use the TYPE command. Remember, you must specify the subdirectory where the **.ABC** files are located. Also remember that you cannot use wildcards with the TYPE command.

Step 4   Key in the following: A:\>**TYPE FEB.TMP** Enter

Step 5   Key in the following: A:\>**TYPE CLASS\FEB.ABC** Enter

```
╔══════════════════════════════════════════════════════════════════════╗
║ ╦╗MS-DOS Prompt                                             _ □ ×     ║
╠══════════════════════════════════════════════════════════════════════╣
║ A:\>TYPE FEB.TMP                                                       ║
║                                                                        ║
║ This is my February file.                                              ║
║ It is my second dummy file.                                            ║
║ This is file 2.                                                        ║
║                                                                        ║
║ A:\>TYPE CLASS\FEB.ABC                                                 ║
║                                                                        ║
║ This is my February file.                                              ║
║ It is my second dummy file.                                            ║
║ This is file 2.                                                        ║
║                                                                        ║
║ A:\>_                                                                  ║
╚══════════════════════════════════════════════════════════════════════╝
```

WHAT'S
HAPPENING?   ➡ The file contents are identical, even though the file names are different
and the files are in different directories.

5.17 USING COPY AND DIR WITH SUBDIRECTORIES

You are going to see how commands work with subdirectories by using the COPY
command to place files in the subdirectories and by using the DIR command to see
that the files were copied.

5.18 ACTIVITY: USING COPY WITH SUBDIRECTORIES

Note: The DATA disk is in Drive A. A:\> is displayed.

Step 1   Key in the following: A:\>**CD POLYSCI\USA** Enter

Step 2   Key in the following: A:\POLYSCI\USA>**DIR** Enter

```
MS-DOS Prompt                                              _ □ ×

A:\>CD POLYSCI\USA

A:\POLYSCI\USA>DIR

 Volume in drive A is DATA
 Volume Serial Number is 3330-1807
 Directory of A:\POLYSCI\USA

 .               <DIR>         07-20-01  5:19p .
 ..              <DIR>         07-20-01  5:19p ..
         0 file(s)               0 bytes
         2 dir(s)        1,442,304 bytes free

A:\POLYSCI\USA>_
```

WHAT'S
HAPPENING?   ➡ You changed the default directory to the **USA** directory, which is under
the **POLYSCI** directory under the root of the DATA disk. The prompt
should display **A:\POLYSCI\USA>** as the default drive and
subdirectory. The prompt is quite lengthy because it shows you the
default drive as well as the default subdirectory. *Remember:* All activities
will occur in the subdirectory **\POLYSCI\USA**, unless you specify
another path. When you keyed in DIR, it showed you the contents of only
the current default directory. The directory is empty of files but has the
two subdirectory markers, dot and double dot.

Step 3   Key in the following:
         A:\POLYSCI\USA>**COPY \CLASS\JAN.PAR FINAL.RPT** Enter

```
MS-DOS Prompt                                              _ □ ×

A:\POLYSCI\USA>COPY \CLASS\JAN.PAR FINAL.RPT
        1 file(s) copied

A:\POLYSCI\USA>_
```

WHAT'S HAPPENING? ➤ The file called **JAN.PAR** in the subdirectory **\CLASS** was successfully copied to the subdirectory **\POLYSCI\USA**, but is now called **FINAL.RPT**. Spacing is very important when keying in commands.

```
command space source (no spaces) space destination (no spaces)
 COPY          \CLASS\JAN.PAR            FINAL.RPT
```

The syntax of the COPY command remained the same—COPY *source destination*. First, you issued the COPY command, but it was not enough to list just the file name **JAN.PAR** as the source. You had to include the path so that the operating system would know in which subdirectory the file was located; hence, the source was **\CLASS\JAN.PAR**. Users often get confused when using \. Here is a simple rule: The first \ in any command line always means the root directory. Any other \ in the command is simply a delimiter.

Thus, in the example, the first \ tells the operating system to go to the root and then go down to **CLASS**. The second \ is the delimiter between the subdirectory name and the file name, **JAN.PAR**. The destination is a file called **FINAL.RPT**. You did not have to key in the path for the destination because the default (**\POLYSCI\USA**) was assumed. Remember, you can always key in the command using the absolute path. In this instance, the command would have read as follows:

```
COPY A:\CLASS\JAN.PAR A:\POLYSCI\USA\FINAL.RPT
```

Next, you are going to make a copy of the file in the current directory, so you do not need to include the absolute path name; here, you can use the relative path name.

Step 4   Key in the following:

A:\POLYSCI\USA>**COPY FINAL.RPT NOTE2.TMP** Enter

Step 5   Key in the following:

A:\POLYSCI\USA>**COPY FINAL.RPT NOTE3.TMP** Enter

```
MS-DOS Prompt                                                  _ □ ✕

A:\POLYSCI\USA>COPY FINAL.RPT NOTE2.TMP
        1 file(s) copied

A:\POLYSCI\USA>COPY FINAL.RPT NOTE3.TMP
        1 file(s) copied

A:\POLYSCI\USA>_
```

WHAT'S HAPPENING? ➤ You copied two files. You did not have to include the absolute path name because the default path was assumed. You used the relative path name. The operating system always assumes the default drive and directory, unless you tell it otherwise. Technically, the commands looked like this:

```
COPY A:\POLYSCI\USA\FINAL.RPT A:\POLYSCI\USA\NOTE2.TMP
COPY A:\POLYSCI\USA\FINAL.RPT A:\POLYSCI\USA\NOTE3.TMP
```

You can see that using the relative path eliminates a lot of keystrokes.

Step 6   Key in the following: A:\POLYSCI\USA>**DIR** [Enter]

```
 MS-DOS Prompt                                                    _ □ ×

 A:\POLYSCI\USA>DIR

  Volume in drive A is DATA
  Volume Serial Number is 3330-1807
  Directory of A:\POLYSCI\USA

 .              <DIR>         07-20-01   5:19p .
 ..             <DIR>         07-20-01   5:19p ..
 FINAL    RPT           73    04-23-00   4:03p FINAL.RPT
 NOTE2    TMP           73    04-23-00   4:03p NOTE2.TMP
 NOTE3    TMP           73    04-23-00   4:03p NOTE3.TMP
          3 file(s)             219 bytes
          2 dir(s)        1,440,768 bytes free

 A:\POLYSCI\USA>_
```

WHAT'S HAPPENING! ▶ You see only the files that are in the default subdirectory. You can create subdirectories from the current directory.

Step 7   Key in the following: A:\POLYSCI\USA>**MD \WORK** [Enter]

Step 8   Key in the following: A:\POLYSCI\USA>**MD \WORK\CLIENTS** [Enter]

Step 9   Key in the following: A:\POLYSCI\USA>**MD \WORK\ADS** [Enter]

```
 MS-DOS Prompt                                                    _ □ ×

 A:\POLYSCI\USA>MD \WORK

 A:\POLYSCI\USA>MD \WORK\CLIENTS

 A:\POLYSCI\USA>MD \WORK\ADS

 A:\POLYSCI\USA>_
```

WHAT'S HAPPENING! ▶ You had to include the first backslash so that the **WORK** directory would be under the root instead of under POLYSCI\USA. **WORK** had to be created before you could create its subdirectories, **CLIENTS** and **ADS**. Now that you have created the directories of interest, you can use wildcards to copy files to them.

Step 10 Key in the following:
         A:\POLYSCI\USA>**COPY *.* \WORK\CLIENTS** [Enter]

```
 MS-DOS Prompt                                                    _ □ ×

 A:\POLYSCI\USA>COPY *.* \WORK\CLIENTS
 FINAL.RPT
 NOTE2.TMP
 NOTE3.TMP
         3 file(s) copied

 A:\POLYSCI\USA>_
```

WHAT'S HAPPENING? ▸ As the files were copied to the **\WORK\CLIENTS** subdirectory, they were listed on the screen. Again, the syntax is the same: the command (COPY), the source (***.*** meaning all the files in the default subdirectory **\POLYSCI\USA**), the destination (**\WORK\CLIENTS**). You had to include the absolute path name in the destination. The first \ in the destination is very important because it tells the OS to go to the top of the tree structure and *then* go down to the **\WORK\CLIENTS** subdirectory. If you had not included that first backslash, the operating system would have looked under the subdirectory **\POLYSCI\USA**. Since you wanted to have the files with the same name in the destination subdirectory, **\WORK\CLIENTS**, you did not have to specify new file names. The operating system used or *defaulted* to the current file names.

Step 11 Key in the following: A:\POLYSCI\USA>**DIR \WORK\CLIENTS** ⌐Enter⌐

```
 MS-DOS Prompt                                              _ □ ×

A:\POLYSCI\USA>DIR \WORK\CLIENTS

 Volume in drive A is DATA
 Volume Serial Number is 3330-1807
 Directory of A:\WORK\CLIENTS

 .                <DIR>         07-24-01   1:10p .
 ..               <DIR>         07-24-01   1:10p ..
 FINAL    RPT           73      04-23-00   4:03p FINAL.RPT
 NOTE2    TMP           73      04-23-00   4:03p NOTE2.TMP
 NOTE3    TMP           73      04-23-00   4:03p NOTE3.TMP
          3 file(s)            219 bytes
          2 dir(s)       1,437,696 bytes free

A:\POLYSCI\USA>_
```

WHAT'S HAPPENING? ▸ You can copy files from anywhere to anywhere provided you give the source and destination locations. If you use the relative path, be sure you are aware of the current default drive and directory.

Step 12 Key in the following: A:\POLYSCI\USA>
COPY \WORK\CLIENTS\NOTE?.TMP \WORK\ADS\EXAM?.QZ ⌐Enter⌐

```
 MS-DOS Prompt                                              _ □ ×

A:\POLYSCI\USA>COPY \WORK\CLIENTS\NOTE?.TMP \WORK\ADS\EXAM?.QZ
A:\WORK\CLIENTS\NOTE2.TMP
A:\WORK\CLIENTS\NOTE3.TMP
        2 file(s) copied

A:\POLYSCI\USA>_
```

WHAT'S HAPPENING? ▸ The operating system displayed the entire path name as it copied all the **.TMP** files from the subdirectory **\WORK\CLIENTS** to the subdirectory **\WORK\ADS**. So that you could retain the number in the source file name in the destination file names, you used the **?** wildcard as a place holder. Thus, **NOTE2.TMP** copied as **EXAM2.QZ**, and

NOTE3.TMP copied as **EXAM3.QZ**. To see if the files were copied correctly, you will use the DIR command.

Step 13   Key in the following: A:\POLYSCI\USA>**DIR \WORK\ADS** Enter

```
MS-DOS Prompt                                                        _ □ X

A:\POLYSCI\USA>DIR \WORK\ADS

 Volume in drive A is DATA
 Volume Serial Number is 3330-1807
 Directory of A:\WORK\ADS

 .                <DIR>          07-24-01  1:10p .
 ..               <DIR>          07-24-01  1:10p ..
 EXAM2    QZ            73       04-23-00  4:03p EXAM2.QZ
 EXAM3    QZ            73       04-23-00  4:03p EXAM3.QZ
          2 file(s)            146 bytes
          2 dir(s)       1,436,672 bytes free

A:\POLYSCI\USA>_
```

WHAT'S HAPPENING? ➡ You successfully copied the files because you used the proper path name. You have been using the COPY and DIR commands to exemplify how to use the path. Any command line command will work if you use the proper syntax and the proper path.

Step 14   Key in the following: A:\POLYSCI\USA>**C:** Enter

Step 15   Key in the following: C:\>**CD \WINDOSBK** Enter

```
MS-DOS Prompt                                                        _ □ X

A:\POLYSCI\USA>C:

C:\>CD \WINDOSBK

C:\WINDOSBK>_
```

Note: The prompt you saw as you began Step 15 (**C:\ >**) may be different on your system if you have been interrupted while following the steps in this chapter. It does not matter; the command **CD \WINDOSBK** specifies to change directories to the root (\) of the current drive, and *then* to the subdirectory **WINDOSBK**. Regardless of what directory you went to when you keyed in Step 14, you will end up in **C:\WINDOSBK** after Step 15.

WHAT'S HAPPENING? ➡ You changed the default drive to C. In this example, you were in the root directory of C. You then changed the default directory to **WINDOSBK**. Note that it took two steps. You must first change drives, then change directories.

Step 16   Key in the following: C:\WINDOSBK>**COPY DRESS.UP A:** Enter

```
┌─ MS-DOS Prompt ───────────────────────────────────────── _□✕ ┐
│                                                               │
│  C:\WINDOSBK>COPY DRESS.UP A:                                 │
│          1 file(s) copied                                     │
│                                                               │
│  C:\WINDOSBK>_                                                │
│                                                               │
└───────────────────────────────────────────────────────────────┘
```

WHAT'S HAPPENING? You executed a simple COPY command. You asked the OS to copy the file called **DRESS.UP** from the **\WINDOSBK** directory to the DATA disk in the A drive, but where on the DATA disk did the file get copied? Since the last place you were on the DATA disk was the **USA** subdirectory (under **POLYSCI**, under the root), that is where the file was copied. You did not specify a destination directory and consequently, the current default directory was used. If you wanted the file copied to the root directory of the DATA disk, you would have had to key in **COPY DRESS.UP A:**.

Step 17　Key in the following: C:\WINDOSBK>**DIR A:DRESS.UP** [Enter]

Step 18　Key in the following: C:\WINDOSBK>**DIR A:\DRESS.UP** [Enter]

```
┌─ MS-DOS Prompt ───────────────────────────────────────── _□✕ ┐
│                                                               │
│  C:\WINDOSBK>DIR A:DRESS.UP                                   │
│                                                               │
│   Volume in drive A is DATA                                   │
│   Volume Serial Number is 3330-1807                           │
│   Directory of A:\POLYSCI\USA                                 │
│                                                               │
│  DRESS    UP           26  10-01-00  4:12p DRESS.UP           │
│          1 file(s)          26 bytes                          │
│          0 dir(s)    1,436,160 bytes free                     │
│                                                               │
│  C:\WINDOSBK>DIR A:\DRESS.UP                                  │
│                                                               │
│   Volume in drive A is DATA                                   │
│   Volume Serial Number is 3330-1807                           │
│   Directory of A:\                                            │
│                                                               │
│  File not found                                               │
│                        1,436,160 bytes free                   │
│                                                               │
│  C:\WINDOSBK>_                                                │
│                                                               │
└───────────────────────────────────────────────────────────────┘
```

WHAT'S HAPPENING? The last place you were on the DATA disk was in the subdirectory **\POLYSCI\USA**. The operating system "remembered" where you last were and copied the file to the **USA** subdirectory (currently, the default directory), not to the root directory. When you asked DIR to locate the file **DRESS.UP** and preceded **DRESS.UP** only with **A:**, the operating system looked in the default directory of A:, which was **\POLYSCI\USA**. In order to look at the root directory, you had to request **A:\DRESS.UP**. When you did, the file was not found because that was not where it was copied.

Step 19   Key in the following: C:\WINDOSBK>**A:** Enter

```
C:\WINDOSBK>A:

A:\POLYSCI\USA>_
```

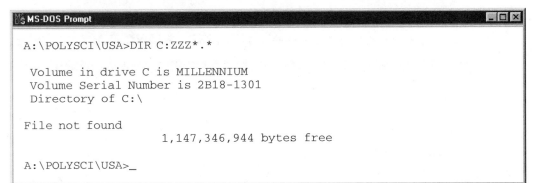

Your default drive is now the A drive where the DATA disk is located. Look at the default directory. Note that you are not in the root directory of the DATA disk but were returned to the **USA** subdirectory (under **POLYSCI**, under the root directory). As you can see, if you change drives during various activities, Windows will remember the last default subdirectory of the drive you were on. On the hard disk, the default directory is still **WINDOSBK**.

Step 20   Key in the following: A:\POLYSCI\USA>**CD C:** Enter

```
A:\POLYSCI\USA>CD C:\

A:\POLYSCI\USA>_
```

You issued the command to change the directory to the root on the hard disk, in this case Drive C, but your prompt shows that you are still in the **USA** subdirectory on the DATA disk. Did you accomplish anything with the command?

Step 21   Key in the following: A:\POLYSCI\USA>**DIR C:ZZZ*.*** Enter

```
A:\POLYSCI\USA>DIR C:ZZZ*.*

 Volume in drive C is MILLENNIUM
 Volume Serial Number is 2B18-1301
 Directory of C:\

File not found
                   1,147,346,944 bytes free

A:\POLYSCI\USA>_
```

You used a made-up file name to see the current default directory on the C drive. Notice the directory line **Directory of C:**. You did, indeed, change directories on C drive. When you issued the command **CD C:**, you changed the default directory from **WINDOSBK** to the root of C on the hard disk without leaving the DATA disk.

5.19 USING SUBDIRECTORY MARKERS WITH THE COPY COMMAND

Because the command line can get unwieldy, using the subdirectory markers dot and double dot is a convenient shorthand way of writing commands. The **..** represents the parent of the current directory. The only directory that does not have a parent is the root directory because it is the ultimate parent of all the directories on a disk. You are going to use COPY as an example, but any system command works with subdirectory markers. Subdirectory markers are sometimes also called dot notation.

5.20 ACTIVITY: USING SHORTCUTS: THE SUBDIRECTORY MARKERS

Note: The DATA disk is in Drive A. A:\POLYSCI\USA> is displayed.

Step 1   Key in the following:

A:\POLYSCI\USA>**COPY FINAL.RPT ..\FIRST.TST** [Enter]

```
┌─────────────────────────────────────────────────────────────────────────┐
│ ▓ MS-DOS Prompt                                               _ □ ✕      │
│                                                                           │
│ A:\POLYSCI\USA>COPY FINAL.RPT ..\FIRST.TST                                │
│         1 file(s) copied                                                  │
│ Z                                                                         │
│ A:\POLYSCI\USA>_                                                          │
│                                                                           │
└─────────────────────────────────────────────────────────────────────────┘
```

WHAT'S HAPPENING? ➤ You copied the file called **FINAL.RPT** located in the current directory, **USA**, to the parent of **USA**, which is **POLYSCI**. You gave it a new name, **FIRST.TST**. Instead of having to key in, as the destination file path, **\POLYSCI\FIRST.TST**, you used the shorthand name for **\POLYSCI**, which is **..** and means the parent of **USA**. You included **** between **..** and **FIRST.TST** as a delimiter.

Step 2   Key in the following:

A:\POLYSCI\USA>**COPY ..\FIRST.TST ..\FRANCE\LAST.TST** [Enter]

```
┌─────────────────────────────────────────────────────────────────────────┐
│ ▓ MS-DOS Prompt                                               _ □ ✕      │
│                                                                           │
│ A:\POLYSCI\USA>COPY ..\FIRST.TST ..\FRANCE\LAST.TST                       │
│         1 file(s) copied                                                  │
│                                                                           │
│ A:\POLYSCI\USA>_                                                          │
│                                                                           │
└─────────────────────────────────────────────────────────────────────────┘
```

WHAT'S HAPPENING? ➤ You copied the file called **FIRST.TST** from the **POLYSCI** subdirectory to the **FRANCE** subdirectory, which is a child directory of **POLYSCI**. The long way to key in the command is to use the absolute path. If you issued the command using the absolute path, it would look like the following:

```
COPY A:\POLYSCI\FIRST.TST A:\POLYSCI\FRANCE\LAST.TST
```

Because you used the subdirectory markers in the source file, the first **..** represented the parent of USA. You did not have to key in **\POLYSCI**. However, you did need to key in the delimiter **** preceding the file name.

You also did not need to key in **\POLYSCI** in the destination file. Instead you used the subdirectory marker, .. (dot dot). You did need to key in \ preceding **FRANCE** and \ preceding **LAST.TST** because they were needed as delimiters to separate subdirectory names and file names. You can use subdirectory markers to save keystrokes. You can now verify that the files are in the **FRANCE** subdirectory.

Step 3   Key in the following: A:\POLYSCI\USA>**DIR ..\FRANCE** [Enter]

```
MS-DOS Prompt                                                    _ □ ✕

A:\POLYSCI\USA>DIR ..\FRANCE

 Volume in drive A is DATA
 Volume Serial Number is 3330-1807
 Directory of A:\POLYSCI\FRANCE

.                  <DIR>         07-20-01  5:21p .
..                 <DIR>         07-20-01  5:21p ..
LAST     TST          73         04-23-00  4:03p LAST.TST
         1 file(s)              73 bytes
         2 dir(s)       1,435,136 bytes free

A:\POLYSCI\USA>_
```

WHAT'S HAPPENING? You used the DIR command with the subdirectory markers to verify that you successfully copied the file using subdirectory markers. The double dot (..) represents the immediate parent directory. If you want to move up the tree structure by two levels, you can use a triple dot (...) to accomplish this.

Step 4   Key in the following: A:\POLYSCI\USA>**CD ...** [Enter]

```
MS-DOS Prompt                                                    _ □ ✕

A:\POLYSCI\USA>CD ...

A:\>_
```

WHAT'S HAPPENING? You have moved two levels up the tree structure to the root directory of the DATA disk using the triple dot.

5.21   OVERWRITING FILES WITH THE COPY COMMAND

When you made copies of files, you gave the files on the same disk and in the same subdirectory unique names. One of the reasons for doing this is that, when you tried to use the same file name on the same disk and directory, you got an error message:

```
File cannot be copied onto itself, 0 file(s) copied.
```

The operating system would not permit you to make that error. However, the rule of unique file names is true only if the files are on the same disk and in the same subdirectory. If you are using more than one disk or more than one subdirectory, the system *will* let you use the same file name. There have been no problems so far because, when you copied the source file from one disk to the destination file on another disk, it was a new file on the destination disk.

    Overwrite means just what it says; it writes over or replaces what used to be in that file. If the contents of the source file are different from the contents of the destination file, when you overwrite the destination file this will change. Both files will now have not only the same file *name* but also the same file *contents*. The previous contents of the destination file will be gone. Overwriting also happens on the same disk when the destination file name already exists. The same rules apply to subdirectories. See Figure 5.4 for a graphic representation of this.

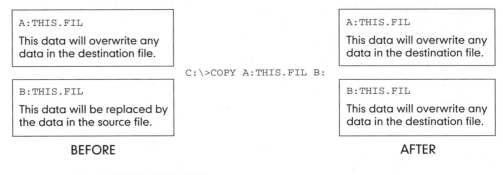

BEFORE   AFTER

FIGURE 5.4 OVERWRITING FILES

    The overwrite process seems dangerous because you will lose the data in the destination file when you replace it with the source file. Why are you not protected from this error? Because, when working with computers, this is typically *not* an error. Usually, you *do* want to overwrite files. That is, you want to replace the old contents of a file with the new, revised contents.

    Data changes all the time. For example, if you have a customer list stored as a file named CUSTOMER.LST on a disk, the information in the file (the data) changes as you add, delete, and update information about customers. When you have completed your work for the day, you want to back up your file or copy it to another disk because you are working with it on a daily basis. Thus, you have a file called CUSTOMER.LST on your source disk and a file called CUSTOMER.LST on your destination disk. Since CUSTOMER.LST is clearly a descriptive file name, you really do not want to create a new file name every time you copy the file to the destination disk because creating new file names and then tracking current files can be time-consuming and confusing. In addition, if you are working with a file on a daily basis, you could end up with hundreds of files. In reality, you do not care about last week's or yesterday's customer information, or the old file; you care about the current version and its backup file. When copying a file for backup purposes, you do want the source file to overwrite the destination file. Windows warns you that this is an overwrite—that you are about to overwrite the data in the older file. The same is true at the command line. In earlier versions of the operating system, prior to DOS 6.2, you were not made aware of the existence of a file on the destination disk that has the same name—DOS simply overwrote the destination file contents with the source file contents without a warning.

5.22 ACTIVITY: OVERWRITING FILES USING THE COPY COMMAND

Note: The DATA disk is in Drive A. A:\> is displayed.

Step 1   Key in the following: A:\>**TYPE GOODBYE.NEW** [Enter]

Step 2   Key in the following: A:\>**TYPE JAN.OLD** [Enter]

```
MS-DOS Prompt                                            _ □ ✕

A:\>TYPE GOODBYE.NEW

THIS IS GOODBYE
AND FAREWELL.

A:\>TYPE JAN.OLD

This is my January file.
It is my first dummy file.
This is file 1.

A:\>_
```

WHAT'S
HAPPENING?   You have displayed the contents of two files and can see that each file
              contains different data.

Step 3   Key in the following: A:\>**COPY GOODBYE.NEW JAN.OLD** [Enter]

```
MS-DOS Prompt                                            _ □ ✕

A:\>COPY GOODBYE.NEW JAN.OLD
Overwrite JAN.OLD (Yes/No/All)?
```

WHAT'S
HAPPENING?   You get a message telling you that you already have a file by the name of
              JAN.OLD.

Step 4   Key in the following: **Y** [Enter]

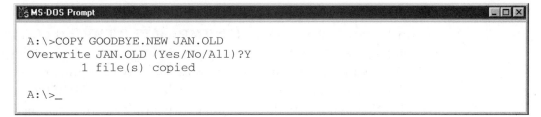

```
MS-DOS Prompt                                            _ □ ✕

A:\>COPY GOODBYE.NEW JAN.OLD
Overwrite JAN.OLD (Yes/No/All)?Y
        1 file(s) copied

A:\>_
```

WHAT'S
HAPPENING?   The file **GOODBYE.NEW** was successfully copied to the file called
              JAN.OLD, but what about the contents of the file? Did anything change?

Step 5   Key in the following: A:\>**TYPE GOODBYE.NEW** [Enter]

Step 6   Key in the following: A:\>**TYPE JAN.OLD** [Enter]

```
MS-DOS Prompt                                                    _ □ ✕

A:\>TYPE GOODBYE.NEW

THIS IS GOODBYE
AND FAREWELL.

A:\>TYPE JAN.OLD

THIS IS GOODBYE
AND FAREWELL.

A:\>_
```

WHAT'S HAPPENING? → The file contents are now identical. What used to be inside the file called **JAN.OLD** located on the DATA disk overwritten or replaced (i.e., is gone forever) by the contents of the file called **GOODBYE.NEW**. You need to be aware of how this procedure works so that you do not accidentally overwrite a file.

The operating system does not allow you to overwrite or copy a file when the source file and the destination file on the same disk and same subdirectory have exactly the same file name.

Step 7   Key in the following: A:\>**COPY JAN.OLD JAN.OLD** [Enter]

```
MS-DOS Prompt                                                    _ □ ✕

A:\>COPY JAN.OLD JAN.OLD
JAN.OLD
File cannot be copied onto itself
        0 file(s) copied

A:\>_
```

WHAT'S HAPPENING? → You tried to copy (overwrite) a file onto itself and got an error message. This process works the same when you are dealing with subdirectories.

In Activity 5.12, you copied **JAN.TMP** and **FEB.TMP** to the **CLASS** directory with the same file names but different extensions, so that in the **CLASS** directory the files were now called **JAN.PAR** and **FEB.PAR**. You are going to use wildcards to copy the rest of the **.TMP** files to the **CLASS** directory. In the process, you will overwrite the existing files.

Step 8   Key in the following: A:\>**COPY *.TMP CLASS*.PAR** [Enter]

```
MS-DOS Prompt                                                    _ □ ✕

A:\>COPY *.TMP CLASS\*.PAR
Overwrite CLASS\JAN.PAR (Yes/No/All)?
```

WHAT'S HAPPENING? → The OS does not know the contents of the file; it only knows you already have a file by that name. Rather than prompting you each time, one of the choices is A for all. Thus, if you intend to overwrite all the .TMP files, you can choose A.

Step 9   Key in the following: **A** Enter

```
┌─────────────────────────────────────────────────────────────┐
│ ▓ MS-DOS Prompt                                    _ □ ☒     │
├─────────────────────────────────────────────────────────────┤
│ A:\>COPY *.TMP CLASS\*.PAR                                    │
│ Overwrite CLASS\JAN.PAR (Yes/No/All)?A                        │
│ FEB.TMP                                                       │
│ MAR.TMP                                                       │
│ APR.TMP                                                       │
│         4 file(s) copied                                      │
│                                                               │
│ A:\>_                                                         │
└─────────────────────────────────────────────────────────────┘
```

WHAT'S
HAPPENING? The OS has overwritten the **JAN.PAR** and **FEB.PAR** files in the
            CLASS directory with the **JAN.TMP** and **FEB.TMP** files in the root
            directory. You can prove this occurred by using the TYPE command.

Step 10   Key in the following: A:\>**TYPE JAN.TMP** Enter

Step 11   Key in the following: A:\>**TYPE CLASS\JAN.PAR** Enter

```
┌─────────────────────────────────────────────────────────────┐
│ ▓ MS-DOS Prompt                                    _ □ ☒     │
├─────────────────────────────────────────────────────────────┤
│ A:\>TYPE JAN.TMP                                              │
│                                                               │
│ This is my January file.                                      │
│ It is my first dummy file.                                    │
│ This is file 1.                                               │
│                                                               │
│ A:\>TYPE CLASS\JAN.PAR                                        │
│                                                               │
│ This is my January file.                                      │
│ It is my first dummy file.                                    │
│ This is file 1.                                               │
│                                                               │
│ A:\>_                                                         │
└─────────────────────────────────────────────────────────────┘
```

WHAT'S
HAPPENING? As you can see, the contents of the two files are identical. You did over-
            write the destination file with the contents of the source file. You can
            verify that all the files have been copied by using the DIR command.

Step 12   Key in the following: A:\>**DIR CLASS*.PAR** Enter

```
┌─────────────────────────────────────────────────────────────┐
│ ▓ MS-DOS Prompt                                    _ □ ☒     │
├─────────────────────────────────────────────────────────────┤
│ A:\>DIR CLASS\*.PAR                                           │
│                                                               │
│  Volume in drive A is DATA                                    │
│  Volume Serial Number is 3330-1807                            │
│  Directory of A:\CLASS                                        │
│                                                               │
│ JAN      PAR          73   04-23-00   4:03p JAN.PAR           │
│ FEB      PAR          75   04-23-00   4:03p FEB.PAR           │
│ MAR      PAR          71   04-23-00   4:03p MAR.PAR           │
│ APR      PAR          72   04-23-00   4:18p APR.PAR           │
│         4 file(s)            291 bytes                         │
│         0 dir(s)       1,434,112 bytes free                   │
│                                                               │
│ A:\>_                                                         │
└─────────────────────────────────────────────────────────────┘
```

WHAT'S HAPPENING?   Now all the **.TMP** files are in the **CLASS** directory. They have the same file names but different file extensions.

5.23 COMBINING TEXT FILES WITH THE COPY COMMAND

Sometimes, but rarely, it is useful to combine the contents of two or more text (ASCII) files. This process is known as the *concatenation* of files. To *concatenate* means to "put together." You might wish to concatenate when you have several short text files that would be easier to work with if they were combined into one file. When you combine files, nothing happens to the original files; they remain intact. You just create a new file from the original files.

However, most often users concatenate files accidentally and are unaware of it until they attempt to retrieve the file. *Concatenation should never be done with either program files or the data files generated by programs.* Programs are binary code and combining any of these files makes the binary code useless and the program incapable of being executed. The same is true for the data files that programs generate. When you create a data file with a program, that program "formats" the data in such a way that the program knows how to interpret that data. That data file format is different for each program. A data file can be read only by the program that created it. If another program can read a foreign data file, it is because the program converts the foreign data into its own native format. The classic example of that is converting data files created in WordPerfect so that these files can be used in Word and the reverse.

Why learn concatenation if you should not use it? You need to learn concatenation because accidental concatenation of files can occur. The clue is to read the messages displayed on the screen. In the following activity you will see the results of concatenation. The COPY command never changes. The syntax never changes. It is always COPY *source destination*. Look at the syntax diagram:

```
COPY [/A : /B] source [/A : /B] [+ source [/A : /B] [+ ...]]
[destination [/A : /B]] [/V] [/Y : /-Y]
```

/A indicates an ASCII file, whereas /B indicates a binary file. In addition, whenever you see the notation in a syntax diagram of two or more items separated by the pipe symbol (¦) as in [/A ¦ /B], it is an either/or choice. Either you may use /A or you may use /B but not both.

5.24 ACTIVITY: COMBINING FILES USING THE COPY COMMAND

Note: The DATA disk is in Drive A. A:\> is displayed.

Step 1   Key in the following: A:\>**TYPE C:\WINDOSBK\EMPLOYEE.ONE** Enter

Step 2   Key in the following: A:\>**TYPE C:\WINDOSBK\EMPLOYEE.TWO** Enter

```
MS-DOS Prompt                                              _ □ ✕

A:\>TYPE C:\WINDOSBK\EMPLOYEE.ONE

This is employee file one.
```

```
It is the first file.

A:\>TYPE C:\WINDOSBK\EMPLOYEE.TWO

This is employee file two.
It is the second file.

A:\>_
```

WHAT'S HAPPENING? You have displayed the contents of two files on the screen. Each file is unique with a different file name and different file contents. You are going to place the contents of these two files into a new file called **JOINED.SAM** that will consist of the contents of the first file, **EMPLOYEE.ONE**, followed by the contents of the second file, **EMPLOYEE.TWO**. The new file will reside on the DATA disk.

Note: In the following step, there are spaces between COPY and the source file specification, (**C:\WINDOSBK\EMPLOYEE.ONE**), before and after the **+** sign, and before the destination file name, (**JOINED.SAM**).

Step 3   Key in the following (press the Enter key only when you see Enter):
A:\>**COPY C:\WINDOSBK\EMPLOYEE.ONE + C:\WINDOSBK\EMPLOYEE.TWO JOINED.SAM** Enter

```
MS-DOS Prompt                                                    _ □ ×

A:\>COPY C:\WINDOSBK\EMPLOYEE.ONE + C:\WINDOSBK\EMPLOYEE.TWO JOINED.SAM
C:\WINDOSBK\EMPLOYEE.ONE
C:\WINDOSBK\EMPLOYEE.TWO
        1 file(s) copied

A:\>_
```

WHAT'S HAPPENING? The message is **1 file(s) copied**. It seems as if you have too many parameters because the syntax is COPY *source destination*. However, you are still following the correct syntax for the COPY command. You are creating one destination file out of two source files. What you did here was say COPY (the command) the contents of the file called **C:\WINDOSBK\EMPLOYEE.ONE** *and* the contents of the file called **C:\WINDOSBK\EMPLOYEE.TWO** (source) to a new file called **JOINED.SAM** that will reside on the DATA disk (destination). The plus sign (**+**) told the operating system that the source had more to it than just one file. It also told the OS that you were joining files. The destination file is the last file name on the command line that does not have a plus sign in front. Look at Step 3 and note that **JOINED.SAM** has just a space in front of it, not a plus sign, making **JOINED.SAM** the destination. Source and destination files in the copy command are separated by a single space delimiter. Multiple source files are separated by a space+space delimiter.

Step 4   Key in the following: A:\>**TYPE JOINED.SAM** Enter

```
MS-DOS Prompt                                              _ □ X

A:\>TYPE JOINED.SAM

This is employee file one.
It is the first file.

This is employee file two.
It is the second file.

A:\>_
```

WHAT'S HAPPENING? The file **JOINED.SAM** consists of the contents of the file **EMPLOYEE.ONE** followed by the contents of the file **EMPLOYEE.TWO**. The contents in **JOINED.SAM** does not show any file names. You do not know where one file ended and the next began. **JOINED.SAM** is a new file, but you did not destroy or in any way alter the two original source files, **EMPLOYEE.ONE** and **EMPLOYEE.TWO**. You can prove this by using the TYPE command.

Step 5   Key in the following: A:\>**TYPE C:\WINDOSBK\EMPLOYEE.ONE** Enter

Step 6   Key in the following: A:\>**TYPE C:\WINDOSBK\EMPLOYEE.TWO** Enter

```
MS-DOS Prompt                                              _ □ X

A:\>TYPE C:\WINDOSBK\EMPLOYEE.ONE

This is employee file one.
It is the first file.

A:\>TYPE C:\WINDOSBK\EMPLOYEE.TWO

This is employee file two.
It is the second file.

A:\>_
```

WHAT'S HAPPENING? As you can see, the source files remain unchanged. You merely created a third file from the contents of two files. You can join many files with the plus sign, but this is useful for text files *only*. If you try to join two data files created by an application program using the COPY command, the application program will no longer be able to read the combined data file.

Step 7   Key in the following: A:\>**C:** Enter

Step 8   Key in the following: C:\>**CD \WINDOSBK\FINANCE** Enter

Step 9   Key in the following (in the next step, do not press the Enter key until you see Enter): C:\WINDOSBK\FINANCE>
COPY BUDGET.TKR + HOMEBUD.TKR A:\TEST.TKR Enter

```
MS-DOS Prompt                                          _ □ ×

A:\>C:

C:\>CD \WINDOSBK\FINANCE

C:\WINDOSBK\FINANCE>COPY BUDGET.TKR + HOMEBUD.TKR A:\TEST.TKR
BUDGET.TKR
HOMEBUD.TKR
        1 file(s) copied

C:\WINDOSBK\FINANCE>_
```

WHAT'S
HAPPENING? → You have changed the drive and directory to the **FINANCE** directory
under the **WINDOSBK** directory on the hard disk. You then concatenated, or combined, the contents of two data files, **BUDGET.TKR** and
HOMEBUD.TKR, generated by the Thinker program and placed the
contents on the DATA disk in one file called **TEST.TKR**. Notice the
message on the screen, **1 file(s) copied**. You are now going to try to
retrieve this joined file, **TEST.TKR**, in the Thinker program.

Step 10   Key in the following: C:\WINDOSBK\FINANCE>**THINK** Enter

Step 11   Press Enter

Step 12   Press /.

Step 13   Press **F**.

Step 14   Press **R**.

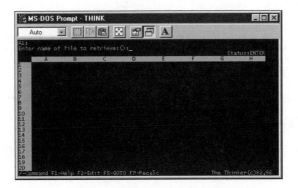

WHAT'S
HAPPENING? → You have loaded the Thinker program and have issued the command to
load a data file. A prompt asks you what data file you wish to load. You
are going to try to load the **TEST.TKR** file on the DATA disk.

Step 15   Key in the following: **A:\TEST.TKR** Enter

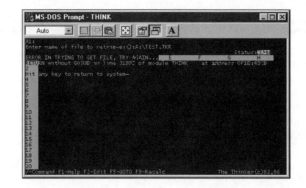

WHAT'S HAPPENING? ➤ The Thinker program cannot recognize the joined data file and informs you of this with the above message message. (*Note:* Sometimes the program finds the error so severe, it kicks you out of the program and returns you to the system level. If that happens to you, simply press **Enter** and proceed to Step 20.)

Step 16   Press **Enter**

Note: Complete Steps 17 through 19 if you have not returned to the command line prompt.

Step 17   Press **/**.

Step 18   Press **Q**.

Step 19   Press **Y**.

```
MS-DOS Prompt                                                    _ □ ×

C:\WINDOSBK\FINANCE>_
```

WHAT'S HAPPENING? ➤ You have exited the program and returned to the MS-DOS Prompt window.

Step 20   Key in the following: C:\WINDOSBK\FINANCE>**CD \ Enter**

Step 21   Key in the following: C:\>**A: Enter**

```
MS-DOS Prompt                                                    _ □ ×

C:\WINDOSBK\FINANCE>CD \

C:\>A:

A:\>_
```

WHAT'S HAPPENING? ➤ You have demonstrated that you should not combine program files or data files created with application programs. You may say to yourself that by never including **+**, you cannot make that mistake. However, there is more to the story. You can also use wildcards to concatenate files, which eliminate the need to use **+** as well as the need to key in all the file names separately. If you wanted to join all the files with a **.TMP**

file extension and place them into a new file called **MONTHS.SAM**, located on the DATA disk, you would have to key in **COPY JAN.TMP + FEB.TMP + MAR.TMP + APR.TMP A:MONTHS.SAM**. You can save many keystrokes by using wildcards.

Step 22 Key in the following: A:\>**COPY *.TMP MONTHS.SAM** Enter

```
MS-DOS Prompt                                                    _ □ ×

C:\>A:

A:\>COPY *.TMP MONTHS.SAM
JAN.TMP
FEB.TMP
MAR.TMP
APR.TMP
        1 file(s) copied

A:\>_
```

WHAT'S HAPPENING? Using the wildcard has the same effect as keying in all the file names and connecting the source files with plus signs. The operating system found each file with a **.TMP** file extension and wrote the contents of those files to a new file called **MONTHS.SAM**. Note the message **1 file(s) copied**. Four files were combined into one.

Step 23 Key in the following: A:\>**TYPE MONTHS.SAM** Enter

```
MS-DOS Prompt                                                    _ □ ×

A:\>TYPE MONTHS.SAM

This is my January file.
It is my first dummy file.
This is file 1.

This is my February file.
It is my second dummy file.
This is file 2.

This is my March file.
It is my third dummy file.
This is file 3.

This is my April file.
It is my fourth dummy file.
This is file 4.

A:\>_
```

WHAT'S HAPPENING? As you can see, you joined together the contents of all the **.TMP** files into a new file called **MONTHS.SAM**. Again, since the **.TMP** files are ASCII files, the text is readable on the screen. How then can you make an error? A typical activity is to copy files from a hard disk to a floppy disk or removable disk such as a Zip drive for backup purposes. Wildcards are very useful for backing up groups of files. You may choose to place the copies in a subdirectory. If you make only a one character error, you will combine the files into one file, making the file useless. Let's say you want to copy all the files in C:\WINDOSBK\FINANCE that begin with a B to the CLASS subdirectory, but you make a typographical error (a "typo") when keying in CLASS.

Step 24   Key in the following:

A:\>**COPY C:\WINDOSBK\FINANCE\B*.TKR CLASX** [Enter]

```
 MS-DOS Prompt                                                    _ □ X

 A:\>COPY C:\WINDOSBK\FINANCE\B*.TKR CLASX
 C:\WINDOSBK\FINANCE\BALANCE.TKR
 C:\WINDOSBK\FINANCE\BUDGET.TKR
         1 file(s) copied

 A:\>_
```

WHAT'S HAPPENING!   The first hint that you made an error is in the message telling you that only one file has been copied. Your intention was to copy the **.TKR** files that begin with B to the **CLASS** directory so you would have a backup copy of each file. You made that one, small typographical error—keying in **CLASX** instead of **CLASS**—so instead of having the BALANCE and BUDGET files backed up into the **CLASS** directory, you now have one useless file called **CLASX**.

Step 25   Key in the following: A:\>**DIR CLASS\B*.*** [Enter]

Step 26   Key in the following: A:\>**DIR CLASX** [Enter]

```
 MS-DOS Prompt                                                    _ □ X

 A:\>DIR CLASS\B*.*

  Volume in drive A is DATA
  Volume Serial Number is 3330-1807
  Directory of A:\CLASS

 File not found
                    1,400,832 bytes free

 A:\>DIR CLASX

  Volume in drive A is DATA
  Volume Serial Number is 3330-1807
  Directory of A:\

 CLASX            15,108  07-24-01  2:18p CLASX
         1 file(s)        15,108 bytes
         0 dir(s)      1,400,832 bytes free

 A:\>_
```

WHAT'S HAPPENING!   There are no files that begin with B in the **CLASS** subdirectory, but there is one file called **CLASX** in the root directory. Once again, the operating system did exactly what you told it to do. In this case, however, what you *said* is not what you *meant*. This is why reading the messages on the screen is so important. The message you should have seen, if you had not made an error, was **2 file(s) copied**. The minute you see the message **1 file(s) copied**, you should realize that you joined the files into one file instead of copying each to the subdirectory called **CLASS**.

5.25   PRINTING FILES

So far, you have not printed the contents of any files. You have redirected the output of the DIR command to the printer, but this printed only file *names*, not file *contents*. You could key in TYPE MY.FIL, and, if you were not on a network that prevented it, print the screen by using the [Shift] + [Print Screen] key combination, but this method of printing has several disadvantages. (*Note:* Remember that in the GUI, this does not work—only when at the command line.) When you print the screen, you get everything displayed on the screen: the prompts, the commands, and the contents of the file. In addition, these text files have been very short and have fit entirely on the screen, but what if the contents of the file were longer than the number of lines available on your screen? There are easier ways to print the contents of text files. However, these techniques work only for ASCII files. Again, data files generated by application programs can be printed only from within the application program because the application program must send special signals to the printer so that the data prints correctly.

There are times you wish to print an ASCII file. You often will want a hard copy of the ASCII files CONFIG.SYS and AUTOEXEC.BAT (you will learn about these later). There are also other reasons for printing text files; for instance, if you have a printer problem from within an application program, the first thing you want to do is verify that it is a software problem, not a hardware problem. To test this, you return to the command line interface level and print an ASCII file. If the ASCII file prints, you now know you have a software problem within the application program and not a connection problem with your printer.

There are three ways to print a text file from the command line:

1. Print the screen.
2. Use redirection as you did in Chapter 2 with the DIR command.
3. Copy the contents of a file to a printer. The destination is a device, not a file. The device is the printer. Since the printer is a device, it has a reserved name: ***PRN***. Sometimes this name causes problems when you are printing on a network, so you will use ***LPT1*** for Line Printer 1. When you use LPT1, be sure to key in the letter L, the letter P, the letter T, and the number 1. You cannot use the letter l ("ell") as the number 1.

Note: Before proceeding with this activity, check with your lab instructor to see if there are any special procedures in your lab or if, in fact, you are able to do the activity at all.

5.26   ACTIVITY: PRINTING FILES

**CAUTION!   DO NOT DO THIS ACTIVITY IF YOU ARE ON A NETWORK
                    UNLESS INSTRUCTED TO DO SO.**

Note 1: The DATA disk is in Drive A. A:\> is displayed.
Note 2: Check with your lab instructor for any special instructions.
Note 3: Remember, many times in a lab environment, you can use **LPT1,** the
hardware name of the printer port. When **LPT1** does not work, you may try **PRN.**
Other times, you need to use the printer object's *URL (Uniform Resource Locator)*, such as **\\SERVER\HP**. Once again, check with your lab instructor for what
is needed in your lab.

Step 1   Key in the following: A:\>**TYPE JANUARY.TXT** Enter

```
MS-DOS Prompt                                                  _ □ ✕

A:\>TYPE JANUARY.TXT

This is my January file.
It is my first dummy file.
This is file 1.

A:\>_
```

WHAT'S
HAPPENING?   The contents of the TYPE command are written to the standard output
              device, the screen. You can redirect the output to another device—the
              printer.

Step 2   Turn the printer on. Make sure the printer is online.

Step 3   Key in the following: A:\>**TYPE JANUARY.TXT > LPT1** Enter

```
MS-DOS Prompt                                                  _ □ ✕

A:\>TYPE JANUARY.TXT > LPT1
A:\>_
```

WHAT'S
HAPPENING?   Nothing was written to the screen because you redirected the output to
              the printer. Now you want to eject the page. Depending on how your
              printer is set up, it may automatically eject the page without your
              having to take the next step. Check your printer. If your page printed
              and ejected, go to Step 5. (*Note:* Remember, the notation Ctrl + **L** means
              press both the Ctrl key and the **L** key at the same time.)

Step 4   Key in the following: A:>**ECHO** Ctrl + L > **LPT1** Enter

```
MS-DOS Prompt                                                  _ □ ✕
A:\>ECHO ^L > LPT1

A:\>_
```

WHAT'S HAPPENING? ➤ The page was ejected. You should get the following printout from your printer.

```
This is my January file.
It is my first dummy file.
This is file 1.
```

It would seem that, if this works as it did, you could also use redirection with the COPY command, but you cannot. The only output that is actually a *product* of the copy command itself is **1 file(s) copied**. If you redirected that output, you would only have the printed message **1 file(s) copied**, not the contents of the file. Instead of using redirection, you copy the file to a device, the printer.

Step 5   Key in the following: A:\>**COPY JANUARY.TXT LPT1** Enter

```
MS-DOS Prompt                                              _ □ ✕
A:\>COPY JANUARY.TXT LPT1
        1 file(s) copied

A:\>_
```

WHAT'S HAPPENING? ➤ Even though you are using a device, the syntax for the COPY command remains the same. COPY is the command, the work you want done. **JANUARY.TXT** is the source, the file you want copied. You do not need to enter a drive designator in front of the file name because the operating system will assume the default. **LPT1** is the device name for the printer. The printer is the destination, where you want the contents of the file to go. As soon as you press Enter, you may hear/see the printer begin to print. If so, it would not be necessary to send the Ctrl + L message to the printer. The hard copy or output is at the printer. Your screen displays the message **1 file(s) copied**. If your page did not eject, take the next step.

Step 6   Key in the following: A:>**ECHO** Ctrl + L > **LPT1** Enter

```
MS-DOS Prompt                                              _ □ ✕
A:\>ECHO ^L > LPT1

A:\>_
```

WHAT'S HAPPENING? ➤ The page was ejected. You see your hard copy.

```
This is my January file.
It is my first dummy file.
This is file 1.
```

CHAPTER SUMMARY

1. One of the major reasons people buy computers is for application programs that assist people in different tasks.

2. Application software usually generates data. Both application software and data are stored as disk files.

3. Usually, only a program can use the data files it creates. A data file without the application program cannot be used.

4. Another component of the operating system is the commands that allow the user to manage and manipulate program and data files.

5. The internal commands DIR, COPY, and TYPE allow you to manage the files on a disk.

6. The file extensions .COM (command file) and .EXE (executable code) tell the operating system that the file is a program.

7. COPY allows you to copy files selectively.

8. The syntax of the copy command is:

```
COPY [drive:][path][filename] [d:][path][filename]
```

A simple way to remember the COPY syntax is

```
COPY source destination
```

Source is what you want to copy. Destination is where you want it copied.

9. The COPY command never changes the source file.

10. When naming files, it is best to stick to alphanumeric characters. Certain characters are illegal, such as the colon (:) and the asterisk (*).

11. When copying a file to a subdirectory, you must include the path name. The path name and the file name are separated by the backslash, which is used as a delimiter. The one exception is that the root directory's name is \ (backslash).

12. Wildcards may be used with the COPY command.

13. Files must have unique names when on the same drive and in the same subdirectory, but files that are copied to different subdirectories may have identical names because the path makes those file names unique.

14. TYPE allows you to display the contents of a file on the screen. The syntax is:

```
TYPE [drive:][path]filename
```

15. Wildcards may not be used with the TYPE command.

16. You may use subdirectory markers with the DIR, COPY, and TYPE commands.

17. If you use *.* with a command, it chooses all the files. Thus, DIR *.* would display all the files. COPY C:\WHAT*.* A:\ would copy all the files in the WHAT directory to the disk in Drive A.

18. When you move between drives, the operating system remembers the last directory you were in.

19. Overwriting files with the COPY command is the process in which the contents of the source file copy over the contents of the destination file.

20. Concatenation means combining the contents of files using the COPY command with either + or a wildcard. There is only one destination file. You should not concatenate program files or data files generated from program files.

21. You may print the contents of ASCII files by using COPY *filename* LPT1 or COPY *filename* PRN.

22. You may also print ASCII files by keying in TYPE *filename* > LPT1 or TYPE *filename* > PRN.

23. You may be required to use the URL (Uniform Resource Locator) of your printer to redirect or copy your ASCII files to the printer.

24. If you wish to eject a page using either COPY *filename* LPT1 or TYPE *filename* > LPT1, you must redirect the Ctrl + L command to the printer as **ECHO Ctrl + L > LPT1**.

KEY TERMS

ASCII	overwrite	Uniform Resource
concatenation	PRN	Locator (URL)
destination file	source file	unformatted text file
LPT1		

DISCUSSION QUESTIONS

1. Explain the function and purpose of internal commands.
2. Give two reasons for making a copy of a file on the same disk.
3. Give the syntax for the COPY command and explain each part of the syntax.
4. Is a file extension mandatory when naming a file?
5. What is the maximum number of characters that may be used when naming a file?
6. List three characters that cannot be used when naming files.
7. List three examples of legal file names.
8. When would you use a wildcard with the COPY command?
9. What is the purpose and function of the TYPE command? Explain each part of the syntax diagram.
10. How can you recognize an executable file?
11. What are ASCII files?
12. What is the purpose and function of dummy files?
13. Every file on a disk must have a unique name. Yet, when you make a copy of a file on the same disk in a different subdirectory, it may have the same file name. Explain.
14. Under what circumstances could a user think that the computer has "lost its files?"
15. Can you use wildcards with the TYPE command? Why or why not?
16. What does the first \ in any command line mean?
17. What does it mean to "overwrite a file?" What are some of the dangers of overwriting files?
18. Why would you make a copy of a file on the same disk? On another disk?
19. What would happen if you tried to copy a file from one disk to another and the destination disk already had a file with the same name?

20. How would you combine the contents of two files? Why would you?
21. What happens to the original files when you combine two or more files?
22. What are some of the dangers of concatenating program files or data files?
23. What message on the screen informs you that you have concatenated several files?
24. What are some of the disadvantages of printing the screen to obtain a printout of an ASCII file?
25. Compare and contrast printing a file using redirection with the TYPE command and with the COPY command.

TRUE/FALSE QUESTIONS

For each question, circle the letter T if the question is true and the letter F if the question is false.

T   F   1. The contents of two files can be identical on the same disk even though the file names are different.
T   F   2. It is a good idea to concatenate text files and program files.
T   F   3. The COPY command is an internal command.
T   F   4. The contents of files are not affected by displaying them with the TYPE command.
T   F   5. To save time when copying multiple files to a different disk, you can use wildcards.

COMPLETION QUESTIONS

Write the correct answer in each blank space.

6. There are two mandatory parameters for the COPY command. They are the _____ and the _____.
7. When you replace the contents of a file with the contents of a different file, this process is known as _____.
8. You can differentiate between a program file and a data file by the file _____.
9. If you wish to display the contents of a text file on the screen, you would use the _____ command.
10. The delimiter that is used to separate a file name from a file extension is _____.

MULTIPLE CHOICE QUESTIONS

For each question, write the letter for the correct answer in the blank space.

11. The COPY command can be used to
   a copy a file from one disk to another.
   b. make a second copy of an existing file on the same disk.
   c. copy a file from one directory to another directory.
   d. all of the above

12. Files may be copied to another disk in order to
    a. make backup copies.
    b. copy a program to another disk.
    c. share data files with others.
    d. all of the above

13. To display the contents of an ASCII file on the screen, you use the
    a. DIR command.
    b. TYPE command.
    c. VIEW command.
    d. SEE command.

14. **COPY *.TXT THE.FIL** will result in
    a. joining together all files with the .TXT extension to a file called
       THE.FIL.
    b. joining THE.FIL to all files with the .TXT extension.
    c. creating a new set of files with the same file name having .FIL as
       an extension.
    d. none of the above

15. **COPY MY.TXT \DATA\OLD.TXT** will
    a. copy the file MY.TXT to a new file called DATA.
    b. copy the file MY.TXT to a new file called OLD.TXT in the
       subdirectory DATA.
    c. copy the file OLD.TXT to a file called MY.TXT in the subdirectory
       DATA.
    d. copy the file called DATA to a file called MY.TXT in the
       subdirectory called OLD.TXT.

WRITING COMMANDS

Write the correct steps or commands to perform the required action as if you were at
the computer. The prompt will indicate the default drive and directory.

16. Copy the file called OLD.FIL from the root of Drive C to the root of Drive A,
    keeping the same file name.
    A:\>

17. Copy all files in the default directory with the .TXT file extension to files with the
    same names but with the .DOC file extension.
    A:\>

18. Copy the file JOE from the root directory to the INFO directory, and call the new
    file NAMES on the default drive.
    A:\>

19. Copy the contents of two files, one named DOG *and* one named CAT from the default directory to a file called ANIMALS in the \MYFILES directory.

    A:\>

20. Copy all files from the default directory with the extension .TXT to the subdirectory TXTFILES.

    A:\>

APPLICATION ASSIGNMENTS

Note 1: Place the APPLICATION disk in Drive A:. Be sure to work on the APPLICATION disk, not the DATA disk.

Note 2: The homework problems will assume Drive C is the hard disk and the APPLICATION disk is in Drive A. If you are using another drive, such as floppy Drive B or hard Drive D, be sure to substitute that drive letter when reading the questions and answers.

Note 3: All subdirectories will be created under the root directory unless otherwise specified.

PROBLEM SET I

PROBLEM A

Note: If the DATA disk is in Drive A, remove it and place it in a safe place. *Do not* use the DATA disk for these application problems.

A-a   Insert the APPLICATION disk into Drive A.

A-b   Copy the file called **GRAMMY.REC** from the **WINDOSBK** subdirectory to the root directory of the APPLICATION disk keeping the same file name.

A-c   Copy the file called **GRAMMY.REC** from the **WINDOSBK** subdirectory to the root directory of the APPLICATION disk but call the new file **GRAMMY.TAP**.

A-d   Execute the DIR command to display only the **GRAMMY** files on the APPLICATION disk.

1. What date is listed for the files?
   a. 10-02-00
   b. 10-10-99
   c. 10-10-00
   d. 10-02-99

2. What is the size of the GRAMMY files in bytes?
   a. GRAMMY.REC = 569 and GRAMMY.TAP = 339
   b. GRAMMY.REC = 596 and GRAMMY.TAP = 496

  c. both files are 569 bytes
  d. GRAMMY.REC = 569 and GRAMMY.TAP = 596

A-e   While in the root of the APPLICATION disk, copy the file **GRAMMY.REC** to **GRAM:.REC**.

  3. What message appears on the screen?
  a. File(s) copied
  b. Invalid file name
  c. Too many parameters
  d. no message was displayed

PROBLEM B

B-a   Copy any files with the file extension **.99** from the **WINDOSBK** subdirectory to the root directory of the APPLICATION disk keeping the same file names.

  4. How many files were copied?
  a. two
  b. four
  c. six
  d. eight

B-b   Execute the DIR command to display only the files with the extension of **.99** on the APPLICATION disk.

  5. What date is displayed for the files?
  a. 11-23-98
  b. 10-23-98
  c. 11-11-99
  d. 10-10-99

B-c   Create a subdirectory on the APPLICATION disk called **FILES**.

B-d   Copy all the files with the extension of **.99** from the root directory of the APPLICATION disk into this subdirectory but give them the new extension of **.FIL**.

B-e   Do a directory display of the FILES directory.

  6. There is a line in the resulting display that states
  a. 2 file(s)   291 bytes
  b. 4 file(s)   291 bytes
  c. 6 file(s)   291 bytes
  d. 8 file(s)   291 bytes

B-f   Create a subdirectory on the APPLICATION disk called **BOOKS**.

B-g   Copy all the files in the **WINDOSBK\MEDIA\BOOKS** directory to the **BOOKS** directory keeping the same file name(s).

7. How many files were copied?
   a. one
   b. three
   c. five
   d. seven

PROBLEM C

C-a   Display the contents of the **GRAMMY.REC** file located in the root directory of the APPLICATION disk.

8. What artist is listed for 1989?
   a. Eric Clapton
   b. Whitney Houston
   c. Bette Midler
   d. Paul Simon

C-b   Display the contents of the **MUSIC.MOV** file located in the **C:\WINDOSBK\MEDIA\MOVIES** directory.

9. What movie title is displayed?
   a. Carousel
   b. Paint Your Wagon
   c. Star Wars
   d. Evita

C-c   Display the contents of the **MYSTERY.BKS** file located in the **BOOKS** directory of the APPLICATION disk.

10. What author's name is NOT displayed?
    a. Sue Grafton
    b. Robert Parker
    c. Elmore Leonard
    d. Donald Westlake

PROBLEM D

D-a   Create a subdirectory called **ROOM** on the APPLICATION disk under the **FILES** directory created in Problem B.

D-b   On the APPLICATION disk change the default directory to **ROOM**.

D-c   Using subdirectory markers, copy the file called **APR.FIL** from the **FILES** directory to the **ROOM** directory keeping the same name but giving it the new extension of **.RMS**.

11. Which command did you use?
    a. COPY \..\APR.FIL \APR.RMS
    b. COPY ..\APR.FIL APR.RMS
    c. COPY ..\APR.FIL \APR.RMS
    d. COPY ..\APR.FIL ..\APR.RMS

PROBLEM E

E-a   Change to the root directory of the APPLICATION disk.

Note: The root directory of the APPLICATION disk is the default drive and directory.

E-b   Copy any file with a **.TMP** extension from the **WINDOSBK** directory to
           the root of the APPLICATION disk, keeping the same file names but
           giving them the extension of **.TRP**.

E-c   Copy the file called **APR.99** from the root directory of the APPLICATION
           disk to the subdirectory called **HISTORY** giving the file the new name of
           APR.ICE.

E-d   Copy any files with a **.99** file extension from the root directory of the
           APPLICATION disk to the **HISTORY** subdirectory but give the files the
           new extension of **.ICE**.

           12. Which command did you use?
                a. COPY *.99 HISTORY
                b. COPY *.99 HISTORY*.ICE
                c. COPY *.99 *.ICE
                d. COPY .ICE \HISTORY\.99

           13. What message was displayed?
                a. 1 file(s) copied
                b. Overwrite HISTORY\APR.ICE (Yes/No/All)?
                c. Overwrite APR.ICE (Yes/No/ALL)?
                d. no message was displayed

E-e   Take any steps necessary to copy the files.

Note: The root directory of the APPLICATION disk is the default drive and directory.

E-f   Overwrite the file **A:\BONJOUR.TRP** with the contents of the file called
           RIGHT.UP, which is located in the **WINDOSBK** directory.

           14. Which command did you use?
                a. COPY C:\BONJOUR.TRP RIGHT.UP
                b. COPY C:\WINDOSBK\RIGHT.UP BONJOUR.TRP
                c. COPY C:\WINDOSBK\BONJOUR.TRP
                   C:\WINDOSBK\RIGHT.UP
                d. COPY C:\WINDOSBK\RIGHT.UP RIGHT.UP

E-g   Display the contents of the file called **BONJOUR.TRP** on the APPLICA-
           TION disk.

           15. What is the first line in the file?
                a. This is a file for me.
                b. This is a file for you.
                c. HELLO, EVERYONE.
                d. BONJOUR, EVERYONE.

PROBLEM F

Note: The root directory of the APPLICATION disk is the default drive and directory.

F-a   Copy all the files that begin with **EMP** and have any file name and
          extension from the **WINDOSBK** directory to the root directory of the
          APPLICATION disk.

Note: The root directory of the APPLICATION disk is the default drive and directory.

F-b   Copy all the files that have a **.MAK** extension from the **WINDOSBK**
          directory to the root directory of the APPLICATION disk.

F-c   Concatenate the files called **EMPLOYEE.THR** and **EMPLOYEE.TWO** (in
          that order) to the root directory of the APPLICATION disk, calling the
          new file **EMPLOYEE.FIL**.

          16. Which command did you use?
               a. COPY EMPLOYEE.THR + EMPLOYEE.TWO EMPLOYEE.FIL
               b. COPY EMPLOYEE*.* EMPLOYEE.FIL
               c. COPY EMPLOYEE.FIL EMPLOYEE.THR
               d. COPY EMP*.* EMP*.*

F-d   Display the contents of the file **EMPLOYEE.FIL** on the APPLICATION disk.

          17. What is the first line in the file?
               a. This is employee file one.
               b. This is employee file two.
               c. This is employee file three.
               d. There are no employees.

Note: The root directory of the APPLICATION disk is the default drive and directory.

F-e   Concatenate all the files that have the extension **.MAK** from the root
          directory of the APPLICATION disk to the subdirectory **FILES** on the
          APPLICATION disk. The new file should be named **AUTOMOB.ILE**. Use
          a wildcard.

          18. Which command did you use?
               a. COPY MAK AUTOMOB.ILE
               b. COPY ?.MAK FILES
               c. COPY *.MAK FILES/AUTOMOB.ILE
               d. COPY *.MAK FILES\AUTOMOB.ILE

Note: The root directory of the APPLICATION disk is the default drive and directory.

F-f   Display the contents of the file called **AUTOMOB.ILE**.

          19. Which make of automobile is displayed?
               a. Lexus LS400
               b. Dodge Caravan
               c. Ford Aerostar
               d. Chevrolet Astrovan

PROBLEM G

Note 1: Check with your lab instructor prior to proceeding with this problem.

Note 2: Remember, use the method of printing (**LPT1**, **PRN**, or the URL of your printer) that works in your particular lab environment.

Note 3: The root directory of the APPLICATION disk is the default drive and directory.

G-a   Print the file called **AME-LIT.BKS** located in the **BOOKS** directory. Use redirection. (*Note:* If you used **PRN** or a URL instead of **LPT1**, substitute what you use for **LPT1** in the answers.)

20. Which command did you use?
     a. TYPE BOOKS\AME-LIT.BKS > LPT1
     b. TYPE BOOKS\AME-LIT.BKS LPT1
     c. COPY LPT1\BOOKS\AME-LIT.BKS
     d. COPY BOOKS\AME-LIT.BKS > LPT1

G-b   Eject the page if it is not automatically ejected.

Note: The root directory of the APPLICATION disk is the default drive and directory.

G-c   Print all the files with the **.BKS** extension located in the **BOOKS** directory, using only one command. Do not use redirection.

21. What message is displayed on the screen?
     a. 1 file(s) copied
     b. 2 file(s) copied
     c. 3 file(s) copied
     d. no message is displayed

PROBLEM H

Note: The root directory of the APPLICATION disk is the default drive and directory.

H-a   Copy all the files from the **WINDOSBK** directory that have the file extension of **.BAT** to the root of the APPLICATION disk.

22. How many files were copied?
     a. two
     b. four
     c. six
     d. eight

H-b   Copy the file called **MARK.FIL** and the file called **GETYN.COM** from the **WINDOSBK** directory to the root of the APPLICATION disk.

23. Is there a way to copy both of these files at the same time with one command?
     a. yes
     b. no

24. What is the size, in bytes, of GETYN.COM?
    a. 326
    b. 226
    c. 126
    d. 26

25. What kind of file is GETYN.COM?
    a. data
    b. text
    c. program
    d. none of the above

PROBLEM SET II—AT THE COMPUTER

Note 1: Before proceeding with these assignments, check with your lab instructor to see if there are any special procedures you should follow.

Note 2: The APPLICATION disk is in Drive A. A:\> is displayed as the default drive and the default directory. All work will occur on the APPLICATION disk.

Note 3: Make sure that **NAME.BAT**, **MARK.FIL**, **GETYN.COM**, and **GO.BAT** are all present in the root directory of the APPLICATION disk before proceeding with these problems.

Note 4: All files with the **.HW** extension *must* be created in the root directory of the APPLICATION disk.

Step 1   Key in the following: A:\>**NAME** [Enter]

Step 2   Here is an example to key in, but your instructor will have other information that applies to your class. Key in the following:
Bette A. Peat [Enter]   (*Your* name goes here.)
CIS 55 [Enter]   (*Your* class goes here.)
T-Th 8-9:30 [Enter]   (*Your* day and time go here.)
Chapter 5 Applications [Enter]

Step 3   Press [F6] [Enter]

Step 4   If the information is correct, press **Y** and you are back to A:\>.

WHAT'S HAPPENING! ➤ You have returned to the system level. You now have a file called **NAME.FIL** with your name and other pertinent information. *Hint:* Remember redirection.

TO CREATE 1.HW

❖   Create a subdirectory called **MOVIES** under the root directory of the APPLICATION disk.

❖   Copy all the files in the **WINDOSBK\MEDIA\MOVIES** directory to the **MOVIES** directory on the APPLICATION disk and keep the same file names.

❖   Locate all the files in the **MOVIES** directory on the APPLICATION disk.

❖   Place the names of the files in a file called **1.HW**.

TO CREATE 2.HW

❖   On the APPLICATION disk, make a copy of all the files in the **MOVIES** directory to the **MOVIES** directory keeping the same file names but having a new extension of **.FLM**.

❖   Locate the files in the **MOVIES** directory that have the extension of **.FLM** on the APPLICATION disk.

❖   Place the names of the files with only an extension of FLM in a file called **2.HW**.

TO CREATE 3.HW

❖   Redirect the contents (not the file name) of the file called **DRAMA.FLM** in the **MOVIES** directory on the APPLICATION disk to a file called **3.HW**.

TO CREATE 4.HW

❖   Overwrite the file called **DRAMA.FLM** in the **MOVIES** directory on the APPLICATION disk with the contents of the files called **APR.99** located in the root directory of the APPLICATION disk.

❖   Redirect the contents (not the file name) of the file called **DRAMA.FLM** in the **MOVIES** directory on the APPLICATION disk to a file called **4.HW**.

TO CREATE 5.HW

❖   Concatenate all the files that have the extension called **.RED** from the **WINDOSBK** directory to the MOVIES directory on the APPLICATION disk.

❖   Call the new file **MYRED.FIL**.

❖   Redirect the contents (not the file name) of the file called **MYRED.FIL** to a file called **5.HW**.

TO PRINT YOUR HOMEWORK

Step 1   Be sure the printer is on and ready to accept print jobs from your computer.

Step 2   Key in the following (be very careful to make no typing errors):
          A:\>**GO NAME.FIL 1.HW 2.HW 3.HW 4.HW 5.HW** Enter

Step 3   Follow the messages on the screen. When you finish, you will return to the A:\> prompt.

Step 4   Execute the shut-down procedure.

PROBLEM SET III—BRIEF ESSAY

Copying and printing files can be done from My Computer or Explorer. Why or why not might you use the command line to accomplish these tasks?

USING DEL, DELTREE, REN, AND MOVE

LEARNING OBJECTIVES

After completing this chapter you will be able to:

1. Explain why it is necessary to eliminate files from a disk.
2. Explain when and how to use wildcards with the DEL command.
3. Explain the use of the /P parameter with the DEL command.
4. Explain the purpose and function of the RENAME/REN command.
5. Explain the purpose and function of the MOVE command.
6. Compare the DELTREE command with the RD command.
7. Explain the importance of backing up data.

STUDENT OUTCOMES

1. Use the DEL command to eliminate files on disks and in directories.
2. Use wildcards appropriately with the DEL command.
3. Use the /P parameter with the DEL command.
4. Use the RENAME/REN command to change the names of file and subdirectories.
5. Use the RENAME/REN command with wildcards to change the names of files and subdirectories.
6. Use the MOVE command to move files and subdirectories.
7. Use DELTREE to delete files and directories.
8. Use the RD command to delete directories.

9.   Back up a data disk using the DISKCOPY command.
10.   Back up files using the COPY command.

CHAPTER OVERVIEW

The more work you do with computers, the more files you create, and the harder it is to manage them. It becomes increasingly difficult to keep track of what disks have which files and which files are needed. In addition, as new data is keyed into existing files, the names given to the files may no longer be appropriate. It is also important to be able to make a copy of an entire disk or specific files on a disk so that data is not lost due to a power failure, power surge, or a bad disk.

In this chapter you will continue to work with commands that help you manage and manipulate your files. This chapter will focus on the DEL command, which allows you to delete files you no longer need or want, the RENAME command, which is used to rename files, and the MOVE command, which allows you to move files and subdirectories from one location to another. In addition, you will look at the DELTREE command, which allows you to eliminate quickly a subdirectory with all its files. You will also learn why and how to back up specific files or an entire disk so that you do not lose important data.

6.1   ELIMINATING FILES WITH THE DEL COMMAND

In the various activities completed previously, you copied many files. The DATA disk began as a disk absent of files. As you have been working, the number of files on the disk has increased dramatically, typical when working with computers. There is a kind of Murphy's Law that says you create as many files as you have disk space. However, you do not want to keep files forever. The more files and/or disks you have, the harder it is to keep track of what disks have which files and which files are the ones you need. If you have floppy disks, you end up with many floppies, and if you have a hard disk, you end up with many subdirectories and many files. Often, you are not quite sure what files are where. By keeping only the files you need on your disk, you will decrease the number of files you have to manage.

Logic should tell you that, if you can copy and create files, you should be able to eliminate files by deleting or erasing them. You can do these tasks with the DEL command. This command is internal, always resident in memory. You do need to be careful with this command. Once you press Enter after the DEL command, the file is gone forever. The operating system does not ask you if this is really the file you want to get rid of; it simply obeys your instructions.

When a file is deleted at the command line, it cannot be recovered except by certain special utility programs. Even then, recovery is not necessarily complete or even possible. Technically, when you delete a file, the file is not actually physically removed from the disk. Instead, the first character of the file name is replaced with a special byte—the symbol s, which marks the file as deleted in the directory entry table. It then places a 0 in each cluster entry in the FAT (file allocation table). The value of 0 in each cluster means to the operating system that the space is now available for reuse by other files, even though, in fact, the data is still on the disk.

When you create the next file, the operating system sees that there is space available in the directory entry table and the FAT and assigns the new file to that space. The old file is overwritten by the new file.

Special utility programs, such as Norton Utilities, can occasionally help you recover deleted files, particularly if you realize immediately that you inadvertently erased a file. In versions of the operating system from MS-DOS version 5.0 through MS-DOS version 6.22, the UNDELETE command was available. UNDELETE was an operating system utility supplied to recover deleted files. However, once a file was overwritten by new data, nothing could recover the previous data. It is gone forever. When you use the DEL command in the Windows operating system, you cannot count on recovering deleted files. Thus, you should consider that, for all practical purposes, when you use DEL you have, indeed, removed the file or files.

When you delete a file from a hard drive using My Computer or Explorer (using the Windows GUI), the file goes to the Recycle Bin, and is then recoverable. You can open the Recycle Bin, select the file you previously deleted, and restore it. However, if you never empty your Recycle Bin, eventually it becomes full and Windows will begin deleting the oldest files in the Recycle Bin. Files are not recoverable if you delete the files from a removable disk such as a Zip drive or a floppy disk. In addition, files deleted from the MS-DOS command line are not placed in the Recycle Bin and cannot be recovered by the operating system.

The syntax of the DEL command is:

```
DEL [drive:][path]filename [/P]
```

When you use the /P parameter, you are prompted before each file is deleted.

6.2   ACTIVITY: USING THE DEL COMMAND

Note 1: When keying in commands, you may use the function keys to correct typographical errors as well as the up and down arrow keys. To edit command lines fully, you may use DOSKEY. For instructions on how to use DOSKEY, see Chapter 7, section 7.11.

Note 2: Be sure the DATA disk, not the APPLICATION disk, is in Drive A.

Note 3: The MS-DOS Prompt window is open and C:\> is displayed as the default drive and directory.

Step 1   Key in the following: C:\>**A:** ⌑Enter⌑

Step 2   Key in the following: A:\>**COPY C:\WINDOSBK*.DOS *.AAA** ⌑Enter⌑

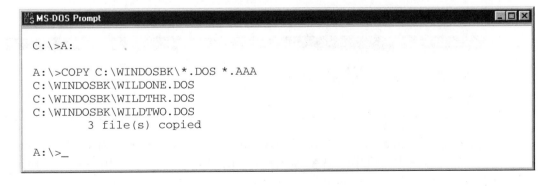

```
MS-DOS Prompt                                         _ □ ×

C:\>A:

A:\>COPY C:\WINDOSBK\*.DOS *.AAA
C:\WINDOSBK\WILDONE.DOS
C:\WINDOSBK\WILDTHR.DOS
C:\WINDOSBK\WILDTWO.DOS
        3 file(s) copied

A:\>_
```

WHAT'S HAPPENING! ➤ You changed the default drive to A. You then copied the files with a **.DOS** extension from the **\WINDOSBK** directory, kept the same file names, but gave them a different extension, (**.AAA**) to the root of the DATA disk.

Step 3   Key in the following: A:\>**DIR *.AAA** [Enter]

```
MS-DOS Prompt                                                    _ □ ✕

A:\>DIR *.AAA

 Volume in drive A is DATA
 Volume Serial Number is 3330-1807
 Directory of A:\

WILDONE   AAA          181  12-31-01   4:32p WILDONE.AAA
WILDTHR   AAA          181  12-31-01   4:32p WILDTHR.AAA
WILDTWO   AAA          182  12-31-01   4:32p WILDTWO.AAA
        3 file(s)              544 bytes
        0 dir(s)        1,399,296 bytes free

A:\>_
```

WHAT'S HAPPENING! ➤ You used the DIR command to confirm that the **.AAA** files are on the DATA disk. The work you wish to do is delete files. The DEL command is an internal command and was installed in memory (RAM) when you booted the system. It will remain in memory until you turn off the power.

Step 4   Key in the following: A:\>**DIR WILDONE.AAA** [Enter]

```
MS-DOS Prompt                                                    _ □ ✕

A:\>DIR WILDONE.AAA

 Volume in drive A is DATA
 Volume Serial Number is 3330-1807
 Directory of A:\

WILDONE   AAA          181  12-31-01   4:32p WILDONE.AAA
        1 file(s)              181 bytes
        0 dir(s)        1,399,296 bytes free

A:\>_
```

WHAT'S HAPPENING! ➤ The DIR command verified that the file called **WILDONE.AAA** is located on the DATA disk.

Step 5   Key in the following: A:\>**DEL WILDONE.AAA** [Enter]

```
MS-DOS Prompt                                                    _ □ ✕

A:\>DEL WILDONE.AAA

A:\>_
```

WHAT'S HAPPENING! ➤ You are asking the DEL command to eliminate the file called **WILDONE.AAA**, located on the DATA disk. You did not need to include the drive letter or \ because the operating system assumed the default drive and directory and looked only for the file called **WILDONE.AAA** on the DATA disk in the root. However, it appears that nothing happened. All you got on the screen was the system prompt.

Step 6   Key in the following: A:\>**DIR WILDONE.AAA** Enter

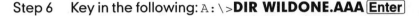

```
MS-DOS Prompt                                                    _ □ X

A:\>DIR WILDONE.AAA

 Volume in drive A is DATA
 Volume Serial Number is 3330-1807
 Directory of A:\

File not found
                          1,399,808 bytes free

A:\>_
```

WHAT'S
HAPPENING?   The DIR command confirmed that the file is gone. You now know that the DEL command was executed and that it removed the file called **WILDONE.AAA**. It is no longer on the DATA disk. What if the file you wanted to delete was not on the disk?

Step 7   Key in the following: A:\>**DEL NOFILE.XXX** Enter

```
MS-DOS Prompt                                                    _ □ X

A:\>DEL NOFILE.XXX
File not found

A:\>_
```

WHAT'S
HAPPENING?   In order for the DEL command to execute, it must be able to find the file to delete. Here, the file was not found.

Step 8   Key in the following: A:\>**DEL** Enter

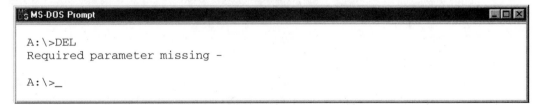

```
MS-DOS Prompt                                                    _ □ X

A:\>DEL
Required parameter missing -

A:\>_
```

WHAT'S
HAPPENING?   Not only must the operating system find the file but it must also know what file to look for. Remember, the syntax is DEL *filename*. The message **Required parameter missing** is the computer's way of saying, "Get rid of what file?"

6.3   DELETING FILES ON OTHER DRIVES AND DIRECTORIES

Using the DEL command to eliminate files works exactly the same on other drives and subdirectories as it did in the previous activity. The syntax of the command remains DEL [*drive*:][*path*]*filename*. The only difference is that you must specify which disk drive and which directory you want to look on. Once again, the operating system follows your instructions exactly as keyed in; it does not check with you to see if you are deleting the correct file. One of the most common mistakes computer users make is placing the drive designator or subdirectory in the wrong place, which can completely change the meaning and results of an instruction. Again, the syntax of the command is:

```
DEL [drive:][path]filename
```

DEL is the command, *drive*: represents the designated drive, *path* represents any subdirectory, and *filename* represents the name of the file you wish to delete. Notice that DEL and *filename* are not in brackets, so are required parts of the command, where [*drive*:][*path*] are in brackets, so are optional. For example, if the file you want to delete is on Drive A, you would substitute A: for [*drive*:]. If the file you want to delete is on Drive C, you would substitute C: for [*drive*:]. If the path name were \FILES, you would substitute \FILES for [*path*]. *filename* is the name of the file—the file specification. For example, if the default drive is A:\> and you want to delete a file on the disk in Drive B called GONE.FIL, a common error is to key in the command as:

```
A:\>DEL GONE.FIL B:
```

This sequence is wrong because you did not use the proper syntax, DEL *path* *filename*. The command should have been keyed in as:

```
A:\>DEL B:GONE.FIL
```

Not only is the first command wrong, but it is also illogical, the equivalent of sending someone to throw away a file folder and not telling that person which file cabinet to look in. What are the results of incorrectly keying in the command? They can vary. If you had keyed in DEL GONE.FIL B:\ you would see:

```
MS-DOS Prompt
A:\>DEL GONE.FIL B:\
Too many parameters - B:\

A:\>_
```

If you had keyed in DEL GONE.FIL B: you would see:

```
MS-DOS Prompt
A:\>DEL GONE.FIL B:
File not found

A:\>_
```

Even though the message is File not found, the OS actually looked for GONE.FIL on the root of the A drive, the default drive and directory, and ignored the

B, but the OS still would not delete the GONE.FIL file as the proper syntax was not provided.

6.4   ACTIVITY: USING THE DEL COMMAND WITH INDIVIDUAL FILES

Note: The DATA disk is in Drive A. A:\> is displayed.

Step 1   Key in the following: A:\>**MD TRIP** [Enter]

Step 2   Key in the following: A:\>**COPY C:\WINDOSBK*.99 TRIP** [Enter]

Step 3   Key in the following: A:\>**COPY C:\WINDOSBK*.JAZ TRIP** [Enter]

```
MS-DOS Prompt                                                    _ □ ✕

A:\>MD TRIP

A:\>COPY C:\WINDOSBK\*.99 TRIP
C:\WINDOSBK\APR.99
C:\WINDOSBK\FEB.99
C:\WINDOSBK\MAR.99
C:\WINDOSBK\JAN.99
        4 file(s) copied

A:\>COPY C:\WINDOSBK\*.JAZ TRIP
C:\WINDOSBK\GREEN.JAZ
C:\WINDOSBK\BLUE.JAZ
        2 file(s) copied

A:\>_
```

WHAT'S HAPPENING?   You created another subdirectory on the DATA disk called **TRIP**. You then copied files from the **\WINDOSBK** subdirectory on the hard disk to the subdirectory called **TRIP** on the DATA disk. You used the COPY command. You had to specify where the source files were located, **C:\WINDOSBK**. However, for the destination of these files, since the default drive is A and the default directory is the root, the OS assumed the default, and you did not have to specify either the destination drive or the root directory in the destination. If you had not included the name of the subdirectory **TRIP**, where you wanted the files copied, the operating system would have assumed the default and copied the files to the root directory of the DATA disk. The longhand or absolute path version of the command is **COPY C:\WINDOSBK*.99 A:\TRIP*.99**.

Step 4   Key in the following: A:\>**DIR TRIP\JAN.99** [Enter]

```
MS-DOS Prompt                                                    _ □ ✕

A:\>DIR TRIP\JAN.99

 Volume in drive A is DATA
 Volume Serial Number is 3330-1807
 Directory of A:\TRIP

JAN      99            73  10-10-99  4:53p JAN.99
        1 file(s)             73 bytes
```

```
            0 dir(s)        1,396,224 bytes free

A:\>_
```

WHAT'S HAPPENING? The file is there. You successfully copied it.

Step 5   Key in the following: A:\>**DEL TRIP\JAN.99** [Enter]

```
MS-DOS Prompt                                    _ □ ✕

A:\>DEL TRIP\JAN.99

A:\>_
```

WHAT'S HAPPENING? You had to provide the proper syntax to tell the DEL command where the **JAN.99** file was located. It was located in the subdirectory **TRIP** under the root directory on the DATA disk. Since the default drive is A, you did not need to include the drive letter. Since the default subdirectory is the root (\), the \ is assumed and does not need to be keyed in. However, the \ between the subdirectory **TRIP** and the file name **JAN.99** does need to be keyed in. In this case \ is used as a delimiter between the subdirectory name and the file name. Has the file been deleted?

Step 6   Key in the following: A:\>**DIR TRIP\JAN.99** [Enter]

```
MS-DOS Prompt                                    _ □ ✕

A:\>DIR TRIP\JAN.99

 Volume in drive A is DATA
 Volume Serial Number is 3330-1807
 Directory of A:\TRIP

File not found
                      1,396,736 bytes free

A:\>_
```

WHAT'S HAPPENING? The file called **JAN.99** is gone from the subdirectory called **TRIP** on the DATA disk. Look at the display. The third line returned by the command, **Directory of A:\TRIP**, tells you that DIR looked only in the subdirectory called **TRIP**.

Step 7   Key in the following: A:\>**C:** [Enter]

Step 8   Key in the following: C:\>**CD \WINDOSBK** [Enter]

Step 9   Key in the following: C:\WINDOSBK>**COPY HELLO.TXT A:** [Enter]

```
MS-DOS Prompt                                    _ □ ✕

A:\>C:

C:\>CD \WINDOSBK

C:\WINDOSBK>COPY HELLO.TXT A:\
```

```
        1 file(s) copied

C:\WINDOSBK>_
```

WHAT'S HAPPENING? You changed the default drive to the hard disk. You then changed the default subdirectory from the root of the hard disk to the subdirectory called **\WINDOSBK**. You then copied the file called **HELLO.TXT** from the **\WINDOSBK** directory to the root directory of the DATA disk. The purpose of this activity is to have two identically named files on different drives.

Step 10 Key in the following: C:\WINDOSBK>**DIR HELLO.TXT** Enter

Step 11 Key in the following: C:\WINDOSBK>**DIR A:\HELLO.TXT** Enter

```
MS-DOS Prompt                                                _ □ ×

C:\WINDOSBK>DIR HELLO.TXT

 Volume in drive C is MILLENNIUM
 Volume Serial Number is 2B18-1301
 Directory of C:\WINDOSBK

HELLO    TXT            53  05-30-00  4:32p HELLO.TXT
        1 file(s)              53 bytes
        0 dir(s)    1,121,550,336 bytes free

C:\WINDOSBK>DIR A:\HELLO.TXT

 Volume in drive A is DATA
 Volume Serial Number is 3330-1807
 Directory of A:\

HELLO    TXT            53  05-30-00  4:32p HELLO.TXT
        1 file(s)              53 bytes
        0 dir(s)       1,396,224 bytes free

C:\WINDOSBK>_
```

WHAT'S HAPPENING? You have two files called **HELLO.TXT**. One file is on the hard disk in the subdirectory **\WINDOSBK**. The other file is on the DATA disk. You want to delete the file on the DATA disk, *not* on the hard disk.

Step 12 Key in the following: C:\WINDOSBK>**DEL A:\HELLO.TXT** Enter

```
MS-DOS Prompt                                                _ □ ×

C:\WINDOSBK>DEL A:\HELLO.TXT

C:\WINDOSBK>_
```

WHAT'S HAPPENING? You asked DEL to erase the file on the DATA disk called **HELLO.TXT**. The file should be gone from the DATA disk, but the file called **HELLO.TXT** on the hard disk (Drive C, subdirectory **\WINDOSBK**) should still be there.

Step 13 Key in the following: C:\WINDOSBK>**DIR HELLO.TXT** Enter

Step 14 Key in the following: C:\WINDOSBK>**DIR A:\HELLO.TXT** Enter

```
MS-DOS Prompt                                                    _ □ X

C:\WINDOSBK>DIR HELLO.TXT

 Volume in drive C is MILLENNIUM
 Volume Serial Number is 2B18-1301
 Directory of C:\WINDOSBK

HELLO    TXT            53  05-30-00  4:32p HELLO.TXT
         1 file(s)              53 bytes
         0 dir(s)    1,121,538,048 bytes free

C:\WINDOSBK>DIR A:\HELLO.TXT

 Volume in drive A is DATA
 Volume Serial Number is 3330-1807
 Directory of A:\

File not found
                   1,396,736 bytes free

C:\WINDOSBK>_
```

WHAT'S HAPPENING! ➤ The file called **HELLO.TXT** is still in the subdirectory **WINDOSBK** on the hard disk, but the file called **HELLO.TXT** on the DATA disk is gone.

Step 15 Key in the following: C:\WINDOSBK>**DIR A:\TRIP\BLUE.JAZ** Enter

```
MS-DOS Prompt                                                    _ □ X

C:\WINDOSBK>DIR A:\TRIP\BLUE.JAZ

 Volume in drive A is DATA
 Volume Serial Number is 3330-1807
 Directory of A:\TRIP

BLUE     JAZ            19  05-30-00  4:32p BLUE.JAZ
         1 file(s)              19 bytes
         0 dir(s)       1,396,736 bytes free

C:\WINDOSBK>_
```

WHAT'S HAPPENING! ➤ There is a file called **BLUE.JAZ** in the subdirectory **TRIP** on the DATA disk. To delete this file, you once again follow the syntax of the DEL command, substituting the values you want for the variable parameters.

Step 16 Key in the following: C:\WINDOSBK>**DEL A:\TRIP\BLUE.JAZ** Enter

```
MS-DOS Prompt                                                    _ □ X

C:\WINDOSBK>DEL A:\TRIP\BLUE.JAZ

C:\WINDOSBK>_
```

WHAT'S HAPPENING? ➡ The syntax is DEL [*drive:*][*path*]*filename*. You substituted the drive letter of the DATA disk for [*drive:*]. You then substituted TRIP for [*path*]. You could have eliminated the first backslash because the root directory of the DATA disk is the default directory on the A drive. In order to ensure that you indeed meant the root directory of the DATA disk, you included \ for the root directory. You then substituted **BLUE.JAZ** for the file name. The second backslash was mandatory because you need a delimiter between the file name and the subdirectory name. This backslash is similar to the period that you used to separate the file name from the file extension. Is the file gone?

Step 17 Key in the following: C:\WINDOSBK>**DIR A:\TRIP\BLUE.JAZ** Enter

```
MS-DOS Prompt                                              _ □ ✕

C:\WINDOSBK>DIR A:\TRIP\BLUE.JAZ

 Volume in drive A is DATA
 Volume Serial Number is 3330-1807
 Directory of A:\TRIP

File not found
                   1,397,248 bytes free

C:\WINDOSBK>_
```

WHAT'S HAPPENING? ➡ The file **BLUE.JAZ** from the directory **TRIP** on the DATA disk is gone.

Step 18 Key in the following: C:\WINDOSBK>**CD ** Enter

Step 19 Key in the following: C:\>**A:** Enter

```
MS-DOS Prompt                                              _ □ ✕

C:\WINDOSBK>CD \

C:\>A:

A:\>_
```

WHAT'S HAPPENING? ➡ You returned to the root directory of the hard disk. You then made the root directory of the DATA disk the default drive and directory.

6.5 USING WILDCARDS WITH THE DEL COMMAND

You have been erasing or deleting files one at a time. Often you want to erase many files. It is tedious to erase many files one at a time. You can use the wildcards with the DEL command to delete several files at one time. Wildcards allow you to erase a group of files with a one-line command. Although you can certainly delete files in My Computer, you must select each file to be deleted, which takes lots of time. It is simply quicker and easier deleting the files from the command line. However, at the command line, be *exceedingly* careful when using wildcards with the DEL command.

Once again, the strength of wildcards is also their weakness. A global file specification means global. You can eliminate a group of files very quickly. If you are not careful, you could erase files you want to keep. In fact, you probably will some day say, "Oh no, those files are gone." However, this does not mean you should never use wildcards. They are far too useful. Just be very, *very* careful.

6.6   ACTIVITY: USING THE DEL COMMAND

Note 1: The DATA disk is in Drive A. A:\> is displayed.
Note 2: If the **.TMP** files are not on the root of the DATA disk, they may be copied from the **\WINDOSBK** subdirectory.

Step 1   Key in the following: A:\>**DIR *.TMP** Enter

```
MS-DOS Prompt
A:\>DIR *.TMP

 Volume in drive A is DATA
 Volume Serial Number is 3330-1807
 Directory of A:\

JAN       TMP        73   04-23-00   4:03p JAN.TMP
FEB       TMP        75   04-23-00   4:03p FEB.TMP
MAR       TMP        71   04-23-00   4:03p MAR.TMP
APR       TMP        72   04-23-00   4:18p APR.TMP
          4 file(s)              291 bytes
          0 dir(s)         1,397,248 bytes free

A:\>_
```

WHAT'S HAPPENING? ➤ You should see four files with **.TMP** as the file extension displayed on the screen. Prior to doing a global erase, it is always wise to key in DIR with the same global file specification you are going to use with the DEL command. In this way, you can see ahead of time *exactly* which files will be deleted. This process allows you to confirm visually that you are not going to erase a file you want to retain.

Step 2   Key in the following: A:\>**DEL *.TMP** Enter

```
MS-DOS Prompt
A:\>DEL *.TMP

A:\>_
```

WHAT'S HAPPENING? ➤ You asked DEL to erase or delete every file on the DATA disk in the root directory that has the file extension **.TMP**. The wildcard * represented any file name. Only the system prompt appears on the screen. The DEL command executed, erasing those *.**TMP** files quickly and permanently. To verify this, use the DIR command.

Step 3   Key in the following: A:\>**DIR *.TMP** Enter

```
MS-DOS Prompt                                                    _ □ ✕

A:\>DIR *.TMP

 Volume in drive A is DATA
 Volume Serial Number is 3330-1807
 Directory of A:\

File not found
                            1,399,296 bytes free

A:\>_
```

WHAT'S HAPPENING? Those ***.TMP** files are, indeed, gone from the root directory on the DATA disk. They are not recoverable by the operating system. Please let it be emphasized that, before you use a wildcard to delete groups of files, you should use the DIR command to see the files you are going to delete. For instance, if you had a file called **TEST.TMP** that you had forgotten about and that you did not want to delete, the directory display would include it as follows:

```
JAN       TMP          72    04-23-98   3:48p JAN.TMP
FEB       TMP          74    04-23-98   3:48p FEB.TMP
MAR       TMP          70    04-23-98   3:48p MAR.TMP
APR       TMP          71    04-23-98   3:48p APR.TMP
TEST      TMP         500    05-01-98   5:00p TEST.TMP

           5 file(s)                787 bytes
```

You would have been made aware of the presence of the **TEST.TMP** file using the DIR command, and would thus have avoided losing a needed file. Using the DIR command with wildcards will let you display on the screen all the files that have been selected by ***.TMP**, which includes the **TEST.TMP** file that you do not want to erase. If you had keyed in **DEL *.TMP**, all those **.TMP** files would have been deleted. Remember, the computer does not come back and tell you, "Oh, by the way, **TEST.TMP** was included with the ***.TMP** files; did you want to erase that file?" The DEL command simply eliminates all the **.TMP** files because that is what you told it to do. You can also use wildcards when files are in a subdirectory.

Step 4   Key in the following: A:\>**DIR TRIP*.99** [Enter]

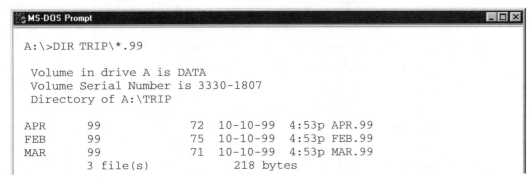

```
MS-DOS Prompt                                                    _ □ ✕

A:\>DIR TRIP\*.99

 Volume in drive A is DATA
 Volume Serial Number is 3330-1807
 Directory of A:\TRIP

APR       99          72    10-10-99   4:53p APR.99
FEB       99          75    10-10-99   4:53p FEB.99
MAR       99          71    10-10-99   4:53p MAR.99
           3 file(s)             218 bytes
```

```
        0 dir(s)        1,399,296 bytes free

A:\>_
```

WHAT'S HAPPENING? → There are three files with the extension **.99** on the DATA disk in the subdirectory **TRIP**. The DEL command works the same way, but you must be sure to include the path name.

Step 5   Key in the following: A:\>**DEL TRIP*.99** (Enter)

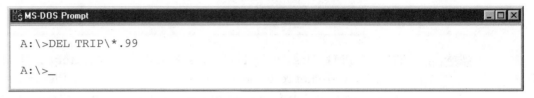

```
A:\>DEL TRIP\*.99

A:\>_
```

WHAT'S HAPPENING? → You asked DEL to erase or delete every file on the DATA disk in the subdirectory **TRIP** that has any file name and has the file extension **.99**. The wildcard ***** represented any file name. Only the system prompt appears on the screen. The DEL command executed, erasing those ***.99** files quickly and permanently. To verify this, you can use the DIR command.

Step 6   Key in the following: A:\>**DIR TRIP*.99** (Enter)

```
A:\>DIR TRIP\*.99

 Volume in drive A is DATA
 Volume Serial Number is 3330-1807
 Directory of A:\TRIP

File not found
                    1,400,832 bytes free

A:\>_
```

WHAT'S HAPPENING? → The *.99 files are indeed gone from the TRIP directory.

6.7   THE /P PARAMETER WITH THE DEL COMMAND

Prior to DOS 4.0, the DEL command provided no way for you to confirm deletions. The file was simply erased. In DOS 4.0 an enhancement was introduced: the /P parameter. This parameter allows you to tell the DEL command to prompt you with the file name prior to deleting the file. The syntax is:

```
DEL [drive:][path]filename [/P]
```

The last statement, /P, is an optional fixed parameter. Its purpose is to display each file name to verify that you really want to delete it. You can think of the P as standing for "prompt you for an answer." This parameter is particularly useful when you are using wildcards. It minimizes the risk of accidental file deletions.

6.8   ACTIVITY: USING /P WITH THE DEL COMMAND

Note: The DATA disk is in Drive A. A:\> is displayed.

Step 1   Key in the following: A:\>**COPY C:\WINDOSBK*.99** [Enter]

```
 MS-DOS Prompt                                                      _ □ X

A:\>COPY C:\WINDOSBK\*.99
C:\WINDOSBK\APR.99
C:\WINDOSBK\FEB.99
C:\WINDOSBK\MAR.99
C:\WINDOSBK\JAN.99
        4 file(s) copied

A:\>_
```

> **WHAT'S HAPPENING?** You have copied the files with the **.99** extension from the **WINDOSBK** directory to the root of the DATA disk and kept the file names the same.

Step 2   Key in the following: A:\>**COPY *.99 TRIP** [Enter]

Step 3   Key in the following: A:\>**DIR TRIP** [Enter]

```
 MS-DOS Prompt                                                      _ □ X

A:\>COPY *.99 TRIP
APR.99
FEB.99
MAR.99
JAN.99
        4 file(s) copied

A:\>DIR TRIP

 Volume in drive A is DATA
 Volume Serial Number is 3330-1807
 Directory of A:\TRIP

.               <DIR>        07-25-01   6:37p .
..              <DIR>        07-25-01   6:37p ..
APR     99              72   10-10-99   4:53p APR.99
FEB     99              75   10-10-99   4:53p FEB.99
MAR     99              71   10-10-99   4:53p MAR.99
JAN     99              73   10-10-99   4:53p JAN.99
GREEN   JAZ             19   05-30-00   4:32p GREEN.JAZ
        5 file(s)           310 bytes
        2 dir(s)      1,396,736 bytes free

A:\>_
```

> **WHAT'S HAPPENING?** You copied the files with the extension of **.99** to the **TRIP** subdirectory on the DATA disk and confirmed that they are there. The file called **GREEN.JAZ** is also in that subdirectory. Next, you are going to choose *some* of the **.99** files to delete.

Step 4   Key in the following: A:\>**DEL TRIP*.99 /P** [Enter]

```
A:\>DEL TRIP\*.99 /P

TRIP\APR.99,    Delete (Y/N)?_
```

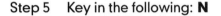 The **/P** parameter, when included in the command line, prompts you by asking if you want to delete the file called **APR.99** in the subdirectory **TRIP** on the DATA disk. When you have a **Y/N** choice, press either **Y** for "Yes" or **N** for "No." Pressing **Enter** takes no action.

Step 5   Key in the following: **N**

```
A:\>DEL TRIP\*.99 /P

TRIP\APR.99,    Delete (Y/N)?N
TRIP\FEB.99,    Delete (Y/N)?_
```

DEL found the next file and asked if you wanted to delete the file called **FEB.99**.

Step 6   Key in the following: **Y**

```
A:\>DEL TRIP\*.99 /P

TRIP\APR.99,    Delete (Y/N)?N
TRIP\FEB.99,    Delete (Y/N)?Y
TRIP\MAR.99,    Delete (Y/N)?_
```

DEL found the next file and asked if you wanted to delete the file called **MAR.99**.

Step 7   Key in the following: **N**

```
A:\>DEL TRIP\*.99 /P

TRIP\APR.99,    Delete (Y/N)?N
TRIP\FEB.99,    Delete (Y/N)?Y
TRIP\MAR.99,    Delete (Y/N)?N
TRIP\JAN.99,    Delete (Y/N)?_
```

DEL found the next file and asked you if you wanted to delete the file called **JAN.99**.

Step 8   Key in the following: **Y**

```
MS-DOS Prompt                                              _ □ ×

TRIP\APR.99,     Delete (Y/N)?N
TRIP\FEB.99,     Delete (Y/N)?Y
TRIP\MAR.99,     Delete (Y/N)?N
TRIP\JAN.99,     Delete (Y/N)?Y

A:\>_
```

WHAT'S HAPPENING? You were returned to the system prompt because there were no more files with the extension **.99** on the DATA disk in the subdirectory **TRIP**. You were able to delete files selectively. You deleted the files **JAN.99** and **FEB.99** but kept the files **MAR.99** and **APR.99**. You can verify this by using the DIR command.

Step 9 Key in the following: A:\>**DIR TRIP** Enter

```
MS-DOS Prompt                                              _ □ ×

A:\>DIR TRIP

 Volume in drive A is DATA
 Volume Serial Number is 3330-1807
 Directory of A:\TRIP

.               <DIR>        07-25-01  6:37p .
..              <DIR>        07-25-01  6:37p ..
APR      99            72    10-10-99  4:53p APR.99
MAR      99            71    10-10-99  4:53p MAR.99
GREEN    JAZ           19    05-30-00  4:32p GREEN.JAZ
         3 file(s)              162 bytes
         2 dir(s)        1,397,760 bytes free

A:\>_
```

WHAT'S HAPPENING? You retained the files **APR.99** and **MAR.99** but deleted **JAN.99** and **FEB.99**. The file **GREEN.JAZ** was not deleted because it did not have the file extension **.99**.

6.9 CHANGING FILE NAMES

Often when working with files, you want to change a file name. For example, you may wish to change the name of a file to indicate an older version. You might also think of a more descriptive file name. As the contents of a file change, the old name may no longer reflect the contents. When you make a typographical error, you want to be able to correct it. One way to change the name of a file is to copy it to a different name. The COPY command can, in this way, help to change the name of a file. You could, for example, copy the file A:\JAN.99 to A:\TRIP\JAN.00. Actually, you did not change the name of an existing file—you created a new file with the same contents under a different name.

The operating system supplies a way to change existing file names using the internal command RENAME. RENAME does exactly what it says; it changes the name of a file. The contents of the file do not change, only the name of the file. The syntax for this command is:

```
RENAME [drive:][path][directoryname1 ¦ filename1] [directoryname2 ¦ filename2]
```

or

```
REN [drive:][path][directoryname1 ¦ filename1] [directoryname2 ¦ filename2]
```

Remember, when you see two or more options within brackets that are separated by the pipe symbol (¦), you can use only one of the options. Note that you *cannot* specify a new drive or path for your destination. RENAME does not let you specify a new drive or path for *filename2* or *directoryname2*. Remember, you are not making a copy of a file. It is like pasting a new label on an existing file folder. That file folder does not get moved in the process. You are dealing with only one file when using REN. In the syntax diagram, *filename1* and *filename2* refer to the same file— *filename1* will be changed to *filename2*. You are changing the file name only, not creating another copy of it with a new name.

The RENAME command has two forms—RENAME or REN—with exactly the same syntax. Most computer users choose REN, simply because it has fewer keystrokes. The syntax is the command REN, the first parameter (the old file name), and the second parameter (the new file name).

Renaming files at the command line is especially useful. In My Computer or Explorer, renaming files is always a two-step process. First, you must select the file; then, you must rename it. At the command line, you can accomplish this task in one step.

6.10   ACTIVITY: USING THE REN COMMAND TO RENAME FILES

Note: The DATA disk is in Drive A. A:\> is displayed.

Step 1   Key in the following: A:\>**COPY C:\WINDOSBK\MEDIA\TV** Enter

```
MS-DOS Prompt                                              _ □ ✕
A:\>COPY C:\WINDOSBK\MEDIA\TV
C:\WINDOSBK\MEDIA\TV\COMEDY.TV
C:\WINDOSBK\MEDIA\TV\DRAMA.TV
        2 file(s) copied
A:\>_
```

WHAT'S HAPPENING?   You copied two files from the hard disk subdirectory **\WINDOSBK\MEDIA\TV** to the root directory of the DATA disk. Notice that after TV you did not have to specify a file name. When you key in a command ending in the name of a directory rather than a file specification, ***.*** is assumed. The destination is also assumed. It is the default drive and directory—in this case the root directory of the DATA disk.

Step 2   Key in the following: A:\>**TYPE COMEDY.TV** Enter

```
MS-DOS Prompt                                                    _ □ ×

A:\>TYPE COMEDY.TV

COMEDY TELEVISION SERIES

Murphy Brown
Suddenly Susan
Caroline in the City
Home Improvement
Seinfeld
I Love Lucy
Roseanne
TAXI
The Mary Tyler Moore Show
Wings
The Dick Van Dyke Show
Frasier
Third Rock From the Sun
A:\>_
```

WHAT'S
HAPPENING?   You are displaying the contents of the file called **COMEDY.TV** located in
the root directory on the DATA disk. You opened the file folder called
COMEDY.TV and looked inside.

Step 3   Key in the following: A:\>**REN COMEDY.TV FUNNY.TV** Enter

```
MS-DOS Prompt                                                    _ □ ×

A:\>REN COMEDY.TV FUNNY.TV

A:\>_
```

WHAT'S
HAPPENING?   Using the command REN changed the name of the file called
COMEDY.TV to **FUNNY.TV**. Since the default was the DATA disk and
the default directory was the root, the operating system looked only on
the root directory of the DATA disk for the file called **COMEDY.TV**.
Once you pressed Enter, you got back only the system prompt. Did
anything happen?

Step 4   Key in the following: A:\>**DIR COMEDY.TV** Enter

```
MS-DOS Prompt                                                    _ □ ×

A:\>DIR COMEDY.TV

 Volume in drive A is DATA
 Volume Serial Number is 3330-1807
 Directory of A:\

File not found
                    1,396,736 bytes free

A:\>_
```

> **WHAT'S HAPPENING!**   Once you have renamed a file, it no longer exists under its old file name.

Step 5   Key in the following: A:\>**DIR FUNNY.TV** [Enter]

```
 MS-DOS Prompt                                                    _ □ ×

A:\>DIR FUNNY.TV

 Volume in drive A is DATA
 Volume Serial Number is 3330-1807
 Directory of A:\

FUNNY    TV             232  03-05-00  4:41p FUNNY.TV
         1 file(s)              232 bytes
         0 dir(s)         1,396,736 bytes free

A:\>_
```

> **WHAT'S HAPPENING!**   The above display demonstrates that the file called **FUNNY.TV** is on the DATA disk in the root directory. You know that the file named **COMEDY.TV** is no longer on the DATA disk. Are the contents of the file **FUNNY.TV** the same as the contents of the file that was named **COMEDY.TV**?

Step 6   Key in the following: A:\>**TYPE FUNNY.TV** [Enter]

```
 MS-DOS Prompt                                                    _ □ ×

A:\>TYPE FUNNY.TV

COMEDY TELEVISION SERIES

Murphy Brown
Suddenly Susan
Caroline in the City
Home Improvement
Seinfeld
I Love Lucy
Roseanne
TAXI
The Mary Tyler Moore Show
Wings
The Dick Van Dyke Show
Frasier
Third Rock From the Sun

A:\>_
```

> **WHAT'S HAPPENING!**   As you can see, you changed the file name from **COMEDY.TV** to **FUNNY.TV**, but the contents of the file did not change. REN works the same way with a file in a subdirectory. You just have to follow the syntax (only partial syntax, that which refers to renaming files, is shown here):

```
REN [drive:][path][filename1] [filename2]
```

Step 7   Key in the following: A:\>**DIR TRIP\GREEN.JAZ** [Enter]

```
MS-DOS Prompt                                                    _ □ ×

A:\>DIR TRIP\GREEN.JAZ

 Volume in drive A is DATA
 Volume Serial Number is 3330-1807
 Directory of A:\TRIP

GREEN    JAZ             19  05-30-00   4:32p GREEN.JAZ
         1 file(s)               19 bytes
         0 dir(s)        1,396,736 bytes free

 A:\>_
```

WHAT'S HAPPENING? The file called **GREEN.JAZ** is in the subdirectory called **TRIP** on the DATA disk. Using REN is different from using COPY. The COPY syntax requires that you place the path name in front of the source file and destination file. You are dealing with two files; thus, each file could be in a separate location. This situation is not true with REN. You are dealing with only one file and are changing only one file name. You are not moving the file; thus, the path name is placed in front of the source file only.

Step 8   Key in the following: A:\>**REN TRIP\GREEN.JAZ TRIP\RED.JAZ** Enter

```
MS-DOS Prompt                                                    _ □ ×

A:\>REN TRIP\GREEN.JAZ TRIP\RED.JAZ
Invalid parameter - TRIP\RED.JAZ

 A:\>_
```

WHAT'S HAPPENING? The message is descriptive. **Invalid parameter** refers to **TRIP\RED.JAZ**. That portion of the command syntax is incorrect. It is incorrect because you placed a subdirectory before the new file name.

Step 9   Key in the following: A:\>**REN TRIP\GREEN.JAZ RED.JAZ** Enter

```
MS-DOS Prompt                                                    _ □ ×

A:\>REN TRIP\GREEN.JAZ RED.JAZ

 A:\>_
```

WHAT'S HAPPENING? You received no error message, indicating that this command was executed. You will use the DIR command to confirm that the file name was changed from **GREEN.JAZ** to **RED.JAZ**.

Step 10   Key in the following: A:\>**DIR TRIP*.JAZ** Enter

```
MS-DOS Prompt                                                      _ □ ×

A:\>DIR TRIP\*.JAZ

 Volume in drive A is DATA
 Volume Serial Number is 3330-1807
 Directory of A:\TRIP

RED        JAZ              19   05-30-00   4:32p RED.JAZ
           1 file(s)                19 bytes
           0 dir(s)          1,396,736 bytes free

A:\>_
```

> **WHAT'S HAPPENING?** You can see that the file in the **TRIP** subdirectory with the extension **.JAZ** is now called **RED.JAZ** instead of **GREEN.JAZ**.

6.11 CHANGING THE NAMES OF SUBDIRECTORIES

In previous versions of MS-DOS, the REN command worked only with files. With the release of Windows 95, it became possible to use the REN command to rename subdirectories. Previously, you used the MOVE command to rename subdirectories. Remember the syntax.

```
REN [drive:][path][directoryname1 ¦ filename1] [directoryname2 ¦ filename2]
```

When renaming subdirectories, the partial syntax is:

```
REN [drive:][path][directoryname1] [directoryname2]
```

6.12 ACTIVITY: USING THE REN COMMAND TO RENAME SUBDIRECTORIES

Note: The DATA disk is in Drive A. A:\> is displayed as the default drive and the default directory.

Step 1   Key in the following: A:\>**MD NAMEONE** [Enter]

Step 2   Key in the following: A:\>**DIR N*.*** [Enter]

```
MS-DOS Prompt                                                      _ □ ×

A:\>MD NAMEONE

A:\>DIR N*.*

 Volume in drive A is DATA
 Volume Serial Number is 3330-1807
 Directory of A:\

NAMEONE        <DIR>            07-25-01   7:14p NAMEONE
           0 file(s)                 0 bytes
           1 dir(s)          1,396,224 bytes free

A:\>_
```

> **WHAT'S HAPPENING?** You have created a new directory called **NAMEONE** on the root of the DATA disk in the A drive. You have verified its existence by using the DIR command. There is only one entry on the root of the DATA disk that begins with the letter **N**.

Step 3   Key in the following: A:\>**REN NAMEONE NAMETWO** [Enter]

```
MS-DOS Prompt                                                    _ □ ✕

A:\>REN NAMEONE NAMETWO

A:\>_
```

> **WHAT'S HAPPENING?** You received no error messages, so the command executed. Was the subdirectory **NAMEONE** actually renamed to **NAMETWO**?

Step 4   Key in the following: A:\>**DIR N*.*** [Enter]

```
MS-DOS Prompt                                                    _ □ ✕

A:\>DIR N*.*

 Volume in drive A is DATA
 Volume Serial Number is 3330-1807
 Directory of A:\

NAMETWO        <DIR>          07-25-01  7:14p NAMETWO
        0 file(s)                 0 bytes
        1 dir(s)         1,396,224 bytes free

A:\>_
```

> **WHAT'S HAPPENING?** You have verified that the REN command successfully renamed the directory **NAMEONE** to **NAMETWO**. **NAMEONE** no longer exists under its original name. It is now **NAMETWO**. You can also rename subdirectories that are within other subdirectories.

Step 5   Key in the following: A:\>**MD NAMETWO\DIRONE** [Enter]

Step 6   Key in the following: A:\>**DIR NAMETWO** [Enter]

```
MS-DOS Prompt                                                    _ □ ✕

A:\>MD NAMETWO\DIRONE

A:\>DIR NAMETWO

 Volume in drive A is DATA
 Volume Serial Number is 3330-1807
 Directory of A:\NAMETWO

.              <DIR>          07-25-01  7:14p .
..             <DIR>          07-25-01  7:14p ..
DIRONE         <DIR>          07-25-01  7:16p DIRONE
        0 file(s)                 0 bytes
        3 dir(s)         1,395,712 bytes free

A:\>_
```

WHAT'S HAPPENING? ➤ You have created a subdirectory called **DIRONE** in the existing subdirectory **NAMETWO**. You have also used the DIR command to display the contents of the **NAMETWO** directory to verify the new subdirectory just created called **DIRONE**. You will now rename the new directory.

Step 7   Key in the following: A:\>**REN NAMETWO\DIRONE DIRTWO** [Enter]

```
MS-DOS Prompt                                                    _ □ ×

A:\>REN NAMETWO\DIRONE DIRTWO

A:\>_
```

WHAT'S HAPPENING? ➤ You have renamed the subdirectory **DIRONE** to **DIRTWO**. Again, you see no error messages, so the command executed. You can verify the change with the DIR command.

Step 8   Key in the following: A:\>**DIR NAMETWO** [Enter]

```
MS-DOS Prompt                                                    _ □ ×

A:\>DIR NAMETWO

 Volume in drive A is DATA
 Volume Serial Number is 3330-1807
 Directory of A:\NAMETWO

.               <DIR>         07-25-01   7:14p .
..              <DIR>         07-25-01   7:14p ..
DIRTWO          <DIR>         07-25-01   7:16p DIRTWO
        0 file(s)                  0 bytes
        3 dir(s)          1,395,712 bytes free

A:\>_
```

WHAT'S HAPPENING? ➤ You have used the DIR command to confirm that you have, indeed, renamed the subdirectory **DIRONE** to the new name of **DIRTWO**. This subdirectory structure will no longer be used. You will use the DELTREE command to remove the entire structure.

Step 9   Key in the following: A:\>**DELTREE NAMETWO** [Enter]

```
MS-DOS Prompt                                                    _ □ ×

A:\>DELTREE NAMETWO
Delete directory "NAMETWO" and all its subdirectories? [yn] _
```

WHAT'S HAPPENING? ➤ The DELTREE command is asking you if you are sure you want to delete the **NAMETWO** subdirectory and all of its contents.

Step 10   Key in the following: **Y** [Enter]

Step 11   Key in the following: A:\>**DIR N*.*** [Enter]

```
MS-DOS Prompt                                                    _ □ ×

A:\>DELTREE NAMETWO
Delete directory "NAMETWO" and all its subdirectories? [yn] y
Deleting NAMETWO...

A:\>DIR N*.*

 Volume in drive A is DATA
 Volume Serial Number is 3330-1807
 Directory of A:\

File not found
                        1,396,736 bytes free

A:\>_
```

WHAT'S HAPPENING? As you can see with the DIR command, you have successfully removed the **NAMETWO** directory structure.

6.13 USING REN WITH WILDCARDS

When you wish to change the name of a single file or directory, you can use My Computer from the GUI. It is easy to do—just right-click the file or folder and choose Rename. If, however, you have numerous files to rename, and they have something in common, such as all the files with the .ABC extension, using the command line is more efficient. You can use the REN or RENAME command with the wildcards ? and *, allowing you to change many file names with a one-line command.

The wildcards or global file specifications are so "global" that, prior to renaming files, it is wise to do a directory display with the wildcards you want to use so that you can see what files are going to be renamed, just as you use a directory display before you use the DEL command with wildcards. You do not want to rename a subdirectory accidentally along with a group of files. This can happen all too easily. Once a file is renamed, you can never find the file under its old name. This rule has caused havoc for users because it seems as if the file is lost. The file is still on the disk, and you can find it, but only under its new name.

6.14 ACTIVITY: USING REN WITH WILDCARDS

Note 1: The DATA disk is in Drive A. A:\> is displayed.
Note 2: This activity assumes you have files on the DATA disk with the file extension **.NEW**. If you do not, you may copy them from **C:\WINDOSBK** to the DATA disk.

Step 1   Key in the following: A:\>**DIR ???.NEW** [Enter]

```
MS-DOS Prompt                                                    _ □ ×

A:\>DIR ???.NEW

 Volume in drive A is DATA
 Volume Serial Number is 3330-1807
 Directory of A:\
```

```
FEB     NEW            75  04-23-00  4:03p FEB.NEW
JAN     NEW            73  04-23-00  4:03p JAN.NEW
MAR     NEW            71  04-23-00  4:03p MAR.NEW
APR     NEW            72  04-23-00  4:18p APR.NEW
        4 file(s)          291 bytes
        0 dir(s)     1,396,736 bytes free

A:\>_
```

WHAT'S HAPPENING! You have four files with file names of three characters and with the extension **.NEW**. You used **???** instead of *****. When you used **???.NEW**, the **???** selected only files that had a file name of three characters. Had you used ***** instead of **???**, you would have selected all file names that had an extension of **.NEW**. That would have included such files as **BONJOUR.NEW**. Your objective is to rename these four files, keeping their file names but changing the file extension from **.NEW** to **.BUD**. You could rename these files one at a time, **REN FEB.NEW FEB.BUD**, then **REN JAN.NEW JAN.BUD**, then **REN MAR.NEW MAR.BUD**, and **REN APR.NEW APR.BUD**. However, this repetition becomes very tiresome. Using wildcards allows you to rename these four files at one time.

Step 2   Key in the following: A:\>**REN ???.NEW *.BUD** Enter

```
MS-DOS Prompt                                      _ □ ×
A:\>REN ???.NEW *.BUD

A:\>_
```

WHAT'S HAPPENING! All that is displayed is the system prompt. Was the work done? Are the files renamed? To verify that you did rename these files, use the DIR command.

Step 3   Key in the following: A:\>**DIR ???.NEW** Enter

Step 4   Key in the following: A:\>**DIR *.BUD** Enter

```
MS-DOS Prompt                                      _ □ ×
A:\>DIR ???.NEW

 Volume in drive A is DATA
 Volume Serial Number is 3330-1807
 Directory of A:\

File not found
                  1,396,736 bytes free

A:\>DIR *.BUD

 Volume in drive A is DATA
 Volume Serial Number is 3330-1807
 Directory of A:\

JAN     BUD            73  04-23-00  4:03p JAN.BUD
MAR     BUD            71  04-23-00  4:03p MAR.BUD
APR     BUD            72  04-23-00  4:18p APR.BUD
```

```
FEB        BUD            75  04-23-00  4:03p FEB.BUD
           4 file(s)           291 bytes
           0 dir(s)     1,396,736 bytes free

A:\>_
```

WHAT'S HAPPENING? Files with file names of three characters and the extension **.NEW** no longer exist on the DATA disk. With the REN command and the use of the wildcards, you renamed four files with one command. You can also use wildcards with subdirectories.

Step 5   Key in the following: A:\>**COPY *.BUD TRIP** Enter

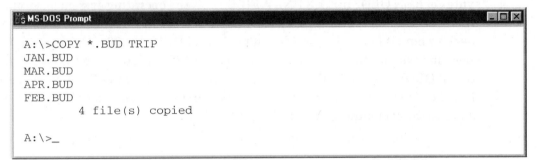

```
A:\>COPY *.BUD TRIP
JAN.BUD
MAR.BUD
APR.BUD
FEB.BUD
        4 file(s) copied

A:\>_
```

WHAT'S HAPPENING? You copied files with the **.BUD** extension from the root directory of the DATA disk to a subdirectory called **TRIP** on the DATA disk.

Step 6   Key in the following: A:\>**REN TRIP*.BUD *.PEN** Enter

Step 7   Key in the following: A:\>**DIR TRIP*.BUD** Enter

Step 8   Key in the following: A:\>**DIR TRIP*.PEN** Enter

```
A:\>REN TRIP\*.BUD *.PEN

A:\>DIR TRIP\*.BUD

 Volume in drive A is DATA
 Volume Serial Number is 3330-1807
 Directory of A:\TRIP

File not found
                 1,394,688 bytes free

A:\>DIR TRIP\*.PEN

 Volume in drive A is DATA
 Volume Serial Number is 3330-1807
 Directory of A:\TRIP

MAR        PEN            71  04-23-00  4:03p MAR.PEN
APR        PEN            72  04-23-00  4:18p APR.PEN
FEB        PEN            75  04-23-00  4:03p FEB.PEN
JAN        PEN            73  04-23-00  4:03p JAN.PEN
           4 file(s)           291 bytes
           0 dir(s)     1,394,688 bytes free

A:\>_
```

> **WHAT'S HAPPENING?** You successfully renamed all the files with the **.BUD** extension in the subdirectory **TRIP** on the DATA disk to a new set of files with the same file name but with the file extension of **.PEN**.

6.15   USING RENAME ON DIFFERENT DRIVES AND DIRECTORIES

Since REN is an internal command, you can use it at any time, for any file, in any drive, and in any directory. If you wish to rename a file on a different drive, you must specify on which drive the old file is located. If you want the file renamed in a different directory, you must specify in which directory the file is located. In the syntax of REN OLDFILE.EXT NEWFILE.EXT, the operating system looks only for OLDFILE.EXT on the designated drive and directory. It renames the file and leaves the file where it found it. If you do not preface OLDFILE.EXT with a drive letter, the operating system looks only on the default drive. When you key in the command REN B:OLDFILE.EXT NEWFILE.EXT, only the disk in Drive B will be searched for the file called OLDFILE.EXT. If a directory is involved, you must also include the name, so the command would read:

```
REN C:\JUNK\OLDFILE.EXT NEWFILE.EXT
```

In addition, there is a substantial difference between the COPY command and the REN command. With the COPY command, you can copy a file from one disk to another disk or one directory to another directory, ending up with two identical files in different locations. You *cannot* do this with the REN command because it changes the names of files in only one directory or disk at a time. Remember, with REN you are changing the name of an existing file in a specific location. REN finds a file by its name, which is the first parameter in the REN command on the designated disk or directory. It knows the file's location; the second parameter must be the new name only, not including a repeat of the location. REN cannot move a file from one location to another, nor can it copy a file. It simply renames a file, leaving it where it found it.

6.16   ACTIVITY: USING RENAME ON DIFFERENT DRIVES

Note: The DATA disk is in Drive A. A:\> is displayed.

Step 1   Key in the following: A:\>**C:** [Enter]

Step 2   Key in the following: C:\>**CD WINDOSBK** [Enter]
Note: If you are at a prompt other than C:\>, such as C:\WINDOWS> you would need to key in CD \WINDOSBK, indicating that WINDOSBK is off the root.

```
MS-DOS Prompt                                              _ □ ✕

A:\>C:

C:\>CD WINDOSBK

C:\WINDOSBK>_
```

> **WHAT'S HAPPENING?** You have changed the default drive to **C:** and have made **WINDOSBK** the default directory.

Step 3   Key in the following: C:\WINDOSBK>**DIR APRIL.TXT** Enter

Step 4   Key in the following: C:\WINDOSBK>**DIR A:\APRIL.TXT** Enter

Note: If you do not have **APRIL.TXT** on your DATA disk, copy it there now.

```
MS-DOS Prompt                                                    _ □ ✕

C:\WINDOSBK>DIR APRIL.TXT

 Volume in drive C is MILLENNIUM
 Volume Serial Number is 2B18-1301
 Directory of C:\WINDOSBK

APRIL    TXT            72  06-16-00  4:32p APRIL.TXT
         1 file(s)              72 bytes
         0 dir(s)   1,121,439,744 bytes free

C:\WINDOSBK>DIR A:\APRIL.TXT

 Volume in drive A is DATA
 Volume Serial Number is 3330-1807
 Directory of A:\

APRIL    TXT            72  04-23-00  4:18p APRIL.TXT
         1 file(s)              72 bytes
         0 dir(s)     1,394,688 bytes free

C:\WINDOSBK>_
```

WHAT'S HAPPENING? ➤ The directory display tells you that the file called **APRIL.TXT** does exist on both the root of the DATA disk in the A drive and in the **\WINDOSBK** subdirectory on the C drive.

Step 5   Key in the following: C:\WINDOSBK>**TYPE A:\APRIL.TXT** Enter

```
MS-DOS Prompt                                                    _ □ ✕

C:\WINDOSBK>TYPE A:\APRIL.TXT

This is my April file.
It is my fourth dummy file.
This is file 4.

C:\WINDOSBK>_
```

WHAT'S HAPPENING? ➤ You used the TYPE command to see the contents of the file called **APRIL.TXT** located on the DATA disk.

Step 6   Key in the following:
          C:\WINDOSBK>**REN A:\APRIL.TXT A:\APR.TST** Enter

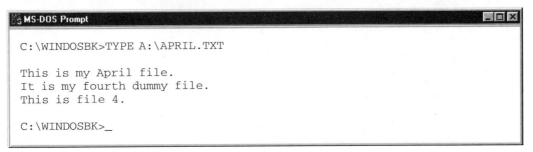

```
MS-DOS Prompt                                                    _ □ ✕

C:\WINDOSBK>REN A:\APRIL.TXT A:\APR.TST
Invalid parameter - A:\APR.TST

C:\WINDOSBK>_
```

WHAT'S
HAPPENING?   Remember, the syntax of this command is:

    REN [*drive:*][*path*]*oldfile*.*ext newfile.ext*

Since the operating system knows you cannot change a file name on any other disk except where the original file is located, it will not allow you to put a drive designator before the new file name.

Step 7   Key in the following: C:\WINDOSBK>**REN A:\APRIL.TXT APR.TST** Enter

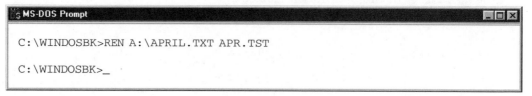

```
C:\WINDOSBK>REN A:\APRIL.TXT APR.TST

C:\WINDOSBK>_
```

WHAT'S
HAPPENING?   You see no messages because the syntax of the command you issued is correct. The file called **APRIL.TXT** is in the root directory of the DATA disk. You requested that REN change the name of this file from **APRIL.TXT** to a new file name **APR.TST**.

Step 8   Key in the following: C:\WINDOSBK>**DIR APRIL.TXT** Enter

Step 9   Key in the following: C:\WINDOSBK>**DIR A:\APRIL.TXT** Enter

```
C:\WINDOSBK>DIR APRIL.TXT

 Volume in drive C is MILLENNIUM
 Volume Serial Number is 2B18-1301
 Directory of C:\WINDOSBK

APRIL    TXT           72  06-16-00  4:32p APRIL.TXT
        1 file(s)              72 bytes
        0 dir(s)   1,121,439,744 bytes free

C:\WINDOSBK>DIR A:\APRIL.TXT

 Volume in drive A is DATA
 Volume Serial Number is 3330-1807
 Directory of A:\

File not found
                1,394,688 bytes free

C:\WINDOSBK>_
```

WHAT'S
HAPPENING?   You did not rename the file **APRIL.TXT** on the hard disk in the **\WINDOSBK** directory, only the one on the DATA disk. You got the message **File not found** for the DATA disk because the file no longer exists under the file name **A:\APRIL.TXT**.

Step 10   Key in the following: C:\WINDOSBK>**DIR A:\APR.TST** Enter

```
MS-DOS Prompt                                                    _ □ ×

C:\WINDOSBK>DIR A:\APR.TST

 Volume in drive A is DATA
 Volume Serial Number is 3330-1807
 Directory of A:\

APR        TST            72   04-23-00  4:18p APR.TST
           1 file(s)              72 bytes
           0 dir(s)       1,394,688 bytes free


C:\WINDOSBK>_
```

WHAT'S HAPPENING? → You successfully renamed the file in the root directory of the DATA disk from **APRIL.TXT** to **APR.TST**. Does the file **APR.TST** have the same contents as **APRIL.TXT**? It should because renaming changes only the file name, not the contents. To verify this, you can use the TYPE command.

Step 11   Key in the following: C:\WINDOSBK>**TYPE A:\APR.TST** [Enter]

```
MS-DOS Prompt                                                    _ □ ×

C:\WINDOSBK>TYPE A:\APR.TST

This is my April file.
It is my fourth dummy file.
This is file 4.

C:\WINDOSBK>_
```

WHAT'S HAPPENING? → If you check the screen display following Step 5, you will see that the file contents are identical. REN works the same way with subdirectories on other drives. In Activity 6.14, you copied the files with the **.BUD** extension to the subdirectory **TRIP** on the DATA disk; you then renamed them with the same file name but with the **.PEN** file extension.

Step 12   Key in the following: C:\WINDOSBK>**DIR A:\TRIP*.PEN** [Enter]

```
MS-DOS Prompt                                                    _ □ ×

C:\WINDOSBK>DIR A:\TRIP\*.PEN

 Volume in drive A is DATA
 Volume Serial Number is 3330-1807
 Directory of A:\TRIP

MAR        PEN            71   04-23-00  4:03p MAR.PEN
APR        PEN            72   04-23-00  4:18p APR.PEN
FEB        PEN            75   04-23-00  4:03p FEB.PEN
JAN        PEN            73   04-23-00  4:03p JAN.PEN
           4 file(s)             291 bytes
           0 dir(s)       1,394,688 bytes free


C:\WINDOSBK>_
```

WHAT'S HAPPENING? The files are there in the subdirectory **TRIP** on the DATA disk.

Step 13 Key in the following: C:\WINDOSBK>**REN A:\TRIP*.PEN *.INK** [Enter]

```
MS-DOS Prompt                                                      _ □ ✕

C:\WINDOSBK>REN A:\TRIP\*.PEN *.INK

C:\WINDOSBK>_
```

WHAT'S HAPPENING? Once again, all that appears is the system prompt. Notice how you placed the drive and path in front of *only* the file names that you wanted to change (the old file names). These files can only be renamed on the DATA disk in the subdirectory **TRIP**. The REN command does not move files; it only changes file names.

Step 14 Key in the following: C:\WINDOSBK>**DIR A:\TRIP*.PEN** [Enter]

Step 15 Key in the following: C:\WINDOSBK>**DIR A:\TRIP*.INK** [Enter]

```
MS-DOS Prompt                                                      _ □ ✕

C:\WINDOSBK>DIR A:\TRIP\*.PEN

 Volume in drive A is DATA
 Volume Serial Number is 3330-1807
 Directory of A:\TRIP

File not found
                      1,394,688 bytes free

C:\WINDOSBK>DIR A:\TRIP\*.INK

 Volume in drive A is DATA
 Volume Serial Number is 3330-1807
 Directory of A:\TRIP

APR      INK         72   04-23-00   4:18p APR.INK
FEB      INK         75   04-23-00   4:03p FEB.INK
JAN      INK         73   04-23-00   4:03p JAN.INK
MAR      INK         71   04-23-00   4:03p MAR.INK
         4 file(s)           291 bytes
         0 dir(s)      1,394,688 bytes free

C:\WINDOSBK>_
```

WHAT'S HAPPENING? You successfully renamed all the **.PEN** files in the subdirectory **TRIP** on the DATA disk. These files no longer exist with the **.PEN** file extension.

Step 16 Key in the following: C:\WINDOSBK>**CD ** [Enter]

Step 17 Key in the following: C:\>**A:** [Enter]

```
MS-DOS Prompt                                                      _ □ ✕

C:\WINDOSBK>CD \

C:\>A:
```

```
A:\>_
```

WHAT'S HAPPENING? ➡ You have returned to the root directory of the hard disk and also changed the default drive to the DATA disk location.

6.17 MOVING FILES AND RENAMING DIRECTORIES

You learned in Chapter 4 that you could use the MOVE command to rename a directory. In this chapter, you learned to use the RENAME command for renaming both files and subdirectories. The REN command renames files and subdirectories; it does not move them from one location to another.

The MOVE command was introduced in DOS 6.0. MOVE allows you to move files and subdirectories from one location to another. If you move a file or subdirectory individually, you can change the name as you move. If you move a group of files and/or subdirectories, you cannot change their names. The MOVE command includes a prompt that will warn you that you are about to overwrite a file. However, if you desire, you can turn off the warning. The full syntax diagram for the MOVE command is:

```
To move one or more files:
MOVE [/Y | /-Y] [drive:][path]filename1[,...] destination

To rename a directory:
MOVE [/Y | /-Y] [drive:][path]dirname1 dirname2

  [drive:][path]filename1   Specifies the location and name of the file or
                            files you want to move.
  destination               Specifies the new location of the file. Destination
                            can consist of a drive letter and colon, a
                            directory name, or a combination. If you are moving
                            only one file, you can also include a filename if
                            you want to rename the file when you move it.
  [drive:][path]dirname1    Specifies the directory you want to rename.
  dirname2                  Specifies the new name of the directory.

  /Y        Suppresses prompting to confirm creation of a directory or
            overwriting of the destination.
  /-Y       Causes prompting to confirm creation of a directory or
            overwriting of the destination.

The switch /Y may be present in the COPYCMD environment variable.
This may be overridden with /-Y on the command line.
```

The MOVE command will not only move files and directories from one directory to another but will also allow you to move them from one drive to another. This feature is especially useful in maintaining your hard disk.

6.18 ACTIVITY: MOVING FILES AND RENAMING DIRECTORIES

Note: The DATA disk is in Drive A. A:\> is displayed.

Step 1   Key in the following: A:\>**MD FILES** Enter

Step 2   Key in the following: A:\>**COPY *.99 FILES*.FIL** Enter

Step 3   Key in the following: A:\>**MD FILES\ROOM** Enter

Step 4   Key in the following: A:\>**COPY GOODBYE.NEW FILES** Enter

```
MS-DOS Prompt                                                    _ □ ×

A:\>MD FILES

A:\>COPY *.99 FILES\*.FIL
APR.99
FEB.99
MAR.99
JAN.99
        4 file(s) copied

A:\>MD FILES\ROOM

A:\>COPY GOODBYE.NEW FILES
        1 file(s) copied

A:\>_
```

 You have created the **FILES** directory with a directory beneath it called **ROOM**. You copied some files from the root directory of the DATA disk into the **FILES** directory.

Step 5   Key in the following: A:\>**DIR FILES** Enter

```
MS-DOS Prompt                                                    _ □ ×

A:\>DIR FILES

 Volume in drive A is DATA
 Volume Serial Number is 3330-1807
 Directory of A:\FILES


.               <DIR>         07-25-01   7:46p .
..              <DIR>         07-25-01   7:46p ..
APR     FIL        72  10-10-99   4:53p APR.FIL
FEB     FIL        75  10-10-99   4:53p FEB.FIL
MAR     FIL        71  10-10-99   4:53p MAR.FIL
JAN     FIL        73  10-10-99   4:53p JAN.FIL
ROOM            <DIR>         07-25-01   7:46p ROOM
GOODBYE NEW        34  01-01-02   4:32a GOODBYE.NEW
        5 file(s)            325 bytes
        3 dir(s)       1,391,104 bytes free

A:\>_
```

 You have a subdirectory called **ROOM** under the **FILES** directory on the DATA disk. You decide that you no longer care for the name **ROOM** and wish to call the directory **MYROOM**.

Step 6   Key in the following: A:\>**MOVE FILES\ROOM FILES\MYROOM** Enter

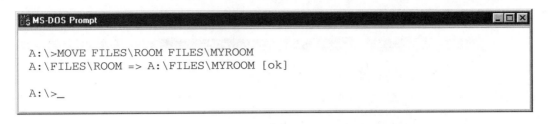

```
MS-DOS Prompt                                              _ □ X

A:\>MOVE FILES\ROOM FILES\MYROOM
A:\FILES\ROOM => A:\FILES\MYROOM [ok]

A:\>_
```

WHAT'S HAPPENING? You have renamed a subdirectory from **FILES\ROOM** to **FILES\MYROOM**. Notice the difference between the MOVE and REN syntax. When using REN, you do not give the path with the new name. When using MOVE to rename a directory, you do give the full path with the new name.

Step 7   Key in the following: A:\>**REN FILES\MYROOM PLACE** Enter

```
MS-DOS Prompt                                              _ □ X

A:\>REN FILES\MYROOM PLACE

A:\>_
```

WHAT'S HAPPENING? You see no **[ok]** message from the REN command, but you can verify that the subdirectory **MYROOM** was, indeed, renamed to **PLACE**.

Step 8   Key in the following: A:\>**DIR FILES** Enter

```
MS-DOS Prompt                                              _ □ X

A:\>DIR FILES

 Volume in drive A is DATA
 Volume Serial Number is 3330-1807
 Directory of A:\FILES

.                <DIR>        07-25-01  7:46p .
..               <DIR>        07-25-01  7:46p ..
APR      FIL         72  10-10-99  4:53p APR.FIL
FEB      FIL         75  10-10-99  4:53p FEB.FIL
MAR      FIL         71  10-10-99  4:53p MAR.FIL
JAN      FIL         73  10-10-99  4:53p JAN.FIL
PLACE            <DIR>        07-25-01  7:46p PLACE
GOODBYE  NEW         34  01-01-02  4:32a GOODBYE.NEW
         5 file(s)           325 bytes
         3 dir(s)      1,391,104 bytes free

A:\>_
```

WHAT'S HAPPENING? The directory name has again changed. Now you want to move a file. You use MOVE to move files from one location to another. If you try to move a file in the same drive and the same directory, it has the effect of eliminating the first file and replacing the contents of the second file with the contents of the first file. In the next steps you will see the results of such a task.

Step 9   Key in the following: A:\>**TYPE FILES\APR.FIL** Enter

Step 10   Key in the following: A:\>**TYPE FILES\JAN.FIL** Enter

```
MS-DOS Prompt                                                      _ □ ×

A:\>TYPE FILES\APR.FIL

This is my April file.
It is my fourth dummy file.
This is file 4.

A:\>TYPE FILES\JAN.FIL

This is my January file.
It is my first dummy file.
This is file 1.

A:\>_
```

WHAT'S
HAPPENING?   You can see that the contents are different as well as the file names.

Step 11   Key in the following: A:\>**MOVE FILES\APR.FIL FILES\JAN.FIL** Enter

```
MS-DOS Prompt                                                      _ □ ×

A:\>MOVE FILES\APR.FIL FILES\JAN.FIL
Overwrite A:\FILES\JAN.FIL (Yes/No/All)?_
```

WHAT'S
HAPPENING?   This warning by the MOVE command tells you that you are about to
              overwrite a file.

Step 12   Press **Y** Enter

```
MS-DOS Prompt                                                      _ □ ×

A:\>MOVE FILES\APR.FIL FILES\JAN.FIL
Overwrite A:\FILES\JAN.FIL (Yes/No/All)?y
A:\FILES\APR.FIL => A:\FILES\JAN.FIL [ok]

A:\>_
```

WHAT'S
HAPPENING?   Because you entered **Y** for yes, the file was overwritten.

Step 13   Key in the following: A:\>**TYPE FILES\APR.FIL** Enter

Step 14   Key in the following: A:\>**TYPE FILES\JAN.FIL** Enter

```
MS-DOS Prompt                                                      _ □ ×

A:\>TYPE FILES\APR.FIL
File not found - FILES\APR.FIL

A:\>TYPE FILES\JAN.FIL

This is my April file.
It is my fourth dummy file.
This is file 4.

A:\>_
```

> **WHAT'S HAPPENING?** The file **APR.FIL** no longer exists. It "moved" to a new file, **JAN.FIL**. Thus, **JAN.FIL** now holds the contents of the old **APR.FIL**. The old contents of **JAN.FIL** are gone. If this sounds confusing, it is. The lesson here is do not use MOVE when you mean REN. The following steps will show you how MOVE is useful when it is used wisely.

Step 15 Key in the following:
        A:\>**MOVE FILES\FEB.FIL FILES\PLACE\FEB.NEW** [Enter]

```
 MS-DOS Prompt                                                  _ □ ×

A:\>MOVE FILES\FEB.FIL FILES\PLACE\FEB.NEW
A:\FILES\FEB.FIL => A:\FILES\PLACE\FEB.NEW [ok]

A:\>_
```

> **WHAT'S HAPPENING?** You have, in essence, accomplished three separate functions with one command. First, you copied the file called **FEB.FIL** located in the **FILES** directory to the **FILES\PLACE** directory. Second, you gave it a new name, **FEB.NEW**. Third, you deleted **FEB.FIL** from the **FILES** directory. All this occurred using one command, MOVE, not three—COPY, REN, and DEL. If you used Explorer, you would have to take two steps—move the file, and then rename it. The command line provided a one-step solution.

Step 16 Key in the following: A:\>**DIR FILES** [Enter]

Step 17 Key in the following: A:\>**DIR FILES\PLACE** [Enter]

```
 MS-DOS Prompt                                                  _ □ ×

A:\>DIR FILES

 Volume in drive  A is DATA
 Volume Serial Number is 3330-1807
 Directory of A:\FILES

.               <DIR>         07-25-01  7:46p .
..              <DIR>         07-25-01  7:46p ..
MAR      FIL           71     10-10-99  4:53p MAR.FIL
JAN      FIL           72     10-10-99  4:53p JAN.FIL
PLACE           <DIR>         07-25-01  7:46p PLACE
GOODBYE  NEW           34     01-01-02  4:32a GOODBYE.NEW
        3 file(s)            177 bytes
        3 dir(s)       1,391,616 bytes free

A:\>DIR FILES\PLACE

 Volume in drive A is DATA
 Volume Serial Number is 3330-1807
 Directory of A:\FILES\PLACE

.               <DIR>         07-25-01  7:46p .
..              <DIR>         07-25-01  7:46p ..
FEB      NEW           75     10-10-99  4:53p FEB.NEW
        1 file(s)             75 bytes
```

```
        2 dir(s)        1,391,616 bytes free

A:\>_
```

WHAT'S HAPPENING?   The file called **FEB.FIL** is no longer in the **FILES** directory. It is, however, in the **FILES\PLACE** directory with the name of **FEB.NEW**. MOVE also works well with wildcards. However, when you use wildcards with the MOVE command, you cannot change file names.

Step 18 Key in the following: A:\>**MOVE FILES*.FIL FILES\PLACE*.TXT** Enter

```
MS-DOS Prompt                                              _ □ ×

A:\>MOVE FILES\*.FIL FILES\PLACE\*.TXT
Make directory "A:\FILES\PLACE\*.TXT"? [yn] _
```

WHAT'S HAPPENING?   The MOVE command thinks that you want to create a directory.

Step 19 Press **Y** Enter

```
MS-DOS Prompt                                              _ □ ×

A:\>MOVE FILES\*.FIL FILES\PLACE\*.TXT
Make directory "A:\FILES\PLACE\*.TXT"? [yn] y
Cannot move multiple files to a single file

A:\>_
```

WHAT'S HAPPENING?   As the message states, MOVE cannot combine the contents of files (concatenate files) and therefore cannot place these files into one file called ***.TXT**.

Step 20 Key in the following: A:\>**MOVE FILES*.FIL FILES\PLACE** Enter

```
MS-DOS Prompt                                              _ □ ×
A:\>MOVE FILES\*.FIL FILES\PLACE
A:\FILES\MAR.FIL => A:\FILES\PLACE\MAR.FIL [ok]
A:\FILES\JAN.FIL => A:\FILES\PLACE\JAN.FIL [ok]

A:\>_
```

WHAT'S HAPPENING?   Now that you have issued the command correctly, the files with the **.FIL** extension are no longer in the **FILES** directory but in the **PLACE** directory.

Step 21 Key in the following: A:\>**DIR FILES** Enter

Step 22 Key in the following: A:\>**DIR FILES\PLACE*.FIL** Enter

```
MS-DOS Prompt                                              _ □ ×

A:\>DIR FILES

 Volume in drive A is DATA
 Volume Serial Number is 3330-1807
```

```
Directory of A:\FILES

.               <DIR>           07-25-01  7:46p .
..              <DIR>           07-25-01  7:46p ..
PLACE           <DIR>           07-25-01  7:46p PLACE
GOODBYE  NEW               34  01-01-02  4:32a GOODBYE.NEW
         1 file(s)              34 bytes
         3 dir(s)        1,391,616 bytes free


A:\>DIR FILES\PLACE\*.FIL

 Volume in drive A is DATA
 Volume Serial Number is 3330-1807
 Directory of A:\FILES\PLACE

MAR      FIL               71  10-10-99  4:53p MAR.FIL
JAN      FIL               72  10-10-99  4:53p JAN.FIL
         2 file(s)             143 bytes
         0 dir(s)        1,391,616 bytes free


A:\>_
```

![WHAT'S HAPPENING?] The files with the **.FIL** extension were successfully moved from one location to another. You can move files from one drive to another and from one directory to another.

Step 23 Key in the following: A:\>**MOVE FILES\PLACE*.FIL CLASS** Enter

```
MS-DOS Prompt                                                          _ □ ×

A:\>MOVE FILES\PLACE\*.FIL CLASS
A:\FILES\PLACE\MAR.FIL => A:\CLASS\MAR.FIL [ok]
A:\FILES\PLACE\JAN.FIL => A:\CLASS\JAN.FIL [ok]

A:\>_
```

![WHAT'S HAPPENING?] The files with the **.FIL** extension are no longer located in the **FILES\PLACE** directory but were moved to the **CLASS** directory, keeping the same file names.

Step 24 Key in the following: A:\>**DIR FILES\PLACE*.FIL** Enter

Step 25 Key in the following: A:\>**DIR CLASS*.FIL** Enter

```
MS-DOS Prompt                                                          _ □ ×

A:\>DIR FILES\PLACE\*.FIL

 Volume in drive A is DATA
 Volume Serial Number is 3330-1807
 Directory of A:\FILES\PLACE

File not found
                     1,391,616 bytes free

A:\>DIR CLASS\*.FIL

 Volume in drive A is DATA
 Volume Serial Number is 3330-1807
 Directory of A:\CLASS
```

```
MAR       FIL            71  10-10-99  4:53p MAR.FIL
JAN       FIL            72  10-10-99  4:53p JAN.FIL
          2 file(s)              143 bytes
          0 dir(s)         1,391,616 bytes free

A:\>_
```

WHAT'S HAPPENING? The files were successfully moved. You can see that the MOVE command is very useful and very powerful. You can move entire subdirectory structures, along with the files in them, with one command.

Step 26 Key in the following: A:\>**MD START** Enter

Step 27 Key in the following: A:\>**MD START\SUBDIR** Enter

Step 28 Key in the following: A:\>**COPY *.FIL START\SUBDIR** Enter

```
MS-DOS Prompt                                              _ □ ×

A:\>MD START

A:\>MD START\SUBDIR

A:\>COPY *.FIL START\SUBDIR
MARCH.FIL
        1 file(s) copied

A:\>_
```

WHAT'S HAPPENING? You have created a new directory, **START**, that contains a child directory, **SUBDIR**, in which there is one file, **MARCH.FIL**. To see everything in the **START** directory structure, you will use the DIR command with two of its parameters: **/S** to view all the contents in the subdirectories and **/B** to see only the file and subdirectory names with none of the other information.

Step 29 Key in the following: A:\>**DIR START /S /B** Enter

```
MS-DOS Prompt                                              _ □ ×

A:\>DIR START /S /B
A:\START\SUBDIR
A:\START\SUBDIR\MARCH.FIL

A:\>_
```

WHAT'S HAPPENING? You can see that with this bare (**/B**) display, you do not see Volume in drive A is DATA, Volume Serial Number is 3330-1807, or Directory of A:\START. Nor do you see the amounts of drive space used or free. The bare display shows you directory names and file names only. You can see that the **START** directory contains only one subdirectory, **SUBDIR**, and no files. The subdirectory **SUBDIR** contains one file, **MARCH.FIL**, but you made a mistake. You actually wanted to place this entire directory structure beginning with **START** under the subdirectory **FILES**. You can move the entire structure with the MOVE command.

Step 30 Key in the following: A:\>**MOVE START FILES** [Enter]

```
MS-DOS Prompt                                                  _ □ ✕

A:\>MOVE START FILES
A:\START => A:\FILES\START [ok]

A:\>_
```

 You see the **[ok]** display, telling you the command has properly executed. What actually happened? You can use the DIR command to verify that the **START** directory is no longer under the root, but that it and all of its contents, is now under the **FILES** directory.

Step 31 Key in the following: A:\>**DIR START** [Enter]

Step 32 Key in the following: A:\>**DIR FILES** [Enter]

```
MS-DOS Prompt                                                  _ □ ✕

A:\>DIR START

 Volume in drive A is DATA
 Volume Serial Number is 3330-1807
 Directory of A:\

File not found
                    1,390,080 bytes free

A:\>DIR FILES

 Volume in drive A is DATA
 Volume Serial Number is 3330-1807
 Directory of A:\FILES

.               <DIR>        07-25-01  7:46p .
..              <DIR>        07-25-01  7:46p ..
START           <DIR>        07-25-01  8:02p START
PLACE           <DIR>        07-25-01  7:46p PLACE
GOODBYE  NEW          34     01-01-02  4:32a GOODBYE.NEW
        1 file(s)              34 bytes
        4 dir(s)      1,390,080 bytes free

A:\>_
```

As you can see, the **START** subdirectory is no longer on the root of the DATA disk. It is now in the **FILES** directory, but has the entire subdirectory structure been moved? You can verify this further with the DIR /S /B command.

Step 33 Key in the following: A:\>**DIR FILES\START /S /B** [Enter]

```
MS-DOS Prompt                                                      _ □ ✕

A:\>DIR FILES\START /S /B
A:\FILES\START\SUBDIR
A:\FILES\START\SUBDIR\MARCH.FIL

A:\>_
```

WHAT'S HAPPENING? You can see that the entire **START** directory structure was moved successfully to the **FILES** directory.

6.19 DELTREE REVISITED

In Chapter 4, you learned two ways to remove a directory. One was by using the RD command. This was the bottom up approach. Since you create directories from the top down, you had to delete directories from the bottom up. If the subdirectory you wished to remove had more subdirectories beneath it, you had to remove those subdirectories first. **DELTREE** allows you to delete directories from the top down with one command. In addition, when you use RD, not only must you remove any subdirectories, but you must first delete any files that are in each subdirectory. Thus, removing directories with RD is a two-step process—first delete files (DEL), then eliminate the directory (RD). Removing directories from the GUI is also a two-step process—delete and empty the Recycle Bin. DELTREE has the advantage that in one fell swoop, you eliminate files and directories—no second step is required. It is a very powerful, but also a very dangerous command.

6.20 ACTIVITY: USING RD AND DELTREE

Note: The DATA disk is in Drive A. A:\> is displayed.

Step 1   Key in the following: A:\>**RD FILES\PLACE** [Enter]

```
MS-DOS Prompt                                                      _ □ ✕

A:\>RD FILES\PLACE
Invalid path, not directory,
or directory not empty

A:\>_
```

WHAT'S HAPPENING? The portion of the message that applies here is that the **FILES\PLACE** directory is not empty of files. Thus, you have to take a step preceding the RD command.

Step 2   Key in the following: A:\>**DEL FILES\PLACE** [Enter]

```
MS-DOS Prompt                                                      _ □ ✕

A:\>DEL FILES\PLACE
All files in directory will be deleted!
```

```
Are you sure (Y/N)?_
```

WHAT'S HAPPENING? You had to use the DEL command to eliminate the files. The command **DEL FILES\PLACE** implied or defaulted to all the files in the **PLACE** directory. You could have keyed in **DEL FILES\PLACE*.***, but ***.*** was not necessary since, if you do not include a value with DEL, the default is all files.

Step 3   Press **Y** [Enter]

Step 4   Key in the following: A:\>**RD FILES\PLACE** [Enter]

Step 5   Key in the following: A:\>**DIR FILES** [Enter]

```
MS-DOS Prompt                                                    _ □ ✕

A:\>RD FILES\PLACE

A:\>DIR FILES

 Volume in drive A is DATA
 Volume Serial Number is 3330-1807
 Directory of A:\FILES

.               <DIR>        07-25-01  7:46p .
..              <DIR>        07-25-01  7:46p ..
START           <DIR>        07-25-01  8:02p START
GOODBYE  NEW           34    01-01-02  4:32a GOODBYE.NEW
        1 file(s)              34 bytes
        3 dir(s)        1,391,104 bytes free

A:\>_
```

WHAT'S HAPPENING? Once you eliminated the files from the **PLACE** directory using DEL, you could remove the directory using RD. If you wanted to eliminate the **FILES** directory using RD, you would still have to delete the files that were in it. In this case, using DELTREE is much faster because it is a one-step process. In addition, if you had any hidden or system files, DELTREE would delete those as well. If you tried that in My Computer, it would tell you it could not delete those files unless you turned on the option of showing all files, thus, again, taking more steps.

Step 6   Key in the following: A:\>**DELTREE FILES** [Enter]

```
MS-DOS Prompt                                                    _ □ ✕

A:\>DELTREE FILES
Delete directory "FILES" and all its subdirectories? [yn] _
```

WHAT'S HAPPENING? As you can see, DELTREE is offering to delete files and directories. **FILES** is the parameter you included with DELTREE.

Step 7   Press **Y** [Enter]

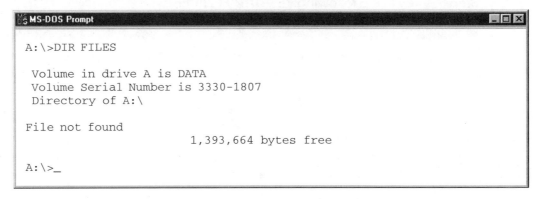

```
A:\>DELTREE FILES
Delete directory "FILES" and all its subdirectories? [yn] y
Deleting FILES...

A:\>_
```

WHAT'S HAPPENING? The message states that the files were deleted. Was the subdirectory also removed?

Step 8   Key in the following: A:\>**DIR FILES** Enter

```
A:\>DIR FILES

 Volume in drive A is DATA
 Volume Serial Number is 3330-1807
 Directory of A:\

File not found
                     1,393,664 bytes free

A:\>_
```

WHAT'S HAPPENING? The directory **FILES** was removed. DELTREE is fast, but keep in mind that "fast" can be "dangerous."

6.21   BACKING UP YOUR DATA DISK

You should get into the habit of backing up your data files so that, if something happens to the original data, you will have a copy of the original material. In data-processing circles, this habit is called "disaster and recovery planning." It means exactly what it says. If there is a disaster—fire, flood, power surge, theft, head crash, coffee spilled on a disk—what is your plan to recover your programs and data?

Most application programs today come on CD-ROM, but there are still programs that come on diskette. Backing up application program disks can be tricky, especially on *copy-protected* disks (which means you cannot back them up with regular operating system commands). You should never back up your program or software application disks until you understand how the application programs work. Application software that comes on diskettes provides documentation that instructs you how to back up the specific application program disk you own.

Backing up a hard disk is a special circumstance, using special operating commands and procedures. You cannot and should not back up the hard disk using the techniques that will be described here because the contents of a hard disk will not fit on one floppy disk.

However, you can and should back up all the data on any data disk with the following techniques. There are three ways to back up data files. One way is to back up the entire data disk—this backs up all the files and all the subdirectories. To do this, you use the DISKCOPY command, which makes an identical copy of a disk, track for track and sector for sector. You can use DISKCOPY on floppy disks.

You can also use the COPY command, which backs up files from floppy disk to floppy disk or specific files in specific directories on the hard disk. The third method, using the XCOPY command, will be discussed later. Never use the MOVE command for backup purposes. The MOVE command, although useful in placing files onto a floppy disk from a hard disk, removes the files from their original location. Thus, you end up with only one copy of your data files, which defeats the purpose of backing up.

Typically, data files are backed up at the end of every work session so that you can keep your data files current. It is very important to acquire a regular backup routine so that it becomes an automatic process.

Usually with application software you are not so worried about backing up the programs. If something happens to the hard disk, you can recover and reinstall the programs from the original purchased CDs or disks. However, the data that you create is unrecoverable unless you have backed it up. A common technique to back up data from a hard disk is to purchase a device called a tape backup. This device allows the user the ease of backing up the hard disk without having to sit in front of the computer and keep inserting blank floppy disks. However, the important message is whatever technique you use, *back up your data files!*

In this text, you have been placing all your data files on a floppy disk. Backing up this disk is the easiest kind of backup to perform. It is also extremely useful. With a backup copy of the DATA disk, if you should have a problem, you would not have to go back to Chapter 2 and redo all the activities and homework. In the next activity, you will back up your DATA disk.

6.22 ACTIVITY: BACKING UP WITH THE DISKCOPY COMMAND

Note 1: The DATA disk is in Drive A. A:\> is displayed.
Note 2: DISKCOPY requires that media types be the same. See Table 6.1.

Data Disk Media Type	Blank Disk to Use
3½-inch, 720KB double-density disk	3½-inch, 720KB double-density disk
3½-inch, 1.44 MB high-density disk	3½-inch, 1.44 MB high-density disk

TABLE 6.1 MATCHING MEDIA TYPES

Step 1   Get either a blank disk, a disk that has not been used, or a disk that has data on it that you no longer want. Label it "BACKUP DATA disk."

Step 2   Key in the following: A:\>**DISKCOPY A: A:** Enter

```
MS-DOS Prompt                                          _ □ ×

A:\>DISKCOPY A: A:

Insert SOURCE diskette in drive A:
```

```
Press any key to continue . . .
```

WHAT'S HAPPENING? You are asked to put the SOURCE disk that you wish to copy in Drive A. In this case, the DATA disk, which you want to copy, is already in Drive A. You keyed in two disk drives, **A** and **A**, to ensure that you do not accidentally copy the hard disk. You are telling DISKCOPY to make a copy from the disk in Drive A to the disk in Drive A.

Step 3   Press **Enter**

```
MS-DOS Prompt                                              _ □ ×

Copying 80 tracks, 18 sectors per track, 2 side(s)

Reading from source diskette . . .
```

WHAT'S HAPPENING? The number of tracks and sectors will vary depending on the disk media type. The DISKCOPY command tells the operating system to copy everything on the disk in Drive A (the SOURCE) to RAM. While this program is doing the copying, the cursor flashes on the screen. When the command is completed or the program has finished executing (copying), you need to take another step. You receive the following prompt:

```
Insert TARGET diskette in drive A:

Press any key to continue . . .
```

This prompt tells you to remove the SOURCE disk from Drive A and insert the blank or TARGET disk in Drive A so that the operating system has a place to copy the information.

Step 4   Remove your original DATA disk from Drive A. Insert the blank disk labeled "BACKUP DATA disk" into Drive A. This is your target disk. Close or latch the drive door. Press **Enter**

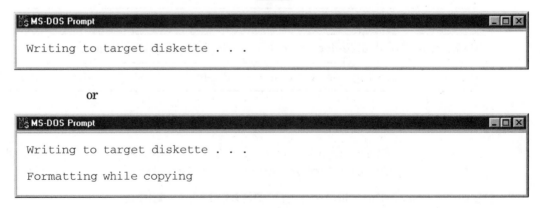

```
MS-DOS Prompt                                              _ □ ×

Writing to target diskette . . .
```

or

```
MS-DOS Prompt                                              _ □ ×

Writing to target diskette . . .

Formatting while copying
```

WHAT'S HAPPENING? Again, you see the flashing cursor. Now whatever was copied into RAM is being copied or written to the blank disk in Drive A. The message you see depends on whether or not the disk has been previously formatted.

```
Do you wish to write another duplicate of this disk (Y/N)? _
```

The prompt tells you that the program has finished executing and now asks you if you want to create another identical copy of the DATA disk? In this case, you do not.

Step 5   Press **N**

```
s MS-DOS Prompt                                                    _ □ ×

Volume Serial Number is 1BE1-201B

Copy another diskette (Y/N)? _
```

WHAT'S
HAPPENING?   You see another question: Do you want to execute DISKCOPY again to copy another disk? In this case, you do not wish to make another copy, so you key in **N**. The Volume Serial Number, by the way, changes each time you use the DISKCOPY command.

Step 6   Press **N**

```
s MS-DOS Prompt                                                    _ □ ×

Copy another diskette (Y/N)? N

A:\>_
```

WHAT'S
HAPPENING?   Because of the DISKCOPY command, you now have two copies of the DATA disk, the original and the backup. At the end of each work session, you should follow these steps to back up your DATA disk. You do not need a new backup disk each time. Keep using the same backup disk over and over. You are merely keeping current by date; you do not need an archival or historical record of each day's work. You should also make a backup copy of your APPLICATION disk. However, if you wish to be prudent, it is wise to have more than one backup copy of your disks. As you can imagine, the only time you need your copy of the data is when something has gone wrong. This is not the time you want to find out that your only copy of the data is bad. It is also a good idea to check your backed up data periodically to ensure that it is good data and that you can recover it if you need to. Remember, DISKCOPY makes an exact duplicate of the source diskette. Anything that was previously on the target diskette is destroyed in this process.

Some organizations, such as banks and the IRS, may need to recreate records, so they will have not only a *disaster and recovery plan* but also *archival data* or an *archival backup*. It is sometimes called a transaction history. Organizations like this need far more than a simple backup copy. For instance, if you go into the bank today and say you are missing the $100.00 deposit you made last week, the bank cannot tell you that they do not know what happened last week. The bank needs to be able to recreate all the transactions that occurred on the day in question.

Just having a backup copy of your account for today or even yesterday is not sufficient. Most PC users, however, do not need archival data. Simply backing up their data is sufficient.

Step 7   Remove the disk labeled "BACKUP DATA disk" and keep it in a safe place until you need it again to make another backup.

WHAT'S HAPPENING!   You now have a backup copy of your DATA disk. You may wish to repeat the steps with another disk to backup your APPLICATION disk too. Every time you complete a chapter, it is a good idea to update your backups so that they are kept current. In this way, if something happens to one of the original disks, you have lost only one chapter's work.

6.23   BACKING UP FILES WITH THE COPY COMMAND

Note: The following material is informational and meant *only to be read*. It is not an activity.

Using the DISKCOPY command backs up an entire floppy disk. More often than not, however, you need to back up only specific files, or you want to back up files from the hard disk to a floppy disk or a removable drive such as a Zip drive. Remember that you can also use the COPY command to back up specific files. The syntax does not change. It is as follows:

```
COPY [drive:][path]source.fil [drive:][path]destination.fil
```

You can also back up files from one floppy disk to another with the COPY command. Be sure that the destination disk is already formatted because COPY does not format a new disk as DISKCOPY does. Furthermore, COPY can be used only if you have two floppy disk drives. Since you are using two disk drives, COPY does not require identical disk media types. For example, you can copy from a 5¼-inch, 360KB disk to a 3½-inch, 1.44 MB disk. You would place the source disk in Drive A and the destination disk in Drive B and key in:

```
A:\>COPY *.*  B:\
```

A:\> is the default drive. COPY is the command. *.* means every file with every file extension—the first * represents any file name, the second * represents any file extension. COPY goes to the source disk to find each file in the root directory. As it copies the source file, it lists the file name on the screen. B:\ represents the root directory of the destination disk. Since you give no file names following B:\, COPY assumes that you want the same file name on the destination disk. If there is a file with the same name on the destination disk, COPY overwrites it.

If you want to back up files from a hard disk, you can also use the COPY command to copy the files in the individual subdirectories. However, you must be sure that there are not too many files in a subdirectory to fit on a floppy disk. Look at the following display:

```
MS-DOS Prompt                                                      _ □ ×

C:\WINDOSBK>DIR *.TMP

 Volume in drive C is MILLENNIUM
 Volume Serial Number is 2B18-1301
 Directory of C:\WINDOSBK

APRIL      TMP          72   04-23-00   4:03p  APRIL.TMP
BONJOUR    TMP          53   04-23-00   4:03p  BONJOUR.TMP
FEB        TMP          75   04-23-00   4:03p  FEB.TMP
GOODBYE    TMP          34   01-01-02   4:32a  GOODBYE.TMP
JANUARY    TMP          73   04-23-00   4:03p  JANUARY.TMP
JAN        TMP          73   04-23-00   4:03p  JAN.TMP
MAR        TMP          71   04-23-00   4:03p  MAR.TMP
MARCH      TMP          71   04-23-00   4:03p  MARCH.TMP
APR        TMP          72   04-23-00   4:18p  APR.TMP
            9 file(s)            594 bytes
            0 dir(s)   1,121,357,824 bytes free

C:\WINDOSBK>_
```

After **9 file(s)**, the number is **594 bytes**. This number tells you that these nine files require only 594 bytes and will easily fit on a floppy disk. On the other hand, you may get a display like the one that follows:

```
MS-DOS Prompt                                                      _ □ ×

 Volume in drive F is BETTES F
 Volume Serial Number is 2F4B-16FD
 Directory of F:\ENCARTA

.                 <DIR>         10-22-97   4:31p  .
..                <DIR>         10-22-97   4:31p  ..
ENCRES97 DLL    2,681,344       08-12-96   8:47p  ENCRES97.DLL
DECO_32  DLL      134,144       08-12-96   2:34p  DECO_32.DLL
E97SPAM  INI        1,434       08-12-96   2:40p  E97SPAM.INI
ENCTITLE DLL      355,328       08-12-96   8:47p  ENCTITLE.DLL
YBBST97A DAT       13,204       08-12-96   2:43p  YBBST97A.DAT
EEUIL10  DLL      526,336       08-12-96   2:34p  EEUIL10.DLL
SUBSCRIB EXE      212,992       08-12-96   2:36p  SUBSCRIB.EXE
DISCS    HLP       17,258       08-12-96   8:45p  DISCS.HLP
ENC97    HLP      863,913       08-12-96   8:46p  ENC97.HLP
ENC97    CNT        6,429       08-12-96   8:45p  ENC97.CNT
WEBTIPS  HLP       60,053       08-12-96   2:36p  WEBTIPS.HLP
README   HLP       84,343       08-12-96   2:34p  README.HLP
INST97A  LOG       20,848       11-16-97   3:42p  INST97A.LOG
ENC97F   STR    1,520,354       08-12-96   8:46p  ENC97F.STR
ENCART97 DAT    3,429,346       08-12-96   8:46p  ENCART97.DAT
UNINSTAL EXE       78,188       08-12-96   8:53p  UNINSTAL.EXE
ENC97    EXE    1,715,200       08-12-96   8:45p  ENC97.EXE
ENCART97 ANN            4       10-05-96  11:49a  ENCART97.ANN
UPDATES          <DIR>          10-22-97   4:31p  UPDATES
           18 file(s)     11,720,718 bytes
            3 dir(s)     921,403,392 bytes free

F:\ENCARTA>_
```

The number is now **18 file(s)** that occupy **11,720,718 bytes**, which will not fit on a single floppy disk. However, the files would fit on a 100 MB Zip cartridge.

Only if the files will fit on a floppy disk can you use the COPY command. Thus, if you wanted to back up the subdirectory \WINDOSBK, the command would be keyed in as:

```
C:\>COPY C:\WINDOSBK\*.* A:
```

This command, however, would not copy files in any subdirectories under the \WINDOSBK subdirectory, only the files in the \WINDOSBK directory. You would have to key in another command such as:

```
C:\>COPY \WINDOSBK\DATA\*.* A:
```

You cannot and must not copy all the files from a hard disk to a floppy disk with the COPY command. There are too many files on the hard disk, and they will not fit on a single floppy disk. There are backup utilities to back up large volumes, but they need a destination other than a floppy disk.

A question that arises is how often should you back up data? If you have backed up files to floppies or a tape and have not changed your original files, you do not need to back them up. The files you are interested in backing up are those that have changed or those that are new. A rule of thumb to follow is how long would it take you to recreate your data. If you think in those terms, you will make regular backups.

CHAPTER SUMMARY

1. DEL eliminates files.
2. Deleting files helps you manage your disks and directories.
3. The syntax for the DEL command is:

    ```
    DEL [drive:][path]filename
    ```

4. Wildcards can be used with DEL.
5. DEL does not eliminate the data on the disk, only the entry in the directory table.
6. Once a file has been deleted, it cannot be recovered except with special utility programs.
7. Before you use wildcards with DEL, it is wise to use the DIR command to see what is going to be erased.
8. The /P parameter prompts you to confirm whether or not you wish to delete a file.
9. You can change the names of files or directories with the RENAME or REN command.
10. The syntax for renaming is:

```
RENAME [drive:][path][directoryname1 | filename1] [directoryname2 | filename2]
REN [drive:][path][directoryname1 | filename1] [directoryname2 | filename2]
```

11. Renaming can be done only on one drive or directory. RENAME does not move files.
12. Renaming changes only file names; not contents of files.
13. With the REN command, you use the path only with the original filename, and do not repeat it with the new filename.
14. Wildcards can be used with the REN command.

15. Before you use wildcards with the REN command, it is wise to use the DIR command to see what files are going to be affected by renaming.

16. Once a file is renamed, it cannot be found under its old name.

17. The MOVE command can be used either to change the name of a subdirectory or to move files from one location to another. When you use MOVE, two steps are taken: the files are copied to the new location and deleted from the old location.

18. You may remove directories with either RD or DELTREE. With RD, you must remove files first and then any directories. DELTREE does it all.

19. It is wise to make backup copies of data files so that, if something happens, you have another source of data.

20. You can back up a floppy disk with the DISKCOPY command, or you can back up files on your disk using the COPY command. The wildcard *.* allows you to back up all the files in a directory.

KEY TERMS

archival backup   copy-protected
archival data   disaster and recovery plan

DISCUSSION QUESTIONS

1. Explain why you may want to eliminate files from a disk.
2. When you delete a file, the file is not actually removed from the disk. What really happens?
3. Give the syntax of the DEL command and explain each part of the syntax.
4. The strength of wildcards is also a weakness. Explain this statement, using DEL.
5. When deleting files, why should you key in DIR with global file specifications first?
6. Explain the purpose and function of the /P parameter with the DEL command.
7. Why would you want to change the name of a file?
8. Explain the purpose and function of the RENAME or REN command.
9. Give the syntax of the REN command and explain each part of the syntax.
10. What is the difference between the REN and RENAME commands?
11. What is the difference between the RENAME and COPY commands?
12. If you are using the REN command and get the message, "Duplicate file name or file in use," what could it mean?
13. What is the function and purpose of the MOVE command?
14. Give the syntax of the MOVE command and explain each part of the syntax.
15. Compare and contrast MOVE and COPY.
16. What is the difference between the MOVE and the REN commands?
17. Compare and contrast the DELTREE command with the RD command.
18. What process could you use to back up specific files?
19. What process could you use to back up a subdirectory?
20. Why would you not copy all the files from the hard disk to a floppy disk with the DISKCOPY command?

21. Why would you not copy all the files from a hard disk to a floppy disk with the COPY command?

TRUE/FALSE QUESTIONS

For each question, circle the letter T if the question is true and the letter F if the question is false.

T F 1. REN and RENAME perform identical functions.

T F 2. It is not possible to find a file that has been renamed if you do not know its new name.

T F 3. When using wildcards with the MOVE command, you cannot change the destination file name.

T F 4. You cannot use REN on subdirectories.

T F 5. If you use the command DEL TRIP and TRIP is a subdirectory name, the default parameter is all files (*.*).

COMPLETION QUESTIONS

Write the correct answer in each blank space.

6. One way to verify that a file has been deleted is to use the _____ command.

7. The REN command does not move files. Its only function is to _____ a file name.

8. The command for making an exact duplicate of a floppy disk is _____.

9. After you complete a work session, an important procedure to follow to ensure not losing your data is to _____ your original disk.

10. The parameter that allows you to confirm whether or not you wish to delete a file is _____.

MULTIPLE CHOICE QUESTIONS

For each question, write the letter for the correct answer in the blank space.

11. DEL is a command that
    a. deletes a subdirectory.
    b. can delete only one file at a time.
    c. can be used with wildcards.
    d. none of the above

12. Prior to using wildcards with the DEL command,
    a. it is a good idea to confirm visually the files to be erased using DIR.
    b. it is wise to remember that wildcards have opposite meanings when used with DIR and COPY.
    c. remember that only data files can be removed with the DEL command.
    d. remember that only program files can be removed with the DEL command.

13. When A:\> is the default and DEL CLASS.DBF is keyed in,
    a. the file CLASS.DBF will be deleted from the default drive.
    b. the file CLASS.DBF will be deleted from Drive C.
    c. nothing will happen.
    d. none of the above

14. Using the command DELTREE *directory_name* only
    a. deletes the files from the specified directory.
    b. deletes the files from the specified directory and its child directories.
    c. deletes the specified directory and all subdirectories and files contained therein.
    d. deletes the subdirectories contained in the specified directory.

15. The MOVE command
    a. can be used to rename a directory.
    b. can be used to make copies of files.
    c. can move an entire directory structure to a new location.
    d. both a and c

WRITING COMMANDS

Write the correct steps or commands to perform the required action as if you were at the computer. The prompt will indicate the default drive and directory.

16. Remove the file called **CATS** in the directory called **ANIMALS** located under the root directory of Drive A.

    `A:\TEST>`

17. Delete all the files with the **.OLD** file extension in the subdirectory **WHAT** located under the current directory on the default drive.

    `C:\JUNK>`

18. Change the extension of the **COLOR** file from **.DOT** to **.DOC**. The file is located in the **PAINT** directory under the root directory on Drive A.

    `C:\>`

19. Change the file extension from **.FIL** to **.TXT** for all the files in the **FURN** subdirectory located under the root directory on Drive C.

    `A:\>`

20. Eliminate the file called **MYFILE.TXT**, located in the subdirectory **JUNK** on Drive C.

    `C:\JUNK>`

APPLICATION ASSIGNMENTS

Note 1: Place the APPLICATION disk in Drive A. Be sure to work on the APPLICA-
TION disk, not the DATA disk.

Note 2: The homework problems will assume Drive C is the hard disk and the
APPLICATION disk is in Drive A. If you are using another drive, such as
floppy Drive B or hard Drive D, be sure and substitute that drive letter when
reading the questions and creating the answers.

Note 3: All subdirectories that are created will be under the root directory unless
otherwise specified.

Note 4: The root directory of the APPLICATION disk is the default drive and directory.

PROBLEM SET I

PROBLEM A

Note: If the DATA disk is in Drive A, remove it and place it in a safe place.

CAUTION!   **DO *NOT* USE THE DATA DISK FOR THESE APPLICATION
PROBLEMS. USE THE APPLICATION DISK.**

A-a   Insert the APPLICATION disk into Drive A.

A-b   Copy all the files from the **WINDOSBK\MEDIA\TV** subdirectory to the
root directory of the APPLICATION disk.

A-c   On the APPLICATION disk, rename the file called **DRAMA.TV** to
SERIOUS.TV.

1. Which command did you use to rename the file?
   a. REN DRAMA.TV SERIOUS.TV
   b. REN SERIOUS.TV DRAMA.TV
   c. COPY DRAMA.TV SERIOUS.TV
   d. COPY SERIOUS.TV DRAMA.TV

A-d   Execute the DIR command looking only for the file called **DRAMA.TV**.

2. What message is displayed?
   a. Invalid File Parameter
   b. File not found
   c. Required parameter missing
   d. no message is displayed

A-e   Rename the filed called **SERIOUS.TV** to **DRAMA.TV**.

3. Which command did you use?
   a. REN DRAMA.TV SERIOUS.TV
   b. REN SERIOUS.TV DRAMA.TV
   c. COPY DRAMA.TV SERIOUS.TV
   d. COPY SERIOUS.TV DRAMA.TV

A-f   Key in the following: **TYPE SERIOUS.TV** Enter

4. What message is displayed?
   a. File not found – SERIOUS.TV
   b. File not found
   c. Required parameter missing
   d. no message is displayed

A-g   Key in the following: **TYPE DRAMA.TV** Enter

5. What television series is displayed?
   a. The Rosie O'Donnell Show
   b. Seinfeld
   c. The Practice
   d. Dallas

PROBLEM B

Note: Remember that the root directory of the APPLICATION disk is the default
drive and directory.

B-a   Copy all files from the **WINDOSBK** subdirectory that have the file
       extension of **.DOS** to the root directory of the APPLICATION disk keeping
       the file names the same.

6. How many files were copied?
   a. one
   b. two
   c. three
   d. four

B-b   Rename all the files on the APPLICATION disk that have a file extension
       of **.DOS** to the same file name but with **.WG** as the file extension
       (remember wildcards).

7. Which command did you use?
   a. COPY *.DOS *.WG
   b. REN *.DOS *.WG
   c. COPY ?.DOS ?.WG
   d. REN ?.DOS ?.WG

B-c   Make copies of all the **.WG** files on the APPLICATION disk keeping the
       same file name but with a new extension of **.RRR**.

8. Which command did you use?
   a. DIR *.RRR
   b. REN *.WG *.RRR
   c. DIR *.WG
   d. COPY *.WG *.RRR

B-d   Make copies of all the **.WG** files on the APPLICATION disk keeping the
       same file names but with a new extension of **.MMM**.

9. What date is listed for the WILDTWO.MMM file?
   a. 02-13-00
   b. 12-31-01
   c. 12-31-00
   d. 02-13-99

B-e   Using the relative path, move all the files with the **.RRR** file extension to
       the **PHONE** subdirectory.

10. What command did you use?
    a. COPY *.RRR PHONE
    b. REN *.RRR PHONE
    c. MOVE *.RRR PHONE
    d. MOVE PHONE *.RRR

B-f   Execute the DIR command looking only for files in the root directory of
       the APPLICATION disk that have the **.RRR** file extension.

11. How many files were located?
    a. one
    b. two
    c. three
    d. no files were located

B-g   Execute the DIR command looking only for files in the **PHONE**
       subdirectory that have the **.RRR** file extension.

12. How many files were located?
    a. one
    b. two
    c. three
    d. no files were located

B-h   Rename all the files that have the extension of **.WG** to the same file
       name but with **.DOS** as the file extension. Use a wildcard.

13. Which command did you use?
    a. COPY *.DOS *.WG
    b. REN *.DOS *.WG
    c. COPY *.WG *.DOS
    d. REN *.WG *.DOS

B-i   Key in the following:
       A:\>**MOVE WILDONE.MMM PHONE\OLD\WILD.MMM** [Enter]

14. What message is displayed?
    a. A:\WILDONE.MMM => a:\phone\old\wild.mmm [ok]
    b. A:\WILDONE.MMM => A:\PHONE\OLD\WILD.MMM [Unable
       to create destination]
    c. A:\WILDONE.MMM => a:\phone\old\wild.mmm [No such
       directory]
    d. no message is displayed

B-j   Delete all the files with the **.MMM** extension. Use a wildcard.

15. Which command did you use?
     a. DEL *.MMM
     b. DEL PHONE*.MMM
     c. RD PHONE*.MMM
     d. MOVE *.MMM

16. What message is displayed when you have finished executing the command?
     a. Duplicate file name
     b. File not found
     c. Duplicate file name or file not found
     d. no message was displayed

B-k   Using the relative path, delete all the files with the **.RRR** extension on the APPLICATION disk. Use a wildcard. (*Hint:* Remember DIR /S.)

17. Which command did you use?
     a. DEL *.RRR
     b. DEL PHONE*.RRR
     c. RD PHONE*.RRR
     d. MOVE *.RRR

PROBLEM C

C-a   Copy the file from the **WINDOSBK\FINANCE** directory called **BALANCE.TKR** to the root of the APPLICATION disk.

C-b   Create a subdirectory called **SERIES** under the root of the APPLICATION disk.

C-c   Copy all the files on the root of the APPLICATION disk with the extension **.99** to the **SERIES** directory.

C-d   Using the relative path, move the file called **BALANCE.TKR** from the root directory of the APPLICATION disk to the **SERIES** directory.

18. Which command did you use with BALANCE.TKR?
     a. COPY BALANCE.TKR SERIES
     b. DEL SERIES\BALANCE.TKR
     c. REN BALANCE.TKR SERIES
     d. MOVE BALANCE.TKR SERIES

19. The file BALANCE.TKR is now in
     a. only the SERIES directory.
     b. only on the root of the APPLICATION disk.
     c. the WINDOSBK\FINANCE directory on the hard drive and SERIES directory on the APPLICATION disk.
     d. none of the above

C-e   From the root of the APPLICATION disk using the relative path, delete the file **BALANCE.TKR** on the APPLICATION disk.

20. Which command did you use?
    a. DEL BALANCE.TKR
    b. DEL SERIES\BALANCE.TKR
    c. MOVE BALANCE.TKR
    d. REN BALANCE.TKR

C-f   Eliminate the **SERIES** directory from the APPLICATION disk *without* using the DELTREE command.

21. Which command did you use *first?*
    a. RD SERIES or RD \SERIES*.*
    b. DEL SERIES or DEL \SERIES*.*
    c. DELETE SERIES or DELETE \SERIES*.*
    d. MOVE SERIES or MOVE \SERIES*.*

PROBLEM D

D-a   You wish to use a wildcard, but you want to select only some files to eliminate in the FILES subdirectory that have the file extension **.FIL**.

22. What parameter would you use with the DEL command?
    a. /K
    b. /P
    c. /S
    d. /T

D-b   Use the correct parameter from the above question with the DEL command to selectively eliminate the files with **JAN** or **FEB** as a file name and **FIL** as a file extension from the **FILES** subdirectory.

23. Beside the file names, which message was displayed?
    a. Delete [ok]?
    b. Delete (Y/N)?
    c. Invalid parameter
    d. no message was displayed

D-c   Rename all the files in the **FILES** subdirectory that have a file extension of **.FIL** to the same file name but with **.AAA** as the file extension.

24. Which command did you use?
    a. REN FILES*.FIL *.AAA
    b. REN FILES*.FIL FILES*.AAA
    c. REN FILES*.AAA FILES*.FIL
    d. REN FILES*.AAA *.FIL

PROBLEM E

E-a   Copy all the files from the **\WINDOSBK** directory that have the file extension of **.TMP** to the root directory of the APPLICATION disk.

25. How many files were copies?
    a. 3
    b. 6
    c. 9
    d. 12

E-b   Rename all the files on the root of the APPLICATION disk with the **.TMP** file extension to have the same names with the file extension of **.FDP**. Use a wildcard.

26. Which command did you use?
    a. REN *.FDP *.TMP
    b. COPY *.FDP *.TMP
    c. REN *.TMP *.FDP
    d. COPY *.TMP *.FDP

E-c   Eliminate all the **.FDP** files *except* **BONJOUR.FDP**.

27. Which command did you use?
    a. DEL *.FDP
    b. DEL *.FDP /P
    c. DEL *.FDP /Y
    d. DEL *.FDP /S

PROBLEM SET II—AT THE COMPUTER

Note 1: Before proceeding with these assignments, check with your lab instructor to see if there are any special procedures you should follow.

Note 2: The APPLICATION disk is in Drive A. The A:\> prompt is displayed as the default drive and the default directory. *All work will occur on the APPLICATION disk.*

Note 3: Make sure that **NAME.BAT**, **MARK.FIL**, **GETYN.COM**, and **GO.BAT** are all present in the root directory of the APPLICATION disk before proceeding with these problems.

Note 4: All files with the **.HW** extension *must* be created in the root directory of the APPLICATION disk.

Step 1   Key in the following: A:\>**NAME** [Enter]

Step 2   Here is an example to key in, but your instructor will have other information that applies to your class. Key in the following:
           Bette A. Peat [Enter]   (*Your* name goes here.)
           CIS 55 [Enter]   (*Your* class goes here.)
           T-Th 8-9:30 [Enter]   (*Your* day and time go here.)
           Chapter 6 Applications [Enter]

Step 3   Press F6 Enter

Step 4   If the information is correct, press **Y** and you are back to A:\>.

WHAT'S
HAPPENING? ➤   You have returned to the system level. You now have a file called
NAME.FIL with your name and other pertinent information. *Hint:*
Remember redirection.

TO CREATE 1.HW

❖   The root directory of the APPLICATION disk is the default drive and
directory.

❖   Key in the following: A:\>**DIR EMP*.* > 1.HW** Enter

❖   Eliminate all the files that begin with **EMP** and have any file extension.

❖   (Note the double **>>** and note that there is no space with between the
two **>>**.) Key in the following: A:\>**DIR EMP*.* >> 1.HW** Enter

TO CREATE 2.HW

❖   The root directory of the APPLICATION disk is the default drive and
directory.

❖   Move all the files with a **.TV** extension to the **PHONE** directory.

❖   Locate only the files in the **PHONE** directory on the APPLICATION disk
that have the extension of **.TV** and place the names of the files in a file
called **2.HW**.

TO CREATE 3.HW

❖   The root directory of the APPLICATION disk is the default drive and
directory.

❖   Locate all the files in the root directory of the APPLICATION disk that
have an extension of **.TV**, if any, placing the output of the command in
a file called **3.HW**.

TO CREATE 4.HW

❖   The root directory of the APPLICATION disk is the default drive and
directory.

❖   Rename all the files in the **FILES** subdirectory that have the extension
.AAA to the same name but with the extension of **.JOB**.

❖   Locate all the files in the **FILES** directory that have an extension of **.JOB**.

❖   Place the output of the command in a file called **4.HW**.

TO CREATE 5.HW

❖   The root directory of the APPLICATION disk is the default drive and directory.

❖   Eliminate all the files in the root directory of the APPLICATION disk that have the **.MAK** extension.

❖   Locate any files in the root directory of the APPLICATION disk with the **.MAK** extension, if any, and place the output of the command in a file called **5.HW**.

TO PRINT YOUR HOMEWORK

Step 1   Be sure the printer is on and ready to accept print jobs from your computer.

Step 2   Key in the following:
A:\>**GO NAME.FIL 1.HW 2.HW 3.HW 4.HW 5.HW** Enter

Step 3   Follow the messages on the screen. When you finish, you will return to the A:\> prompt.

Step 4   Execute the shut-down procedure.

PROBLEM SET III—BRIEF ESSAY

What are the advantages of using the commands REN, DEL, COPY, and MOVE from the command line instead of using Windows Explorer. What are the disadvantages?

USING ATTRIB, SUBST, XCOPY, DOSKEY, AND THE MS-DOS TEXT EDITOR

LEARNING OBJECTIVES

After finishing this chapter, you will be able to:
1. Explain the purpose and function of the ATTRIB command.
2. Explain the purpose and function of the SUBST command.
3. Explain the purpose and function of the XCOPY command.
4. Compare and contrast XCOPY and XCOPY32.
5. Explain the purpose and function of DOSKEY.
6. Use the MS-DOS text editor to create and edit text files.

STUDENT OUTCOME

1. Use the ATTRIB command to protect files.
2. Use the SUBST command to simplify long path names.
3. Use XCOPY to copy files and subdirectories.
4. Use the XCOPY parameters to copy hidden files and retain file attributes.
5. Use DOSKEY to be more efficient at the command line.
6. Create text files using the MS-DOS text editor.

CHAPTER OVERVIEW

By using different utility commands and programs, you can manipulate files and subdirectories to help make tasks at the command line much easier. You can make the DEL *.* command safer by using the ATTRIB command to hide files that you don't want to delete. You will learn what file attributes are and how to manipulate them with the ATTRIB command. You can copy files and subdirectories at the same time with the XCOPY command. You can even copy hidden files and empty subdirectories. By using DOSKEY, you can streamline command line operations. By using the MS-DOS text editor, you can quickly create simple text files. In this chapter, you will take a look at these commands and programs.

7.1   FILE ATTRIBUTES AND THE ATTRIB COMMAND

The root directory keeps track of information about every file on a disk. This information includes the file name, file extension, file size, date and time the file was last modified, and a pointer to the file's starting cluster in the file allocation table. In addition, each file in the directory has attributes. Each attribute is a "bit" of information that is either on or off. A bit is 1/8 of a byte, and can store only a 1 or a 0, representing True or False, Yes or No, or On or Off. These attributes describe the status of a file. The attributes are represented by a single letter and depict whether or not a file is a system file (S), a hidden file (H), a read-only file (R), or an archived file (A). Attributes are sometimes called flags.

The *system attribute* is a special signal to the operating system that the file is a system file. Files with this attribute are usually operating system files, but some application programs may set a bit to indicate that a particular program is a system file. The *hidden attribute* means that, when you use the DIR command, the file name is not displayed. Hidden files cannot be deleted with the DEL command, copied with the COPY command, or renamed. For example, hidden files such as the operating system files IO.SYS and MSDOS.SYS are on a disk, but when you execute DIR, they are not displayed. The same is true in Explorer or My Computer. Unless you change the folder options, hidden files are not displayed.

When a file is marked as read-only, it means exactly that. A user can only read the file, not modify or delete it. Sometimes application programs will set the *read-only attribute* bit to "on" for important files so that a user cannot delete them. Finally, the *archive attribute* is used to indicate the backup history (archive status) of a file. When you create or modify a file, an archive bit is turned on or set. When a file has its archive bit turned on, that signifies that it has not been backed up. Certain commands and programs, such as those which back up, can modify the archive bit and reset it (turn off or on).

The ATTRIB command allows you to manipulate *file attributes*. You can view, set, and reset all the file attributes for one file or many files. ATTRIB is an external command. The syntax for the ATTRIB command is:

```
ATTRIB [+R ¦ -R] [+A ¦ -A] [+S ¦ -S] [+H ¦ -H] [[drive:][path]filename] [/S]
```

When you see a parameter in brackets, as you know, it is an optional parameter. When you see a parameter displayed as [+R ¦ -R], the bar (called a pipe) signifies that there is a choice. The parameter can be one thing or the other, not both.

Thus, you can set a file with +R or -R, but not both at the same time. The parameters are as follows:

+	Sets an attribute.
-	Clears an attribute.
R	Read-only file attribute.
A	Archive file attribute.
S	System file attribute.
H	Hidden file attribute.
/S	Processes files in all directories in the specified path.

The attributes that you will find most useful to set or unset are read-only (R) and hidden (H). By making a file read-only, no one, including you, will be able to delete or overwrite the file accidentally. If a data file is marked read-only, even when you are in an application program, you cannot alter the data.
When you use the H attribute to make a file hidden, it will not be displayed when using the DIR command. If you cannot see a file displayed in the directory listing, you also cannot copy, delete, or rename it. This feature, as you will see, will allow you great flexibility in manipulating and managing files.

The A attribute is called the archive bit. The A attribute is a signal that the file has not been backed up. However, merely using the COPY command does not turn off the A attribute. For instance, when you used the COPY command in previous chapters, simply copying a file to another location did not turn off the archive attribute. You must use certain programs, such as XCOPY, which can read and manipulate the archive bit. Unlike COPY, XCOPY will determine whether or not a file has changed since the last time it was backed up, based on whether or not the archive bit is set. Then, XCOPY can make a decision on whether or not the file needs to be backed up. Rarely, if ever, will you use the ATTRIB command to change the attribute of a file marked as a system file (S).

You will find that, although you can change file attributes from Explorer, it is much easier to do these kinds of tasks from the command prompt.

7.2   ACTIVITY: USING ATTRIB TO MAKE FILES READ-ONLY

Note 1: Be sure you have opened the MS-DOS Prompt window.
Note 2: Be sure the DATA disk is in Drive A and A:\> is displayed.
Note 3: If specified files are not on your DATA disk, you can copy them from the \WINDOSBK subdirectory.

Step 1   Key in the following: A:\>**ATTRIB *.99** Enter

```
MS-DOS Prompt                                                    _ □ ×

A:\>ATTRIB *.99
   A            APR.99           A:\APR.99
   A            FEB.99           A:\FEB.99
   A            MAR.99           A:\MAR.99
   A            JAN.99           A:\JAN.99

A:\>_
```

WHAT'S HAPPENING? ➤ You asked the ATTRIB command to show you all the files with the **.99** extension in the root directory of the DATA disk. The only file attribute that is visible or "on" for these files is A, the archive bit. The display tells you that the archive bit is set for each file that has a **.99** file extension.

Step 2   Key in the following: A:\>**ATTRIB C:*.*** Enter

```
MS-DOS Prompt                                                    _ □ ✕

A:\>ATTRIB C:\*.*
   A   H      BOOTLOG.TXT     C:\BOOTLOG.TXT
       SH     COMMAND.COM     C:\COMMAND.COM
       SHR    MSDOS.SYS       C:\MSDOS.SYS
   A   SH     SETUPLOG.TXT    C:\SETUPLOG.TXT
       SH     DETLOG.TXT      C:\DETLOG.TXT
       SH     SUHDLOG.DAT     C:\SUHDLOG.DAT
   A   SH     NETLOG.TXT      C:\NETLOG.TXT
   A   SH     BOOTLOG.PRV     C:\BOOTLOG.PRV
   A          CONFIG.SYS      C:\CONFIG.SYS
       HR     CLASSES.1ST     C:\CLASSES.1ST
   A          AUTOEXEC.BAT    C:\AUTOEXEC.BAT
       SH     COMMAND.DOS     C:\COMMAND.DOS
       SH     SYSTEM.1ST      C:\SYSTEM.1ST
       SHR    IO.SYS          C:\IO.SYS
       HR     ASD.LOG         C:\ASD.LOG

A:\>_
```

WHAT'S HAPPENING? ➤ You are looking at the files in the root directory of C. Your display will be different depending on what files are in your root directory. Also, if you are using a network drive instead of a local hard disk, you may not be able to access the root directory of the network drive. If you cannot access the root directory of Drive C on your system, just look at the above example. You can see that in this display, **IO.SYS** and **MSDOS.SYS** are marked with an S for the system attribute, an H for the hidden attribute, and an R for the read-only attribute. Since you cannot boot the computer from the hard disk without these files, they are triple protected. In addition, other critical files are marked with one or more of the S, H, and R attributes.

Step 3   Key in the following: A:\>**COPY C:\WINDOSBK*.FIL** Enter
Note: Overwrite any files if you are prompted to do so.

```
MS-DOS Prompt                                                    _ □ ✕

A:\>COPY C:\WINDOSBK\*.FIL
C:\WINDOSBK\CASES.FIL
C:\WINDOSBK\STEVEN.FIL
C:\WINDOSBK\CAROLYN.FIL
C:\WINDOSBK\SECOND.FIL
C:\WINDOSBK\PERSONAL.FIL
C:\WINDOSBK\MARK.FIL
C:\WINDOSBK\FRANK.FIL
C:\WINDOSBK\NEWPRSON.FIL
C:\WINDOSBK\Y.FIL
        9 file(s) copied
```

```
A:\>_
```

WHAT'S HAPPENING? ➤ You have copied all the files with the .FIL extension from the **\WINDOSBK** subdirectory to the DATA disk.

Step 4   Key in the following: A:\>**ATTRIB *.FIL** Enter

```
MS-DOS Prompt                                                    _ □ ✕

A:\>ATTRIB *.FIL
   A           MARCH.FIL      A:\MARCH.FIL
   A           CASES.FIL      A:\CASES.FIL
   A           STEVEN.FIL     A:\STEVEN.FIL
   A           CAROLYN.FIL    A:\CAROLYN.FIL
   A           SECOND.FIL     A:\SECOND.FIL
   A           PERSONAL.FIL   A:\PERSONAL.FIL
   A           MARK.FIL       A:\MARK.FIL
   A           FRANK.FIL      A:\FRANK.FIL
   A           NEWPRSON.FIL   A:\NEWPRSON.FIL
   A           Y.FIL          A:\Y.FIL

A:\>_
```

WHAT'S HAPPENING? ➤ The only attribute that is set (turned on) for these files is the archive bit (A).

Step 5   Key in the following: A:\>**ATTRIB +R STEVEN.FIL** Enter

```
MS-DOS Prompt                                                    _ □ ✕

A:\>ATTRIB +R STEVEN.FIL

A:\>_
```

WHAT'S HAPPENING? ➤ You asked the ATTRIB command to make **STEVEN.FIL** a read-only file.

Step 6   Key in the following: A:\>**ATTRIB STEVEN.FIL** Enter

```
MS-DOS Prompt                                                    _ □ ✕

A:\>ATTRIB STEVEN.FIL
   A    R     STEVEN.FIL     A:\STEVEN.FIL

A:\>_
```

WHAT'S HAPPENING? ➤ Now you have flagged or marked **STEVEN.FIL** as a read-only file.

Step 7   Key in the following: A:\>**DEL STEVEN.FIL** Enter

```
MS-DOS Prompt                                                    _ □ ✕

A:\>DEL STEVEN.FIL
Access denied

A:\>_
```

WHAT'S HAPPENING? ➤ You cannot delete this file because it is marked read-only. You can also protect against other kinds of file destruction. Once a file is marked read-only, even when you are in an application program, the operating system will stop you from overwriting the file.

Step 8 Key in the following: A:\>**C:** [Enter]

Step 9 Key in the following: C:\>**CD \WINDOSBK\FINANCE** [Enter]

Step 10 Key in the following:
C:\WINDOSBK\FINANCE>**COPY HOMEBUD.TKR A:** [Enter]

Step 11 Key in the following:
C:\WINDOSBK\FINANCE>**ATTRIB +R A:\HOMEBUD.TKR** [Enter]

Step 12 Key in the following:
C:\WINDOSBK\FINANCE>**ATTRIB A:\HOMEBUD.TKR** [Enter]

```
MS-DOS Prompt                                                    _ □ X

A:\>C:

C:\>CD\WINDOSBK\FINANCE

C:\WINDOSBK\FINANCE>COPY HOMEBUD.TKR A:\
        1 file(s) copied

C:\WINDOSBK\FINANCE>ATTRIB +R A:\HOMEBUD.TKR

C:\WINDOSBK\FINANCE>ATTRIB A:\HOMEBUD.TKR
  A     R       HOMEBUD.TKR    A:\HOMEBUD.TKR

C:\WINDOSBK\FINANCE>_
```

WHAT'S HAPPENING? ➤ You have taken several steps. You changed your default drive to the hard disk. You changed directories. You then copied the **HOMEBUD.TKR** file to the DATA disk and made it a read-only file. Although you can alter the data in the file, if you try to save the altered file, the read-only attribute will prohibit you from overwriting the original data.

Step 13 Key in the following: C:\WINDOSBK\FINANCE>**THINK** [Enter]

Step 14 Press [Enter]

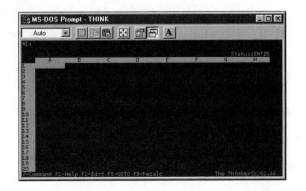

WHAT'S HAPPENING? You are in the Thinker program. You are going to load the read-only file from the DATA disk.

Step 15 Press **/**.

Step 16 Press **F**.

Step 17 Press **R**.

WHAT'S HAPPENING? You issued the command to retrieve a file. Now you must enter the file name.

Step 18 Be sure to include the DATA disk drive letter in front of the file name. Key in the following: **A:\HOMEBUD** [Enter]

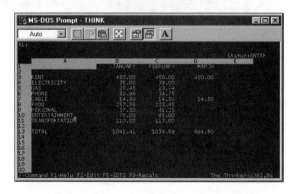

WHAT'S HAPPENING? You have loaded the data file **HOMEBUD.TKR** from the DATA disk. You are going to change the file and try to save the changed file to the DATA disk.

Step 19 Key in the following: **tttt** [Enter]

WHAT'S HAPPENING? You have keyed in some characters, tttt, changing the data file.

Step 20 Press **/**.

Step 21 Press **F**.

Step 22 Press **S**.

Step 23   Press [Enter] to accept the current file name.

WHAT'S HAPPENING? This program asks if you want to replace an existing file.

Step 24   Press **R**.

WHAT'S HAPPENING? The message indicates that on the DATA disk, the data file A:\HOMEBUD.TKR was flagged with the read-only attribute and cannot be overwritten.

Step 25   Press **/**.

Step 26   Press **Q**.

Step 27   Press **Y**.

```
MS-DOS Prompt                                          _ □ ×

C:\WINDOSBK\FINANCE>_
```

WHAT'S HAPPENING? You have exited Thinker and returned to the system level. Your data file has not been changed on the DATA disk.

Step 28   Key in the following: C:\WINDOSBK\FINANCE>**CD ** [Enter]

Step 29   Key in the following: C:\>**A:** [Enter]

```
MS-DOS Prompt                                          _ □ ×

C:\WINDOSBK\FINANCE>CD \

C:\>A:

A:\>_
```

WHAT'S HAPPENING? You have returned to the root directory of the DATA disk.

7.3   USING THE HIDDEN AND ARCHIVE ATTRIBUTES WITH ATTRIB

The purpose of the H attribute is to hide a file so that when you use the DIR command, you will not see it displayed. Why would you want to hide a file? The most likely person you are going to hide the file from is yourself, and this seems to make no sense. The real advantage to using the hidden attribute is that it allows you to manipulate files. For instance, when you use the COPY or the MOVE command with wildcards, you may not want to move or copy specific files. When you hide files, neither COPY nor MOVE can see them so they are protected from manipulation. These are tasks you cannot perform in Windows Explorer. Although you can hide files and folders by right-clicking the file name, then clicking Properties, and then choosing the Hide attribute, it is much more difficult to perform file operations on groups of files simultaneously in Windows Explorer.

The A attribute uses certain commands to flag a file as changed since the last time you backed it up. These commands can read the attribute bit (A) and can identify if it has been set. If it is set (on), the commands that can read the archive bit know whether the file has changed since the last time it was copied. With the ATTRIB command, you can set and unset this flag to help identify what files you changed since the last time you backed them up. The following activity will demonstrate how you can use the H and A attributes.

7.4 ACTIVITY: USING THE H AND THE A ATTRIBUTES

Note: The DATA disk is in Drive A. A:\> is displayed.

Step 1   Key in the following: A:\>**COPY C:\WINDOSBK\FI*.*** [Enter]

```
MS-DOS Prompt                                                        _ □ ✕

A:\>COPY C:\WINDOSBK\FI*.*
C:\WINDOSBK\FILE3.FP
C:\WINDOSBK\FILE3.SWT
C:\WINDOSBK\FILE4.FP
C:\WINDOSBK\FILE2.CZG
C:\WINDOSBK\FILE2.FP
C:\WINDOSBK\FILE2.SWT
C:\WINDOSBK\FILE3.CZG
        7 file(s) copied

A:\>_
```

Step 2   Key in the following: A:\>**DIR F*.*** [Enter]

```
MS-DOS Prompt                                                        _ □ ✕

A:\>DIR F*.*

 Volume in drive A is DATA
 Volume Serial Number is 3330-1807
 Directory of A:\

FEB        99          75   10-10-99   4:53p  FEB.99
FEBRUARY   TXT         75   04-23-00   4:03p  FEBRUARY.TXT
FEB        BUD         75   04-23-00   4:03p  FEB.BUD
FUNNY      TV         232   03-05-00   4:41p  FUNNY.TV
FRANK      FIL         44   07-31-99  12:53p  FRANK.FIL
FILE3      FP          19   12-06-00   2:45p  FILE3.FP
FILE3      SWT         19   12-06-00   2:45p  FILE3.SWT
FILE4      FP          19   12-06-00   2:45p  FILE4.FP
FILE2      CZG         19   12-06-00   2:45p  FILE2.CZG
FILE2      FP          19   12-06-00   2:45p  FILE2.FP
FILE2      SWT         19   12-06-00   2:45p  FILE2.SWT
FILE3      CZG         19   12-06-00   2:45p  FILE3.CZG
        12 file(s)              634 bytes
         0 dir(s)        1,372,672 bytes free

A:\>_
```

WHAT'S HAPPENING? ➤ You copied all the files that begin with **FI** from the **WINDOSBK** subdirectory to the root directory of the DATA disk. Now you want to move all the files that begin with **F** to the **TRIP** subdirectory, but you do not want to move the files you just copied. The problem is that, if you use **MOVE F*.* TRIP**, all the files that begin with **F** will be moved, not just the ones you desire. You cannot say, "Move all the files that begin with F except the files that begin with FI." Here, the ability to hide files is useful.

Step 3   Key in the following: A:\>**ATTRIB +H FI*.*** [Enter]

Step 4   Key in the following: A:\>**DIR F*.*** [Enter]

```
MS-DOS Prompt                                                    _ □ ✕

A:\>ATTRIB +H FI*.*

A:\>DIR F*.*

 Volume in drive A is DATA
 Volume Serial Number is 3330-1807
 Directory of A:\

FEB         99          75  10-10-99  4:53p FEB.99
FEBRUARY  TXT          75  04-23-00  4:03p FEBRUARY.TXT
FEB        BUD          75  04-23-00  4:03p FEB.BUD
FUNNY      TV          232  03-05-00  4:41p FUNNY.TV
FRANK      FIL          44  07-31-99 12:53p FRANK.FIL
            5 file(s)              501 bytes
            0 dir(s)        1,372,672 bytes free

A:\>_
```

WHAT'S HAPPENING? ➤ The files that begin with **FI** are hidden and will not be displayed by the DIR command. Now when you use the MOVE command, none of the hidden files, the **FI*.*** files, will be moved.

Step 5   Key in the following: A:\>**MOVE F*.* TRIP** [Enter]

```
MS-DOS Prompt                                                    _ □ ✕

A:\>MOVE F*.* TRIP
A:\FEB.99 => A:\TRIP\FEB.99 [ok]
A:\FEBRUARY.TXT => A:\TRIP\FEBRUARY.TXT [ok]
A:\FEB.BUD => A:\TRIP\FEB.BUD [ok]
A:\FUNNY.TV => A:\TRIP\FUNNY.TV [ok]
A:\FRANK.FIL => A:\TRIP\FRANK.FIL [ok]
Cannot move FILE3.FP - Permission denied
Cannot move FILE3.SWT - Permission denied
Cannot move FILE4.FP - Permission denied
Cannot move FILE2.CZG - Permission denied
Cannot move FILE2.FP - Permission denied
Cannot move FILE2.SWT - Permission denied
Cannot move FILE3.CZG - Permission denied

A:\>_
```

WHAT'S HAPPENING? ➤ You see that you accomplished your mission. The files you hid were not moved. The "Permission denied" message told you that you are not allowed to move hidden files. What if you forget which files you hid? The / A parameter, which can be used with the DIR command, allows you to specify the kind of file you want to look for. The attribute choices are:

D   Directories

R   Read-only files

H   Hidden files

A   Files ready to archive

Step 6   Key in the following: A:\>**DIR /AH** [Enter]

```
MS-DOS Prompt                                                    _ □ ×

A:\>DIR /AH

 Volume in drive A is DATA
 Volume Serial Number is 3330-1807
 Directory of A:\

FILE3        FP              19  12-06-00  2:45p FILE3.FP
FILE3        SWT             19  12-06-00  2:45p FILE3.SWT
FILE4        FP              19  12-06-00  2:45p FILE4.FP
FILE2        CZG             19  12-06-00  2:45p FILE2.CZG
FILE2        FP              19  12-06-00  2:45p FILE2.FP
FILE2        SWT             19  12-06-00  2:45p FILE2.SWT
FILE3        CZG             19  12-06-00  2:45p FILE3.CZG
             7 file(s)              133 bytes
             0 dir(s)        1,372,672 bytes free

A:\>_
```

WHAT'S HAPPENING? ➤ The attribute you wanted to use was the hidden attribute (H). As you can see, the DIR /AH command displays only the hidden files. Now you can "unhide" the files.

Step 7   Key in the following: A:\>**ATTRIB -H FI*.*** [Enter]

```
MS-DOS Prompt                                                    _ □ ×
A:\>ATTRIB -H FI*.*

A:\>_
```

WHAT'S HAPPENING? ➤ The **FI*.*** files are no longer hidden. You can manipulate other file attributes to assist you in managing your files. You can indicate what files have changed since the last time you copied them by changing the A or archive bit. When you create a file, the operating system automatically turns on the A attribute or "flags" it as new and not backed up. When you use certain commands, such as XCOPY, that specific command will turn off the A flag to indicate that the file has been backed up. Whenever you make a change to a file, the A attribute bit is turned on again or "re-flagged" to indicate that there has been a change since the last time you backed it up. You will learn later how this works when using the XCOPY command. However, you can also manipulate the archive bit directly with the ATTRIB command to let you know if you changed a file.

Step 8   Key in the following: A:\>**TYPE STEVEN.FIL** Enter

Step 9   Key in the following: A:\>**ATTRIB STEVEN.FIL** Enter

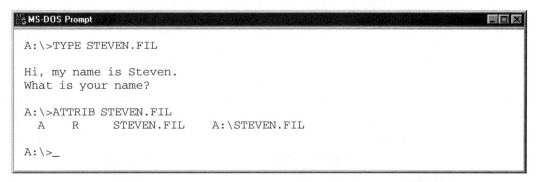

```
MS-DOS Prompt                                                    _ □ ×

A:\>TYPE STEVEN.FIL

Hi, my name is Steven.
What is your name?

A:\>ATTRIB STEVEN.FIL
   A    R      STEVEN.FIL     A:\STEVEN.FIL

A:\>_
```

WHAT'S HAPPENING? ▶ This file is protected with the R attribute. You can see the contents of it using the TYPE command. You set the R attribute. The operating system automatically set the A attribute.

Step 10   Key in the following: A:\>**ATTRIB -A -R STEVEN.FIL** Enter

Step 11   Key in the following: A:\>**ATTRIB STEVEN.FIL** Enter

```
MS-DOS Prompt                                                    _ □ ×

A:\>ATTRIB -A -R STEVEN.FIL

A:\>ATTRIB STEVEN.FIL
            STEVEN.FIL     A:\STEVEN.FIL

A:\>_
```

WHAT'S HAPPENING? ▶ You have turned off all the attributes of this file.

Step 12   Key in the following: A:\>**COPY TRIP\FRANK.FIL STEVEN.FIL** Enter

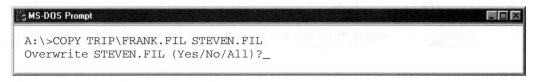

```
MS-DOS Prompt                                                    _ □ ×

A:\>COPY TRIP\FRANK.FIL STEVEN.FIL
Overwrite STEVEN.FIL (Yes/No/All)?_
```

WHAT'S HAPPENING? ▶ Since the file is no longer read-only, you are asked if you want to over-write the contents of **STEVEN.FIL** with **FRANK.FIL**.

Step 13   Press **Y** Enter

Step 14   Key in the following: A:\>**TYPE STEVEN.FIL** Enter

```
MS-DOS Prompt                                               _ □ ×

A:\>COPY TRIP\FRANK.FIL STEVEN.FIL
Overwrite STEVEN.FIL (Yes/No/All)?Y
        1 file(s) copied

A:\>TYPE STEVEN.FIL

Hi, my name is Frank
What is your name?

A:\>_
```

WHAT'S
HAPPENING! ➤ The file contents have clearly changed. This file is an ASCII or text file and can be read on the screen with the TYPE command. If this were a data file generated by a program, you could not use the TYPE command to see if the contents had changed. By looking at the attributes of a data file, you could see that the file had changed.

Step 15   Key in the following: A:\>**ATTRIB STEVEN.FIL** Enter

```
MS-DOS Prompt                                               _ □ ×

A:\>ATTRIB STEVEN.FIL
  A             STEVEN.FIL    A:\STEVEN.FIL

A:\>_
```

WHAT'S
HAPPENING! ➤ The A attribute or archive bit is once again turned on so that you know the file has changed. Another way of saying it is that **STEVEN.FIL** is flagged by the archive bit. If you had protected **STEVEN.FIL** with the read-only attribute, you would be protected from accidentally overwriting the file. Other operations do not work the same way. If you rename a file, it keeps the same file attributes, but if you copy the file, it does not carry the read-only attribute to the copy. Since this is a "new" file, the archive bit will be set automatically.

Step 16   Key in the following: A:\>**ATTRIB +R -A STEVEN.FIL** Enter

Step 17   Key in the following: A:\>**ATTRIB STEVEN.FIL** Enter

```
MS-DOS Prompt                                               _ □ ×

A:\>ATTRIB +R -A STEVEN.FIL

A:\>ATTRIB STEVEN.FIL
      R       STEVEN.FIL    A:\STEVEN.FIL

A:\>_
```

WHAT'S
HAPPENING! ➤ STEVEN.FIL is now read-only and has had the A flag turned off.

Step 18   Key in the following: A:\>**REN STEVEN.FIL BRIAN.FIL** Enter

Step 19 Key in the following: A:\>**ATTRIB BRIAN.FIL** [Enter]

```
┌─────────────────────────────────────────────────────────────────────────────┐
│ ▓ MS-DOS Prompt                                              [_][□][×]        │
├─────────────────────────────────────────────────────────────────────────────┤
│                                                                               │
│  A:\>REN STEVEN.FIL BRIAN.FIL                                                 │
│                                                                               │
│  A:\>ATTRIB BRIAN.FIL                                                         │
│       R     BRIAN.FIL    A:\BRIAN.FIL                                          │
│                                                                               │
│  A:\>_                                                                         │
│                                                                               │
└─────────────────────────────────────────────────────────────────────────────┘
```

WHAT'S HAPPENING?   Even though you renamed **STEVEN.FIL** to **BRIAN.FIL**, **BRIAN.FIL** retained the same file attributes that **STEVEN.FIL** had. It is the same file; you just renamed it. However, things change when you copy a file because you are creating a new file.

Step 20 Key in the following: A:\>**COPY BRIAN.FIL STEVEN.FIL** [Enter]

Step 21 Key in the following: A:\>**ATTRIB STEVEN.FIL** [Enter]

Step 22 Key in the following: A:\>**ATTRIB BRIAN.FIL** [Enter]

```
┌─────────────────────────────────────────────────────────────────────────────┐
│ ▓ MS-DOS Prompt                                              [_][□][×]        │
├─────────────────────────────────────────────────────────────────────────────┤
│                                                                               │
│  A:\>COPY BRIAN.FIL STEVEN.FIL                                                │
│        1 file(s) copied                                                       │
│                                                                               │
│  A:\>ATTRIB STEVEN.FIL                                                        │
│    A          STEVEN.FIL    A:\STEVEN.FIL                                      │
│                                                                               │
│  A:\>ATTRIB BRIAN.FIL                                                         │
│       R     BRIAN.FIL    A:\BRIAN.FIL                                          │
│                                                                               │
│  A:\>_                                                                         │
│                                                                               │
└─────────────────────────────────────────────────────────────────────────────┘
```

WHAT'S HAPPENING?   When you copied **BRIAN.FIL**, which had a read-only file attribute, to a new file called **STEVEN.FIL**, the operating system removed the read-only attribute of the new file. **STEVEN.FIL** is not a read-only file. Thus, setting the read-only attribute is really most valuable for protecting you against accidental erasure of a file, not for any particular security reason. The same was true for the A attribute. When you renamed the file **STEVEN.FIL** to **BRIAN.FIL**, the A attribute was not set, but, when you copied **BRIAN.FIL** to **STEVEN.FIL**, **STEVEN.FIL** had the A attribute set. Remember that you set file attributes with the plus sign (+). You can unset file attributes with the minus sign (-). You can eliminate or add several file attributes with a one-line command, but there must be a space between each parameter, so follow the spacing of the command syntax carefully.

7.5   THE SUBST COMMAND

SUBST is an external command that allows you to substitute a drive letter for a path name. This command can be used to avoid having to key in a long path name. It can also be used to install programs that do not recognize a subdirectory but do recognize a disk drive. You can also use SUBST if you need information from a drive that a program does not recognize.

CAUTION!   **BE CAUTIOUS WHEN YOU USE SUBST WITH A NETWORK DRIVE. YOU MAY NOT BE ABLE TO USE SUBST ON THE NETWORK. AS NETWORKS USE LETTER DRIVE SPECIFICATION, BE SURE TO CHECK WITH YOUR LAB ADMINISTRATOR TO SEE IF YOU CAN USE THIS COMMAND SUCCESSFULLY, AND IF SO, WHAT DRIVE LETTER YOU ARE FREE TO USE.**

On a stand-alone system, when you use SUBST and while a substitution is in effect, you should not use the commands MD, RD, PATH, LABEL, CHKDSK, FORMAT, DISKCOPY, or FDISK. These commands expect a drive letter to represent an actual disk drive. The syntax for the SUBST command is:

```
SUBST [drive1: [drive2:]path]
```

or to undo a substitution:

```
SUBST drive1: /D
```

and to see what you have substituted:

```
SUBST
```

7.6   ACTIVITY: USING SUBST

Note 1: You have the DATA disk in Drive A with A:\> displayed.
Note 2: If you have a Drive E on your own computer system you should pick a drive letter that is not being used, such as H: or K:. Remember that if you are in a lab environment you must check with your instructor to see if you can do this activity.

Step 1   Key in the following: A:\>**TYPE POLYSCI\USA\DRESS.UP** Enter

```
MS-DOS Prompt                                                    _ □ ×

A:\>TYPE POLYSCI\USA\DRESS.UP

This is a file for me.

A:\>_
```

WHAT'S HAPPENING?   You displayed the contents of the file called **DRESS.UP** in the subdirectory called **USA** under the subdirectory called **POLYSCI** in the root directory. Even though you left the first backslash off, since the default directory is the root, you still have a lot of keying in to do. If you use the SUBST command, you need to key in only the logical or virtual drive letter. In this example, E: is selected.

You are creating a virtual drive, one that exists temporarily. A virtual drive is also known as a logical drive. You are letting a drive letter represent an actual physical drive and path. Thus, you must be sure to use a drive letter that is not being used by an actual physical disk drive. If you have a floppy disk Drive A; a floppy disk Drive B; a hard disk that is logically divided into Drives C, D, and E; a removable drive such as a Zip drive that is Drive G; and a CD-ROM that is Drive H; your first available letter would be I. If, on the other hand, you had all the above drives except an actual physical Drive B, you could use B. Conceptually, this is how networks operate—a network takes a path name and substitutes a drive letter for the path. It appears to the user as a "real" drive and behaves like a real drive for COPY, MOVE, and other file and directory commands. However, since it is not a "real" drive, you cannot perform disk actions on it such as SCANDISK, format, or DISKCOPY. (*Note:* If you have a Drive E on your own computer system, you should pick a drive letter that is not being used, such as H: or K:. Remember, if you are in a lab environment, you must check with your instructor to see if you can do this activity.) Often, Drive B is not assigned to a drive letter and you may use B: instead of E:

Step 2   Key in the following: A:\>**SUBST E: A:\POLYSCI\USA** [Enter]

Step 3   Key in the following: A:\>**TYPE E:DRESS.UP** [Enter]

```
MS-DOS Prompt                                                    _ □ X

A:\>SUBST E: A:\POLYSCI\USA

A:\>TYPE E:DRESS.UP

This is a file for me.

A:\>_
```

WHAT'S HAPPENING! You first set up the substitution. You said substitute the letter **E** for the path name **A:\POLYSCI\USA**. Now, every time you want to refer to the subdirectory called **A:\POLYSCI\USA**, you can just use the letter **E**, which refers to logical Drive E. You can use this logical drive just like a physical drive. You can use the DIR command, the COPY command, the DEL command, and just about any other command you wish.

Step 4   Key in the following: A:\>**SUBST** [Enter]

```
MS-DOS Prompt                                                    _ □ X

A:\>SUBST
E: => A:\POLYSCI\USA

A:\>_
```

WHAT'S HAPPENING! SUBST, when used alone, tells you what substitution you have used.

Step 5   Key in the following: A:\>**SUBST E: /D** [Enter]

Step 6   Key in the following: A:\>**SUBST** [Enter]

```
MS-DOS Prompt                                              _ □ ✕

A:\>SUBST E: /D

A:\>SUBST

A:\>_
```

WHAT'S HAPPENING? ➤   The /D parameter disabled or "undid" the SUBST command so that
logical Drive E no longer refers to the subdirectory **A:\POLYSCI\USA**.
The SUBST that was keyed in with no parameters showed that no
substitution was in effect. Most software today is quite sophisticated. For
instance, if you have an older program that comes on a 5¼-inch disk and
insists on running from Drive A, but Drive A is a 3½-inch disk drive, you
can solve the problem with SUBST. The biggest offenders are game
programs and older installation programs. The solution would be as
follows:

```
SUBST A: B:\
```

This command would reroute every disk request intended for Drive A to
Drive B. The only thing tricky about this command is that you must
include \ after B:. SUBST does not recognize a drive letter alone as a
destination, so it must include the path.

7.7   THE XCOPY COMMAND

Although COPY is a useful internal command, it has some drawbacks, as you have
seen. COPY copies one file at a time, even with wildcards, so it is a slow command.
In addition, you cannot copy a subdirectory structure. If you have disks with different formats such as 3½ inch and 5¼ inch, you cannot use DISKCOPY because the
media types must be the same. You can, however, use XCOPY. Unlike COPY,
XCOPY is an external command that allows you to copy files that exist in different
subdirectories as well as the contents of a subdirectory including both files and
subdirectories beneath a parent subdirectory. It allows you to specify a drive as a
source and assumes you want to copy all files on the drive in the default directory.
With XCOPY you can copy files created on or after a certain date, or files with the
archive bit set. XCOPY provides overwrite protection so that, if there is a file with
the same name, XCOPY will request permission before overwriting the destination
file with the source file. Furthermore, XCOPY operates faster than the COPY
command. The COPY command reads and copies one file at a time, even if you use
wildcards. XCOPY first reads all the source files into memory and subsequently
copies them as one group of files. XCOPY will not, by default, copy system or hidden
files.

There are two versions of XCOPY—XCOPY.EXE and XCOPY32.EXE. XCOPY.EXE is a 16-bit version. Fortunately, you do not have to be concerned with which version to use. If, for some reason, you are unable to boot to the full 32-bit Windows operating system, or if you use your startup disk to boot from the A drive, you cannot use XCOPY32. As a 32-bit version of the command, it requires the full operating system to be loaded. When you key in XCOPY, the operating system knows whether or not the 32-bit operations are available. If the full 32-bit operating system is not loaded, the 16-bit version of XCOPY will be used. If the full system is loaded, when you key in XCOPY, you will actually be using XCOPY32.EXE, which uses the module file XCOPY32.MOD to provide the additional functions available with 32-bit operation.

XCOPY is a very powerful and useful command. With it you can copy files and subdirectories that have any attributes. You can also specify that the files and subdirectories copied retain their attributes. As you remember, when you use COPY to make a copy of a file, the copy does not have the same attributes as the source file. The attributes are lost when the file is copied. There are further advantages to using the command line over using Explorer. When dragging and dropping to copy files and directory structures, it is easy to "miss" your destination. If you want to be specific, it is easier to key in commands than to drag and drop. In addition, you can perform file operations on a group of files rather than one file at a time.

There are many parameters available when using the XCOPY command. The full syntax is:

```
XCopies files and directory trees.

XCOPY source [destination] [/A ¦ /M] [/D[:date]] [/P] [/S [/E]] [/W] [/C] [/I]
                           [/Q] [/F] [/L] [/H] [/R] [/T] [/U] [/K] [/N]
  source       Specifies the file(s) to copy.
  destination  Specifies the location and/or name of new files.
  /A           Copies files with the archive attribute set, doesn't change
               the attribute.
  /M           Copies files with the archive attribute set, turns off the
               archive attribute.
  /D:date      Copies files changed on or after the specified date. If no date
               is given, copies only those files whose source time is newer
               than the destination time.
  /P           Prompts you before creating each destination file.
  /S           Copies directories and subdirectories except empty ones.
  /E           Copies directories and subdirectories, including empty ones.
               Same as /S /E. May be used to modify /T.
  /W           Prompts you to press a key before copying.
  /C           Continues copying even if errors occur.
  /I           If destination does not exist and copying more than one file,
               assumes that destination must be a directory.
  /Q           Does not display file names while copying.
  /F           Displays full source and destination file names while copying.
  /L           Displays files that would be copied.
  /H           Copies hidden and system files also.
  /R           Overwrites read-only files.
  /T           Creates directory structure, but does not copy files. Does not
               include empty directories or subdirectories. /T /E includes
               empty directories and subdirectories.
  /U           Updates the files that already exist in destination.
  /K           Copies attributes. Normal Xcopy will reset read-only attributes.
  /Y           Overwrites existing files without prompting.
  /-Y          Prompts you before overwriting existing files.
  /N           Copy using the generated short names.
```

These parameters give XCOPY a great deal of versatility.

7.8 ACTIVITY: USING THE XCOPY COMMAND

Note: You have the DATA disk in Drive A with A:\> displayed.

Step 1   Key in the following: A:\>**DIR C:\WINDOSBK\MEDIA** Enter

Step 2   Key in the following: A:\>**DIR C:\WINDOSBK\MEDIA\BOOKS** Enter

```
MS-DOS Prompt                                            _ □ ✕

A:\>DIR C:\WINDOSBK\MEDIA

Directory of C:\WINDOSBK\MEDIA

.               <DIR>        07-20-01   4:26p .
..              <DIR>        07-20-01   4:26p ..
BOOKS           <DIR>        07-20-01   4:26p BOOKS
TV              <DIR>        07-20-01   4:26p TV
MOVIES          <DIR>        07-20-01   4:26p MOVIES
        0 file(s)                 0 bytes
        5 dir(s)     1,028,886,528 bytes free

A:\>DIR C:\WINDOSBK\MEDIA\BOOKS

 Volume in drive C is MILLENNIUM
 Volume Serial Number is 2B18-1301
 Directory of C:\WINDOSBK\MEDIA\BOOKS

.               <DIR>        07-20-01   4:26p .
..              <DIR>        07-20-01   4:26p ..
MYSTERY  BKS         233     08-08-00   1:39p MYSTERY.BKS
AME-LIT  BKS         184     08-08-00   1:39p AME-LIT.BKS
PULITZER BKS         662     08-08-00   1:39p PULITZER.BKS
        3 file(s)             1,079 bytes
        2 dir(s)     1,028,886,528 bytes free

A:\>_
```

WHAT'S HAPPENING? As you can see, the **MEDIA** subdirectory has three subdirectories: **BOOKS, TV,** and **MOVIES**. Each subdirectory has files in it as well. If you were going to use the COPY command to recreate this structure on your DATA disk, you would have to create the directories with the MD command and then copy the files in the **BOOKS, TV,** and **MOVIES** subdirectories. XCOPY can do all this work for you. You are still copying files, but you can consider XCOPY as a smart COPY command. When working with computers, you want the computer to do all the work, when possible.

Step 3   Key in the following:
          A:\>**XCOPY C:\WINDOSBK\MEDIA MEDIA /S** Enter

```
MS-DOS Prompt                                              _ □ ×

A:\>XCOPY C:\WINDOSBK\MEDIA MEDIA /S
Does MEDIA specify a file name
or directory name on the target
(F = file, D = directory)?_
```

WHAT'S HAPPENING! You asked XCOPY to copy all the files from the **WINDOSBK\MEDIA** subdirectory located on the hard disk to the **\MEDIA** subdirectory under the root directory of the DATA disk. In this case, XCOPY is a smart command. It asks you if you want to place all these files in one file or to create a subdirectory structure. In this case, you want to create the subdirectory structure. The /S parameter means to copy all the subdirectories and their files to the **MEDIA** subdirectory on the DATA disk. XCOPY is a command that does not care where you place /S. The command could have been written as **XCOPY /S C:\WINDOSBK \MEDIA MEDIA**, and it would also have been correct.

Step 4   Key in the following: **D**

```
MS-DOS Prompt                                              _ □ ×

(F = file, D = directory)?D
BOOKS\MYSTERY.BKS
BOOKS\AME-LIT.BKS
BOOKS\PULITZER.BKS
TV\COMEDY.TV
TV\DRAMA.TV
MOVIES\DRAMA.MOV
MOVIES\MUSIC.MOV
MOVIES\OTHER.MOV
        8 File(s) copied

A:\>_
```

WHAT'S HAPPENING! Since you included the /S parameter, XCOPY copied all the files from the subdirectory **\WINDOSBK\MEDIA**, including the subdirectories called **BOOKS**, **TV**, and **MOVIES** and their contents.

Step 5   Key in the following: A:\>**DIR MEDIA** Enter

Step 6   Key in the following: A:\>**DIR MEDIA\BOOKS** Enter

```
MS-DOS Prompt                                              _ □ ×

A:\>DIR MEDIA

 Volume in drive A is DATA
 Volume Serial Number is 3330-1807
 Directory of A:\MEDIA

 .              <DIR>         07-30-01 11:14a .
 ..             <DIR>         07-30-01 11:14a ..
 BOOKS          <DIR>         07-30-01 11:14a BOOKS
 TV             <DIR>         07-30-01 11:14a TV
```

```
MOVIES          <DIR>           07-30-01 11:14a MOVIES
        0 file(s)                     0 bytes
        5 dir(s)          1,365,504 bytes free

A:\>DIR MEDIA\BOOKS

 Volume in drive A is DATA
 Volume Serial Number is 3330-1807
 Directory of A:\MEDIA\BOOKS

.               <DIR>           07-30-01 11:14a .
..              <DIR>           07-30-01 11:14a ..
MYSTERY BKS         233         08-08-00  1:39p MYSTERY.BKS
AME-LIT BKS         184         08-08-00  1:39p AME-LIT.BKS
PULITZER BKS        662         08-08-00  1:39p PULITZER.BKS
        3 file(s)                 1,079 bytes
        2 dir(s)          1,365,504 bytes free

A:\>_
```

WHAT'S HAPPENING? All the files and subdirectories were copied, and the subdirectory structure was retained. As you can see, XCOPY is a smart command with many useful parameters. One of the more useful ones is copying files modified or created after a certain date.

Step 7 Key in the following: A:\>**DIR C:\WINDOSBK*.TXT** Enter

```
MS-DOS Prompt                                              [_][□][X]

A:\>DIR C:\WINDOSBK\*.TXT

 Volume in drive C is MILLENNIUM
 Volume Serial Number is 2B18-1301
 Directory of C:\WINDOSBK

GOODBYE   TXT          34   01-01-02  4:32a GOODBYE.TXT
APRIL     TXT          72   06-16-00  4:32p APRIL.TXT
JANUARY   TXT          73   06-16-00  4:32p JANUARY.TXT
FEBRUARY  TXT          75   06-16-00  4:32p FEBRUARY.TXT
MARCH     TXT          71   06-16-00  4:32p MARCH.TXT
HELLO     TXT          53   05-30-00  4:32p HELLO.TXT
BYE       TXT          45   05-30-00  4:32p BYE.TXT
DANCES    TXT          72   12-11-99  4:03p DANCES.TXT
TEST      TXT          65   12-11-99  4:03p TEST.TXT
SANDYA~1  TXT          53   11-16-00 12:00p Sandy and Nicki.txt
SANDYA~2  TXT          59   11-16-00 12:00p Sandy and Patty.txt
        11 file(s)             672 bytes
         0 dir(s)    1,028,874,240 bytes free

A:\>_
```

WHAT'S HAPPENING? You want to copy all the **.TXT** files that were created on or after 05-01-00 to the root directory of the DATA disk. You do not want to copy the files **TEST.TXT** and **DANCES.TXT**. The XCOPY command allows you to make choices by date. In the following step, overwrite files if necessary.

Step 8 Key in the following:
A:\>**XCOPY C:\WINDOSBK*.TXT /D:05-01-00** Enter

```
MS-DOS Prompt                                              _ □ ×

A:\>XCOPY C:\WINDOSBK\*.TXT /D:05-01-00
GOODBYE.TXT
APRIL.TXT
Overwrite JANUARY.TXT (Yes/No/All)?_
```

WHAT'S HAPPENING? Remember the default for XCOPY is to confirm overwrites. The command is telling you that **JANUARY.TXT** already exists. In this case, you want to overwrite all the files.

Step 9   Press **A**

```
MS-DOS Prompt                                              _ □ ×

Overwrite JANUARY.TXT (Yes/No/All)?A
FEBRUARY.TXT
MARCH.TXT
HELLO.TXT
BYE.TXT
Sandy and Nicki.txt
Sandy and Patty.txt
        9 File(s) copied

A:\>_
```

WHAT'S HAPPENING? You copied only the nine files of interest and not all 11 files that were in the **WINDOSBK** subdirectory. Furthermore, you can use the XCOPY command to copy only files that have changed since the last time you copied them with XCOPY. Remember, XCOPY can manipulate the A attribute (archive bit).

Step 10   Key in the following: A:\>**ATTRIB *.BUD** [Enter]

Note: Do not be concerned if your files display in a different order than shown here.

```
MS-DOS Prompt                                              _ □ ×

A:\>ATTRIB *.BUD
  A             JAN.BUD        A:\JAN.BUD
  A             MAR.BUD        A:\MAR.BUD
  A             APR.BUD        A:\APR.BUD

A:\>_
```

WHAT'S HAPPENING? The files with the extension of .BUD have the archive attribute turned on.

Step 11   Key in the following: A:\>**XCOPY /M *.BUD CLASS** [Enter]

Step 12   Key in the following: A:\>**ATTRIB *.BUD** [Enter]

```
MS-DOS Prompt                                              _ □ ×

A:\>XCOPY /M *.BUD CLASS
JAN.BUD
```

```
MAR.BUD
APR.BUD
        3 File(s) copied

A:\>ATTRIB *.BUD
            JAN.BUD        A:\JAN.BUD
            MAR.BUD        A:\MAR.BUD
            APR.BUD        A:\APR.BUD

A:\>_
```

WHAT'S HAPPENING? When you used the /M parameter, it read the attribute bit for the ***.BUD** files and, as it copied each file to the **CLASS** directory, it turned off the archive bit on the source file.

To see how XCOPY can use the archive bit, you are going to make a change to the **APR.BUD** file by using COPY to copy over the contents of **APR.BUD** with the contents of **FILE2.FP**. You will then use the ATTRIB command to see that the A bit is back on because the file contents changed. When you next use XCOPY with the /M parameter, it will copy only the file that changed.

Step 13　Key in the following: A:\>**COPY FILE2.FP APR.BUD** Enter

Step 14　Press **Y** Enter

Step 15　Key in the following: A:\>**ATTRIB *.BUD** Enter

```
MS-DOS Prompt                                           _ □ ✕

A:\>COPY FILE2.FP APR.BUD
Overwrite APR.BUD (Yes/No/All)?Y
        1 file(s) copied

A:\>ATTRIB *.BUD
            JAN.BUD        A:\JAN.BUD
            MAR.BUD        A:\MAR.BUD
   A        APR.BUD        A:\APR.BUD

A:\>_
```

WHAT'S HAPPENING? Since **APR.BUD** already existed, COPY asked if you really wanted to overwrite it. You keyed in Y for Yes. The **APR.BUD** file has changed since the last time you used XCOPY. When you used the ATTRIB command, you saw that the A bit for **APR.BUD** was turned back on.

Step 16　Key in the following: A:\>**XCOPY *.BUD CLASS /M** Enter

Step 17　Press **Y**

Step 18　Key in the following: A:\>**ATTRIB *.BUD** Enter

```
MS-DOS Prompt                                           _ □ ✕

A:\>XCOPY *.BUD CLASS /M
Overwrite APR.BUD (Yes/No/All)?Y
        1 File(s) copied
```

```
A:\>ATTRIB *.BUD
            JAN.BUD        A:\JAN.BUD
            MAR.BUD        A:\MAR.BUD
            APR.BUD        A:\APR.BUD

A:\>_
```

WHAT'S HAPPENING? ➤ Once again, XCOPY informed you that you were about to overwrite an existing file in the **CLASS** subdirectory. You told XCOPY you wanted to do that. Notice that only one file was copied, **APR.BUD**, to the **CLASS** subdirectory. XCOPY read the attribute bit, saw that only **APR.BUD** had changed, and copied only one file, not all of the **.BUD** files. The XCOPY command then turned off the A attribute so that, if you make any further changes to any of the **.BUD** files, XCOPY will know to copy only the files that changed. XCOPY can also copy files that are hidden.

Step 19 Key in the following: A:\>**COPY C:\WINDOSBK*.TXT** Enter

Step 20 Key in the following: **A** Enter

```
▓ MS-DOS Prompt                                                  _ □ ×

A:\>COPY C:\WINDOSBK\*.TXT
Overwrite A:GOODBYE.TXT (Yes/No/All)?A
C:\WINDOSBK\APRIL.TXT
C:\WINDOSBK\JANUARY.TXT
C:\WINDOSBK\FEBRUARY.TXT
C:\WINDOSBK\MARCH.TXT
C:\WINDOSBK\HELLO.TXT
C:\WINDOSBK\BYE.TXT
C:\WINDOSBK\DANCES.TXT
C:\WINDOSBK\TEST.TXT
C:\WINDOSBK\Sandy and Nicki.txt
C:\WINDOSBK\Sandy and Patty.txt
      11 file(s) copied

A:\>_
```

WHAT'S HAPPENING? ➤ You have copied all the files with the extension .TXT from the WINDOSBK directory to the root of the DATA disk.

Step 21 Key in the following: A:\>**DIR *.TXT** Enter

Step 22 Key in the following: A:\>**ATTRIB +H SAN*.TXT** Enter

```
▓ MS-DOS Prompt                                                  _ □ ×

A:\>DIR *.TXT

 Volume in drive A is DATA
 Volume Serial Number is 3330-1807
 Directory of A:\

SANDYA~1 TXT           53  11-16-00  12:00p Sandy and Nicki.txt
MARCH    TXT           71  06-16-00   4:32p MARCH.TXT
JANUARY  TXT           73  06-16-00   4:32p JANUARY.TXT
GOODBYE  TXT           34  01-01-02   4:32a GOODBYE.TXT
APRIL    TXT           72  06-16-00   4:32p APRIL.TXT
FEBRUARY TXT           75  06-16-00   4:32p FEBRUARY.TXT
```

```
HELLO      TXT          53  05-30-00   4:32p HELLO.TXT
BYE        TXT          45  05-30-00   4:32p BYE.TXT
SANDYA~2   TXT          59  11-16-00  12:00p Sandy and Patty.txt
DANCES     TXT          72  12-11-99   4:03p DANCES.TXT
TEST       TXT          65  12-11-99   4:03p TEST.TXT
          11 file(s)              672 bytes
           0 dir(s)         1,359,872 bytes free


A:\>ATTRIB +H SAN*.TXT


A:\>_
```

WHAT'S HAPPENING? You have used the DIR command to display all 11 files ending in **.TXT**. You have set the H attribute on for the two **.TXT** files that begin with **SAN**. Those files will no longer be listed by the DIR command.

Step 23 Key in the following: A:\>**DIR *.TXT** [Enter]

```
MS-DOS Prompt                                                    _ □ ✕

A:\>DIR *.TXT

 Volume in drive A is DATA
 Volume Serial Number is 3330-1807
 Directory of A:\

MARCH      TXT          71  06-16-00   4:32p MARCH.TXT
JANUARY    TXT          73  06-16-00   4:32p JANUARY.TXT
GOODBYE    TXT          34  01-01-02   4:32a GOODBYE.TXT
APRIL      TXT          72  06-16-00   4:32p APRIL.TXT
FEBRUARY   TXT          75  06-16-00   4:32p FEBRUARY.TXT
HELLO      TXT          53  05-30-00   4:32p HELLO.TXT
BYE        TXT          45  05-30-00   4:32p BYE.TXT
DANCES     TXT          72  12-11-99   4:03p DANCES.TXT
TEST       TXT          65  12-11-99   4:03p TEST.TXT
           9 file(s)              560 bytes
           0 dir(s)         1,359,872 bytes free


A:\>_
```

WHAT'S HAPPENING? You have displayed all the files ending with **.TXT**, but only nine files are displayed. The DIR command does not display hidden files.

Step 24 Key in the following: A:\>**MD HIDDEN** [Enter]

Step 25 Key in the following: A:\>**COPY *.TXT HIDDEN** [Enter]

```
MS-DOS Prompt                                                    _ □ ✕

A:\>MD HIDDEN

A:\>COPY *.TXT HIDDEN
MARCH.TXT
JANUARY.TXT
GOODBYE.TXT
APRIL.TXT
FEBRUARY.TXT
HELLO.TXT
BYE.TXT
DANCES.TXT
```

```
TEST.TXT
        9 file(s) copied

A:\>_
```

WHAT'S HAPPENING? Only nine files were copied. The two hidden files were not copied.

Step 26 Key in the following: A:\>**XCOPY *.TXT HIDDEN /H** [Enter]

Step 27 Key in the following: **A**

```
MS-DOS Prompt                                            _ □ ×
A:\>XCOPY *.TXT HIDDEN /H
Sandy and Nicki.txt
Overwrite MARCH.TXT (Yes/No/All)?A
JANUARY.TXT
GOODBYE.TXT
APRIL.TXT
FEBRUARY.TXT
HELLO.TXT
BYE.TXT
Sandy and Patty.txt
DANCES.TXT
TEST.TXT
        11 File(s) copied

A:\>_
```

WHAT'S HAPPENING? All the files ending with .TXT were copied, including the two files with the H attribute set.

Step 28 Key in the following: A:\>**CD HIDDEN** [Enter]

Step 29 Key in the following: A:\HIDDEN>**DEL *.*** [Enter]

Step 30 Key in the following: **Y** [Enter]

Step 31 Key in the following: A:\HIDDEN>**DIR** [Enter]

```
MS-DOS Prompt                                            _ □ ×
A:\>CD HIDDEN

A:\HIDDEN>DEL *.*
All files in directory will be deleted!
Are you sure (Y/N)?Y

A:\HIDDEN>DIR

 Volume in drive A is DATA
 Volume Serial Number is 3330-1807
 Directory of A:\HIDDEN

.            <DIR>        07-30-01 11:53a .
..           <DIR>        07-30-01 11:53a ..
        0 file(s)              0 bytes
        2 dir(s)      1,357,824 bytes free

A:\HIDDEN>_
```

WHAT'S HAPPENING? It would appear that all the files have been deleted.

Step 32   Key in the following: A:\HIDDEN>**DIR /AH** Enter

```
MS-DOS Prompt                                                      _ □ ✕

A:\HIDDEN>DIR /AH

 Volume in drive A is DATA
 Volume Serial Number is 3330-1807
 Directory of A:\HIDDEN

SANDYA~1 TXT              53  11-16-00 12:00p Sandy and Nicki.txt
SANDYA~2 TXT              59  11-16-00 12:00p Sandy and Patty.txt
         2 file(s)             112 bytes
         0 dir(s)       1,357,824 bytes free

A:\HIDDEN>_
```

WHAT'S HAPPENING? You have used the DIR command, asking it to display all files with the hidden attribute (/AH). You can see that there are still two files in the HIDDEN subdirectory. You did not delete them.

7.9   MULTIPLE XCOPY PARAMETERS

One of the advantages of using XCOPY is the ability to perform file operations on hidden, system, and even read-only files. You can use XCOPY to manipulate files that have one or more attributes set. As you become a more sophisticated computer user, you will find that you need to troubleshoot different kinds of computer problems to protect your Windows environment. Here you will find commands like XCOPY invaluable because you can accomplish tasks at the command line that you cannot accomplish in the graphical user interface.

In the last activity, there were two files in the A:\HIDDEN directory that had the hidden attribute set. Now you want to copy these files to a new directory without removing the H attribute.

7.10   ACTIVITY: USING MULTIPLE XCOPY PARAMETERS

Note: The DATA disk is in Drive A and A:\HIDDEN> is displayed.

Step 1   Key in the following: A:\HIDDEN>**MD HOLD** Enter

Step 2   Key in the following: A:\HIDDEN>**XCOPY *.TXT HOLD /H** Enter

```
MS-DOS Prompt                                                      _ □ ✕

A:\HIDDEN>MD HOLD

A:\HIDDEN>XCOPY *.TXT HOLD /H
Sandy and Nicki.txt
Sandy and Patty.txt
        2 File(s) copied

A:\HIDDEN>_
```

WHAT'S HAPPENING? ➤ You can see from the display that the two hidden files were copied to the new HOLD directory. Did the copies of the files retain the hidden attribute?

Step 3   Key in the following: A:\HIDDEN>**DIR HOLD** [Enter]

```
MS-DOS Prompt                                                        _ □ ✕

A:\HIDDEN>DIR HOLD

 Volume in drive A is DATA
 Volume Serial Number is 3330-1807
 Directory of A:\HIDDEN\HOLD

.               <DIR>           07-30-01 11:59a .
..              <DIR>           07-30-01 11:59a ..
        0 file(s)                     0 bytes
        2 dir(s)          1,356,288 bytes free

A:\HIDDEN>_
```

WHAT'S HAPPENING? ➤ There are no visible files in the HOLD directory.

Step 4   Key in the following: A:\HIDDEN>**DIR HOLD /AH** [Enter]

```
MS-DOS Prompt                                                        _ □ ✕

A:\HIDDEN>DIR HOLD /AH

 Volume in drive A is DATA
 Volume Serial Number is 3330-1807
 Directory of A:\HIDDEN\HOLD

SANDYA~1 TXT            53  11-16-00 12:00p Sandy and Nicki.txt
SANDYA~2 TXT            59  11-16-00 12:00p Sandy and Patty.txt
        2 file(s)                 112 bytes
        0 dir(s)          1,356,288 bytes free

A:\HIDDEN>_
```

WHAT'S HAPPENING? ➤ The hidden attribute was retained. You can manipulate files with other attributes.

Step 5   Key in the following: A:\HIDDEN>**COPY \FILE*.*** [Enter]

```
MS-DOS Prompt                                                        _ □ ✕

A:\HIDDEN>COPY \FILE*.*
A:\FILE3.FP
A:\FILE3.SWT
A:\FILE4.FP
A:\FILE2.CZG
A:\FILE2.FP
A:\FILE2.SWT
A:\FILE3.CZG
        7 file(s) copied

A:\HIDDEN>_
```

WHAT'S HAPPENING? You have copied all the files that begin with FILE from the root directory to the HIDDEN subdirectory.

Step 6 Key in the following: A:\HIDDEN>**ATTRIB *.FP +R** [Enter]

Step 7 Key in the following: A:\HIDDEN>**ATTRIB +S *.CZG** [Enter]

Step 8 Key in the following: A:\HIDDEN>**ATTRIB *.SWT +S +H +R** [Enter]

```
MS-DOS Prompt                                                    _ □ ×

A:\HIDDEN>ATTRIB *.FP +R

A:\HIDDEN>ATTRIB +S *.CZG

A:\HIDDEN>ATTRIB *.SWT +S +H +R

A:\HIDDEN>_
```

WHAT'S HAPPENING? You have applied different attributes to the files you copied from the root directory. Notice that in Step 7, the file specification is listed last, while in Steps 6 and 8, it is listed first. Though not the case with most commands, with the ATTRIB command, the order of the parameters does not matter.

Step 9 Key in the following: A:\HIDDEN>**DIR** [Enter]

```
MS-DOS Prompt                                                    _ □ ×

A:\HIDDEN>DIR

 Volume in drive A is DATA
 Volume Serial Number is 3330-1807
 Directory of A:\HIDDEN

.              <DIR>         07-30-01 11:53a .
..             <DIR>         07-30-01 11:53a ..
HOLD           <DIR>         07-30-01 11:59a HOLD
FILE3    FP           19     12-06-00  2:45p FILE3.FP
FILE4    FP           19     12-06-00  2:45p FILE4.FP
FILE2    FP           19     12-06-00  2:45p FILE2.FP
         3 file(s)             57 bytes
         3 dir(s)       1,352,704 bytes free

A:\HIDDEN>_
```

WHAT'S HAPPENING? Only the files ending with .FP are displayed. You can verify that all the files are there, as well as look at all the file attributes.

Step 10 Key in the following: A:\HIDDEN>**ATTRIB** [Enter]

```
MS-DOS Prompt                                                    _ □ ×

A:\HIDDEN>ATTRIB
  A    R      FILE3.FP      A:\HIDDEN\FILE3.FP
  A   SHR     FILE3.SWT     A:\HIDDEN\FILE3.SWT
  A    R      FILE4.FP      A:\HIDDEN\FILE4.FP
  A   S       FILE2.CZG     A:\HIDDEN\FILE2.CZG
```

```
    A   R       FILE2.FP        A:\HIDDEN\FILE2.FP
    A   SHR     FILE2.SWT       A:\HIDDEN\FILE2.SWT
    A   S       FILE3.CZG       A:\HIDDEN\FILE3.CZG
    A   H       SANDYA~1.TXT    A:\HIDDEN\Sandy and Nicki.txt
    A   H       SANDYA~2.TXT    A:\HIDDEN\Sandy and Patty.txt

A:\HIDDEN>_
```

WHAT'S HAPPENING? ➤ You can see that all but five of the files have the hidden attribute set. You have discovered that files with only the S attribute set (the system attribute) are also hidden. Can you manipulate all of these files with different attributes at the same time?

Step 11 Key in the following: A:\HIDDEN>**CD ** [Enter]

Step 12 Key in the following: A:\>**MD HIDDEN2** [Enter]

```
⌘ MS-DOS Prompt                                             _ □ ✕

A:\HIDDEN>CD \

A:\>MD HIDDEN2

A:\>_
```

WHAT'S HAPPENING? ➤ You have returned to the root of the DATA disk and created a new subdirectory named HIDDEN2.

You are going to copy the HIDDEN subdirectory with all its files and subdirectories to the new subdirectory HIDDEN2. To do this, you will use multiple parameters with the XCOPY command. The parameters you will use are:

/S Copies directories and subdirectories except empty ones.

/H Copies hidden and system files.

/E Copies directories and subdirectories, including empty ones.

/R Overwrites read-only files.

/K Copies attributes. XCOPY will automatically reset read-only attributes.

These five parameters used together will copy everything, retaining all attributes. It may help you to remember them as SHERK. (Rhymes with JERK!)

Step 13 Key in the following:
A:\>**XCOPY HIDDEN HIDDEN2 /S /H /E /R /K** [Enter]

```
⌘ MS-DOS Prompt                                             _ □ ✕

A:\>XCOPY HIDDEN HIDDEN2 /S /H /E /R /K
FILE3.FP
FILE3.SWT
FILE4.FP
FILE2.CZG
FILE2.FP
FILE2.SWT
```

```
FILE3.CZG
Sandy and Nicki.txt
Sandy and Patty.txt
HOLD\Sandy and Nicki.txt
HOLD\Sandy and Patty.txt
      11 File(s) copied

A:\>_
```

WHAT'S HAPPENING? ➡ You copied all the files and subdirectories with one command. Did the copies of the files retain their attributes?

Step 14 Key in the following: A:\>**CD HIDDEN2** Enter

Step 15 Key in the following: A:\HIDDEN2>**ATTRIB /S** Enter

```
MS-DOS Prompt                                                   _ □ ✕
A:\HIDDEN2>ATTRIB /S
   A    H      SANDYA~1.TXT   A:\HIDDEN2\HOLD\Sandy and Nicki.txt
   A    H      SANDYA~2.TXT   A:\HIDDEN2\HOLD\Sandy and Patty.txt
   A    R      FILE3.FP       A:\HIDDEN2\FILE3.FP
   A  SHR      FILE3.SWT      A:\HIDDEN2\FILE3.SWT
   A    R      FILE4.FP       A:\HIDDEN2\FILE4.FP
   A  S        FILE2.CZG      A:\HIDDEN2\FILE2.CZG
   A    R      FILE2.FP       A:\HIDDEN2\FILE2.FP
   A  SHR      FILE2.SWT      A:\HIDDEN2\FILE2.SWT
   A  S        FILE3.CZG      A:\HIDDEN2\FILE3.CZG
   A    H      SANDYA~1.TXT   A:\HIDDEN2\Sandy and Nicki.txt
   A    H      SANDYA~2.TXT   A:\HIDDEN2\Sandy and Patty.txt

A:\HIDDEN2>_
```

WHAT'S HAPPENING? ➡ You have verified that all the files you copied from the **HIDDEN** subdirectory to the **HIDDEN2** subdirectory have retained their attributes.

Step 16 Key in the following: A:\HIDDEN2>**CD ** Enter

Step 17 Key in the following: A:\>**DELTREE HIDDEN** Enter

Step 18 Key in the following: **Y** Enter

Step 19 Key in the following: A:\>**DELTREE HIDDEN2** Enter

Step 20 Key in the following: **Y** Enter

```
MS-DOS Prompt                                                   _ □ ✕
A:\ HIDDEN2>CD \

A:\>DELTREE HIDDEN
Delete directory "HIDDEN" and all its subdirectories? [yn] y
Deleting HIDDEN...

A:\>DELTREE HIDDEN2
Delete directory "HIDDEN2" and all its subdirectories? [yn] y
Deleting HIDDEN2...

A:\>_
```

> **WHAT'S HAPPENING?** You returned to the root of the DATA disk and deleted the **HIDDEN** and **HIDDEN2** subdirectories along with all the files and subdirectories they contained.

7.11 DOSKEY

DOSKEY is a much-needed tool for working with commands. You may already have used it to correct keystroke errors. DOSKEY is an external, memory-resident command that in Windows Millennium is loaded automatically when you open an MS-DOS window. This is a new feature with the Millennium Edition. In Windows 95 and Windows 98, you had to load DOSKEY into memory manually. Once it was loaded into memory, it remained in memory during that entire session. Once you closed the MS-DOS screen and return to the desktop, DOSKEY was no longer in memory, so in order to use it during the next session, you had to reload it.

DOSKEY, though an external command, acts like an internal command. This means that you need not reload it from disk each time you wish to use it. **_Memory-resident commands_** are also referred to as **_TSR_** commands (Terminate Stay Resident). The normal process with any external command (program) is to execute it by keying in the command name. The operating system goes to the disk and looks for a program with that name, loads it into memory, and executes that program. When loaded, that program occupies and uses RAM. When you exit the program, the operating system reclaims the memory.

When you load a TSR, the process works initially as it does with any external command. You execute it by keying in the command name. The operating system goes to the specified or default drive and path and looks for the program with that name. The program is loaded into memory and executed. However, a TSR holds on to the memory it occupies, even while it is not actually being used or accessed. It does not release the memory for the duration of the MS-DOS work session. Thus, the "external" command acts like an internal command. You may still load other programs, but the other programs will not use the memory that the TSR has claimed. DOSKEY is a TSR that is loaded into memory when an MS-DOS window is opened. It remains there until you close the MS-DOS window. DOSKEY lets you recall command lines, edit them, keep a command history, and write macros. The full syntax is as follows:

```
Edits command lines, recalls command lines, and creates macros

DOSKEY [/switch ...] [macroname=[text]]

    /BUFSIZE:size  Sets size of macro and command buffer        (default:512)
    /ECHO:on|off   Enables/disables echo of macro expansions     (default:on)
    /FILE:file     Specifies file containing a list of macros
    /HISTORY       Displays all commands stored in memory
    /INSERT        Inserts new characters into line when typing
    /KEYSIZE:size  Sets size of keyboard type-ahead buffer       (default:15)
    /LINE:size     Sets maximum size of line edit buffer         (default:128)
    /MACROS        Displays all DOSKey macros
    /OVERSTRIKE    Overwrites new characters onto line when typing (default)
    /REINSTALL     Installs a new copy of DOSKey
    macroname      Specifies a name for a macro you create
```

```
    text              Specifies commands you want to assign to the macro

  UP,DOWN arrows recall commands
      Esc clears current command
       F7 displays command history
   Alt+F7 clears command history
[chars]F8 searches for command beginning with [chars]
       F9 selects a command by number
  Alt+F10 clears macro definitions

The following are special codes you can use in DOSKey macro definitions:
    $T     Command separator: allows multiple commands in a macro
    $1-$9 Batch parameters: equivalent to %1-%9 in batch programs
    $*     Symbol replaced by everything following macro name on the command line
```

7.12 ACTIVITY: LOADING AND USING DOSKEY

Note 1: A:\> is displayed and the path is set to C:\WINDOWS\COMMAND. The DATA disk is in Drive A.

Note 2: If you are on a network, you may not be able to increase the buffer size without rebooting. Check with your lab instructor.

Step 1   Key in the following: A:\>**DOSKEY /REINSTALL /BUFSIZE=2048** Enter

```
┌──────────────────────────────────────────────────────────────────────┐
│ MS-DOS Prompt                                              _ □ ✕       │
├──────────────────────────────────────────────────────────────────────┤
│ A:\>DOSKEY /REINSTALL /BUFSIZE:2048                                    │
│ DOSKey installed                                                       │
│                                                                        │
│ A:\>_                                                                  │
│                                                                        │
└──────────────────────────────────────────────────────────────────────┘
```

WHAT'S HAPPENING?   You have increased the buffer size of DOSKEY. The default value allocated in memory is 512 bytes. To change the size of the memory buffer, you used the REINSTALL and the BUFSIZE parameters. Since 512 bytes is really not enough to use DOSKEY effectively, you increased the size to 2KB.

Step 2   Key in the following:
          A:\>**DIR *.TXT** Enter
          A:\>**DIR C:\WINDOSBK*.99** Enter
          A:\>**TYPE PERSONAL.FIL** Enter
          A:\>**VOL** Enter
          A:\>**DIR C:\WINDOSBK\SPORTS\B*.TMS** Enter

```
┌──────────────────────────────────────────────────────────────────────┐
│ MS-DOS Prompt                                              _ □ ✕       │
├──────────────────────────────────────────────────────────────────────┤
│ JONES     JERRY    244 East     Mission Viejo CA Systems Analyst       │
│ Lo        Ophelia  1213 Wick    Phoenix       AZ Writer                │
│ Jones     Ervin    15 Fourth    Santa Cruz    CA Banker                │
│ Perez     Sergio   134 Seventh  Ann Arbor     MI Editor                │
│ Yuan      Suelin   56 Twin Leaf Orange        CA Artist                │
│ Markiw    Nicholas 12 Fifth     Glendale      AZ Engineer              │
│                                                                        │
│ A:\>VOL                                                                │
│                                                                        │
│  Volume in drive A is DATA                                             │
```

```
 Volume Serial Number is 3330-1807

A:\>DIR C:\WINDOSBK\SPORTS\B*.TMS

 Volume in drive C is MILLENNIUM
 Volume Serial Number is 2B18-1301
 Directory of C:\WINDOSBK\SPORTS

BSBALL-N TMS            222  02-24-00 11:36a BSBALL-N.TMS
BASKETBL TMS            222  10-31-00  4:43p BASKETBL.TMS
BSBALL-A TMS            211  02-24-00 11:36a BSBALL-A.TMS
          3 file(s)              655 bytes
          0 dir(s)   1,027,289,088 bytes free

A:\>_
```

WHAT'S HAPPENING? → You have executed several commands and can now use the DOSKEY editing keys to recall and edit commands. The following tables illustrate the keys you may use to edit a command history.

F7	Displays a list of commands.
Alt + **F7**	Clears the list of commands.
↑	Allows you to scroll up through the commands.
↓	Allows you to scroll down through the commands.
F8	Searches the list for the command that starts with the text you provide.
F9	Selects the command from the list by number.
PgUp	Displays the oldest command in the list.
PgDn	Displays the newest command in the list.
Esc	Erases the displayed command from the screen.
Alt + **F10**	Clears the macros.

TABLE 7.1 DOSKEY COMMAND SUMMARY

Home	Moves cursor to beginning of displayed command.
End	Moves cursor to end of displayed command.
←	Moves cursor back one character.
→	Moves cursor forward one character.
Ctrl + **←**	Moves cursor back one word.
Ctrl + **→**	Moves cursor forward one word.
Backspace	Moves cursor back one character. If you are in insert mode, it will also delete the character preceding the cursor.

Delete	Deletes the character at the cursor.
Ctrl + End	Deletes all characters from the cursor to the end of the line.
Ctrl + Home	Deletes all characters from the cursor to the beginning of the line.
Esc	Clears the command.
Insert	Toggles between insert and overstrike mode.

TABLE 7.2 EDITING KEY COMMAND SUMMARY

Step 3   Press the ⬆ key three times.

```
MS-DOS Prompt                                              _ □ ✕

A:\>TYPE PERSONAL.FIL_
```

> **WHAT'S HAPPENING?** You have recalled, in reverse order, the commands you previously entered.

Step 4   Press the Backspace key to delete **PERSONAL.FIL**, leaving **TYPE**.

Step 5   Key in **JANUARY.TXT** Enter

```
MS-DOS Prompt                                              _ □ ✕

A:\>TYPE JANUARY.TXT

This is my January file.
It is my first dummy file.
This is file 1.

A:\>_
```

> **WHAT'S HAPPENING?** You edited the line by deleting **PERSONAL.FIL** and keying in **JANUARY.TXT**.

Step 6   Press F7

```
MS-DOS Prompt                                              _ □ ✕

A:\>
1: DIR *.TXT
2: DIR C:\WINDOSBK\*.99
3: TYPE PERSONAL.FIL
4: VOL
5: DIR C:\WINDOSBK\SPORTS\B*.TMS
6: TYPE JANUARY.TXT
A:\>_
```

> **WHAT'S HAPPENING?** Pressing the F7 key lists all the commands that you have keyed in. You may edit any line you wish by selecting the line number, but you must press the F9 key first.

Step 7   Press F9. Press **5**.

```
MS-DOS Prompt                                          _ □ ✕

A:\>Line number: 5
```

WHAT'S
HAPPENING?   By pressing F9, you saw the Line number: prompt. You then keyed in
the line number (5) of the command you wished to edit.

Step 8   Press Enter

```
MS-DOS Prompt                                          _ □ ✕

A:\> DIR C:\WINDOSBK\SPORTS\B*.TMS
```

WHAT'S
HAPPENING?   You can edit this line or simply execute it again.

Step 9   Press the ← key to until it is under the **B** in **B*.TMS**. Key in **F** Enter

```
MS-DOS Prompt                                          _ □ ✕

A:\>DIR C:\WINDOSBK\SPORTS\F*.TMS

 Volume in drive C is MILLENNIUM
 Volume Serial Number is 2B18-1301
 Directory of C:\WINDOSBK\SPORTS

FOOT-COL TMS            227   12-25-99 11:36a FOOT-COL.TMS
FOOT-PRO TMS            207   12-25-99 11:36a FOOT-PRO.TMS
         2 file(s)            434 bytes
         0 dir(s)    1,031,483,392 bytes free

A:\>_
```

WHAT'S
HAPPENING?   You displayed the list of commands in numerical order. You selected a
command that you were interested in by number. You then edited the
line. You did not have to return to the end of the line before pressing
Enter to execute the command. If you wish to delete a line quickly, there
is a shortcut—the Esc key.

Step 10   Press ↑ once.

Step 11   Press Esc

```
MS-DOS Prompt                                          _ □ ✕

A:\>_
```

WHAT'S
HAPPENING?   You quickly deleted the command. You can also search for a previously
entered command by pressing the first letter or letters of the command
you are interested in.

Step 12   Press **D**. Press F8

```
MS-DOS Prompt                                          _ □ X

A:\>DIR C:\WINDOSBK\SPORTS\F.TMS
```

WHAT'S HAPPENING? You selected a command by keying in the first letter and then pressing **F8**. With DOSKEY, you can also have more than one command on a line. In order to do this, you must use special keys—you must press the **Ctrl** + **T** key combination between commands.

Step 13 Press **Esc**

Step 14 Key in the following:

A:\>**CD CLASS** **Ctrl** + **T DIR *.BUD** **Ctrl** + **T CD** \ **Enter**

```
MS-DOS Prompt                                          _ □ X

A:\>CD CLASS ¶ DIR *.BUD ¶ CD\
A:\>CD CLASS

A:\CLASS>DIR *.BUD

 Volume in drive A is DATA
 Volume Serial Number is 3330-1807
 Directory of A:\CLASS

JAN      BUD          73   04-23-00   4:03p JAN.BUD
MAR      BUD          71   04-23-00   4:03p MAR.BUD
APR      BUD          19   12-06-00   2:45p APR.BUD
         3 file(s)              163 bytes
         0 dir(s)        1,359,872 bytes free

A:\CLASS>CD \

A:\>_
```

WHAT'S HAPPENING? You executed three commands on one command line by separating each command with **Ctrl** + **T**. If you want to clear all the commands from the buffer, you may do so.

Step 15 Press **Alt** + **F7**

Step 16 Press ⬆ once.

```
MS-DOS Prompt                                          _ □ X

A:\>_
```

WHAT'S HAPPENING? You cleared all the commands that were in the buffer. There are no remaining commands to scroll through.

7.13   THE MS-DOS TEXT EDITOR

There is no doubt that, for your writing needs, you will use a word-processing program such as Word or WordPerfect. Word-processing programs are extremely sophisticated and allow you full flexibility in creating and editing documents, including inserting graphics or using different fonts such as Century Schoolbook or Times New Roman. In order to retain all of your selections in your word-processing documents, there are special codes that only the word-processing program can read. These codes are entered as the document is formatted. Most word-processing programs will, however, allow you to save your document files as ASCII text, also referred to as DOS text or as unformatted text, by stripping the formatting and saving only the keyed in text. This may puzzle you since, if you are creating a letter or a report, you want the formatting included when you print it. However, you will find that sometimes you need to "talk" to your computer. The only way you can talk to it or give the operating system instructions is by using a text file. Now you know why every operating system includes a *text editor*.

The Windows operating system includes the applet called Notepad, which allows you to create text documents. If you are having troubles with Windows, you may need to edit certain text documents that the Windows operating system requires to operate, such as AUTOEXEC.BAT or MSDOS.SYS. In addition, you will want to write batch files. These can be written only with a text editor. The command-line interface contains a text editor called Edit. It is a full-screen text editor for use in the MS-DOS window. It is not a word processor—it has no ability to format the data in documents. Edit cannot manipulate the environment with margin-size or page-length adjustments.

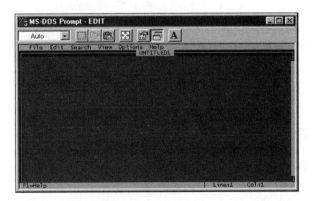

The Edit screen has a menu bar at the top and a status bar at the bottom. The status bar shows you the column and line where the cursor is currently positioned. Each menu contains further choices.

From the File menu, you can begin a new document, open an existing document, save a document, save a document under a new name (Save As), print a document, and exit the editor.

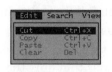

From the Edit menu, you can cut selected text, copy selected text, paste previously cut or copied text, or clear (delete) selected text.

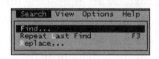

From the Search menu, you can find a specified string of text, repeat the last find, and search for a specified string of text and replace it with another specified string of text.

From the View menu, you can split, size, or close the Edit window.

From the Options menu, you can change the printer port or the tab settings and choose the colors for the Edit window.

From the Help menu, you can click Commands to get a list of all available Edit commands and click About to view the version information for Edit.

Aside from using the menus, there are many keystrokes you can use to edit a text file in the Edit window. The following table lists most of the cursor movement keys and shortcuts.

Desired Cursor Movement	Key(s) to Use	Keyboard Shortcuts
Character left	◄	**Ctrl** + **S**
Character right	►	**Ctrl** + **D**
Word left	**Ctrl** + ►	**Ctrl** + **A**
Word right	**Ctrl** + ◄	**Ctrl** + **F**
Line up	▲	**Ctrl** + **E**

Line down	$\downarrow$	
Beginning of current line	**Home**	**Ctrl** + **Q, S**
End of current line	**End**	**Ctrl** + **Q, D**
Top of file	**Ctrl** + **Home**	
End of file	**Ctrl** + **End**	

7.14 ACTIVITY: USING THE MS-DOS TEXT EDITOR

Note: The DATA disk is in the A drive. A:\> is displayed.

Step 1   Key in the following: A:\>**EDIT** **Enter**

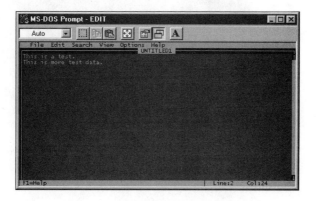

WHAT'S HAPPENING?   This is the opening screen to the editor. If this is the first time the program has been executed, you will see a welcome message in the middle of the screen, with instructions on how to remove the welcome message.

Step 2   If necessary, close the welcome message so your screen is blank.

Step 3   Key in the following:
This is a test. Enter
This is more test data.

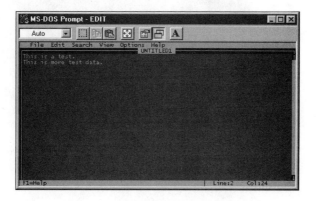

WHAT'S
HAPPENING?   You have keyed in some data. If you did not press Enter and kept keying in data, you would move to character column 25. If you look at the bottom of the screen, you see that the status line tells you what line and what character position you are in. As you can see, you are on the second line, and the cursor is in the 24th position.

You have two modes of operation: insert mode and overstrike mode. Insert mode is the default. You can tell you are in insert mode because the cursor is a small blinking line. *Insert mode* means that, as you key in data on an existing line, any data following the cursor will not be replaced, just pushed along.

Step 4   Press Ctrl + Home

Step 5   Key in the following: **THIS IS MORE DATA.**

WHAT'S
HAPPENING?   The new data is there in front of the old data. *Overstrike mode* permits you to replace the characters that are there. You can toggle between overstrike mode and insert mode by pressing the Insert key.

Step 6   Press the Insert key.

Step 7   Key in the following: **My second**

WHAT'S
HAPPENING?   Notice the shape of the cursor. It is a vertical rectangle. This cursor shape indicates that you are in overstrike mode. You have replaced old text data with new.

Step 8   Press the [Insert] key to return to insert mode.

WHAT'S HAPPENING? ➤ Full-screen editing can be done either with the cursor keys or with the mouse. You can position the mouse and click to reposition the point of insertion. You can select text by clicking the mouse at the beginning of the text you wish to select, holding down the left mouse button, and dragging it to the end of the text you wish to select.

Step 9   Click under the first **t** in the phrase **text data**.

Step 10   Hold down the left mouse button and drag to the end of the sentence.

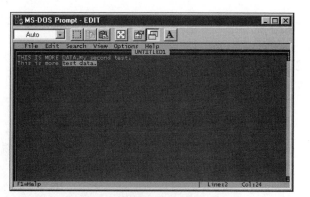

WHAT'S HAPPENING? ➤ You have selected the phrase **text data**.

Step 11   Press the [Delete] key.

Step 12   Key in the following: **meaningless data.**

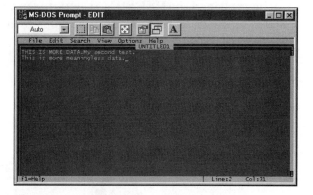

WHAT'S HAPPENING? ➤ You have used the mouse to edit data. You can also use the MS-DOS editor to edit existing files.

Step 13   On the menu bar at the top of the editor, click **File**.

Step 14   Click **Open**.

Step 15   Key in the following: **A:\PERSONAL.FIL**

WHAT'S HAPPENING? You have chosen to open the **PERSONAL.FIL** file from the DATA disk in the A drive.

Step 16 Click **OK**.

WHAT'S HAPPENING? You have opened the **PERSONAL.FIL** file in the editor. You can search for text strings in the editor. You are going to look for Ervin Jones.

Step 17 On the menu bar, click **Search**.

Step 18 Click **Find**.

Step 19 In the Find What area, key in **Jones**.

Step 20 Click **OK**.

WHAT'S HAPPENING? You found a Jones, but not the right one. You can repeat the search with a function key.

Step 21   Press the **F3** key three times.

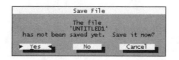

```
MS-DOS Prompt - EDIT                                        _ □ ×
  Auto          ▼  ☐ ⬚ ⬚ ☒ ⬚ ⬚ A
    File  Edit  Search  View  Options  Help
                              A:\PERSONAL.FIL
Halm        Milton    333 Meadow    Sherman Oaks    CA  Consultant
Suzuki      Charlene  567 Abbey     Rochester       MI  Day Care Teacher
Markiw      Nicholas  354 Bell      Phoenix         AZ  Engineer
Markiw      Emily     10 Zion       Sun City West   AZ  Retired
Nyles       John      12 Brooks     Sun City West   AZ  Retired
Nyles       Sophie    12 Brooks     Sun City West   CA  Retired
Markiw      Nick      10 Zion       Sun City West   AZ  Retired
Washington  Tyrone    245 Newport   Orange          CA  Manager
Jones       Steven    32 North      Phoenix         AZ  Buyer
Smith       David     120 Collins   Orange          CA  Chef
Babchuk     Walter    12 View       Thousand Oaks   CA  President
Babchuk     Deana     12 View       Thousand Oaks   CA  Housewife
Jones       Cleo      355 Second    Ann Arbor       MI  Clerk
Gonzales    Antonio   40 Northern   Ontario         CA  Engineer
JONES       JERRY     244 East      Mission Viejo   CA  Systems Analyst
Lo          Ophelia   1213 Wick     Phoenix         AZ  Writer
Jones       Erwin     15 Fourth     Santa Cruz      CA  Banker
Perez       Sergio    134 Seventh   Ann Arbor       MI  Editor
Yuan        Suelin    56 Twin Leaf  Orange          CA  Artist
Markiw      Nicholas  12 Fifth      Glendale        AZ  Engineer

 F1=Help                                           Line:35    Col:1
```

WHAT'S HAPPENING? ➤ You have cycled from Jones to Jones until you reached the one you were looking for. You can also add text to the file.

Step 22   Press the **↓** key four times.

Step 23   Key in the following (use **Space Bar** to line the entries up with the lines above):

Peat	**Brian**	**125 Second**	**Vacaville**	**CA**	**Athlete** **Enter**
Farneth	**Nichole**	**237 Arbor**	**Vacaville**	**CA**	**Dancer**

Step 24   On the menu bar, click **File**.

Step 25   Click **Exit**.

```
                    Save File
                    The file
                   'UNTITLED1'
        has not been saved yet.  Save it now?
        ▶ Yes ◀        No          Cancel
```

WHAT'S HAPPENING? ➤ A dialog box appears asking you if you want to save the file **UNTITLED1**. This file has the first data you keyed in. You do not want this file.

Step 26   Click **No**.

```
                    Save File
                    The file
                 'A:\PERSONAL.FIL'
        has not been saved yet.  Save it now?
        ▶ Yes ◀        No          Cancel
```

WHAT'S HAPPENING? ➤ You are now asked if you want to save **A:\PERSONAL.FIL**. You do want to save the changes you made.

Step 27   Click **Yes**.

```
MS-DOS Prompt                                               _ □ ×

A:\>EDIT

A:\>_
```

WHAT'S HAPPENING? ➤ You have exited the editor and returned to the MS-DOS window.

Step 28 Open the MS-DOS editor.

Step 29 Click **File**. Click **Open**.

Step 30 Key in **A:\STEVEN.FIL** Enter

Step 31 Click **View**.

Step 32 Click **Split Window**.

WHAT'S HAPPENING? ➤ You can see the file data displayed in two windows.

Step 33 Change the word "Frank" in the top screen to "Steven."

WHAT'S HAPPENING? ➤ You can see that the word was changed in both sections. When you split the screen, you can look at the same file data in both windows.

Step 34 Click **File**. Click **Save**.

Step 35 Click **File**. Click **Close**.

Step 36 Place your cursor in the top window.

Step 37 Click **File**. Click **Open**.

Step 38 Key in **A:\APR.99**.

Step 39 Click **OK**.

Step 40 Place your cursor in the bottom window.

Step 41   Click **File**. Click **Open**.

Step 42   Key in **A:\BYE.TXT**.

Step 43   Click **OK**.

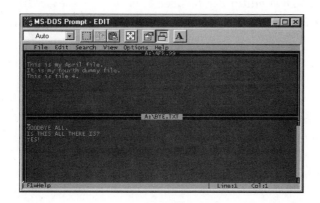

WHAT'S HAPPENING? You have opened two separate files and can view them simultaneously on the split screen.

Step 44   Close both files.

Step 45   Exit the MS-DOS editor.

CHAPTER SUMMARY

1. File attributes are tracked by the operating system.
2. There are four file attributes: A (archive), H (hidden), S (system), and R (read-only).
3. The ATTRIB command allows you to manipulate file attributes.
4. The SUBST command allows you to substitute an unused drive letter for a long, unwieldy path name.
5. The XCOPY command allows you to copy files and subdirectories.
6. There are many parameters available to the XCOPY command. Among them are parameters which enable you to:
    a. copy by date (/D)
    b. copy hidden files (/H)
    c. copy subdirectories (/S)
    d. overwrite read-only files (/R)
    e. copy empty directories (/E)
    f. keep file attributes (/K)
7. DOSKEY is an external memory-resident program that loads automatically (in Windows Millennium) when an MS-DOS window is open. DOSKEY allows you to correct keystroke errors.
8. A memory-resident program is commonly referred to as a TSR program. Once loaded into memory, it remains in memory for the duration of the session.
9. The arrow and function keys in DOSKEY allow you to do command-line editing by recalling and listing the previously keyed in commands.

10. DOSKEY allows you to place more than one command on a line provided each command is separated by the [Ctrl] + T keystroke combination.

11. On the desktop, you use Notepad to edit text files. In the MS-DOS window, you use the MS-DOS editor.

12. The MS-DOS editor can be used to edit or create ASCII text files.

13. In the MS-DOS editor, you can use menus, the mouse, and keystrokes to edit text.

KEY TERMS

archive attribute	memory-resident	system attribute
file attribute	command	text editor
hidden attribute	overstrike mode	TSR
insert mode	read-only attribute	

DISCUSSION QUESTIONS

1. What is the purpose and function of the ATTRIB command?
2. Give two parameters for the ATTRIB command and describe the function and purpose of each.
3. What are file attributes?
4. What effect does a file marked "hidden" have for a user? How can you "unhide" the file?
5. What does a file marked "read-only" mean to a user?
6. What is the function of the archive bit?
7. What is the purpose of the SUBST command?
8. Under what circumstances would the SUBST command be useful?
9. What is the purpose of the XCOPY command?
10. What advantages does the XCOPY command have over the COPY command?
11. List four XCOPY parameters and explain their function and their syntax.
12. Explain the purpose and function of the DOSKEY command.
13. What is a memory-resident program, and how does it work?
14. List and explain five of the DOSKEY editing keys that can be used to edit the command history.
15. Explain how to recall the DOSKEY command line. Discuss how to execute commands from the history list.
16. Compare and contrast a word-processing program, Notepad, and the MS-DOS text editor.

TRUE/FALSE QUESTIONS

For each question, circle the letter T if the question is true and the letter F if the question is false.

T   F   1. The ATTRIB command allows you to add and remove file attributes.

T   F   2. You should not use the DIR command when the drive letter has been assigned with the SUBST command.

T   F   3. You cannot copy empty subdirectories with the XCOPY command.
T   F   4. DOSKEY is a TSR program.
T   F   5. The MS-DOS editor can be used in place of Notepad.

COMPLETION QUESTIONS

Write the correct answer in each blank space.

6. If you key in the command ATTRIB +H THIS.ONE, you have marked the file
    THIS.ONE as _____.

7. The XCOPY parameter(s) that allow(s) you to copy hidden, system, and read-only
    files is/are _____.

8. When you are using DOSKEY, to display a previously entered command press
    the _____ key.

9. If you have to key in a long path name repeatedly, you can use the _____
    command to assign a drive letter to the path.

10. In the MS-DOS editor, to go to the beginning of a file press _____.

MULTIPLE CHOICE QUESTIONS

For each question, write the letter for the correct answer in the blank space.

11. Once installed, a TSR acts like an
    a. external command.
    b. internal command.
    c. both a and b
    d. neither a nor b

12. The /D parameter of the SUBST command
    a. displays the true name of the logical drive.
    b. will have no effect on the SUBST command.
    c. will confirm that the substitution has occurred.
    d. will disable the SUBST command.

13. XCOPY will copy _____ than COPY.
    a. faster, with more options
    b. slower, with more options
    c. with fewer options
    d. none of the above

14. If you want to protect the file MY.FIL from being accidentally erased,
    you would key in the following:
    a. ATTRIB -R MY.FIL
    b. ATTRIB +R MY.FIL
    c. ATTRIB +S MY.FIL
    d. ATTRIB -S MY.FIL

15. To xcopy a file marked read-only and to be sure that the destination file retains the read-only attribute, you would use the parameters
   a. /S /R
   b. /R /K
   c. /R /E
   d. /T /E

WRITING COMMANDS

Write the correct step(s) or command(s) necessary to perform the action listed as if you were at the keyboard.

16. Copy all the files and subdirectories, regardless of their attributes, from the TEMP directory on the root of the default directory to the OLDTEMP directory on the root directory of the disk in the A drive.
   C:\>

17. Change the size of the TSR that will save you re-keying in commands to 2K.
   C:\>

18. Allow the letter J to stand for C:\WINDOSBK\SPORTS.
   C:\>

19. Prevent the DIR command from seeing all the files ending with .99 in the root directory of the disk in the A drive.
   C:\>

20. In the MS-DOS text editor, view and edit two text files simultaneously.
   A:\>

APPLICATION ASSIGNMENTS

Note 1: Be sure to work on the APPLICATION disk, not the DATA disk.

Note 2: The homework problems will assume Drive C is the hard disk and the APPLICATION disk is in Drive A. If you are using another drive, such as floppy drive B or hard drive D, be sure to substitute that drive letter when reading the questions and answers.

Note 3: All subdirectories that are created will be under the root directory unless otherwise specified.

PROBLEM SET I

Note: The prompt is A:\>.

PROBLEM A

A-a If necessary, remove the DATA disk and insert the APPLICATION disk in Drive A.

A-b Copy any files with the **.TV** extension from the **PHONE** directory to the root directory of the APPLICATION disk.

A-c Copy the file in the root directory called **DRAMA.TV** to a new file called **GRAVE.TV**, also in the root directory.

A-d Using the relative path, display the attributes of the **GRAVE.TV** file.

    1. Which command did you use?
      a. DIR GRAVE.TV
      b. ATTRIB GRAVE.TV
      c. ATTRIB +R GRAVE.TV or ATTRIB GRAVE.TV +R
      d. ATTRIB -R GRAVE.TV or ATTRIB GRAVE.TV -R

    2. What file attribute is not displayed?
      a. S
      b. H
      c. both a and b
      d. neither a nor b

A-e Make the **GRAVE.TV** file read-only.

    3. Which command did you use?
      a. DIR GRAVE.TV
      b. ATTRIB GRAVE.TV
      c. ATTRIB -R GRAVE.TV or ATTRIB GRAVE.TV -R
      d. ATTRIB +R GRAVE.TV or ATTRIB GRAVE.TV +R

A-f Key in the following: A:\>**DEL GRAVE.TV**

    4. What message is displayed?
      a. Access denied
      b. This is a read-only file
      c. This file is read-only, delete anyway?
      d. no message is displayed

A-g Display the attributes of the **GRAVE.TV** file.

    5. Which attributes are set on the GRAVE.TV file?
      a. A and S
      b. A and R
      c. A and H
      d. A, H, and R

A-h   Copy **GRAVE.TV** to **GRAVEST.TV**.

A-i   Delete **GRAVE.TV** with the DEL command.

    6. Which command did you use first?
        a. ATTRIB GRAVE.TV +R or ATTRIB +R GRAVE.TV
        b. ATTRIB GRAVE.TV +S or ATTRIB +S GRAVE.TV
        c. ATTRIB GRAVE.TV -R or ATTRIB -R GRAVE.TV
        d. ATTRIB GRAVE.TV -S or ATTRIB -S GRAVE.TV

A-j   Make **GRAVEST.TV** a hidden, read-only file.

    7. Which command did you use?
        a. ATTRIB +A +R GRAVEST.TV
        b. ATTRIB +H +A GRAVEST.TV
        c. ATTRIB +H +R GRAVEST.TV
        d. ATTRIB +S +H +R GRAVEST.TV

A-k   Use the DIR command (with no parameters) to display **GRAVEST.TV**.

    8. Which of the following lines do you see on the screen?
        a. GRAVEST.TV is a hidden file
        b. File not found
        c. Not found - GRAVEST.TV
        d. none of the above

PROBLEM B

B-a   Make a subdirectory on the root of the APPLICATION disk called **FIRST**.

B-b   From the root of the APPLICATION disk, make a subdirectory under **FIRST** called **SECOND**.

B-c   From the root of the APPLICATION disk, make a subdirectory under **SECOND** called **THIRD**.

    9. Which command did you use to make the THIRD subdirectory?
        a. MD THIRD
        b. MD FIRST\THIRD
        c. MD FIRST\SECOND\THIRD
        d. MD SECOND\THIRD

B-d   Copy all the files ending in **.99** from the **WINDOSBK** directory on the C drive to **FIRST**.

B-e   Copy the files in the **FIRST** subdirectory to the **SECOND** subdirectory keeping the same names but with the new file extension of **.BRI**.

B-f   Copy the files in the **SECOND** subdirectory to the **THIRD** subdirectory keeping the same names but with the new file extension of **.NIC**.

B-g   From the root of the APPLICATION disk, display all the files and subdirectories in and under the **FIRST** subdirectory, but not the entire disk.

10. Which command did you use?
   a. DIR /S
   b. DIR FIRST SECOND THIRD
   c. DIR FIRST /S
   d. DIRvFIRST/SECOND/THIRD

B-h   Make all the files in the **FIRST** directory read-only.

B-i   Make all the files in the **THIRD** directory hidden.

11. Which command did you use to mark the files in the THIRD subdirectory as hidden?
   a. ATTRIB +H THIRD
   b. ATTRIB THIRD +H
   c. ATTRIB FIRST\SECOND\THIRD*.* +H
   d. either a or b

B-j   With the root directory of the APPLICATION disk as the default, make a directory called **FIRST-2**.

B-k   With the root directory of the APPLICATION disk as the default, dupli-cate the **FIRST** subdirectory, including all files and subdirectories beneath it, to the subdirectory **FIRST-2**. (Be sure to duplicate all files and retain their attributes in **FIRST-2**.)

12. Which command and parameters did you use?
   a. XCOPY FIRST FIRST-2 /S /E
   b. XCOPY FIRST FIRST-2 /S /H /E /R /K
   c. XCOPY FIRST FIRST-2 /R /H /K
   d. XCOPY FIRST FIRST-2 /S /E

13. How many files were copied?
   a. 4
   b. 8
   c. 12
   d. 16

PROBLEM C

Note: Check with your lab administrator before proceeding with the next step.

C-a   With the root directory of the APPLICATION disk as the default, assign the letter E to represent the path to the **THIRD** subdirectory on the APPLICATION disk under **FIRST**.

Note: If Drive E is not available, choose another drive letter and substitute it in the answers.

14. Which command did you use?
    a. SUBST E FIRST\SECOND\THIRD
    b. SUBST E: FIRST\SECOND\THIRD
    c. SUBST E THIRD
    d. SUBST E: THIRD

C-b　Key in the following: A:\>**SUBST** Enter

15. What line is displayed on the screen?
    a. E: => A:\FIRST\SECOND\THIRD
    b. E = A:\FIRST\SECOND\THIRD
    c. E: = THIRD
    d. none of the above

C-c　With the root directory of the APPLICATION disk as the default, display the directory of the E drive.

16. How many files are listed?
    a. zero
    b. two
    c. four
    d. eight

C-d　With the root directory of the APPLICATION disk as the default and without using the ATTRIB command to determine which attributes are set, issue a command that will remove the attributes from the files in the THIRD directory.

17. Which command did you use?
    a. ATTRIB -A -S -R --H -E:
    b. ATTRIB -ALL E:
    c. ATTRIB -*.* E:
    d. none of the above

C-e　Remove the virtual Drive E.

18. Which command did you use?
    a. SUBST /D
    b. SUBST E: /D
    c. SUBST E /D
    d. SUBST /D E

PROBLEM D

D-a　Clear the DOSKEY memory buffer.

D-b　Key in the following: A:\>**DIR** Enter

D-c　Key in the following: A:\>**DIR FIRST** Enter

D-d　Key in the following: A:\>**DIR FIRST\SECOND** Enter

D-e   Key in the following: A:\>**DIR FIRST\SECOND\THIRD** Enter

D-f   Key in the command to display DOSKEY's history on the screen.

19. Which key did you press?
   a. F9
   b. F8
   c. F7
   d. F6

D-g   Bring up the **Line number:** prompt.

20. Which key did you press?
   a. F9
   b. F8
   c. F7
   d. F6

D-h   At the **Line number:** prompt, key in the following: **3** Enter

21. Which command line is displayed?
   a. A:\>DIR FIRST
   b. A:\>DIR FIRST\SECOND
   c. A:\>DIR FIRST\SECOND\THIRD
   d. A:\>DIR

D-i   Remove the command from the line without executing it.

22. Which key did you press?
   a. F2
   b. F4
   c. Esc
   d. Ctrl + End

PROBLEM E

Note: The APPLICATION disk is in the A drive and A:\> is the default drive.

E-a   Copy **FRANK.FIL** from the **WINDOSBK** directory to the root of the A drive.

E-b   Copy **CAROLYN.FIL** from the **WINDOSBK** directory to the root of the A drive.

E-c   With the MS-DOS editor, edit **FRANK.FIL** to say "Hi, my name is Bob." instead of "Hi, my name is Frank."

E-d   Save the file as **BOB.FIL**.

23. To save the file as BOB.FIL,
    a. you clicked File and then Save As, keyed in BOB.FIL, and clicked OK.
    b. you clicked File and then Save, keyed in BOB.FIL, and clicked OK.
    c. you clicked Edit and then Save As, keyed in BOB.FIL, and clicked OK.
    d. you clicked Edit and then Save, keyed in BOB.FIL, and clicked OK.

E-e   Close the file.

E-f   Open **CAROLYN.FIL** with the MS-DOS editor.

E-g   Edit the file to read:
       Hi, my name is Bette.
       I like learning about operating systems.
       I hope you like it too.

E-h   Save the file as **BETTE.FIL**.

E-i   Close the editor.

24. The current contents of CAROLYN.FIL are:
    a. Hi, my name is Carolyn.
       What is your name?
    b. Hi, my name is Bette.
       What is your name?
    c. Hi, my name is Bette.
       I like learning about operating systems.
       I hope you like it too.
    d. none of the above

E-j   Copy any files with the name **BYE** and any extension from the **\WINDOSBK** directory to the root of the A drive.

E-k   Open the MS-DOS editor and split the window into two sections.

25. After the editor was open, which procedure did you follow?
    a. Click File, click Two Windows.
    b. Click Edit, click Split Screen.
    c. Click View, click Split Window.
    d. Click Options, click Split View.

E-l   With the cursor in the top window, open the file **APR.99** from the root of the A drive.

E-m   Move the cursor to the bottom window and open the file **BYE.TYP** from the root of the A drive.

26. What is the last line in the bottom window?
    a. This is file 4.
    b. This is my April file.
    c. GOODBYE ALL
    d. YES!

E-n   Close the MS-DOS editor.

PROBLEM SET II

Note 1: Before proceeding with these assignments, check with your lab instructor to see if there are any special procedures you should follow.

Note 2: The APPLICATION disk is in Drive A. The A:\> prompt is displayed as the default drive and the default directory. All work will occur on the APPLICATION disk.

Note 3: Make sure that NAME.BAT, MARK.FIL, GETYN.COM, and GO.BAT are all present in the root directory of the APPLICATION disk before proceeding with these problems.

Note 4: All files with the .HW extension must be created in the root directory of the APPLICATION disk.

Step 1   Key in the following: A:\>**NAME** [Enter]

Step 2   Here is an example to key in, but your instructor will have other information that applies to your class. Key in the following:

         Bette A. Peat [Enter]   (Your name goes here.)
         CIS 55 [Enter]   (Your class goes here.)
         T-Th 8-9:30 [Enter]   (Your day and time go here.)
         Chapter 7 Applications [Enter]

Step 3   Press [F6] [Enter]

Step 4   If the information is correct, press **Y** and you are back to A:\>.

WHAT'S HAPPENING? ➡ You have returned to the system level. You now have a file called NAME.FIL with your name and other pertinent information. (*Hint:* Remember redirection.)

TO CREATE 1.HW

❖   Display the names of all files in only the root of the APPLICATION disk that are hidden and redirect the output of the command to a file called 1.HW.

TO CREATE 2.HW

❖   Remove the hidden attribute from files in only the root directory of the APPLICATION disk.

❖   Remove the FIRST-2 subdirectory from the root of the APPLICATION disk.

❖   Change the default directory to A:\FIRST>.

❖   Remove all the attributes from all files and subdirectories under the FIRST subdirectory but not in the FIRST subdirectory.

❖   Key in the following: A:\FIRST>**ATTRIB /S > \2.HW** [Enter]

TO CREATE 3.HW

❖   Change the default directory to A:\>.

❖   Perform the step necessary to be able to refer to the directory A:\FIRST\SECOND\THIRD as E: or a drive letter you can use.

❖   Key in the following: A:\>**DIR E: > 3.HW** Enter

❖   Remove the virtual Drive E.

TO CREATE 4.HW

❖   Concatenate the files BETTE.FIL and BOB.FIL to a new file named PEAT.FIL.

❖   Open the file PEAT.FIL with the MS-DOS editor and make sure there is a blank line between "I hope you like it too." and "Hi, my name is Bob."

❖   Add a new blank line to the bottom of the file, then add another line that reads "Are we having fun yet?"

❖   Save the file and exit the MS-DOS editor.

❖   Display the contents of PEAT.FIL and redirect it to a file called 4.HW.

TO CREATE 5.HW

❖   From the root of the A drive, set the read-only and hidden attributes for all the files in the FILES subdirectory.

❖   Make an exact duplicate of the FILES subdirectory and any subdirectories to another subdirectory off of the root called MORFILES. (*Hint:* You need to copy all files, regardless of their attributes, and the new files should retain their attributes.)

❖   Create a new file with the MS-DOS editor on the root of the APPLICA-TION disk called 5.HW. In the file, key in the command you used to copy FILES to MORFILES in the previous step.

TO PRINT YOUR HOMEWORK

Step 1   Be sure the printer is on and ready to accept print jobs from your computer.

Step 2   Key in the following:
A:\>**GO NAME.FIL 1.HW 2.HW 3.HW 4.HW 5.HW** Enter

Step 3   Follow the messages on the screen. When you finish, you will return to the A:\> prompt.

Step 4   Execute the shut-down procedure.

PROBLEM SET III—BRIEF ESSAY

1. The attributes most often set by the user are H and R. Describe two scenarios where you might find it advantageous to set the hidden and/or read-only attributes to a file or group of files.

2. The XCOPY command's many parameters make it a versatile command. Choose two of the parameters and describe, in detail, how, why, and when you would use them.

ORGANIZING AND MANAGING YOUR HARD DISK

LEARNING OBJECTIVES

After completing this chapter, you will be able to:

1. Explain the purpose of organizing a hard disk.
2. List criteria for organizing a hard disk efficiently and logically.
3. Explain the role XCOPY can play in organizing a hard disk.
4. Explain the difference between contiguous and noncontiguous files.
5. Explain when and how to use the /F parameter with the CHKDSK command.
6. Explain the purpose and function of the ScanDisk command.
7. Compare and contrast the CHKDSK and ScanDisk commands.
8. Explain the purpose and function of the DEFRAG command.
9. Explain the function and purpose of a logical disk drive.
10. Understand the purpose of backing up your hard disk.

STUDENT OUTCOMES

1. Reorganize the DATA disk.
2. Use the XCOPY command with its parameters to copy files.
3. Use the CHKDSK command to elicit statistical information about disks and memory.
4. Interpret the statistical information obtained by using the CHKDSK command.

5. Use the desktop system tools ScanDisk and Disk Defragmenter.
6. Use the CHKDSK/ScanDisk commands to determine if files are contiguous or noncontiguous.

CHAPTER OVERVIEW

The more efficiently and logically a hard disk is organized, the easier it becomes for you to know where to store a new file or how to access an existing one. Subdirectories (folders that group files together under one heading) help you organize a hard disk so that you can easily locate a specific file.

An inefficient but typical hard-disk organizational scheme is to divide the disk into major application programs (i.e., word-processing program, spreadsheet program, etc.) and place the data files for those applications in the same subdirectory. This organizational scheme can create problems when you try to locate a specific data file. To locate a specific data file, you have to remember under which program the data file was listed. It makes sense to never place program files and data files in the same subdirectory. Program files rarely change, and data files are always changing. The majority of computer users are working with application programs to help them do their work projects more easily and efficiently. It makes better sense to organize the disk the way most people work—by project, not by software application.

This chapter demonstrates ways to use the hard disk efficiently. You will learn how to organize a hard disk to serve your specific needs, use directories to keep track of the files on your disk, and determine the best command to use to locate a specific file. You will learn what a logical disk is and what commands can be used with a logical disk. In addition, you will learn some useful commands to manage the hard disk itself and keep it healthy.

8.1 WHY ORGANIZE A HARD DISK?

The initial response of most people with a hard disk, no matter what size, is to place program files and/or data files into the root directory. When they purchase a new program, such as Microsoft Office, there will be a default directory, My Documents, where the data files will be stored. All the files created with Word, Excel, and PowerPoint will end up in this directory. Within a relatively short period of time, there will be many, many files listed in that directory. Other application programs use the now-standard setup or install routines to place the application program on the hard disk. These routines are programs that usually create a subdirectory for that application program and then copy the files from the floppy disks to the named subdirectory on the hard disk. Many application programs have such huge files that, when they are placed on the disk by the manufacturer, the files are compressed. In the process of copying the files to the named subdirectory, the setup or install programs must first decompress those program files. As part of the installation, these programs may or may not create a directory for data. If not, your data files may, by default, end up being saved to the directory that holds the application program files.

If, when you use the DIR command or when you use Windows Explorer, the many files and subdirectory names in the root directory scroll by endlessly, it becomes very difficult to know what files are on the hard disk and where they are located. You spend your time looking for data files instead of doing work with data files. This problem does not change with the Windows GUI. Even in a graphical environment, a disorganized disk does not look pretty.

If you install program files to the root directory of the hard disk instead of to a subdirectory, you are going to have a major problem knowing to which program those files belong. There are also technical reasons for not placing all files in the root directory on a hard disk if you are using FAT16. No matter what size a hard disk is, the root directory can hold only a limited number of file entries when using FAT16. If all files are placed in the root directory, it quickly becomes full. When the root directory table is full, then the operating system thinks the disk is full, even if there is actually room on the disk.

Remember, when you create a subdirectory, it counts as only one entry in the root directory, even though the subdirectory itself may hold hundreds of files. Your only storage limitation becomes the physical size of your hard disk. Most programs written for the Windows environment install themselves to the C:\Program Files subdirectory. As you can imagine, this directory fills rapidly. Other setup programs handle it differently. For example, when you install a program like WordPerfect using the setup program, a subdirectory is created called C:\Corel, and all products written by Corel are installed in that same directory. Most setup programs allow you to change the directory you wish to install in, and if you have a second drive or partition with extra space on it, you will often want to install to a subdirectory of your own choosing. Perhaps you have three drawing programs, PCDraw, PCPaint, and PCPic. You might want to create a subdirectory called DRAW, and then install the programs in C:\DRAW\PCDraw, C:\DRAW\PCPaint, and C:\DRAW\PCPic, respectively. In this way, all your drawing programs would be in one place.

There can be, however, one disadvantage to choosing your own installation location. If you have technical problems with an installed program, and need to call that company's tech support, the person you speak to will undoubtedly expect the software to be installed to the setup program's default directory. If you have installed it somewhere else, the support person may have difficulty helping you.

You typically have more than one program on your computer system. The programs may have come with the computer when you purchased it, or you may have purchased additional programs. For instance, a typical user might have a word-processing program (Word), a spreadsheet program (Lotus 1-2-3), a database program (FoxPro), the operating system (Windows Me), and a checkbook management program (Quicken). If you were that user, your hard disk might look like Figure 8.1.

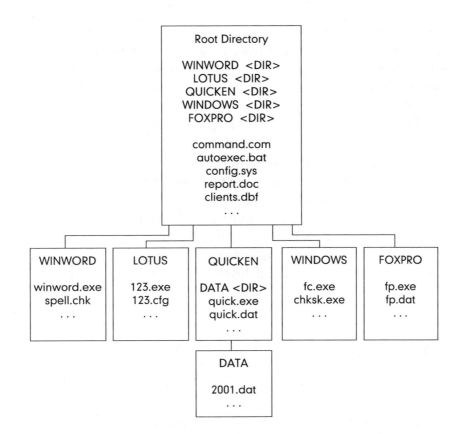

FIGURE 8.1   A TYPICAL HARD-DISK CONFIGURATION

In the above figure, the ellipsis (...) represents the rest of the files. You or the program would create each subdirectory and place the program files that belong to the application program in the proper subdirectory. Notice the Quicken program has automatically created a subdirectory for data files.

The point is, you want to use the programs to do work. As an example, you are a salesperson, and you have two products to sell: widgets and bangles. You use Word to write letters to clients and to make proposals. You use Lotus 1-2-3 to do budget projections for clients. You use Quicken to manage your expenses. You use the operating system to manage your files and disks. You use FoxPro to manage your client's names and addresses (a database) and to work with those data files. You know enough that you know you do not want the data files (such as REPORT.DOC or CLIENTS.DBF) in the root directory. You could use the MOVE command to move the REPORT.DOC file to the WINWORD subdirectory and to move CLIENTS.DBF to the FOXPRO subdirectory.

However, you now know that you do not want to place your data files in the program subdirectory. There are several reasons for this. The major reason is that program files do not change. Data files are always changing as you add or delete information. Within this process you are also adding and deleting files. Thus, when you want to back up your data files, you would have to sort through many program files to do so. Furthermore, part of the rationale for subdirectories is to categorize information—data files are information. It is easier to locate the file of interest if you know what subdirectory it might be in.

When creating file names, you always attempt to create a meaningful name. You want to have a naming convention so that when you create new files that fit into your scheme, you know what name you are going to give them. For example, you are using your database program and you want to keep track of your clients for the bangles product line. You name the data file CLIENTS.DBF. However, you have two products to sell, bangles and widgets. Each product has different clients, so each product requires a separate client file. Since CLIENTS.DBF is a meaningful file name, and you can use CLIENTS for your files, you now have two files you want to call CLIENTS.DBF. You do not want to overwrite one file with another, so you must uniquely identify each file. An efficient way to do this is to create a subdirectory called BANGLES and a subdirectory called WIDGETS and place each CLIENTS.DBF file in the appropriate subdirectory. It is the subdirectory name that clarifies which product client file you work with. An example of an inefficient but typical hard disk organizational scheme with subdirectories for data might look like Figure 8.2.

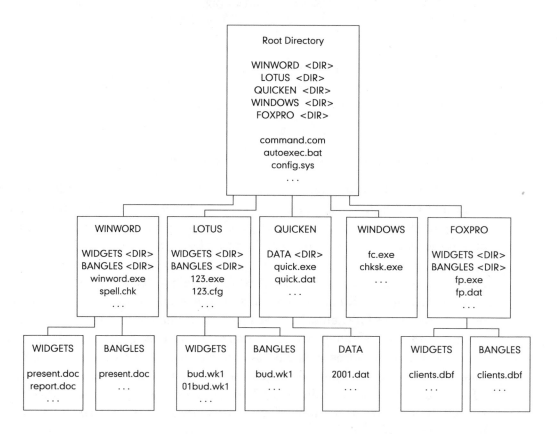

FIGURE 8.2   ORGANIZING A DISK BY SOFTWARE APPLICATION PACKAGE

Although this organizational scheme is better than placing the data files in the root directory or in the program subdirectories, it is still very inefficient. There are too many repeated subdirectory names. In addition, every time you want a data file, you will have to remember not only what application you are working on, but also where the appropriate data file is located. Furthermore, at this point you must key in long path names. For example, when you want to retrieve REPORT.DOC in Word, you need to key in C:\WINWORD\WIDGETS\REPORT.DOC. In addition, when you need to find a file two or three levels down the hierarchical tree, the operating system must look at every subdirectory on the way down. The heads on the disk drive are constantly going back and forth reading the entries and looking for the files.

As you become a more sophisticated user, you will find that you can use data files in conjunction with different application programs. For instance, you can use FoxPro to generate a mailing list from your CLIENTS.DBF file so that you can use it with Word to send out a form letter. When you begin doing this, you end up with data in two places: the word-processing subdirectory and the database subdirectory. More importantly, when you find a new program you want to purchase, such as a presentation package like Harvard Graphics, you need to add a new subdirectory for that program, and you need to add further subdirectories for your products, bangles and widgets. Or you could decide that you want a different word processor such as WordPerfect. How do you handle those data files in the WIDGETS and BANGLES subdirectories? You do not want to delete them because WordPerfect will be able to read them. An even worse nightmare is if, as in this example, you pick up a new product line such as beads. Now you have to create a BEADS subdirectory under each application program. You have created a logistic nightmare for finding out where the files are located and deciding what data files should be kept.

The real problem with this all-too-typical organizational scheme is the logic behind it. Remember, programs are tools. Before computers, you still used tools—a pencil, a calculator, a typewriter. But did you file your output from these tools by the tool name? When you wrote a letter using a typewriter, did you file it in a folder labeled TYPEWRITER? When you calculated some numbers with your calculator, did you place your totals in a file folder called CALCULATOR? Of course not. It sounds silly to even suggest that. But in the above organizational scheme, that is exactly what you are doing!

Programs are simply tools. People do not work by software package; they work by projects. Software is a tool to help do work easily and efficiently. Hence, it makes much better sense to organize a hard disk by the way you work rather than by the application package—the tool. In addition, with an efficient organizational scheme, it is easier to add and delete projects and software. The following section will recommend some guidelines to assist you in organizing your hard disk. However, you must always remember that any organizational scheme you devise is to assist you in saving, retrieving, and backing up your data files easily. A good organizational scheme for one user will not necessarily work for another.

8.2   METHODS OF ORGANIZING A HARD DISK

Certain criteria can give a hard disk an efficient and logical organization. These include the following suggestions:

- The root directory should be a map to the rest of the disk. The only files that should be in the root directory are the files placed there by the operating system, and perhaps AUTOEXEC.BAT and CONFIG.SYS. All other files in the root directory should be subdirectory listings. Look at the root directory as the index or table of contents to your entire hard disk. Ideally, when you execute the DIR command, you should not see more than a screenful of information. With today's very large hard disks, it is difficult to keep to this ideal. In reality, you may have thirty or more subdirectories off the root, which cannot fit on one screen. Nonetheless, the principle remains valid. Keep the root directory clear of unnecessary files.

- Create subdirectories that are shallow and wide instead of compact and deep. The reason is that it is easier for the operating system to find files that are not buried several levels down. Also, it is much easier for you to keep track of the subdirectories when the organizational scheme is simple. Remember the old programmer's principle: "KISS—Keep It Simple, Stupid." Short path names are easier to key in than long path names.

- Plan the organization of your hard disk. Think about the work you do and how it would be easiest for you to find your work files. This is especially true prior to installing new software.

- Do not place data files in the same subdirectory as program files. Although you are constantly changing, creating, and deleting data files, you rarely, if ever, create or delete program files.

- Many small subdirectories with few files are better than a large subdirectory with many files. Remember, you are categorizing data. If you begin to get too many files in a subdirectory, think about breaking the subdirectory into two or more subdirectories. It is easier to manage and update a subdirectory with a limited number of files because there is less likelihood of having to determine on a file-by-file basis which file belongs where. In addition, if you have too few files in many subdirectories, think about combining them into one subdirectory.

- Keep subdirectory names short but descriptive. Try to stay away from generic and meaningless subdirectory names such as DATA. The shorter the subdirectory name, the less there is to key in. For instance, using the subdirectory name WIDGETS for your widgets data files is easy. If you simply use W, that is too short and cryptic for you to remember easily what the W subdirectory holds. On the other hand, using the name WIDGETS.FIL is a little long to key in. You rarely, if ever, use extensions with subdirectory names. Again, remember you will be keying in these path names.

- Create a separate subdirectory for batch files. Batch files are files that you will learn to write to help automate processes you do often. Place the subdirectory for batch files under the root directory. A popular name for this subdirectory is BATCH.

- Create a subdirectory called UTILS (utilities) in which you will create further separate subdirectories for each utility program you own or purchase. As you work with computers, you start collecting utility software. Utility software programs provide commonly needed services. An example of this is Norton Utilities. Utility software would also include any shareware utilities that you might acquire from a download site on the World Wide Web. In many instances, utility software and shareware packages have similar file names, making it imperative that each has its own separate and readily identifiable subdirectory. You can place these subdirectories under the UTILS directory.

- Learn how to install programs to your hard drive. Typically, programs will have a setup or install command. For instance, if you were going to install a file-compression program called WinZip, you would key in SETUP, and the setup program would tell you that it is going to install the program to C:\WINZIP. You can change that to C:\UTILS\WINZIP or D:\WINZIP. In other words, you can create your own organizational scheme and do not have to let the installation programs put the programs anywhere they wish.

- Learn how to use the application package, and also learn how the application package works. For instance, find out if the application package assigns a file extension. Lotus 1-2-3 assigns an extension of .WK1 for its files, whereas WordPerfect assigns a file extension of .WPD. If an application does not assign file extensions to data files, you can be extremely flexible and create file extensions that will apply to the work that you do with that application program's data files. For instance, you could assign the file extension .LET to letter files that deal with all your correspondence or .MYS for data files that deal with a mystery book you are writing. Most Windows programs will assign file extensions. With the addition of long file names introduced in Windows 95, you can name a file CHAPTER8.MYS in Word, and the .DOC extension will be added, leaving the full file name as CHAPTER8.MYS.DOC.

- Find out how the application package works with subdirectories. For instance, does it recognize subdirectories for data files? Very few programs today do not recognize subdirectories. However, most programs will have a default subdirectory where that program saves its data files. You should know what that subdirectory is and if you can change the default directory.

- Analyze the way you work. If you always use an application program's default data directory when you save and retrieve files, then organizing your hard disk around projects will not work for you. In that case, perhaps you do want to create data directories. Figure 8.3 is another way to organize your hard disk.

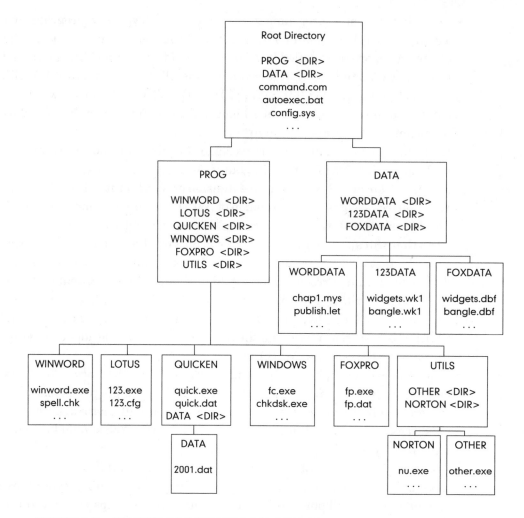

FIGURE 8.3   ANOTHER ORGANIZATIONAL SCHEME

- Analyze your environment. If, for instance, you are in an educational environment, organization by application package makes sense. You are teaching only that one application package, and all data created by students will be saved to floppy disks. Hence, your focus is the package, and organizing around the application package in this instance is logical.

An organizational scheme for a project-oriented environment based on our salesperson scenario could look something like Figure 8.4.

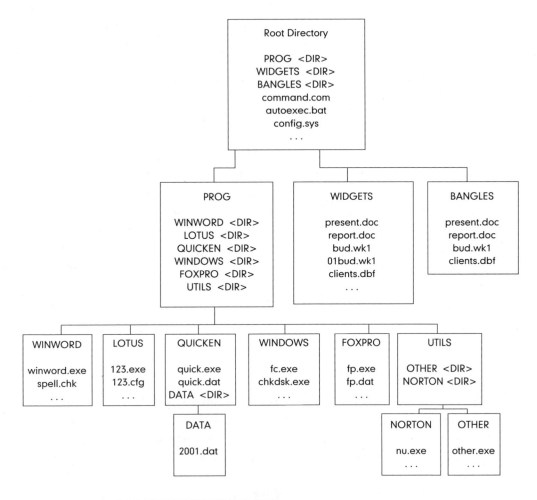

FIGURE 8.4 ORGANIZATION BY PROJECT

In this organizational scheme, you know where all your software application programs are located. In addition, it is much easier to add a new software package or to update an existing one because all the program files are located in one place. For instance, when you want to add a presentation software application program, such as Harvard Graphics, you can create a subdirectory called C:\PROG\HG and install all the files in that location. If you have a suite of software, such as Corel Perfect Office or Microsoft Office, their installation makes subdirectories that act like PROG in the example. Microsoft creates MICROSOFT OFFICE under Program Files, and Corel creates COREL. Under these directories are subdirectories holding the individual programs. Also, since this scheme is organized by project, it is easy to add a new project or delete an old one. If, for example, you are now selling beads, you can create a subdirectory called C:\BEADS. If you no longer are selling widgets, you can use DELTREE and eliminate the WIDGETS subdirectory. It is also easy to know which data files belong to what project. You also can tell which data file belongs to which program by virtue of the file extension. In this example, if you look at the subdirectory called WIDGETS, you know that the data files PRESENT.DOC and REPORT.DOC were created with Word. You know that the data files BUD.WK1 and 98BUD.WK1 were created with Lotus 1-2-3, whereas CLIENTS.DBF was created with FoxPro. The same would be true for the BANGLES subdirectory. This example also shows that you leave the DATA subdirectory as is for Quicken because that is where Quicken prefers the data files.

This, of course, is not the only way to organize a hard disk. You can organize your hard disk any way you wish, but there should be organization. Although it may take some time in the beginning, ultimately organization will make more effective use of the hard disk. Primarily you want to organize your data files into meaningful directories. You do not want to save all your data files to a subdirectory called My Documents. You want to be able to go directly to the subdirectory that holds the files you wish to work on. Except when you create a new file, you will find that if you properly organize your data files, you will rarely use the Start/Programs menu. Instead, you will go directly to the directory that holds the files you wish to work on. For instance, if you were working with the bangles product line, you could open the directory bangles which would have all of your files that deal with bangles, regardless of the application program that created them. The two major considerations for any organizational scheme are first, how do you work, and second, how do the application programs work?

8.3   ORGANIZING A DISK

Most users do not begin with an organized hard disk. What may seem organized to one user is chaos to another. In this instance the user needs to reorganize the hard disk, a process that can be done without reformatting the hard disk. To master this process, you are going to take the DATA disk and reorganize it. This exercise will give you some idea of how the process works without having to worry about inadvertently deleting files from the hard disk. Prior to reorganizing it, however, you will update your backup copy of the DATA disk.

8.4   ACTIVITY: MAKING A COPY OF THE DATA DISK

Note 1: You are in Windows and have not shelled out to the MS-DOS prompt.
Note 2: You will use My Computer to create a copy of the DATA disk.

Step 1   Double-click **My Computer**.

Step 2   Place the DATA disk in the A drive.

Step 3   Right-click the A drive icon.

Step 4   Point to **Copy Disk**.

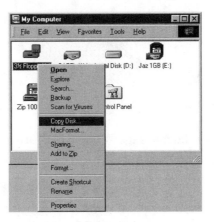

WHAT'S HAPPENING? ➤ You have started the process to copy a disk.

Step 5   Click **Copy Disk**.

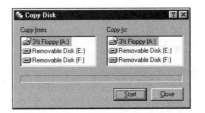

Step 6   Be sure both the Copy from and Copy to boxes have floppy Drive A selected.

Step 7   Click **Start**.

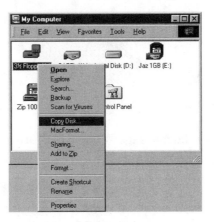

WHAT'S HAPPENING? ➤ The copy process has started. Soon you will see:

The information from the DATA disk is now in memory, and the operating system is waiting for the target disk.

Step 8   Replace the DATA disk with the BACKUP DATA disk you created in Chapter 6. Do not use the ACTIVITIES disk or the APPLICATION disk.

Step 9   Click the **OK** button.

 You see the message Writing to destination disk. When the writing to disk is completed, you will see the following:

The copy process is completed.

Step 10 Click the **Close** button.

Step 11 Remove the BACKUP DATA disk from Drive A.

 You now have updated your BACKUP DATA disk. Now you can safely work on the DATA disk because you have a current backup copy of it.

Step 12 Place the BACKUP DATA disk in a safe place. Insert the DATA disk into Drive A.

8.5 ORGANIZING THE DATA DISK

The DATA disk has minimal organization. The ellipsis (...) in the following figure represent file names. (*Note:* If you did not do all the chapter activities, your disk could look different. It is not important that your disk is exactly as the one pictured. If you have additional files, or are missing some files, you can delete, copy, or create files as needed. The contents of the text files do not matter.) Its structure is as follows:

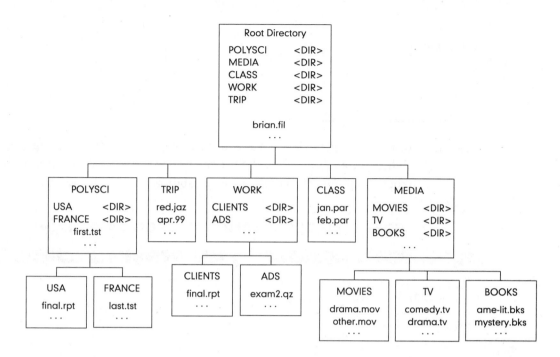

In addition to organizing this disk, you are also going to copy some programs from the \WINDOSBK directory to the disk so that there will be programs as well as data files on it. At this moment, you really cannot tell what is on this disk. In addition, there are so many files in the root directory that when you key in DIR, you see many, many files scrolling by on the screen. Therefore, you are going to reorganize the disk so that it will be easier to manage. You are going to create the necessary subdirectories and copy the appropriate files to the correct subdirectories. You will create a PROG subdirectory which will be the map to the programs on the DATA disk. In the PROG subdirectory you will have the subdirectory GAMES for the different games you will copy from the \WINDOSBK directory and UTILS for the RNS.EXE program. (*Warning:* If you have installed programs on your hard disk, you do not move or copy them elsewhere. You may do so here, as these are special examples.)

8.6   ACTIVITY: SETTING UP THE PROG SUBDIRECTORY

Note: The DATA disk is in Drive A. C:\WINDOWS> is displayed as the default drive and the default directory.

Step 1   Key in the following: C:\WINDOWS>**A:** [Enter]

Step 2   Key in the following: A:\>**MD PROG** [Enter]

Step 3   Key in the following: A:\>**MD PROG\GAMES** [Enter]

Step 4   Key in the following: A:\>**MD PROG\UTILS** [Enter]

```
MS-DOS Prompt                                    _ □ ✕

C:\WINDOWS>A:
```

```
A:\>MD PROG

A:\>MD PROG\GAMES

A:\>MD PROG\UTILS

A:\>_
```

WHAT'S HAPPENING? You created a generic program subdirectory and identified the specific subdirectories that reflect the programs on the DATA disk. Now you need to copy the proper files to the proper subdirectory for this example.

Step 5   Key in the following:
A:\>**COPY C:\WINDOSBK\GAMES\M*.* PROG\GAMES** Enter

```
MS-DOS Prompt                                                _□×

A:\>COPY C:\WINDOSBK\GAMES\M*.* PROG\GAMES
C:\WINDOSBK\GAMES\MLSHUT.EXE
C:\WINDOSBK\GAMES\MLSHUT.DOC
C:\WINDOSBK\GAMES\MAZE.EXE
        3 file(s) copied

A:\>_
```

WHAT'S HAPPENING? You copied all the programs that begin with **M** from the **\WINDOSBK\GAMES** directory to the **PROG\GAMES** subdirectory on the DATA disk.

Step 6   Key in the following: A:\>**DIR C:\WINDOSBK\GAMES** Enter

```
MS-DOS Prompt                                                _□×

A:\>DIR C:\WINDOSBK\GAMES

 Volume in drive C is MILLENNIUM
 Volume Serial Number is 2B18-1301
 Directory of C:\WINDOSBK\GAMES

.               <DIR>         07-20-01   4:25p .
..              <DIR>         07-20-01   4:25p ..
LS       DOC       2,611      06-23-89  11:34p LS.DOC
3DTICTAC EXE      37,760      10-08-85  11:13p 3DTICTAC.EXE
LS       EXE      12,576      06-23-89  11:40p LS.EXE
ARGH     DOC       8,729      08-19-90   4:00a ARGH.DOC
ARGH     EXE      69,728      08-19-90   4:00a ARGH.EXE
MLSHUT   EXE      43,776      08-14-89  10:31p MLSHUT.EXE
MLSHUT   DOC      15,049      08-14-89  10:48p MLSHUT.DOC
MAZE     EXE      34,645      05-09-89   3:51p MAZE.EXE
LS       PAS       8,404      06-23-89  11:41p LS.PAS
CHEK            <DIR>         07-20-01   4:25p CHEK
MLINK           <DIR>         07-20-01   4:25p MLINK
        9 file(s)        233,278 bytes
        4 dir(s)   1,012,719,616 bytes free

A:\>_
```

WHAT'S HAPPENING? You used the COPY command in Step 5 to request all the files that begin with M to be copied to the **PROG\GAMES** subdirectory, but the subdirectory called **MLINK** and the files in it were not copied to the DATA disk. COPY copies only files, not subdirectories. If you had wanted to copy everything that begins with **M** including the **MLINK** subdirectory, you would have used the XCOPY command.

Step 7   Key in the following: A:\>**DIR C:\WINDOSBK*.TXT** [Enter]

```
MS-DOS Prompt                                                    _ □ X

A:\>DIR C:\WINDOSBK\*.TXT

 Volume in drive C is MILLENNIUM
 Volume Serial Number is 2B18-1301
 Directory of C:\WINDOSBK

GOODBYE    TXT            34  01-01-02   4:32a  GOODBYE.TXT
APRIL      TXT            72  06-16-00   4:32p  APRIL.TXT
JANUARY    TXT            73  06-16-00   4:32p  JANUARY.TXT
FEBRUARY   TXT            75  06-16-00   4:32p  FEBRUARY.TXT
MARCH      TXT            71  06-16-00   4:32p  MARCH.TXT
HELLO      TXT            53  05-30-00   4:32p  HELLO.TXT
BYE        TXT            45  05-30-00   4:32p  BYE.TXT
DANCES     TXT            72  12-11-99   4:03p  DANCES.TXT
TEST       TXT            65  12-11-99   4:03p  TEST.TXT
SANDYA~1 TXT             53  11-16-00  12:00p  Sandy and Nicki.txt
SANDYA~2 TXT             59  11-16-00  12:00p  Sandy and Patty.txt
          11 file(s)            672 bytes
           0 dir(s)   1,012,707,328 bytes free

A:\>_
```

WHAT'S HAPPENING? You displayed all the **.TXT** files in the **WINDOSBK** directory. You want to copy all the **.TXT** files that were created on or after 05-30-00 to the root directory of the DATA disk. You do not want to copy the files **TEST.TXT** or **DANCES.TXT**. XCOPY allows you to make choices by date.

Step 8   Key in the following: A:\>**ATTRIB -S -H -R A:*.*** [Enter]

```
MS-DOS Prompt                                                    _ □ X

A:\>ATTRIB -S -H -R A:\*.*

A:\>_
```

WHAT'S HAPPENING? You removed any system, hidden, and read-only attributes that were set for the files on the root of the A drive.

Step 9   Key in the following:
          A:\>**XCOPY C:\WINDOSBK*.TXT /D:05-30-00** [Enter]

```
MS-DOS Prompt                                                    _ □ X

A:\>XCOPY C:\WINDOSBK\*.TXT /D:05-30-00
Overwrite GOODBYE.TXT (Yes/No/All)?_
```

WHAT'S
HAPPENING? ➤ Remember the default for XCOPY is to confirm overwrites. The command is telling you that **GOODBYE.TXT** already exists. In this case, you do want to overwrite all the files.

Step 10 Press **A**

```
A:\>XCOPY C:\WINDOSBK\*.TXT /D:05-30-00
Overwrite GOODBYE.TXT (Yes/No/All)?A
APRIL.TXT
JANUARY.TXT
FEBRUARY.TXT
MARCH.TXT
HELLO.TXT
BYE.TXT
Sandy and Nicki.txt
Sandy and Patty.txt
        9 File(s) copied

A:\>_
```

WHAT'S
HAPPENING? ➤ You copied only the nine files of interest, and not all eleven that were in the \WINDOSBK subdirectory.

8.7   THE MOVE COMMAND REVISITED

When reorganizing your hard disk, you sometimes do need to copy files and/or subdirectory structures from one place to another and replace existing files. In terms of reorganizing your hard disk, you do not necessarily want to copy files and directories. Most often, what you really want to do is either move files from one location to another or simply rename the subdirectory.

You have used the MOVE command in previous chapters to move files from one directory to another. Clearly, using the MOVE command is an easy way to manipulate your files. However, there is an important warning prior to moving files and directories wholesale. Moving data files and data directories is usually a fairly safe and foolproof procedure that seldom impacts how your programs work. However, moving program files and renaming program directories is not "safe." Windows registers program files, their names, and their locations in the Registry. If they are moved or renamed at the MS-DOS prompt, the Registry will not be able to find them, causing major problems. Program files are not generally copied to a location—they are installed in a location with a setup program. Files pertaining to the program are placed in many different locations. Moving or renaming these Windows program files and directories will almost certainly cause the program to fail.

When dealing with small programs that are completely contained within one directory and were created to run under DOS rather than Windows, problems can still occur. Moving the entire directory or renaming it may be safe—the program may still run. If you do decide to manipulate program files and directories, be sure to take note of which directory the program files are in before you start. Does this mean that you should not organize your hard disk? It does not, but you must do it with caution. You can and will be primarily concerned with organzing your data files. These files can be easily and safely rearranged to meet your needs.

In the next activity you will move files and rename subdirectories so you can see how easy it is with data files.

8.8   ACTIVITY: USING MOVE TO ORGANIZE YOUR DISK

Note: You have the DATA disk in Drive A with A:\> displayed.

Step 1   Key in the following: A:\>**MOVE BON*.* POLYSCI\FRANCE** (Enter)

```
MS-DOS Prompt                                                    _ □ ✕

A:\>MOVE BON*.* POLYSCI\FRANCE
A:\BONJOUR.NEW => A:\POLYSCI\FRANCE\BONJOUR.NEW [ok]

A:\>_
```

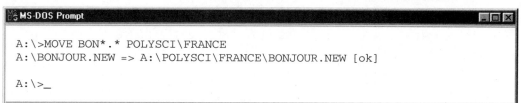 You quickly copied the **BONJOUR.NEW** file to the **POLYSCI\FRANCE** subdirectory and deleted it from the root directory at the same time. That is what the MOVE command does.

Step 2   Key in the following: A:\>**DIR M*.*** (Enter)

```
MS-DOS Prompt                                                    _ □ ✕

A:\>DIR M*.*

 Volume in drive A is DATA
 Volume Serial Number is 3330-1807
 Directory of A:\

MAR        99           71  10-10-99  4:53p MAR.99
MARCH      FIL          71  04-23-00  4:03p MARCH.FIL
MAR        BUD          71  04-23-00  4:03p MAR.BUD
MARCH      NEW          71  04-23-00  4:03p MARCH.NEW
MARCH      TXT          71  06-16-00  4:32p MARCH.TXT
MONTHS     SAM         292  07-24-01  2:15p MONTHS.SAM
MEDIA           <DIR>          07-30-01 11:14a MEDIA
MARK       FIL          73  08-12-00  4:12p MARK.FIL
          7 file(s)            720 bytes
          1 dir(s)       1,264,128 bytes free

A:\>_
```

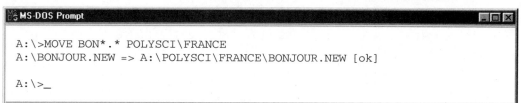 You want to move all the files that begin with **M** to the **POLYSCI\USA** directory. But you don't want to move the **MEDIA** subdirectory. If you use the command **MOVE M*.***, the **MEDIA** subdirectory will also be moved. How can you avoid this?

Step 3   Key in the following: A:\>**ATTRIB +H MEDIA** (Enter)

Step 4   Key in the following: A:\>**DIR M*.*** (Enter)

```
MS-DOS Prompt                                                    _ □ X

A:\>ATTRIB +H MEDIA

A:\>DIR M*.*

 Volume in drive A is DATA
 Volume Serial Number is 3330-1807
 Directory of A:\

MAR      99            71  10-10-99  4:53p MAR.99
MARCH    FIL           71  04-23-00  4:03p MARCH.FIL
MAR      BUD           71  04-23-00  4:03p MAR.BUD
MARCH    NEW           71  04-23-00  4:03p MARCH.NEW
MARCH    TXT           71  06-16-00  4:32p MARCH.TXT
MONTHS   SAM          292  07-24-01  2:15p MONTHS.SAM
MARK     FIL           73  08-12-00  4:12p MARK.FIL
         7 file(s)              720 bytes
         0 dir(s)        1,264,128 bytes free

A:\>_
```

WHAT'S HAPPENING? You have hidden the **MEDIA** subdirectory. Now you can use the MOVE command to move all files beginning with M without disturbing the **MEDIA** subdirectory.

Step 5   Key in the following: A:\>**MOVE M*.* POLYSCI\USA** [Enter]

```
MS-DOS Prompt                                                    _ □ X

A:\>MOVE M*.* POLYSCI\USA
A:\MAR.99 => A:\POLYSCI\USA\MAR.99 [ok]
A:\MARCH.FIL => A:\POLYSCI\USA\MARCH.FIL [ok]
A:\MAR.BUD => A:\POLYSCI\USA\MAR.BUD [ok]
A:\MARCH.NEW => A:\POLYSCI\USA\MARCH.NEW [ok]
A:\MARCH.TXT => A:\POLYSCI\USA\MARCH.TXT [ok]
A:\MONTHS.SAM => A:\POLYSCI\USA\MONTHS.SAM [ok]
Cannot move MEDIA - Permission denied
A:\MARK.FIL => A:\POLYSCI\USA\MARK.FIL [ok]

A:\>_
```

WHAT'S HAPPENING? Notice that the MEDIA subdirectory was not moved. You see the message Cannot move MEDIA - Permission denied.

Step 6   Key in the following: A:\>**ATTRIB -H MEDIA** [Enter]

WHAT'S HAPPENING? You have removed the hidden attribute from the **MEDIA** subdirectory. In the next step, you are going to move the **BOOKS** subdirectory, which is under the **MEDIA** subdirectory, to the **TRIP** subdirectory with its directory name and files intact.

Step 7   Key in the following:
              A:\>**MOVE MEDIA\BOOKS*.* TRIP\BOOKS** [Enter]

```
MS-DOS Prompt                                          _ □ ×

A:\>MOVE MEDIA\BOOKS\*.* TRIP\BOOKS
Make directory "A:\TRIP\BOOKS"? [yn] _
```

WHAT'S HAPPENING? The MOVE command knows that you do not have a subdirectory called **BOOKS** under **TRIP**, so it is asking you if you want to create one.

Step 8   Press **Y** **Enter**

```
MS-DOS Prompt                                          _ □ ×

A:\>MOVE MEDIA\BOOKS\*.* TRIP\BOOKS
Make directory "A:\TRIP\BOOKS"? [yn] y
A:\MEDIA\BOOKS\MYSTERY.BKS => A:\TRIP\BOOKS\MYSTERY.BKS [ok]
A:\MEDIA\BOOKS\AME-LIT.BKS => A:\TRIP\BOOKS\AME-LIT.BKS [ok]
A:\MEDIA\BOOKS\PULITZER.BKS => A:\TRIP\BOOKS\PULITZER.BKS [ok]

A:\>_
```

WHAT'S HAPPENING? It seems that the move was successful. Well, was it?

Step 9   Key in the following: A:\>**DIR TRIP\BOOKS** **Enter**

Step 10   Key in the following: A:\>**DIR MEDIA** **Enter**

```
MS-DOS Prompt                                          _ □ ×

Directory of A:\TRIP\BOOKS

.              <DIR>        08-01-01  8:29p .
..             <DIR>        08-01-01  8:29p ..
MYSTERY  BKS        233     08-08-00  1:39p MYSTERY.BKS
AME-LIT  BKS        184     08-08-00  1:39p AME-LIT.BKS
PULITZER BKS        662     08-08-00  1:39p PULITZER.BKS
         3 file(s)          1,079 bytes
         2 dir(s)       1,263,616 bytes free

A:\>DIR MEDIA

 Volume in drive A is DATA
 Volume Serial Number is 3330-1807
 Directory of A:\MEDIA

.              <DIR>        07-30-01 11:14a .
..             <DIR>        07-30-01 11:14a ..
BOOKS          <DIR>        07-30-01 11:14a BOOKS
TV             <DIR>        07-30-01 11:14a TV
MOVIES         <DIR>        07-30-01 11:14a MOVIES
         0 file(s)               0 bytes
         5 dir(s)       1,263,616 bytes free

A:\>_
```

WHAT'S HAPPENING? The files in the **BOOKS** subdirectory did get moved, but why is **BOOKS** still in the **MEDIA** subdirectory? What is in it?

Step 11   Key in the following: A:\>**DIR MEDIA\BOOKS** **Enter**

```
MS-DOS Prompt                                                          _ □ X

A:\>DIR MEDIA\BOOKS

 Volume in drive A is DATA
 Volume Serial Number is 3330-1807
 Directory of A:\MEDIA\BOOKS

 .              <DIR>          07-30-01  11:14a  .
 ..             <DIR>          07-30-01  11:14a  ..
          0 file(s)                    0 bytes
          2 dir(s)         1,263,616 bytes free

A:\>_
```

WHAT'S HAPPENING? The files were moved successfully. Moving files is easy, and so was creating the subdirectory called **BOOKS** under the **TRIP** subdirectory. Nonetheless, the MOVE command has no way of removing a directory after you empty it. You must use a separate command to remove the **BOOKS** directory under **MEDIA**. You must understand how a command works. The bad news is that a command does not always do what you expect or want it to do. The MOVE command did not remove the **BOOKS** directory, but the good news is the command will always behave in the exact same way. Once you know what the "way" is, you will always know what to expect. Now you know that if you move files, you will need to issue another command to remove the empty directory.

You can use the MOVE command to rename a subdirectory, but the REN command works on subdirectories as well as files.

Step 12 Key in the following: A:\>**REN TRIP NEWSTUFF** ⌈Enter⌉

Step 13 Key in the following: A:\>**DIR TRIP** ⌈Enter⌉

```
MS-DOS Prompt                                                          _ □ X

A:\>REN TRIP NEWSTUFF

A:\>DIR TRIP

 Volume in drive A is DATA
 Volume Serial Number is 2415-16DD
 Directory of A:\

File not found
                   1,263,616 bytes free

A:\>_
```

WHAT'S HAPPENING? You successfully renamed the **TRIP** directory **NEWSTUFF**. In versions of DOS previous to Windows 95, the REN command would not rename subdirectories; you had to use the MOVE command. Using the MOVE command for this purpose was confusing given that, if you keyed it in one way, you moved files, but, if you keyed it another way, you renamed subdirectories. Because this was so confusing, there were utility programs created that rename subdirectories. One such program is **RNS.EXE**.

8.9 A UTILITY PROGRAM—RNS.EXE

There is always something that users want to do that cannot be done easily with the commands that come with the operating system. This is how third-party utilities are born. Some of these utility programs are given away, others are released as shareware, and others are commercially packaged and sold. One of the better-known commercial utility programs is Norton Utilities. Why do computer users buy utility programs? Each program does something useful that the operating system does not allow you to do.

The program RNS.EXE was written by Nick Markiw. It was written for versions of DOS previous to Windows 95 when the REN command could not be used to rename subdirectories. It is included on the ACTIVITIES disk. This program was given to you when you purchased this textbook to demonstrate how third-party utility programs can work with the operating system. The syntax for this program is as follows:

```
RNS [drive:][path]oldname [drive:][path]newname
```

8.10 ACTIVITY: USING RNS, A RENAME SUBDIRECTORY UTILITY

Note 1: You have the DATA disk in Drive A with A:\> displayed.
Note 2: You previously created the PROG\UTILS subdirectory on your DATA disk. If you do not have this directory structure, create it now.

Step 1   Key in the following:
          A:\>**COPY C:\WINDOSBK\RNS.EXE PROG\UTILS** Enter

Step 2   Key in the following: A:\>**DIR PROG\UTILS** Enter

```
MS-DOS Prompt                                              _ □ ×

A:\>COPY C:\WINDOSBK\RNS.EXE PROG\UTILS
        1 file(s) copied

A:\>DIR PROG\UTILS

 Volume in drive A is DATA
 Volume Serial Number is 3330-1807
 Directory of A:\PROG\UTILS

.              <DIR>         08-01-01  8:12p .
..             <DIR>         08-01-01  8:12p ..
RNS       EXE       7,269    11-22-89 10:35p RNS.EXE
        1 file(s)            7,269 bytes
        2 dir(s)         1,255,936 bytes free

A:\>_
```

WHAT'S HAPPENING?   You copied the file **RNS.EXE** from the **\WINDOSBK** subdirectory to the **PROG\UTILS** subdirectory on the DATA disk. You should recognize any file with an **.EXE** extension as a program. You decide that **NEWSTUFF** is not a descriptive name for the subdirectory and want to change the subdirectory name from **NEWSTUFF** to **TRIP**.

Step 3   Key in the following: A:\>**CD PROG\UTILS** [Enter]

Step 4   Key in the following: A:\PROG\UTILS>**RNS \NEWSTUFF \TRIP** [Enter]

```
MS-DOS Prompt                                                    _ □ ✕

A:\>CD PROG\UTILS

A:\PROG\UTILS>RNS \NEWSTUFF \TRIP
RNS  VER. 1.05

A:\PROG\UTILS>_
```

WHAT'S HAPPENING?   You first changed the directory to the place where the program **RNS.EXE** is located so that you could execute it. You could have changed the path, but since this is a one-time experiment, you do not want to do that. Then you executed the RNS program to change the directory names. This seemed easy enough. Did it work?

Step 5   Key in the following: A:\PROG\UTILS>**DIR \TRIP** [Enter]

Step 6   Key in the following: A:\PROG\UTILS>**DIR \NEWSTUFF** [Enter]

```
MS-DOS Prompt                                                    _ □ ✕

A:\PROG\UTILS>DIR \TRIP

 Volume in drive A is DATA
 Volume Serial Number is 3330-1807
 Directory of A:\TRIP

.              <DIR>        07-25-01  6:37p .
..             <DIR>        07-25-01  6:37p ..
APR      99           72    10-10-99  4:53p APR.99
RED      JAZ          19    05-30-00  4:32p RED.JAZ
MAR      99           71    10-10-99  4:53p MAR.99
APR      INK          72    04-23-00  4:18p APR.INK
FEB      INK          75    04-23-00  4:03p FEB.INK
JAN      INK          73    04-23-00  4:03p JAN.INK
MAR      INK          71    04-23-00  4:03p MAR.INK
FEB      99           75    10-10-99  4:53p FEB.99
FEBRUARY TXT          75    04-23-00  4:03p FEBRUARY.TXT
FEB      BUD          75    04-23-00  4:03p FEB.BUD
FUNNY    TV          232    03-05-00  4:41p FUNNY.TV
FRANK    FIL          44    07-31-99 12:53p FRANK.FIL
BOOKS          <DIR>        08-01-01  8:28p BOOKS
        12 file(s)          954 bytes
         3 dir(s)     1,255,936 bytes free

A:\PROG\UTILS>DIR \NEWSTUFF

 Volume in drive A is DATA
 Volume Serial Number is 3330-1807
```

```
  Directory of A:\

File not found
                           1,255,936 bytes free

A:\PROG\UTILS>_
```

WHAT'S HAPPENING? The RNS command did rename the subdirectory **NEWSTUFF** to **TRIP**. It is, of course, not necessary to use this command, as the REN command works as well. The RNS command is used here as an example of a third-party utility. People write utility programs like RNS to extend the power of the operating system. You will find that this is also true with Windows utilities. There are third-party utility programs available for Windows that extend and expand its capabilities. Although utility programs often have overlapping commands, users often purchase more than one utility program because each one has certain useful functions.

Step 7   Key in the following: A:\PROG\UTILS>**CD \ [Enter]**

```
MS-DOS Prompt                                              _ □ ✕

A:\PROG\UTILS>CD \

A:\>_
```

WHAT'S HAPPENING? You have returned to the root of the A drive.

8.11   CHECKING A DISK AND MEMORY

CHKDSK is an operating system utility that dates back to very early versions of MS-DOS. CHKDSK is an external command stored in the C:\WINDOWS \COMMAND subdirectory. Although CHKDSK can only be used fully on disks partitioned with 16-bit file allocation tables (FAT) and not 32-bit (FAT32), it is still a viable utility. ScanDisk is the replacement for CHKDSK. It can detect and repair many disk problems on both disk formats, but does not report the same information that CHKDSK will. CHKDSK will report disk-space usage information, and can list all files on floppy disks, zip disks, and FAT hard drive partitions. On FAT32 partitions, CHKDSK will report total and remaining space, total number of allocation units and remaining allocation units, and the number of bytes per allocation unit on the disk. It will also report on conventional memory. This is information you need to know about your disks. You need to know how much room is left on the disk so that you can add a new file.

8.12   ACTIVITY: USING CHKDSK ON A FAT32 DRIVE

Note: The DATA disk is in Drive A. A:\> is displayed.

Step 1   Key in the following: A:\>**C: [Enter]**

Step 2   Key in the following: C:\WINDOWS>**CHKDSK [Enter]**

```
MS-DOS Prompt                                                    _ □ ×

A:\>C:

C:\WINDOWS>CHKDSK

CHKDSK has NOT checked this drive for errors.
You must use SCANDISK to detect and fix errors on this drive.

Volume MILLENNIUM created 07-19-2001 9:02a
Volume Serial Number is 2B18-1301

2,107,691,008 bytes total disk space
  999,366,656 bytes available on disk

        4,096 bytes in each allocation unit
      514,573 total allocation units on disk
      243,986 available allocation units on disk

      655,360 total bytes memory
      593,840 bytes free

C:\WINDOWS>_
```

WHAT'S HAPPENING?   The operating system tells you that CHKDSK has not checked this drive for errors. But, nonetheless, valuable information has been provided. You know the total disk capacity, (2,107,691,008 bytes) the remaining space, (999,366,656 bytes) the total number of allocation units, (514,573) allocation units available for use, (243,986) and the number of bytes in each allocation unit, (4,096). Conventional memory usage in the MS-DOS session is also provided. Memory is covered in a later chapter.

8.13 CHKDSK ON FAT AND FLOPPY DRIVES

You want to know if there are any bad spots on a disk, which can mean the loss of a file. Bad spots can come from a variety of sources, such as a mishandled disk or a manufacturing defect. You may want to know if the files are being stored efficiently on a disk. On non-FAT32 format drives, these tasks can be accomplished with CHKDSK. The CHKDSK command analyzes the directory on a disk, making sure that the directory entries match the location and lengths of files with the file allocation table on the default drive (or designated drive). It makes sure that all the directories are readable. After checking the disk, CHKDSK reports any errors and gives information about the disk's total capacity—how many files are on a disk and how much space is taken. CHKDSK establishes the space left on the disk for additional files and displays the size of the computer's conventional memory in terms of bytes. Thus, the command supplies a disk and memory status report. You should occasionally run the CHKDSK command for each non-FAT32 disk to ensure that your file structures have integrity.

CHKDSK informs you of errors. The two kinds of errors are cross-linked files and lost clusters. *Cross-linked files* result when two files claim the same sectors in the file allocation table. Different files cannot share clusters. *Lost clusters* indicate sectors that have no directory entry and are "orphans"; that is, they do not belong to any file that the operating system knows about.

The syntax for CHKDSK is:

```
CHKDSK [drive:][[path]filename] [/F] [/V]

   [drive:][path]  Specifies the drive and directory to check.
   filename        Specifies the file(s) to check for fragmentation.
   /F              Fixes errors on the disk.
   /V              Displays the full path and name of every file on the disk.
Type CHKDSK without parameters to check the current disk.
```

As previously stated, ScanDisk is intended as a replacement for CHKDSK, and it is better at fixing the disk problems mentioned above. ScanDisk scans the surface of the disk, looks for bad sectors, and fixes other disk problems as well. However, ScanDisk does not really replace CHKDSK because ScanDisk does not report the information that CHKDSK does. So, although ScanDisk may be a better command for repairing disk errors, CHKDSK still is a viable command because of its reporting functions.

8.14 ACTIVITY: USING CHKDSK ON A FAT DRIVE

Step 1   Key in the following: C:\WINDOWS>**CD COMMAND** [Enter]

Step 2   Key in the following: C:\WINDOWS\COMMAND>**DIR CHKDSK.*** [Enter]

```
MS-DOS Prompt                                              _ □ ✕

C:\WINDOWS>CD COMMAND

C:\WINDOWS\COMMAND>DIR CHKDSK.*

 Volume in drive C is MILLENNIUM
 Volume Serial Number is 2B18-1301
 Directory of C:\WINDOWS\COMMAND

CHKDSK    EXE       27,968  06-08-00  5:00p CHKDSK.EXE
          1 file(s)          27,968 bytes
          0 dir(s)    1,012,600,832 bytes free

C:\WINDOWS\COMMAND>_
```

WHAT'S HAPPENING? → The DIR command told you that the program CHKDSK.EXE is indeed stored as a file in the \WINDOWS\COMMAND subdirectory.

Step 3   Key in the following: C:\WINDOWS\COMMAND>**CHKDSK** [Enter]

```
MS-DOS Prompt                                              _ □ ✕

 Volume in drive C is MILLENNIUM
 Volume Serial Number is 2B18-1301

 2,146,631,680 bytes total disk space
    15,204,352 bytes in 133 hidden files
    11,534,336 bytes in 350 directories
   734,363,648 bytes in 7,498 user files
 1,385,529,344 bytes available on disk
```

```
32,768 bytes in each allocation unit
65,510 total allocation units on disk
42,283 available allocation units on disk

655,360 total bytes memory
627,184 bytes free
```

WHAT'S HAPPENING? ▶ Do not worry if you do not see the same numbers displayed on your screen. These numbers are related to how the disk was formatted, the size of the hard disk, and how much internal memory is installed in a specific computer. What is important is what the status report is telling you. Let us look at this example, line for line.

2,146,631,680 bytes total disk space	This number is the entire capacity of a specific disk.
15,204,352 bytes in 133 hidden files	What are hidden files? On Drive C, in order to boot from the disk, there must be at least two hidden files: IO.SYS and MSDOS.SYS. The Registry files are also hidden files. Many help files are hidden files, as well as system and information files from both the operating system and software applications. The number of hidden files will vary from disk to disk.
11,534,336 bytes in 350 directories	Nearly all hard disks have subdirectories. This number is for subdirectory entries only.
734,363,648 bytes in 7,498 user files	A user file is any file that is stored on the disk. It does not have to be a file that you, the user, created. User files include all program or application files you have on a disk.
1,385,529,344 bytes available on disk	This line establishes how much room remains on the disk in Drive C for new data or program files in bytes. A byte is one character. It can be the letter b, the letter c, the number 3, or the punctuation mark ?, for example. To give you a rough idea of what a byte means, a page of a printed novel contains about 3,000 bytes. Thus, a disk with a total capacity of 360,000 bytes could hold or store a maximum of about 120 pages of a novel. If you had a 20 MB hard disk (1 megabyte means 1,000,000 bytes) it would hold approximately 20,000,000 bytes or 6,667 pages of text, and if the average novel has about 400 pages, you could store about 16½

	novels. A 2 GB hard drive could hold about 1,800 books! This approximation is not entirely accurate because it does not take into account that often information is stored in such a way as to be compressed. However, it does give you an idea of the disk capacity in "human terms." As you work with computers, you become accustomed to thinking in bytes.
32,768 bytes in each allocation unit	As discussed earlier, the smallest unit that the OS actually reads is a cluster. A cluster is made up of sectors. A cluster is also referred to as an allocation unit. The number of sectors that make up a cluster (allocation unit) vary depending on the type of disk. For small hard drives, a cluster is comprised of 16 sectors (512 * 16 = 8,192). For larger drives, a cluster is comprised of 64 sectors (512 * 64 = 32,768).
65,510 total allocation units on disk	This indicates the total number of clusters available. If you multiply 65,510 by 32,768, you get 2,146,631,680—or the capacity of this hard disk, a 2 GB hard disk.
42,283 available allocation units on disk	This line tells you how much room is available on the disk by cluster.
655,360 total bytes memory	After all these numerical lines on the display screen, there are two blank lines followed by the next two lines of information. This second group of numbers discloses the conventional internal memory (RAM) of the personal computer you are using. Although today we talk of computer memory in gigabytes, memory and disk space are still measured in bytes. Bytes are expressed in the context of the binary numbering system, as 20, 21, 22, and so on. Rather than being stated individually, bytes are grouped in kilobytes (KB). One kilobyte is 210 or 1,024. The odd 24 per 1,000 is dropped to simplify calculations. For all practical purposes the value of 1 GB is equal to 1,000 MB. Thus, 32 GB of RAM memory would be 32 * 1,024 * 1,000 bytes.
627,184 bytes free	Conventional memory available to the system.

Sometimes you will see a line reporting how many bad sectors a disk may have. Having bad sectors is not uncommon on hard disks. If you had bad sectors, the line might read "65,536 bytes in bad sectors." The number would, of course, vary depending on the disk that is checked. On a 1 GB hard disk, for instance, 65,536 bytes in bad sectors is not that significant. However, if you had a smaller hard disk, the number would be significant and you might want to determine if your hard disk needs to be replaced.

This informs you of the ScanDisk command, which does a better job of fixing problems than CHKDSK, but, as you will see, ScanDisk does not give you the reports CHKDSK does.

Step 4   Key in the following: C:\WINDOWS\COMMAND>**CHKDSK A:** Enter

```
MS-DOS Prompt

C:\WINDOWS\COMMAND>CHKDSK A:

Volume DATA         created 07-20-2001 4:55p
Volume Serial Number is 3330-1807

    1,457,664 bytes total disk space
        8,192 bytes in 16 directories
      193,536 bytes in 97 user files
    1,255,936 bytes available on disk

          512 bytes in each allocation unit
        2,847 total allocation units on disk
        2,453 available allocation units on disk

      647,168 total bytes memory
      585,552 bytes free

C:\WINDOWS\COMMAND>_
```

WHAT'S HAPPENING?   In Step 3, CHKDSK checked out the disk on the default drive, Drive C. Since here you wanted to know about the status of the DATA disk located in Drive A, you had to ask specifically for that information by telling CHKDSK which disk to check. In other words, you added a parameter (the parameter A:). This display looks similar to the first screen. You have 1,457,664 bytes total disk space because this is a 1.44 MB disk. If you had formatted this disk with an operating system, you would have seen two hidden files. Since you did not, you did not see this information. The files and bytes available will vary based on what is on the DATA disk. The last two lines displayed on the screen do not change because you are still using the same computer and the amount of internal memory (RAM) on a specific computer does not vary. However, the statistical information about the disk does change because you asked for information about a different disk. If you placed another disk in Drive A, you would get different information about files and free bytes remaining on the disk.

Step 5   Key in the following: C:\WINDOWS\COMMAND>**CD \ [Enter]**

Step 6   Key in the following: C:\>**A: [Enter]**

```
MS-DOS Prompt                                                    _ □ ✕

C:\WINDOWS\COMMAND>CD \

C:\>A:

A:\>_
```

WHAT'S HAPPENING?   ➤ You have made the root directory of the DATA disk the default.

8.15 THE VERBOSE PARAMETER WITH THE CHKDSK COMMAND

The CHKDSK command has a very useful parameter, /V. Using /V is known as
running in verbose mode. This parameter, in conjunction with the CHKDSK command, not only gives the usual status report, but also lists every file on the disk
including hidden files. An important thing to remember about parameters is that
they are associated with specific commands and perform specific tasks for those
commands. The same parameter does not do the same thing with other commands.
For instance, if you use the parameter /V with the FORMAT command, it means put
a volume label on the disk. However, when you use /V with the CHKDSK command,
it displays all the files on the disk. Again, this parameter only works on disks that
are FAT16.

8.16 ACTIVITY: USING THE /V PARAMETER; USING DIR PARAMETERS

Note 1: The DATA disk is in Drive A. A:\> is displayed.
Note 2: When you press **[Enter]** in Step 1, the screen display will scroll by too fast to
see. Even hitting the **[Pause]** key immediately will not stop the screen.
Note 3: Your files may appear in a different order.

Step 1   Key in the following: A:\>**CHKDSK /V [Enter]**

```
MS-DOS Prompt                                                    _ □ ✕

A:\FILE2.CZG
A:\FILE2.FP
A:\FILE2.SWT
A:\FILE3.CZG
A:\APRIL.TXT
A:\FEBRUARY.TXT
A:\HELLO.TXT
A:\BYE.TXT
A:\SANDYA~2.TXT
A:\DANCES.TXT
A:\TEST.TXT
Directory A:\PROG
Directory A:\PROG\GAMES
A:\PROG\GAMES\MLSHUT.EXE
A:\PROG\GAMES\MLSHUT.DOC
```

```
A:\PROG\GAMES\MAZE.EXE
Directory A:\PROG\UTILS
A:\PROG\UTILS\RNS.EXE

  1,457,664 bytes total disk space
      8,192 bytes in 16 directories
    193,536 bytes in 97 user files
  1,255,936 bytes available on disk

        512 bytes in each allocation unit
      2,847 total allocation units on disk
      2,453 available allocation units on disk

    647,168 total bytes memory
    585,552 bytes free

A:\>_
```

WHAT'S HAPPENING? The output from the command you entered scrolled by so quickly that you were unable to see that all the files on the disk were listed. You can see only the last few files and the statistical and memory information at the end of the display. In order to view the information returned by this command, you are going to use an operating system feature that will be covered in the next chapter—redirection. You have, however, used this feature in previous chapters to direct the Application Assignments to the printer. You will redirect the output of the CHKDSK /V command to a file instead of the screen, and then use the MS-DOS editor to see it.

Step 2   Key in the following: A:\>**CHKDSK /V > CHKDSK.TXT** (Enter)

```
MS-DOS Prompt                                                    _ □ ✕

A:\>CHKDSK /V > CHKDSK.TXT

A:\>_
```

WHAT'S HAPPENING? Nothing is displayed on the screen. You have redirected the display to the file CHKDSK.TXT on the default drive.

Step 3   Key in the following: A:\>**EDIT CHKDSK.TXT** (Enter)

WHAT'S HAPPENING? You can see the output of the CHKDSK /V command that you have redirected to the CHKDSK.TXT file.

Step 4   Move the scroll bar at the right edge of the screen approximately halfway down the screen, as shown in the following screen.

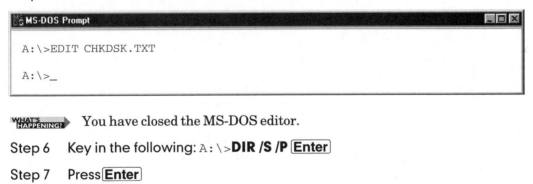

Notice the subdirectory names are displayed, along with all the files each subdirectory contains. You can use this command on any non-FAT32 drive. If you have a FAT16 hard drive, you could, for instance, key in A:\>CHKDSK C: /V. However, since the display on a hard disk is typically large, it is not as useful as you would like. The DIR command has the /S parameter, which allows you to look at all your subdirectories on any disk. Furthermore, the DIR command has the /P parameter to pause the display, and CHKDSK does not.

Step 5   On the MS-DOS menu bar, click **File**. Click **Exit**.

```
MS-DOS Prompt                                              _ □ ×

A:\>EDIT CHKDSK.TXT

A:\>_
```

You have closed the MS-DOS editor.

Step 6   Key in the following: A:\>**DIR /S /P** [Enter]

Step 7   Press[Enter]

Step 8   Press[Enter]

```
MS-DOS Prompt                                              _ □ ×

 (continuing A:\)
 FILE3     CZG         19  12-06-00   2:45p  FILE3.CZG
 HELLO     TXT         53  05-30-00   4:32p  HELLO.TXT
 BYE       TXT         45  05-30-00   4:32p  BYE.TXT
 SANDYA~2  TXT         59  11-16-00  12:00p  Sandy and Patty.txt
 DANCES    TXT         72  12-11-99   4:03p  DANCES.TXT
 TEST      TXT         65  12-11-99   4:03p  TEST.TXT
 PROG           <DIR>      07-24-01  12:26p  PROG
        42 file(s)       49,920 bytes

 Directory of A:\CLASS

 .              <DIR>      07-24-01  12:26p  .
 ..             <DIR>      07-24-01  12:26p  ..
```

```
JAN       PAR         73   04-23-00   4:03p JAN.PAR
FEB       PAR         75   04-23-00   4:03p FEB.PAR
JAN       ABC         73   04-23-00   4:03p JAN.ABC
FEB       ABC         75   04-23-00   4:03p FEB.ABC
MAR       ABC         71   04-23-00   4:03p MAR.ABC
APR       ABC         72   04-23-00   4:18p APR.ABC
MAR       PAR         71   04-23-00   4:03p MAR.PAR
APR       PAR         72   04-23-00   4:18p APR.PAR
Press any key to continue . . .
```

WHAT'S HAPPENING? This parameter allows you to view the files in all your directories and pause the display. You can also view specific files in all subdirectories.

Step 9 Press **Enter** until you reach the A:\> prompt.

Step 10 Key in the following: A:\>**DIR *.NEW /S** **Enter**

```
MS-DOS Prompt                                              _ □ ✕

 Volume in drive A is DATA
 Volume Serial Number is 3330-1807

Directory of A:\

APRIL     NEW         72   04-23-00   4:03p APRIL.NEW
GOODBYE   NEW         34   01-01-02   4:32a GOODBYE.NEW
JANUARY   NEW         73   04-23-00   4:03p JANUARY.NEW
          3 file(s)              179 bytes

Directory of A:\POLYSCI\FRANCE

BONJOUR   NEW         53   04-23-00   4:03p BONJOUR.NEW
          1 file(s)               53 bytes

Directory of A:\POLYSCI\USA

MARCH     NEW         71   04-23-00   4:03p MARCH.NEW
          1 file(s)               71 bytes

Total files listed:
          5 file(s)              303 bytes
          0 dir(s)         1,252,864 bytes free

A:\>_
```

WHAT'S HAPPENING? This command allows you to be even more specific and locate a file anywhere on the disk by searching all the subdirectories. Thus, DIR /S supplants CHKDSK /V in its ability to show every file on the disk in every subdirectory.

The CHKDSK /V command will also show you any hidden files, but again the parameters in the DIR command are better for that purpose. By using the /A parameter (attribute) with the attribute you wish, you can determine what you will see. You can use D (directories), R (read-only files), H (hidden files), S (system files), A (files ready to archive), or, if you use the - sign before an attribute, you will select all the files except those that have that attribute.

Step 11   Key in the following: A:\>**DIR /AD** Enter

```
MS-DOS Prompt                                              _ □ ✕

A:\>DIR /AD

 Volume in drive A is DATA
 Volume Serial Number is 3330-1807
 Directory of A:\

POLYSCI       <DIR>         07-20-01   4:57p POLYSCI
TRIP          <DIR>         07-25-01   6:37p TRIP
CLASS         <DIR>         07-24-01  12:26p CLASS
WORK          <DIR>         07-24-01   1:10p WORK
MEDIA         <DIR>         07-30-01  11:14a MEDIA
PROG          <DIR>         08-01-01   8:12p PROG
        0 file(s)               0 bytes
        6 dir(s)        1,252,864 bytes free

A:\>_
```

WHAT'S HAPPENING?   You selected the /A parameter and used the D attribute for directories only to control the output of the DIR command. Remember, the order in which your directories and files are displayed may vary.

8.17   CONTIGUOUS AND NONCONTIGUOUS FILES

Contiguous means being in contact with or touching. What does this have to do with files? As far as the operating system is concerned, data is a string of bytes that it keeps track of by grouping the data into a file. In order to manage storing and retrieving files, a disk is divided into numbered blocks called sectors. Sectors are then grouped into clusters. A cluster is the smallest unit that the operating system deals with, and it is always a set of contiguous sectors. Clusters on a 1.44 MB floppy disk consist of one 512-byte sector. The number of sectors that make up a cluster on a hard disk varies depending on the size of the hard disk and FAT (file allocation table) being used. On a 2 GB hard disk, a sector consists of 32,768 bytes. Most often, a data file will take up more space on a disk than one cluster. Thus, the operating system has to keep track of the location of all the parts of the file that are on the disk. It does so by means of the directory and the FAT.

The original release of Windows 95 used the standard FAT—a 16-bit version. A 32-bit FAT was introduced with release B of Windows 95. From that version through Millennium, you have the choice—use the standard FAT or the 32-bit version, referred to as FAT32. The decision on which FAT to use is made when the disk volume is originally partitioned. See Figure 8.5 to see the differences between FAT and FAT32.

Feature	FAT	FAT32
Maximum partition size	2 GB	2,048 GB
Cluster size for 2-GB partition	32K	4K

Accessible locally from	Windows (all versions), Windows NT, and MS-DOS	Windows 95-B, 98, and Me
Accessible remotely by	Windows (all versions), Windows NT, and MS-DOS	Windows (all versions), Windows NT, and MS-DOS
Drive space compression	Yes	No

FIGURE 8.5   FAT VS. FAT32

The FAT keeps a record of the cluster numbers each file occupies. As the operating system begins to write files on a new disk, it makes an entry in the disk's directory for that file and updates the FAT with the cluster numbers used to store that file. Data is written to disk based on the next empty cluster. Files being written to disk are written in adjacent clusters. The operating system wants all the file information to be next to each other and tries to write to adjacent clusters whenever possible because it is easier to retrieve or store information when it is together. When this occurs, the file is considered contiguous. For example, if you began writing a letter to your United States senator, it would be stored on your disk in the manner shown in Figure 8.6.

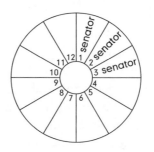

FIGURE 8.6   ONE FILE IN CLUSTERS

The clusters with nothing in them are simply empty spaces on the disk. If you now decide to write a letter to your mother, this new file is written to the next group of adjacent clusters, which would begin with cluster 4 as shown in Figure 8.7.

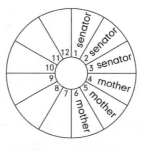

FIGURE 8.7   CONTIGUOUS FILES IN CLUSTERS

These two files, SENATOR and MOTHER, are contiguous. Each part of each file follows on the disk. Now you decide to add a comment to your senator letter, making the SENATOR file bigger. When the operating system goes to write the letter file to disk, the FAT looks for the next empty clusters, which are clusters 7 and 8. The FAT would appear as shown in Figure 8.8.

FIGURE 8.8 NONCONTIGUOUS FILES IN CLUSTERS

The parts of the file named SENATOR are separated, making this file noncontiguous or fragmented. The process becomes more complicated as you add and delete files. For example, if you delete the file SENATOR, the FAT marks clusters 1, 2, 3, 7, and 8 as available even though the data actually remains on the disk. You then decide to develop a PHONE file, shown in Figure 8.9.

FIGURE 8.9 ADDING A FILE

Next, you decide to write a letter to your friend Joe, to write a letter to your friend Mary, to add to the PHONE file, and to add to the letter to your mother. The disk would look like Figure 8.10.

FIGURE 8.10 ADDING MORE FILES

The parts of these files are broken up and are no longer stored in adjacent clusters. They are now known as noncontiguous or *fragmented files*. If the disk is comprised of noncontiguous files, it can be called a fragmented disk. It will take longer to read noncontiguous files because the read/write heads must move around the disk to find all the parts of a file. You can see if files are contiguous or noncontiguous by using a parameter with the CHKDSK command.

8.18 ACTIVITY: USING CHKDSK TO SEE IF FILES ARE CONTIGUOUS

Note: The DATA disk is in Drive A. A:\> is displayed.

Step 1   Key in the following: A:\>**CHKDSK GOODBYE.TXT** Enter

```
MS-DOS Prompt                                                    _ □ ✕

A:\>CHKDSK GOODBYE.TXT

Volume DATA          created 07-20-2001 4:55p
Volume Serial Number is 3330-1807

    1,457,664 bytes total disk space
        8,192 bytes in 16 directories
      196,608 bytes in 98 user files
    1,252,864 bytes available on disk

          512 bytes in each allocation unit
        2,847 total allocation units on disk
        2,447 available allocation units on disk

      647,168 total bytes memory
      585,552 bytes free

All specified file(s) are contiguous

A:\>_
```

WHAT'S
HAPPENING?
The screen display supplies all the statistical information about the
DATA disk and computer memory. In addition, the last line states **All
specified file(s) are contiguous**. By adding the parameter of the file
name **GOODBYE.TXT** after the CHKDSK command, you asked not only
to check the disk but also to look at the file **GOODBYE.TXT** to see if all
the parts of this file are next to one another on the DATA disk. Are they
contiguous? The message indicates that they are.

Step 2   Key in the following: A:\>**CHKDSK *.TXT** Enter

```
MS-DOS Prompt                                                    _ □ ✕

A:\>CHKDSK *.TXT

Volume DATA          created 07-20-2001 4:55p
Volume Serial Number is 3330-1807

    1,457,664 bytes total disk space
        8,192 bytes in 16 directories
      196,608 bytes in 98 user files
    1,252,864 bytes available on disk

          512 bytes in each allocation unit
        2,847 total allocation units on disk
        2,447 available allocation units on disk
```

```
        647,168 total bytes memory
        585,552 bytes free

All specified file(s) are contiguous

A:\>_
```

WHAT'S HAPPENING? CHKDSK not only gave you the usual statistical information but also checked to see if all the files that have **.TXT** as an extension are contiguous in the root directory of the DATA disk. By using wildcards, you can check a group of files with a common denominator. In this case, the common denominator is the file extension **.TXT**. The message on the screen verifies that all the files with the extension **.TXT** are contiguous.

Step 3   Key in the following: A:\>**CHKDSK *.*** [Enter]

```
MS-DOS Prompt                                                    _ □ ✕

A:\>CHKDSK *.*                                                    ʄ

Volume DATA          created 07-20-2001 4:55p
Volume Serial Number is 3330-1807

    1,457,664 bytes total disk space
        8,192 bytes in 16 directories
      196,608 bytes in 98 user files
    1,252,864 bytes available on disk

          512 bytes in each allocation unit
        2,847 total allocation units on disk
        2,447 available allocation units on disk

      647,168 total bytes memory
      585,552 bytes free

A:\NEWPRSON.FIL Contains 4 non-contiguous blocks

A:\>_
```

WHAT'S HAPPENING? The screen display shows one noncontiguous file. In this example, **NEWPRSON.FIL** has four noncontiguous blocks (your screen display can vary). If you have no fragmented files, you would receive the message, All specified file(s) are contiguous. The CHKDSK command, followed by star dot star (*.*), checked every file in the root directory on the DATA disk to see if all the files were contiguous. The *.* represents all files in the root directory.

Step 4   Key in the following: A:\>**CHKDSK CLASS*.*** [Enter]

```
MS-DOS Prompt                                                    _ □ ✕

A:\>CHKDSK CLASS\*.*

Volume DATA          created 07-20-2001 4:55p
Volume Serial Number is 3330-1807
```

```
      1,457,664 bytes total disk space
          8,192 bytes in 16 directories
        196,608 bytes in 98 user files
      1,252,864 bytes available on disk

            512 bytes in each allocation unit
          2,847 total allocation units on disk
          2,447 available allocation units on disk

        647,168 total bytes memory
        585,552 bytes free

All specified file(s) are contiguous

A:\>_
```

WHAT'S
HAPPENING! You are checking to see if all the files in the subdirectory **CLASS** are
contiguous. In this case, they are. If a subdirectory had noncontiguous
files, the screen display might look as follows:

```
 MS-DOS Prompt                                              _ □ ×

A:\>CHKDSK CLASS\*.*

Volume DATA         created 07-20-2001 4:55p
Volume Serial Number is 3330-1807

      1,457,664 bytes total disk space
          8,192 bytes in 16 directories
        196,608 bytes in 98 user files
      1,252,864 bytes available on disk

            512 bytes in each allocation unit
          2,847 total allocation units on disk
          2,447 available allocation units on disk

        647,168 total bytes memory
        585,552 bytes free

A:\CLASS\JAN.PAR   Contains 2 non-contiguous blocks
A:\CLASS\FEB.PAR   Contains 1 non-contiguous blocks


A:\>_
```

What difference does it make if files are contiguous or not? It matters to
the extent that noncontiguous files or a fragmented disk can slow performance. In other words, if a file is contiguous, all of its parts can be found
quickly, minimizing the amount of time the head needs to read and write
to the disk. If files are noncontiguous, the operating system has to look
for all the parts of the file, causing the read/write heads to fly about the
disk. The longer the disk is used, the more fragmented it becomes,
slowing its performance. However, there is a way to solve the problem
with a floppy-based system—format a new disk. Then place the newly
formatted disk in Drive B and the old, fragmented disk in Drive A, and
key in A:\>COPY *.* B:. As the COPY command is executed, it finds the

first file, including all the associated clusters, on the disk in Drive A and copies that file contiguously to the disk in Drive B. Next, it goes to the second file and so on. Remember, the disk in Drive B must be newly formatted. Furthermore, do not use the DISKCOPY command. DISKCOPY makes an identical, track for track, cluster for cluster, sector for sector copy of a disk. You want to make your newly formatted disk a contiguous copy of the old, noncontiguous disk. However, performance on a floppy disk is usually not that important because most of the time you are working on the hard disk.

Where you notice a big decline in performance is on a hard disk system. The solution most hard disk users opt for is to use **DEFRAG.EXE**, a utility program that is included with the system utility files. This program is listed as Disk Defragmenter on the Start menu, under Accessories, under System Tools. This program, referred to generically as a ***disk-optimization program***, rearranges the storage on the hard disk so that each file is stored in sequentially numbered clusters. Before using disk optimization, the disk must be free of errors. Errors can be detected and many can be repaired automatically with the ScanDisk program, also found on the Start menu, under Accessories, under System Tools.

8.19   USING CHKDSK TO REPAIR DISK PROBLEMS

The file allocation table (FAT) and directory work in conjunction. Every file has an entry in the directory table. The file entry in the directory table points to the starting cluster in the FAT. If the file is longer than one cluster, which it usually is, the file allocation table has a pointer that leads it to the next cluster, then the next cluster, and so on. These pointers ***chain*** all the data together in a file. If the chain is broken (i.e., there is a lost pointer), the disk ends up with lost clusters, which means that these clusters are marked as used in the FAT and not available for new data. Look at Figure 8.11: clusters 3, 4, and 6 are a chain, but the FAT does not know to which file this chain belongs. There is no entry in the root directory. Hence, these are lost clusters.

Root Directory Table

File Name	File Extension	Date	Time	Other Info	Starting Cluster Number
MY	FIL	5-7-99	11:23a		1
HIS	DOC	5-7-99	11:50a		5
					3

File Allocation Table

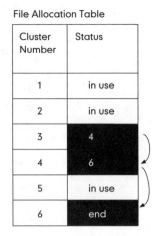

Cluster Number	Status
1	in use
2	in use
3	4
4	6
5	in use
6	end

Clusters 3, 4, and 6 have data, are linked together,
but have no file entry in the directory table.

FIGURE 8.11   LOST CLUSTERS

Since these lost clusters belong to no specific file, they cannot be retrieved. The data becomes useless, yet the operating system cannot write other data to these lost clusters. Thus, you lose space on the disk. This phenomenon occurs for a variety of reasons, the most common being a user who does not exit a program properly. If you simply turn off the computer, you are interrupting the shut-down process of the application program. Often, when you interrupt this process, the data will not be properly written to the disk. Other times power failures or power surges are the cause. Not exiting an application properly can be damaging to the operating system and can leave lost clusters on the hard disk.

If one of these events happens, you may not be able to boot back into Windows. You would then boot with your Windows startup disk that was made during installation. From this 16-bit version of Windows, on a non-FAT32 hard drive, you can run CHKDSK with the /F parameter and attempt to repair disk errors. When you execute the CHKDSK command, you will get a message at the beginning of the CHKDSK display similar to this:

```
MS-DOS Prompt                                                    _ □ ×

Volume DATA     created 12-29-1997 3:07p
Volume Serial Number is 2158-16D4

Errors found, F parameter not specified
Corrections will not be written to disk
```

This message means that if you run CHKDSK with the /F parameter, CHKDSK will turn these lost clusters into files with the file name FILE000*n*.CHK (where *n* is a number such as 1, 2 or 3).

CAUTION!   **YOU SHOULD NOT RUN CHKDSK ON A HARD DRIVE WITH THE /F PARAMETER FROM A NORMAL WINDOWS BOOT UP. TO REPAIR HARD DISK PROBLEMS FROM WITHIN WINDOWS, YOU SHOULD USE SCANDISK.**

8.20 SCANDISK

ScanDisk is not only a replacement for CHKDSK, but is also an enhancement to CHKDSK. CHKDSK does a better job of displaying information about how much conventional memory you have, as well as the total number of files on a disk. ScanDisk, however, does a much better job fixing disk problems. Most importantly, ScanDisk works on the newer, larger FAT32 hard drives. The only thing CHKDSK can do is fix a lost cluster when booting to the MS-DOS prompt. ScanDisk can find and repair errors in the following:

* file allocation table (FAT)
* file system structure (lost clusters, cross-linked files)
* directory tree structure
* physical surface of the drive (bad clusters)

Both hard drives and floppy disks can be checked by ScanDisk. CD-ROM drives and network drives cannot.

CAUTION!   **ABOUT SCANDISK: DO NOT USE SCANDISK WHEN OTHER PROGRAMS ARE RUNNING. IT IS DESIGNED FOR USE WHEN FILES ON A DISK ARE IN AN UNCHANGING STATE. WHEN YOU ARE USING A FILE, THE OPERATING SYSTEM UPDATES THE FILE ALLOCATION TABLE (FAT) AND THE DIRECTORY STRUCTURE TO REFLECT CHANGES. SUCH UPDATES ARE NOT ALWAYS MADE IMMEDIATELY. IF YOU RUN SCANDISK WHEN OTHER PROGRAMS ARE RUNNING, FILES MIGHT STILL BE OPEN. SCANDISK INTERPRETS DIFFERENCES BE-TWEEN THE DIRECTORY STRUCTURE AND THE FILE ALLOCA-TION TABLE AS ERRORS. THIS CAN RESULT IN CORRUPTION OR LOSS OF DATA.**

It should be clear to you that you must close all application programs before running ScanDisk on your hard drive. However, you can run ScanDisk safely on a floppy disk regardless of whether you have a program running.

Cross-linked files are two files that claim the same cluster.

Root Directory Table

File Name	File Extension	Date	Time	Other Info	Starting Cluster Number
MY	FIL	4-15-94	11:23		1
HIS	FIL	4-15-94	11:23		3

File Allocation Table

Cluster Number	Status
1	MY.FIL
2	MY.FIL
3	HIS.FIL
4	MY.FIL HIS.FIL
5	HIS FIL
6	MY.FIL

FIGURE 8.12   CROSS-LINKED FILES

In Figure 8.12, MY.FIL thinks it owns clusters 1, 2, 4 and 6. HIS.FIL thinks it owns clusters 3, 4, and 5. Thus, both MY.FIL and HIS.FIL think that cluster 4 is part of their chain. If you edit MY.FIL, the files will contain their own data as well as some part of HIS.FIL. Even worse, if you delete MY.FIL, you will be deleting part of the HIS.FIL data. Usually, to recover data from cross-linked files, you copy each file to a new name. One of the files is usually bad, but at least you have one file that is good. ScanDisk automates this process and will create two separate files for you.

Another error-fixing ability that needs to be understood is detection of DriveSpace errors. As you work with computers, you will discover that you always seem to need more hard disk space as programs and files get bigger and bigger. On smaller non-FAT32 hard drives, one of the ways to increase disk space, other than purchasing a new hard disk, is through disk-compression programs. A ***disk-compression program*** is software that increases disk space. This program does not actually make your hard disk larger, but instead pulls some software tricks to make it seem as if your disk is larger. For instance, if you take the following sentence, "What is the cost of the newest hard disk and the newest software?" the word "the" is repeated many times. A disk-compression program essentially takes that redundant, repetitive data in a file, stores it one time and makes a note to itself how many times and where the data needs to be repeated. When you need the data, it is uncompressed. This is known as on-the-fly compression. You, as the user, only see and manipulate uncompressed data.

Microsoft includes a program called DriveSpace, which you can use to access information or allocate disk space on compressed drives and to decompress floppy disks for those disks that used previous versions of DriveSpace. Windows Millennium Edition does not use DriveSpace 3 to compress drives. With the rapid decrease in the cost of large hard drives, DriveSpace is rarely used, and the utility is only included for backwards compatibility if you compressed a drive in an earlier version of Windows.

8.21 ACTIVITY: USING SCANDISK ON THE DATA DISK

Note: The DATA disk is in the A drive. A:\> is displayed.

Step 1   Key in the following: A:\>**EXIT** [Enter]

WHAT'S
HAPPENING! ➡ You have exited from the MS-DOS Prompt window and returned to the desktop.

Step 2   Click **Start**.

Step 3   Point to **Programs**.

Step 4   Point to **Accessories**.

Step 5   Point to **System Tools**.

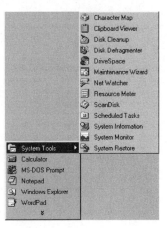

WHAT'S HAPPENING? ➤ You have opened the System Tools menu. The items on the menu are listed in alphabetic order.

Step 6   Click **ScanDisk**.

WHAT'S HAPPENING? ➤ You have opened the main ScanDisk dialog box. You can choose which disk to check, if the test will be standard (which checks areas on the disk that have been written to) or thorough (which checks the entire surface of the disk), and whether or not to automatically fix errors. Notice the Advanced button in the lower-right corner of the dialog box. There are more options available to you here.

Step 7   Click the **Automatically fix errors** check box.

Step 8   Select the **Standard** test type.

Step 9   Select the A drive.

Step 10 Click the **Advanced** button.

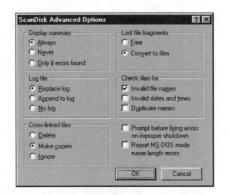

WHAT'S HAPPENING? You have opened the ScanDisk Advanced Options dialog box. Here you can decide problems to check for; what to do with cross-linked files; whether or not to create a new log, append an old log, or create no log at all; what sort of summary of information you want ScanDisk to display; and how you want ScanDisk to deal with lost file fragments, invalid or duplicate file names, invalid dates and times, and MS-DOS name length.

Step 11   Make the following selections:

Display summary	**Always**
Log file	**Replace log**
Cross-linked files	**Make copies**
Lost file fragments	**Free**
Check files for	Check both **Invalid file names** and **Invalid dates and times**

Step 12   Click **OK**.

Step 13   Click **Start**.

WHAT'S HAPPENING? ScanDisk checked the DATA disk for errors. If it found errors, it repaired them and reported to you that it had done so.

Step 14   Click **Close**.

Step 15   Click **Close**.

Step 16   Shell out to the MS-DOS window.

Step 17   Key in the following: C:\WINDOWS>**CD ** Enter

Step 18   Key in the following: C:\>**DIR SCANDISK.LOG** Enter

```
MS-DOS Prompt                                                        _ □ X

C:\WINDOWS>CD \

C:\>DIR SCANDISK.LOG

 Volume in drive C is MILLENNIUM
 Volume Serial Number is 2B18-1301
 Directory of C:\

SCANDISK LOG               493  08-03-01  2:08p SCANDISK.LOG
        1 file(s)                493 bytes
        0 dir(s)        900,849,664 bytes free
C:\>_
```

WHAT'S HAPPENING?   You closed the ScanDisk program and shelled out to the MS-DOS screen. You changed to the root of the C drive and issued a DIR command to find the log file left by the ScanDisk program. What is in the log file? (*Note:* If you are on a network you may not be able to save a file to Drive C.)

Step 19   Key in the following: C:\>**EDIT SCANDISK.LOG** Enter

WHAT'S HAPPENING?   You have used the MS-DOS editor to display the contents of the ScanDisk log file. Notice the note on the screen that information may appear incorrectly. Nonetheless, the information is clear enough so that you can read it and discover any information logged by the ScanDisk program.

Step 20   Click **File**.

Step 21   Click **Exit**.

Step 22   Key in the following: C:\>**A:** Enter

```
MS-DOS Prompt                                                        _ □ X

C:\>EDIT SCANDISK.LOG

C:\>A:

A:\>_
```

WHAT'S HAPPENING? ➤ You have closed the MS-DOS editor and returned to the A:\> prompt.

Step 23 Key in the following: A:\>**EXIT** [Enter]

WHAT'S HAPPENING? ➤ You have returned to the desktop.

8.22 DEFRAGMENTING YOUR DISK

To make your programs run faster and better, you need to perform disk maintenance. One way to maintain your disk is to regularly run the Disk Defragmenter
program to rearrange files and unused space on your hard disk. You first make sure
that you have no lost clusters or cross-linked files by running ScanDisk. You repair
any errors on the DATA disk. Then you are ready to run Disk Defragmenter. Although the Windows operating system allows you to run Disk Defragmenter without
closing all your programs, it is better, faster, and safer to close any open programs
you have running, including any screen savers or virus-protection programs.

8.23 ACTIVITY: DEFRAGMENTING YOUR DISK

Step 1 Click **Start**.

Step 2 Point to **Programs**.

Step 3 Point to **Accessories**.

Step 4 Point to **System Tools**.

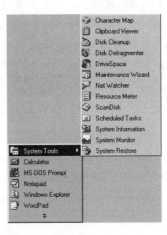

WHAT'S HAPPENING? ➤ You have once again opened the System Tools menu. This time you will
choose Disk Defragmenter.

Step 5 Click **Disk Defragmenter**.

 You have started the Disk Defragmenter program. You need to tell the program which disk you want to defragment.

Step 6   In the drop-down list box, click the down arrow and select Drive A.

Step 7   Click the **Settings** button.

 In previous versions of Windows, Disk Defragmenter would report the amount of fragmentation on the selected disk. In Windows Millennium, this is not the case. The Disk Defragmenter Settings allow you choices of what is to be done, and if you want to use the settings every time, or just this time.

Step 8   Click **This time only**.

Step 9   Click both **Rearrange program files so my programs start faster** and **Check the drive for errors** as shown above.

Step 10   Click **OK**.

Step 11   Click **OK**.

 You have started the defragmentation process. Notice the Pause and Show Details buttons at the bottom. On slower computers, you may pause the process, or see a graphical representation of the process, but on today's fast computers, there is not enough time. The process will complete too quickly. If you had time to click the Show Details button, you

could then see a legend explaining the meaning of the details shown. The details screen would appear similar to what is shown below.

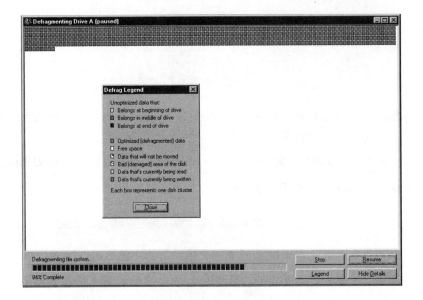

Looking at the above figure, you can see a graphical representation of the defragmentation process.

Step 12 Read the legend to familiarize yourself with the meanings of the different squares.

Step 13 Click **Yes** in the box to close Disk Defragmenter.

WHAT'S HAPPENING? The DATA disk is now error-free and fully optimized.

CHAPTER SUMMARY

1. All disks should be organized. All programs and data should not be in the root directory.
2. The root directory of a hard disk holds only 512 files if you are using FAT16..
3. Many users inefficiently organize their disk by application programs. This often leads to a repetition of subdirectory names, forcing users to remember where they placed their files and key in long path names. The operating system must search every subdirectory when accessing a file. It is difficult to add and delete application programs and data files in this scheme.
4. One way to organize a hard disk is by project.
5. Some guidelines to organizing a disk:
    a. The root directory is a map to the rest of the disk.
    b. Subdirectories should be shallow and wide.
    c. Plan the organization before installing software.
    d. Do not place data files in program subdirectories.
    e. It is better to have small subdirectories with only a few files.
    f. Keep subdirectory names short and descriptive.
    g. Create a separate subdirectory for utility programs.

h. Learn how each application program works.

i. Analyze the way you work.

6. If a disk is unorganized, you can organize it by planning it, creating the new organizational scheme and any necessary subdirectories, copying files to the new subdirectories, and deleting those files from the old subdirectories.

7. The XCOPY command allows you to copy files and the subdirectories beneath them. You may choose:

a. to be prompted (/P).

b. to copy by date (/D).

c. to be instructed to insert another disk (/W).

d. to copy subdirectories and the files in them (/S).

e. to create an empty subdirectory (/E).

f. to verify that sectors are written correctly (/V).

g. to copy files whose archive bit is set (/M).

h. to copy only files that have been created or modified since the last backup (/A).

i. to copy hidden files (/H).

j. to keep file attributes (/K).

k. to keep the read-only attribute (/R).

8. The MS-DOS editor is a full-screen editor that allows you to modify text files. It is a menu-driven program.

9. MOVE is used to move files. Although it can rename directories, it is better to use the REN command to rename objects and the MOVE command to move these objects. You must be cautious when you use MOVE to ensure you are performing the task that you wish.

10. Utility programs include the ones that come with the operating system, such as the external command MOVE.

11. There are software packages that add enhancements to the operating system. These are either given away, sold commercially, or are shareware.

12. RNS (rename subdirectory) is an example of a third-party utility program that does not come with the operating system.

13. ScanDisk is an intended replacement for CHKDSK. ScanDisk can repair more types of disk errors than CHKDSK, but ScanDisk does not give the statistical information that CHKDSK does.

14. You cannot use CHKDSK to check or repair FAT32 hard drives.

15. You must not use ScanDisk or CHKDSK /F while on a network drive or on any substituted drives.

16. Do not run ScanDisk when there are any other programs running.

17. Disk Defragmenter is a program used to optimize performance of a disk by rewriting files so the clusters are contiguous. When files are contiguous, computer performance is enhanced.

KEY TERMS

chain	disk-compression program	fragmented file
cross-linked files	disk-optimization program	lost cluster

DISCUSSION QUESTIONS

1. Why would you want to organize a hard disk?
2. What are the advantages and disadvantages of organizing a hard disk by application program rather than by project?
3. Why would you not want to place data files in a program subdirectory?
4. List five criteria that can be used for organizing a hard disk and explain the rationale for each.
5. What are two major considerations for any disk organizational scheme?
6. What are some of the drawbacks of using the COPY command for organizing your disk?
7. Why is moving program files and renaming program directories not as safe as moving data files and renaming data file directories?
8. What steps would you take to move a directory?
9. Why would you want to own utility programs that do not come with the operating system?
10. What is the purpose and function of programs like RNS.EXE?
11. What type of statistical information about a disk and about computer memory might be useful to you?
12. What is the function and purpose of the CHKDSK command?
13. CHKDSK informs you of two types of errors. Explain.
14. What is a lost cluster? a cross-linked file? What impact does either of these have on available disk space?
15. Give the syntax for CHKDSK and explain each part of the syntax.
16. What is verbose mode? Explain the use of the /V parameter with the CHKDSK command.
17. Compare and contrast contiguous files with noncontiguous (fragmented) files.
18. Why would you use the parameter of the file name with the CHKDSK command?
19. What is the purpose and function of the /F parameter when it is used with the CHKDSK command, and under what circumstances would you use it?
20. Explain the purpose and function of the ScanDisk command.
21. Compare the ScanDisk and CHKDSK commands.
22. Explain the function and purpose of disk-optimization programs.
23. What should you do before executing the Disk Defragmenter program?

TRUE/FALSE QUESTIONS

For each statement, circle the letter T if the statement is true, and the letter F if the statement is false.

T　F　1. The number of files that can be stored in the root of a hard drive is unlimited if the file system is FAT16.

T　F　2. It is a good idea to have your data files and program files in the same subdirectory so you can keep track of your files easily.

T　F　3. To repair FAT32 drives, you should use CHKDSK.

T　F　4. The operating system writes files to disk based on the next available cluster.

T　F　5. To optimize a disk, you should use ScanDisk.

COMPLETION QUESTIONS

Write the correct answer in each blank space.

6. To change the name of a subdirectory, you can use the _____ command or the _____ command.

7. Two commands that can help you organize your disk are _____ and _____.

8. When you use the MOVE *.* command, subdirectories contained in the default directory _____ (*are* or *are not*) moved.

9. When you use the CHKDSK command, the parameter that will list every file on the disk, including hidden files, is the _____ parameter.

10. To solve the problem of having noncontiguous files on a disk, first use _____ and then use _____.

MULTIPLE CHOICE QUESTIONS

For each question, write the letter for the correct answer in the blank space.

11. A good rule of thumb when organizing a hard disk is
    a. to create compact and deep subdirectories rather than shallow and wide ones.
    b. to place data files in the same subdirectories with their associated program files.
    c. to use the root directory as a map to the rest of the disk.
    d. to have no files, only subdirectories in the root directory.

12. When organizing a hard disk, XCOPY is _____ to use than COPY.
    a. faster
    b. slower
    c. neither faster nor slower
    d. less reliable

13. CHKDSK will not
    a. tell how many files are on a floppy disk.
    b. tell whether or not a floppy disk has hidden files.
    c. remove damaged files from a floppy disk.
    d. tell how much room is left on a floppy disk.

14. A noncontiguous file is one that
    a. occupies more than one cluster.
    b. occupies nonconsecutive clusters.
    c. has a directory entry table that is missing certain numbers.
    d. contains a document that hasn't been finished.

15. To help your disk perform quickly and reliably, you should
    a. rename the directories that hold program files after they have been installed, so that they are all in the same directory.
    b. use deep subdirectories.
    c. run ScanDisk and then Disk Defragmenter.
    d. use long file names.

WRITING COMMANDS

Write the correct steps or commands to perform the required action as if you were at the computer. The prompt will indicate the default drive and directory. If there is no prompt indicated, assume you are at the desktop and not in the MS-DOS window.

16. You need statistical information about the disk in Drive A.

    C:\WINDOWS\COMMAND>

17. You want to see if the file called MARCH.TXT in the POLYSCI\USA directory on the disk in Drive A is contiguous.

    C:\WINDOWS\COMMAND>

18. You want to fix lost clusters and cross-linked files on the disk in Drive A.

    C:\WINDOWS\COMMAND>

19. You want to make all files on the disk in Drive A contiguous.

20. You want to display all the files on the disk in Drive A. (Do not use the DIR command.)

    C:\>

APPLICATION ASSIGNMENTS

Note 1: Place the APPLICATION disk in Drive A. Be sure to work on the APPLICATION disk, not the DATA disk.

Note 2: The homework problems will assume that Drive C is the hard disk and the APPLICATION disk is in Drive A. If you are using another drive, such as floppy Drive B or hard Drive D, be sure and substitute that drive letter when reading the questions and answers.

Note 3: All subdirectories that are created will be under the root directory unless otherwise specified.

PROBLEM SET 1

PROBLEM A

A-a   On the APPLICATION disk, under the subdirectory called **HISTORY**, create a subdirectory called **ROMAN**.

A-b   With the root directory of the APPLICATION disk as the default, use the XCOPY command with the relative path to copy all the files in the root directory that begin with **W** to the subdirectory called **ROMAN** that you just created.

1. Which command did you use?
   a. XCOPY W*.* HISTORY
   b. XCOPY W*.* HISTORY\ROMAN
   c. XCOPY W*.* ROMAN\HISTORY
   d. XCOPY W*.* ROMAN

2. What message(s) was/were displayed on the screen?
   a. Reading source file(s)
   b. Copying source file(s)
   c. 3 File(s) copied
   d. none of the above

3. Are there any files that begin with W in the root directory of the
   APPLICATION disk?
   a. yes
   b. no

A-c   With the root directory of the APPLICATION disk as the default, move all
       the files that begin with **W** to the subdirectory called **ROMAN** you
       created above.

4. Which command did you use?
   a. MOVE W*.* HISTORY\ROMAN
   b. MOVE W*.* ROMAN\HISTORY
   c. MOVE W*.* ROMAN
   d. none of the above

A-d   Take the necessary steps to complete the move.

5. Are there any files that begin with W in the root directory of the
   APPLICATION disk?
   a. yes
   b. no

PROBLEM B

B-a   With the root directory of the APPLICATION disk as the default, under
       the subdirectory called **PHONE** create a subdirectory called **FILES**.

B-b   With the root directory of the APPLICATION disk as the default, move all
       the files in the root directory that begin with **F** to the subdirectory called
       PHONE\FILES that you just created without moving the two
       subdirectories that begin with **F**.

6. Which command(s) did you use first?
   a. ATTRIB +H FILES and ATTRIB +H FIRST
   b. ATTRIB -H FILES and ATTRIB -H FIRST
   c. ATTRIB +S FILES and ATTRIB +H FIRST
   d. ATTRIB -S FILES and ATTRIB -S FIRST

7. Which command did you use second?
   a. MOVE F*.* FILES\PHONE
   b. MOVE F*.* PHONE\FILES
   c. MOVE F*.* FILES
   d. none of the above

8. What message was displayed regarding the FIRST subdirectory?
   a. FIRST is hidden - cannot be moved
   b. Cannot move FIRST - Permission denied
   c. [ok]
   d. none of the above

B-c   Do what is necessary to make the **FILES** and **FIRST** subdirectories on the root directory visible.

B-d   With the root directory of the APPLICATION disk as the default, move all the files in the root directory that have the file extension of **.FIL** to the **PHONE\FILES** subdirectory.

9. How many files were moved?
   a. one
   b. two
   c. five
   d. six

PROBLEM C

Note: The root directory of the APPLICATION disk is the default.

C-a   Copy from the **WINDOSBK** directory the **LEVEL-1**, **LEVEL-2**, and **LEVEL-3** subdirectories and all the files in those directories to the root directory of the APPLICATION disk. There are no empty directories. Maintain the hierarchical structure.

10. Which of the following commands did you use?
    a. XCOPY C:\WINDOSBK\LEVEL-1*.* LEVEL-1
    b. XCOPY C:\WINDOSBK\LEVEL-1*.*
    c. XCOPY C:\WINDOSBK\LEVEL-1*.* LEVEL-1 /S
    d. XCOPY C:\WINDOSBK\LEVEL-1*.* LEVEL-1 /D

11. What is the first message displayed?
    a. Reading source file(s) . . .
    b. Does LEVEL-1 specify a file name or directory name on the target?
    c. LEVEL-1 directory being created
    d. no message was displayed

C-b   Complete the command. Then, with the root directory of the APPLICA-TION disk as the default, use the MS-DOS editor to create a new file called **DOWN.RED**. The contents of the file will be as follows:

This is a new red file.
I like the color red.
I like the softness of down.

C-c   Make a directory called **TRAVEL** on the root of the APPLICATION disk.

C-d   Copy all the files from the **WINDOSBK** directory ending with the extension **.RED** to the **TRAVEL** subdirectory on the APPLICATION disk.

C-e   With the root directory of the APPLICATION disk as the default, move the **DOWN.RED** file to the **TRAVEL** subdirectory on the APPLICATION disk.

C-f   With the root directory of the APPLICATION disk as the default, use the MS-DOS editor to alter and save the **DOWN.RED** file so that the contents read:
This is the last red file.
I am not so sure I like the color red.

C-g   With the root directory of the APPLICATION disk as the default, use the MS-DOS editor to create a new file in the **TRAVEL** directory called **UP.RED**. The contents should read:
Maybe it wasn't the last red file after all!

12. How many files are on the root of the APPLICATION disk with the file extension of .RED?
  a. one
  b. two
  c. three
  d. zero

13. How many files are in the TRAVEL subdirectory with the file extension of .RED?
  a. two
  b. three
  c. four
  d. five

C-h   With the root of the APPLICATION disk as the default, rename the file called **UP.RED** to **UPPER.RED** in the **TRAVEL** subdirectory.

C-i   With the root of the APPLICATION disk as the default, copy all the files from the **TRAVEL** directory to the **BOOKS** subdirectory.

14. What is the total number of files with the extension .RED on the APPLICATION disk?
  a. 3
  b. 5
  c. 8
  d. 10

15. What command did you use to answer question 14?
    a. CHKDSK A:
    b. DIR *.RED
    c. DIR *.RED /S
    d. DIR *.RED TRAVEL BOOKS

PROBLEM D

D-a   Run ScanDisk on the APPLICATION disk, creating a log file.

D-b   Use the Disk Defragmenter on the APPLICATION disk.

D-c   Move the **SCANDISK.LOG** file, created on the root of the C drive when you ran ScanDisk, to the root of the APPLICATION disk. (*Note:* If your lab does not allow you to save files to Drive C, you will not be able to do this.)

PROBLEM SET II

Note 1: Before proceeding with these assignments, check with your lab instructor to see if there are any special procedures you should follow.

Note 2: The APPLICATION disk is in Drive A. A:\> is displayed as the default drive and the default directory. All work will occur on the APPLICATION disk.

Note 3: Make sure that NAME.BAT, MARK.FIL, GETYN.COM, GO.BAT, and NAME.FIL are all present in the root directory of the APPLICATION disk before proceeding with these problems. (MARK.FIL was moved from the root directory as part of a homework exercise—you will need to copy it to the root of the A drive from WINDOSBK.)

Note 4: All files with the .HW extension must be created in the root directory of the APPLICATION disk.

Step 1   Key in the following: A:\>**NAME** Enter

Step 2   Here is an example to key in, but your instructor will have other information that applies to your class. Key in the following:

Bette A. Peat Enter   (Your name goes here.)
CIS 55 Enter   (Your class goes here.)
T-Th 8-9:30 Enter   (Your day and time go here.)
Chapter 8 Applications Enter

Step 3   Press F6 Enter

Step 4   If the information is correct, press Y and you are back to A:\>.

WHAT'S HAPPENING?   You have returned to the system level. You now have a file called **NAME.FIL** with your name and other pertinent information. (*Hint:* Remember redirection.)

TO CREATE 1.HW

❖   Locate all of the files ending with .RED on the APPLICATION disk and place the results of the command in a file called 1.HW.

TO CREATE 2.HW

❖   Copy only the files with the .TXT extension that were created on or after 5-30-00 in the WINDOSBK subdirectory to the root of the APPLICATION disk.

❖   Locate only the files in the root of the APPLICATION disk that have the extension .TXT. Place the names of the files in a file called 2.HW.

TO CREATE 3.HW

❖   Copy all the files that have the extension .RED from the BOOKS subdirectory to the root of the APPLICATION disk.

❖   Edit the file DOWN.RED in the TRAVEL directory. Add the following line to the bottom of the file:
      Does a down red file come from a red goose?

❖   Display the contents (not the file name) of the DOWN.RED file you just edited to a file called 3.HW.

TO CREATE 4.HW

❖   Locate all the files that have the extension .TXT on the APPLICATION disk and place the results of the command in a file called 4.HW.

TO PRINT YOUR HOMEWORK

Step 1   Be sure the printer is on and ready to accept print jobs from your computer.

Step 2   Key in the following:
         A:\>**GO NAME.FIL 1.HW 2.HW 3.HW 4.HW SCANDISK.LOG** Enter

Step 3   Follow the messages on the screen. When you finish, you will return to the A:\> prompt.

Step 4   Execute the shut-down procedure.

PROBLEM SET III—BRIEF ESSAY

Plan and organize the APPLICATION disk on paper only. Write a brief explanation to justify your organizational scheme.

PIPES, FILTERS, AND REDIRECTION

LEARNING OBJECTIVES

After completing this chapter you will be able to:
1. List the standard input and output devices.
2. Explain redirection.
3. Explain what filters are and when they are used.
4. Formulate and explain the syntax of the filter commands SORT, FIND, and MORE.
5. Explain when and how to use the SORT, FIND, and MORE commands.
6. Explain what pipes are and how they are used.

STUDENT OUTCOMES

1. Use > and >> to redirect standard output.
2. Use < to redirect standard input.
3. Use filter commands to manipulate information.
4. Combine commands using pipes, filters, and redirection.

CHAPTER OVERVIEW

The operating system usually expects to read information from the keyboard. The keyboard is the standard input device. The standard output device, where the results of commands and the output of programs is displayed, is the screen. However, there are times when it is desirable to *redirect* input and output. Changing the standard input or output from one device to another is a process known as redirection. There are three external commands, called filters, which allow the user to manipulate data input and output. Pipes, used with filters, allow the user to link commands. Pipes, filters, and redirection give the user choices in determining where information is read from (input) and written to (output).

In this chapter you will learn how to use redirection. You will learn to use pipes to connect programs and filters to manipulate data.

9.1   REDIRECTION OF STANDARD I/O (INPUT/OUTPUT)

You have already used input and output. When you keyed in something on the keyboard, the operating system recognized it as input. After the input was processed, it was written to an output device—usually the screen. In other words, if you key in TYPE MYFILE.TXT, the input is what you key in. The output is the content of the file that is displayed on the screen. See Figure 9.1.

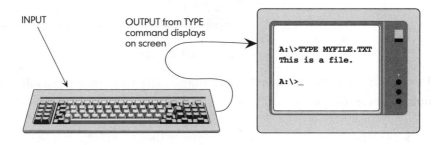

FIGURE 9.1   INPUT AND OUTPUT DEVICES

In the data processing world, this *input/output* process is commonly referred to as *I/O*.

The operating system gets information from or sends information to three places: standard input, standard output, and standard error. **Standard input** is the keyboard. **Standard output** is the display screen. **Standard error** is the place from which the operating system writes error messages to the screen, e.g., "File not found."

Not all commands deal with standard input and standard output. For instance, the result or output of many of the commands you have used has been some action that occurred, such as copying a file with the COPY command. There is no standard input or output except the messages written to the screen. See Figure 9.2.

```
A:\> COPY MY.TXT ONE.FIL          ◄──── INPUT from user
              1 file(s) copied     ◄──── OUTPUT from COPY command
A:\>
```

FIGURE 9.2   RESULTS OF COPY COMMAND

On the other hand, the output of commands like DIR has been a screen display of all the files on a disk. The information was received from the standard input device, the keyboard, and the results of the DIR command were sent to the standard output device, the screen. I/O *redirection* means that you tell the operating system you want information read from or written to a device *other than* the standard ones. With the DIR command, you can write the output to some other device such as a printer or another file. This process is called redirecting the output of a command. See Figure 9.3.

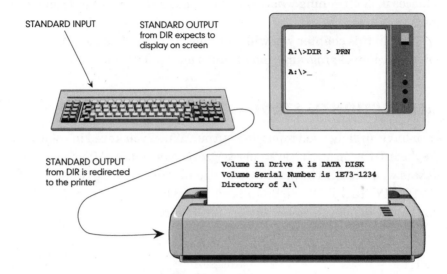

FIGURE 9.3   REDIRECTING STANDARD OUTPUT

Redirection works only when the command expects to send its results to the standard output device or receive the information from the standard input device.

The symbols used for redirection are:

>   The greater-than symbol redirects the output of a command to some other device or file.

<   The less-than symbol tells the operating system to get its input from somewhere other than the keyboard.

>>   The double greater-than symbol redirects the output of a command but does not overwrite the existing file. It appends the output to the bottom of the existing file.

As a matter of fact, you have already used these redirection principles if you did the Application Assignments in prior chapters. You redirected output to a file, appended the files together, and redirected the output to the printer.

9.2   ACTIVITY: USING THE > TO REDIRECT STANDARD OUTPUT

Note: The DATA disk is in Drive A with A:\> displayed.

Step 1   Key in the following: A:\>**DIR C:\WINDOSBK*.TXT** [Enter]

```
MS-DOS Prompt                                                    _ □ ×

A:\>DIR C:\WINDOSBK\*.TXT

 Volume in drive C is MILLENNIUM
 Volume Serial Number is 2B18-1301
 Directory of C:\WINDOSBK

GOODBYE   TXT           34  01-01-02  4:32a GOODBYE.TXT
APRIL     TXT           72  06-16-00  4:32p APRIL.TXT
```

```
JANUARY   TXT              73  06-16-00   4:32p JANUARY.TXT
FEBRUARY  TXT              75  06-16-00   4:32p FEBRUARY.TXT
MARCH     TXT              71  06-16-00   4:32p MARCH.TXT
HELLO     TXT              53  05-30-00   4:32p HELLO.TXT
BYE       TXT              45  05-30-00   4:32p BYE.TXT
DANCES    TXT              72  12-11-99   4:03p DANCES.TXT
TEST      TXT              65  12-11-99   4:03p TEST.TXT
SANDYA~1  TXT              53  11-16-00  12:00p Sandy and Nicki.txt
SANDYA~2  TXT              59  11-16-00  12:00p Sandy and Patty.txt
           11 file(s)              672 bytes
            0 dir(s)       624,193,536 bytes free

A:\>_
```

WHAT'S HAPPENING? → This command behaved in the "normal" way. You asked for a display of all the files in the **WINDOSBK** directory that had a **.TXT** file extension. The selected files were displayed on the screen. Because the DIR command writes its results to the screen, the standard output device, redirection can be used with this command.

Step 2   If you are on a network, check with your lab instructor to see if you can do this activity in the lab. Be sure the printer is turned on. Key in the following: A:\>**DIR C:\WINDOSBK*.TXT > LPT1** Enter

```
MS-DOS Prompt                                                    _ □ ×
A:\>DIR C:\WINDOSBK\*.TXT > LPT1
A:\>_
```

WHAT'S HAPPENING? → The output of the command has been sent to the printer. Nothing appears on the screen. When you key in **DIR C:\WINDOSBK*.TXT**, you normally see the directory listing of all the ***.TXT** files on the screen, as you did in the display following Step 1. The **>** sign tells the operating system that instead of sending the standard output to the screen, you want to redirect that output elsewhere. LPT1 is the name of the port device where most printers are connected, so the operating system redirected the output to the printer. Redirection is very useful. For example, if you wanted a hard copy of the directory of a disk, you could not key in **COPY DIR LPT1** because DIR is a command, not a file. You cannot copy a *command* to the printer. COPY is for files only. Redirection used properly gets you that printed copy.

On some printers, the output that you send to the printer will not fill an entire page. Again, if this is so, you can use the technique you have learned to send a form feed to the printer. On some networks you use PRN instead of LPT1. On some networks, a form feed is automatically sent to the printer, so you may not have to do the following step. Check with your lab administrator before doing Step 3.

Step 3   Key in the following: A:\>**ECHO** Ctrl **+ L > LPT1** Enter
           (*Remember:* Ctrl + L means to hold down the Ctrl key while you press the **L** key.)

```
 MS-DOS Prompt                                          _ □ ✕

 A:\>ECHO ^L > LPT1

 A:\>_
```

WHAT'S HAPPENING? → You have ejected the printed page.

9.3   ACTIVITY: USING THE < TO REDIRECT STANDARD INPUT

Note: The DATA disk is in Drive A with A:\> displayed.

Step 1   Key in the following: A:\>**MD TEST** Enter

Step 2   Key in the following: A:\>**COPY C:\WINDOSBK*.NEW TEST** Enter

```
 MS-DOS Prompt                                          _ □ ✕

 A:\>MD TEST

 A:\>COPY C:\WINDOSBK\*.NEW TEST
 C:\WINDOSBK\JAN.NEW
 C:\WINDOSBK\APR.NEW
 C:\WINDOSBK\FEB.NEW
 C:\WINDOSBK\MAR.NEW
         4 file(s) copied

 A:\>_
```

WHAT'S HAPPENING? → You have a created a subdirectory called **TEST** on the DATA disk and copied four files into it.

Step 3   Key in the following: A:\>**DEL TEST*.*** Enter

```
 MS-DOS Prompt                                          _ □ ✕

 A:\>DEL TEST\*.*
 All files in directory will be deleted!
 Are you sure (Y/N)?_
```

WHAT'S HAPPENING? → You asked the DEL command to delete all the files in the **TEST** subdirectory. DEL is asking you if you are really sure that you want to delete these files. DEL is expecting input from the standard input device, the keyboard.

Step 4   Key in the following: **N** Enter

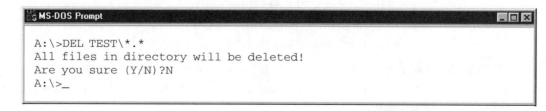

```
 MS-DOS Prompt                                          _ □ ✕

 A:\>DEL TEST\*.*
 All files in directory will be deleted!
 Are you sure (Y/N)?N
 A:\>_
```

> **WHAT'S HAPPENING?** You were returned to the system prompt without deleting the files in the **TEST** subdirectory because you answered **N** for "No, don't delete." As you can see, the operating system took no action until it received input from you via the keyboard, **N**. The input was **N**. You can prove that the files are still there by keying in **DIR TEST**.

Step 5   Key in the following: A:\>**DIR TEST** [Enter]

```
 MS-DOS Prompt                                              _ □ ☒

  A:\>DIR TEST

   Volume in drive A is DATA
   Volume Serial Number is 3330-1807
   Directory of A:\TEST

  .                <DIR>        08-05-01  3:19p .
  ..               <DIR>        08-05-01  3:19p ..
  JAN     NEW           73      10-01-99  2:53p JAN.NEW
  APR     NEW           74      10-01-99  2:53p APR.NEW
  FEB     NEW           75      10-01-99  2:53p FEB.NEW
  MAR     NEW           71      10-01-99  2:53p MAR.NEW
          4 file(s)            293 bytes
          2 dir(s)       1,250,304 bytes free

  A:\>_
```

> **WHAT'S HAPPENING?** From the display you can see that you did not delete the files in the **TEST** directory.

Step 6   Key in the following: A:\>**TYPE Y.FIL** [Enter]

```
 MS-DOS Prompt                                              _ □ ☒

  A:\>TYPE Y.FIL
  Y

  A:\>_
```

> **WHAT'S HAPPENING?** The **Y.FIL** file is a simple file that contains the letter Y followed by a carriage return ([Enter]). If you do not have this file on the DATA disk, you can copy it from the **WINDOSBK** directory to the DATA disk.

Step 7   Key in the following: A:\>**DEL TEST*.* < Y.FIL** [Enter]

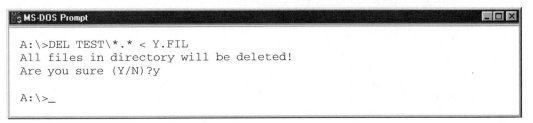

```
 MS-DOS Prompt                                              _ □ ☒

  A:\>DEL TEST\*.* < Y.FIL
  All files in directory will be deleted!
  Are you sure (Y/N)?y

  A:\>_
```

> **WHAT'S HAPPENING?** This time you told the operating system to get input from a file called **Y.FIL** (**< Y.FIL**), instead of from the standard input device, the keyboard. When **DEL TEST*.*** was executed and displayed the message **Are you**

sure (Y/N)? it still needed input, a **Y** or **N** followed by Enter. The operating system found the file you told it to look for, **Y.FIL**, which had the "**Y** Enter" answer. This file provided a response to the question, so the operating system proceeded to delete the files in the subdirectory **TEST**.

You must be very careful with redirection of input. When you tell the operating system to take input from a file, any input from the keyboard will be ignored. In this example, if the **Y.FIL** contents were "X," this would not be a valid answer to the question posed, **Are you sure (Y/N)?** Only **Y** or **N** are acceptable responses. Any other letter would be unacceptable, and the question would be asked again, and then the system would seem to freeze up. You could not correct the problem by keying in **Y** or **N** because the operating system would never look to the keyboard. Remember, you told it not to. If you ever get into this situation, you may not be able to use Ctrl + Break or Ctrl + **C** because no input from the keyboard would be recognized. Sometimes pressing Ctrl + Break will allow you to "break" into your command and will release the keyboard. Otherwise, your only recourse would be to close the MS-DOS window by clicking the Close button at the top right of the screen, which may open the following screen:

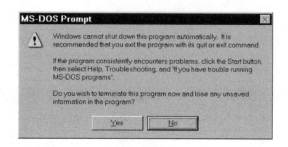

Then you would click the **Yes** button.

Step 8   Key in the following: A:\>**DIR TEST** Enter

```
MS-DOS Prompt

A:\>DIR TEST

 Volume in drive A is DATA
 Volume Serial Number is 3330-1807
 Directory of A:\TEST

 .            <DIR>        08-05-01  3:19p .
 ..           <DIR>        08-05-01  3:19p ..
        0 file(s)               0 bytes
        2 dir(s)       1,252,352 bytes free
A:\>_
```

WHAT'S HAPPENING? The files were deleted. You did it with one command line, and you did not have to key in the **Y**. The Y came from the file **Y.FIL**.

9.4   ACTIVITY: USING THE >> TO ADD REDIRECTED OUTPUT TO A FILE

Note: The DATA disk is in Drive A with A:\> displayed.

Step 1   Key in the following: A:\>**TYPE JANUARY.TXT** [Enter]

Step 2   Key in the following: A:\>**TYPE FEBRUARY.TXT** [Enter]

```
MS-DOS Prompt                                                    _ □ ×

A:\>TYPE JANUARY.TXT

This is my January file.
It is my first dummy file.
This is file 1.

A:\>TYPE FEBRUARY.TXT

This is my February file.
It is my second dummy file.
This is file 2.

A:\>_
```

WHAT'S HAPPENING?   You have two separate files. You want to add **FEBRUARY.TXT** to the end of **JANUARY.TXT**. If you keyed in **TYPE FEBRUARY.TXT >** **JANUARY.TXT**, you would *overwrite* the contents of **JANUARY.TXT** with the contents of **FEBRUARY.TXT**. To *append* to the end of an existing file, you use the double redirection symbol, >>.

Step 3   Key in the following: A:\>**TYPE FEBRUARY.TXT >> JANUARY.TXT** [Enter]

Step 4   Key in the following: A:\>**TYPE JANUARY.TXT** [Enter]

```
MS-DOS Prompt                                                    _ □ ×

A:\>TYPE FEBRUARY.TXT >> JANUARY.TXT

A:\>TYPE JANUARY.TXT

This is my January file.
It is my first dummy file.
This is file 1.

This is my February file.
It is my second dummy file.
This is file 2.

A:\>_
```

WHAT'S HAPPENING?   Instead of overwriting the contents of **JANUARY.TXT** with the contents of **FEBRUARY.TXT**, the contents of **FEBRUARY.TXT** were added to the end of the **JANUARY.TXT** file.

9.5   FILTERS

Filter commands manipulate information. ***Filters*** read information from the keyboard (standard input), change the input in a specified way, and write the results to the screen (standard output). Filter commands function like filters in a water purification system. They remove the unwanted elements from the water (data) and send the purified water (data) on its way. There are three filters, all of which are external commands:

SORT	Arranges lines in ascending or descending order.
FIND	Searches for a particular group of characters, also called a ***character string***.
MORE	Temporarily halts the screen display after each screenful.

The operating system creates temporary files while it "filters" data, so during this process it is important that there be access to the disk and the filters. You must be sure that the floppy disk is not write-protected. If a disk is write-protected, the operating system will not be able to execute filter commands.

9.6   THE SORT COMMAND

The SORT filter command arranges or sorts lines of input (text) and sends them to standard output (the screen), unless you redirect it. The default SORT is in ascending order (A to Z or lowest to highest numbers), starting in the first column. The syntax for the command is:

```
SORT [/R] [/+n] [[drive1:][path1]filename1] [> [drive2:][path2]filename2]
[command ¦] SORT [/R] [/+n] [> [drive2:][path2]filename2]

 /R                         Reverses the sort order; that is, sorts Z to A,
                            then 9 to 0.
 /+n                        Sorts the file according to characters in
                            column n.
 [drive1:][path1]filename1  Specifies file(s) to be sorted
 [drive2:][path2]filename2  Specifies a file where the sorted input is to be
                            stored.
 command                    Specifies a command whose output is to be sorted.
```

9.7   ACTIVITY: USING SORT

Note 1: The DATA disk is in Drive A with A:\> displayed.

Note 2: Remember when you see **F6**, it means to press the **F6** key.

Step 1   Key in the following: A:\>**SORT** **Enter**
          BETA **Enter**
          OMEGA **Enter**
          CHI **Enter**
          ALPHA **Enter**
          F6 **Enter**

```
MS-DOS Prompt                                                    _ □ ×

A:\>SORT
BETA
OMEGA
CHI
ALPHA
^Z
ALPHA
BETA
CHI
OMEGA

A:\>_
```

WHAT'S HAPPENING? → As you can see, the SORT command took input from the keyboard. When you pressed the F6 key (identical to pressing Ctrl + Z), you told the SORT command that you were finished entering data. Then, the SORT command "filtered" the data and wrote the keyboard input alphabetically to the standard output device (the screen). See Figure 9.4 for a graphical representation of this filter.

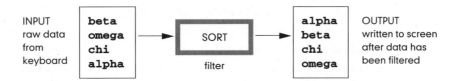

INPUT raw data from keyboard — **beta omega chi alpha** → SORT → **alpha beta chi omega** — OUTPUT written to screen after data has been filtered

filter

FIGURE 9.4   FILTERING DATA

Step 2   Key in the following: A:\>**SORT** [Enter]
          333 [Enter]
          3 [Enter]
          23 [Enter]
          124 [Enter]
          [F6] [Enter]

```
MS-DOS Prompt                                                    _ □ ×

A:\>SORT
333
3
23
124
^Z
124
23
3
333

A:\>_
```

WHAT'S HAPPENING? → The SORT command does not seem very smart because these numbers are certainly not in order. Numbers, in this case, are really character data and not numeric values that are manipulated mathematically. Numbers are often used as character data. For instance, a zip code or a phone number, although they use numbers, really are character data and are not treated mathematically. You would not think of adding your address to your phone number and dividing by your zip code, for example.

Character data is sorted from left to right. Numeric data is sorted by units. Thus, if you look at "Smith" and "Smythe," you read character data from left to right and would place "Smith" before "Smythe." If you had the numbers "124," "222," "22," "23," "31," "9," and "6," the numeric order would be, of course, 6, 9, 22, 23, 31, 124, and 222. You first sort all the single-digit numbers—based on the number on the *right*. You then sort the two-digit numbers by looking at the first digit—thus you know that 22 and 23 come before 31. Since 22 and 23 have the same first digit, you then go to the second digit to determine that the 2 in 22 comes before the 3 in 23.

A human knows that "12" comes before "13" because a person has learned how numbers work. The operating system is different. It relies on something called the ***ASCII sort sequence***. ASCII is a standard code that assigns values to letters, numbers, and punctuation marks—all the characters—from the *left*, in the same way we read characters. The ASCII sort sequence is determined by the number assigned to the ASCII character. The sort order is punctuation marks (including the space), then numbers, then letters (lowercase preceding uppercase). If you had a series of characters such as BB, aa, #, 123, bb, 13, and AA, the ASCII sort order would be:

```
#    123    13    aa    AA    bb    BB
```

Notice that with the new sort sequence the relative position of aa and AA did not change, but the relative position of BB and bb did change.

There is another point about using the SORT command. Not only does it follow the ASCII sort sequence, but it also sorts entire lines from left to right. Thus, the sort sequence of "Carolyn Smith" and "Robert Nesler" is:

```
Carolyn Smith
Robert Nesler
```

Because the SORT command looks at the entire line, "Carolyn" comes before "Robert."

In our numeric example, SORT looked at the entire line, and, since the "1" in "124" preceded the "2" in "23," it placed the "124" before the "23." You can force the operating system to sort numbers correctly using the spacebar to add the space character.

Step 3   Key in the following: A:\>**SORT** [Enter]
         333 [Enter]
         [Space Bar] [Space Bar] **3** [Enter]
         [Space Bar] **23** [Enter]

124 [Enter]
[F6] [Enter]

```
MS-DOS Prompt                                        _ □ ✕
A:\>SORT
333
  3
 23
124
^Z
  3
 23
124
333

A:\>_
```

> **WHAT'S HAPPENING?** By entering spaces, you forced the lines to be the same length, placing the number digits in their proper position. Since spaces precede numbers in the ASCII sort sequence, the SORT command could sort the entire line and place it in proper numeric order. Indeed, you made numeric data character data. Essentially, you left-justify character data and right-justify numeric data.

9.8 FILTERS AND REDIRECTION

The standard output of filters is a screen display. Hence, you can redirect both the output and input of these filter commands. The filter commands are not usually used with actual keyboard input, but with input redirected from a file, a device, or another command.

9.9 ACTIVITY: USING THE SORT COMMAND WITH REDIRECTION

Note: The DATA disk is in Drive A with A:\> displayed.

Step 1   Key in the following: A:\>**COPY C:\WINDOSBK\STATE.CAP** [Enter]

Step 2   Key in the following: A:\>**SORT < STATE.CAP** [Enter]

```
MS-DOS Prompt                                        _ □ ✕
A:\>COPY C:\WINDOSBK\STATE.CAP
       1 file(s) copied

A:\>SORT < STATE.CAP

Arizona         Phoenix
California      Sacramento
Colorado        Denver
Florida         Tallahassee
Louisiana       Baton Rouge
Michigan        Lansing
Nebraska        Lincoln
New York        Albany
```

```
Ohio            Columbus
Oregon          Salem

A:\>_
```

WHAT'S HAPPENING? You copied the **STATE.CAP** file from the **WINDOSBK** directory to the DATA disk. You then keyed in the SORT command. You used the symbol **<** for taking data from a source other than the keyboard, the file called **STATE.CAP**, and fed it into the SORT command. Displayed on your screen (the standard output) is the **STATE.CAP** file arranged in alphabetical order, with **ARIZONA** and **PHOENIX** at the top. Another SORT command feature is the /R parameter, which allows you to sort in reverse or descending order (Z to A).

Step 3　Key in the following: A:\>**SORT /R < STATE.CAP** [Enter]

```
MS-DOS Prompt                                                    _ □ ×

A:\>SORT /R < STATE.CAP
Oregon          Salem
Ohio            Columbus
New York        Albany
Nebraska        Lincoln
Michigan        Lansing
Louisiana       Baton Rouge
Florida         Tallahassee
Colorado        Denver
California      Sacramento
Arizona         Phoenix


A:\>_
```

WHAT'S HAPPENING? The file **STATE.CAP** that the SORT command used as input is displayed on the screen in reverse alphabetical order. The standard output, the results of the SORT command, is written to the screen. The SORT parameter that sorts by a column number is /+n. (A column, on the screen, is the place occupied by one character.)

Step 4　Key in the following: A:\>**SORT /+17 < STATE.CAP** [Enter]

```
MS-DOS Prompt                                                    _ □ ×

A:\>SORT /+17 < STATE.CAP

New York        Albany
Louisiana       Baton Rouge
Ohio            Columbus
Colorado        Denver
Michigan        Lansing
Nebraska        Lincoln
Arizona         Phoenix
California      Sacramento
Oregon          Salem
Florida         Tallahassee


A:\>_
```

WHAT'S HAPPENING? This time you sorted by column number, the seventeenth position in the list in this example. The first letter of the city is in the seventeenth column. The file is now ordered by city rather than by state. It is important to note that the SORT command does not understand columns in the usual sense. A person would say that the "city column" is the second column going from left to right. The SORT command counts each character (letters and spaces) from left to right and counts each character as a column. Thus, "city" is located by counting the number of characters to the ones you want to sort, *including the spaces between the characters.* The total number was 17.

In these examples, you have been "massaging the data." The actual data in **STATE.CAP** has not changed at all. It remains exactly as it was written. The only thing that has changed is the way it is displayed—the way you are *looking* at the data. This alphabetic arrangement is temporary. If you want to change the data in the file, you need to save the altered data to a new file.

Step 5   Key in the following: `A:\>`**SORT < STATE.CAP > SORTED.CAP** [Enter]

Step 6   Key in the following: `A:\>`**TYPE SORTED.CAP** [Enter]

```
MS-DOS Prompt                                                    _ □ ×

A:\>SORT < STATE.CAP > SORTED.CAP

A:\>TYPE SORTED.CAP

Arizona        Phoenix
California     Sacramento
Colorado       Denver
Florida        Tallahassee
Louisiana      Baton Rouge
Michigan       Lansing
Nebraska       Lincoln
New York       Albany
Ohio           Columbus
Oregon         Salem

A:\>_
```

WHAT'S HAPPENING? You saved the sorted output to a new file called **SORTED.CAP**. The standard output of the command **SORT < STATE.CAP** will normally be written to the screen (standard output device). Since standard output is written to the screen, you can redirect it to a file called **SORTED.CAP**, or the command line **SORT < STATE.CAP > SORTED.CAP**. If you did not want a permanent file copy of it but wanted a printed copy of the file, you could have written the command as **SORT < STATE.CAP > LPT1**, directing the output of the **SORT < STATE.CAP** command to the printer.

9.10   THE FIND FILTER

The FIND command allows you to search a file for a specific character string by enclosing them in quotation marks. Although intended for use with ASCII text files, this command can be useful with some data files produced by application software. For example, let's say you used a program to create five documents. One of the documents was a paper on law enforcement in which you know you used the word "indictment" but you can't remember the name of the file. You could, of course, open each one of the five documents, or you could use the FIND command to search for the word "indictment." Although much of the document would appear as funny characters if you used the TYPE command, the FIND command might be able to tell you whether or not the word "indictment" is in the file.

On the desktop, there is a Search option in the Start menu, which can search files for text as well. In this text you are using the command line. Using the FIND command at the command line can help you find a file based on content.

The FIND command is **case sensitive** unless you use the parameter /I, which means ignore case. The syntax is:

```
FIND [/V] [/C] [/N] [/I] "string" [[drive:][path]filename[ ...]]

  /V           Displays all lines NOT containing the specified string.
  /C           Displays only the count of lines containing the string.
  /N           Displays line numbers with the displayed lines.
  /I           Ignores the case of characters when searching for the string.
  "string"     Specifies the text string to find.
  [drive:][path]filename   Specifies a file or files to search.
```

If a pathname is not specified, FIND searches the text typed at the prompt or piped from another command.

9.11   ACTIVITY: USING THE FIND FILTER

Note 1: The DATA disk is in Drive A with the A:\> displayed.
Note 2: If PERSONAL.FIL is not on the DATA disk, it can be copied from the WINDOSBK directory to the DATA disk.
Note 3: You *must* use double quotes. Single quotes (apostrophes) are invalid.

Step 1   Key in the following: A:\>**FIND "Smith" PERSONAL.FIL** [Enter]

```
MS-DOS Prompt                                                    _ □ ✕

A:\>FIND "Smith" PERSONAL.FIL

---------- PERSONAL.FIL
Smith      Gregory  311 Orchard    Ann Arbor     MI   Engineer
Smith      Carolyn  311 Orchard    Ann Arbor     MI   Housewife
Smith      David    120 Collins    Orange        CA   Chef

A:\>_
```

WHAT'S HAPPENING?   The FIND command found every occurrence of the character string **Smith** in **PERSONAL.FIL** on the DATA disk. A character string must be enclosed in quotation marks. Since FIND is case sensitive, you must key in the word exactly as it appears in the file. The character string SMITH would not be found because FIND would be looking for uppercase letters. If you use the parameter /I, the command would find SMITH, smith, or Smith. The FIND command "filtered" the file **PERSONAL.FIL** to extract the character string that matched the specification. With the use of the /V parameter, you can search a file for anything *except* what is in quotation marks.

Step 2   Key in the following: A:\>**FIND /V "Smith" PERSONAL.FIL** Enter

```
MS-DOS Prompt                                                    _ □ ✕

Babchuk    Bianca    13 Stratford  Sun City West  AZ  Professor
Rodriguez  Bob       20 Elm        Ontario        CA  Systems Analyst
Helm       Milton    333 Meadow    Sherman Oaks   CA  Consultant
Suzuki     Charlene  567 Abbey     Rochester      MI  Day Care Teacher
Markiw     Nicholas  354 Bell      Phoenix        AZ  Engineer
Markiw     Emily     10 Zion       Sun City West  AZ  Retired
Nyles      John      12 Brooks     Sun City West  AZ  Retired
Nyles      Sophie    12 Brooks     Sun City West  CA  Retired
Markiw     Nick      10 Zion       Sun City West  AZ  Retired
Washingon  Tyrone    345 Newport   Orange         CA  Manager
Jones      Steven    32 North      Phoenix        AZ  Buyer
Babchuk    Walter    12 View       Thousand Oaks  CA  President
Babchuk    Deana     12 View       Thousand Oaks  CA  Housewife
Jones      Cleo      355 Second    Ann Arbor      MI  Clerk
Gonzales   Antonio   40 Northern   Ontario        CA  Engineer
JONES      JERRY     244 East      Mission Viejo  CA  Systems Analyst
Lo         Ophelia   1213 Wick     Phoenix        AZ  Writer
Jones      Ervin     15 Fourth     Santa Cruz     CA  Banker
Perez      Sergio    134 Seventh   Ann Arbor      MI  Editor
Yuan       Suelin    56 Twin Leaf  Orange         CA  Artist
Markiw     Nicholas  12 Fifth      Glendale       AZ  Engineer
Peat       Brian     125 Second    Vacaville      CA  Athlete
Farneth    Nichole   237 Arbor     Vacaville      CA  Dancer

A:\>_
```

WHAT'S HAPPENING?   Though the output is so long it scrolled off the screen, you can see that FIND located everyone *except* Smith. Furthermore, you can find the specific line number of each occurrence by using the /N parameter.

Step 3   Key in the following: A:\>**FIND /N "Smith" PERSONAL.FIL** Enter

```
MS-DOS Prompt                                                    _ □ ✕

A:\>FIND /N "Smith" PERSONAL.FIL

---------- PERSONAL.FIL
[7]Smith     Gregory  311 Orchard  Ann Arbor    MI  Engineer
[8]Smith     Carolyn  311 Orchard  Ann Arbor    MI  Housewife
[28]Smith    David    120 Collins  Orange       CA  Chef

A:\>_
```

WHAT'S HAPPENING?   Displayed on the screen are not only all the people named **Smith** but also the line numbers where their names appear in the file. You can also have a numeric count of the number of times a specific character string appears in a file. The FIND command will not display the actual lines, but it will tell you how many occurrences there are of that specific string.

Step 3   Key in the following: A:\>**FIND /C "Smith" PERSONAL.FIL** (Enter)

```
MS-DOS Prompt                                                   _ □ X

A:\>FIND /C "Smith" PERSONAL.FIL

---------- PERSONAL.FIL: 3

A:\>_
```

WHAT'S HAPPENING?   The number **3** follows the file name. The name **Smith** appears three times in the file **PERSONAL.FIL**. You can also tell the FIND command to ignore case.

Step 4   Key in the following: A:\>**FIND /I "Jones" PERSONAL.FIL** (Enter)

```
MS-DOS Prompt                                                   _ □ X

A:\>FIND /I "Jones" PERSONAL.FIL

---------- PERSONAL.FIL
Jones      Steven    32 North     Phoenix        AZ  Buyer
Jones      Cleo      355 Second   Ann Arbor      MI  Clerk
JONES      JERRY     244 East     Mission Viejo  CA  Systems Analyst
Jones      Ervin     15 Fourth    Santa Cruz     CA  Banker

A:\>_
```

WHAT'S HAPPENING?   By using the /I parameter, which told the FIND command to ignore the case, you found both **Jones** and **JONES**.

9.12 PIPES

Pipes allow the standard output of one program to be used as the standard input to the next program. When you use pipes, you are not limited to two programs. You may pipe together many programs. The term *pipe* reflects the flow of information from one command to the next. Pipes are used with filter commands. You may take any command that has standard output and pipe it to a filter. The filter will "do" something to the standard output of the previous command, such as sort it. Since filters always write to standard output, you may use pipes and filters to further refine your data. Essentially, you may use filters to transform data to meet your needs.

The pipe symbol is the vertical broken bar ¦ used between two commands. The standard output from a command is written to a temporary file. Then the next command in the pipeline, typically a filter, reads the temporary file as standard input. See Figure 9.5.

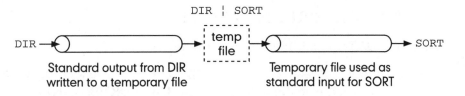

FIGURE 9.5 PIPING COMMANDS

On the original IBM-PC keyboard, the pipe symbol is located between the
Shift key and the letter Z. On some computers, the pipe symbol is located along with
the backslash. Some other keyboards have the ¦ symbol next to the **Ctrl** and **Alt**
keys on the right side of the keyboard. The location of the ¦ symbol is not standard
and could appear in other locations. The symbol ¦ is the connection between two
commands, like a pipe in a water system. Since filters are external commands, the
operating system must be able to access the commands. If a disk is write-protected,
filter commands will not work because these commands read and write temporary
files to the disk.

After using pipes with filters, you may see some strange files on the directory
listing labeled:

```
%PIPE1.$$$
%PIPE2.$$$
%PIPE3.$$$
```

or

```
11002649
1100274E
```

All files must be named—even temporary files. These are the names the operating
system gives for the files that it creates when you use piping. These temporary files
"hold" the data until the next command can process it. These temporary files are
automatically deleted by the operating system when you have finished your chain of
commands. You will not see these names displayed on the screen, and probably will
not see them at all.

9.13 THE MORE FILTER

The MORE command displays one screenful of data at a time with a prompt that
reads **-- More --**. The MORE command pauses after the screen is full. When any key
is pressed, the MORE command displays the next screenful of information, once
again pausing so you can read the screen display. When there is no more data in the
file, the MORE command finishes by returning you to the system prompt. The
purpose of the MORE command is to allow you to be able to read a long text file, one
that would not fit onto the screen, one screenful at a time. The syntax is:

```
MORE [drive:][path]filename
MORE < [drive:][path]filename
command-name ¦ MORE [drive:][path][filename]

  [drive:][path]filename    Specifies file(s) to display one screen at a time
  command-name              Specifies a command whose output will be displayed.
```

As the syntax diagram indicates, MORE can be both redirected and used with a pipe.

9.14 ACTIVITY: USING THE MORE FILTER

Note: The DATA disk is in Drive A with the A:\> displayed.

Step 1　　You will use the pipe symbol ¦, so be sure you locate it on the keyboard. Key in the following: A:\>**DIR ¦ MORE** [Enter]

```
MS-DOS Prompt                                                    _ □ ×

A:\>DIR ¦ MORE

 Volume in drive A is DATA
 Volume Serial Number is 3330-1807
 Directory of A:\

POLYSCI       <DIR>           07-20-01   4:57p POLYSCI
APR      99              72   10-10-99   4:53p APR.99
BRIAN    FIL             44   07-31-99  12:53p BRIAN.FIL
CHKDSK   TXT          2,663   08-02-01   4:13p CHKDSK.TXT
JAN      99              73   10-10-99   4:53p JAN.99
TRIP          <DIR>           07-25-01   6:37p TRIP
SANDYA~1 TXT             53   11-16-00  12:00p Sandy and Nicki.txt
APRIL    NEW            72    04-23-00   4:03p APRIL.NEW
TEST          <DIR>           08-05-01   3:19p TEST
JAN      BUD            73    04-23-00   4:03p JAN.BUD
GOODBYE  NEW            34    01-01-02   4:32a GOODBYE.NEW
JANUARY  NEW            73    04-23-00   4:03p JANUARY.NEW
STATE    CAP           260    07-31-01   4:32p STATE.CAP
APR      BUD            19    12-06-00   2:45p APR.BUD
SORTED   CAP           260    08-05-01   3:44p SORTED.CAP
APR      TST            72    04-23-00   4:18p APR.TST
JAN      OLD            34    01-01-02   4:32a JAN.OLD
JANUARY  TXT           148    08-05-01   3:26p JANUARY.TXT
-- More --
```

WHAT'S HAPPENING?　　Your file listing may vary. By using the pipe symbol, you asked that the output of the DIR command be used as input to the MORE command. The **-- More --** on the bottom of the screen tells you that there are more screens of data. Press any key and the next screen of data will display.

Step 2　　Press any key until you are back at the system prompt. You may have to press several times until you are returned to the system prompt.

```
MS-DOS Prompt                                                    _ □ ×

PERSONAL FIL         2,428   07-30-01   1:46p PERSONAL.FIL
GOODBYE  TXT            34   01-01-02   4:32a GOODBYE.TXT
NEWPRSON FIL         2,672   07-31-99  12:53p NEWPRSON.FIL
Y        FIL             3   08-12-01   4:12p Y.FIL
HOMEBUD  TKR         8,064   01-01-99   5:00a HOMEBUD.TKR
FILE3    FP             19   12-06-00   2:45p FILE3.FP
FILE3    SWT            19   12-06-00   2:45p FILE3.SWT
FILE4    FP             19   12-06-00   2:45p FILE4.FP
FILE2    CZG            19   12-06-00   2:45p FILE2.CZG
-- More --

FILE2    FP             19   12-06-00   2:45p FILE2.FP
FILE2    SWT            19   12-06-00   2:45p FILE2.SWT
FILE3    CZG            19   12-06-00   2:45p FILE3.CZG
APRIL    TXT            72   06-16-01   4:32p APRIL.TXT
```

```
FEBRUARY TXT                75  06-16-01  4:32p FEBRUARY.TXT
HELLO    TXT                53  05-30-01  4:32p HELLO.TXT
BYE      TXT                45  05-30-01  4:32p BYE.TXT
SANDYA~2 TXT                59  11-16-00 12:00p Sandy and Patty.txt
DANCES   TXT                72  12-11-99  4:03p DANCES.TXT
TEST     TXT                65  12-11-99  4:03p TEST.TXT
         44 file(s)         50,515 bytes
          7 dir(s)       1,251,328 bytes free

A:\>_
```

Note: The size (number of bytes) listed may be different from the display due to the difference in files you created and the size of the ScanDisk log.

WHAT'S HAPPENING? You returned to the system level. You may ask why do this when I get the same effect by using DIR /P? There are two reasons. The first is that you can connect several commands with pipes and filters. The second is that /P works only with the DIR command.

Step 3   Key in the following: A:\>**DIR ¦ SORT ¦ MORE** Enter

```
┌─ MS-DOS Prompt ─────────────────────────────────────────────── _ □ ✕ ┐
│                                                                         │
│           7 dir(s)       1,251,328 bytes free                          │
│          44 file(s)         50,515 bytes                               │
│  Directory of A:\                                                      │
│  Volume in drive A is DATA                                             │
│  Volume Serial Number is 3330-1807                                     │
│ APR      99                72  10-10-99  4:53p APR.99                  │
│ APR      BUD               19  12-06-00  2:45p APR.BUD                 │
│ APR      TST               72  04-23-00  4:18p APR.TST                 │
│ APRIL    NEW               72  04-23-00  4:03p APRIL.NEW               │
│ APRIL    TXT               72  06-16-00  4:32p APRIL.TXT               │
│ BRIAN    FIL               44  07-31-99 12:53p BRIAN.FIL               │
│ BYE      TXT               45  05-30-00  4:32p BYE.TXT                 │
│ CAROLYN  FIL               47  07-31-99 12:53p CAROLYN.FIL             │
│ CASES    FIL              314  08-12-00  4:12p CASES.FIL               │
│ CHKDSK   TXT            2,663  08-02-01  4:13p CHKDSK.TXT              │
│ CLASS         <DIR>            07-24-01 12:26p CLASS                   │
│ CLASX               15,108    07-24-01  2:18p CLASX                   │
│ DANCES   TXT               72  12-11-99  4:03p DANCES.TXT              │
│ DRAMA    TV               213  07-03-00  1:24p DRAMA.TV                │
│ FEBRUARY TXT               75  06-16-00  4:32p FEBRUARY.TXT            │
│ FILE2    CZG               19  12-06-00  2:45p FILE2.CZG               │
│ -- More --                                                            │
└─────────────────────────────────────────────────────────────────────┘
```

WHAT'S HAPPENING? You now have an alphabetically sorted directory. The reason the blank lines, volume label, files, and numbers are at the top is that, as we discussed in the ASCII sort sequence, spaces are listed before numbers.

Step 4   Continue pressing any key until you have returned to the system prompt.

```
┌─ MS-DOS Prompt ─────────────────────────────────────────────── _ □ ✕ ┐
│                                                                         │
│ JANUARY  TXT              148  08-05-01  3:26p JANUARY.TXT             │
│ JOINED   SAM              108  07-24-01  1:48p JOINED.SAM              │
│ MEDIA         <DIR>            07-30-01 11:14a MEDIA                   │
│ NEWPRSON FIL            2,672  07-31-99 12:53p NEWPRSON.FIL            │
└─────────────────────────────────────────────────────────────────────┘
```

```
         PERSONAL FIL           2,428   07-30-01  1:46p PERSONAL.FIL
         POLYSCI         <DIR>           07-20-01  4:57p POLYSCI
         PROG            <DIR>           08-01-01  8:12p PROG
         SANDYA~1 TXT              53    11-16-00 12:00p Sandy and Nicki.txt
         SANDYA~2 TXT              59    11-16-00 12:00p Sandy and Patty.txt
         -- More --

         SECOND   FIL              75    08-12-00  4:12p SECOND.FIL
         SORTED   CAP             260    08-05-01  3:44p SORTED.CAP
         STATE    CAP             260    07-31-00  4:32p STATE.CAP
         STEVEN   FIL              44    07-30-01  2:52p STEVEN.FIL
         TEST            <DIR>           08-05-01  3:19p TEST
         TEST     TKR          16,516    07-24-01  1:52p TEST.TKR
         TEST     TXT              65    12-11-99  4:03p TEST.TXT
         TRIP            <DIR>           07-25-01  6:37p TRIP
         WILDTHR  AAA             181    12-31-01  4:32p WILDTHR.AAA
         WILDTWO  AAA             182    12-31-01  4:32p WILDTWO.AAA
         WORK            <DIR>           07-24-01  1:10p WORK
         Y        FIL               3    08-12-00  4:12p Y.FIL


         A:\>_
```

WHAT'S HAPPENING? You returned to the system prompt. Pipes are extremely useful with long ASCII text files. Often a program will come with a **Read.me** or **Readme.txt** file, and this command can be used to read the file. A Readme file holds late-breaking information about the program. If you have a text file that is more than one screenful of data, you cannot use **TYPE /P filename.ext** because /P is not a valid TYPE parameter. You can use the MORE command with a file as input. You can either redirect the input of any text file to the MORE command, or you can pipe it. In the next step, redirection will be used first.

Step 5   Key in the following: A:\>**MORE < PERSONAL.FIL** Enter

```
 MS-DOS Prompt                                                     _ □ ✕

Gillay      Carolyn    699 Lemon      Orange         CA  Professor
Panezich    Frank      689 Lake       Orange         CA  Teacher
Tuttle      Steven     356 Embassy    Mission Viejo  CA  Juggler
Maurdeff    Kathryn    550 Traver     Ann Arbor      MI  Teacher
Maurdeff    Sonia      550 Traver     Ann Arbor      MI  Student
Smith       Gregory    311 Orchard    Ann Arbor      MI  Engineer
Smith       Carolyn    311 Orchard    Ann Arbor      MI  Housewife
Winter      Jim        333 Pick       Garden Grove   CA  Key Grip
Winter      Linda      333 Pick       Garden Grove   CA  Teacher
Tran        Tai Chan   345 Lakeview   Orange         CA  Doctor
Golden      Jane       345 Lakeview   Orange         CA  Nurse
Chang       Wendy      356 Edgewood   Ann Arbor      MI  Librarian
Brogan      Lloyd      111 Miller     Santa Cruz     CA  Vice-President
Brogan      Sally      111 Miller     Santa Cruz     CA  Account Manager
Babchuk     Nicholas    13 Stratford  Sun City West  AZ  Professor
Babchuk     Bianca      13 Stratford  Sun City West  AZ  Professor
Rodriguez   Bob         20 Elm        Ontario        CA  Systems Analyst
Helm        Milton     333 Meadow     Sherman Oaks   CA  Consultant
Suzuki      Charlene   567 Abbey      Rochester      MI  Day Care Teacher
Markiw      Nicholas   354 Bell       Phoenix        AZ  Engineer
Markiw      Emily       10 Zion       Sun City West  AZ  Retired
Nyles       John        12 Brooks     Sun City West  AZ  Retired
-- More --
```

WHAT'S HAPPENING? ➡ You asked that the file from the DATA disk called **PERSONAL.FIL** be redirected (<) as input into the command MORE. The MORE command then displayed a screenful of this file.

Step 6   Continue to press any key until you have returned to the system prompt.

```
MS-DOS Prompt                                                    _ □ ✕

Suzuki     Charlene 567 Abbey      Rochester      MI  Day Care Teacher
Markiw     Nicholas 354 Bell       Phoenix        AZ  Engineer
Markiw     Emily    10 Zion        Sun City West  AZ  Retired
Nyles      John     12 Brooks      Sun City West  AZ  Retired
— More —

Nyles      Sophie   12 Brooks      Sun City West  CA  Retired
Markiw     Nick     10 Zion        Sun City West  AZ  Retired
Washingon  Tyrone   345 Newport    Orange         CA  Manager
Jones      Steven   32 North       Phoenix        AZ  Buyer
Smith      David    120 Collins    Orange         CA  Chef
Babchuk    Walter   12 View        Thousand Oaks  CA  President
Babchuk    Deana    12 View        Thousand Oaks  CA  Housewife
Jones      Cleo     355 Second     Ann Arbor      MI  Clerk
Gonzales   Antonio  40 Northern    Ontario        CA  Engineer
JONES      JERRY    244 East       Mission Viejo  CA  Systems Analyst
Lo         Ophelia  1213 Wick      Phoenix        AZ  Writer
Jones      Ervin    15 Fourth      Santa Cruz     CA  Banker
Perez      Sergio   134 Seventh    Ann Arbor      MI  Editor
Yuan       Suelin   56 Twin Leaf   Orange         CA  Artist
Markiw     Nicholas 12 Fifth       Glendale       AZ  Engineer
Peat       Brian    125 Second     Vacaville      CA  Athlete
Farneth    Nichole  237 Arbor      Vacaville      CA  Dancer

A:\>_
```

WHAT'S HAPPENING? ➡ You returned to the system prompt. There is an alternative way to produce the same results. You can pipe the output of the file to the MORE command.

Step 7   Key in the following: A:\>**TYPE PERSONAL.FIL ¦ MORE** [Enter]

```
MS-DOS Prompt                                                    _ □ ✕

Gillay     Carolyn  699 Lemon      Orange         CA  Professor
Panezich   Frank    689 Lake       Orange         CA  Teacher
Tuttle     Steven   356 Embassy    Mission Viejo  CA  Juggler
Maurdeff   Kathryn  550 Traver     Ann Arbor      MI  Teacher
Maurdeff   Sonia    550 Traver     Ann Arbor      MI  Student
Smith      Gregory  311 Orchard    Ann Arbor      MI  Engineer
Smith      Carolyn  311 Orchard    Ann Arbor      MI  Housewife
Winter     Jim      333 Pick       Garden Grove   CA  Key Grip
Winter     Linda    333 Pick       Garden Grove   CA  Teacher
Tran       Tai Chan 345 Lakeview   Orange         CA  Doctor
Golden     Jane     345 Lakeview   Orange         CA  Nurse
Chang      Wendy    356 Edgewood   Ann Arbor      MI  Librarian
Brogan     Lloyd    111 Miller     Santa Cruz     CA  Vice-President
Brogan     Sally    111 Miller     Santa Cruz     CA  Account Manager
Babchuk    Nicholas 13 Stratford   Sun City West  AZ  Professor
Babchuk    Bianca   13 Stratford   Sun City West  AZ  Professor
Rodriguez  Bob      20 Elm         Ontario        CA  Systems Analyst
```

```
Helm       Milton     333 Meadow   Sherman Oaks    CA  Consultant
Suzuki     Charlene   567 Abbey    Rochester       MI  Day Care Teacher
Markiw     Nicholas   354 Bell     Phoenix         AZ  Engineer
Markiw     Emily      10 Zion      Sun City West   AZ  Retired
Nyles      John       12 Brooks    Sun City West   AZ  Retired
-- More --
```

WHAT'S HAPPENING?→ You took the output from the TYPE command, which is normally a screen display, and piped it as input to the MORE command. The MORE command then displayed a screenful of this file. Remember that there must be a command on either side of the pipe. You could not key in **PERSONAL.FIL | MORE** because **PERSONAL.FIL** is a file and not a command.

Step 8   Continue to press any key until you have returned to the system prompt.

```
MS-DOS Prompt                                                     _ □ ✕

Suzuki     Charlene   567 Abbey    Rochester       MI  Day Care Teacher
Markiw     Nicholas   354 Bell     Phoenix         AZ  Engineer
Markiw     Emily      10 Zion      Sun City West   AZ  Retired
Nyles      John       12 Brooks    Sun City West   AZ  Retired
-- More --

Nyles      Sophie     12 Brooks    Sun City West   CA  Retired
Markiw     Nick       10 Zion      Sun City West   AZ  Retired
Washingon  Tyrone     345 Newport  Orange          CA  Manager
Jones      Steven     32 North     Phoenix         AZ  Buyer
Smith      David      120 Collins  Orange          CA  Chef
Babchuk    Walter     12 View      Thousand Oaks   CA  President
Babchuk    Deana      12 View      Thousand Oaks   CA  Housewife
Jones      Cleo       355 Second   Ann Arbor       MI  Clerk
Gonzales   Antonio    40 Northern  Ontario         CA  Engineer
JONES      JERRY      244 East     Mission Viejo   CA  Systems Analyst
Lo         Ophelia    1213 Wick    Phoenix         AZ  Writer
Jones      Ervin      15 Fourth    Santa Cruz      CA  Banker
Perez      Sergio     134 Seventh  Ann Arbor       MI  Editor
Yuan       Suelin     56 Twin Leaf Orange          CA  Artist
Markiw     Nicholas   12 Fifth     Glendale        AZ  Engineer
Peat       Brian      125 Second   Vacaville       CA  Athlete
Farneth    Nichole    237 Arbor    Vacaville       CA  Dancer

A:\>_
```

WHAT'S HAPPENING?→ You returned to the system prompt.

9.15   COMBINING COMMANDS WITH PIPES AND FILTERS

You can use the pipe symbol to join commands where the standard output of one command is the standard input of the next command. The pipe symbol allows you to connect two or more programs and create a flow of data. When you use the pipe symbol, there must be a command on both sides of the actual symbol. If you use redirection with the "pipeline," a command does not have to be on either side of the > or >>. Remember, when you are redirecting output from a command, it is an "instead of" process. For instance, *instead* of writing the output of a command to the screen, you are redirecting the output to a file or a device. When you combine the use of pipes and the >, the redirection becomes the end of the pipeline, the last step in the process.

9.16 ACTIVITY: COMBINING COMMANDS

Note: The DATA disk is in Drive A. A:\> is displayed.

Step 1   Key in the following:
          A:\>**FIND "Teacher" PERSONAL.FIL ¦ FIND "CA"** Enter

```
MS-DOS Prompt                                                    _ □ X

A:\>FIND "Teacher" PERSONAL.FIL ¦ FIND "CA"
Panezich   Frank     689 Lake      Orange        CA  Teacher
Winter     Linda     333 Pick      Garden Grove  CA  Teacher

A:\>_
```

> **WHAT'S HAPPENING?**   You asked the FIND command to locate the lines that contained "Teacher" in the PERSONAL.FIL, and to take the output from that command and pipe it back through the FIND command again, locating the lines from that output that contained "CA." The results were that only the teachers who live in California were displayed. Remember, the data in **PERSONAL.FIL** has not changed. You have merely searched that data so you could display only those lines, or records, that met your requirements. If you want to save the data you displayed, you must save it to a file.

Step 2   Key in the following: A:\>
          FIND "Teacher" PERSONAL.FIL ¦ FIND "CA" > TEACHER.FIL Enter

Step 3   Key in the following: A:\>**TYPE TEACHER.FIL** Enter

```
MS-DOS Prompt                                                    _ □ X

A:\>FIND "Teacher" PERSONAL.FIL ¦ FIND "CA" > TEACHER.FIL

A:\>TYPE TEACHER.FIL
Panezich   Frank     689 Lake      Orange        CA  Teacher
Winter     Linda     333 Pick      Garden Grove  CA  Teacher

A:\>_
```

> **WHAT'S HAPPENING?**   You used FIND to locate all the teachers in California in the same way you did in Step 1. Since the FIND command sends its output to the screen, you were able to redirect it. The results of the command did not appear on the screen because you redirected the output to a file called **TEACHER.FIL**. You then used the TYPE command to display that file on the screen. You can use the same filter more than once in the same

command line. You can also use filters in combination in the same command line.

Step 4   Key in the following:

A:\>**FIND "Professor" PERSONAL.FIL ¦ FIND "AZ" ¦ SORT** Enter

```
┌─ 🖳 MS-DOS Prompt ─────────────────────────────────────── _ □ ✕ ┐
│                                                                  │
│ A:\>FIND "Professor" PERSONAL.FIL ¦ FIND "AZ" ¦ SORT             │
│ Babchuk    Bianca    13 Stratford   Sun City West   AZ  Professor│
│ Babchuk    Nicholas  13 Stratford   Sun City West   AZ  Professor│
│                                                                  │
│ A:\>_                                                            │
│                                                                  │
└──────────────────────────────────────────────────────────────── ┘
```

WHAT'S HAPPENING?   You asked FIND to locate all occurrences of **Professor** in the file called **PERSONAL.FIL**. You then piped (had the standard output of the FIND command sent as standard input to the next FIND command) to select only those who lived in Arizona (**AZ**). You then piped the standard output of FIND to the SORT command because you wanted all the professors who live in Arizona sorted in alphabetical order.

If you wanted a permanent copy of this list, you could have redirected the standard output (normally displayed on the screen) to a file. If you wanted only a printout, you could have redirected the standard output (normally displayed on the screen) to the printer. You could not do both. For instance, if you had keyed in the command as **FIND "Professor" PERSONAL.FIL ¦ FIND "AZ" ¦ SORT > AZ.FIL > LPT1**, you would have only a hard copy of the output, *not* a saved file called **AZ.FIL**. You can consider the > as the "end of the line." The secret, when combining filters and redirection, is to break the command line down into separate components and determine whether each part of the command works. Furthermore, you should know that if you keyed in **AZ.FIL > LPT1** at the system prompt, it would not work. You would get an error message of "Bad command or file name" because no command was issued. **AZ.FIL** is not a command and neither is **LPT1**. Just because you use pipes, filters, and redirection, the rules of the operating system are not suspended. You must always begin with a command. Similarly, the command line **FIND "Professor" PERSONAL.FIL ¦ FIND "AZ" ¦ SORT ¦ LPT1** also would not work. Again, you should know that if you keyed in **SORT ¦ LPT1** at the system prompt, it would not work because, although SORT is a command, **LPT1** is a device. What is SORT supposed to sort? You have given the SORT command no data. It cannot sort the printer.

Perhaps the easiest way to remember the rules of pipes, filters, and redirection is that, when you use a pipe, there must be a command on either side of the pipe. Remember, you are taking the standard output of a command and using it as standard input to the next command. Remember also that not every command has standard output. For instance, when you key in **DEL filename** at the system level, there is no output that appears or is written to the screen. The file is simply deleted. When you key in **COPY MYFILE YOURFILE**, the only item written to the screen is the message **1 file(s) copied**. The standard output from the COPY command is the message **1 file(s) copied**. Nothing else is written to the screen.

Conversely, when you use redirection, it is an "instead of" action. Instead of the standard output being written to the screen, you are redirecting (sending) it somewhere else, such as a file or a device. You only get "one" somewhere else. Since it is an "instead of" action, you cannot say instead of displaying the output of the DIR command on the screen, redirect the output to a file and redirect the output to the printer. Your choice is either the printer or a file, not both. The primary use of pipes and filters is manipulating the standard output and standard input of commands. You rarely use pipes and filters to sort or find data in text or data files.

Step 5   Key in the following: A:\>**DIR ¦ SORT /+9 ¦ MORE** [Enter]

```
 MS-DOS Prompt                                                    _ □ ✕

  CLASX                  15,108   07-24-01   2:18p  CLASX
  POLYSCI         <DIR>            07-20-01   4:57p  POLYSCI
  WORK            <DIR>            07-24-01   1:10p  WORK
  CLASS           <DIR>            07-24-01  12:26p  CLASS
  TRIP            <DIR>            07-25-01   6:37p  TRIP
  MEDIA           <DIR>            07-30-01  11:14a  MEDIA
  PROG            <DIR>            08-01-01   8:12p  PROG
  TEST            <DIR>            08-05-01   3:19p  TEST
            7 dir(s)       1,250,816 bytes free
  APR       99              72     10-10-99   4:53p  APR.99
  JAN       99              73     10-10-99   4:53p  JAN.99
  WILDTHR   AAA            181     12-31-01   4:32p  WILDTHR.AAA
  WILDTWO   AAA            182     12-31-01   4:32p  WILDTWO.AAA
  APR       BUD             19     12-06-00   2:45p  APR.BUD
  JAN       BUD             73     04-23-00   4:03p  JAN.BUD
  STATE     CAP            260     07-31-01   4:32p  STATE.CAP
  SORTED    CAP            260     08-05-01   3:44p  SORTED.CAP
  FILE2     CZG             19     12-06-00   2:45p  FILE2.CZG
  FILE3     CZG             19     12-06-00   2:45p  FILE3.CZG
  Y         FIL              3     08-12-00   4:12p  Y.FIL
  BRIAN     FIL             44     07-30-01   2:52p  BRIAN.FIL
  -- More --
```

Note: Your screen display will vary based on the work you did as well as the date and time you created the files.

WHAT'S HAPPENING!➡   You took the directory display and piped the output to the SORT command. You then sorted by the file extension. How did you know that the file extension was in the ninth column? Since you know that all files can have no more than eight characters, the extension must start at nine. You then piped the output to the MORE command so that you could see the output one screenful at a time. You can perform the same task with the parameters of the DIR command. The command line **DIR /ON /P** would provide the same results.

Step 6   Continue pressing **Enter** until you have returned to the system prompt.

Step 7   Key in the following: A:\>**DIR ¦ FIND "<DIR>" ¦ SORT** **Enter**

```
MS-DOS Prompt                                          _ □ ✕

A:\>DIR ¦ FIND "<DIR>" ¦ SORT
CLASS           <DIR>        07-24-01 12:26p  CLASS
MEDIA           <DIR>        07-30-01 11:14a  MEDIA
POLYSCI         <DIR>        07-20-01  4:57p  POLYSCI
PROG            <DIR>        08-01-01  8:12p  PROG
TEST            <DIR>        08-05-01  3:19p  TEST
TRIP            <DIR>        07-25-01  6:37p  TRIP
WORK            <DIR>        07-24-01  1:10p  WORK

A:\>_
```

WHAT'S HAPPENING? You sent the output of DIR to FIND. You were looking for any file that had **<DIR>** in it. You used uppercase letters since everything in the directory is in uppercase. You had to use quotation marks to enclose **<DIR>**. Had you not done that, the command line would have read the < and the > as redirection symbols. By enclosing them, you ensured those symbols were read as character data. You then sent that output to the SORT command. Now you have an alphabetical list of the subdirectories on your DATA disk. Again, you can do the same task with the parameters of the DIR command. The command line **DIR /AD /ON** would provide the same results, except you would see information about bytes and volume label.

CHAPTER SUMMARY

1. The redirection symbols are the >, the <, and the >>.
2. The >> appends output to the end of a file.
3. Redirection, pipes, and filters have to do with standard input and standard output.
4. Any command that expects its input from the keyboard has standard input.
5. Any command that normally displays its output on the screen has standard output.
6. Standard error means that the operating system writes error messages to the screen.
7. You can redirect standard input and output to and from devices or files.
8. The pipe symbol is ¦.
9. The pipe takes standard output from one command and uses it as standard input for the next command.
10. You can pipe many programs together.
11. Filters take data, change it in some fashion, and send the output to the screen.
12. The three filters are SORT, FIND, and MORE.
13. SORT has two parameters: /R for reverse order and /+n for column number.

14. FIND has four parameters: /V for everything except the specified item, /C for counting occurrences of the item, /N for line number where the item appears in the file, and /I for ignore case.

15. MORE lets you look at any text file one screenful at a time. It has no parameters.

16. You must have a command on both ends of the pipe.

17. Redirection is the last action you can take. You either write to the screen or to a file or device. You either accept input from the keyboard or from a file.

18. You can string together pipes and filters to create your own commands.

19. Each part of a command must be able to stand alone on the command line.

20. Redirection performs an "instead of" action.

KEY TERMS

ASCII sort sequence	input/output	standard error
case sensitive	I/O	standard input
character string	pipe	standard output
filters	redirection	

DISCUSSION QUESTIONS

1. Explain redirection.
2. Explain the terms standard input, standard output, and standard error.
3. Does every operating system command use standard input and standard output? If not, why not?
4. What is the difference between > and >> when redirecting output?
5. Explain how the symbol < is used.
6. Keying in COPY DIR LPT1 will not give you a printout of the directory. Why?
7. What are filters?
8. Give the syntax of the SORT command.
9. What do the parameters in the SORT syntax represent?
10. Explain how the SORT command works. Describe any limitations of the SORT command.
11. Identify one place to which standard output can be written.
12. Give the syntax for the FIND command.
13. What is the purpose of the FIND command?
14. What are the four parameters that can be used with the FIND command, and what do they represent?
15. Why must a character string be enclosed in quotation marks when using the FIND command?
16. What are pipes?
17. Are there any restrictions on the use of pipes? If so, what are they?
18. How is the MORE command used? What is the syntax?

TRUE/FALSE QUESTIONS

For each statement, circle the letter T if the statement is true or the letter F if the statement is false.

T   F   1. All system commands use standard input and standard output.

T   F   2. Standard output can be directed to a file.

T   F   3. There are only two filter commands: FIND and SORT.

T   F   4. You can use the FIND command to find data either *with* or *without* a specified word.

T   F   5. The MORE command allows you to enter more data from the keyboard.

COMPLETION QUESTIONS

Write the correct answer in each blank space.

6. The standard input device is the _____.

7. The standard output device is the _____.

8. In the syntax SORT [/R] [/+n], the letter *n* represents a(n) _____.

9. The filter command used to display information one screenful at a time is the _____ command.

10. The redirection symbols are _____, _____, and _____.

MULTIPLE CHOICE QUESTIONS

For each question, write the letter for the correct answer in the blank space.

11. The command that redirects the output of the DIR command to the printer is:
    a. DIR ¦ LPT1
    b. DIR < LPT1
    c. DIR > LPT1
    d. COPY DIR LPT1

12. If you redirect a command to expect the input from a file instead of standard input, and the information in the file is incorrect, you may be able to correct the problem by
    a. pressing Ctrl + Shift.
    b. pressing Ctrl + Break or Ctrl + C.
    c. closing the MS-DOS window.
    d. both b and c

13. The parameter used with the command SORT to sort a list by the fifth column of data in a file (where the fifth column begins with character number 25) would be:
    a. /+5
    b. /+25
    c. /+5-25
    d. /+R=25

14. To display MYFILE.FIL one screenful at a time, you would use:
    a. MORE < MYFILE.FIL
    b. TYPE MYFILE.FIL ¦ MORE
    c. COPY MYFILE.FIL > MORE
    d. either a or b

15. When using the SORT command, if you key in 1234, 96, 4, and 789, the order returned would be:

a.	4	96	789	1234
b.	1234	789	96	4
c.	1234	4	789	96
d.	96	789	4	1234

WRITING COMMANDS

Note: If you find it necessary to perform some of the steps in order to write your answer, do the work on a new disk. If so, copy the files \WINDOSBK\STATES.USA, \WINDOSBK\PERSONAL.FIL, and \WINDOSBK\CASES.FIL to the root of the DATA disk.

Write the steps or command(s) to perform the required action as if you were at the computer. The prompt will indicate the default drive and directory.

16. Sort the file called STATES.USA by chief crops, and send the output to the printer. The chief crops are located in the 40th column.
    C:\>

17. Locate every occurrence of "Teacher" in the file PERSONAL.FIL located in the root directory of the disk in the A drive, and send the output to a file called TEACHER.FIL, which is in the WORK directory of the disk in the A drive.
    A:\>

18. Display the contents of PERSONAL.FIL, located on the root of the disk in the A drive, one screenful at a time.
    C:\TEMP>

19. Append the contents of BRIAN.FIL to the file called CASES.FIL. Both files are on the root of the disk in Drive A.
    C:\>

20. Find out how many occurrences of "Teacher" appear in the file PERSONAL.FIL, which is located on the root of the disk in Drive A.
    C:\>

APPLICATION ASSIGNMENTS

Note 1: Place the APPLICATION disk in Drive A. Be sure to work on the APPLICA-
TION disk, not the DATA disk.

Note 2: The homework problems assume that Drive C is the hard disk and that the
APPLICATION disk is in Drive A. If you are using another drive, such as
floppy Drive B or hard Drive D, be sure to substitute that drive letter when
reading the questions and answers.

Note 3: All subdirectories that are created will be under the root directory unless
otherwise specified.

Note 4: The homework problems will use C:\WINDOWS\COMMAND as the directory where the system utility files are located.

Note 5: It is assumed that the path includes C:\WINDOWS\COMMAND.

Note 6: Do not save the output from the commands to a file unless specified.

PROBLEM SET I

PROBLEM A

A-a Place the APPLICATION disk in Drive A.

A-b Copy all the files from the **WINDOSBK\SPORTS** directory to the APPLI-
CATION disk, maintaining the same directory structure on the APPLICA-
TION disk. (*Hint:* Remember XCOPY /S.)

A-c With the root directory of the A drive as the default directory and using
the relative path, sort the file called **BASKETBL.TMS** in the **SPORTS**
subdirectory.

    1. Which command(s) could you have used?
      a. SORT < SPORTS\BASKETBL.TMS
      b. TYPE BASKETBL.TMS ¦ SORT
      c. both a and b
      d. neither a nor b

    2. What team is listed first?
      a. Atlanta Hawks
      b. Boston Celtics
      c. Charlotte Hornets
      d. Los Angeles Lakers

A-d Key in the following:
    A:\>**COPY \SPORTS*.TMS \SPORTS\ALL.SPT** Enter

A-e With the root directory of the APPLICATION disk as the default and
using the relative path, display the contents of the **SPORTS\ALL.SPT** file
one screenful at a time. Use redirection.

    3. Which command did you use?
      a. TYPE SPORTS\ALL.SPT < MORE
      b. TYPE SPORTS\ALL.SPT /P

      c. MORE < SPORTS\ALL.SPT

      d. MORE < TYPE SPORTS\ALL.SPT

A-f   Press [Enter] until you have displayed all of the file.

A-g   Sort the **ALL.SPT** file in reverse order and display the output one screenful at a time.

      4. What team appeared first on the first screen display?

        a. Utah Jazz

        b. Washington Bullets

        c. USC Trojans

        d. Washington Redskins

A-h   Press [Enter] until you have displayed all of the file.

A-i   In the **ALL.SPT** file, find all the teams that have "Los" in their names.

      5. What team *does not* appear?

        a. Los Angeles Lakers

        b. Los Angeles Dodgers

        c. neither a nor b appears

        d. both a and b appear

PROBLEM B

B-a   Be sure you have the ALL.SPT file from Problem A above. In the **ALL.SPT** file, find all the teams that have "go" in their names.

      6. What team appears that *is not* from Chicago?

        a. Michigan Gophers

        b. San Diego Padres

        c. San Diego Chargers

        d. all teams are from Chicago

B-b   Copy **PERSONAL.FIL** from the **C:\WINDOSBK** to the **TRAVEL** directory.

B-c   Sort the **TRAVEL\PERSONAL.FIL** file in alphabetical order.

      7. What name appears last?

        a. Winter

        b. Wyse

        c. Yuan

        d. Zola

B-d   From **TRAVEL\PERSONAL.FIL**, create a file sorted by city (the city starts in column 34) called **CALIF.FIL** that will be saved to the **TRAVEL** subdirectory. This file will contain only people who live in **CA**. Begin your command with the FIND command.

8. What street name is listed *last* in **CALIF.FIL**?
   a. Brooks
   b. Lake
   c. Pick
   d. View

B-e   Find anyone who is an engineer in **PERSONAL.FIL** but exclude anyone who lives in **CA**.

9. What state(s) is/are displayed?
   a. AZ
   b. CO
   c. MI
   d. both a and c

B-f   Copy the **STATES.USA** file from the **WINDOSBK** directory to the subdirectory called **TRAVEL** on the APPLICATION disk keeping the same file name.

B-g   In the **STATES.USA** file, find all the states that are located in the south and sort the output in reverse alphabetical order.

10. What state is displayed first?
    a. South Carolina
    b. North Carolina
    c. Louisiana
    d. Florida

PROBLEM SET II

Note 1: Before proceeding with these assignments, check with your lab instructor to see if there are any special procedures you should follow.

Note 2: The APPLICATION disk is in Drive A. A:\> is displayed as the default drive and the default directory. *All work will occur on the APPLICATION disk.*

Note 3: Make sure that NAME.BAT, MARK.FIL, GETYN.COM, GO.BAT, and NAME.FIL are all present in the root directory of the APPLICATION disk before proceeding with these problems.

Note 4: All files with the .HW extension *must* be created in the root directory of the APPLICATION disk.

Step 1   Key in the following: A:\>**NAME** [Enter]

Step 2   Here is an example to key in, but your instructor will have other information that applies to your class. Key in the following:
Bette A. Peat [Enter]   (*Your* name goes here.)
CIS 55 [Enter]   (*Your* class goes here.)
T-Th 8-9:30 [Enter]   (*Your* day and time go here.)
Chapter 9 Applications [Enter]

Step 3   Press [F6] [Enter]

Step 4   If the information is correct, press **Y** and you are back to A:\>.

WHAT'S HAPPENING! ▶ You have returned to the system level. You now have a file called **NAME.FIL** with your name and other pertinent information. (*Hint*: Remember redirection.)

TO CREATE 1.HW

❖   While the root directory of the APPLICATION disk is the default, locate all the people who live in Orange in the **TRAVEL\PERSONAL.FIL** file and sort them in descending order (Z to A).

❖   Save the output to a file called **1.HW**.

TO CREATE 2.HW

❖   Sort the **TRAVEL** directory of the APPLICATION disk and save the output to a file called **2.HW**.

❖   Sort the **SPORTS** directory of the APPLICATION disk and append the output to the file called **2.HW**.

TO CREATE 3.HW

❖   In the **SPORTS\ALL.SPT** file, find all the teams that have "in" within their names, and direct the output to a file called **3.HW**.

TO CREATE 4.HW

❖   In the **TRAVEL\PERSONAL.FIL**, find all occurrences, regardless of case, of the name "Jones," and direct the output to a file called **4.HW**.

TO PRINT YOUR HOMEWORK

Step 1   Be sure the printer is on and ready to accept print jobs from your computer.

Step 2   Key in the following: A:\>**GO NAME.FIL 1.HW 2.HW 3.HW 4.HW** [Enter]

Step 3   Follow the messages on the screen. When you finish, you will return to the A:\> prompt.

Step 4   Execute the shut-down procedure.

PROBLEM SET III—BRIEF ESSAY

List and explain the syntax and various parameters for the three filter commands (FIND, SORT, and MORE). Also explain how redirection and piping can work with each of them.

INTRODUCTION TO BATCH FILES

LEARNING OBJECTIVES

After completing this chapter you will be able to:

1. Compare and contrast batch and interactive processing.
2. Explain how batch files work.
3. Explain the purpose and function of the REM, ECHO, and PAUSE commands.
4. Explain how to stop or interrupt the batch file process.
5. Explain the function and use of replaceable parameters in batch files.
6. Explain the function of pipes, filters, and redirection in batch files.
7. Explain the purpose and function of AUTOEXEC.BAT.
8. Explain the purpose and function of interactive booting.
9. Explain how to selectively execute CONFIG.SYS and AUTOEXEC.BAT files.
10. Explain how to use batch files from the desktop.

STUDENT OUTCOMES

1. Use Edit to write batch files.
2. Use COPY CON to write batch files.
3. Write and execute a simple batch file.
4. Write a batch file to load an application program.
5. Use the REM, PAUSE, and ECHO commands in batch files.
6. Terminate a batch file while it is executing.

7. Write batch files using replaceable parameters.
8. Write a batch file using pipes, filters, and redirection.
9. Write and use AUTOEXEC.BAT.
10. Be able to selectively execute AUTOEXEC.BAT.
11. Write a batch file for use from the desktop.

CHAPTER OVERVIEW

You have used many command line commands throughout this textbook. Many of these commands are repeated in the same sequence. If more than one command is needed to execute a program, you have to key in each command at the system prompt. This repetitive, time-consuming process increases the possibility of human error.

A batch file is a text file that contains a series of commands stored in the order the user wants them carried out. It executes a series of commands with a minimum number of keystrokes. Batch files allow you to automate a process and, at the same time, create more powerful commands, which increases productivity.

In this chapter you will learn to create batch files to automate a sequence of commands, to write and use batch files for complex tasks, to use batch file subcommands, to halt the execution of a batch file, and to write batch files using replaceable parameters. You will also learn how batch files can be used from the desktop.

10.1 CONCEPTS OF BATCH AND INTERACTIVE PROCESSING

Operating system commands used at the MS-DOS command line are programs that are executed or run when you key in the command name. If you wish to run more than one command, you need to key in each command at the system prompt. You can, however, customize and automate the sequence of commands by writing a command sequence, called a ***batch file*** or a command file, to be executed with a minimum number of keystrokes. Any command you can enter at the system prompt can be included in a batch file. You can even execute an application program from a batch file. When you string together a sequence of steps in an application program, it is called a macro, which is conceptually similar to a batch file.

A batch file contains one or more commands. To create this file of commands, you write a text file using Edit, COPY CON, or a text editor such as Notepad. You can also use a word processor providing it has a "Save as text file" option. The file that you write and name will run any command that the operating system can execute. This file *must* have the file extension .BAT and must be an ASCII file. Once you have written this command file, you execute or run it by simply keying in the name of the batch file, just as you key in the name of a command. The operating system reads and executes each line of the batch file, as if you were sitting at the terminal and separately keying in each command line. Once you start running a batch file, your attention or input is not needed until the batch file has finished executing.

Batch files are used for several reasons. They allow you to minimize keystrokes, and they minimize the possibility of errors, as you don't have to key in the commands over and over. Batch files are used to put together a complex sequence of commands and store them under an easily remembered name. They automate any frequent and/or consistent procedures that you always want to do in the same manner, such as backing up critical data to an alternate location. In addition, you can execute application programs by calling them with a batch file.

Batch is an old data-processing term. In the early days of computing, work was done by submitting a job (or all the instructions needed to run the job successfully) to a data-processing department, which would run these jobs in *batches*. There was no chance for anyone to interact with the program. The job was run, and the output was delivered. Thus, when you run a batch job, you are running a computer routine without interruption.

Batch jobs are still run today. An example of a batch job would be running a payroll—issuing paychecks. The computer program that calculates and prints paychecks is run without interruption. The output or results are the paychecks. This job can be run at any time. If a company decides that payday will be Friday, the data-processing department can run the payroll Thursday night. If the company decides payday will be Monday, the data processing department can run the payroll Sunday night. This is ***batch processing***.

Batch processing is in contrast to an interactive mode of data processing. Sometimes called online or real-time mode, interactive means interacting directly with the computer. An automated teller machine (ATM) that a bank uses so that you can withdraw or deposit money without human intervention is an example of ***interactive processing***. The bank needs instant updating of its records. It cannot wait until next week to run a batch job to find out how much money you have deposited or withdrawn. If you withdraw $100, the bank first wants to be sure that you have $100 in your account, and then it wants the $100 subtracted immediately from your balance. You are dealing with the computer in an interactive, real-time mode—the data is processed without delay.

In the PC world, you can work in interactive mode, but this usually requires a connection to another computer, often over phone lines. The Internet allows you to communicate directly with other computers and perform such functions as reviewing airline flight schedules. Although interactive mode can be exciting, most of the time you are working one-on-one with your computer and are not in interactive mode. Hence, the batch mode is the area of emphasis.

10.2 HOW BATCH FILES WORK

You will be creating and executing batch files in this chapter. By now you should know that data and programs are stored as files, but how does the operating system know the difference between a data file and a program file? As mentioned in previous chapters, it knows the difference based on the file extension. When you key in something at the prompt, the operating system first checks in RAM to compare what you keyed in to the internal table of commands. If it finds a match, the program is executed. If what you keyed in does not match an internal command, the operating system first looks on the default drive and directory for the extension .COM, meaning command file. Then the operating system looks for the file extension .EXE, meaning executable file (this extension is used for system utility programs and most application software).

If what you keyed in does not match either .COM or .EXE, the operating system finally looks on the default drive and directory for the file extension .BAT, meaning batch file. If it finds a match, it loads and executes the batch file, one line at a time. If what you keyed in does not match any of the above criteria, you see the message "Bad command or file name."

What if you had files on a disk that had the same file name but three different file extensions, such as CHKDSK.COM, CHKDSK.EXE, and CHKDSK.BAT? How would the operating system know which program to load and execute? Priority rules are followed. The operating system looks for the program with the .COM file extension first and, if found, would never get to the other files. However, if you were more specific and keyed in both the file name *and* the file extension, such as CHKDSK.BAT, the operating system would then execute the file name you specified.

Remember that, since the batch file is a program, either the .BAT file must be on the default drive and directory or the path must be set to the location of the batch file so you may invoke it. Most importantly, each line in a batch file must contain only one command.

10.3 USING EDIT TO WRITE BATCH FILES

To write batch files, you need a mechanism to create an ASCII text file, since that is what a batch file is. You should remember that ASCII is a code used by the operating system to interpret the letters, numbers, and punctuation marks that you key in. In simple terms, if you can read a file with the TYPE command, it is an ASCII text file. You can use a word-processing program to write a batch file if it has a non-document or text mode. However, most word-processing programs are quite large and take time to load into memory. Most batch files are not very long, nor do they need the features of a word processor. Using a word processor to write a batch file is like using a sledgehammer to kill a fly.

Having a small, simple text editor is so important that the operating system includes one as part of the system utility programs. This is the MS-DOS editor, called Edit. Edit is simple to use and universal. You will write some batch files using Edit. Remember, Edit is only a tool to create the file; it does not run or execute it. You execute the file when you key in the file name at the system prompt in the MS-DOS window. Each line in a batch file must contain only one command. A batch file can have any legal file name but the file extension must always be .BAT.

If you are in the Windows interface, the text editor is Notepad. Like Edit, Notepad creates text-only files and may be used to write batch files. However, if you are having problems with Windows, you will not have Notepad available to you because you need a graphical user interface to use Notepad. Edit, on the other hand, can work at the command line. In fact, you will later see that when you create your startup disk, Edit is on the disk, but not Notepad. Thus, in the following activities, you will be using Edit.

10.4 ACTIVITY: WRITING AND EXECUTING A BATCH FILE

Note 1: The DATA disk is in Drive A. A: \> is displayed.

Note 2: Although you may use a mouse with the MS-DOS editor, the instructions will show the keystroke steps, not the mouse steps.

Note 3: The amount of space shown as remaining on the disk will vary, depending on the size and placement of the batch files on your disk.

Step 1   Key in the following: A: \>**EDIT EXAMPLE.BAT** [Enter]

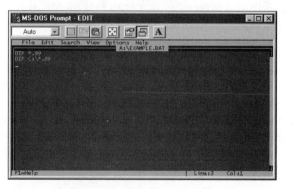

WHAT'S HAPPENING?   You are now using the MS-DOS editor. You are going to create a batch file named **EXAMPLE**. The file extension must be **.BAT**.

Step 2   Key in the following: **DIR *.99** [Enter]

Step 3   Key in the following: **DIR C:*.99** [Enter]

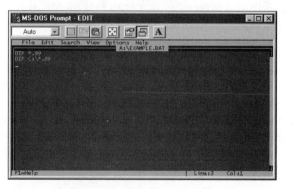

WHAT'S HAPPENING?   Look at each line. Each one is a legitimate operating system command that could be keyed in at the prompt. Each command is on a separate line. The first line asks for a listing of all the files on the disk in the default drive that have the file extension **.99**. The second line asks for all the files in the root directory of C that have the file extension **.99**. At this point, you have written the batch file. Next, you need to exit Edit and save the file to disk.

Step 4   Press [Alt] + **F**.

Step 5   Press **X**.

 Since you have not saved the file, Edit reminds you with a dialog box that, if you want this file on the disk, you must save it.

Step 6   Press **Y**.

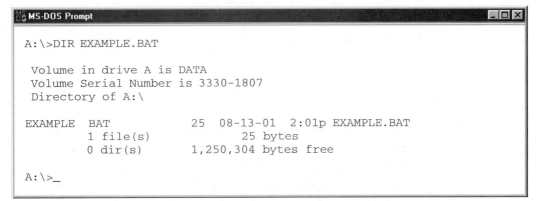

 You have saved your file, exited the MS-DOS editor, and returned to the system prompt.

Step 7   Key in the following: A:\>**DIR EXAMPLE.BAT** Enter

```
MS-DOS Prompt                                                    _ □ X

A:\>DIR EXAMPLE.BAT

 Volume in drive A is DATA
 Volume Serial Number is 3330-1807
 Directory of A:\

EXAMPLE   BAT           25   08-13-01  2:01p EXAMPLE.BAT
        1 file(s)                 25 bytes
        0 dir(s)       1,250,304 bytes free

A:\>_
```

 The **DIR EXAMPLE.BAT** command shows that there is a file on the DATA disk called **EXAMPLE.BAT**. It looks like any other text file.

How do you make the operating system treat it like a program so that you can execute it? You simply key in the name of the file at the prompt. You do not need to key in the extension, just the name. The operating system first looks for a file in its internal table called **EXAMPLE**. It does not find it. It then looks for a file called **EXAMPLE.COM** on the default disk, the DATA disk. No file exists called **EXAMPLE.COM**. Next, it looks for a file on the default disk called **EXAMPLE.EXE**. No file exists called **EXAMPLE.EXE**. Finally, the operating system looks for a file called **EXAMPLE.BAT** on the default disk. It does find a file by this name. It loads it into memory and executes each line, one at a time. Thus, to execute the batch file called **EXAMPLE**, key in the name of the file at the prompt. Watch what happens on the screen after you key in the file name.

Step 8   Key in the following: A:\>**EXAMPLE** Enter

```
MS-DOS Prompt                                                    _ □ ×

A:\>EXAMPLE


A:\>DIR *.99

 Volume in drive A is DATA
 Volume Serial Number is 3330-1807
 Directory of A:\

APR       99              72  10-10-99  4:53p APR.99
JAN       99              73  10-10-99  4:53p JAN.99
          2 file(s)              145 bytes
          0 dir(s)         1,250,304 bytes free

A:\>DIR C:\*.99

 Volume in drive C is MILLENNIUM
 Volume Serial Number is 2B18-1301
 Directory of C:\

File not found
                     640,512,000 bytes free

A:\>
A:\>

A:\>_
```

WHAT'S HAPPENING? (*Note:* Part of the display may have scrolled off of your screen.) The operating system read and executed each line of the batch file you wrote, one line at a time. The screen displayed each command line and the results of the command line as it executed. Each line executed as if you had sat in front of the keyboard and keyed in each command individually. You did key in the commands when you wrote the batch file, but you had to key them in only once. The first line was **DIR *.99**. When the operating system read that line, it executed it and showed on the screen both files on the DATA disk with the file extension **.99**. It read the next line of the batch file and looked in the root directory of Drive C for any file that had the file extension **.99**. Since there were no files on that drive with the extension **.99**, it gave the message **File not found**. Now that you have written the file **EXAMPLE.BAT**, you can execute this batch file's commands over and over again by keying in **EXAMPLE** at the prompt.

10.5 WRITING AND EXECUTING A BATCH FILE TO SAVE KEYSTROKES

The previous example showed you how to write and execute a batch file, but that file is not especially useful. The next batch file to be written will allow you to key in only one keystroke instead of seven. As you know, the command DIR /AD will quickly show you any subdirectories on the DATA disk. The /A switch means attribute, and the attribute you want displayed is D for directories. This command is composed of seven keystrokes, and you must have the proper parameters. With a batch file, you can do the same task by pressing only one key.

The DIR command has other parameters that are very useful. One of these is O for order. There are many kinds of order you can achieve. One kind that is useful is the arrangement of files by size. The command line would be DIR /OS. The O is for order, and the S is to arrange by size from the smallest to the largest file. If you wanted to reverse the order so that the files would be displayed from the largest to smallest, the command would be DIR /O-S. The O is still for order, but the - is for reverse order, placing smallest files at the end of the listing. The S is for file size. This command would take eight keystrokes. You can reduce it to one.

These batch files you are going to write are very small—one line. It seems like a lot of trouble to load Edit just to accomplish this task. If you would rather not load Edit, you can use the COPY command to write a simple ASCII file. The syntax is:

```
COPY CON filename
```

What you are doing here is copying what you key in (CON) to a file name. CON is the operating system's name for the keyboard/console devices of your computer. You are still following the syntax of the COPY command; it is just that now you are copying from a device—the console (CON)—to a file. Remember that in an early chapter, you copied to a device, the printer (COPY filename PRN). Just as PRN, LPT1, and LPT2 are reserved device names, so is CON.

When you are done keying in text, you must tell the COPY command you are finished. You do this by pressing the **F6** key and then the **Enter** key. This writes the data you keyed in to the file name you specified. This is what you have been doing in your application assignments when you have entered data in NAME.FIL. The only problem with COPY CON, as it is informally referred to, is that you cannot correct errors once you press **Enter** at the end of a command line. Nor can you use COPY CON to correct errors in an existing file. To do that, you need an editor, such as Edit. But nothing is faster than using COPY CON.

10.6   ACTIVITY: WRITING AND EXECUTING A ONE-LETTER BATCH FILE

Note 1: The DATA disk is in Drive A. A:\> is displayed.
Note 2: For these examples, the use of COPY CON will be shown. If you make errors, you can either use COPY CON and key in all the data again or use the MS-DOS editor to correct the errors.
Note 3: In earlier chapters you may have used DOSKEY and the function keys to correct errors. Either of these methods will work with COPY CON.

Step 1   Key in the following: A:\>**COPY CON D.BAT** [Enter]

```
MS-DOS Prompt                                              _ □ ✕

A:\>COPY CON D.BAT
_
```

> **WHAT'S HAPPENING?** When you keyed in **COPY CON D.BAT**, you were informing the COPY command that you wanted to make the keyboard the source. The cursor is blinking right below the prompt, and the screen is blank.

Step 2   Key in the following: **DIR /AD** Enter

```
MS-DOS Prompt                                                    _ □ ✕
A:\>COPY CON D.BAT
DIR /AD
_
```

> **WHAT'S HAPPENING?** You have one line. You are finished keying in data and you wish this line to be saved to a file called **D.BAT**. First, however, you must tell COPY you are finished.

Step 3   Press F6 Enter

```
MS-DOS Prompt                                                    _ □ ✕
A:\>COPY CON D.BAT
DIR /AD
^Z
        1 file(s) copied

A:\>_
```

> **WHAT'S HAPPENING?** By pressing F6 and then Enter, you sent a signal to COPY that you were done. The F6 appeared on the screen as **^Z**. Pressing Ctrl + Z will produce the same results as F6. You then got the message **1 file(s) copied** and were returned to the system level.

Step 4   Key in the following: A:\>**TYPE D.BAT** Enter

```
MS-DOS Prompt                                                    _ □ ✕
A:\>TYPE D.BAT
DIR /AD

A:\>_
```

> **WHAT'S HAPPENING?** You wrote a one-line batch file named **D.BAT** with **COPY CON** and saved the file **D.BAT** to disk. Once you returned to the system prompt, you displayed the contents of **D.BAT** with the TYPE command. The fact that you could display this file with the TYPE command is another indication that it is indeed an ASCII file. All COPY CON did was allow you to create the file, and TYPE merely displayed what is inside the file. To execute the file, you must key in the file name. Now, whenever you want to see the subdirectories on the DATA disk in Drive A, you only have to key in one letter to execute this command.

Step 5   Key in the following: A:\>**D** Enter

```
MS-DOS Prompt                                              _ □ ×

A:\>D

A:\>DIR /AD

 Volume in drive A is DATA
 Volume Serial Number is 3330-1807
 Directory of A:\

POLYSCI        <DIR>        07-20-01  4:57p POLYSCI
TRIP           <DIR>        07-25-01  6:37p TRIP
TEST           <DIR>        08-05-01  3:19p TEST
CLASS          <DIR>        07-24-01 12:26p CLASS
WORK           <DIR>        07-24-01  1:10p WORK
MEDIA          <DIR>        07-30-01 11:14a MEDIA
PROG           <DIR>        08-01-01  8:12p PROG
          0 file(s)              0 bytes
          7 dir(s)       1,249,792 bytes free

A:\>

A:\>_
```

WHAT'S HAPPENING? ➤ Your display may vary based on what subdirectories are on the DATA disk and in what order they were created. As you can see, you set up a command sequence in a batch file called **D.BAT**. You can run this batch file whenever the need arises, simply by keying in the name of the batch file at the system prompt. You can also display the files by size, with the smallest file at the end of the list.

Step 6   Key in the following: A:\>**COPY CON S.BAT** Enter
                              DIR /O-S Enter
                              F6 Enter

```
MS-DOS Prompt                                              _ □ ×

A:\>COPY CON S.BAT
DIR /O-S
^Z
        1 file(s) copied

A:\>_
```

WHAT'S HAPPENING? ➤ You have written another simple one-line batch file and saved it to the default directory.

Step 7   Key in the following: A:\>**TYPE S.BAT** Enter

```
MS-DOS Prompt                                              _ □ ×

A:\>TYPE S.BAT
DIR /O-S

A:\>_
```

WHAT'S HAPPENING? ➤ After saving the file to disk, you looked at its contents with the TYPE command. To execute the batch file, you must key in the batch file name (**S**) at the system prompt.

Step 8   Key in the following: A:\>**S** Enter

```
MS-DOS Prompt                                                    _ □ ×

    EXAMPLE  BAT            25   08-13-01   2:01p  EXAMPLE.BAT
    APR      BUD            19   12-06-00   2:45p  APR.BUD
    FILE3    FP             19   12-06-00   2:45p  FILE3.FP
    FILE3    SWT            19   12-06-00   2:45p  FILE3.SWT
    FILE4    FP             19   12-06-00   2:45p  FILE4.FP
    FILE2    CZG            19   12-06-00   2:45p  FILE2.CZG
    FILE2    FP             19   12-06-00   2:45p  FILE2.FP
    FILE2    SWT            19   12-06-00   2:45p  FILE2.SWT
    FILE3    CZG            19   12-06-00   2:45p  FILE3.CZG
    S        BAT            10   08-13-01   3:17p  S.BAT
    D        BAT             9   08-13-01   2:05p  D.BAT
    Y        FIL             3   08-12-00   4:12p  Y.FIL
    POLYSCI       <DIR>          07-20-01   4:57p  POLYSCI
    TRIP          <DIR>          07-25-01   6:37p  TRIP
    TEST          <DIR>          08-05-01   3:19p  TEST
    CLASS         <DIR>          07-24-01  12:26p  CLASS
    WORK          <DIR>          07-24-01   1:10p  WORK
    MEDIA         <DIR>          07-30-01  11:14a  MEDIA
    PROG          <DIR>          08-01-01   8:12p  PROG
           48 file(s)          50,681 bytes
            7 dir(s)        1,249,280 bytes free

    A:\>

    A:\>_
```

WHAT'S HAPPENING? ➤ The files are listed by size, and all the subdirectories are grouped at the bottom of the display. Because directories have no size, they are listed last as the smallest files.

10.7 USING BATCH FILES TO LOAD APPLICATION SOFTWARE

Today, in the Windows environment, you typically launch application programs such as Word or Excel by either selecting from a menu, clicking the program icon, or using a toolbar. These are, of course, application programs written for the Windows world. If you had an older program that was written for the DOS world only, it would have none of these choices. Thus, you could write a batch file to launch it, and then create an icon for your desktop. You will also find that there will be system activities you will want to run from the command line. Some of these activities will launch certain programs. The techniques you learn here can assist you in these matters.

You will first look at the use of batch files to load application software written to run under MS-DOS. Usually, application software programs are stored in a subdirectory. When you want to use a program, you have to change the directory to the proper subdirectory, load the program, and, when you are finished using the application program, return to the system level. You usually want to change the default subdirectory to the root directory. This process can be easier with a batch file.

First you will run through the process of working with application software, and then you will create a batch file to load the application software.

10.8 ACTIVITY: USING THE HPB APPLICATION PACKAGE

Note: The DATA disk is in Drive A. A:\> is displayed.

Step 1   Key in the following:
A:\>**XCOPY C:\WINDOSBK\PHONE*.* HPB** [Enter]

```
MS-DOS Prompt                                              _ □ ×

A:\>XCOPY C:\WINDOSBK\PHONE\*.* HPB
Does HPB specify a file name
or directory name on the target
(F = file, D = directory)?_
```

WHAT'S HAPPENING?   You are copying the **PHONE** directory and its files from the **\WINDOSBK** subdirectory to the DATA disk. You are placing the files in a subdirectory you called **HPB**.

Step 2   Press **D**.

```
MS-DOS Prompt                                              _ □ ×

A:\>XCOPY C:\WINDOSBK\PHONE\*.* HPB
Does HPB specify a file name
Or directory name on the target
(F = file, D = directory)?D
README.HPB
FILE_ID.DIZ
HPB.DAT
HPB.CFG
HPB.EXE
HPB.SLC
        6 File(s) copied

A:\>_
```

WHAT'S HAPPENING?   You have copied the files to the new **HPB** subdirectory on the DATA disk.

Step 3   Key in the following: A:\>**CD HPB** [Enter]

Step 4   Key in the following: A:\HPB>**DIR HPB.EXE** [Enter]

Step 5   Key in the following: A:\HPB>**DIR HPB.DAT** [Enter]

```
MS-DOS Prompt                                              _ □ ×

A:\>CD HPB

A:\HPB>DIR HPB.EXE

 Volume in drive A is DATA
 Volume Serial Number is 3330-1807
 Directory of A:\HPB
```

```
HPB        EXE       164,420  01-04-99  3:48a HPB.EXE
           1 file(s)         164,420 bytes
           0 dir(s)        1,060,864 bytes free


A:\HPB>DIR HPB.DAT

 Volume in drive A is DATA
 Volume Serial Number is 3330-1807
 Directory of A:\HPB

HPB        DAT         4,368  01-04-99  3:48a HPB.DAT
           1 file(s)           4,368 bytes
           0 dir(s)        1,060,864 bytes free

A:\HPB>_
```

WHAT'S HAPPENING?   You are looking at the file **HPB.EXE** in the subdirectory **HPB** on the DATA disk. You are going to load the program called **HPB.EXE**, which is a simple address book. You are going to use the data file called **HPB.DAT**, also in the subdirectory **HPB**. This program automatically loads its data file when you load the program.

Step 6   Key in the following: A:\HPB>**HPB** [Enter]

WHAT'S HAPPENING?   You see the opening screen introducing you to shareware and to the details for registering the program.

Step 7   Press [Enter]

WHAT'S HAPPENING?   You see a quick message that this program is automatically loading the data file. The data file is called **HPB.DAT**. Then the above screen appears. This is a database program called Home Phone Book. It has a menu bar across the top with specific choices. To access the menu, you press the **Alt** key and the first letter of your menu choice.

Step 8   Press **Alt** + **O**.

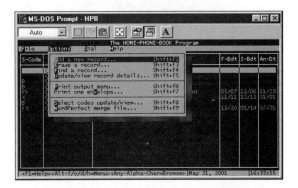

 You dropped down the Options menu, which has many choices. A database program is comprised of records and fields. A record is a new entry in the file. **Add a new record** is already highlighted and is the default choice, so it is not necessary to select it. To add a new record, there is also a keyboard shortcut—pressing the **Shift** + **F2** keys.

Step 9   Press **Shift** + **F2**

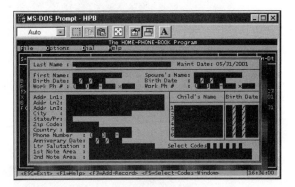

You are presented with a screen in which you can fill out information. Each item on the screen is a field. A collection of fields makes up a record, and a collection of records is the data file.

Step 10   In the **Last Name :** field, key in your last name.

Step 11   Press the **Tab** key. That will move you to **First Name :**.

Step 12   Key in your first name.

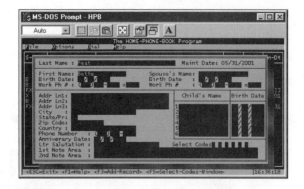

WHAT'S HAPPENING?   You have keyed in some information in the appropriate fields. At the bottom of the screen are the instructions for using this program. You are going to choose **Add Record**. This means that you will save the information you just keyed in.

Step 13   Press the **F3** key.

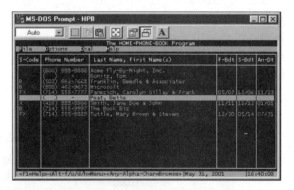

WHAT'S HAPPENING?   You returned to the main screen. Your name should be highlighted. Now you are going to exit the program.

Step 14   Press **Alt** + **F**.

WHAT'S HAPPENING?   You have dropped down the File menu. From this menu, you know you simply press **X** to exit the program.

Step 15   Press **X**.

> **WHAT'S HAPPENING?** You briefly see what is called a "housekeeping detail" on the screen. The housekeeping here is placing the records in the file in order. Then you are returned to the MS-DOS window. However, you are still in the HPB subdirectory.

Step 16 Key in the following: A:\HPB>**CD ** [Enter]

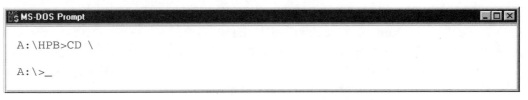

> **WHAT'S HAPPENING?** You returned to the root directory of the DATA disk so that you can do other work.

10.9 WRITING A BATCH FILE TO LOAD AN APPLICATION PROGRAM

In the previous activity, in order to execute the database program called HPB, you needed to take three steps. First (Step 3), you went from the root directory to the subdirectory called HPB. Second (Step 6), you had to load HPB.EXE, and third (Step 16), after you exited HPB, you returned to the root directory. A batch file is an ideal place to put all of these commands.

10.10 ACTIVITY: WRITING A BATCH FILE TO EXECUTE HPB

Note 1: The DATA disk is in Drive A. A:\> is displayed.
Note 2: You may use any text editor you wish for creating the batch files. You may use COPY CON, but when you have more than one line, using an editor is easier. Remember, you cannot edit lines when you use COPY CON. The Edit instructions for keyboard use will be shown, but if you prefer using a mouse, do so.

Step 1 Key in the following: A:\>**EDIT HPB.BAT** [Enter]

Step 2 Key in the following: **CD \HPB** [Enter]
                                                HPB [Enter]
                                                **CD **

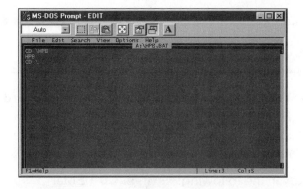

WHAT'S HAPPENING?   You have just written a batch file to load the HPB application program. You can give the file the name **HPB.BAT**, because it is in the root directory and HPB is in a subdirectory. The two file names will not conflict, and you will not have to be specific and key in **HPB.BAT**. Furthermore, the first line states **CD \HPB**. Although the backslash is not necessary in this instance, you want the batch file to run no matter where you are, so the CD command includes the \.

Step 3   Press `Alt` + **F**.

Step 4   Press **X**.

Step 5   Press **Y**.

Step 6   Key in the following: A:\>**TYPE HPB.BAT** `Enter`

```
MS-DOS Prompt

A:\>TYPE HPB.BAT
CD \HPB
HPB
CD \

A:\>_
```

WHAT'S HAPPENING?   You created the batch file **HPB.BAT** in Edit and then returned to the system prompt. Now you can execute this file.

Step 7   Key in the following: A:\>**HPB** `Enter`

Step 8   Press `Enter`

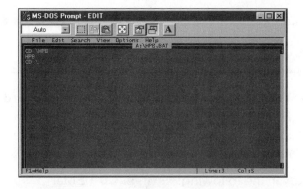

> **WHAT'S HAPPENING?** When you keyed in HPB at the root directory, the operating system looked for **HPB.BAT** and found it. It read the first line, which said to change the directory to the **HPB** subdirectory. It then read the second line, which told it to look for a program called **HPB.EXE**, and then it loaded HPB. The program HPB then appeared on the screen.

Step 9   Press Alt +**F**.

Step 10   Press **X**.

```
MS-DOS Prompt                                              _ □ ×

A:\HPB>CD \

A:\>

A:\>_
```

> **WHAT'S HAPPENING?** It does not matter if you are in the application program one minute, one hour, or one entire day. Whenever you exit the application program, the operating system continues with the batch file where it last was and simply reads and executes the next line. The operating system finished executing your batch file by changing the directory to the root.

10.11 CREATING SHORTCUTS FOR BATCH FILES ON THE DESKTOP

Any batch file can be run from the Windows environment. One way to do it is to locate the batch file name in Windows Explorer or My Computer, then double-click the file name. You can also create a shortcut for it and place it on the desktop or in a folder. Again, once it is a shortcut, the shortcut can be clicked to execute the batch file. However, there are things that you can do with the shortcut that you cannot do in the command line interface. One of the things you may have noticed is that if you run a batch file from the GUI, it will open a DOS window and leave you in the DOS window. You can change the properties of a shortcut so the DOS window is automatically closed. You can also change the icon for the shortcut.

10.12 ACTIVITY: CREATING A SHORTCUT ON THE DESKTOP

Note: The DATA disk is in Drive A. A:\> is displayed.

Step 1   Key in A:\>**EXIT** Enter

Step 2   On the desktop, double-click **My Computer**. Double-click the A drive icon to see the contents of the DATA disk.

WHAT'S HAPPENING?   You are looking at the contents of the DATA disk.

Step 3   Scroll down using the horizontal scroll bar until you locate **HPB.BAT**. Double-click it.

WHAT'S HAPPENING?   You have just executed **HPB.BAT**.

Step 4   Press **Enter**. Press **Alt** + **F**. Press **X**.

WHAT'S HAPPENING?   The title of the DOS window is **Finished**. To return to the desktop, you must close the window.

Step 5   Click ☒ on the MS-DOS title bar.

Step 6   Select **HPB.BAT** in the My Computer window. Point to the HPB icon and hold down the right mouse button.

Step 7   Drag the icon to the desktop and release the right mouse button.

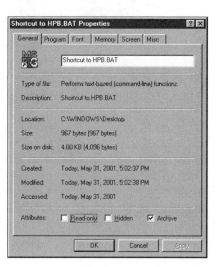

WHAT'S
HAPPENING? ➡   The shortcut menu has **Copy Here** highlighted. You want a shortcut,
              not a copy.

Step 8   Click **Create Shortcut(s) Here**.

WHAT'S
HAPPENING? ➡   You now have a shortcut to the batch file you created. If you clicked it, it
              would execute. But you would still have to take the step of closing the
              command prompt window.

Step 9   Close the My Computer window. Right-click the shortcut.

Step 10   Click **Properties**.

WHAT'S
HAPPENING? ➡   You have opened the property sheet for the shortcut to **HPB.BAT**.

Step 11   Click the **Program** tab.

WHAT'S HAPPENING?　You can see the command line listed in the **Cmd line** text box. In addition, there is a check box for **Close on exit**. By enabling this option, the DOS window will automatically close when the program has finished.

Step 12　Click in the **Close on exit** box. Click the **Change Icon** button.

WHAT'S HAPPENING?　As you can see, you have different icons to choose from.

Step 13　Click the apple icon. Click **OK**. Click **OK**.

WHAT'S HAPPENING?　Now your shortcut to HPB is represented by the apple icon.

Step 14　Double-click the apple icon.

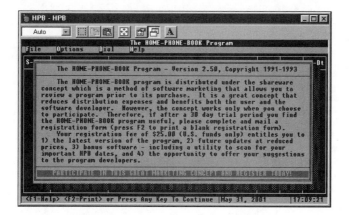

You have opened the HPB program.

Step 15 Press ⟨Enter⟩. Press ⟨Alt⟩ + **F**. Press **X**.

You have returned to the desktop. The DOS window closed automatically.

Step 16 Drag the shortcut to HPB to the Recycle Bin.

Step 17 Open the MS-DOS window. Key in the following:
   C:\WINDOWS>**A:** ⟨Enter⟩

You have returned to the MS-DOS window with the A:\> prompt.

10.13 BATCH FILES TO RUN WINDOWS PROGRAMS

You can use a batch file to run the small programs that come with Windows, such as
Notepad or Calculator. Perhaps you prefer to use Notepad when writing batch files,
but find it bothersome to have to return to the GUI to start the Notepad program.
You can create a batch file that will allow you to run the program without having to
return to the desktop.

10.14 ACTIVITY: CREATING A BATCH FILE TO RUN NOTEPAD

Note: The DATA disk is in Drive A. A:\> is displayed.

Step 1 Key in the following: A:\>**EDIT N.BAT** ⟨Enter⟩
                                   C:\WINDOWS\NOTEPAD.EXE ⟨Enter⟩
                                   A: ⟨Enter⟩

Step 2 Key in the following: ⟨Alt⟩ + **F**. Press **X**.

Step 3 Key in the following: **Y** ⟨Enter⟩

```
 MS-DOS Prompt                                          _ □ ×

 A:\>EDIT N.BAT

 A:\>_
```

You have written a batch file to start the Windows applet, Notepad.

Step 4   Key in the following: **N** [Enter]

WHAT'S HAPPENING? ➤ You have opened Notepad without returning to the desktop.

Step 5   Click **File**. Click **Exit**.

```
MS-DOS Prompt                                                    _ □ ×

A:\>N

A:\>C:\WINDOWS\NOTEPAD.EXE

A:\>A:

A:\>
A:\>

A:\>_
```

WHAT'S HAPPENING? ➤ You have closed Notepad and returned to the MS-DOS window.

10.15 SPECIAL BATCH FILE COMMANDS

There are commands specifically designed to be used in batch files. These commands can make batch files extremely versatile. They are listed in Table 10.1 below:

Command	Purpose
CALL	Calls one batch program from another without causing the first batch program to stop.
CHOICE	Prompts the user to make a choice in a batch program. Displays a prompt that you can specify and pauses for the user to choose from among a specified set of keystrokes.
ECHO	Displays or hides the text in batch programs while the program is running. Also used to determine whether or not commands will be *echoed* to the screen while the program file is running.

FOR	Runs a specified command for each file in a set of files. This command can also be used at the command line.
GOTO	Directs the operating system to a new line in the program that you specify with a label.
IF	Performs conditional processing in a batch program, based on whether or not a specified condition is true or false.
PAUSE	Suspends processing of a batch file and displays a message prompting the user to press a key to continue.
REM	Used to document your batch files. The operating system ignores any line that begins with REM, allowing you to place lines of information in your batch program or to prevent a line from running.
SHIFT	Changes the position of the replaceable parameter in a batch program.

TABLE 10.1   BATCH FILE COMMANDS

You will examine and use some of these commands in the following activities.

10.16 THE REM COMMAND

The REM command, which stands for remarks, is a special command that allows the user to key in explanatory text that will be displayed on the screen. Nothing else happens. REM does not cause the operating system to take any action, but it is very useful. When a line begins with REM, the operating system knows that anything following the REM is not a command and, thus, is not supposed to be executed, just displayed on the screen. REM allows a batch file to be *documented*. In a data-processing environment, "to document" means to give an explanation about the purpose of a program. This process can be very important when there are many batch files on a disk, especially when someone who did not write the batch file would like to use it. The REM statements should tell anyone what the purpose of the batch file is. The remarks can also include the name of the batch file, the time and date it was last updated, and the author of the batch file.

10.17 ACTIVITY: USING REM

Note 1: The DATA disk is in Drive A. A:\> is displayed.
Note 2: If **JAN.BUD** is not on the DATA disk, you can copy **\WINDOSBK\JAN.TMP** to the DATA disk as **JAN.BUD**.

Step 1   Key in the following: A:\>**EDIT TEST.BAT** Enter
                                 REM This is a test file Enter
                                 REM to see how the REM Enter
                                 REM command works. Enter

TYPE JAN.BUD Enter
COPY JAN.BUD JAN.XYZ

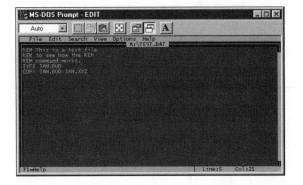

 You are using Edit to write another batch file called **TEST.BAT**. You have inserted some text with **REM** preceding each line. You keyed in two command line commands, TYPE and COPY. Now you want to save this file to disk and return to the system level.

Step 2   Press **Alt** + **F**.

Step 3   Press **X**.

Step 4   Press **Y**.

Step 5   Key in the following: A:\>**TYPE TEST.BAT** Enter

```
A:\>EDIT TEST.BAT

A:\>TYPE TEST.BAT
REM This is a test file
REM to see how the REM
REM command works.
TYPE JAN.BUD
COPY JAN.BUD JAN.XYZ

A:\>_
```

 This batch file was created to be used as a test case. The remarks just keyed in explain the purpose of this batch file. You created **TEST.BAT** in Edit and returned to the system prompt. You then displayed **TEST.BAT** with the TYPE command. To execute the **TEST.BAT** batch file, you must run it.

Step 6   Key in the following: A:\>**TEST** Enter

```
A:\>TEST

A:\>REM This is a test file

A:\>REM to see how the REM
```

```
A:\>REM command works.

A:\>TYPE JAN.BUD

This is my January file.
It is my first dummy file.
This is file 1.

A:\>COPY JAN.BUD JAN.XYZ
        1 file(s) copied

A:\>

A:\>_
```

WHAT'S HAPPENING? ➤ When you keyed in **TEST**, the batch file was executed. The operating system read the first line of the batch file, **REM This is a test file**. It knew that it was supposed to do nothing but display the text following REM on the screen. Then the next line in the batch file was read, **REM to see how the REM**, and the same procedure was followed. The operating system kept reading and displaying the REM lines until it got to the line that had the command TYPE. To the operating system, TYPE is a command, so it executed or ran the TYPE command with the parameter **JAN.BUD**. Then the next line was read, which was another command, COPY, so it was executed. The file **JAN.BUD** was copied to a new file called **JAN.XYZ**. Then the operating system looked for another line in the batch file but could find no more lines, so it returned to the system level. The purpose of REM is to provide explanatory remarks about the batch file.

10.18 THE ECHO COMMAND

Notice in the above activity, when you ran TEST.BAT you saw the command on the screen, and then the command executed. You saw TYPE JAN.BUD and then saw the typed out file. Both the command and the output of the command were "echoed" to the screen. ECHO is a command that means "display to the screen." The default value for ECHO is on. The only time it is off is if you turn it off. In a batch file, you can turn off the display of the command and see only the output of a command—not the command itself. For instance, COPY THIS.FIL THAT.FIL is a command. The output of the command is **1 file(s) copied**. The work of the command is the actual copying of the file. See Table 10.2.

	Echo On Display	**Echo Off Display**
Command:	**COPY THIS.FIL THAT.FIL**	
Output:	1 file(s) copied	1 file(s) copied

TABLE 10.2 ECHO ON OR OFF

If the purpose of the REM command is to document a batch file, what is the purpose of the ECHO command? One of the purposes you saw in an earlier chapter was to redirect a special character to the printer so that the printer would eject a page. Another purpose of the ECHO command is to minimize screen clutter. For instance, although you want to use the REM command to document your batch file, you really do not need to see your documentation on the screen every time you run the batch file. ECHO OFF allows you to suppress the display of the commands.

10.19 ACTIVITY: USING ECHO

Note: The DATA disk is in Drive A. A:\> is displayed.

Step 1   Key in the following: A:\>**COPY TEST.BAT TESTING.BAT** [Enter]

```
MS-DOS Prompt                                              _ □ ✕

A:\>COPY TEST.BAT TESTING.BAT
        1 file(s) copied

A:\>_
```

WHAT'S HAPPENING?   You made a copy of the file **TEST.BAT**.

Step 2   Key in the following: A:\>**EDIT TESTING.BAT** [Enter]
                              ECHO OFF [Enter]

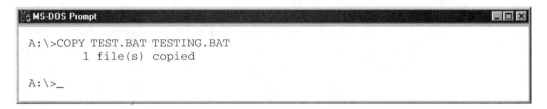

WHAT'S HAPPENING?   You are using a copy of the batch file from the previous activity. The only difference is that you added one line at the top of the batch file to turn ECHO off. You are going to run the batch file so that only the output of each command is displayed, not the actual commands. First you must exit Edit and save the file to disk.

Step 3   Press [Alt] + **F**. Press **X**.

Step 4   Press **Y**.

Step 5   Key in the following: A:\>**TYPE TESTING.BAT** [Enter]

```
MS-DOS Prompt                                              _ □ ✕

 A:\>TYPE TESTING.BAT
```

```
ECHO OFF
REM This is a test file
REM to see how the REM
REM command works.
TYPE JAN.BUD
COPY JAN.BUD JAN.XYZ

A:\>_
```

WHAT'S
HAPPENING?   You saved the file as **TESTING.BAT** and displayed the contents on the
screen. Now you wish to execute the file.

Step 6   Key in the following: A:\>**TESTING** [Enter]

```
MS-DOS Prompt                                              _ □ ×

A:\>TESTING

A:\>ECHO OFF

This is my January file.
It is my first dummy file.
This is file 1.
        1 file(s) copied
A:\>_
```

WHAT'S
HAPPENING?   The batch file **TESTING.BAT** has the same commands as **TEST.BAT**,
but this time you saw only the output of the commands, not the actual
commands themselves. You saw the ECHO OFF command on the screen,
but you did not see the REM command displayed on the screen. You saw
the results of the **TYPE JAN.BUD** command, the contents of the file on
the screen, but you never saw the **TYPE JAN.BUD** command on the
screen. You also did not see the **COPY JAN.BUD JAN.XYZ** command,
only the results of the command—the message **1 file(s) copied**.

You already have a file by the name of **JAN.XYZ**, but, even though you
are using the COPY command, it did not tell you that the file already
exists (overwrite protection). The purpose of using a batch program would
be defeated if there were interaction required by the user, so the warning
is not there. The differences between ECHO ON and ECHO OFF are
shown in Table 10.3.

	TEST.BAT—ECHO ON Display	**TESTING.BAT—ECHO OFF Display**
Command:	ECHO ON	ECHO OFF
Command:	REM This is a test file	
Command:	REM to see how the REM	
Command:	REM command works.	
Command:	TYPE JAN.BUD	

Output:	This is my January file.	This is my January file.
	It is my first dummy file.	It is my first dummy file.
	This is file 1.	This is file 1.
Command:	COPY JAN.BUD JAN.XYZ	
Output:	1 file(s) copied	1 file(s) copied

(*Note:* Although commands and file names are shown as uppercase letters, the case does not matter.)

TABLE 10.3   ECHO ON AND ECHO OFF: A COMPARISON OF SCREEN DISPLAYS

The batch files **TEST.BAT** and **TESTING.BAT** executed the same commands. The only difference is that when ECHO was on, which it was for **TEST.BAT**, you saw the remarks as well as the commands. When you executed **TESTING.BAT**, you saw only the output of the commands displayed on the screen, not the actual commands, because ECHO was off. If you did not want to see ECHO OFF on the screen, you could have entered the command as @ECHO OFF. The @ suppresses the display of ECHO OFF.

10.20 THE PAUSE COMMAND

Another batch file command is PAUSE, which does *exactly* what its name implies: it tells the batch file to stop executing until the user takes some action. No other batch command will be executed until the user presses a key. The PAUSE command will wait forever until the user takes some action.

10.21 ACTIVITY: USING PAUSE

Note: The DATA disk is in Drive A. A:\> is displayed.

Step 1   Key in the following: A:\>**EDIT TEST.BAT** Enter

Step 2   Press Ctrl + End

Step 3   Key in the following: **PAUSE You are going to delete JAN.XYZ** Enter
DEL JAN.XYZ

WHAT'S HAPPENING? You edited the batch file **TEST.BAT**. When the file is executed, the first three lines of the file, the **REM** statements, explain the purpose of **TEST.BAT**. Then the batch file displays the contents of **JAN.BUD** on the screen and copies the file **JAN.BUD** to a new file, **JAN.XYZ**. The PAUSE statement tells you that the file is going to be deleted and gives you a chance to change your mind. After you take action by pressing a key, the file **JAN.XYZ** is erased.

Step 4   Press **Alt** + **F**. Press **X**. Press **Y**.

Step 5   Key in the following: A:\>**TYPE TEST.BAT** **Enter**

```
MS-DOS Prompt                                             _ □ X

A:\>TYPE TEST.BAT
REM This is a test file
REM to see how the REM
REM command works.
TYPE JAN.BUD
COPY JAN.BUD JAN.XYZ
PAUSE You are going to delete JAN.XYZ
DEL JAN.XYZ

A:\>_
```

WHAT'S HAPPENING? You saved the file to disk with the changes you made. You then looked at the contents of the file with the TYPE command. To execute **TEST.BAT**, you must key in **TEST** at the prompt.

Step 6   Key in the following: A:\>**TEST** **Enter**

```
MS-DOS Prompt                                             _ □ X

A:\>TEST

A:\>REM This is a test file

A:\>REM to see how the REM

A:\>REM command works.

A:\>TYPE JAN.BUD

This is my January file.
It is my first dummy file.
This is file 1.

A:\>COPY JAN.BUD JAN.XYZ
        1 file(s) copied

A:\>PAUSE You are going to delete JAN.XYZ
Press any key to continue . . .
```

WHAT'S HAPPENING? The batch file TEST has stopped running, or "paused." It has halted execution until some action is taken. When you press a key, the operating system will read and execute the next line of the batch file. PAUSE just stops; it is not an order. If ECHO were off, all you would see is the message, **Press any key to continue**. You would not see the message **You are going to delete JAN.XYZ**.

Step 7 Press the Space Bar

```
 MS-DOS Prompt                                                    _ □ ✕

A:\>PAUSE You are going to delete JAN.XYZ
Press any key to continue . . .


A:\>DEL JAN.XYZ

A:\>

A:\>_
```

WHAT'S
HAPPENING? The batch file continued executing all the steps and deleted the file called **JAN.XYZ**.

Step 8 Key in the following: A:\>**DIR JAN.XYZ** Enter

```
 MS-DOS Prompt                                                    _ □ ✕

A:\>DIR JAN.XYZ

 Volume in drive A is DATA
 Volume Serial Number is 3330-1807
 Directory of A:\

File not found
                        1,053,184 bytes free

A:\>_
```

WHAT'S
HAPPENING? The file **JAN.XYZ** was deleted.

10.22 STOPPING A BATCH FILE FROM EXECUTING

In the above activity, you pressed a key after the PAUSE command was displayed so that the batch file continued to execute. What if you wanted to stop running the batch file? You can do this by interrupting or exiting from a running batch file. You do this by pressing the Ctrl key, and while pressing the Ctrl key, pressing the letter C (Ctrl + C or Ctrl + Break). At whatever point Ctrl + C is pressed, you leave the batch file and return to the system prompt. The rest of the lines in the batch file do not execute.

10.23 ACTIVITY: QUITTING A BATCH FILE

Note: The DATA disk is in Drive A. A:\> is displayed.

Step 1 Key in the following: A:\>**TEST** Enter

```
MS-DOS Prompt                                                    _ □ X

A:\>TEST

A:\>REM This is a test file

A:\>REM to see how the REM

A:\>REM command works.

A:\>TYPE JAN.BUD

This is my January file.
It is my first dummy file.
This is file 1.

A:\>COPY JAN.BUD JAN.XYZ
        1 file(s) copied

A:\>PAUSE You are going to delete JAN.XYZ
Press any key to continue . . .
```

WHAT'S HAPPENING! ➤ You are at the same point as you were in the last activity. The batch file reached the PAUSE command. It has momentarily stopped running. You do not want to erase **JAN.XYZ**. You want the batch file to cease operation. The previous experience with the PAUSE command showed that pressing any key would continue running the program. If any key were pressed here, the next line in the file, **DEL JAN.XYZ**, would execute and the file **JAN.XYZ** would be erased. To stop this from happening, another action must be taken to interrupt the batch file process.

Step 2   Hold down the **Ctrl** key, and while it is down, press the letter **C**, then release both keys.

```
MS-DOS Prompt                                                    _ □ X

A:\>PAUSE You are going to delete JAN.XYZ
Press any key to continue . . .
^C

Terminate batch job (Y/N)?_
```

WHAT'S HAPPENING! ➤ The message is giving you a choice: either stop the batch file from running (**Y** for yes) or continue with the batch file (**N** for no). If you press **Y** for yes, the last line in the batch file, **DEL JAN.XYZ**, will not execute.

Step 3   Press **Y**.

```
MS-DOS Prompt                                                    _ □ X

A:\>PAUSE You are going to delete JAN.XYZ
Press any key to continue . . .
^C

Terminate batch job (Y/N)?Y

A:\>_
```

WHAT'S
HAPPENING? The system prompt is displayed. If the batch file was interrupted properly, **JAN.XYZ** should not have been deleted because the line **DEL JAN.XYZ** should not have executed.

Step 4　　Key in the following: A:\>**DIR JAN.XYZ** Enter

```
 MS-DOS Prompt                                                    _ □ ×

A:\>DIR JAN.XYZ

 Volume in drive A is DATA
 Volume Serial Number is 3330-1807
 Directory of A:\

JAN       XYZ             73  04-23-00  4:03p JAN.XYZ
          1 file(s)              73 bytes
          0 dir(s)        1,052,672 bytes free

A:\>_
```

WHAT'S
HAPPENING? The file **JAN.XYZ** is still on the DATA disk. Pressing Ctrl + **C** at the line **PAUSE You are going to delete JAN.XYZ** broke into the batch file **TEST.BAT** and stopped it from running. Because **TEST.BAT** stopped executing and returned you to the system prompt, it never got to the command line **DEL JAN.XYZ**. Therefore, the file **JAN.XYZ** is still on the DATA disk. Although in this activity you broke into the batch file at the PAUSE statement, you can press Ctrl + **C** any time during the execution of a batch file. The batch file will stop when it has completed the current command before executing the next one. The problem is, with the speed of today's computers, it is difficult to ascertain how many lines of the batch file have been read by the operating system when you press Ctrl + **C**.

10.24 REPLACEABLE PARAMETERS IN BATCH FILES

In the same way that you use parameters with system commands, parameters can be used effectively in batch files. For instance, look at the command DIR A: W.

Command	Command Line Parameter
DIR	A: /W

In the above example, the space and the / are delimiters. DIR is the command. A: and W are parameters that tell the operating system that you want a directory of A: and that you want it displayed in a wide mode. Parameters give the command additional instructions on what to do. When you use the DIR command as used above, the /W parameter is *fixed*; you cannot choose another letter to accomplish a wide mode display.

Many commands use *variable* or *replaceable parameters*. An example of a command that uses a replaceable parameter is TYPE. TYPE requires one parameter—a file name, but the file name you use will vary; hence, it is a *variable parameter*. The TYPE command uses the parameter that you keyed in to choose the file to display on the screen. You can key in TYPE THIS.FIL or TYPE TEST.TXT or whatever file name you want. You replace the file name for the parameter—hence the term *replaceable parameter*.

Command	Replaceable command line parameter
TYPE	THIS. FIL

or

Command	Replaceable command line parameter
TYPE	TEST.TXT

Batch files can also use a replaceable parameters, also called a ***dummy parameter***, a ***substitute parameter***, or a ***positional parameter***. When you key in the name of the batch file to execute, you can also key in, at the same time, additional information on the command line that your batch file can use. What you are doing is parsing a command. To parse is to analyze something in an orderly way. In linguistics, to parse is to divide word and phrases into different parts in order to understand relationships and meanings. In computers, to parse is to divide the computer language statement into parts that can be made useful for the computer. In the above example, the TYPE command had the argument TEST.TXT passed to it so that it can display the contents of that variable. When you write the batch file, you supply the markers or placeholders to let the batch file know that something, a variable, will be keyed in with the batch file name. The placeholder, marker, or blank parameter used in a batch file is the percent sign (%) followed by a number from 0 through 9. The % sign is the signal to the operating system that a parameter is coming. The numbers indicate what position the parameter is on the command line. Whatever is first is %0, usually the command itself. Thus, the command occupies %0.

The batch files that you have written so far deal with specific commands and specific file names, but the real power of batch files is their ability to use replaceable parameters. You are going to write a batch file in the usual way with specific file names, and then use the batch file to see how replaceable parameters work.

10.25 ACTIVITY: USING REPLACEABLE PARAMETERS

Note: The DATA disk is in Drive A. A:\> is displayed.

Step 1   Key in the following: A:\>**TYPE JAN.XYZ** [Enter]

Step 2   Key in the following: A:\>**DIR JAN.XYZ** [Enter]

```
MS-DOS Prompt                                              _ □ ×

A:\>TYPE JAN.XYZ

This is my January file.
It is my first dummy file.
This is file 1.

A:\>DIR JAN.XYZ

 Volume in drive A is DATA
 Volume Serial Number is 3330-1807
```

```
 Directory of A:\

JAN      XYZ          73  04-23-00  4:03p JAN.XYZ
         1 file(s)                73 bytes
         0 dir(s)         1,052,672 bytes free

A:\>_
```

WHAT'S HAPPENING?   This file was created in the last activity. It has data in it and occupies 73 bytes of space on the disk. (Your file size may differ slightly.) If you remember, when you delete a file, the data is still on the disk. What if you wanted a way to delete the data completely so that it cannot ever be recovered? You can effectively *fool* most data recovery programs. One of the pieces of information that they use to recreate the data is the length of the file. If you can set the length of the file to 0 bytes, prior to deleting the file, most recovery programs have no way to recover the data. You have an "empty" file. How can you make a file 0 bytes long? You can redirect the output of the REM command (REM creates nothing) to your file, making it 0 bytes long. You are going to first try this at the command line.

Step 3   Key in the following: A:\>**REM > JAN.XYZ** (Enter)

Step 4   Key in the following: A:\>**TYPE JAN.XYZ** (Enter)

Step 5   Key in the following: A:\>**DIR JAN.XYZ** (Enter)

```
MS-DOS Prompt                                          _ □ ✕

A:\>REM > JAN.XYZ

A:\>TYPE JAN.XYZ

A:\>DIR JAN.XYZ

 Volume in drive A is DATA
 Volume Serial Number is 3330-1807
 Directory of A:\

JAN      XYZ           0  08-20-01  2:18p JAN.XYZ
         1 file(s)                 0 bytes
         0 dir(s)         1,053,184 bytes free

A:\>_
```

WHAT'S HAPPENING?   As you can see, it worked. You have really deleted this file. There is no data in the file to recover. This command would be useful when deleting files of a confidential nature. It would prevent most data recovery programs from being able to recover the data from your file. It can also be used in a batch file.

Step 6   Key in the following: A:\>**EDIT KILLIT.BAT** (Enter)
                                         REM > JAN.XYZ (Enter)
                                         DEL JAN.XYZ

Step 7   Press Alt + **F**. Press **X**.

Step 8   Press **Y**.

WHAT'S HAPPENING?   Edit is the tool you used to write the batch file. You created a simple batch file that sends 0 bytes to **JAN.XYZ** and then deletes the file called **JAN.XYZ**. You then used Edit's menu to exit and save **KILLIT.BAT** to your disk.

Step 9   Key in the following: A:\>**TYPE KILLIT.BAT** Enter

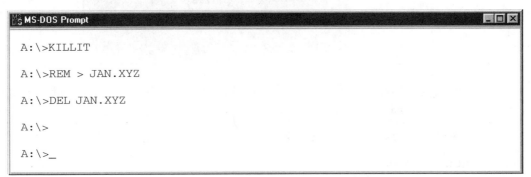

WHAT'S HAPPENING?   You displayed the contents of the **KILLIT.BAT** file. To execute this batch file, you must *call* it, which is another way of saying key in the command name—the name of the batch file.

Step 10   Key in the following: A:\>**KILLIT** Enter

```
MS-DOS Prompt                                    _ □ ✕

A:\>KILLIT

A:\>REM > JAN.XYZ

A:\>DEL JAN.XYZ

A:\>

A:\>_
```

WHAT'S HAPPENING?   The batch file called **KILLIT** ran successfully. However, this batch file can only be used for the file called **JAN.XYZ**. You have deleted **JAN.XYZ** so now **KILLIT.BAT** is no longer useful.

What if you wanted to do the same sequence of commands for a file called **JAN.TMP** or **PERSONAL.FIL** or any other file on the disk? Until now, you would have to create another batch file using **JAN.TMP** instead of **JAN.XYZ**. You would write another batch file for **PERSONAL.FIL**. You can quickly clutter up your disks with many batch files, all doing the same thing but using different file names and having no value after they have executed. An easier way is to have a batch file that does the same steps—a generic batch file. When you execute it, you supply the specific parameter or file name that interests you. When you write this batch file, you need to supply a place for the name of the file. These places are called *replaceable parameters*. They are percent signs followed by numbers.

You are going to edit **KILLIT.BAT** so that it uses replaceable parameters. In addition, you will document it and add some protection for yourself. When you key in the replaceable parameters, be sure to use the percent sign (%), then the number 1, and not the lowercase of the letter L (l). Also note that there is no space between % and the number 1.

Step 11 Key in the following:

    A:\>**EDIT KILLIT.BAT** Enter
    REM This batch file will make Enter
    REM the data in a file unrecoverable. Enter
    DIR %1 Enter
    PAUSE You are going to kill the file, %1. Are you sure? Enter

Step 12 Replace **REM > JAN.XYZ** with **REM > %1**.

Step 13 Replace **DEL JAN.XYZ** with **DEL %1**.

WHAT'S HAPPENING? Your edited file should look like the above screen. Remember, you must save the file to disk.

Step 14 Press Alt + **F**. Press **X**.

Step 15 Press **Y**.

Step 16 Key in the following: A:\>**TYPE KILLIT.BAT** Enter

```
A:\>TYPE KILLIT.BAT
REM This batch file will make
REM the data in a file unrecoverable.
DIR %1
PAUSE You are going to kill the file, %1. Are you sure?
REM > %1
DEL %1


A:\>_
```

WHAT'S
HAPPENING? → You used Edit to edit the file **KILLIT.BAT**. You then saved it to disk. You displayed the contents of the file on the screen. The contents of the batch file **KILLIT.BAT** are different from the previous version of **KILLIT.BAT**. By using the place holder **%1**, instead of a specific file name, you are saying that you do not yet know what file name (**%1**) you want these commands to apply to. When you run the batch file **KILLIT**, you will provide a value or parameter on the command line that the batch file will substitute for **%1**. For instance, if you key in on the command line, **KILLIT MY.FIL**, **KILLIT** is in the zero position on the command line (**%0**) and **MY.FIL** is in the first position on the command line (**%1** replaceable parameter).

For you to understand the purpose of replaceable parameters, it is helpful to view them as *positional* parameters, their other name. The operating system gets the information or knows what to substitute by the position on the command line. The first piece of data on the command line is always in position 0; the second piece of data on the command line is always in position 1; the third piece of data on the command line is always in position 2, and so on.

Step 17   Key in the following: A:\>**KILLIT JAN.BUD** Enter

```
MS-DOS Prompt                                               _ □ X

A:\>KILLIT JAN.BUD

A:\>REM This batch file will make

A:\>REM the data in a file unrecoverable.

A:\>DIR JAN.BUD

 Volume in drive A is DATA
 Volume Serial Number is 3330-1807
 Directory of A:\

JAN      BUD            73  04-23-00  4:03p JAN.BUD
         1 file(s)             73 bytes
         0 dir(s)       1,052,672 bytes free

A:\>PAUSE You are going to kill the file, JAN.BUD. Are you sure?
Press any key to continue . . .
```

WHAT'S
HAPPENING? → In the command line **KILLIT JAN.BUD**, **KILLIT** is position 0 and **JAN.BUD** is position 1. The batch file **KILLIT** executed each command line. However, when it found **%1** in the batch file, it looked for the first position after **KILLIT** on the command line, which was **JAN.BUD**. It substituted **JAN.BUD** every time it found **%1**. You placed the **DIR %1** in the batch file to confirm that it is on the disk. The PAUSE statement allows you to change your mind. The **%1** in the PAUSE line identifies which file is to be killed.

Step 18   Press Enter

```
MS-DOS Prompt                                              _ □ ×

A:\>PAUSE You are going to kill the file, JAN.BUD. Are you sure?
Press any key to continue . . .


A:\>REM > JAN.BUD

A:\>DEL JAN.BUD

A:\>

A:\>_
```

WHAT'S HAPPENING? ➡ You have deleted the file. Even if you, or anyone else, try to recover it, the data is truly gone. You have written a generic or "plain wrap" batch file that allows you to use the same batch file over and over. All you have to supply is a value or parameter after the batch file name on the command line. Thus, you could key in **KILLIT BUSINESS.APP**, **KILLIT SALES.LET**, **KILLIT FEB.99**, **KILLIT TELE.SET**, or any other file name. The batch file will execute the same commands over and over, using the position 1 value (the file name) you key in after the batch file name. You can see that because this file is versatile, it is infinitely more useful than it was without positional parameters.

10.26 MULTIPLE REPLACEABLE PARAMETERS IN BATCH FILES

In the above example, you used one replaceable parameter. What happens if you need more than one parameter? For instance, if you want to include the COPY command in a batch file, COPY needs two parameters: *source* and *destination*. Many commands require more than one parameter. You may also use multiple parameters in batch files. You can have up to 10 dummy parameters (%0 through %9). Remember, replaceable parameters are sometimes called positional parameters because the operating system uses the position number in the command line to determine which parameter to use. The parameters are placed in order from left to right. For example, examine the command line:

```
COPY MYFILE.TXT YOUR.FIL
```

COPY is in the first position, %0 (computers always count beginning with 0, not 1) MYFILE.TXT is in the second position, %1, and YOUR.FIL is in the third position, %2.

The next activity will allow you to create a simple batch file with multiple replaceable parameters so you will see how the positional process works. Then you will write another batch file, and in it you will create a command that the operating system does not have. Your new command will copy all files *except* the ones you specify.

10.27 ACTIVITY: USING MULTIPLE REPLACEABLE PARAMETERS

Note: The DATA disk is in Drive A. A:\> is displayed.

Step 1   Key in the following:

A:\>**EDIT MULTI.BAT** Enter
REM This is a sample batch file Enter
REM using more than one replaceable parameter. Enter
TYPE %3 Enter
COPY %1 %2 Enter
TYPE %1

Step 2   Press Alt + **F**. Press **X**.

Step 3   Press **Y**.

Step 4   Key in the following: A:\>**TYPE MULTI.BAT** Enter

```
MS-DOS Prompt                                                   _ □ ✕

A:\>EDIT MULTI.BAT

A:\>TYPE MULTI.BAT
REM This is a sample batch file
REM using more than one replaceable parameter.
TYPE %3
COPY %1 %2
TYPE %1

A:\>_
```

WHAT'S HAPPENING?   You keyed in and saved a batch file called **MULTI.BAT** on the root of the DATA disk. You then displayed the contents of **MULTI.BAT** on the screen. To execute it you must not only key in the command name **MULTI** but must also provide the command with the positional parameters that are referred to in the file. In the next step, you will key in **MULTI APR.99 LAST.ONE FILE2.SWT**. The batch file knows what to put in each percent sign because it looks at the position on the command line. It does not matter which order you use the %1 or %2 or %3 in the batch file, only the order you use on the command line. See Table 10.4.

Position 0 on the command line	Position 1 on the command line	Position 2 on the command line	Position 3 on the command line
MULTI	**APR.99**	**LAST.ONE**	**FILE2.SWT**
When batch file needs a value for %0, it uses	When batch file needs a value for %1, it uses	When batch file needs a value for %2, it uses	When batch file needs a value for %3, it uses
MULTI	**APR.99**	**LAST.ONE**	**FILE2.SWT**
Command	**Parameter**	**Parameter**	**Parameter**

TABLE 10.4   POSITIONAL PARAMETERS

Step 5   Key in the following: A:\>**MULTI APR.99 LAST.ONE FILE2.SWT** Enter

```
 MS-DOS Prompt                                                    _ □ ✕

 A:\>MULTI APR.99 LAST.ONE FILE2.SWT

 A:\>REM This is a sample batch file

 A:\>REM using more than one replaceable parameter.

 A:\>TYPE FILE2.SWT

 This is file 2.

 A:\>COPY APR.99 LAST.ONE
         1 file(s) copied

 A:\>TYPE APR.99

 This is my April file.
 It is my fourth dummy file.
 This is file 4.

 A:\>

 A:\>_
```

WHAT'S
HAPPENING?   Each time the batch file came to a command line and needed a value for
a replaceable parameter (**%1**, **%2**, or **%3**), it looked to the command line
as it was keyed in by you, and it counted over until it found the value to
replace for the percent sign. **MULTI.BAT** is actually in the first position,
which is counted as **%0**. The command itself is always first, or **%0**. Thus,
to indicate the position of the replaceable parameters, **%1** refers to the
first position after the command, not the first item on the command line.
%2 refers to the second position after the command, not the second item
on the command line, and so on. Hence, when you refer to **%1**, you are
referring to the first position after the command. When it needed a value
for **%1**, it used **APR.99** because that was in the first position on the
command line. When it needed a value for **%2**, it used **LAST.ONE**
because that was in the second position on the command line, and, when
it needed a value for **%3**, it used **FILE2.SWT** because that was in the
third position on the command line. Instead of calling them replaceable
parameters, it is easier to remember them as positional parameters
because it is the position on the command line that matters, not where it
occurs in the batch file. Although this batch file may show you how the
positional parameters work, it is not very useful. It does not accomplish
any logical task. You are going to use the same principle to create a
command that the operating system does not have.

Step 6   Key in the following: A:\>
          EDIT NOCOPY.BAT Enter
          REM This batch file, NOCOPY.BAT, will hide specified files, Enter
          REM then copy all other files from one location to another, Enter

REM then unhide the original files. `Enter`
ATTRIB +H %1 `Enter`
COPY %3*.* %2 `Enter`
ATTRIB -H %1

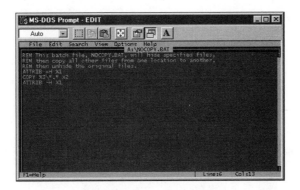

WHAT'S HAPPENING? You created a batch file called **NOCOPY.BAT** using multiple positional parameters. You have created a command that the operating system does not have. It copies files selectively, allowing you to copy all files except those you hide. You must save the file to disk.

Step 7   Press `Alt` + **F**. Press **X**.

Step 8   Press **Y**.

Step 9   Key in the following: A:\>**TYPE NOCOPY.BAT** `Enter`

```
A:\>TYPE NOCOPY.BAT
REM This batch file, NOCOPY.BAT, will hide specified files,
REM then copy all other files from one location to another,
REM then unhide the original files.
ATTRIB +H %1
COPY %3\*.* %2
ATTRIB -H %1

A:\>_
```

WHAT'S HAPPENING? You are displaying the contents of **NOCOPY.BAT**. To execute it, you must not only key in the command name—NOCOPY—but also provide the command with values for all the positional parameters. You want to copy all the files from the **CLASS** directory to the **TRIP** subdirectory except the files that have the **.ABC** file extension. Remember, parameters are separated by a space. On the command you will key in **NOCOPY CLASS*.ABC TRIP CLASS**. The value **CLASS*.ABC** replaces parameter **%1**, **TRIP** replaces **%2**, and **CLASS** replaces **%3**. Notice that **%1** will be used to represent a subdirectory and files ending with **.ABC**, while **%2** and **%3** will represent subdirectory names only.

Step 10   Key in the following: A:\>**NOCOPY CLASS*.ABC TRIP CLASS** `Enter`

```
MS-DOS Prompt                                                    _ □ ✕

A:\NOCOPY CLASS\*.ABC TRIP CLASS

A:\>REM This batch file, NOCOPY.BAT, will hide specified files,

A:\>REM then copy all other files from one location to another,

A:\>REM then unhide the original files.

A:\>ATTRIB +H CLASS\*.ABC

A:\>COPY CLASS\*.* TRIP
CLASS\JAN.PAR
CLASS\FEB.PAR
CLASS\MAR.PAR
CLASS\APR.PAR
CLASS\MAR.FIL
CLASS\JAN.FIL
CLASS\JAN.BUD
CLASS\MAR.BUD
CLASS\APR.BUD
        9 file(s) copied

A:\>ATTRIB -H CLASS\*.ABC

A:\>

A:\>_
```

WHAT'S HAPPENING?　(*Note:* You may not see the command line you keyed in, as it may scroll off the screen.) You ran the batch file called **NOCOPY**. You substituted or provided the values: **CLASS*.ABC** (**%1**), **TRIP** (**%2**), and **CLASS** (**%3**). To check that the ***.ABC** files are not hidden in the **CLASS** directory and that they have not been copied to the **TRIP** directory, do the following:

Step 11　Key in the following: A:\>**DIR CLASS*.ABC** Enter

Step 12　Key in the following: A:\>**DIR TRIP*.ABC** Enter

```
MS-DOS Prompt                                                    _ □ ✕

A:\>DIR CLASS\*.ABC

 Volume in drive A is DATA
 Volume Serial Number is 3330-1807
 Directory of A:\CLASS

JAN      ABC            73   04-23-00  4:03p JAN.ABC
FEB      ABC            75   04-23-00  4:03p FEB.ABC
MAR      ABC            71   04-23-00  4:03p MAR.ABC
APR      ABC            72   04-23-00  4:18p APR.ABC
        4 file(s)             291 bytes
        0 dir(s)       1,046,528 bytes free

A:\>DIR TRIP\*.ABC

 Volume in drive A is DATA
```

```
Volume Serial Number is 3330-1807
Directory of A:\TRIP

File not found
                          1,046,528 bytes free

A:\>_
```

WHAT'S HAPPENING? Your goal was achieved. To the operating system, the command sequence or string of commands looked like this:

ATTRIB +H CLASS*.ABC
COPY CLASS*.* TRIP
ATTRIB -H CLASS*.ABC

When you keyed in **NOCOPY CLASS*.ABC TRIP CLASS**, you asked the operating system to load the batch file called **NOCOPY.BAT**. The first position after **NOCOPY** has the value of **CLASS*.ABC**. The second position has the value of **TRIP**, and the third position has the value of **CLASS**. Then the lines were executed in order:

1. **REM This batch file, NOCOPY.BAT, will hide specified files,**
   This line is documentation for you to know why you wrote this batch file.

2. **REM then copy all other files from one location to another,**
   This line is a continuation of the documentation for you to know why you wrote this batch file.

3. **REM then unhide the original files.**
   This line is a continuation of the documentation for you to know why you wrote this batch file.

4. **ATTRIB +H CLASS*.ABC**
   This line tells ATTRIB to hide all the files in the **CLASS** directory with the file extension of **.ABC**. The operating system knew which file and which directory were %1 and could substitute **CLASS*.ABC** for %1 because **CLASS*.ABC** held the first position (%1) after the command NOCOPY.

5. **COPY CLASS*.* TRIP**
   This line tells the operating system to copy files in a directory. It knew in which directory to get the files because **CLASS** was %3, so it substituted **CLASS** for %3. The operating system knew it could substitute **CLASS** for %3 because **CLASS** was in the third position after NOCOPY. It knew to copy all the files because you included ***.***. It knew which directory to copy the files to because it substituted **TRIP** for %2. It could substitute **TRIP** for %2 because **TRIP** was in the second position after NOCOPY.

6. **ATTRIB -H CLASS*.ABC**
   This line tells the operating system to unhide all the files in the **CLASS** directory with the file extension of **.ABC**. It knew which files and which directory were %1 and could substitute **CLASS*.ABC** for %1 because **CLASS*.ABC** held the first position after the command NOCOPY.

This command, which you just wrote as a batch file with replaceable parameters, can be very useful. You can use it to copy files selectively from one disk to another or from one subdirectory to another. You do not need to take separate steps because all the steps are included in the batch file.

10.28 CREATING USEFUL BATCH FILES

Batch files are used to automate processes that otherwise take numerous commands in succession. With batch files you can, in essence, create new commands—commands that are not provided with the operating system.

The next batch file you will write will solve a problem. For backup purposes, you often have the same files on more than one subdirectory or floppy disk. You may want to compare which files are in which directory or on which disk. This normally would involve using the DIR command to view each directory or disk, or redirecting the output of the DIR command to the printer and comparing them. Why not let the computer do the work? To be sure the DATA disk contains all the necessary files, first you will copy the files from the \WINDOSBK\GAMES directory to the PROG\GAMES directory on the DATA disk.

10.29 ACTIVITY: WRITING USEFUL BATCH FILES

Note: The DATA disk is in Drive A with A:\> displayed.

Step 1   Key in the following:
A:\>**COPY C:\WINDOSBK\GAMES*.* A:\PROG\GAMES** [Enter]

Step 2   Press **A** [Enter] to overwrite files when necessary.

```
MS-DOS Prompt                                          _ □ ✕
A:\>COPY C:\WINDOSBK\GAMES\*.* A:\PROG\GAMES
C:\WINDOSBK\GAMES\LS.DOC
C:\WINDOSBK\GAMES\3DTICTAC.EXE
C:\WINDOSBK\GAMES\LS.EXE
C:\WINDOSBK\GAMES\ARGH.DOC
C:\WINDOSBK\GAMES\ARGH.EXE
Overwrite A:\PROG\GAMES\MLSHUT.EXE (Yes/No/All)?A
C:\WINDOSBK\GAMES\MLSHUT.DOC
C:\WINDOSBK\GAMES\MAZE.EXE
C:\WINDOSBK\GAMES\LS.PAS
        9 file(s) copied

A:\>_
```

WHAT'S HAPPENING?   Though you have not copied all the files needed to play the games, you have copied all the files you will need to use with the batch file you will write.

Step 3   Key in the following: A:\>
EDIT DCOMP.BAT [Enter]

REM This batch file will compare the file names [Enter]
REM in two directories. [Enter]
DIR /A-D /B /ON %1 > SOURCE.TMP [Enter]
DIR /A-D /B /ON %2 > OTHER.TMP [Enter]
FC SOURCE.TMP OTHER.TMP ¦ MORE [Enter]
PAUSE You are about to delete SOURCE.TMP and OTHER.TMP [Enter]
DEL SOURCE.TMP [Enter]
DEL OTHER.TMP

Step 4   Press [Alt] + **F**. Press **X**.

Step 5   Press **Y**.

WHAT'S
HAPPENING?   This batch file will compare file names in directories. Rather than writing the command line as **DIR ¦ SORT > SOURCE.TMP**, the command line was written as **DIR /A-D /B /ON %1 > SOURCE.TMP**. Why? We will examine each part of the line:

DIR /A-D   This is the command used to display files that do not have the directory attribute—so any subdirectory names will not be displayed.

/B   The /B parameter will eliminate all information in the directory display, such as
                      Volume in drive A is DATA
                      Volume Serial Number is 3330-1807
                      Directory of A:
                      as well as the file size, date, time, and long file name information.

/ON   This parameter will order the display by name—sorting the display alphabetically.

> SOURCE.TMP   This redirectional character will send the output of the command line to the specified file, first SOURCE.TMP, and then OTHER.TMP. The files can now be compared to each other.

In addition, you took care to clean up by deleting both **SOURCE.TMP** and **OTHER.TMP** when the program finished executing. You are now going to test this batch file.

Step 6   Key in the following:
         A:\>**DCOMP PROG\GAMES C:\WINDOSBK\GAMES** [Enter]

```
MS-DOS Prompt                                          _ □ ×

A:\>DCOMP PROG\GAMES C:\WINDOSBK\GAMES

A:\>REM This batch file will compare the file names

A:\>REM in two directories.

A:\>DIR /A-D /B /ON PROG\GAMES > SOURCE.TMP
```

```
A:\>DIR /A-D /B /ON C:\WINDOSBK\GAMES > OTHER.TMP

A:\>FC SOURCE.TMP OTHER.TMP ¦ MORE

Comparing files SOURCE.TMP and OTHER.TMP
FC: no differences encountered


A:\>PAUSE You are about to delete SOURCE.TMP and OTHER.TMP
Press any key to continue . . .
```

WHAT'S
HAPPENING?   The same files are on the DATA disk in the **PROG\GAMES**
              subdirectory and in the **C:\WINDOSBK\GAMES** subdirectory.

Step 7   Press Enter

```
MS-DOS Prompt                                                    _ □ ✕

A:\>PAUSE You are about to delete SOURCE.TMP and OTHER.TMP
Press any key to continue . . .


A:\>DEL SOURCE.TMP

A:\>DEL OTHER.TMP

A:\>

A:\>_
```

WHAT'S
HAPPENING?   You have deleted the **SOURCE.TMP** and **OTHER.TMP** files. What if
              there were differences?

Step 8   Key in the following: A:\>**DCOMP HPB C:\WINDOSBK\PHONE** Enter

```
MS-DOS Prompt                                                    _ □ ✕

A:\>REM This batch file will compare the file names

A:\>REM in two directories.

A:\>DIR /A-D /B /ON HPB > SOURCE.TMP

A:\>DIR /A-D /B /ON C:\WINDOSBK\PHONE > OTHER.TMP

A:\>FC SOURCE.TMP OTHER.TMP ¦ MORE

Comparing files SOURCE.TMP and OTHER.TMP
****** SOURCE.TMP
HPB.SLC
HPB.OLD
README.HPB
****** OTHER.TMP
HPB.SLC
README.HPB
******

A:\>PAUSE You are about to delete SOURCE.TMP and OTHER.TMP
Press any key to continue . . .
```

WHAT'S HAPPENING? ➡ There are differences. The DATA disk has one more file (**HPB.OLD**) than the **C:\WINDOSBK\PHONE** subdirectory.

Step 9   Press Enter

```
MS-DOS Prompt                                                    ▢ ▢ ✕

A:\>PAUSE You are about to delete SOURCE.TMP and OTHER.TMP
Press any key to continue . . .


A:\>DEL SOURCE.TMP

A:\>DEL OTHER.TMP

A:\>

A:\>_
```

WHAT'S HAPPENING? ➡ You have deleted the temporary files. You now have an easy way to compare the files in directories or on disks. You could add an @ECHO OFF statement at the beginning of the batch file so you would not see the REM statements and would see only the results of the command.

10.30 UNDERSTANDING AUTOEXEC.BAT

AUTOEXEC.BAT, which means automatically execute, is a unique batch file. When the system is booted and the operating system is loaded into memory, one of the last things the operating system does before it loads the 32-bit Windows graphical user interface is look for a file called AUTOEXEC.BAT on the booting disk. If it finds a file by that name, it is AUTOmatically EXECuted. The AUTOEXEC.BAT file is just a batch file. The only thing special about it is the time that it runs. It always runs when you boot the system. Thus, only one AUTOEXEC.BAT file can be on any one booting disk. In order for AUTOEXEC.BAT to be automatic, it must be on the booting disk, Drive C, Drive A, the CD, or which ever disk is specified as the booting disk. It must also be located in the root directory of the booting disk.

The AUTOEXEC.BAT file is typically used for startup routines that are necessary to operate a particular program that was not written for a Windows ME or newer operating system. In Windows Millennium, very little adjustment by the user to the autoexec.bat file on the hard drive is permitted. Typically the AUTOEXEC.BAT file could contain a PATH statement required by this older, legacy software. Also, you can SET the values for environmental variables in the AUTOEXEC.BAT file. (Environmental variables will be examined in a later chapter.) In MS-DOS 6.2, a new feature (that has remained a feature of the Windows operating systems) was added. It is called *interactive booting*. In Windows 95 and 98, these were two ways to use interactive booting. One was a clean boot. A clean boot meant that both your CONFIG.SYS file and your AUTOEXEC.BAT files were bypassed and none of the commands were executed. The CONFIG.SYS file is a file that configures your system and sets up different hardware and software specific to your computer. This first choice is no longer available in Windows Me. The second choice, however, is available, and is truly interactive. You will be asked by the operating system if you want to see each item in the boot process and be able to choose if you do or do not want a particular action to take place. This is called *step-by-step conformation*. If you are having trouble with your computer, this allows you to troubleshoot the problem by trying out different combinations of commands so that you can pinpoint the troublemaker. Before doing the next activity, you should check with your lab instructor. If you are on a network, it may not be possible for you to do this activity. If you are working on your own computer, you may proceed.

You are going to create an AUTOEXEC.BAT file on a newly created bootable floppy disk. With floppy disks, you can manipulate the CONFIG.SYS and AUTOEXEC.BAT files freely. In previous versions of the Windows operating system, you could use the SYS command to copy the minimum required booting files to any drive. In Windows Me, that option is not available. To create a simple boot disk, you will have to use a "work-around." You will place the bootable floppy in Drive A and then boot from Drive A. Computers can be set to boot from different drives. This activity will work only if your computer is set to look to the A drive first. In older computers, the A drive was always the default drive—if there was a bootable disk in the A drive, the system booted from there. With newer computers, you can set the order in which you want the computer to look for system files to boot. This is done in the CMOS of your system.

CMOS is an acronym for complementary metal-oxide semiconductor. CMOS, maintained by battery pack, is memory that is used to store parameter values, such as the size and type of hard disk, the number and type of floppy drives, keyboard, and display type, that are used to boot PCs. The CMOS setup also allows you to set password protection on a system. The CMOS battery is also what keeps the internal clock running when the computer is off. If your computer is set to look to the A drive first, you may be able to complete the following activity, but please read the warning below before you continue.

CAUTION!   CHECK WITH YOUR INSTRUCTOR BEFORE PROCEEDING. YOU MAY BE INSTRUCTED TO READ THE ACTIVITY AND NOT DO IT.

10.31 ACTIVITY: CREATING A SIMPLE BOOTABLE FLOPPY DISK

Note: You will need the startup disk you created in Chapter 3 in the A drive. The A:\> is displayed.

Step 1   Key in the following: A:\>**DISKCOPY A: A:** Enter

```
MS-DOS Prompt
A:\>DISKCOPY A: A:

Insert SOURCE diskette in drive A:

Press any key to continue . . .
```

WHAT'S HAPPENING?   You started the process to make a copy of the startup disk.

Step 2   Press the [Enter] key.

```
MS-DOS Prompt                                                    _ □ X

Copying 80 tracks, 18 sectors per track, 2 side(s)

Reading from source diskette . . .

Insert TARGET diskette in drive A:

Press any key to continue . . .
```

WHAT'S HAPPENING? The source disk has been read, and the operating system is ready to write to the target disk.

Step 3   Remove the startup disk from the A drive.

Step 4   Insert a blank disk, or a disk with unwanted data into the A drive.

Step 5   Press the [Enter] key.

```
MS-DOS Prompt                                                    _ □ X

Insert TARGET diskette in drive A:

Press any key to continue . . .

Writing to target diskette . . .

Do you wish to write another duplicate of this disk (Y/N)? _
```

WHAT'S HAPPENING? The OS has finished writing to the target disk and is asking if you want another copy of the same disk. When you enter N for no, it will ask if you wish to copy another disk.

Step 6   Key in the following: **N**

Step 7   Key in the following: **N**

```
MS-DOS Prompt                                                    _ □ X

Do you wish to write another duplicate of this disk (Y/N)? N

Volume Serial Number is 1AE5-2527

Copy another diskette (Y/N)? N

A:\>_
```

WHAT'S HAPPENING? You now have a duplicate copy of the Windows startup disk you created in Chapter 3.

Step 8   Remove the disk from the drive, and write **Simple Boot** on the label.

Step 9   Return the Simple Boot disk to the A drive.

Step 10   Key in the following: A:\>**DIR /W** [Enter]

Step 11   Key in the following: A:\>**DIR /AH /W** Enter

```
MS-DOS Prompt                                                           _ □ ✕

A:\>DIR /W

 Volume in drive A has no label
 Volume Serial Number is 1AE5-2527
 Directory of A:\

AUTOEXEC.BAT    CONFIG.SYS      SETRAMD.BAT     README.TXT      FINDRAMD.EXE
FIXIT.BAT       RAMDRIVE.SYS    ASPI4DOS.SYS    BTCDROM.SYS     ASPICD.SYS
BTDOSM.SYS      ASPI2DOS.SYS    ASPI8DOS.SYS    ASPI8U2.SYS     FLASHPT.SYS
EXTRACT.EXE     FDISK.EXE       COMMAND.COM     HIMEM.SYS       OAKCDROM.SYS
EBDUNDO.EXE     CHECKSR.BAT     HIBINV.EXE      EBD.CAB
        24 file(s)          902,291 bytes
         0 dir(s)           432,640 bytes free

A:\>DIR /AH /W

 Volume in drive A has no label
 Volume Serial Number is 1AE5-2527
 Directory of A:\

IO.SYS          MSDOS.SYS       EBD.SYS
         3 file(s)          116,745 bytes
         0 dir(s)           432,640 bytes free

A:\>_
```

WHAT'S HAPPENING?   You have displayed all the files on the Simple Boot disk, including the hidden files IO.SYS, MSDOS.SYS, and EBD.SYS. Aside from these hidden files, the only file you need on this disk is COMMAND.COM.

Step 12   Key in the following: A:\>**ATTRIB +H COMMAND.COM** Enter

Step 13   Key in the following: A:\>**DIR COMMAND.COM** Enter

```
MS-DOS Prompt                                                           _ □ ✕

A:\>ATTRIB +H COMMAND.COM

A:\>DIR COMMAND.COM

 Volume in drive A has no label
 Volume Serial Number is 1AE5-2527
 Directory of A:\

File not found
                    432,640 bytes free

A:\>_
```

WHAT'S HAPPENING?   You have hidden the COMMAND.COM file, and issued a DIR command to be sure it is not there.

Step 14   Key in the following: A:\>**DEL *.*** Enter

Step 15   Key in the following: **Y** Enter

Step 16 Key in the following: A:\>**ATTRIB –H COMMAND.COM** [Enter]

Step 17 Key in the following: A:\>**DIR** [Enter]

Step 18 Key in the following: A:\>**DIR /AH** [Enter]

```
MS-DOS Prompt                                              _ □ ✕

A:\>DEL *.*
All files in directory will be deleted!
Are you sure (Y/N)?Y

A:\>ATTRIB -H COMMAND.COM

A:\>DIR

 Volume in drive A has no label
 Volume Serial Number is 1AE5-2527
 Directory of A:\

COMMAND  COM        93,040  06-08-00  5:00p COMMAND.COM
        1 file(s)           93,040 bytes
        0 dir(s)         1,247,232 bytes free

A:\>DIR /AH

 Volume in drive A has no label
 Volume Serial Number is 1AE5-2527
 Directory of A:\

IO       SYS       116,736  06-08-00  5:00p IO.SYS
MSDOS    SYS             9  07-15-01  8:14a MSDOS.SYS
EBD      SYS             0  07-15-01  8:14a EBD.SYS
        3 file(s)          116,745 bytes
        0 dir(s)         1,247,232 bytes free

A:\>_
```

WHAT'S HAPPENING?   You deleted all the non-hidden files, removed the hidden attribute from COMMAND.COM, and then, by using the DIR command twice, viewed all the files on the Simple Boot disk. You now have a bootable floppy, ready for an AUTOEXEC.BAT file.

10.32 ACTIVITY: WRITING AND USING AN AUTOEXEC.BAT FILE

Note: The Simple Boot disk is in Drive A. A:\> is displayed.

Step 1   Key in the following: A:\>**EDIT A:\AUTOEXEC.BAT** [Enter]

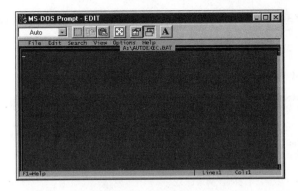

WHAT'S HAPPENING? ➤ You should have a blank Edit screen with **A:\AUTOEXEC.BAT** showing at the top of the screen area as shown above. If it is not blank, *exit now* and repeat Step 1, being *extremely* careful that you are at the A:\> prompt when you begin.

Step 2   Key in the following:
PATH A:\GAMES;C:\WINDOWS\COMMAND Enter
DIR Enter
VER

Step 3   Press Alt + **F**. Press **X**.

Step 4   Press **Y**.

Step 5   Key in the following: A:\>**TYPE AUTOEXEC.BAT** Enter

```
MS-DOS Prompt

A:\>EDIT A:\AUTOEXEC.BAT

A:\>TYPE AUTOEXEC.BAT
PATH A:\GAMES;C:\WINDOWS\COMMAND
DIR
VER

A:\>_
```

WHAT'S HAPPENING? ➤ You have written a simple **AUTOEXEC.BAT** file with Edit and saved the file to your disk. You have typed the file to the screen to verify the contents of the file. When you boot your computer with this disk, the **AUTOEXEC.BAT** file will execute. The first line will set the path to **GAMES** on Drive A. Next, the second line will execute and you will see a DIR of the root directory. Last, the third and final line will execute and show you the version of the operating system you are working with. What makes **AUTOEXEC.BAT** unique is that it executes automatically when you boot the system. However, before you do that, you are going to create the **GAMES** directory on the disk and copy the files from the **C:\WINDOSBK\GAMES** subdirectory to the **GAMES** directory on the bootable floppy disk.

Step 6   Key in the following:

A:\>**XCOPY C:\WINDOSBK\GAMES*.* GAMES /S /E** Enter

```
MS-DOS Prompt                                              _ ☐ ✕

A:\>XCOPY C:\WINDOSBK\GAMES\*.* GAMES /S /E
Does GAMES specify a file name
or directory name on the target
(F = file, D = directory)?_
```

WHAT'S HAPPENING? ➤ You are using XCOPY to copy the games and to create a directory called **GAMES**.

Step 7   Press **D**.

```
MS-DOS Prompt                                              _ ☐ ✕

A:\>XCOPY C:\WINDOSBK\GAMES\*.* GAMES /S /E
Does GAMES specify a file name
or directory name on the target
(F = file, D = directory)?D
3DTICTAC.EXE
LS.EXE
ARGH.DOC
ARGH.EXE
MLSHUT.EXE
MLSHUT.DOC
MAZE.EXE
LS.PAS
CHEK\CHEKKERS.EXE
MLINK\MLLOYD.DOC
MLINK\MLLOYD.EXE
MLINK\MLOTRA.DOC
MLINK\MLPUSH.DOC
MLINK\MLOTRA.EXE
MLINK\MLPUSH.EXE
MLINK\MLYAHT.EXE
MLINK\MLYAHT.DOC
MLINK\MLCRUX.DOC
MLINK\MLCRUX.EXE
        20 File(s) copied

A:\>_
```

WHAT'S HAPPENING? ➤ Using XCOPY, you created a subdirectory and copied files to it. *Be sure you have the permission of your lab supervisor before continuing with this activity.*

Step 8   Exit the MS-DOS window.

Step 9   Click **Start**. Click **Shut Down**.

Step 10   Select **Restart**.

Step 11   Click **OK**.

WHAT'S HAPPENING?   The system will restart. With the bootable system disk in the A drive, the system will boot from A. BIOS information and information about your hardware will scroll across the screen, followed by:

```
MS-DOS Prompt                                                    _ □ ×

Starting Windows Millennium Emergency Boot. . . .

A:\>PATH A:\GAMES;C:\WINDOWS\COMMAND

A:\>DIR

 Volume in drive A has no label
 Volume Serial Number is 1AE5-2527
 Directory of A:\

GAMES          <DIR>          08-20-00  8:14p GAMES
AUTOEXEC BAT            46    08-20-00  8:13p AUTOEXEC.BAT
COMMAND  COM        93,040    06-08-00  5:00p COMMAND.COM
         2 file(s)          93,086 bytes
         1 dir(s)          624,128 bytes free

A:\>VER

Windows millennium [Version 4.90.3000]

A:\>
A:\>

A:\>_
```

You did not have to key in the file name **AUTOEXEC** to execute this batch file because **AUTOEXEC.BAT** always automatically executes when you boot the system. It followed the instructions you included in it. It set the path, ran the command DIR, and indicated what version of the OS you are running. Since the last command in **AUTOEXEC.BAT** was VER, you are returned to the MS-DOS prompt A:\>, and the operating system is ready for you to key in the next command.

It is always good to have a Simple Boot disk on hand. Booting to the GUI, or even booting with an emergency startup disk is time consuming. If you computer is off, and you suddenly realize you need a copy of a file to take to work with you, you have to go through the boot process, waiting...waiting! If you have a Simple Boot disk, it will boot your computer in the minimum possible time. You can copy your file, shut off the power, and be on your way!

If you have a problem with your computer, you would not use a Simple Boot disk, you would use an emergency startup disk. When you install the Windows operating system, you are afforded the opportunity to create a startup disk—and you should always do so. But it can be very handy to have a quick way to get to your files.

10.33 CONTROLLING THE BOOT PROCESS

When you are experiencing problems with your computer (while booting from your hard disk) that may be related to the statements in the CONFIG.SYS or AUTOEXEC.BAT file, you want a way to prevent the computer from following the instructions in either CONFIG.SYS or AUTOEXEC.BAT.

There is a procedure that allows you to select which lines in the files you want to execute and which lines you do not. This procedure involves pressing certain keys and holding them down. On most computers, pressing and holding down the Ctrl key while the system is booting will bring up the menu. On some computers, you must use the F8 key.

CAUTION! **CHECK WITH YOUR INSTRUCTOR BEFORE PROCEEDING. YOU MAY BE INSTRUCTED TO READ THE ACTIVITY ONLY.**

10.34 ACTIVITY: BYPASSING AUTOEXEC.BAT

Note: The bootable Simple Boot disk has been removed from the A drive.

Step 1   Reboot the computer by using the reset button, pressing Ctrl + Alt + Delete, or cycling the power off and on again, depending on the requirements of your lab equipment, holding the Ctrl key (or the F8 key) down during the process until you see a screen similar to the one below:

```
MS-DOS Prompt                                                _□×

Microsoft Windows Millennium Startup


   1.   Normal
   2.   Logged (\BOOTLOG.TXT)
   3.   Safe mode
   4.   Step-by-step conformation


Enter a choice:1









   F5=Safe mode    Shift+F8=Step-by=step confirmation [N]

```

Step 2　Immediately press the down arrow. This will stop the countdown of 30 seconds. If you don't stop it, the default choice, Normal, will execute.

WHAT'S HAPPENING? ➤ As soon as you press the down arrow, the automatic 30-second countdown stops, giving you a chance to look at the choices. If you choose Step-by-step confirmation, each element of the CONFIG.SYS file, the AUTOEXEC.BAT file, and all the normal drivers loading during the boot process will be listed with a Y/N? choice. If you were, for example, unable to boot to the desktop due to a corrupt video driver, you could choose N when the video driver started to load. In this way, Windows would load the default standard monitor driver, allowing you to get to the GUI where you would have the chance to fix the problem.

Step 3　Choose **Normal**.

WHAT'S HAPPENING? ➤ Windows continues the bootup process.

CHAPTER SUMMARY

1. Batch processing means running a series of instructions without interruption.
2. Interactive processing allows the user to interface directly with the computer and update records immediately.
3. Batch files allow a user to put together a string of commands and execute them with one command.
4. Batch files must have the .BAT file extension.
5. Windows first looks internally for a command, then for a .COM file extension, then for an .EXE file extension, and finally for a .BAT file extension.
6. Edit is a full-screen text editor used to write batch files.
7. A word processor, if it has a means to save files in ASCII, can be used to write batch files. ASCII files are also referred to as unformatted text files.
8. Batch files must be in ASCII.
9. A quick way to write an ASCII file is to use COPY CON. You copy from the console to a file.
10. Batch files are executed from the system prompt by keying in the batch file name.
11. Batch files are used for many purposes, such as to save keystrokes.
12. To "document" means to explain the purpose a file serves.
13. REM allows the user to document a batch file.
14. When the operating system sees REM, it displays on the screen whatever text follows REM. REM is not a command that executes.
15. ECHO OFF turns off the display of commands. Only the messages from the commands are displayed on the screen.
16. PAUSE allows the user to take some action before the batch file continues to execute.
17. PAUSE does not force the user to do anything. The batch file just stops running until the user presses a key.
18. To stop a batch file from executing, press the Ctrl key and the letter **C** (Ctrl + **C**).

19. Replaceable parameters allow the user to write batch files that can be used with many different parameters. The replaceable parameters act as place holders for values that the user will substitute when executing the batch file.

20. Replaceable parameters are sometimes called dummy, positional, or substitute parameters.

21. The percent (%) sign followed immediately by a numerical value, 0 to 9, indicates a replaceable parameter in a batch file.

22. A batch file called AUTOEXEC.BAT can be created.

23. An AUTOEXEC.BAT file will execute automatically when the system is booted.

24. There can only be one AUTOEXEC.BAT file per booting disk.

25. You may control the boot process.

26. By pressing and holding the [Ctrl] key (or [F8]), during the booting process, you will be able to selectively execute lines in the CONFIG.SYS and AUTOEXEC.BAT files.

KEY TERMS

batch file	fixed	step-by-step confirma-
batch processing	interactive booting	tion
CMOS	interactive processing	substitute parameter
documented	positional parameter	variable parameter
dummy parameter	replaceable parameter	

DISCUSSION QUESTIONS

1. Explain the purpose and function of batch files.

2. Compare and contrast batch processing with interactive processing.

3. You have a batch file called **CHECK.BAT**. You key in **CHECK** at the prompt. Where does it look for the file? What does the operating system then do?

4. What is an ASCII file? Why is it important in batch processing?

5. Under what circumstances can a word processor be used to write batch files?

6. Compare and contrast using Edit and COPY CON to write batch files.

7. Explain the purpose and function of the O and A parameters when used with the DIR command.

8. Explain the purpose and function of the REM command. What happens when the operating system sees REM in a batch file?

9. In a data processing environment, what does it mean to document a batch file? Why would it be important to document a batch file?

10. Explain the purpose and function of the ECHO command.

11. Explain the purpose and function of the PAUSE command.

12. Why does the PAUSE command require user intervention?

13. How can you stop a batch file from executing once it has begun?

14. What are parameters?

15. What is a replaceable parameter? Describe how it might be used.

16. What indicates to the operating system that there is a replaceable parameter in a file?

17. What advantages are there to using replaceable parameters in a batch file?
18. Replaceable parameters are sometimes called positional parameters. Explain.
19. There appear to be two prompts when you do not use the ECHO OFF. Explain.
20. Explain the purpose and function of an **AUTOEXEC.BAT** file.
21. Why can only one **AUTOEXEC.BAT** file be on any booting disk?
22. Explain what is accomplished with interactive booting.

TRUE/FALSE QUESTIONS

For each question, circle the letter T if the question is true and the letter F if the question is false.

T   F   1. Any command that can be keyed in at the system prompt can be included in a batch file.

T   F   2. Each command in a batch file is on a separate line.

T   F   3. Batch files should be written to complete a multicommand process that will need to be done one time only.

T   F   4. The PAUSE command, when used in a batch file, requires user intervention.

T   F   5. In the batch file line COPY MYFILE YOURFILE, COPY would be %1.

COMPLETION QUESTIONS

Write the correct answer in each blank space.

6. A word-processing program can be used to write batch files if it has a(n) _____ output mode.

7. The name of the custom batch file that can be placed on a booting floppy disk and is run when you boot the system is _____.

8. In a data-processing environment, to explain the purpose of a batch file is to _____ it.

9. Pressing the [Ctrl] and **C** keys simultaneously during the execution of a batch file will cause the file execution to _____.

10. The two possible keys to press and hold to initiate the interactive boot process are _____ or _____.

MULTIPLE CHOICE QUESTIONS

For each question, write the letter for the correct answer in the blank space.

11. When searching a disk for an external command, the operating system will
   a. choose the command with the extension .COM before one with the extension .BAT.
   b. choose the command with the extension .BAT before one with the extension .COM.
   c. know automatically which file extension you are seeking.
   d. choose the command with the extension .BAT before one with the extension .EXE.

12. To execute a batch file called THIS.BAT at the prompt, key in:
    a. THIS %1
    b. %1
    c. THIS
    d. RUN BATCH THIS

13. In a batch file, to display the output of the command but not the command itself, use:
    a. ECHO ON
    b. ECHO OFF
    c. DISPLAY ON
    d. none of the above

14. Which of the following statements is true?
    a. Batch files cannot use variable parameters.
    b. Ctrl + Pause interrupts the execution of a batch file.
    c. The PAUSE command will wait until the user takes some action.
    d. either b or c

15. Quitting a batch file by using Ctrl + C
    a. erases all the lines of the batch file that came after you quit.
    b. can be done only at a PAUSE during the batch file run.
    c. erases the batch files from the disk.
    d. can be done at any time while the batch file is running.

WRITING COMMANDS

Write five lines that would perform the following items in a batch file. Each question represents one line in the file.

16. Document the batch file, explaining that it is a demonstration file.

17. List the files in the A:\TEMP directory.

18. Display the contents of a file in the A:\TEMP directory that is specified when the batch file is called.

19. Rename the above file to NAME.NEW.

20. Display the contents of the NAME.NEW file.

APPLICATION ASSIGNMENTS

PROBLEM SET I

Note 1: Place the APPLICATION disk in Drive A. Be sure to work on the APPLICA-
TION disk, not the DATA disk. On each batch file you write, be sure to
include *your name*, the *name of the batch file*, and the *date* as part of the
documentation.

Note 2: The homework problems will assume Drive C is the hard disk and the
APPLICATION disk is in Drive A. If you are using another drive, such as
floppy drive B or hard drive D, be sure to substitute that drive letter when
reading the questions and answers.

Note 3: Test all of your batch files before submitting them to be sure they work
correctly.

Note 4: To save a file with Edit under a new name, press Alt + **F** and choose **Save
As**.

Note 5: It will be assumed that the root of the APPLICATION disk is the default
drive and directory, unless otherwise specified.

Note 6: There can be more than one way to write a batch file. If your batch file works
correctly, it is most likely written correctly.

PROBLEM A

TO CREATE DD.BAT

A-a   Create a batch file called **DD.BAT**. This batch file should display the
files on the root of the APPLICATION disk in date order with the most
current date displayed first, and should pause so that the user may
view the display one screenful at a time.

A-b   Document **DD.BAT**. Remember to include *your name*, the *name of the
batch file*, and the *date* as part of the documentation.

TO CREATE DDA.BAT

A-c   Edit the batch file called **DD.BAT** and save it under the new name of
DDA.BAT.

A-d   Edit **DDA.BAT** so that it will look on any drive for files, using a replaceable parameter. It will still be displaying files in date order, with the
most current date displayed first.

A-e   Update the documentation.

TO CREATE SD.BAT

A-f   Create a batch file called **SD.BAT** that will display subdirectories only,
in order by name, on the root of the A drive.

A-g   Document the file. Remember to include your name, the name of the
         batch file, and the date as part of the documentation.

TO CREATE SDD.BAT

A-h   Edit **SD.BAT** created above and save the edited file as **SDD.BAT**. The
         SDD.BAT file will display subdirectories on a specified drive\directory in
         order by name.

A-i   Use replaceable parameters.

A-j   Document the file.

TO PRINT YOUR HOMEWORK

Step 1   Be sure the printer is on and ready to accept print jobs from your
         computer.

Step 2   Key in the following: A:\>**NAME** Enter

Step 3   You will be given an example to key in, but your instructor will have
         other information that applies to your class. Key in the following:
         Bette A. Peat Enter   (*Your* name goes here.)
         CIS 55 Enter   (*Your* class goes here.)
         T-Th 8-9:30 Enter   (*Your* day and time go here.)
         Chapter 10 Applications Enter
         Problem A Enter

Step 4   Press F6 Enter

Step 5   If the information is correct, press **Y** and you are back to A:\>.

Step 6   Key in the following:
         A:\>**GO NAME.FIL DD.BAT DDA.BAT SD.BAT SDD.BAT** Enter
         (These files will not be deleted from your disk after printing.)

PROBLEM B

TO CREATE EXTRA.BAT

B-a   Copy all the files with the **.TXT** extension from the **WINDOSBK**
         subdirectory to the root directory of the APPLICATION disk. (Overwrite
         existing files.)

B-b   Create a batch file named **EXTRA.BAT** that will do the following:
         ❖ Clear the screen.
         ❖ Display the root directory of the APPLICATION disk for any file that
           has **.TXT** as a file extension.
         ❖ Make a copy of the file called **DANCES.TXT** and call the copy
           NEWEST.DAN.
         ❖ Display the contents of the file called **NEWEST.DAN**.

> ❖ Give the user time to read the file.
> ❖ Erase the file called **NEWEST.DAN**.

B-c   Document **EXTRA.BAT**, including your name, the name of the file, and the date.

TO CREATE EXTRA2.BAT

B-d   Edit **EXTRA.BAT**. **EXTRA2.BAT** will do all that **EXTRA.BAT** does but will
> ❖ use replaceable parameters so that the user may choose what files to display. (Use only one parameter to represent the entire file specification, such as *.fil or my.fil)
> ❖ allow any existing file to be copied to a new file that the user names.
> ❖ display the contents of the newly created file.
> ❖ provide a way for the user to change her or his mind and not delete any files.

B-e   Save the edited file as **EXTRA2.BAT**.

TO PRINT YOUR HOMEWORK

Step 1   Be sure the printer is on and ready to accept print jobs from your computer.

Step 2   Use Edit to edit **NAME.FIL**. Change the last line from Problem A to Problem B.

Step 3   Key in the following: A:\>**GO NAME.FIL EXTRA.BAT EXTRA2.BAT** [Enter]

PROBLEM C

TO CREATE CHECKIT.BAT

C-a   Write and document a batch file using replaceable parameters called **CHECKIT.BAT** that will
> ❖ check the status of a specified disk.
> ❖ see if any files are noncontiguous on that disk.
> ❖ do a wide display of the root directory of that disk.
> ❖ pause as necessary so users can view all of *each display*.

TO CREATE LIST.BAT

C-b   Write and document a batch file called **LIST.BAT** that will use replaceable parameters to display the contents of three files, using the TYPE command, instead of only one file. (*Hint*: Remember that TYPE can use only one parameter, so think about how many replaceable parameters you will want to use.) Use **JAN.99**, **MAR.99**, and **APR.99** to test your file.

TO PRINT YOUR HOMEWORK

Step 1   Be sure the printer is on and ready to accept print jobs from your computer.

Step 2   Use Edit to edit **NAME.FIL**. Change the last line from Problem B to Problem C.

Step 3   Key in the following: A:\>**GO NAME.FIL CHECKIT.BAT LIST.BAT** [Enter]

PROBLEM D—CHALLENGE ASSIGNMENTS

The following three batch file assignments use commands in combination that may not have been specifically discussed or shown by example in the chapter. Research and experimentation may be required in order to write these batch files.

TO CREATE CDD.BAT

D-a   Write and document a batch file called **CDD.BAT** that will allow you to change drives and directories on one line (the line used to run the batch file).

TO CREATE NODEL.BAT

D-b   Using **NOCOPY.BAT**, created in this chapter, as a model, write and document a batch file called **NODEL.BAT** that will
   ❖ allow you to delete all the files *except* the file(s) you hide in a specified subdirectory.
   ❖ view the files you are about to delete.
   ❖ clear the screen when necessary to make it easy for the user to read what is happening in the file.
   ❖ give the user an opportunity to cancel prior to deleting the files.
   ❖ delete the files.
   ❖ unhide the files.
   ❖ view which files remain.

D-c   Document the batch file completely, explaining precisely what the file will do, and giving an example of how to run the file.

Hint 1: Create a practice subdirectory, such as \TEMP, on the APPLICATION disk. Use the NODEL batch file with the files that you copy into this temporary subdirectory, such as the *.RED files and the *.FIL files. If you make a mistake, you will not delete all the files on your APPLICATION disk.

Hint 2: If you do not want to be asked for conformation from the DEL command, you can use the command DEL *.* < Y.FIL. You will need to copy Y.FIL from \WINDOSBK to the root directory of the APPLICATION disk.

TO CREATE NEWSUB.BAT

D-d Write and document a batch files called **NEWSUB.BAT**, using replaceable parameters that will accomplish what is specified in the following documentation:

```
REM This file will allow the user to create a subdirectory
REM on a drive specified by the user, and with a name specified
REM by the user and then copy files (both location and
REM file names specified by the user) to the new subdirectory.
REM This batch file is flexible, so any of the elements can be
REM changed by the user when executing this file.(Elements are
REM DESTINATION FOR NEW SUBDIRECTORY, NEW SUBDIRECTORY NAME,
REM LOCATION OF FILES TO BE COPIED, and FILES TO BE COPIED).
REM The newly created subdirectory with its files will then be
REM displayed on the screen.
```

D-e Include the above lines in the documentation of the file.

D-f You may want to delete the TEMP directory created with the NODEL.BAT assignment, and use it again to write and debug NEWSUB.BAT.

TO PRINT YOUR HOMEWORK

Step 1 Be sure the printer is on and ready to accept print jobs from your computer.

Step 2 Use Edit to edit **NAME.FIL**. Change the last two lines to read:
Chapter 10 Challenge Assignments
Problem D

Step 3 Key in the following:
A:\>**GO NAME.FIL CDD.BAT NODEL.BAT NEWSUB.BAT** Enter

CAUTION! **IF YOU CREATED A TEMP DIRECTORY ON THE APPLICATION DISK, DELETE THAT DIRECTORY BEFORE GOING ON TO CHAPTER 11.**

PROBLEM SET II—BRIEF ESSAY

Discuss replaceable parameters, including how they work and why they are useful. Include the number of parameters available and the numbering sequence used to represent the command in your discussion.

ADVANCED BATCH FILES

LEARNING OBJECTIVES

After completing this chapter you will be able to:

1. List commands used in batch files.
2. List and explain batch file rules.
3. Explore the function of the REM, PAUSE, and ECHO commands.
4. Explain the purpose and function of the CTTY command.
5. Explain the use of batch files with shortcuts.
6. Explain the purpose and function of the GOTO command.
7. Explain the purpose and function of the SHIFT command.
8. Explain the purpose and function of the IF command.
9. Explain the purpose and function of the IF EXIST/IF NOT EXIST command.
10. Explain the purpose and function of the IF ERRORLEVEL command.
11. Explain the purpose and function of writing programs.
12. Explain the purpose and function of the CHOICE command.
13. Explain the purpose and function of the environment and environmental variables.
14. Explain the use of the SET command.
15. Explain the purpose and function of the FOR...IN...DO command.
16. Explain the purpose and function of the CALL command.

STUDENT OUTCOMES

1. Use the ECHO command to place a blank line in a batch file.
2. Use the GOTO command in conjunction with a label to create a loop.
3. Use the CTTY command to suppress unwanted display.
4. Use a batch file with a shortcut.
5. Use the SHIFT command to move parameters.
6. Use the IF command with strings for conditional processing.
7. Test for null values in a batch file.
8. Use the IF EXIST/IF NOT EXIST command to test for the existence of a file or a subdirectory.
9. Use the SET command.
10. Use the environment and environmental variables in batch files.
11. Use the IF ERRORLEVEL command with XCOPY to write a batch file for testing exit codes.
12. Use the CHOICE command in a batch file.
13. Use the FOR...IN...DO command for repetitive processing.
14. Use the CALL command in a batch file.

CHAPTER OVERVIEW

You learned in Chapter 10 how to write simple batch files, use replaceable parameters, and write a simple AUTOEXEC.BAT file. Some commands allow you write even more powerful batch files that act like sophisticated programs.

This chapter focuses on the remaining batch file commands, which will allow you to write sophisticated batch files. You will further refine your techniques in working with the environment.

11.1   BATCH FILE COMMANDS

A quick summary of batch file rules tells us that any batch file must have the file extension of .BAT, it must always be an ASCII file, and it must include legitimate commands. In addition, you can use replaceable or positional parameters to create generic batch files. Batch file commands are not case sensitive. You may use any command in a batch file that you can use on the command line, as well as some specific batch file commands, in batch files. Only one batch file has a predetermined name, AUTOEXEC.BAT. This batch file executes when you initially boot the system. You may create or alter an AUTOEXEC.BAT file on a floppy disk. Table 11.1 lists the specific batch file commands.

Command	Purpose
CALL	Calls one batch program from another without causing the first batch program to stop.
CHOICE	Prompts the user to make a choice in a batch program. Displays a prompt that you can specify and pauses for the user to choose from among a specified set of keystrokes.
ECHO	Displays or hides the text in batch programs while the program is running. Also used to determine whether commands will be "echoed" to the screen while the program file is running.
FOR	Runs a specified command for each file in a set of files. This command can also be used at the command line.
GOTO	Directs the operating system to a new line that you specify with a label.
IF	Performs conditional processing in a batch program, based on whether or not a specified condition is true or false.
PAUSE	Suspends processing of a batch file and displays a message prompting the user to press a key to continue.
REM	Used to document your batch files. The operating system ignores any line that begins with REM, allowing you to place lines of information in your batch program or to prevent a line from running.
SHIFT	Changes the position of the replaceable parameter in a batch program.

TABLE 11.1   BATCH FILE COMMANDS

You have already used ECHO, PAUSE, and REM. You will now learn the remaining batch file commands, which allow you to create complex batch files. Using these commands is similar to using a programming language. Batch files have a limited vocabulary (the commands listed above), a syntax, and programming logic. Batch files are also limited in the kinds of programming they can do. They do not have the power or the flexibility of a "real" programming language such as Visual Basic or C++. Batch files, however, accomplish many things in the Windows environment.

11.2   A REVIEW OF THE REM, PAUSE, AND ECHO COMMANDS

The REM command in a batch file indicates to the operating system that whatever text follows is to be displayed, but only if ECHO has *not* been turned off. If a command follows REM, it will be displayed but not executed. Remarks can be a string of up to 123 characters, and typically they document batch files. Placing REM in front of a command will allow you to execute a batch file or the CONFIG.SYS file without executing the command that follows it. This allows you to disable a line or lines without having to actually delete them.

The PAUSE command stops a batch file from continuing to execute until you press any key. It informs you to press any key to continue, but does not do any *conditional processing*.

Remember, to interrupt a batch file, you can always press **Ctrl** + **C** or **Ctrl** + **Break**. Pressing this key combination will interrupt the execution of the batch file. There is one warning—if the batch file has called an external command and the operating system is in the middle of executing a command such as FORMAT or DISKCOPY, it will finish executing the command before exiting the batch file. **Ctrl** + **C** stops the execution of the batch file itself—it will not stop the execution of a .exe or .com program.

The ECHO command can be used either on a command line or in a batch file. It is a special command that turns on or turns off the echoing of commands to the screen. If you key in the command ECHO by itself on the command line or include it in a batch file, it will return the status of ECHO: either ECHO on or ECHO off. When ECHO is on, all the commands in a batch file are displayed on the screen. When ECHO is off, you see the output of the command, but not the command itself. Normally ECHO is on, which is particularly useful when you want to track the operation of a batch file. However, when a batch file runs successfully, the display of commands can clutter the screen.

In a batch file, if you do not wish to see each command on the screen, you can issue the command ECHO OFF. The batch file commands are not displayed, but any messages that a command such as COPY issues will be displayed; for example, "1 file(s) copied." Depending on your preferences, you can key in ECHO ON or ECHO OFF within the batch file to display or not display the commands. In addition, if you precede ECHO OFF with @, the words ECHO OFF will not appear on the screen.

11.3 ADVANCED FEATURES OF ECHO AND REM

There are some interesting features and variations you can implement with both REM and ECHO. One problem with REM is that the operating system recognizes it as a command and must take time to process it. A shortcut is to use a double colon (::) instead of REM in front of a remark, or documentation line. This will save valuable processing time because the operating system treats all lines beginning with a colon as a label and ignores them unless they are "called" elsewhere in the batch file. This will be further explained later.

When you turn ECHO off, you still get the display of messages such as "1 file(s) copied." Sometimes you do not wish to see messages. You can use redirection with standard output to redirect the output of a command to a device called NUL. As the name implies, NUL means send it to "nothing." When you send the output to NUL, it goes nowhere, and it is not displayed on the screen.

Although redirecting the output of a command to the NUL device will suppress messages such as "1 file(s) copied," it will not suppress a message generated by the operating system like "File not found."

You can suppress those messages by using another command, CTTY. This command allows you to specify what device the operating system will use as the console (the place where you input commands and where output is sent). Usually it is the keyboard and the monitor. The combination of the keyboard and the monitor has a reserved name—CON. You can use the NUL device with the CTTY command by using the command CTTY NUL. When you use this command in a batch file, you are essentially telling the operating system to accept what you key in and send all the screen output to nowhere. *You should use this command only in a batch file because if you use it at the command line, you will not be able to enter any other commands. This could force you to reboot.* You should also use CTTY NUL in tandem with CTTY CON. CTTY CON passes control back to the console so when you exit the batch file, you have control of the console.

CAUTION!   **WHENEVER YOU USE CTTY NUL, *BE SURE* THE LAST LINE IN THE FILE IS ALWAYS CTTY CON TO ENSURE THAT CONTROL IS RETURNED TO THE CONSOLE.**

You often want to place a blank line in a batch file for aesthetic purposes or to highlight particular commands. There is, of course, no such thing as a blank line. In the word-processing world, when you want a blank line, you press the **Enter** key, which places a carriage return in the document and prints as a blank line. This does not work in batch files. In a batch file, the operating system simply ignores it when you press **Enter**. Pressing **Enter** does not leave a blank line. If you use REM, you will see nothing if ECHO is off. If you place the word ECHO in the batch file, it will report whether ECHO is on or off. An easy method to get a blank line is to key in ECHO followed by a period. There can be no space between ECHO and the period.

11.4   ACTIVITY: USING :, ECHO, CTTY, AND NUL

Note 1: The DATA disk is in Drive A. A:\> is displayed.

Step 1   Use an editor to create and save the following batch file called **ONE.BAT**, pressing the **Enter** key where indicated only.
:: This is a test of a batch file using **Enter**
:: different features. **Enter**
COPY CAROLYN.FIL BOOK.FIL **Enter**
Enter
TYPE BOOK.FIL **Enter**
ECHO **Enter**
DEL BOOK.FIL **Enter**
COPY NO.FIL BOOK.FIL **Enter**

Step 2   Close the editor and then key in the following:
A:\>**TYPE ONE.BAT** **Enter**

```
MS-DOS Prompt                                              _ □ ×

A:\>TYPE ONE.BAT
:: This is a test of a batch file using
```

```
:: different features.
COPY CAROLYN.FIL BOOK.FIL

TYPE BOOK.FIL
ECHO
DEL BOOK.FIL
COPY NO.FIL BOOK.FIL


A:\>_
```

Step 3   Key in the following: A:\>**ONE** Enter

```
MS-DOS Prompt                                              _ □ X

A:\>ONE

A:\>COPY CAROLYN.FIL BOOK.FIL
        1 file(s) copied

A:\>
A:\>TYPE BOOK.FIL

Hi, my name is Carolyn.
What is your name?

A:\>ECHO
ECHO is on

A:\>DEL BOOK.FIL

A:\>COPY NO.FIL BOOK.FIL
File not found - NO.FIL
        0 file(s) copied

A:\>
A:\>

A:\>_
```

WHAT'S
HAPPENING?   You see messages as well as the output. Your blank line presented only
             the prompt.

Step 4   Edit and save **ONE.BAT** so it looks as follows:
             @ECHO OFF
             :: This is a test of a batch file using
             :: different features.
             COPY CAROLYN.FIL BOOK.FIL > NUL
             ECHO.
             TYPE BOOK.FIL
             ECHO.
             DEL BOOK.FIL
             COPY NO.FIL BOOK.FIL > NUL

Step 5   Key in the following: A:\>**ONE** Enter

```
MS-DOS Prompt                                              _ □ ✕

A:\>ONE


Hi, my name is Carolyn.
What is your name?

File not found - NO.FIL
A:\>_
```

WHAT'S HAPPENING? ➤ You now do not see your messages or remarks. You also get some blank lines. The COPY command could not find **NO.FIL**, and you did not suppress the display of the message **File not found - NO.FIL**.

Step 6   Edit and save **ONE.BAT** so it looks as follows:
@ECHO OFF
:: This is a test of a batch file using
:: different features.
COPY CAROLYN.FIL BOOK.FIL > NUL
ECHO.
TYPE BOOK.FIL
ECHO.
DEL BOOK.FIL
CTTY NUL
COPY NO.FIL BOOK.FIL > NUL
CTTY CON

Step 7   Key in the following: A:\>**ONE** Enter

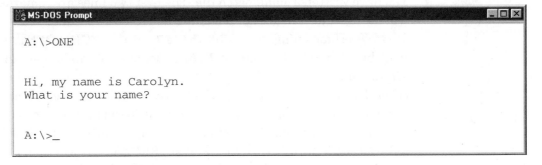

```
MS-DOS Prompt                                              _ □ ✕

A:\>ONE


Hi, my name is Carolyn.
What is your name?


A:\>_
```

WHAT'S HAPPENING? ➤ You no longer display any messages. Note that **CTTY CON** is at the end of the batch file. Some of these techniques will be used in the batch files you are going to create.

11.5   THE GOTO COMMAND

By using the GOTO command, a batch file can be constructed to behave like a program written in a programming language such as BASIC or C++. The GOTO command will branch to a specific part within a batch file, creating a loop. A *loop* is an operation that will repeat steps until you stop the loop either by using an IF statement or by breaking into the batch file with [Ctrl] + C.

The GOTO command works in conjunction with a label. This label is not to be confused with a volume label on a disk. A label is any name you choose to flag a location in a batch file. A label is preceded by a colon (:) and is ignored by the operating system until called with the GOTO command. A double colon (::), used earlier for REM statements, ensures that the operating system will always disregard the line since a colon may not be used as a label name. A label can be no longer than eight characters. The label itself is not a command, it just identifies a location in a batch file. When a batch file goes to a label, it carries out whatever command follows on the line after the label. GOTO has one parameter, GOTO label. Although it is not necessary that labels be exactly the same; i.e., the same case, it is still wise to make them the same case.

11.6   ACTIVITY: USING THE GOTO COMMAND

Note: The DATA disk should be in Drive A with A:\> displayed.

Step 1   Use any text editor to create and save a batch file called **REPEAT.BAT**. Key in the following using exactly the same case:
REM This file displays many times the contents [Enter]
REM of a file. [Enter]
:REPEAT [Enter]
TYPE %1 [Enter]
PAUSE [Enter]
GOTO REPEAT

WHAT'S HAPPENING?   You have written a small batch file. The first two lines are remarks that will not execute. You are not including ECHO OFF, because you want to see what is happening in your batch file. Omitting ECHO OFF is a way to "debug" a batch file program. *Debug* means to see and repair any errors. The third line (:REPEAT) is a label which must be preceded by a colon. The fourth line is a simple TYPE command with a replaceable parameter. The PAUSE command is placed on the fifth line so you may see what is happening. The sixth and last line is the loop. The GOTO tells the batch file to return to the label (:REPEAT). It will then return to line three and execute the TYPE command. It will then read lines 5 and 6 and continually repeat the process.

Step 2   You must be at the system prompt, not in the editor. Key in the following: A:\>**REPEAT APRIL.TXT** [Enter]

```
MS-DOS Prompt                                        _ □ X

A:\>REPEAT APRIL.TXT

A:\>REM This file displays many times the contents

A:\>REM of a file.
```

```
A:\>TYPE APRIL.TXT

This is my April file.
It is my fourth dummy file.
This is file 4.

A:\>PAUSE
Press any key to continue . . .
```

WHAT'S HAPPENING? ➤ The first two lines displayed are remarks. The label was ignored, but the TYPE command was executed. The next line has paused the batch file. You need to press **Enter** to continue.

Step 3 Press **Enter**

```
MS-DOS Prompt                                              _ □ ✕

A:\>PAUSE
Press any key to continue . . .


A:\>GOTO REPEAT

A:\>TYPE APRIL.TXT

This is my April file.
It is my fourth dummy file.
This is file 4.

A:\>PAUSE
Press any key to continue . . .
```

WHAT'S HAPPENING? ➤ The next line in the batch file was GOTO REPEAT. The batch file was sent back to the label :REPEAT. The batch file read the next line after the label, which was the TYPE command, then the next line, which is PAUSE. When you press a key, you will again be returned to the label. Now you see a loop in action.

Step 4 Press **Enter** a few times to see the loop in action. Then press **Ctrl** + **C** to break out of the batch file. It will ask you if you want to terminate the batch job. Key in **Y** for yes. You will be returned to the A:\> prompt.

WHAT'S HAPPENING? ➤ A loop can be very useful. For instance, if you wanted to delete all the files from many floppy disks, you could write a batch file that would look like this:

```
@ECHO OFF
:TOP
CLS
ECHO Place the disk with the files you no longer want ECHO in Drive A.
PAUSE
ECHO Y | DEL A:*.*
ECHO Press Ctrl + C to stop executing this batch file.
ECHO Otherwise, press any key to continue deleting
ECHO files.
PAUSE > NUL
GOTO TOP
```

The **ECHO Y ¦ DEL A:*.*** is a way to send the Y character to the prompt that DEL A:*.* will ask for. You could have used **DEL A:*.* < Y.FIL**, but the ECHO method has the advantage of not requiring a file called **Y.FIL.** You did not want to see the output of the PAUSE command, so you redirected it to the NUL device.

11.7   THE SHIFT COMMAND

When you have written a batch file with positional parameters, you key in the batch file name followed by a series of values. When the batch file is executed, the operating system looks to the command line for the values it needs to plug into the batch file. It does this based on the position of particular parameters in the command line. In the case of a batch file called LIST.BAT with the lines TYPE %1, TYPE %2, and TYPE %3, you would key in the following command line:

```
LIST  ARPIL.TXT  MAY.TXT  JUNE.TXT
```

With this generic batch file, you could key in only three file names. If you wanted more file names, you would have to re-execute the batch file. You are limited to 10 parameters on a command line—%0 through %9. Since %0 actually represents the batch file name itself, you can have only nine parameters. The SHIFT command allows you to shift the parameters to the left, one by one, making the number of parameters on a line limitless. As the SHIFT command shifts the contents of the parameters to the left, parameter 2 becomes parameter 1, parameter 3 becomes parameter 2, and so on. This allows the batch file to process all the parameters on the command line.

11.8   ACTIVITY: USING THE SHIFT COMMAND

Note: The DATA disk should be in Drive A with A:\> displayed.

Step 1   Key in the following: A:\>**ECHO a b c d e** [Enter]

```
MS-DOS Prompt                                                    _ □ ×
A:\>ECHO a b c d e
a b c d e

A:\>_
```

ECHO on a command line just "echoed" what you keyed in. Thus, the parameters a, b, c, d, and e on the command line were repeated on the screen. If you wanted to display more than five parameters and place the echoing parameters in a batch file, you would need to use the SHIFT command.

Step 2   Use any text editor to create and save the file **ALPHA.BAT** as follows:
@ECHO OFF
ECHO %0 %1 %2 %3

SHIFT
ECHO %0 %1 %2 %3
SHIFT
ECHO %0 %1 %2 %3
SHIFT
ECHO %0 %1 %2 %3

WHAT'S
HAPPENING? ▶ You have created a batch file with replaceable parameters. The purpose of the batch file is to demonstrate the SHIFT command. Remember that ECHO just echoes what you keyed in. In your command line, however, even though you have only four parameters (0 through 3), you want to key in more than four values.

Step 3   Remember, you must be at the system prompt, not in the editor. Key in the following: A:\>**ALPHA a b c d e f** [Enter]

```
MS-DOS Prompt                                              _ □ ×
A:\>ALPHA a b c d e f
ALPHA a b c
a b c d
b c d e
c d e f
A:\>_
```

WHAT'S
HAPPENING? ▶ Notice the output. In each case, when the batch file read SHIFT, it moved each parameter over by one position. You had keyed in **ALPHA a b c d e f**.

Batch File	Supplied Value from Command Line	Screen Display
@ECHO OFF		
ECHO %0 %1 %2 %3	ALPHA is %0 a is %1 b is %2 c is %3	ALPHA a b c
SHIFT	ALPHA is dropped as %0 a becomes %0 b becomes %1 c becomes %2 d becomes %3	
ECHO %0 %1 %2 %3	a is %0 b is %1 c is %2 d is %3	a b c d

SHIFT	a is dropped as %0	
	b becomes %0	
	c becomes %1	
	d becomes %2	
	e becomes %3	
ECHO %0 %1 %2 %3	b is %0	b c d e
	c is %1	
	d is %2	
	e is %3	
SHIFT	b is dropped as %0	
	c becomes %0	
	d becomes %1	
	e becomes %2	
	f becomes %3	
ECHO %0 %1 %2 %3	c is %0	c d e f
	d is %1	
	e is %2	
	f is %3	

You should see that you are indeed shifting parameters, but how is this useful? You will write some batch files that use SHIFT so you can see how this technique can be used.

As you know, the operating system stamps each file with the current date and time when it is created or modified. Most often, this means that each file has a unique time and date based on the last time you modified or created the file. Sometimes, you want to place a specific time and date stamp on a file or group of files. For example, if you sell software and you have customers to whom you send files, you might like to ascertain which version of the file they have. By having a particular date and/or time on the file, you can easily keep a date log that is not dependent on the file modification date. Commands such as XCOPY can back up files after or before a certain date. To ensure that you are backing up all the files you want, you can set the date and update the date stamp on your files. Then you can back up from that date. You need a way to update the dates. You can do this by using the following command:

```
COPY filename /b +
```

Remember, the + sign tells the operating system to concatenate files. The first thing that happens when copying files is a file name is created with the current time and date in the destination directory. At first, the new file is empty. Since there is no specific destination file name, COPY will default to the source file name. It then proceeds to concatenate (add) the existing file to the "new" file name and the new date and time. In essence, it is copying a file onto itself. Since it is a new entry in the directory table, it has the current date and time.

The /b switch tells the operating system to copy the file in binary mode. When you concatenate files with no switches, the files are copied in text mode. The COPY command knows the contents of the file has ended when it sees a special mark called an *EOF (end-of-file) mark*. Typically, the EOF mark is Ctrl + Z. The instant COPY sees this special signal, it thinks there is no more information to copy and will place its own EOF mark at the end of the file—another Ctrl + Z. Unfortunately, this "extra" EOF mark is sometimes interpreted by a program or a data file as something other than the end of the file. Thus, you could be in the situation of not copying the entire file. The alternative is to copy the file in binary mode. When you choose this option—the /b switch—COPY will not read the file but will copy everything in the file, ensuring that the entire file contents are copied without adding an extra Ctrl + Z. An extra Ctrl + Z can create problems when you are trying to use the copied file.

Now that you know how and why to update file dates and times, it is easy to place these commands in a batch file. Since you may have more than one file you wish to "stamp," you want to allow for many file names by using the SHIFT command.

Step 4   Use any text editor to create a new file. Name the file **UPDATE.BAT** and then key in the following:
:DOIT Enter
COPY %1 /b + > NUL Enter
SHIFT Enter
PAUSE Enter
GOTO DOIT

Step 5   Key in the following: A:\>**DIR APR.99** Enter

Step 6   Key in the following: A:\>**DIR APR.BUD** Enter

```
 MS-DOS Prompt                                                    _ □ ✕

 A:\>DIR APR.99

  Volume in drive A is DATA
  Volume Serial Number is 3330-1807
  Directory of A:\

 APR       99          72  10-10-99  4:53p APR.99
          1 file(s)              72 bytes
          0 dir(s)         902,144 bytes free

 A:\>DIR APR.BUD

  Volume in drive A is DATA
  Volume Serial Number is 3330-1807
  Directory of A:\

 APR       BUD         19  12-06-00  2:45p APR.BUD
          1 file(s)              19 bytes
```

```
        0 dir(s)          902,144 bytes free

A:\>_
```

WHAT'S HAPPENING? ➤ You want the files **APR.99** and **APR.BUD** to have today's date and time on them.

Step 7   Key in the following: A:\>**UPDATE APR.99 APR.BUD** Enter

```
MS-DOS Prompt                                               _ □ X

A:\>UPDATE  APR.99  APR.BUD

A:\>COPY APR.99 /b + > NUL

A:\>SHIFT

A:\>PAUSE
Press any key to continue . . .
```

WHAT'S HAPPENING? ➤ The batch file copied **APR.99**, went to SHIFT, and is now going to copy the next parameter it shifted, **APR.BUD**.

Step 8   Press Enter

```
MS-DOS Prompt                                               _ □ X

A:\>UPDATE  APR.99  APR.BUD

A:\>COPY APR.99 /b + > NUL

A:\>SHIFT

A:\>PAUSE
Press any key to continue . . .


A:\>GOTO DOIT

A:\>COPY APR.BUD /b + > NUL

A:\>SHIFT

A:\>PAUSE
Press any key to continue . . .
```

WHAT'S HAPPENING? ➤ It copied **APR.BUD**.

Step 9   Press Enter

```
MS-DOS Prompt                                               _ □ X

A:\>COPY  /b + > NUL
Required parameter missing

A:\>SHIFT

A:\>PAUSE
Press any key to continue . . .
```

WHAT'S HAPPENING? ➤ This batch file seemed to work effectively when you first initiated it. It copied **APR.99**. It then shifted over to **APR.BUD** and copied that. However, you created an endless loop. When the batch file finished copying **APR.BUD**, it again shifted parameters, but there was nothing to shift to. The batch file informed you that the file name is missing (**Required parameter missing**). It will continue to do this forever. There is something missing here: a condition that you need to insert. First, though, you must break into the batch file.

Step 10 Press **Ctrl** + **C** and answer **Y** to the prompt.

Step 11 Key in the following: A:\>**DIR APR.99** **Enter**

Step 12 Key in the following: A:\>**DIR APR.BUD** **Enter**

```
MS-DOS Prompt                                                    _ □ X

Terminate batch job (Y/N)?Y

A:\>DIR APR.99

 Volume in drive A is DATA
 Volume Serial Number is 2415-16DD
 Directory of A:\

APR      99            72  12-26-01  9:43a APR.99
         1 file(s)              72 bytes
         0 dir(s)          902,144 bytes free

A:\>DIR APR.BUD

 Volume in drive A is DATA
 Volume Serial Number is 2415-16DD
 Directory of A:\

APR      BUD           19  12-26-01  9:43a APR.BUD
         1 file(s)              19 bytes
         0 dir(s)          902,144 bytes free

A:\>_
```

WHAT'S HAPPENING? ➤ The file worked—the date and time should be the current date and time. You can create a batch file and use SHIFT to identify the size and number of files in a directory so you can determine whether the files will fit on a floppy disk.

Step 13 Use any text editor to create and save a file named **SIZE.BAT** that contains the following:

:TOP
DIR %1 ¦ FIND "Directory" >> TEMP.FIL
DIR %1 ¦ FIND "bytes" ¦ FIND /V "free" >> TEMP.FIL
SHIFT
GOTO TOP
TYPE TEMP.FIL

```
PAUSE
DEL TEMP.FIL
```

WHAT'S HAPPENING? ➤ Since you do not care about the names of the files, only the size and the directory they are in, you filtered the output from the DIR command to include only the items that you wanted. You used the double >> so that you would see both the name of the directory and the bytes in the directory. Had you not used >>, you would have *overwritten* **TEMP.FIL**. At the end of your work, delete **TEMP.FIL** so it will not take space on your disk.

Step 14   Key in the following: A:\>**SIZE CLASS TRIP** Enter

```
┌─ MS-DOS Prompt ──────────────────────────────────── _ □ X ─┐
│                                                             │
│ A:\>GOTO TOP                                                │
│                                                             │
│ A:\>DIR TRIP ¦ FIND "Directory" >>  TEMP.FIL                │
│                                                             │
│ A:\>DIR TRIP ¦ FIND "bytes" ¦ FIND /V "free" >> TEMP.FIL    │
│                                                             │
│ A:\>SHIFT                                                   │
│                                                             │
│ A:\>GOTO TOP                                                │
│                                                             │
│ A:\>DIR  ¦ FIND "Directory" >>  TEMP.FIL                    │
│                                                             │
│ A:\>DIR  ¦ FIND "bytes" ¦ FIND /V "free" >> TEMP.FIL        │
│                                                             │
└─────────────────────────────────────────────────────────────┘
```

WHAT'S HAPPENING? ➤ Your batch file is running endlessly. You again created an endless loop.

Step 15   Press Ctrl + **C** and answer **Y** to the prompt.

```
┌─ MS-DOS Prompt ──────────────────────────────────── _ □ X ─┐
│                                                             │
│ A:\>DIR  ¦ FIND "bytes" ¦ FIND /V "free" >> TEMP.FIL        │
│                                                             │
│ A:\>SHIFT                                                   │
│                                                             │
│ A:\>GOTO TOP                                                │
│                                                             │
│ A:\>DIR  ¦ FIND "Directory" >>  TEMP.FIL                    │
│                                                             │
│ A:\>DIR  ¦ FIND "bytes" ¦ FIND /V "free" >> TEMP.FIL        │
│ ^C                                                          │
│                                                             │
│ Terminate batch job (Y/N)?Y                                 │
│                                                             │
│ A:\>_                                                       │
│                                                             │
└─────────────────────────────────────────────────────────────┘
```

WHAT'S HAPPENING? ➤ Your display may look different depending on where you broke into the batch file.

Step 16   Key in the following: A:\>**TYPE TEMP.FIL ¦ MORE** Enter

```
 MS-DOS Prompt                                                    _ □ ✕

    Directory of A:\CLASS
          13 file(s)                 888 bytes
    Directory of A:\TRIP
          21 file(s)               1,551 bytes
    Directory of A:\
          62 file(s)              52,485 bytes
    Directory of A:\
          62 file(s)              52,545 bytes
    Directory of A:\CLASS
          13 file(s)                 888 bytes
    Directory of A:\TRIP
          21 file(s)               1,551 bytes
    Directory of A:\
          62 file(s)              52,672 bytes
    Directory of A:\
          62 file(s)              52,732 bytes
    Directory of A:\
          62 file(s)              52,792 bytes
    Directory of A:\
          62 file(s)              52,852 bytes
    Directory of A:\
          62 file(s)              52,912 bytes
    Directory of A:\
    -- More --
```

WHAT'S HAPPENING? Your file may be shorter or longer, depending on the length of time before you "broke out" with **Ctrl** + **C**. In any case, you got more information than you wanted. You now know the size of the **CLASS** and **TRIP** directories, but the other information is useless. You are missing conditional processing. (The size of your directories may be different, depending on the work you have done on your DATA disk.)

Step 17   Press **Ctrl** + **C** to stop the processing, if necessary.

11.9   THE IF COMMAND

The IF command allows for conditional processing. Conditional processing is a powerful tool in programming. Conditional processing allows a comparison between two items to determine whether the items are identical or whether one is greater than another. A comparison test will yield one of only two values—*true* or *false*. If the items are identical, the condition is true. If the items are not identical, the condition is false. Once you establish a true or false value, you can then direct the program to do something based on that value. Conditional processing is often expressed as IF the condition is true, THEN do something; IF the condition is false, THEN do nothing.

In batch files, the IF command will test for some logical condition and then, if the condition is true, the batch file will execute the command. If the test is false, the command will not be executed and the batch file will fall through to the next command line in the batch file. The IF command in batch file processing can check for three conditions:

1. Whether two sets of characters are or are not identical. The characters are called a string, as in a string of data (sometimes referred to as a character string).
2. Whether or not a file exists.
3. The value of the variable in ERRORLEVEL. ERRORLEVEL is a number that a program can set depending on the outcome of a process, such as checking a true/false condition. ERRORLEVEL can check that number.

The syntax for IF/IF NOT ERRORLEVEL is:

```
Performs conditional processing in batch programs.

IF [NOT] ERRORLEVEL number command
IF [NOT] string1==string2 command
IF [NOT] EXIST filename command

  NOT                   Specifies that Windows should carry out the command only
                        if the condition is false.
  ERRORLEVEL number     Specifies a true condition if the last program run
                        returned an exit code equal to or greater than the number
                        specified.
  command               Specifies the command to carry out if the condition is
                        met.
  string1==string2      Specifies a true condition if the specified text strings
                        match.
  EXIST filename        Specifies a true condition if the specified filename
                        exists.
```

11.10 IF COMMAND USING STRINGS

You can use the IF command with character strings to test whether or not one string is exactly the same as another. You can tell the IF statement to GOTO a label or to perform an operation when the strings match and the condition is true. Conversely, you can tell the IF statement to GOTO a label or perform an operation when the strings do *not* match and the condition is false. What is to be compared is separated by two equal signs (==).

11.11 ACTIVITY: USING THE IF COMMAND WITH STRINGS

Note: The DATA disk should be in Drive A. The default drive and directory should be A:\>.

Step 1   Use any text editor to create and save a file called **GREET.BAT**. (*Note:* There are no spaces between the two equal signs.) Key in the following:
IF %1==Carolyn GOTO Carolyn Enter
IF %1==Bette GOTO Bette Enter
ECHO Isn't anyone there? Enter
GOTO FINISH Enter
:Carolyn Enter
ECHO Greetings, Ms. Carolyn. Enter
GOTO FINISH Enter
:Bette Enter

ECHO Greetings, Ms. Bette. [Enter]
:FINISH

WHAT'S HAPPENING? ➤ You have created a batch file to test the IF statement using character strings. You did not place the **ECHO OFF** at the beginning of the file so you can see what happens when it executes.

Step 2   Key in the following: A:\>**GREET Carolyn** [Enter]

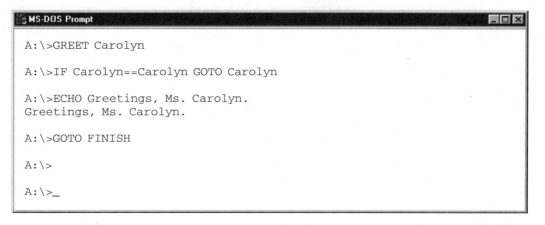

```
MS-DOS Prompt                                              _ □ ×

A:\>GREET Carolyn

A:\>IF Carolyn==Carolyn GOTO Carolyn

A:\>ECHO Greetings, Ms. Carolyn.
Greetings, Ms. Carolyn.

A:\>GOTO FINISH

A:\>

A:\>_
```

WHAT'S HAPPENING? ➤ You keyed in **GREET Carolyn**. The first line in the batch file was executed. When **Carolyn** took the place of **%1**, the line read **IF Carolyn==Carolyn**, which is a true statement because the strings of data matched exactly. Since it is true, it performed the GOTO Carolyn command. The line after the label **:Carolyn** was then displayed: **Greetings, Ms. Carolyn.** The line following said **GOTO FINISH**, which it did. After the label **:FINISH**, there were no more lines, and you were returned to the system prompt.

Step 3   Key in the following: A:\>**GREET Bette** [Enter]

```
MS-DOS Prompt                                              _ □ ×

A:\>GREET Bette

A:\>IF Bette==Carolyn GOTO Carolyn

A:\>IF Bette==Bette GOTO Bette

A:\>ECHO Greetings, Ms. Bette.
Greetings, Ms. Bette.

A:\>

A:\>_
```

WHAT'S HAPPENING? ➤ When you keyed in **GREET Bette**, it read the first line as **IF Bette==Carolyn GOTO Carolyn**. **Bette** does not equal **Carolyn**, so it is a false statement. Therefore, the batch file did not go to the label **:Carolyn** but fell through to the next line. The line then read as **IF Bette==Bette**, which is a true statement because the strings of data match exactly. Since it is true, it performed the GOTO Bette command. The line after the label **:Bette** was then displayed: **Greetings, Ms. Bette.** The line following said **:FINISH**, which it did. After the label **:FINISH**, there were no more lines, and you were returned to the system prompt.

Step 4   Key in the following: A:\>**GREET Juan** Enter

```
MS-DOS Prompt                                                    _ □ ×

A:\>GREET Juan

A:\>IF Juan==Carolyn GOTO Carolyn

A:\>IF Juan==Bette GOTO Bette

A:\>ECHO Isn't anyone there?
Isn't anyone there?

A:\>GOTO FINISH

A:\>

A:\>_
```

WHAT'S HAPPENING? ➤   You keyed in **GREET Juan**. It read the first line as **IF Juan==Carolyn GOTO Carolyn**. Juan does not equal Carolyn, so it is a false statement. The batch file did not go to the label **:Carolyn** but fell through to the next line. The line then read as **IF Juan==Bette**. This is another false statement, so the batch file did not go to the label **:Bette** but fell through to the next line. The line following said **ECHO Isn't anyone there?** Thus, **Isn't anyone there?** was displayed (echoed) to the screen. It then fell through to the next line, which was **GOTO FINISH**. After the label **:FINISH**, there were no more lines, and you were returned to the system prompt.

Step 5   Key in the following: A:\>**GREET BETTE** Enter

```
MS-DOS Prompt                                                    _ □ ×

A:\>GREET BETTE

A:\>IF BETTE==Carolyn GOTO Carolyn

A:\>IF BETTE==Bette GOTO Bette

A:\>ECHO Isn't anyone there?
Isn't anyone there?

A:\>GOTO FINISH

A:\>

A:\>_
```

WHAT'S HAPPENING? ➡ You keyed in **GREET BETTE**. It read the first line as **IF BETTE==Carolyn GOTO Carolyn**. BETTE does not equal Carolyn, so it is a false statement. The batch file did not go to the label **:Carolyn** but fell through to the next line. The line then read **IF BETTE==Bette**, which is another false statement. Even though the word is the same, the case is different. Both sides of == must match *exactly*. Because it was not an exact match, the batch file did not go to the label **:Bette**, but fell through to the next line. The line following said **ECHO Isn't anyone there?** Thus, **Isn't anyone there?** was displayed (echoed) to the screen. It then fell through to the next line, which was **GOTO FINISH**. It did. After the label **:FINISH**, there were no more lines, and you were returned to the system prompt.

11.12 TESTING FOR NULL VALUES

In the above example, you tested for an exact match of character strings. What if you have nothing to test for? For example, in the batch files you wrote, UPDATE.BAT and SIZE.BAT, you used SHIFT. SHIFT kept shifting parameters until all of them were used. When there were no more parameters, you were in an endless loop. You can test to see if a string matches, but what if nothing is there? This is called testing for a ***null value***. You are literally testing for nothing. You must have "something" to test for "nothing." Thus, you place a value in the test that will give you nothing.

There are a variety of methods for testing for null values. One method is to use quotation marks so that your statement becomes IF "%1"=="" GOTO LABEL. The second set of quotation marks is keyed in with no spaces. This statement says, "If nothing is there, GOTO somewhere else." You may also make the line read IF %1void==void GOTO LABEL. If you keyed in GREET Carolyn, your line would then look like Carolynvoid==void. This is not true, so it would proceed to the next line. If there were no value, your line would look like void==void. Now this is true, and the GOTO label would execute. You may use any word; "void" was used in this example. Another method is to use \ so that the statement would become IF \%1\==\\ GOTO LABEL. If you keyed in GREET Carolyn, your line would then look like \Carolyn\==\\. This is not true, so it would proceed to the next line. If there were no value, your line would look like \\==\\. Now this *is* true and the GOTO label would execute.

11.13 ACTIVITY: USING NULL VALUES

Note: The DATA disk should be in Drive A. The default drive and directory should be A:\>.

Step 1   Edit and save the file called **UPDATE.BAT** to look as follows:

```
:DOIT
IF "%1"=="" GOTO END
COPY %1 /b + > NUL
SHIFT
```

```
PAUSE
GOTO DOIT
:END
```

Step 2   Key in the following: `A:\>`**DIR CAROLYN.FIL** `Enter`

```
MS-DOS Prompt                                              [_][□][X]

A:\>DIR CAROLYN.FIL

 Volume in drive A is DATA
 Volume Serial Number is 3330-1807
 Directory of A:\

CAROLYN  FIL            47  07-31-99 12:53p CAROLYN.FIL
         1 file(s)              47 bytes
         0 dir(s)          899,584 bytes free

A:\>_
```

WHAT'S HAPPENING?   The file called **CAROLYN.FIL** has a date of 7-31-99. You are going to update only the date on this file. SHIFT will still work and will shift "nothing" to %1, but now you are testing for a null value. Once the file is updated, you will go to :END.

Step 3   Key in the following: `A:\>`**UPDATE CAROLYN.FIL** `Enter`

```
MS-DOS Prompt                                              [_][□][X]

A:\>UPDATE CAROLYN.FIL

A:\>IF "CAROLYN.FIL"=="" GOTO END

A:\>COPY CAROLYN.FIL /b + > NUL

A:\>SHIFT

A:\>PAUSE
Press any key to continue . . .
```

WHAT'S HAPPENING?   The batch file updated the file **CAROLYN.FIL**. Prior to your testing for a null value, the file looped endlessly. Now you will see if your test for "nothing" works. Remember, there is a SHIFT that will shift over nothing.

Step 4   Press `Enter`

```
MS-DOS Prompt                                              [_][□][X]

A:\>PAUSE
Press any key to continue . . .


A:\>GOTO DOIT

A:\>IF ""=="" GOTO END
```

```
A:\>

A:\>_
```

WHAT'S HAPPENING? ➤ Since nothing, or a null value, was there, it was a true condition, and GOTO told it to go to the label called :END. Thus, it skipped the lines and went directly to the end of the batch file.

Step 5 Key in the following: A:\>**DIR CAROLYN.FIL** [Enter]

```
┌─────────────────────────────────────────────────────────────────────┐
│ ▓ MS-DOS Prompt                                           _ □ ×       │
├─────────────────────────────────────────────────────────────────────┤
│ A:\>DIR CAROLYN.FIL                                                   │
│                                                                       │
│  Volume in drive A is DATA                                            │
│  Volume Serial Number is 3330-1807                                    │
│  Directory of A:\                                                     │
│                                                                       │
│ CAROLYN  FIL              47  12-26-01  8:06p CAROLYN.FIL             │
│         1 file(s)              47 bytes                               │
│         0 dir(s)          899,584 bytes free                         │
│                                                                       │
│ A:\>_                                                                 │
└─────────────────────────────────────────────────────────────────────┘
```

WHAT'S HAPPENING? ➤ The date did change to the current date (your date will be different), and you were not in an endless loop. You are now going to try another technique to test for a null value.

Step 6 Edit and save the file called **SIZE.BAT** to look as follows:
:TOP
IF %1nothing==nothing GOTO END
DIR %1 ¦ FIND "Directory" >> TEMP.FIL
DIR %1 ¦ FIND "bytes" ¦ FIND /V "free" >> TEMP.FIL
SHIFT
GOTO TOP
TYPE TEMP.FIL
PAUSE
DEL TEMP.FIL
:END

Step 7 Key in the following: A:\>**DEL TEMP.FIL** [Enter]

WHAT'S HAPPENING? ➤ You wanted to eliminate **TEMP.FIL**, because the last time you ran this batch file, you were stuck in a loop and **TEMP.FIL** did not get deleted. You never reached that line in the batch file.

Step 8 Key in the following: A:\>**SIZE CLASS TRIP** [Enter]

```
┌─────────────────────────────────────────────────────────────────────┐
│ ▓ MS-DOS Prompt                                           _ □ ×       │
├─────────────────────────────────────────────────────────────────────┤
│ A:\>IF CLASSnothing==nothing GOTO END                                 │
│                                                                       │
│ A:\>DIR CLASS ¦ FIND "Directory" >> TEMP.FIL                          │
│                                                                       │
│ A:\>DIR CLASS ¦ FIND "bytes" ¦ FIND /V "free" >> TEMP.FIL             │
└─────────────────────────────────────────────────────────────────────┘
```

```
A:\>SHIFT

A:\>GOTO TOP

A:\>IF TRIPnothing==nothing GOTO END

A:\>DIR TRIP | FIND "Directory" >> TEMP.FIL

A:\>DIR TRIP | FIND "bytes" | FIND /V "free" >> TEMP.FIL

A:\>SHIFT

A:\>GOTO TOP

A:\>IF nothing==nothing GOTO END

A:\>

A:\>_
```

> **WHAT'S HAPPENING!** You did not have the problem of an endless loop, but, when you tested for a null value and there was a null value, you told the batch file to GOTO END. It did so, but, by going to the label :END, it never processed the other three lines in the batch file—the lines beginning with TYPE, PAUSE, and DEL. This is why writing batch files (and programs) is a complicated task. You have to think through what you are trying to do and what consequences your instructions will have.

Step 9   Key in the following: A:\>**TYPE TEMP.FIL** [Enter]

```
MS-DOS Prompt                                                  _ □ ✕
A:\>TYPE TEMP.FIL
 Directory of A:\CLASS
        13 file(s)              888 bytes
 Directory of A:\TRIP
        21 file(s)            1,551 bytes

A:\>_
```

> **WHAT'S HAPPENING!** The batch file **SIZE.BAT** worked, to some degree. You got the information in the file **TEMP.FIL**, but the file was never displayed or deleted. Thus, you must find another solution to the problem.

11.14 THE IF EXIST/IF NOT EXIST COMMAND

The IF EXIST command uses a file specification for the test. If the file exists, then the condition is true. Processing then passes to the specified GOTO location or to the command that follows the IF statement. If the file does not exist, the condition is false and the batch process reads the next line in the file. When you use IF NOT EXIST and the file does not exist, then the condition is true. Processing then passes to the specified GOTO location or to the command that follows the IF NOT statement. If the file does exist, the condition is false and the batch process will fall through to the next line in the batch file. *Note:* IF EXIST/IF NOT EXIST works only with file names and *not with directory names*.

11.15 ACTIVITY: USING IF EXIST TO TEST FOR A FILE

Note: The DATA disk should be in Drive A. The displayed prompt is A:\>.

Step 1   Use any text editor and create and save a file called **RENDIR.BAT**. Key in the following:
IF \%1\==\\ GOTO end [Enter]
IF NOT \%2\==\\ GOTO next [Enter]
ECHO You must include a destination name [Enter]
ECHO for the new directory name. [Enter]
GOTO end [Enter]
:next [Enter]
IF EXIST %1 GOTO message [Enter]
REN %1 %2 [Enter]
GOTO end [Enter]
:message [Enter]
ECHO This is a file, not a directory. [Enter]
:end

WHAT'S
HAPPENING?   This batch file will ensure that you are renaming a directory and not a file. The following table analyzes the batch file one line at a time:

Batch File by Line Number	Test TRUE	Processing	Test FALSE
1. IF \%1\==\\ GOTO end	User keys in nothing for %1. Since test is true, action is to go to line 12.	Testing for null value.	User keys in value for %1. Since test is false, action is to go to line 2.
2. IF NOT \%2\==\\ GOTO next	User keys in nothing for %2. Since test is true, action is to go to line 3.	Testing for null value.	User keys in value for %2. Since test is false, action is to go to line 6.
3. ECHO You must include a destination name		Message for user that he or she did not include a value.	
4. ECHO for the new directory name.		Continuation of the message.	

5. GOTO end		Falls through to the GOTO end statement. Action is to go to line 12.
6. :next		Label referred to in line 2.
7. IF EXIST %1 GOTO message	User keys in file name for %1. Since test is true, action is to go to line 10. / Testing for value for %1. Is it a file or a directory? / User keys in directory for %1. Since test is false, action is to go to line 8.	
8. REN %1 %2		Since %1 test is false (not a file), renaming directory can proceed.
9. GOTO end		After directory is renamed, falls through to GOTO end.
10. :message		Label referred to in line 2.
11. ECHO This is a file, not a directory.		Message that user used a file name, not a directory name.
12. :end		

Step 2   Key in the following: A:\>**RENDIR JAN.99 LAST** Enter

```
MS-DOS Prompt                                                    _ □ ×

A:\>RENDIR JAN.99 LAST

A:\>IF \JAN.99\==\\ GOTO end

A:\>IF NOT \LAST\==\\ GOTO next

A:\>IF EXIST JAN.99 GOTO message

A:\>ECHO This is a file, not a directory.
This is a file, not a directory.
```

```
A:\>

A:\>_
```

WHAT'S HAPPENING? Since **JAN.99** is a file, the line **IF EXIST JAN.99** is true. Since it is true, the batch file executed GOTO and went to the label **:message**. What if it is a directory and not a file?

Step 3   Key in the following: A:\>**RENDIR TEST OLDER** Enter

```
MS-DOS Prompt                                                    _ □ ✕

A:\>RENDIR TEST OLDER

A:\>IF \TEST\==\\ GOTO end

A:\>IF NOT \OLDER\==\\ GOTO next

A:\>IF EXIST TEST GOTO message

A:\>REN TEST OLDER

A:\>GOTO end

A:\>

A:\>_
```

WHAT'S HAPPENING? Each of the tests was false, so the batch file fell through to the REN line and successfully renamed the **TEST** directory to **OLDER**. Using the logic you just learned, you can correct (debug) **SIZE.BAT** so that it processes all the lines in the batch file. There is one more piece of information you need. You cannot use IF EXIST to check for the existence of a directory, as it only works with files. There is a way around this—you can "fool" the IF EXIST command. To check for the existence or nonexistence of a directory, you must use NUL. NUL is a device that discards anything sent to it. By using %1\NUL, you force IF EXIST/IF NOT EXIST to check for a directory name and not a file name. IF looks for a NUL file (or the non-existence of a nothing file) in the directory represented by %1. If it cannot get through %1 to look for NUL, then %1 does not exist.

Step 4   Edit and save the file called **SIZE.BAT** to look as follows:
IF EXIST TEMP.FIL DEL TEMP.FIL
:TOP
IF %1nothing==nothing GOTO END
IF NOT EXIST %1\NUL GOTO NEXT
DIR %1 ¦ FIND "Directory" >> TEMP.FIL
DIR %1 ¦ FIND "bytes" ¦ FIND /V "free" >> TEMP.FIL
:NEXT
SHIFT

GOTO TOP
:END
TYPE TEMP.FIL
PAUSE
DEL TEMP.FIL

WHAT'S
HAPPENING?   The first line IF EXIST TEMP.FIL DEL TEMP.FIL will look for the file
called **TEMP.FIL** and delete it if it exists. Then when you create
TEMP.FIL, it will be a new file every time. The next addition, IF NOT
EXIST %1\NUL GOTO NEXT, will see if a directory exists. That is the
purpose of %1\NUL. If it is a file, the batch file will go to the :NEXT
label, SHIFT, and go back to the :TOP label. The :TOP label is not at the
top of the batch file because you want to delete **TEMP.FIL** only the first
time you execute the batch file. Notice that you had to move the :END
label. In its previous batch file location, you would not have been able to
read **TEMP.FIL**.

Step 5   Key in the following: A:\>**SIZE CLASS JAN.99 TRIP** [Enter]

```
MS-DOS Prompt                                                    _ □ ×

A:\>GOTO TOP

A:\>IF TRIPnothing==nothing GOTO END

A:\>IF NOT EXIST TRIP\NUL GOTO NEXT

A:\>DIR TRIP | FIND "Directory" >> TEMP.FIL

A:\>DIR TRIP | FIND "bytes" | FIND /V "free" >> TEMP.FIL

A:\>SHIFT

A:\>GOTO TOP

A:\>IF nothing==nothing GOTO END

A:\>TYPE TEMP.FIL
 Directory of A:\CLASS
       13 file(s)              888 bytes
 Directory of A:\TRIP
       21 file(s)            1,551 bytes

A:\>PAUSE
Press any key to continue . . .
```

WHAT'S
HAPPENING?   Your batch file worked correctly. It used **JAN.99**, knew it was a file, and
did not include it in the output. The more complicated you want a batch
file to be, the more you will have to analyze the logic of what you want to
do and how to accomplish it.

Step 6   Press [Enter]

```
MS-DOS Prompt                                        _ □ ✕

A:\>PAUSE
Press any key to continue . . .


A:\>DEL TEMP.FIL

A:\>
A:\>

A:\>_
```

> **WHAT'S HAPPENING?** ➤ You have executed your batch file and returned to the system level.

11.16 THE IF ERRORLEVEL COMMAND TESTING

A program can set an ***exit code*** when it finishes executing. A batch file can test this exit code with the IF ERRORLEVEL statement. Actually, the name ERRORLEVEL is a misnomer because the number returned does not necessarily mean there was an error. For instance, the test IF ERRORLEVEL 3 will be true if the exit code is greater than or equal to 3. Thus, an exit code is not tested for a match with ERRORLEVEL, but to determine if it is greater than or equal to it. The test IF ERRORLEVEL 0 will *always* be true since every possible exit code is greater than or equal to 0. The trickiest thing about testing ERRORLEVELs in batch files is that the exit codes must be listed in *descending* order when you use IF ERRORLEVEL and in *ascending* order when you use IF NOT ERRORLEVEL. For instance, XCOPY will set one of the following five exit codes:

```
0    Files were copied without error.
1    No files were found to copy.
2    The user pressed CTRL + C to terminate XCOPY.
4    Initialization error occurred. There is not enough memory
     or disk space, or you entered an invalid drive name or
     invalid syntax on the command line.
5    Disk write error occurred.
```

You can write a batch file testing for exit codes.

11.17 ACTIVITY: USING IF ERRORLEVEL WITH XCOPY

Note: The DATA disk should be in Drive A. The displayed prompt is A:\>.

Step 1   Use any text editor to create and save a file called **ERROR.BAT**. Key in the following:

                  XCOPY %1 %2 [Enter]
                  IF ERRORLEVEL 2 GOTO message [Enter]
                  IF ERRORLEVEL 1 GOTO NOTOK [Enter]
                  IF ERRORLEVEL 0 GOTO OK [Enter]
                  :message [Enter]
                  ECHO You used Ctrl + Break and did not copy any files. [Enter]

GOTO END [Enter]
:NOTOK [Enter]
ECHO There are no %1 files. Try again. [Enter]
GOTO END [Enter]
:OK [Enter]
ECHO You copied the %1 files successfully. [Enter]
:END

Step 2   Key in the following: A:\>**ERROR *.TXT OLDER** [Enter]

```
MS-DOS Prompt                                                    _ □ ✕

CHKDSK.TXT
Sandy and Nicki.txt
JANUARY.TXT
GOODBYE.TXT
APRIL.TXT
FEBRUARY.TXT
HELLO.TXT
BYE.TXT
Sandy and Patty.txt
DANCES.TXT
TEST.TXT
        11 File(s) copied

A:\>IF ERRORLEVEL 2 GOTO message

A:\>IF ERRORLEVEL 1 GOTO NOTOK

A:\>IF ERRORLEVEL 0 GOTO OK

A:\>ECHO You copied the *.TXT files successfully.
You copied the *.TXT files successfully.

A:\>

A:\>_
```

WHAT'S
HAPPENING!   You successfully copied the **.TXT** files to the **OLDER** subdirectory. The
              exit code that was generated by XCOPY gave you the message that the
              copy was successful.

Step 3   Key in the following: A:\>**ERROR *.NON OLDER** [Enter]

```
MS-DOS Prompt                                                    _ □ ✕

A:\>ERROR *.NON OLDER

A:\>XCOPY *.NON OLDER
File not found - *.NON
        0 File(s) copied

A:\>IF ERRORLEVEL 2 GOTO message

A:\>IF ERRORLEVEL 1 GOTO NOTOK

A:\>ECHO There are no *.NON files. Try again.
There are no *.NON files. Try again.
```

```
A:\>GOTO END

A:\>

A:\>_
```

**WHAT'S
HAPPENING?**　　Again, the exit code was correctly read. As you can see, you can use the exit codes successfully in a batch file. Since programs like XCOPY give you a message anyway when it could not find the file or files, you may ask yourself, why go to the trouble of writing a batch file? The reason is that you can write a small program to test for other kinds of information.

11.18 WRITING PROGRAMS TO TEST FOR KEY CODES

Rather than being limited to the exit codes that are set by operating system programs, you can write a small program that will create an exit code based on some activity. For instance, a program can be written that will identify which key was pressed and report which key it was. You can do this because every time you press a key, it is identified by a one- or two-digit *scan code*. Actually, two things are reported when you press any key on the keyboard. First, that you pressed a key. Second, that you released the key. The keyboard controller tells the CPU that some keyboard activity is occurring. The stream of bytes is converted into the scan code, which identifies the specific key (see Appendix C for a list of scan codes for all the keys).

You are going to write a program that will report the scan code for any key that is pressed on the keyboard. Once you know the reported code, you can test for a specific key using ERRORLEVEL in the batch file. The batch file can then act based on the reported code. In order to do this, you must write a program. Remember, to be executed, a program must be in "bits and bytes"—the 0s and 1s the computer understands.

There are several ways to write a program. One is to know a programming language and be able to turn the programming language program (source code) into executable code (object code). This is called compiling a program—turning a language into code. That task is beyond the scope of this text. Fortunately, there is an easier way that you can create a small program—using an operating system utility program called DEBUG.

DEBUG can directly modify bytes in a file. DEBUG allows you to test and debug executable files—those with a .COM or .EXE file extension. Remember, you cannot use TYPE to look at a file with the extension of .EXE or .COM because those file extensions indicate programs that are not ASCII-readable files. DEBUG is a small program that has its own commands and syntax. If you know the commands of the DEBUG program and the rules of programming, you could write a .COM program directly with DEBUG. Unless you are a programming expert, you will probably not want to do this.

The easiest way to use DEBUG is to create a script or a *script file*. A script is a set of instructions that you can write in any ASCII editor. Once you have written the script, you can "feed" it to the DEBUG program via redirection (DEBUG <

SCRIPT.FIL). DEBUG will then convert the script file to an executable program with a .COM file extension. Once you have a .COM file, you can execute it as you do any program. This process is the simplest way to create a file that will report the scan code for any key that is pressed. The program you create will be called REPLY.COM.

Since using DEBUG directly can be tricky, the example below shows a .COM program written with DEBUG that will return the scan code of a pressed key. If you want to try to use DEBUG directly, what appears on the screen in this example will be in `this typeface` and what you key in will be in **this typeface**. The hyphen (-) and the colon (:) are prompts presented to you by the DEBUG program. Instructions such as 100 assemble the program at memory address 100 (hexadecimal). 12B3 will vary from machine to machine. In the example shown here, 12B3:0100 represents segment/offset memory address. You must press Enter after each line and also when Enter is specified. Following is a summary of commands available within the DEBUG program.

```
assemble     A [address]
compare      C range address
dump         D [range]
enter        E address [list]
fill         F range list
go           G [=address] [addresses]
hex          H value1 value2
input        I port
load         L [address] [drive] [firstsector] [number]
move         M range address
name         N [pathname] [arglist]
output       O port byte
proceed      P [=address] [number]
quit         Q
register     R [register]
search       S range list
trace        T [=address] [value]
unassemble   U [range]
write        W [address] [drive] [firstsector] [number]

allocate expanded memory       XA [#pages]
deallocate expanded memory     XD [handle]
map expanded memory pages      XM [Lpage] [Ppage] [handle]
display expanded memory status XS
```

The following is shown as an example of how to use DEBUG, but you do not have to do this. If you do, note the differences between the letter l and the number 1. Be sure and check with your lab administrator before attempting to key in this example. Be very sure you are at the A:\> prompt.

```
A:\>DEBUG

A:\>DEBUG
-a 100 Enter
158E:0100 mov ah,8 Enter
158E:0102 int 21 Enter
158E:0104 cmp al,0 Enter
158E:0106 jnz 10a Enter
158E:0108 int 21 Enter
158E:010A mov ah,4c Enter
```

```
158E:010C  int 21 [Enter]
158E:010E  [Enter]
-r cx [Enter]
CX 0000
:e [Enter]
-n reply.com [Enter]
-w [Enter]
Writing 0000E bytes
-q [Enter]
```

An easier way to create REPLY.COM is to create a script file. Again, a script file is merely a text file that contains a series of commands that can be redirected into DEBUG to create a .COM file. The script file is not the program. You use any text editor, name the file, in this case REPLY.SCR, and key in the following commands. Then, to make REPLY.SCR an executable program, you redirect it into DEBUG to create REPLY.COM. The next activity will show you how to create REPLY.SCR and REPLY.COM. (*Note:* You may want to check with your instructor to see if he or she has created REPLY.COM for you.)

11.19 ACTIVITY: WRITING A SCRIPT FILE

Note: The DATA disk should be in Drive A. The displayed prompt is A:\>.

Step 1   Use any text editor to create and save a file called **REPLY.SCR**. Key in the following:

e 100 b4 08 cd 21 3c 00 75 02 cd 21 b4 4c cd 21 [Enter]

rcx [Enter]

e [Enter]

n reply.com [Enter]

w [Enter]

q

WHAT'S HAPPENING? ➤ Now that you have written **REPLY.SCR**, you must now "assemble" it or convert it into the bytes that make it a program. You do this by redirecting the script file into DEBUG.

Step 2   Key in the following: A:\>**DEBUG < REPLY.SCR** [Enter]

```
MS-DOS Prompt                                          _ □ ✕

A:\>DEBUG < REPLY.SCR
-e 100 b4 08 cd 21 3c 00 75 02 cd 21 b4 4c cd 21
-rcx
CX 0000
:e
-n  reply.com
-w
Writing 0000E bytes
-q

A:\>_
```

WHAT'S HAPPENING? You have compiled **REPLY.SCR** into a program called **REPLY.COM**.

Step 3   Key in the following: A:\>**DIR REPLY.COM** Enter

```
MS-DOS Prompt                                                    _ □ ×

A:\>DIR REPLY.COM

 Volume in drive A is DATA
 Volume Serial Number is 3330-1807
 Directory of A:\

REPLY     COM             14  12-26-01  8:55p REPLY.COM
          1 file(s)              14 bytes
          0 dir(s)          890,368 bytes free

A:\>_
```

WHAT'S HAPPENING? Now that you have written a program, you want to use it in a batch file.

Step 4   Use any text editor to create and save a file called **KEYS.BAT** that
          contains the following:
          ECHO PRESS F1 TO CLEAR THE SCREEN.
          ECHO PRESS F2 TO DISPLAY THE DIRECTORY.
          ECHO PRESS ANY OTHER KEY TO EXIT.
          REPLY
          IF ERRORLEVEL 61 GOTO END
          IF ERRORLEVEL 60 GOTO F2
          IF ERRORLEVEL 59 GOTO F1
          GOTO END
          :F1
          CLS
          GOTO END
          :F2
          DIR
          :END

WHAT'S HAPPENING? This is a simple batch file that checks the scan codes you generate by
          pressing a key. Checking IF ERRORLEVEL codes in descending order is
          critical because the command is tested to determine if the error code is
          equal to or greater than the value specified. In this program, if you press
          a key that returns a value of 61 or above, you exit the program. If you
          press F2, it returns a code of 60. If you press F1, it returns a code of 59.
          If none of those conditions exist, then you exit the batch file.

Step 5   Key in the following: A:\>**KEYS** Enter

```
MS-DOS Prompt                                                    _ □ ×

A:\>KEYS

A:\>ECHO PRESS F1 TO CLEAR THE SCREEN.
PRESS F1 TO CLEAR THE SCREEN.
```

```
A:\>ECHO PRESS F2 TO DISPLAY THE DIRECTORY
PRESS F2 TO DISPLAY THE DIRECTORY

A:\>ECHO PRESS ANY OTHER KEY TO EXIT.
PRESS ANY OTHER KEY TO EXIT.

A:\>REPLY
_
```

WHAT'S HAPPENING? ➤ You have executed the **KEYS** batch file. The program called **REPLY.COM** is waiting for you to press a key.

Step 6   Press [F1]

```
MS-DOS Prompt                                                    _ □ ✕

A:\>GOTO END

A:\>

A:\>_
```

WHAT'S HAPPENING? ➤ Pressing [F1] cleared the screen.

Step 7   Key in the following: A:\>**KEYS** [Enter]

Step 8   Press [F2]

```
MS-DOS Prompt                                                    _ □ ✕

KILLIT    BAT          94  08-20-01  2:28p  KILLIT.BAT
TESTING   BAT         115  08-20-01  2:00p  TESTING.BAT
HPB       BAT          19  08-13-01  4:12p  HPB.BAT
N         BAT          30  08-13-01  4:40p  N.BAT
TEST      BAT         157  08-20-01  2:04p  TEST.BAT
LAST      ONE          72  10-10-99  4:53p  LAST.ONE
ALPHA     BAT         104  08-26-01  7:16p  ALPHA.BAT
UPDATE    BAT          89  12-26-00  8:06p  UPDATE.BAT
NOCOPY    BAT         203  08-20-01  2:47p  NOCOPY.BAT
DCOMP     BAT         253  08-20-01  3:05p  DCOMP.BAT
ONE       BAT         198  08-26-01  7:04p  ONE.BAT
REPEAT    BAT         104  08-26-01  7:13p  REPEAT.BAT
SIZE      BAT         258  12-26-01  8:41p  SIZE.BAT
REPLY     COM          14  12-26-01  8:55p  REPLY.COM
GREET     BAT         191  08-26-01  7:56p  GREET.BAT
RENDIR    BAT         244  12-26-01  8:11p  RENDIR.BAT
OLDER         <DIR>       08-05-01  3:19p  OLDER
REPLY     SCR          90  12-26-01  8:55p  REPLY.SCR
KEYS      BAT         243  12-26-01  8:56p  KEYS.BAT
       67 file(s)          53,529 bytes
        8 dir(s)          889,856 bytes free

A:\>

A:\>_
```

WHAT'S HAPPENING? ➤ Pressing [F2] gave you a directory of your disk. As you can see, **REPLY.COM** checked the scan code returned by the key you pressed and followed the instruction in the batch file based on the key you pressed. Writing **.COM** programs can be difficult. Thus, the CHOICE command was introduced in DOS 6.0.

11.20 THE CHOICE COMMAND

The CHOICE command is an external command. It will display an optional message and wait for the user to press a key. If you do not specify which keys you want the user of the batch file to choose from, CHOICE uses **Y** or **N** by default. But you can choose your own values. You can make CHOICE case sensitive, but by default it is not case sensitive. When you use CHOICE, ERRORLEVEL is set to indicate which key is pressed. You can even specify a time-out period ranging from 0 to 99 seconds. Time-out means that if the time elapses and the user has not pressed a key, CHOICE will end and set ERRORLEVEL to the default key.

CHOICE does have drawbacks. Although CHOICE accepts most keys on the keyboard, it does not support the [Space Bar], any function keys, or any key combinations such as [Ctrl] + **J**. There is no easy way to set CHOICE to accept any key or to accept a word or phrase. In addition, CHOICE supports only a single pressed key. Nonetheless, CHOICE can still be useful. The syntax is:

```
CHOICE [/C[:]choices] [/N] [/S] [/T[:]c,nn] [text]

/C[:]choices   Specifies allowable keys. Default is YN
/N             Do not display choices and ? at end of prompt string.
/S             Treat choice keys as case sensitive.
/T[:]c,nn      Default choice to c after nn seconds
text           Prompt string to display

ERRORLEVEL is set to offset of key user presses in choices.
```

11.21 ACTIVITY: USING CHOICE

Note: The DATA disk should be in Drive A. The displayed prompt is A:\>.

Step 1   Key in the following: A:\>**COPY KEYS.BAT KEYTWO.BAT** [Enter]

```
┌─────────────────────────────────────────────────────────────────┐
│ MS-DOS Prompt                                          _ □ ×      │
├─────────────────────────────────────────────────────────────────┤
│ A:\>COPY KEYS.BAT KEYTWO.BAT                                      │
│         1 file(s) copied                                          │
│                                                                   │
│ A:\>_                                                             │
│                                                                   │
└─────────────────────────────────────────────────────────────────┘
```

WHAT'S HAPPENING?   You have made a copy of the **KEYS.BAT** file. You are going to edit **KEYTWO.BAT**.

Step 2   Use any text editor to edit and save **KEYTWO.BAT** so it looks as follows:
ECHO PRESS 1 TO CLEAR THE SCREEN.
ECHO PRESS 2 TO DISPLAY THE DIRECTORY.
ECHO PRESS 3 TO EXIT.
CHOICE /C123
IF ERRORLEVEL 3 GOTO END

```
IF ERRORLEVEL 2 GOTO DISP
IF ERRORLEVEL 1 GOTO CLEAR
GOTO END
:CLEAR
CLS
GOTO END
:DISP
DIR
:END
```

WHAT'S HAPPENING? ➤ You have written a batch file using CHOICE. Notice that 1 and 2 and 3 do not need to be separated by any punctuation.

Step 3   Key in the following: A:\>**KEYTWO** [Enter]

```
MS-DOS Prompt                                              _ □ ×

A:\>KEYTWO

A:\>ECHO PRESS 1 TO CLEAR THE SCREEN.
PRESS 1 TO CLEAR THE SCREEN.

A:\>ECHO PRESS 2 TO DISPLAY THE DIRECTORY.
PRESS 2 TO DISPLAY THE DIRECTORY.

A:\>ECHO PRESS 3 TO EXIT.
PRESS 3 TO EXIT.

A:\>CHOICE /C123
[1,2,3]?_
```

WHAT'S HAPPENING? ➤ The choices are displayed as **[1,2,3]?_**. The CHOICE command formats the choices by placing the brackets around the choices as well as including the question mark. You simply press a number as directed.

Step 4   Press **1**

```
MS-DOS Prompt                                              _ □ ×

A:\>GOTO END

A:\>

A:\>_
```

WHAT'S HAPPENING? ➤ Your batch file ran successfully. There is another way to use CHOICE with an IF and IF NOT ERRORLEVEL test, which saves the trouble of using a GOTO statement. You can also customize what the choice will look like. You may also use letters of the alphabet in your choice statement.

Step 5   Use any text editor to create and save a batch file called **MYDIR.BAT**. Key in the following:

CLS [Enter]
ECHO How do you want your directory displayed? [Enter]
ECHO. [Enter]
ECHO 1. Files only arranged by file name.   **A to Z** [Enter]
ECHO 2. Files only arranged by file name.   **Z to A** [Enter]
ECHO 3. Files only arranged by file extension.   **A to Z** [Enter]
ECHO e. Files only arranged by file extension.   **Z to A** [Enter]
ECHO. [Enter]
CHOICE /N /C123e Please select a number or letter. [Enter]
IF ERRORLEVEL 1 IF NOT ERRORLEVEL 2 DIR /ON /A-D /P [Enter]
IF ERRORLEVEL 2 IF NOT ERRORLEVEL 3 DIR /O-N /A-D /P [Enter]
IF ERRORLEVEL 3 IF NOT ERRORLEVEL 4 DIR /OE /A-D /P [Enter]
IF ERRORLEVEL 4 IF NOT ERRORLEVEL 5 DIR /O-E /A-D /P

WHAT'S
HAPPENING? ► There are several interesting items in this batch file. First, observe the
IF ERRORLEVEL statement. You must test IF ERRORLEVEL state-
ments in descending order but test IF NOT ERRORLEVEL statements in
ascending order. Because you specified a range (if 1 but not 2) you have
limited your choice to one answer. Hence, you can write the batch file as
above. In addition, you can place the command immediately after the
ERRORLEVEL statement.

Now look at the **CHOICE** line. The **/N** suppresses the default format—
brackets and a question mark. You supplied the format you wanted. The
Please select a number or letter is your replacement for the default
message and format. You also included the letter **e** to show you that you
may use letters as well as numbers in a CHOICE menu.

Step 6   Key in the following: A:\>**MYDIR** [Enter]

```
MS-DOS Prompt                                                    _ □ ✕

A:\>ECHO How do you want your directory displayed?
How do you want your directory displayed?

A:\>ECHO.

A:\>ECHO 1. Files only arranged by file name.          A to Z
1. Files only arranged by file name.          A to Z

A:\>ECHO 2. Files only arranged by file name.          Z to A
2. Files only arranged by file name.          Z to A

A:\>ECHO 3. Files only arranged by file extension.   A to Z
3. Files only arranged by file extension.     A to Z

A:\>ECHO e. Files only arranged by file extension.   Z to A
e. Files only arranged by file extension.     Z to A

A:\>ECHO.

A:\>CHOICE /N /C123e  Please select a number or letter.
Please select a number or letter._
```

WHAT'S HAPPENING? Your choices are ready.

Step 7   Press **E**

```
MS-DOS Prompt                                                    _ □ ×

    Volume in drive A is DATA
    Volume Serial Number is 3330-1807
    Directory of A:\

    CHKDSK    TXT        2,663   08-02-01   4:13p  CHKDSK.TXT
    SANDYA~1  TXT           53   11-16-00  12:00p  Sandy and Nicki.txt
    JANUARY   TXT          148   08-05-01   3:26p  JANUARY.TXT
    GOODBYE   TXT           34   01-01-02   4:32a  GOODBYE.TXT
    APRIL     TXT           72   06-16-00   4:32p  APRIL.TXT
    FEBRUARY  TXT           75   06-16-00   4:32p  FEBRUARY.TXT
    HELLO     TXT           53   05-30-00   4:32p  HELLO.TXT
    BYE       TXT           45   05-30-00   4:32p  BYE.TXT
    SANDYA~2  TXT           59   11-16-00  12:00p  Sandy and Patty.txt
    DANCES    TXT           72   12-11-99   4:03p  DANCES.TXT
    TEST      TXT           65   12-11-99   4:03p  TEST.TXT
    DRAMA     TV           213   07-03-00   1:24p  DRAMA.TV
    APR       TST           72   04-23-00   4:18p  APR.TST
    TEST      TKR       16,516   07-24-01   1:52p  TEST.TKR
    HOMEBUD   TKR        8,064   01-01-99   5:00a  HOMEBUD.TKR
    FILE3     SWT           19   12-06-00   2:45p  FILE3.SWT
    FILE2     SWT           19   12-06-00   2:45p  FILE2.SWT
    REPLY     SCR           90   12-26-01   8:55p  REPLY.SCR
    JOINED    SAM          108   07-24-01   1:48p  JOINED.SAM
    Press any key to continue . . .
```

WHAT'S HAPPENING? Your files are arranged in reverse order by file extension. To "clean up" any of these batch files, you would simply place @ECHO OFF as the first line of the file, and CLS as the second. For demonstration purposes, it is better not to add these lines, as we want to see how the file is working.

Step 8   Press **Enter** until you have returned to the prompt.

11.22 THE ENVIRONMENT

The environment is an area that the operating system sets aside in memory. It is like a scratch pad where notes are kept about important items that the operating system needs to know. The environment is like post-it notes. Application programs can read any items in the environment and can post their own messages there. What the operating system places and keeps in the environment is the location of the file COMMAND.COM. It also keeps track of the path, if one is set, and the prompt, if it is changed. You can also leave messages there via the AUTOEXEC.BAT file, other batch files, or from the command line. You do this with the SET command. Environmental variables set by the operating system, or in the AUTOEXEC.BAT file will remain in effect throughout the entire work session at the computer. Those set in the MS-DOS window or in batch files executed in the MS-DOS window will remain in effect *only* during that MS-DOS session. While values are in effect, you can use the syntax *%variablename%*, which will use the value of the environment variable.

The internal command SET allows you to display what is currently in the environment, set environmental variables, or delete environmental variables. The syntax is:

```
SET [variable=[string]]

variable  Specifies the environment-variable name.
string    Specifies a series of characters to assign to the
          variable.

Type SET without parameters to display the current environment
variables.
```

11.23 ACTIVITY: USING SET AND THE ENVIRONMENT IN BATCH FILES

Note: The DATA disk should be in Drive A. The displayed prompt is A:\>.

Step 1   Close the MS-DOS window, and reopen it to begin a new DOS session. Return to the A:\> prompt.

Step 2   Key in the following: A:\>**SET** [Enter]

```
MS-DOS Prompt                                                    _ □ ×

A:\>SET
COMSPEC=C:\WINDOWS\COMMAND.COM
PATH=C:\WINDOWS;C:\WINDOWS\COMMAND
PROMPT=$P$G
TEMP=C:\WINDOWS\TEMP
TMP=C:\WINDOWS\TEMP
winbootdir=C:\WINDOWS
windir=C:\WINDOWS
BLASTER=A220 I5 D1 T4 P330
CMDLINE=doskey /insert

A:\>_
```

WHAT'S HAPPENING?   Your environment will vary based on how your computer is set up. However, you will have a **winbootdir** statement, a **COMSPEC** statement, a **windir** statement, and most likely a **PATH** statement and a **PROMPT** statement. These statements represent information the operating system needs to know.

Step 3   Write and save the following batch file called **TESTIT.BAT**.
          @ECHO OFF
          ECHO %PATH%
          ECHO.

Step 4   Key in the following: A:\>**TESTIT** [Enter]

```
MS-DOS Prompt                                                    _ □ ×

A:\>TESTIT
C:\WINDOWS;C:\WINDOWS\COMMAND

A:\>_
```

WHAT'S HAPPENING? ▶ The screen display created by this batch file showed the path used in an MS-DOS Prompt window on your system. Notice that it did not return the word PATH but the value stored in the environmental variable "PATH." You can set an environmental value and then use it in a batch file.

Step 5   Key in the following: A:\>**SET TODAY=C:\WINDOSBK*.99** [Enter]

Step 6   Key in the following: A:\>**SET** [Enter]

```
MS-DOS Prompt                                                    _ □ ✕

A:\>SET TODAY=C:\WINDOSBK\*.99

A:\>SET

COMSPEC=C:\WINDOWS\COMMAND.COM
PATH=C:\WINDOWS;C:\WINDOWS\COMMAND
PROMPT=$P$G
TEMP=C:\WINDOWS\TEMP
TMP=C:\WINDOWS\TEMP
winbootdir=C:\WINDOWS
windir=C:\WINDOWS
BLASTER=A220 I5 D1 T4 P330
CMDLINE=doskey /insert
TODAY=C:\WINDOSBK\*.99_
```

WHAT'S HAPPENING? ▶ You now have a value for TODAY, which you set in the environment as **C:\WINDOSBK*.99**. Now, as long as you do not close the MSDOS window, you can use it in a batch file. When you close the MS-DOS window, the environmental variables you set there will disappear.

Step 7   Write and save the following batch file called **SETTING.BAT**. Key in the following:
DIR %today% [Enter]
ECHO %TODAY%

Step 8   Key in the following: A:\>**SETTING** [Enter]

```
MS-DOS Prompt                                                    _ □ ✕

A:\>SETTING

A:\>DIR C:\WINDOSBK\*.99

 Volume in drive C is MILLENNIUM
 Volume Serial Number is 2B18-1301
 Directory of C:\WINDOSBK

APR      99              72   10-10-99  4:53p APR.99
FEB      99              75   10-10-99  4:53p FEB.99
MAR      99              71   10-10-99  4:53p MAR.99
JAN      99              73   10-10-99  4:53p JAN.99
         4 file(s)            291 bytes
         0 dir(s)     593,924,096 bytes free

A:\>ECHO C:\WINDOSBK\*.99
C:\WINDOSBK\*.99
```

```
A:\>

A:\>_
```

WHAT'S HAPPENING! ⮞ Your batch file needed a value for %today%. The percent signs indicate that the value was in the environment. It substituted **C:\WINDOSBK*.99** for %today% and for %TODAY%. Case does not matter with environmental variables. You can use another value.

Step 9 Key in the following: A:\>**SET today=C:\WINDOSBK*.TMP** Enter

Step 10 Key in the following: A:\>**SETTING** Enter

```
MS-DOS Prompt                                                    _ □ ×

A:\>DIR C:\WINDOSBK\*.TMP

 Volume in drive C is MILLENNIUM
 Volume Serial Number is 2B18-1301
 Directory of C:\WINDOSBK

APRIL     TMP              72   04-23-00   4:03p APRIL.TMP
BONJOUR   TMP              53   04-23-00   4:03p BONJOUR.TMP
FEB       TMP              75   04-23-00   4:03p FEB.TMP
GOODBYE   TMP              34   01-01-02   4:32a GOODBYE.TMP
JANUARY   TMP              73   04-23-00   4:03p JANUARY.TMP
JAN       TMP              73   04-23-00   4:03p JAN.TMP
MAR       TMP              71   04-23-00   4:03p MAR.TMP
MARCH     TMP              71   04-23-00   4:03p MARCH.TMP
APR       TMP              72   04-23-00   4:18p APR.TMP
         9 file(s)              594 bytes
         0 dir(s)       593,924,096 bytes free

A:\>ECHO C:\WINDOSBK\*.TMP
 C:\WINDOSBK\*.TMP

A:\>

A:\>_
```

WHAT'S HAPPENING! ⮞ Since you changed the value of %today% from **C:\WINDOSBK*.99** to **C:\WINDOSBK*.TMP**, the batch file knew to get only the value in the environment called %today%. To eliminate the value, you must set it to nothing.

Step 11 Key in the following: A:\>**SET TODAY=** Enter

Step 12 Key in the following: A:\>**SET** Enter

```
MS-DOS Prompt                                                    _ □ ×

A:\>SET TODAY=

A:\>SET
COMSPEC=C:\WINDOWS\COMMAND.COM
PATH=C:\WINDOWS;C:\WINDOWS\COMMAND
PROMPT=$P$G
TEMP=C:\WINDOWS\TEMP
```

```
TMP=C:\WINDOWS\TEMP
winbootdir=C:\WINDOWS
windir=C:\WINDOWS
BLASTER=A220 I5 D1 T4 P330
CMDLINE=EDIT SETTING.BAT

A:\>_
```

WHAT'S HAPPENING? Notice the last program you executed is recorded under the variable CMDLINE. The first time you issued the SET command, if you were at the beginning of a new DOS session, the CMDLINE variable reflected the automatic loading of DOSKEY. You had run no previous programs. CMDLINE now reflects the use of the Edit program. You no longer have an environmental value called TODAY. That environmental variable would have been eliminated automatically if you had closed and reopened the MS-DOS window.

Step 13   Key in the following: A:\>**SET TODAY=FRIDAY** Enter

Step 14   Key in the following: A:\>**ECHO %TODAY%** Enter

Step 15   Key in the following: A:\>**SET** Enter

```
MS-DOS Prompt                                        _ □ ×

A:\>SET TODAY=FRIDAY

A:\>ECHO %TODAY%
FRIDAY

A:\>SET
COMSPEC=C:\WINDOWS\COMMAND.COM
PATH=C:\WINDOWS;C:\WINDOWS\COMMAND
PROMPT=$P$G
TEMP=C:\WINDOWS\TEMP
TMP=C:\WINDOWS\TEMP
winbootdir=C:\WINDOWS
windir=C:\WINDOWS
BLASTER=A220 I5 D1 T4 P330
CMDLINE=EDIT SETTING.BAT
TODAY=FRIDAY

A:\>_
```

WHAT'S HAPPENING? You have set a new environmental variable with the value of FRIDAY. You have used the variable syntax *%variablename%* to display the value of the variable. You have also used the SET command to see the current environment.

Step 16   Close the MS-DOS window.

Step 17   Reopen the MS-DOS window and return to the A prompt.

Step 18   Key in the following: A:\>**SET** Enter

```
MS-DOS Prompt                                                    _ □ ×

A:\>SET
COMSPEC=C:\WINDOWS\COMMAND.COM
PATH=C:\WINDOWS;C:\WINDOWS\COMMAND
PROMPT=$P$G
TEMP=C:\WINDOWS\TEMP
TMP=C:\WINDOWS\TEMP
winbootdir=C:\WINDOWS
windir=C:\WINDOWS
BLASTER=A220 I5 D1 T4 P330
CMDLINE=doskey /insert

A:\>_
```

WHAT'S HAPPENING? ▶ The TODAY variable is no longer there. (If you wanted an environmental variable to be available during all DOS sessions, you would make the assignment in the AUTOEXEC.BAT file.) Once again, the CMDLINE variable reflects the insertion of DOSKEY, as no other programs have been executed from the command line since this MS-DOS window was opened. You can create a useful batch file that you can use during a DOS session. You don't often want to add a directory to your PATH statement, but perhaps you will be doing a lot of work at the MS-DOS prompt using files that are in the root of the A drive. To do this by hand would involve keying in the entire path you currently have and adding your new directory to the end. There is an easier way to do it using the environment.

Note: The default prompt is A:\>.

Step 19 Write and save the following batch file called **ADD.BAT**. Key in the following:
> **IF "%1"=="" GOTO END** Enter
> **PATH > OLDPATH.BAT** Enter
> **:TOP** Enter
> **PATH %PATH%;%1** Enter
> **SHIFT** Enter
> **IF NOT \%1\==\\ GOTO TOP** Enter
> **:END**

Step 20 Key in the following: A:\>**PATH > ORIGPATH.BAT** Enter

Step 21 Key in the following: A:\>**ADD A:\PROG\GAMES** Enter

```
MS-DOS Prompt                                                    _ □ ×

A:\>PATH > ORIGPATH.BAT

A:\>ADD A:\PROG\GAMES

A:\>IF "A:\PROG\GAMES"=="" GOTO END

A:\>PATH > OLDPATH.BAT
```

```
A:\>PATH C:\WINDOWS;C:\WINDOWS\COMMAND;A:\PROG\GAMES

A:\>SHIFT

A:\>IF NOT \\==\\ GOTO TOP

A:\>

A:\>_
```

WHAT'S HAPPENING? To preserve your default path, you saved it to a file called **ORIGPATH.BAT**. You then used your new batch file, **ADD.BAT**, and added the games directory to the path. You can add more than one directory.

Step 22   Key in the following: A:\>**ORIGPATH** Enter

Step 23   Key in the following: A:\>**ADD A:\PROG\UTILS OLDER CLASS** Enter

```
MS-DOS Prompt                                                      _ □ ×

A:\>IF "A:\PROG\UTILS"=="" GOTO END

A:\>PATH > OLDPATH.BAT

A:\>PATH C:\WINDOWS;C:\WINDOWS\COMMAND;A:\PROG\UTILS

A:\>SHIFT

A:\>IF NOT \OLDER\==\\ GOTO TOP

A:\>PATH C:\WINDOWS;C:\WINDOWS\COMMAND;A:\PROG\UTILS;OLDER

A:\>SHIFT

A:\>IF NOT \CLASS\==\\ GOTO TOP

A:\>PATH C:\WINDOWS;C:\WINDOWS\COMMAND;A:\PROG\UTILS;OLDER;CLASS

A:\>SHIFT

A:\>IF NOT \\==\\ GOTO TOP

A:\>

A:\>_
```

WHAT'S HAPPENING? You have quickly added new directories to your path.

Step 24   Key in the following: A:\>**PATH** Enter

```
MS-DOS Prompt                                                      _ □ ×

A:\>PATH
PATH=C:\WINDOWS;C:\WINDOWS\COMMAND;A:\PROG\UTILS;OLDER;CLASS

A:\>_
```

WHAT'S HAPPENING? ▶ You keyed in **PATH** to confirm that you added subdirectories. To return to your original path, you created **ORIGPATH.BAT**.

Step 25 Key in the following: A:\>**ORIGPATH** [Enter]

```
  MS-DOS Prompt                                                      _ □ ×

 A:\>ORIGPATH

 A:\>PATH=C:\WINDOWS;C:\WINDOWS\COMMAND

 A:\>

 A:\>_
```

11.24 THE DIRCMD ENVIRONMENTAL VARIABLE

The environment is an area that is set aside in memory. In addition to being able to place and use variables in the environment, you can preset DIR command parameters and switches by including the SET command with the DIRCMD environmental variable. This means that if you prefer the DIR command to display your files in alphabetic order by name every time, you can place a SET DIRCMD in AUTOEXEC.BAT. Keying in SET by itself will tell you what is in the environment. You can use the DIRCMD variable and ERRORLEVEL to write a batch file that will allow you to change the way DIR displays information for the current MS-DOS work session.

11.25 ACTIVITY: USING DIRCMD

Note: The DATA disk should be in Drive A. The displayed prompt is A:\>.

Step 1 Key in the following: A:\>**COPY MYDIR.BAT MY.BAT** [Enter]

```
  MS-DOS Prompt                                                      _ □ ×

 A:\>COPY MYDIR.BAT MY.BAT
        1 file(s) copied

 A:\>_
```

WHAT'S HAPPENING? ▶ You have made a copy of the **MYDIR.BAT** file. You are going to edit **MY.BAT**.

Step 2 Use any text editor to edit and save **MY.BAT** so it looks as follows:
@ECHO OFF
CLS
ECHO How do you want your directory displayed?
ECHO.
ECHO 1. Files only arranged by file name.   **A to Z**
ECHO 2. Files only arranged by file name.   **Z to A**

ECHO 3. Files only arranged by file extension.   A to Z
ECHO 4. Files only arranged by file extension.   Z to A
ECHO 5. Directory displays in default mode.
ECHO.
CHOICE /N /C12345 Please select a number.
IF ERRORLEVEL 1 IF NOT ERRORLEVEL 2 SET DIRCMD=/ON /A-D
IF ERRORLEVEL 2 IF NOT ERRORLEVEL 3 SET DIRCMD=/O-N /A-D
IF ERRORLEVEL 3 IF NOT ERRORLEVEL 4 SET DIRCMD=/OE /A-D
IF ERRORLEVEL 4 IF NOT ERRORLEVEL 5 SET DIRCMD=/O-E /A-D
IF ERRORLEVEL 5 IF NOT ERRORLEVEL 6 SET DIRCMD=

WHAT'S HAPPENING?   You have created a batch file to set the DIRCMD environmental variable.

Step 3   Key in the following: A:\>**MY** [Enter]

```
MS-DOS Prompt                                                    _ □ ×

How do you want your directory displayed?

1. Files only arranged by file name.       A to Z
2. Files only arranged by file name.       Z to A
3. Files only arranged by file extension.  A to Z
4. Files only arranged by file extension.  Z to A
5. Directory displays in default mode.

Please select a number._
```

WHAT'S HAPPENING?   So far this looks very similar to **MYDIR.BAT**.

Step 4   Key in the following: **4**

Step 5   Key in the following: A:\>**SET** [Enter]

```
MS-DOS Prompt                                                    _ □ ×

A:\>SET
COMSPEC=C:\WINDOWS\COMMAND.COM
PROMPT=$P$G
TEMP=C:\WINDOWS\TEMP
TMP=C:\WINDOWS\TEMP
winbootdir=C:\WINDOWS
windir=C:\WINDOWS
BLASTER=A220 I5 D1 T4 P330
PATH=C:\WINDOWS;C:\WINDOWS\COMMAND
CMDLINE=CHOICE /N /C12345  Please select a number.
DIRCMD=/O-E /A-D

A:\>_
```

WHAT'S HAPPENING?   Now during this MS-DOS prompt session, whenever you key in **DIR**, it will automatically arrange the files by extension in reverse order. You can see that you have established the environmental variable for DIRCMD to equal the switch /O-E and /A-D. The CMDLINE variable reflects the last program used at the command line—CHOICE.

Step 6   Key in the following: A:\>**DIR CLASS** [Enter]

```
MS-DOS Prompt                                                    _ □ ×

A:\>DIR CLASS

 Volume in drive A is DATA
 Volume Serial Number is 3330-1807
 Directory of A:\CLASS

JAN      PAR          73   04-23-00   4:03p JAN.PAR
FEB      PAR          75   04-23-00   4:03p FEB.PAR
MAR      PAR          71   04-23-00   4:03p MAR.PAR
APR      PAR          72   04-23-00   4:18p APR.PAR
MAR      FIL          71   10-10-99   4:53p MAR.FIL
JAN      FIL          72   10-10-99   4:53p JAN.FIL
JAN      BUD          73   04-23-00   4:03p JAN.BUD
MAR      BUD          71   04-23-00   4:03p MAR.BUD
APR      BUD          19   12-06-00   2:45p APR.BUD
JAN      ABC          73   04-23-00   4:03p JAN.ABC
FEB      ABC          75   04-23-00   4:03p FEB.ABC
MAR      ABC          71   04-23-00   4:03p MAR.ABC
APR      ABC          72   04-23-00   4:18p APR.ABC
         13 file(s)             888 bytes
          0 dir(s)          884,736 bytes free

A:\>_
```

WHAT'S HAPPENING! ➤ The files are arranged by file extension in reverse alphabetical order.
Until you change the values, or close this MS-DOS session, every time
you issue the DIR command it will display file names in reverse alphabetical order by file extension.

Step 7   Key in the following: A:\>**MY** [Enter]

Step 8   Press **5**

Step 9   Key in the following: A:\>**SET** [Enter]

```
MS-DOS Prompt                                                    _ □ ×

How do you want your directory displayed?

1. Files only arranged by file name.        A to Z
2. Files only arranged by file name.        Z to A
3. Files only arranged by file extension.   A to Z
4. Files only arranged by file extension.   Z to A
5. Directory displays in default mode.

Please select a number.5
A:\>SET
COMSPEC=C:\WINDOWS\COMMAND.COM
PROMPT=$P$G
TEMP=C:\WINDOWS\TEMP
TMP=C:\WINDOWS\TEMP
winbootdir=C:\WINDOWS
windir=C:\WINDOWS
BLASTER=A220 I5 D1 T4 P330
PATH=C:\WINDOWS;C:\WINDOWS\COMMAND
CMDLINE=CHOICE /N /C12345  Please select a number.

A:\>_
```

WHAT'S HAPPENING? ➡ You returned the default DIRCMD environmental variable.

11.26 THE FOR..IN..DO COMMAND

The FOR...IN...DO command can be issued at the command line or placed in a batch file. This command allows repetitive processing. FOR allows you to use a single command to issue several commands at once. The command can DO *something* FOR every value in a specified set. The syntax at the command line is:

```
FOR %variable IN (set) DO command [command-parameters]

%variable            Specifies a replaceable parameter.
(set)                Specifies a set of one or more files. Wildcards
                     may be used.
command              Specifies the command to carry out for each file.
command-parameters   Specifies parameters or switches for the
                     specified command.

To use the FOR command in a batch program, specify %%variable instead
of %variable.
```

The batch file variable is an arbitrary single letter. The double percent sign with a letter (%%a) distinguishes the batch file variable from the replaceable parameter (%1). The difference between a variable and a parameter is not complicated. The FOR statement tells the operating system to get a value from the set you have chosen. After it executes the command that appears after DO, the FOR command looks for the next value in the set. If it finds another value, %%a will represent something new, and the command will be executed with the new value. If there are no more values in the set, the FOR command stops processing.

If you consider the GOTO label as a *vertical* loop, you can consider the FOR..IN..DO as a *horizontal* loop. You do not need to use the letter a. You may use any letter—a, c, x, etc. The parameter value, on the other hand, is set before the batch file begins processing. Remember, the operating system gets the value from the position in the command line. The set is always enclosed in parentheses. The values in the set, either data or file names, will be used to DO some command. The items in the set must be separated by spaces or commas. You may also use wildcards in a set.

11.27 ACTIVITY: USING THE FOR..IN..DO COMMAND

Note 1: The DATA disk should be in Drive A. The displayed prompt is A:\>.
Note 2: Look at the command line you are going to use in Step 1. In English, the command says: Using the variable %a to hold each value in the set (what is in parentheses), do the command (TYPE) to each value in the set (%a).

Step 1   Key in the following: A:\>**FOR %a IN (*.99) DO TYPE %a** Enter

```
MS-DOS Prompt                                              _ □ ✕

A:\>FOR %a IN (*.99) DO TYPE %a

A:\>TYPE APR.99

This is my April file.
```

```
It is my fourth dummy file.
This is file 4.

A:\>TYPE JAN.99

This is my January file.
It is my first dummy file.
This is file 1.

A:\>_
```

WHAT'S HAPPENING? ➤ FOR...IN...DO processed every item in the set as indicated below. Besides using wildcards, you can also be specific.

Step 2　Key in the following:
　　　　A:\>**FOR %x IN (APR.BUD NOFILE.EXT D.BAT) DO TYPE %x** Enter

Step 3　Key in the following:
　　　　A:\>**FOR %y IN (APR.BUD,NOFILE.EXT,D.BAT) DO TYPE %y** Enter

```
 MS-DOS Prompt                                            _ □ ✕

A:\>FOR %x IN (APR.BUD NOFILE.EXT D.BAT) DO TYPE %x

A:\>TYPE APR.BUD

This is file 2.

A:\>TYPE NOFILE.EXT
File not found - NOFILE.EXT

A:\>TYPE D.BAT
DIR /AD

A:\>FOR %y IN (APR.BUD,NOFILE.EXT,D.BAT) DO TYPE %y

A:\>TYPE APR.BUD

This is file 2.

A:\>TYPE NOFILE.EXT
File not found - NOFILE.EXT

A:\>TYPE D.BAT
DIR /AD

A:\>_
```

WHAT'S HAPPENING? ➤ There are some important things to notice about these command lines. First, both a space and a comma between items in a set work the same way. Second, the variable letter you choose is not important. In the first case, x was chosen—in the second, y. This command line is case sensitive. If you had keyed in **FOR %b IN (APR.BUD NOFILE.EXT D.BAT) DO TYPE %B**, the difference between b and B would have made the command line invalid. Even when there was an invalid file (**NOFILE.EXT**), the command line continued processing the other file names in the command. You did not need to worry about testing for null values. This command works the same when placed in a batch file, only you must use %%.

Step 4   Create and save the following batch file called **DO.BAT** and key in the following:
FOR %%v IN (Patty Nicki Sandy Brian) DO ECHO %%v

Step 5   Key in the following: A:\>**DO** [Enter]

```
MS-DOS Prompt                                            _ □ ✕

A:\>DO

A:\>FOR %v IN (Patty Nicki Sandy Brian) DO ECHO %v

A:\>ECHO Patty
Patty

A:\>ECHO Nicki
Nicki

A:\>ECHO Sandy
Sandy

A:\>ECHO Brian
Brian


A:\>

A:\>_
```

WHAT'S HAPPENING? ➡   As you can see, the ECHO command was carried out for each item in the set. It substituted each value (**Patty**, **Nicki**, **Sandy**, and **Brian**) for the replaceable parameter in the ECHO command. In this example, spaces were used to separate the values, but you could have also used commas. The advantage to using this command is that you do not have to write it with a command on each line, as in:

```
ECHO Patty
ECHO Nicki
ECHO Sandy
ECHO Brian
```

Another advantage of the FOR..IN..DO method is that you can also set values in the environment and then use them in a batch file. Remember, the environmental variables need to be set either in the **AUTOEXEC.BAT** file or during the current MS-DOS session.

Step 6   Write and save a batch file called **PASS.BAT** that contains the following:
FOR %%a IN (%USERS%) DO IF "%1"=="%%a" GOTO OKAY
:NO
ECHO You, %1, are NOT allowed in the system.
GOTO END
:OKAY

ECHO Welcome %1 to my world of computers.
:END

> WHAT'S
> HAPPENING! You have combined several features in this FOR..IN..DO statement. You have used an environmental variable in the set (%USERS%). The percent signs surrounding the value tell the FOR command to use the environmental variable called USERS. You have also used an IF statement. If what the user keys in is in the environment, then it is a true statement and the batch file will go to the :OKAY label. If what the user keys in is false and not equal to the environmental variable, then the batch file falls through to the next line. First, you need to set the environmental variable. (Use upper and lower case exactly as shown.)

Step 7   Key in the following: A:\>**SET USERS=Carolyn,Bette** Enter

Step 8   Key in the following: A:\>**PASS Bette** Enter

```
MS-DOS Prompt                                          _ □ ×

A:\>PASS Bette

A:\>FOR %a IN (Carolyn,Bette) DO IF "Bette"=="%a" GOTO OKAY

A:\>IF "Bette"=="Carolyn" GOTO OKAY

A:\>IF "Bette"=="Bette" GOTO OKAY


A:\>ECHO Welcome Bette to my world of computers.
Welcome Bette to my world of computers.

A:\>

A:\>_
```

> WHAT'S
> HAPPENING! You set the environmental values for USERS. You then executed the **PASS.BAT** batch file. It worked as directed because the statement was true. What if it were false?

Step 9   Key in the following: A:\>**PASS Denzel** Enter

```
MS-DOS Prompt                                          _ □ ×

A:\>PASS Denzel

A:\>FOR %a IN (Carolyn,Bette) DO IF "Denzel"=="%a" GOTO OKAY

A:\>IF "Denzel"=="Carolyn" GOTO OKAY

A:\>IF "Denzel"=="Bette" GOTO OKAY


A:\>ECHO You, Denzel, are NOT allowed in the system.
You, Denzel, are NOT allowed in the system.

A:\>GOTO END
```

```
A:\>

A:\>_
```

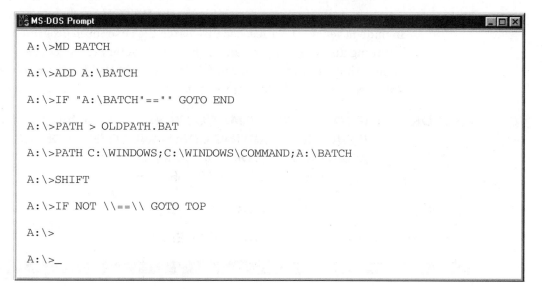

WHAT'S HAPPENING? The statement was false and the batch file behaved accordingly. FOR..IN..DO can also be used with replaceable parameters, file names, and wildcards. You are going to take another look at **UPDATE.BAT**.

Step 10 Use any text editor and edit and save the **UPDATE.BAT** file so it looks as follows:

:DOIT
IF "%1"=="" GOTO END
FOR %%v IN (%1) DO COPY %%v /b + > NUL
SHIFT
PAUSE
GOTO DOIT
:END

WHAT'S HAPPENING? You now can process any number of parameters that appear in the command line. There can be a problem with this batch file. As written, this batch file will copy the newly updated files to the current default directory. Thus, it is a good idea, in general, to place all your batch files in a subdirectory called **BATCH** and set your path to include the **BATCH** directory.

Step 11 Key in the following: A:\>**MD BATCH** Enter

Step 12 Key in the following: A:\>**ADD A:\BATCH** Enter

```
MS-DOS Prompt                                                        _ □ ✕

A:\>MD BATCH

A:\>ADD A:\BATCH

A:\>IF "A:\BATCH"=="" GOTO END

A:\>PATH > OLDPATH.BAT

A:\>PATH C:\WINDOWS;C:\WINDOWS\COMMAND;A:\BATCH

A:\>SHIFT

A:\>IF NOT \\==\\ GOTO TOP

A:\>

A:\>_
```

WHAT'S HAPPENING? You have created a subdirectory called **BATCH** and added it to your current path. Now you will move all the batch files, as well as the **REPLY** files into the **BATCH** subdirectory.

Step 13 Key in the following: A:\>**MOVE *.BAT BATCH** Enter

Step 14 Key in the following: A:\>**MOVE REPLY.* BATCH** [Enter]

```
┌──────────────────────────────────────────────────────────────────────┐
│ ▓ MS-DOS Prompt                                          _ □ X        │
├──────────────────────────────────────────────────────────────────────┤
│                                                                        │
│  A:\HPB.BAT => A:\BATCH\HPB.BAT [ok]                                   │
│  A:\N.BAT => A:\BATCH\N.BAT [ok]                                       │
│  A:\TEST.BAT => A:\BATCH\TEST.BAT [ok]                                 │
│  A:\ALPHA.BAT => A:\BATCH\ALPHA.BAT [ok]                               │
│  A:\UPDATE.BAT => A:\BATCH\UPDATE.BAT [ok]                             │
│  A:\NOCOPY.BAT => A:\BATCH\NOCOPY.BAT [ok]                             │
│  A:\DCOMP.BAT => A:\BATCH\DCOMP.BAT [ok]                               │
│  A:\ONE.BAT => A:\BATCH\ONE.BAT [ok]                                   │
│  A:\REPEAT.BAT => A:\BATCH\REPEAT.BAT [ok]                             │
│  A:\SIZE.BAT => A:\BATCH\SIZE.BAT [ok]                                 │
│  A:\GREET.BAT => A:\BATCH\GREET.BAT [ok]                               │
│  A:\RENDIR.BAT => A:\BATCH\RENDIR.BAT [ok]                             │
│  A:\KEYS.BAT => A:\BATCH\KEYS.BAT [ok]                                 │
│  A:\KEYTWO.BAT => A:\BATCH\KEYTWO.BAT [ok]                             │
│  A:\MYDIR.BAT => A:\BATCH\MYDIR.BAT [ok]                               │
│  A:\TESTIT.BAT => A:\BATCH\TESTIT.BAT [ok]                             │
│  A:\SETTING.BAT => A:\BATCH\SETTING.BAT [ok]                           │
│  A:\ADD.BAT => A:\BATCH\ADD.BAT [ok]                                   │
│  A:\ORIGPATH.BAT => A:\BATCH\ORIGPATH.BAT [ok]                         │
│  A:\OLDPATH.BAT => A:\BATCH\OLDPATH.BAT [ok]                           │
│  A:\MY.BAT => A:\BATCH\MY.BAT [ok]                                     │
│  A:\DO.BAT => A:\BATCH\DO.BAT [ok]                                     │
│  A:\PASS.BAT => A:\BATCH\PASS.BAT [ok]                                 │
│                                                                        │
│  A:\>MOVE REPLY.* BATCH                                                │
│  A:\REPLY.COM => A:\BATCH\REPLY.COM [ok]                               │
│  A:\REPLY.SCR => A:\BATCH\REPLY.SCR [ok]                               │
│                                                                        │
│  A:\>_                                                                 │
│                                                                        │
└──────────────────────────────────────────────────────────────────────┘
```

WHAT'S HAPPENING? You have moved all your batch files to the **BATCH** subdirectory and you included the **REPLY** files, because batch files use these programs. This grouping allowed you to clean up the root directory of the DATA disk. To ensure that you can use your batch files, you first added the **BATCH** subdirectory to the PATH statement.

CAUTION!   **IF YOU CLOSE THE MS-DOS WINDOW, YOU WILL HAVE TO ISSUE THE FOLLOWING COMMAND TO INCLUDE THE A:\BATCH DIRECTORY IN YOUR PATH:**
C:\WINDOWS>A:\BATCH\ADD A:\BATCH

Step 15 Key in the following: A:\>**DIR *.SWT** [Enter]

Step 16 Key in the following: A:\>**DIR *.CAP** [Enter]

```
┌──────────────────────────────────────────────────────────────────────┐
│ ▓ MS-DOS Prompt                                          _ □ X        │
├──────────────────────────────────────────────────────────────────────┤
│                                                                        │
│  A:\>DIR *.SWT                                                         │
│                                                                        │
│   Volume in drive A is DATA                                           │
│   Volume Serial Number is 3330-1807                                   │
│   Directory of A:\                                                    │
│                                                                        │
│  FILE3     SWT            19  12-06-00  2:45p FILE3.SWT               │
└──────────────────────────────────────────────────────────────────────┘
```

```
FILE2      SWT              19  12-06-00   2:45p FILE2.SWT
           2 file(s)                 38 bytes
           0 dir(s)            882,176 bytes free


A:\>DIR *.CAP

 Volume in drive A is DATA
 Volume Serial Number is 3330-1807
 Directory of A:\

STATE      CAP             260  07-31-00   4:32p STATE.CAP
SORTED     CAP             260  08-05-01   3:44p SORTED.CAP
           2 file(s)                520 bytes
           0 dir(s)            882,176 bytes free


A:\>_
```

WHAT'S HAPPENING! You can see the dates on these files. Now you are going to update them to the current date.

Step 17 Key in the following: A:\>**UPDATE *.SWT *.CAP** Enter

```
┌─────────────────────────────────────────────────────────────────────┐
│ MS-DOS Prompt                                              [_][□][×]   │
├─────────────────────────────────────────────────────────────────────┤
│                                                                       │
│  Volume in drive A is DATA                                            │
│  Volume Serial Number is 3330-1807                                    │
│  Directory of A:\                                                     │
│                                                                       │
│ STATE      CAP             260  07-31-00   4:32p STATE.CAP            │
│ SORTED     CAP             260  08-05-01   3:44p SORTED.CAP           │
│            2 file(s)                520 bytes                          │
│            0 dir(s)            882,176 bytes free                      │
│                                                                       │
│ A:\>UPDATE *.SWT *.CAP                                                │
│                                                                       │
│ A:\>IF "*.SWT"=="" GOTO END                                           │
│                                                                       │
│ A:\>FOR %v IN (*.SWT) DO COPY %v /b + > NUL                           │
│                                                                       │
│ A:\>COPY FILE3.SWT /b +                                               │
│                                                                       │
│ A:\>COPY FILE2.SWT /b +                                               │
│                                                                       │
│                                                                       │
│ A:\>SHIFT                                                             │
│                                                                       │
│ A:\>PAUSE                                                             │
│ Press any key to continue . . .                                       │
└─────────────────────────────────────────────────────────────────────┘
```

WHAT'S HAPPENING! You can see how FOR processed each item in the set, which it got from the command line (**%1** was ***.SWT**). Each file that had an **.SWT** file extension was updated. Now the batch file is going to SHIFT and process the new item in the set (***.CAP**).

Step 18 Keep pressing Enter until you are back at the command prompt.

Step 19 Key in the following: A:\>**DIR *.SWT** Enter

Step 20 Key in the following: A:\>**DIR *.CAP** Enter

```
 MS-DOS Prompt                                                    _ □ ×

 A:\>DIR *.SWT

  Volume in drive A is DATA
  Volume Serial Number is 3330-1807
  Directory of A:\

 FILE3     SWT              19  12-26-01   9:59p FILE3.SWT
 FILE2     SWT              19  12-26-01   9:59p FILE2.SWT
           2 file(s)             38 bytes
           0 dir(s)         882,176 bytes free

 A:\>DIR *.CAP

  Volume in drive A is DATA
  Volume Serial Number is 3330-1807
  Directory of A:\

 STATE     CAP             260  12-26-01 10:00p STATE.CAP
 SORTED    CAP             260  12-26-01 10:00p SORTED.CAP
           2 file(s)            520 bytes
           0 dir(s)         882,176 bytes free

 A:\>_
```

WHAT'S HAPPENING? ➤ Your dates will be different, but you have successfully changed the dates of the files. You have successfully used the FOR.. IN..DO command.

11.28 THE CALL COMMAND

You sometimes need to be able to execute one batch file from within another. If the second batch file is the last line in the original batch file, there is no problem. The second batch file is "invoked" from the first batch file. But invoking a second batch file, executing it, and upon completion of the second file, returning to the first batch file, is not so simple. When the operating system finishes executing a batch file, it returns control to the system level and never returns to the original batch file. There is a solution to this problem: the CALL command. It allows you to call (execute) another batch file and then return control to the next line in the first (calling) batch file.

11.29 ACTIVITY: USING CALL

Note: The DATA disk should be in Drive A. The displayed prompt is A:\>. You have executed the command A:\BATCH\>**ADD A:\BATCH** at some point during the current MS-DOS session.

Step 1　Key in the following: A:\>**CD BATCH** [Enter]

```
 MS-DOS Prompt                                                    _ □ ×

 A:\>CD BATCH

 A:\BATCH>_
```

WHAT'S HAPPENING? ➤ Your default directory is now the **BATCH** subdirectory. One of the things that you can create is a "noise" to get a user's attention. In the same way you used **Ctrl** + **L** to eject a page, you can use **Ctrl** + **G** to make a noise. All computers will not make a noise—most do. Although the noise you create sounds like a beep, it is referred to as a bell because, in the ASCII character set, the **Ctrl** + **G** is labeled BEL. By using **Ctrl** + **G** with ECHO you "ring a bell." Remember that when you see **Ctrl** + **G**, it means press the **Ctrl** key and the letter **G**, and, when you see **F6**, it means press the **F6** function key. Today's computers are very fast; 200–400 MHz is commonplace. The beep sound is very short, and may be difficult to hear. Therefore, we will repeat the beep command four times, making it easier for you to hear the generated sound. Even if you cannot hear the sound, you will not get an error message.

Step 2 Key in the following: A:\BATCH>**COPY CON BELL.BAT** **Enter**
 ECHO **Ctrl** + **G** **Enter**
 ECHO **Ctrl** + **G** **Enter**
 ECHO **Ctrl** + **G** **Enter**
 ECHO **Ctrl** + **G** **Enter**
 F6 **Enter**

```
MS-DOS Prompt                                              _ □ ✕

A:\BATCH>COPY CON BELL.BAT
ECHO ^G
ECHO ^G
ECHO ^G
ECHO ^G
^Z
        1 file(s) copied

A:\>BATCH_
```

WHAT'S HAPPENING? ➤ Now that you have written **BELL.BAT**, you can execute it.

Step 3 Key in the following: A:\BATCH>**BELL** **Enter**

```
MS-DOS Prompt                                              _ □ ✕

A:\BATCH>BELL

A:\BATCH>ECHO

A:\BATCH>ECHO

A:\BATCH>ECHO

A:\BATCH>ECHO

A:\BATCH>

A:\BATCH>_
```

WHAT'S HAPPENING? You should have heard the bell beeping or clicking as you ran the program.

Step 4   Use any text editor to create and save a batch file called **BELLING.BAT**. Key in the following:
COPY *.99 *.XYZ [Enter]
DEL *.XYZ [Enter]
BELL [Enter]
(Be sure to hit [Enter] after **BELL**.)

WHAT'S HAPPENING? This batch file will copy the **.99** files to the **BATCH** subdirectory, delete them, and then ring a bell.

Step 5   Key in the following: A:\BATCH>**BELLING** [Enter]

```
MS-DOS Prompt                                          _ □ ×

A:\BATCH>BELLING

A:\BATCH>COPY \*.99 *.XYZ
A:\JAN.99
A:\APR.99
        2 file(s) copied

A:\BATCH>DEL *.XYZ

A:\BATCH>BELL

A:\BATCH>ECHO

A:\BATCH>ECHO

A:\BATCH>ECHO

A:\BATCH>ECHO

A:\BATCH>

A:\BATCH>_
```

WHAT'S HAPPENING? You called one batch file from another. You ran **BELLING**. Its last line was **BELL**. **BELL** was called and it executed as expected. However, perhaps you would like the bell to sound before the files are deleted.

Step 6   Edit and save **BELLING.BAT** to look as follows:
COPY *.99 *.XYZ
BELL
REM You are about to delete the *.XYZ files. Are you sure?
PAUSE
DEL *.XYZ

Step 7   Key in the following: A:\BATCH>**BELLING** [Enter]

```
MS-DOS Prompt                                          _ □ ×

A:\BATCH>BELLING
```

```
A:\BATCH>COPY \*.99 *.XYZ
A:\JAN.99
A:\APR.99
        2 file(s) copied

A:\BATCH>BELL

A:\BATCH>ECHO

A:\BATCH>ECHO

A:\BATCH>ECHO

A:\BATCH>ECHO

A:\BATCH>

A:\BATCH>_
```

WHAT'S HAPPENING? ▶ When the **BELLING** batch file reached the line **BELL**, it called and executed **BELL**. It turned control over to **BELL.BAT**. Once **BELL.BAT** had control, it never returned to **BELLING**. Since it never returned to **BELLING.BAT**, your ***.XYZ** files were not deleted, nor did you see a message.

Step 8   Key in the following: A:\BATCH>**DIR *.XYZ** [Enter]

```
MS-DOS Prompt                                          _ □ ✕

A:\BATCH>DIR *.XYZ

 Volume in drive A is DATA
 Volume Serial Number is 2415-16DD
 Directory of A:\BATCH

JAN      XYZ          73   10-10-99  4:21p JAN.XYZ
APR      XYZ          72   06-28-01  9:43a APR.XYZ
         2 file(s)             145 bytes
         0 dir(s)          880,128 bytes free

A:\BATCH>_
```

WHAT'S HAPPENING? ▶ Indeed, the files are there. This is why you need the CALL command. CALL will process the batch file **BELL**, but it will then return control to **BELLING** so that the other commands in **BELLING** can be executed.

Step 9   Edit and save **BELLING.BAT** to look as follows:
COPY *.99 *.XYZ
CALL BELL
REM You are about to delete the *.XYZ files. Are you sure?
PAUSE
DEL *.XYZ

Step 10 Key in the following: A:\BATCH>**BELLING** [Enter]

```
 MS-DOS Prompt                                                    _ □ ✕

 A:\JAN.99
 A:\APR.99
        2 file(s) copied

 A:\BATCH>CALL BELL

 A:\BATCH>ECHO


 A:\BATCH>ECHO


 A:\BATCH>ECHO


 A:\BATCH>ECHO


 A:\BATCH>

 A:\BATCH>REM You are about to delete the *.XYZ files. Are you sure?

 A:\BATCH>PAUSE
 Press any key to continue . . .
```

WHAT'S HAPPENING?   Since you added **CALL** in front of **BELL**, the bell sounded. Once **BELL** was finished executing, it passed control back to **BELLING** so that the next commands could be executed.

Step 11   Press **Enter**

Step 12   Key in the following: A:\BATCH>**DIR *.XYZ** **Enter**

```
 MS-DOS Prompt                                                    _ □ ✕

 A:\BATCH>DIR *.XYZ

  Volume in drive A is DATA
  Volume Serial Number is 3330-1807
  Directory of A:\BATCH

 File not found
                        881,152 bytes free

 A:\BATCH>_
```

WHAT'S HAPPENING?   The CALL command worked as promised. Your **.XYZ** files are gone. A more practical example of using CALL can be seen in the next group of batch files you are going to write. You may find, as you move among directories, that you want to go "home" again. In other words, you want to return to the directory where you were previously. You can create a series of batch files that will remember the directory you were in and return you to it.

Note: In the next file, it is important to press the F6 immediately after the command *before* you press Enter. Do not press Enter, then F6.

Step 13 Use **COPY CON** to create and save **HOME.DAT**. Key in the following:
A:\>**COPY CON HOME.DAT** Enter
        SET HOME=F6 Enter

Step 14 Use any editor to create and save a batch file called **HOMETO.BAT**. Key in the following:
COPY A:\BATCH\HOME.DAT A:\BATCH\HOMESAVE.BAT Enter
CD >> A:\BATCH\HOMESAVE.BAT Enter
CALL HOMESAVE.BAT Enter
DEL A:\BATCH\HOMESAVE.BAT

> **WHAT'S HAPPENING?**   The **HOME.DAT** data file you created will create an environmental variable called HOME. The batch file, **HOMETO.BAT,** that you just created will be used to set the environmental variable to wherever you want HOME to be. The batch file, line by line, breaks down as follows:

Line 1: copies the contents of the data file to the batch file	HOME.DAT contains SET HOME= HOMESAVE.BAT now contains SET HOME=
Line 2: takes whatever directory you are in and appends it to HOMESAVE.BAT	If your current directory is GAMES, HOMESAVE.BAT now has contents of SET HOME=A:\GAMES
Line 3: executes the batch file and sets the environmental of HOME to A:\GAMES	HOMESAVE.BAT now executes
Line 4: deletes the batch file	now that you have set the environmental variable, you no longer need the batch file HOMESAVE.BAT

Step 15 Use any editor to create and save a batch file called **HOME.BAT** that contains the following:
CD %HOME%

> **WHAT'S HAPPENING?**   The batch file **HOME.BAT** will change your directory to whatever value in the environmental variable called **HOME** at the time the batch file is executed. In order for this procedure to work correctly, you must include **A:\BATCH** in your path statement.

Step 16 Key in the following: **PATH** Enter

```
MS-DOS Prompt                                                      _ □ ✕

A:\BATCH>PATH
PATH=C:\WINDOWS;C:\WINDOWS\COMMAND;A:\BATCH

A:\BATCH>_
```

 In this example, **A:\BATCH** is indeed included in the path. If it is not included in your path, run ADD A:\BATCH before proceeding.

Step 17 Key in the following: A:\BATCH>**SET** `Enter`

```
MS-DOS Prompt                                                      _ □ X

A:\BATCH>SET
COMSPEC=C:\WINDOWS\COMMAND.COM
PROMPT=$P$G
TEMP=C:\WINDOWS\TEMP
TMP=C:\WINDOWS\TEMP
winbootdir=C:\WINDOWS
windir=C:\WINDOWS
BLASTER=A220 I5 D1 T4 P330
USERS=Carolyn,Bette
PATH=C:\WINDOWS;C:\WINDOWS\COMMAND;A:\BATCH
CMDLINE=edit belling.bat

A:\BATCH>_
```

 **A:\BATCH** is included in the path. There is no environmental variable HOME displayed. You are now ready to test "going home."

Step 18 Key in the following: A:\BATCH>**CD ** `Enter`

Step 19 Key in the following: A:\>**CD WORK\ADS** `Enter`

Step 20 Key in the following: A:\WORK\ADS>**HOMETO** `Enter`

```
MS-DOS Prompt                                                      _ □ X

A:\BATCH>CD \
A:\>CD WORK\ADS

A:\WORK\ADS>HOMETO

A:\WORK\ADS>COPY A:\BATCH\HOME.DAT A:\BATCH\HOMESAVE.BAT
        1 file(s) copied

A:\WORK\ADS>CD >> A:\BATCH\HOMESAVE.BAT

A:\WORK\ADS>CALL HOMESAVE.BAT

A:\WORK\ADS>SET HOME=A:\WORK\ADS

A:\WORK\ADS>

A:\WORK\ADS>DEL A:\BATCH\HOMESAVE.BAT

A:\WORK\ADS>

A:\WORK\ADS>_
```

 You want the subdirectory **\WORK\ADS** to be your home directory, so you keyed in **HOMETO** to set up your home directory.

Step 21 Key in the following: A:\WORK\ADS>**SET** `Enter`

```
MS-DOS Prompt                                                _ □ ×

A:\WORK\ADS>SET
COMSPEC=C:\WINDOWS\COMMAND.COM
PROMPT=$P$G
TEMP=C:\WINDOWS\TEMP
TMP=C:\WINDOWS\TEMP
winbootdir=C:\WINDOWS
windir=C:\WINDOWS
BLASTER=A220 I5 D1 T4 P330
USERS=Carolyn,Bette
PATH=C:\WINDOWS;C:\WINDOWS\COMMAND;A:\BATCH
CMDLINE=edit belling.bat
HOME=A:\WORK\ADS

A:\WORK\ADS>_
```

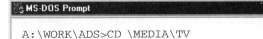 You now have an environmental variable named HOME whose value is **A:\WORK\ADS**. You will go to another directory and then return to **A:\WORK\ADS** by using the HOME command you just wrote.

Step 22 Key in the following: A:\WORK\ADS>**CD \MEDIA\TV** [Enter]

```
MS-DOS Prompt                                                _ □ ×

A:\WORK\ADS>CD \MEDIA\TV

A:\MEDIA\TV>_
```

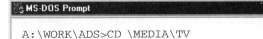 Your default directory is now **A:\MEDIA\TV**. You want to return home, which is **A:\WORK\ADS**.

Step 23 Key in the following: A:\MEDIA\TV>**HOME** [Enter]

```
MS-DOS Prompt                                                _ □ ×

A:\MEDIA\TV>HOME

A:\MEDIA\TV>CD A:\WORK\ADS

A:\WORK\ADS>

A:\WORK\ADS>_
```

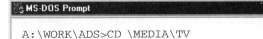 You went home—home being the value set in the HOME variable. At any time during the MS-DOS window session, you can change the value of home by running HOMETO while in the directory you want home to be, and return to it at any time by simply keying in **HOME**.

Step 24 Key in the following: A:\WORK\ADS>**CD ** [Enter]

Step 25 Key in the following: A:\>**ORIGPATH** [Enter]

```
MS-DOS Prompt                                                    _ □ ✕

A:\WORK\ADS>CD\

A:\>ORIGPATH

A:\>PATH=C:\WINDOWS;C:\WINDOWS\COMMAND

A:\>

A:\>_
```

> **WHAT'S HAPPENING?** → You have returned to the root directory of the DATA disk and reset the default path.

CHAPTER SUMMARY

1. You may substitute a double colon (::) for the REM statement.
2. You can suppress the display of any messages by using the command CTTY NUL. You return control to the console by keying in CTTY CON. These commands are always used together.
3. To place a blank line in a batch file, use the ECHO command followed immediately by a period (ECHO.).
4. The GOTO command used in conjunction with a label creates a loop. The GOTO will process the command following the label.
5. The label in a batch file is not a command but identifies a location in the batch file.
6. The SHIFT command shifts over command line parameters to the left one position at a time.
7. The SHIFT command is typically used in conjunction with GOTO and a label.
8. The IF command will test for some logical condition. If the condition is true, the command is processed. If the condition is false, the batch file will fall through to the next line of the batch file.
9. The IF command can test whether or not two character strings are identical.
10. The IF command can test whether or not a file exists.
11. The IF command checks ERRORLEVEL.
12. You may also use IF with NOT. The IF NOT command will test for a NOT condition. If a condition is not true, then the command will process. If the command is true, then the batch file will fall through to the next line in the batch file.
13. You can test for a null value by using quotation marks, by using a word, or by using backslashes.
14. To use IF EXIST and to test for the existence of a subdirectory, you may use IF %1\NUL.
15. Many programs set an exit code when finished executing. The IF ERRORLEVEL in a batch file will test if an exit code is equal to or greater than the one in the test.

16. When you use IF ERRORLEVEL in a batch file, the codes must be listed in descending order.

17. When you use IF NOT ERRORLEVEL in a batch file, the codes must be listed in ascending order.

18. You may write programs with DEBUG to set exit codes.

19. You can write programs directly in DEBUG, or you may write a script file that supplies input for DEBUG to create a program.

20. The CHOICE command is an external command that can be used to set exit codes for input from the keyboard.

21. Each key, when pressed, issues a scan code that can be checked by the CHOICE command or by a program written in DEBUG.

22. The environment is an area in memory where the operating system leaves messages to itself, including the path and the prompt values.

23. You can create environmental variables that can be used in batch files. When using the variable in a batch file, the syntax is *%variable%*.

24. The SET command lets you view what is currently in the environment.

25. Environmental variables set in the AUTOEXEC.BAT file remain in effect throughout the entire work session.

26. Environmental variables set in other batch files, or at the command line, remain in effect only during the current MS-DOS window session. When the MS-DOS window is closed, the variable disappears.

27. The DIRCMD command can be used to preset the DIR command parameters and switches.

28. The FOR...IN...DO command allows repetitive processing. The command will execute some command for every value in a specified set.

29. When you use FOR...IN...DO at the command line, the syntax is FOR *%variable* IN (*set*) DO *command* [*command-parameter*].

30. The CALL command allows you to call one batch file from another and when the second batch file is finished executing, it returns control to the first batch file.

KEY TERMS

debug	conditional processing	scan code
EOF (end-of-file) mark	loop	script file
exit code	null value	

DISCUSSION QUESTIONS

1. What is the function of the REM, ECHO, and PAUSE commands?
2. What happens in a batch file if ECHO is set to OFF?
3. What happens in a batch file if you precede the ECHO OFF switch with @?
4. What is the purpose and function of the CTTY command?
5. What is a NUL device? Why would you use a NUL device?
6. Why should you use the CTTY NUL command only in a batch file and not at the command line?

7. Why should you use CTTY NUL in tandem with CTTY CON?
8. How can you place a blank line in a batch file?
9. How can you create a loop in a batch file? How can you stop a loop from processing in a batch file?
10. What is the purpose and function of the GOTO command?
11. What is a label in a batch file?
12. What is the purpose and function of the SHIFT command?
13. Why is it useful to shift parameters?
14. How can you determine whether or not a file exists?
15. What is the purpose and function of the IF command?
16. Give the syntax of the IF command and explain each part of the syntax.
17. What does it mean to test for a null value?
18. How can you test for a null value? Why would you test for a null value?
19. What is the purpose and function of the IF EXIST/IF NOT EXIST command?
20. Explain the purpose and function of the IF ERRORLEVEL command.
21. What is a script file? How can you create one?
22. What is a scan code?
23. What is the purpose and function of the CHOICE command?
24. Give the syntax of the CHOICE command and explain each part of the syntax.
25. What are some of the drawbacks of using CHOICE?
26. Give the syntax of the SET command and explain each part of the syntax.
27. Explain the purpose and function of the DIRCMD environmental variable.
28. What is the purpose and function of the FOR..IN..DO command?
29. Give the syntax of the FOR..IN..DO command and explain each part of the syntax.
30. Explain the purpose and function of the CALL command.

TRUE/FALSE QUESTIONS

For each question, circle the letter T if the question is true and the letter F if the question is false.

T F 1. The SHIFT command may be used only in batch files.
T F 2. Environmental variables set at the command line remain in effect until the computer is turned off.
T F 3. You may alter the way DIR displays by changing the values in DIRCMD.
T F 4. Keying in SET at the command line shows the correct date and time.
T F 5. In order to run a batch file from another batch file and then return to the original batch file, you must use the CALL command.

COMPLETION QUESTIONS

Write the correct answer in each blank space.

6. In a batch file, to see whether or not the file called MY.FIL is a valid file, you must have the line IF _____ MY.FIL.

7. In a batch file, the line IF "%1"=="" GOTO END, is testing for a(n) _____.

8. The operating system batch file command that allows decisions to be made based on user input from the keyboard is _____.

9. When you key in SET THIS=DIR *.TXT, you are setting a(n) _____.

10. When you use the GOTO command, you must also use a(n) _____.

MULTIPLE CHOICE QUESTIONS

For each question, write the letter for the correct answer in the blank space.

11. If **ECHO.** (ECHO followed immediately by a period) is entered into a batch file, it will
   a. display the status of ECHO.
   b. create a blank line.
   c. do nothing.
   d. cause the following command not to execute.

12. ECHO %PATH% (keyed in at the command line) will
   a. produce an error message.
   b. display the contents of the file named PATH.
   c. display the path for the current session.
   d. display the environmental variables set in the current session.

13. The following command in a batch file—IF %1none==none GOTO TOP—will
   a. test for a null value.
   b. test for the existence of a file.
   c. test for ERRORLEVEL.
   d. all of the above

14. A valid batch file label consists of a
   a. percent sign (%) and text chosen by the user.
   b. colon (:) and text chosen by the user.
   c. double colon (::) and text chosen by the user.
   d. any of the above

15. So that %3 becomes %2, and %2 becomes %1, you must use the _____ command in a batch file.
   a. ROTATE %1
   b. SHIFT %1
   c. SHIFT
   d. none of the above

WRITING COMMANDS

The following batch file provides options for the user. She or he may use one of three commands: VER, CHKDSK, or SORT. Complete the missing (numbered) lines that will make this batch file work.

```
        @ECHO OFF
        REM A simple program using choice
        CHOICE /N Select Version(V), CHKDSK(C)or SORT list(S) /CVCS
        IF ERRORLEVEL 3 GOTO SORTLIST
16.     IF _____
17.     IF _____
        :VERSION
        VER
        GOTO END
        :CHECK
18.     _____
        GOTO END
19.     :_____
        SORT
20.     :_____
```

APPLICATION ASSIGNMENTS

Note 1: Place the APPLICATION disk in Drive A. Be sure to work on the APPLICA-TION disk, not the DATA disk.

Note 2: The homework problems will assume Drive C is the hard disk and the APPLICATION disk is in Drive A. If you are using another drive, such as floppy drive B or hard drive D, be sure and substitute that drive letter when reading the questions and answers.

Note 3: Test all of your batch files before submitting them to be sure they work correctly.

Note 4: To save a file under a new name with Edit, press [Alt] + **F** and choose **Save As**.

Note 5: There can be more than one way to write a batch file. If your batch file works correctly, it is most likely written correctly.

SETUP

Step 1   Place the APPLICATION disk in Drive A.

Step 2   Create a **BATCH** subdirectory on the APPLICATION disk and move any batch files from the root directory, except for **GO.BAT** and **NAME.BAT**, into the **BATCH** subdirectory.

Step 3   Make sure that **GO.BAT** and **NAME.BAT** are in the root of the APPLICA-TION disk.

Step 4   Create a subdirectory called **CHAP11** off the root directory of the APPLICATION disk.

PROBLEM SET I

PROBLEM A

A-a   Make **CHAP11** the default directory.

A-b   Create and save a batch file in the **CHAP11** subdirectory called
             DELBAK.BAT that has the following line in it:
             FOR %%h IN (*.BAK) DO IF EXIST %%h DEL %%h

        1. The DELBAK.BAT file will
          a. delete any file in the default drive and directory.
          b. delete any file in the default drive and directory with the .BAK
              extension.
          c. first check whether or not any files with the .BAK file extension
              exist in the current drive and directory.
          d. both b and c

        2. If you wanted to use the previous batch file command on the command
           line, what would you have to do?
          a. change %%h to %h
          b. change %%h to %h%
          c. change *.BAK to %h%
          d. none of the above

A-c   Create and save the following batch file called **LIST.BAT** in the **CHAP11**
             subdirectory.
             @ECHO OFF
             ECHO.
             FOR %%v IN (%PATH%) DO ECHO %%v
             ECHO.
             ECHO.

        3. The LIST.BAT file will
          a. display the directory names in the current path.
          b. use an environmental variable.
          c. both a and b
          d. neither a nor b

PROBLEM B

B-a   Be sure that **CHAP11** is the default directory on the APPLICATION disk.

B-b   In the **CHAP11** subdirectory, create and save a batch file called **DT.BAT**
             that has the following lines in it. (*Note:* Piping ECHO to MORE to a
             command sends an Enter in a batch file.)
             @ECHO OFF
             CLS
             ECHO ¦ MORE ¦ DATE ¦ FIND /V "new"
             ECHO ¦ MORE ¦ TIME ¦ FIND /V "new"

B-c   Execute **DT.BAT**.

        4. When you used DT.BAT you
          a. changed the current system date and time.
          b. viewed the current system date and time.

PROBLEM C

C-a   Be sure that **CHAP11** is the default directory on the APPLICATION disk.

Note: The following batch file is called SWAP.BAT. Its purpose is to allow the user to swap file names between two existing files. If the user keyed in SWAP MY.OLD MY.NEW, the file MY.OLD would then be named MY.NEW and the file MY.NEW would then be named MY.OLD. However, this batch file has a problem and does not work properly.

C-b   In the **CHAP11** subdirectory, create and save a batch file called
        SWAP.BAT that has the following lines in it:
        @ECHO OFF
        IF NOT EXIST %1 GOTO NOFILE1
        IF NOT EXIST %2 GOTO NOFILE2
        REN %1 HOLD
        REN %2 %1
        REN HOLD %2
        GOTO END
        :NOFILE1
        ECHO Cannot find file %1
        :NOFILE2
        ECHO Cannot find file %2
        :END

C-c   If you do not have a subdirectory called **\SPORTS**, create it now. Then
        copy any file with a **.99** extension from the **WINDOSBK** subdirectory to
        the **\SPORTS** subdirectory on the APPLICATION disk.

C-d   Key in the following: A:\CHAP11>**SWAP \SPORTS\APR.99**
        \SPORTS\JAN.99 ⌈Enter⌋

        5. When you used **SWAP.BAT**, you received an error message and
            SWAP.BAT did not work. Why?
            a. You cannot name a file **HOLD**.
            b. The file **\SPORTS\APR.99** does not exist.
            c. The syntax of the REN command is incorrect.
            d. You were immediately sent to the :END label.

        6. Did any file get renamed in the **\SPORTS** directory?
            a. yes
            b. no

PROBLEM SET II

Note 1: The APPLICATION disk is in drive A and the A:\> is displayed as the default drive and the default directory. All work will occur on the APPLICATION disk.

Note 2: If NAME.BAT, MARK.FIL, GETYN.COM, and GO.BAT are not in the root directory, copy them from the WINDOSBK directory before proceeding.

Step 1   Key in the following: A:\>**NAME** Enter

Step 2   Here is an example to key in, but your instructor will have other infor-
          mation that applies to your class. Key in the following:
          Bette A. Peat Enter   (*Your* name goes here.)
          CIS 55 Enter   (*Your* class goes here.)
          T-Th 8-9:30 Enter   (*Your* day and time go here.)
          Chapter 11 Applications Enter
          Problem A Enter

Step 3   Press F6 Enter

Step 4   If the information is correct, press **Y** and you are back to A:\>.

Step 5   Begin a new MS-DOS session by closing any existing MS-DOS window
          and opening a new window.

Step 6   Make A:\> the default directory.

Step 7   Key in the following: A:\>**PATH > MYPATH.BAT** Enter

PROBLEM A

A-a   Make **CHAP11** the default directory.

A-b   The following batch file is called **SETPATH.BAT**. Its purpose is to allow
       the user to add a path to either the front or the back of the existing
       path. Any number of subdirectory names can be added. When the
       user keys in **SETPATH /F subdirectory1 subdirectory2** or **SETPATH /f
       subdirectory1 subdirectory2**, the /F or /f tells the batch file to add the
       subdirectory name in front of the existing path. If the SETPATH com-
       mand is keyed in without /F or /f, each subdirectory listed will be
       added to the end of the path.

A-c   Analyze the following batch file:
```
IF "%1"=="" GOTO DEFAULT
IF "%1"=="/f" GOTO FRONT
IF "%1"=="/F" GOTO FRONT
:ADD
IF "%1"=="" GOTO END
PATH= %PATH%;%1
SHIFT
GOTO ADD
:FRONT
SHIFT
IF "%1"=="" GOTO END
PATH=%1;%PATH%
GOTO FRONT
:DEFAULT
PATH=C:\WINDOWS\COMMAND
:END
```

A-d   In the **CHAP11** subdirectory, create and edit a batch file called **SETPATH.BAT** based on the model above.

A-e   Document it with your name and date, and explain the purpose of the batch file.

A-f   Begin the batch file with **CHOICE** so you may give the user the opportunity to choose help on how to use this command. If the user chooses help, provide help on syntax as well as a description on how to use **SETPATH.BAT**. After displaying help, the user should exit from the batch file.

A-g   Change the :DEFAULT section so that it calls whatever your original path was, rather than **PATH C:\WINDOWS\COMMAND**. (*Hint*: Remember, **MYPATH.BAT** is in the root directory of the APPLICATION disk.)

A-h   How can you be sure that **MYPATH.BAT** is always the path that is set when you boot up? Place your answer in a text file called **SETPATH.TXT** in the **CHAP11** subdirectory of the APPLICATION disk.

A-i   Key in the following: A:\CHAP11>**CD** Enter

A-j   Key in the following: A:\>
       GO NAME.FIL CHAP11\SETPATH.BAT \CHAP11\SETPATH.TXT Enter

PROBLEM B

B-a   Make **CHAP11** the default directory.

B-b   Use SETPATH created in Problem A to add the A:**CHAP11** and the A:\BATCH subdirectories to the path.

B-c   Using as a model **MYDIR.BAT** in Activity 11.21, create and save a batch file called **DIRS.BAT** in the **CHAP11** subdirectory.

B-d   Document it with your name and date and explain the purpose of the batch file.

B-e   Have the following choices in **DIRS.BAT**:
       ❖ Look at directories only, arranged alphabetically by name in the root directory. (Call this **Root Directory Only**.)
       ❖ Look at directories only, arranged alphabetically by name on the entire disk. (Call this **All Disk Directories**.)
       ❖ Look at file names only—no dates, no directory information, on the root directory in reverse alphabetic order (*Hint:* Remember /b). (Call this **Filenames Only**.)
       ❖ Remove any other choices.
       ❖ Be sure no command lines are displayed, only the results of the commands.

B-f   Key in the following: A:\CHAP11>**CD** Enter

B-g   Use Edit to modify **NAME.FIL**, changing Problem A to Problem B.

B-h   Key in the following: A:\>**GO NAME.FIL CHAP11\DIRS.BAT** Enter

PROBLEM C

C-a   Make **CHAP11** the default directory.

C-b   Check the path to see if **CHAP11** is in the path. If not, use SETPATH created in Problem A to add the **A:\CHAP11** subdirectory to the path and add the **A:\BATCH** subdirectory to the path as well.

Note: The following batch file is called WORD.BAT. Its purpose is to allow the user to key in WORD *filename.ext.* If the file already exists, the user is immediately taken into Edit with the named file. If, however, the file is a new file, the user will be told to key in WORD and the new file name at the command line. This batch file, as written, has a fatal flaw. Every time the user keys in WORD *new.fil* he or she is kicked out of the batch file.

C-c   Analyze the following batch file:
```
:START
IF EXIST %1 GOTO PROCEED
IF NOT EXIST %1 GOTO NEWFILE
:PROCEED
EDIT %1
GOTO END
:NEWFILE
ECHO This is a new file, %1. If you
ECHO wish to create a new file, you must
ECHO key in WORD and the new file name at the command line.
ECHO The syntax is:
ECHO WORD new.fil
:END
```

C-d   Edit and save a batch file called **WORD.BAT** in the **CHAP11** subdirectory based on the above model. Document it with your name and date and explain the purpose of the batch file.
   ❖ If the user keys in WORD with no file name, the batch file should tell the user what was done wrong and return the user to the system level.
   ❖ If the user keys in WORD *filename.ext* and it is an existing file, the file should go directly into Edit using that file name. However, if the file does not exist, offer the user two choices—either not to create a new file and exit the batch file or to create a new file and be taken back to the PROCEED label. You will use CHOICE and ERRORLEVEL so this choice can be made.

C-e   Key in the following: A:\CHAP11>**CD ** Enter

C-f   Use Edit to modify **NAME.FIL**, changing Problem B to Problem C.

C-g   Key in the following: A:\>**GO NAME.FIL CHAP11\WORD.BAT** Enter

PROBLEM D—CHALLENGE ASSIGNMENT

The following batch file change is difficult, so do it only if you want a challenge.

D-a   Make **CHAP11** the default directory.

D-b   Copy **SWAP.BAT** (created in Problem Set I—Problem C) to a new file called **SWAP2.BAT**.

D-c   Document it with your name and date and explain the purpose of the batch file.

D-d   The batch file should perform as follows:
- ❖ When you key in SWAP2 *dirname filename1 filename2*, the file names will be reversed in a specific directory. The batch file will change to the specified directory prior to performing the "swap."
- ❖ One of the items you wish to test for is the existence of a directory. (*Hint*: Remember %1\Nul.) If you key in a subdirectory name where a file name is expected, the batch file should take you to a message that tells you that you keyed in a directory name, not a file name.
- ❖ If you key in only SWAP2, the batch file will take you to a message that tells the user how to use the command correctly.
- ❖ Be sure the batch file returns the user to the **CHAP11** subdirectory.

D-e   Key in the following: A:\CHAP11>**CD ** Enter

D-f   Use Edit to modify **NAME.FIL**, changing Problem C to Problem D.

D-g   Key in the following: A:\>**GO NAME.FIL \CHAP11\SWAP2.BAT** Enter

PROBLEM E—CHALLENGE ASSIGNMENT

The following batch file change is very difficult, so do it only if you want a *real* challenge.

E-a   In the Chap11 directory, copy **SWAP2.BAT** to **SWAP3.BAT**.

E-b   Change **SWAP3.BAT** to allow the user to key in either SWAP3 *dirname file1 file2* or SWAP3 *file1 file2 dirname*.

E-c   Use Edit to modify **NAME.FIL**, changing Problem D to Problem E.

E-d   Key in the following: A:\>**GO NAME.FIL \CHAP11\SWAP3.BAT** Enter

PROBLEM SET III—BRIEF ESSAY

1. The following is a batch file called **TEST.BAT**.

```
@ECHO OFF
:AGAIN
IF \%1\==\\ GOTO END
IF %1==LIFE ECHO LIFE
IF %1==MINE ECHO MINE
IF %1==YOURS ECHO YOURS
IF \%1\==\\ GOTO END
```

```
IF NOT EXIST %1 GOTO NEXT
TYPE %1
:NEXT
SHIFT
GOTO AGAIN
:END
```

LIFE, MINE and YOURS are variables. MY.FIL is a file that is on the disk. Analyze this file and describe what will happen and why when you key in each of the following at the command line:

  a. **TEST LIFE**
  b. **TEST MINE**
  c. **TEST YOURS**
  d. **TEST MY.FIL**
  e. **TEST life**
  f. **TEST my.fil**

CONNECTIVITY

LEARNING OBJECTIVES

After completing this chapter, you will be able to:

1. Explain the terms client, server, and resources, and how they relate to networks.
2. Compare and contrast server-based networks and peer-to-peer networks.
3. List and explain two reasons for setting up a network.
4. Explain how to set up a peer-to-peer network using Windows.
5. Explain the purpose of sharing printers and/or an entire hard drive.
6. Explain the purpose and function of a mapped drive.
7. Explain the purpose and function of the Internet.
8. Compare and contrast the Internet and the World Wide Web.
9. List the three standards that the Web uses to access information on the Internet.
10. List and explain ways that a computer user can connect to the Internet.
11. Explain the roles that TCP/IP can play in computer communication.
12. Explain the purpose and function of an IP address.
13. Explain the function and purpose of the Domain Name System.
14. Explain the purpose and function of a URL.
15. Explain how the TCP/IP utilities can be used to troubleshoot problems and offer connections to non-Microsoft hosts.

STUDENT OUTCOMES

1. If you have the appropriate hardware, you will set up a peer-to-peer network.
2. If you have a peer-to-peer network, you will share a printer on the network.
3. If you have a peer-to-peer network, you will share a drive on the network.
4. If you have a peer-to-peer network, you will map a drive.
5. If you have an Internet connection, you will access the Internet and use your browser to visit two sites.
6. Use two TCP/IP Utilities.

CHAPTER OVERVIEW

In the computer world of today, connectivity is the reality. Connectivity can mean connecting to other computers in your home or office. It can mean sharing resources such as printers or files on your computer, or accessing those resources from another computer. It can also mean connecting to resources throughout the world using the Internet. Networks provide these connections. Windows is designed for networking and allows you to network with others to collect information, to exchange files, and to share resources.

This chapter introduces you to the basic concepts of networking. It explains the terminology used in the networking world such as client/server, peer-to-peer, LAN, and WAN. If you have the appropriate hardware, this chapter will show you how to set up a peer-to-peer network and how to share resources on your network.

Networking also encompasses the Internet. If you have the appropriate connections, you will learn how to connect to and navigate through the Internet. You will be introduced to the basic protocol of the Internet, TCP/IP. You will learn about the command line utilities included with TCP/IP that allow you to troubleshoot simple problems as well as connect to non–Web-based computers.

12.1 NETWORKS (LANS AND WANS)

Today it is more and more common for small businesses or even users at home to have more than one computer. In a world of so many computers, you will probably want to connect these computers together. When you connect computers together, it is called a *LAN* (*local area network*). In a network, there are servers and clients. A *server* is a computer that provides shared *resources* to network users. A *client* is a computer that accesses the shared network resources provided by the server. Resources are the parts of the computer that you wish to share, such as a disk drive, a printer, a file, or a folder. A *server-based network* is one in which security and other network functions are provided by one computer that is a dedicated server.

Server-based networks have become the standard model for networks serving more than 10 users. The key here is 10 or more users. There are many environments that have fewer than 10 users, but would still benefit from a network. Thus, there is an alternative to the server-based network. It is called a *peer-to-peer* network, or sometimes a *workgroup*. A peer-to-peer network has no dedicated servers or hierarchy among the computers. All the computers are equal and therefore peers. Each computer can function as either a client or a server.

There are many advantages to setting up a network. If you have only one printer, CD-ROM drive, or Zip drive, every computer in the LAN can use that hardware. If you and others are working on the same document, users can access the document without having to copy it to their own computers. If you have several people working on the same data, such as a customer list, you can keep all that information on one computer, and every user will be able to access that information. Users then know that they are working with the most current information. You can set up local email so that you can send messages to any user on the network. If you have any notebook computers (portables), you can attach or detach them from the network and update information as you need. If you are away from the office, you can dial in to your network and access the resources you need.

You may also hear the term **WAN** (*wide area network*). A WAN consists of computers that use long-range telecommunications links such as modems or satellites to connect the networked computers over long distances. The *Internet* is a WAN. It is a worldwide network of networks that connects millions of computers.

In order to have any kind of network, including a peer-to-peer network, you must have a **network interface card,** referred to as a **NIC**, installed into a slot in each computer so that the LAN connecting all the computers can be installed. The most common NIC card is an Ethernet card. The card must also fit the bus architecture slot you have available, typically a PCI (peripheral component interconnect) slot on a Pentium, an ISA (Industry Standard Architecture) on an older desktop computer or, or a PCMCIA (Personal Computer Memory Card International Association) slot on a notebook computer. The card must support the type of cable you will be using to connect the computers.

There are two common ways to set up a peer-to-peer network. One type of networking uses a single coaxial cable, commonly called **Thinnet,** Thin-Ethernet or 10Base2. If you use this method, you also need **T-connectors** and **terminator plugs**. In this case, all the computers connect to a single cable. The T-connector has one end plugged into the network card and two open ends (like a T) for connecting the cables that go to the computers. Once the cables are connected to the computers using the T-connector, each end of the cable uses a terminator plug to complete the network. Every cable must be plugged into the network or have a terminator to complete the connection. There can be no end that is unattached. See Figure 12.1.

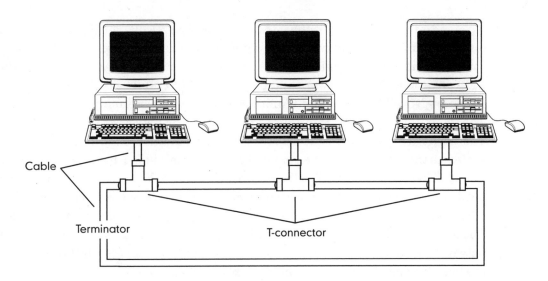

Cable

Terminator

T-connector

FIGURE 12.1   PEER-TO-PEER NETWORK USING T-CONNECTORS

The other way to create a peer-to-peer network is to use an Ethernet hub. Each connection is like a spoke of a bicycle; one end connected to the hub and the other end connected to a computer. In this case, you would use the type of cable called *twisted-pair cable*, also known as 10BaseT, 10BT, twisted pair, twisted-pair Ethernet, TPE, or RJ-45. See Figure 12.2.

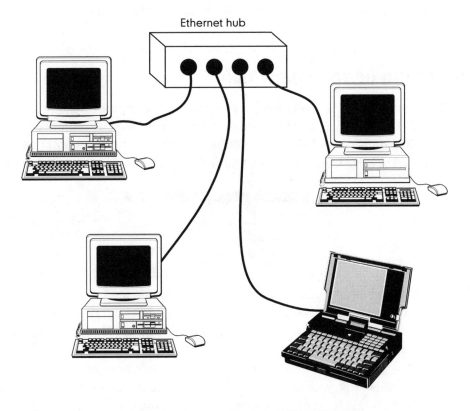

Ethernet hub

FIGURE 12.2   PEER-TO-PEER NETWORK USING AN ETHERNET HUB

You not only must connect the computers physically and have a network interface card in each computer, but you must also have software that tells the computers how to communicate with one another. In a server-based network, the software is known as a network operating system (NOS). The two most popular NOSs are Novell NetWare and Windows 2000 Server, also known as Microsoft NT5. The computer that serves the other computers on the network uses this software. Those who are served are called clients. In a generic sense, a network operating system is the software you need to make your networked hardware communicate.

There is a third part to the networking trilogy. You have been introduced to hardware and software. The third component is the ***network administrator***. The administrator is the person who decides how the hardware and software will be used. The administrator decides who will have access to what devices and resources on the network. The administrator also manages the day-to-day operation of the hardware, the network operating system, and resources of the network.

A server-based network is beyond the scope of this text. However, peer-to-peer networking is not. Any computer that is running Windows has the built-in peer-to-peer software to create and administer a small network. A small network still needs the appropriate hardware, software and an administrator. In a peer-to-peer network, users can administer their own computers, or there can be a single administrator. The selection of the network card and the cable is beyond the scope of this text. This text makes the assumption that these hardware decisions have been made. In this chapter you will set up a LAN with the built-in networking software that comes with Windows.

12.2 SETTING UP YOUR NETWORK

In order to install the software, you will need your original Windows installation disk because, when you boot with the new network card in your computer, Windows will normally detect it and ask for the Windows CD files it needs for networking. You will be asked to reboot the computer. You will then see the following dialog box:

Each user will have a logon name. Common user names are first initial and last name such as Cgillay or Bpeat. If you like, you could use your entire name, such as Carolyn Z. Gillay or Bette Peat. You will also be asked to key in a password. Select one that you will not forget. You will then be asked to key in your password a second time to confirm its spelling and case. Passwords are case-sensitive. If you have security concerns, your password should be difficult to guess, but not so difficult that you might forget it. For this reason, you should avoid obvious passwords such as children's names, your address, or your social security number. Too often a user creates a password and then tapes it on the computer—obviously defeating the purpose of any security.

Once you have logged on, you will see a new icon on your desktop, My Network Places, shown below.

My Network Places is your map to your network. The activities that follow are based on a specific computer configuration. These activities are meant to act as a guide to accomplishing these tasks on your system. You will have to interpret the screen examples to match your specific computer needs. Unfortunately, most schools do not have the hardware, software, or staff support to allow you to do these tasks in a lab environment. If this is the case, you will only be able to read the activities, not do them. *Again, do not attempt to do these activities in a lab environment.*

12.3 ACTIVITY: IDENTIFYING A COMPUTER TO THE NETWORK

Note 1: It is assumed that you have successfully installed the necessary software and hardware.
Note 2: The following activity is based on a specific computer configuration. Your display will be different.

Step 1   Right-click **My Network Places**. Click **Properties**.

The Network dialog box appears. In this example, there are more things listed than you might need. This computer system is on a peer-to-peer network, and it also has a DSL connection to the Internet. Regardless, the Network dialog box will be the same. It has three tabs: Configuration, Identification, and Access Control. The dialog box lists the network clients, adapters, **protocols**, and services that are installed on your computer. The client software allows you to use files and printers shared on other networked computers. The adapter is the network interface card that physically connects you to the network. A protocol is a set of rules that allows computers to connect with one another and to exchange information. Computers on a network must use the same protocol in order to communicate. Services allow you to share your files and printers with other computers on the network. Besides sharing files and printers, there are other services as well, such as an automatic system backup and remote administration of the Registry. In a peer-to-peer network, you want to be sure that at least the following items are listed in the Configuration tab:

- Client for Microsoft Networks
- NetBEUI (pronounced "net booey")
- Your network card (in the above example, DFE-530TX+ 10/100 PCI Fast Ethernet NIC is the NIC)

If any item is missing, you would select the item of interest, then click the **Add** button.

Step 2   Click the **Add** button.

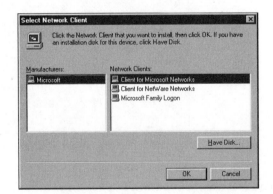

WHAT'S HAPPENING!   As you can see, the icon identifies what type of component you need to install to complete your network setup.

Step 3   Click **Client**. Click **Add**. Click **Microsoft**.

WHAT'S HAPPENING!   In this case, if **Client for Microsoft Networks** were not in the dialog box, you would choose to add it. **Client for NetWare Networks** is needed if you are dealing with a Novell network. The **Microsoft Family Logon** was introduced with Windows 98. If user profiles are enabled and this option has been chosen, users will be able to select their name from a list rather than keying it in.

Step 4   Click **Cancel**. Click **Cancel**.

Step 5   In the Primary Network Logon drop-down list box, be sure **Client for Microsoft Networks** is chosen. Click the **File and Print Sharing** button.

WHAT'S HAPPENING? Here is where you give others access to both your files and printers.

Step 6   Be sure both boxes are checked. Click **OK**.

Step 7   Click the **Identification** tab.

WHAT'S HAPPENING? There are three boxes to fill in: the **Computer name**, the **Workgroup**, and the **Computer Description**. The computer name can be any name you wish, but each computer on the network needs to have a unique name. The name can be up to 15 characters with no spaces. You may use the brand of computer, the operating system, or, perhaps, you might prefer to use the name of the person who most often uses the computer. Choose a name that will clearly identify which computer is which on the network. Here, this computer is identified by its operating system. All computers on your network must use the same workgroup name. It must be identical in case and spelling. Again, you can have up to 15 characters with no spaces. Only computers with the same workgroup name can share resources. In this example, the workgroup name is **HOME**. It is your choice whether you wish to add any more identifying information in the Computer Description text box; The wisdom in selecting names is KISS: Keep It Simple, Stupid. You may key in anything that might help you identify the computer. In this case, to keep it simple, the processor name is listed.

Step 8   Click the **Access Control** tab.

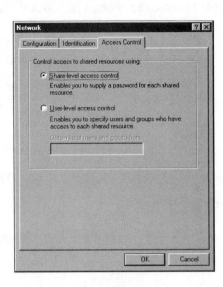

   Here you have two choices: the first, **Share-level access control**, is
simpler to select, since you assign one password to each resource; and the
second, **User-level access control**, is where you must list the name of
every member of your network who is allowed to use every shared device.
Only in unique situations is this choice used.

Step 9   Click **Cancel**.

Step 10   Repeat these steps for each computer on the network.

Step 11   Be sure that all your computers are turned on. Choose one computer.
Double-click **My Network Places**. Double-click **Entire Network**.
Double-click the workgroup name, in this example **HOME**.

   You see the names for every computer on your network. Be a little
patient. It takes some time for the computers to see one another. Each is
broadcasting its availability. In this example, there are two computers—
Millennium, just created, and Server. (*Note:* If you do not see **My Network Places** or **My Network Places** is empty, chances are you have a
problem with your network installation, either with the hardware or
with the protocols and services. This problem is beyond the scope of this
text. However, a simple mistake that users make is that they have a

different workgroup name. You can correct this easily by right-clicking **My Network Places**, clicking the **Identification** tab, and ensuring that the Workgroup is the same on all networked computers.)

Step 12   *(Note:* Remember that this activity refers to a specific computer configuration. Your computer network will not look exactly like this example.) Double-click the **Server** computer.

WHAT'S HAPPENING? ➡ Windows uses the Internet Explorer-type window. Internet Explorer is a *browser* (tool to search the Internet). In this example, the Server window contains two printers and two folders that have been "shared" previously. The **Server** computer is a computer running Windows 95. It is acting as a print server and additional storage for the **Millennium** computer. There are two printers, one drive, and a CDROM that are shared on the Server computer. Note the name in the window. Server is named as **Server**. The double backslash is the *UNC (universal naming convention)* for locating the path to a network resource. It specifies the share name on a particular computer. The computer name is limited to 15 characters, and the share name is usually limited to 15 characters. It takes the format of **computername\sharename\optional path**.

Step 13   Close My Network Places.

12.4   SHARING DEVICES ON YOUR NETWORK

There are always two parts to sharing resources—the client and the server. The server is the computer that has the resource you wish to share. The client is the computer that wishes to access the resource. The most common items to share are a printer, a folder on a hard drive, or an entire hard drive. In a peer-to-peer network, the sharing can go both ways. The Server computer is already sharing two printers and two directories. The Millennium computer has as yet not shared anything. A common device that you might want to share is your CD, particularly if one of your computers on your network does not have a CD. In this day and age, most software is installed using a CD. If you had a computer that did not have a CD, you could not install any software that came on a CD. By sharing a CD, you overcome this limitation .You could install your software on the computer without a CD using the CD on the other computer.

12.5   ACTIVITY: SHARING DEVICES ON THE NETWORK

Note 1: The following activity is based on a specific computer configuration. Your display will be different.

Note 2: This activity also assumes that you have a CD ROM on your local computer.

Step 1   Go to the computer that physically has the device you want to share attached to it. (In this case, the CD ROM).

Step 2   Open **My Computer**. Right-click the CD-ROM drive you wish to share.

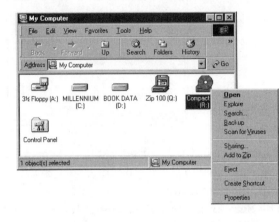

WHAT'S HAPPENING?   You need to share this CD-ROM drive. The context menu has a menu choice, **Sharing**.

Step 3   Click **Sharing**. Click the **Shared As** button.

WHAT'S HAPPENING?   Here is where you give a name to your shared device. You again must use the same name across the network. The name showing is the drive letter assigned to the CD-ROM on the local computer, but that is not very descriptive.

Step 4   In this example, you key in **MILL-CD**.

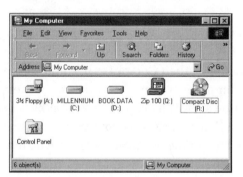

WHAT'S HAPPENING? You have named your shared CD-ROM. If you wanted, you could include a password. However, if you did that, any user who wanted to use this CD would need to know the password.

Step 5   Click **OK**.

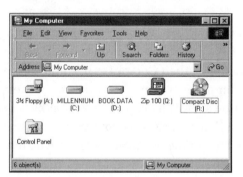

WHAT'S HAPPENING? Your CD-ROM drive now has a hand icon under it. This icon indicates that the drive is shared.

12.6   SHARING A PRINTER ON YOUR NETWORK

Another common device that is shared is a printer. You may have only one printer and wish any computer on the network to be able to use it. Another common scenario is that you have two printers, a color printer and a laser printer. Again, you want the ability so that any computer on the network can use any of the available printers without having to physically leave the computer you are working on and move to the computer that has the printer you want to use.

When you share a printer, any computer on the network can use that printer. The printer, of course, needs to be connected physically to a computer on the network. This computer then becomes the print server. Often, in a large network, there will be one computer dedicated to handling printing, and it will be called the print server. In a small network, the *print server* is not dedicated only to printing.

It can be any computer on the network. Furthermore, if you have more than one printer, each can be shared. Look at Figure 12.3.

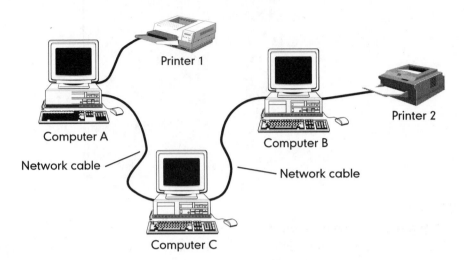

Printer 1

Computer A

Network cable

Computer B

Printer 2

Network cable

Computer C

FIGURE 12.3   PRINTER SHARING ON A NETWORK

Computers A, B and C are networked. Computer A has Printer 1 attached to it. If you are sitting at Computer C, you are the client who wants to use the resources (Printer 1) of Computer A. Computer A in this case is the print server because Printer 1 is attached to Computer A. If you wanted to use the printer attached to Computer B, then Computer B would be the print server because Printer 2 is attached to Computer B. Any computer on this network can use any printer attached to it. However, the print server must be turned on. If you were sitting at Computer C and Computer A was not turned on, you would not be able to use the printer attached to Computer A. However, you do have the choice of using a printer *locally*. If you were sitting at Computer A, you could use Printer 1 locally. Locally means that you are not using the network. You use the printer as usual because it is physically attached to the computer. You do not need to be on the network.

If you do not wish to have to turn on a computer to use a printer, there is another alternative. You need to purchase a piece of hardware called a *hub*. A hub is common connection point for devices on a network. If you have a printer that can have its own network card, you can attach the printer to the hub as well as all your computers. Then, the printer is simply a device on the network that is always available. It does not need to be connected to a computer because it is connected to the hub.

12.7   ACTIVITY: SHARING A PRINTER ON YOUR NETWORK

Note: The following activity is based on a specific computer configuration. Your display will be different. A new printer, an HP 1200C, has been attached to the Millennium computer, it will be shared so it can be used from the Server computer.

Step 1   Click **Start**. Click **Settings**. Click **Printers**.

Printers window showing:
File   Edit   View   Favorites   Tools   »
Back   Forward   Up   Search   »
Address Printers   Go

Add Printer   HP LaserJet III   Canon Bubble-Jet

HP DeskJet 1220C Printer

4 object(s)

WHAT'S HAPPENING? You have opened the printer folder. You can see three printers. The HP LaserJet III and the Canon Bubble-Jet are physically installed on the Server computer and shared for use by the Millennium computer. This time, you will do the opposite. You will share the HP 1220C.

Step 2   Right-click the **HP DeskJet 1220C Printer**.

Context menu:
Open
Pause Printing
Set as Default
Purge Print Documents
Sharing...
Create Shortcut
Delete
Rename
Properties

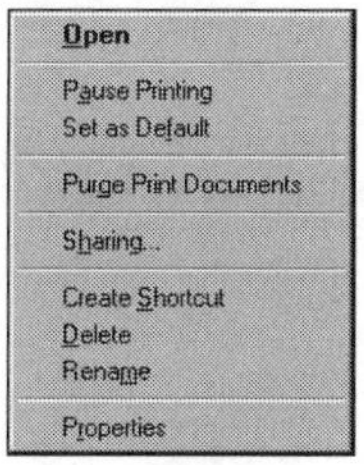

WHAT'S HAPPENING? The fifth item on the menu that appears is Sharing. This is what you want.

Step 3   Click **Sharing**.

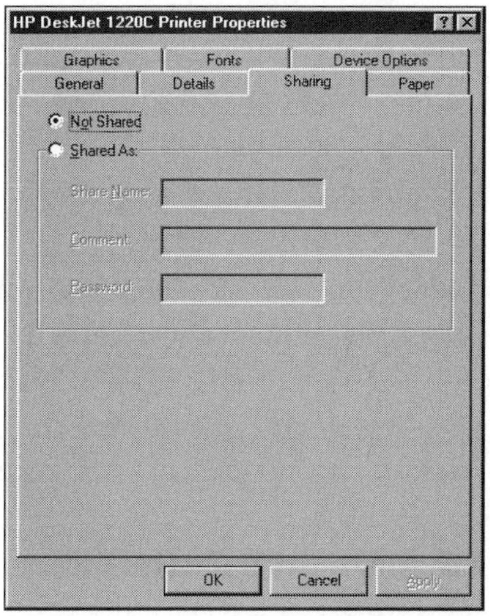

HP DeskJet 1220C Printer Properties dialog:
Graphics   Fonts   Device Options
General   Details   Sharing   Paper
• Not Shared
○ Shared As:
Share Name:
Comment:
Password:
OK   Cancel   Apply

WHAT'S HAPPENING? You opened the Properties box to the Sharing tab. Not Shared is the current selection.

Step 4   Change the selection to Shared As.

Step 5   Change the Share Name to a name that will be certain to identify the printer to the user.

▶ You have completed the sharing process.

Step 6   Click **Apply**. Click **OK**.

▶ You can see that the HP DeskJet is now a shared device by the sharing hand on the icon.

This is half of the process of sharing a printer. You now need to go to all other computers on the network and install the new printer as a network printer.

Step 7   Close the Printer window.

12.8   CONNECTING TO A SHARED PRINTER

In the example you are following, it has been decided that the HP DeskJet 1220 should replace the Cannon Bubble-Jet. This will mean deleting the HP printer from the Millennium computer, physically disconnecting it from Millennium. It will also require deleting the Cannon from both the Server computer and the Millennium computer, and physically disconnecting it. Finally, the HP 1220 will need to be connected and installed on the Server computer. As you can see, planning is important. However, you should be aware that networks, even simple home networks, are rarely static. As you change operating systems, and replace hardware, your network will continue to evolve.

As the example continues, the hardware and software changes required to move the HP 1220C printer have been completed. The HP DeskJet 1220C printer is now physically connected to the Server computer, and has been shared. You now want to connect to that printer from the Millennium computer so you can use it no matter which computer you are using. This is accomplished by installing a Network Printer.

12.9 ACTIVITY: CONNECTING TO A SHARED PRINTER

Step 1   Click **Start**. Click **Settings**. Click **Printers**.

WHAT'S
HAPPENING!   As you can see, both the Cannon printer and the local HP 1200C printer
                are no longer available.

Step 2   Double-click **Add Printer**.

Step 3   Click **Next** in the opening Add Printer Wizard window.

Step 4   Select **Network Printer**.

Step 5   Click **Next**.

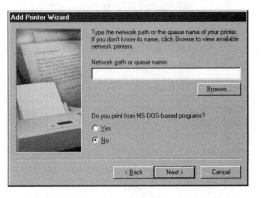

WHAT'S HAPPENING? You have to provide two pieces of information to this dialog box. First, Do you print from MS-DOS-based programs? During the activities in this book, and also for many printouts from the utility programs you have learned to use, you most certainly do. Second, the Network path name. If you know the name you can key it in. In this example that would be \\Server\HP-1220C. You can also click the Browse button.

Step 6   Click **Browse**.

Step 7   Click the **+** by Entire Network.

Step 8   Click the **+** by HOME.

Step 9   Click the **+** by Server.

WHAT'S HAPPENING? You can see the new printer HP-1220C. This is the printer you want to install.

Step 10   Click on the hp-1220c and click **OK**.

WHAT'S HAPPENING? A printer name, usually provided in the driver by the manufacturer, is inserted in the Printer name box. You can change it if you wish. Notice that No is selected for default printer, as you have already chosen the HP Laser for default. You could change default printers by selecting Yes, but in this case you will keep the current default printer.

In this example, You were not asked for Windows CD or the CD that came with the printer to install the drivers, as the printer drivers are already on the hard drive from a previous installation. If that had not been the case, the Add Printer Wizard would have prompted you to insert the disk containing the drivers, and then the installation would continue as follows.

Step 11   Click **Next**.

> **Add Printer Wizard**
>
> After your printer is installed, Windows can print a test page so you can confirm that the printer is set up properly.
>
> Would you like to print a test page?
>
> ○ Yes (recommended)
> ○ No
>
> < Back   Finish   Cancel

 You are asked if you want to print a test page, which is always a good idea on a new installation.

Step 12   Select **Yes (recommended)** and click **Finish**.

> **HP DeskJet 1220C Printer**
>
> Printer test page completed!
>
> A test page is now being sent to the printer. Depending on the speed of your printer, it may take a minute or two before the page is printed.
>
> The test page briefly demonstrates the printer's ability to print graphics and text, as well as providing technical information about the printer driver.
>
> Did the test page print correctly?
>
> Yes   No

 If you did not receive a test page, you would click No and then be guided through a troubleshooting wizard to help solve the problem.

Step 13   Click **Yes**.

Step 14   Close all open windows

Step 15   Click **Start**. Click **Settings**. Click **Printers**.

> **Printers**
>
> File   Edit   View   Favorites   Tools   »
>
> Back   Forward   Up   Search   »
>
> Address Printers   ▾   Go
>
> Add Printer   HP LaserJet III   HP DeskJet 1220C Printer
>
> 3 object(s)

 You have successfully installed the network printer.

12.10 SHARING HARD DRIVES AND FOLDERS ON YOUR NETWORK

Remember that there are two parts to sharing resources—the client and the server. The server is the computer that has the resource you wish to share. The client is the computer that wishes to access the resource. When you share a hard drive, just like a CD-ROM or printer, any computer on the network can look into that drive and use the folders and files on that drive. The computer with the drive you wish to share takes on the roll of *file server*. Again, in a large network, often there will be one computer dedicated to being a file server. In a small network, typically, there is no dedicated file server.

In a peer-to-peer network any computer that has installed File and Print Services, as was shown in Activity 12.3, can share its drives. You have the choice of sharing the entire drive or selected folders. Again, the process requires two steps. You must go to the server computer, which contains the drive you wish to share. You then set up the drive so you can share it. When you go to the client computer, you access the shared drive via My Network Places. You can also access the drive and/or folder by using the command prompt, but you must know the path to the computer. You can also assign a drive letter to the drive.

·12.11 ACTIVITY: SHARING DRIVES AND FOLDERS OVER THE NETWORK

Note: The following activity is based on a specific computer configuration. Your display will be different.

Step 1   Go to the computer on which the drive you wish to share is located.

Step 2   Open **My Network Places**. Double-click **Entire Network**. Double-click **HOME**.

WHAT'S HAPPENING?   In this example, you are logged onto the Millennium computer.

Step 3   Double-click **Millennium**.

WHAT'S HAPPENING? All you see is the shared CD. No other drives are available through My Network Places, as this is currently the only share on the Millennium computer.

Step 4 Close the Millennium window.

Step 5 Open My Computer.

Step 6 Double-click the C drive icon.

Step 7 Right-click the folder you want to share, in this case **TEMP**.

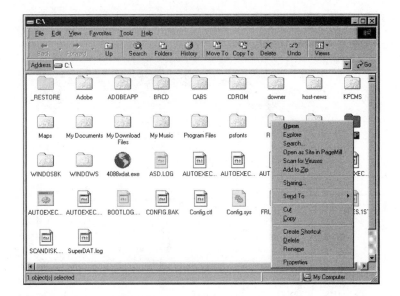

WHAT'S HAPPENING? The sharing option is available for the folders too.

Step 8 Click **Sharing**. In the TEMP Properties box, choose **Shared as:**.

Step 9 In the Share Name box, key in **MILL-TEMP**.

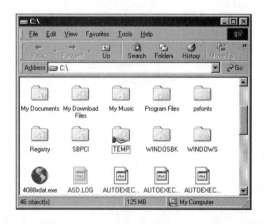

WHAT'S HAPPENING? You have chosen a name for the shared folder. Always make your share names descriptive. Notice the default Access Type is Read-Only. You want to be able to access this drive for not only reading from, but also for writing to.

Step 10   Select **Full** under the Access type.

Step 11   Click **Apply**. Click **OK**.

WHAT'S HAPPENING? The **TEMP** directory now has the Share hand under the icon.

Step 12   Close My Computer. Open **My Network Places**. Double-click **Entire Network.**

Step 13   Double-click **Home**. Double-click **Millennium**.

WHAT'S HAPPENING! ➡ Now you see your **mill-temp** folder icon along with the shared CD.

Step 14   Close My Network Places.

12.12 USING SHARED DRIVES: MAPPING

Once a drive or folder is shared, you may map a drive letter to the shared drive or shared folder. A *mapped drive* is a network drive or folder (one that has been shared) that you assign a local drive letter. When you map a drive or a folder, it appears as a drive on your client computer in Explorer and My Computer. You no longer need to browse My Network Places to have access to that shared drive or folder.

In order to see the mapped drive icon on the toolbar, you need to add the Map Network Drive icon. You can also right-click My Network Places to go through this process. The third option is to use the command NET USE, either at the command line or in a batch file. All three methods will be demonstrated.

For the following activity, the Server computer has two printers and two drives, and the Temp directory on Server drive C is shared, as shown below. The Temp directory share has been given full access, and the ddrive on Server has been given Read-Only access.

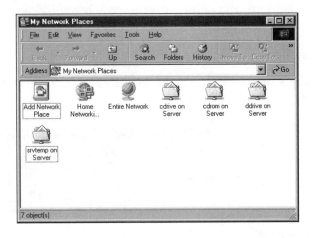

12.13 ACTIVITY: MAPPING DRIVES ON THE NETWORK FROM THE GUI

Note 1: The following activity is based on the above-mentioned specific computer configuration. Your display will be different.

Note 2: In these examples, the Server computer is running Windows 95 and the Millennium computer is running Windows Me.

Step 1   You are going to be working from the Millennium computer. Right-click **My Network Places**.

WHAT'S
HAPPENING?   You see a shortcut menu listing your choices. The one you are interested in is Map Network Drive.

Step 2   Click **Map Network Drive**.

WHAT'S
HAPPENING?   The drive listed, in this case, is E, the first available drive letter not assigned to any real device on this computer. The entry required in the path box is the UNC (Universal Naming Convention) path to the drive that you want. If you check the **Reconnect at logon** box, Drive E on your local computer (Millennium in this example) would actually point to the path you enter each time you boot up. You can, however, choose another drive.

STEP 3   In the Path box, key in: **\\SERVER\SVRTEMP**

Step 4   Click the down arrow in the Drive box, scroll down and select the letter **T.**

Step 5   Click **OK**.

WHAT'S
HAPPENING?   You may see a window with the contents of the newly mapped drive appear.

Step 6   Close all open windows. Open **My Computer**.

WHAT'S HAPPENING? ➤ You can see that Drive T appears in My Computer as if it were a drive on your system. You may access it in the usual way, by clicking on it. You can tell it is a network drive by the icon that is setting on a cable, indicating a network connection. You can access the Add Network Drive dialog box by adding its icon to the toolbar.

Step 7   Click **View** on the My Computer menu bar. Click **Toolbars**. Click **Customize**.

Step 8   Click **Map Drive** in the **Available toolbar buttons** window.

Step 9   Click **Add**.

WHAT'S HAPPENING? ➤ The dialog box shows you that you have added the Map Drive button to your toolbar. Notice the Move Up and Move Down buttons on the right. Use them to place the icon where you want it to be on the toolbar.

Step 10 Click **Close**.

Step 11 Close all open windows.

Step 12 Open **My Computer**. Double-click **Srvtemp on 'Server' (T:)**.

WHAT'S HAPPENING? The Mapped drive "T" displays the same way it would if it were an actual, local drive. There are two files on that drive, a text file and a batch file.

Step 13 Double-click **OnServer.txt**.

WHAT'S HAPPENING? You can open the text file with Notepad, just as if it resided locally.

Step 14 Close Notepad.

Step 15 Double-click the **RUNME.BAT** icon.

WHAT'S HAPPENING? The batch file executed in the same way it would have had it been located on a local drive. As you can see, when dealing with a network drive to which you have been granted Full Access, there is no noticeable difference from dealing with a local drive.

Step 16 Close all open windows.

Step 17 Right-click **My Network Places**. Click **Disconnect Network Drive**.

WHAT'S
HAPPENING? The T drive is the only available mapped drive to disconnect.

Step 18   Click **OK** to disconnect.

12.14 ACTIVITY: MAPPING DRIVES WITH THE NET USE COMMAND

The NET USE command is a very powerful command that gives you information and allows you to manipulate your shares. Some of the options are applicable to larger Local Area Networks, and are in reference to passwords and HOME directories. Those options are outside the scope of this text. The following abbreviated syntax and options are applicable to a small peer-to-peer network.

```
Connects or disconnects your computer from a shared resource or
displays information about your connections.

NET USE [drive: ¦ *] [\\computer\directory [/YES] [/NO]
NET USE [port:] [\\computer\printer [/YES] [/NO]

NET USE drive: ¦ \\computer\directory /DELETE [/YES]
NET USE port: ¦ \\computer\printer /DELETE [/YES]
NET USE * /DELETE [/YES]

NET USE drive: ¦ * /HOME

  drive        Specifies the drive letter you assign to a shared
               directory.
  *            Specifies the next available drive letter. If used with
               /DELETE, specifies to disconnect all of your connections.
  port         Specifies the parallel (LPT) port name you assign to a
               shared printer.
  computer     Specifies the name of the computer sharing the resource.
  directory    Specifies the name of the shared directory.
  printer      Specifies the name of the shared printer.

  /YES         Carries out the NET USE command without first prompting
               you to provide information or confirm actions.
  /DELETE      Breaks the specified connection to a shared resource.
  /NO          Carries out the NET USE command, responding with NO
               automatically when you are prompted to confirm actions.

To list all of your connections, type NET USE without options.

To see this information one screen at a time, type the following at
the command prompt:

NET USE /? ¦ MORE    or    NET HELP USE ¦ MORE


NET USE can be used at the command line or, as with all command line
commands, in a batch file.
```

Note 1: This activity is based on a specific computer network. Your own environment will be significantly different.

Note 2: Be sure to check with your instructor and/or lab technician before attempting to use NET USE in a lab environment.

Step 1   Open a MS-DOS window. You are at the C:\WINDOWS> prompt.

Step 2   Key in the following: **NET USE** Enter

```
 MS-DOS Prompt                                                      _ □ ×

C:\WINDOWS>NET USE

Status          Local name      Remote name
--------------------------------------------------------------
OK                              \\SERVER\HP
The command was completed successfully.

C:\WINDOWS>_
```

WHAT'S HAPPENING?   You see nothing under Local name, as you have no drives mapped, but the name of the connected printer device HP, which has been accessed during this session, is visible. Remember that there are two printers connected to this network. A test page will be printed from the second printer, and then the NET USE command will be reissued.

```
 MS-DOS Prompt                                                      _ □ ×

C:\WINDOWS>NET USE

Status          Local name      Remote name
--------------------------------------------------------------
OK                              \\SERVER\HP-1220C
The command was completed successfully.

C:\WINDOWS>_
```

The Remote name now displays the recently used HP-1220C printer. Now we will use the NET USE command to map some drives.

Step 3   Key in the following: C:\WINDOWS>**NET USE T: \\Server\srvtemp** [Enter]

```
 MS-DOS Prompt                                                      _ □ ×

C:\WINDOWS>NET USE T: \\Server\srvtemp
The command was completed successfully.

C:\WINDOWS>_
```

WHAT'S HAPPENING?   You see confirmation that the command worked. Also, a window will open to the mapped drive T.

Step 4   Key in the following: C:\WINDOWS>**T:** [Enter]

Step 5   Key in the following: T:\>**DIR** [Enter]

```
 MS-DOS Prompt                                                      _ □ ×

C:\WINDOWS>T:

T:\>DIR

 Volume in drive T is SERVER-C
 Directory of T:\
```

```
     .           <DIR>         03-29-96   7:26p .
    ..           <DIR>         03-29-96   7:26p ..
ONSERVER TXT               171  11-11-00  10:15a OnServer.txt
RUNME    BAT               226  11-11-00  12:29p RUNME.BAT
             2 file(s)             397 bytes
             2 dir(s)   1,025,540,096 bytes free

T:\>_
```

WHAT'S HAPPENING? ➤ As you can see, you can access a mapped drive from the command line prompt just as if it were a local drive.

Step 6   Key in the following: `T:\>`**C:** [Enter]

Step 7   Key in the following: `C:\WINDOWS>`**NET USE T: /DELETE** [Enter]

Step 8   Key in the following: `C:\WINDOWS>`**DIR T:** [Enter]

```
┌─────────────────────────────────────────────────────────────────┐
│ 🄼 MS-DOS Prompt                                        _ □ ✕    │
├─────────────────────────────────────────────────────────────────┤
│ T:\>C:                                                            │
│                                                                   │
│ C:\WINDOWS>NET USE T: /DELETE                                     │
│ The command was completed successfully.                           │
│                                                                   │
│ C:\WINDOWS>DIR T:                                                 │
│ Invalid drive specification                                       │
│                                                                   │
│ C:\WINDOWS>_                                                      │
└─────────────────────────────────────────────────────────────────┘
```

WHAT'S HAPPENING? ➤ You have successfully disconnected the drive mapping of T: to \\Server\srvtemp. However, it is ever so much more convenient to place drive-mapping commands in batch files, and place shortcuts to the batch files on the desktop.

Step 9   Place the DATA disk in the A drive.

Step 10   Key in the following: `C:\WINDOWS>`**A:** [Enter]

Step 11   Key in the following: `A:\>`**MD CHAP12** [Enter]

Step 12   Key in the following: `A:\>`**CD CHAP12** [Enter]

Step 13   Using the MS-DOS text editor, create the following two batch files in the CHAP12 subdirectory on the DATA disk:

MAP-T.BAT: UNMAP-T.BAT:
@ECHO OFF   **@ECHO OFF**
NET USE T: \\SERVER\SRVTEMP   **NET USE T: /DELETE**
PAUSE   **PAUSE**

Step 14   Close the MS-DOS prompt window.

Step 15   Right-click the desktop. Click **New** and then click **Shortcut**.

Step 16   Click **Browse**. Go to the A drive. Go to the CHAP12 directory.

WHAT'S HAPPENING? You can see both of the batch files.

Step 17   Click on **MAP-T.BAT** and click **Open**.

Step 18   Click **Next** twice.

WHAT'S HAPPENING? You are shown a group of icons from which to choose.

Step 19   Select an icon and click **Finish**.

WHAT'S HAPPENING? You have a new icon on the desktop, pointing to the batch file that will map the T drive to the Temp directory on the Server Computer's C drive.

Step 20   Right-click the **MAP-T.BAT** icon.

Step 21   Click **Properties**. Click the **Program** tab.

MAP-T.BAT Properties

General | Program | Font | Memory | Screen | Misc

MAP-T

Cmd line: A:\CHAP12\MAP-T.BAT

Working: A:\CHAP12

Batch file:

Shortcut key: None

Run: Normal window

☐ Close on exit

☐ Prevent MS-DOS-based programs from detecting Windows

Change Icon...

OK   Cancel   Apply

WHAT'S HAPPENING? ➤ You have opened the property sheet for the **MAP-T.BAT** file.

Step 22   Click in the **Close on exit** box. (Now the MS-DOS window will close when the batch file has completed execution.)

Step 23   Click **OK**.

Step 24   Repeat Steps 15 through 23 for the UNMAP-T.BAT file, choosing a different icon.

MAP-T.BAT

UNMAP-T.BA
T

WHAT'S HAPPENING? ➤ You now have icons to both map and disconnect the T: drive mapping.

Step 25   Double click the **MAP-T.BAT** icon.

MAP-T

Auto

The command was completed successfully.
Press any key to continue . . .

T:\

File Edit View Favorites Tools »

Back   Forward   Up

Address 🖳 T:\   ⟳ Go

OnServer.txt   RUNME.BAT

2 object   1.42 MB   🖳 Local intranet

WHAT'S HAPPENING? ➤ Two things happen very quickly. First, you get the message that the command was successfully completed, and then the T drive window opens. The MS-DOS window has not closed, as there is a PAUSE command holding the batch file for user intervention. If not for the PAUSE command, the window would close immediately. If there had been a problem with the mapping, you would have no opportunity to view the error message.

Step 26   Close the T: drive window.

Step 27   Make sure the MS-DOS window is active and press any key.

WHAT'S HAPPENING? ➤   The batch file finishes, and the window closes.

Step 28   Open My Computer.

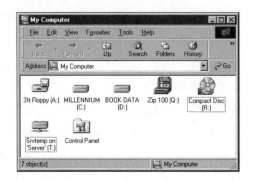

WHAT'S HAPPENING? ➤   The T drive is available.

Step 29   Open an MS-DOS window and issue the NET USE command.

```
MS-DOS Prompt

C:\WINDOWS>NET USE

Status          Local name       Remote name
-------------------------------------------------------------
OK              T:               \\SERVER\SRVTEMP
The command was completed successfully.

C:\WINDOWS>_
```

WHAT'S HAPPENING? ➤   The NET USE command registers the drive mapping T:

Step 30   Close the MS-DOS window.

Step 31   Double-click the **UNMAP-T.BAT** icon. (You may need to move the My Computer window to see the icon.)

Step 32   Press [Space Bar] when you see the message that the command was successful.

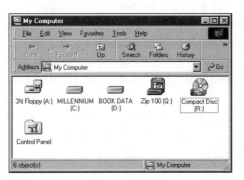

<image>WHAT'S
HAPPENING!</image> The batch file window closed, and the T drive disappeared from the My Computer window.

Step 33 Close all open windows.

<image>WHAT'S
HAPPENING!</image> There are endless combinations of useful ways to use drive letter mappings to shared devices. If you have a graphics package with two CDs, you could place one in each computer, map a drive letter to the second computer, and be able to access them quickly without switching disks. You can make backups of critical data "on the fly" by mapping a letter to a subdirectory on the remote computer, and doing a second save to the remote drive. Each situation is different, and only you know the optimum method for your system.

12.15 THE INTERNET

The Internet is an enormous, worldwide network of computers. Most simply stated, it is the network of networks. More than 350 million people and organizations are connected to the Internet (**http://www.nua.ie/suverys/how_many_online/world.html**), and by accessing this network, you can communicate with all the people who sit at those computers. You can connect to various public and private institutions in order to gather information, do research, explore new ideas, and purchase items. You can access the government, museums, companies, colleges, and universities.

The Internet is part of the ***information superhighway***, a term popularized by the media. The Internet is also referred to as ***cyberspace***. William Gibson, who coined the term *cyberspace* in his book *Neuromancer*, defined it as "a consensual hallucination experienced daily by billions of legitimate operators, in every nation, by children being taught mathematical concepts. A graphic representation of data abstracted from the banks of every computer in the human system. Unthinkable complexity. Lines of light ranged in the nonspace of the mind, clusters and constellations of data. Like city lights, receding . . ."

When you log on to the Internet, you are in cyberspace. You can use the Internet to communicate by email (electronic mail), chat lines, and forums, which are like bulletin boards where you leave notes or read information about a topic of interest. Email allows you to send letters and notes instantly. Chat lines let you talk to people around the world on any subject of interest, such as computers, sewing, or

Ukrainian culture. You are sure to find people who share your interests on the "net." You may connect to the **World Wide Web** (**WWW**) through the Internet. You may even publish your own documents.

For most people, the best-known aspect of the Internet is the Web, an informal expression for the World Wide Web. The Web is a collection of standards and protocols used to access information on the Internet. It is an interconnected collection of more than 15 million **Web sites**. It is a virtual space accessible from the Internet that holds pages of text and graphics in a format recognizable by Web browsers. These pages are linked to one another and to individual files. Using the Web requires a browser to view and navigate through links. The most popular browsers today are Netscape Navigator and Microsoft Internet Explorer.

The World Wide Web is the graphical interface developed at the European Laboratory for Particle Physics in Geneva, Switzerland, by Tim Berners-Lee as a means for physicists to share papers and data easily. Tim Berners-Lee disseminated these tools for free, not taking any personal profit from this world-changing event. He even won a MacArthur "genius" award for the development of the WWW.

The Web and the Internet are not synonymous. The Internet is the actual network used to transport information. The Web is a graphical interface to the Internet. The Web uses three standards: **URLs** (**uniform resource locators**), which tell the location of documents; **HTML** (**Hypertext Markup Language**), which is the programming language used to create Web documents; and the protocols used for information transfer. Most Web traffic uses the protocol **HTTP** (**Hypertext Transfer Protocol**).

URLs are a standard means for identifying locations on the Internet. URLs specify three types of information needed to retrieve a document—the protocol to be used, the server address with which to connect, and the path to the information. The URL syntax is *protocol://servername/path*; examples of URLs are **http://www .netscape.com/netcenter** and **ftp://microsoft.com**. **FTP** stands for **File Transfer Protocol**, and it is used to download or upload files. HTTP is the major protocol used to transfer information within the World Wide Web.

A Web site resides on a server. It is both the virtual and the physical location of a person's or an organization's Web pages. A **Web page** is a single screen of text and graphics that usually has links to other pages. A Web site has an address, its URL. A **home page** is the first page of a Web site. A home page can be thought of as a gateway page that starts you on your search through that Web site.

Web pages usually have hypertext links, referred to as hyperlinks or links. A hypertext link is a pointer to a Web page on the same site or on a different site anywhere in the world. When you click on a link, your browser takes you to the page indicated by the link. If you were at a site about companies that provide electronic commerce solutions for businesses and saw a link called Reference Desk, you could click it to see what references were available. From the Reference Desk page, you could see a hypertext link to a document called "United States Government Electronic Commerce Policy." Clicking that would take you to the Web site of the Department of Commerce, where you could read the article "Surfing the Net."

A Web site's type is indicated by the "dot" part of its address. Common types include commercial sites, which end in .com; educational sites, which end in .edu;

government sites, which end in .gov; military sites, which end in .mil; and most nonprofit organizations' sites, which end in .org. Since addresses are being depleted by the rapid growth of the Internet, new "dots" are being developed, even ones longer than three characters.

Since so much information exists on the Internet, a category of sites called search engines has been developed to help you find what you want. These are essentially indexes to indexes. Popular search engines include Yahoo! (**http://www.yahoo .com**), AltaVista (**http://altavista.com**), Infoseek (**http://www.guide.infoseek .com**), Google (**http://www.google.com**), Ask Jeeves (**http://www.askjeeves.com**), Lycos (**http://www.lycos.com**), and WebCrawler (**http://www.webcrawler.com**). Many companies and organizations position themselves as ***portals***. A portal is an entry to the Web. Yahoo! and AOL (America Online) are now expanding beyond being just search engines and are positioning themselves as portals.

There are many ways to access information on the Internet. One common way is to have a modem, communication software, and an online provider. You may set up your dial-up network using the Dial Up Networking icon found in the Control Panel window with the Add/Remove Program icon, also located in Control Panel; or you may install when you install Windows Millennium. You use your modem to dial out through your telephone line. In order to establish your dial-up account, you have to decide what service you were going to use. You could choose to connect to the Internet by belonging to a service such as MSN (Microsoft Network) or AOL (America Online). Each of these providers would give you detailed instructions on how to set up your dial-up account and would supply you with a local telephone number. If you used a service such as AOL or MSN, you would probably use its preferred browser, although you certainly could use any browser. Both MSN and AOL are now considered portals.

Another popular way to connect to the Internet is to use an ISP. ***ISPs*** (***Internet service providers***), also called *access providers* or *service providers,* are companies or organizations that provide a gateway or link to the Internet for a fee. EarthLink and Concentric Network are examples of these kinds of companies. You would be given explicit instructions from your provider how to create your dial-up account. You may choose your browser. Most people choose either Netscape Navigator or Microsoft Internet Explorer. The ISP is simply the link to the Internet. On your browser, you could have a home page, the first page that would open when you launched your browser. With some ISPs you can have your own Web site, with a home page and one or more Web pages. Many ISPs charge a fee to create a Web site, but some provide this service at no additional cost.

There are other ways to connect to the Internet. Some cable companies provide direct cable connections. In this case, you would not use your telephone line. You would always be connected to the Internet and would not have to dial up when you wished to surf the Net. You could use Netscape Navigator or Internet Explorer as your browser, or you could use the cable company's supplied browser. The advantage of a cable connection is speed. Some people joke that when the Internet is accessed over a telephone line, WWW stands for World Wide Wait. A cable connection, on the other hand, is extremely fast.

Another choice is to use an ISDN (Integrated Services Digital Network), which is a high-speed digital phone line that transfers data at a rate five to six times faster than that of a 28.8-kilobits-per-second modem. The phone company must lay the ISDN line to your home or business, and you must have a special modem. A DSL (digital subscriber line) is yet another choice, if available. To use DSL, you must be close enough geographically to a telephone company's central office and a local loop. In telephony, a local loop is the wired connection from a telephone company's central office in a locality to its customers' telephones at homes and businesses. The system was originally designed for voice transmission only. Today, your computer's modem makes the conversion between analog signals and digital signals. With Integrated Services Digital Network or Digital Subscriber Line, the local loop can carry digital signals directly and at a much higher bandwidth than they do for voice only. It is anticipated that DSL will replace ISDN lines. Here a user can purchase bandwidth that is potentially 10 times faster than an ISDN line but still slower than cable. You may be fortunate enough to have your connection through a business or educational institution that has a T1 or T3 leased line, which provides a faster connection than any of the above choices. Another way, not that common yet, is connecting via satellites. This connection provides truly high-speed communications, but it is, at this point, not readily available.

DSL is becoming more and more popular. In many areas there are waiting lists to have DSL installed. When you have DSL installed, the company will usually provide you with a special modem, and will run a line directly that looks just like a normal telephone line into your house. They may also provide the Network Interface card. The installers will "activate" your line with the local company. Some companies will do the software installation, as well as the hardware installation.

To your computer, the DSL connection is just another link on a LAN. The company will provide you with the IP addresses that you require.

The Millennium computer is on a static DSL connection. "Static" refers to the fact that the IP address of the Millennium computer does not change. This is not the usual home connection, however. Most companies assign a temporary IP address to your computer as you connect.

12.16 ABOUT DSL

The acronym "DSL" stands for Digital Subscriber Line. It is used to refer to both categories of DSL—ADSL and SDSL. Both operate over existing copper telephone lines and both need to be relatively close to a central telephone office. Usually you are required to be within 20,000 feet.

ADSL stands for Asymmetrical Digital Subscriber Line. It uses a special modem and a technology that allows more data be sent on existing phone lines. This is the type that is currently extremely popular.

SDSL stands for Symmetrical Digital Subscriber Line. It also requires a special modem. This technology is being used primarily in Europe. It uses high frequency digital pulsing, and since high frequencies are not used by the human voice, SDSL can operate simultaneously with voice on the same line.

When you speak on a phone line, your voice is transmitted on analog signals. Computers "speak" digital, not analog. Old modems MOdulated digital signal from a computer into analog signal to transmit, and then, at the other end DEModulated back to digital for the receiving computer. Hence the word *modem*. DSL knows that the data does not require change into analog form and back, but can be transmitted directly as sent from one computer into another. This technology allows for speeds up to 50 times greater than over a 56k modem. For example, to download a needed upgrade for software on a 56k modem would take over 45 minutes. Using DSL, the same upgrade would take less than 2 minutes.

12.17 SETTING UP A DSL ACCOUNT

Note 1: This is a read only activity, and is presented here for demonstration purposes.

Note 2: It is assumed that the TCP/IP protocol has been added to the Network properties, as demonstrated previously in this chapter.

Step 1   Right-click **My Network Places**.

Step 2   Click **Properties**.

WHAT'S HAPPENING?   You have opened the Network properties box and are looking at the Configuration tab. There are two NIC's (Network Interface Cards) installed—3Com Etherlink III and LNE 100 TX. And there are two protocols are installed—TCP/IP and NetBEUI. When protocols are installed, they are installed to a specific NIC, not to the network in general. This is referred to as *binding* the protocol to the NIC. The 3Com card has two protocols bound to it, both TCP/IP and NetBEUI. This is the card that is used to connect Millennium to Server, the two PCs on the LAN. The LNE card is the card provided by the DSL provider, and has only TCP/IP bound to it.

Step 3   Click **TCP/IP->LNE100TX Fast Ethernet Adapter** to select it.

Step 4   Click the **Properties** button. Click the **IP Address** tab.

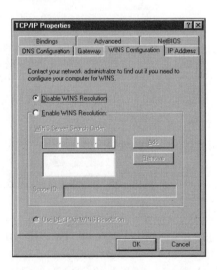

WHAT'S HAPPENING? You are looking at the TCP/IP properties sheet for the DSL NIC. **Specify an IP address** is selected. In most cases, you would choose **Obtain an IP address automatically**. The Subnet Mask is used to mask off a portion of the IP address so that TCP/IP can distinguish the network ID from the host ID. The most common is 255.255.255.0. This number will be given to you by your provider.

Step 5   Click the **WINS Configuration** tab.

WHAT'S HAPPENING? WINS is not required for DSL home connections. Disable should be selected.

Step 6   Click the **Gateway** tab.

> **WHAT'S HAPPENING?** The default gateway will be given by your provider. This is the address of the router used to handle the packets of information sent to remote networks—destinations not physically connected to each other.

Step 7   Click the **DNS Configuration** tab.

> **WHAT'S HAPPENING?** DNS (Domain Name System) has to be enabled. Your local computer is the "host" and has the name Millennium. The exact name you have given your computer is entered here. The "Domain" is the name of the provider, in this example **pacbell.net**. Two addresses were provided for the host to reach the domain. They are keyed into the DNS Server Search Order box. Then the Add button is clicked. The numbers, and the order to enter them will be provided by the DSL service provider, as well as the Domain Suffix Search Order, which is simply the search order to use by default.

Step 8   At this point, you would click **OK** to return to the properties box, and click **OK** again to start the process of implementing your changes. You would be told you needed to re-boot your computer for the changes to take effect.

WHAT'S HAPPENING? ▶ This has been a demonstration of the installation of DSL as provided by a specific company. Details may vary slightly from different providers, but the basic principles will remain the same.

12.18 ACTIVITY: A BRIEF LOOK AT INTERNET EXPLORER

Step 1   Click **Start**. Point to **Settings**. Click **Dial-Up Networking**.
Note: In a lab environment or if you have DSL, your connection is already established. If so, go directly to your browser, key in the address shown in Step 6, and go on to Step 8.

WHAT'S HAPPENING? ▶ In this example, there are two dial-up accounts. **Deltanet** is the name of an Internet service provider. Look above the Dial-Up Networking window. You see a shortcut. Rather than having to open this window, using the shortcut is easier and faster. Once you have chosen your type of connection, you must access it.

Step 2   Double-click **Deltanet**.

WHAT'S HAPPENING? ▶ You see the Connect To dialog box.

Step 3   Click **Connect**.

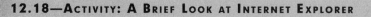

WHAT'S HAPPENING? ➥ A dialog box indicates that you are connecting to the service.

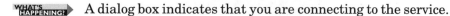

> You have connected. If you look at the status bar, you can see an icon indicating that you are connected. You can right-click this icon at any time to either disconnect or to see the status of your connection.

Step 4   Open your browser. In this case, it is Internet Explorer.

The Book Biz

The Book Biz, Inc. is the business name and website for Carolyn Z. Gillay (czg@bookbiz.com) and Frank Panezich. Carolyn teaches at Saddleback Community College (http://saddleback.cc.ca.us) in the Computer Information Management Department, Business Science Division in Mission Viejo, CA. (http://iserver.saddleback.cc.ca.us/div/bus) She was one of the earliest developers of the DOS class and curriculum at Saddleback. From that first class, she has been a key player in developing the curriculum for as well as teaching classes in various operating systems, including Windows 3.1, Windows 95, Windows 98, Windows NT, and in fall, 2000 will begin teaching Linux. She also teaches various application software such as Quicken. She holds both her B.A. and M.A. from the University of Michigan. She was a manager of software development in industry before making the move to education 16 years ago. In addition, she is the author of 15 college textbooks on operating systems, all published by Franklin, Beedle and Associates. (http://www.fbeedle.com). She also participates in a Windows information site. (http://www.clubwin.com)

Frank Panezich (fdp@bookbiz.com) teaches Latin and Auto Tech at California High School in Whittier, CA. He has been a key player in developing the Latin program at California High School, which now offers Latin I, Latin II and Latin III. He has also been instrumental in the auto tech program at California High School. He has also done extensive coaching in golf and football at both public and private schools. He holds his B.A. degree from California State University at Long Beach. He has also, during his teaching career, been involved in managing and running different

WHAT'S HAPPENING? ➥ You have opened Internet Explorer and you have connected to the Internet. You can now explore the Internet. The **Address** text box shows my "home," which is **http://www.bookbiz.com**, the address that I will come home to.

Step 5   Click **File** on the menu bar. Click **Open**.

Open

Type the Internet address of a document or folder, and Internet Explorer will open it for you.

Open: [   ]

☐ Open as Web Folder

    [OK]   [Cancel]   [Browse...]

WHAT'S HAPPENING? ➥ If you know where you want to go, you can key in the address here.

Step 6   In the **Open** text box, key in the following: **http://www.yahoo.com**

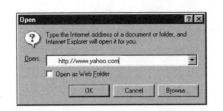

WHAT'S
HAPPENING? You will find that Internet Explorer can complete a URL address once
you start keying it in if you have previously visited the site. You have
keyed in the URL.

Step 7   Click **OK**.

WHAT'S
HAPPENING? You have gone to the Yahoo! Web site. Yahoo! is an index to the different
sites on the net. Each time you click an underlined term, called a
hypertext link, you will be taken to an index of sites.

Step 8   Click **Computers & Internet**.

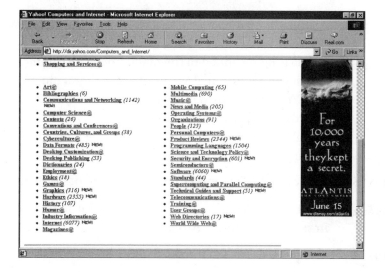

> **WHAT'S HAPPENING?** You have gone to the page of your selected topic, **Computers and Internet**.

Step 9   Scroll down until you see the topic **Humor**.

> **WHAT'S HAPPENING?** Each one of these topics will take you to another topic. You can tell because it is underlined. The number in parentheses after the site name tells you the number of entries.

Step 10   Click **Humor**.

> **WHAT'S HAPPENING?** As you can see, each click takes you to another site. You can also back up one page at a time. You are backed up in the reverse order in which you accessed the pages.

Step 11   Click the **Back** button twice.

> **WHAT'S HAPPENING?** You have returned to the first page, **yahoo.com**. If you wanted to go here often, you could add it to your favorites.

Step 12 Click **Favorites**. Click **Add**.

WHAT'S HAPPENING?   Yahoo is being added to the menu under its common name (**Yahoo!**), which you can use instead of having to remember the URL of the Web site. You can see in Windows Me that you have more choices. If you want to add a new favorite, whenever you find a page you like you click **Add**. To delete or change your favorites, you would choose **Organize**. You can also quickly return to your home page.

Step 13 Click **Cancel**. Click the **Home** button on the toolbar.

WHAT'S HAPPENING?   You have returned to your home page. To go to another site, you can key in the address in the **Address** text box.

Step 14 Select the address in the **Address** text box, in this case **bookbiz.com**

Address http://www.book-biz.com

WHAT'S HAPPENING?   You need to select only the part you wish to change because typing will replace what is highlighted, leaving the unhighlighted portion as it is.

Step 15 Key in the following: **fbeedle.com**

Address http://www.fbeedle.com

WHAT'S HAPPENING?   You have the URL of the home page of the publisher of this book, Franklin, Beedle and Associates.

Step 16 Press Enter

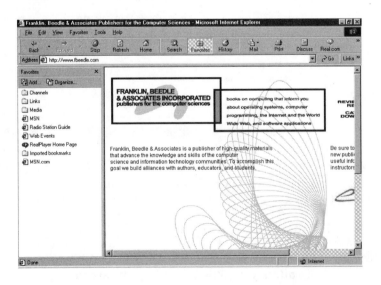

WHAT'S HAPPENING? ➤ You can write to the publisher, see the available books, and order books on the Franklin, Beedle and Associates Web site.

Step 17 Click the **Home** button.

WHAT'S HAPPENING? ➤ You have returned to your home page.

Step 18 Close the browser window.

WHAT'S HAPPENING? ➤ You are returned to the desktop. Remember, although you no longer have the browser open, you are still connected. *If your lab environment is set to connect you automatically, you should not do Steps 19 through 21.*

Step 19 Right-click the communications icon on the status bar. Click **Status**.

```
Connected to Deltanet                    ? X
   Connected at 44,000 bps        [   OK   ]
   Duration: 000:26:08
   Bytes received: 537,724        [Disconnect]
   Bytes sent: 95,019             [Details >>]
```

WHAT'S HAPPENING? ➤ As you can see, you are still connected.

Step 20 Click **Details**.

```
Connected to Deltanet                    ? X
   Connected at 44,000 bps        [   OK   ]
   Duration: 000:27:48
   Bytes received: 537,724        [Disconnect]
   Bytes sent: 95,019             [No Details]

Modem: U.S. Robotics 56K Voice Win
Server type:  PPP: Internet, Windows 2000/NT, Windows
Protocols:
Password authentication protocol
TCP/IP
```

WHAT'S HAPPENING? ➤ You see your speed and how long you have been connected, as well as your protocols and server types.

Step 21 Click **Disconnect**.

WHAT'S HAPPENING? ➤ You have returned to the desktop.

12.19 AN OVERVIEW OF TCP/IP

When discussing communication, and especially the Internet, you will hear the term TCP/IP (Transmission Control Protocol/Internet Protocol). TCP/IP are truly the protocols of the Internet. Data is transferred over the Internet through the protocols called TCP/IP.

Using the Internet is like making a telephone call. For example, you are in Los Angeles and you need to call your mother in Phoenix. You know that you do not have a direct phone line connection to your mother's home. You dial her telephone number, and the phone company decides the best way to route your call. If Los Angeles is very busy, the phone company may send your call to Phoenix through

Denver if Denver is not as busy and can process the data faster. It is not important to you how the phone company manages the communication as long as you can talk to your mother.

On the Internet, data usually travels through several networks before it gets to its destination. Each network has a *router*, a device that connects networks. Data is sent in *packets*, units of information. A router transfers a packet to another network only when the packet is addressed to a station outside of its own network. The router can make intelligent decisions as to which network provides the best route for the data.

The rules for creating, addressing, and sending packets are specified by the TCP/IP protocols. TCP and IP have different jobs and are actually two different protocols. TCP is what divides the data into packets and then numbers each packet so it can be reassembled correctly at the receiving end. IP is responsible for specifying the addresses of the sending and receiving computers and sending the packets on their way. An *IP address* tells routers where to route the data. Data is divided into packets for two major reasons. The first is to ensure that sending a large file will not take up all of a network's time, and the second is to ensure that the data will be transferred correctly. Each packet is verified as having been received correctly. If a packet is corrupt, only the corrupted packet has to be resent, not the entire file.

A large company, college, or university will maintain a permanent open connection to the Internet (a T1 or T3 line), but this is not the case for a small office or a stand-alone PC. As mentioned previously, a single user often accesses the Internet through a dial-up connection. This procedure provides a temporary connection known as a *PPP* (*Point-to-Point Protocol*) connection. Another older protocol that accomplishes the same task is *SLIP* (*Serial Line Internet Protocol*). This connection provides full access to the Internet as long as you are online. However, if you are using a cable modem or a DSL connection, you do not need to "dial up"; you are always connected to your provider (the cable company or phone company). The connection is more like a LAN. You are always connected to the server, which in turn is connected or the gateway to the Internet.

Each computer connected to the Internet must have the TCP/IP protocols installed, as well as a unique IP address. The IP address identifies the computer on the Internet. If you are connected to the Internet through a permanent connection, the IP address remains a static (constant) address. If you have a dial-up account, a cable modem account, or other type of connection, you typically get a dynamic (temporary) IP address. It is a leased address and will change depending on how long the hosting server runs its leases for.

The Internet Corporation for Assigned Names and Numbers (ICANN), **http://www.icann.org/general/abouticann.htm**, is the nonprofit corporation that was formed to assume responsibility for the IP address space allocation, protocol parameter assignment, domain name system management, and root server system management functions previously performed under U.S. Government contract by IANA (Internet Assigned Numbers Authority), **http://www.ican.org**, and other entities. It is a nonprofit organization established for the purpose of administration and registration of IP numbers for the geographical areas previously managed by Network Solutions, Inc. When an organization applies for IP addresses, ICANN assigns a range of addresses appropriate to the number of hosts on the asking organization's network.

An IP address is made up of four numbers separated by periods. An IP address is 32 bits long, making each of the four numbers 8 bits long. These 8-bit numbers are called *octets*. The largest possible octet is 11111111. In decimal notation, that is equal to 255. So the largest possible IP address is 255.255.255.255. This format is called dotted decimal notation, also referred to as "dotted quad." See Figure 12.4.

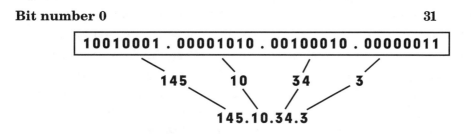

Bit number 0 **31**

10010001 . 00001010 . 00100010 . 00000011

145   10   34   3

145.10.34.3

FIGURE 12.4   A DOTTED QUAD ADDRESS

As originally designed, IP address space was divided into three different address classes: Class A, Class B, and Class C. A Class A network receives a number that is used in the first octet of the address. Class A network numbers range from 0 to 127. If an organization were assigned 95 as its network address, the hosts in the network would have IP addresses like 95.0.0.1, 95.0.0.2, 95.0.0.3, and so forth. There are no Class A network addresses remaining. Class A networks are now referred to as /8 (pronounced "slash eight") or sometimes just 8 since they have an 8-bit network prefix.

A Class B network has its network address assigned as the first two octets. The first octet can range between 128 and 191. The second octet can range between 0 and 255. If an organization were assigned 145.21, the hosts in the network would have IP addresses like 145.21.0.1, 145.21.0.2, 145.21.0.3, and so on. Class B networks are now referred to as /16 since they have a 16-bit network prefix. There are also no Class B network addresses remaining.

Today, Class C network addresses are still available. These are assigned the first three octets as their network address. The first octet can range from 192 to 254. If an organization were assigned 199.91.14, the hosts in the network would have IP addresses like 199.91.14.1, 199.91.14.2, 199.91.14.3, and so on. Class C networks are now referred to as /24 since they have a 24-bit network prefix.

There are two additional classes: Class D, which is used to support multicasting, and Class E, which is reserved for experimental use. With the explosive expansion of the Internet, IP addresses are going to be depleted. The appropriate parties are working on a solution to this problem by developing a new standard, called IP Next Generation (IPv6). In the meantime, the current system remains in place.

Even with the current system, if you had an organization with a large number of computers, you would still run out of IP addresses fairly quickly. A solution is to not assign a permanent (static) IP address to a computer, but rather assign an IP address to be used for the current work session only when the computer goes online (a dynamic—temporary—IP address). In this system, when you log off, your IP address is returned to the list of available addresses, and, since not everyone is online at the same time, not as many IP addresses are needed. The server that manages dynamic IP addresses is called a Dynamic Host Configuration Protocol (DHCP) server. Some ISPs use this method to assign IP addresses to their dial-up or cable clients. Others assign the address to the modem you dial into.

It would be difficult for most people to remember a numeric IP address. People remember names better than numbers. Phone numbers such as 1-800-FLOWERS or 1-800-URENTIT became popular for this very reason. Although you may not name your personal computer, computers in organizations are named so one computer can be distinguished from another. Organizations may choose names such as *pc1*, *pc2*, *mac1*, *mac2* or do it by department such as *sales*. Often, a computer's name will reflect its major role in the company. Thus, a computer devoted to handling electronic mail is often named *mail*, whereas a computer devoted to running the company's World Wide Web service is often called *www*. Both are easy-to-remember host names. These are in-house business names, not IP addresses for the Internet. If the computer is on the Internet, it has an IP address. An IP address can change, but typically it is not an organization's name. To give Internet addresses easy-to-remember names like this, the Internet is divided into domains. A domain is a general category that a computer on the Internet belongs to. A domain name is an easy-to-understand name given to an Internet host, as opposed to the numerical IP address. A user or organization applies for a ***domain name*** through the Internet Network Information Center (InterNIC) to ensure that each name is unique. InterNIC is now not the only organization responsible for assigning domain names. Some examples of domain names are saddleback.cc.ca.us, solano.cc.ca.us, fbeedle.com, unl.edu, loyola.edu, ces.sdsu.edu, printnation.com, bookbiz.com, dell.com, and microsoft.com.

Fully qualified domain names (FQDNs) are alphabetic aliases to IP addresses. A fully qualified domain name is a host name plus a domain name. As an example, a host named *mail* with the domain name *fbeedle.com* would have the FQDN mail.fbeedle.com. Another host name could be *www* with a domain name of *microsoft.com*; the FQDN would be *www.microsoft.com*. A fully qualified domain name must be resolved into its numeric IP address in order to be communicated across the Internet.

The ***DNS (Domain Name System)*** provides this name resolution. It ensures that every site on the Internet has a unique address. Large domains are divided into smaller domains, with each domain responsible for maintaining unique addresses in the next lower domain (subdomain). DNS maintains a distributed database. When a new domain name is assigned, the domain name and its IP address are placed into a database on a top-level domain name server (also called a domain root server), which is a special computer that keeps information about addresses in its domain. When a remote computer tries to access a domain name and does not know the IP address, it queries its DNS server. If that DNS server does not have the IP address in its database, it contacts a domain root server for the authoritative server responsible for that domain. Then, the DNS server goes directly to the authoritative server to get the IP address and other needed information, updates its database, and informs the remote computer of the IP address of the domain name.

When you use a browser to access a site on the Internet, you key in its URL. The browser contacts the remote server for a copy of the requested page. The server on the remote system returns the page, tells the browser how to display the information, and gives a URL for each item on the page that can be clicked. Figure 12.5 describes the parts of a URL.

name of computer on
which server is running

http://www.microsoft.com/support

name of protocol to   name of item to
use when accessing   request from server
the server

FIGURE 12.5   THE PARTS OF A URL

The URL in the above figure is for the page that gives you support for Microsoft products.

This somewhat technical discussion is not intended to confuse you, but to give you some idea of Internet jargon. Terms like IP address, URL, and domain name are commonly used in conjunction with the Internet. Having some understanding and familiarity with the terms will help you navigate the Internet.

12.20 TCP/IP UTILITIES—THE COMMAND LINE INTERFACE WITH THE INTERNET

Although you will normally use a browser such as Netscape Navigator to surf the net, Windows also provides a series of commands, also called utility programs, that run at the command line. These commands are a set of tools that can help you troubleshoot problems as well as offer you connections to computers not connected to the Web, such as Unix system computers. These utilities are automatically installed when you install the TCP/IP network protocol. These tools are:

Command	Purpose
arp	Displays and modifies the IP to Ethernet translation tables.
IPCONFIG	Command line utility that displays the IP address and other configuration information.
FTP	Transfers files to and from a node running FTP services.
Nbstat	Displays protocol statistics and current TCP/IP connections using NetBIOS over TCP/IP.
Netstat	Displays protocol statistics and current TCP/IP connections.
ping	Verifies connections to a remote host or hosts.

Route	Manually controls network-routing tables.
Telnet	Starts terminal emulation with a remote system running a Telnet service. Windows provides a graphical version of this utility, as well as the MS-DOS-based service.
Tracert	Determines the route taken to a destination.
WINIPCFG	Graphical utility that displays IP address and other configuration information.

TABLE 12.1   COMMAND LINE COMMANDS FOR THE INTERNET

If you want help on any of these commands, at the command line you key in the command name, a space, and then **-?**, such as **ping -?**. In the next activities, you will look at some of these utilities.

12.21 IPCONFIG AND WINIPCFG

IPCONFIG and WINIPCFG are two programs that display the current TCP/IP configurations and allow you to request a release or renewal of a DHCP-assigned IP address. In order to use DHCP, you must have a computer running Windows NT Server or Windows 2000 (networked-based operating systems) and the DHCP server software that comes with Windows NT. Windows can be a DHCP client, but not a DHCP server. Thus, if you are on a peer-to-peer network, you cannot use this portion of the utility.

This tool presents all the TCP/IP configuration settings in one place. If you have a dial-up service and you dial in, you are assigned an IP address that you might need to know if you are trying to telnet into a restricted server. Telnet is the utility that emulates a video display terminal. You use it to connect to character-based computers on a TCP/IP network, typically a computer running the Unix operating system. When you telnet, you log in and use a remote computer interactively. A restricted server denies everyone entry except those who are explicitly permitted into the system. The administrator of the remote system might need to know your IP address in order to allow you into the system.

12.22 ACTIVITY: USING IPCONFIG AND WINIPCFG

Step 1   Point to **Start**. Click **Run**. Key in: **winipcfg** Enter

WHAT'S HAPPENING? ▶ This display shows the peer-to-peer network card. In each case, the card has an address.

Step 2   Click the down arrow in the drop-down list box. Click **Linksys LNE100TX Fast Ethernet Adapter**.

WHAT'S HAPPENING? ▶ Now you are looking at the configuration of the adapter that is connected to the DSL line. Notice, there is a Default Gateway.

Step 3   Click **OK**.

Step 4   Open an MS-DOS window. Key in: **ipconfig** [Enter]

```
C:\WINDOWS>ipconfig

Windows IP Configuration

0 Ethernet adapter :

        IP Address. . . . . . . . . : 90.0.0.2
        Subnet Mask . . . . . . . . : 255.255.255.0
        Default Gateway . . . . . . :

1 Ethernet adapter :

        IP Address. . . . . . . . . : 207.202.137.14
        Subnet Mask . . . . . . . . : 255.255.255.0
        Default Gateway . . . . . . : 207.202.137.14

C:\WINDOWS>_
```

WHAT'S HAPPENING? ▶ You can see all the information on both adapters. This computer is on a static DSL connection, so is always on the Web. Also, it is always logged on to the server computer. Consequently, it always has an IP addresses. If you were not connected and logged on, no IP addresses would be reported.

Step 5   Close the MS-DOS window.

12.23 PING

If you are using your browser and cannot connect to a site, ping is an easy diagnostic tool for checking to see if the computer you are trying to reach is up and running. You can use ping (Packet InterNet Groper) to check out your connection to your service provider or to another computer. Ping sends out a request to see if a computer at the address you specified is there. It affirms whether that computer is up and running. You can ping either the IP address or the host name of the computer you are trying to reach. Ping sends four packets of data to the specified computer. If your ping is successful, you see four replies on the screen display. If any of the packets did not successfully reach their destination or were returned to your computer, you will see a "Request timed out" message. If the IP address is verified but the host name is not, there is some kind of name resolution problem. You can also ping yourself using the special loopback address, 127.0.0.1. However, you should be aware that pings are not always reliable. Some servers do not allow themselves to be pinged, because the server would then be wasting its time responding to pings. Furthermore, some organizations also do not respond to pings for security reasons.

12.24 ACTIVITY: USING PING

Note: It is assumed you are logged on.

Step 1   Open an MS-DOS window.

Step 2   Key in the following: **ping fbeedle.com** Enter

```
MS-DOS Prompt                                                    _ □ X

C:\WINDOWS>ping fbeedle.com

Pinging fbeedle.com [207.202.148.200] with 32 bytes of data:

Reply from 207.202.148.200: bytes=32 time=68ms TTL=243
Reply from 207.202.148.200: bytes=32 time=68ms TTL=243
Reply from 207.202.148.200: bytes=32 time=83ms TTL=243
Reply from 207.202.148.200: bytes=32 time=82ms TTL=243

Ping statistics for 207.202.148.200:
    Packets: Sent = 4, Received = 4, Lost = 0 (0% loss),
Approximate round trip times in milli-seconds:
    Minimum = 68ms, Maximum =  83ms, Average =  75ms

C:\WINDOWS>_
```

WHAT'S HAPPENING?   You have successfully pinged the publisher of this book. Note the IP address.

Step 3   Key in the following: **ping 207.202.148.200** Enter

```
MS-DOS Prompt                                                    _ □ X

C:\WINDOWS>ping 207.202.148.200

Pinging 207.202.148.200 with 32 bytes of data:
```

```
Reply from 207.202.148.200: bytes=32 time=69ms TTL=243
Reply from 207.202.148.200: bytes=32 time=83ms TTL=243
Reply from 207.202.148.200: bytes=32 time=82ms TTL=243
Reply from 207.202.148.200: bytes=32 time=83ms TTL=243

Ping statistics for 207.202.148.200:
    Packets: Sent = 4, Received = 4, Lost = 0 (0% loss),
Approximate round trip times in milli-seconds:
    Minimum = 69ms, Maximum =  83ms, Average =   79ms

C:\WINDOWS>_
```

WHAT'S
HAPPENING?   You have pinged both the IP address and the host name. You now know
              this site is up and running.

Step 4   Key in the following: **ping 127.0.0.1** Enter

```
⌗ MS-DOS Prompt                                              _ □ ✕

C:\WINDOWS>ping 127.0.0.1

Pinging 127.0.0.1 with 32 bytes of data:

Reply from 127.0.0.1: bytes=32 time<10ms TTL=128
Reply from 127.0.0.1: bytes=32 time<10ms TTL=128
Reply from 127.0.0.1: bytes=32 time<10ms TTL=128
Reply from 127.0.0.1: bytes=32 time<10ms TTL=128

Ping statistics for 127.0.0.1:
    Packets: Sent = 4, Received = 4, Lost = 0 (0% loss),
Approximate round trip times in milli-seconds:
    Minimum = 0ms, Maximum =  0ms, Average =   0ms

C:\WINDOWS>_
```

WHAT'S
HAPPENING?   You have just "pinged" yourself. Remember that 127.0.0.1 is the loopback
              address and is the IP address of your computer.

Step 5   Key in the following: **ping microsoft.com**

```
⌗ MS-DOS Prompt                                              _ □ ✕

C:\WINDOWS>ping microsoft.com

Pinging microsoft.com [207.46.230.229] with 32 bytes of data:

Request timed out.
Request timed out.
Request timed out.
Request timed out.

Ping statistics for 207.46.230.229:
    Packets: Sent = 4, Received = 0, Lost = 4 (100% loss),
Approximate round trip times in milli-seconds:
    Minimum = 0ms, Maximum =  0ms, Average =   0ms

C:\WINDOWS>_
```

WHAT'S
HAPPENING! ➡   Microsoft has "blocked" your ping. However, you did attain some information, as the ping did resolve the address (207.46.230.229).

Step 6   Close the MS-DOS window.

Step 7   If you are going to continue with the activities, remain logged on.
Otherwise, log off the system.

12.25 TRACERT

Tracert, pronounced "trace route," is a utility that traces the route on which your
data is moving. It is a diagnostic utility that determines the route to the destination
computer by sending packets containing time values (TTL—Time to Live). Each
router along the path is required to decrease the time value by 1 before forwarding it.
When the value of the TTL is 0, the router is supposed to send back a message to the
originating computer. When you use the command, it returns a five-column display.
The first column is the hop number, which is the TTL value. Each of the next three
columns contains the round-trip times in milliseconds. The last column is the host
name and IP address of the responding system. An asterisk (*) means that the
attempt timed out. If nothing else, it is fascinating to see the way your data travels.
Since tracert uses pings, you may not be able to trace a route if the server you are
looking for does not allow pinging.

12.26 ACTIVITY: USING TRACERT

Note: It is assumed you are logged on.

Step 1   Open an MS-DOS window.

Step 2   Key in the following: **tracert www.bookbiz.com** Enter

```
MS-DOS Prompt                                                    _ □ ✕

C:\WINDOWS>tracert www.bookbiz.com

Tracing route to www.bookbiz.com [204.210.20.241]
over a maximum of 30 hops:

  1     28 ms     13 ms     42 ms   adsl-63-199-16-254.dsl.snfc21.pacbell.net
[63.199.16.254]
  2     28 ms     13 ms     14 ms   core4-g3-0.snfc21.pbi.net [216.102.187.130]
  3     27 ms     14 ms     14 ms   edge1-ge1-0.snfc21.pbi.net [209.232.130.20]
  4    467 ms       *         *     sfra1sr3-so-1-1-0-0.ca.us.prserv.net
[165.87.161.6]
  5    480 ms    481 ms    467 ms   sfra1sr4-ge-1-2-0-0.ca.us.prserv.net
[165.87.33.120]
  6      *       466 ms       *     agns-gw.sffca.ip.att.net [192.205.32.193]
  7    454 ms       *         *     gbr4-p50.sffca.ip.att.net [12.123.13.70]
  8      *       384 ms       *     gbr3-p10.la2ca.ip.att.net [12.122.2.169]
  9      *         *         *      Request timed out.
 10      *       480 ms       *     gbr2-p30.sd2ca.ip.att.net [12.122.2.121]
 11    481 ms    494 ms       *     gar1-p370.sd2ca.ip.att.net [12.123.145.25]
 12    481 ms       *         *      12.124.23.6
 13    412 ms    398 ms    398 ms   ubr3-POS2-0.san.rr.com [24.25.192.53]
```

```
14    494 ms       *          *        mcr3.san.rr.com [24.25.192.58]
15    508 ms    522 ms    522 ms       dt031nf1.san.rr.com [204.210.20.241]

Trace complete.

C:\WINDOWS>_
```

WHAT'S HAPPENING? Your display will be different. In this example, the sending computer is in Fairfield, California. The Web site, **bookbiz.com**, is on a computer in San Diego. It is part of the **bookbiz.net** domain. If you look at the rightmost column, you can see what computers the packets are traveling on. The packets go out first on **pacbell.net**, which is this user's ISP. Notice the **adsl** notation, reporting the use of ADSL by this computer. It then goes to "pbi" network, then to some connections in San Francisco, then to Los Angeles, and eventually to San Diego. As you can see, the packets traveled up and down the California coast in milliseconds.

Step 3   Key in: **tracert www.fbeedle.com** [Enter]

```
┌─────────────────────────────────────────────────────────────────────────┐
│ MS-DOS Prompt                                                  _ □ ×      │
├─────────────────────────────────────────────────────────────────────────┤
│ Tracing route to www.fbeedle.com [207.202.148.200]                       │
│ over a maximum of 30 hops:                                               │
│                                                                           │
│    1      *          *          *        Request timed out.              │
│    2    146 ms    145 ms    144 ms       gw-backbone.delta.net [199.171.190.11] │
│    3    144 ms    151 ms    144 ms       Hssi5-1-0.GW1.LAX1.ALTER.NET [137.39.134.41] │
│    4    144 ms    144 ms    142 ms       103.ATM2-0-0.XR1.LAX2.ALTER.NET │
│ [146.188.248.18]                                                          │
│                                                                           │
│    5    142 ms    141 ms    139 ms       100.ATM3-0-0.TR1.LAX2.ALTER.NET │
│ [146.188.248.118]                                                         │
│    6    179 ms    184 ms    182 ms       111.ATM5-0-0.TR1.SEA1.ALTER.NET │
│ [146.188.137.150]                                                         │
│    7    185 ms    181 ms    183 ms       100.ATM5-0-0.XR1.SEA1.ALTER.NET │
│ [146.188.200.101]                                                         │
│    8    185 ms    179 ms    182 ms       195.ATM1-0-0.CR2.SEA1.ALTER.NET │
│ [146.188.200.25]                                                          │
│                                                                           │
│    9    188 ms    187 ms    184 ms       110.Hssi9-0-0.GW1.POR2.Alter.Net │
│ [137.39.58.61]                                                            │
│                                                                           │
│   10    189 ms    192 ms    192 ms       europa-gw.customer.ALTER.NET [157.130.176.86] │
│   11    200 ms    201 ms    199 ms       www.fbeedle.com [199.2.194.43]  │
│                                                                           │
│ Trace complete.                                                           │
│                                                                           │
│ C:\WINDOWS>_                                                              │
└─────────────────────────────────────────────────────────────────────────┘
```

WHAT'S HAPPENING? In this example, your route goes from Orange, California, to Portland, Oregon.

Step 4   Close the MS-DOS window.

12.27 FTP

FTP (file transfer protocol) servers store files that Internet users can download (copy) to their own computers. FTP is the communications protocol that these computers use to transfer files. It allows you to transfer text and binary files between a host computer and your computer. FTP requires you to log on to the remote host for user identification. Many FTP servers, however, let you log on as anonymous and use your email address as your password so that you can acquire free software and documents. Most FTP servers contain text files that describe the layout of their entire directory structure to help you find what you need. You can transfer files in either text or binary mode but you must first choose the mode. Text (ASCII) is the default.

One of the major advantages to FTP is that you do not care what operating system is on these remote computers because they all have TCP/IP. The ability to transfer files to and from computers running different operating systems is one of the greatest benefits of FTP. There are still computers out there that only have the character-based interface.

FTP has many commands. To get help from within FTP, you key in **help** *command*, where *command* is the name of the command for which you seek help. For a list of the commands, you simply key in **help**.

12.28 ACTIVITY: USING FTP

Note: It is assumed you are logged on.

Step 1   Open an MS-DOS window.

Step 2   Key in the following: **ftp ftp.microsoft.com** Enter

```
MS-DOS Prompt                                                        _ □ ✕

C:\WINDOWS>ftp ftp.microsoft.com
Connected to ftp.microsoft.com.
220 CPMSFTFTPA06 Microsoft FTP Service (Version 5.0).
User (ftp.microsoft.com:(none)): _
```

WHAT'S HAPPENING?   You have just contacted the FTP server at Microsoft. It is asking for a user name. This server allows anonymous logins.

Step 3   Key in: **anonymous** Enter

```
MS-DOS Prompt                                                        _ □ ✕

User (ftp.microsoft.com:(none)): anonymous
331 Anonymous access allowed, send identity (e-mail name) as password.
Password: _
```

WHAT'S HAPPENING?   It asks for your password and tells you that your email name can be used. When you key in your email address, you will not see it on the screen. You may key in anything for the password; you do not really need to key in your email address.

Step 4   Key in: **aaaa** [Enter]

Note: The cursor will appear frozen when you key this in, but when you press [Enter]
you will continue on.

```
MS-DOS Prompt                                                    _ □ ×

  230-This is FTP.MICROSOFT.COM  Please see the dirmap.txt
  230-file for more information.
  230 Anonymous user logged in.
  ftp> _
```

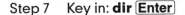 You are logged into the site.

Step 5   Key in: **help** [Enter]

```
MS-DOS Prompt                                                    _ □ ×

ftp> help
Commands may be abbreviated.   Commands are:

!               delete          literal         prompt          send
?               debug           ls              put             status
append          dir             mdelete         pwd             trace
ascii           disconnect      mdir            quit            type
bell            get             mget            quote           user
binary          glob            mkdir           recv            verbose
bye             hash            mls             remotehelp
cd              help            mput            rename
close           lcd             open            rmdir
ftp> _
```

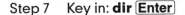 These are the FTP commands. For syntax on any command, you would
key in **help** plus the command name.

Step 6   Key in: **help bye** [Enter]

```
MS-DOS Prompt                                                    _ □ ×

ftp> help bye
bye             Terminate ftp session and exit
ftp> _
```

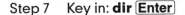 The command bye is how you can terminate the FTP session. You can
use commands you are familiar with already, like DIR, to see what is in
the directory.

Step 7   Key in: **dir** [Enter]

```
MS-DOS Prompt                                                    _ □ ×

ftp> dir
200 PORT command successful.
150 Opening ASCII mode data connection for /bin/ls.
dr-xr-xr-x   1 owner     group                 0 Feb 13 20:02 bussys
dr-xr-xr-x   1 owner     group                 0 May 21 15:41 deskapps
dr-xr-xr-x   1 owner     group                 0 Apr 20 15:41 developr
-r-xr-xr-x   1 owner     group                 0 Nov 27  2000 dirmap.htm
```

```
dr-xr-xr-x   1 owner     group            0 Feb 25   2000 kbhelp
dr-xr-xr-x   1 owner     group            0 Jan 20  23:04 misc
dr-xr-xr-x   1 owner     group            0 Feb 25   2000 peropsys
dr-xr-xr-x   1 owner     group            0 Jan  2  14:43 products
dr-xr-xr-x   1 owner     group            0 Sep 21   2000 reskit
dr-xr-xr-x   1 owner     group            0 Feb 25   2000 services
dr-xr-xr-x   1 owner     group            0 Feb 25   2000 softlib
dr-xr-xr-x   1 owner     group            0 Feb 25   2000 solutions
226 Transfer complete.
ftp: 820 bytes received in 0.01Seconds 82.00Kbytes/sec.
ftp> _
```

WHAT'S HAPPENING? You see a list of files and directories. You can recognize directories by locating a **dr** on the far left. **Softlib** is a directory that contains Microsoft software files. Files that have a **.ZIP** extension are compressed. You need a utility like PKZIP to unpack the file. If you key in the command **get** *filename*, it will transfer the file to your default directory. If you key in **get** *filename* **-**, the file name followed by a hyphen acts just like the TYPE command. These commands are Unix commands. As you can see, MS-DOS commands borrow much from Unix commands. If you wanted to transfer a binary file (**.EXE**), you would key in

binary
get file.exe
ascii

You key in **ascii** to return to text-file mode.

Step 8   Key in: **cd deskapps** [Enter]

Step 9   Key in: **dir** [Enter]

```
MS-DOS Prompt                                                          _ □ ✕
ftp> cd deskapps
250 CWD command successful.
ftp> dir
200 PORT command successful.
150 Opening ASCII mode data connection for /bin/ls.
dr-xr-xr-x   1 owner     group            0 Feb 25   2000 access
dr-xr-xr-x   1 owner     group            0 Feb 25   2000 dosword
dr-xr-xr-x   1 owner     group            0 Feb 25   2000 excel
dr-xr-xr-x   1 owner     group            0 Mar 20   2000 games
dr-xr-xr-x   1 owner     group            0 Feb 25   2000 gen-info
dr-xr-xr-x   1 owner     group            0 Feb 25   2000 homeapps
dr-xr-xr-x   1 owner     group            0 Feb 25   2000 ie
dr-xr-xr-x   1 owner     group            0 Feb 25   2000 kids
dr-xr-xr-x   1 owner     group            0 May 21  16:08 macofficeten
dr-xr-xr-x   1 owner     group            0 Feb 25   2000 miscapps
dr-xr-xr-x   1 owner     group            0 Feb 25   2000 mmapps
dr-xr-xr-x   1 owner     group            0 Feb 25   2000 money
dr-xr-xr-x   1 owner     group            0 Feb 25   2000 office
dr-xr-xr-x   1 owner     group            0 Feb 25   2000 powerpt
dr-xr-xr-x   1 owner     group            0 Feb 25   2000 project
dr-xr-xr-x   1 owner     group            0 Feb 25   2000 publishr
-r-xr-xr-x   1 owner     group         1791 Aug 30   1994 readme.txt
dr-xr-xr-x   1 owner     group            0 Feb 25   2000 word
dr-xr-xr-x   1 owner     group            0 Feb 25   2000 works
226 Transfer complete.
```

```
ftp: 1282 bytes received in 0.13Seconds 9.86Kbytes/sec.
ftp> _
```

WHAT'S HAPPENING? ➤ You changed directories to **deskapps**, and are now seeing the contents of that directory.

Step 10 Key in: **get readme.txt** [Enter]

```
MS-DOS Prompt                                            _ □ ×

ftp> get readme.txt
200 PORT command successful.
150 Opening ASCII mode data connection for readme.txt (1791 bytes).
226 Transfer complete.
ftp: 1791 bytes received in 0.01Seconds 179.10Kbytes/sec.
ftp> _
```

WHAT'S HAPPENING? ➤ You have downloaded the readme.txt file to the default directory.

Step 11 Key in: **bye** [Enter]

```
MS-DOS Prompt                                            _ □ ×

ftp> bye
221 Thank You for using Microsoft Products!

C:\WINDOWS>_
```

WHAT'S HAPPENING? ➤ You have logged off from the FTP site at Microsoft as well as quit the FTP program.

Step 12 Key in the following: C:\WINDOWS>**TYPE README.TXT ¦ MORE** [Enter]

```
MS-DOS Prompt                                            _ □ ×

Welcome to the Microsoft FTP Server. This machine offers the following
materials and information for systems and network  products:

- Selected knowledge-base articles
- Selected product fixes
- Updated drivers
- Utilities
- Documentation

The deskapps directory is maintained by Microsoft Product Support.
Products represented here are Access, Word (for MS-DOS and Windows),
Excel, Flight Simulator, Creative Writer, Fine Artist, Office,
PowerPoint, Project, Publisher, Works and Money.

Each has its own directory, with appropriate sub-directories below.
See the readme.txt in each directory for more information.

Please report any problems with this area to "ftp@microsoft.com".
Sorry, individual replies to this alias may not be possible, but all
mail will be read. Please, this is not a product support alias!

                    f-- More --
```

WHAT'S
HAPPENING? ➤ You are seeing the file you downloaded from Microsoft's ftp site.

Step 13 Press **Enter** until you reach the bottom of the file.

Step 14 Close the MS-DOS window.

12.29 TELNET

Telnet is a connection to a remote computer which makes your computer act like a terminal on the remote machine. This connection type is used for real time exchange of text. Telnet makes your computer into a dumb terminal. It is called a dumb terminal because each time your press a key on your computer, your computer does nothing except transmit your keystroke to some other computer on the Internet. The software performing the commands actually runs at the remote computer and not on your computer. Telnet operates in a client/server environment in which one host (the computer you are using running Client Telnet) negotiates opening a session on another computer (the remote host, running Server Telnet). During the behind-the-scenes negotiation process, the two computers agree on the parameters governing the session. Technically Telnet is the protocol and is the terminal handler portion of the TCP/IP protocol suite. It tells the remote computer how to transfer commands from the local computer, on which you are working, to another computer in a remote location. Thus, Telnet lets you become a user on a remote computer. Both computers must support the Telnet protocol. The incoming user must have permission to use the remote computer by providing a user name and password. Telnet can be used by a system administrator or other professionals to log on to your computer and trouble-shoot problems on your computer. However, Telnet is also most commonly used for connecting to libraries and other informational public databases. You can use a Telnet client to access hundreds of library and government databases. Windows Me includes a Telnet client. You begin the session in a DOS window which opens the Telnet window.

12.30 ACTIVITY—USING TELNET

Step 1 Open an MS-DOS window.

Step 2 Key in the following: C:\WINDOWS>**TELNET**

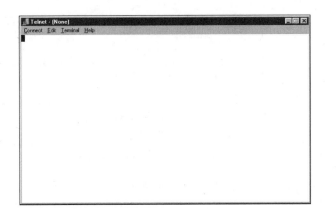

WHAT'S HAPPENING? ▶ You have opened the Telnet window. You must now connect to the site that you are interested in.

Step 3   Click **Connect**. Click **Remote System**.

WHAT'S HAPPENING? ▶ The Host Name is where you key in the site you wish to use. The Port is the connection and the TermType is the terminal type that Windows will use. Normally, you use the default settings.

Step 4   In Host Name, key in the following: **antpac.lib.uci.edu**

Step 5   Click **Connect**.

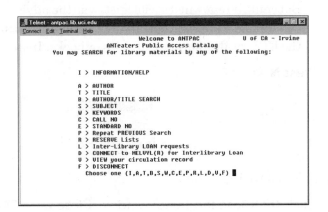

WHAT'S HAPPENING? ▶ You have just connected to the University of California at Irvine (UCI) Library Catalog. You are in the public access area and can look up information and make requests to this library.

Step 6   Press **A**.

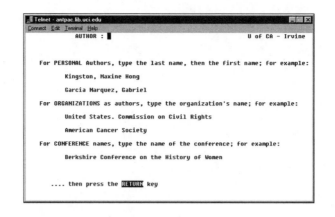

WHAT'S HAPPENING? You are on the Author page.

Step 7   At AUTHOR, key in the following: **Babchuk, Nicholas** Enter

WHAT'S HAPPENING? You have found a book, *Fraternal Organizations*, where Dr. Nicholas Babchuk, a renowned sociologist, was the advisory editor. You see the call number, the location, and the status. You could continue to search the UCI catalog for more articles or books. Instead, you will log out.

Step 8   Press **N**. Press **F**.

WHAT'S HAPPENING? You have logged out.

Step 9   Click **OK**. Close the Telnet window. Close the DOS window.

WHAT'S HAPPENING? You have had a brief introduction to Telnet.

CHAPTER SUMMARY

1. When you connect computers together, it is known as a LAN (local area network).

2. A server is a computer that provides shared resources. A client is a computer that accesses the shared resources provided by the server. Resources are the parts of the computer you share.

3. The standard model for networks with more than 10 users is a server-based network. It is one in which network functions are provided by a computer that is a dedicated server.

4. For networks with fewer than 10 users, the model is a peer-to-peer network, in which all computers are equal. Each computer can function as either a client or server.

5. A WAN (wide area network) consists of computers that use long-range telecommunications links to connect the networked computers over long distances.

6. A network interface card (NIC) is required to set up a network.

7. The NIC must match your bus architecture slot as well as the type of cable used to connect your network.

8. You must have the proper networking software for your network to work.

9. A simple network has three parts: the hardware, the software, and the network administrator.

10. Setting up a peer-to-peer network using Windows usually requires that you have the original system disk.

11. You must install the correct protocols. All computers on the network must use the same protocol. A protocol is a set of rules that allows computers to connect with one another and exchange information.

12. In a peer-to-peer network, you must have these settings in the Configuration tab of the Network dialog box: Client for Microsoft Networks, NetBEUI, and your network card. You may add or delete items in the My Network Places property sheet.

13. In a peer-to-peer network, you must be sure to enable file and print sharing.

14. In a peer-to-peer network, you must name your computer as well as your workgroup. The workgroup name must be identical on all computers in the workgroup.

15. There are two parts to sharing resources: the client and the server. The server has the resource. The client is the computer that wishes to access the resource.

16. When you share devices, any computer on the network can use that device.

17. Common shared devices include printers, drives, and folders.

18. The computer that has the resource must first share it so that others on the network can access it. You must name your shared resource. Others on the network will access it by its shared name.

19. My Network Places is a tool to browse the network.

20. Once a drive has been shared, you may assign a drive letter to it. This act is called mapping a drive. If you map a drive, you can access it through My Computer or Explorer and need not use My Network Places.

21. You can use the NET USE command to map drives.

22. The Internet is a network of networks. You can use the Internet to use email and access chat lines and forums. You may connect to the World Wide Web.

23. The Web is an interconnected collection of Web sites that holds pages of text and graphics in a form recognized by the Web. These pages are linked to one another and to individual files. The Web is a collection of standards and protocols used to access information on the Internet. Using the Web requires a browser.

24. The Web uses three standards: URL (uniform resource locator), HTML (hypertext markup language), and a method of access such as HTTP (hypertext transfer protocol).

25. URLs are a standard format for identifying locations on the Internet.

26. A Web site is both the physical and virtual location of a person's or organization's Web page(s).

27. A Web page is a single screen of text and graphics that usually has hypertext links to other pages.

28. In order to access the Internet, you usually need a modem, communication software, and an online provider.

29. Online providers include services such as AOL (America Online) or MSN (Microsoft Network). You may also use an ISP (Internet service provider).

30. You can connect to the Internet using a phone line, a special phone line (ISDN), through your cable company, or via satellite.

31. TCP/IP is the protocol of the Internet.

32. Protocols are "bound" to specific Network Interface Cards.

33. Each network has a router, which is a device that connects networks. A router can make intelligent decisions on which network to use to send data.

34. TCP protocol divides data into packets and numbers each packet.

35. Internet Protocol (IP) specifies the addresses of the sending and receiving computers and sends the packets on their way.

36. A single user will typically access the Internet thorough a dial-up connection. This provides a temporary connection, usually a PPP (point-to-point protocol) connection.

37. Each computer on the Internet uses TCP/IP and must have a unique IP address.

38. An IP address is made up of four numbers separated by periods. This format is called dotted-decimal notation. Each section is called an octet.

39. IP address space is divided into three major address classes: A, B, and C.

40. Each site attached to the Internet belongs to a domain. A user or organization applies for a domain name so that each domain name is unique.

41. Fully qualified domain names are an alphabetic alias to the IP address.

42. The DNS (domain name system) resolves the domain name into the IP address.

43. When you connect to the Internet, you use the URL of the site to which you wish to connect. If you know the IP address, you may use that as well.

44. Included with TCP/IP is a set of command line utilities that can help you troubleshoot problems as well as offer you connections to computers not connected to the Web, such as Unix system computers. These tools are as follows:

Command	Purpose
arp	Displays and modifies the IP to Ethernet translation tables.
IPCONFIG	Command line utility that displays the IP address and other configuration information (Windows 98 only).
FTP	Transfers files to and from a node running FTP services.
Nbstat	Displays protocol statistics and current TCP/IP connections using NetBIOS over TCP/IP.
Netstat	Displays protocol statistics and current TCP/IP connections.
ping	Verifies connections to a remote host or hosts.
Route	Manually controls network-routing tables.
Telnet	Starts terminal emulation with a remote system running a Telnet service. Windows Millennium provides a graphical version of this utility
Tracert	Determines the route taken to a destination.
WINIPCFG	Graphical utility that displays IP address and other configuration information.

If you want help on any of these commands, at the command line you key in the command name, a space, and then **-?**.

KEY TERMS

binding
browser
client
cyberspace
DNS (domain name
    system)
domain name
file server
FTP (file transfer
    protocol)
home page
HTML (Hypertext
    Markup Language)
HTTP (Hypertext Trans-
    fer Protocol)
hub
information
    superhighway
Internet

IP address
ISP (Internet service
    provider)
LAN (local area network)
locally
mapped drive
network administrator
NIC (network interface
    card)
octet
packet
peer-to-peer
portal
PPP (point-to-point
    protocol)
print server
protocol
resources

router
server
server-based network
SLIP (serial-line Internet
    protocol)
T-connectors
terminator plug
Thinnet
twisted-pair cable
UNC (universal naming
    convention)
URL (uniform
    resource locator)
WAN (wide area network)
Web page
Web site
workgroup
World Wide Web (WWW)

DISCUSSION QUESTIONS

1. Define the following terms: *client, server, resources,* and *LAN.*
2. Compare and contrast a client computer with a server computer.
3. Compare and contrast a server-based network with a peer-to-peer network.
4. List and explain three reasons why you might set up a network.
5. Compare and contrast a LAN and a WAN.
6. What is the purpose and function of a network interface card?
7. List the steps necessary to set up a peer-to-peer network.
8. Explain the purpose and function of the network clients, adapters, protocols, and services found in the Configuration tab of the Network dialog box.
9. Explain the purpose and function of a protocol. Why must computers on a network use the same protocol?
10. Why is it important that all computers in a peer-to-peer network use the same workgroup name?
11. Compare and contrast a print server and a file server on a server-based network and a peer-to-peer network.
12. List and explain the steps you need to take in order to share your drive on a peer-to-peer network.
13. Give the syntax of the network path and explain each part of the syntax.
14. When sharing your drive with another computer, why is it not wise for your share name to be C?
15. Explain the purpose and function of a mapped drive.
16. What is the purpose and function of the Internet?
17. How can the Internet be used?
18. Compare and contrast the Internet and the World Wide Web.
19. Explain the purpose of URLs, HTML, and HTTP.
20. List the three types of information a URL needs to retrieve a document.
21. What is a Web site?
22. Compare and contrast a Web site with a Web page.
23. The type of Web site is indicated by its "dot" address. Explain.
24. What is a hypertext link?
25. List and explain three ways a computer user can connect to the Internet.
26. Why is TCP/IP considered the protocol of the Internet?
27. What is a router?
28. Compare and contrast the purposes and functions of TCP and IP.
29. Data is divided into packets when it is transferred over the Internet. Why?
30. What is the purpose of an IP address?
31. Compare and contrast a static versus a dynamic IP address.
32. Why is the format of an IP address called dotted-decimal notation?
33. Describe the format of a Class A, Class B, and Class C IP address.
34. What is a loopback address?
35. Explain the purpose and function of the domain name system.
36. What is the purpose of name resolution?
37. What is a fully qualified domain name?
38. Why can computers have both an IP address and a domain name?
39. Define each part of the following URL: **http://www.amazon.com/books**.

40. Explain the purposes and functions of two utilities that are automatically installed when TCP/IP network protocol is installed.
41. How can you receive help on the TCP/IP utilities?
42. What is the purpose and function of IPCONFIG?
43. What is the purpose and function of ping?
44. What is the purpose and function of tracert?
45. What is the purpose and function of FTP?

TRUE/FALSE QUESTIONS

For each question, circle the letter T if the question is true or the letter F if the question is false.

T F 1. My Network Places allows you to browse all the resources on your network.

T F 2. On a peer-to-peer network, anyone may access any resource on the network, even if it has not been shared.

T F 3. Netscape Navigator is an example of a protocol.

T F 4. You may map both folders and drives.

T F 5. The World Wide Web (WWW) and the Internet are synonyms.

COMPLETION QUESTIONS

Write the correct answer in each blank space.

6. The global system of networked computers is called the _____.
7. In order to connect to a Web site on the WWW, you must key in the address, known as the _____.
8. An IP address expressed in terms of 121.22.34.44 is called _____ notation.
9. A TCP/IP utility that allows you to check out your connection to another computer is the _____ utility.
10. A network in which security and other network functions are provided by a dedicated computer is called a(n) _____ network.

MULTIPLE CHOICE QUESTIONS

For each question, write the letter for the correct answer in the blank space.

11. What protocol is used to connect Windows to the Internet?
    a. PPP
    b. NetBIOS
    c. NetBEUI
    d. TCP/IP

12. If you wish to access information in a folder on another computer, you must, on the server computer, first _____.
    a. map the folder
    b. share the folder
    c. open My Network Places
    d. both a and c

13. In the URL **http://www.yahoo.com/computers**, **www.yahoo.com** is an example of the
    a. protocol used.
    b. name of the computer on which the server is running.
    c. name of the computer on which the client is running.
    d. name of the item to request from the server.

14. Many FTP servers allow you to log on as
    a. anonymous.
    b. user.
    c. an email address.
    d. none of the above

15. You can connect to an ISP using
    a. DSL.
    b. cable.
    d. telephone lines with a modem.
    e. all of the above

APPLICATION ASSIGNMENTS

PROBLEM SET I—AT THE COMPUTER

Note: To do these two activities, you must have access to the Internet as well as a browser to access the World Wide Web.

1. If you have access to the Internet, visit the site of the magazine *Scientific American* (**http://www.sciam.com**). You will be taken to the home page. Click **Past Issues**. Click **Issues from 1999**. Click **Dec. 1999**. Scroll till you see "Technology and Business." Read the article entitled **Cable-Free** and write a brief report on what it says.

2. To know where things are going, it is helpful to know where they have been. Visit the Web site at **http://www.zakon.org**. Once you reach the site, click on **Hobbes' Internet Timeline**. Scroll through the page. Find **1993**. Read it. Write a brief report describing one 1993 happening (from the timeline, not your memory).

PROBLEM SET II—BRIEF ESSAY

1. You are a small advertising company with three employees: Mary Brown, Jose Rodriquez, and Jin-Li Yu. The office has three computers, a scanner, a laser printer, and a color printer. You have already set up a peer-to-peer network. Mary's computer is connected to the laser printer. Jose's computer is connected to the color printer and Jin-Li's computer is attached to the scanner. Mary needs to access the color printer but not the scanner. Jose needs only the color printer. Jin-Li needs access to the color printer. Describe what you need to do to accomplish these goals.

2. Briefly describe the importance and use of an IP address. Describe what it is and how it is used. Include in your discussion why a domain name must be resolved. Describe how a name is resolved.

PROTECTING YOUR SYSTEM

LEARNING OBJECTIVES

After completing this chapter, you will be able to:
1. Explain the need for a Startup disk.
2. Explain the purpose and function of Disk Cleanup.
3. Explain why it is necessary to back up your data and system files.
4. Explain the purpose and function of the Backup Wizard.
5. Explain the purpose and function of the initialization files.
6. Explain the purpose and function of the Registry.
7. Explain the purpose and function of System Restore.
8. Explain the purpose and function of the Registry Checker.
9. Describe the boot process.
10. Explain the different types of memory.
11. List two tools to determine the amount of memory on a Windows Millennium Edition computer.
12. Explain the purpose and function of a swap file.

STUDENT OUTCOMES

After completing this chapter, students will:
1. Know how to create a Startup disk for their system.
2. Use Disk Cleanup to remove unnecessary files.
3. Be able to back up and restore files using the Backup Wizard.
4. Create a restore point with System Restore.
5. Use ScanRegW to check for Registry errors.

6. Have an understanding of the boot process.
7. Understand the different types of memory.
8. Use the MEM command and System Information to check on the computer's memory.
9. Configure virtual memory for optimum performance.

CHAPTER OVERVIEW

You will discover why creating a Startup disk is essential to solving problems with and maintaining the health of your computer system. Furthermore, you will discover ways to clean up your disk so that you can gain more space for your files. Backing up your data and programs is a critical function. In this chapter, you will learn how to back up and restore files using the Backup program, and you will learn other ways to protect your files.

The Registry stores all of the configuration information about the hardware on your computer. It also tracks and contains all of the preferences for each user of the computer. Typically, you do not have to deal directly with the Registry. Making changes through the use of the Control Panel is the preferred method of changing your Registry. However, if your Registry became corrupt, you would need to be able to restore it. Windows Millennium provides tools to do this such as the Registry Checker. Another new tool was introduced in Windows Millennium called System Restore. If you add new software or hardware that causes your computer to become inoperable, System Restore allows you to roll back your computer system to a previous time when your computer was working correctly. You will also learn about command line tools such as ScanRegW, which you can use to restore your Registry. You will also learn about the boot process in Windows Millennium.

The Windows operating system manages memory for you. Most of the time, you need not be concerned with the particulars of how this is done—you can let Windows handle it. However, understanding the concepts of the different types of memory, as well as how physical memory works and how virtual memory is implemented, is necessary to a good overall understanding of the Windows operating system.

13.1   THE STARTUP DISK

Sometimes you may have trouble with your computer system and your computer may not start. You have the option, when you boot up, to hold down the **Ctrl** key or, on some systems, the **F8** key. This procedure is supposed to take you into a menu system where you can use Safe Mode or other menu choices to troubleshoot. However, sometimes even that does not work, and you need another option. You need to be able to boot your system.

Windows Millennium provides a mechanism for booting from a floppy disk, also called the *Startup disk*. A Startup disk will at the very least boot you to an MS-DOS Prompt so that you may repair the system. The Startup disk for Windows Millennium includes the most common drivers for CD-ROM drives so that, if necessary, you may reinstall Windows Millennium. If you installed or upgraded to Windows Millennium, when you did so, the installation process asked you to create a Startup disk. If you did not do so then, or if your computer came with Windows Millennium already installed, you can still make a Startup disk at any time. It is a good idea to have more than one Startup disk, in case a floppy disk goes bad on you. When you have a problem with your computer, Murphy's Law seems to come into play all too often, and sometimes even your Startup disk will not boot your system. Having another copy of the Startup disk can be valuable.

13.2 ACTIVITY: MAKING AND USING A STARTUP DISK IN WINDOWS MILLENNIUM

Note: Be sure you have a blank disk. Label your blank disk "Windows Me Startup Disk" with the current date. You may need your Windows Millennium CD.

Step 1   Click **Start**. Point to **Settings**. Click **Control Panel**. Double-click **Add/Remove Programs**. Click the **Startup Disk** tab.

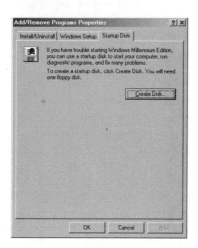

WHAT'S HAPPENING?   You are ready to make your Startup disk.

Step 2   Click **Create Disk**.

WHAT'S HAPPENING?   When you see this message, you are ready to create your Startup disk. If you see a message to insert your Windows Me CD, do so and follow the instructions.

Step 3   Insert your labeled floppy disk into Drive A. Click **OK**.

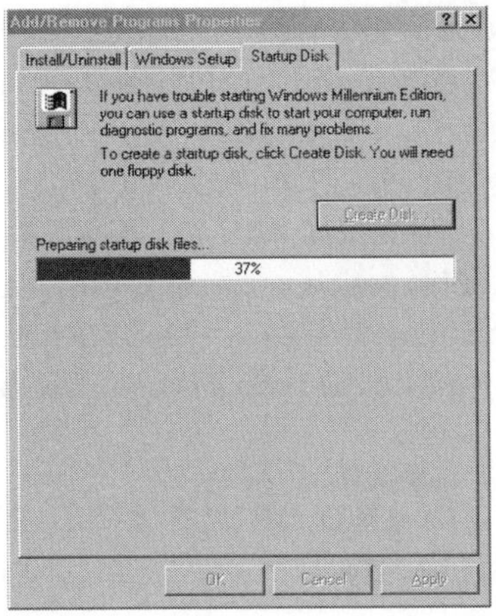

WHAT'S HAPPENING? You see a progress screen as Windows begins creating your Startup disk. When it is finished, you see the following screen.

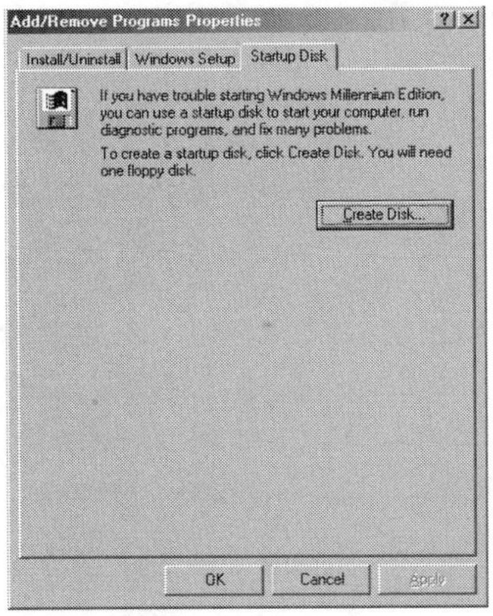

Step 4 Click **OK**.

Step 5 Close the Control Panel window.

Step 6 If necessary, remove the Windows Me CD.

Step 7 With the Startup disk in Drive A, click **Start**. Click **Shut Down**.

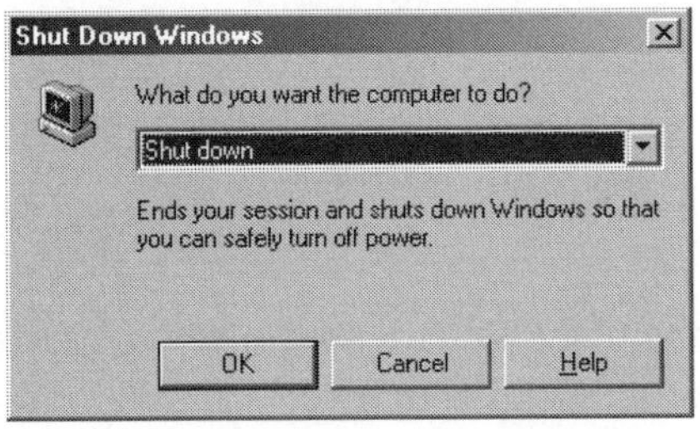

WHAT'S HAPPENING? The Shut Down Windows dialog box appears.

Step 8 Click the down arrow in the dialog box.

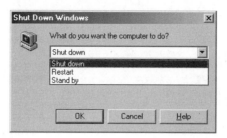

> **WHAT'S HAPPENING?** You may have more choices available to you. The choice you want is Restart.

Step 9   Click **Restart**. Click **OK**.

```
MS-DOS Prompt                                                        _ □ ✕

Microsoft Windows Millennium Startup Menu

1.         Help
2.         Start computer with CD-ROM support.
3.         Start computer without CD-ROM support.
4.         Minimal Boot

Enter a choice: 1                    Time remaining: 3

F5=Safe mode Shift+F5=Command prompt Shift+F8=Step-by-Step confirmation [N]
```

> **WHAT'S HAPPENING?** You may have more choices available if you upgraded from Windows 98. You restarted your computer with the Startup disk in Drive A. Note that Windows Millennium gives you CD-ROM support. However, if you have a Zip drive or other devices, you will not be able to access them, because Windows Millennium will not load the drivers for those devices. The default choice is 1. If you do not enter a different number, the clock (Time remaining) will default to choice 1.

Step 10   Press **2** [Enter]

> **WHAT'S HAPPENING?** You see messages on your screen telling you what Windows Millennium is doing. One of the items you will see is Windows Millennium creating a RAM drive (virtual drive). Note the assigned drive letter. A RAM drive is space that Windows Millennium borrows from memory and treats as a drive. This RAM drive is where Windows Millennium uncompresses the various utility files that you need. It needs to do this because the files are too large to fit on one floppy disk.

Step 11   After you see the MS-DOS Prompt, key in the following, substituting your RAM drive letter if it is not H: A:\>**DIR H:** [Enter]

```
MS-DOS Prompt                                                        _ □ ✕

A:\>DIR H:

 Volume in drive H is MS-RAMDRIVE
 Directory of H:\

ATTRIB    EXE          15,252   06-07-00   8:05p
```

```
CHKDSK      EXE        27,968   06-07-00    8:05p
COMMAND     COM        93,040   06-08-00    5:00p
DEBUG       EXE        20,490   06-07-00    8:07p
EDIT        COM        69,854   06-07-00    8:17p
EXT         EXE        13,299   02-04-98    6:09p
EXTRACT     EXE        53,767   06-08-00    5:00p
FORMAT      COM        49,415   06-07-00    9:13p
HELP        BAT            36   02-06-98    5:47p
MSCDEX      EXE        25,473   06-07-00    5:00p
README      TXT        12,661   06-08-00    5:00p
SCANDISK    EXE       245,324   06-07-00   11:04p
SCANDISK    INI         7,329   03-03-99   04:22p
SYS         COM        21,943   06-07-00    8:14p
         14 file(s)         655,851 bytes
          0 dir(s)       1,427,456 bytes free

A:\>_
```

WHAT'S
HAPPENING?   As you can see, here are typical program files, such as ATTRIB.EXE and
              SCANDISK.EXE, that you would use to repair errors. One file that is
              often used in troubleshooting is SYS.COM. This program copies the
              operating system files to a boot disk; this process is referred to as *SYSing
              a disk*. The syntax is SYS *d*: where *d*: represents the drive letter of
              interest, such as SYS C: or SYS A:. However, there are no tools here for
              repairing the Registry.

Step 12   Key in the following: A:\>**DIR /P** Enter

```
┌─────────────────────────────────────────────────────────────────────────┐
│ MS-DOS Prompt                                                    _ □ ✕   │
├─────────────────────────────────────────────────────────────────────────┤
│ Volume in drive A has no label                                            │
│  Volume Serial Number is 2970-56C1                                        │
│  Directory of A:\                                                         │
│                                                                           │
│ AUTOEXEC BAT         1,253   06-08-00    5:00p AUTOEXEC.BAT               │
│ CONFIG   SYS           847   06-08-00    5:00p CONFIG.SYS                 │
│ SETRAMD  BAT         1,443   06-08-00    5:00p SETRAMD.BAT                │
│ README   TXT        12,661   06-08-00    5:00p README.TXT                 │
│ FINDRAMD EXE         6,855   06-08-00    5:00p FINDRAMD.EXE               │
│ FIXIT    BAT         1,247   06-08-00    5:00p FIXIT.BAT                  │
│ RAMDRIVE SYS        12,663   06-08-00    5:00p RAMDRIVE.SYS               │
│ ASPI4DOS SYS        14,386   06-08-00    5:00p ASPI4DOS.SYS               │
│ BTCDROM  SYS        21,971   06-08-00    5:00p BTCDROM.SYS                │
│ ASPICD   SYS        29,606   06-08-00    5:00p ASPICD.SYS                 │
│ BTDOSM   SYS        30,955   06-08-00    5:00p BTDOSM.SYS                 │
│ ASPI2DOS SYS        35,330   06-08-00    5:00p ASPI2DOS.SYS               │
│ ASPI8DOS SYS        37,564   06-08-00    5:00p ASPI8DOS.SYS               │
│ ASPI8U2  SYS        44,828   06-08-00    5:00p ASPI8U2.SYS                │
│ FLASHPT  SYS        64,425   06-08-00    5:00p FLASHPT.SYS                │
│ EXTRACT  EXE        53,767   06-08-00    5:00p EXTRACT.EXE                │
│ FDISK    EXE        66,060   06-08-00    5:00p FDISK.EXE                  │
│ COMMAND  COM        93,040   06-08-00    5:00p COMMAND.COM                │
│ HIMEM    SYS        33,191   06-08-00    5:00p HIMEM.SYS                  │
│ Press any key to continue . . .                                          │
└─────────────────────────────────────────────────────────────────────────┘
```

WHAT'S
HAPPENING?   The files on the Startup disk are also necessary to starting your com-
              puter.

Step 13   Press Enter

```
MS-DOS Prompt                                                    _ □ ✕

RAMDRIVE  SYS       12,663   06-08-00   5:00p  RAMDRIVE.SYS
ASPI4DOS  SYS       14,386   06-08-00   5:00p  ASPI4DOS.SYS
BTCDROM   SYS       21,971   06-08-00   5:00p  BTCDROM.SYS
ASPICD    SYS       29,606   06-08-00   5:00p  ASPICD.SYS
BTDOSM    SYS       30,955   06-08-00   5:00p  BTDOSM.SYS
ASPI2DOS  SYS       35,330   06-08-00   5:00p  ASPI2DOS.SYS
ASPI8DOS  SYS       37,564   06-08-00   5:00p  ASPI8DOS.SYS
ASPI8U2   SYS       44,828   06-08-00   5:00p  ASPI8U2.SYS
FLASHPT   SYS       64,425   06-08-00   5:00p  FLASHPT.SYS
EXTRACT   EXE       53,767   06-08-00   5:00p  EXTRACT.EXE
FDISK     EXE       66,060   06-08-00   5:00p  FDISK.EXE
COMMAND   COM       93,040   06-08-00   5:00p  COMMAND.COM
HIMEM     SYS       33,191   06-08-00   5:00p  HIMEM.SYS
Press any key to continue . . .

(continuing A:\)
OAKCDROM  SYS       41,302   06-08-00   5:00p  OAKCDROM.SYS
EBDUNDO   EXE       29,843   06-08-00   5:00p  EBDUNDO.EXE
CHECKSR   BAT          922   06-08-00   5:00p  CHECKSR.BAT
HIBINV    EXE        3,501   06-08-00   5:00p  HIBINV.EXE
EBD       CAB      264,631   06-08-00   5:00p  EBD.CAB
          24 file(s)        902,291 bytes
           0 dir(s)         432,640 bytes free

A:\>_
```

WHAT'S HAPPENING? All of these files are necessary to restart your computer with the Startup disk.

Step 14 Remove the Startup disk and put it in a safe place.

Step 15 Reboot the computer to return to Windows.

13.3 CLEANING UP YOUR DISK

How well your computer system performs depends a great deal on your hard drive. Remember, all of your files (programs and data files) are stored on the hard disk. You need to access these files easily and quickly, and you need space for new files. In addition, many programs create temporary files while they are working. You must have sufficient disk space to allow the creation of these temporary files. For example, when you print a document, it is sent to the hard disk where it is queued in a temporary file until the printer is ready. Also, if you use the Internet, Web browsers cache files on the hard disk to improve your access speed to the sites you frequently visit. A *cache* is a storage area for often-used information. When you delete files from the hard disk, they are sent to the Recycle Bin, which is also an area on the hard disk.

As you can see, you need hard disk space. You will find that many programs do not automatically delete their temporary files. You may forget to empty the Recycle Bin or to delete your cached Internet files. All of these items will not only cause your hard disk to run out of space, but will also slow down your system performance. To assist you, Windows Millennium provides a tool to help you maintain your disk. It is a utility called Disk Cleanup. Disk Cleanup is intended to be run on your hard drives. Although Disk Cleanup can be run on removable disks such as floppies or Zip disks, it serves little purpose to run it there. It cannot be run on network or CD-ROM drives. Disk Cleanup gives you several options to assist you in recovering disk space.

13.4 ACTIVITY: USING DISK CLEANUP

Step 1   Click **Start**. Point to **Accessories**. Point to **System Tools**. Click **Disk Cleanup**.

WHAT'S HAPPENING?   A message box appears asking you which drive you want to clean up.

Step 2   Click **OK**.

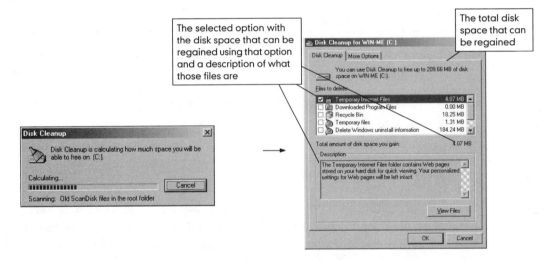

WHAT'S HAPPENING?   A quick message box appears telling you that your system is being analyzed. Then the property sheet appears with the complete analysis. Your computer's analysis will be different. In the example, almost 210 MB can be regained in disk space. You can choose which types of files to remove.

Step 3   If the **Recycle Bin** check box in the Disk Cleanup property sheet is not selected, check it now. Then click the **Details** command button in the Disk Cleanup property sheet.

WHAT'S HAPPENING? ➤ Before you eliminate files, you can look at them to confirm that you want to eliminate them. The files in your Recycle Bin will vary.

Step 4   Close the Recycle Bin window. Clear the **Recycle Bin** check box. Click the **More Options** tab.

WHAT'S HAPPENING? ➤ Other options are available to free up disk space. You can remove Windows Millennium components or programs that you do not use. You may also reduce the amount of space used for System Restore. System Restore is a new feature in Windows Millennium Edition. If you make changes to your hardware, software, or settings on your computer (including new program installations, new hardware, or many other types of changes to your system or system settings) and you start having problems, if you have enabled System Restore, you can use it to undo the changes made to your computer. However, this feature does not restore your data files.

Step 5   Click the **Clean up** command button in the System Restore area.

WHAT'S HAPPENING? ➡ In this example, System Restore is using 400 MB of space on the hard disk. You could reduce this amount. However, System Restore needs at least 200 MB of free disk space to run.

Step 6   Click **Cancel**. Click **Cancel**. Close the Disk Cleanup property sheet.

Step 7   Place the DATA disk in Drive A.

Step 8   Click **Start**. Point to **Programs**. Point to **Accessories**. Point to **System Tools**. Click **Disk Cleanup**.

Step 9   Click the down arrow in the drop-down list box. Select Drive A. Click **OK**.

WHAT'S HAPPENING? ➡ Although normally you only clean up your hard drive, you can actually select any drive you wish. However, there is really nothing to clean up on a removable drive. In fact, there is no Recycle Bin on a removable drive. So there is little reason to try to reclaim space on a removable disk such as a floppy or Zip disk. Usually, if you needed space on these types of disks, you would simply format them or delete the files. As you can see, you gain 0.00 MB on your floppy disk by using Disk Cleanup.

Step 10   Click **Cancel**.

WHAT'S HAPPENING? ➡ You have returned to the desktop.

13.5   BACKING UP YOUR DATA

Backing up data is a critical task that users often neglect. When things go wrong, either through your error or the computer's, it is easier to reclaim your lost data from backups than to try to recreate it; however, this only works if you have created backups. A *backup* is nothing more than a duplicate of the file or files that are on a disk copied to a medium such as a floppy disk or a tape. You retrieve the files by restoring them, which means copying them back to the original medium. When you copy a file to a floppy disk, a Zip disk, or a read-write CD, you are in effect backing it up. You usually want to back up your entire hard disk, which includes all of your files and all of your folders. Although you can back up your entire hard disk to floppy disks, it is a very tedious and time-consuming process in this era of 10-GB or larger hard drives. Thus, most users opt to have a tape backup unit or a removable drive such as a Zip or Jaz drive. Special tapes must be purchased for use in a tape drive, special cartridges for a removable drive.

As you use your computer and programs, you create data. For instance, imagine that you are writing a book. You create your first chapter and save it as a file on the hard disk. You back up your hard disk in January. Fast forward to April; you have now completed 10 chapters. One day, you accidentally delete the folder that contains your chapters. You do not want to rewrite those chapters and, furthermore, you cannot. You turn to your backup, but you have a major problem. The only file that you can restore is the first chapter, which you created in January. The rest of your work is gone. To say the least, backing up your data files regularly is critical. The reason for backing up your entire hard drive may not be as obvious, but it is equally important.

However, although backing up your data files is critical for ensuring that you have your information, there is another area to consider, which is backing up the files needed to run your computer. As you work with Windows Millennium, you create settings, install new programs, and delete old programs. You are also adding and making changes to the system Registry that controls the Windows Millennium environment. If the Registry becomes corrupt, you will not be able to boot Windows Millennium. The system itself is ever-changing. If, for instance, you install a new program and it does something to your hard drive, such as cause another program not to work (or worse), you would like to return to the system you had prior to the installation. If the problem is serious, you might have to reformat your hard drive. It can literally take hours, if not days, to reinstall all of your software. If you have backed up your system, you can simply restore what you had before, and a major catastrophe becomes a minor inconvenience. Although Windows Millennium provides tools to restore your Registry, these tools do not back up your data.

There are two major backup types: full and incremental. A *full backup* copies all of the files from the hard drive to the backup media, regardless of when or whether anything has changed. Full backup is the "back up all files" option. After the files are backed up, the archive bit is turned off. Remember, the archive bit is a file attribute, also called the archive flag. Backup uses the archive bit to determine whether or not a file needs to be backed up. If the bit is on, the file needs to be backed up. After the file is backed up, the archive bit is set to off so that Backup knows that the file has been backed up. When you make any changes to the file, the archive bit is turned on, indicating that the file has changed since the last backup. To do a full backup, you must choose all of your drives and also choose the option to back up your Registry. If you choose "all files," the Registry will not automatically be backed up— unless you select the Windows folder. In that case, the Registry is backed up. A full backup is slower to perform because you are backing up your entire system. How-ever, it is faster to restore your files since you only need to use the most current full backup tape.

You can also back up incrementally, in stages. In this case, you are choosing to back up only some files. A *differential backup* backs up all selected files that have changed since the last time you did an "all selected files" backup. All files that have the archive bit on are backed up. When the backup is complete, the archive bit is left on. This type of backup is faster to perform since you only back up what has changed, but restoration is slower since you need the original backup and all the tapes or disks that have the daily changes on them.

An *incremental backup* only copies the files that have changed since the most recent "All selected files" backup or incremental backup was done. All files that have the archive bit turned on are backed up. When the backup is complete, the archive bits are turned off. In this case as well, the backup is faster to perform but restoration takes more time.

Windows Millennium does not automatically install the backup program. In fact, you cannot install the backup program using the Add/Remove Programs in Control Panel. Instead, you must place the original Windows Millennium CD in your CD-Drive and choose "Browse This CD." You then go to the add-ons folder, then choose the MSBackup folder. In the MSBackup folder, you will see an icon called "msbexp.exe." This file is a self-executing or self-extracting program. *A self-executing* or *self-extracting* program is one that, when you double-click it, it will "extract" itself and install the program. Most self-extracting programs are compressed, and many programs you download from the Internet are self-extracting programs. In this case, double-clicking the msbexp.exe icon will install the Backup program and add the Backup menu item to the System Tools menu. If you want a different backup program, you may purchase a third-party backup program. Often, when you purchase a device, such as tape backup, it will come with its own backup program. However, even if you choose not to install a backup program, you should still back up your data. You may back up your data files and folders by copying them to removable media such as a Zip disk or a CD-ROM (if you have a read/write CD). Something that is very important, regardless of how you back up, is that you DO back up. You should have a regular backup schedule. The timing of your backups depends on how much you use your computer and how often you change things. This is another reason that organizing your disk is important. If you organize your disk by project, for instance, it is easy, once you have finished for the day, to copy the folder to your backup media.

If you are using Backup, you may choose to do a full or incremental backup of your hard drive. A typical backup schedule might include a weekly full backup and a daily incremental backup. If you needed to restore your data, you would need all of the backups, both the full and the incremental. If you are on a network, the network administrator will usually back up the system. However, depending on the network policies, your data may or may not be backed up. It is good insurance, regardless of the network policy, to make your own backups of your data. If the network administrator takes care of the full backup, you need only be concerned about backing up your data files.

When you do backups, it is a good idea to have more than one copy of your backup or backup set. For instance, if you are backing up your data to Zip disks, it would be good to have two Zip disks and alternate them during your backup cycle. If you are using the Backup program and you did a full system backup weekly and incremental backups daily, you would want at least two sets of backups. One week, you would back up on one set; the following week, you would use the other set. Thus, if Murphy's law was in effect for you—your hard disk and your backup were both corrupted—you would be able to restore files from the other week's backup. The files would not be the most current, but at least you would not have to recreate everything from scratch. Another word of warning: Store at least one copy of your backup away from your computer. If you have your backup tapes at the office and you have a fire or theft, you will lose everything. If you have another set at home, you can recover what was lost at work. The most important thing about backing up is to *do it*. Not only do it, but do it on a regularly scheduled basis.

Once Backup is installed, you can access it from System Tools. Backup is licensed from Seagate, the manufacturer of many tape backup units. Using Backup, you can back up your files to QIC (quarter-inch cartridge) tape drives or new larger tape sizes, to local or remote hard drives, or even to floppy disks. You can create a file set (list of files) that describes the files you want to back up. Once you have created a file set, you can drag and drop it onto the Backup icon. With Backup, you can do full backups or incremental backups, or you can back up only those files that have changed since a certain date, regardless of whether they have changed since your last backup.

Backup also has other uses. You can use Backup to ***archive data***. If your hard disk starts filling up and you want to make more room on it, you can use Backup to copy seldom-used files to a backup medium and then delete them from the hard drive. If you need these files at a later date, you can restore them. You can also use Backup to transfer programs and files to other computers. If you purchase a new computer, you can back up your old computer and restore to your new computer. This way, your new system will look the same as your old system, including the arrangement of your desktop.

The first time you use Backup, it automatically creates a file set to be backed up that includes your entire hard drive and the Registry. All file sets are saved to the hard disk.

13.6 ACTIVITY: USING BACKUP

Note 1: Since Backup requires writing information to the hard disk, and since each system is unique, these steps are only one example of how to use Backup. Should you choose to complete this activity on your own computer, be aware that you are going to do only an incremental backup of some files. Under no circumstances should you do this activity if you are on a network, nor are you able to do it on a network.

Note 2: You should have a formatted floppy disk. Do not use your Data or Homework disks for this activity.

Note 3: If Backup is not available on your System Tools menu, you did not install it. To install it, see Appendix D.

Step 1   Click **Start**. Point at **Programs**. Point at **Accessories**. Point at **System Tools**. Click **Backup**.

WHAT'S HAPPENING? If you have never used Microsoft Backup, the first time you run it, it is looking for a backup device such as a tape backup. If you have installed such a device, you would follow the instructions and use the Add New Hardware Wizard. However, even if you do not have such a device, you may still use Backup and back up to a Zip drive or floppy disk. In this activity, it is assumed you have no backup device and will use a floppy disk. If you have used Backup before, you will be taken to the screen below Step 2.

Step 2   If you see the Microsoft Backup dialog box above, click **No**.

WHAT'S HAPPENING? The introductory screen tells you what Backup does and that the Backup Wizard will lead you through the steps to backing up files. Currently, **Create a new backup job** is selected. If you did not want to use the wizard, you would click **Close**. In this case, you will use it.

Step 3   Click **OK**.

WHAT'S HAPPENING? The default setting is to back up your entire hard drive or drives (My Computer). Since this is an activity, you are going to choose the other option, **Back up selected files, folders and drives**.

Step 4   Click **Back up selected files, folders and drives**. Click **Next**.

WHAT'S HAPPENING? You see the drives on your system. The Backup Wizard window looks somewhat like the Windows Explorer window. The left pane is the structure of your disk, and the right pane shows the files in the folders. In front of each item is an empty check box. To select an item, click in the check box. To expand an entry, double-click it or click the plus sign next to it.

Step 5   Click the plus sign next to Drive C: to expand it. Scroll in the left window until you locate the **WINDOSBK** folder. Click on the plus sign to expand it. Click **WINDOSBK** in the left pane. Be sure not to place a check mark in the box. You merely want to select the **WINDOSBK** folder.

WHAT'S HAPPENING? The left pane shows the structure of the WINDOSBK directory. The right pane shows the contents of the WINDOSBK directory. If you had placed a check mark in the check box, that would have indicated that you wanted to back up the entire WINDOSBK directory.

Step 6   Scroll in the right pane until you can see the April files. Click the check box in front of **APR.99**, **APR.NEW**, **APR.TMP**, **APRIL.TMP**, and **APRIL.TXT**.

WHAT'S HAPPENING? You have selected the files you wish to back up by placing a check mark in the box preceding each file.

Step 7   Click **Next**.

WHAT'S HAPPENING? The Backup Wizard wants to know if you want to back up all of the files that you selected or only those that are new or have changed since your last backup. In this case, you are going to back up all five of the files you selected.

Step 8   Click **Next**.

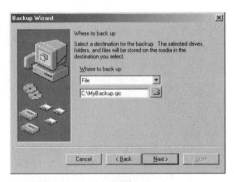

WHAT'S HAPPENING? The wizard wants to know where to back up the files. If you had a tape drive or another backup media type, you could select it here. In this case, since you are backing up to a floppy disk, your only choice is **File**. Backup creates a file, and you need to tell it what device and what file name you are going to use. Currently, the default is **C:\MyBackup.qic**. If you had previously used Backup, the last file you created would be listed here.

Step 9   Click the folder icon next to **C:\MyBackup.qic**.

WHAT'S
HAPPENING? ⮞ You now have your choice of where to back up the files and what to call
               the file.

Step 10   Place a blank, formatted disk in Drive A. Click the **3½ Floppy (A:)** icon
              in the Look in drop-down list box.

WHAT'S
HAPPENING? ⮞ You have chosen your location, Drive A. Now you are going to name the
               backup file.

Step 11   In the File name text box, key in: **April.qic**

WHAT'S
HAPPENING? ⮞ You have named your backup set.

Step 12   Click **Open**.

WHAT'S
HAPPENING? ⮞ You are returned to the **Where to back up** screen of the Backup Wiz-
               ard.

Step 13   Click **Next**.

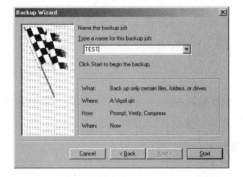   You have more choices—the defaults are to compare the original and backup files and to compress the data to save space. Both should be checked. If you choose to compare, your backup will take about twice as long.

Step 14   Click **Next**.

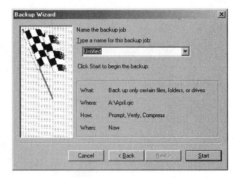

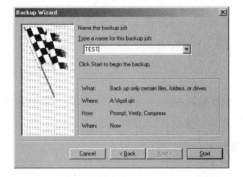   You are asked to name the backup job. The default name is **Untitled**. The backup job is a file that defines your backup. It includes a list of the files you want to include in your backup and any Backup options you selected, including the kind of backup you want to use and the destination drive and folder for the backup files. This is what is listed in the What, Where, How, and When areas.

Step 15   In the text box, key in **TEST**

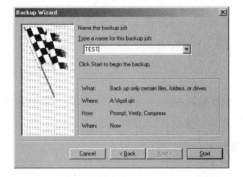   You have named the backup job.

Step 16   Click **Start**.

WHAT'S HAPPENING? A window tells you that Backup is getting ready to do its job. Another window shows the progress of the backup. When it is complete, you see the following information box:

Step 17   Click **OK**.

WHAT'S HAPPENING? You see a status report on the backup you just created.

Step 18   Click the **Report** button.

WHAT'S HAPPENING? ➡ You have opened a document in Notepad that has all of the information about your backup in it.

Step 19   Close **Notepad**. Click **OK**.

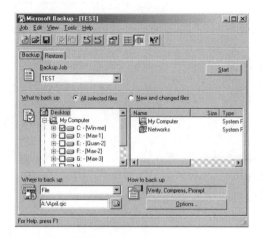

WHAT'S HAPPENING? ➡ You are in the Backup program. At this point, you could choose to restore your files or to do another backup.

Step 20   Close the window. Open Windows Explorer. Open My Computer. Open Drive A.

WHAT'S HAPPENING? ➡ Here is your backup file set called **April.qic**. You have successfully backed up the APRIL files. However, you cannot use this file or open it except with the Restore portion of the Backup utility.

Step 21   Close the Drive A window.

WHAT'S HAPPENING? ➡ Your backup is complete. You have returned to the desktop.

13.7   RESTORE

Backup has an option called Restore, which you can use to copy some or all of your files to your original disk, to another disk, or to another directory. Restore lets you choose which backup set to copy your files. Restoring files is as easy as backing them up with the Backup program. You merely choose Restore and choose the kind of restoration you want. You can use the Restore Wizard, which will lead you through the process of restoring your system.

13.8 ACTIVITY: RESTORING FILES

Note 1: Since using Restore requires writing information to the hard disk and since each system is unique, these steps will look different on your computer. Be aware that you are only going to do an incremental restoration of some files. Under no circumstances should you do this activity if you are on a network, nor are you able to do it on a network.

Note 2: You should have the disk to which you just backed up your files in Drive A.

Step 1   Click **Start**. Point at **Programs**. Point at **Accessories**. Point at **System Tools**. Click **Backup**.

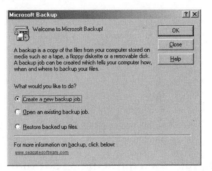

WHAT'S HAPPENING? ➤ This screen is the same introduction you saw in the last activity. In this case, you are going to restore the files on the floppy disk to the hard disk.

Step 2   Click **Restore backed up files**. Click **OK**.

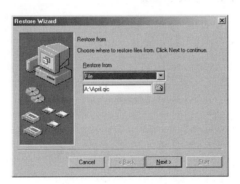

WHAT'S HAPPENING? ➤ The Restore Wizard is asking you from where you want to restore your files. Since you just backed them up to the floppy disk in Drive A, it remembers that location.

Step 3   Click **Next**.

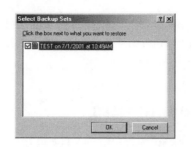

WHAT'S HAPPENING?   You saw a quick dialog box that told you that Restore was loading the information. You then were presented with the Select Backup Sets window. In the Select Backup Sets window, you have only one listed, TEST, and it is the one you wish to select.

Step 4   Click **OK**.

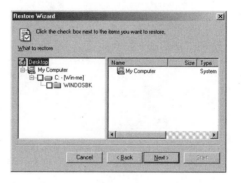

WHAT'S HAPPENING?   Again, you saw a quick dialog box that told you that Restore was loading the information. You were then presented with the Restore Wizard window. The Restore Wizard asks you where you want the files restored to.

Step 5   Click **+** in front of **C:**.

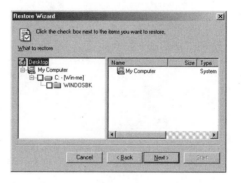

WHAT'S HAPPENING?   As you can see, Restore remembers which drive and folder the files came from.

Step 6   Click **WINDOSBK** to place a check mark in the check box. Click **Next**.

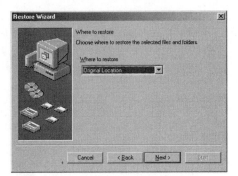

WHAT'S HAPPENING? Here you may select another location rather than the original. In this case, you will accept the default.

Step 7   Click **Next**.

WHAT'S HAPPENING? The default selection is **Do not replace the files on my computer (recommended)**. The assumption here is that the files on your hard drive are the most current. In this case, you are going to select **Always replace the file on my computer** so that you can see how Restore works.

Step 8   Click **Always replace the file on my computer**. Click **Start**.

WHAT'S HAPPENING? The program is telling you that it needs the required media for the TEST backup.

Step 9   Be sure your backup disk is in Drive A. Click **OK**.

WHAT'S HAPPENING? There was a progress report, but, since there were only five files to replace, the operation was quickly completed.

Step 10   Click **OK**. Click **Report**.

WHAT'S HAPPENING? You have successfully restored the files to the hard disk.

Step 11   Close Notepad. Click **OK**.

WHAT'S HAPPENING? You used the wizard to back up and restore your files. However, you do not need to use the wizard. You can use the Backup program. In fact, there are items that you can select when you use Backup that you cannot select when you use the wizard.

Step 12   Click the **Backup** tab. Click **Job** on the menu. Click **Options**.

WHAT'S HAPPENING? As you can see, you have many choices. You can have a password, or you can exclude certain types of files.

Step 13   Click the **Advanced** tab.

WHAT'S HAPPENING? Here you can select to back up the Registry. Note that it is not selected, because backing up the Registry is not the default option.

Step 14   Click **Cancel**. Close the Backup window. Remove the disk from Drive A.

13.9   INITIALIZATION FILES

As you are aware, the Windows Millennium environment is very customizable. You may have different users on one computer, each with his or her own desktop settings, menus, and icons. When you install new hardware, the operating system must know about the new hardware and must have any necessary drivers for those hardware devices. You can double-click a document icon in Windows to open the correct application program, because, when you install an application program, the program "registers" its extension with Windows. As you can see, the operating system has much information to keep track of. All of this information is called the ***configuration information***.

In previous versions of Windows, the operating system and most application programs used .INI files to store information about the users, environmental parameters, and necessary drivers. The .INI extension is derived from ***initialization files***. The initialization files were broken into two types: the system initialization files and private initialization files. Windows created the system .INI files such as WIN.INI and SYSTEM.INI, and application programs created the private .INI files. These configuration files contain the information that Windows needed to run itself as well as to run the programs that are installed on a specific computer. The private .INI files were often added to the Windows directory and kept track of the state of the application, containing such information as the screen position or the last-used files.

The .INI files can specify many items that will vary from one computer to the next. Thus, there cannot be "one" set of .INI files that is common to all users. These files contain such items as the name and path of a specific file that is required by Windows, some user-defined variable, or some hardware or software configuration.

Windows itself had two primary initialization files, WINI.INI and SYSTEM.INI. WIN.INI was the primary location for information pertaining to the software configuration and specific system-wide information added by application software. The SYSTEM.INI file was the primary location for system information that had to do with the computer hardware. One might say that WIN.INI had information for how your system behaved, whereas SYSTEM.INI pointed the Windows operating system to the correct hardware and software components, such as device drivers. In order to run Windows, these two files had to be present. The other initialization files that Windows used were PROGMAN.INI, WINFILE.INI, CONTROL.INI, and PROTOCAL.INI. PROGMAN.INI contained the settings for Program Manager. WINFILE.INI contained the settings for File Manager. CONTROL.INI contained such items as driver and pattern descriptions. These files were not required to start Windows, as was the case with WIN.INI and SYSTEM.INI. PROTOCAL.INI was added to Windows for Workgroups and contained the information for Windows networking.

The last file that Windows used was a file called REG.DAT. This file was the ***registration database***, but it was not an ASCII file and could only be edited by using a special application program called REGEDIT. It contained information about how various applications would open, how some of them would print, the information that was needed about file extension associations, and how OLE (object linking and embedding) objects were handled.

13.10 THE REGISTRY

Instead of using SYSTEM.INI for hardware settings, WIN.INI for user settings, REG.DAT for file associations and object linking and embedding, and all of the various private initialization files, Windows Millennium uses a single location, called the ***Registry***, for hardware, system software, and application configuration information. The Registry data is kept in two files, USER.DAT and SYSTEM.DAT. SYSTEM.DAT contains all of the system configuration information and data settings. These are required during system startup to load the device drivers, to determine what hardware you have, and to handle the registration of file types. If you are on a network, SYSTEM.DAT is always on the local machine in the Windows directory. USER.DAT contains all the user-specific settings such as your logon name, desktop preferences, Start menus, and so forth. If there is only one user on the system, this file is also kept in the Windows directory. If, however, you have enabled user profiles so that different users can maintain their own settings, USER.DAT is stored in the WINDOWS\PROFILES directory under the user's name. USER.DAT and SYSTEM.DAT are hidden files.

To see them, you must set Show all files.

WITH PROFILES

WITHOUT PROFILES

If you are on a network, USER.DAT may be stored on a central server so that, when users dial in or log on from another location, they will retain the same settings. In addition, if you are on a network, the system administrator may have established system policies. *System policies* are designed to provide an override to any settings contained in SYSTEM.DAT and USER.DAT. System policies often contain additional information specific to a particular company and are established by the system administrator. These policies are contained in a file called POLICY.POL and are created with the Policy Editor.

The Registry is absolutely critical to the operation of Windows Millennium. If you have a corrupt or bad Registry, you cannot start Windows Millennium. Windows Millennium also creates a backup file called SYSTEM.1ST. This file is a copy of SYSTEM.DAT that was created at the successful conclusion of your Windows Millennium setup. It is *not* updated, and it is stored in the root of C:\ as a hidden file.

Windows Millennium provides even more protection for the Registry. This protection is called the ***Registry Checker***, which was introduced in Windows 98; it is a system maintenance program that finds and fixes Registry problems and also regularly backs up the Registry, keeping five copies of it. Every time you start up your computer, a new .CAB file is created. These are kept in the hidden WINDOWS\SYSBCKUP folder.

The file name starts with *rb000.cab*, and one is added to the file name each day until five is reached. At that point, the new file replaces the oldest file. Registry Checker always maintains at least the last configuration from which the system was successfully booted. In addition to the Windows-based program, Windows Millennium also provides an MS-DOS-based program for scanning the Registry, backing it up, and restoring the Registry and system configuration files. Given that the Registry is so critical to the operation of Windows Millennium, it is imperative that it be backed up.

Windows Millennium has also introduced a new feature to protect your system and the Registry called ***System Restore***, which is used to undo changes to your computer. If you install a program or device and your computer no longer works properly, you may return your computer to a state prior to when your problems began.

13.11 SYSTEM RESTORE

If you make changes to your hardware such as adding new hardware, installing a new driver for your hardware, or installing or removing software, you are making changes to your system settings. Any of these changes can cause your computer or your devices to no longer work or to work incorrectly. Sometimes, even removing the hardware and the drivers or uninstalling a program still does not solve your problem. As Windows Millennium Edition states, your computer is now in an "undesirable state." You would like to be able to go back in time to when your system was working properly, when you were in a "desirable state." System Restore allows you to undo the changes that you made to your computer. System Restore does all of the following:

- Rolls back your computer to a more stable state. System Restore keeps track of changes made at specific times. It also tracks certain events such as when you install a new software program. These times are called *restore points*. You may also create your own personal restore points. Restore points allow you to "roll back" your computer system to a time when everything was working correctly.
- System Restore will save your email messages, browsing history, and so on. However, be forewarned–System Restore *does not* save or restore your documents. System Restore is not a substitute for backing up your data files. System Restore is for your computer system files, not for your data files. System Restore restores Windows and your programs to a restore point–not your data files.
- System Restore saves about one to three weeks of changes depending on how much you use your computer, your hard disk size, and how much space has been allocated to store the System Restore information.
- You may select which dates you want to restore to by using a calendar.
- System Restore provides several restore points. It creates an initial system checkpoint when your upgrade or install Windows Millennium. Even if you have not made any changes to your system, regular checkpoints are created at specific time intervals, either every 10 hours your computer is on or every 24 hours in real time. It also creates restore points based on programs that you have installed. If you use Windows Automatic Update, restore points are created prior to the update.
- System Restore is reversible so that if the restore point you selected is not successful, you can undo it.

13.12 ACTIVITY: USING SYSTEM RESTORE

Note: If you are in a lab environment, you will not be able to do this activity.

Step 1   Click **Start**. Point to **Programs**. Point to **Accessories**. Point to **System Tools**. Click **System Restore**.

WHAT'S HAPPENING? The System Restore wizard window opens. You may either create a restore point or restore your computer to an earlier time.

Step 2   Click **Create a restore point**. Click **Next**.

WHAT'S HAPPENING? Here you name your restore point. The date and time are automatically added. Make your description brief but meaningful. For instance, if you wanted to install a new program called Wonder Program, you would want to create a restore point prior to your installation; you might call this point Pre-Wonder.

Step 3   Key in the following: **Pre-Wonder**. Click **Next**.

WHAT'S HAPPENING? The system takes a few minutes to create the restore point then presents you with a confirmation window. You may either go back to change your description (Back), return to the opening screen of the System Restore wizard (Home), or continue on (OK).

Step 4   Click **OK**.

WHAT'S HAPPENING? You are returned to the desktop.

Step 5   Click **Start**. Point to **Programs**. Point to **Accessories**. Point to **System Tools**. Click **System Restore**.

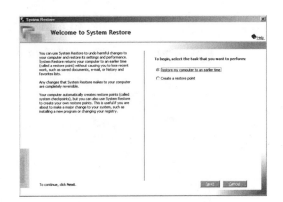

WHAT'S HAPPENING? You again opened the System Restore wizard. Now you are going to look at your restore points.

Step 6   Be sure that **Restore my computer to an earlier time** is selected. Click **Next**.

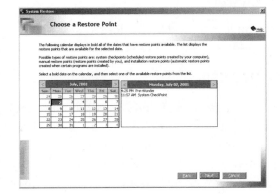

WHAT'S HAPPENING? You are presented with a calendar with available restore points. In this example, there are two restore points—one created by this user (Pre-Wonder) and a System Checkpoint created by Windows Millennium Edition. Only dates that are bold have a check point.

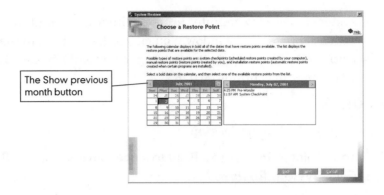

The Show previous month button

Step 7   Click the **Show previous month** button to look at an earlier month.

WHAT'S HAPPENING? In this example, there is only one restore point, one created by Windows Millennium. However, any date that is in bold on the calendar holds a restore point.

Step 8   Click **Cancel**.

WHAT'S HAPPENING? You have returned to the desktop.

13.13 REGISTRY CHECKER

In addition to System Restore, Windows Millennium provides a utility called Registry Checker that was introduced in Windows 98. Each time you start your computer, it will automatically scan the Registry. It maintains one backup for each day. It maintains up to five compressed backups of the Registry that have been successful in booting the system. Five is the default value, but it can be increased to 99 copies. When you start your system, Registry Checker automatically scans the Registry for errors. If it finds a problem, it will automatically restore the most recent Registry from a backup copy. Registry Checker also performs other functions. The Registry grows in size, which decreases performance. Registry Checker determines the amount of free space in the Registry and compacts it, if necessary.

In addition to running automatically, you can run Registry Checker manually. It has two flavors: ScanRegW, which is the Windows-based program, and ScanReg, which is the command line, MS-DOS-based program. ScanRegW scans the Registry for corruption and determines if it requires optimization. It backs up USER.DAT, SYSTEM.DAT, WIN.INI, and SYSTEM.INI. If ScanRegW finds a problem, it will prompt you to restart your computer to fix the problem. This restart causes ScanReg to run and either restore the Registry from a known good backup or, if it can find no good backup, to repair the current Registry. It will also optimize the Registry. Table 13.1 compares the differences between the two programs.

Function	ScanRegW	ScanReg
Has real or protected mode	Protected mode	Real mode
Scans the Registry	Yes	Yes
Fixes the Registry	No	Yes
Backs up the Registry	Yes	Yes
Runs in Safe Mode	Yes	Yes
Compresses the backup	Yes	No
Runs automatically	Yes—every time you start the computer	Yes—if a Registry problem is found
Restores the Registry	No	Yes

TABLE 13.1 SCANREGW VERSUS SCANREG

Both programs also have command line options that allow you further control over your environment. Table 13.2 lists those options.

Option	Description	Can Be Used With
/backup	Backs up the Registry with no prompts to the user.	ScanReg, ScanRegW
/restore	Displays a list of backup files available, sorted by the date and time of the backup.	ScanReg
"/comment"	Specifies that a comment be attached to the backup and displayed with /restore. For instance, "/comment=This is a backup comment."	ScanReg, ScanRegW
/fix	Repairs the Registry files.	ScanReg
/autoscan	Scans the Registry files every time it is run but backs up the Registry only once a day.	ScanRegW
/scanonly	Scans the Registry files and returns an error code. Does not back up the Registry.	ScanRegW

TABLE 13.2 OPTIONS AVAILABLE IN SCANREGW AND SCANREG

One of the functions of the Startup disk is to allow you to boot to the MS-DOS Prompt. When you do so, you can run ScanReg from the MS-DOS Prompt to repair or restore a corrupt Registry.

13.14 ACTIVITY: USING SCANREGW

Step 1　Click **Start**. Click **Run**.

Step 2　Key in the following: **SCANREGW**

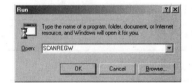

WHAT'S HAPPENING? You are running the Windows Millennium version of Registry Checker. If you did not want to see the dialog box but just the program, you could have keyed in **ScanRegW /autoscan**.

Step 3　Click **OK**.

WHAT'S HAPPENING? In this example, no errors were found. Since the Registry has already been backed up, you are given a choice of whether you want to do it again.

Step 4　Click **No**. Click **Start**. Point to **Programs**. Point to **Accessories**. Point to **System Tools**. Click **System Information**.

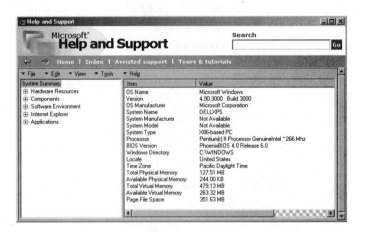

WHAT'S HAPPENING? You can also run the Registry Checker and other utilities from here.

Step 5　Click **Tools**.

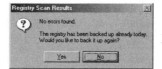

WHAT'S HAPPENING? You are presented with many tools to help you manage your computer. System Restore is also one of the choices.

Step 6   Click **Registry Checker**.

WHAT'S HAPPENING? ScanRegW automatically executed and, in this example, found no errors.

Step 7   Click **No**. Close the System Information window.

13.15 RESTORING THE REGISTRY

The only time you will need to choose which Registry to restore is in case you install something on your computer that keeps it from booting and the Registry is not corrupt. You would, in this case, use ScanReg /restore, which will provide a list of known good .CAB files and will indicate whether the system configuration files stored in the .CAB files have successfully started Windows Millennium. You should choose the .CAB file that was most recently used to start Windows Millennium unless you are *certain* that a specific .CAB file will successfully start Windows Millennium (for instance, one you created by manually running ScanRegW). There are two scenarios: a "no boot" and a "boot." If the computer failed to boot because the Registry was corrupt, ScanReg automatically fixes the problem. However, if the Registry is not corrupt and your computer did not boot because of a change in the Registry, then you would use the ScanReg /restore.

If you have a "no boot" situation, you would take the following steps:

- Restart Windows Millennium. Hold the **Ctrl** key until you see the Startup menu.

- Select **Command Prompt only**.

- Key in: **ScanReg /restore**

Your Backup Sets screen would appear. You would then select your backup.

If your system boots and you want to restore a former Registry, you would take the following steps:

- Shut down Windows. Choose **Restart** in MS-DOS mode.

- At the MS-DOS Prompt, key in: **ScanReg /restore**

Your Backup Sets screen would appear. You would then select your backup.

You may also boot with your Startup disk. If you are working on your own computer and have not yet created one, do so now. (See Appendix C.) If your system is so corrupt that you cannot even boot to these menus, you may always boot with the floppy Startup disk. It will take you to the MS-DOS Prompt, where you can run Scanreg /Restore and select the Registry you wish to restore from there.

13.16 BOOTING WINDOWS

It is beyond the scope of this text to examine all the technical details of the Windows operating system, but some understanding of the interaction between the operating system, the hardware, and the configuration files is necessary.

There are four files necessary to boot the Windows operating system: IO.SYS, MSDOS.SYS, COMMAND.COM, and WIN.COM. To understand the boot process, you need to understand the two modes of operation—real mode and protected mode—and the difference between them. You also need to understand what a process is and what a thread is.

PROCESSES AND THREADS

A *process*, quite simply, is an executable program or part of a program. The process consists of the program itself, the memory address space it uses, the system resources it uses, and at least one *thread*.

Threads are a subset of a process. A thread is a set of commands that does a specific task within a process. It runs in the process' allocated space using the process' allocated system resources.

MS-DOS-based or 16-bit Windows-based programs have only one thread each. But 32-bit programs—programs written for the 32-bit operating systems such as Windows 95/98, Windows Millennium, Windows NT, or Windows 2000 Professional—can have multiple threads. For example, one thread writes to a file while another modifies the screen output. Another example of a thread is Windows itself. Although the shell (the desktop or GUI interface) is a Win32-based process, each folder window that opens is a separate thread of execution. As a result, when you open two folder windows and initiate a copy operation from one window to the other, the copy operation is performed on the thread of the target or destination window. Because of this, you can use the source or original folder window without interruption, or you can even open another copy of the folder.

Windows 95/98 and Windows Millennium are preemptive *multitasking* operating systems. Each thread is executed within a certain set period of time or until a thread with a higher priority is ready and preempts the currently running thread. Because of this system, one malfunctioning thread will not bring the entire system down.

Previous versions of Windows running under MS-DOS operated in a cooperative multitasking environment. Each thread continued to use the processor until it voluntarily gave way to another. In this way, one thread that malfunctioned could bring the operating system to a halt.

REAL MODE

When Windows is running in real mode, only a 16-bit version of the operating system is loaded instead of the full 32-bit operating system. This mode of operation is necessary to run older 16-bit software that wants to make direct calls to the *kernel*. The kernel is the core of the operating system. It is the portion of the system that manages memory, files, and peripheral devices; maintains the time and date; launches applications; and allocates system resources. Long file names are not supported in this mode, and some commands are not fully functional. For example, the /H and /K parameters cannot be used with XCOPY in the 16-bit environment. Older programs or processes not written for the Windows operating system run in a (KT) virtual machine—a VM—of their own. No matter how many of these 16-bit programs are running at the same time, they all use the same message path, or *queue*, to the processor. If one of the threads of one of the 16-bit programs (perhaps the spell checker in a word-processing program) becomes inoperable, all of the programs running in real mode stop responding until the problem program is cleared. In real mode, the processor can execute only one program at a time.

PROTECTED MODE

When Windows is running in protected mode, the full 32-bit operating system is loaded. This mode recognizes all commands and long file names. A *virtual machine (VM)* is an environment in memory, which, from the application's point of view, looks like a separate computer, complete with all of the resources available on a physical computer that an application needs to run. There is a System VM in which all system processes run. In addition, each Win32-based and MS-DOS application runs in its own VM, while Win16-based applications share a single Win16 VM. Each of these 32-bit programs has its own separate queue for each thread of the program running. Thus, if a particular task fails, such as a spell checker, the other parts of the program and any other 32-bit programs that are running are not affected.

THE BOOT PROCESS

The term *boot* comes from bootstrap—starting from the beginning. The Windows boot process is broken down into the following five categories or steps:

- ***BIOS Bootstrap***
- ***Master Boot Record (MBR)*** and Boot Sector
- Real Mode Boot
- Read Mode Configuration
- Protected Mode Load

These categories are explained in sequence in the table below:

BIOS Bootstrap	This occurs before booting. The program that controls this process is in the BIOS chip and the CMOS setup of the computer. The POST (power on self-test) is performed, where the computer checks its physical health. Plug-and-play devices are identified and configured, and a bootable partition is executed.
MBR and Boot Sector	This portion also occurs before booting. It is controlled by programs that are on the hard disk. It determines the location of the bootable partition of the hard disk and gives control over to it. Then IO.SYS is loaded into memory.
Real Mode Boot	Now the Windows boot process begins. A minimal FAT is loaded, MSDOS.SYS is loaded, and you see "Starting Windows" on the screen. The operating system waits (two seconds, by default) to see if the user presses a function key. Then the Windows image is loaded and displayed. A check on the integrity of the Registry files is then performed, SYSTEM.DAT is loaded, and information about the hardware is obtained.
Real Mode Configuration	Although the AUTOEXEC.BAT file is not necessary, if it is there, IO.SYS will process it.
Protected Mode Load	Now WIN.COM is executed, and the 32-bit operating system is fully loaded. The 32-bit drivers are loaded along with the Explorer shell and any network support that is installed.

TABLE 13.3   THE WINDOWS BOOT PROCESS

As you can see, it is a very complicated process. The full Windows 32-bit operating system (the protected-mode operation) is not loaded until the end.

13.17 MEMORY

There are two different types of memory: ***physical memory***, the actual memory chips in the computer; and ***virtual memory***, which is logical memory—it does not physically exist. This section will examine physical memory.

Memory is organized so that it can be addressed. It is much like a bank of mailboxes at the post office. Each box has a unique address. You do not know if there is anything in the mailboxes, but you can locate any mailbox by its address. The same is true with memory. It also has addresses that represent specific locations.

Personal computers use different microprocessor chips identified by number. Very early personal computers used the 8086 or 8088 Intel chip, which had 20 address pins. These address pins connect electrically to the rest of the system. Each of these address pins, when combined with other pins, can "map" or look at many addresses. Remember, all work on a computer deals with only 0s or 1s; this is a binary numbering system. The number of available addresses becomes 2^{20}. The calculation is based on the base-2 number system "powered" to the number of address pins. If you multiply out 2^{20}, your final total is 1,048,576 unique addresses (1 MB of address space). The Intel 80386 chip had 30 lines, so the mathematical calculation is 2^{30}. This computes to 4 gigabytes. A gigabyte is a billion bytes; 4 GB is 4 billion bytes. Though 4 GB of memory seems to be more than we will ever use, it was once thought that no one would ever need more than 640K of RAM! Today, 128 MB is commonplace.

However, one is still left with the legacy of the original CPU 1 MB limit. The 20-bit address bus allows for addresses between 00000H and FFFFFH (0 and 1,048,575). The addresses are expressed in hexadecimal notation, meaning a base-16 number system. One reason for using hexadecimal notation is that binary numbers become extremely cumbersome. Base-16 uses the digits 0 through 9 and the letters A through F to represent numbers. As you know, the later processors can access up to 4 GB of addresses with their 32-bit addresses. When running MS-DOS, all of these processors must use a mode that emulates the original 8086 processor, which is in real mode. Only when the processor can access all available memory does it run in protected mode.

The real-mode processors divide addressable memory into segments. The 8086 and 286 processors and 486-and-above virtual 8086 mode were 16-bit processors with 16-bit registers. All addresses had to fit into 16-bit quantities. The processors used two registers to hold the address of the memory item being used—one to hold the segment address, the other to hold the offset in the segment that the particular addresses occupied. Addresses in this form are expressed as the segment address listed first, separated from the offset by a colon, as in CFFF:A3F1. The segmented form of an address can be converted to a physical address by shifting the segment address to the left and adding in the offset.

Why should you care about this "techno-geek" discussion? Memory is your work area. The larger the work area, the more you can put there. More memory means your computer can handle enormous spreadsheets or large documents. It means you can use larger and much more powerful application programs.

When you are running the MS-DOS Prompt in real mode, memory comes in three flavors: conventional, extended, and expanded.

CONVENTIONAL MEMORY

Conventional memory is the first 640 KB of memory on the computer. All DOS application programs must think they are running in conventional memory. In the Windows operating system, they run in a VM, so the program thinks it has its own 640K of conventional memory.

Conventional memory cannot exceed 640K. The area of memory which begins at the end of conventional memory (640K) and ends at the beginning of *extended memory* (over 1 MB) is called the *adapter segment*. Today, it is more commonly called the *upper memory area* or *UMA*. It is also sometimes referred to as reserved memory.

The adapter segment, or upper memory area, contains room for such things as ROM-BIOS routines, display adapters, and network adapters. Before DOS 5.0, this is where memory ended.

EXTENDED MEMORY

Extended memory is the region above the high memory area (covered later) through the end of physical memory. Extended memory is memory above 1 MB, which could not be directly addressed until the release of DOS 5.0. Extended memory is required by the Windows operating system. An 8086 or 8088 cannot have extended memory, nor can it handle the Windows operating system. Extended memory is managed by a real-mode *memory manager*. This manager is called HIMEM.SYS.

EXPANDED MEMORY

Windows Millennium will allot extended memory as *expanded memory* if it is required to do so by legacy software. An expanded memory manager is usually not required, but one is provided (EMM386.EXE). EMM386.EXE establishes a *page frame* in an empty area of the upper memory area. Each 16 KB is called a "page," and the area of memory that receives the page is called a "page frame." The page frame is the storage place for the addresses in extended memory that contain data. EMM386.EXE manages these pages with a page register and updates the page register to make the page frame point to the data in extended memory. The data then becomes available via the page frame so that older DOS programs can access it. This process is called *bank switching*. Very few programs today actually require bank switching but will use instead the expanded memory allotted by the Windows operating system directly.

UPPER MEMORY AREA

Another kind of memory becomes important if you boot to the MS-DOS Prompt to use MS-DOS based programs. It is called the upper memory area, the area immediately adjacent to the 640 KB of conventional memory. This area in reserved memory is not considered part of conventional memory. It is normally reserved for running hardware such as the monitor or a network card. However, information can be mapped from another kind of memory to the upper memory areas that are unused by your system. The unused portions are called *upper memory blocks (UMBs)*. To use UMBs, you must have an expanded memory manager, such as EMM386.EXE, loaded. You can use the upper memory area for device drivers and memory-resident programs that you need when you are using your computer in MS-DOS mode.

Upper memory addresses are also one of the critical system resources that are managed by plug and play. Memory between A0000H and C0000H is usually used for video memory.

HIGH MEMORY

The *high memory area* is the first 64 KB of extended memory. By enabling this area of memory, a portion of the operating system that in real mode would be resident in conventional memory can be loaded into the HMA (high memory area).

MEMORY MANAGER—HIMEM.SYS

In order to use extended, expanded, or upper memory, Windows Millennium installs a memory manager called HIMEM.SYS. A memory manager is a software program that controls the access to the kind of memory you have.

HIMEM.SYS provides access to the memory above 1 MB on your computer. HIMEM.SYS ensures that no two programs will simultaneously use the same portion of extended memory. The Windows operating system will not load in protected mode without HIMEM.SYS.

How can you learn about the memory in your system? You can check the documentation for your computer to see what you have, but there is also a utility that will help you. There is an external command called MEM that will tell you about the memory in your machine when you are in the MS-DOS window.

13.18 THE MEM COMMAND

The CHKDSK command gives you a report about disks and conventional memory. Because users always need more information about memory, the MEM command was introduced in DOS 4.0. The MEM command reports the amount of used and unused memory. It will report extended memory if memory above 1 MB is installed and will report all memory available for allotment as expanded memory. The syntax is:

```
Displays the amount of used and free memory in your system.

MEM [/CLASSIFY | /DEBUG | /FREE | /MODULE modulename] [/PAGE]

  /CLASSIFY or /C  Classifies programs by memory usage. Lists the size of
                   programs, provides a summary of memory in use, and lists
                   largest memory block available.
  /DEBUG or /D     Displays status of all modules in memory, internal drivers,
                   and other information.
  /FREE or /F      Displays information about the amount of free memory left
                   in both conventional and upper memory.
```

```
/MODULE or /M    Displays a detailed listing of a module's memory use.
                 This option must be followed by the name of a module,
                 optionally separated from /M by a colon.
/PAGE or /P      Pauses after each screenful of information.
```

The MEM command displays the amount of used and free memory in your system.

13.19 ACTIVITY: USING THE MEM COMMAND

Note: You are in the MS-DOS Prompt window with C:\> displayed as the default drive and directory.

Step 1   Key in the following: C:\>**MEM** [Enter]

```
┌─────────────────────────────────────────────────────────────────────┐
│ MS-DOS Prompt                                               _ □ ×     │
├─────────────────────────────────────────────────────────────────────┤
│                                                                       │
│  C:\>MEM                                                              │
│                                                                       │
│  Memory Type        Total       Used        Free                      │
│  ---------------   --------    --------    --------                    │
│  Conventional         636K        60K        576K                     │
│  Upper                  0K         0K          0K                     │
│  Reserved               0K         0K          0K                     │
│  Extended (XMS)     65,535K          ?     129,864K                   │
│  ---------------   --------    --------    --------                    │
│  Total memory       66,171K          ?     130,440K                   │
│                                                                       │
│  Total under 1 MB     636K        60K        576K                     │
│                                                                       │
│  Total Expanded (EMS)               64M (67,108,864 bytes)            │
│  Free Expanded (EMS)                16M (16,777,216 bytes)            │
│                                                                       │
│  Largest executable program size   576K (589,760 bytes)              │
│  Largest free upper memory block      0K      (0 bytes)              │
│  MS-DOS is resident in the high memory area.                         │
│                                                                       │
│  C:\>_                                                                │
│                                                                       │
└─────────────────────────────────────────────────────────────────────┘
```

WHAT'S HAPPENING? ➤ Your display will vary depending on the amount of RAM in your machine, the version of Windows you are using, and how your configuration files load. Compare the lines showing conventional and extended memory. In this example, you have a lot of extended memory, and very little of it is being used. This computer has 64 MB of RAM. Notice that MEM is reporting all of the memory in the computer as expanded memory (EMS). Windows will provide all of the expanded memory needed by most programs without actually having the expanded memory manager EMM386.EXE loaded.

Step 2   Key in the following: C:\>**MEM /C** [Enter]

```
┌─────────────────────────────────────────────────────────────────────┐
│ MS-DOS Prompt                                               _ □ ×     │
├─────────────────────────────────────────────────────────────────────┤
│    VMM32      3,136    (3K)      3,136    (3K)       0     (0K)        │
│    COMMAND    7,264    (7K)      7,264    (7K)       0     (0K)        │
│    DOSKEY     4,688    (5K)      4,688    (5K)       0     (0K)        │
│    Free     589,904  (576K)    589,904  (576K)      0     (0K)        │
│                                                                       │
└─────────────────────────────────────────────────────────────────────┘
```

```
Memory Summary:

  Type of Memory        Total          Used            Free
  ----------------   -----------    -----------     -----------
  Conventional           651,264         61,360         589,904
  Upper                        0              0               0
  Reserved                     0              0               0
  Extended (XMS)      67,107,840              ?     132,980,736
  ----------------   -----------    -----------     -----------
  Total memory        67,759,104              ?     133,570,640

  Total under 1 MB       651,264         61,360         589,904

  Total Expanded (EMS)               67,108,864         (64M)
  Free Expanded (EMS)                16,777,216         (16M)
  Largest executable program size       589,760        (576K)
  Largest free upper memory block             0          (0K)
  MS-DOS is resident in the high memory area.

C:\>_
```

WHAT'S HAPPENING? ➡ Notice that the display scrolls off the screen. You can stop the display by adding a /P parameter.

Step 3 Key in the following: C:\>**MEM /C /P** Enter

```
MS-DOS Prompt                                                    _ □ ✕

Modules using memory below 1 MB:

  Name        Total              Conventional         Upper Memory
  --------  ----------------   ----------------     ----------------
  MSDOS      46,016   (45K)      46,016   (45K)            0    (0K)
  VMM32       3,136    (3K)       3,136    (3K)            0    (0K)
  COMMAND     7,264    (7K)       7,264    (7K)            0    (0K)
  DOSKEY      4,688    (5K)       4,688    (5K)            0    (0K)
  Free      589,904  (576K)     589,904  (576K)            0    (0K)

Memory Summary:

  Type of Memory        Total          Used            Free
  ----------------   -----------    -----------     -----------
  Conventional           651,264         61,360         589,904
  Upper                        0              0               0
  Reserved                     0              0               0
  Extended (XMS)      67,107,840              ?     132,980,736
  ----------------   -----------    -----------     -----------
  Total memory        67,759,104              ?     133,570,640

  Total under 1 MB       651,264         61,360         589,904

Press any key to continue . . .
```

WHAT'S HAPPENING? ➡ By looking at these reports, you can see that on this computer there is 64 MB of memory. If you look at the line, Largest executable program size, you see that you have only 576KB to run programs because you have taken up 61KB of conventional memory with MSDOS, VMM32, COMMAND, and DOSKEY. (Your numbers will vary based on how much memory you have on your computer and what you have loaded.) Notice

the VMM32 entry. This is the virtual machine manager loaded by
Windows.

13.20 WINDOWS TOOLS FOR LOOKING AT MEMORY

Windows Millennium Edition also has tools that you can use in the GUI. These
include the Device Manager, which is located in the property sheet of My Computer,
and System Information, which is located in the Programs/Accessories/System Tools
menu. Each of these tools gives you information about memory and other areas of
your computer.

13.21 ACTIVITY: LOOKING AT THE GUI TOOLS

Step 1   Right-click **My Computer**.

Step 2   Click **Properties**. Click **Device Manager**.

WHAT'S HAPPENING?   You are looking at the devices on your system. **Computer** should be
highlighted.

Step 3   Click **Properties**. Click the **Memory** check box.

WHAT'S HAPPENING?   You can see the memory and what pieces of hardware are using which
memory locations.

Step 4   Click **Cancel**. Click **Cancel**.

Step 5   Click **Start**. Point to **Programs**. Point to **Accessories**. Point to **System Tools**. Click **System Information**.

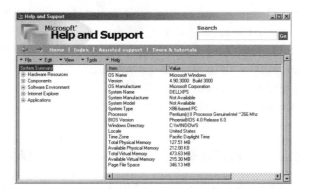

WHAT'S HAPPENING? ▶ Windows Millennium provides additional tools to assist you in learning about your computer and its resources.

Step 6   Click the plus sign next to Hardware Resources to expand it.

Step 7   Click **Memory**.

WHAT'S HAPPENING? ▶ Once again, you have a view of what hardware resources are occupying which areas in memory.

Step 8   Close the System Information window.

13.22 THE SWAP FILE

Windows Millennium uses space on the hard drive as virtual memory when it runs out of physical memory. Called a virtual memory *swap file*, this file is dynamic—it can shrink and/or grow as needed. Let's say you are writing a book and have an 80-page chapter with color pictures. Such a document can be 20 to 24 MB in size. Even a computer with 128 MB of RAM does not have that much memory available—with the drivers going, the program running, and other overhead—to keep a document of that size in memory. So while you are looking at pages 7 and 8, pages 60 through 80 may be written out to the swap file to free up needed RAM. The swap does slow down performance, but it gives the user more "room" in which to operate.

It is possible to set the place and size of the swap file yourself, but it is strongly recommended by Microsoft that you let Windows manage the swap file. There are, however, some instances where it may be advisable to specify where you want the swap file to be. Perhaps you have a second hard drive that is free of executable programs. There would be little I/O (input/output) to this drive. You may want to place your swap file on that drive, freeing up the read/write heads on your main drive. Or you may have a large hard drive that has very little information on it; in that case, you may wish to place the swap file on that drive. Also, if you elect to modify the placement of your swap file, be sure you are placing it on your fastest hard drive (the drive with the fastest access time).

13.23 READ-ONLY ACTIVITY: SETTING UP YOUR SWAP FILE

Note: The following activity is read-only. It is specific to the machines used for the demonstration. **Do not do this activity.**

Step 1   Right-click **My Computer**.

Step 2   Click **Properties**.

Step 3   Click the **Performance** tab.

WHAT'S HAPPENING?   You are looking at the property sheet for your system.

Step 4   Click **Virtual Memory**.

WHAT'S HAPPENING? As you can see, it is recommended that you let Windows manage your virtual memory.

Step 5 Select **Let me specify my own virtual memory settings**.

Step 6 Change the selection to a faster or larger hard drive.

WHAT'S HAPPENING? You have selected an alternate drive on which to place your swap file. In this example, D: is a faster drive, has fewer files on it, has little I/O, and has no often-used executable files.

Step 7 Click **OK**.

WHAT'S HAPPENING? As you can see, Windows is really reluctant to let you change your virtual memory settings. If you were sure, you would click **Yes**, and then you would have to reboot your system for the settings to take effect. Most users will not find it necessary to make any adjustments to virtual memory settings, but, if you frequently have numerous programs open at the same time or deal with very large data files, placing your swap file on a second, faster hard drive could significantly improve performance.

Step 8 Click **No**.

Step 9 Click **Cancel**. Click **Cancel**.

WHAT'S HAPPENING? You have, in this instance, let Windows manage the swap file.

CHAPTER SUMMARY

1. You should have a Startup disk for your system. It is a good idea to have more than one, as floppy disks can easily fail.
2. You create the Startup disk in Control Panel in the Add/Remove Programs tab.

3. Windows Millennium creates a RAM drive (an area of memory), which it treats as a disk. On that RAM drive is where Windows uncompresses and copies the utility files needed to start your computer.

4. To free up space on your hard disk, you may use Disk Cleanup. Disk Cleanup is for use on hard drives.

5. Backing up data is critical. A backup is a duplicate of what is on your hard disk.

6. A full backup copies all of the files from the hard drive to the backup media, regardless of whether the files have changed.

7. A differential backup backs up all of the selected files that have changed since the last time you used the "all selected files" backup.

8. An incremental backup copies only the files that have changed since the most recent "all selected files" backup or incremental backup was done.

9. You should have a regular backup schedule, as well as having more than one copy of your backup media. Furthermore, at least one copy should be stored off-site.

10. The Microsoft backup and restore program is called Backup and is located in System Tools.

11. Archiving data is removing data from the hard drive and keeping the data on an alternate media source. You may use the Backup program for this procedure.

12. You may back up selected files or all files.

13. You may use the Backup Wizard, which leads you through the steps you need to take to use the Backup program.

14. Restoring files allows you to copy your files back to your hard drive from your backup media.

15. The information used to run your system is called the configuration information.

16. Previous versions of Windows used initialization files to track configuration information.

17. Windows Millennium uses a single location, called the Registry, for all hardware, system software, and application configuration information.

18. The Registry data is kept in two files called USER.DAT and SYSTEM.DAT.

19. SYSTEM.DAT contains all of the system configuration and setting data. It is machine-specific and is contained in the WINDOWS directory.

20. USER.DAT contains all user-specific settings and is also kept in the WINDOWS directory, unless there are user profiles set up. In that case, there is a USER.DAT for each user, and each file is kept in the WINDOWS\PROFILE\USERNAME directory.

21. System Restore allows you to undo changes you made to your computer.

22. You may create a restore point to indicate a point when your computer was stable.

23. Windows Millennium provides more protection for the Registry with the Registry Checker tool. This tool automatically keeps at least five backup copies of the Registry.

24. When you start your system, the Registry Checker automatically scans the Registry for problems. If it finds any, it will automatically restore the most recent Registry. It also compacts any free space.

25. You can run the Registry Checker manually. The Windows version is ScanRegW. The MS-DOS-based program is ScanReg.

26. ScanRegW can be run from the MS-DOS Prompt. It can also be run from the System Information tool.

27. The only time you choose which Registry to restore is whenever the Registry is not corrupt but something you installed keeps the machine from booting. You then would use ScanReg /restore. You would then choose which .CAB file to restore.

28. Four files are necessary to boot the Windows operating system: IO.SYS, MSDOS.SYS, COMMAND.COM, and WIN.COM.

29. Newer software written for Windows 95 and later runs in protected mode—the full 32-bit operating system is loaded. Multiple programs run in the same VM (virtual machine).

30. A process is an executable program consisting of the program, its memory address space, required system resources, and a minimum of one thread.

31. A thread is a subset of a process. It is a set of commands that perform a specific task within the process.

32. Windows Millennium is a preemptive, multitasking operating system.

33. The boot process can be broken into five categories: BIOS Bootstrap, MBR and boot sector, real mode boot, real mode configuration, and protected mode load.

34. BIOS bootstrap occurs before booting. The power on self-test (POST) is performed, along with a check of the hardware.

35. The MBR and boot sector process also occurs before booting. This section determines the location of the bootable hard disk and turns control over to it.

36. The Windows boot begins with the real mode boot. The integrity of the Registry files is checked and the SYSTEM.DAT information is loaded, which includes information about the hardware.

37. During the last phase of the boot process, the protected mode load, WIN.COM is executed and the full 32-bit Windows operating system is loaded.

38. There are three types of memory: conventional, extended, and expanded.

39. Conventional memory is the first 640 KB of memory.

40. Extended memory is memory above the first 1 MB.

41. To manage extended memory, the memory manager HIMEM.SYS is used. It is loaded by default.

42. The expanded memory driver, EMM386.EXE, makes use of the adapter segment area to create a page frame so information can be switched in and out of extended memory to simulate expanded memory. This process is called bank switching.

43. The UMA (upper memory area) is the area between conventional memory and extended memory. Unused portions of this memory are called memory blocks (UMB).

44. The high memory area (HMA) is the first 64 KB of extended memory. When enabled, a portion of the operating system can be loaded into this area.

45. The MEM command makes it possible for you to display information about the memory available in a system.

46. You may use System Information in the GUI to explore information about memory.

47. Virtual memory is space on a hard drive used to simulate an environment in which more RAM is made available than actually exists on the system board.

48. Additional RAM is simulated by means of a virtual swap file on the hard disk.

49. It is advisable to let Windows manage your virtual memory swap file if you have only one hard drive on your system.

50. If you have a second, faster hard drive on your system, you may consider taking over the management of the virtual memory swap file and moving it to the faster drive.

KEY TERMS

adapter segment
archive data
backup
bank switching
BIOS Bootstrap
cache
configuration
   information
conventional
   memory
differential backup
expanded
   memory
extended
   memory
full backup

high memory area
   (HMA)
incremental backup
initialization files
kernel
master boot record
   (MBR)
memory manager
multitasking
page frame
physical memory
process
queue
registration database
Registry
Registry Checker

restore point
self-extracting
   or self-executing
Startup disk
swap file
system policies
System Restore
thread
upper memory
   area (UMA)
upper memory
   blocks (UMB)
virtual machine
   (VM)
virtual memory

DISCUSSION QUESTIONS

1. What is a Startup disk?
2. What is the purpose and function of Disk Cleanup? What benefits do you gain from running it?
3. Why is it important to back up data? Programs?
4. Compare and contrast full and incremental backups.
5. Why is it wise to have more than one copy of your backup data? Programs?
6. Explain the purpose and function of the Backup program.
7. Explain how you restore files.
8. What is the purpose and function of System Restore?
9. What is a restore point?
10. If you use System Restore, it is still necessary to back up your data files? Why or why not?
11. What is the purpose and function of the Registry Checker?
12. Why is it important to back up the Registry?
13. When and where would you use the Registry Checker?

14. Compare and contrast the SYSTEM.DAT and USER.DAT files.
15. Compare and contrast ScanRegW and ScanReg.
16. What is a process?
17. What is a thread?
18. Compare and contrast real and protected mode.
19. List and explain the five steps of the Windows boot process.
20. What is physical memory?
21. What is the purpose and function of conventional memory?
22. What is the purpose and function of extended memory?
23. What two memory managers are provided by the Windows operating system?
24. What is the purpose and function of HIMEM.SYS?
25. What is the purpose and function of EMM386.EXE?
26. What is the purpose and function of the MEM command?
27. How might you check memory using the Windows GUI tools?
28. Define virtual memory.
29. What is a swap file?
30. Describe a set of circumstances in which you would take over the management of your machine's virtual memory swap file.

TRUE/FALSE QUESTIONS

For each question, circle the letter T if the statement is true and the letter F if the statement is false.

T   F   1. It is critical to create a Windows Startup disk.
T   F   2. It is only important to back up your data.
T   F   3. The MEM command provides information on the existence and usage of your computer's memory.
T   F   4. If you install a new driver and your computer system no longer works, you may use the System Restore tool to return you to an operational version of your computer system.
T   F   5. Virtual memory means additional memory chips on the system board.

COMPLETION QUESTIONS

Write the correct answer in each blank space.

6. When you boot with the Windows Startup disk, it creates a disk out of memory. This is called a(n) _____ or a(n) _____ drive.
7. A ____ is a storage area for often-used information.
8. A backup that only backs up files that have changed since the last full backup is called a(n) _____ backup.
9. To restore files, you would open the ____ program, located in the ____ menu.
10. The Registry is made up of two files: _____ and _____.

MULTIPLE CHOICE QUESTIONS

For each question, write the letter for the correct answer in the blank space.

11. Which of the following statements is true?
    a. Using Backup will automatically back up the Registry.
    b. The Registry is used for configuration information.
    c. The Registry has been replaced by .INI files.
    d. all of the above

12. Which of the following is false about System Restore?
    a. It will roll your computer back to a more stable state because System Restore keeps track of changes made at specific times.
    b. You may select which dates you want to restore to by using a calendar.
    c. System Restore will save and restore your documents.
    d. System Restore creates an initial system checkpoint when you upgrade or install Windows Millennium.

13. The Registry is comprised of two files. These are
    a. SYSTEM.DAT and USER.DAT.
    b. SYSTEM.DA0 and USER.DA0.
    c. WIN.INI and SYSTEM.INI.
    d. SYSTEM.1ST and USER.1ST.

14. The memory manager that is loaded by default is
    a. EMM386.EXE.
    b. UMA.
    c. HIMEM.SYS.
    d. VMA.EXE.

15. Virtual memory is
    a. disk space used as memory where data is swapped in and out of RAM.
    b. memory space used as storage where data is swapped on and off of the hard drive.
    c. chips on the system board.
    d. none of the above

APPLICATION ASSIGNMENTS

1. Describe how you create a Startup disk. Explain the purpose and function of a Startup disk.

2. Develop a plan for backing up your system, including your data files and the Registry. Describe the time sequencing, i.e., how often you would back up which files. Describe the tools and media you would use.

3. The following files can be deleted in Disk Cleanup. Briefly describe the purpose of deleting each group of files. Determine and explain which options you think are best when using Disk Cleanup.

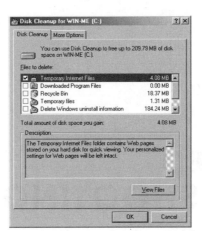

4. *Windows Millennium includes two new tools, Registry Checker and System Restore. These tools are critical features for all users.* Compare and contrast Registry Checker and System Restore. Then, agree or disagree with these statements. Give your reasons for your choices.

5. Compare and contrast virtual memory with physical memory.

6. Compare and contrast conventional memory, upper memory, high memory, extended memory, and expanded memory.

7. Explain the meaning of the lines shown in the following excerpt from the output of the MEM /C command:

```
MS-DOS Prompt                                                    _ □ ×

Modules using memory below 1 MB:

Name          Total            Conventional       Upper Memory
--------   --------------    ----------------    ----------------
MSDOS        46,016  (45K)      46,016  (45K)            0   (0K)
VMM32         3,136   (3K)       3,136   (3K)            0   (0K)
COMMAND       7,264   (7K)       7,264   (7K)            0   (0K)
DOSKEY        4,688   (5K)       4,688   (5K)            0   (0K)
Free        589,904 (576K)     589,904 (576K)            0   (0K)

Memory Summary:

Type of Memory       Total          Used          Free
----------------   -----------   -----------   -----------
Conventional          651,264        61,360       589,904
Upper                       0             0             0
Reserved                    0             0             0
Extended (XMS)     67,107,840             ?   132,980,736
----------------   -----------   -----------   -----------
Total memory       67,759,104             ?   133,570,640

Total under 1 MB      651,264        61,360       589,904

Total Expanded (EMS)              67,108,864   (64M)
Free Expanded (EMS)               16,777,216   (16M)
Largest executable program size     589,760  (576K)
Largest free upper memory block           0    (0K)
MS-DOS is resident in the high memory area.
```

8. Define and explain the use of a swap file. When and why would you want to change the settings?

ADVANCED TROUBLESHOOTING

LEARNING OBJECTIVES

1. List the steps to take when troubleshooting your computer.
2. Describe the purpose and function of a Utility disk.
3. List the steps that occur during the boot process.
4. Compare and contrast the different options when booting into Safe Mode.
5. Explain the importance of the CMOS Setup Utility.
6. Explain the purpose and function of FDISK.
7. Explain the purpose and function of the Registry.
8. Explain the structure of the Registry.
9. Explain how to modify the Registry using REGEDIT.

STUDENT OUTCOMES

1. Create a Utility disk.
2. Boot into Safe Mode, if permitted.
3. Use the CMOS Setup Utility, if permitted.
4. Run FDISK to look at your partitions, if permitted.
5. Use REGEDIT to modify the Registry, if permitted.

CHAPTER OVERVIEW

This chapter will help you in troubleshooting your computer system and give you a procedure for solving your problems. You will create a Utility disk that will assist you when you have problems. You will understand how the boot process works. In addition, you will learn about Safe Mode and the different menu options available to you should you have a problem with your system. A complementary metal-oxide semiconductor (CMOS, pronounced "sea moss") is a computer chip built into your computer system. It is specific to your computer system. It is powered by a battery and retains all of your computer settings. Since the CMOS settings are so critical to the operation of your computer, it is a good idea to know how to access the CMOS and how to make changes to the settings. Furthermore, you will look at FDISK, a crucial utility in setting up your computer system.

The Registry stores all of the configuration information about the hardware on your specific computer. It also tracks and contains all of the preferences for each user of the computer system. Typically, you do not deal directly with the Registry. The preferred method is to make changes using tools such as the Control Panel. Nonetheless, even though you can corrupt the Registry by editing it, there are some problems that can be solved only by editing or modifying the Registry. Also, if your Registry becomes corrupt, you need to be able to restore it.

14.1   TROUBLESHOOTING

When your computer will not start or your programs are not working correctly, you have several options to get back in business. First you have to be able to define your problem. Is it hardware? Is it software? Is the problem that you cannot boot or that you have corrupt files or drivers? Is it a software program that is the problem, or is it Windows itself? It is beyond the scope of this text to describe all of the possible software, hardware, or network problems that you might have. However, if it is a Windows problem, there are several tools you can use to get Windows back up and running. There is a logical troubleshooting order you go through from the simplest to the most drastic. Some of these you have already learned, and others you will learn in this chapter. A suggested order might be:

1. Use System Restore, covered in Chapter 13.
2. Use Backup and Restore, covered in Chapter 13.
3. If you think it is Registry problem, restore the Registry to a prior working version, sometimes known as "last known good configuration." This was also covered in Chapter 13.
4. Boot into Safe Mode and see if you can make Windows operational so that you may repair your problem.
5. Boot with your Startup disk, created in Chapter 13.
6. Boot into CMOS and see if you have a hardware problem.
7. Create a Utility disk to boot into a C:\> prompt to see if you can repair the system.
8. If your system is damaged beyond repair, you may have to partition and FDISK your drive and reinstall Windows as well as all your software. This is the most drastic measure, as you will destroy everything on your drive (and this is, of course, the reason that you back up, back up, and back up!). This is also why you would want a Utility disk, so at least you could boot.

You may also use some of the above tools to fix problems on a current operating system. Here is where you might modify the Registry. You might also need a tool such as FDISK if you add a new drive to your system.

14.2   CREATING A UTILITY DISK FROM THE STARTUP DISK

There may be times when you would like to do a "vanilla" boot on your computer. A *vanilla boot* is a boot with the minimum files necessary to bring you to the C\:> prompt. Perhaps you purchased a second hard drive, and want to partition and format it. Perhaps you have a great many floppy disks to format, and want to write a batch file to do this at the MS-DOS Prompt. You do not need the entire operating system present to do this. When you boot with the Millennium Startup disk, there are many files loaded into memory that are not necessary for a minimum boot. If you look at your Millennium Startup disk using My Computer with the Folder Options/View Options changed so no files are hidden, you would see that there are many files on the disk.

The only files that are *necessary* to bring you to the C:\> are IO.SYS, MSDOS.SYS, and COMMAND.COM. Also, you might like to have some other useful files on your Utility disk. This disk can also be used to boot if you suspect you might have a virus. Once you create your Utility disk, you should be sure that it does not have a virus by using a virus checking program. You would then lock the disk and place it in a safe location. You should do the same for your Startup disk.

14.3   ACTIVITY: MAKING A UTILITY DISK

Note 1: You will need to either make a copy of the Startup disk you made in
Chapter 13 or create another Startup disk following Activity 13.2.
Note 2: Your system is up and running, the MS-DOS window is closed, and you are
at the Desktop.

Step 1   Place the extra Startup disk in the A: drive.

Step 2   Double-click **My Computer**. Double-click the A drive icon.

Step 3 On the My Computer Menu, click **Tools**. Click **Folder Options**. Click **View**.

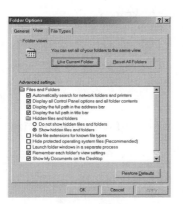

WHAT'S HAPPENING? You are looking at the window where you can set the folder options.

Step 4 Set the **Display** and **Hide** options to match those above. Click **OK**.

WHAT'S HAPPENING? Your display will include the hidden files.

Step 5 Hold down the Ctrl key and press the **A** key.

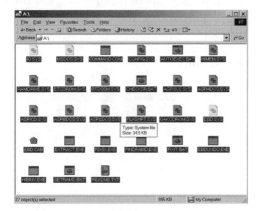

WHAT'S HAPPENING? You have selected all of the files on the disk.

Step 6 Hold down the Ctrl key and click on the three necessary files: **COMMAND.COM**, **MSDOS.SYS**, and **IO.SYS**.

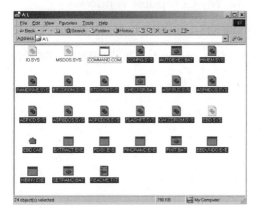

WHAT'S HAPPENING? You now have all the files that are *not* necessary for a vanilla boot selected.

Step 7   Press the [Delete] key.

Confirm Multiple File Delete   ×

Are you sure you want to delete these 24 items?

Yes   No

WHAT'S HAPPENING? You are presented with the Confirm Multiple File Delete dialog box.

Step 8   Click **Yes** to begin the delete process.

Confirm File Delete   ×

The file 'EBD.SYS' is a system file.

If you remove it, your computer or one of your programs may no longer work correctly. Are you sure you want to delete it?

Yes   Yes to All   No   Cancel

WHAT'S HAPPENING? Soon you are presented with another Confirm File Delete dialog box. This message warns you that the **EBD.SYS** file is a system file, and removing it may cause problems. This file is used to extract cab files on the Startup disk that we will not be using on our Utility disk, so it is not needed.

Step 9   Click **Yes to All**.

WHAT'S HAPPENING? Now there are only the three necessary files remaining on the floppy disk in the A drive.

Step 10 Close the My Computer window.

Step 11 Open the MS-DOS Prompt window.

Step 12 Change directories to **C:\WINDOWS\COMMAND:>**

```
MS-DOS Prompt                                              _ □ ×

C:\WINDOWS\COMMAND>_
```

WHAT'S HAPPENING? You have changed directories to the **COMMAND** directory, where the external command files are located. You are going to copy some of these files to the root of the A drive.

Step 13 Execute the following commands:

COPY FORMAT.COM A:
COPY EDIT.COM A:
COPY DOSKEY.COM A:
COPY FDISK.EXE A:
COPY LABEL.EXE A:
COPY MOVE.EXE A:
COPY CHKDSK.EXE A:
COPY XCOPY.EXE A:
COPY DELTREE.EXE A:
COPY MEM.EXE A:

```
MS-DOS Prompt                                              _ □ ×

C:\WINDOWS\COMMAND>COPY FORMAT.COM A:
        1 file(s) copied

C:\WINDOWS\COMMAND>COPY EDIT.COM A:
        1 file(s) copied

C:\WINDOWS\COMMAND>COPY DOSKEY.COM A:
        1 file(s) copied

C:\WINDOWS\COMMAND>COPY FDISK.EXE A:
        1 file(s) copied

C:\WINDOWS\COMMAND>COPY LABEL.EXE A:
        1 file(s) copied

C:\WINDOWS\COMMAND>COPY MOVE.EXE A:
        1 file(s) copied

C:\WINDOWS\COMMAND>COPY CHKDSK.EXE A:
        1 file(s) copied

C:\WINDOWS\COMMAND>COPY XCOPY.EXE A:
        1 file(s) copied

C:\WINDOWS\COMMAND>COPY DELTREE.EXE A:
        1 file(s) copied

C:\WINDOWS\COMMAND>COPY MEM.EXE A:
        1 file(s) copied

C:\WINDOWS\COMMAND>_
```

WHAT'S HAPPENING?　You have copied some utility files to the disk in the A drive.

Step 14 Key in the following:

C:\WINDOWS\COMMAND>**LABEL　A:UTILITY** [Enter]

Step 15 Key in the following: C:\WINDOWS\COMMAND>**DIR** [Enter]

```
MS-DOS Prompt                                                    _ □ ✕

C:\WINDOWS\COMMAND>LABEL  A:UTILITY

C:\WINDOWS\COMMAND>DIR  A:

 Volume in drive A is UTILITY
 Volume Serial Number is 2AE3-5E61
 Directory of A:\

FORMAT    COM        49,415  06-08-00   5:00p FORMAT.COM
EDIT      COM        69,854  06-08-00   5:00p EDIT.COM
DOSKEY    COM        15,495  06-08-00   5:00p DOSKEY.COM
FDISK     EXE        66,060  06-08-00   5:00p FDISK.EXE
LABEL     EXE         9,324  06-08-00   5:00p LABEL.EXE
MOVE      EXE        27,315  06-08-00   5:00p MOVE.EXE
CHKDSK    EXE        27,968  06-08-00   5:00p CHKDSK.EXE
XCOPY     EXE         3,878  06-08-00   5:00p XCOPY.EXE
DELTREE   EXE        19,083  06-08-00   5:00p DELTREE.EXE
MEM       EXE        32,146  06-08-00   5:00p MEM.EXE
COMMAND   COM        93,040  06-08-00   5:00p COMMAND.COM
          11 file(s)        413,578 bytes
           0 dir(s)         923,648 bytes free

C:\WINDOWS\COMMAND>_
```

WHAT'S HAPPENING?　You can see the disk is electronically labeled as UTILITY and contains the useful file that you copied.

Step 16 Remove the Utility disk from the drive, and write "Millennium Utility Boot Disk" on the label.

WHAT'S HAPPENING?　Your Utility disk is complete.

14.4　THE BOOT PROCESS

When you power on a computer, the processor locates and executes startup routines (programs) that are stored in BIOS (Basic Input/Output System). These essential routines test your hardware at startup, beginning with the loading of the operating system. BIOS controls and supports the transfer of data among your hardware devices. It is stored in a chip called ROM-BIOS in ROM (Read-only memory) so that these tasks can be executed.

When you turn on your computer, the POST (power-on self-test) checks for hardware errors such as a bad keyboard or memory errors. If it finds an error, it lets you know by either a series of beeps or a numeric error code. You would need to either have a reference manual for your computer to interpret the meaning of these codes or use the Internet to locate this information.

The next startup routine checks the first boot device for the operating system. Normally this is Drive A. The booting order of your drives is set in the CMOS (complementary metal-oxide semiconductor), which is a semiconductor chip that stores your system settings such as what hardware you have installed as well as the boot order of your disks. The boot order simply determines the order in which drives will be searched for the operating system.

If you have a system disk (***boot disk***) in Drive A, the system is started from Drive A. A boot disk contains the most basic of the operating system files to get your computer started. This is the purpose of the Startup disk and the Utility disk you just created. If you have computer problems, such as your computer not starting or a virus, you will want a bootable floppy disk and will boot from Drive A. Normally, however, your system boots from Drive C.

When you boot from Drive C, the BIOS locates and loads the MBR (Master Boot Record) into memory. The MBR, which is located on the first sector of the hard disk, contains a small amount of executable code and the partition table, which stores information about the disk's primary and extended partitions. A ***boot loader***, the executable code in the MBR, locates the boot partition and then starts the process of loading the operating system. The process then switches operation from real mode to protected mode. Real mode remains from the original PC's operation and can address up to only 1 MB of memory. It cannot use extended memory. Real mode was used with DOS and allowed other programs to directly deal with memory and communicating with devices. This could cause problems in running programs. Alternately, protected mode "protects" the system, forcing all programs to use the operating system to gain access to memory or devices. In addition, protected mode allows addressing of more than 1 MB of memory, supports virtual memory (the ability to use hard disk space as memory), protects memory so that no two programs can access the same address space in memory, uses 32-bit processing instead of the old 16-bit processing, and supports multitasking.

14.5   INTERACTIVE BOOTING—SAFE MODE

When you start Windows, you have an opportunity to interrupt the boot process. The minute you boot your computer, you may press different keys to either boot into Safe Mode or boot into the Startup menu. However, you must your press and hold your key choice(s) very quickly or Windows will boot. In addition, when you press F8, you must be patient as it takes a very long time to boot into the Startup menu. On some systems, holding the Ctrl key provides the same function as holding the F8 key.

F5	Windows boots into Safe Mode.
F8	This key activates the Windows Millennium Edition Startup menu.

Shift + **F8** Windows processes your startup files, one line at a time, asking you for conformation before executing each line. This is known as interactive booting.

If you press **F8** while the system is starting to boot, you will see the following screen:

```
MS-DOS Prompt                                                    _ □ X

Microsoft Windows Millennium Startup Menu

1.    Normal
2.    Logged (\BOOTLOG.TXT)
3.    Safe mode
4.    Step-by-step confirmation




F5=Safe mode   Shift+F8=Step-by-step confirmation [N]
```

You can also use the function key options from this area. Note the menu at the bottom of the screen. This menu provides a list of booting choices and gives you different ways to boot your computer. Choices on this menu can vary depending on your computer. In addition, remember that booting will be very slow.

Safe Mode will boot into Safe Mode and immediately take you to the Help and Support window. See Figure 14.1 Help and Support Screen.

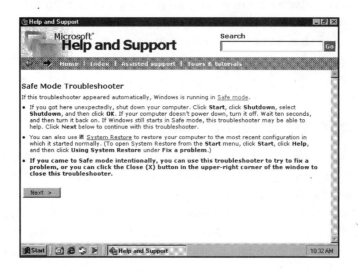

FIGURE 14.1 HELP AND SUPPORT SCREEN

You may then use the Troubleshooter or close the Help and Support screen. When you close the Help and Support window, you see that Windows is in Safe Mode. In Safe Mode, you will see the Desktop in the lowest resolution, 640 by 480. See Figure 14.2 GUI Desktop in Safe Mode.

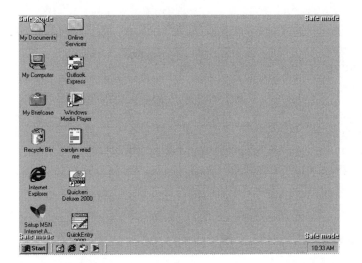

FIGURE 14.2 GUI DESKTOP IN SAFE MODE

In Safe Mode, only the bare minimum set of files and drivers are loaded. Windows Millennium may boot to Safe Mode if there is a problem with newly installed software or with an upgrade of the operating system or with newly installed hardware. Using Safe Mode, you may change settings in hardware or software and then attempt to reboot to see if you boot normally into Windows Millennium Edition. If you do, then you have solved your problem. Booting in Safe Mode is particularly valuable when newly installed software or device drivers do not allow your system to boot normally. It gives you an opportunity to repair the problem. It is also valuable when you are booting and the booting process stalls for an extended period of time or when Windows Millennium Edition is not behaving correctly.

The Logged (BOOTLOG.TXT) choice is booting normally, but when you boot Windows Millennium Edition, you create or update a hidden file called BOOTLOG.TXT, which is saved in the root of C:\ that tracks all device drivers and services that it loads or does not load. A *service* is a program or process that provides support to other programs. By creating this file, you can look at it in any text editor and potentially identify any problem areas. An example of the partial contents of a BOOTLOG.TXT file is shown in Figure 14.3 BOOTLOG.TXT file.

```
MS-DOS Prompt                                              _ □ ×

[0009F399] Loading Vxd = VMM
(Logo disabled)
[0009F399] LoadSuccess = VMM
[0009F3F7] Loading Vxd = vnetsup.vxd
[0009F3F8] LoadSuccess = vnetsup.vxd
[0009F407] Loading Vxd = ndis.vxd
[0009F409] LoadSuccess = ndis.vxd
[0009F417] Loading Vxd = JAVASUP.VXD
[0009F418] LoadSuccess = JAVASUP.VXD
[0009F418] Loading Vxd = CONFIGMG
[0009F418] LoadSuccess = CONFIGMG
[0009F418] Loading Vxd = VPOWERD
[0009F419] LoadSuccess = VPOWERD
[0009F419] Loading Vxd = NTKERN
[0009F41A] LoadSuccess = NTKERN
[0009F41A] Loading Vxd = VWIN32
```

```
[0009F41B]  LoadSuccess = VWIN32
[0009F41B]  Loading Vxd = VFBACKUP
```

FIGURE 14.3 BOOTLOG.TXT FILE

If you choose the Step-by-step confirmation, you are prompted before Windows loads each driver. Thus, if you were having a problem with a piece of hardware, you could load drivers one by one until you isolated the problem. Boot Normal is the default option and boots Windows Millennium Edition in the usual way. When you reboot from Safe Mode, Windows automatically goes to Restart rather than Shut Down.

14.6 AN OVERVIEW OF CMOS

A *CMOS (complementary metal-oxide semiconductor)* is a computer chip built into your computer system. It is specific to your computer system. It is powered by a battery and retains all of your computer settings. It is battery-powered so that even if there is a power outage, your computer retains its settings. The batteries usually last five to seven years. The CMOS contains the settings that identify the type and specifications of your disk drives—how many and what kind, as well as the assigned drive letters and any password options. It also includes the *boot sequence*, which is the order in which the BIOS searches drives to locate and load the operating system. The normal boot sequence is to search for the operating system on Drive A, then Drive C, and then, on some systems, the CD-ROM. This order can be changed. However, if, for instance, Drive C is set as the only drive to be searched and your system cannot boot, you cannot use floppies to boot the system since it will never look on Drive A. The CMOS also contains any settings for power management, language, and so on.

Since the CMOS settings are so critical to the operation of your computer, it is a good idea to know how to access the CMOS, as well as how to change the settings. You should also either print the settings, if you can, or write them down. If your battery should ever fail or you have other problems, knowing the CMOS settings allows you to repair your system.

Accessing CMOS varies from computer to computer, as CMOS is hardware-dependent, not software-dependent. Usually, when you boot your system, you will see a message telling you what key or combination of keys to press to enter the CMOS utility program, often called Setup. Common keys used are the ⎡Delete⎤ key, the ⎡F2⎤ key, or the ⎡Ctrl⎤ and ⎡Alt⎤ keys. On some computer systems, you see no information displayed on your monitor during the POST (power on self-test) as you boot until the system displays the Starting Windows screen. Once you have started Windows, you no longer have access to the CMOS utility. If this is the case on your system, and you want to see the POST, often pressing the ⎡Esc⎤ key when your computer starts to boot will display the POST information and the key or keys necessary to launch the CMOS utility. Some computer systems even require you to insert a special Startup disk in Drive A to access the CMOS utility.

When you launch the CMOS utility, you must be exceedingly careful. You do not want to accidentally change settings that might stop your computer from working or even booting. In most lab environments, the computers will have their CMOS utility programs password-protected so no one except the network administrator can make changes to the system. Because of this, the next activity is a read-only activity. The activity will describe the steps and some functions of two CMOS utilities, but you will not do the activity. You are going to look at the opening screen and the screen that allows you to change the boot order. Then you will see how you exit from the CMOS utility.

14.7 ACTIVITY: LOOKING AT CMOS (A READ-ONLY ACTIVITY)

Step 1   Turn your computer on.

Step 2   Immediately press the [F2] key (or watch the screen for which key(s) to press).

```
    Dell Computer Corporation (www.dell.com) - PowerEdge 1400

Intel® Pentium® III Processor: 1000 MHz     BIOS Version: A03
Level 2 Cache: 256 KB Integrated            Service Tag : 95YPJ01

System Time ......................................... 14:05:20        ▲
System Date ......................................... Fri Jun 29, 2001

Diskette Drive A: ................................... 3.5 inch, 1.44 MB

System Memory ....................................... 512 MB ECC SDRAM
Video Memory ........................................ 4 MB SDRAM
CPU Information ...................................... <ENTER>

Boot Sequence ....................................... <ENTER>
Hard-Disk Drive Sequence ............................ <ENTER>

Integrated Devices .................................. <ENTER>
PCI IRQ Assignment .................................. <ENTER>

System Security ..................................... <ENTER>        ▼

 ←↑↓→ to select  |  SPACE,+,- to change  |  ESC to exit  |  F1-Help
```

PENTIUM BIOS

```
              ROM PCI/ISA BIOS (2A69KD4F)
                  CMOS SETUP UTILITY
                 AWARD SOFTWARE, INC.

   STANDARD CMOS SETUP          INTEGRATED PERIPHERALS

   BIOS FEATURES SETUP          SUPERVISOR PASSWORD

   CHIPSET FEATURES SETUP       USER PASSWORD

   POWER MANAGEMENT SETUP       IDE HDD AUTO DETECTION

   PNP/PCI CONFIGURATION        SAVE & EXIT SETUP

   LOAD FAIL-SAFE SETTINGS      EXIT WITHOUT SAVING

   LOAD OPTIMAL SETTINGS

Esc : Quit                    ↑ ↓ → ←  : Select Item
F10 : Save & Exit Setup       (Shift)F2 : Change Color

              Time, Date, Hard Disk Type...
```

AWARD BIOS

WHAT'S HAPPENING? ➡ Shown above are two common BIOS setup screens. The Pentium BIOS Setup Utility opening screen display gives you information about memory, the language you are using, the system, and other information that is computer-specific. In the Award BIOS Setup Utility, you must use the up and down arrow keys (⬆ and ⬇) to select an item. To see memory information and so on, you would select CHIPSET FEATURES SETUP. In both cases, you are interested in the boot order.

Step 3   In a Pentium Processor, arrow over to the boot choice on the menu. In the Award BIOS, down arrow to **BIOS FEATURE SETUP** and press Enter.

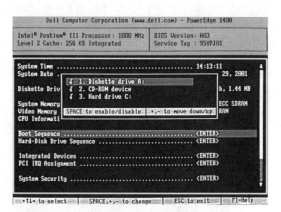

PENTIUM BIOS BOOT SCREEN

AWARD BIOS BOOT SCREEN

WHAT'S HAPPENING! ➤ The Pentium BIOS screen shows you the boot order on this computer. You then would use the ⬇ and ⬆ to select an item, and then use the + and – keys to cycle through the available choices. Once you have made your selection, you would press Esc to exit.

In the Award BIOS window, the boot order is listed. In this example, the boot order is first Drive A, then Drive C, then a SCSI drive. In this utility, you would use the ⬇ and ⬆ arrow keys to move to the item of interest, then use PgUp and PgDn within that item to make changes. Once you had selected an item, the PgUp and PgDn keys would cycle through the available choices for that item. In either example, you could change the boot order so that, for instance, it would check Drive C first, then Drive A. However, you always want to be able to check Drive A for the operating system so that if you have a problem with Drive C, you can use the different recovery tools available from Drive A.

Step 4   Using either BIOS Setup Utility screen, press Esc.

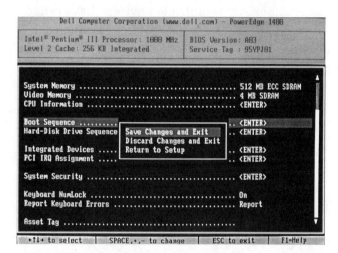

PENTIUM BIOS

AWARD BIOS

In the Pentium Exit screen, the default choice is to save the changes. If you want to save the changes, you would press Enter. In the Award BIOS, the **Save & Exit** choice is selected. This will automatically save the changes you made. Note that regardless of the type of BIOS Setup Utility you have, you may restore the default settings. Since you are only looking at the CMOS, you do not want to make any changes.

Step 5   In the Pentium Processor Exit Screen, use the down arrow key to select **Discard Changes and Exit**. Press ⌷Enter⌷. In the Award BIOS Exit Screen, down arrow to **Exit without Saving** and press ⌷Enter⌷.

WHAT'S HAPPENING! ➤ Your system will reboot.

14.8 PARTITIONING THE HARD DISK

A hard disk is comprised of multiple physical disks called drive platters. Each platter is divided into concentric rings (tracks), and each track is divided into sectors. On a hard disk, a three-dimensional cylinder is formed by connecting the track-sector "pie wedges" from all the platters.

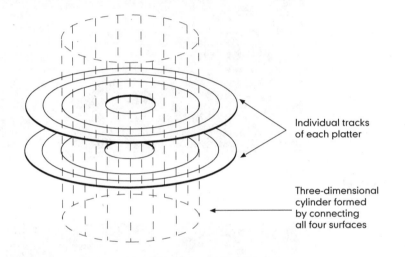

Individual tracks of each platter

Three-dimensional cylinder formed by connecting all four surfaces

Low-level formatting tells where the cylinders and sectors lie on the disk. This process creates the sectors and cylinders by writing the ID numbers of the sectors to the disk surface so that each sector is located and numbered. This identification or address tells the hard-disk controller where the requested information is on the disk.

The numbering of each sector provides two primary benefits besides the obvious one of giving the controller a place to find the information on the disk. These include the sector *interleave* and marking the bad sectors on a disk. The sector interleave matches the rotation of the disk to the rate at which the disk controller can physically process data passing underneath the drive head. Thus, sectors will not be consecutively numbered on the disk. This occurs because computers cannot read a sector, write the data to RAM, and get ready to read the next sector by the time the next consecutively numbered sector appears to the drive head. Rather than waiting for another entire revolution, the sectors are spaced so that when the head is ready to read the next sector, the next consecutively numbered sector is under the drive head. In this way, when the controller is ready to ready to read, it is in the proper place.

Low-level formatting also marks any bad sectors on the disk so that they will not be written to. Usually, a disk is low-leveled only once, at the factory. Rarely, if ever, will an end user have to deal with low-level formatting.

14.9 FDISK

After low-level formatting, and before formatting and installing the operating system, the hard disk must be partitioned. A ***partition*** defines what part of the hard disk belongs to which operating system. With some operating systems, you may choose to have more than one operating system on a hard disk. For instance, you could have both DOS and Windows Millennium Edition on the same disk, in · different partitions. They "get along" very well. However, note that only one operating system can be active at one time.

There are three types of partitions: the ***primary DOS partition***, the ***extended DOS partition***, and the non-DOS partition. If you wish to use the Windows operating system on a hard disk, at least one partition is required and is called the primary DOS partition. The primary DOS partition *must* exist in order to boot from the hard disk. It is the first partition on the disk. Using FAT (FAT16), the primary partition is limited in size to 2 GB. Using FAT32 (in Windows 95B, 95C, OSR2, Windows 98, and Windows Me), the primary partition not limited. (*Note:* In older computers, the hardware may limit the partition size to 7.9 GB.)

Many recommend that when creating the primary booting partition, FAT16 be used as opposed to FAT32. The reason is that DOS 6.22 and below does not recognize a disk partitioned to FAT32, and if there is "trouble," you would be unable to boot to DOS on a floppy and "see" the C drive. However, if you use a boot disk created with the same computer you are trying to boot, this should not be a problem.

After a hard disk is partitioned, you can either format it or allow the Windows Installation Setup program to format for you. Please note, however, that formatting the partitions prior to the installation of the Windows operating system speeds up the installation process considerably.

14.10 ACTIVITY: USING FDISK (A READ-ONLY ACTIVITY)

Note 1: These steps are an example *only*. The specifics will vary, depending on the exact version of the OS you are using and the size of your hard drive.

Note 2: This example assumes you have a brand new drive in a computer that contains no other hard drives. You will need to have a boot disk that contains the FDISK.EXE file and the FORMAT.EXE file. Your Startup disk does not, by default, include the FDISK.EXE file. As previously recommended, you should have available your Utility disk that contains these and other utility files. However, you will not be able to "see" your CD-ROM drive.

Step 1   Boot with your boot disk.

Step 2   Key in the following: **FDISK** [Enter]

```
MS-DOS Prompt                                                    _ □ ×

  Your computer has a disk larger than 512 MB. This version of Windows
  includes improved support for large disks, resulting in more efficient
  use of disk space on large drives, and allowing disks over 2 GB to be
  formatted as a single drive.
```

```
IMPORTANT: If you enable large disk support and create any new drives
on this disk, you will not be able to access the new drive(s) using
other operating systems, including some versions of Windows 95 and
Windows NT, as well as earlier versions of Windows and MS-DOS. In
addition, disk utilities that were not designed explicitly for the
FAT32 file system will not be able to work with this disk. If you need
to access this disk with other operating systems or older disk
utilities, do not enable large drive support.

Do you wish to enable large disk support (Y/N)...........? [Y]
```

WHAT'S HAPPENING? Here, you need to decide whether or not you wish to use FAT32. The question, Do you wish to enable large disk support is really asking if you want to use FAT32 or FAT 16. Note that FAT32 or Yes is the default.

Step 3   Press **Y**.

```
 MS-DOS Prompt                                                    _ □ ×

                      Microsoft Windows Millennium
                        Fixed Disk Setup Program
                   (C)Copyright Microsoft Corp. 1983 - 2000

                            FDISK Options

      Current fixed disk drive: 1

      Choose one of the following:

      1. Create DOS partition or Logical DOS Drive
      2. Set active partition
      3. Delete partition or Logical DOS Drive
      4. Display partition information


      Enter choice: [1]




      Press Esc to exit FDISK
```

WHAT'S HAPPENING? If you had more than one hard drive in your computer, there would be a fifth option, as shown below:

```
 MS-DOS Prompt                                                    _ □ ×

      5. Change current fixed disk drive
```

Step 4   Select number **4**.

WHAT'S HAPPENING? Number 4 displays your partition information. Using 4 does not do any damage to your system. Since this is a new drive, you will get a message telling you that no partitions are defined.

Step 5   Press Esc to return to the main menu.

Step 6   Choose **1** to create a primary partition.

WHAT'S
HAPPENING? ➤ You will be asked if you wish to use the maximum size for a DOS partition and make the partition active.

Step 7   Press **N** for no.

WHAT'S
HAPPENING? ➤ At this point, you will be told the size of the drive, and you can key in what size (either in bytes of percentage of total drive space) you wish to use for the primary partition. At this point, you must decide how much space you wish to allocate to each partition. In this example, you will partition the hard drive into two equal halves, and then split the second partition into two equal logical drives.

Step 8   Key in **50%** Enter

WHAT'S
HAPPENING? ➤ You will now see a choice on the menu to set the active partition. The *active partition* is where you boot from.

Step 9   Choose **Set the active partition** and set the number **1** partition as the active (booting) partition.

Step 10   Select **Create DOS partition or Logical DOS Drive** once again.

Step 11   Select **Create Extended DOS partition**.

Step 12   Choose all the available space.

WHAT'S
HAPPENING? ➤ Once the partition is created, you will get a message saying "No logical drives defined." At this point, you will divide the space you have created as an extended DOS partition into more than one *logical drive* (as opposed to *physical drive*). You will split this partition into the logical drives D and E, using 50 percent of the available space for each logical drive.

Step 13   Press Esc to exit from FDISK.

WHAT'S
HAPPENING? ➤ You need to reboot the system. Your boot disk is still in Drive A.

Step 14   Reboot the system.

WHAT'S
HAPPENING? ➤ You have partitioned or "FDISKED" the drive. You now need to format the drive. This is why you placed the FORMAT command on your Utility disk.

Step 15   Key in the following: A:\>**FORMAT C:/S** Enter

WHAT'S
HAPPENING? ➤ If you were going to prepare the installation of the OS, you would not need to place the OS on Drive C. When you installed Windows, the installation process would do this. But for purposes of this demonstration, you placed the system on the C: drive during formatting.

Step 16   Key in the following: A:\>**FORMAT D:** Enter

At this point, since you formatted Drive C, you would be able to boot the computer from the Primary DOS partition (drive C) of the new drive. As the Millennium Operating System is on a CD disk, you will have to create an **AUTOEXEC.BAT** and **CONFIG.SYS** file on either the booting C drive or the booting disk that loads the driver and **MSCDEX.EXE** files necessary to "spin" the CD-ROM drive. If you had created a Startup disk, you would be able to boot from that disk. It would then allow you to see the CD-ROM drive.

14.11 PROCEDURES

Working with the Registry can be, to say the least, fraught with danger. It is not for the faint of heart. If you in any way damage the Registry files, you will not be able to boot into Windows Millennium Edition. Your entire computer system will be inoperable.

Nonetheless, Windows Millennium Edition provides tools so that you may change the Registry files. This feature seems to be a contradictory position on the part of Microsoft. What Microsoft knows is what all computer users know. At one point or other, something will happen to your computer, and it will not work. Your only alternative would be to take it to a repair facility (at $100 or more an hour) and hope for the best.

However, with the techniques you learn here, you will find that there is much you can do yourself to solve your computer problems. You will also find that, as you use your computer, there will be things that you will want to fix. For instance, if you want to delete a program, you will find that it is not as simple as deleting the directory that holds the files. Windows Millennium Edition application programs leave footprints all over the Registry. To remove a program completely from your disk, you will need to delete the files and modify the Registry to remove all references to the program. There will also be certain types of customizations you will like to do that can only be done by modifying the Registry. For instance, Windows Millennium Edition will remember your desktop as you last left it when you exited Windows. If you leave any windows open, the next time you start Windows those open windows will be on the desktop. If you want to create a desktop that always appears, regardless of what you leave open, you will need to modify the Registry.

This section differs from most of the others in this textbook. It will provide activities with step-by-step instructions, but, if you are in a lab environment or on a network, you will not be able to, nor should you, do any of these activities. No system administrator would ever let changes be made to the system, since one change could bring down the entire lab or the entire network in a company. This activity is intended only to be read. *Read this section, but do not do any of the activities*. If you are using your own computer, you can do the activities. However, remember, until you know what you are doing, you run a great risk of destroying your computer system and making it totally inoperable. So if you choose to do the activities, proceed at your own risk!

14.12 BACKING UP THE REGISTRY

Given that the Registry is so critical to the operation of Windows Millennium Edition, it is imperative that it be backed up. Although Windows Millennium Edition does make backup copies of the Registry, you can still have problems. Although most of the time the Registry and, hence, Windows Millennium Edition, works successfully, the Registry can become corrupted in many ways. How does the Registry become corrupted or "go bad"? The three most common ways the Registry becomes corrupted are as follows:

1. You add new application programs or new drivers to your system.
2. You (or the hardware installation software) make hardware changes from new settings, or your hardware fails.
3. You make changes to the Registry.

Your best protection is to back up the Registry.

14.13 ALTERNATIVES TO EDITING THE REGISTRY

The *Registry* is the central storage for all *configuration information*, including the system configuration, the hardware configuration, configuration of any Windows-based applications, and all user preferences. Although the Registry is logically one database, it is physically stored in three files: USER.DAT, SYSTEM.DAT, and CLASSES.DAT. The CLASSES.DAT file contains software settings, essential information about OLE, and file-association mappings to support drag-and-drop features, Windows shortcuts, and core aspects of the Windows user interface. The USER.DAT file contains user-specific information such as logon names, desktop settings, and so on. During setup, the USER.DAT file is automatically stored as a hidden file in the Windows folder. If you enable user profiles, user settings are then stored in the \WINDOWS\PROFILE folder for each user. If you are on a network, these file(s) could be stored on a central server. The SYSTEM.DAT file contains any hardware-specific or computer-specific settings. This file contains all hardware configuration, plug-and-play settings, and program settings. This file is always stored as a hidden file on the local computer in the Windows folder.

The simplest, safest, and recommended way to make changes to the Registry is to use Control Panel. When you activate any icon in Control Panel and make changes to an object, you are indeed making changes to the Registry. When you use Add/Remove Hardware or run setup programs for hardware, this information is placed in the Registry. When you use the Open With dialog box, you may change the registered file type. This method is an easy way to update the Registry. When you open Windows Explorer and use Tools/Folder Options/File Types, you may alter Registry settings for registered file types.

Also, some application programs store their settings in the Registry. You can update these settings by changing the options in the application program's property sheet. You may use Device Manager to make changes to system hardware and resource settings. Device Manager displays all of the hardware on your computer. It gets this information directly from the Registry. There is also a tool provided by Microsoft called "Tweak UI," which lets you set some of the most popular entries, such as an entry that controls window animation. This tool is located in the \TOOLS\RESKIT\POWERTOY folder on the Windows CD in Windows 98. It is not on the Windows Millennium Edition CD. You may also go the Microsoft Web site to locate and download Tweak UI.

The last choice, and the most dangerous, is to modify the Registry by using the provided tool Registry Editor. When you install Windows, Registry Editor is automatically installed in the Windows directory. Again, if you are going to modify the Registry, back it up first!

14.14 STRUCTURE OF THE REGISTRY

The Registry is designed as a hierarchical structure, not unlike Windows Explorer. *Keys* and subkeys are similar in concept to folders and subfolders in Windows Explorer. The Registry contains three types of objects: keys, values, and data. At the top of the hierarchy are the *Registry keys*. Registry keys can also have several keys or subkeys. Keys can contain one or more other keys and values. When this occurs, it is known as *nesting*. Each key and value must have a unique name within a key or subkey. Keys are case-aware but not case-sensitive. A key name cannot use backslashes. Backslashes are used as delimiters.

Keys and subkeys contain at least one value with a special name (Default). If the default value has no data, it is read as "value not set." *Values* have three parts: the *data type*, the *data name*, and the *data value* itself. A value has data, just as a file has data. There are three types of data: binary, strings, and DWORD values. *DWORD* values are data that are represented by numbers four bytes long.

Only applications use the binary and DWORD value types. A *string* of data is a variable-length set of characters. String values are always enclosed in quotation marks. Whereas DWORD and binary data are not readable, string data is. String data can be easily changed. For instance, if you wanted to call the My Computer icon Carolyn's Computer or Bette's Computer, you could make this change in the Registry. My Computer is string data. It is listed as "My Computer." A *binary* value is a variable-length set of hexadecimal digits. It appears under the data heading of Registry Editor. Each byte is represented by two hexadecimal digits. A DWORD (double word) value is a single 32-bit value (eight hexadecimal digits) and appears in the Registry as an eight-digit hexadecimal number.

When you open Registry Editor, you can see the structure of the Registry. My Computer is at the top. In the left pane, you see displayed the hierarchy of the structure with the keys and subkeys. The plus or minus in front of each entry indicates, as in Windows Explorer, whether an item is expanded or collapsed. The right pane shows the current setting of the selected entry or the value. See Figure 14.4 Registry Organization.

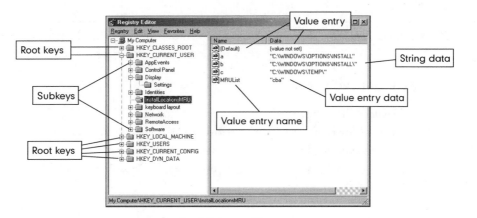

FIGURE 14.4   REGISTRY ORGANIZATION

There are six root keys. Each root key begins with HKEY. *HKEY* is an acronym for "Handle to a KEY." Although there are six HKEYs that appear, in reality, there are only two keys: HKEY_LOCAL_MACHINE and HKEY_USERS. The other HKEYs are aliases for those two keys. Any change that is made in the aliases is changed in either HKEY_LOCAL_MACHINE or HKEY_USERS. Table 14.1 lists the root keys.

Root Key	Description
HKEY_LOCAL_MACHINE	This contains configuration data that is specific to your computer, such as what hardware you have installed and what your program settings are. The information in this key applies to every user who uses this computer.
HKEY_CLASSES_ROOT	This is an alias for HKEY_LOCAL_MACHINE. It contains settings for shortcuts, dragging and dropping, and file associations.
HKEY_CURRENT_CONFIG	This is also an alias for HKEY_LOCAL_MACHINE, which contains the current configuration for your computer.
HKEY_DYN_DATA	This is also an alias for HKEY_LOCAL_MACHINE, which contains information that is changeable, such as the status of a plug-and-play device.
HKEY_USERS	This is the other major key that contains the configuration information for any user who logs onto the computer. In addition to maintaining information that applies to all users on the machine, it also contains information that is specific to each user. There will be a subkey for each user who has a profile.

HKEY_CURRENT_USER   This is an alias for the branch in HKEY_USERS that applies to the user who is currently logged on.

TABLE 14.1   ROOT KEYS

HKEY_CLASSES_ROOT is an alias for HKEY_LOCAL_MACHINE. An alias is needed for backward compatibility. Windows 3.1 programs use this alias. In this branch, you will see the file associations that associate specific classes with different file extensions. In the example shown below, WinZip is associated with the .ARC file extension.

This key also includes class definitions that describe all of the actions associated with a file's class, such as open or print. In addition, you will find information about the icon that is used, any shell extensions installed, and that class's OLE information.

HKEY_CURRENT_USER is an alias for the current user in HKEY_USERS. If there is only one user on a computer, this will point to the Default subkey. If there is more than one user who maintains a configuration, this key will indicate who is currently logged on.

HKEY_LOCAL_MACHINE relates to the configuration data for this specific machine. This root key information applies to the computer itself, not to each user. This relationship is the reason you would never want to copy the Registry files from one computer to another. In this key, you will find individual program settings, such as the path to a program, that would apply to any user who logs on. You would find information about the drive letter assignments for your CD-ROM and removable drives. You would also find information about all the hardware on the computer. Furthermore, you would find data indicating where a program was installed from—the installation path. There are many subkeys which are also aliased by other root keys.

Some of the major keys include the Config subkey, which contains information for any alternate hardware configurations. The Enum subkey contains device information for every device on your computer, including the type of device, the device driver, and other such information. In Windows 98, it contains specific information about such items as your processor. The Network subkey contains any information about the network when a computer is configured for networking. The Security subkey contains information about network security. The Software subkey contains all the information about the software installed on the computer, including file associations and program settings.

HKEY_USERS contains the Default subkey, as well as a subkey for each user when you have multiple user profiles.

Each of the subkeys contains preferences that are specific to that user. Information is written here when you use Control Panel to make changes or when you create settings for specific programs.

HKEY_CURRENT_CONFIG is an alias for the currently-used hardware configuration found in HKEY_LOCAL_MACHINE. You will not have multiple configurations unless you have also set up hardware profiles.

HKEY_DYN_DATA is an alias for HKEY_LOCAL_MACHINE. This key holds information that Windows needs to update quickly. Some of the Registry is kept in memory for quick access to it.

14.15 FILES AND THE REGISTRY

One of the ways you are impacted by the Registry is in the way that Windows handles files. When you click a registered file icon, a program automatically opens. For example, if you click on a text file, Notepad opens with the text file in place. This "magic" happens because of the way the Registry operates. When you click a registered file, such as CAROLYN.TXT, Windows looks up the .TXT extension in HKEY_CLASSES_ROOT. When it does, it sees the following entry:

      Windows knows the type of file associated with the .TXT extension—txtfile. Txtfile is the ProgID. With this information, Windows looks up the ProgID (txtfile) in HKEY_CLASSES_ROOT to find the default action that should occur when the user clicks the file name. Every file association actually has two entries in the key. The .TXT associates the file extension to a ProgID. The ProgID tells what application operates on the files as ProgId\shell\action\command. Using Notepad as an example, it finds the entry txtfile\shell\open\command. It then sees that its value is C:\WINDOWS\NOTEPAD.EXE %1. This statement says to load Notepad using what value (file name) the user keyed in for %1. As you can see, the variable parameters work the same throughout the programming world. If you looked up the Notepad entry in the Registry, under its ProgID of txtfile, it would look as follows:

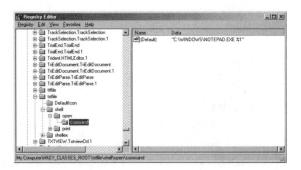

      When you install an application, the application typically registers any file extensions it wants Windows to handle. By handle, it means that the icon will behave in a typical Windows fashion; i.e., when you click the registered document icon, Windows opens the program and loads the data file. The most common subkey is ShellNew, which defines what happens when you right-click a folder, choose New, and pick an entry from the list. The most common values are:

- Command, which will be executed to edit newly created files.
- Filename, which defines a template file that will be copied to create a new file.
- NullFile, to indicate that an empty file will be created.
- Data, to indicate that the value entry's contents should be copied into the new file.

     Note: Filename, NullFile, and Data are mutually exclusive.

Although application programs are free to create subkeys under a file type, there are common subkeys you will find for file types. For instance, if you looked at the Folder subkey for Windows Explorer, you would see the following:

Common subkeys include CLSID, DefaultIcon, EditFlags, Shell, ShellEx, and QuickView.

The CLSID (class ID) subkey looks particularly mysterious. If you opened the CLSID subkey and then opened a specific CLSID in the Registry, you would see the following:

Each one of these subkeys represents a software object. The name of the key is called the class ID (the number in the left pane). In the right pane is the default value entry or the name of the software object, in this case Control Panel. Class IDs are also known as globally unique identifiers (GUIDs). They are 16-byte numbers formatted into 32 individual hexadecimal digits in the format of 8-4-4-4-12. The first 8 digits are simply random numbers. The next four digits come from the date and time. The last 20 digits come from the characteristics of your computer's hardware. There may also be subkeys for each CLSID.

DefaultIcon defines how a file type's icon appears in Explorer or on the desktop. This entry usually includes the name of the icon file (.DLL, .EXE, or .ICO) and the index of the icon in the file. Icon files include WINDOWS\MORICONS.DLL, \WINDOWS\SYSTEM\COOL.DLL, \WINDOWS \SYSTEM\PIFMGR.DLL, \WINDOWS\PROGMAN.EXE, and \WINDOWS \SYSTEM\SHELL32.DLL.

EditFlags tells Windows which controls are available to you in the Windows Explorer File Types dialog box. An entry such as the following:

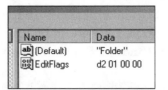

is a 4-byte hexadecimal number, which is converted into its binary equivalent. Then, each bit is either on or off and has an associated action with that state. For example, if bit 4 in byte 1 is on, it means to disable the Remove button.

The Shell subkey defines the actions that are possible for a specific file type. It contains a number of subkeys under it that define verbs. Each verb contains a subkey whose default entry value defines the command. The following is a menu with the items identified as they appear in the Registry.

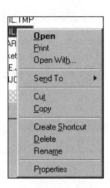

The ShellEx subkey for a file type defines any shell extensions available for the file type. Each shell extension is described by a subkey under ShellEx. These subkeys include icon handlers, context menu handlers, drag-drop handlers, property-sheet handlers, drop handlers, and copy-hook handlers. An icon handler allows a software object to create icons dynamically for the specified file type. A context menu handler allows a software object to add menu items to a context menu dynamically. Drag-drop handlers allow software objects to add menu items to drag-and-drop context (shortcut) menus. Property-sheet handlers allow software objects to add pages to property sheets. Drop handlers allow software objects to handle files that are dropped onto their file type. Copy-hook handlers allow software objects to refuse when you try to copy, move, delete, or rename specific file types.

Although this presentation is a complex subject that you have only been briefly introduced to, if you look at the Edit File Type dialog box, you can see where all the entries are in the Registry.

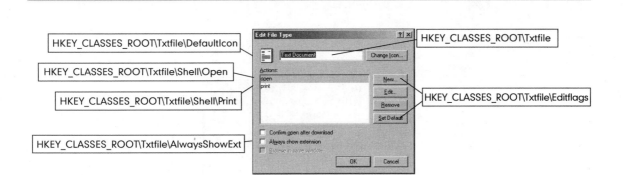

14.16 REGEDIT

Although Microsoft feels that changes should not be made directly to the Registry, there is a tool to make changes. Remember that Microsoft technical support will not help you if you have used this tool. The tool is REGEDIT.EXE, which is automatically copied to the Windows directory when you install Windows. ***REGEDIT*** offers a particular view of the Registry. It is the best general-purpose tool for browsing and modifying the Registry.

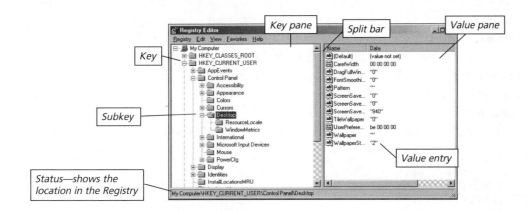

As you can see, the left pane displays the keys, and the right pane displays the values for a key. The status line shows where you are in the Registry. The split bar allows you to alter the size of the left and right panes. In the value pane one of two icons is displayed. The 🔤 icon indicates the text data type, whereas the 🔢 icon indicates the binary data type. The display of data in REGEDIT is static rather than dynamic. In other words, the display is showing you the Registry at the specific moment in time that REGEDIT was opened. Any changes made to the Registry after you have opened REGEDIT will not be reflected in the display.

There are only five menu choices—Registry, Edit, View, Favorites, and Help.

14.16.1 REGISTRY MENU

You can import and export the entire Registry or a branch of the Registry to a text file by using the Import and Export commands. There are reasons for doing so. One of these is that, if you export the Registry to a text file, you can safely edit it. You can then import the altered file back into the Registry. These files have the .REG extension. This process can be *very* dangerous. If you double-click any file with a .REG extension, the file will *automatically* update the Registry whether you want it to or not. You can also export the Registry before you install a program or make changes, and then export it again after you have made these changes to see the differences. Exporting the Registry is another way to back up the Registry. The Registry can also be imported or exported in real mode at the command line.

When you run REGEDIT from Windows, it is a graphical program. When you run it from the MS-DOS mode, it is a command line utility for importing and exporting .REG files. As a real-mode utility, it is useful for correcting a seriously damaged or corrupted Registry. REGEDIT is included on a startup disk. The syntax is displayed below. Table 14.2 further explains the command line switches.

```
REGEDIT [/L:system] [/R:user] [/T:classes] filename1
REGEDIT [/L:system] [/R:user] [/T:classes] /C filename2
REGEDIT [/L:system] [/R:user] [/T:classes] /E filename3 [regpath1]
REGEDIT [/L:system] [/R:user] [/T:classes] /D regpath2

    /L:system     Specifies the location of the SYSTEM.DAT file.
    /R:user       Specifies the location of the USER.DAT file.
    /T:classes    Specifies the location of the CLASSES.DAT file.
    filename1     Specifies the file(s) to import into the registry.
    /C filename2  Specifies the file to create the registry from.
    /E filename3  Specifies the file to export the registry to.
    regpath1      Specifies the starting registry key to export from.
                  (Defaults to exporting the entire registry).
    /D regpath2   Specifies the registry key to delete.
```

Switch	Description
/?	Displays the syntax of REGEDIT.
/L:system	Displays the path and file name of SYSTEM.DAT.
/R:user	Displays the path and file name of USER.DAT.

/E filename *\<regpath\>*	Generates a .REG file. The *regpath* specifies which branch of the Registry you wish to export. If you do not include the regpath, the entire Registry will be exported.
/C filename	Replaces the entire Registry with the contents of the specified file.

TABLE 14.2 COMMAND LINE SWITCHES

Thus, to generate a .REG file that contains the entire contents of the Registry called WHOLE.REG at the command line, you would key in

```
REGEDIT /L:system /R:user /T: classes /E whole.reg
```

And to import a .REG file that contains the entire contents of the Registry called WHOLE.REG at the command line, you would key in

```
REGEDIT /L:system /R:user /T:classes whole.reg
```

And to replace the existing Registry with the contents of a .REG file that contains the entire contents of the Registry called WHOLE.REG at the command line, you would key in

```
REGEDIT /L:system /R:user /T:/classes /C whole.reg
```

Remember, these commands are used only in case of dire emergency.

"Connect Network Registry" and "Disconnect Network Registry" allow an administrator to make changes to the Registry remotely. "Print," of course, prints the Registry.

14.16.2 EDIT MENU

This menu allows you to delete or rename an existing key, copy a key, and find a value, key, or data in the Registry. The New option has a submenu.

The submenu allows you to create a new key as well as the items listed above.

14.16.3 VIEW MENU

The View menu allows you to turn the status bar on or off, to adjust the size of the panes with the keyboard, and to force a rereading of the Registry (Refresh).

14.16.4 FAVORITES MENU

The Favorites menu allows you to quickly return to an item that you often use in the Registry. In this example, there is a favorite—Desktop. You add or remove favorites with the items on the menu.

14.17 USING REGEDIT TO ADD ACTIONS TO A CONTEXT MENU

You can use REGEDIT to add items to context menus. A common reason for this is that only one file extension can be associated with a specific application program. As an example, if you have WordPad but also have Word, the .DOC extension is assigned to Word first. If you double-click a WordPad document icon, you will open Word, not WordPad. If you right-click the document icon, your menu choices will include Open With. Then you must open the submenu to choose which program to use to open your document. Then you choose among programs that are installed on your system. You can add another choice to the context menu, Open With WordPad, so you do not have to use the submenus. Then you will have the choice of opening Word or WordPad. This problem occurs especially with graphic packages that have common file extensions such as JPEG, TIF, and so on.

14.18 ACTIVITY: USING REGEDIT TO OPEN WORDPAD

Note: The following activity assumes that you have Office 97 or Office 2000 (Word 8). Also, remember that if you make a mistake working with the Registry, you can make your system inoperable. If you have not backed up the Registry, do so now.

Step 1   Place your Data disk in Drive A. Open WordPad.

Step 2   Key in the following: **This is a test of altering the Registry**.

Step 3   Click **File**. Click **Save**. In the Save As dialog box, in the File Name box, key in **A:\MaryB.doc**.

Step 4   Close WordPad.

Step 5   Click **Start**. Point to **Search**. Click **Files or Folders**. In the Search for Files and Folders named text box, key in **A:\MaryB.doc**.

Step 6   Click **Search Now**.

Step 7   Right-click the **MaryB.doc** file.

WHAT'S HAPPENING? ➤ On the context (shortcut) menu, only Open is available. Open opens this document in Word. You cannot choose WordPad. You could also choose Open With, then choose WordPad. You cannot choose Open With WordPad from this menu.

Step 8   Close the Search Results dialog box. Click **Start**. Click **Run**. In the Run dialog box, key in **REGEDIT**. Click **OK**.

Step 9   Press [Ctrl] + [Home] and collapse the tree. Highlight My Computer.

WHAT'S HAPPENING? ➤ You have opened REGEDIT, moved to the top of the tree, and collapsed any open keys.

Step 10   Click **Edit**. Click **Find**.

WHAT'S HAPPENING? ➡ The Find dialog box is going to look at all the keys, values, and data for whatever you key in the Find what text box.

Step 11 Clear the **Values** and **Data** check boxes. In the Find what text box, key in **Word.Document.8**.

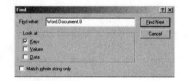

WHAT'S HAPPENING? ➡ You are going to look for your key. Word.Document.8 is Office 97 or Office 2000. If you had an earlier version of Office, you would use Word.Document.7 or Word.Document.6.

Step 12 Click **Find Next**.

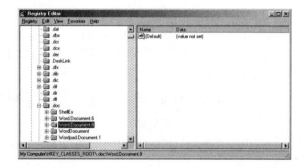

WHAT'S HAPPENING? ➡ Find found the first occurrence of Word.Document.8. This is *not* the one you want. This is the .DOC file extension. You need to go to the shell.

Step 13 Click **Edit**. Click **Find Next** or press the F3 key.

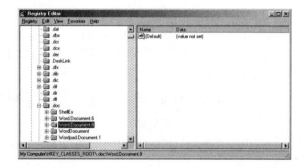

WHAT'S HAPPENING? ➡ Here is the key you are looking for.

Step 14 Click the **+** sign next to Word.Document.8 to expand it. Click the **+** sign next to Shell to expand it. Click **Shell** to select it.

WHAT'S HAPPENING? You are ready to add your new subkey.

Step 15 Click **Edit**. Point to **New**. Click **Key**.

WHAT'S HAPPENING? You can now create your subkey.

Step 16 In the text box, key in **Open With WordPad** and press **Enter**. (Note that if there is not a dotted line for New Key #1, right-click it and click **Rename**).

WHAT'S HAPPENING? Now you need to create the action.

Step 17 Click **Open with WordPad** to select it. Click **Edit**. Point to **New**. Click **Key**.

WHAT'S HAPPENING? You now want to create the action.

Step 18 In the New Key #1 text box, key in **command** and press Enter

WHAT'S HAPPENING? Now you have to tell it what value you want.

Step 19 In the value pane, double-click **(Default)**.

WHAT'S HAPPENING? You are going to tell it what program you want to use.

Step 20 In the Value data text box, key in the following:
         C:\Program Files\Accessories\WordPad.exe "%1"

WHAT'S HAPPENING? You told the value which program to use and where it is located, and you used the variable parameter %1, enclosed by quotation marks so that WordPad will substitute your file name for %1.

Step 21 Click **OK**. Close the Registry.

Step 22 Click **Start**. Point to **Search**. Click **Files or Folders**. In the Search for Files named text box, key in **A:\MaryB.doc** and press Enter

Step 23 Right-click **A:\MaryB.doc**.

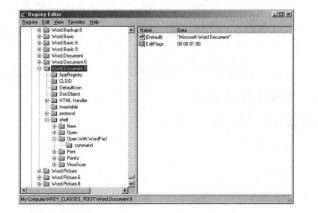

WHAT'S HAPPENING? ➤ Notice your new choice on the context menu—**Open With WordPad**. Now you can choose to open any file that has the .DOC extension in either Word or WordPad.

Step 24 Click **Open with WordPad**.

WHAT'S HAPPENING? ➤ Indeed, your file opened with WordPad, not Word. Now you are going to remove the key you just created.

Step 25 Close WordPad. Close the Search Results dialog box.

Step 26 Click **Start**. Click **Run**. In the Run dialog box, key in **REGEDIT**. Click **OK**.

Step 27 Press [Ctrl] + [Home]. Collapse the tree and select My Computer.

Step 28 Click **Edit**. Click **Find**.

Step 29 Clear the Values and Data check boxes. In the Find what text box, key in **Word.Document.8**.

Step 30 Click **Find Next**.

Step 31 Click **Edit**. Click **Find Next**.

WHAT'S HAPPENING? Find found the first occurrence of Word.Document.8. Remember, this was *not* the one you want. Find Next found the shell, the key you were looking for.

Step 32 If necessary, click the **+** sign next to Word.Document.8 to expand it. If necessary, click the **+** sign next to Shell to expand it. Click **Shell** to select it. Click **Open With WordPad** to select it.

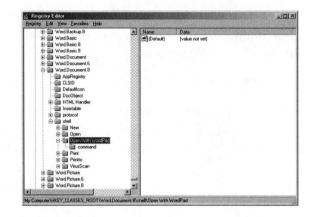

WHAT'S HAPPENING? You are going to delete this key that you created. Be sure that **Open With WordPad** is selected.

Step 33 Click **Edit**. Click **Delete**.

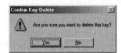

WHAT'S HAPPENING? You are being asked to confirm your key deletion.

Step 34 Click **Yes**.

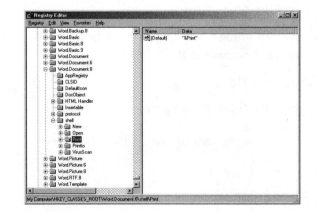

WHAT'S HAPPENING? Your key is gone.

Step 35 Close the Registry Editor.

14.19 USING REGEDIT TO SEE YOUR BITMAP ICONS

If you have many bitmap files, you will have to open many files to see your pictures. You can change this so that the icon will be a small representation of the image rather than just a generic .BMP icon.

14.20 ACTIVITY: USING REGEDIT TO SEE YOUR BITMAP ICONS

Step 1   Open **Explorer**. Open **My Computer**. Open the C drive. Open the **\WINDOWS** directory.

Step 2   Click **View**. Click **Large Icons**.

Step 3   Click **View**. Click **Arrange Icons**. Click by **Type**.

Step 4   Click **Tools**. Click **Folder Options**. Click **View**. Remove the check mark from **Hide file extensions for known file types**.

WHAT'S HAPPENING? You have set up options to enable you to see the necessary information on the bitmap files.

Step 5   Click **OK**.

Step 6   Scroll down until you can see the files with the **.BMP** extension.

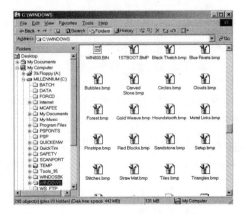

WHAT'S HAPPENING? You can see that the icons for your bitmap image files are all the same.

Step 7   Close **Explorer**. Open **REGEDIT**.

Step 8   Hold down the Ctrl key and press the Home key to take you to the top of the order to begin your search.

Step 9   Click **Edit**. Click **Find**. Clear the **Values and Data** check boxes. Key in the following: **Paint.Picture**

WHAT'S HAPPENING?   You are looking for a subkey.

Step 10   Click **Find Next**.

WHAT'S HAPPENING?   Here is the entry you are looking for.

Step 11   Click the plus sign next to **Paint.Picture** to expand it. Click **DefaultIcon** to select it.

WHAT'S HAPPENING?   The quoted information under Data may be different on your computer, depending on the graphic programs installed.

Step 12   Be *sure* to write down the value listed under Data *exactly* as it appears, as you will need this to return to default values when you are finished.

Step 13   Double-click **Default**.

WHAT'S HAPPENING? ▶ You have opened the dialog box where you can edit the data for the subkey.

Step 14 In the **Value data** box, key in **%1**

WHAT'S HAPPENING? ▶ You have changed the data.

Step 15 Click **OK**. Close **REGEDIT**.

WHAT'S HAPPENING? ▶ In order for your change to take effect, you need to restart Windows.

Step 16 Click **Start**. Click **Shut Down**. Select **Restart**. Click **OK**.

Step 17 Once at the Desktop, right-click the Desktop.

Step 18 Click **Properties**. Click **Effects**. Check **Use large icons**. Click **OK**.

Step 19 Open **Explorer**. Open **My Computer**. Open the C drive. Open the \ **WINDOWS** directory. Scroll down to the files ending in .**BMP**.

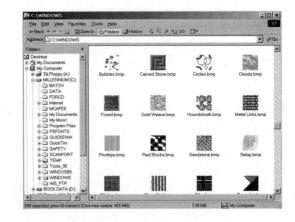

WHAT'S HAPPENING?   Now you can see the actual image instead of the Paint program icon. Now, you will replace the original values.

Step 20   Close Explorer. Open **REGEDIT**.

Step 21   Hold down the Ctrl key and press the Home key to return to the top of the Registry.

Step 22   Click **Edit**. Click **Find**. Clear the **Values** and **Data** check boxes if necessary. Key in the following: **Paint.Picture**

WHAT'S HAPPENING?   You are finding the subkey.

Step 23   Click **Find Next**.

WHAT'S HAPPENING?   You have found the key where you made the change.

Step 24   Click the plus sign next to **Paint.Picture** to expand it. Click **DefaultIcon** to select it.

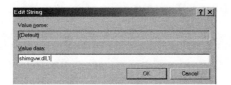

WHAT'S HAPPENING? Now you are going to put the value back to the original value.

Step 25 Double-click **(Default)** in the Value Name box.

WHAT'S HAPPENING? Refer to the value you wrote down prior to changing it.

Step 26 Key in the original value.

WHAT'S HAPPENING? You have replaced the value.

Step 27 Click **OK**.

Step 28 Close **REGEDIT**.

Step 29 Right-click the Desktop. Click **Properties**. Click **Effects**.

Step 30 Remove the check from **Use large icons**. Click **OK.**

WHAT'S HAPPENING? You have returned to the desktop and returned the icon size to normal. Remember, for the .BMP icon appearance to take effect, you need to restart your computer.

CHAPTER SUMMARY

1. When you troubleshoot your computer, there is a logical series of steps to take, starting with the simplest and moving to the most complex.
2. Creating a vanilla boot disk is helpful so that if you have computer problems, you have a way to boot your system.
3. You can create and modify a Startup disk to create a Utility disk.
4. You may access your system by booting into Safe Mode, either by pressing the **F8** or the **F5** keys.

5. If you boot into Safe Mode, you load a minimal set of drivers to get your system up and running.

6. You may choose to boot using a step-by-step confirmation so that you can load or not load individual drivers.

7. If you create a BOOTLOG.TXT file, you may open it in a text editor and see what items loaded or did not load.

8. A CMOS (complementary metal-oxide semiconductor) is a computer chip built into your computer system and is specific to your computer system.

9. The CMOS contains the settings that identify the type and specifications of your disk drives, the assigned drive letters, and any password options. It also includes the boot sequence.

10. The boot sequence is the order in which the BIOS searches drives in order to locate and load the operating system.

11. CMOS is hardware-dependent. When you boot your system, you will see a message that tells you what keys you must press to enter the CMOS Setup utility program.

12. Before you can use a new drive you must partition it. The tool you may use is FDISK.

13. FDISK is a dangerous utility, as it will delete everything on your hard drive.

14. Working with the Registry, if improperly done, can cause your system not to boot.

15. There are many changes that can be done only by editing the Registry.

16. Windows Millennium Edition uses a single location, called the Registry, for all hardware, system software, and application configuration information.

17. The Registry data is kept in two files called USER.DAT and SYSTEM.DAT.

18. SYSTEM.DAT contains all the system configuration and setting of data. It is machine-specific and is contained in the WINDOWS directory.

19. USER.DAT contains all user-specific settings and is also kept in the WINDOWS directory, unless there are user profiles set up. In that case, there is a USER.DAT for each user and each file is kept in the WINDOWS\PROFILE\USERNAME directory.

20. You may alter file types in Windows Explorer by using the View/Folder/Options/File Type menu choice.

21. You may alter the Registry by making changes in an application's property sheets.

22. The Registry is a tree-shaped hierarchy.

23. The Registry maintains three types of objects: keys, values, and data. The Registry keys can have subkeys, a procedure known as nesting.

24. Keys and subkeys contain at least one value with a special name called (Default).

25. Values have three parts: the data type, the name, and the value. A value can have three types of data: binary, string, or DWORD.

26. String data is enclosed in quotation marks and is a variable length set of characters.

27. Binary and DWORD values are binary and not readable.

28. There are six root keys: HKEY_LOCAL_MACHINE, HKEY_CLASSES_ROOT, HKEY_CURRENT_CONFIG, HKEY_DYN_DATA, HKEY_USERS, and HKEY_CURRENT_USER. There are actually only two keys— HKEY_LOCAL_MACHINE and HKEY_USERS. The other keys are aliases for these two keys.

29. HKEY_LOCAL_MACHINE contains configuration information specific to the computer.

30. HKEY_USER contains the .Default subkey that is used for user preferences unless profiles have been enabled. In that case, there is a subkey for each user.

31. When you click a registered file extension, Windows looks up the extension in the HKEY_CLASSES_ROOT. It finds the ProgID with which it can find the default action to take with a file.

32. The most common subkey is ShellNew, which defines what happens when you right-click a folder, choose New, and select an entry from the list.

33. REGEDIT is the tool that allows you to change the Registry directly.

34. The Registry Editor has the keys in the left pane with the values in the right pane.

35. The data type is either text or binary, and the type is indicated by an icon.

36. The Registry Editor has only five menu choices: Registry, Edit, View, Favorites, and Help.

37. Common subkey types include the CLSID (ClassID), DefaultIcon, EditFlags, and ShellEx.

38. Class IDs are also known as globally unique identifiers (GUIDs).

39. You can import and export the entire Registry or a branch to a text file by using the Import/Export command. If you have a text file of the Registry, you can edit it safely and import back into the Registry.

40. In Windows, REGEDIT is a graphical program. At the MS-DOS Prompt, it is a command-line utility.

KEY TERMS

active partition	DWORD	nesting
binary	extended DOS	partition
boot disk	partition	physical drive
boot loader	HKEY	primary DOS
boot sequence	HKEY_CLASSES_ROOT	partition
CMOS (complemen-	HKEY_CURRENT_CONFIG	REGEDIT
tary metal-oxide	HKEY_CURRENT_USER	Registry
semiconductor)	HKEY_DYN_DATA	Registry keys
configuration	HKEY_LOCAL_MACHINE	service
information	HKEY_USERS	string
data name	interleave	values
data type	keys	vanilla boot
data value	logical drive	

DISCUSSION QUESTIONS

1.   If you cannot boot your system, in what order would you try to troubleshoot your system?
2.   What is a Utility disk? How do you create one?
3.   Why would you want or need a Utility disk?
4.   Briefly describe the boot process.
5.   What is a boot disk? Why would you want a boot disk?
6.   What purpose does Safe Mode provide? How can you boot to Safe Mode?
7.   Compare and contrast the options on the Windows Startup menu.
8.   Describe the purpose and function of the CMOS.
9.   Describe the steps you would take to use the CMOS Setup Utility.
10. Why is it necessary to partition a disk?
11. Compare and contrast the primary DOS partition and the extended DOS partition.
12. What is the active partition and why is it important?
13. How and when would you use the FDISK utility program?
14. Why is it important to understand the purpose and function of the Registry?
15. Compare and contrast the safest and most dangerous methods of modifying the Registry.
16. Describe the structure of the Registry.
17. List the major keys of the Registry.
18. List and explain at least two types of objects found in the Registry.
19. What is nesting?
20. Explain the purpose of two of the major keys found in the Registry.
21. List and explain the function of values in the Registry.
22. List and identify the three parts of a value.
23. Explain one type of data found in a value.
24. Explain the purpose and function of a Registry Editor.
25. Explain how to add an item to a context menu using REGEDIT.

TRUE/FALSE QUESTIONS

For each question, circle the letter T if the statement is true and the letter F if the statement is false.

T   F   1.   The first step to take when your computer will not boot is to run FDISK and partition your hard drive.

T   F   2.   The POST checks for hardware errors when you boot the system.

T   F   3.   To boot to Safe Mode, you hold down the [F8] key when your computer begins to boot.

T   F   4.   To change the booting sequence, you must use the CMOS setup utility.

T   F   5.   You may edit the Registry using REGEDIT.

COMPLETION QUESTIONS

Write the correct answer in each blank space.

6. When you boot from the hard disk, the BIOS locates the _____(first sector on the hard disk) and reads it into memory.

7. The computer chip that retains the boot sequence of your computer is the _____.

8. If you wish to load drivers one at a time, you can choose _____ from the _____ menu.

9. The Registry is organized by _____, each of which usually has _____.

10. HKEY_CURRENT_CONFIG is an alias for _____.

MULTIPLE CHOICE QUESTIONS

For each question, write the letter for the correct answer in the blank space.

11. If your system is not working correctly or it will not boot, what can you do?
    a. Format your hard drive.
    b. Boot into Safe Mode and choose Boot Normally.
    c. Boot into Safe Mode.
    d. none of the above

12. If you want to protect your system and always be sure you can boot into your system, you should
    a. Create a Startup disk.
    b. Create a Utility disk.
    c. both a and b
    d. neither a nor b

13. To change the boot sequence, you must
    a. use FDISK.
    b. the CMOS Utility program.
    c. boot into Safe Mode.
    d. boot with your Utility disk.

14. REG_DWORD is an example of a
    a. registry.
    b. key.
    c. value.
    d. data type.

15. Which key stores the configuration data that is specific to your computer, such as what hardware you have installed and what your program settings are?
    a. HKEY_CLASSES_ROOT
    b. HKEY_USERS
    c. HKEY_LOCAL_MACHINE
    d. HKEY_CURRENT_USER

APPLICATION ASSIGNMENTS

For all essay questions, use Notepad or WordPad for your answer. Print your answer.

1. Your computer will not boot. Describe the steps you would take so that you could make your computer operational.

2. *It is critical to create a Startup disk and a Utility disk.* Agree or disagree with this statement. Give your reasons for your choice. In your discussion, include what you would use each disk for.

3. Briefly describe the purpose and function of the CMOS utility program. Describe why you might use it.

4. When and how might you use FDISK? Why is it an important utility?

5. You have files that have the .BMP file extension. Every time you double-click a document with that extension, the Paint program opens. However, now you also have another program that you would like double-clicking a file with the .BMP extension to be able to open instead of Paint. What could you do to solve this problem? Describe the steps you would take.

INSTALLING THE WINDOSBK DIRECTORY AND SHAREWARE REGISTRATION

A.1 THE WINDOSBK DIRECTORY

The disk supplied with this textbook provides programs and files for you to use as you work through the book. The textbook assumes that the **WINDOSBK** directory has been installed on Drive C. If you wish to install the **WINDOSBK** directory on a hard drive other than Drive C, you must substitute the correct drive letter in these instructions. If you are working on your own computer, you must be in MS-DOS at the command line, not in Windows. You must be at the root of C and the default drive and directory must be A:\.

If you are in a lab environment, the lab instructors should have installed the **WINDOSBK** directory on the hard disk. The lab instructors, particularly if the lab is on a network, will have to give you instructions as to the location of the **WINDOSBK** directory if it is not on Drive C. The instructor will inform you if you need to install the **WINDOSBK** directory.

A.2 INSTALLING THE WINDOSBK DIRECTORY

Step 1   Have no disk in any drive. Turn on the monitor and computer.

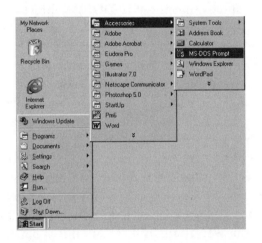

WHAT'S HAPPENING? You are at the Windows desktop.

Step 2 Click **Start**. Point to **Programs**. Point to **Accessories**. Point to **MS-DOS Prompt**.

WHAT'S HAPPENING? You are going to open the command line window.

Step 3 Click **MS-DOS Prompt**.

WHAT'S HAPPENING? You have opened a DOS window. Your directory may differ. In this example, it is C: \WINDOWS>.

Step 4 Key in the following: C: \WINDOWS>**CD \ Enter**

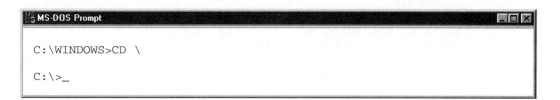

```
MS-DOS Prompt                                                    _ ☐ ✕

C:\WINDOWS>CD \

C:\>_
```

 You are now at the root of Drive C. If you wanted this folder to be on a drive other than C, you would substitute that drive letter for C.

Step 5   Place the ACTIVITIES disk that came with the textbook into Drive A.

Step 6   Key in the following: C:\>**A:** `Enter`

```
MS-DOS Prompt                                                    _ ☐ ✕

C:\>A:

A:\>_
```

 You have made the root of A the default drive and directory.

Step 7   Key in the following: A:>**XCOPY A:*.* /S /E C:\WINDOSBK**

```
MS-DOS Prompt                                                    _ ☐ ✕

C:\>A:

A:\>XCOPY A:*.*  /S /E C:\WINDOSBK_
```

 Be sure that this is what you have keyed in. Now you can begin executing the program by pressing `Enter`.

Step 8   Press `Enter`

```
MS-DOS Prompt                                                    _ ☐ ✕

A:\>XCOPY A:*.*  /S /E C:\WINDOSBK
Does WINDOSBK specify a file name
or directory name on the target
(F = file, D = directory)?_
```

 The XCOPY command is asking you if you want to create a directory or file called **WINDOSBK**. In this case you want to create a directory so you must specify that by pressing the letter **D**. Once you press **D**, the files will be copied to Drive C to the directory called **WINDOSBK**.

Step 9   Press **D** `Enter`

```
MS-DOS Prompt                                                    _ ☐ ✕

FINANCE\ORDER
FINANCE\GO.BAT
FINANCE\SHAREWAR.DOC
FINANCE\README.BAT
FINANCE\THINK.DOC
```

```
FINANCE\THINK.HLP
LEVEL-1\HELLO.TXT
LEVEL-1\LEVEL-2\HELLO.TXT
LEVEL-1\LEVEL-2\LEVEL-3\HELLO.TXT
SPORTS\FOOT-COL.TMS
SPORTS\FOOT-PRO.TMS
SPORTS\BSBALL-N.TMS
SPORTS\BASKETBL.TMS
SPORTS\BSBALL-A.TMS
MEDIA\BOOKS\PULITZER.BKS
MEDIA\BOOKS\AME-LIT.BKS
MEDIA\BOOKS\MYSTERY.BKS
MEDIA\TV\COMEDY.TV
MEDIA\TV\DRAMA.TV
MEDIA\MOVIES\OTHER.MOV
MEDIA\MOVIES\DRAMA.MOV
MEDIA\MOVIES\MUSIC.MOV
        152 File(s) copied

A:\>_
```

WHAT'S HAPPENING? You now have a directory on Drive C called **WINDOSBK**. You need to have this directory placed on Drive C in order to complete the exercises, activities, and homework.

Step 10 Key in the following: A:\>**C:** [Enter]

Step 11 Key in the following: C:\>**DIR WINDOS*.*** [Enter]

```
MS-DOS Prompt                                                    _ □ ×

C:\>DIR WINDOS*.*

 Volume in drive C has no label
 Volume Serial Number is 07CE-0212
 Directory of C:\

WINDOSBK       <DIR>         06-23-01  8:43p WINDOSBK
        0 file(s)                0 bytes
        1 dir(s)      824,082,432 bytes free

C:\>_
```

WHAT'S HAPPENING? You have successfully installed the **WINDOSBK** directory on Drive C. Installed means that you created the **WINDOSBK** directory on Drive C and copied all the files on the disk in Drive A to the newly created directory called **WINDOSBK**.

Step 12 Key in the following: C:\>**EXIT** [Enter]

WHAT'S HAPPENING? You have closed the MS-DOS Prompt window and returned to the Windows desktop.

A.3   REMOVING THE WINDOSBK DIRECTORY FROM THE HARD DISK

Note 1: If you are working in a lab environment, do not take these steps. However, if you are working on your own computer, when you have completed the textbook you will probably want to take the **WINDOSBK** directory and the files it contains off your hard drive. You may, of course, use Explorer. You would select the **WINDOSBK** folder, then press the Delete key. You may use the DELTREE command in the command prompt window.

Note 2: It is assumed that you have booted the system and are on the Windows desktop.

Step 1   Click **Start**. Point to **Programs**. Point to **Accessories**. Click **MS-DOS Prompt**.

Step 2   Key in the following: C:\WINDOWS>**CD \ Enter**

```
MS-DOS Prompt                                                    _ □ ×

C:\WINDOWS>CD \

C:\>_
```

WHAT'S HAPPENING?   You are now at the root of Drive C.

Step 3   Key in the following: C:\>**DELTREE \WINDOSBK**

```
MS-DOS Prompt                                                    _ □ ×

C:\>DELTREE \WINDOSBK
```

WHAT'S HAPPENING?   Be sure you have correctly keyed in the directory name.

Step 4   Press **Enter**

```
MS-DOS Prompt                                                    _ □ ×

C:\>DELTREE \WINDOSBK
Delete directory "\WINDOSBK" and all its subdirectories? [yn] _
```

WHAT'S HAPPENING?   You are being asked to confirm if you really want to delete the directory called **WINDOSBK** and all the files and directories that are in it.

Step 5   Press **Y Enter**

Step 6   Key in the following: C:\>**DIR WINDOS*.* Enter**

```
MS-DOS Prompt                                                    _ □ ×

C:\>DIR WINDOS*.*

 Volume in drive C has no label
 Volume Serial Number is 07CE-0212
 Directory of C:\

File not found
```

```
                        830,013,440 bytes free

 C:\>_
```

WHAT'S HAPPENING? → You have successfully deleted the **WINDOSBK** directory.

Step 7 Key in the following: C:\>**EXIT** [Enter]

WHAT'S HAPPENING? → You have closed the MS-DOS Prompt window and returned to the Windows desktop.

A.4   SHAREWARE PROGRAMS PROVIDED WITH THE TEXTBOOK

Several programs on the ACTIVITIES disk that are installed to the **WINDOSBK** directory are shareware programs. Shareware programs are for trial purposes only. If you find you like the programs and would like to keep them, you must register them and pay the registration fee.

HOME PHONE BOOK SHAREWARE PROGRAM

Home Phone Book, Version 2.5
This shareware program is provided by:

Thomas E. Bonitz
7903 Kona Circle
Papillion, NE 68046

If you like Home Phone Book, please send $20.00 to Thomas E. Bonitz at the above address.

THE THINKER SHAREWARE PROGRAM

The Thinker, Version 3.0-0788
This shareware program is provided by:

Alan C. Elliott
TexaSoft
P.O. Box 1169
Cedar Hill, TX 75104

If you like The Thinker, please send $35.00 plus shipping and handling to Alan C. Elliott at the above address. Phone orders: (214) 291–2115 or 1–800–955–TEXAS; FAX: (214) 291–3400. You may also print a copy of the order form by keying in PRINT \WINDOSBK\FINANCE\ORDER. The order form will allow you to specify your desired disk size.

MICROLINK SHAREWARE PROGRAMS

SHUT THE BOX, YAHT, OTRA, LOYD, PUSH YOUR LUCK, AND CRUX

These shareware programs are provided by:

Bob Lancaster
P. O. Box 5612
Hacienda Heights, CA 91745

If you like any of these games, please send $5.00 for each game to Bob Lancaster at the above address.

CHEKKERS SHAREWARE PROGRAM

CHEKKERS, Version 4.1
This shareware program is provided by:

J & J Software
P.O. Box 254
Matamoras, PA 18336

If you like CHEKKERS, please send $15.00 to J & J Software at the above address.

ARGH SHAREWARE PROGRAM

ARGH, Version 4.0
This shareware program is provided by:

David B. Howorth
1960 S.W. Palatine Hill Road
Portland, OR 97219

If you like ARGH, please send $10.00 to David B. Howorth at the above address.

COMMAND SUMMARY

APPEND   Allows programs to open data files in specified directories as if they were in the current directory.

      APPEND   [[drive:]path[;...]] [/X[:ON ¦ :OFF]] [/PATH:ON ¦ /PATH:OFF] [/E] APPEND ;

[drive:]path	Specifies a drive and directory to append.
/X:ON	Applies appended directories to file searches and application execution.
/X:OFF	Applies appended directories only to requests to open files. /X:OFF is the default setting.
/PATH:ON	Applies appended directories to file requests that already specify a path. /PATH:ON is the default setting.
/PATH:OFF	Turns off the effect of /PATH:ON.
/E	Stores a copy of the appended directory list in an environment variable named APPEND. /E may be used only the first time you use APPEND after starting your system.

      Type APPEND ; to clear the appended directory list. Type APPEND without parameters to display the appended directory list.

— —

ARP   Displays and modifies the IP-to-Physical address translation tables used by address resolution protocol (ARP).

      ARP -s inet_addr eth_addr [if_addr]
      ARP -d inet_addr [if_addr]
      ARP -a [inet_addr] [-N if_addr]

-a	Displays current ARP entries by interrogating the current protocol data. If inet_addr is specified, the IP and Physical addresses for only the specified computer are displayed. If more than one network interface uses ARP, entries for each ARP table are displayed.
-g	Same as -a.
inet_addr	Specifies an Internet address.
-N if_addr	Displays the ARP entries for the network interface specified by if_addr.

-d	Deletes the host specified by inet_addr. inet_addr may be wildcarded with * to delete all hosts.
-s	Adds the host and associates the Internet address inet_addr with the Physical address eth_addr. The Physical address is given as 6 hexadecimal bytes separated by hyphens. The entry is permanent.
eth_add	Specifies a physical address.
if_addr	If present, this specifies the Internet address of the interface whose address translation table should be modified. If not present, the first applicable interface will be used.

Example:
> arp -s 157.55.85.212 00-aa-00-62-c6-09 .... Adds a static entry.
> arp -a .... Displays the ARP table.

_____

ASSOC   Displays or modifies file extension associations.

ASSOC [.ext[=[fileType]]]

.ext	Specifies the file extension to associate the file type with.
fileType	Specifies the file type to associate with the file extension.

Type ASSOC without parameters to display the current file associations. If ASSOC is invoked with just a file extension, it displays the current file association for that file extension. Specify nothing for the file type and the command will delete the association for the file extension.

_____

AT   Schedules commands and programs to run on a computer at a specified time and date. The Schedule service must be running to use the AT command.

AT [\\computername] [[id] [/DELETE] ¦ /DELETE [/YES]]
AT [\\computername] time [/INTERACTIVE] [/EVERY:date[,...] ¦ /NEXT:date[,...]] "command"

\\computername	Specifies a remote computer. Commands are scheduled on the local computer if this parameter is omitted.
id	Is an identification number assigned to a scheduled command.
/DELETE	Cancels a scheduled command. If id is omitted, all the scheduled commands on the computer are canceled.
/YES	Used with cancel all jobs command when no further confirmation is desired.
time	Specifies the time when command is to run.
/INTERACTIVE	Allows the job to interact with the desktop of the user who is logged on at the time the job runs.
/EVERY:date[,...]	Runs the command on each specified day of the week or month. If date is omitted, the current day of the month is assumed.
/NEXT:date[,...]	Runs the specified command on the next occurrence of the day (for example, next Thursday). If date is omitted, the current day of the month is assumed.
"command"	Is the command or batch program to be run.

_____

ATMADM   Monitors connections and addresses registered by the ATM Call Manager on an asynchronous transfer mode (ATM) network. You can use the utility to display statistics for incoming and outgoing calls on ATM adapters.

Usage: atmadm [options]
where options are one or more of the following:
-c   Lists all connections.
-a   Lists all registered addresses.
-s   Displays Statistics.

_____

ATTRIB   Displays or changes file attributes.

ATTRIB [+R ¦ -R] [+A ¦ -A] [+S ¦ -S] [+H ¦ -H] [[drive:] [path] filename][/S [/D]]

+   Sets an attribute.
-     Clears an attribute.
R   Read-only file attribute.
A   Archive file attribute.
S   System file attribute.
H   Hidden file attribute.
/S   Processes matching files in the current folder and all subfolders.
/D   Processes folders as well.

BREAK   Sets or clears extended Ctrl+C–checking on DOS systems.

This is present for compatibility with DOS systems. It has no effect under Windows 2000.

If Command Extensions are enabled, on the Windows 2000 platform, the BREAK command will enter a hard coded breakpoint if being debugged by a debugger.

CACLS   Displays or modifies access control lists (ACLs) of files.

CACLS filename [/T] [/E] [/C] [/G user:perm] [/R user [...]]
              [/P user:perm [...]] [/D user [...]]

filename   Displays ACLs.
/T   Changes ACLs of specified files in the current directory and all subdirectories.
/E   Edits ACL instead of replacing it.
/C   Continues on access denied errors.
/G user:perm Grants specified user access rights.
             perm can be: R   Read
                          W   Write
                          C   Change (write)
                          F   Full control
/R user   Revokes specified user's access rights (only valid with /E).
/P user:perm Replaces specified user's access rights.
             perm can be: N   None
                          R   Read
                          W   Write
                          C   Change (write)
                          F   Full control
/D user   Denies specified user access.

Wildcards can be used to specify more than one file in a command. You can specify more than one user in a command.

CALL   Calls one batch program from another.

CALL [drive:][path]filename [batch-parameters]

batch-parameters   Specifies any command line information required by the batch program.

If Command Extensions are enabled CALL changes as follows:

The CALL command now accepts labels as the target of the CALL. The syntax is the following:

CALL :label arguments

A new batch file context is created with the specified arguments and control is passed to the statement after the label specified. You must "exit" twice by reaching the end of the batch script file twice. The first time you read the end, control will return to just after the CALL statement.

The second time you will exit the batch script. Type GOTO /? for a description of the GOTO :EOF extension that will allow you to "return" from a batch script.

In addition, expansion of batch script argument references (%0, %1, etc.) have been changed as follows:

%* in a batch script refers to all the arguments (e.g., %1 %2 %3 %4 %5 ...)

Substitution of batch parameters (%n) has been enhanced. You can now use the following optional syntax:

%~1	Expands %1 removing any surrounding quotes (").
%~f1	Expands %1 to a fully qualified path name.
%~d1	Expands %1 to a drive letter only.
%~p1	Expands %1 to a path only.
%~n1	Expands %1 to a file name only.
%~x1	Expands %1 to a file extension only.
%~s1	Expanded path contains short names only.
%~a1	Expands %1 to file attributes.
%~t1	Expands %1 to date/time of file.
%~z1	Expands %1 to size of file.
%~$PATH:1	Searches the directories listed in the PATH environment variable and expands %1 to the fully qualified name of the first one found. If the environment variable name is not defined or the file is not found by the search, then this modifier expands to the empty string.

The modifiers can be combined to get compound results:

%~dp1	Expands %1 to a drive letter and path only.
%~nx1	Expands %1 to a file name and extension only.
%~dp$PATH:1	Searches the directories listed in the PATH environment variable for %1 and expands to the drive letter and path of the first one found.
%~ftza1	Expands %1 to a DIR-like output line.

In the above examples %1 and PATH can be replaced by other valid values. The %~ syntax is terminated by a valid argument number. The %~ modifiers may not be used with %*.

_____

CD or CHDIR   Displays the name of or changes the current directory.

     CHDIR [/D] [drive:][path]
     CHDIR [..]
     CD [/D] [drive:][path]
     CD [..]

     .. Specifies that you want to change to the parent directory.

Type CD drive: to display the current directory in the specified drive. Type CD without parameters to display the current drive and directory.

Use the /D switch to change the current drive in addition to changing the current directory for a drive.

If Command Extensions are enabled CHDIR changes as follows:

The current directory string is converted to use the same case as the on-disk names. So CD C:\TEMP would actually set the current directory to C:\Temp if that is the case on the disk.

The CHDIR command does not treat spaces as delimiters, so it is possible to CD into a subdirectory name that contains a space without surrounding the name with quotes. For example:

cd \winnt\profiles\username\programs\start menu

is the same as

cd "\winnt\profiles\username\programs\start menu"

which is what you would have to type if extensions were disabled.

CHCP   Displays or sets the active code page number.

CHCP [nnn]

nnn   Specifies a code page number.

Type CHCP without a parameter to display the active code page number.

CHKDSK   Checks a disk and displays a status report.

CHKDSK [volume[[path]filename]] [/F] [/V] [/R] [/X] [/I]
[/C] [/L[:size]]

volume	Specifies the drive letter (followed by a colon), mount point, or volume name.
filename	FAT only: Specifies the files to check for fragmentation.
/F	Fixes errors on the disk.
/V	On FAT/FAT32: Displays the full path and name of every file on the disk. On NTFS: Displays cleanup messages if any.
/R	Locates bad sectors and recovers readable information (implies /F).
/L:size	NTFS only: Changes the log file size to the specified number of kilobytes. If size is not specified, displays current size.
/X	Forces the volume to dismount first if necessary. All opened handles to the volume would then be invalid (implies /F).
/I	NTFS only: Performs a less vigorous check of index entries.
/C	NTFS only: Skips checking of cycles within the folder structure.

The /I or /C switch reduces the amount of time required to run CHKDSK by skipping certain checks of the volume.

CHKNTFS   Displays or modifies the checking of a disk at boot time.

CHKNTFS volume [...]
CHKNTFS /D
CHKNTFS /T[:time]
CHKNTFS /X volume [...]
CHKNTFS /C volume [...]

volume	Specifies the drive letter (followed by a colon), mount point, or volume name.
/D	Restores the machine to the default behavior; all drives are checked at boot time and CHKDSK is run on those that are dirty.
/T:time	Changes the AUTOCHK initiation countdown time to the specified amount of time in seconds. If time is not specified, displays the current setting.
/X	Excludes a drive from the default boot-time check. Excluded drives are not accumulated between command invocations.
/C	Schedules a drive to be checked at boot time; CHKDSK will run if the drive is dirty.

If no switches are specified, CHKNTFS will display if the specified drive is dirty or scheduled to be checked on next reboot.

CIPHER   Displays or alters the encryption of directories (files) on NTFS partitions.

CIPHER [/E ¦ /D] [/S:dir] [/A] [/I] [/F] [/Q] [/H] [/K] [pathname [...]]

/E	Encrypts the specified directories. Directories will be marked so that files added afterward will be encrypted.

/D	Decrypts the specified directories. Directories will be marked so that files added afterward will not be encrypted.
/S	Performs the specified operation on directories in the given directory and all subdirectories.
/A	Operation for files as well as directories. The encrypted file could become decrypted when it is modified if the parent directory is not encrypted. It is recommended that you encrypt the file and the parent directory.
/I	Continues performing the specified operation even after errors have occurred. By default, CIPHER stops when an error is encountered.
/F	Forces the encryption operation on all specified objects, even those that are already encrypted. Already-encrypted objects are skipped by default.
/Q	Reports only the most essential information.
/H	Displays files with the hidden or system attributes. These files are omitted by default.
/K	Create new file encryption key for the user running CIPHER. If this option is chosen, all the other options will be ignored.
pathname	Specifies a pattern, file, or directory.

Used without parameters, CIPHER displays the encryption state of the current directory and any files it contains. You may use multiple directory names and wildcards. You must put spaces between multiple parameters.

CLUSTER   You can use cluster commands to administer server clusters from the Windows 2000 command prompt.

```
CLUSTER /LIST[:domain-name]
CLUSTER [[/CLUSTER:]cluster-name] <options>

<options> =
  /PROP[ERTIES] [<prop-list>]
  /PRIV[PROPERTIES] [<prop-list>]
  /PROP[ERTIES][:propname[,propname ...] /USEDEFAULT]
  /PRIV[PROPERTIES][:propname[,propname ...] /USEDEFAULT]
  /REN[AME]:cluster-name
  /VER[SION]
  /QUORUM[RESOURCE][:resource-name] [/PATH:path] [/MAXLOGSIZE:max-size-kbytes]
  /SETFAIL[UREACTIONS][:node-name[,node-name ...]]
  /REG[ADMIN]EXT:admin-extension-dll[,admin-extension-dll ...]
  /UNREG[ADMIN]EXT:admin-extension-dll[,admin-extension-dll ...]
  NODE [node-name] node-command
  GROUP [group-name] group-command
  RES[OURCE] [resource-name] resource-command
  {RESOURCETYPE ¦ RESTYPE} [resourcetype-name] resourcetype-command
  NET[WORK] [network-name] network-command
  NETINT[ERFACE] [interface-name] interface-command

<prop-list> =
  name=value[,value ...][:<format>] [name=value[,value ...][:<format>] ...]

<format> =
  BINARY ¦ DWORD ¦ STR[ING] ¦ EXPANDSTR[ING] ¦ MULTISTR[ING] ¦ SECURITY ¦ ULARGE
```

CMD   Starts a new instance of the Windows 2000 command interpreter.

```
CMD [/A ¦ /U] [/Q] [/D] [/E:ON ¦ /E:OFF] [/F:ON ¦ /F:OFF] [/V:ON ¦ /V:OFF] [[/S] [/C ¦ /K]
string]
```

/C	Carries out the command specified by the string and then terminates.
/K	Carries out the command specified by the string but remains.
/S	Modifies the treatment of the string after /C or /K (see below).
/Q	Turns echo off.
/D	Disables the execution of AutoRun commands from the Registry (see below).
/A	Causes the output of internal commands to a pipe or file to be ANSI.

/U	Causes the output of internal commands to a pipe or file to be Unicode.
/T:fg	Sets the foreground/background colors (see COLOR /?).
/E:ON	Enables command extensions (see below).
/E:OFF	Disables command extensions (see below).
/F:ON	Enables file and directory name completion characters (see below).
/F:OFF	Disables file and directory name completion characters (see below).
/V:ON	Enables delayed environment variable expansion using c as the delimiter. For example, /V:ON would allow !var! to expand the variable var at execution time. The var syntax expands variables at input time, which is quite a different thing when inside of a FOR loop.
/V:OFF	Disables delayed environment expansion.

Note that multiple commands separated by the command separator '&&' are accepted for string if surrounded by quotes. Also, for compatibility reasons, /X is the same as /E:ON, /Y is the same as /E:OFF, and /R is the same as /C. Any other switches are ignored.

If /C or /K is specified, then the remainder of the command line after the switch is processed as a command line, where the following logic is used to process quote (") characters:

1. If all of the following conditions are met, then quote characters on the command line are preserved:

    - no /S switch
    - exactly two quote characters
    - no special characters between the two quote characters, where special is one of:
    &<>()@^ ¦
    - there are one or more whitespace characters between the two quote characters
    - the string between the two quote characters is the name of an executable file

2. Otherwise, old behavior is to see if the first character is a quote character and if so, strip the leading character and remove the last quote character on the command line, preserving any text after the last quote character.

If /D was NOT specified on the command line, then when CMD.EXE starts, it looks for the following REG_SZ/REG_EXPAND_SZ registry variables, and if either or both are present, they are executed first.

HKEY_LOCAL_MACHINE\Software\Microsoft\Command Processor\AutoRun

and/or

HKEY_CURRENT_USER\Software\Microsoft\Command Processor\AutoRun

Command Extensions are enabled by default. You may also disable extensions for a particular invocation by using the /E:OFF switch. You can enable or disable extensions for all invocations of CMD.EXE on a machine and/or user logon session by setting either or both of the following REG_DWORD values in the registry using REGEDT32.EXE:

HKEY_LOCAL_MACHINE\Software\Microsoft\Command Processor\EnableExtensions

and/or

HKEY_CURRENT_USER\Software\Microsoft\Command Processor\EnableExtensions

to either 0x1 or 0x0. The user-specific setting takes precedence over the machine setting. The command line switches take precedence over the Registry settings.

The command extensions involve changes and/or additions to the following commands:

DEL or ERASE
COLOR
CD or CHDIR
MD or MKDIR
PROMPT
PUSHD

POPD
SET
SETLOCAL
ENDLOCAL
IF
FOR
CALL
SHIFT
GOTO
START (also includes changes to external command invocation)
ASSOC
FTYPE

To get specific details, type commandname /?.

Delayed environment variable expansion is NOT enabled by default. You can enable or disable delayed environment variable expansion for a particular invocation of CMD.EXE with the /V:ON or /V:OFF switch. You can enable or disable completion for all invocations of CMD.EXE on a machine and/or user logon session by setting either or both of the following REG_DWORD values in the Registry using REGEDT32.EXE:

HKEY_LOCAL_MACHINE\Software\Microsoft\Command Processor\DelayedExpansion

and/or

HKEY_CURRENT_USER\Software\Microsoft\Command Processor\DelayedExpansion

to either 0x1 or 0x0. The user-specific setting takes precedence over the machine setting. The command line switches take precedence over the Registry settings.

If delayed environment variable expansion is enabled, then the exclamation character can be used to substitute the value of an environment variable at execution time.

File and directory name completion is NOT enabled by default. You can enable or disable file name completion for a particular invocation of CMD.EXE with the /F:ON or /F:OFF switch. You can enable or disable completion for all invocations of CMD.EXE on a machine and/or user logon session by setting either or both of the following REG_DWORD values in the Registry using REGEDT32.EXE:

HKEY_LOCAL_MACHINE\Software\Microsoft\Command Processor\CompletionChar
HKEY_LOCAL_MACHINE\Software\Microsoft\Command Processor\PathCompletionChar

and/or

HKEY_CURRENT_USER\Software\Microsoft\Command Processor\CompletionChar
HKEY_CURRENT_USER\Software\Microsoft\Command Processor\PathCompletionChar

with the hex value of a control character to use for a particular function (e.g., 0x4 is Ctrl-D and 0x6 is Ctrl-F). The user-specific settings take precedence over the machine settings. The command line switches take precedence over the Registry settings.

If completion is enabled with the /F:ON switch, the two control characters used are Ctrl-D for directory name completion and Ctrl-F for file name completion. To disable a particular completion character in the Registry, use the value for space (0x20) as it is not a valid control character.

Completion is invoked when you type either of the two control characters. The completion function takes the path string to the left of the cursor, appends a wildcard character to it if none is already present, and builds up a list of paths that match. It then displays the first matching path. If no paths match, it just beeps and leaves the display alone. Thereafter, repeated pressing of the same control character will cycle through the list of matching paths. Pressing the Shift key with the control character will move through the list backwards. If you edit the line in any way and press the control character again, the saved list of matching paths is discarded and a new one generated. The same occurs if you switch between file and directory name completion. The only difference between the two control characters is that the file completion character matches both file and directory names, while the directory completion character only matches directory names. If file completion is used on any of the built-in directory commands (CD, MD, or RD) then directory completion is assumed.

The completion code deals correctly with file names that contain spaces or other special characters by placing quotes around the matching path. Also, if you back up and then invoke completion from within a line, the text to the right of the cursor at the point completion was invoked is discarded.

COLOR   Sets the default console foreground and background colors.

COLOR [attr]

attr Specifies color attribute of console output.

Color attributes are specified by TWO hex digits. The first corresponds to the background; the second the foreground. Each digit can be any of the following values:

0 = Black	8 = Gray
1 = Blue	9 = Light Blue
2 = Green	A = Light Green
3 = Aqua	B = Light Aqua
4 = Red	C = Light Red
5 = Purple	D = Light Purple
6 = Yellow	E = Light Yellow
7 = White	F = Bright White

If no argument is given, this command restores the color to what it was when CMD.EXE started. This value comes from the current console window, the /T command line switch, or the DefaultColor Registry value.

The COLOR command sets ERRORLEVEL to 1 if an attempt is made to execute the COLOR command with a foreground and background color that are the same.

Example: "COLOR fc" produces light red on bright white

COMP   Compares the contents of two files or sets of files.

COMP [data1] [data2] [/D] [/A] [/L] [/N=number] [/C]

data1	Specifies location and name of first file to compare.
data2	Specifies location and name of second file to compare.
/D	Displays differences in decimal format.
/A	Displays differences in ASCII characters.
/L	Displays line numbers for differences.
/N=number	Compares only the first specified number of lines in each file.
/C	Disregards case of ASCII letters when comparing files.

To compare sets of files, use wildcards in the data1 and data2 parameters.

COMPACT   Displays or alters the compression of files on NTFS partitions.

COMPACT [/C ¦ /U] [/S[:dir]] [/A] [/I] [/F] [/Q] [filename [...]]

/C	Compresses the specified files. Directories will be marked so that files added afterward will be compressed.
/U	Uncompresses the specified files. Directories will be marked so that files added afterward will not be compressed.
/S	Performs the specified operation on files in the given directory and all subdirectories. By default, "dir" is the current directory.
/A	Displays files with the hidden or system attributes. These files are omitted by default.

/I   Continues performing the specified operation even after errors have occurred. By default, COMPACT stops when an error is encountered.

/F   Forces the compress operation on all specified files, even those that are already compressed. Already-compressed files are skipped by default.

/Q   Reports only the most essential information.

filename   Specifies a pattern, file, or directory.

Used without parameters, COMPACT displays the compression state of the current directory and any files it contains. You may use multiple file names and wildcards. You must put spaces between multiple parameters.

CONVERT   Converts FAT volumes to NTFS.

CONVERT volume /FS:NTFS [/V]

volume   Specifies the drive letter (followed by a colon), mount point, or volume name.
/FS:NTFS   Specifies that the volume be converted to NTFS.
/V   Specifies that CONVERT should be run in verbose mode.

COPY   Copies one or more files to another location.

COPY [/V] [/N] [/Y ¦ /-Y] [/Z] [/A ¦ /B] source [/A ¦ /B]
[+ source [/A ¦ /B] [+ ...]] [destination [/A ¦ /B]]

source   Specifies the file or files to be copied.
/A   Indicates an ASCII text file.
/B   Indicates a binary file.
destination   Specifies the directory and/or file name for the new file(s).
/V   Verifies that new files are written correctly.
/N   Uses the short file name, if available, when copying a file with a non-8.3
name.
/Y   Suppresses prompting to confirm you want to overwrite an existing
destination file.
/-Y   Causes prompting to confirm you want to overwrite an existing destination
file.
/Z   Copies networked files in restartable mode.

The switch /Y may be preset in the COPYCMD environment variable. This may be overridden with /-Y on the command line. The default is to prompt on overwrites unless the COPY command is being executed from within a batch script.

To append files, specify a single file for destination, but multiple files for source (using wildcards or file1+file2+file3 format).

CSCRIPT   Runs scripts using the command line–based script host.

CSCRIPT scriptname.extension [option...] [arguments...]

Options:
//B   Batch mode: Suppresses script errors and prompts from displaying.
//D   Enables Active Debugging.
//E:engine   Uses engine for executing script.
//H:CScript   Changes the default script host to CScript.exe.
//H:WScript   Changes the default script host to WScript.exe (default).
//I   Activates interactive mode (default, opposite of //B).
//Job:xxxx   Executes a WS job.
//Logo   Displays logo (default).
//Nologo   Prevents logo display: No banner will be shown at execution time.
//S   Saves current command line options for this user.
//T:nn   Times out in seconds: Maximum time a script is permitted to run.
//X   Executes script in debugger.
//U   Uses Unicode for redirected I/O from the console.

DATE   Displays or sets the date.

DATE [/T ¦ date]

Type DATE without parameters to display the current date setting and a prompt for a new one. Press Enter to keep the same date.

If Command Extensions are enabled the DATE command supports the /T switch, which tells the command to just output the current date, without prompting for a new date.

DEBUG   Runs DEBUG, a program testing and editing tool.

DEBUG [[drive:][path]filename [testfile-parameters]]

[drive:][path]filename Specifies the file you want to test.
testfile-parameters   Specifies the command line information required by the file you want to test.

After DEBUG starts, type ? to display a list of debugging commands.

DEL or ERASE   Deletes one or more files.

DEL [/P] [/F] [/S] [/Q] [/A[[:]attributes]] names
ERASE [/P] [/F] [/S] [/Q] [/A[[:]attributes]] names

names   Specifies a list of one or more files or directories. Wildcards may be used to delete multiple files. If a directory is specified, all files within the directory will be deleted.
/P   Prompts for confirmation before deleting each file.
/F   Forces the deletion of read-only files.
/S   Deletes specified files from all subdirectories.
/Q   Activates quiet mode—does not ask if okay to delete on global wildcard.
/A   Selects files to delete based on attributes.
attributes R Read-only files   S System files
            H Hidden files   A Files ready for archiving
            - Prefix meaning not

If Command Extensions are enabled DEL and ERASE change as follows:

The display semantics of the /S switch are reversed in that it shows you only the files that are deleted, not the ones it could not find.

DIR   Displays a list of files and subdirectories in a directory.

DIR [drive:][path][filename] [/A[[:]attributes]] [/B] [/C] [/D] [/L] [/N] [/O[[:]sortorder]] [/P] [/Q] [/S]
[/T[[:]timefield]] [/W] [/X] [/4]

[drive:][path][filename] Specifies the drive, directory, and/or files to list.
/A   Displays files with specified attributes.
attributes D Directories   R Read-only files
            H Hidden files A Files ready for archiving
            S System files
            - Prefix meaning not
/B   Uses bare format (no heading information or summary).
/C   Displays the thousand separator in file sizes. This is the default. Use /-C to disable display of separator.
/D   Same as wide but files are sorted by column.
/L   Uses lowercase.
/N   Displays in new long list format where file names are on the far right.
/O   Lists by files in sorted order.

	sortorder	N By name (alphabetic)	S By size (smallest first)
		E By extension (alphabetic)	D By date/time (oldest first)
		G Group directories first	- Prefix to reverse order

/P	Pauses after each screenful of information.
/Q	Displays the owner of the file.
/S	Displays files in the specified directory and all subdirectories.
/T	Controls which time field is displayed or used for sorting.
timefield	C Creation
	A Last Access
	W Last Written
/W	Uses wide list format.
/X	Displays the short names generated for non-8.3 file names. The format is that of /N with the short name inserted before the long name. If no short name is present, blanks are displayed in its place.
/4	Displays four-digit years.

Switches may be preset in the DIRCMD environment variable. Override preset switches by prefixing any switch with - (hyphen), for example, /-W.

DISKCOMP   Compares the contents of two floppy disks.

DISKCOMP [drive1: [drive2:]]

DISKCOPY   Copies the contents of one floppy disk to another.

DISKCOPY [drive1: [drive2:]] [/V]

/V   Verifies that the information is copied correctly.

The two floppy disks must be the same type. You may specify the same drive for drive1 and drive2.

DISKPERF   Controls the types of counters that can be viewed using System Monitor.

DISKPERF [-Y[D ¦ V] ¦ -N[D ¦ V]] [\\computername]

-Y	Sets the system to start all disk performance counters when the system is restarted.
-YD	Enables the disk performance counters for physical drives when the system is restarted.
-YV	Enables the disk performance counters for logical drives or storage volumes when the system is restarted.
-N	Sets the system to disable all disk performance counters when the system is restarted.
-ND	Disables the disk performance counters for physical drives.
-NV	Disables the disk performance counters for logical drives.
\\computername	Is the name of the computer you want to see set disk performance counter use.

DOSKEY   Edits command lines, recalls Windows 2000 commands, and creates macros.

DOSKEY [/REINSTALL] [/LISTSIZE=size] [/MACROS[:ALL ¦ :exename]] [/HISTORY] [/INSERT ¦ /OVERSTRIKE] [/EXENAME=exename] [/MACROFILE=filename] [macroname=[text]]

/REINSTALL	Installs a new copy of DOSKEY.
/LISTSIZE=size	Sets the size of the command history buffer.
/MACROS	Displays all DOSKEY macros.
/MACROS:ALL	Displays all DOSKEY macros for all executables that have DOSKEY macros.
/MACROS:exename	Displays all DOSKEY macros for the given executable.

/HISTORY	Displays all commands stored in memory.
/INSERT	Specifies that new text you type is inserted in old text.
/OVERSTRIKE	Specifies that new text overwrites old text.
/EXENAME=exename	Specifies the executable.
/MACROFILE=filename	Specifies a file of macros to install.
macroname	Specifies a name for a macro you create.
text	Specifies commands you want to record.

Up and down arrows recall commands; Esc clears command line; F7 displays command history; Alt+F7 clears command history; F8 searches command history; F9 selects a command by number; Alt+F10 clears macro definitions.

The following are some special codes in DOSKEY macro definitions:

$T	Command separator. Allows multiple commands in a macro.
$1–$9	Batch parameters. Equivalent to %1–%9 in batch programs.
$*	Symbol replaced by everything following macro name on command line.

ECHO   Displays messages or turns command-echoing on or off.

ECHO [ON ¦ OFF]
ECHO [message]

Type ECHO without parameters to display the current echo setting.

EDLIN   Starts EDLIN, a line-oriented text editor.

EDLIN [drive:][path]filename [/B]

/B   Ignores end-of-file (Ctrl+Z) characters.

ENDLOCAL Ends localization of environment changes in a batch file. Environment changes made after ENDLOCAL has been issued are not local to the batch file; the previous settings are not restored on termination of the batch file.

ENDLOCAL

If Command Extensions are enabled ENDLOCAL changes as follows:

If the corresponding SETLOCAL enabled or disabled command extensions using the new ENABLEEXTENSIONS or DISABLEEXTENSIONS options, then after the ENDLOCAL, the enabled/disabled state of command extensions will be restored to what it was prior to the matching SETLOCAL command execution.

EXIT   Quits the CMD.EXE program (command interpreter) or the current batch script.

EXIT [/B] [exitCode]

/B	Specifies to exit the current batch script instead of CMD.EXE. If executed from outside a batch script, it will quit CMD.EXE.
exitCode	Specifies a numeric number. If /B is specified, sets ERRORLEVEL to that number. If quitting CMD.EXE, sets the process exit code with that number.

EXPAND   Expands one or more compressed files.

EXPAND [-r] source destination
EXPAND -r source [destination]
EXPAND -D source.cab [-F:files]
EXPAND source.cab -F:files destination

-r	Renames expanded files.
-D	Displays a list of the files in source.
source	Source file specification. Wildcards may be used.
-F:files	Name of files to expand from a .CAB.
destination	Destination file ¦ path specification. Destination may be a directory.

If source is multiple files and -r is not specified, destination must be a directory.

FC Compares two files or sets of files and displays the differences between them.

FC [/A] [/C] [/L] [/LBn] [/N] [/T] [/U] [/W] [/nnnn]
    [drive1:][path1]filename1
    [drive2:][path2]filename2
FC /B [drive1:][path1]filename1 [drive2:][path2]filename2

/A	Displays only first and last lines for each set of differences.
/B	Performs a binary comparison.
/C	Disregards the case of letters.
/L	Compares files as ASCII text.
/LBn	Sets the maximum consecutive mismatches to the specified number of lines.
/N	Displays the line numbers on an ASCII comparison.
/T	Does not expand tabs to spaces.
/U	Compare files as Unicode text files.
/W	Compresses white space (tabs and spaces) for comparison.
/nnnn	Specifies the number of consecutive lines that must match after a mismatch.

FIND Searches for a text string in a file or files.

FIND [/V] [/C] [/N] [/I] "string" [[drive:][path]filename[...]]

/V	Displays all lines NOT containing the specified string.
/C	Displays only the count of lines containing the string.
/N	Displays line numbers with the displayed lines.
/I	Ignores the case of characters when searching for the string.
"string"	Specifies the text string to find.
[drive:][path]filename	Specifies a file or files to search.

If a path is not specified, FIND searches the text typed at the prompt or piped from another command.

FINDSTR Searches for strings in files.

FINDSTR [/B] [/E] [/L] [/R] [/S] [/I] [/X] [/V] [/N] [/M] [/O] [/P] [/F:file] [/C:string] [/G:file] [/D:dir list]
[/A:color attributes] [strings] [[drive:][path]filename[...]]

/B	Matches pattern if at the beginning of a line.
/E	Matches pattern if at the end of a line.
/L	Uses search strings literally.
/R	Uses search strings as regular expressions.
/S	Searches for matching files in the current directory and all subdirectories.
/I	Specifies that the search is not to be case-sensitive.
/X	Prints lines that match exactly.
/V	Prints only lines that do not contain a match.
/N	Prints the line number before each line that matches.
/M	Prints only the file name if a file contains a match.
/O	Prints character offset before each matching line.
/P	Skip files with nonprintable characters
/A:attr	Specifies color attribute with two hex digits. See "color /?".
/F:file	Reads file list from the specified file (/ stands for console).
/C:string	Uses specified string as a literal search string.
/G:file	Gets search strings from the specified file (/ stands for console).

/D:dir	Searches a semicolon-delimited list of directories.
strings	Text to be searched for.
[drive:][path]filename	Specifies a file or files to search.

Use spaces to separate multiple search strings unless the argument is prefixed with /C. For example, 'FINDSTR "hello there" x.y' searches for "hello" or "there" in file x.y. 'FINDSTR / C:"hello there" x.y' searches for "hello there" in file x.y.

Regular expression quick reference:

.	Wildcard: any character
*	Repeat: zero or more occurances of previous character or class
^	Line position: beginning of line
$	Line position: end of line
[class]	Character class: any one character in set
[^class]	Inverse class: any one character not in set
[x-y]	Range: any characters within the specified range
\x	Escape: literal use of metacharacter x
\<xyz	Word position: beginning of word
xyz\>	Word position: end of word

For full information on FINDSTR regular expressions refer to the online Command Reference.

_____

FOR   Runs a specified command for each file in a set of files.

FOR %variable IN (set) DO command [command-parameters]

%variable	Specifies a replaceable parameter.
(set)	Specifies a set of one or more files. Wildcards may be used.
command	Specifies the command to carry out for each file.
command-parameters	Specifies parameters or switches for the specified command.

To use the FOR command in a batch program, specify %%variable instead of %variable. Variable names are case sensitive, so %i is different from %I.

If Command Extensions are enabled, the following additional forms of the FOR command are supported:

FOR /D %variable IN (set) DO command [command-parameters]

If set contains wildcards, then it specifies to match against directory names instead of file names.

FOR /R [[drive:]path] %variable IN (set) DO command [command-parameters]

Walks the directory tree rooted at [drive:]path, executing the FOR statement in each directory of the tree. If no directory specification is specified after /R then the current directory is assumed. If set is just a single period (.) character then it will just enumerate the directory tree.

FOR /L %variable IN (start,step,end) DO command [command-parameters]

The set is a sequence of numbers from start to end, by step amount. So (1,1,5) would generate the sequence 1 2 3 4 5 and (5,-1,1) would generate the sequence (5 4 3 2 1).

FOR /F ["options"] %variable IN (file-set) DO command [command-parameters]
FOR /F ["options"] %variable IN ("string") DO command [command-parameters]
FOR /F ["options"] %variable IN ('command') DO command [command-parameters]

or, if usebackq option present:

FOR /F ["options"] %variable IN (file-set) DO command [command-parameters]
FOR /F ["options"] %variable IN ('string') DO command [command-parameters]
FOR /F ["options"] %variable IN (`command`) DO command [command-parameters]

filenameset is one or more file names. Each file is opened, read, and processed before going on to the next file in filenameset. Processing consists of reading in the file, breaking it up into individual lines of text, and then parsing each line into zero or more tokens. The body of the for loop is then called with the variable value(s) set to the found token string(s). By default, /F passes the first blank separated token from each line of each file. Blank lines are skipped. You can override the default parsing behavior by specifying the optional "options" parameter. This is a quoted string that contains one or more keywords to specify different parsing options. The keywords are the following:

eol=c	Specifies an end-of-line comment character (just one).
skip=n	Specifies the number of lines to skip at the beginning of the file.
delims=xxx	Specifies a delimiter set. This replaces the default delimiter set of space and tab.
tokens=x,y,m-n	Specifies which tokens from each line are to be passed to the for body for each iteration. This will cause additional variable names to be allocated. The m-n form is a range, specifying the mth through the nth tokens. If the last character in thetokens= string is an asterisk, then an additional variable is allocated and receives the remaining text on the line after the last token parsed.
usebackq	Specifies that the new semantics are in force, where a back quoted string is executed as a command and a single quoted string is a literal string command and allows the use of double quotes to quote file names in filenameset.

FORCEDOS Starts the specified program in the MS-DOS subsystem. This command is necessary only for those MS-DOS programs not recognized as such by Windows 2000.

FORCEDOS [/D directory] filename [parameters]

/D directory	Specifies the current directory for the specified program to use.
filename	Specifies the program to start.
parameters	Specifies parameters to pass to the program.

FORMAT Formats a disk for use with Windows 2000.

FORMAT volume [/FS:file-system] [/V:label] [/Q] [/A:size] [/C] [/X]
FORMAT volume [/V:label] [/Q] [/F:size]
FORMAT volume [/V:label] [/Q] [/T:tracks /N:sectors]
FORMAT volume [/V:label] [/Q] [/1] [/4]
FORMAT volume [/Q] [/1] [/4] [/8]

volume	Specifies the drive letter (followed by a colon), mount point, or volume name.
/FS:filesystem	Specifies the type of the file system (FAT, FAT32, or NTFS).
/V:label	Specifies the volume label.
/Q	Performs a quick format.
/C	Files created on the new volume will be compressed by default.
/X	Forces the volume to dismount first if necessary. All opened handles to the volume would no longer be valid.
/A:size	Overrides the default allocation unit size. Default settings are strongly recommended for general use. NTFS supports 512, 1024, 2048, 4096, 8192, 16K, 32K, 64K. FAT supports 512, 1024, 2048, 4096, 8192, 16K, 32K, 64K (128K, 256K for sector size > 512 bytes). FAT32 supports 512, 1024, 2048, 4096, 8192, 16K, 32K, 64K (128K, 256K for sector size > 512 bytes).

Note that the FAT and FAT32 file systems impose the following restrictions on the number of clusters on a volume:
    FAT: Number of clusters <= 65526
    FAT32: 65526 < Number of clusters < 268435446

Format will immediately stop processing if it decides that the above requirements cannot be met using the specified cluster size.

	NTFS compression is not supported for allocation unit sizes above 4096.
/F:size	Specifies the size of the floppy disk to format (160, 180, 320, 360, 640, 720, 1.2, 1.23, 1.44, 2.88, or 20.8).
/T:tracks	Specifies the number of tracks per disk side.
/N:sectors	Specifies the number of sectors per track.
/1	Formats a single side of a floppy disk.
/4	Formats a 5.25-inch 360K floppy disk in a high-density drive.
/8	Formats eight sectors per track.

FTP   Transfers files to and from a computer running an FTP server service (sometimes called a daemon). FTP can be used interactively. This command is available only if the TCP/IP protocol has been installed. FTP is a service, that, once started, creates a sub-environment in which you can use FTP commands, and from which you can return to the Windows 2000 command prompt by typing the QUIT subcommand. When the FTP sub-environment is running, it is indicated by the FTP command prompt.

FTP [-v] [-n] [-i] [-d] [-g] [-s:filename] [-a]
[-w:windowsize] [computer]

-v	Suppresses display of remote server responses.
-n	Suppresses auto-login upon initial connection.
-i	Turns off interactive prompting during multiple file transfers.
-d	Enables debugging, displaying all FTP commands passed between the client and server.
-g	Disables file-name globbing, which permits the use of wildcard characters (* and ?) in local file and path names. (See the GLOB command in the online Command Reference.)
-s:filename	Specifies a text file containing FTP commands; the commands automatically run after FTP starts. No spaces are allowed in this parameter. Use this switch instead of redirection (>).
-a	Uses any local interface when binding data connection.
-w:windowsize	Overrides the default transfer buffer size of 4096.
computer	Specifies the computer name or IP address of the remote computer to connect to. The computer, if specified, must be the last parameter on the line.

FTYPE   Displays or modifies file types used in file extension associations.

FTYPE [fileType[=[openCommandString]]]

fileType	Specifies the file type to examine or change.
openCommandString	Specifies the open command to use when launching files of this type.

Type FTYPE without parameters to display the current file types that have open command strings defined. When FTYPE is invoked with just a file type, it displays the current open command string for that file type. Specify nothing for the open command string and the FTYPE command will delete the open command string for the file type. Within an open command string %0 or %1 are substituted with the file name being launched through the association. %* gets all the parameters and %2 gets the 1st parameter, %3 the second, etc. %~n gets all the remaining parameters starting with the *n*th parameter, where *n* may be between 2 and 9, inclusive. For example:

ASSOC .pl=PerlScript
FTYPE PerlScript=perl.exe %1 %*

would allow you to invoke a Perl script as follows:

script.pl 1 2 3

If you want to eliminate the need to type the extensions, then do the following:

set PATHEXT=.pl;%PATHEXT%

and the script could be invoked as follows:

script 1 2 3

GOTO   Directs CMD.EXE to a labeled line in a batch program.

GOTO label

label   Specifies a text string used in the batch program as a label.

You type a label on a line by itself, beginning with a colon.

If Command Extensions are enabled GOTO changes as follows:

The GOTO command now accepts a target label of :EOF, which transfers control to the end of the current batch script file. This is an easy way to exit a batch script file without defining a label. Type CALL /? for a description of extensions to the CALL command that make this feature useful.

GRAPHICS Loads a program that can print graphics.

GRAPHICS [type] [[drive:][path]filename] [/R] [/B] [/LCD]
[/PRINTBOX:STD ¦ /PRINTBOX:LCD]

type	Specifies a printer type (see User's Guide and Reference).
[drive:][path]filename	Specifies the file containing information on supported printers.
/R	Prints white on black as seen on the screen.
/B	Prints the background in color for COLOR4 and COLOR8 printers.
/LCD	Prints using LCD aspect ratio.
/PRINTBOX:STD ¦ /PRINTBOX:LCD	
	Specifies the print-box size, either STD or LCD.

HELP   Provides help information for Windows 2000 commands.

HELP [command]

command   Displays help information on that command.

IF   Performs conditional processing in batch programs.

IF [NOT] ERRORLEVEL number command
IF [NOT] string1==string2 command
IF [NOT] EXIST filename command

NOT the	Specifies that Windows 2000 should carry out the command only if
	condition is false.
ERRORLEVEL number code	Specifies a true condition if the last program run returned an exit
	equal to or greater than the number specified.
string1==string2	Specifies a true condition if the specified text strings match.
EXIST filename	Specifies a true condition if the specified file name exists.
command command can	Specifies the command to carry out if the condition is met. The
	be followed by the ELSE command, which will execute the command
after	
	the ELSE keyword if the specified condition is FALSE.

The ELSE clause must occur on the same line as the command after the IF. For example:

```
IF EXIST filename. (
del filename.
) ELSE (
echo filename. missing.
)
```

The following would NOT work because the del command needs to be terminated by a newline:
```
IF EXIST filename. del filename. ELSE echo filename. missing
```

Nor would the following work, since the ELSE command must be on the same line as the end of the IF command:
```
IF EXIST filename. del filename.
ELSE echo filename. missing
```

The following would work if you want it all on one line:
```
IF EXIST filename. (del filename.) ELSE echo filename. missing
```

If Command Extensions are enabled IF changes as follows:
```
IF [/I] string1 compare-op string2 command
IF CMDEXTVERSION number command
IF DEFINED variable command
```

where compare-op may be one of the following:
```
EQU     Equal
NEQ     Not equal
LSS     Less than
LEQ     Less than or equal
GTR     Greater than
GEQ     Greater than or equal
```

and the /I switch, if specified, says to do case-insensitive string compares. The /I switch can also be used on the string1==string2 form of IF. These comparisons are generic, in that if both string1 and string2 are comprised of all numeric digits, then the strings are converted to numbers and a numeric comparison is performed.

The CMDEXTVERSION conditional works just like ERRORLEVEL, except it is comparing against an internal version number associated with the Command Extensions. The first version is 1. It will be incremented by one when significant enhancements are added to the Command Extensions.
CMDEXTVERSION conditional is never true when Command Extensions are disabled.

The DEFINED conditional works just like EXISTS except it takes an environment variable name and returns true if the environment variable is defined.

%ERRORLEVEL% will expand into a string representation of the current value of ERRORLEVEL, provided that there is not already an environment variable with the name ERRORLEVEL, in which case you will get its value instead. After running a program, the following illustrates ERRORLEVEL use:
```
goto answer%ERRORLEVEL%
:answer0
echo Program had return code 0
:answer1
echo Program had return code 1
```

You can also using the numerical comparisons above:
```
IF %ERRORLEVEL% LEQ 1 goto okay
```

%CMDCMDLINE% will expand into the original command line passed to CMD.EXE prior to any processing by CMD.EXE, provided that there is not already an environment variable with the name CMDCMDLINE, in which case you will get its value instead.

%CMDEXTVERSION% will expand into a string representation of the current value of CMDEXTVERSION, provided that there is not already an environment variable with the name CMDEXTVERSION, in which case you will get its value instead.

_____

IPCONFIG   Displays all current TCP/IP network configuration values.

Windows 2000 IP Configuration

IPCONFIG [/? ¦ /all ¦ /release [adapter] ¦ /renew [adapter] ¦ /flushdns ¦ /registerdns
¦ /showclassid adapter ¦ /setclassid adapter [classidtoset]]

adapter	Full name or pattern with '*' and '?' to 'match', * matches any character, ? matches one character.

Options:

/?	Displays this help message.
/all	Displays full configuration information.
/release	Releases the IP address for the specified adapter.
/renew	Renews the IP address for the specified adapter.
/flushdns	Purges the DNS Resolver cache.
/registerdns	Refreshes all DHCP leases and re-registers DNS names.
/displaydns	Displays the contents of the DNS Resolver Cache.
/showclassid	Displays all the dhcp class IDs allowed for adapter.
/setclassid	Modifies the dhcp class id.

The default is to display only the IP address, subnet mask, and default gateway for each adapter bound to TCP/IP.

For Release and Renew, if no adapter name is specified, then the IP address leases for all adapters bound to TCP/IP will be released or renewed.

For SetClassID, if no class id is specified, then the classid is removed.

Examples:

> ipconfig	Shows information.
> ipconfig /all	Shows detailed information.
> ipconfig /renew	Renews all adapaters.
> ipconfig /renew EL*	Renews adapters named EL...
> ipconfig /release *ELINK?21*	Releases all matching adapters, e.g., ELINK-21, myELELINKi21adapter.

_____

JVIEW   Runs a command line Loader for Java.

Usage: JView [options] <classname> [arguments]

Options:

/?	Displays usage text.
/cp <classpath>	Sets class path.
/cp:p <path>	Prepends path to class path.
/cp:a <path>	Appends path to class path.
/n <namespace>	Namespace in which to run.
/p	Pauses before terminating if an error occurs.
/v	Verifies all classes.
/d:<name>=<value>	Defines system property.
/a	Executes AppletViewer.
/vst	Prints verbose stack traces (requires debug classes).
/prof[:options]	Enables profiling (/prof:? for help).
classname:	.CLASS file to be executed.
arguments:	Command-line arguments to be passed on to the class file.

_____

LABEL   Creates, changes, or deletes the volume label of a disk.

LABEL [drive:][label]
LABEL [/MP] [volume] [label]

drive:	Specifies the drive letter of a drive.
label	Specifies the label of the volume.

/MP   Specifies that the volume should be treated as a mount point or volume name.
volume   Specifies the drive letter (followed by a colon), mount point, or volume name. If
volume

                       name is specified, the /MP flag is unnecessary.

LOADFIX   Loads a program above the first 64K of memory, and runs the program.

                       LOADFIX [drive:][path]filename

                       Use LOADFIX to load a program if you have received the message "Packed file corrupt" when
                       trying to load it in low memory.

LPQ   Displays the state of a remote lpd queue.

                       Usage: lpq -S server -P printer [-l]

                       Options:
                       -S server   Name or ipaddress of the host providing lpd service.
                       -P printer   Name of the print queue.
                       -l   Verbose output.

LPR   Sends a print job to a network printer.

                       Usage: lpr -S server -P printer [-C class] [-J job][-o option][-x][-d] filename

                       Options:
                       -S server   Name or ipaddress of the host providing lpd service.
                       -P printer   Name of the print queue.
                       -C class   Job classification for use on the burst page.
                       -J job   Job name to print on the burst page.
                       -o option   Indicates type of the file (by default assumes a text file)
                                          Use "-o l" for binary (e.g., PostScript) files.
                       -x   Compatibility with SunOS 4.1.x and prior.
                       -d   Sends data file first.

MAKECAB   Loads Cabinet Maker.

                       MAKECAB [/V[n]] [/D var=value ...] [/L dir] source [destination]
                       MAKECAB [/V[n]] [/D var=value ...] /F directive_file [...]

                       source   File to compress.
                       destination   File name to give compressed file.
                                          If omitted, the last character of the source file name is replaced with an
                       underscore
                                          (_) and used as the destination.
                       /F directive_file A file with MakeCAB directives (may be repeated).
                       /D var=value   Defines variable with specified value.
                       /L dir   Location to place destination (default is current directory).
                       /V[n]   Verbosity level (1–3).

MEM   Displays the amount of used and free memory in your system.

                       MEM [/PROGRAM ¦ /DEBUG ¦ /CLASSIFY]

                       /PROGRAM or /P   Displays status of programs currently loaded in memory.
                       /DEBUG or /D   Displays status of programs, internal drivers, and other information.
                       /CLASSIFY or /C   Classifies programs by memory usage. Lists the size of programs,
                                          provides a summary of memory in use, and lists largest memory block
                                          available.

MKDIR or MD   Creates a directory.

        MKDIR [drive:]path
        MD [drive:]path

        If Command Extensions are enabled MKDIR changes as follows:

        MKDIR creates any intermediate directories in the path, if needed.
        For example, assume \a does not exist then:

          mkdir \a\b\c\d

        is the same as:

          mkdir \a
          chdir \a
          mkdir b
          chdir b
          mkdir c
          chdir c
          mkdir d

        which is what you would have to type if extensions were disabled.

MODE   Configures system devices.

        Serial port: MODE COMm[:] [BAUD=b] [PARITY=p] [DATA=d] [STOP=s] [to=on¦off]
        [xon=on¦off] [odsr=on¦off] [octs=on¦off] [dtr=on¦off¦hs] [rts=on¦off¦hs¦tg] [idsr=on¦off]

        Device status: MODE [device] [/STATUS]
        Redirect printing: MODE LPTn[:]=COMm[:]
        Select code page: MODE CON[:] CP SELECT=yyy
        Code page status: MODE CON[:] CP [/STATUS]
        Display mode:MODE CON[:] [COLS=c] [LINES=n]
        Typematic rate: MODE CON[:] [RATE=r DELAY=d]

MORE   Displays output one screen at a time.

        MORE [/E [/C] [/P] [/S] [/Tn] [+n]] < [drive:][path]filename
        command-name ¦ MORE [/E [/C] [/P] [/S] [/Tn] [+n]]
        MORE /E [/C] [/P] [/S] [/Tn] [+n] [files]

        [drive:][path]filename Specifies a file to display one screen at a time.
        command-name   Specifies a command whose output will be displayed.
        /E   Enables extended features.
        /C   Clears screen before displaying page.
        /P   Expands FormFeed characters.
        /S   Squeezes multiple blank lines into a single line.
        /Tn   Expands tabs to n spaces (default 8).

        Switches can be present in the MORE environment variable.

        +n   Starts displaying the first file at line n.
        files   List of files to be displayed. Files in the list are separated by blanks.

        If extended features are enabled, the following commands are accepted at the --More-- prompt:

        P n   Displays next n lines.
        S n   Skips next n lines.
        F   Displays next file.
        Q   Quits.
        =   Shows line number.

?	Shows help line.
\<space\>	Displays next page.
\<ret\>	Displays next line.

MOVE   Moves files and renames files and directories.

To move one or more files:
MOVE [/Y ¦ /-Y] [drive:][path]filename1[,...] destination

To rename a directory:
MOVE [/Y ¦ /-Y] [drive:][path]dirname1 dirname2

[drive:][path]filename1 to	Specifies the location and name of the file or files you want
	move.
destination of a	Specifies the new location of the file. Destination can consist
	drive letter and colon, a directory name, or a combination. If
you	are moving only one file, you can also include a file name if
you	
	want to rename the file when you move it.
[drive:][path]dirname1	Specifies the directory you want to rename.
dirname2	Specifies the new name of the directory.
/Y existing	Suppresses prompting to confirm you want to overwrite an
	destination file.
/-Y existing	Causes prompting to confirm you want to overwrite an
	destination file.

The switch /Y may be present in the COPYCMD environment variable. This may be overridden with
/-Y on the command line. The default is to prompt on overwrites unless the MOVE command is being executed from within a batch script.

NBTSTAT   Displays protocol statistics and current TCP/IP connections using NBT (NetBIOS over TCP/IP).

NBTSTAT [[-a RemoteName] [-A IP address] [-c] [-n] [-r] [-R] [-RR] [-s] [-S] [interval]]

-a (adapter status)	Lists the remote machine's name table given its name.
-A (Adapter status)	Lists the remote machine's name table given its IP address.
-c (cache)	Lists NBT's cache of remote [machine] names and their IP addresses.
-n (names)	Lists local NetBIOS names.
-r (resolved)	Lists names resolved by broadcast and via WINS.
-R (Reload)	Purges and reloads the remote cache name table.
-S (Sessions)	Lists sessions table with the destination IP addresses.
-s (sessions) NETBIOS	Lists sessions table converting destination IP addresses to computer
	names.
-RR (ReleaseRefresh)	Sends Name Release packets to WINs and then starts Refresh.
RemoteName	Remote host machine name.
IP address	Dotted decimal representation of the IP address.
interval	Redisplays selected statistics, pausing interval seconds between each
display.	
	Press Ctrl+C to stop redisplaying statistics.

NET   Many Windows 2000 networking commands begin with the word NET. These NET commands have some common properties. You can see a list of all available NET commands by typing net / ?.

NET /? results in:

NET [ACCOUNTS ¦ COMPUTER ¦ CONFIG ¦ CONTINUE ¦ FILE ¦ GROUP ¦ HELP ¦ HELPMSG ¦ LOCALGROUP ¦ NAME ¦ PAUSE ¦ PRINT ¦ SEND ¦ SESSION ¦ SHARE ¦ START ¦ STATISTICS ¦ STOP ¦ TIME ¦ USE ¦ USER ¦ VIEW]

You can get syntax help at the command line for a NET command by typing NET HELP *command*. For example, for help with the NET USE command, type NET HELP USE. See results of this command below. (For help with the other commands listed above, key in NET HELP *command* at the command line.)

_____

NET USE
Connects a computer to a shared resource or disconnects a computer from a shared resource. When used without options, it lists the computer's connections.

NET USE [devicename ¦ *] [\\computername\sharename[\volume] [password ¦ *]]
[/USER:[domainname\]username]
[/USER:[dotted domain name\]username]
[/USER:[username@dotted domain name]
[[/DELETE] ¦ [/PERSISTENT:{YES ¦ NO}]]

NET USE {devicename ¦ *} [password ¦ *] /HOME

NET USE [/PERSISTENT:{YES ¦ NO}]

devicename	Assigns a name to connect to the resource or specifies the device to be disconnected. There are two kinds of device names: disk drives (D:
through Z:)	
specific	and printers (LPT1: through LPT3:). Type an asterisk instead of a
	device name to assign the next available device name.
\\computername	The name of the computer controlling the shared resource. If computername contains blank characters, enclose the double backslash
(\\)	
	and computername in quotation marks (" "). The computername may be from 1 to 15 characters long.
\sharename	The network name of the shared resource.
\volume	Specifies a NetWare volume on the server. You must have Client
Services for	
	Netware (Windows Workstations) or Gateway Service for Netware
(Windows	
	Server) installed and running to connect to NetWare servers.
password	The password needed to access the shared resource.
*	Produces a prompt for the password. The password is not displayed
when you	
	type it at the password prompt.
/USER	Specifies a different user name with which the connection is made.
domainname	Specifies another domain. If domain is omitted, the current logged on
domain is	
	used.
username	Specifies the user name with which to log on.
/HOME	Connects a user to the home directory.
/DELETE	Cancels a network connection and removes the connection from the list
of	
	persistent connections.
/PERSISTENT	Controls the use of persistent network connections. The default is the
setting	
	used last.
YES	Saves connections as they are made, and restores them at next logon.
NO	Does not save the connection being made or subsequent connections; existing connections will be restored at next logon. Use the /DELETE switch to remove persistent connections.

_____

NETSH   The NetShell utility (NETSH) is a command line, scripting interface for configuring and
             monitoring Windows 2000.

             Usage: NETSH [-a AliasFile] [-c Context] [-r RemoteMachine] [Command ¦ -f ScriptFile]

             The following commands are available:

             ?   Displays a list of commands.
             add   Adds a configuration entry to a list of entries.
             delete   Deletes a configuration entry from a list of entries.
             dump   Displays a configuration script.
             exec   Runs a script file.
             help   Displays a list of commands.
             interface   Changes to the "interface" context.
             ras   Changes to the "ras" context.
             routing   Changes to the "routing" context.
             set   Updates configuration settings.
             show   Displays information.

             _

NETSTAT   Displays protocol statistics and current TCP/IP network connections.

             NETSTAT [-a] [-e] [-n] [-s] [-p proto] [-r] [interval]

             -a   Displays all connections and listening ports.
             -e   Displays Ethernet statistics. This may be combined with the -s option.
             -n   Displays addresses and port numbers in numerical form.
             -p proto   Shows connections for the protocol specified by proto; proto may be TCP or UDP.
             If used
                          with the -s option to display per-protocol statistics, proto may be TCP, UDP, or IP.
             -r   Displays the routing table.
             -s   Displays per-protocol statistics. By default, statistics are shown for TCP, UDP, and
             IP; the
                          -p option may be used to specify a subset of the default.
             interval   Redisplays selected statistics, pausing interval seconds between each display.
             Press
                          Ctrl+C to stop redisplaying statistics. If omitted, NETSTAT will print the current
                          configuration information once.

             _

PATH   Displays or sets a search path for executable files.

             PATH [drive:]path[;...][;%PATH%]
             PATH ;

             Type PATH ; to clear all search-path settings and direct CMD.EXE to search only in the current
             directory.
             Type PATH without parameters to display the current path.
             Including %PATH% in the new path setting causes the old path to be appended to the new
             setting.

             _

PATHPING   Loads a route-tracing tool.

             Usage: pathping [-n] [-h maximum_hops] [-g host-list] [-p period]
             [-q num_queries] [-w timeout] [-T] [-R] [-r] target_name

             Options:
             -n   Do not resolve addresses to host names.
             -h maximum_hops Maximum number of hops to search for target.
             -g host-list   Loose source route along host-list.
             -p period   Wait period milliseconds between pings.
             -q num_queries   Number of queries per hop.
             -w timeout   Wait timeout milliseconds for each reply.

-T	Test connectivity to each hop with Layer-2 priority tags.
-R	Test if each hop is RSVP-aware.

PAUSE — Suspends processing of a batch program and displays the message "Press any key to continue . . ."

PENTNT — Reports on whether the local computer exhibits Intel Pentium floating point division error.

pentnt [-?] [-H] [-h] [-C] [-c] [-F] [-f] [-O] [-o]

Run without arguments this program will tell you if the system exhibits the Pentium floating point division error and whether floating point emulation is forced and whether floating point hardware is disabled.

-?	Prints this help message.
-c	Turns on conditional emulation. This means that floating -C point emulation will be forced on if and only if the system detects the Pentium floating point division error at boot. Rebooting is required before this takes effect. This is what should generally be used.
-f	Turns on forced emulation. This means that floating -F point hardware is disabled and floating point emulation will always be forced on, regardless of whether the system exhibits the Pentium division error. Useful for testing software emulators and for working around floating point hardware defects unknown to the OS. Rebooting is required before this takes effect.
-o	Turns off forced emulation. Re-enables floating point hardware if present. Rebooting is required before this takes effect.

The floating point division error that this program addresses only occurs on certain Intel Pentium processors. It only affects floating point operations. The problem is described in detail in a white paper available from Intel. If you are doing critical work with programs that perform floating point division and certain related functions that use the same hardware (including remainder and transcendental functions), you may wish to use this program to force emulation.

PING — Verifies connections to a remote computer or computers. This command is available only if the TCP/IP protocol has been installed.

ping [-t] [-a] [-n count] [-l size] [-f] [-i TTL] [-v TOS] [-r count] [-s count] [[-j host-list] ¦ [-k host-list]] [-w timeout] destination-list

-t	Pings the specified host until stopped. To see statistics and continue, type Ctrl+Break; to stop, type Ctrl+C.
-a	Resolves addresses to host names.
-n count	Number of echo requests to send.
-l size	Sends buffer size.
-f	Sets Don't Fragment flag in packet.
-i TTL	Time To Live.
-v TOS	Type Of Service.
-r count	Records route for count hops.
-s count	Timestamp for count hops.
-j host-list	Loose source route along host-list.
-k host-list	Strict source route along host-list.
-w timeout	Timeout in milliseconds to wait for each reply.

PRINT — Prints a text file.

PRINT [/D:device] [[drive:][path]filename[...]]

/D:device   Specifies a print device.

POPD   Changes to the directory stored by the PUSHD command.

                POPD

                If Command Extensions are enabled the POPD command will delete any temporary drive letter
                created by PUSHD when you POPD that drive off the pushed directory stack.

PROMPT   Changes the CMD.EXE command prompt.

                PROMPT [text]

                text   Specifies a new command prompt.

                Prompt can be made up of normal characters and the following special codes:

                $A   & (Ampersand)
                $B   ¦ (Pipe)
                $C   ((Left parenthesis)
                $D   Current date
                $E   Escape code (ASCII code 27)
                $F   ) (Right parenthesis)
                $G   > (Greater-than sign)
                $H   Backspace (erases previous character)
                $L   < (Less-than sign)
                $N   Current drive
                $P   Current drive and path
                $Q   = (Equal sign)
                $S   (Space)
                $T   Current time
                $V   Windows 2000 version number
                $_   Carriage return and linefeed
                $$ $ (Dollar sign)

                If Command Extensions are enabled the PROMPT command supports the following additional
                formatting characters:

                $+   zero or more plus sign (+) characters depending upon the depth of the PUSHD directory
                stack,   one character for each level pushed.

                $M Displays the remote name associated with the current drive letter or the empty string if
                current   drive is not a network drive.

PUSHD   Stores the current directory for use by the POPD command, then changes to the specified
                directory.

                PUSHD [path ¦ ..]

                path   Specifies the directory to make the current directory.

                If Command Extensions are enabled the PUSHD command accepts network paths in addition to
                the normal drive letter and path. If a network path is specified, PUSHD will create a temporary
                drive letter that points to that specified network resource and then change the current drive
                and directory, using the newly defined drive letter. Temporary drive letters are allocated from
                Z: on down, using the first unused drive letter found.

RCP   Copies files to and from a computer running the RCP service.

                RCP [-a ¦ -b] [-h] [-r] [host][.user:]source [host][.user:] path\destination

-a   Specifies ASCII transfer mode. This mode converts the EOL characters to a carriage return for UNIX and a carriage return/line feed for personal computers. This is the default transfer mode.
-b   Specifies binary image transfer mode.
-h   Transfers hidden files.
-r   Copies the contents of all subdirectories; destination must be a directory.
host   Specifies the local or remote host. If host is specified as an IP address or if the host name contains dots, you must specify the user.
.user: Specifies a user name to use, rather than the current user name.
source   Specifes the files to copy.
path\destination   Specifies the path relative to the logon directory on the remote host. Use the escape characters (\ , ", or ') in remote paths to use wildcard characters on the remote host.

RECOVER   Recovers readable information from a bad or defective disk.

                 RECOVER [drive:][path]filename

                 Consult the online Command Reference in Windows 2000 Help before using the RECOVER command.

REM   Records comments (remarks) in a batch file or CONFIG.SYS.

                 REM [comment]

REN or RENAME   Renames a file or files.

                 RENAME [drive:][path]filename1 filename2
                 REN [drive:][path]filename1 filename2

                 Note that you cannot specify a new drive or path for your destination file.

REPLACE   Replaces files.

                 REPLACE [drive1:][path1]filename [drive2:][path2] [/A] [/P] [/R] [/W]
                 REPLACE [drive1:][path1]filename [drive2:][path2] [/P] [/R] [/S] [/W] [/U]

                 [drive1:][path1]filename   Specifies the source file or files.
                 [drive2:][path2]   Specifies the directory where files are to be replaced.
                 /A   Adds new files to the destination directory. Cannot use with the /S or /U switch.
                 /P   Prompts for confirmation before replacing a file or adding a source file.
                 /R   Replaces read-only files as well as unprotected files.
                 /S   Replaces files in all subdirectories of the destination directory. Cannot use with the /A switch.
                 /W   Waits for you to insert a disk before beginning.
                 /U   Replaces (updates) only files that are older than source files. Cannot use with the /A switch.

RMDIR or RD Removes (deletes) a directory.

                 RMDIR [/S] [/Q] [drive:]path
                 RD [/S] [/Q] [drive:]path

                 /S   Removes all directories and files in the specified directory in addition to the directory itself. Used to remove a directory tree.
                 /Q   Quiet mode, do not ask if okay to remove a directory tree with /S.

ROUTE   Manipulates network routing tables.

ROUTE [-f] [-p] [command] [destination]
[MASK netmask] [gateway] [METRIC metric] [IF interface]

-f   Clears the routing tables of all gateway entries. If this is used in conjunction with
one
               of the commands, the tables are cleared prior to running the command.
-p   When used with the ADD command, makes a route persistent across boots of the
               system. By default, routes are not preserved when the system is restarted.
Ignored for
               all other commands, which always affect the appropriate persistent routes. This
option is
               not supported in Windows 95.
command   PRINT   Prints a route.
               ADD   Adds a route.
               DELETE   Deletes a route.
               CHANGE   Modifies an existing route.
destination   Specifies the host.
MASK   Specifies that the next parameter is the netmask value.
netmask   Specifies a subnet mask value for this route entry. If not specified, it defaults to
               255.255.255.255.
gateway   Specifies gateway.
interface   The interface number for the specified route.
METRIC   Specifies the metric, i.e., the cost for the destination.

All symbolic names used for destination are looked up in the network database file
NETWORKS. The symbolic names for gateway are looked up in the host name database file
HOSTS.

If the command is PRINT or DELETE. Destination or gateway can be a wildcard (wildcard is
specified as a star "*"), or the gateway argument may be omitted.

If Dest contains a * or ?, it is treated as a shell pattern, and only matching destination routes are
printed. The "*" matches any string, and "?" matches any one char. Examples: 157.*.1, 157.*,
127.*, *224*.

Diagnostic Notes:
Invalid MASK generates an error, that is when (DEST & MASK) != DEST.
Example> route ADD 157.0.0.0 MASK 155.0.0.0 157.55.80.1 IF 1
The route addition failed: The specified mask parameter is invalid. (Destination & Mask) !=
Destination.

Examples:

> route PRINT
     > route ADD 157.0.0.0 MASK 255.0.0.0 157.55.80.1 METRIC 3 IF 2
     destination^   ^mask   ^gateway   metric^ ^ interface^
If IF is not given, it tries to find the best interface for a given gateway.
> route PRINT
> route PRINT 157*   .... Only prints those matching 157*
> route DELETE 157.0.0.0
> route PRINT

- -

RSH   Runs commands on remote hosts running the RSH service.

RSH host [-l username] [-n] command

host   Specifies the remote host on which to run the command.
-l username   Specifies the user name to use on the remote host. If omitted, the logged on user
               name is used.
-n   Redirects the input of RSH to NULL.
command   Specifies the command to run.

———

RUNAS   Allows a user to run specific tools and programs with different permissions than the user's current logon provides.

RUNAS USAGE:
RUNAS [/profile] [/env] [/netonly] /user:<UserName> program

/profile	If the user's profile needs to be loaded.
/env	Uses current environment instead of user's.
/netonly	Use if the credentials specified are for remote access only.
/user	<UserName> should be in form USER@DOMAIN or DOMAIN\USER.
program	Command line for EXE. See below for examples.

Examples:
> runas /profile /user:mymachine\administrator cmd
> runas /profile /env /user:mydomain\admin "mmc %windir%\system32\dsa.msc"
> runas /env /user:user@domain.microsoft.com "notepad \"my file.txt\""

Note: Enter user's password only when prompted.
Note: USER@DOMAIN is not compatible with /netonly.

———

SET   Displays, sets, or removes CMD.EXE environment variables.

SET [variable=[string]]

variable	Specifies the environment variable name.
string	Specifies a series of characters to assign to the variable.

Type SET without parameters to display the current environment variables.

If Command Extensions are enabled SET changes as follows:

The SET command invoked with just a variable name, no equal sign or value, will display the value of all variables whose prefix matches the name given to the SET command. For example:

SET P would display all variables that begin with the letter 'P'

The SET command will set the ERRORLEVEL to 1 if the variable name is not found in the current
environment.

The SET command will not allow an equal sign to be part of the name of a variable.

Two new switches have been added to the SET command:

SET /A expression
SET /P variable=[promptString]

The /A switch specifies that the string to the right of the equal sign is a numerical expression that is evaluated. The expression evaluator is pretty simple and supports the following operations, in decreasing order of precedence:

()	grouping
* / %	arithmetic operators
+ -	arithmetic operators
<< >>	logical shift
&	bitwise and
^	bitwise exclusive or
¦	bitwise or
= *= /= %= += -=	assignment
&= ^= ¦= <<= >>=,	expression separator

If you use any of the logical or modulus operators, you will need to enclose the expression string in quotes. Any non-numeric strings in the expression are treated as environment variable names whose values are converted to numbers before using them. If an environment variable name is specified but is not defined in the current environment, then a value of zero is used. This allows you to do arithmetic with environment variable values without having to type all those % signs to get their values. If SET /A is executed from the command line outside of a command script, then it displays the final value of the expression. The assignment operator requires an environment variable name to the left of the assignment operator. Numeric values are decimal numbers, unless prefixed by 0x for hexadecimal numbers, and 0 for octal numbers. So 0x12 is the same as 18 is the same as 022. Please note that the octal notation can be confusing: 08 and 09 are not valid numbers because 8 and 9 are not valid octal digits.

The /P switch allows you to set the value of a variable to a line of input entered by the user. Displays the specified promptString before reading the line of input. The promptString can be empty.

Environment variable substitution has been enhanced as follows:

    %PATH:str1=str2%

would expand the PATH environment variable, substituting each occurrence of "str1" in the expanded result with "str2". "str2" can be the empty string to effectively delete all occurrences of "str1" from the expanded output. "str1" can begin with an asterisk, in which case it will match everything from the begining of the expanded output to the first occurrence of the remaining portion of str1.

May also specify substrings for an expansion.

    %PATH:~10,5%

would expand the PATH environment variable, and then use only the five characters that begin at the eleventh (offset 10) character of the expanded result. If the length is not specified, then it defaults to the remainder of the variable value. If either number (offset or length) is negative, then the number used is the length of the environment variable value added to the offset or length specified.

    %PATH:~-10%

would extract the last 10 characters of the PATH variable.

    %PATH:~0,-2%

would extract all but the last two characters of the PATH variable.

Finally, support for delayed environment variable expansion has been added. This support is always disabled by default, but may be enabled/disabled via the /V command line switch to CMD.EXE.
See CMD /?.

Delayed environment variable expansion is useful for getting around the limitations of the current expansion that happens when a line of text is read, not when it is executed. The following example demonstrates the problem with immediate variable expansion:

```
set VAR=before
if "%VAR%" == "before" (
set VAR=after;
if "%VAR%" == "after" @echo If you see this, it worked
)
```

would never display the message, since the %VAR% in both IF statements is substituted when the first IF statement is read, since it logically includes the body of the IF, which is a compound statement. So the IF inside the compound statement is really comparing "before" with "after," which will never be equal. Similarly, the following example will not work as expected:

```
set LIST=
for %i in (*) do set LIST=%LIST% %i
echo %LIST%
```

in that it will not build up a list of files in the current directory, but instead will just set the LIST variable to the last file found. Again, this is because the %LIST% is expanded just once when the FOR statement is read, and at that time the LIST variable is empty. So the actual FOR loop we are executing is:

```
for %i in (*) do set LIST= %i
```

which just keeps setting LIST to the last file found.

Delayed environment variable expansion allows you to use a different character (the exclamation mark) to expand environment variables at execution time. If delayed variable expansion is enabled, the above examples could be written as follows to work as intended:

```
set VAR=before
if "%VAR%" == "before" (
set VAR=after
if "!VAR!" == "after" @echo If you see this, it worked
)

set LIST=
for %i in (*) do set LIST=!LIST! %i
echo %LIST%
```

If Command Extensions are enabled, then there are several dynamic environment variables that can be expanded but which don't show up in the list of variables displayed by SET. These variable values are computed dynamically each time the value of the variable is expanded. If the user explicitly defines a variable with one of these names, then that definition will override the dynamic one described below:

%CD%	Expands to the current directory string.
%DATE%	Expands to current date using same format as DATE command.
%TIME%	Expands to current time using same format as TIME command.
%RANDOM%	Expands to a random decimal number between 0 and 32767.
%ERRORLEVEL%	Expands to the current ERRORLEVEL value.
%CMDEXTVERSION% number.	Expands to the current Command Processor Extensions version
%CMDCMDLINE% Processor.	Expands to the original command line that invoked the Command

- -

SETLOCAL   Begins localization of environment changes in a batch file. Environment changes made after SETLOCAL has been issued are local to the batch file. ENDLOCAL must be issued to restore the previous settings. When the end of a batch script is reached, an implied ENDLOCAL is executed for any outstanding SETLOCAL commands issued by that batch script.

SETLOCAL

If Command Extensions are enabled SETLOCAL changes as follows:

SETLOCAL batch command now accepts optional arguments:
ENABLEEXTENSIONS / DISABLEEXTENSIONS: Enables or disables command processor extensions. See CMD /? for details.
ENABLEDELAYEDEXPANSION / DISABLEDELAYEDEXPANSION: Enables or disables delayed environment variable expansion. See SET /? for details.

These modifications last until the matching ENDLOCAL command, regardless of their setting prior to the SETLOCAL command.

The SETLOCAL command will set the ERRORLEVEL value if given an argument. It will be zero if one of the two valid arguments is given and one otherwise. You can use this in batch scripts to determine if the extensions are available, using the following technique:

VERIFY OTHER 2>nul
SETLOCAL ENABLEEXTENSIONS
IF ERRORLEVEL 1 echo Unable to enable extensions

This works because on old versions of CMD.EXE, SETLOCAL does NOT set the ERRORLEVEL value. The VERIFY command with a bad argument initializes the ERRORLEVEL value to a non-zero value.

SETVER   Sets the version number that MS-DOS reports to a program.

Display current version table: SETVER [drive:path]
Add entry: SETVER [drive:path] filename n.nn
Delete entry: SETVER [drive:path] filename /DELETE [/QUIET]

[drive:path]	Specifies location of the SETVER.EXE file.
filename	Specifies the file name of the program.
n.nn	Specifies the MS-DOS version to be reported to the program.
/DELETE or /D	Deletes the version-table entry for the specified program.
/QUIET	Hides the message typically displayed during deletion of version-table entry.

SHIFT   Changes the position of replaceable parameters in a batch file.

SHIFT [/n]

If Command Extensions are enabled the SHIFT command supports the /n switch, which tells the command to start shifting at the nth argument, where n may be between zero and eight. For example:

SHIFT /2

would shift %3 to %2, %4 to %3, etc., and leave %0 and %1 unaffected.

SORT   Reads input, sorts data, and writes the results to the screen, to a file, or to another device.

SORT [/R] [/+n] [/M kilobytes] [/L locale] [/RE recordbytes]
[[drive1:][path1]filename1] [/T [drive2:][path2]]
[/O [drive3:][path3]filename3]

/+n indicates	Specifies the character number, n, to begin each comparison. /+3 indicates
	that each comparison should begin at the third character in each line.
Lines	
	with fewer than n characters collate before other lines. By default comparisons start at the first character in each line.
/L[OCALE] locale	Overrides the system default locale with the specified one. The ""C""
locale	
	yields the fastest collating sequence and is currently the only
alternative. The	
	sort is always case insensitive.
/M[EMORY] kilobytes	Specifies amount of main memory to use for the sort, in kilobytes. The memory size is always constrained to be a minimum of 160 kilobytes. If
the	
	memory size is specified the exact amount will be used for the sort,
regardless	
	of how much main memory is available.

The best performance is usually achieved by not specifying a memory size. By default the sort will be done with one pass (no temporary file) if it fits in the default maximum memory size. Otherwise the sort will be done in two passes (with the partially sorted data being stored in a temporary file) such that the amounts of memory used for both the sort and merge passes are equal. The default maximum memory size is 90% of available main memory if both the input and output are files, and 45% of main memory otherwise.

/REC[ORD_MAXIMUM] characters record	Specifies the maximum number of characters in a (default 4096, maximum 65535).
/R[EVERSE] 0.	Reverses the sort order; that is, sorts Z to A, then 9 to
[drive1:][path1]filename1 input.	Specifies the file to be sorted. If not specified, the standard input is sorted. Specifying the input file is faster than redirecting the same file as standard
/T[EMPORARY] working	Specifies the path of the directory to hold the sort's
[drive2:][path2] The	storage, in case the data does not fit in main memory. default is to use the system's temporary directory.
/O[UTPUT] stored.	Specifies the file where the sorted input is to be
[drive3:][path3]filename3 redirecting	If not specified, the data is written to the standard output. Specifying the output file is faster than standard output to the same file.

START   Starts a separate window to run a specified program or command.

START ["title"] [/Dpath] [/I] [/MIN] [/MAX] [/SEPARATE ¦ /SHARED] [/LOW ¦ /NORMAL ¦ /
HIGH ¦
/REALTIME ¦ /ABOVENORMAL ¦ /BELOWNORMAL] [/WAIT] [/B] [command/program]
[parameters]

"title"	Title to display in window title bar.
path	Starting directory
B	Starts application without creating a new window. The application has ^C handling ignored. Unless the application enables ^C processing, ^Break
is the	only way to interrupt the application.
I	The new environment will be the original environment passed to the
CMD.EXE	and not the current environment.
MIN	Starts window minimized.
MAX	Starts window maximized.
SEPARATE	Starts 16-bit Windows program in separate memory space.
SHARED	Starts 16-bit Windows program in shared memory space.
LOW	Starts application in the IDLE priority class.
NORMAL	Starts application in the NORMAL priority class.
HIGH	Starts application in the HIGH priority class.
REALTIME	Starts application in the REALTIME priority class.
ABOVENORMAL	Starts application in the ABOVENORMAL priority class.
BELOWNORMAL	Starts application in the BELOWNORMAL priority class.
WAIT	Starts application and wait for it to terminate command/program.

If it is an internal command or a batch file, then the command processor is run with the /K switch to CMD.EXE. This means that the window will remain after the command has been run.

If it is not an internal command or batch file then it is a program and will run as either a windowed application or a console application.

parameters   These are the parameters passed to the command program

If Command Extensions are enabled, external command invocation through the command line or the START command changes as follows:

Nonexecutable files may be invoked through their file association just by typing the name of the file as a command. (For example, WORD.DOC would launch the application associated with the .DOC file extension.) See the ASSOC and FTYPE commands for how to create these associations from within a command script.

When executing an application that is a 32-bit GUI application, CMD.EXE does not wait for the application to terminate before returning to the command prompt. This new behavior does NOT occur if executing within a command script.

When executing a command line whose first token is the string "CMD" without an extension or path qualifier, then "CMD" is replaced with the value of the COMSPEC variable. This prevents picking up CMD.EXE from the current directory.

When executing a command line whose first token does NOT contain an extension, then CMD.EXE uses the value of the PATHEXT environment variable to determine which extensions to look for and in what order. The default value for the PATHEXT variable is:

.COM;.EXE;.BAT;.CMD

Notice the syntax is the same as the PATH variable, with semicolons separating the different elements.

When searching for an executable, if there is no match on any extension, then looks to see if the name matches a directory name. If it does, the Start command launches Explorer on that path. If done from the command line, it is the equivalent to doing a CD /D to that path.

SUBST   Associates a path with a drive letter.

SUBST [drive1: [drive2:]path]
SUBST drive1: /D

drive1:   Specifies a virtual drive to which you want to assign a path.
[drive2:]path   Specifies a physical drive and path you want to assign to a virtual drive.
/D   Deletes a substituted (virtual) drive.

Type SUBST with no parameters to display a list of current virtual drives.

TELNET   Provides user support for the Telnet protocol, a remote access protocol you can use to log on to a remote computer, network device, or private TCP/IP network.

telnet [host [port]]

host   Specifies the host name or IP address of the remote computer to connect to.
port   Specifies the port number or service name.

TIME   Displays or sets the system time.

TIME [/T ¦ time]

Type TIME with no parameters to display the current time setting and a prompt for a new one. Press Enter to keep the same time.

If Command Extensions are enabled the TIME command supports the /T switch, which tells the command to just output the current time, without prompting for a new time.

TITLE   Sets the window title for the command prompt window.

TITLE [string]

string   Specifies the title for the command prompt window.

TRACERT   This diagnostic utility determines the route taken to a destination by sending Internet Control Message Protocol (ICMP) echo packets with varying Time-To-Live (TTL) values to the destination. Each router along the path is required to decrement the TTL on a packet by at least

1 before forwarding it, so the TTL is effectively a hop count. When the TTL on a packet reaches 0, the router is supposed to send back an ICMP Time Exceeded message to the source system. Tracert determines the route by sending the first echo packet with a TTL of 1 and incrementing the TTL by 1 on each subsequent transmission until the target responds or the maximum TTL is reached. The route is determined by examining the ICMP Time Exceeded messages sent back by intermediate routers. However, some routers silently drop packets with expired TTL values and are invisible to TRACERT.

tracert [-d] [-h maximum_hops] [-j computer-list] [-w timeout] target_name

-d	Specifies not to resolve addresses to computer names.
-h maximum_hops	Specifies maximum number of hops to search for target.
-j computer-list	Specifies loose source route along computer-list.
-w timeout	Waits the number of milliseconds specified by timeout for each reply.
target_name	Name of the target computer.

TREE   Graphically displays the folder structure of a drive or path.

TREE [drive:][path] [/F] [/A]

/F	Displays the names of the files in each folder.
/A	Uses ASCII instead of extended characters.

TYPE   Displays the contents of a text file or files.

TYPE [drive:][path]filename

VER   Displays the Windows 2000 version number.

VER

VERIFY   Tells CMD.EXE whether to verify that your files are written correctly to a disk.

VERIFY [ON ¦ OFF]

Type VERIFY without a parameter to display the current VERIFY setting.

VOL   Displays the disk volume label and serial number, if they exist.

VOL [drive:]

XCOPY   Copies files and directory trees.

XCOPY source [destination] [/A ¦ /M] [/D[:date]] [/P] [/S [/E]] [/V] [/W] [/C] [/I] [/Q] [/F] [/L] [/H]
[/R] [/T] [/U]
[/K] [/N] [/O] [/X] [/Y] [/-Y] [/Z] [/EXCLUDE:file1[+file2][+file3]...]

source	Specifies the file(s) to copy.
destination	Specifies the location and/or name of new files.
/A	Copies only files with the archive attribute set, doesn't change the attribute.
/M	Copies only files with the archive attribute set, turns off the archive attribute.
/D:date	Copies files changed on or after the specified date. If no date is given, copies only those files whose source time is newer than the destination time.
/EXCLUDE:file1[+file2][+file3]...	
	Specifies a list of files containing strings. When any of the strings match any part of the absolute path of the file to be copied, that file will be excluded from being copied.

For example, specifying a string like \obj\ or .obj will exclude all files underneath the directory obj or all files with the .obj extension, respectively.

/P	Prompts you before creating each destination file.
/S	Copies directories and subdirectories except empty ones.
/E	Copies directories and subdirectories, including empty ones. Same as /S /E. May be used to modify /T.
/V	Verifies each new file.
/W	Prompts you to press a key before copying.
/C	Continues copying even if errors occur.
/I	If destination does not exist and copying more than one file, assumes that destination must be a directory.
/Q	Does not display file names while copying.
/F	Displays full source and destination file names while copying.
/L	Displays files that would be copied.
/H	Copies hidden and system files also.
/R	Overwrites read-only files.
/T	Creates directory structure, but does not copy files. Does not include empty directories or subdirectories. /T /E includes empty directories and subdirectories.
/U	Copies only files that already exist in destination.
/K	Copies attributes. Normal XCOPY will reset read-only attributes.
/N	Copies using the generated short names.
/O	Copies file ownership and ACL information.
/X	Copies file audit settings (implies /O).
/Y	Suppresses prompting to confirm you want to overwrite an existing destination file.
/-Y	Causes prompting to confirm you want to overwrite an existing destination file.
/Z	Copies networked files in restartable mode.

The switch /Y may be preset in the COPYCMD environment variable. This may be overridden with /-Y on the command line.

ANSI.SYS KEYBOARD SCANCODE VALUES

APPENDIX

C

Key	Standard	With Shift	With Ctrl	With Alt
A	97	65	1	0;30
B	98	66	2	0;48
C	99	67	3	0;46
D	100	68	4	0;32
E	101	69	5	0:18
F	102	70	6	0;33
G	103	71	7	0;34
H	104	72	8	0;35
I	105	73	9	0;23
J	106	74	10	0;36
K	107	75	11	0;37
L	108	76	12	0;38
M	109	77	13	0;50
N	110	78	14	0;49
O	111	79	15	0;24
P	112	80	16	0;25
Q	113	81	17	0;16
R	114	82	18	0;19
S	115	83	19	0;31

Key	Standard	With Shift	With Ctrl	With Alt
T	116	84	20	0;20
U	117	85	21	0;22
V	118	86	22	0;47
W	119	87	23	0;17
X	120	88	24	0;45
Y	121	89	25	0;21
Z	122	90	26	0;44
1	49	33	N/A	0;120
2	50	64	0	0;121
3	51	35	N/A	0;122
4	52	36	N/A	0;123
5	53	37	N/A	0;124
6	54	94	30	0;125
7	55	38	N/A	0;126
8	56	42	N/A	0;126
9	57	40	N/A	0;127
0	48	41	N/A	0;129
–	45	95	31	0;130
=	61	43	N/A	0;131
[	91	123	27	0;26
]	93	125	29	0;27
Space Bar	92	124	28	0;43
;	59	58	N/A	0;39
'	39	34	N/A	0;40
,	44	60	N/A	0;51
.	46	62	N/A	0;52
/	47	63	N/A	0;53
`	96	126	N/A	0;41
Enter (keypad)	13	N/A	10	0;166
/ (keypad)	47	47	0;142	0;74

Key	Standard	With Shift	With Ctrl	With Alt
* (keypad)	42	0;144	0;78	N/A
- (keypad)	45	45	0;149	0;164
+ (keypad)	43	43	0;150	0;55
5 (keypad)	0;76	53	0;143	N/A
F1	0;59	0;84	0;94	0;104
F2	0;60	0;85	0;95	0;105
F3	0;61	0;86	0;96	0;106
F4	0;62	0;87	0;97	0;107
F5	0;63	0;88	0;98	0;108
F6	0;64	0;89	0;99	0;109
F7	0;65	0;90	0;100	0;110
F8	0;66	0;91	0;101	0;111
F9	0;67	0;92	0;102	0;112
F10	0;68	0;93	0;103	0;113
F11	0;133	0;135	0;137	0;139
F12	0;134	0;136	0;138	0;140
Home	0;71	55	0;119	N/A
↑	0;72	56	0;141	N/A
PgUp	0;73	57	0;132	N/A
←	0;75	52	0;115	N/A
→	0;77	54	0;116	N/A
End	0;79	49	0;117	N/A
↓	0;80	50	0;145	N/A
PgDn	0;81	51	0;118	N/A
Insert	0;82	48	0;146	N/A
Delete	0;83	46	0;147	N/A
Print Screen	N/A	N/A	0;114	N/A
Pause	N/A	N/A	0;0	N/A
Backspace	8	8	127	0
Enter	13	N/A	10	0

Key	Standard	With Shift	With Ctrl	With Alt
Tab	9	0;5	0;148	0;165
Home (directional keypad)	224;71	224;71	224;119	224;151
↑ (directional keypad)	224;72	224;72	224;141	224;152
PgUp (directional keypad)	224;73	224;73	224;132	224;153
← (directional keypad)	224;75	224;75	224;115	224;155
→ (directional keypad)	224;77	224;77	224;116	224;157
End (directional keypad)	224;79	224;79	224;117	224;159
↓ (directional keypad)	224;80	224;80	224;145	224;154
PgDn (directional keypad)	224;81	224;81	224;118	224;161
Insert (directional keypad)	224;82	224;82	224;146	224;162
Delete (directional keypad)	224;83	224;83	224;147	224;163

ADDING WINDOWS MILLENNIUM EDITION COMPONENTS

Windows Millennium Edition is very customizable. How Windows Millennium Edition looks and what is installed depends on what choices you, or someone else, made when Windows Millennium Edition was installed. You may add the missing components later, but you must use the original CD-ROM to load them. If you purchased your computer with Windows Millennium Edition already installed on it and you did not get a Windows Millennium Edition CD-ROM, you have two choices: (1) contact the manufacturer of your computer to find out how you can get the missing components, or (2) purchase the Windows Millennium Edition upgrade. The following activity will demonstrate how to identify and add missing components. If you are in a lab environment, read but do not do this activity.

D.1   ACTIVITY—ADDING AND REMOVING WINDOWS COMPONENTS

Step 1   Click **Start**. Click **Help**.

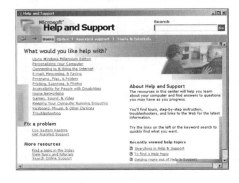

WHAT'S
HAPPENING?   You have opened the help window. Help remembers the topics that you
viewed and lists them in the lower part of the Help window.

Step 2   Click **Programs, Files, & Folders**.

Step 3   Click **Running programs & utilities**.

Step 4   Click **Starting a Windows game**.

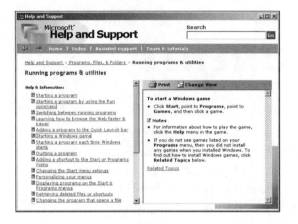

WHAT'S
HAPPENING?   You see the instructions for how to start a game. You are told that, if
you tried to follow the instructions and found no games to play on your
system, you can click Related Topics.

Step 5   Click **Related Topics**.

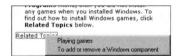

WHAT'S
HAPPENING?   There are two choices here—to play the game or to add or remove a
Windows component.

Step 6   Click **To add or remove a Windows component**.

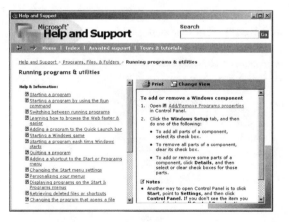

WHAT'S
HAPPENING?   Here are instructions for how to install a missing component. This
procedure is an example of hypertext. Remember, hypertext allows you

to jump from one logically related topic to another. You did not have to return to the categories as you would have had to do in a sequential search for information. In addition, when you see a link with a right-bent arrow, clicking it will take you to the appropriate place so you make your changes.

Step 7   Click the right-bent arrow next to the link.

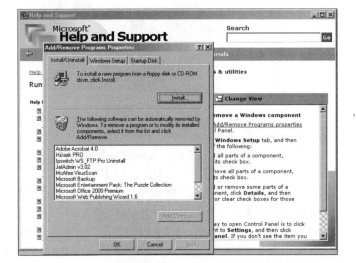

WHAT'S HAPPENING?   Windows Millennium Edition took you to the property sheets that deal with adding and removing programs. You could click the Change View button in the help window so that you could follow the help directions while you were in the Add/Remove Programs Properties sheets.

Step 8   Click the **Windows Setup** tab.

WHAT'S HAPPENING?   Windows Millennium Edition first looks to see what components are installed on your computer. When it determines this, you see the following screen:

You were taken to the correct property sheet—Add/Remove Programs Properties. (You may also access this property sheet by double-clicking My Computer, double-clicking the Control Panel folder, and then double-clicking the Add/Remove Programs icon.) Your entries may differ in the Add/Remove Programs Properties dialog box, depending on what was installed on your system. If you look at the property sheet in this example, you see that the highlighted entry Accessibility has a check mark in its check box. The check mark means that Accessibility Options was installed on this system. If you do not see a check mark in this check box, Accessibility Options was not installed. If installed, Accessibility Options occupies 4.7 MB of disk space. If you look in the Description box at the bottom of the dialog box, you see a description of the option indicating that two out of two components were selected.

If you look at the fourth entry, Communications, you see a check mark in the check box, but the check box is grayed, . A check box with a check mark but grayed check indicates that some of the options were installed, but not all.

Note: **Working on your own computer.** The following steps will demonstrate how to add missing Windows Millennium Edition components. If you want to take steps to add a component, you may need to have the Windows Millennium Edition CD-ROM available.

Working in a lab. If you are in a lab environment, you must not take these steps. Simply read the steps so that you understand how to complete the procedure.

Step 9   Click **Communications**.

WHAT'S HAPPENING? In this example, the Description area tells you that only 8 of 10 components were installed. Your Description might be different.

Step 10 Click **Details**. Click the down arrow in the scroll box.

WHAT'S HAPPENING? In this example, Internet Connection Sharing is one of the items not installed.

Step 11 Do not click the check box; instead, click the words **Internet Connection Sharing**.

The description tells you that this feature would allow you to share a single Internet connection if you had several computers.

Step 12 Click **Cancel**. Click **Accessories**. Click **Details**.

 In this example, all the items have a check mark, indicating that all components were installed. If you clear a check mark in a box, you will remove the item. If you click an empty box and add a check mark, you will add the item. The items to choose from are in a list box. A ***list box*** is exactly what you would think, a list of items from which you can select what interests you. Sometimes the list will not fit into one window. If the entries do not fit into one window, a scroll bar appears. The scroll bar allows you to move up or down through the list so you can see all the items. If you click the up arrow, you move up one entry, and, if you click the down arrow, you move down one entry. In addition, there is a scroll box that allows you to drag the box to move rapidly through the list, rather than move one item at a time.

Step 13 Click the check box for **Desktop Wallpaper.**

 Since this item was installed on this example, clearing the check box would remove Desktop Wallpaper from the system. You see that .6 MB would be freed up on your hard drive.

Step 14 Click the check box for **Desktop Wallpaper** so that there is a check mark in it. Scroll through the list until you are at the bottom of the list.

What's Happening? As you can see in this example, all the Accessories components have been installed.

Step 15 Click **Cancel**.

What's Happening? Using this process, you could go through each item on the list, choosing to add or remove components. Once you made your selections, you would click OK. At that point, you would be asked to insert the correct disc. If programs were to be removed, Windows Millennium Edition would give you a message that it was deleting programs. If you were adding programs, you would see a progress bar indicating that the necessary files were being copied to the hard drive. You would then be returned to the desktop. You would have completed the installation or removal of the components. The most important thing to remember is that to add or remove components you *must* have the Windows Millennium Edition CD-ROM.

Step 16 Click **Cancel**. Close Help.

What's Happening? You have returned to the desktop.

GLOSSARY

Absolute path The direct route from a root directory to the subdirectory of interest; the hierarchical structure of a directory tree.

Active window The window that is currently in use when multiple windows are open.

Adapter cards Printed circuit boards that are installed in a computer to allow the installation and use of some type of device, such as a monitor.

Adapter segment The area between the end of conventional memory and the beginning of extended memory. See also *Upper memory area*.

Add-on An accessory or utility program designed to work with, extend, and increase the capabilities of an original product.

All folders pane The left pane of the Explorer window.

Allocation unit See *Cluster*.

Alphanumeric keys The keys on the keyboard that include the letters (A to Z), the digits (0 to 9), and other characters such as the punctuation characters.

ALU Arithmetic logic unit. It is the circuitry that a computer uses for mathematical and logical functions and is an integral part of the microprocessor chip.

Applets Smaller, less powerful versions of application software. They frequently have expanded features a user needs.

Application packages See *Application software*.

Application program See *Application software*.

Application software Computer programs that are user-oriented and are usually for a specific job, such as word processing. Application packages are also called packages, off-the-shelf software, canned software, or apps.

Application window The window of an application that is currently open and on the desktop. An application window may also contain a document window.

Apps See *Application software*.

Archival backup Backup procedure in which all the files on the hard disk are copied to floppy disks or some other backup medium.

Archival data Information that is stored in archive files.

Archive attribute See *Archive bit*.

Archive bit File attribute that gives the backup history of a file, telling whether or not a file has been backed up since the last time it changed. Usually refers to long-term storage.

Archive files Remove files from the hard disk and store them on another medium.

ASCII An acronym for American Standard Code for Information Interchange. It is a coding scheme used for transmitting data between a computer and peripherals. Each character has its own numerical equivalent in ASCII.

ASCII sort sequence The order in which data is sorted based on assigned decimal numbers.

Associate Save time by associating a set of files that are all generated by the same program.

Asynchronous Not synchronized or not happening at regular time intervals.

Asynchronous communication Form of data transmission that comes into play when only two wires are used for communication between computers (generally via modems). Data is transmitted by sending one character at a time with variable time intervals between characters and a start bit and a stop bit to mark the beginning and end of the data.

AUTOEXEC.BAT Batch file (set of specific commands) that automatically executes every time the system is booted.

AutoPlay Whenever an audio CD is placed in a CD-ROM drive, it will automatically play. To bypass this, hold the Shift key down when inserting a disk.

AutoRun Whenever a program CD is placed in a CD-ROM drive, it will automatically begin executing the program on the CD. To bypass this, hold the Shift key down when inserting a disk.

Background printing Printing a document in one program while another program is active.

Background program In Windows, which has multitasking capabilities, background program refers to a program that executes in the background while the user is working with another program in the foreground. For example, printing one document (in the background program) while editing another document (in the foreground program).

Backup Copy of an original file or files made by a user for safekeeping.

Bank switching Method of expanding an operating system's memory by switching rapidly between two banks of memory chips.

Batch file Text file of DOS commands. When its name is keyed in at the DOS system level, the commands in the batch file are executed sequentially.

Batch processing Manner of running programs without interruption. Programs to be executed are collected and placed into prioritized batches, and then the programs are processed one after another without user interaction or intervention.

Baud rate Measure of how fast a modem can transmit data. Named after the French telegrapher and engineer Jean-Maurice-Emile Baudot.

Beta testing Formal process of pretesting hardware and software that is still under development with selected "typical" users to see whether any operational or utilization errors (bugs) still exist in the program before it is released to the general public.

Binary value Variable length set of hexadecimal digits.

BIOS An acronym for Basic Input/Output System. It is a program that controls input/output devices.

BIOS bootstrap The program that controls this process is in the BIOS chip and the CMOS setup of the computer. The POST (power-on self-test) is performed before booting to check the physical health of the computer. Plug-and-Play devices are identified and configured, and a bootable partition is executed.

Bit The smallest unit of information, expressed in binary numbers 0 and 1, that a computer can measure. Eight bits make a byte.

Bitmapped font Fonts from the screen and printer that are created from a series of dots. When displayed on the monitor, bitmapped fonts are created from a series of pixels.

Boot Start the computer by loading the operating system files, from the booting disk, into memory.

Boot record Record that contains disk information such as the type of media, number of tracks and sectors, and so forth. If a disk is a system disk, the boot record contains the bootstrap routine used for loading. Otherwise, the disk will present a message that the disk is a non-system disk. Every disk has a boot record.

Boot sector virus Virus that replaces a disk's original boot sector with its own and then loads the virus into memory. Once in memory, it infects other disks.

Bootable disk Disk containing the operating system files.

Booting the system Process of powering on the computer and loading the operating system into memory.

Bootstrap The process a computer uses to get itself ready for loading the operating system into memory. The OS pulls itself up by its "bootstraps."

Browser An application software package that allows you to easily explore the Internet and the World Wide Web.

Buffer Temporary holding area in memory for data.

Bug Error in software that causes programs to malfunction or produce incorrect results.

Built-in font Resident font that comes with a printer.

Bulletin Board Service (BBS) A service that users link to by using their modems. Some BBSs allow users to read and post messages, download program fixes or other programs, and much more.

Bundled One or more programs included with a larger program to make the larger program more attractive or functional. With hardware, the software necessary to install the device.

Bus A set of hardware lines (wires) that are used for data transfer among the elements of a computer system.

Business resumption plan Disaster and recovery plan that covers the entire business spectrum.

Byte A unit of measurement that represents one character (a letter, number, or punctuation symbol). A byte is comprised of eight bits. Computer storage and memory are measured in bytes.

Cache memory A place in memory where data can be stored for quick access.

Caching A process where the OS sets up a reserved area in RAM where it can quickly access frequently used data prior to reading from or writing to the disk.

Cascade Layer windows one on top of another.

Cascading menu A menu that opens another menu. Thus, a secondary menu will open as a result of a command issued on the first, or primary, menu. A right-pointing arrow next to the primary menu indicates that a cascading menu is available.

Case-sensitive Describes a program that distinguishes between upper- and lowercase characters.

CD-ROM Acronym for compact disc read-only memory. Usually refers to the disc that plays in a CD-ROM device.

Central processing unit See *CPU*.

Chaining Process of linking together two or more batch files.

Chains When referring to the file allocation table, pointers link clusters together to form chains.

Character device Computer device (i.e., keyboard or printer) that receives or sends information one character at a time.

Character string Set of letters, symbols, and/or control characters that are treated as a unit.

Checkbox A box that is clicked to either set or unset a feature.

Child directory An offshoot (subdirectory) of any root directory or subdirectory.

Child menu In a hierarchical menu structure, a menu that is under the parent menu. Each subsequent child menu becomes a parent to the next menu down in the hierarchy.

Child window A window that belongs to a parent window. A child window can have only one parent window but one or more child windows of its own.

Clean boot When the CONFIG.SYS and AUTOEXEC.BAT files are bypassed during the boot process.

Click Press and release the left mouse button once.

Client In networking, a computer that accesses the shared network resources provided by the server.

Close button A button that shuts down a document window, application window, or dialog box.

Cluster The smallest unit of disk space that DOS or Windows 95/98 can write to or read from. It is comprised of one or more sectors. A cluster can also be called an allocation unit.

Cluster overhang Since clusters are made up of one or more 512-byte sectors and Windows 95/98 reads from or writes to an entire cluster at a time, a file will occupy more space than it needs for its data, causing cluster overhang.

CMOS An acronym for complimentary metal-oxide semiconductor. CMOS, maintained by battery pack, is memory that is used to store parameter values, such as the size and type of hard disk(s), the number and type of floppy drive(s) and keyboard and display information, that are used to boot PCs.

Coaxial cable A type of cable used in connecting network components.

Combo box A combination text box and interdependent list box.

Command An instruction, which is a program, that the user keys in at the command line prompt. This instruction then executes the selected program.

Command button A button that, when selected by the user, carries out a command.

Command interpreter See *Command processor*.

Command processor That portion of an operating system that interprets what the user keys in.

Command specification (comspec) The location of COMMAND.COM; information needed by DOS to reload the transient portion of COMMAND.COM. The default is the root directory of the booting disk unless altered by the user in CONFIG.SYS.

Command syntax The vocabulary, order, and punctuation necessary to execute a command properly.

COMMAND.COM That part of the OS that the user actually communicates and interacts with. It processes and interprets what has been keyed in. Also known as the command processor or command interpreter.

Communication protocol Set of communication rules that enable computers to exchange information.

Compact disc See *CD-ROM*.

Compound document A document that contains information or other objects created from more than one application program.

Compressed file File written by a file-compression utility program that minimizes the amount of storage space needed.

Compressed volume file (CVF) A single file, created and compressed by DriveSpace, that contains all the data for a drive.

Computer virus A computer program designed as a prank or as sabotage that can replicate itself by attaching to other programs and spreading unwanted and harmful operations. A virus can be spread to other computers by floppy disk and/or through electronic bulletin boards.

Comspec See *Command specification (comspec)*.

CON Device name that is reserved by the OS for the keyboard and the monitor.

Concatenate Put together. See also *Concatenate files*.

Concatenate files Combine the contents of two or more text files into a new file.

Conditional processing A comparison of two items that yields a true or false value. Once the value is determined, a program can be directed to take some action based on the results of the test.

Configuration data Information about your system such as the hardware and user preferences.

Connection profile When you first set up a remote computer connection, you will save settings for the connection and assign an icon. This icon can then be double-clicked to connect you based on those settings.

Context menu See *Pop-up menu*.

Contiguous Next to each other. Contiguous files are written to adjacent clusters on a disk.

Control A means by which a user can provide input for available choices. A control is a way to initiate an action, display information, or set values. Examples of controls include command buttons, options buttons, drop-down list boxes, and text boxes.

Control key Key labeled Ctrl on the keyboard that, when held down with another key, causes that key to have another meaning.

Control menu An icon located in the left corner of a window that can be opened to provide commands to manipulate the window.

Controller Board that goes into the computer and is needed to operate a peripheral device.

Control-menu icon In Windows, the icon that can be clicked to provide a drop-down menu with commands. Also called the Control-menu box.

Conventional memory The first 640KB of memory where programs and data are located while the user is working.

Copy-protected disks Disks that cannot be backed up with regular DOS commands.

CPU Acronym for central processing unit. The CPU is the brain of the computer that carries out the instructions or commands given to it by a program.

Cross-linked files Two files that claim the same sectors in the file allocation table (FAT).

CRT Cathode-ray tube. Another name for the monitor.

Current directory The default directory.

Cursor The location where the user can key in information.

Customized prompt A prompt that has been modified to suit the needs or preferences of the user.

Cyberspace A term that refers to the Internet; interconnected computers create this virtual place where individuals or organizations can communicate.

Cylinder The vertical measurement of two or more disk platters that have aligned tracks. Used when referring to hard disks.

Daisy-wheel printer Computer printer that uses a rotating plastic wheel as a printing element. The quality of print is comparable to that of a carbon-ribbon typewriter. Daisy-wheel printers were considered high quality printers until laser printers became available.

Data Information in the widest possible sense. Usually it refers to the numbers and text entered into a computer by a user.

Data bits Group of bits used to represent a single character for transmission over a modem. A start bit and stop bit must be used in transmitting a group of data.

Data files Files composed of related data that are created by the user with an application program. They are organized in a specific manner and usually can be used only by the program that created them.

Database   Collection of related information (data) organized, structured, and stored on a computer so that the information can be easily manipulated.

Database-management programs   Application programs that allow for manipulation of information in a database.

Debug   Find and correct problems in a program. Also a program at the command line interface.

Default   The value that the computer system or computer program falls back to if no other specific instructions are given.

Default drive   Disk drive that the OS looks on to locate commands or files if no other instructions are given.

Default folder   The folder that will be automatically used unless you change the default.

Default subdirectory   Subdirectory that the computer falls back to when no other specific instructions are given.

Delimiter   A special character used to separate information so that an OS can recognize where one part of a parameter ends and the next part begins.

Designated drive   See *Default drive*.

Desktop   In Windows, an onscreen work area that simulates the work area of a desk.

Destination file   File location to which data is sent.

Device   A piece of computer equipment, such as a disk drive or a printer, that performs a specific job.

Device driver   Software necessary for the use of hardware devices. The program controls the specific peripheral devices.

Device icons   A small graphic that represents a device, such as a printer or a disk drive.

Device name   Reserved name that the OS assigns to a device, such as PRN for printer.

Dialog box   In a graphical user interface, a box that either conveys a message to or requests information from the user.

DIB (device-independent bitmap)   Format that allows you to display any graphic file no matter what video mode you are using.

Differential backup   A process that backs up all the selected files that have changed since the last time you used the "All selected files" backup choice.

Direct read   When an application program bypasses the OS and reads information directly from a disk.

Direct write   When an application program bypasses the OS and writes information directly to a disk.

Directional keys   Keys used to move the cursor in various directions.

Directive   Used in the CONFIG.SYS file to refer to the available commands.

Directory   Index or list of files that the OS maintains for each disk. The DIR command displays this list, as does Explorer.

Directory tree   The structure of a disk drive.

Dirty data   The result of a failed attempt, in write-caching, to save a file to disk. Instead of the file being saved to disk, it is written back to cache memory.

Disaster and recovery plan   A plan for backing up data files in case something happens to the original data.

Disk   Magnetically coated disk that allows permanent storage of computer data.

Disk buffer   Acts as the go-between for the disk and RAM.

Disk caching   An area in memory where Windows 95 looks for information prior to reading from or writing to the disk for the purpose of optimizing performance.

Disk compression　A means to increase disk space by using special programs that fool the operating system into thinking that there is more space on the disk than actually exists.

Disk drive　A device that rotates a disk so that the computer can read information from and write data to the disk.

Disk files　Files that are stored on a disk.

Disk intensive　A description of programs that are constantly reading records from and writing records to a disk.

Disk optimization　A means for enhancing performance on a disk, it is usually accomplished by running the Disk Defrag program that rearranges the storage of files on a disk so that they are contiguous.

Docucentric　Describes a paradigm or model that designs a computer system or program based on the fact that what is most important to the user is his or her data (document), not the program that created it.

Document　Write the purpose of and instructions for a computer program.

Document file　A data file that was created in an application program and then saved to disk.

Documentation　Written instructions that inform a user how to use hardware and/or software.

Documents　Saved files that store the data created in applications.

Domain name　An alphabetic alias to the IP address. Some examples of domain names are **saddleback.cc.ca.us** or **daedal.net**.

Domain name system (DNS)　The system by which domain names are translated into their numeric IP addresses.

DOS　Acronym for Disk Operating System, which refers to the character-based operating system commonly used on microcomputers. It is also a short-

hand way of referring to the command line interface.

Dot　A subdirectory marker; the . for the specific subdirectory name.

Dot-matrix printer　A printer that produces text characters and graphics by creating them with a series of closely spaced dots. It uses a print-head, platen, and ribbon to print the characters.

Double dot　A subdirectory marker; the . . for the parent directory of the current subdirectory.

Double-click　Press and release the mouse button twice in rapid succession.

Download　Receive a file from a remote computer using a modem.

Downward compatibility　Characteristic of software/hardware that can be used on older computer systems.

Drag　Move or manipulate objects on the screen by holding down the left mouse button.

Drag and drop　A feature that enables the user to move or manipulate an object or document and drop it at another location.

Drive letter　Letter of the alphabet that identifies a specific disk drive.

Drop-down combo box　A box that combines the characteristics of a text box with those of a drop-down list box.

Drop-down list box　A box that contains a default selection. A user can click on the down arrow to drop down a list box that displays further choices.

Drop-down menus　Menus on the menu bar that, when clicked, drop down a list of choices and remain open on the screen until the user chooses a menu item or closes the menu.

Dummy files　Files without particular meaning, usually created for test purposes.

Dummy parameters　See *Replaceable parameters*.

DVD　An enhancement to CD-ROM technology. It provides the next generation of optical disc storage technology. It encompasses audio, video, and computer data. DVD is not an acronym but a trademark.

DWORD In the Registry, DWORD values are data that are represented by a number four bytes long.

Dynamic Data Exchange (DDE) A set of standards that supports data exchange among application programs.

Edit Alter the contents of a file. Also the text editor that was introduced in DOS 5.0.

Electronic bulletin board Forum where people exchange ideas or solve computer problems. Usually accessed by a modem.

Ellipsis Three dots that appear after a menu item. If you choose the item, a dialog box will open.

Email An acronym for electronic mail. Notes or messages sent among different computers that use telecommunications services or are on a network.

Embed Take data (an object) from a document in one application and place it in another document in a different application.

Enhancements Hardware and/or software added or updated to increase the capabilities of a computer.

Environment Area in memory that stores a list of specifications that the OS and other application programs can read.

EOF (end of file) A symbol that alerts the OS when a file has no more data.

Event An action performed by you or by your program that your computer can notify you of. Usually the notification is a sound, such as a beep if you press an incorrect key.

Executables Programs that place instructions in memory. The instructions are followed by the computer.

Executing the program The process during which instructions for running a program are placed in memory and then followed by the computer.

Exit code A program that sets a code when it finishes executing, indicating some condition.

Expanded memory Additional hardware added to the computer that makes more memory available. Only programs that are designed to use expanded memory can take advantage of it.

Expanded memory emulator A memory manager that uses extended memory to emulate expanded memory.

Expanded memory manager (EMM) A software program that must be installed in order to use expanded memory.

Expansion slots Empty slots or spaces inside the system unit that can be used for adding new boards or devices to expand the computer's capabilities.

Export Send the data from one file to another file.

Extended memory Memory above 1 MB. Most programs do not know how to access extended memory.

Extended memory manager (XMS) A software program that must be installed prior to using extended memory.

Extension See *File extension*.

External command Program that resides on a disk and must be read into RAM before it can be used.

External storage media Storage that is outside the computer system. Floppy disks, CD-ROMs, or removable disks (such as Jaz or Zip disks) are the most common external storage media.

FAT (file allocation table) A map of a disk that keeps track of all the clusters on the disk. Used in conjunction with the directory table.

File Collection of related information stored on a disk.

File allocation table (FAT) See *FAT (file allocation table)*.

File attributes Characteristics that describe and/or supply other information about a file. File attributes can be viewed in a file's directory entry.

File extension   The portion of a file name that follows the last period. Usually the last three letters of the file name. File extensions indicate the type of data in the file.

File format   A special format used to construct a file so an application program can read the data. It consists of special codes understandable only by the application program that created the file.

File handle   Two-byte number DOS uses to refer to an open file or device.

File infector virus   Virus that adds programming instructions to files that run programs. The virus then becomes active when you run the program.

File name   A label used to identify a file. When most users refer to the file name, they are referring to the file specification.

File server   On a network, a file storage device that stores files. On a large network, a file server is a sophisticated device that not only stores files but manages them and maintains order as network users request files and make changes to the files.

File specification   Complete name of a file, including the file name and the file extension (file type).

File type   See *File extension*.

Filters   Commands that alter input by reading the information, changing the input, and writing the results to the screen.

Firmware   Software and hardware that are designed for specific tasks and have been permanently stored in ROM (read-only memory) rather than on a disk. Firmware usually cannot be modified by the user.

Fixed disk   See *Hard disk*.

Fixed parameters   Parameters whose values are specific and limited.

Flag   A marker of some type used to process information. File attributes are commonly called flags because they indicate a particular condition of a file.

Floating   Description of a toolbar or taskbar that can be positioned anywhere on the screen and does not have to be anchored to a window.

Floppy disk drive   See *Disk drive*.

Floppy disks   Magnetically coated disks that allow permanent storage of data. A removable medium.

Flushing the buffer   A process in which the OS writes information to a disk after a buffer has been filled.

Folder icon   The graphic representation of a folder that opens the folder when you double-click on it.

Folder   Location or container where documents, program files, devices, and other folders are stored on your disk. The terms folders and directories are synonymous.

Font   A typeface (set of characters) that consists of several parts, such as the type size and weight, (i.e., bold or italic).

Foreground   The area of the desktop where the user is currently working.

Foreground application   An application or window that the user is currently working on.

Foreground window   See *Foreground application*.

Form feed   Operation that advances the printer to a new page at the end of a print job.

Format   Prepare a disk for use. Can also be used to refer to the layout of data in a document.

Formatting   See *Format*.

Four-color printers   Printers that use a combination of four colors, each of which is printed separately. These printers produce high-quality color output.

Fragmented   See *Fragmented disks*.

Fragmented disks   Disks that have many noncontiguous files on them.

Fragmented files Files that are written to disk in noncontiguous clusters. See also *Noncontiguous (files)*.

Free system resources Resources that are left over after the operating system manages system resources, such as screen redraw or the status of available memory. Not to be confused with available memory.

FTP (file transfer protocol) A protocol that allows files to be transferred to and from a node running FTP services.

Full backup A backup procedure that backs up every file on a disk, regardless of whether or not a file has changed.

Full system backup A backup procedure that backs up every file on a disk including special system files, regardless of whether or not a file has changed.

Function keys Programmable keys on a keyboard. F1 and F2 are examples of function keys. Function keys are program dependent.

Gig A colloquial term for gigabyte.

Gigabyte (GB) A unit of measurement equal to approximately one billion bytes.

Glide pad An input device that is a small, smooth object on which you move your finger to control the action of the pointer.

Global file specifications The symbols * and ?, also called wildcards, are used to represent a single character (?) or a group of characters (*) in a file name.

Graphical user interface (GUI) Display format that allows the user to manage computer resources and work with application programs by using pictorial representations and menu choices.

Graphics Pictures and drawings that can be produced on the screen or printer.

GUI See *Graphical user interface (GUI)*.

Hard copy The printed paper copy of information that is created when using the computer. Can also be referred to as printouts.

Hard disk A disk that is permanently installed in a computer system and has a larger capacity to store files than a floppy disk. Hard disks are measured in megabytes or gigabytes.

Hard disk drive See *Hard disk*.

Hardware Physical computer components.

Hardware interrupts A request for service or a signal from peripherals to the CPU for attention so the device may be serviced.

Head slot Exposes the disk surface to the read/write heads via an opening in the jacket of a floppy disk.

Heap Thirty-two-bit region of memory that is used by Windows to manage system resources.

Hexadecimal A numbering system that uses a base of 16 consisting of the digits 0–9 and the letters A–F.

Hidden attribute The characteristic of a file that prevents the OS from displaying the file in a directory list.

Hidden file File that is not displayed when the DIR command is used. In MS-DOS, the two hidden files are IO.SYS and MSDOS.SYS. In IBM PC-DOS, the two hidden files are IBMBIO.COM and IBMDOS.COM.

Hierarchical menu See *Cascading menu*.

Hierarchical structure The logical grouping of files and programs based on pathways between root directories and their subsequent directories. Also called a tree structure.

Hierarchy A dependent relationship where one folder is dependent on the folder above it. Every disk begins with the root directory (folder), with subsequent folders branching from the root.

High memory area (HMA) High memory is the first 64KB of extended memory. DOS 5.0 and above can be installed in high memory.

High-capacity disks See *High-density disks.*

High-density disks Floppy disks that can store up to 1.2 MB on a 5¼-inch disk or 1.44 MB on a 3½-inch disk.

High-level formatting Also known as logical formatting. The process that the OS uses to structure a disk so that files can be stored and retrieved.

Highlight Select an object, text, or icon. Objects must be selected before they can be acted upon. Highlighting is indicated by reverse video.

HKEY In the Registry, HKEY is an acronym for Handle to a KEY.

HKEY_CLASSES_ROOT In the Registry, this is an alias for HKEY_LOCAL_MACHINE. It contains settings for shortcuts, drag and drop, and file associations.

HKEY_CURRENT_CONFIG In the Registry, this is also an alias for HKEY _LOCAL_MACHINE, which contains the current configuration for your computer.

HKEY_CURRENT_USER In the Registry, this is an alias for the branch in HKEY_USERS that applies to the user who is currently logged on.

HKEY_DYN_DATA In the Registry, this is also an alias for HKEY_LOCAL_MACHINE, which contains variable information such as the status of a Plug-and-Play device.

HKEY_LOCAL_MACHINE In the Registry, this contains configuration data that is specific to your computer such as what hardware you have installed and your program settings. The information in this key applies to every user who uses your computer.

HKEY_USERS In the Registry, this is the other major key that contains the configuration information for any user who logs on to the computer. In addition to maintaining information that applies to all users on that machine, it also contains information that is specific to each user. There is a subkey for each user who has a profile.

Home page The first screen that appears when you access a Web site.

Housekeeping tasks Any number of routines to keep the computer system in good working order.

HTML (hypertext markup language) The programming language with which Web documents are created.

HTTP (hypertext transfer protocol) A method of access used on the Internet.

Hypertext link A means to easily jump from one logically related topic to the next.

IAP Internet access provider.

I/O See *Input/output.*

Icon Symbol that, when clicked, provides access to a program file or task.

Impact printer A printer that creates images with a mechanism that strikes a ribbon and transfers the images to paper. Uses a process similar to that of a typewriter.

Import Retrieve an existing file and insert it into another file.

Incremental backup A backup process that only backs up files that have changed since the last full or incremental backup.

Information superhighway A term that refers to the Internet. A worldwide network or set of networks that allows users to gather information, do research, explore ideas, purchase items, send email, and chat with people around the world. See *Cyberspace.*

.INI files In previous versions of Windows, the operating system and most application programs stored information about users, environmental parameters, and necessary drivers in .INI files. The .INI extension is derived from the term initialization files.

Initialization files Files that initialize a program or process.

Initializing The process of getting a medium (disks or files) ready for use.

Inkjet printer A nonimpact printer that prints by spraying a matrix of dots onto the paper.

In-place editing The process of altering an object created in another document without having to open that document. The menus and toolbars of the current program are temporarily replaced with the menus and toolbars of the program that created the object being edited.

Input Data or information entered into the computer.

Input buffer Portion of computer memory that has been set aside to store data before it is processed.

Input device A means to get information into RAM by communicating with the computer. Typical input devices include the keyboard or the mouse.

Input/output The process of data and program instructions going into and out of the CPU (central processing unit). Also referred to as I/O.

Insert mode A mode that allows a user to enter data so that new text is inserted at the cursor and pushes all text that follows to the right.

Install Place files (programs) from a CD or floppy disk onto the hard disk.

Integrated circuit Electronic device that combines thousands of transistors on a small wafer of silicon (chip). Such devices are the building blocks of computers.

Integrated pointing device An input device on the keyboard that is shaped like an eraser and that you can manipulate to control cursor movement.

Interactive Describes the ability to update data instantaneously within the computer system.

Interactive booting Process of loading the OS into memory during which you will be asked by the operating system if you want to execute each line in the CONFIG.SYS and AUTOEXEC.BAT files.

Interactive processing Manner of running programs in which the user must intervene or enter input. Sometimes called online or real-time mode.

Interface Hardware and/or software needed to connect computer components. Also used as a synonym for the computer environment with which the user interacts.

Internal commands A part of the operating system file, COMMAND.COM, that includes commands loaded into memory when the operating system is booted and remain resident in memory until the computer is turned off.

Internet A network that connects computer users around the world.

IO.SYS One of the hidden system files that make up the operating system of MS-DOS. This file manages the input/output devices.

IP address A unique numeric address that identifies a computer on the Internet.

ISP Internet service provider.

Keyboard Main device used for entering data into a computer. It consists of a typewriter-like collection of labeled keys.

Keyboard buffer See *Input buffer*.

Keys In the Registry, keys and subkeys are similar in concept to folders and subfolders in Explorer. At the top of the Registry's hierarchy are the keys. Registry keys can also have several keys or subkeys. This phenomenon is known as nesting.

Kilobyte (KB) A unit of measurement equal to 1,024 bytes. Abbreviated as KB or K.

LAN Acronym for local area network. Network of computer equipment and connected by a communication link that enables any device to interact with any other device in the network. Enables users to exchange information, share peripherals, and draw on common resources.

Landscape Printing orientation in which the paper is printed horizontally (sideways).

Laser printer A high-resolution, nonimpact printer that provides letter-quality output of text and graphics. Characters are formed by a laser and are made visible by the same technology used by photocopy machines.

Last known good A shorthand way of saying that USER.DAT and SYSTEM.DAT were saved the last time you successfully booted.

Left justified Describes text that is lined up on the left side of the page.

Legacy hardware Hardware that is not Plug-and-Play compatible.

Legacy software Older versions of software that were designed to run on earlier versions of an operating system, such as DOS.

Light pen A pointing device that is connected to the computer by a cable and resembles a pen. It is used to provide input to the computer when the user writes, sketches, or selects commands on a special monitor designed to respond to the light pen.

LIM EMS standard An acronym for Lotus Intel Microsoft Expanded Memory Specifications. Standards designed for adding memory to DOS-based systems. Called LIM EMS because it was developed as the result of a Lotus/Intel/Microsoft collaboration.

Line editor Text-editing program that numbers each line of text and then allows the user to edit the text only one line at a time. EDLIN is a line editor that was included with DOS.

Line feed Operation that advances the hard copy to the next line of text whether or not the line is full.

Link Establish a connection between two applications and their data.

Linked object In object linking and embedding, an object that is automatically updated in the destination

document whenever any changes are made to the object in the source document.

List box A box that presents a user with a list of options. Used in menus and dialog boxes.

Loaded Describes information (data or programs) that has been retrieved and placed into memory.

Loading See *Loaded.*

Local area network See *LAN.*

Local bus See *Bus.*

Locally In a networked environment, describes a process that bypasses the network and accesses only your own computer.

Logged drive See *Default drive.*

Logical device Device named by the logic of a software system regardless of its physical relationship to the system.

Logical disk drives Drives named by the logic of the software (operating) system. Imaginary drives that act exactly like real disk drives.

Logical formatting See *High-level formatting.*

Logical view A view in which items are represented by icons rather than according to their hierarchical structure.

Long file names (LFNs) The term used in Windows to indicate that file names are no longer limited by the 8.3 naming rules. In Windows, file names cannot exceed 255 characters.

Look-ahead buffer A secondary buffer cache used to store contents of files being accessed by programs.

Loop A set of statements executed repeatedly within a program.

Loop back The address 127.0.0.1, which is used to send data to your own computer without using the network card. The data "loops back."

Lost clusters Clusters that have no directory entry in the directory table and do not belong to any file. They are debris that result from incomplete data and should be cleaned up periodically with ScanDisk.

Low-level formatting Also known as physical formatting. The process of numbering the tracks and sectors of a disk sequentially so that each can be identified. On a hard disk, this process is done by the manufacturer of the hard disk.

Macro A user-defined keyboard command that executes a sequence of saved instructions to accomplish a given task.

Main memory See *RAM (random access memory)*.

Mandatory parameters Parameters that must be used with a command.

Manual links In object linking and embedding, a linked object that is not updated automatically when changes are made in the source document. The user must choose to update the object.

Mapped drive A shared network drive or folder that you may assign a local drive letter.

Master boot record (MBR) Used before booting, it determines the location of the bootable partition of the hard disk and gives control over to it.

Maximize button A button that makes the current window fill the entire screen.

Meg A colloquial term for megabyte.

Megabyte (MB) A unit of measurement that is roughly equal to one million bytes. Abbreviated as MB.

Megahertz (MHz) A unit of measurement used to compare clock speeds of computers.

Memory The temporary workspace of the computer where data and programs are kept while they are being worked on. Also referred to as RAM (random access memory). Information in RAM is lost when the computer is turned off, which is why memory is considered volatile.

Memory manager Utility program that controls and allocates memory resources.

Memory resident See *Memory-resident program*.

Memory-resident program Program that remains in the computer memory after being loaded from disk. See also *Terminate-and-stay-resident (TSR) program*.

Menu A list of choices (selections) displayed on the screen from which the user chooses a course of action.

Menu bar A rectangular bar, usually in a program, in which the names of the available menus are shown. The user chooses one of these menus, and a list of choices for that menu is shown.

Menu-driven programs Programs that make extensive use of menus to present command choices and available options.

Message Text that appears on the screen to provide information to assist the user in completing a task, suggest an action, or inform the user of an error.

Message box A type of dialog box that informs the user of a condition.

Metastring Symbol used with the PROMPT command that returns a value for the symbol. For example, using the metastring "d" will return the system date.

Microcomputer A personal computer that is usually used by one person. Also referred to as a desktop computer or a stand-alone computer.

Microfloppy disk A 3½-inch floppy disk encased in a hard plastic shell.

MIDI (Musical Instrument Digital Interface) Used to get input from musical instruments into a computer and then modify and store the sounds recorded.

Minicomputer Mid-level computer larger than a microcomputer but smaller than a mainframe computer. Usually used to meet the needs of a small company or department.

Minifloppy disk A 5¼-inch floppy disk.

Minimize button A button that reduces the current window to a button on the taskbar.

Modem Short for modulator/demodulator. A device that provides communications among computers using phone lines. Modems are typically used to access online services, such as AOL (America Online) or an ISP to gain access to the Internet.

Monitor A device similar to a television screen that displays the input and output of the computer. Also called the screen, display screen, CRT (cathode-ray tube), or VDT (video display terminal).

Monospaced typeface A typeface that spaces all characters in the set evenly, regardless of character width.

Motherboard The main computer board that holds the memory and CPU, as well as slots for adapter cards. The power supply plugs directly into the motherboard.

Mouse A small, hand-held device that is equipped with one or more control buttons. It is used to control cursor movement.

Mouse pointer An onscreen pointer that is controlled by the movement of the mouse.

Mouse trails Ghost-pointer shapes of mouse pointers that follow the movement of the mouse around the screen. Used to improve visibility of the cursor.

MPC (Multimedia Personal Computer) A consortium that sets standards for multimedia.

MPC-2 The latest standard from the MPC (Multimedia Personal Computer) consortium.

MS-DOS Abbreviation for Microsoft Disk Operating System, which is a character-based operating system for computers that use the 8086 (or above) microprocessor.

MSDOS.SYS Hidden system file that is one of the files that makes up the operating system of MS-DOS. This file manages the disks.

Multitasking Term for the ability to work on more than one task or application program at a time.

Multithreading Term for the ability to work on more than one thread (small task) at a time.

Nesting In the Registry, this occurs when Registry keys have several keys or subkeys.

Net A colloquial name for the Internet.

Network A group of computers connected by a communication facility called a server, so that data can be shared and transmitted. The server also allows resources to be shared, such as a hard drive or a printer.

Network administrator The person who decides how the hardware and software will be used. The administrator decides who will have access to what devices on the network.

Nonbootable disk Disk that does not contain the operating system files; the computer cannot boot from it.

Noncontiguous (files) Files that are written to the disk in nonadjacent clusters.

Nonimpact printer A type of printer that transfers images onto paper by means of inkjet sprayers, melting ink, or lasers.

Notepad A text editor available in Windows.

Null value A user-defined value equivalent to nothing (no data).

Numeric keypad Separate set of keys, next to the main set of keys, that contain the digits 0 through 9. Also includes an alternate set of commands that correspond to Pg Up, the arrow keys, and so on. These functions are program dependent.

Object Most items in Windows are considered objects. Objects have properties, settings, and parameters and can be opened and manipulated.

Object linking and embedding (OLE) A method of allowing application programs to share information without needing to copy the physical data into each application.

Octet One of the four sections of the dotted decimal notation address.

Offline Describes a printer that is probably attached to the computer, but is not activated and ready to print.

OLE-aware Describes Windows application programs that support and recognize OLE.

OLE-compliant See *OLE-aware*.

Online Describes a printer that is not only attached to the computer, but also activated and ready for operation.

Online help Onscreen assistance that can be accessed on the computer without interrupting the work session. Consists of advice or instructions on utilizing a program's features.

On-the-fly compression See *Real-time compression*.

Operating system (OS) A master control program (set of programs) that manages the operation of all the parts of a computer. An operating system is loaded into memory when the computer is booted and is known as system software. It must be loaded prior to loading any application software.

Optimize a disk Make files contiguous on the disk. A function of utility programs.

Option button Shown in a list of choices that the user can choose from. Only one option can be selected at a time. Option buttons provide mutually exclusive choices.

Optional parameters Parameters that may be used with a command but are not mandatory.

Overhead Information that provides support to a computing process but often increases processing time.

Overlay files Segments of a large program that get loaded into memory as the program needs them. This allows a large program to fit into a limited amount of memory.

Overtype See *Typeover*.

Overwrite Replace old data with new data. When you copy a file from one location to another, the file that is copied usually overwrites the file that was there.

Overwrite mode Mode in which newly typed characters replace existing characters to the right of the cursor.

Packet A unit of information transferred between computers via network or modem connection.

Page The section of expanded memory that can be swapped in and out of the page frame.

Page frame Physical address in conventional memory where a page of expanded memory may be stored.

Pane When a window is divided, each division is considered a pane.

PANOSE file A file that is created for a particular font and stores information about the font's size, attributes, and design.

Parallel In data transmission, it describes the sending of one byte (eight bits) at one time.

Parameter A qualifier or modifier that can be added to a command to specify the action to be taken.

Parent directory The directory or subdirectory above the current subdirectory. The parent directory is always one step closer to the root than the child is.

Parent menu A menu in a hierarchical menu structure that is the top of the menu system. A parent menu may have a child menu; a child menu may become a parent and have child menus of its own.

Parent window A window that is the owner of any objects in it. If there is a folder in the window, it is a child to that parent. A child window can have only one parent, but it can have one or more child windows of its own.

Parity A simple method for checking for transmission errors. An extra bit is added to be sure that there is always either an even or an odd number of bits.

Partitioning Process of physically dividing a section of the hard disk from the other sections of the disk and then having the operating system treat that section as if it were a separate unit.

Password A unique string of text or numbers that identifies a user. Passwords are used for logging on to networks or when Windows 95 has been set up with user profiles.

Path The route that the OS must follow to locate programs and files on a disk that has more than one directory.

Path name Information that tells the OS where to look for the programs and files on a disk that has more than one folder (directory).

Pattern A design made up of a grid of dots that is repeated to fill the screen so that the desktop is decorated.

Pause Temporarily stop the execution of a program or a command by pressing Pause on the keyboard. Also a batch file subcommand.

PC-DOS A disk operating system that manages the computer's resources and allows the user to manage the files and devices of a computer. Developed for IBM Personal Computer by Microsoft. Virtually identical to MS-DOS.

Peer-to-peer network A network that has no dedicated servers and no hierarchy among the networked computers. All the computers are equal or peers. Each computer can function as either client or server.

Pels See *Pixel*.

Peripheral device Any device, such as a keyboard, monitor, or printer, that is connected to and controlled by the CPU.

Physical formatting See *Low-level formatting*.

Physical memory The actual memory chips in the computer.

Physical view The view of your folders that shows you the hierarchy of your file system, indicating what drives you have and where they are located.

Pipe Symbol used to string two or more programs together so that the output of one program becomes the input of another program. The pipe symbol is the ¦.

Pixel Smallest element on the display screen grid that can be stored or displayed. Pixels are used to create and/or print letters, numbers, or graphics. The more pixels there are per inch, the higher the resolution.

Plug and Play Feature of Windows that is supposed to automatically detect and configure a new hardware device when it is added to a computer system.

Point Position the tip of the mouse pointer over an object.

Pointer An arrow on the screen that represents the current cursor (mouse) location.

Points Fonts are measured in points. The more points, the larger the font. A point is $1/72$ of an inch.

Pop-up menu A menu that opens when the mouse pointer is positioned over an object and the right mouse button is clicked. See also *Shortcut menu*.

Port A location or place on the CPU to connect other devices to a computer. It allows the computer to send information to and from the device.

Portrait The most common printing mode for letters and other documents. The printing orientation that prints a page vertically.

Positional parameters See *Replaceable parameters*.

PPP (point-to-point protocol) A temporary dial-up connection uses this protocol, which provides full access to the Internet as long as the user is online.

Primary mouse button Usually the left mouse button.

Print buffer The section of memory where print output is sent for temporary storage until the printer is ready to print. It helps the print spooler compensate for differences between rates of data flow by storing the print output while the print spooler receives data at high speed from the computer and passes it along at the much slower rate required by the printer. Thus, it frees the computer for other tasks.

Print queue A list of files that have been sent to the printer. The print manager sends the files to the printer as the printer becomes available.

Print server On a network, a computer that is dedicated only to printing.

Print spooler A program that compensates for differences between rates of data flow by temporarily storing data in memory and then doling it out to the printer at the proper speed.

Printer A computer peripheral that produces a copy of text or graphics on paper.

Printer driver Software that is used to send correct codes to the printer. Called driver software since it drives the printer.

Printer fonts Fonts that a printer is capable of printing; built-in fonts that come with a printer.

Process An executable program or part of a program. The process consists of the program itself, the memory address space it uses, the system resources it uses, and at least one thread.

Program A set of step-by-step instructions that tell the computer what to do.

Program approach A paradigm of treating programs as central. In order to use your data, you must first open your program, and then open your file. See *Docucentric*.

Program files Files containing executable computer programs. See also *Application software*.

Programming language processor A tool for writing programs so that users can communicate with computers.

Progress bar control See *Progress indicator*.

Progress indicator A control that is a visual representation of the progress of a task.

Prompt A symbol on the screen that tells the user that the computer is ready for the next command. The prompt consists of the letter of the current drive followed by a greater-than sign (A>, B>, C>).

Property sheet A special kind of dialog box that allows the user to view or change the properties (characteristics) of an object.

Proportional typefaces Typefaces that vary the space given to each character based on character width.

Protected mode Operating mode in which different parts of memory are allocated to different programs so that when programs are running simultaneously they can access only their own memory space and cannot invade each other's memory space.

Protocol A set of rules or standards designed to enable computers to connect with one another and to exchange information.

Queue A line of items waiting for processing.

RAM Random access memory. See *Memory*.

RAM drive A disk drive created in memory that emulates a physical disk drive.

Read-cache A mechanism that intercepts, makes a copy of, and places whatever file has been read into memory. When a program makes a request, Windows checks to see if the data is already in the read-cache. Read-cache is used to optimize performance.

Read-only attribute A characteristic of a file that prevents it from being changed or deleted.

Real mode A single-task working environment. DOS runs in real mode.

Real time Actual amount of time the computer uses to complete an operation.

Real-time compression A background program that compresses and uncompresses files as you use them.

Reboot Reload the operating system from disk.

Redirection A process in which the OS takes input or output from standard devices and sends the data to a nonstandard input or output device. The redirection symbol is >.

Registration database In older versions of Windows, a file called REG.DAT was the registration database. It contained information about how various applications would open, how some of them would print, how file extensions would be associated, how OLE (object linking and embedding) objects would be handled, and so forth.

Registry A mechanism in Windows that centralizes and stores user information, application program information, and information about the specific computer being used. The Registry is critical to the running of Windows. It is comprised of two files, USER.DAT and SYSTEM.DAT.

Registry keys In the Registry, keys can contain one or more other keys and values. Each key and value must have a unique name within a key or subkey.

Relative path The path from where you are to where you want to go in regards to the directory tree hierarchical structure.

Repeat delay The length of time that Windows waits before it repeats a character.

Repeat rate How fast a key repeats when held down.

Replaceable parameters Place holders for values. They allow the user to write batch files that can be used with many different parameters.

Required parameters See *Mandatory parameters*.

Reserved memory A synonym for the adapter area or upper-memory area.

Resident commands See *Internal commands*.

Resident font A font stored in the printer.

Resize tab A spot located on the corner of a window that allows you to resize the length and width of a window at the same time.

Resources In a networked environment, resources are what are provided by the server. Resources are the shared parts of the computer such as a device or file.

Restore Copy some or all of your files to your original disk, another disk, or another directory from your backup media.

Restore button A button on a window's title bar that returns the window to its previous size.

Retry The operation that tells MODE what to do when it gets a busy signal from a device.

Rich Text Format (RTF) A file format that allows different applications to open formatted documents.

Right-click Press and release the right mouse button.

Right-dragg Drag an object while holding the right mouse button.

Right justified Describes text that is lined up at the right margin.

ROM Acronym for read-only memory. Memory that contains programs that are written on ROM chips. ROM is retained when the computer is turned off. ROM often controls the startup routines of the computer.

ROM-BIOS (read-only memory basic input/output system) Chip built into the hardware of the system unit. Its functions include running self-diagnostics, loading the boot record, and handling low-level system tasks.

Root directory The directory that Windows or DOS creates on each disk when the disk is formatted. The backslash symbol (\) is used to represent the root directory.

Router Each network has a router, which is a device that connects networks. A router can make intelligent decisions about which network to use to send data.

Sample box In a dialog box, the box where a preview of your selections can be seen.

Sans serif font A typeface with no serifs. See also *Serif font*.

Scaled Describes fonts that can be made to print in various sizes.

Scan code Code number transmitted when a key is pressed or released. Each key on the keyboard has a unique scan code.

Scanners Device that enables a handwritten or printed page to be input to a computer.

Screen capture A "snapshot" of a computer screen. To capture the screen to the Clipboard, you press the Print Screen key. To capture the active window, you press Alt+Print Screen.

Screen dump A printed copy of what is displayed on a monitor.

Screen fonts Fonts that are used to display text and graphics on the monitor.

Screen saver An image that prevents screen burn-in and provides a modicum of security if passwords are used.

Script Instructions that tell a program what to do.

Script file A script that is saved as a file. In DOS, a script file can be redirected into DEBUG to create a .COM program.

Scroll bar When an entire list will not fit on the screen, the element that allows you to access the parts of the list that are not in view.

Scroll box A box in a scroll bar that shows the current location in a window

or document. It can be dragged with the mouse to move rapidly through a document.

Scroll Move vertically through text.

Search path The set path for searching directories.

Secondary storage media Data storage media other than RAM. Includes disks, tapes, or removable drives such as ZIP drives.

Sector A portion of a track on a disk. A sector is 512 bytes long.

Serial port The communications port to which a device, such as a modem or a serial printer, can be attached. The data is transmitted and/or received one bit at a time.

Serif font Font with a small step at the end of each letter.

Server On a network, a computer that provides shared resources to network users. Also used to refer to an application that provides the data or object in object linking and embedding.

Server application An application program that provides data (an object) in object linking and embedding.

Server-based network A network model in which security and other network functions are provided by a dedicated server.

Shareware Software that is free on a trial basis, with the option to either purchase it or remove it from your hard disk.

Shortcut An icon that represents commonly used objects. The icon is placed on the desktop or other location for easy access. A shortcut provides a pointer to an actual object, and it can be recognized by its right-bent arrow on top of the object's normal icon.

Shortcut button In Help, an icon with a purple arrow pointing to the upper-left corner. When clicked, it will take you directly to the proper location to accomplish the task for which you requested help.

Shortcut menu A menu that opens when you right-click the mouse over an object. See *Pop-up menu*.

Sizing buttons Buttons on a window's title bar that allow the user to minimize or maximize the window.

Slider A control that allows you to adjust or set values when there is a range of values. You move the slider with the mouse.

SLIP (serial-line Internet protocol) An older protocol used in a temporary dial-up connection that provides full access to the Internet as long as you are online.

Soft return A code that is automatically inserted when the end of a line is reached in a document. Unlike a hard return, if text is inserted or removed, software will automatically readjust text to fit within margins.

Soft sectored Describes a floppy disk whose sectors are marked with recorded data marks rather than punched holes.

Software Program files that tell the computer what to do.

Software packages See *Application software*.

Source document In object linking and embedding, the document in which a linked or embedded object was created.

Source file The file from which data is read in the transfer-of-data process.

Spin box A control that allows you to either key in a number or click on the up or down arrow to increase or decrease a quantity. A control that contains numeric options is usually represented as a spin box.

Split bar In Explorer, a bar dividing the window into two panes that display the structure of a disk (left) and the disk's contents (right).

Spreadsheet programs Programs that allow for budget management and financial projections.

Standard A set of detailed technical guidelines used to establish conformity in software or hardware development.

Standard error Error messages written to the screen by the OS.

Standard input Where the OS expects to receive information, usually the keyboard.

Standard output Where the OS expects to send information, usually the screen. Also refers to a command that normally writes its output to the screen.

Start button The first button on the taskbar. When you click the Start button, it opens the Start menu, which opens further menus so that you can access programs and data on your system.

Startup disk A bootable disk that has critical system files on it.

Static exchange Relationship that occurs when data created in one application is copied or moved to a different document created with a different application program and cannot be edited or changed in the new document.

Status area The area that is located at the right side of the taskbar where Windows and other programs to place information or notification of events. For instance, if you were printing, an icon of the printer would appear in the status area.

Status bar A bar that supplies information about the current window.

Stop bit Marker that indicates the end of asynchronous serial transmission.

String (of data) A variable length set of characters. String values are always enclosed in quotation marks.

Stroke weight The thickness of a font.

Subdirectories Manageable portions that allow the user to organize a disk into a hierarchical filing system. Subdirectories have names and contain files. Windows uses the term folder for directories and subdirectories.

Subdirectory markers Symbols used to move easily through the hierarchical structure. See also *Dot* and *Double dot*.

Subfolder A folder beneath a folder. It can also be called a child folder.

Subkeys In the Registry, a key can have a key beneath it, which is known as a subkey.

Substitute parameters See *Replaceable parameters*.

Support Refers to a program's ability to read from and write to a specific file format. The program is described as supporting that file format.

Surf the net Explore the Internet by moving from topic to topic.

Swap file When you are running several programs and running out of memory, Windows moves programs or data from memory to a swap file, which is space on the hard disk. When memory is freed up, Windows returns what is in the swap file to memory.

Switch Modifier that controls the execution of a command; typically the forward slash (/) is used to indicate a switch. See also *Parameter*.

Syntax The proper order or sequence of a computer's language and/or command.

Syntax diagram A graphic representation of a command and its syntax.

SYSing a disk Placing the operating system files on a disk without removing the data that is there. The command used to di this is called SYS.

System attribute A special signal that the OS interprets to recognize a system file.

System board Also known as a motherboard, it is the main circuit board to control the major components of a computer system.

System configuration The components that comprise a specific computer system.

System date The current date indicated by the computer system.

System disk See *Bootable disk*.

System level The point when the operating system has been loaded and no application programs are open.

System policies Policies designed to provide an override to any settings contained in SYSTEM.DAT and USER.DAT. System policies often contain company information that is specified by the system administrator. These policies are contained in a file called POLICY.POL and are created with the Policy Editor.

System prompt A symbol on the screen that tells the user that the computer is ready for the next command. Used in the command line interface, it usually consists of the current drive letter followed by a colon, backslash, and greater-than sign, as in C:\>.

System resources An area in memory that Windows uses for critical operating system tasks, such as drawing the windows on the screen, using fonts, or running many applications. See also *Free system resources*.

System software A set of programs that coordinates the operations of the hardware components.

System time The current time indicated by the computer.

System utilities Programs that carry out specific, vital functions to assist in the operation of a computer or software. DOS utility programs include such programs as FORMAT and CHKDSK. Windows also includes system utilities such as ScanReg. There are also commercial utility programs such as Norton Utilities. See also *External commands*.

Taskbar The bar on the screen that provides buttons to move between tasks in any open programs, files, folders, or windows. The taskbar includes the Start button as well as the status area where Windows and other programs can notify a user of events.

Taskbar button Button on the taskbar that indicates an open program, file, or window. Clicking a specific button on the taskbar will activate that choice.

T-connector A device used in a network that has one end plugged into the network card and two open ends (like a T) for connecting cables to computers in the network.

Terminate-and-stay-resident (TSR) program Program that remains in memory after it has been initially loaded from disk. See also *Memory-resident program.*

Terminator plug A device used with T-connectors so that there is no unplugged end in a network's cable.

Text box A place where a user can key in information.

Text editor A program that is similar to a word processor but is unable to perform any special editing, such as embedded codes. Text editors can only edit ASCII text files, which are also called text files or unformatted text files.

Text file File that contains text as opposed to a program. It consists of data that can be read, such as letters and numbers, with the TYPE command. A text file does not contain any special symbols. Also referred to as an unformatted text file.

Thermal printer A nonimpact printer that prints by using heat to melt wire particles that contain ink on heat-sensitive paper.

Thinnet A single coaxial cable.

Thread A subset of a process; a set of commands that does a specific task within a process. A thread runs in the process's allocated space using the process's allocated system resources.

Tiled Describes a display mode that divides the screen equally among the open windows.

Title bar A bar that contains the name of the program.

Toggle switch A switch that turns a function on or off.

Token A binary shorthand for repetitive words or phrases. When a file is decompressed, the tokens are read and the original characters are restored.

Toolbar A bar in a window or on the desktop that provides shortcuts for menu commands. Rather than accessing the command through a menu, you click a button on the toolbar.

ToolTip Text that provides the name or function of a button. ToolTips are activated by pausing the mouse pointer over a button on a toolbar or the taskbar.

Trackball A device used to move the cursor on the monitor. It usually consists of a stationary box containing a ball that the user rotates to move the cursor.

Tracking speed The rate at which the mouse pointer moves across the screen.

Track Concentric circle on a disk where data is stored. Each track is divided into sectors. All tracks and sectors are numbered so that the operating system can quickly locate information.

Transient commands See *External commands.*

Transparent to the user Describes a program or process that works so smoothly and easily that it is invisible to the user.

Tree structure An organizational scheme based on the branches of a tree, relating to the structure of a disk from the root directory down to the subdirectories.

Trojan horse virus A virus proffered as a legitimate program that, when run, begins a destructive process that unequivocally destroys data and programs on a disk.

TrueType fonts Fonts that are provided with Windows and can be printed on any printer. The screen display of the fonts usually matches the printed output. See *WYSIWYG*.

TSR Terminate-and-stay-resident program. See *Memory-resident programs*.

Tweak the system Make final changes and fine-tune a system to improve performance.

Twisted pair cable A type of cable also known as 10BaseT, 10BT, twisted pair, Ethernet, TPE, or RJ-45.

Typeface The design of a set of letters, numbers, and punctuation, such as Arial or Times New Roman.

Typematic rate Rate or speed at which MS-DOS repeats a character when the key for that character is held down on the keyboard.

Typeover A mode that allows a user to delete characters one by one as each new character is keyed in.

Typing replaces selection The process of deleting existing characters by selecting them and keying in data. What you key in replaces your selection.

UNC (universal naming convention) A convention used to locate the path to a network resource. It specifies the share name on a particular computer. The computer name is limited to 15 characters, and the share name is usually limited to 15 characters. It uses the format \\computer name\share name[\optional path].

Undocumented command A command that exists but is not listed in the OS manual.

Unformatted text file See *Text file*.

Unfragment a disk See *Optimize a disk*.

Uniform resource locator (URL) A standard format for identifying locations on the Internet. URLs specify three types of information needed to retrieve a document—the protocol to be used, the server address to which to connect, and the path to the information. The URL syntax is protocol/servername/path; an

example of a URL address would be **http://www.netscape.com**.

Universal Serial Bus (USB) The latest bus standard. It is an external bus standard for a computer that uses Plug-and-Play. Plug-and-Play technology eliminates the need to install cards into dedicated computer slots and reconfigure the system.

Upgrade Purchase the latest version of software and replace your existing version with it.

Upload Send a file to another computer while connected by a modem or on a network.

Upper memory area Area reserved for running a system's hardware. Programs cannot store information in this area. Also called adapter area and reserved area.

Upper memory blocks (UMBs) Unused parts of the upper memory area. Can be used for device drivers and TSRs if the computer is a 386 and is running DOS 5.0 or above.

User profiles Saved settings in Windows that allow more than one user to use the same computer and let each user retain his or her own personal settings on the desktop.

Utility programs Programs whose purpose it is to carry out specific, vital functions that assist in the operation of a computer or software.

Values In the Registry, keys and subkeys contain at least one value with the special name (Default). If the default value has no data, it is read as "value not set." Values have three parts—the data type, the name, and the value itself. Values are like files— each contains data. There are three types of data: binary, string, and DWORD values.

Variable parameters Value/information provided by the user.

Verbose Parameter used in conjunction with CHKDSK that gives the status report and lists every file on the disk, including hidden ones.

Verbs In the Registry, the Shell subkey defines the action that is possible for a specific file type. It contains a number of subkeys under it that define verbs. Each verb contains a subkey whose default entry value defines the command.

Verify Parameter that "double-checks" a file or program and ensures that sectors have been recorded correctly.

Version Number that indicates the progressive enhancements and improvements to a particular program. Successive releases of a program have increasingly higher version numbers.

VFAT (virtual file allocation table) An extension of the file allocation table. It provides the ability to handle long file names. See also *FAT (file allocation table)*.

Video card A circuit board that controls the capabilities of the video display.

Virtual disk drive See *RAM drive*.

Virtual drive See *RAM drive*.

Virtual machine (VM) An environment in memory that, from the application's point of view, looks like a separate computer, complete with all the resources available on a physical computer that an application needs to run.

Virtual memory Memory that does not actually exist. It is part of a method to extend a computer's memory by using a disk to simulate memory space.

Volume label Electronic label for a disk that a user can assign at the time of formatting a disk.

Volume serial number Random number assigned to a disk when it is formatted.

Wallpaper A graphic image file that serves as a background on the desktop behind all open windows.

WAN (wide area network) Consists of computers that use long-range telecommunication links to connect the networked computers over long distances.

Web A colloquial expression for the World Wide Web (WWW). See *World Wide Web (WWW)*.

Web page A single screen of text and graphics that usually has hypertext links to other pages.

Web site The physical and virtual location of a person's or organization's Web page(s).

Widow In word processing, the last line of a paragraph that appears on the top of a page rather than staying with the rest of the paragraph.

Wildcards The symbols * and ?, also called global file specifications, that are used to represent a character (?) or a group of characters (*) in a file name.

Window border Outline of a window that separates it from other windows or objects on the screen.

Wizard Program that uses step-by-step instructions to lead the user through the execution of a Windows task.

Word-processing programs Software that facilitates writing by allowing the user to write, edit, and print text.

Word wrap Feature in word-processing or other software that automatically moves text to the next line when the end of the line is reached.

Workgroup Another name for a peer-to-peer network.

World Wide Web (WWW) An interconnected collection of Web sites. It is a virtual space accessible from the Internet and holds pages of text and graphics in a format recognizable by a WWW browser. These pages are linked to one another and to individual files. The WWW is a collection of standards and protocols used to access information on the Internet. Also referred to informally as the Web.

Write-cache A mechanism that intercepts, copies, and places into memory the data a program has tried to write to disk. At a specified time or when the system is less busy, it writes what is in memory to disk. Write-caching is more dangerous than read-caching. It is used to optimize performance.

Write-protect notch   A cutout on the side of a 5¼-inch floppy disk that, when covered, keeps programs and data from being written to the disk. On a 3½-inch floppy disk, there is a write-protect slider.

Write-protected disk   Floppy disk that can only be read from, not written to.

WYSIWYG   Acronym for What You See Is What You Get. It means that something displays on the screen in the manner in which it will be printed.

INDEX